MW01014884

Carli
Caps: Albany
Stu03

CASES, COMMENT, QUESTIONS

CRIMINAL LAW

SEVENTH EDITION

by

LLOYD L. WEINREB
Dane Professor of Law, Harvard University

FOUNDATION PRESS
NEW YORK, NEW YORK
2003

COPYRIGHT © 1969, 1975, 1980, 1986, 1993, 1998 FOUNDATION PRESS
COPYRIGHT © 2003 By FOUNDATION PRESS

    395 Hudson Street
    New York, NY 10014
    Phone Toll Free 1–877–888–1330
    Fax (212) 367–6799
    fdpress.com

ISBN 1–58778–540–4

 TEXT IS PRINTED ON 10% POST CONSUMER RECYCLED PAPER

PREFACE

The five parts of this book are intended collectively to present criminal law as a body of law worth studying for "its own sake." Those who practice in the area of criminal law have, of course, need of a thorough grounding in its fundamental principles and contours; and lawyers who do not practice in the area also ought to have an acquaintance with it as part of their general professional competence. This book, studied in a course on the subject, will satisfy those demands. It seeks also, however, to present criminal law as intellectually demanding and rewarding aside from its practical value.

Part One sets out the framework of criminal law by showing how its basic concepts and theories function in the law of homicide. In Part Two, the manner in which criminal law develops is illustrated by aspects of the past and current development of the law of theft. Part Three uses the crime of rape to present explicitly the relationship between law and its social context. Part Four includes some of the general part of criminal law in a sequence from harmful acts for which the actor claims an excuse to (criminal) acts that may not be harmful but for which the actor can claim no excuse; concepts considered for the most part in Part One are reexamined in a context shaped to emphasize the tension in criminal law between attention to the actor and attention to the act. Part Five briefly notes constitutional limitations on aspects of criminal law that were previously considered without specific reference to the Constitution, provides two actual presentence reports for concrete discussion of issues about punishment that were raised earlier, and then opens the discussion outward to embrace individual liberty fully generally. There is a Bibliography keyed to sections of the text.

It is evident from the structure of the book that I believe that most of the general concepts used in criminal law, such as "act" and "mens rea," are best considered in the context of a specific crime. Analysis of such concepts illuminates the most important problems of criminal law; nevertheless, they are generalizations of the specific requirements of substantive offenses. No doubt the general and the particular interact and have reciprocal influence on one another. Still, if one direction is to be preferred, it is far more likely that in the development of the law, the direction of thought has been from the offenses to the generalizations, both historically and analytically. It seems to me also that one is less likely to suppose mistakenly that concepts like "mens rea" refer to elements of crimes independent of and different from the particular elements of particular crimes, if the concepts are first encountered in a specific form. That is, furthermore, the form in which they almost always appear in the world outside the classroom. All of the general concepts, therefore, are presented in this way in Part One. Teachers may take the occasion there or later in Part Four, when problems cutting across the substantive offenses are discussed, to acquaint students with the general terminology.

In order to keep the book to manageable length and still to include materials of other kinds, I have limited the number of cases presented in their full factual setting. The value of the case method is unquestionable, but it does not depend on endlessly distinguishing an endless collection of cases. I have often substituted questions that make distinctions among cases explicit and focus attention on the relevance of the distinctions to specific issues. I have generally not provided and have tried not to predetermine answers to questions that involve normative judgments and considerations of policy. Asking as many questions as I have, it has seemed particularly important to leave most of them for students to answer.

The space allotted to various topics reflects the significance of the issues they present for an understanding of the criminal law generally, rather than their incidence in actual cases. The topic of insanity, for example, is given much more space then the number of cases in which the insanity defense is presented would warrant, because it focuses attention starkly on the issue of the state's responsibility toward those whom the community rejects. More space is allotted to topics like provocation as an element of voluntary manslaughter, the requirement of retreat as an element of self defense, and felony murder than they require simply as doctrine, because they have been the subject of great controversy and expose fundamental choices of value that the law has to make. The use of extensive questions and problems in place of cases has provided the space to do this, without scanting doctrine.

The book is designed roughly for a three- or four-hour course. With some abbreviation or the use of lectures or assignments for reading without discussion, it should be suitable for a shorter course or for part of a course in which the procedural part of criminal law is studied also. The five parts of the book are designed to serve complementary purposes, and there are frequent cross-references. It should not, however, be difficult to omit some of the materials or to rearrange them in another order.

Preparing this seventh edition, I find that, although there are things that I should do differently were I to begin again, in general the conception of the book that guided me when I prepared the first edition 35 years ago has stood up well. Students sometimes feel along the way that they have rather a heavy dose of the law of homicide; but I still find value in the focus on a more or less constant factual setting—a "stiff on the floor," as I have come to call it in class—while different parts of the conceptual structure of the law are being surveyed. Students apply the concepts readily to other facts, with a degree of comprehension that reflects their having acquired the concepts in a concrete context. The historical material in Part Two has proved to be more difficult to teach and more difficult for students to absorb than I had expected. Although I continue to believe that the current law of theft and problems in the law are greatly illuminated by its history, the constraint of time has led me usually to lecture about the historical material and to concentrate on a few topics in the law of theft that exemplify the general issues. Part Three, which appeared for the first time in the fourth edition, is an integral part of the course that I teach. Whatever may have been true in the past, the crime of rape now has social significance that makes its inclusion in a course on criminal law obvious and essential. The approach in Part Four seems to me about right, although other teachers will no doubt have their own views about how much time to spend on each of the topics considered. By that point in the course, especially because of the extended consideration of the basic concepts in Part One, students have been able to master the essential issues quickly, without extensive discussion of individual cases.

In place of the large number of short passages from works about the philosophy and theory of punishment that appeared in the first four editions, I have provided a short essay, with references to a few of the most important sources, and placed it along with material about capital punishment near the end of Part One. The important issues arise in the discussion about homicide in any case; and placing the more abstract material there, in a readily accessible form, has served the purpose of an introductory course on criminal law better than more obscure and inevitably truncated excerpts from original works.

Notes containing comments, additional materials, and questions are numbered consecutively through the book. Footnotes are numbered consecutively in each Part. I have generally omitted footnotes in reproduced materials. Those that appear are renumbered but are in the original materials unless the footnote number is enclosed in brackets. I have corrected obvious typographical and similar errors and have made a few other small changes in reproduced materials not affecting their sense. Information about defendants' post-conviction history and similar material for which no source is given was obtained by correspondence with the appropriate officials or lawyers.

Copyright acknowledgments. I am grateful to the following for permission to reproduce extracts from the works indicated: The American Law Institute: The Model Penal Code, copyright 1985, as adopted at the 1962 Annual Meeting of the American Law Institute; Model Penal Code and Commentaries Part I, copyright 1985; and Model Penal Code and Commentaries Part II, copyright 1980. Her Majesty's Stationery Office: Royal Commission on Capital Punishment (Cmd. 8932) (1953). The Fresno Bee: articles, April 1 and 2, May 29, and June 24, 25, 26, 27, and 29, 1946. The New York Times: articles March 27 and 28, 1964, March 17, 1966, August 19, 1968, and November 7, 1971, copyright 1964/1966/1968/1971 by The New York Times Company. Sweet & Maxwell, Ltd.: Brown, Self-Defense in Homicide from Strict Liability to Complete Exculpation, 1958 Crim.L.Rev. 583. The Wall Street Journal: There Is This Store in Queens That's Not the Best Place to Rob, copyright Dow Jones & Company, Inc. (1971). The University of Chicago Press: A. Simpson, Cannibalism and the Common Law

(1984). The Selden Society: Anon. v. The Sheriff of London, 64 Selden Society 30 (1948). The University of Pennsylvania Law Review: Pearce, Theft by False Promises, 101 U.Pa.L.Rev. 967 (1953). The Belknap Press of Harvard University Press: O. Holmes, The Common Law (M. Howe ed. 1963). The Women's Press, Toronto: L. Clark & D. Lewis, Rape: The Price of Coercive Sexuality (1977). Women's Rights Law Reporter: Leigh Bienen, Rape I, 3 Women's Rights L.Rep. 53 (1976); Leigh Bienen, Rape III—National Developments in Rape Reform Legislation, 6 Women's Rights L.Rep. 170 (1981). B. Wootton, Social Science and Social Pathology (1959). The University of Chicago Law Review: Guttmacher, The Psychiatrist as an Expert Witness, 22 U.Chi.L.Rev. 325 (1955). Cressey, The Differential Association Theory and Compulsive Crimes, 45 J.Crim.L.C. & P.S. 29 (1954), copyright 1954 by the Northwestern University School of Law. The American Bar Foundation: Matthews, Mental Illness and the Criminal Law: Is Community Health an Answer? (Research Contribution of the American Bar Foundation No. 2) (1967). The Yale Law Journal Company and Fred B. Rothman & Company: Dession, Psychiatry and the Conditioning of Criminal Justice, 47 Yale L.J. 319 (1938); Goldstein & Katz, Abolish the "Insanity Defense"—Why Not? 72 Yale L.J. 853 (1963). Harvard Civil Rights Civil Liberties Law Review, A. Stone, The Insanity Defense and the Civil Libertarian, 20 Harv.C.R.–C.L.L.Rev. 525 (1985). Stanford University Press: H.L.A. Hart, Law, Liberty and Morality (1963), copyright 1963 by the Board of Trustees of the Leland Stanford Junior University.

Donald Lacey, while a student at Harvard Law School, worked with me on this edition and made substantial research and editorial contributions. Melinda Eakin did extensive copy-editing and was closely involved in every stage of preparation of the manuscript. Her assistance was invaluable. As in the past, I am grateful to Raymond S. Andrews ("Sherwood") for his precise illustrations of the fine points of criminal law.

LLOYD L. WEINREB

May 2003

SUMMARY OF CONTENTS

PART FIVE. LIMITATIONS

TABLE OF CONTENTS

PART ONE

THE STRUCTURE OF CRIMINAL LAW

HOMICIDE

PART TWO

DEVELOPMENT OF THE LAW

THEFT

PART THREE

LAW IN SOCIAL CONTEXT

RAPE

PART FOUR

ACTOR AND ACT

PART FIVE

LIMITATIONS

TABLE OF CASES

Principal cases are in bold type. Non-principal cases are in roman type. References are to Pages.

*

CASES, COMMENT, QUESTIONS

CRIMINAL LAW

*

PART ONE

THE STRUCTURE OF CRIMINAL LAW

The materials in Part One are designed to display the structure and conceptual apparatus of criminal law. To be effective, criminal law must operate with a limited number of concepts that are consistent with each other and with the facts they describe. Together the concepts must give the facts an order meaningfully related to the policies we intend to promote.

As you read the materials in this Part, consider which concepts of criminal law are basic, which are subsidiary or derivative, and which are not independent concepts at all but "fictions." Consider whether the concepts are used consistently and whether they accurately reflect our perception of the facts they order. Consider whether the order that they impose on the facts serves the purposes for which we have criminal law. The materials in this Part are unified by the overriding theme of the law of homicide, the value of human life.

At the back of the book, at pp. 789–824, there is a bibliography, keyed to the text, for further study.

---

1. THE PROBLEM OF DEFINITION

People v. Chavez

77 Cal.App.2d 621, 176 P.2d 92 (1947)

■ BARNARD, PRESIDING JUSTICE. The defendant was charged with the murder of her newborn baby. A jury found her guilty of manslaughter and she has appealed from the judgment.

The defendant was an unmarried woman about 21 years of age. She had previously had an illegitimate child, and at about 12:30 A.M. on March 31, 1946, she gave birth to the child here in question. She lived with her

1

mother and sisters in a small house having two bedrooms, with a bath room off the kitchen porch. On this night the mother slept in the back bed room, and the defendant occupied the front bedroom with her two sisters. She had attempted to conceal the fact of her pregnancy from her family by wearing a girdle and loose sweaters.

The circumstances surrounding the birth of this baby are disclosed by the testimony of the defendant alone, as there were no other eyewitnesses. After going to bed on the evening of March 30, she had several attacks of what she called "cramps." Apparently, she mistook her labor pains for cramps. Twice she arose and went through the kitchen and back porch to the bath room, and then returned to her bed. She made a third trip about 12:30 A.M., the other members of her family being asleep. She left the doors open and no lights were turned on. As she was sitting on the toilet she "felt a little pressure on the lower bones. Then I knew the baby was going to be born." She had not expected it to be born until the latter part of April. She did not call for help and, so far as she knew, no one was awake. She testified that "It came out rather slow. Next, the head was out, and it sort of dropped out real fast." She knew from her previous experience that the placenta had to be removed and so, after the baby was in the toilet "a little while," she expelled the placenta by putting pressure on her stomach. She did not notice whether the baby's head was under water, because the afterbirth fell over its head. It took two to three minutes for the placenta to come out. She then turned on the light and found a napkin and pinned it on herself. She then removed the baby from the toilet, picking it up by the feet, and cut the cord with a razor blade. She testified that the baby was limp and made no cry; that she thought it was dead; and that she made no attempt to tie the cord as she thought there was no use. She then laid the baby on the floor and proceeded to take further care of herself and clean up the room. The baby remained on the floor about fifteen minutes after which she wrapped it in a newspaper and placed it under the bath tub to conceal it from her mother. She then returned to bed and the next day went about as usual, going to a carnival that evening. On the next day, April 1, her mother discovered the body of the infant under the bath tub.

An autopsy was performed by a physician. He testified that the cord on the baby was about eighteen inches long, untied and depleted of blood; that the baby would live until it bled to death, in this case about an hour; that the baby appeared to be a full nine-month child and weighed about six and one-half pounds; that it appeared normal in every respect; that the lips were dark and swollen, but blood had been extravasated out of the vessels into the tissues of the lips and cheeks; that the tongue was dark and appeared hemorrhaged; that he opened the chest and stomach; that the lungs appeared normal and had air in them, the texture of which could be followed; that there was "crepitation"; that the heart and liver and other internal organs appeared normal; and that the body had very little blood in it, indicating hemorrhage. He expressed the opinion that the child was born alive, based on conditions he found and the fact that the lungs contained air and the blood was extravasated or pushed back into the tissues, indicating heart action. Although he admitted, on cross examination, that certain things were possible, he gave his reasons for excluding them here and reaffirmed his opinion that this baby was born alive and that it had had independent lung and heart action.

The appellant first contends that there is no substantial evidence to support the verdict in that it does not sufficiently appear from the evidence that this infant was born alive and became a human being; that it appears from the testimony of another doctor, called by the defense, that the doctor performing the autopsy did not use certain tests which might have been used and did not open the infant's head and heart which this other doctor thought might disclose some possibilities; and that it follows that the question of whether this infant was born alive and became a human being rests entirely on pure speculation.

While the autopsy surgeon expressed the firm opinion that this child was born alive, giving his reasons therefor, he admitted that it was possible that the main factors on which he based his opinion, the inflation of the lungs and the evidence of heart action, could have resulted from the child's breathing after presentation of the head but before the birth was completed. In other words, before there was a complete separation of the child from the mother. The respondent has presented a very able review and analysis of the leading cases along this line from the older and the modern common law of England . . . and from other states in this country which still closely follow the common law rules in this regard. . . . Some of these cases involve situations where an injury inflicted upon the mother resulted in the death of an unborn child. Others seem to be based upon such theories as that unattended childbirth is so violent a proceeding that the life of the child is in natural jeopardy or that the mother, because of momentary insanity or because of physical disability, should not be held responsible for a premeditated killing in the act of birth or for a death resulting from neglect after birth. For these and similar reasons, very stringent rules were developed at common law and have been largely followed in common law states in this country. Most of these jurisdictions have bridged the gap thus resulting by adopting various forms of infanticide statutes making the destruction of unborn infants or of infants not completely born a crime, but providing for a lesser punishment. While the matter was variously stated in these cases, and while some of them are somewhat inconsistent with others, it was generally held under the older common law that a child did not become a human being and could not be the subject of a homicide until it was completely born alive, was entirely separated from its mother and had an entirely independent life, with the cord cut and with its own breathing and heart action. Some of the cases have gone to ridiculous lengths, and others have varied some of the requirements, but these rules have largely been retained in the modern common law and in common law states in this country. While there have been some modifications of the rules these jurisdictions still require a rather complete separation from the mother and a rather complete demonstration that there was an entirely independent existence in the child before considering the infant as a human being, although in some of the more modern cases it has been held that the cutting of the cord was not necessary to this end.

Beyond question, it is a difficult thing to draw a line and lay down a fixed general rule as to the precise time at which an unborn infant, or one in the process of being born, becomes a human being in the technical sense. There is not much change in the child itself between a moment before and a moment after its expulsion from the body of its mother, and normally, while still dependent upon its mother, the child, for some time before it is born, has not only the possibility but a strong probability of an ability to live an independent life. It is well known that a baby may live and grow when removed from the body of its dead mother by a Caesarian operation. The mere removal of the baby in such a case or its birth in a normal case does not, of itself and alone, create a human being. While before birth or removal, it is in a sense dependent upon its mother for life, there is another sense in which it has started an independent existence after it has reached a state of development where it is capable of living and where it will, in the normal course of nature and with ordinary care, continue to live and grow as a separate being. While it may not be possible to draw an exact line applicable to all cases, the rules of law should recognize and make some attempt to follow the natural and scientific facts to which they relate. As Judge Cardozo once said: "Let the facts be known as they are, and the law will sprout from the seed and turn its branches toward the light." There is no sound reason why an infant should not be considered a human being when born or removed from the body of its mother, when it has reached that stage of development where it is capable of living an independent life as a separate being, and where in the natural course of events it will so live if given normal and reasonable care. It should equally be held that a viable child in the process of being born is a human being within the meaning of the homicide statutes, whether or not the process has been fully completed. It should at least be considered a human being where it is a living baby and where in the natural course of events a birth which is already started would naturally be successfully completed. While the question of whether death by criminal means has resulted while the process of birth was being carried out, or shortly thereafter, may present difficult questions of fact, those questions should be met and decided on the basis of whether or not a living baby with the natural possibility and probability of growth and development was being born, rather than on any hard and fast technical rule establishing a legal fiction that the infant being born was not a human being because some part of the process of birth had not been fully completed.

The question presented has not been decided in this state. Section 192 of the Penal Code provides: "Manslaughter is the unlawful killing of a human being, without malice . . . ." In Scott v. McPheeters, 33 Cal. App. 2d 629, it was pointed out that the theory under another statute that an unborn child is a human being separate and distinct from its mother is something more than a fiction and is based upon scientific fact, common experience and knowledge. In fact, it would be a mere fiction to hold that a child is not a human being because the process of birth has not been fully completed, when it has reached that state of viability when the destruction of the life of its mother would not end its existence and when, if separated from the mother naturally or by artificial means, it will live and grow in the normal manner. In practical effect, the rules that have developed at common law furnish a presumption that the baby in question is, or will be, born dead. This presumption is not only contrary to common experience and the ordinary course of nature, but it is contrary to the usual rule with respect to presumptions followed in this state. Section 1963(28) of the Code of Civil Procedure provides that, while it may be disputed, it is to be presumed "That things have happened according to the ordinary course of nature and the ordinary habits of life." While this presumption may not be sufficient for every purpose it is not only some evidence, but it suggests the proper manner of approach in considering all of the evidence.

Without drawing a line of distinction applicable to all cases, we have no hesitation in holding that the evidence is sufficient here to support the implied finding of the jury that this child was born alive and became a human being within the meaning of the homicide statutes. That it became a human being does not rest upon pure speculation. The evidence is sufficient to support a finding, beyond a reasonable doubt, that a live child was actually born here, and that it died because of the negligence of the appellant in failing to use reasonable care in protecting its life, having the duty to do so. This baby was completely removed from its mother and even the placenta was removed. A factual question was presented and the opinion of the autopsy physician was evidence which could be considered by the jury. His opinion was that the baby was born alive and that it breathed and had heart action. He gave good reasons for that opinion and while he admitted that there could be a possible doubt his evidence justifies the inference that there was no valid ground for a reasonable doubt. While he admitted that he had not used certain tests suggested by the other doctor he stated that he knew of these tests but did not consider them necessary here. With respect to the test most relied upon by the defense, it was stated by both doctors that this test would show only what the autopsy physician testified he had discovered by other means. The doctor called by the defense had not seen the baby's body and his testimony was based upon his general laboratory experience. While it may be said that there was some conflict between the testimony of these two doctors no more than a conflict appears. The question was one of fact for the jury and, in our opinion, the evidence is sufficient to support its findings. If it could be said that there might be a possible doubt with respect to this phase of the case, it cannot be said that there was necessarily a reasonable doubt. The finding of the jury is sufficiently supported, and the implied finding that this was a human being rests on a factual basis and not upon speculation.

The appellant further contends that the evidence is insufficient to issue #2 show that the death of this infant was caused by a criminal act. It is argued, in this connection, that the autopsy surgeon was unable to state precisely what caused the death of the infant and that it follows that the question as to the cause of the death rests on speculation and conjecture. It is pointed out that this doctor gave as the cause of death both suffocation and hemorrhage from an untied umbilical cord, and that he admitted that it was very difficult to determine which of these actually caused the death. He described the conditions he found in the body of the infant, including certain things which indicated that suffocation had taken place and other things which indicated an excessive hemorrhage. While he testified that the cause of death was very likely hemorrhage he later stated that it could be both of these things. He reaffirmed his opinion that one or both of these things caused the death although he admitted the possibility that the baby could have died of brain hemorrhage, saying "anything is possible." This doctor expressed a fixed opinion that the death resulted from one or both of these things and gave substantial reasons for that opinion. The fact that he was unable or unwilling to attribute the death to one of these causes alone does not make this evidence mere speculation or conjecture, and does not affect the question as to whether the death resulted from a criminal act.

There is ample evidence that such was the case. Penal Code section 192 defines involuntary manslaughter as the unlawful killing of a human being "In the commission of a lawful act which might produce death . . . without due caution and circumspection." The failure to use due care in the treatment of another where a duty to furnish such care exists is sufficient to constitute that form of manslaughter which results from an act of omission. . . . While the circumstances here are distressing, the evidence indicates a complete failure on the part of the appellant to use any of the care towards this infant which was necessary for its welfare and which was naturally required of her. While it is conceivable that in some such cases the mental and physical condition of a mother, at the time, might prevent her from exercising that reasonable care which would ordinarily be required, and thus excuse her from blame for the consequences of her failure to act, no such situation here appears. The appellant's own testimony discloses not only that she had a full realization of the situation but that she was able to think clearly and act with definite ends in view. With plenty of assistance near at hand she intentionally chose not to call for any help. Although she knew that the baby had dropped into the toilet she made no effort to rescue it or care for it for some time. Knowing that the placenta should be removed she gave her first attention to that. Even after that was accomplished she got up, turned on the light and proceeded to care for herself. Only after this was done and some seven minutes after the baby was born did she pick up the infant and make any effort to observe its condition. Even then her actions were very perfunctory and she made no effort to do anything, or to call for aid, in order to take care of the baby and attempt to preserve its life. She then let it remain on the floor in a cold room for some fifteen minutes while she attended to other things, after which she put it in a newspaper and hid it under the tub. Even the appellant's own medical expert testified that a child born under these circumstances would die. The evidence is entirely sufficient to show that the death of this infant was caused by a criminal act.

The judgment is affirmed.

Singleton v. State

33 Ala.App. 536, 35 So.2d 375 (1948)

■ HARWOOD, JUDGE. The appellant was indicted for murder in the first degree. Her jury trial resulted in a verdict of guilty of murder in the second degree, her punishment being fixed at imprisonment in the penitentiary for a term of twenty years.

. . .

The prosecution below revolved around the discovery of the body of a new born baby.

On a Monday morning in January, 1946, the body of a new born Negro male infant was found in or near the white cemetery in Jackson, Alabama. The child had been born within the previous twenty-four hours. Adhering to the body was a section of newspaper, The Mobile Press Register, in which the body had been wrapped. . . .

. . .

[There was evidence that on the previous night, the appellant had given birth to a baby on a bed in her home, about a quarter of a mile from where the body was found. She had apparently carried the body to the cemetery and thrown it over a wire fence. She had two children. She operated a small cafe in which she worked on the day before and the day on which the body was discovered.]

[A]ppellant's counsel attacks the sufficiency of the evidence to establish that the child, if born to appellant, was born alive and had an existence separate from its mother.

In infanticide cases an element additional to the required elements of the usual homicide case must be established by the State beyond a reasonable doubt, namely that the deceased babe was born alive, it being *Rule* axiomatic that one cannot kill something already dead. Rough and rule of thumb tests were applied by the earlier cases, and the question of the viability of the child seems to have revolved around whether the child breathed and had a circulation independent of its mother. . . .

Some of the cases dealing with infanticide, erring it is true because of the inherent humaneness of the common law, have been blinded by overzealous charity to the extent that all reasonable inferences to be gathered from the evidence are ignored and the State is required to prove that the baby was born alive beyond any possible doubt rather than beyond all reasonable doubt.

It was early established that proof that the child had breathed was insufficient to prove that it had lived, as a child often breathes during the process of its birth and prior to complete delivery. See Cyc. of Law and

Proc., Vol. 21, p. 663, and cases there cited. The earlier cases also required a complete separation of the infant from the mother and the establishment of an independent circulatory existence. In the relatively later cases it has been held however that severance of the umbilical cord is not requisite to establish such condition.

The desired and rational view as to the burden placed on the State in proving that the deceased child was born alive is reflected in an enlightened opinion by the District Court of Appeal of California, Fourth District, in People v. Chavez. . . .

The views expressed above by the California Court of Appeal in our opinion present a logical approach and invite a rational conclusion to determining the viability of a new born child. Adopting such view it is our conclusion that the State met the burden of proof cast upon it to establish that the infant in the present case was born alive.

We now come to consider the basic and fundamental elements usually arising in determining the sufficiency of the proof of the corpus delicti. Not only must the State establish by the required proof the fact of the death of the infant, but also that a criminal agency caused the death.

> *State must also prove infant's death by criminal act.*

. . .

Mr. Grubbs, the State Toxicologist, testified that from his tests he concluded that the baby in this case had breathed. As to the cause of its death he had no opinion. Dr. Chapman's testimony can only be interpreted to mean that the baby died from hemorrhage resulting from non ligation of the umbilical cord.

Thus the sum total of the evidence presented by the State as to the cause of this infant's death, insofar as this appellant is concerned, is that she may have been guilty of non-feasance in failing to tie the severed umbilical cord of her just delivered baby. Certainly there is not one scintilla of evidence indicating any positive wrongful acts on her part.

True, the principle is well settled that where a duty grows out of a close relationship, such as parent and child, then non-feasance on the part of one so obligated which results in the death of the one to whom such duty is owed may well amount to manslaughter, or possibly even murder. Cases enunciating the above principles have chiefly arisen where the parent has failed to secure medical aid for a sick child, or has permitted such child to die from starvation, or exposure. . . .

Our research has however not uncovered any case where a court has been willing to hold that non-feasance of a mother in the throes of childbirth or its immediate aftermath, resulting in death to the new born babe, should be considered of sufficient criminality to sustain a homicide conviction growing out of the death of the child.

Clearly there is a vast difference between the studied non-feasance of a parent failing to call medical aid for a sick child, and the non-feasance present in omissions by an unattended mother beset with the pangs and travail of childbirth. The possibility and probability that maternal non-feasance under the latter conditions springs from ignorance, pain, or physical incapacity is too great to permit the inference of constructive criminal intent.

The rigid requirements of the earlier cases as to proof of the viability of the child we think represent a groping recognition of the dangers inherent in a nonliberal approach to the doubtful question of the mother's criminality in such cases. Tables of infant mortality during birth bespeak the natural dangers accompanying and besetting the delivery of a child even when attended by skilled obstetricians and under the most favorable conditions.

. . .

[T]his court is unwilling to attach criminality to non-feasant acts of a mother resulting during the travail of childbirth even though such non action result in the death of the baby. Particularly is such view correct where, as in this case the mother is ignorant, uneducated, and unattended.

We are clear to the conclusion therefore that the State has failed to meet to the required degree the burden of establishing that this infant's death was caused by the criminal agency of this appellant. The State has therefore failed to prove the corpus delicti, without which no conviction can stand.

. . .

———

1. In the *Chavez* case, what is the first contention of the appellant? What is the issue that the court had to decide in order to resolve this contention?

2. The court states that it is difficult to fix the precise moment during birth when an infant becomes "a human being in the technical sense," p. 4. What is "the technical sense"?

3. The court states that there is a point during birth after which an infant will live and grow "in the normal course of nature and with ordinary care," p. 4. What is "the normal course of nature"? What is "ordinary care"?

4. The court observes that "the rules of law should recognize and make some attempt to follow the natural and scientific facts to which they relate," p. 4. On which "natural and scientific facts" does the court rely?

5.   Why is it a "legal fiction" or a "mere fiction" that "a child is not a human being because the process of birth has not been fully completed," p. 4? Compare Allaire v. St. Luke's Hospital, 56 N.E. 638, 640 (Ill.1900) (overruled by Amann v. Faidy, 114 N.E.2d 412 (Ill.1953)), in which the Supreme Court of Illinois, holding that there could be no recovery of damages for a prenatal injury, said: "That a child before birth is, in fact, a part of the mother and is only severed from her at birth, cannot, we think, be successfully disputed. The doctrine . . . that an unborn child may be regarded as *in esse* for some purposes . . . is a mere legal fiction . . . ." In Kelly v. Gregory, 125 N.Y.S.2d 696, 697 (App.Div.1953), the court concluded that there was a right to recover damages for a prenatal injury; it observed that "legal separability should begin where there is biological separability . . . and what we know ['of the actual process of conception and foetal development now'] makes it possible to demonstrate clearly that separability begins at conception."

With respect to viability, which the court in *Chavez* thought so significant, the Supreme Court of Rhode Island, allowing parents an action for wrongful death of a fetus, observed: "If we profess allegiance to reason, it would be seditious to adopt so arbitrary and uncertain a concept as viability as a dividing line between those persons who shall enjoy the protection of our remedial laws and those who shall become, for most intents and purposes, non-entities. It seems that if live birth is to be characterized, as it so frequently has been, as an arbitrary line of demarcation, then viability, when enlisted to serve that same purpose, is a veritable *non sequitur*." Presley v. Newport Hospital, 365 A.2d 748, 754 (R.I.1976). (All the same, so far as wrongful death actions are concerned, viability remains critical. See note 10 below.)

In People v. Hall, 557 N.Y.S.2d 879 (App.Div.1990), the defendant was prosecuted for the homicide of an infant who was born prematurely by caesarian delivery; the early delivery was necessary because the mother had been shot by the defendant. The baby had no congenital defects but was in a precarious condition from birth. She was placed on a respirator, fed intravenously, and attached to a cardiac monitor. After 36 hours, she died. The court observed:

> Defendant . . . appears to advance the novel proposition that someone who requires the assistance of modern medical technology to survive, even temporarily, is not really alive. However, it is unclear whether this theory is to be applied only to the newborn or to all people irrespective of age. Perhaps defendant is suggesting that only those persons who have first been the beneficiaries of good health can be considered alive if they subsequently develop medical problems necessitating technological intervention but that sick babies are not fully alive until they recover or their condition improves both significantly and permanently. . . . In short, defendant seems to claim that although Atallia may not have been completely dead at birth, she was not sufficiently alive to be deemed a "person" under Penal Law 125.00 et seq. This position is untenable. Illness is not equivalent to the absence of life, and the fact that Atallia was very sick at birth scarcely means that she was not alive. Notwithstanding defendant's concerted attempt

to depict her as the victim of a feticide, resulting in a miscarriage or stillbirth, she was, by any reasonable measure, born alive.

Id. at 882–83.

6. The court says that "the question" was "one of fact for the jury," p. 5. What question is that?

7. What kind of question did the court have before it?

8. What kind of tools should the court have used to decide the question? Consider the following:

(i) " 'Person,' when referring to the victim of a homicide, means a human being who has been born and is alive." N.Y. Penal Law § 125.05(1).

(ii) " '[H]uman being' means a person who has been born and is alive . . . ." Model Penal Code § 210.0(1).[1]

(iii) "Homicide is the killing of a human being by a human being." Royal Commission on Capital Punishment, Report (Cmd. 8932) 25 (1953).

Would any of these provisions have helped the court?

9. In Roe v. Wade, 410 U.S. 113, 164–65 (1973), the Supreme Court held that the Due Process Clause of the Fourteenth Amendment requires

1. Model Penal Code. The Model Penal Code was prepared by the American Law Institute. Its purpose, as its name suggests, was to provide a model for statutory codification of the criminal law in the United States. Drafting of the code was started in 1952. Tentative drafts accompanied by extensive commentaries culminated with the Institute's adoption of a "Proposed Official Draft" of the Code in 1962. After 1962 the Model Penal Code and its commentaries became a significant factor in legislative revisions of the criminal law in 40 or more states.

In 1976 the American Law Institute began work on final publication of the Code accompanied by revised and updated commentaries. In 1980, Part II of the Code and Commentaries, covering the definition of specific crimes, was published in three volumes. In 1985, the official draft of the Code with brief explanatory notes was published in a single volume. Also in 1985, Part I of the Code and Commentaries, covering general provisions of culpability, inchoate crimes, and disposition, was published in three volumes. No plans to republish the commentaries to Parts III and IV of the Code, covering respectively Treatment and Correction and Organization of Correction, have been announced. Commentary to those provisions can be found in Tentative Drafts No. 2 (1954), 5 (1956), 7 (1957), and 12 (1960).

The person principally responsible for the planning and execution of the entire project was Herbert Wechsler, Professor of Law at Columbia Law School. Professor Wechsler was the Chief Reporter for the Code and was Director of the American Law Institute from 1963 to 1984.

The revised volumes of the Code are cited hereafter as MPC, MPC Commentaries Part I, and MPC Commentaries Part II.

that during approximately the first trimester of pregnancy, the decisions whether and how to have an abortion be "left to the medical judgment of the pregnant woman's attending physician"; during the subsequent stage until viability of the fetus, "the State, in promoting its interest in the health of the mother, may, if it chooses, regulate the abortion procedure in ways that are reasonably related to maternal health"; and after the fetus becomes viable, "the State, in promoting its interest in the potentiality of human life may, if it chooses, regulate, and even proscribe, abortion except where it is necessary, in appropriate medical judgment, for the preservation of the life or health of the mother." (The Court observed that it was an essential part of its reasoning for the conclusion protecting the right to have an abortion "that the word 'person,' as used in the Fourteenth Amendment, does not include the unborn." Id. at 158.)

At the time of the *Chavez* case, California law prohibited abortions except in very limited circumstances. See California Penal Code §§ 274, 275; Health and Safety Code §§ 25950–54. See generally, People v. Barksdale, 503 P.2d 257 (Cal.1972). The penalty for a woman who solicited and submitted to any means to procure an abortion was imprisonment for one to five years. Penal Code § 275. Do legislative provisions prescribing when and how an abortion can be obtained and penalties for obtaining an abortion in other circumstances have a bearing on the problem in the *Chavez* case? See Hollis v. Commonwealth, 652 S.W.2d 61 (Ky.1983) (considering relevance of Roe v. Wade).

10. Should the court have looked to definitions of "human being" elsewhere than in the criminal law? Section 29 of the California Civil Code, for example, provides that a "child conceived, but not yet born, is to be deemed an existing person, so far as may be necessary for its interests in the event of its subsequent birth . . . ." In Scott v. McPheeters, 92 P.2d 678 (Cal.Dist.Ct.App.1939), mentioned in the *Chavez* opinion, p. 4, the court construed § 29 to allow recovery of damages for the negligent infliction of injuries on an unborn child, by a suit brought following the child's birth.[2] And in Lavell v. Adoption Institute, 8 Cal.Rptr. 367 (Dist.Ct. App.1960), the court held that under § 29 the father of a child who would otherwise be illegitimate when born could receive the child into his family and treat it as legitimate while yet unborn, thereby "adopting" and legitimating it from the time of its birth. Does § 29 alone or as construed in these cases have any bearing on the proper outcome of the *Chavez* case? Is it relevant that in Scott v. McPheeters the court acknowledged that at common law "an unborn child, in contemplation of law, has no existence as a human being separate from its mother," 92 P.2d at 680?

The courts have generally rejected the claim of a child to recover damages for the infliction of a wrong that both gave the child life or

---

2. The right to recover belongs to the child, not the fetus; no right attaches unless and until the child is born alive. See Wilson v. Kaiser Foundation Hospitals, 190 Cal.Rptr. 649 (Ct.App.1983).

sustained its life and harmed it in some way, sometimes called an action for "wrongful life." See, e.g., Gildiner v. Thomas Jefferson University Hospital, 451 F.Supp. 692 (E.D.Pa.1978) (child with Tay/Sachs disease; doctor advised that child would be free of disease); Stills v. Gratton, 127 Cal.Rptr. 652 (Ct.App.1976) (illegitimate child; abortion ineffective); Zepeda v. Zepeda, 190 N.E.2d 849 (Ill.Ct.App.1963) (illegitimate child; mother induced to have relations with father by false promise of marriage); Williams v. State, 223 N.E.2d 343 (N.Y.1966) (illegitimate child; mother raped while a patient in state mental hospital, sued state for negligence). See Miller v. Duhart, 637 S.W.2d 183 (Mo.Ct.App.1982) (normal child; ineffective sterilization operation). The parents of the child, however, may have an independent cause of action for medical expenses and/or emotional pain and suffering arising from the birth of the child. E.g., *Gildiner*; *Stills*. See Cockrum v. Baumgartner, 447 N.E.2d 385 (Ill.1983) (costs of rearing healthy child following unwanted pregnancy not recoverable; additional cases cited); Weintraub v. Brown, 470 N.Y.S.2d 634 (App.Div.1983) (same). But see Ochs v. Borrelli, 445 A.2d 883 (Conn.1982). In Procanik v. Cillo, 478 A.2d 755, 757 (N.J.1984), the New Jersey court overruled its earlier rejection of a wrongful-life action and concluded, in light of Roe v. Wade, p. 11 above, that a child born with an affliction in such a case can recover "the extraordinary medical expenses attributable to his affliction but . . . not . . . general damages for emotional distress or for an impaired childhood." See also Hummel v. Reiss, 608 A.2d 1341 (N.J.1992) (*Procanik* inapplicable to child born before decision in Roe v. Wade). In Turpin v. Sortini, 643 P.2d 954, 966 (Cal.1982), parents of a child born with a hereditary ailment alleged that they would not have conceived the child if they had been properly advised about the ailment; the court concluded that "while a plaintiff-child in a wrongful life action may not recover general damages for being born impaired as opposed to not being born at all, the child—like his or her parents—may recover special damages for the extraordinary expenses necessary to treat the hereditary ailment."

Are such decisions relevant to the issue in *Chavez*?

It has been held that a child, after its birth, can recover for injuries caused by acts on the mother before the child was conceived. See Bergstreser v. Mitchell, 577 F.2d 22 (8th Cir.1978) (allegedly negligent operation performed on mother before conception of child).

Had the Chavez baby died *in utero* due to the wrongful act of some person not its mother, its mother could not have maintained an action for the death. Justus v. Atchison, 565 P.2d 122 (Cal.1977). A majority of states allow such an action (but only after the fetus has become viable). See, e.g., Coveleski v. Bubnis, 571 A.2d 433 (Pa.Super.Ct.1990). Does this have a bearing on the *Chavez* case?

11. In *Chavez*, how does the court resolve the issue underlying the appellant's first contention? What is the court's precise answer to the appellant's first contention?

12.

Petitioner and Teresa Keeler obtained an interlocutory decree of divorce on September 27, 1968. They had been married for 16 years. Unknown to petitioner, Mrs. Keeler was then pregnant by one Ernest Vogt, whom she had met earlier that summer. She subsequently began living with Vogt in Stockton, but concealed the fact from petitioner. Petitioner was given custody of their two daughters, aged 12 and 13 years, and under the decree Mrs. Keeler had the right to take the girls on alternate weekends.

On February 23, 1969, Mrs. Keeler was driving on a narrow mountain road in Amador County after delivering the girls to their home. She met petitioner driving in the opposite direction; he blocked the road with his car, and she pulled over to the side. He walked to her vehicle and began speaking to her. He seemed calm, and she rolled down her window to hear him. He said, "I hear you're pregnant. If you are you had better stay away from the girls and from here." She did not reply, and he opened the car door; as she later testified, "He assisted me out of the car. . . . [I]t wasn't roughly at this time." Petitioner then looked at her abdomen and became "extremely upset." He said, "You sure are. I'm going to stomp it out of you." He pushed her against the car, shoved his knee into her abdomen, and struck her in the face with several blows. She fainted, and when she regained consciousness petitioner had departed.

Mrs. Keeler drove back to Stockton, and the police and medical assistance were summoned. She had suffered substantial facial injuries, as well as extensive bruising of the abdominal wall. A Caesarian section was performed and the fetus was examined *in utero*. Its head was found to be severely fractured, and it was delivered stillborn. The pathologist gave as his opinion that the cause of death was skull fracture with consequent cerebral hemorrhaging, that death would have been immediate, and that the injury could have been the result of force applied to the mother's abdomen. There was no air in the fetus' lungs, and the umbilical cord was intact.

Upon delivery the fetus weighed five pounds and was 18 inches in length. Both Mrs. Keeler and her obstetrician testified that fetal movements had been observed prior to February 23, 1969. The evidence was in conflict as to the estimated age of the fetus;[3] the expert testimony on the point, however, concluded "with reasonable medical certainty" that the fetus had developed to the stage of viability, i.e.,

---

3. Mrs. Keeler testified, in effect, that she had no sexual intercourse with Vogt prior to August 1968, which would have made the fetus some 28 weeks old. She stated that the pregnancy had reached the end of the seventh month and the projected delivery date was April 25, 1969. The obstetrician, however, first estimated she was at least 31½ weeks pregnant, then raised the figure to 35 weeks in the light of the autopsy report of the size and weight of the fetus. Finally, on similar evidence an attending pediatrician estimated the gestation period to have been between 34½ and 36 weeks. The average full-term pregnancy is 40 weeks.

that in the event of premature birth on the date in question it would have had a 75 percent to 96 percent chance of survival.

Keeler v. Superior Court of Amador County, 470 P.2d 617, 618–19 (Cal. 1970).

The petitioner Keeler was charged with murder. He sought a writ of prohibition on the ground that the facts stated above did not support the charge. Following *Chavez*, what should be the result?

Relying primarily on its construction of the murder statute, the court concluded that the writ of prohibition should issue.

Following the decision in *Keeler*, the California legislature amended the provisions of Penal Code § 187, which defines murder, to include killing "a fetus," except in cases of legal abortion and certain other special cases or when the killing was with the consent of the mother. The legislature did not, however, include killing a fetus within the crime of manslaughter. Accordingly, where the other elements of murder are not satisfied, killing a fetus is not a criminal homicide at all. See People v. Apodaca, 142 Cal.Rptr. 830 (Ct.App.1978).

The great majority of state courts that have considered the question have agreed with the *Keeler* court that a fetus before the process of birth has begun cannot be the victim of a homicide. See State v. Soto, 378 N.W.2d 625 (Minn.1985). For further discussion and citation of additional cases and scholarly discussion, see Commonwealth v. Booth, 766 A.2d 843 (Pa.2001) (vehicular homicide). Responding sometimes to the argument that medical developments have made the requirement of live birth obsolete, the courts have said that such a change, if it is desirable, is the responsibility of the legislature. E.g., State v. McCall, 458 So.2d 875 (Fla.Dist.Ct.App.1984) (vehicular homicide); Hollis v. Commonwealth, 652 S.W.2d 61 (Ky.1983) (murder). The "born alive" rule has been rejected in Massachusetts, Commonwealth v. Cass, 467 N.E.2d 1324 (Mass.1984) (vehicular homicide; prospective only), Oklahoma, Hughes v. State, 868 P.2d 730 (Okla.Crim.App.1994) (manslaughter; prospective only), and South Carolina, State v. Horne, 319 S.E.2d 703 (S.C.1984) (voluntary manslaughter, prospective only). See State v. Ard, 505 S.E.2d 328 (S.C.1998) (fetus carried by mother who was victim of homicide is a person for purpose of statute making killing of more than one person an aggravating sentencing factor). A number of states, like California, have enacted legislation specifically making it a crime to kill an unborn child. E.g., Ill. Rev. Stat. ch. 38, ¶ 9–1.2 (specifically excluding abortion with consent of the mother); Minn. Stat. Ann. § 609.266–.2665.

13. In People v. Davis, 872 P.2d 591 (Cal.1994), the defendant shot a woman who was 23–25 weeks pregnant, in the course of a robbery. Following surgery on the woman, the fetus was stillborn the next day. At that stage of development, the fetus had only a small possibility of survival. The defendant was prosecuted for murder pursuant to § 187 of the Penal

[handwritten margin notes: "Probability fetus could survive on its own"; "Ct's decision"; "New California legislation as a result of this case."]

Code. At trial, following some earlier California cases, the judge instructed the jury that viability was required for conviction under the statute; and he defined viability as a possibility of survival. On appeal, following the Supreme Court's analysis in Roe v. Wade, 410 U.S. 113 (1973), the defendant argued that viability meant that there was a probability of survival. The Supreme Court of California concluded that viability was not required under § 187. Roe v. Wade, it said, was not dispositive, since the mother's individual liberty (or privacy) interest is not at stake in a case under § 187. It concluded that the statutory reference to a fetus referred to an unborn in the "post-embryonic" stage of development, which begins "seven or eight" weeks after conception. (Because the prior law had apparently been that viability meant a probability of survival, however, the court concluded that its holding should not apply to the defendant's case.) Dissenting, Judge Mosk observed that at seven weeks, a human fetus is "slightly over half an inch" in length and weighs "about one-tenth of an ounce"; "its appearance remains less than human"; "its paddle-like hands and feet are still webbed; and it retains a vestigial tail." Id. at 614–15. "I cannot believe," he said, "the Legislature intended to make it murder— indeed, capital murder—to cause the death of an object the size of a peanut." Id. at 615.

Cases in which a newborn baby has been discarded and is found, alive or dead, in a trash container are reported frequently in the press. Occasionally, sensational factors of such an occurrence attract more attention. In 1996, for example, the body of a newborn baby was found in a trash container outside a motel where it had been born. The baby's mother and father, who were raised in comfortable circumstances and were still in their teens, were indicted for first-degree murder. See The New York Times, Nov. 18, 1996, at B1; Dec. 18, 1996, at B4. In 1997, a young woman who was attending a high school prom gave birth in the school bathroom and after discarding the baby, returned to the prom. She was charged with murder. See The New York Times, June 9, 1997, at B4; Sept. 18, 1997, at A37. The number of reported cases suggests that the number of cases that are not reported is much larger. Most often, the baby is born to a woman who, like the defendant in *Chavez*, has concealed her pregnancy and is unattended during the birth. Some commentators have observed that a woman who gives birth in such circumstances following an unwanted pregnancy may perceive the baby not as a human being but rather as a threatening foreign object that has invaded her body and that her instinctive response may be to get rid of it. The individual's perception of the event and the public perception may, therefore, be profoundly discordant.

14. The defendant shot a woman who was in the eighth month of pregnancy. She delivered twin fetuses by a caesarian operation. One, who received a bullet wound across his back as the bullet passed through his mother, died about three hours after birth; the cause of death was the bullet wound. The other twin died 15 hours after birth. He had not been struck by the bullet; the cause of death was "immaturity." The caesarian operation would not have been necessary but for the injury to the mother. The defendant was charged with two counts of murder. State v. Anderson, 413 A.2d 611 (N.J.Super.Ct.App.Div.1980).

What result? How does the problem in this case differ from that presented in *Keeler*, note 12 above?

See also United States v. Spencer, 839 F.2d 1341 (9th Cir.1988) (baby born alive, lived for ten minutes); State v. Cotton, 5 P.3d 918 (Ariz.App. 2000) (baby born alive, died next day; additional cases cited); Jones v. Commonwealth, 830 S.W.2d 877 (Ky.1992) (*Hollis*, note 12 above, distinguished).

15. Do you agree with the Alabama Court of Appeals in *Singleton* that the opinion in *Chavez* is an "enlightened opinion" expressing views which "present a logical approach and invite a rational conclusion to determining the viability of a new born child," p. 8?

16. In *Singleton*, the court states that it has been unable to find "any case where a court has been willing to hold that non-feasance of a mother in the throes of childbirth or its immediate aftermath, resulting in death to the new born babe, should be considered of sufficient criminality to sustain a homicide conviction growing out of the death of the child," p. 8. Can you help the court out?

17. In *Chavez*, how satisfactory is the court's explanation of its answer to the appellant's contention that there was not sufficient evidence to show that the child's death had been caused by a criminal act? Does the *Singleton* court give a more satisfactory explanation of its resolution of the same issue?

18. Suppose one of the sisters of the appellant in *Chavez* had heard noises in the bathroom and guessed what was happening in time to aid both the appellant and the baby, but had turned over and gone back to sleep. Would she be guilty of criminal homicide? Suppose she had walked to the bathroom, observed what was happening, and then gone back to bed without aiding the appellant or the child. What then?

19. Do the opinions in *Chavez* and *Singleton* contain hints of an explanation for the fact that the two courts reached contrary answers to what was essentially the same question, on a matter as important as a homicide conviction?

20. In State v. Osmus, 276 P.2d 469, 477 (Wyo.1954), a case similar to *Chavez* and *Singleton*, the court observed: "[O]ne cannot help but feel that, for the most part, courts have been hesitant in applying Draconian laws; have felt that as much consideration is due to the party accused of infanticide as is due to a new born child whose very existence as a human being may be in the twilight zone; have applied the rule of reasonable doubt fairly strictly and many times have reversed convictions on account of indefiniteness and unreliability of the evidence produced by the state, even in cases in which there was testimony of a confession on the part of the accused."

Commenting on the expression of concern in *Singleton* for "an unattended mother beset with the pangs and travail of childbirth," p. 8, which the court in *Osmus* quoted with approval, another court observed: "Sensitivity to the capabilities of a sixteen year old girl who has recently endured an unattended childbirth . . . does not require a conclusion that a mother owes no duty of care to her newborn child. . . . Recognition that a legal duty exists will not prevent consideration of a mother's physical or mental capabilities in assessing her willfulness, malice, deliberation, premeditation, or degree of negligence in failing to care for her baby. We therefore hold that although a court may consider the mother's condition in determining the degree of criminal culpability, if any, arising from a failure to attend to her newborn baby, the sole fact that she has recently experienced childbirth does not excuse her from a legal duty to care for the baby." Vaughan v. Commonwealth, 376 S.E.2d 801 (Va.Ct.App.1989).

In *Vaughan*, the circumstances of the birth resembled those in *Chavez*. The defendant was 16 years old and gave birth for the first time. Several hours after giving birth, she went to a neighbor's house to borrow a paper bag. She put the dead baby into the bag and walked to a dumpster, where she deposited it. The neighbor testified that the defendant behaved normally, laughing and talking. Reversing the defendant's conviction of first-degree murder, the court said that her concealment of her pregnancy and the birth and her failure to arrange for adoption of the baby did not support beyond a reasonable doubt an inference of intent to kill the baby. "Although this evidence may be consistent with the behavior of a person who intends to kill a baby at birth, it is also consistent with the behavior of an unwed young girl who is frightened, enveloped in shame, and embarrassed about her pregnancy and labor. Disposing of the baby's body is behavior that is as consistent with shame, an attempt to avoid embarrassment, and fear of incurring the anger of one's parents as it is consistent with an attempt to conceal a murder." Id. at 807. The court noted that the defendant could be prosecuted for involuntary manslaughter.

21. On August 31, 1978, The Boston Globe reported that in Kentucky, Maria Pitchford, a 22-year-old former university student, had been found not guilty by reason of temporary insanity of a charge of performing an illegal abortion on herself with a knitting needle. Pitchford went to a clinic when she was between 20 and 24 weeks pregnant. Doctors at the clinic refused to perform the abortion. She was charged under a statute that made it a crime for a woman to perform an abortion on herself without the advice of a physician; the crime carried a possible sentence of imprisonment for 10–20 years. (She was charged also with manslaughter; the judge dismissed the charge on the ground that a fetus is not a person under the manslaughter statute.)

The father of the child testified that he had suggested an abortion because he was unable to support a child. A legal psychologist testified for the defense that after the abortion, Pitchford had exhibited "symptoms of rejection and self-hatred and depression." Another psychologist testified that she was "in an emotional state" on the day of the abortion, and that statements she had given to the police at the hospital following the abortion should be discounted because of medication that had been administered to her. Under those conditions of stress, he said, "the mind . . . steps outside the body, and the emotions take over."

The judge instructed the jury that the defendant should be found guilty if they were convinced that she gave herself an abortion without the advice of a physician, and that the defense of temporary insanity was available only if she was not in control of her own emotions at the time. The jury deliberated for less than an hour. The Boston Globe, Aug. 31, 1978, at 2.

Might a defense of temporary insanity have been available to Chavez? Might the answer to that question be affected by her socio-economic background? If so, how?

22. It is clear, isn't it, that the defendants in *Chavez* and *Singleton* did something "bad" in some sense of that word, although we might not all agree about the characteristic(s) of their conduct that made it bad or about the standards (and the source of the standards) that we are applying? Since we *can* probably agree that they have done something bad, why is it so important to define precisely what it is that they have done?

23. Would the best solution to the problem presented in the *Chavez* and *Singleton* cases be to treat the killing of a child during or immediately following birth as a special category of homicide, or to create some other crime related to the facts of such cases which is distinct from homicide altogether?

Some states, mindful of the difficulties of proof in cases like *Chavez* and *Singleton* as well as their special nature, have made concealment of the death of an illegitimate child a misdemeanor. E.g., Mass. Gen. L. ch. 272, § 22. In England, the Infanticide Act, 1 & 2 Geo. 6, ch. 36 (1938), provides that if a woman, disturbed by the effects of giving birth to a child, kills the child within a year of its birth in circumstances that would otherwise constitute murder, she is guilty of infanticide and shall be punished as if guilty of manslaughter. See also the Infant Life (Preservation) Act, 19 & 20 Geo. 5, ch. 34 (1929).

24.   Recent developments in medical technology have made it possible for some vital bodily functions to be performed temporarily or permanently by a machine attached to the body. For purposes of the law of homicide, when a vital organ of the body has ceased permanently to function and its function is carried on by a machine, how should we determine when life has ended?

Considering cases in which the victim of an assault was subsequently treated at a hospital, where heart and lung action was temporarily maintained mechanically after the cessation of brain activity, the New York Court of Appeals concluded: "[W]hen a determination has been made according to accepted medical standards that a person has suffered an irreversible cessation of heartbeat and respiration, or, when these functions are maintained solely by extraordinary mechanical means, an irreversible cessation of all functions of the entire brain, including the brain stem, no life traditionally recognized by the law is present in that body." People v. Eulo, 472 N.E.2d 286, 296 (N.Y.1984). That definition of death is generally accepted.

In In re Quinlan, 355 A.2d 647 (N.J.1976), the court declared:

[U]pon the concurrence of the guardian and family of Karen, should the responsible attending physicians conclude that there is no reasonable possibility of Karen's ever emerging from her present comatose condition to a cognitive, sapient state and that the life-support apparatus now being administered to Karen should be discontinued, they shall consult with the hospital "Ethics Committee" or like body of the institution in which Karen is then hospitalized. If that consultative body agrees that there is no reasonable possibility of Karen's ever emerging from her present comatose condition to a cognitive, sapient state, the present life-support system may be withdrawn and said action shall be without any civil or criminal liability therefor on the part of any participant, whether guardian, physician, hospital or others.

By the above ruling we do not intend to be understood as implying that a proceeding for judicial declaratory relief is necessarily required for the implementation of comparable decisions in the field of medical practice.

Id. at 672. See Barber v. Superior Court, 195 Cal.Rptr. 484 (Ct.App.1983) (doctor's removal of intravenous tubes providing nourishment from comatose patient in permanent vegetative state, in accordance with direction of family and person's previously expressed wishes, was not an unlawful failure to perform duty); Matter of Welfare of Colyer, 660 P.2d 738 (Wash. 1983) (same).

Following the decision of the New Jersey Supreme Court, in 1976 Karen Quinlan was taken off the respirator that had helped her to breathe. She continued to be fed through feeding tubes. In that condition, she lived until 1985.

———

THE CHAVEZ CASE

The Fresno Bee

Monday, April 1, 1946.

Unwed Fresno Mother Slays Newborn Baby

A 20 year old unwed Fresno mother today is being sought on a murder charge after the discovery of the body of a newborn boy which had been wrapped in newspapers and stuffed under the bathtub in her home at 339 G Street.

The girl is Miss Josephine Chavez, 20, the daughter of Mrs. Josephine P. Chavez, who discovered the infant's body at 10 o'clock yesterday morning and notified the authorities after her daughter left the house.

Born Alive Over Weekend

District Attorney James M. Thuesen and Detective Sergeant J. B. Wilson said the baby probably was born alive late Friday night or early Saturday morning in the bathroom of the home without the knowledge of any of the other occupants of the house.

Coroner A. M. Yost ordered an autopsy by Dr. George Sciaroni, who reported the child probably was suffocated by having its lips held together and its nostrils closed shortly after birth.

Mrs. Chavez told the investigating officers she suspected her daughter was pregnant, but that the girl denied it when she asked her about it.

Has 1½ Year Old Boy

Police detectives said the missing girl also is the mother of a 1½ year old boy, being cared for by Miss Chavez' mother in their G Street home. The officers describe the girl as a Pachuco and said she associates with hoodlum gangs in West Fresno.

Detective Sergeant Jack McCoy, the head of the police department special service bureau, said the girl was placed on probation by the bureau three years ago.

At that time, McCoy said, she was out of the control of her mother and was associating with undesirable companions. Later she was turned over to the county probation department as a juvenile delinquent, but was released from their supervision when she became 18 years old.

Thuesen said none of the six persons who were in the house Friday night and Saturday morning knew of the birth of the child. They were Mrs. Chavez, a brother, a 15 year old sister and three smaller children, one of them Josephine's small son.

The mother said Josephine arose and had breakfast with other members of the family at the usual hour Saturday morning. She spent most of the day lying down, but got up at noon and in the evening for other meals.

Saturday night she attended a carnival, returning home at about 11 P.M. She got up at about 9 o'clock yesterday morning and was in the house at the time the body of the dead infant was discovered.

Flees When Body Is Found

Mrs. Chavez said Josephine threw her hands over her head and fled from the house when she was confronted with the discovery.

The mother immediately asked a friend to telephone Mrs. Frances F. Hancock, assistant county probation officer under whose charge the girl had been and Mrs. Hancock notified the police.

Wilson said questioning of acquaintances of the girl failed to reveal any trace of her. Her brother, Mike Banias, a recently discharged soldier, told the officers he loaned Josephine $5 Saturday night and gave her $5 more yesterday morning before he learned of the discovery of the body.[4]

---

[4] The dates given here conflict with the dates given in the court's opinion, p. 1 above. The baby was evidently born on Friday night, March 29–30, rather than on the night of March 30–31, as the opinion indicates.

COMPLAINT

In the Police Court of the City of Fresno
County of Fresno, State of California

The People of the State of California,
Plaintiff___

vs.

___JOSEPHINE CHAVEZ___

Defendant___

COMPLAINT—CRIMINAL

P. C. Sec. 1426

1203/-2

Personally appeared before me, this __1st__ day of _____ April _____, 19__46__

_____ A. B. MC CREARY _____

in the City of Fresno, who first being duly sworn, complains and accuses the above named defendant _____ JOSEPHINE CHAVEZ _____

of the crime of __a felony, to-wit: MURDER_____

_____ committed as follows:

The said defendant on or about the __30__ day of _____ March _____ A. D. 1946

in the City of Fresno, County of Fresno, State of California, murdered one infant, a human being.

All of which is contrary to the form, force and effect of the Statute in such case made and provided, and against the peace and dignity of the people of the State of California.

Said Complainant therefore prays that a warrant may be issued for the arrest of the said defendant___ and that __she__ may be dealt with according to law.

Subscribed and sworn to before me this __1st__ day of _____ April _____, 19__46__

A B McCreary

Albert Myer
act. Police Judge

Attest _W. H. Sheek_, Clerk

By _Beth Locke_, Deputy Clerk

The State of California started criminal proceedings against Josephine Chavez for the death of her newborn son on Monday, April 1, 1946, when A.B. McCreary, a member of the City of Fresno Police Department, swore out a complaint against her in the Fresno Police Court. "The complaint is the allegation in writing made to a court or magistrate that a person has been guilty of some designated offense."[5] The maximum penalty for murder, the offense charged against Josephine Chavez, was death or imprisonment for life.[6]

The complaint was prepared in the office of the district attorney. Officer McCreary knew nothing about the case. He was the complaining witness because he was the police officer in charge of the booking desk when the complaint was obtained.

California Penal Code

813. When warrant may issue. If the magistrate is satisfied therefrom that the offense complained of has been committed, and that there is reasonable ground to believe that the defendant has committed it, he must issue a warrant of arrest.[7]

Acting Police Judge Albert Myer, who signed the complaint, also issued a warrant for Josephine Chavez's arrest. The decision to arrest Josephine Chavez, like the decision to file a complaint, was made in the office of the district attorney, on the basis of the investigative reports of the Homicide Squad of the Fresno Police Department.[8]

The warrant was not served.

---

5. Cal. Penal Code § 806. This and all subsequent references to the California Penal Code in this discussion state the provisions of the code at the time of the *Chavez* case. Section 806 has since been amended, Penal Code § 806.

The notation "P.C. Sec. 1426" at the top of the complaint form, p. 23, refers to the section of the code, since repealed, which governed the form of complaints charging offenses triable in the police court. Evidently the same form was used for all complaints filed in the police court. For the form of a complaint charging an offense triable in the superior court, which is used as a pleading, see Cal. Penal Code § 806.

6. Cal. Penal Code § 190, since amended.

[7] Since amended.

8. Although § 813 indicates that the magistrate issuing the warrant must be satis-

fied that the offense charged has been committed, the California practice was to rely on the decision of the district attorney's office to file a complaint. The Supreme Court of California has since declared that this violates the rights of an accused under the Fourth Amendment to the Constitution, which, the court said, requires that the magistrate determine independently that there is probable cause to arrest the accused. People v. Sesslin, 439 P.2d 321 (Cal.1968).

The notation "P.C. Sec. 1427" at the top of the warrant of arrest, p. 25, refers to the section of the Penal Code, since amended, that governed the form of arrest warrants issued by the police court for offenses triable in the police court. Evidently the same form was used for all warrants issued by the police court. The form of arrest warrants for offenses triable in the superior court is prescribed by § 814 of the code, as amended.

WARRANT OF ARREST

In the Police Court of the City of Fresno
County of Fresno, State of California

The People of the State of California,
Plaintiff—

vs.

JOSEPHINE CHAVEZ

_____

_____

_____
Defendant—

Warrant of Arrest
P. C. Sec. 1427

1203/-2

THE PEOPLE OF THE STATE OF CALIFORNIA:

To the Sheriff or any Constable,
or Marshall or Policeman of the State of California.
Information on oath having been this day laid before me by A.B.McCREARY
that the crime of

a felony, t -wit: MURDER

having been committed and accusing SAID DEFENDANT
thereof, YOU ARE THEREFORE COMMANDED, forthwith to arrest the above
named DEFENDANT and bring HER before me,
forthwith, at my office, in the City of Fresno, in said County of Fresno.

WITNESS MY HAND at said City of Fresno, this 1st
day of APRIL, 194 6, and directed that this warrant
may be served at any hour of the night.

The defendant is to be

admitted to bail in the   Attest: W.H. Shick

sum of $_____.   By Beth McNeill

Albert Myers
Police Judge

Clerk
Deputy Clerk

I HEREBY CERTIFY that I received the within warrant on the_____day of
_____, 194__, _____ and served the said
Warrant by arresting the said named defendant on the_____day of_____,194__,

and bringing_____into Court, this_____day of_____, 194__.

Police Officer of the City of Fresno

The said Defendant_ having been brought before me under this Warrant, declare
true name_ to be_____

and _he_ hereby committed to the Sheriff of County of Fresno, until_he_ can be tried
or examined on said charge, _he_ admitted to bail in the sum of $_____and stand
_____committed until _he_ give such bail.

Police Judge

Dated this 3/ day of may, 194 6

Attest:
Clerk

By:_____
Deputy Clerk

Held with out Bond.

The Fresno Bee

Tuesday, April 2, 1946.

Family Asserts
Suspected Slayer Was Remorseless

The members of the family of Miss Josephine Chavez, 20 year old West Fresno woman who is sought for murdering her infant son shortly after his birth, today declared the girl showed no remorse either before or after the body of the child was discovered Sunday.

Her mother, Mrs. Josephine Chavez, who found the infant's body stuffed under the bathtub in the family home at 339 G Street, and the girl's half brother, Mike Banias, a veteran of the South Pacific campaign, declared they saw nothing unusual in her demeanor either Saturday or Sunday.

Attended Carnival

Saturday night, Banias said, she accompanied him and a group of friends to a carnival. In spite of the fact she had given birth to the child Friday night or Saturday morning, she rode on the various amusement devices during the evening with no apparent ill effects, and joined the other members of the party in a meal before going home.

"I did not know she was pregnant," said Banias. "My mother suspected it and accused her of it. She denied it and so my mother just took her word for it.

"I have only been home a little while and I did not notice anything was wrong. She did not act worried. I did not pay much attention to her because I did not know anything was wrong, but I can't remember that she ever seemed to be worried about anything."

Banias said he and his sister had left the house Sunday morning when their mother called Miss Chavez back. He asserted Josephine was gone for a few minutes and then returned to walk down the street with him. He said he did not notice her appearance particularly but he knew she was not crying and gave no other indication she might have been disturbed or worried.

When they parted at Kern and G Streets she asked him if he had any money and he gave her $5. He said he thought she wanted it for spending money, and she gave no indication she planned to remain away from home.

Mrs. Chavez said she called the girl back after finding the body and asked her what she had to say about the baby.

"She just said 'Oh' and went out of the house," said Mrs. Chavez. She declared the daughter did not cry and was not hysterical.

Planned Flight

Banias said it is possible Josephine had prepared to leave and had taken clothing and other articles to the house of a friend and would pick it up when she desired.

He said neither he nor his mother knew very much concerning her associates, most of whom she met in places other than her home.

Banias added his sister apparently believed she had succeeded in concealing her condition from the family and friends up to the time of the birth of the child. She may have thought, he said, that by doing away with the infant, no one would know that she had been pregnant.

He said he knew nothing of the birth of the child or the recovery of its body until he returned home late Sunday.

Inquest Is Scheduled

Coroner A. M. Yost said he is planning an inquest tomorrow into the death of the infant.

In the meantime, the police reported no progress in their search for the girl, who fled from her home at 10 o'clock Sunday morning after her mother discovered the child's body.

Friends of the girl were questioned by the police, but none admitted seeing her since last Saturday. Information that she may have gone to Los Angeles could not be verified. The Los Angeles officers checked two places where it was thought she might seek refuge, but she had not been seen there. The homes of relatives in the San Francisco area also are being watched.

California Penal Code

1510. Coroner's jury: when called. When a coroner is informed that a person has been killed, or has committed suicide, or has suddenly died under such circumstances as to afford a reasonable ground to suspect that his death has been occasioned by the act of another by criminal means, he must go to the place where the body is, cause it to be exhumed if it has been interred, and make an investigation and if the circumstances warrant it he shall hold an inquest and summon not less than nine nor more than fifteen persons, qualified by law to serve as jurors, to appear before him forthwith, either at the place where the body of deceased is, or at some other convenient place within the county to be designated by the coroner, at his discretion, or at the request of the district attorney to inquire into the cause of the death. . . .[9]

At the inquest conducted by Coroner Yost, Dr. George H. Sciaroni testified concerning the results of an autopsy which he had performed on the infant's body. The coroner's jury concluded that the death had occurred by criminal means.

Josephine Chavez was in Oakland where she was working for the Grandma Baking Company. Among the exhibits at the trial was an earnings statement which showed her wages ($25.40) for the pay period ending on May 25.[10] Between May 25 and May 27, she returned to Fresno and went to see her brother. On Monday, May 27, he called a friend, J.J. Nagel, and told him the story. Nagel was 33 years old, a member of the California Bar since 1942. About a month before, he had formed a law partnership with another, somewhat older lawyer, Gerald W. Stutsman. Nagel told her brother to bring her to their offices at the end of the day. The four of them discussed the case far into the night and decided that she should surrender herself. She had returned to Fresno with that in mind and made no objection.

The next day, Josephine Chavez bought a new dress and had her hair done. Nagel and Stutsman called the office of the district attorney and arranged with an assistant district attorney to bring her to the Fresno County Jail, where she would surrender herself that night. To counteract some of the unfavorable press reports of the case, they also called an editor of The Fresno Bee and told him what was to take place.

[9] Now contained as amended in Cal. Gov't Code §§ 27491.–.7, 27492. For the conduct of the coroner's inquest generally, see Cal. Gov't Code §§ 27490–27513.

10. The statement did not show the length of the pay period. The defense introduced the statement to show that the defendant had been working in Oakland under her real name. This, it was argued, showed that she was not in flight and therefore that her leaving Fresno did not indicate consciousness of guilt.

BOOKING FORMS

BOOKING NO.	NAME									DATE		A.M.	TANK NO.
COUNTY	CITY	FEDERAL	ENROUTE	CASE NO.		ORDER NO.		ALIAS				P.M.	

ADDRESS		DATE OF ARREST	TIME	WHERE ARRESTED

WRITE SPECIFIC CHARGES - CODE AND SECTION

ARRESTING OFFICER		SO	PD	CONST.	C.H.P.	FED.	LOCATION

DATE OF BIRTH	PLACE OF BIRTH	DESCENT OF	CITIZEN OF	PREVIOUS ARRESTS	
				YES	NO

MARKS - SCARS - TATOOS

RACE	SEX	HAIR	EYES	HEIGHT	WEIGHT	AGE	COUNTY	STATE	US	CONDITION AT TIME OF ARREST (SOBER - DRUNK - NARCOTICS)

FORMER HOME ADDRESS	OCCUPATION
NAME AND ADDRESS OF NEAREST RELATIVE OR FRIEND	SOCIAL SECURITY NO.
ILLNESS OR INJURY AT TIME OF ARREST OR BOOKING	CALIF. DRIVER'S LICENSE NO.

EMPLOYER	(NAME)	(ADDRESS)	SELECTIVE SERVICE CARD (AGE 18-35)	YES	NO

BOOKING OFFICER	SEARCHED BY	BOOKED INTO JAIL BY

HOW ARRESTED	WARRANT	PICK-UP	TELETYPE	LETTER	TELEGRAM	RADIO	JUDICIAL DISTRICT AND JUDGE - WARRANT NO.

ADDITIONAL INFORMATION ON WARRANTS AND COMMITMENTS

PROPERTY SLIP

AMT. OF COIN	BANK CHECK	WALLET	WATCH	RING	GLASSES	LIGHTER	SUIT CASE	KEYS	PACKAGE	BED ROLL	MISCELLANEOUS

MISCELLANEOUS

TELEPHONE CALL MADE	TELEPHONE CALL NOT WANTED	O.K. FOR N.C.F.	DO NOT RELEASE

REMARKS

I HEREBY AUTHORIZE THE SHERIFF OR JAILERS TO RECEIVE AND OPEN ALL MY MAIL WHILE I AM CONFINED IN THE FRESNO COUNTY JAIL. SIGNATURE IS NOT AN ACKNOWLEDGMENT OF GUILT.	I HEREBY ACKNOWLEDGE RECEIPT OF ALL PROPERTY HELD BY THE FRESNO COUNTY JAIL DURING MY CONFINEMENT.
BY	BY

PROPERTY RELEASED BY	DATE
JAILER OR CLERK	

OFFICE COPY

Records

COUNTY OF FRESNO - SHERIFF'S DEPT.
SECURITY DIVISION

20M SETS; MOORE; P. C. #8492:11-57

BOOKING FORMS

FRESNO COUNTY SHERIFF'S DEPARTMENT
DIVISION OF IDENTIFICATION AND RECORDS
FRESNO, CALIFORNIA

Name...Classification..
  Surname   Given Name   Middle Name

Alias...

No.........................Color...Sex.........................Reference..

RIGHT HAND

(1) Thumb	(2) Index Finger	(3) Middle Finger	(4) Ring Finger	(5) Little Finger

LEFT HAND

(6) Thumb	(7) Index Finger	(8) Middle Finger	(9) Ring Finger	(10) Little Finger

IMPRESSIONS TAKEN BY

.... Signature of person fingerprinted ....
(SIGNATURE OF OFFICIAL TAKING PRINTS)

DATE

Four fingers taken simultaneously	See reverse side for description and data	Four fingers taken simultaneously
Left Hand		Right Hand

Left Thumb	Right Thumb

A reporter and a photographer from the Bee were present at the jail that evening. Josephine Chavez was received into custody and booked. She spent the night at the jail. Her lawyers had advised her not to discuss the case.

The Fresno Bee

Wednesday, May 29, 1946.

Girl Suspected Of Baby Murder Surrenders Self

Miss Josephine Chavez, 21 year old unwed mother, last night was surrendered by her attorneys to Assistant District Attorney Harold Thompson and today is booked in the Fresno County Jail on a charge of murdering the son born to her on the night of March 29th.

The girl fled on March 31st, when her mother, Mrs. Josephine Chavez, found the infant's body wrapped in a newspaper and stuffed behind the bathtub in the family home at 339 G Street.

Although she has been sought by the police since that time, Miss Chavez said she worked in an Oakland bakery under her own name since leaving Fresno, and returned here voluntarily.

Refuses Answers

Her attorneys, J. J. Nagel and Gerald W. Stutsman, refused to permit her to answer questions but agreed to meet with Thompson today to discuss the case.

A coroner's jury found the infant died of strangulation and bleeding from an untied umbilical cord but the attorneys for the girl denied she murdered the child in the following statement:

"Miss Chavez gave birth to a baby. At no time after the child's birth did she observe any life or motion of the body, and as far as she knows the baby was born dead. She did not strangle the baby, nor in any way molest it. When she left the baby she believed it was dead."

They left unexplained the charge made by the police that she wrapped the body in a newspaper and hid it behind the bathtub, and likewise had no comment to make on her reason for leaving Fresno after the discovery of the body.

Seeks To Clear Self

She returned, she said, to "clear herself" of the murder charge.

Miss Chavez and her attorneys were accompanied by the girl's half brother, Mike Banias, an army veteran of several Pacific campaigns.

Immediately after Miss Chavez fled, Banias said he believed her act may have been caused by fear of him. He said he did not suspect she was an expectant mother, and thought she may have deduced that since she had concealed her condition she would be able to dispose of the child without suspicion.

However, her attorneys today described him as "the best friend she has in the world" and declared he is backing her in her attempt to clear herself of the murder charge.

The California Penal Code provided that Josephine Chavez be taken before a judge of the police court "without unnecessary delay," and, in any event, within two days after her arrest,[11] to be informed of the charges against her and advised of her right to the aid of counsel.[12] The code pro-

---

11. Cal. Penal Code §§ 821, 825, since amended.

12. Cal. Penal Code § 858, since amended.

vided also that a preliminary examination should promptly be held in the police court to determine whether there was "sufficient cause to believe the defendant guilty of a public offense";[13] if there were not, she was entitled to be discharged. The state could present witnesses against her at the examination, and she was entitled to compulsory process to obtain witnesses in her own behalf.[14]

On May 31, she was brought before Police Judge Walton, who signed an order on the bottom of the warrant of arrest that she be held without bail pending the examination, which was scheduled for June 6.

The defense attorneys had already decided that the main defense would be based on the lack of proof that a child had been born alive, and concluded that their client could gain nothing from a preliminary examination. The California Penal Code provided that a defendant represented by counsel could waive her right to an examination.[15] On June 6 Josephine Chavez was again brought before Judge Walton. The examination was waived. As then required,[16] the judge entered an order on the back of the complaint that Josephine Chavez be held to answer the charges against her.

A defendant charged with an offense not punishable with death was entitled "as a matter of right" to be admitted to bail and released from custody before conviction, upon giving satisfactory assurance that she would appear as required.[17] A defendant charged with a capital offense, however, could not be admitted to bail "when the proof of his guilt is evident or the presumption thereof great."[18] No attempt was made to secure Josephine Chavez's release before trial. Judge Walton ordered that she be held without bail. She was never again out of custody until her final release from prison.

The police court did not have jurisdiction to conduct a trial for murder, a felony, which was within the jurisdiction of the superior court. The district attorney was required to file an information in the superior court within fifteen days after entry of an order that a defendant charged with a felony be held for trial.[19]

---

13. Cal. Penal Code § 871, since amended.

14. The conduct of the hearing is described generally in Cal. Penal Code §§ 858–83, since amended.

15. Cal. Penal Code § 860, since amended.

16. Id.

17. Cal. Penal Code § 1271, since amended.

18. Cal. Penal Code § 1270, since amended.

19. Cal. Penal Code § 809 (following examination), now contained as amended in § 739, § 860 (following waiver of examination), since amended.

BACK OF COMPLAINT

It appearing to me that the offense OF a felony, to-wit: MURDER

has been committed; and that there is sufficient cause to believe that the within named

JOSEPHINE CHAVEZ

guilty thereof, I order that he be held to answer the same, and committed to the Sheriff of the County of FRESNO and that she be admitted to bail

be held without bail

C T Walton

Police Judge

Dated June-6th , 19 46 .

No. 9010

Docket 30 3 Page 110

Police Court
CITY OF FRESNO
COUNTY OF FRESNO

The People of the State of California
Plaintiff

vs.

JOSEPHINE CHAVEZ

Defendant

COMPLAINT—CRIMINAL

Filed
Police Judge
Police Judge

JKT:DAT

CW: A. E. McCreary. (N/W)
F.P.D.

OW: J. B. Wilson
F.P.D.

Wm. Mortland
F.P.D.

Dr. Geo. H. Sciaroni
Pac. SW Bldg.
Fresno

Josephine Chavez
(Mother of Defendant)
(See Police)

Margarete Chavez
Same as above

INFORMATION

FILED
JUN 17 1946
E. _____ CLERK
BY _____ DEPUTY

No. 12031 Dept. 2

The People of the State of California
AGAINST
JOSEPHINE CHAVEZ

In the Superior Court of the State of California
In and for the County of Fresno

The District Attorney of the County of Fresno hereby accuses...

JOSEPHINE CHAVEZ

of a....felony............to-wit:..MURDER..

....

in that on or about the.....30th.....day of............March............19 46; in the County of Fresno, State of California, s he murdered one infant, a human being.

JAMES M. THUESEN
District Attorney in and for the County of Fresno,
State of California

By....Clarko Savory..
Deputy District Attorney

On June 17, the District Attorney for the County of Fresno began proceedings in the Superior Court of the State of California in and for the County of Fresno by filing an information accusing Josephine Chavez of murder. On the same day, she was brought before the superior court for arraignment.

California Penal Code

988.   Arraignment of defendant. The arraignment must be made by the court, or by the clerk or district attorney under its direction, and consists in reading the indictment or information to the defendant and delivering to him a true copy thereof, and of the endorsements thereon, including the list of witnesses, and asking him whether he pleads guilty or not guilty to the indictment or information.[20]

Both defense counsel were present. She pleaded not guilty and requested a trial by jury. The trial was scheduled to begin one week later, on Monday, June 24. Three days were set aside on the court calendar for the trial.

California Penal Code

1093.   Order of trial. The jury having been impaneled and sworn, the trial must proceed in the following order, unless otherwise directed by the court:

1.   If the indictment or information be for a felony, the clerk must read it, and state the plea of the defendant to the jury, and in cases where it charges a previous conviction, and the defendant has confessed the same, the clerk in reading it shall omit therefrom all that relates to such previous conviction. In all other cases this formality may be dispensed with.

2.   The district attorney, or other counsel for the people, must open the cause and offer the evidence in support of the charge.

3.   The defendant or his counsel may then open the defense, and offer his evidence in support thereof.

4.   The parties may then respectively offer rebutting testimony only, unless the court, for good reason, in furtherance of justice, permit them to offer evidence upon their original case.

5.   When the evidence is concluded, unless the case is submitted to the jury on either side, or on both sides, without argument, the district attorney, or other counsel for the people, and counsel for the defendant, may argue the case to the court and jury; the district attorney, or other counsel for the people, opening the argument and having the right to close.

[20] Substantially unchanged.

6. The judge may then charge the jury, and must do so on any points of law pertinent to the issue, if requested by either party; and he may state the testimony, and may comment on the failure of the defendant to explain or deny by his testimony any evidence or facts in the case against him, whether the defendant testifies or not, and he may make such comment on the evidence and the testimony and credibility of any witness as in his opinion is necessary for the proper determination of the case and he may declare the law. If the charge be not given in writing, it must be taken down by the phonographic reporter.[21]

Mother Goes On Trial
For Murder Of Newborn Baby

A jury is being selected today in Superior Judge Dan F. Conway's court, to try Josephine Chavez, 21 year old unwed mother on a charge of murdering her infant child March 29th and stuffing the body, wrapped in newspapers, behind a bathtub.

Miss Chavez, who fled her home March 30th, has pleaded not guilty and, through her attorneys, maintained she was unaware of life in the child when it was born in the home of her mother, Mrs. Josephine Chavez, 339 G Street.

Body Found By Mother

The body was found by her mother. She said she was unaware of the birth of the child to her daughter, and notified authorities immediately. Miss Chavez fled and was unheard of for approximately a month, when she surrendered to the district attorney. She said she believed the child was dead when born.

District Attorney James M. Thuesen asserted an autopsy performed by Dr. George H. Sciaroni indicated the baby was strangled to death. Dr. Sciaroni declared this might have been done by holding the lips of the child together. He will be one of the principal witnesses for the prosecution.

Circumstantial Evidence Cited

Indications were that a jury would not be impaneled before late today. Both the prosecution and defense attorneys questioned prospective jurors closely on their feelings toward circumstantial evidence. Each side can exercise 20 peremptory challenges in the selection of the jury.

Thuesen said he will not ask for the death penalty. He has submitted instructions to the court on both first degree murder, with a recommendation by the jurors, and second degree murder.

---

[21] Since amended. On comment by the court on a defendant's failure to testify, see p. 59 n.30 below.

Miss Chavez showed no emotion when she appeared in the courtroom. She was dressed in attractive blue, print dress, with brown shoes and stockings and wore a simple gold necklace.

Her mother, subpœnaed as a prosecution witness, was in the rear of the courtroom when the trial commenced. She will testify about finding the body and notifying the authorities.

———

The state's case was straightforward. As a policeman involved in the case put it, "Jim Thuesen just put the baby in the toilet and rested."

Mother Tells Of Finding Dead Body Of Baby

Spectators filled every seat and lined the walls in the courtroom of Superior Judge Dan F. Conway today as Mrs. Josephine P. Chavez testified as the first witness for the state in the trial of her unwed daughter, Josephine Chavez, 21, accused of slaying her new born child by strangulation the night of March 28th in the family home.

Through an interpreter, Mrs. Chavez declared she learned about a month before the child was born that her daughter was pregnant but there never was a discussion of the situation. She said that the morning before the dead baby was found Josephine arose about 9 o'clock and complained of a headache and stomach trouble, but that she was well enough to help her sister, Lupe, clean the house.

Goes To Carnival

"Josephine asked her brother, Mike, to take her to the carnival that night," said Mrs. Chavez, "and they got home some time about midnight. The next morning I happened to look under the bathtub and found the baby, wrapped in a newspaper."

"I told Lupe I had found the baby in the bathroom," said Mrs. Chavez. "A little while before that she and Josephine had an argument, but I didn't know what it was about.

"Josephine got ready and went to town with my son. She never said goodbye or anything. Her other little baby wanted to go along with her, but Lupe would not let her take the child."

Has Another Child

Mrs. Chavez disclosed the other baby, a year and a half old boy, was born before Josephine was employed in the Oakland shipyards. Thuesen said the child also is illegitimate.

Under cross examination, Mrs. Chavez said Josephine's brother had asked her to go to the carnival earlier in the day. She said her attention was drawn to the bundle under the bathtub when she saw a foot sticking out.

During the lengthy examination of Mrs. Chavez, she declared her daughter on the morning following the birth of the child asked for an aspirin. She said Josephine, after helping with the house work, lay down.

The mother said that when she questioned her daughter about the body of the infant the girl went into a closet, put on her coat and fled from the home. Josephine returned home about three weeks ago and surrendered.

Dr. George H. Sciaroni, who conducted an autopsy on the baby's body, testified he found what appeared to be burns on the top of the head, left jaw and under the right ear, probably caustic in nature. He said the umbilical cord had not been tied but looked as though it had been torn.

"The lips were swollen and dark and so was the tongue," said the physician. "This indicates some pressure had been applied to lips and side of the face.

"The baby had the appearance of Negro blood from the texture of the hair and color of the skin, although I made no blood test."

Dr. Sciaroni attributed death to suffocation and hemorrhage, and said it was possible the burns could have been caused by contact with a caustic. He said the condition of the lungs and other vital organs was normal and that the baby was born alive.

Defense attorney sought to break down his testimony by inferring the physician did not use recognized medical tests. He admitted death might have been due to a brain hemorrhage.

The prosecution is expected to complete its case today and the defense anticipates concluding tomorrow in time to submit the case to the jury late in the afternoon.

Members of the jury are:

George M. Pauls, 4826 Nevada Avenue; William E. Ferguson, Orange Cove; Ray D. Wharton, 915 Clinton Avenue; Mrs. Mamie C. Bacon, 2645 Merced Street; Mrs. Healon Williams, 1521 Amador Street; Mrs. Anna Shireff, 1479 Wilson Avenue; Vera Pettitt, 1266 Poplar Avenue; Thomas Cooper, 5824 Van Ness Boulevard; Earl W. Nevins, Route 1, Box 71, Clovis; Jesse M. Peoples, 1048 Simpson Avenue; Catherine Pellegrino, 1443 Belmont Avenue; and Mrs. Myrtle L. Brown, 458 Thesta Street.

When the state rested, defense counsel made a motion for dismissal on the ground that the state had failed to establish its case. Judge Conway denied the motion.

Defense counsel opened with a statement explaining the defense to the jury and then presented evidence. The defendant did not contest that the baby was hers. She took the stand and described the circumstances of the birth. She did not think that the baby was about to be born when she went into the bathroom; she had eaten pickles that day and thought that the cramps were a stomachache attributable to the pickles. She had not intended that the child die, but had been surprised by the sudden delivery. The major witness for the defense was Dr. Clarence D. Newell, a pathologist at the county hospital, who criticized the methods which Dr. Sciaroni had used in the autopsy and said that Dr. Sciaroni's findings did not prove that the baby had been born alive.

The Fresno Bee

Wednesday, June 26, 1946.

Jury Will Get Baby Slaying Case Late Today

The murder trial of Josephine Chavez, 21 year old unmarried Fresno mother, accused of killing her infant child in the early morning hours of March 30th, will go to the jury in Superior Judge Dan F. Conway's court late today.

The defense closed this morning after an attack upon the medical testimony of Dr. George H. Sciaroni, autopsy surgeon, designed to cast doubt upon the prosecution theory the infant was born alive. The theory that Miss Chavez intended to go to Los Angeles to have the child was emphasized with the testimony of her half brother that he had planned to take her to Los Angeles.

She held up under the rapid fire cross examination of District Attorney James M. Thuesen, who sought to show the baby was alive at birth.

Pathologist Testifies

Dr. Clarence D. Newell, Fresno pathologist, testified that it is possible for gas to develop and cause an expansion of the lungs, but under cross examination he admitted that if the infant was born alive and allowed to remain in the toilet bowl, where it was born, for seven minutes, as admitted by the defendant, it would have died.

Dr. Newell mentioned a number of scientific tests desirable in determining whether the child was born alive, among them cutting open the heart and head and removal of the stomach. He said many children are born with hearts incapable of sustaining life.

Identifies Father

Against repeated objections by defense attorneys, Miss Chavez identified the father as Bobby Rodriguez, who lives near the Chandler Municipal Airport.

"As far as I know, the baby was Mexican," said Miss Chavez under cross examination. "He might have had some Indian blood. I'd rather not say his name since he recently was married."

Thuesen said he insisted upon the name of the father for impeachment purposes and intends to prove no such relationship existed. He said the autopsy indicated the possibility there might be some Negro blood involved.

Miss Chavez admitted she has another child about two years of age, born while she was unmarried. She said she planned to go to Los Angeles early in April to stay with friends until the second child was born.

Concealed Pregnancy

"I never told anyone about my pregnancy and wore a girdle for six months to conceal the fact from my family," said the girl. "I wanted to keep it from my family for I already had one baby that way and did not want to bring further disgrace."

Relating the circumstances surrounding the birth of the child, Miss Chavez explained, "It all happened so fast I was taken by surprise. I looked at the baby and it was limp and there was no sign of life. I laid the baby on the floor and later wrapped it in a newspaper and put it under the bathtub.

"I did not know what to do then, for I did not want my sister, Lupe, to know about it."

Baby Is Found

It was on March 31st, Miss Chavez explained, that her sister, Lupe, told her the baby had been found by their mother. She said Lupe told her to pack up and get out.

Miss Chavez testified her brother, who was not aware of the baby's birth, took her to town about 11 A.M. and that she went to Oakland the same day.

After the defense rested, defense counsel made a motion for a directed verdict of acquittal. Judge Conway denied the motion.

(The Fresno Bee, June 26, 1946, continued)

Complete Arguments

Arguments were completed early in the afternoon after which Judge Conway instructed the jury at length on the law pertaining to the case.

District Attorney James M. Thuesen submitted instructions covering first degree, second degree murder and manslaughter.

He said in his opinion manslaughter is the least the prosecution could ask. In his opening argument, he flayed the young mother for alleged neglect in failure to call for help, permitting the child to be born in the toilet and allowing it to remain there.

G. W. Stutsman, one of the defense counsel, opening the argument for the defense, criticised the method employed by Dr. Sciaroni in his autopsy and concentrated upon reasonable doubt which he contends exists as to whether the baby was born dead or alive.

The closing defense argument was given by J. J. Nagel.

Counsel for the state and for the defense submitted requests for instructions. Judge Conway instructed the jury.[22]

INSTRUCTIONS

FILED
JUN 26 1946
E. DUSENBERRY CLERK
BY _____ DEPUTY

\# 12031

IN THE SUPERIOR COURT OF THE STATE OF CALIFORNIA,

IN AND FOR THE COUNTY OF FRESNO.

--:--

THE PEOPLE OF THE STATE OF CALIFORNIA, Plaintiff, vs. JOSEPHINE CHAVEZ, Defendant.	No. 12031 Dept. II INSTRUCTIONS

GENTLEMEN OF THE JURY:

You are instructed that the defendant, is charged in the information, which has been read to you by the Clerk of this Court, with the crime therein alleged to have been committed at the time and in the manner therein specified.

Upon the charge in the information the defendant has been arraigned before this Court, and has entered a plea of not guilty thereto, and upon the issue thus raised you have been selected and sworn as jurors to determine from the evidence adduced before you on this trial, under the instructions that the Court will now give you as to the law, whether the defendant is guilty or innocent of the offense charged.

---

22. See Cal. Penal Code § 1093.5, added in 1957: "In any criminal case which is being tried before the court with a jury, all requests for instructions on points of law must be made to the court and all proposed instructions must be delivered to the court before commencement of argument. Before the commencement of the argument, the court, on request of counsel, must: (1) decide whether to give, refuse, or modify the proposed instructions; (2) decide which instructions shall be given in addition to those proposed, if any; and (3) advise counsel of all instructions to be given. However, if, during the argument, issues are raised which have not been covered by instructions given or refused, the court may, on request of counsel, give additional instructions on the subject matter thereof."

INSTRUCTIONS—Continued

INSTRUCTION NO._____

If you are convinced to a moral certainty and beyond a reasonable doubt that the defendant's child was born wholly alive, and had established a circulation independent of its mother, but conclude from the evidence that the death of the child resulted from accidental causes, then you must acquit the defendant.

Requested by the defendant and
Given _____
                      Judge.

Given as modified _____
                      Judge.

Refused _____
                      Judge.

INSTRUCTION NO._____

The defendant cannot be found guilty of manslaughter until the prosecution has proved to a moral certainty and beyond a reasonable doubt, First, that the defendant's child was born wholly alive and had established a circulation independent of its mother, and Second, that the death of the baby resulted from the failure of the defendant to exercise due caution and circumspection under all of the attendant circumstances.

Requested by the defendant and
Given _____
                      Judge.

Given as modified _____
                      Judge.

Refused _____ as covered _____
                      Judge.

INSTRUCTIONS—Continued

INSTRUCTION NO. _____

Accordingly, as you may find and determine the facts to be, you may bring in either one of the following verdicts:

We, the Jury, find the defendant guilty of Murder of the first degree, and recommend that she be imprisoned for life;

or

We, the Jury, find the defendant guilty of Murder of the second degree;

or

We, the Jury, find the defendant guilty of Manslaughter;

or

We, the Jury, find the defendant not guilty.

Whatever your verdict may be, it must be concurred in by all of the jurors and signed by your Foreman.

_____ Conway
                Judge

_____

The jury was out for 70 minutes.

VERDICT

FILED
JUN 26 1946
E. DUSENBERRY, CLERK
BY _____ DEPUTY

In the Superior Court of the State of California
In and for the County of Fresno

The People of the State of California, *Plaintiff,* *vs.* JOSEPHINE CHAVEZ *Defendant.*	No. 12031 Dept. 2 **VERDICT** P. C., SEC. 1151

WE, the jury in the above entitled action, find the defendant _____ JOSEPHINE CHAVEZ _____

_____ guilty OF MANSLAUGHTER _____

June 25 1946   *Ray D Wharton*

Foreman.

Unwed Mother Is Found Guilty Of Slaying Baby

A jury of five men and seven women late yesterday found Miss Josephine Chavez, 21 year old unwed mother, guilty of manslaughter for the killing of her newborn baby during the early morning hours of March 30th.

Superior Judge Dan F. Conway continued the case until Saturday at 10 A.M. for sentence. The offense carries punishment of from one to 10 years in the State Institution for Women at Tehachapi.

Gerald W. Stutsman and J. J. Nagel, defense attorneys, announced they will petition for a new trial.

Accepts Verdict Calmly

Miss Chavez calmly accepted the verdict which was reached after one hour and 10 minutes of deliberation by the jury.

She talked with her attorneys briefly before she was led back to the jail.

The verdict allows either of two conclusions—that she took the life of the infant almost immediately after its birth in the bathroom in the home of her mother at 339 G Street, or that its death was attributable to criminal negligence.

District Attorney James M. Thuesen argued that her admission she left the child unattended for approximately 10 minutes, and then allowed it to lie on the linoleum covered floor without covering during the 45 degree temperature of the early morning hours amounted to criminal negligence.

Termed Murder

He also argued that the taking of the life under California law is murder, despite the fact that the infant lived only a few minutes. He relied on the expert testimony of Dr. George H. Sciaroni, the autopsy surgeon, that the baby was born alive.

The defense contended the baby was still born and attacked the testimony of Dr. Sciaroni. Stutsman and Nagel argued that life within the child was highly problematical.

Miss Chavez testified that after the infant was born she could observe no signs of life, and that she laid the child on the floor. She said she then wrapped the infant in a newspaper and placed it behind the bathtub.

She is the mother of another illegitimate child approximately 18 months old.

The prosecution argued her asserted unfitness to care for her older child by citing her conduct after the birth of the second baby. According to Miss Chavez' testimony, she got up for breakfast the following morning, helped with the housework and, after resting a while, went to a carnival with her brother and the following day left for Oakland after being confronted by her sister with the dead body of her baby.

Josephine Chavez remained in the county jail. On June 29, Judge Conway pronounced judgment.

California Penal Code

3200. Establishment of Institution for Women. There is and shall continue to be within the State an institution for the punishment, treatment, supervision, custody and care of females convicted of felonies to be known as "The California Institution for Women."

The Fresno Bee

Saturday, June 29, 1946.

Miss Chavez Gets Prison Term In Child Death Case

Superior Judge Dan F. Conway today sentenced Miss Josephine Chavez, 21 year old unwed Fresno mother, to the California Institution for Women at Tehachapi for manslaughter resulting from the death of her infant child in the home of her mother, Mrs. Josephine Chavez, last March 29th.

Gerald W. Stutsman and J. J. Nagel, defense attorneys, announced they will appeal the decision on the legal question of whether a human being was born.

Cite Legal Authorities

"It has never been decided by our higher courts at what stage during the birth of a child it becomes a living human being, which must be fully proven before a conviction of homicide can be sustained," Stutsman and Nagel said. "The general, common law in America and England requires that it be proven that the child was wholly born alive and had established a circulation independent and apart from its mother.

"It is our opinion that if the California courts accept this general rule of law, there has been no substantial evidence introduced in this case to support the charge that the child in question became a living human being."

The prosecution not only maintained a human being was born, but that it had life, and relied upon the medical testimony of Dr. George H. Sciaroni, the autopsy surgeon, who testified the infant was alive and normal in every respect.

Believed Child Was Dead

Confronted by her sister and mother the day following the birth of the child, Miss Chavez left Fresno and was in Oakland for more than a month before she returned and surrendered herself to the authorities. She testified she believed the child to be dead when she wrapped it in a newspaper and stuffed the body behind the bathtub in the Chavez home.

The prosecution contended the defendant was guilty of criminal negligence in leaving the child unattended for several minutes following the birth before she inspected the infant to see whether or not it had life.

Under the California law, Miss Chavez must serve one calendar year before she is eligible to go before the Tehachapi prison board to have the length of her confinement determined.

3201.   Purpose. The purpose of said institution shall be to provide custody, care, protection, industrial, vocational, and other training, and reformatory help, for women confined therein.[23]

Defense counsel filed notice of appeal to the District Court of Appeal for the Fourth Appellate District, accompanied by an application stating the grounds of appeal and a request for the transcription of the trial reporter's notes.

[23] Unchanged.

JUDGMENT

IN THE

Superior Court of the State of California
In and for the County of Fresno

The Court Convened

Fresno, Calif.,................June 29........., 194.6

Present: Hon.........Dan F. Conway................Judge·

................Ray Esheim........ Deputy Sheriff

................A. F. Gregory..... Deputy·Clerk

................J. Price.................Reporter

The People of the State of California
Against

JOSEPHINE CHAVEZ

No. 12031

Judgment

her
The District Attorney with the defendant and ~~his~~ *counsel* G. W. Stutsman and
J. J. Kagel .... *came into court, this being the time heretofore fixed*
for rendering judgment herein. The defendant was duly informed by the Court of the nature
of the .... information .... *filed against* her *for the crime*
of .... MRUDER ...., *committed on the*
30th *day of* .... March ...., 1946, as charged in this
information

...... and *of* her *arraignment and plea of* NOT GUILTY as charged; and of
her trial June 24th, 1946 before a jury of Women and women of her
own selection; and of the verdict of the jury finding the defendant
guilty of the crime of MANSLAUGHTER

The defendant was then asked if____s.he had any legal cause to show why judgment should not be pronounced against____her____ to which defendant replied that____she had____none

And no sufficient cause being shown or appearing to the Court, thereupon the Court renders its judgment:

THAT WHEREAS, The said ____JOSEPHINE CHAVEZ____ *having* BEEN FOUND GUILTY ____*of the crime of* MANSLAUGHTER____

IT *IS THEREFORE ORDERED, ADJUDGED AND DECREED, That the said* ____JOSEPHINE CHAVEZ____ *be punished by imprisonment in the California State Prison at* detained in the CALIFORNIA INSTITUTION FOR WOMEN AT TEHACHAPI

Until legally discharged. The defendant was then remanded to the custody of the Sheriff of the County of Fresno, to be by him delivered into the custody of the proper officers of said State Prison at ____Tehachapi____*, California.*

Josephine Chavez's precise sentence of imprisonment was to be determined by the Adult Authority of the Department of Corrections.[24] The maximum sentence that could be imposed was imprisonment for ten years.[25] Both the district attorney and the trial judge were required to file a statement of views regarding sentence, to aid the Adult Authority.[26] The district attorney's statement, dated July 5, recited the circumstances of the crime and added: "This defendant has a reputation of being a member of a Pachuco gang, and showed little remorse or consideration for the baby." Before judgment was pronounced in court on June 29, Judge Conway asked if the defendant would provide information that he could use to make a recommendation on sentence. Defense counsel, preferring not to disclose information which might prejudice the defendant on appeal or at a new trial if the appeal were successful, stated that she preferred to give such information directly to the sentencing authority. Accordingly, on August 1, Judge Conway certified that he had no information "of the history or antecedents of said defendant and [had] no recommendation to make in the premises."

The Attorney General of California and defense counsel submitted briefs and argued the case before the district court of appeal. On January 10, 1947, the court affirmed the judgment of the superior court, and filed its opinion, p. 1 above. On February 13, 1947, the Adult Authority determined that Josephine Chavez's sentence of imprisonment should be six years. She was released on parole on February 16, 1949, and was finally discharged from custody on July 11, 1950.

While she was imprisoned, Josephine Chavez completed her high school education and was trained as a laboratory technician. After her release, Dr. Newel hired her as a technician at the county hospital, where she did good work. While she was working there, she voluntarily made some payments to her defense counsel, whose original fee had not covered the costs of her defense. Later, she undertook the care of her first child. She married and had several more children. The California Corrections Agency has had no further contact with her.

---

24. Cal. Penal Code § 3020, since repealed. The Adult Authority was abolished in 1977. Its authority and powers are exercised by the Board of Prison Terms, Cal. Penal Code § 5078.

25. Cal. Penal Code § 193, since amended (involuntary manslaughter punishable by imprisonment for two, three, or four years).

26. Cal. Penal Code § 1192a, since repealed. Following conviction of a felony for which probation is authorized, a probation officer makes an investigation and reports the findings to the court before sentence is imposed. Cal. Penal Code § 1203(b). (See presentence reports, pp. 721–39 below.) See Cal. Penal Code § 1203.01, providing that the judge and district attorney may file a statement of their views for transmission to the Department of Corrections.

REMITTITUR

IN THE

District Court of Appeal, Fourth Appellate District, State of California

FILED
FEB 18 1947
E. QUEENBERRY CLERK
BY .... DEPUTY

4 Crim. No. 579

12031 - -

The People of the State of
California,

     Plaintiff and Respondent,

vs.

Josephine Chavez,

     Defendant and Appellant.

On Appeal from the Superior Court in

and for the County of   Fresno.

The above entitled cause having been heretofore fully argued, and submitted and taken under advisement, and all and singular the law and premises having been fully considered,

It is Ordered, Adjudged, and Decreed by the Court that the

-----Judgment-----

of the Superior Court in and for the County of   Fresno

in the above entitled cause, be and the same is   hereby   affirmed.

E. J. VERDECKBERG
I, M. C. VAN ALLEN, Clerk of the District Court of Appeal, Fourth Appellate District, State of California, do hereby certify that the foregoing is a true copy of an original judgment entered in the above entitled cause on the   10th   day of   January,   , 19 47, and now remaining of record in my office.

Witness my hand and the seal of the Court, affixed at my office, this   10th   day of   February,   , A. D. 19 47.

E. J. VERDECKBERG
M. C. VAN ALLEN, Clerk

By   *Lloyd E. Hidden*
                     Deputy

25. A year and a day. Events (or verbs, if you like) are as hard to pin down as objects (nouns). See L. Carroll, Through the Looking Glass, ch. 6, at 118 (1902 ed.). According to the common law, a death that occurred more than a year and a day after the act that (so it appeared) caused it was not a homicide, or at least not a homicide for which the actor could be held criminally responsible. Stephen said that this was "an arbitrary rule for criminal purposes" which reflected the fact that the connection between an injury to a person and his death is generally obscured by the passage of time. 3 J. Stephen, A History of the Criminal Law of England 8 (1883).[27] The rule has been followed in most of the states and in some has been enacted by statute. The history and rationale of the rule are discussed in Commonwealth v. Ladd, 166 A.2d 501 (Pa.1960).

Should the rule be regarded as specifying an element of the crime of homicide or as prescribing a rule of evidence or procedure? Does it make any difference? In *Ladd*, the court concluded that the rule was one of evidence, which the court could (and did) abolish "without being guilty of judicial legislation."

> The rule does not change the legal concept of the facts of the case but only prevents process being had upon them under certain conditions. It should not be considered part of the definition of the crime any more than should the rule of venue: it is no less murder that prosecution of it may be had in county A but not in county B. It is clear . . . that the reason for the rule lay in the primitive state of medical knowledge at the time, or it may have been . . . that it was designed to mitigate the rigor of the old law that exacted a life for murder and manslaughter indiscriminately.

> . . . A rule becomes dry when its supporting reason evaporates: cessante ratione legis cessat lex. There is now no more reason for a rule of a year and a day than there is for one of a hundred days or a thousand and one nights.

> . . . A modern rule should be based on causation in the light of current knowledge. Society is free to prosecute murderers without a statutory limitation, and it is possible that evidence and witnesses may be lost during a long interval between crime and trial. It is therefore not a strange idea to put no restriction of time upon the death of the

---

27. Sir James Fitzjames Stephen (1829–1894) was an outstanding member of the nineteenth-century English bar. He was a judge of the Court of Queen's Bench from 1879 to 1891. He was a prolific writer, and wrote articles on a wide variety of subjects. His book Liberty, Equality, Fraternity (1873), see pp. 768–87 below, displays his utilitarian philosophy coupled with conservative and antidemocratic attitudes. Aside from that book, his major works were in the area of criminal law. He was a leading proponent of codification of the criminal law. A History of the Criminal Law of England remains the standard work in the field. It is cited hereafter as Stephen, History.

Stephen may have had another connection with criminal law, of an entirely different kind. For an elaborate argument that Stephen's son, James Kenneth Stephen, who was a friend and adviser to His Royal Highness the Duke of Clarence, was Jack the Ripper, see M. Harrison, Clarence (1972).

victim and to require only proof of causation of conventional quality at the trial.

Id. at 506.[28]

The rule has been abolished judicially in Massachusetts as well. Commonwealth v. Lewis, 409 N.E.2d 771 (Mass.1980). The court observed: "[T]he rule appears anachronistic upon a consideration of the advances of medical and related science in solving etiological problems as well as in sustaining or prolonging life in the face of trauma or disease. . . . Thus the relatively short time limit is seen as not only capricious but as senselessly indulgent toward homicidal malefactors. It is reckoned a sufficient safeguard for defendants that the prosecution, quite apart from the rule, must establish the connection between act and death by proof beyond a reasonable doubt." Id. at 773. It has also been abolished in New Jersey. State v. Young, 390 A.2d 556 (N.J.1978). Reasoning that the rule was "a constituent element of the crime of murder, not a mere rule of evidence," id. at 559, the court concluded that its abolition could not be applied retroactively to sustain the defendant's conviction for murder, even though he had not relied on the rule. The Massachusetts court agreed that the change in the law should be prospective, but for different reasons. *Lewis*, above, 409 N.E.2d at 775.

The year-and-a-day rule has been abolished or questioned in about half the states, including the vast majority of those in which the rule has recently been considered. See Rogers v. Tennessee, 532 U.S. 451, 463 (2001) (5–4). In Commonwealth v. Casanova, 708 N.E.2d 86 (Mass.1999), the court rejected the defendant's argument that, the rule having been abolished, due process of law required that it be replaced with some other rule lest a person be indefinitely under the threat of a prosecution for homicide. The court said:

> Institution of a new time period between injury and death beyond which a defendant may not be prosecuted for murder is appropriate only if there is a time past which there is no significant number of cases in which the prosecution could satisfy its burden of proof. We have no basis for estimating what such a time may be, if, indeed, one exists at all. Although it will undoubtedly be difficult in many cases for the prosecution to prove causation where death is remote in time from the allegedly precipitating injury, in cases where this link can be proved, such as where a slow-acting poison is used or where a person purposely infects another with a virus such as HIV, prosecution should not be barred by some arbitrary time limit.

708 N.E.2d at 90. The California and Washington legislatures at one time adopted a three-year-and-a-day rule; both now have no such limitation.

---

28. See also People v. Brengard, 191 N.E. 850 (N.Y.1934), in which the court, relying on the *statutory* definition of murder, affirmed a conviction of first degree murder for a death resulting from a bullet wound inflicted almost four years earlier.

The Maryland Court of Special Appeals, on the other hand, concluded that if the year-and-a-day rule was to be abolished, it should be done by the legislature:

> It is patent that major advances have been made in medical science and that improvements have been attained in scientific crime detection. The trier of fact need not, as did the early English juries, find a verdict upon its own knowledge or merely give expression to the community conviction on the question, but today may place reliance on the testimony of expert witnesses. But even so, we are not prepared to say that the rule of a year and a day is presently anachronistic, or that such period, after which death is conclusively presumed to result from natural causes, is no longer realistic. Abolition of the rule may well result in imbalance between the adequate protection of society and justice for the individual accused, and there would remain a need for some form of limitation on causation.

State v. Brown, 318 A.2d 257, 261 (Md.Ct.Spec.App.1974). The Maryland legislature subsequently abolished the rule. Md. Code Ann. art. 27, § 415 (2002 Supp.).

In United States v. Chase, 18 F.3d 1166 (4th Cir.1994), the defendant had struck the victim on the side of her head. She survived but suffered from epileptic seizures caused by the blow and, after 17 years, died of a seizure. The defendant was convicted of murder. On appeal, the court reversed the conviction. It said that the year-and-a-day rule was a "substantive legal principle" that had been applied by the Supreme Court, albeit more than 100 years ago (Ball v. United States, 140 U.S. 118 (1891)), and not abrogated by Congress and that, although the court acknowledged reasons for rejecting the rule, it is "alive and controlling, until Congress or the Supreme Court instructs us otherwise." Id. at 1173. In Rogers v. Tennessee, above, the defendant claimed that the retroactive abolition of the year-and-a-day rule to his case violated the Due Process Clause. Upholding the defendant's conviction, the Court concluded that abolition of the rule by the state court was neither unexpected nor indefensible. The rule, it said, "is widely viewed as an outdated relic of the common law." 532 U.S. at 462.

26. Statutes of limitations. As the passage from *Ladd*, note 25 above, indicates, the year-and-a-day rule should be distinguished from statutes of limitations, which provide that a crime must be prosecuted, if at all, within a certain period after its commission. There is typically no statute of limitations applicable to the more extreme forms of criminal homicide. So long as there is compliance with the relevant statute of limitations, if the year-and-a-day rule precludes a prosecution for homicide, it may be possible to prosecute the person thought to be responsible for the death for some other offense, such as assault, arising out of the same facts. See, e.g., Ball v. United States, 140 U.S. 118, 133, 136 (1891).

2. THE PROBLEM OF PROOF

English case — *the Queen*

Regina v. Onufrejczyk *(if it was the King it would say RES v. ...)*

[1955] 1 Q.B. 388, [1955] 1 All E.R. 247 (C.C.A.)

■ LORD GODDARD, C.J. The appellant, a Pole, who has been in this country since 1947, was convicted before Oliver J. at the last assizes for Swansea of the murder of his partner, another Pole, named Sykut. The trial lasted for some 12 days and was summed up with meticulous care by the judge, who analysed the evidence in what I think I might describe as a masterly fashion, and the principal question argued on this appeal is whether there was proof of what the law calls a corpus delicti. For the remarkable fact about this case—and it has remained remarkable and unexplained—is that the body of Sykut who was last seen, so far as anybody knows, on December 14, 1953, has completely disappeared, and there is no trace whatever either of him or his clothes or his ashes.

Rule — It has been submitted to us that unless the body can be found or an account given of the death, the law is that there is no proof of a corpus delicti. Corpus delicti means, first, that a crime has been committed, that is to say, that the man is dead, and that his death has been caused by a crime. . . .

Now it is perfectly clear that there is apparently no reported case in English law where a man has been convicted of murder when there has been no trace of the body at all. But it is equally clear that the fact of death, like any other fact, can be proved by circumstantial evidence, that is to say, evidence of facts which lead to one conclusion, provided that the jury are satisfied and are warned that it must lead to one conclusion only. Oliver J. began and ended his summing up to the jury with the direction which he took from Rex v. Horry[29] before the New Zealand Court of Appeal, saying that it was as clear a direction as he could give. The headnote of that case, which he took as stating the law, is as follows: "At the trial of a person charged with murder, the fact of death is provable by circumstantial evidence, notwithstanding that neither the body nor any trace of the body has been found and that the accused has made no confession of any participation in the crime. Before he can be convicted, the fact of death should be proved by such circumstances as render the commission of the crime moral-

29.   [1952] N.Z.L.R. 111.

ly certain and leave no ground for reasonable doubt: the circumstantial evidence should be so cogent and compelling as to convince a jury that upon no rational hypothesis other than murder can the facts be accounted for."

Speaking for myself I entirely agree with that as a statement of the law except that I would not have used the words "morally certain"; I would prefer "such circumstances as render the commission of the crime certain." It is always a pity, when dealing with evidence, to use epithets either to increase or decrease its value; and when cases in the books use expressions such as "a high degree of certainty" or "strong evidence" and so on, they really add nothing to what the law requires. The law requires a case to be proved, and a jury is warned and told that its members have to be satisfied on the evidence that the crime is proved, that the prisoner is guilty of the crime; and they should be told that if when they have heard the evidence they are not satisfied, and do not feel sure that the crime has been committed or that the prisoner has committed the crime, their verdict should be "not guilty." Let us leave out of account, if we can, any expression such as "giving the prisoner the benefit of the doubt." It is not a question of giving him the benefit of the doubt, for if the jury are left with any degree of doubt that the prisoner is guilty, the case has not been proved.

Oliver J., having read that statement of the law contained in the headnote to Rex v. Horry, said to the jury: "It is indeed a grave step to find a murder proved when there is no body; but it is not the law, and I do not believe it has ever been the law—it is certainly not the law today—that if a body can be got rid of so that no trace of it can be found, a murderer who has done so is not to be convicted. That is not the law. But, of course, the burden of proving everything against the man is on the Crown. There is no burden on him to disprove anything. I think the most helpful way I can bring this to your minds is to say this. If Onufrejczyk had not given evidence at all in this case, and all you had was the case for the Crown, would you be satisfied with that case unanswered, the case for the Crown? If you would, then you will proceed. But if you were, for instance, to come to the conclusion that the case for the Crown standing uncontradicted was not good enough—suppose you took that view—then you need not go on to consider Onufrejczyk's explanation; there is no burden on him." A little later, before turning to the details of this remarkable case, the judge said: "If he did not die by natural causes, he was killed. Members of the jury, if he was killed his body was concealed or destroyed and has not been found. If he is dead and was killed and the body was destroyed or concealed, he was murdered, was he not? That is the point. I want you to apply your minds to that set of circumstances, and decide for yourselves whether, in the light of those facts, and many more to which I shall have to draw your attention, you can say that you are satisfied that no rational hypothesis except that he is dead, dead by violence, is open. If you are driven to that conclusion, that would be a verdict of murder; but if you think that that would be going too far, and that you could not safely say that no rational explanation of his death except murder could be conceived, why then it will mean that you have a doubt about it, and you will acquit him." I do not

think that [defense counsel], for whose assistance and forceful and temper-
ate argument in this case the court is much indebted, would quarrel with
that direction of the judge, which seems to me as ample and as fair to the
accused man as it is possible to conceive.

. . .

facts

The case against the prisoner was this: He and Sykut had a farm. The
farm was a failure, and the appellant had come to the end of his resources.
He was in dire need of money; of that there cannot be any doubt, for his
own letters show it. He was trying to borrow money from this person and
that, that relation and near friend; and he failed every time. He had
actually got to the point when he was obviously considering fraud, for he
was hoping to find a valuer who would overvalue the farm so that he might
be able to raise more money on mortgage from his bank. Meanwhile, Sykut
wanted to break off his association with the appellant. There was a
suggestion that he should be paid out. Sykut had invested his money in the
farm and was willing to sell his share in it for £ 700 if he could get it from
the appellant; otherwise, Sykut had said, the farm must be put up for sale.
They had been to Mr. Roberts, a solicitor of Llandilo, and their difficulties
had been discussed before him. There was evidence—though for myself I do
not think that it was anything like so strong or convincing, as was much of
the other evidence, as to point towards murder—that the men had quarrelled; but by December 14 nothing had happened for any conclusion to be
reached between the two men about the sale of the farm. Whether or not
the appellant had at that time any money beyond perhaps a few shillings or
a few pounds it seems clear that he had nothing at all to enable him to buy
out his partner. He, the appellant, was very anxious to avoid the sale by
auction and wanted to get the whole farm, because presumably he thought
that if he had the whole of it he could make a satisfactory business out of
it.

On December 14 Sykut disappeared, not only from Carmarthenshire,
not only from England but, so far as is known, from the face of the earth.
Letters came from Poland from his wife after his complete disappearance
when there would have been ample time for him to have got back to Poland
and to have got into touch with his friends, which would seem to show that
he had not gone back to Poland; and the last person who is known to have
seen Sykut is the appellant.

The appellant's activities after December 14 were certainly very remarkable. There was evidence, and very strong evidence, that the appellant
must have posted a letter to a Polish woman living not very far away not
later than a quarter to five, or possibly five o'clock, on December 18. In
that letter he said: "My case is already completed, but I must if only for a
few hours pop in to London to take from my acquaintances money. I gave
my partner the gross of the money"—I suppose that means the larger part
of the money—"because I borrowed for a few weeks, only I must sell what
is possible. So beg you very much to help me in this matter and I will be
very grateful, at the moment this is all for now, the rest we talk over when
Mrs. comes over. Beg you to inquire whether it is possible to sell the

poultry alive before the holidays, as I must have at least part of the money to begin something and may be some of the cattle. Hand kisses, expecting as soon as possible to see you because my partner is leaving for 14 days and might change his mind. Please don't wait a moment because it might be too late." There he is saying that he has fixed up matters with his partner, that he has paid him most of the money and that he is expecting him to go away for a few days. What we know is that the appellant went to London and that he was trying by every means in his power to borrow money from relatives there to enable him to pay off his partner. He was getting a woman, who gave evidence and who evidently impressed the judge, to forge—there is no other word for it, though she may not have known that she was forging—documents purporting to be agreements, and then adding a signature to them which purported to be the signature of Sykut, and he was giving all sorts of contradictory accounts. When he was required to give an account of how his partner disappeared, he told the sort of story that might well be found in a magazine or a detective story, or a story by the late Phillips Oppenheim, as to how a large, dark car, sometimes described as black and sometimes as green, had arrived at this lonely farm at 7.30 at night, finding its way up a dreadful rocky path; that there were three men, one of whom had had a revolver; and that the unfortunate Sykut was put into the car at the point of the revolver and driven away. That was the kind of story that was told; and yet, remarkably enough, on December 18, when a sheriff's officer had gone to the farm before 7 p.m. to levy an execution against the appellant alone, and in order to ensure that he was not levying on partnership property the officer had asked: "Where is Mr. Sykut?" he was told: "Oh, Sykut has gone to a doctor at Llandilo." According to the evidence that was given he never went to a doctor at Llandilo, but at 7.30 that night he was supposed to have been kidnapped and taken to London. The appellant said in his evidence that he was expecting his partner back at the farm, and yet all the letters which he wrote at that time seem to say that his partner had gone to Poland and that he would not see him back; his letters can only be explained on the footing that he knew perfectly well that his partner could never appear again.

It seems to me that one of the matters of the greatest possible importance is that when the appellant was in London, telling all sorts of contradictory stories to the people from whom he was trying to borrow money, he made two remarkable proposals. First, he asked Mrs. Pokora, with whom he was evidently on terms of close friendship, to send him sham registered letters, that is to say, to get registered envelopes, put sheets of paper in them, and send them to him, purporting to send him a couple of hundred pounds. Another more remarkable proposal was that he actually asked that Mrs. Pokora's husband should go with him to see a solicitor at Llandilo and impersonate his partner. Could he have done that—would he have dared to do that, if he had thought that there was the smallest chance of this man appearing again? Yet he said in his evidence that he did expect Sykut to come back again. Sykut had new clothes and other property, and yet, if the appellant's story is true, he went off with these people, whether to Poland or somewhere else, leaving his clothes and everything behind and never came back or made any attempt to come back. Indeed, the appellant said that he knew one of the men, Jablonski—which I daresay is as good as any other name if one is using a Polish name—and that Mr. Jablonski had arranged to meet his partner at Paddington Station at 3 o'clock, on which day does not matter; that he went there and waited till 3 o'clock and that nobody came. Later, he said that he met Jablonski and Sykut at a Polish club and that there a document was signed; and that the signature said by the prosecution to be a forgery was affixed by Sykut in the presence of Jablonski and another gentleman; but nobody was called from the Polish club to say that these people ever existed at all.

I do not propose to go all through the evidence called, but one very remarkable piece of evidence cannot possibly be accounted for in any way other than that the appellant was deliberately trying to manufacture evidence with regard to the life of Sykut. That was the evidence of the local blacksmith. On December 14, the last day on which anyone saw Sykut alive, the appellant had taken a horse from the farm to the blacksmith for shoeing; the horse had been fetched away from the forge by Sykut, and the blacksmith had charged 17s. 6d. for shoeing the horse. The blacksmith's evidence was perfectly clear about that. He said that there was no doubt in his mind at all about it. Whether he referred to his books or not I do not know, but I think that he did; and it was on December 14 that Sykut came and took away the horse. Later in the month, at the end of December, when the police were beginning to make inquiries, the appellant visited the blacksmith and paid him the money, and he then tried to persuade the blacksmith to say that it was on December 17 that Sykut had gone there to take the horse away. The case for the prosecution was that Sykut was dead by the 17th, having been killed either on or immediately after the 14th. December 14 was the last day on which anybody had seen that unhappy man alive. Yet here was the appellant, at the end of December, when the police had begun to make inquiries, trying to get a man whose evidence on one point was vital, to give untrue evidence as to the date on which Sykut had fetched the horse. There can be no doubt about it; the blacksmith's evidence was either true or untrue. If it was true, the appellant was trying to get him to say something untrue.

Those are all matters which were pointed out to the jury by the judge, matters on which they had the advantage of hearing counsel on both sides. It is true that the judge did not point out to the jury all the matters. A judge does very often say to a jury: "It is very remarkable that such a point has not been proved, and if it could be, it ought to have been proved." The case for the prosecution was: this man has disappeared: he has completely gone from the ken of mankind; it is impossible to believe that he is alive now. I suppose that it would have been possible for him to have got out of the country and become immured behind what is sometimes called the "iron curtain"; but here there are facts which point inevitably, as it is said irresistibly, towards the appellant being the person who knows what happened to the missing man and who disposed of that man in one way or another. It may be that it would have been desirable to emphasize to the jury that the first thing to which they must apply their minds was whether a murder had been committed; but, speaking for myself, I think that the way the judge put it in the two passages which I have read did sufficiently direct the attention of the jury to the fact that they had to be satisfied of that, and that if they were satisfied of the death, the violent death, of this man, they need not go any further. It is no doubt true that the prosecution relied considerably on certain minute spots in the kitchen—a minute quantity on the wall and a minute quantity on the ceiling—which were found to be blood when scientifically examined; spots so small that they might easily have escaped the attention of somebody who was trying to wash or wipe up blood. The appellant did not deny that the blood which was found was that of his partner. He said that it was due to the fact that his partner had cut his hand in the field, on one of the tractors, and that on coming in he must have shaken his hand and shaken off some blood. That, of course, was a possibility, and it was put to the jury. It was also a possibility that Sykut was disposed of in the kitchen; but there is no evidence that he was; indeed, as Mr. Elwyn Jones has very properly stressed, there is no evidence at all as to how the man met his death. But this court is of opinion that there was evidence on which the jury could infer that he did meet his death, and that he was dead; and if he was dead, the circumstances of the case point to the fact that his death was not a natural one. If that establishes, as it would, a corpus delicti, the evidence was such that the jury were entitled to find that the appellant murdered his partner.

For these reasons, we have been unable to find any misdirection by the judge, or anything in the summing up which would justify us in saying that the case was not properly presented to the jury. We have come to the conclusion that there was evidence on which the jury were entitled to find that the appellant's partner was murdered and that the appellant was the murderer, and accordingly this appeal is dismissed.

————

27. If you were a member of the jury at Onufrejczyk's trial, how would you have voted?

28. The Home Secretary commuted Onufrejczyk's sentence of death to life imprisonment. He was imprisoned at Wormwood Scrubbs Prison until May 31, 1965, when he was released on parole. He was killed in a road accident in 1967. Sykut has not been found alive (or dead) since the trial.

One commentator has observed that since it seems clear that if Onufrejczyk was guilty of killing Sykut at all, he was guilty of a premeditated murder for gain, the reprieve must have been based on doubt of his guilt, and "if such a doubt remains that the prisoner has to be reprieved, then he ought never to be convicted and sentenced." Coaker, *"Corpus*

Delecti Murder with No Trace of a Body,'' 73 S. Afr. L.J. 181, 185 (1956). Do you agree? Doubt that Onufrejczyk should have been convicted is expressed also in a comment in 33 Can. B. Rev. 603 (1955), in which the author notes that Sykut had been gone for only 11 months when Onufrejczyk was charged with murder.

29.   In The King v. Horry, [1952] N.Z.L.R. 111, to which the court referred in *Onufrejczyk*, the defendant was convicted of murdering his wife, who disappeared very soon after she married him. There was no direct evidence that she was dead, but there was abundant evidence of the kind produced in *Onufrejczyk* that the defendant had profited by her disappearance and had tried to obscure the facts surrounding it. The court said in part: "In this case, there is neither the body nor traces of the body, nor anything in the form of a confession, but, in our opinion, that does not exhaust the possibilities. There may be other facts so incriminating and so incapable of any reasonable explanation as to be incompatible with any hypothesis other than murder. It is in accord both with principle and with authority that the fact of death should be provable by such circumstances as render it morally certain and leave no ground for reasonable doubt—that the circumstantial evidence should be so cogent and compelling as to convince a jury that upon no rational hypothesis other than murder can the facts be accounted for." [1952] N.Z.L.R. at 123.

Professor Norval Morris has suggested that although in *Horry* the court said that circumstantial evidence was sufficient to establish the corpus delicti, by requiring that the victim's death be proved to a "moral certainty" it "set up a different standard of proof of the fact of death as one aspect of the crime of murder; a standard lying somewhere between the burden of proving guilt beyond all reasonable doubt, as in all criminal cases, and proof positive of guilt, which is never available in human affairs." Although proof *beyond all reasonable doubt* and proof *to a moral certainty* are different degrees of proof and both differ from proof *to an absolute certainty*, the "fine shades of distinction are extremely elusive," and we must ultimately "rely on the good sense of juries . . . [although] we know virtually nothing of the reasoning processes applied in the jury room." Morris, "Corpus Delicti and Circumstantial Evidence," 68 L. Q. Rev. 391, 394, 396 (1952).

People v. Scott, 1 Cal.Rptr. 600 (Ct.App.1959), is another case in which a man was convicted of the murder of his wife, who had disappeared. The court stated that circumstantial evidence could sustain a conviction provided "the facts found and the reasonable inferences from them proved the nonexistence of any reasonable hypothesis of innocence. . . . All that is required to prove death is circumstantial evidence sufficient to convince the minds of reasonable men of the existence of the fact. The law employs the judgment of reasonable minds as the only means of arriving at the truth by inference from the circumstances in evidence. If this were not true, an infinite number of crimes involving the element of a specific intent would go unpunished." Id. at 619.[30]

See also People v. Manson, 139 Cal.Rptr. 275, 298 (Ct.App.1977), in which the court observed: "The fact that a murderer may successfully dispose of the body of the victim does not entitle him to an acquittal. That is one form of success for which society has no reward. Production of the body is not a condition precedent to the prosecution for murder."

A conviction of murder was affirmed, although the victim's body was not found, in Gilchrist v. State, 466 So.2d 988 (Ala.Crim.App.1984). "[T]he defendant's statements indicated that he struck the victim several times in the head with a large stick and then hid her body. Additionally, evidence was introduced that the offense had been committed. These facts included: (1) that Christina Zane, the victim, had been missing for almost five months, contrary to her habit of contacting her parents regularly; (2) that Zane's friends and neighbors had not seen her since the day she disappeared; (3) that Zane had not shown up at work since the day she disappeared, although she usually did show up or call when she could not work; (4) her small dog was found inside her abandoned car, although she was in the habit of keeping the dog with her at all times; (5) Zane had little money and 'lived from paycheck to paycheck'; yet, she had not picked up her last

30. An appeal to the Supreme Court was dismissed. 364 U.S. 471 (1960). Justice Douglas dissented, saying in part: "A reading of the report shows that the entire evidence against the defendant was circumstantial. It was not even shown directly that his wife, whom he is now convicted of murdering, is dead. Proof of the *corpus delicti*, as well as proof of petitioner's criminal agency, was to be inferred from his wife's inexplicable disappearance coupled with his unnatural behavior thereafter. A prominent aspect of this unnatural behavior was his silence. At the trial, the petitioner did not take the stand." Id. at 471–72. Justice Douglas argued that the trial judge's adverse comment on the defendant's failure to take the stand was a denial of his constitutional right not to be required to testify against himself, and that the case showed how "utterly devastating" the rule permitting such comment can be. Id. at 473. Such comment was declared unconstitutional in 1965, in Griffin v. California, 380 U.S. 609 (1965).

paycheck, something she was likely to do absent foul play; (6) Zane was not unhappy and had not told anyone that she was going to leave town; and (7) her purse and driver's license were found in her abandoned car." Id. at 991. In State v. Garner, 699 P.2d 468 (Kan.1985), also, the court gives a lengthy account of details, somewhat similar to those in *Onufrejczyk*, which pointed beyond a reasonable doubt to homicide as the explanation for a person's complete disappearance. See Government of the Virgin Islands v. Harris, 938 F.2d 401 (3d Cir.1991), citing many other cases.

30.   In Commonwealth v. Webster, 59 Mass. (5 Cush.) 295 (1850), a famous murder case in which the defendant was professor of chemistry at the medical school of Harvard University, parts of a body presumed to be that of the victim were found but there was no direct evidence of the alleged killing. Chief Justice Shaw of the Supreme Judicial Court said in his charge to the jury:

> This case is to be proved, if proved at all, by circumstantial evidence; because it is not suggested that any direct evidence can be given, or that any witness can be called to give direct testimony, upon the main fact of the killing. It becomes important, therefore, to state what circumstantial evidence is; to point out the distinction between that and positive or direct evidence; and to give some idea of the mode in which a judicial investigation is to be pursued by the aid of circumstantial evidence.

> The distinction, then, between direct and circumstantial evidence, is this. Direct or positive evidence is when a witness can be called to testify to the precise fact which is the subject of the issue on trial; that is, in a case of homicide, that the party accused did cause the death of the deceased. Whatever may be the kind or force of the evidence, this is the fact to be proved. But suppose no person was present on the occasion of the death, and of course that no one can be called to testify to it; is it wholly unsusceptible of legal proof? Experience has shown that circumstantial evidence may be offered in such a case; that is, that a body of facts may be proved of so conclusive a character, as to warrant a firm belief of the fact, quite as strong and certain as that on which discreet men are accustomed to act, in relation to their most important concerns. It would be injurious to the best interests of society, if such proof could not avail in judicial proceedings. If it was necessary always to have positive evidence, how many criminal acts committed in the community, destructive of its peace and subversive of its order and security, would go wholly undetected and unpunished?

> The necessity, therefore, of resorting to circumstantial evidence, if it is a safe and reliable proceeding, is obvious and absolute. Crimes are secret. Most men, conscious of criminal purposes, and about the execution of criminal acts, seek the security of secrecy and darkness. It is therefore necessary to use all other modes of evidence besides that of direct testimony, provided such proofs may be relied on as leading to safe and satisfactory conclusions; and, thanks to a beneficent providence, the laws of nature and the relations of things to each other are

so linked and combined together, that a medium of proof is often thereby furnished, leading to inferences and conclusions as strong as those arising from direct testimony.

. . .

Each of these modes of proof has its advantages and disadvantages; it is not easy to compare their relative value. The advantage of positive evidence is, that it is the direct testimony of a witness to the fact to be proved, who, if he speaks the truth, saw it done; and the only question is, whether he is entitled to belief. The disadvantage is, that the witness may be false and corrupt, and that the case may not afford the means of detecting his falsehood.

But, in a case of circumstantial evidence where no witness can testify directly to the fact to be proved, it is arrived at by a series of other facts, which by experience have been found so associated with the fact in question, that in the relation of cause and effect, they lead to a satisfactory and certain conclusion; as when footprints are discovered after a recent snow, it is certain that some animated being has passed over the snow since it fell; and, from the form and number of footprints, it can be determined with equal certainty, whether they are those of a man, a bird, or a quadruped. Circumstantial evidence, therefore, is founded on experience and observed facts and coincidences, establishing a connection between the known and proved facts and the fact sought to be proved. The advantages are, that, as the evidence commonly comes from several witnesses and different sources, a chain of circumstances is less likely to be falsely prepared and arranged, and falsehood and perjury are more likely to be detected and fail of their purpose. The disadvantages are, that a jury has not only to weigh the evidence of facts, but to draw just conclusions from them; in doing which, they may be led by prejudice or partiality, or by want of due deliberation and sobriety of judgment, to make hasty and false deductions; a source of error not existing in the consideration of positive evidence.

. . .

One other general remark on the subject of circumstantial evidence is this; that inferences drawn from independent sources, different from each other, but tending to the same conclusion, not only support each other, but do so with an increased weight. To illustrate this, suppose the case . . . of the wad of a pistol consisting of part of a ballad, the other part being in the pocket of the accused; it is not absolutely conclusive, that the accused loaded and wadded the pistol himself; he might have picked up the piece of paper in the street. But suppose that by another and independent witness it were proved, that that individual purchased such a ballad at his shop; and further, from another witness, that he purchased such a pistol at another shop. Here are circumstances from different and independent sources, bearing upon the same conclusion, to wit, that the accused loaded and used the pistol; and they, therefore, have an increased weight in establishing the proof of the fact.

. . .

Another rule is, that the circumstances taken together should be of a conclusive nature and tendency, leading on the whole to a satisfactory conclusion, and producing in effect a reasonable and moral certainty, that the accused, and no one else, committed the offense charged. It is not sufficient that they create a probability, though a strong one; and if, therefore, assuming all the facts to be true which the evidence tends to establish, they may yet be accounted for upon any hypothesis which does not include the guilt of the accused, the proof fails. It is essential, therefore, that the circumstances taken as a whole, and giving them their reasonable and just weight, and no more, should to a moral certainty exclude every other hypothesis. The evidence must establish the *corpus delicti*, as it is termed, or the offence committed as charged; and, in case of homicide, must not only prove a death by violence, but must, to a reasonable extent, exclude the hypothesis of suicide, and a death by the act of any other person. This is to be proved beyond reasonable doubt.

Then, what is reasonable doubt? It is a term often used, probably pretty well understood, but not easily defined. It is not mere possible doubt; because every thing relating to human affairs, and depending on moral evidence, is open to some possible or imaginary doubt. It is that state of the case, which, after the entire comparison and consideration of all the evidence, leaves the minds of jurors in that condition that they cannot say they feel an abiding conviction, to a moral certainty, of the truth of the charge. The burden of proof is upon the prosecutor. All the presumptions of law independent of evidence are in favor of innocence; and every person is presumed to be innocent until he is proved guilty. If upon such proof there is reasonable doubt remaining, the accused is entitled to the benefit of it by an acquittal. For it is not sufficient to establish a probability, though a strong one arising from the doctrine of chances, that the fact charged is more likely to be true than the contrary; but the evidence must establish the truth of the fact to a reasonable and moral certainty; a certainty that convinces and directs the understanding, and satisfies the reason and judgment, of those who are bound to act conscientiously upon it. This we take to be proof beyond reasonable doubt; because if the law, which mostly depends upon considerations of a moral nature, should go further than this, and require absolute certainty, it would exclude circumstantial evidence altogether.

59 Mass. at 310–20.[31]

31. Shaw's instructions concerning "reasonable doubt," which were widely adopted elsewhere, are discussed and criticized at length in the concurring opinion of Justice Mosk, in People v. Brigham, 599 P.2d 100, 106–21 (Cal.1979).

Is the standard of proof which Chief Justice Shaw said must be met in *Webster* the same as that prescribed in *Onufrejczyk* and *Horry*? If so, in which of the cases is the standard described best? If not, what are the differences among them? Would Lord Goddard, who wrote the opinion in *Onufrejczyk*, have approved Chief Justice Shaw's instruction? Is it wise for the law to employ distinctions as fine as that which Professor Morris thought was established in *Horry*?

For an imaginative recreation of the *Webster* case, see S. Schama, Dead Certainties (1991).

31. Counsel for the defendant in *Horry* argued that the Crown's case had not been proved to a moral certainty because where there is moral certainty "contemplation of the contrary possibility ought to shake reason," and if the victim were to walk into the court during argument of the appeal, "it would contradict no part of the evidence, and would not shock reason," [1952] N.Z.L.R. at 114. Counsel for Onufrejczyk made a similar argument: "If Sykut were to walk into this court now, not one word of the case for the Crown would be proved wrong." [1955] 1 Q.B. at 389. What sort of "contradiction" did counsel have in mind? Might the victim's appearance in court have shocked reason because it would have contradicted the *whole* of the evidence even though it did not contradict any *part* of the evidence? Is that what circumstantial evidence is all about?

32. Does Chief Justice Shaw's statement that direct evidence "is when a witness can be called to testify to the precise fact which is the subject of the issue on trial," p. 60 above, satisfactorily distinguish direct and circumstantial evidence? Does all direct evidence involve testimony of an eyewitness? What about the testimony of an "earwitness" who hears the sounds of an argument, a gunshot, a scream, and a thud, in sequence? Is what the witness heard direct evidence of a homicide? If not, why not? See, e.g., People v. Manson, 139 Cal.Rptr. 275, 287 (Ct.App.1977) ("direct 'ear witness' evidence" of murder). Cf. Guidi v. Superior Court of Los Angeles County, 513 P.2d 908 (Cal.1973) ("plain smell" of contraband as basis for search and seizure).

33. "The myth of innate superiority of direct testimonial evidence was exploded long ago. . . . Indeed, circumstantial evidence is generally stronger, at least when it depends, as it often does, upon undisputed evidentiary facts about which human observers are less likely to err as a matter of accuracy or to distort as a matter of motivation, emotional shock, or external suggestion." People v. Cleague, 239 N.E.2d 617, 619 (N.Y.1968). On what kind of evidence do you base most of your judgments?

34. At the time of the *Scott* case, p. 59 above, there was a statutory rebuttable presumption in California that "a person not heard from in seven years" is dead. Cal. Evid. Code § 667 (since amended; now five years). The defendant in *Scott* was indicted for the murder of his wife less than two years after she disappeared and was tried well within the seven-year period. Was he entitled to an instruction to the jury that his wife was presumed to be alive unless direct evidence of her death were produced, or to any other instruction based on the presumption? See *Scott*, 1 Cal.Rptr. at 626, 628–29.

35. In People v. Hayner, 90 N.E.2d 23, 25 (N.Y.1949), the court reversed a conviction for the murder of a child during birth and observed that in the absence of "an eye or ear witness . . . evidence of live birth precedent to speedy death is of a nature practically impossible to medical science." Do the *Chavez* and *Singleton* cases in effect simply establish contrary presumptions about live birth in cases of that type, which prevail in the absence of evidence to overcome them? See generally People v. Wang, 490 N.Y.S.2d 423 (Sup.Ct.1985) (discussing *Hayner*).

36. Corpus delicti. It is clear that the corpus delicti is not, as is commonly supposed, the body of the victim in a homicide case. It is the "body of the crime," facts which indicate that a crime has been committed. Generally, proof of the corpus delicti requires proof that there has been an injury or a loss (in homicide, a death), and proof that the injury or loss had a criminal rather than noncriminal (e.g., accidental) cause. E.g., People v. Cullen, 234 P.2d 1 (Cal.1951) (murder); State v. Hepburn, 460 So.2d 422 (Fla.Dist.Ct.App.1984) (driving while intoxicated; leaving scene of accident); State v. Pyle, 532 P.2d 1309 (Kan.1975) (murder); People v. Murray, 353 N.E.2d 605 (N.Y.1976) (felony murder). See United States v. Woods, 484 F.2d 127 (4th Cir.1973), holding that proof of prior similar occurrences is admissible to prove criminal agency. Wigmore argued that "corpus delicti" should be construed more narrowly and that proof only of the injury or loss should be required, since the danger against which rules requiring special proof of the corpus delicti are intended to guard is conviction of a man for a crime when no injury or loss has occurred. 7 J. Wigmore, Evidence § 2072 (Chadbourn rev. 1978).

The corpus delicti is of significance nowadays primarily in cases in which part of the evidence is an extrajudicial confession of the defendant. It is generally the rule that a person may not be convicted on the basis of such a confession alone and that corroboration is needed. Many jurisdictions require corroboration specifically of the corpus delicti. See, e.g., People v. Alvarez, 46 P.3d 372 (Cal.2002); People v. McMahan, 548 N.W.2d 199 (Mich.1996). The federal courts and some state courts follow the rule stated by the Supreme Court in Opper v. United States, 348 U.S. 84 (1954), which requires corroboration of the confession sufficient to warrant belief in its truth but beyond that does not require that facts establishing the corpus delicti be corroborated. See generally, *McMahan* above. The amount of independent proof that is required varies. Generally, it is enough if there is "substantial independent evidence which would tend to establish the trustworthiness of the statement," *Opper*, 348 U.S. at 93. See also Smith v. United States, 348 U.S. 147 (1954). In DeJesus v. State, 655 A.2d 1180 (Del.1995), the court held, contrary to the prevailing view, that in a case of felony murder, the corpus delicti requirement applies to both the homicide and the underlying felony.

Mistrust of confessions furnishes adequate basis for requiring corroboration of a confession and, in particular, corroboration of the fact that the crime in question has been committed; independent proof of the corpus delicti may *also* be probative of the defendant's guilt. It is less easy to see why corroboration of the defendant's statement that *he* committed the crime should not be required. A well publicized crime may prompt "confessions" from disturbed people. False confessions to crimes known to have been committed have sometimes been elicited by pressure of one form or another. Various unconvincing explanations have been suggested for requiring corroboration only of the fact that a crime has been committed, such as the greater "shock" of convicting an innocent person of a nonexistent crime compared with convicting him of a crime committed by someone else or the greater likelihood that a person will be mistaken about having committed a *crime* compared with being mistaken about *his* having committed a crime. Part of a rationalization for the rule may lie in the facts (1) that corroboration of a confession that did *not* furnish any proof of the corpus delicti (e.g., corroboration of the defendant's admission that he had a motive for the crime) would be weak corroboration of the charge as a whole, and (2) that all elements of the charge including the guilt of the defendant must be proved beyond a reasonable doubt, so that corroboration of that element of a confession will be required in appropriate circumstances. See generally State v. Lucas, 152 A.2d 50, 57–63 (N.J.1959); Green v. State, 304 N.E.2d 845 (Ind.Ct.App.1973).

37. For the literary possibilities of the corpus delicti rule, see Lord Dunsany's story, "The Two Bottles of Relish," in 101 Years Entertainment 464 (E. Queen ed. 1945).

3.   The Problem of Sorting

Consider the following cases:

(i) A soldier shoots and kills an enemy soldier in combat;

(ii) A policeman shoots and kills an escaping felon;

(iii) An escaping felon shoots and kills a policeman;

(iv) A woman discovers her husband and his lover committing an act of adultery and shoots and kills the lover;

(v) A woman surprises her husband and his lover committing an act of adultery and is shot and killed by the lover;

(vi) A woman shoots and kills her husband in order to be free to marry another man;

(vii) A householder shoots and kills a burglar whom she has caught at the safe;

(viii) A burglar shoots and kills a householder who has caught him at the safe;

(ix) A householder shoots and kills his butler whom he has mistaken for a burglar;

(x) A householder who is polishing his rifle rubs too hard on the trigger and shoots and kills his butler;

(xi) A householder tells his cook that the meat is overdone and is shot and killed by the cook.

Not all homicides are alike.

The problem is to decide which differences are relevant and which are not. In many respects situations (vii) and (viii) above are alike. In both cases, one person is killed, and the method of killing is the same. It is reasonable to suppose that the burglar was every bit as startled, irritated, and provoked at being discovered as the householder was at discovering him. Should the law react to the two homicides in the same way, and penalize the burglar for his burglary as a separate matter?

No one would suggest that homicides committed on Thursdays should be treated differently from homicides committed on Tuesdays. Why not? All sorts of activities used to be prohibited on Sunday that were permitted during the rest of the week.

Very few people would suggest that we should punish the murder of a businessman more severely than the murder of a bricklayer (or the reverse). Why not? Suppose the businessman were a philanthropist and the bricklayer a bully. Suppose there were a great shortage of businessmen. Suppose the businessman were elected President. See, for example, 18 U.S.C. § 1751, making it a crime to kill or kidnap or assault the President or Vice-President of the United States and other designated persons. At one time under English law "murder" (*murdrum*) referred to the killing of a Frenchman but not an Englishman. Before that, murder may have referred to the killing of a Dane.[32]

Should the policeman in situation (ii) be punished more severely than the felon in situation (iii)? Why not? Didn't the felon have more to lose by

---

32. See Regina v. Mawgridge, Kel. 119, 84 Eng. Rep. 1107 (1707); 1 W. Hawkins, Pleas of the Crown 78 (1716); 3 Stephen, History 30–40. "Englishry," proof that the dead man was an Englishman, as a basis for distinguishing murder from other homicides was abolished by statute in 1340. 14 Edw. 3, st. 1, ch. 4.

holding his fire than the policeman? Would it make a difference in situation (ii) if the policeman could easily and safely have stopped the felon without shooting? Would it be of any relevance at all in situation (iii) that the felon could easily and safely have escaped without shooting? Or that he was certain to be captured if he did not shoot?[33] Would it make any difference if the policeman shot (was shot by) a misdemeanant rather than a felon? Would it make any difference in situation (iii) if the felon reasonably mistook the policeman for his sworn enemy, who had vowed to kill him, and the felon shot only to avoid what he thought would be certain death?

What features of a homicidal situation are likely to be relevant? Why?

Is the problem of sorting which we face here the same as the problem of definition considered in the *Chavez* case? If not, how is it different?

Do we have to do any sorting in advance? Would it be preferable to acknowledge in the law what is true in fact: that every case is unique in some respect(s)? Should the process of the law be designed simply to bring out all relevant facts (leaving it to advocacy, perhaps, to omit nothing that may be relevant) and then, on the basis of the "total event" decide on a response? Isn't all sorting inevitably distorting? Doesn't sorting imply abstracting, and isn't abstracting a movement away from what "actually happened," whatever that means? Or is it more accurate to say that sorting (abstracting) is precisely how we do find out "what happened"? Is it significantly true that every case is unique in some respect(s)? Or is it true but trivial?

Is the only reason to differentiate among homicides that the law must respond and we can indicate what response or range of responses is appropriate for a particular homicide by placing it in a class of homicides for which a particular response or range of responses is prescribed? Or do classifications like "murder" and "manslaughter" (and, indeed, "homicide") have significance—a function—apart from indicating a response?

The concepts we employ (the labels we affix) reflect our interests. As you read the materials that follow, consider what interests are reflected by (1) the fact that we do differentiate among homicides, and (2) the factors on which we rely to differentiate.

MURDER AND VOLUNTARY MANSLAUGHTER

"Malice aforethought" is the characteristic mark of all murder, as distinguished from the lesser crime of manslaughter which lacks it. It

---

33. Cf. State v. Tyson, 323 S.E.2d 770 (S.C.1984), in which the defendant, convicted of armed robbery and murder, argued (unsuccessfully) that the resistance of the victim of the robbery constituted provocation that could reduce an intentional killing from murder to voluntary manslaughter (see pp. 72–92 below).

does not mean simply hatred or particular ill will, but extends to and embraces the state of mind with which one commits a wrongful act. It may be discoverable in a specific deliberate intent to kill. It is not synonymous with premeditation, however, but may also be inferred from circumstances which show a wanton and depraved spirit, a mind bent on evil mischief without regard to its consequences. It includes all those states of mind in which a homicide is committed without legal justification, extenuation or excuse.

Government of the Virgin Islands v. Lake, 362 F.2d 770, 774 (3d Cir.1966).

Although, as the court in *Lake*, above, says, the phrase "malice aforethought" is traditionally used to refer to the "characteristic mark of all murder," it is considerably misleading, because it does not necessarily signify either malice or forethought. Rather, as the court's further comment indicates, it is simply a way of referring collectively to the states of mind that, accompanied by a homicide, characterize the homicide as murder. In the succeeding pages of this section, through p. 184, those states of mind are developed.

[I]f the act of killing, though intentional, be committed under the influence of passion or in heat of blood, produced by an adequate or reasonable provocation, and before a reasonable time has elapsed for the blood to cool and reason to resume its habitual control, and is the result of the temporary excitement, by which the control of reason was disturbed, rather than of any wickedness of heart or cruelty or recklessness of disposition; then the law, out of indulgence to the frailty of human nature, or rather, in recognition of the laws upon which human nature is constituted, very properly regards the offense as of a less heinous character than murder, and gives it the designation of manslaughter.

Maher v. People, 10 Mich. 212, 219 (1862).

Here and elsewhere, the names used for the categories of homicide, like "murder" and "voluntary manslaughter" or "murder in the first degree" and "murder in the second degree," pp. 110–39 below, are rooted in the common law or, in the case of the degree formula, an old statute, and are still widely used. Current statutory codifications in some jurisdictions, however, may use different terms for one or another category. The Model Penal Code, for example, uses only the two general rubrics, murder, § 210.2, and manslaughter, § 210.3, the latter crime including both voluntary manslaughter, discussed here, and reckless homicide, discussed below, pp. 251–305, as involuntary manslaughter. There are also many small variations in the substantive law of different jurisdictions, whatever the term used. Notes and questions indicate the significant substantive issues and the ways in which they are resolved.

38. Chance-medley. Among the antecedents of the crime of voluntary manslaughter is killing by chance-medley. The term was used to refer to killings which occurred in a sudden fight, which were often also described, as in the quotations from Kelyng and East below, as manslaughter. See W. Lambard, Eirenarcha 248 (1614 ed.). Such a killing was distinguished from murder without regard to the nature of the provocation which caused the fight; the fight, not the provocation, was what showed absence of the malice aforethought that would have made the killing murder.

> Agreed, that no words, be what they will, are in law such a Provocation, as if a Man kill another for words only will diminish the Offence of killing a Man from Murder to Manslaughter: as suppose one call another son of a Whore, or give him the Lie, and thereupon he to whom the words are given, kill the other, this is Murder. But if upon ill words, both the Parties suddainly Fight, and one kill the other, this is but Manslaughter, for it is a combat betwixt two upon a suddain heat, which is the legal description of Manslaughter. . . .

Kel. 55, 84 Eng. Rep. 1080 (1666). Of this kind of case, East said: "[W]here upon words of reproach, or indeed any other sudden provocation, the parties come to blows, and a combat ensues, no undue advantage being taken or sought on either side: if death ensue, this amounts to manslaughter. And here it matters not what the cause be, whether real or imagined, or who draws or strikes first; provided the occasion be sudden, and not urged as a cloak for pre-existing malice." 1 Pleas of the Crown 241 (1803). The killing was a felony; but it was a "clergyable offense," which avoided capital punishment.[34] The killer's goods were forfeited, and a deodand, forfeiture to the crown of any personal chattel that was the instrumentality of a death, was exacted.[35]

The doctrine of killing by chance-medley developed in the sixteenth and seventeenth centuries, when "fights with deadly weapons . . . were no doubt the common occasions of death. . . . The old law on this subject is adjusted at every point to a state of things in which men habitually carried deadly weapons and used them on very slight occasions." 3 Stephen, History 59.[36] Before the boundaries between noncriminal and criminal homicide and between murder and manslaughter were clear, killing by

---

34. The curious institution of benefit of clergy, which was originally an exemption of the clergy from the jurisdiction of lay courts and evolved into a general mitigation of punishment for "clergyable" offenses, is described briefly in Mullaney v. Wilbur, 421 U.S. 684 (1975), p. 99 below. For a fuller account, see 1 Stephen, History 458–72.

35. Parliament abolished forfeiture for a nonfelonious homicide in 1828, 9 Geo. 4, ch. 31, § 10, and abolished forfeiture altogether in 1870, 33 & 34 Vict., ch. 23, § 1; it abolished deodands in 1846, 9 & 10 Vict., ch. 62.

36. In 1604 Parliament made an effort to control such conduct by providing that

chance-medley was easily confused with a killing in self-defense or a killing provoked by an assault, and it was finally effectively absorbed by them.[37]

Oddly, although the rationale for chance-medley has generally been discarded, an apparent reference to it survives in the federal statute, which defines voluntary manslaughter as a killing "upon a sudden quarrel or heat of passion," 18 U.S.C. § 1112(a), and a few state statutes. For the most part, however, notwithstanding that "sudden quarrel" and "heat of passion" are stated in the disjunctive, courts in those jurisdictions have treated the former simply as one of the circumstances that might give rise to the requisite hot state of mind. See United States v. Martinez, 988 F.2d 685 (7th Cir.1993), for a thorough discussion.

As you read the materials on voluntary manslaughter that follow, consider:

(i) whether some of the rules surrounding the crime of voluntary manslaughter in its modern form are not most easily understood as traces of the law on killing by chance-medley;

(ii) whether the basis for distinguishing murder from killing by chance-medley was not more sensible than the justifications offered for some of the rules now surrounding the crime of voluntary manslaughter;

someone who stabbed and killed a person who had no weapon drawn and had not struck first should be guilty of murder, even if malice aforethought could not be proved. 2 Jac. 1, ch. 8. The habits of the times were stronger than Parliament, however, and the so-called Statute of Stabbing was not given its intended effect. See Kel. 55, 84 Eng. Rep. 1080 (1789). See generally 3 Stephen, History 47–49.

37. The process was completed and made official in Rex v. Semini, [1949] 1 K.B. 405 (Crim. App.).

(iii) whether the law should not now recognize as a distinct category of homicide killing by chance-medley, by whatever name.

———

Girouard v. State
321 Md. 532, 583 A.2d 718 (1991)

■ Cole, Judge.

In this case we are asked to reconsider whether the types of provocation sufficient to mitigate the crime of murder to manslaughter should be limited to the categories we have heretofore recognized, or whether the sufficiency of the provocation should be decided by the factfinder on a case-by-case basis. Specifically, we must determine whether words alone are provocation adequate to justify a conviction of manslaughter rather than one of second degree murder.

facts

married
2 months at time of death.

The Petitioner, Steven S. Girouard, and the deceased, Joyce M. Girouard, had been married for about two months on October 28, 1987, the night of Joyce's death. Both parties, who met while working in the same building, were in the army. They married after having known each other for approximately three months. The evidence at trial indicated that the marriage was often tense and strained, and there was some evidence that after marrying Steven, Joyce had resumed a relationship with her old boyfriend, Wayne.

On the night of Joyce's death, Steven overheard her talking on the telephone to her friend, whereupon she told the friend that she had asked her first sergeant for a hardship discharge because her husband did not love her anymore. Steven went into the living room where Joyce was on the phone and asked her what she meant by her comments; she responded, "nothing." Angered by her lack of response, Steven kicked away the plate of food Joyce had in front of her. He then went to lie down in the bedroom.

Joyce provokes arguement/ anger
insults him, says marriage was a mistake, ask for divorce

Joyce followed him into the bedroom, stepped up onto the bed and onto Steven's back, pulled his hair and said, "What are you going to do, hit me?" She continued to taunt him by saying, "I never did want to marry you and you are a lousy fuck and you remind me of my dad." The barrage of insults continued with her telling Steven that she wanted a divorce, that the marriage had been a mistake and that she had never wanted to marry him. She also told him she had seen his commanding officer and filed charges against him for abuse. She then asked Steven, "What are you going to do?" Receiving no response, she continued her verbal attack. She added that she had filed charges against him in the Judge Advocate General's Office (JAG) and that he would probably be court martialed.

He gets kitchen knife

When she was through, Steven asked her if she had really done all those things, and she responded in the affirmative. He left the bedroom with his pillow in his arms and proceeded to the kitchen where he procured a long handled kitchen knife. He returned to Joyce in the bedroom with the knife behind the pillow. He testified that he was enraged and that he kept waiting for Joyce to say she was kidding, but Joyce continued talking. She said she had learned a lot from the marriage and that it had been a mistake. She also told him she would remain in their apartment after he moved out. When he questioned how she would afford it, she told him she would claim her brain-damaged sister as a dependent and have the sister move in. Joyce reiterated that the marriage was a big mistake, that she did not love him and that the divorce would be better for her.

After pausing for a moment, Joyce asked what Steven was going to do. What he did was lunge at her with the kitchen knife he had hidden behind the pillow and stab her 19 times. Realizing what he had done, he dropped the knife and went to the bathroom to shower off Joyce's blood. Feeling like he wanted to die, Steven went back to the kitchen and found two steak knives with which he slit his own wrists. He lay down on the bed waiting to die, but when he realized that he would not die from his self-inflicted wounds, he got up and called the police, telling the dispatcher that he had just murdered his wife.

When the police arrived they found Steven wandering around outside his apartment building. Steven was despondent and tearful and seemed detached, according to police officers who had been at the scene. He was unconcerned about his own wounds, talking only about how much he loved his wife and how he could not believe what he had done. Joyce Girouard was pronounced dead at the scene.

At trial, defense witness, psychologist, Dr. William Stejskal, testified that Steven was out of touch with his own capacity to experience anger or express hostility. He stated that the events of October 28, 1987, were entirely consistent with Steven's personality, that Steven had "basically reach[ed] the limit of his ability to swallow his anger, to rationalize his wife's behavior, to tolerate, or actually to remain in a passive mode with that. He essentially went over the limit of his ability to bottle up those strong emotions. What ensued was a very extreme explosion of rage that was intermingled with a great deal of panic." Another defense witness, psychiatrist, Thomas Goldman, testified that Joyce had a "compulsive need to provoke jealousy so that she's always asking for love and at the same time destroying and undermining any chance that she really might have to establish any kind of mature love with anybody."

Steven Girouard was convicted, at a court trial in the Circuit Court for Montgomery County, of second degree murder and was sentenced to 22 years incarceration, 10 of which were suspended. Upon his release, Petitioner is to be on probation for five years, two years supervised and three years unsupervised. The Court of Special Appeals affirmed the judgment of the circuit court in an unreported opinion. We granted certiorari to determine whether the circumstances of the case presented provocation adequate to mitigate the second degree murder charge to manslaughter.

Petitioner relies primarily on out of state cases to provide support for his argument that the provocation to mitigate murder to manslaughter should not be limited only to the traditional circumstances of: extreme assault or battery upon the defendant; mutual combat; defendant's illegal arrest; injury or serious abuse of a close relative of the defendant's; or the

mitigate to make less severe or intense

sudden discovery of a spouse's adultery. Petitioner argues that manslaughter is a catchall for homicides which are criminal but that lack the malice essential for a conviction of murder. Steven argues that the trial judge did find provocation (although he held it inadequate to mitigate murder) and that the categories of provocation adequate to mitigate should be broadened to include factual situations such as this one.

State's argument

society is not ready to recognize this provocative act as Reasonable.

The State counters by stating that although there is no finite list of legally adequate provocations, the common law has developed to a point at which it may be said there are some concededly provocative acts that society is not prepared to recognize as reasonable. Words spoken by the victim, no matter how abusive or taunting, fall into a category society should not accept as adequate provocation. According to the State, if abusive words alone could mitigate murder to manslaughter, nearly every domestic argument ending in the death of one party could be mitigated to manslaughter. This, the State avers, is not an acceptable outcome. Thus, the State argues that the courts below were correct in holding that the taunting words by Joyce Girouard were not provocation adequate to reduce Steven's second degree murder charge to voluntary manslaughter.

definition of manslaughter

Initially, we note that the difference between murder and manslaughter is the presence or absence of malice. . . . Voluntary manslaughter has been defined as "an *intentional* homicide, done in a sudden heat of passion, caused by adequate provocation, before there has been a reasonable opportunity for the passion to cool" (emphasis in original). Cox v. State, 311 Md. 326, 331 (1988). . . .

[acceptable provocations]

There are certain facts that may mitigate what would normally be murder to manslaughter. For example, we have recognized as falling into that group: (1) discovering one's spouse in the act of sexual intercourse with another; (2) mutual combat; (3) assault and battery. . . . There is also authority recognizing injury to one of the defendant's relatives or to a third party, and death resulting from resistance of an illegal arrest as adequate provocation for mitigation to manslaughter. . . . Those acts mitigate homicide to manslaughter because they create passion in the defendant and are not considered the product of free will. . . .

In order to determine whether murder should be mitigated to manslaughter we look to the circumstances surrounding the homicide and try to discover if it was provoked by the victim. Over the facts of the case we lay the template of the so-called "Rule of Provocation." The courts of this State have repeatedly set forth the requirements of the Rule of Provocation:

[Rule of provocation]

1. There must have been adequate provocation;

2. The killing must have been in the heat of passion;

3. It must have been a sudden heat of passion—that is, the killing must have followed the provocation before there had been a reasonable opportunity for the passion to cool;

4. There must have been a causal connection between the provocation, the passion, and the fatal act.

. . .

We shall assume without deciding that the second, third, and fourth of the criteria listed above were met in this case. We focus our attention on an examination of the ultimate issue in this case, that is, whether the provocation of Steven by Joyce was enough in the eyes of the law so that the murder charge against Steven should have been mitigated to voluntary manslaughter. For provocation to be "adequate," it must be "'calculated to inflame the passion of a reasonable man and tend to cause him to act for the moment from passion rather than reason.'" Carter v. State, 66 Md. App. at 572, quoting R. Perkins, Perkins on Criminal Law at p. 56 (2d ed. 1969). The issue we must resolve, then, is whether the taunting words uttered by Joyce were enough to inflame the passion of a *reasonable* man so that that man would be sufficiently infuriated so as to strike out in hot-blooded blind passion to kill her. Although we agree with the trial judge that there was needless provocation by Joyce, we also agree with him that the provocation was not adequate to mitigate second degree murder to voluntary manslaughter.

Although there are few Maryland cases discussing the issue at bar, those that do hold that words alone are not adequate provocation. Most recently, in Sims v. State, 319 Md. 540, we held that "[i]nsulting words or gestures, no matter how opprobrious, do not amount to an affray, and standing alone, do not constitute adequate provocation." Id. at 552, 573 A.2d 1317. That case involved the flinging of racial slurs and derogatory comments by the victim at the defendant. That conduct did not constitute adequate provocation.

In Lang v. State, 6 Md. App. 128 (1969), the Court of Special Appeals stated that it is "generally held that mere words, threats, menaces or gestures, however offensive and insulting, do not constitute adequate provocation." Id. at 132. Before the shooting, the victim had called the appellant "a chump" and "a chicken," dared the appellant to fight, shouted obscenities at him and shook his fist at him. Id. The provocation, again, was not enough to mitigate murder.

The court in *Lang* did note, however, that words can constitute adequate provocation if they are accompanied by conduct indicating a present intention and ability to cause the defendant bodily harm. Id. Clearly, no such conduct was exhibited by Joyce in this case. While Joyce did step on Steven's back and pull his hair, he could not reasonably have feared bodily harm at her hands. This, to us, is certain based on Steven's testimony at trial that Joyce was about 5'1" tall and weighed 115 pounds, while he was 6'2" tall, weighing over 200 pounds. Joyce simply did not have the size or strength to cause Steven to fear for his bodily safety. Thus, since there was no ability on the part of Joyce to cause Steven harm, the words she hurled at him could not, under the analysis in *Lang*, constitute legally sufficient provocation.

Other jurisdictions overwhelmingly agree with our cases and hold that words alone are not adequate provocation. . . . One jurisdiction that does allow provocation brought about by prolonged stress, anger and hostility caused by marital problems to provide grounds for a verdict of voluntary manslaughter rather than murder is Pennsylvania. See Commonwealth v. Nelson, 514 Pa. 262 (1987). The Pennsylvania court left the determination of the weight and credibility of the testimony regarding the marital stress and arguments to the trier of fact.

Ct. Explains why Penn. Ct. is wrong.

We are unpersuaded by that one case awash in a sea of opposite holdings, especially since a Maryland case counters *Nelson* by stating that "the long-smoldering grudge . . . may be psychologically just as compelling a force as the sudden impulse but it, unlike the impulse, is a telltale characteristic of premeditation." Tripp v. State, 36 Md. App. at 471–72. Aside from the cases, recognized legal authority in the form of treatises supports our holding. . . .

Holding

Thus, with no reservation, we hold that the provocation in this case was not enough to cause a reasonable man to stab his provoker 19 times. Although a psychologist testified to Steven's mental problems and his need for acceptance and love, we agree with the Court of Special Appeals speaking through Judge Moylan that "there must be not simply provocation in psychological fact, but one of certain fairly well-defined classes of provocation recognized as being adequate as a matter of law." Tripp v. State, 36 Md. App. at 473. The standard is one of reasonableness; it does not and should not focus on the peculiar frailties of mind of the Petitioner. That standard of reasonableness has not been met here. We cannot in good conscience countenance holding that a verbal domestic argument ending in the death of one spouse can result in a conviction of manslaughter. We agree with the trial judge that social necessity dictates our holding. Domestic arguments easily escalate into furious fights. We perceive no reason for a holding in favor of those who find the easiest way to end a domestic dispute is by killing the offending spouse.

We will leave to another day the possibility of expansion of the categories of adequate provocation to mitigate murder to manslaughter. The facts of this case do not warrant the broadening of the categories recognized thus far.

———

39. The prosecution argued that "if abusive words alone could mitigate murder to manslaughter, nearly every domestic argument ending in the death of one party could be mitigated to manslaughter," which, it said, was not "an acceptable outcome," p. 74. This is evidently what the court meant by "social necessity," p. 76. Is that sound? Including abusive words among the categories of adequate provocation does not mean that a jury *must* find the provocation in a particular case to be adequate but only that it may so find. Would that be undesirable? For what reason? In a famous English case decided soon after the end of World War II, the defendant killed his wife after she told him that she had been unfaithful (and incidentally accused him of infidelity as well). Arguing along the same lines as the prosecution in *Girouard*, the Crown urged that during the war, wives' adultery might have been more common than usual and that it would be unfortunate if returning soldiers regarded a wife's confession of adultery as "something like a license to kill." Holmes v. Director of Public Prosecutions, [1946] App. Cas. 588, 593 (H.L.). The penalty for manslaughter in England when *Holmes* was decided included the possibility of life imprisonment. In *Girouard* the maximum penalty was ten years' imprisonment, Md. Ann. Code art. 27, § 387, not much less than the effective sentence actually imposed for second-degree murder. Exposure to a sentence of that seriousness is hardly a "license to kill," is it? Just the same, did the prosecution in both cases have a point?

40. Although for a time after the promulgation of the Model Penal Code in 1962, see p. 89 note 56 below, there was a trend to open up the element of adequate provocation, e.g., People v. Berry, 556 P.2d 777 (Cal.1976), more recently courts have generally adhered to the traditional rule that "mere words" are never adequate provocation. In addition to *Girouard*, see, e.g., Hunter v. State, 349 S.E.2d 389 (Ga.1986) ("salvo of curse words"); People v. Batson, 495 N.E.2d 154 (Ill.App.Ct.1986) (accusation that defendant had stolen victim's cigarette lighter); State v. Best, 340 S.E.2d 524 (N.C.App.1986) ("black son of a bitch"). Courts have sometimes held, however, that words accompanied by provocative conduct, including gestures, may be adequate. For example, in Hambrick v. State, 353 S.E.2d 177, 179 (Ga.1987), the court observed: "While it is a correct statement of the law that provocation by *words* alone is inadequate to reduce murder to manslaughter . . . the issue of whether a reasonable person acts as the result of an irresistible passion may be raised by words which are connected to *provocative conduct* by the victim. . . . [P]rovocative conduct might in some instances include actions which could be described as gestures . . . ."

For a case applying in rather extreme circumstances the rule that "words and gestures alone, where no assault is made or threatened, regardless of how insulting or inflammatory those words or gestures may be, does not constitute adequate provocation for the taking of a human life," see State v. Watson, 214 S.E.2d 85, 89 (N.C.1975). See also Commonwealth v. Griffin, 472 N.E.2d 1354 (Mass.App.Ct.1985) (giving defendant "the finger").

For a middle position, that insulting or scandalous words are not sufficient provocation but "words conveying information of a fact which constitutes adequate provocation when that fact is observed" may be, see Commonwealth v. Berry, 336 A.2d 262, 264 (Pa.1975). To the same effect, stating that "it is well recognized that informational words, as distinguished from mere insulting words, may constitute adequate provocation," is Sells v. State, 653 P.2d 162, 164 (N.M.1982) (disclosure of adulterous relationship). If this middle position had been the law in Maryland, would the wife's words in *Girouard* have been within the bounds of adequate provocation? Would you have found that the provocation was adequate? Cf.

Brennon v. State, 319 S.E.2d 841 (Ga.1984), in which the defendant stabbed and killed a law enforcement agent conducting a lawful search of his house for contraband. To support his claim of provocation, the defendant testified that he had thought the victim was his friend and was angered to learn that he was an undercover agent and that the victim had told him he would be imprisoned for 100 years and lose his home and family. The court held that there was not enough evidence to require an instruction on provocation.

41. In *Girouard*, the prosecution asserted that "although there is no finite list of legally adequate provocations . . . there are some concededly provocative acts that society is not prepared to recognize as reasonable," p. 74 [sic—presumably, a homicidal response to which is not reasonable]. Do you agree that society should establish categorically, without regard to the circumstances of the case, that some "concededly provocative acts" are nevertheless inadequate, to reduce an intentional killing to manslaughter? Why (not)?

42. Does the court's list of the kinds of provocation that may be adequate to reduce a killing to manslaughter include all the categories that ought to be included? Does it include any that ought not to be included?

What should be the basis of inclusion? Aside from precedent, the principle on which the court apparently relies is evidently that only those kinds of provocation should be included that are "enough to inflame the passion of a *reasonable* man so that the man would be sufficiently infuriated so as to strike out in hot-blooded blind passion to kill," p. 75. Is that sound? Glanville Williams has observed that "it seems absurd to say that the reasonable man will commit a felony the possible punishment for which is imprisonment for life." Williams, "Provocation and the Reasonable Man," 1954 Crim. L. Rev. 740, 742. Is the proposition any more reasonable if the maximum punishment for voluntary manslaughter is only 20 years' imprisonment, or ten?

43. Among the categories of adequate provocation, the court in *Girouard* listed "extreme assault or battery." Elsewhere it referred simply to "assault and battery," p. 74. How extreme must the battery be? According to the defendant's testimony, his wife climbed on top of him and pulled his hair. Should that have been enough? The court concluded that it was not, evidently because the battery could not reasonably have put him in fear of bodily harm. Is that the only significance of a battery? Does the court's reasoning confuse the mitigation of provocation with so-called "imperfect self-defense," p. 195 note 114 below? Compare Commonwealth v. Cisneros, 113 A.2d 293, 296 (Pa.1955) (victim emphasized remarks by "sticking her finger" at defendant's shoulder; legal "battery," combined with words, was "of no moment in reducing the crime to manslaughter"), and State v. Owens, 308 S.E.2d 494 (N.C.Ct.App.1983) (victim threw cigarette butt at defendant; same), with State v. Wright, 336 S.W.2d 714, 717 (Mo.1960) (victim's "amorous advance by way of actually putting his arm around defendant and unzipping his trousers" satisfied requirement of a battery).

Suppose a person's eyeglasses have fallen on the ground and another person deliberately steps on them and crushes them. May that be adequate provocation for homicide? See R. v. Raney, 29 Crim.App. 14 (1942) (victim delivered blow to crutch of defendant, who had one leg).

With the above cases, compare Byrd v. State, 354 S.E.2d 428 (Ga.1987). "Appellant was sentenced to life imprisonment for murder following a jury trial. The evidence showed that he shot Clifford Lee Wilson after demanding a return of $20.00. Witnesses testified that when he alighted from a car and demanded the money, he hit the victim. Another person then got out of the car and began to fight with the victim. When the victim struck back, this person told appellant to get the gun. Appellant took a shotgun from the car and shot the victim in the back. When the victim ran, appellant pursued him and shot him in the back of the head." Upholding the conviction, the court said: "The 'boxing' or fighting prior to the homicide does not constitute the kind of provocation which would warrant a charge of voluntary manslaughter." Id. Why not? Would the law of chance-medley have been applicable here? If so, would that result be preferable?

44. Is an assault on a member of one's family that would clearly be adequate provocation if committed on oneself adequate provocation? See Collins v. United States, 150 U.S. 62 (1893). "The threatened or immediate infliction of serious injury upon a parent, spouse or child because of the relationship of the parties and the expected concern of one for the well being of the other, has occasioned courts to hold this conduct may be sufficient provocation to reduce the killing to voluntary manslaughter." Commonwealth v. Berry, 336 A.2d 262, 264 (Pa.1975).

What about a good friend? See Commonwealth v. Paese, 69 A. 891 (Pa.1908).

Is an assault not involving a battery sufficient provocation to reduce a killing to manslaughter? Most courts would probably agree with the Supreme Court in Stevenson v. United States, 162 U.S. 313, 322 (1896): "It seems to us quite plain, that an assault upon another by means of firing a pistol at him, is naturally calculated to excite some kind of passion in the one upon whom such an assault is made. It might be one of anger or it might be terror. If either existed to a sufficient extent to render the mind of a person of ordinary temper incapable of cool reflection, it might be plausibly claimed that the act which followed such an assault was not accompanied by the malice necessary to constitute the killing murder." But see State v. Brookshire, 368 S.W.2d 373 (Mo.1963).

45. In *Girouard*, the court states the well-established rule that "the sudden discovery of a spouse's adultery," pp. 73–74, is provocation that may mitigate an intentional homicide to manslaughter. How far should this recognition of the *crime passionel* extend? Does anything depend on the circumstances, the relationship of the persons, or, perhaps, the fact that the defendant had himself or herself also committed adultery? It is sometimes suggested that the jury should be instructed that the discovery of a spouse's adultery is adequate provocation as a matter of law. See, e.g., Holmes v. Director of Public Prosecutions, [1946] App. Cas. 588 (H.L.).[38] Is that sound? Or is this like other kinds of provocation, the adequacy of which in the particular circumstances is for the jury to determine? Does the much-talked-about "sexual revolution" starting in the 1960s or debate about "family values" in the 1990s have a bearing on this issue?

Suppose a husband reasonably but mistakenly believes that his wife is committing adultery. See State v. Yanz, 50 A. 37 (Conn.1901). Suppose a man discovers his fiancée with another man. See King v. Palmer, [1913] 2 K.B. 29 (Crim. App.). What of a mistress? In People v. McDonald, 212 N.E.2d 299, 302 (Ill.Ct.App.1965), the court said that it would not apply the "exculpatory features of *crime passionel* to the killing of a mistress, regardless of the duration of the relationship." Cf. People v. Eagen, 357 N.W.2d 710 (Mich.Ct.App.1984) (former girlfriend; inadequate provocation).

Should the discovery of one's spouse (or fiancé or lover) *in flagrante* be treated differently from a confession or report of such conduct in the recent or remote past? Should such a confession or report be treated like informational words generally or is the fact in this instance (aside from the discovery *in flagrante*) special? In Commonwealth v. Bermudez, 348 N.E.2d 802, 805 (Mass.1976), the court said that although in an appropriate case words conveying information might be adequate provocation, an unspecific confession of past adultery was not: "Past adultery lacks the peculiarly immediate and intense offense to a spouse's sensitivities which has led courts to recognize present adultery as adequate provocation . . . ." On what can this conclusion of the court be based? Suppose the defendant is informed that the deceased raped the defendant's wife, see State v. Flory, 276 P. 458 (Wyo.1929), or daughter, see Toler v. State, 260 S.W. 134

---

38. Cf. Scroggs v. State, 93 S.E.2d 583, 585 (Ga.Ct.App.1956), in which the court declared that "if a wife kills another woman to prevent sexual relations between such other woman and her husband, the killing is justified under Code, § 26–1016 . . . provided the killing was apparently necessary to prevent the commission of such sexual act. . . . On the other hand, if the killing, although apparently necessary to prevent adultery, was actually done by the defendant under a violent and sudden impulse of passion engendered by the circumstances and not to prevent the adultery, the offense is that of manslaugh-ter." Understating the fact somewhat, the court acknowledged that the reason for the killing in such circumstances was "elusive." Id. "The gist of such holdings is that where a continuing adulterous affair exists, as opposed to mere past acts of misconduct, if a jury believes the killing was done to prevent future misconduct, an acquittal is authorized." Brown v. State, 184 S.E.2d 655, 658 (Ga.1971). What sense does such a legal distinction make? Would it be preferable simply to give the jury discretion to acquit after considering "all the circumstances"?

(Tenn.1924), or girlfriend, see Commonwealth v. Leate, 225 N.E.2d 921 (Mass.1967) (attempted rape). Should such information be treated like informational words generally or should it be given the same special status, if any, of being informed about adultery?

46. May it be adequate provocation that the deceased was a trespasser on the defendant's property and refused to leave, or that he was taking goods belonging to the defendant over the defendant's objection? See, e.g., Pearce v. State, 18 So.2d 754 (Fla.1944); State v. Matthews, 49 S.W. 1085 (Mo.1899); State v. Clark, 41 S.E. 204 (W.Va.1902).

47. Should fear or terror engendered by the conduct of the deceased have the same effect in reducing a killing to manslaughter as anger or rage?

> Passion, of course, takes many forms. The most important characteristic of a truly impassioned mind is its inability to function rationally. Webster's Third New International Dictionary (unabridged) defines "passion" as "the state of being subjected to or acted on by what is external or foreign to one's true nature; a state of desire or emotion that represents the influence of what is external and opposes thought and reason as the true activity of the human mind." Rage and sudden resentment are the states of mind most often associated with manslaughter. However, fear is clearly a reason-obscuring state of mind and courts have held that fear, adequately provoked, will reduce murder to manslaughter.

Dickens v. State, 295 N.E.2d 613, 618 (Ind.1973). See LaPierre v. State, 734 P.2d 997 (Alaska Ct.App.1987) (distinguishing between fear as "heat of passion" and as the ground of (perfect or imperfect) self-defense). See further, notes 111–114, pp. 195–96 below.

48. Cooling time. After a homicidal passion has been aroused, how much time ought the law allow "for the blood to cool and reason to resume its habitual control," *Maher*, p. 69 above? "The question of reasonable time is whether, under all the circumstances and conditions connected with the killing the ordinary, average man would have brought himself under control." Shorter v. Commonwealth, 67 S.W.2d 695, 696 (Ky.1934).

> The law, in its wisdom, extenuates certain killings by lowering the degree of blameworthiness because it recognizes human frailty when one is in the clutches of blind and sudden fury. The long-smoldering grudge, by way of contrast, may be psychologically just as compelling a force as the sudden impulse but it, unlike the impulse, is a telltale characteristic of premeditation. The law extenuates certain killings not

simply because they have been provoked but because there has also been the lack of time between the provoking cause and the impulsive response to think about the consequences or the alternatives. In the case of the spontaneous explosion, reason has no opportunity to intervene; in the case of the "slow burn," it has. We demand that it intervene whenever it can.

Tripp v. State, 374 A.2d 384, 392 (Md.Ct.Spec.App.1977). See United States v. Bordeaux, 980 F.2d 534 (8th Cir.1992), holding that cooling time precluded a finding of provocation; it was revealed to the defendant that the victim had raped the defendant's mother 20 years ago and the defendant killed the victim much later on the same day.

To what extent should the law acknowledge a passion that gathers slowly from an accumulation of provocations and is set off by a final incident insufficient in itself?

In R. v. Duffy, [1949] 1 All E.R. 932, 933 (Crim. App.), the court described as "a classic direction given to a jury in a case in which the sympathy of everyone would be with the accused person and against the dead man," instructions on provocation which included the following:

> Circumstances which merely predispose to a violent act are not enough. Severe nervous exasperation or a long course of conduct causing suffering and anxiety are not by themselves sufficient to constitute provocation in law. Indeed, the further removed an incident is from the crime, the less it counts. A long course of cruel conduct may be more blameworthy than a sudden act provoking retaliation, but you are not concerned with blame here—the blame attaching to the dead man. You are not standing in judgment on him. He has not been heard in this court. He cannot now ever be heard. He has no defender here to argue for him. It does not matter how cruel he was, how much or how little he was to blame, except in so far as it resulted in the final act of the appellant. What matters is whether this girl [the appellant] had the time to say: "Whatever I have suffered, whatever I have endured, I know that Thou shalt not kill." That is what matters.

In State v. Hoyt, 128 N.W.2d 645 (Wis.1964), however, the court said that the cumulative effect of ill treatment and humiliation over a long period of time might magnify the immediate provocation for a killing enough to meet the test of reasonable provocation. See, to the same effect, State v. Lamb, 366 A.2d 981 (N.J.1976).

49. Should the provocation that reduces an intentional killing from murder to manslaughter be limited to conduct of the victim? If A is extremely disturbed because of something that B has done or because of something that has happened without anyone's fault and he intentionally kills C, should her crime be reduced to manslaughter? See People v. Spurlin, 202 Cal.Rptr. 663 (Ct.App.1984) (provocation limited to conduct of victim); Tripp v. State, 374 A.2d 384 (Md.Ct.Spec.App.1977) (same).

If we determine that it is reasonable for A to be disturbed, is it of no relevance how she responds to the disturbance? Suppose she intentionally kills C, D, E, and F? Cf. R. v. Souva (No. 2), [1951] V.L.R. 298. Should we perhaps distinguish between A, who kills C because she mistakenly believes that C is the cause of her woe, and H, who purposely kills J knowing that it is K (or the gods) and not J that is the cause of her woe? See Rex v. Manchuk, [1937] 4 D.L.R. 737 (Can.); cf. Claxton v. State, 288 S.W. 444 (Tex.Crim.App.1926); State v. Michael, 82 S.E. 611 (W.Va.1914). Or should we distinguish in advance in this situation only on the basis of the cause and intensity of the killer's emotion, and leave it to the sentencing authority to make appropriate distinctions based on the nature of the response? Or is it simply that no distinction on such basis would be appropriate?

m P C
Provocation

The Model Penal Code (see p. 89 note 56 below) does not limit "provocation" to acts of the person killed. The commentary states: "Under the Code, mitigation may be appropriate where the actor believes that the deceased is responsible for some injustice to another or even where he strikes out in a blinding rage and kills an innocent bystander. In some such cases, the cause and intensity of the actor's emotion may be less indicative of moral depravity than would be a homicidal response to a blow to one's person. By eliminating any reference to provocation in the ordinary sense of improper conduct by the deceased, the Model Code avoids arbitrary exclusion of some circumstances that may justify reducing murder to manslaughter." 1 MPC Commentaries Part II, 61 (comment to § 210.3). See State v. Huber, 361 N.W.2d 236 (N.D.1985). Compare the Illinois formula, by which the mitigating effect of provocation is available only if the provocation is attributable to the person killed or to "another whom the offender endeavors to kill, but he negligently or accidentally causes the death of the individual killed." Ill. Rev. Stat. ch. 38, ¶ 9–2(a)(2). So also *Tripp*, above, 374 A.2d at 389: "Except for rare instances of 'transferred intent,' where one aims at A, misses and hits B by mistake, a defendant seeking to extenuate an intentional killing upon the theory that he killed in hot-blooded rage brought on by the provocative acts of his victim is limited to those killings where the victim is the provocateur." (On "transferred intent," see p. 109 note 63 below.) Suppose the defendant claims that he fired at the victim because he mistook the victim for the person who had provoked him. See State v. Mauricio, 568 A.2d 879 (N.J.1990) (provocation available). Should we distinguish between A, who is provoked by B and striking out in a blind rage kills C, and H, who is provoked by K and wildly striking out at K kills J? Cf. R. v. Porritt, [1961] 1 W.L.R. 1372 (Crim. App.).

50. To what extent should the particular characteristics of the defendant be taken into account when the adequacy of provocation is assessed? In Bedder v. Director of Public Prosecutions, [1954] 1 W.L.R. 1119 (H.L.), the defendant, who was 18 years old, was convicted of the murder of a prostitute. He was sexually impotent.

> On the night of the crime he saw the prostitute with another man and when they had parted went and spoke to her and was led by her to a quiet court off a street in Leicester. There he attempted in vain to have intercourse with her, whereupon—and I summarise the evidence in the way most favourable to him—she jeered at him and attempted to get away. He tried still to hold her, and then she slapped him in the face and punched him in the stomach: he grabbed her shoulders and pushed her back from him whereas (I use his words), "She kicked me in the privates. Whether it was her knee or foot, I do not know. After that I do not know what happened till she fell." She fell, because he had taken a knife from his pocket and stabbed her with it twice, the second blow inflicting a mortal injury.

Id. at 1120.

The trial judge instructed the jury that when it considered the effect of the victim's conduct on the defendant, it should consider "the reasonable person, the ordinary person," and that the defendant's sexual impotence did not entitle him "to rely on provocation which would not have led an ordinary person to have acted" as he did. The defendant appealed on the ground that the jury should have been instructed to consider his particular physical defect when it considered the adequacy of the provocation. In the House of Lords, the appeal was dismissed.

> It would be plainly illogical not to recognize an unusually excitable or pugnacious temperament in the accused as a matter to be taken into account but yet to recognize for that purpose some unusual physical characteristic, be it impotence or another. Moreover, the proposed distinction appears . . . to ignore the fundamental fact that the temper of a man which leads him to react in such and such a way to provocation, is or may be itself conditioned by some physical defect. It is too subtle a refinement for my mind or, I think, for that of a jury to grasp that the temper may be ignored but the physical defect taken into account.

> [The] purpose [of the hypothetical reasonable man test] is to invite the jury to consider the act of the accused by reference to a certain standard or norm of conduct and with this object the "reasonable" or the "average" or the "normal" man is invoked. If the reasonable man is then deprived in whole or in part of his reason or the normal man endowed with abnormal characteristics, the test ceases to have any value.

Id. at 1121, 1123.

The court concluded not to follow *Bedder* in Director of Public Prosecutions v. Camplin, [1978] App. Cas. 705 (H.L.), in which it relied on languages in the Homicide Act of 1957.[39] In *Camplin*, the defendant was a

---

39. The Act retained the "reasonable man" test but provided that the nature of the   provocation, as distinct from its degree, was immaterial: "Where on a charge of murder

15-year-old boy, who claimed that he killed the victim after the victim had assaulted him sexually and then laughed at him. The court said that the legislation was intended to mitigate the harshness of the law relating to provocation; to that end it had abolished all rules, including the "mere words" rule, as to what can and what cannot amount to sufficient provocation, and it would contradict that intention not to allow the jury to "take into consideration all those factors which in their opinion would affect the gravity of taunts or insults when applied to the person to whom they are addressed." It concluded that the "reasonable man" to which the statute refers should be described to the jury as "a person having the power of self-control to be expected of an ordinary person of the sex and age of the accused, but in other respects sharing such of the accused's characteristics as they think would affect the gravity of the provocation to him." Id. at 717–18.

In a subsequent case, Newell, 71 Crim. App. 331 (1980), the defendant was a chronic alcoholic. While drunk, he killed a friend who made a derogatory remark about his girlfriend and evidently suggested that the defendant engage in a homosexual act. The judge charged the jury to consider the adequacy of the provocation, from the perspective of "a reasonable man, sober." The defendant contended that a proper instruction would have been: "Do you consider that the accused, being emotionally depressed and upset, as he was, and in the physical condition of a chronic alcoholic, was reasonably provoked by the words used and reacted in a way in which he might reasonably be expected to have acted, on the basis that he had had a very large amount to drink and had had a suicidal overdose of drugs four days previously, and that he was in a state of toxic confusion?" Id. at 335, 338.

Affirming the conviction, the court quoted from a New Zealand case, McGregor, [1962] N.Z.L.R. 1069, as follows:

> The Legislature [in a statute referring to "a person having the power of self-control of an ordinary person, but otherwise having the characteristics of the offender"] has given us no guide as to what limitations might be imposed, but perforce there must be adopted a construction which will ensure regard being had to the characteristics of the offender without wholly extinguishing the ordinary man. The

there is evidence on which the jury can find that the person charged was provoked (whether by things done or by things said or by both together) to lose his self-control, the question whether the provocation was enough to make a reasonable man do as he did shall be left to be determined by the jury; and in determining that question the jury shall take into account everything both done and said according to the effect which, in their opinion, it would have on a reasonable man." 5 & 6 Eliz. 2, ch.11, § 3. Thus, Bedder would have been no better off. Holmes, however, whose claim that his wife's confession of adultery provoked him to kill was rejected, see p. 76 note 39 above, might not have been a murderer had the Homicide Act been in effect in 1946.

(Bedder's sentence was commuted to life imprisonment. He was imprisoned for eight years and released on parole in 1962. Holmes was executed at Lincoln Prison on May 28, 1946. The Homicide Act abolished capital punishment for a crime like Holmes's.)

offender must be presumed to possess in general the power of self-control of the ordinary man, save in so far as his power of self-control is weakened because of some particular characteristic possessed by him. It is not every trait or disposition of the offender that can be invoked to modify the concept of the ordinary man. The characteristic must be something definite and of sufficient significance to make the offender a different person from the ordinary run of mankind, and have also a sufficient degree of permanence to warrant its being regarded as something constituting part of the individual's character or personality. A disposition to be unduly suspicious or to lose one's temper readily will not suffice, nor will a temporary or transitory state of mind such as a mood of depression, excitability or irascibility. These matters are either not of sufficient significance or not of sufficient permanency to be regarded as "characteristics" which would enable the offender to be distinguished from the ordinary man. . . . Still less can a self-induced transitory state be relied upon, as where it arises from the consumption of liquor. The word "characteristics" in the context of this section is wide enough to apply not only to physical qualities but also to mental qualities and such more indeterminate attributes as colour, race and creed. It is to be emphasised that of whatever nature the characteristic may be, it must be such that it can fairly be said that the offender is thereby marked off or distinguished from the ordinary man of the community. Moreover, it is to be equally emphasised that there must be some real connection between the nature of the provocation and the particular characteristic of the offender by which it is sought to modify the ordinary man test. The words or conduct must have been exclusively or particularly provocative to the individual because, and only because, of the characteristic. In short, there must be some direct connection between the provocative words or conduct and the characteristic sought to be invoked as warranting some departure from the ordinary man test. Such a connection may be seen readily enough where the offender possesses some unusual physical peculiarity. Though he might in all other respects be an ordinary man, provocative words alluding for example to some infirmity or deformity from which he was suffering might well bring about a loss of self-control. So too, if the colour, race or creed of the offender be relied on as constituting a characteristic, it is to be repeated that the provocative words or conduct must be related to the particular characteristic relied upon. Thus, it would not be sufficient, for instance, for the offender to claim merely that he belongs to an excitable race, or that members of his nationality are accustomed to resort readily to the use of some lethal weapon. Here again, the provocative act or words require to be directed at the particular characteristic before it can be relied upon. Special difficulties, however, arise when it becomes necessary to consider what purely mental peculiarities may be allowed as characteristics.

In our opinion it is not enough to constitute a characteristic that the offender should merely in some general way be mentally deficient or weak-minded. To allow this to be said would, as we have earlier indicated, deny any real operation to the reference made in the section to the ordinary man. . . .

71 Crim. App. at 339.

Compare People v. Washington, 130 Cal.Rptr. 96 (Ct.App.1976), in which the defendant killed his homosexual lover after a quarrel in which the latter said that he wanted to end the relationship. The court rejected the defendant's claim that the adequacy of the provocation should be tested by the standard of an average homosexual. See also Taylor v. State, 452 So.2d 441, 449 (Miss.1984), holding that the defendant's "emotional background" is not relevant to the adequacy of provocation. The facts of *Taylor* are set forth in p. 135 note 79 below.

51.

Stated in its most general form . . . [the defendant's argument] amounts to this: that because the mind usually receives provocation with an intensity proportioned to its own excitement or excitability, therefore the act of provocation must be measured, not by its own character and its ordinary effect, but by the state and habit of the mind that receives it. Then, measured by this rule, the crimes of a proud, or captious, or selfish, or habitually ill-natured man, or of one who eats or fasts too much, or of one who is habitually quarrelsome, covetous, dishonest, or thievish, or who, by any sort of indulgence, fault, or vice, renders himself very easily excitable, or very subject to temptation, are much less criminal than those of a moderate, well-tempered, and orderly citizen, because to the former a very small provocation or temptation becomes adequate to excuse or palliate any crime. If such were the rule, a defendant would be much more likely to injure than to benefit his case by showing a good character, and the law would present no inducement to men to try to rise to the standard of even ordinary social morality.

Of course, it is impossible that such a principle can be a rule of law. If it were admitted, it could not be administered, for no judicial tribunal can have time or competence for such a thorough investigation of the special character or state of each individual mind as the rule requires, and therefore it would necessarily jump to a conclusion, such as the caprice, or prejudice, or other influence of the moment would dictate.

Indeed, if we admit the principle, and carry it out logically, we shall abolish law entirely as a compulsory rule of civil conduct; for we shall measure all crime and all duty by the conscience of the individual, and not by the social conscience, and no contract could be binding, no debt collected, no duty enforced, and no crime punished, unless when the defendant's conscience feels that it ought to be, and thus courts would be useless, and social organization impossible. No such principle can stand before man's natural tendency to social organization, or before the power and the right of an organized society. Individual or even social charity may often act upon the principle, but law excludes it from its sphere. Very few persons practically admit it. . . .

In most matters, what is usual and ordinary in any given society is the law of that society. All, therefore, must come up to the standard of the usual and ordinary, or take the consequences. Those who, in their conduct, fall below this standard must, to that extent, submit to the condemnation of society, either legally or morally, according as the rules transgressed are civil or only moral. And those whose conduct rises above that standard, and yet harmonizes with it, must always be accepted as highly meritorious citizens. And this principle applies here; for men who degrade themselves below the ordinary level of social morality, by bad conduct or habits, do not thereby relieve themselves from having their acts and duties judged by the ordinary rules of social action. They cannot set up their own vices as a reason for being set into a special class that is to be judged more favorably than other persons.

Keenan v. Commonwealth, 44 Pa. 55, 58–59 (1863).

52. It has been much debated whether the rules by which an intentional killing is reduced from murder to manslaughter should be regarded as a matter of excuse, focusing on the *explanation* for the defendant's act regarded from his perspective, or as a matter of justification, focusing on the conduct of the victim (or another) that is said to constitute provocation. See, e.g., Dressler, "Rethinking Heat of Passion: A Defence in Search of a Rationale," 73 J. Crim. L. & Criminology 421 (1982); Ashworth, "The Doctrine of Provocation," 35 Cambridge L.J. 292 (1976). Look again at the rules elaborated in *Girouard* and the preceding notes. Which view of voluntary manslaughter do they support? Do you agree with that approach to the issue? If not, how would you change any of the rules to reflect your view?

53. What relationship is there between a rule limiting the kinds of provocation that the law will recognize as adequate and a rule that the adequacy of the provocation in a particular case must be considered without regard to unusual characteristics of the defendant?

54. In *Bedder*, note 50, above, would it have been "plainly illogical" to take into account an "unusual physical characteristic" like impotence but not "an unusually excitable or pugnacious temperament"? Logical or not, don't we make similar distinctions for similar purposes all the time? If Bedder had been blind rather than impotent, would the distinction between that physical defect and the temper of a man have been "too subtle a refinement . . . for . . . a jury to grasp," p. 84?

It may be difficult to imagine the criminal law employing an army of reasonable persons, each invested with the physical defect or combination of defects of some actual or potential defendant in a homicide case: the reasonable impotent man, the reasonable nearsighted woman, the reasonable nearsighted bald man, and so forth. Might it be preferable not to refer to a "reasonable person" at all, but to a killing in "circumstances in which it is reasonable" (or "understandable") that a person should be extremely provoked? If the test were so phrased might Bedder's counsel have argued successfully that Bedder's impotence was a "circumstance" to be taken into account?

55. When it assesses the adequacy of provocation, should a jury be instructed to consider (or not to consider) the defendant's racial or ethnic group identification? If the claimed provocation is a racial or ethnic epithet, for example, is it relevant that the defendant is (not) a member of the group named?

See Gonzales v. State, 689 S.W.2d 900, 903 (Tex.Crim.App.1985), in which the court rejected the defendant's contention that "because he is an Hispanic farm worker who was living with a Caucasian woman [the homicide victim] on a low income he should be granted more latitude in the degree of insult, etc., sufficient to enrage him." The court said that the defendant's argument "fails to recognize that the standard of the reasonable man, the person of ordinary temper, is employed precisely to avoid different applications of the law of manslaughter to defendants of different races, creed, color, sex or social status." Id. A concurring opinion noted that the facts to which the defendant referred could be considered among the "facts and circumstances going to show *the condition of the mind of the accused at the time of the offense*," as provided by the statute. Id. at 904.

56. Model Penal Code § 210.3. "Manslaughter. (1) Criminal homicide constitutes manslaughter when: . . . . (b) a homicide which would otherwise be murder is committed under the influence of extreme mental or emotional disturbance for which there is reasonable explanation or excuse. The reasonableness of such explanation shall be determined from the viewpoint of a person in the actor's situation under the circumstances as he believes them to be." *this say common Law approach is to rigid*

The Model Penal Code's formulation has been adopted in a number of jurisdictions and rejected in others. Recently, there are indications of a trend back to the traditional formulation limiting "adequate provocation" to certain categories.

Commenting on its provision, the Reporters for the Model Penal Code said:

There is a larger element of subjectivity in the standard than there was under prevailing law, though it is only the actor's "situation" and "the circumstances as he believes them to be," not his scheme of moral values, that are thus to be considered. The ultimate test, however, is objective; there must be "reasonable" explanation or excuse for the actor's disturbance. This is to state in fair and realistic terms the criteria by which the mitigating import of mental or emotional distress should be appraised when it is a factor in so grave a crime as homicide. . . .

The critical element in the Model Code formulation is the clause requiring that reasonableness be assessed "from the viewpoint of a person in the actor's situation." The word "situation" is designedly ambiguous. On the one hand, it is clear that personal handicaps and some external circumstances must be taken into account. Thus, blindness, shock from traumatic injury, and extreme grief are all easily read into the term "situation." This result is sound, for it would be morally obtuse to appraise a crime for mitigation of punishment without reference to these factors. On the other hand, it is equally plain that idiosyncratic moral values are not part of the actor's situation. An assassin who kills a political leader because he believes it is right to do so cannot ask that he be judged by the standard of a reasonable extremist. Any other result would undermine the normative message of the criminal law. In between these two extremes, however, there are matters neither as clearly distinct from individual blameworthiness as blindness or handicap nor as integral a part of moral depravity as a belief in the rightness of killing. Perhaps the classic illustration is the unusual sensitivity to the epithet "bastard" of a person born illegitimate. An exceptionally punctilious sense of personal honor or an abnormally fearful temperament may also serve to differentiate an individual actor from the hypothetical reasonable man, yet none of these factors is wholly irrelevant to the ultimate issue of culpability. The proper role of such factors cannot be resolved satisfactorily by abstract definition of what may constitute adequate provocation. The Model Code endorses a formulation that affords sufficient flexibility to differentiate in particular cases between those special aspects of the actor's situation that should be deemed material for purpose of grading and those that should be ignored. There thus will be room for interpretation of the word "situation," and that is precisely the flexibility desired. There will be opportunity for argument about the reasonableness of explanation or excuse, and that too is a ground on which argument is required. In the end, the question is whether the actor's loss of self-control can be understood in terms that arouse sympathy in the ordinary citizen. Section 210.3 faces this issue squarely and leaves the ultimate judgment to the ordinary citizen in the function of a juror assigned to resolve the specific case.

1 MPC Commentaries Part II, 49–50, 62–63 (comment to § 210.3).

How would the following cases have been decided under the provision of the Model Penal Code?

In Roberts v. State, 717 P.2d 1115 (Nev.1986) the statute provided that "in cases of voluntary manslaughter, there must be a serious and highly provoking injury inflicted upon the person killing, sufficient to excite an irresistible passion in a reasonable person." Concluding that the trial judge had erred in refusing to give an instruction on voluntary manslaughter, the court said:

> [T]he defendant and the victim had a long-standing relationship. He continued after their separation to provide her with financial support and to see her romantically. He said that he considered the victim and her children to be his family. The day of the killing was to a large degree dedicated to her convenience. He had taken a half day off from his job to furnish her son with a truck. He ran an errand for her and expected to spend that evening with her. He would have been justified in viewing her "standing him up" as a calloused insult, greatly aggravated by her taking up sexually with another man on the night of his planned get-together with her.

Id. at 1117 n.2.

In Cole v. State, 329 S.E.2d 146 (Ga.1985), the defendant, who had worked in law enforcement against the use of illegal drugs, killed his stepson after an argument about the latter's use of drugs. The statutory definition of voluntary manslaughter required that the killing be the result of passion caused by "serious provocation sufficient to excite such passion in a reasonable person." The court held that "the desire to prevent a drug user from using drugs again is not sufficient provocation." Id. at 148.

In People v. Gjidoda, 364 N.W.2d 698 (Mich.Ct.App.1985), the defendant was charged with killing one of his daughters and seriously wounding another, when he learned that they would testify against him in a trial for murder. Responding to his claim that he should have been allowed the defense of provocation, the court said: "Defendant's decision to shoot the victims was induced by their intention to testify against him. Although defendant was provoked, in a broad sense, that provocation is not one which we recognize as 'adequate' for the purposes of the law of manslaughter. . . . Rather, the claimed 'provocation' is nothing but the motive for the shootings. That defendant was enraged by the prospect of his daughters' testimony furnishes no basis for a manslaughter conviction." Conceding that the law may appear to be harsh, "especially to one who becomes subjectively enraged at the prospect of his daughters' adverse testimony," the court rejected the defendant's argument that "the standards of the law should look only to the rage which was boiling within him at the moment of the events and not at an objective standard which is externally imposed by society." Id. at 700.

If "in the end, the question is" how much sympathy we have for the defendant, Model Penal Code, p. 90 above, why is it better to rely on the sympathy level of the jury (presumably aided by the judge) than on that of the governor? Is the question really how much sympathy we (meaning one, or some, of us selected somehow) have for the defendant or how much sympathy we ought to have? In fact, doesn't the Model Penal Code require that our sympathy be rationally grounded on the facts of the case and not simply on sympathy for someone who was provoked enough to kill another human being? See generally State v. Ott, 686 P.2d 1001 (Or.1984).

57. For the limits (and literary possibilities) of a rule of provocation, see J. Collier, "The Touch of Nutmeg Makes It," in Fancies and Goodnights 48 (1951).

————

United States v. Alexander
471 F.2d 923 (D.C.Cir.1972)

. . .

■ BAZELON, CHIEF JUDGE.

. . . On the evening of June 4, 1968, five men and a woman—all white—walked into a hamburger shop, stood by the take-out counter, and ordered some food. The men were United States Marine Lieutenants in formal dress white uniforms; the woman was a friend of one of them. They noticed three Negro men sitting at the other end of the counter; these were appellants Alexander and Murdock and one Cornelius Frazier.

What ensued in the restaurant had the tragic result that both Alexander and Murdock drew guns on the group, and that shots were fired that left two of the Marines dead and another and the woman seriously wounded. At a joint trial by jury in February, 1969, Alexander and Murdock were each found guilty of carrying a dangerous weapon, and of four counts of assault with a dangerous weapon. Murdock, in addition, was found guilty of two counts of second-degree murder. A separate hearing for Murdock on the issue of insanity was held in November, 1969, at the close of which the jury returned a verdict of guilty on all counts. Appellants received consecutive sentences as to several counts, totalling five to twenty-three years for Alexander, and twenty years to life for Murdock.

. . .

Five United States Marine Lieutenants—Ellsworth Kramer, Thaddeus Lesnick, William King, Frank Marasco, and Daniel LeGear—attended a dinner at the Marine Corps Base in Quantico, Virginia, on the evening of June 4, 1968, in celebration of their near-completion of basic officers' training. After dinner, they drove to Washington, arriving about midnight, still wearing their formal dress white uniforms. They stopped for about an hour-and-a-half at a nightclub, where they each had a drink. They were well-behaved and "conducted themselves like gentlemen." At the nightclub they met Barbara Kelly, a good friend of Lieutenant Kramer. They accompanied her to her apartment, which she shared with another young woman, and visited there with the two women until about 2:40 a.m. When the five

Marines departed, Miss Kelly accompanied them, intending to return to the nightclub to meet another friend. Along the way, they decided to stop at a hamburger shop to get some coffee and sandwiches before the trip back to Quantico. The six of them entered the shop, stood by the take-out counter, and ordered their food. They noticed three Negro males sitting at the other end of the counter. As described by Lieutenant Kramer, "[T]heir hair was in Afro-bush cut, wearing medallions, jersey knit shirts, sport jackets. . . . [T]hey were what I consider in eccentric dress." The three men were Alexander, Murdock, and Cornelius Frazier. The critical events which subsequently took place in the restaurant were described by the four survivors of the Marine group and by Murdock and Frazier. Alexander chose not to take the stand.

According to the prosecution witnesses, Lieutenant Kramer realized that appellant Alexander was staring at him, and he returned the stare. "[I]t was on the order of a Mexican stand-off type thing where you just keep staring at one another for an indefinite period of time." No words were exchanged between the two men, and Lieutenant Kramer soon turned and faced the counter. Shortly thereafter Frazier, Murdock, and Alexander got up from where they were sitting and walked to the door behind the Marines. Murdock and Frazier left the shop, but Alexander stopped in the doorway. He tapped Lieutenant Kramer on the shoulder. When the Marine turned around, Alexander poked his uniform name tag and said, "You want to talk about it more? You want to come outside and talk about it more?" When Lieutenant Kramer replied, "Yes, I am ready to come out" or "Yes, I guess so," Alexander added, "I am going to make you a Little Red Ridinghood." At this point, Lieutenant King stepped up beside Lieutenant Kramer and made a remark variously reported by the prosecution witnesses as "What you God-damn niggers want?", "What do you want, you nigger?", "What do you want, dirty nigger bastard?", and "Get out of here nigger." Thereupon Alexander abruptly drew a long-barrelled .38 caliber revolver, cocked it, and pointed it at the group or directly into Lieutenant King's chest, saying, "I will show you what I want," or "This is what I want."

The Marines possessed no weapons whatsoever and, according to their testimony, were not advancing toward Alexander. As they stood there, shocked at the sight of the gun, Murdock reentered the shop at Alexander's left and rear, and drew a short-barrelled .38 caliber revolver. A series of shots suddenly rang out, and the Marines and Miss Kelly fell or dived to the floor. None attempted to retaliate because they all were taking cover and trying to get out of the line of fire. Alexander and Murdock withdrew from the shop, but one of them stuck his arm back into the shop and attempted—unsuccessfully—to fire his weapon several times more. Only Lieutenant Kramer attempted to identify this man, and he said it was Murdock.

Lieutenants King and Lesnick were mortally wounded in the fusillade; they died within minutes. Lieutenant Kramer was wounded in the head, but he remained conscious, as did Miss Kelly, who had been shot in the hip. Only Lieutenants LeGear and Marasco were not hit.

Alexander, Murdock, and Frazier fled to Alexander's automobile and drove off rapidly in the wrong direction on a one-way street. Alexander was driving, and as the car drove off, Murdock fired three more shots from the window of the car, at the door of the hamburger shop, and at people in the street. A nearby scout car raced after the fleeing car and stopped them within a few blocks. Two revolvers were recovered from the front floor-board of Alexander's automobile.

For the defense, Frazier and appellant Murdock testified that the Marines in the restaurant had been drunk and loud. Frazier testified that they had obstructed his exit as he left. He walked around them and left the restaurant just ahead of Murdock, but when he looked back, Murdock had gone back inside. He then heard shots and ran to Alexander's car.

Murdock testified that when he realized that Alexander had not followed him out of the restaurant, he returned, and as he entered he heard someone say, "Get out, you black bastards." He then saw the Marine advancing towards him. Murdock called to Alexander to leave with him, and Alexander turned as if to go. Murdock then heard a "sound like all the feet in the place were moving," turned around himself, and saw Alexander's drawn gun. Murdock pulled his own gun, as a reflex, and testified that he "commenced firing about the time one of them was actually right up on me. . . . [M]aybe a foot away." He testified that the other Marines were advancing toward him fast, and he felt they were going to kill him. On cross-examination he admitted that he emptied his fully-loaded revolver at the Marine group in the restaurant, testified that he didn't know if Alexander had fired, and admitted that he fired three shots from Alexander's gun from the window of the car as it was driven off.

Who fired the bullets inside the restaurant was an issue of some importance during the trial, but because of the testimony of the Government's firearms expert, both sides seem now to agree that Alexander did not fire his revolver inside the restaurant, and that Murdock—as he testified himself—emptied his gun at the Marines and Miss Kelly, picked up Alexander's gun in the automobile, and fired three shots with it from the window.

. . .

Turning to Murdock's contentions, we consider first his claim that the evidence was insufficient to permit the jury to find him guilty of second degree murder rather than manslaughter. Though the question is a close one—as it must almost invariably be when a defendant's state of mind is at issue—the panel agrees that the evidence presented in this case justifies a finding of malice.

While it appears that Murdock was inside the restaurant or close enough to the door to hear Lieutenant King's racial remark, the surviving Marines and Miss Kelly all denied that any other provocative conduct took place.[40] According to their testimony, they were all standing motionless—in shock—staring at Alexander's gun when Murdock came in, drew his gun, and began firing. We think, therefore, that the jury was presented with sufficient evidence to find that Murdock was not adequately provoked to justify the deadly force with which he retaliated.

But though we resolve the sufficiency of the evidence question against Murdock, our study of the record in this case has brought to our attention a difficulty with the existing instructions on manslaughter. To present the problem in the context of a concrete example, we quote in the margin the entire instruction on manslaughter given by the able trial judge in this case.[41] Paragraphs have been lettered for ease of reference. We note that

40. Appellant Murdock does not attempt to attack the traditional rule that "mere words standing alone, . . . no matter how insulting, offensive, or abusive, are not adequate to reduce a homicide from murder to manslaughter." D.C. Bar Ass'n, Criminal Jury Instructions for the District of Columbia, No. 87 (1966). . . .

41. [Instruction on manslaughter]

Now, ladies and gentlemen, there is involved in count one and count two [the second degree murder counts] what is known in law as a lesser included offense.

[A] If the jury determines that neither defendant is guilty of murder in the second degree, then the jury is required to consider whether or not one defendant or both defendants are guilty of a lesser included offense known in law as manslaughter. And, the Court will now instruct the members of the jury as to the elements of manslaughter.

[B] Manslaughter is the unlawful killing of a human being without malice.

[C] Manslaughter is committed when a human being is killed unlawfully *in the sudden heat of passion caused by adequate provocation.*

[D] The essential elements of the offense of manslaughter, each of which the Government must prove beyond a reasonable doubt are:

(1) That the defendant inflicted an injury or injuries upon the deceased from which the deceased died; and

(2) That the defendant so injured the deceased in the heat of passion; and

(3) That the heat of passion was caused by *adequate provocation*; and

(4) That the homicide was committed without legal justification or excuse.

[E] It is necessary that the defendant have inflicted an injury or injuries upon the deceased, and that the deceased have died as a result of such injury.

[F] The defendant must have injured the deceased in the heat of passion, caused by *adequate provocation* and without malice.

[G] If *a homicide is committed in the heat of passion, caused by adequate provocation, the offense is manslaughter rather than murder in the second degree.* In addition to adequate provocation, there must be heat of passion caused by that provocation. Both the provocation and the passion must exist at the time the injury or injuries causing the death of the deceased are inflicted.

[H] "Heat of passion" includes rage, resentment, anger, terror, and fear. Heat of passion may be produced by fear as well as by rage.

[I] Provocation, *in order to be adequate to reduce the offense from murder in the second degree to manslaughter*, must be such as might naturally induce a reasonable man in the passion of the moment to lose self-control and commit the act on impulse and without reflection.

[J] A blow or other personal violence may constitute adequate provocation. But a trivial or slight provocation, entirely disproportionate to the violence of the retaliation, is *not adequate provocation to reduce the offense from murder in the second degree to manslaughter.* Mere words standing alone, however, no matter how insulting, no matter how offensive, no matter how abusive, are *not adequate to reduce a homicide from murder in the second degree to manslaughter.*

[K] It must be such provocation as would arouse a reasonable, sober man. If the provocation aroused the defendant because

the instruction follows closely the Junior Bar Section's Model Instruction No. 88.

Two different themes run through this instruction. The first concerns the essential elements of manslaughter. Assuming a defendant is charged only with manslaughter, what should the jury be told they must find to convict him? Reflecting this theme are paragraphs A, B, most of D, E, and L. The second theme, however, concerns the distinction between manslaughter and second degree murder—with the factors that will *reduce* the offense from murder to manslaughter. This theme, of course, is appropriate only when, as in this case, the defendant is charged with second degree murder as well as manslaughter. The paragraphs which clearly reflect this second theme are paragraphs C, D (2) & (3), F, G, H, I, J, and K.

The intermingling of these different themes has extraordinary results, the most striking of which is paragraph D. According to that paragraph, it is an element of manslaughter that the defendant injured the deceased in the heat of passion caused by adequate provocation, and the Government must prove this beyond a reasonable doubt. Taken literally, this has the ludicrous result that a jury which finds the evidence in balance on the question of provocation can convict the defendant *neither* of second degree murder *nor* of manslaughter. Of course the law does not require the Government to run the risk of thus falling between two stools. Manslaughter, as paragraph B quite properly states, is "the unlawful [that is, unexcused] killing of a human being without malice." If malice is proved beyond a reasonable doubt and no affirmative defense applies, the defendant is guilty of murder; if malice is not proved, he is guilty of manslaughter. The only defense to a charge of causing another's death—aside from self-defense, insanity, duress, and so forth—is that the homicide was inadvertent and that defendant's negligence, if any, was not sufficient to convict him of involuntary manslaughter.

From what we have said, it would seem that the confusing nature of the instruction leads only to a risk that guilty men might be acquitted of both manslaughter and second degree murder. But juries are likely to have enough common sense to avoid the conclusion that a man who has intentionally shot another, without legal justification, is innocent of any crime. There is a danger, accordingly, that a jury might resolve the confusion in another way: by thinking that in some sense the burden of proof is on the *defendant* to show that the provocation was adequate to reduce murder to manslaughter. Over and over again, the instruction repeats that the provocation must be *adequate* before defendant can be acquitted of second degree murder and convicted instead of manslaughter. Since the Government is clearly trying to get the more severe verdict, the jury might therefore conclude that the defendant, as the only party really interested in showing provocation, must persuade it of the adequacy of the provocation.

he was intoxicated, and would not have aroused a sober man, *it does not reduce the offense to manslaughter.*

[L] It is necessary that the homicide have been committed without legal justification or excuse. [Emphasis added.]

All it takes to cure this defect, of course, is to tell the jury plainly what the law is: that when the defendant, or the Government, has introduced evidence of provocation, then the Government must prove the *absence* or *inadequacy* of the provocation beyond a reasonable doubt. To make this as clear as possible to the jury, it should be explained that provocation is *not* an element of manslaughter (whether voluntary or involuntary), but a *defense* to second degree murder. The Government is not required to disprove provocation in its case in chief, unless its own evidence would support a finding of adequate provocation. If the defense introduces some evidence of provocation, the Government will have the opportunity to rebut. Once some evidence of provocation is in the case—whether introduced by the Government or the defense—defendant is entitled to an instruction on provocation and manslaughter, the burden of persuading the jury of the absence of provocation is on the Government, and the jury is entitled to a clear instruction to that effect.

With these considerations in mind, paragraph A of the manslaughter instruction in this case reads quite peculiarly. It says:

> *If* the jury determines that neither defendant is guilty of murder in the second degree, *then* the jury is required to consider whether or not one defendant or both defendants are guilty of . . . manslaughter. And, the Court will now instruct the members of the jury as to the elements of manslaughter. [Emphasis added.]

What follows, as we have already indicated, is not just a concise statement of the law of manslaughter, but a detailed statement of several issues which it is clearly important for the jury to consider when it is deciding whether to convict defendant of second degree murder.

However startling we find the confusions present in the instructions in this case, we do not think that they require reversal of this conviction. The confusion, we have suggested, may prejudice the Government as well as the defendant. More important, we cannot ignore that instructions of this form have for years gone uncriticized by scholars, defense lawyers, experienced trial judges, and—we do not hesitate to add—appellate judges with many years on the bench. Therefore, we make our holding on this issue prospective only. In trials held after the date of this opinion, in which the defendant is entitled to a charge on the lesser included offense of manslaughter, the instructions must take a form which, first, distinguishes clearly between those factors which constitute defenses to second degree murder and those which constitute the elements of manslaughter, and second, clearly instructs the jury that when a defense to second degree murder—adequate provocation, for example—has been put in issue, the Government must prove its absence beyond a reasonable doubt. . . .

. . .

[Murdock's convictions were affirmed. Some of Alexander's convictions were vacated, on other grounds.]

---

58. The killings in *Alexander* occurred on the night of June 4, 1968. The assassination of Martin Luther King, Jr. had occurred two months earlier, on April 4, 1968. Is that fact relevant to the issue of "malice aforethought" in *Alexander*? Would you as defense counsel (or as prosecutor) have wanted to bring that fact to the attention of the jury? What advantages or risks would you foresee? Should such facts, which indicate the general "social context" in which a killing like those in *Alexander* occurred, be admissible on the issue of provocation (or any other issue)?

For a case similar in some respects to *Alexander*, in which, after a "senseless" brawl left one person dead, another person was convicted of second-degree murder, see Commonwealth v. Bray, 477 N.E.2d 596 (Mass. Ct.App.1985).

59. Are the critical factors that led to the killings in *Alexander* brought out as well by the rules regarding provocation as they might have been by the rules that defined the ancient crime of chance-medley, see p. 70 note 38, above, or something similar?

Consider in that connection the observation of Judge McGowan in a separate opinion in *Alexander*: "The tragic and senseless events giving rise to these appeals are a recurring by-product of a society which, unable as yet to eliminate explosive racial tensions, appears equally paralyzed to deny easy access to guns. Cultural infantilism of this kind inevitably exacts a high price, which in this instance was paid by the two young officers who were killed. The ultimate responsibility for their deaths reaches far beyond these appellants." 471 F.2d at 965. Upholding the conviction, Judge McGowan went on to observe that the courts "administer a system of justice which is limited in its reach" and "deal only with those formally accused under laws which define criminal accountability narrowly." Id.

In jurisdictions that adhere to the rule that words alone are inadequate provocation, how do the ancient and modern crimes differ?

60. The issue about instructions to the jury on the burden of proving provocation or absence of provocation, which is discussed in the second half of the *Alexander* opinion, has been troubling elsewhere as well. See State v. Grunow, 488 A.2d 1098 (N.J.Super.Ct.App.Div.1985). The larger issue is who ought to have the burden of proof in the first place, prosecution or defense. That issue is presented in the materials immediately following.

Mullaney v. Wilbur

421 U.S. 684, 95 S.Ct. 1881, 44 L.Ed.2d 508 (1975)

■ MR. JUSTICE POWELL delivered the opinion of the Court.

The State of Maine requires a defendant charged with murder to prove that he acted "in the heat of passion on sudden provocation" in order to reduce the homicide to manslaughter. We must decide whether this rule comports with the due process requirement, as defined in In re Winship, 397 U.S. 358, 364 (1970), that the prosecution prove beyond a reasonable doubt every fact necessary to constitute the crime charged.

I

In June 1966 a jury found respondent Stillman E. Wilbur, Jr., guilty of murder. The case against him rested on his own pretrial statement and on circumstantial evidence showing that he fatally assaulted Claude Hebert in the latter's hotel room. Respondent's statement, introduced by the prosecution, claimed that he had attacked Hebert in a frenzy provoked by Hebert's homosexual advance. The defense offered no evidence, but argued that the homicide was not unlawful since respondent lacked criminal intent. Alternatively, Wilbur's counsel asserted that at most the homicide was manslaughter rather than murder, since it occurred in the heat of passion provoked by the homosexual assault.

The trial court instructed the jury that Maine law recognizes two kinds of homicide, murder and manslaughter, and that these offenses are not subdivided into different degrees. The common elements of both are that the homicide be unlawful—i.e., neither justifiable nor excusable—and that it be intentional. The prosecution is required to prove these elements by proof beyond a reasonable doubt, and only if they are so proved is the jury to consider the distinction between murder and manslaughter.

In view of the evidence the trial court drew particular attention to the difference between murder and manslaughter. After reading the statutory definitions of both offenses,[42] the court charged that "malice aforethought is an essential and indispensable element of the crime of murder," App. 40, without which the homicide would be manslaughter. The jury was further instructed, however, that if the prosecution established that the homicide was both intentional and unlawful, malice aforethought was to be conclusively implied unless the defendant proved by a fair preponderance of the evidence that he acted in the heat of passion on sudden provocation. The

---

42. The Maine murder statute, Me. Rev. Stat. Ann., Tit. 17, § 2651 (1964), provides:

"Whoever unlawfully kills a human being with malice aforethought, either express or implied, is guilty of murder and shall be punished by imprisonment for life."

The manslaughter statute, Me. Rev. Stat. Ann., Tit. 17, § 2551 (1964), in relevant part provides:

"Whoever unlawfully kills a human being in the heat of passion, on sudden provocation, without express or implied malice aforethought . . . shall be punished by a fine of not more than $1,000 or by imprisonment for not more than 20 years . . . ."

court emphasized that "malice aforethought and heat of passion on sudden provocation are two inconsistent things," id., at 62; thus, by proving the latter the defendant would negate the former and reduce the homicide from murder to manslaughter. The court then concluded its charge with elaborate definitions of "heat of passion" and "sudden provocation."

After retiring to consider its verdict, the jury twice returned to request further instruction. It first sought reinstruction on the doctrine of implied malice aforethought, and later on the definition of "heat of passion." Shortly after the second reinstruction, the jury found respondent guilty of murder.

Respondent appealed to the Maine Supreme Judicial Court, arguing that he had been denied due process because he was required to negate the element of malice aforethought by proving that he had acted in the heat of passion on sudden provocation. He claimed that under Maine law malice aforethought was an essential element of the crime of murder—indeed that it was the sole element distinguishing murder from manslaughter. Respondent contended, therefore, that this Court's decision in *Winship* requires the prosecution to prove the existence of that element beyond a reasonable doubt.

The Maine Supreme Judicial Court rejected this contention, holding that in Maine murder and manslaughter are not distinct crimes but, rather, different degrees of the single generic offense of felonious homicide. . . . The court further stated that for more than a century it repeatedly had held that the prosecution could rest on a presumption of implied malice aforethought and require the defendant to prove that he had acted in the heat of passion on sudden provocation in order to reduce murder to manslaughter. With respect to *Winship*, which was decided after respondent's trial, the court noted that it did not anticipate the application of the *Winship* principle to a factor such as the heat of passion on sudden provocation.

Respondent next successfully petitioned for a writ of habeas corpus in Federal District Court. Wilbur v. Robbins, 349 F. Supp. 149 (D.Me.1972). The District Court ruled that under the Maine statutes murder and manslaughter are distinct offenses, not different degrees of a single offense. The court further held that "[m]alice aforethought is made the distinguishing element of the offense of murder, and it is expressly excluded as an element of the offense of manslaughter." Id., at 153. Thus, the District Court concluded, *Winship* requires the prosecution to prove malice aforethought beyond a reasonable doubt; it cannot rely on a presumption of implied malice, which requires the defendant to prove that he acted in the heat of passion on sudden provocation.

The Court of Appeals for the First Circuit affirmed, subscribing in general to the District Court's analysis and construction of Maine law. 473 F.2d 943 (1973). Although recognizing that "within broad limits a state court must be the one to interpret its own laws," the court nevertheless ruled that "a totally unsupportable construction which leads to an invasion of constitutional due process is a federal matter." Id., at 945. The Court of

Appeals equated malice aforethought with "premeditation," id., at 947, and concluded that *Winship* requires the prosecution to prove this fact beyond a reasonable doubt.

Following this decision, the Maine Supreme Judicial Court decided the case of State v. Lafferty, 309 A.2d 647 (1973), in which it sharply disputed the First Circuit's view that it was entitled to make an independent determination of Maine law. The Maine court also reaffirmed its earlier opinion that murder and manslaughter are punishment categories of the single offense of felonious homicide. Accordingly, if the prosecution proves a felonious homicide the burden shifts to the defendant to prove that he acted in the heat of passion on sudden provocation in order to receive the lesser penalty prescribed for manslaughter.

In view of the *Lafferty* decision we granted certiorari in this case and remanded to the Court of Appeals for reconsideration. . . . On remand, that court again applied *Winship*, this time to the Maine law as construed by the Maine Supreme Judicial Court. . . . Looking to the "substance" of that law, the court found that the presence or absence of the heat of passion on sudden provocation results in significant differences in the penalties and stigma attaching to conviction. For these reasons the Court of Appeals held that the principles enunciated in *Winship* control, and that to establish murder the prosecution must prove beyond a reasonable doubt that the defendant did not act in the heat of passion on sudden provocation.

Because of the importance of the issues presented, we again granted certiorari. . . . We now affirm.

II

. . . [W]e accept as binding the Maine Supreme Judicial Court's construction of state homicide law.

III

The Maine law of homicide, as it bears on this case, can be stated succinctly: Absent justification or excuse, all intentional or criminally reckless killings are felonious homicides. Felonious homicide is punished as murder—i.e., by life imprisonment—unless the defendant proves by a fair preponderance of the evidence that it was committed in the heat of passion on sudden provocation, in which case it is punished as manslaughter—i.e., by a fine not to exceed $1,000 or by imprisonment not to exceed 20 years. The issue is whether the Maine rule requiring the defendant to prove that he acted in the heat of passion on sudden provocation accords with due process.

A

Our analysis may be illuminated if this issue is placed in historical context. At early common law only those homicides committed in the enforcement of justice were considered justifiable; all others were deemed unlawful and were punished by death. Gradually, however, the severity of the common-law punishment for homicide abated. Between the 13th and

16th centuries the class of justifiable homicides expanded to include, for example, accidental homicides and those committed in self-defense. Concurrently, the wide-spread use of capital punishment was ameliorated further by extension of the ecclesiastic jurisdiction. Almost any person able to read was eligible for "benefit of clergy," a procedural device that effected a transfer from the secular to the ecclesiastic jurisdiction. And under ecclesiastic law a person who committed an unlawful homicide was not executed; instead he received a one-year sentence, had his thumb branded and was required to forfeit his goods. At the turn of the 16th century, English rulers, concerned with the accretion of ecclesiastic jurisdiction at the expense of the secular, enacted a series of statutes eliminating the benefit of clergy in all cases of "murder of malice prepensed." Unlawful homicides that were committed without such malice were designated "manslaughter," and their perpetrators remained eligible for the benefit of clergy.

Even after ecclesiastic jurisdiction was eliminated for all secular offenses the distinction between murder and manslaughter persisted. It was said that "manslaughter, when voluntary, arises from the sudden heat of the passions, murder from the wickedness of the heart." 4 W. Blackstone, Commentaries *190. Malice aforethought was designated as the element that distinguished the two crimes, but it was recognized that such malice could be implied by law as well as proved by evidence. Absent proof that an unlawful homicide resulted from "sudden and sufficiently violent provocation," the homicide was "presumed to be malicious." Id., at *201. In view of this presumption, the early English authorities . . . held that once the prosecution proved that the accused had committed the homicide, it was "incumbent upon the prisoner to make out, to the satisfaction of the court and jury" "all . . . circumstances of justification, excuse, or alleviation." 4 W. Blackstone, Commentaries *201. . . . Thus, at common law the burden of proving heat of passion on sudden provocation appears to have rested on the defendant.

In this country the concept of malice aforethought took on two distinct meanings: in some jurisdictions it came to signify a substantive element of intent, requiring the prosecution to prove that the defendant intended to kill or to inflict great bodily harm; in other jurisdictions it remained a policy presumption, indicating only that absent proof to the contrary a homicide was presumed not to have occurred in the heat of passion. . . . In a landmark case, Commonwealth v. York, 50 Mass. (9 Met.) 93 (1845), Chief Justice Shaw of the Massachusetts Supreme Judicial Court held that the defendant was required to negate malice aforethought by proving by a preponderance of the evidence that he acted in the heat of passion. Initially, York was adopted in Maine as well as several other jurisdictions. In 1895, however, in the context of deciding a question of federal criminal procedure, this Court explicitly considered and unanimously rejected the general approach articulated in York. Davis v. United States, 160 U.S. 469. And, in the past half century, the large majority of States have abandoned York and now require the prosecution to prove the absence of the heat of passion on sudden provocation beyond a reasonable doubt. . . .

This historical review establishes two important points. First, the fact at issue here—the presence or absence of the heat of passion on sudden provocation—has been, almost from the inception of the common law of homicide, the single most important factor in determining the degree of culpability attaching to an unlawful homicide. And, second, the clear trend has been toward requiring the prosecution to bear the ultimate burden of proving this fact. . . .

B

Petitioners, the warden of the Maine Prison and the State of Maine, argue that despite these considerations *Winship* should not be extended to the present case. They note that as a formal matter the absence of the heat of passion on sudden provocation is not a "fact necessary to constitute the *crime*" of felonious homicide in Maine. In re Winship, 397 U.S., at 364 (emphasis supplied). This distinction is relevant, according to petitioners, because in *Winship* the facts at issue were essential to establish criminality in the first instance, whereas the fact in question here does not come into play until the jury already has determined that the defendant is guilty and may be punished at least for manslaughter. In this situation, petitioners maintain, the defendant's critical interests in liberty and reputation are no longer of paramount concern since, irrespective of the presence or absence of the heat of passion on sudden provocation, he is likely to lose his liberty and certain to be stigmatized. In short, petitioners would limit *Winship* to those facts which, if not proved, would wholly exonerate the defendant.

This analysis fails to recognize that the criminal law of Maine, like that of other jurisdictions, is concerned not only with guilt or innocence in the abstract but also with the degree of criminal culpability. Maine has chosen to distinguish those who kill in the heat of passion from those who kill in the absence of this factor. Because the former are less "blameworth[y]," State v. Lafferty, 309 A.2d, at 671, 673 (concurring opinion), they are subject to substantially less severe penalties. By drawing this distinction, while refusing to require the prosecution to establish beyond a reasonable doubt the fact upon which it turns, Maine denigrates the interests found critical in *Winship*.

The safeguards of due process are not rendered unavailing simply because a determination may already have been reached that would stigmatize the defendant and that might lead to a significant impairment of personal liberty. The fact remains that the consequences resulting from a verdict of murder, as compared with a verdict of manslaughter, differ significantly. Indeed, when viewed in terms of the potential difference in restrictions of personal liberty attendant to each conviction, the distinction established by Maine between murder and manslaughter may be of greater importance than the difference between guilt or innocence for many lesser crimes.

Moreover, if *Winship* were limited to those facts that constitute a crime as defined by state law, a State could undermine many of the interests that decision sought to protect without effecting any substantive change in its law. It would only be necessary to redefine the elements that constitute different crimes, characterizing them as factors that bear solely on the extent of punishment. An extreme example of this approach can be fashioned from the law challenged in this case. Maine divides the single generic offense of felonious homicide into three distinct punishment categories— murder, voluntary manslaughter, and involuntary manslaughter. Only the first two of these categories require that the homicidal act either be intentional or the result of criminally reckless conduct. . . . But under Maine law these facts of intent are not general elements of the crime of felonious homicide. . . . Instead, they bear only on the appropriate punishment category. Thus, if petitioners' argument were accepted, Maine could impose a life sentence for any felonious homicide—even those that traditionally might be considered involuntary manslaughter—unless the *defendant* was able to prove that his act was neither intentional nor criminally reckless.

Winship is concerned with substance rather than this kind of formalism. The rationale of that case requires an analysis that looks to the "operation and effect of the law as applied and enforced by the State," St. Louis S. W. R. Co. v. Arkansas, 235 U.S. 350, 362 (1914), and to the interests of both the State and the defendant as affected by the allocation of the burden of proof.

In *Winship* the Court emphasized the societal interests in the reliability of jury verdicts:

> The requirement of proof beyond a reasonable doubt has [a] vital role in our criminal procedure for cogent reasons. The accused during a criminal prosecution has at stake interests of immense importance, both because of the possibility that he may lose his liberty upon conviction and because of the certainty that he would be stigmatized by the conviction. . . .

> Moreover, use of the reasonable-doubt standard is indispensable to command the respect and confidence of the community in applications of the criminal law. It is critical that the moral force of the criminal law not be diluted by a standard of proof that leaves people in doubt whether innocent men are being condemned.

397 U.S., at 363, 364. These interests are implicated to a greater degree in this case than they were in *Winship* itself. Petitioner there faced an 18-month sentence, with a maximum possible extension of an additional four and one-half years . . . whereas respondent here faces a differential in sentencing ranging from a nominal fine to a mandatory life sentence. Both the stigma to the defendant and the community's confidence in the administration of the criminal law are also of greater consequence in this case, since the adjudication of delinquency involved in *Winship* was "benevolent" in intention, seeking to provide "a generously conceived program of compassionate treatment." Id., at 376 (Burger, C.J., dissenting).

Not only are the interests underlying *Winship* implicated to a greater degree in this case, but in one respect the protection afforded those interests is less here. In *Winship* the ultimate burden of persuasion remained with the prosecution, although the standard had been reduced to proof by a fair preponderance of the evidence. In this case, by contrast, the State has affirmatively shifted the burden of proof to the defendant. The result, in a case such as this one where the defendant is required to prove the critical fact in dispute, is to increase further the likelihood of an erroneous murder conviction. Such a result directly contravenes the principle articulated in Speiser v. Randall, 357 U.S. 513, 525–526 (1958):

> [W]here one party has at stake an interest of transcending value— as a criminal defendant his liberty—th[e] margin of error is reduced as to him by the process of placing on the [prosecution] the burden . . . of persuading the factfinder at the conclusion of the trial. . . .
>
> . . .

C

It has been suggested . . . that because of the difficulties in negating an argument that the homicide was committed in the heat of passion the burden of proving this fact should rest on the defendant. No doubt this is often a heavy burden for the prosecution to satisfy. The same may be said of the requirement of proof beyond a reasonable doubt of many controverted facts in a criminal trial. But this is the traditional burden which our system of criminal justice deems essential.

Indeed, the Maine Supreme Judicial Court itself acknowledged that most States require the prosecution to prove the absence of passion beyond a reasonable doubt. . . . Moreover, the difficulty of meeting such an exacting burden is mitigated in Maine where the fact at issue is largely an "objective, rather than a subjective, behavioral criterion." State v. Rollins, 295 A.2d [914 (1972)], at 920. In this respect, proving that the defendant did not act in the heat of passion on sudden provocation is similar to proving any other element of intent; it may be established by adducing evidence of the factual circumstances surrounding the commission of the homicide. And although intent is typically considered a fact peculiarly within the knowledge of the defendant, this does not, as the Court has long recognized, justify shifting the burden to him. . . .

Nor is the requirement of proving a negative unique in our system of criminal jurisprudence. Maine itself requires the prosecution to prove the absence of self-defense beyond a reasonable doubt. . . . Satisfying this burden imposes an obligation that, in all practical effect, is identical to the burden involved in negating the heat of passion on sudden provocation. Thus, we discern no unique hardship on the prosecution that would justify requiring the defendant to carry the burden of proving a fact so critical to criminal culpability.

IV

Maine law requires a defendant to establish by a preponderance of the evidence that he acted in the heat of passion on sudden provocation in order to reduce murder to manslaughter. Under this burden of proof a defendant can be given a life sentence when the evidence indicates that it is *as likely as not* that he deserves a significantly lesser sentence. This is an intolerable result in a society where . . . it is far worse to sentence one guilty only of manslaughter as a murderer than to sentence a murderer for the lesser crime of manslaughter. . . . We therefore hold that the Due Process Clause requires the prosecution to prove beyond a reasonable doubt the absence of the heat of passion on sudden provocation when the issue is properly presented in a homicide case. . . .[43]

---

61. Without quite saying so, the Court in Mullaney v. Wilbur came near to holding in effect that murder and voluntary manslaughter are *inherently* (or, at any rate, historically) different crimes, so that a state could not rationally include them in the same category. If that is indeed what the Court intended, it is a very strong statement about sorting homicides. The Washington statute, for example, provides simply that an intentional killing is murder. Wash. Rev. Code § 9A.32.050. It is irrelevant that the defendant may have been strongly provoked. As the Washington Supreme Court put it, "The makers of our Criminal Code, having steeled themselves against the feeling of tenderness for the frailty of human nature, no longer palliate the offense, and all killings not excusable or justifiable, done with a design to effect death, constitute murder in one of its degrees." State v. Palmer, 176 P. 547, 549 (Wash.1918). See State v. Johnson, 418 P.2d 238 (Wash.1966). Under the reasoning of Mullaney v. Wilbur, is such a provision consistent with due process of law?

62. Patterson v. New York. Two years after it decided Mullaney v. Wilbur, the Supreme Court decided Patterson v. New York, 432 U.S. 197 (1977) (5–3), in which it considered the New York statutory formula for distinguishing second-degree murder and (voluntary) manslaughter. The statute provided that a person is guilty of murder when, "with intent to cause the death of another person, he causes the death of such person or of a third person." It provided further that it was an affirmative defense to the charge of murder that the defendant "acted under the influence of extreme emotional disturbance for which there was a reasonable explanation or excuse . . . ." Manslaughter was defined as intentionally causing the death of another person under the circumstances constituting an affirmative defense to murder. At Patterson's trial, the jury was instructed that the prosecution had to prove the facts establishing an intentional killing beyond a reasonable doubt, but that the defendant had the burden of proving the affirmative defense by a preponderance of the evidence. In the Supreme Court, the defendant argued that these instructions were incorrect under Mullaney v. Wilbur.

---

[43] Justice Rehnquist wrote a concurring opinion, which Chief Justice Burger joined.

The Court affirmed the conviction. It noted that the New York law was "a considerably expanded version of the common-law defense of heat of passion on sudden provocation" and that at common law the burden of proving such an affirmative defense was on the defendant. It noted also that its prior decisions had upheld the constitutionality of a state requirement that a defendant prove the defense of insanity beyond a reasonable doubt. It said:

> We cannot conclude that Patterson's conviction under the New York law deprived him of due process of law. The crime of murder is defined by the statute, which represents a recent revision of the state criminal code, as causing the death of another person with intent to do so. The death, the intent to kill, and causation are the facts that the State is required to prove beyond a reasonable doubt if a person is to be convicted of murder. No further facts are either presumed or inferred in order to constitute the crime. The statute does provide an affirmative defense—that the defendant acted under the influence of extreme emotional disturbance for which there was a reasonable explanation—which, if proved by a preponderance of the evidence, would reduce the crime to manslaughter, an offense defined in a separate section of the statute. It is plain enough that if the intentional killing is shown, the State intends to deal with the defendant as a murderer unless he demonstrates the mitigating circumstances.

> Here, the jury was instructed in accordance with the statute, and the guilty verdict confirms that the State successfully carried its burden of proving the facts of the crime beyond a reasonable doubt. Nothing in the evidence, including any evidence that might have been offered with respect to Patterson's mental state at the time of the crime, raised a reasonable doubt about his guilt as a murderer; and clearly the evidence failed to convince the jury that Patterson's affirmative defense had been made out. It seems to us that the State satisfied the mandate of *Winship* that it prove beyond a reasonable doubt "every fact necessary to constitute the crime with which [Patterson was] charged." 397 U.S., at 364.

> . . .

> . . . Here, in revising its criminal code, New York provided the affirmative defense of extreme emotional disturbance, a substantially expanded version of the older heat-of-passion concept; but it was willing to do so only if the facts making out the defense were established by the defendant with sufficient certainty. The State was itself unwilling to undertake to establish the absence of those facts beyond a reasonable doubt, perhaps fearing that proof would be too difficult and that too many persons deserving treatment as murderers would escape that punishment if the evidence need merely raise a reasonable doubt about the defendant's emotional state. It has been said that the new criminal code of New York contains some 25 affirmative defenses which exculpate or mitigate but which must be established by the defendant to be operative. The Due Process Clause, as we see it, does

not put New York to the choice of abandoning those defenses or undertaking to disprove their existence in order to convict of a crime which otherwise is within its constitutional powers to sanction by substantial punishment.

. . .

[I]n each instance of a murder conviction under the present law, New York will have proved beyond a reasonable doubt that the defendant has intentionally killed another person, an act which it is not disputed the State may constitutionally criminalize and punish. If the State nevertheless chooses to recognize a factor that mitigates the degree of criminality or punishment, we think the State may assure itself that the fact has been established with reasonable certainty. To recognize at all a mitigating circumstance does not require the State to prove its nonexistence in each case in which the fact is put in issue, if in its judgment this would be too cumbersome, too expensive, and too inaccurate.

432 U.S. at 205–209.

Mullaney v. Wilbur, the Court said, was distinguishable because according to the definition of murder under Maine law, "malice, in the sense of the absence of provocation, was part of the definition of that crime. Yet malice, i.e., lack of provocation, was presumed and could be rebutted by the defendant only by proving by a preponderance of the evidence that he acted with heat of passion upon sudden provocation." Id. at 216.

A dissenting opinion argued that the Maine and New York statutes were indistinguishable, on the basis of Mullaney v. Wilbur, and that the distinctions drawn in *Patterson* were "formalistic rather than substantive." Id. at 216, 221 (dissenting opinion of Justice Powell, which Justice Brennan and Justice Marshall joined). According to the dissenters, the legislature could assign the burden of proof as it wished, except when "the factor at issue makes a substantial difference in punishment and stigma," *and* "in the Anglo–American legal tradition the factor in question historically has held that level of importance." Id. at 226. If both those conditions were met, the state should be required to prove the fact beyond a reasonable doubt.

For further discussion of the burden of proof in a homicide prosecution, this time in the context of self-defense, see Martin v. Ohio, 480 U.S. 228 (1987) (5–4). In *Martin*, the Court distinguished evidence that the defendant acted in self-defense to contradict a specific intent to kill "with prior calculation and design," as an element of the offense, and such evidence to establish the affirmative defense of self-defense. With respect to the former, the Court said that the prosecution must meet the burden of proof beyond a reasonable doubt, and with respect to the latter, that the defendant can be required to prove the defense by a preponderance of the evidence. In practice, will juries be able to replicate the subtlety of the Court's reasoning? See also Montana v. Egelhoff, 518 U.S. 37 (1996) (5–4), in which the Court held that a state law excluding evidence of (voluntary) intoxication to show that defendant did not kill "knowingly" or "purposely" as an element of the crime of deliberate homicide was not unconstitutional. The Court made another foray into the thicket of determining what counts as an element of a crime in Apprendi v. New Jersey, 530 U.S. 466, 490 (2000) (5–4), in which it held: "Other than the fact of a prior conviction, any fact that increases the penalty for a crime beyond the prescribed statutory maximum must be submitted to a jury, and proved beyond a reasonable doubt." The case involved a so-called "sentencing factor"—in this case the fact that the purpose of the crime was to intimidate a person because of his race—for which, if found by a judge, an increased sentence is authorized.

63. "Transferred intent." When a defendant's conduct would make him guilty of some form of intentional criminal homicide (voluntary manslaughter or murder) except for the fact that the person killed is someone other than the person intended, the usual result is that the defendant is guilty of the crime that he would have committed had he killed the person intended. The doctrine of "transferred intent," as it is called, is explained in the following jury instruction: "What is the situation where a person intends to kill one person but instead kills another person? To put it a different way, what is the situation when the deceased is not the intended victim? The law is that such a homicide partakes of the quality of the original act so that the guilt of an accused is exactly what it would have been had the shots been fired at the intended victim instead of the person actually killed. The fact that the person actually killed was killed instead of the intended victim is immaterial and the only question is what would have been the degree of guilt if the result intended had actually been accomplished. The intent is transferred to the person whose death has been caused." Gladden v. State, 330 A.2d 176, 177–78 (Md.1974).

Should the doctrine of transferred intent apply to an assault with intent to kill that injures but does not kill a third person? If A fires a gun at B with intent to kill and the bullet wounds C, is A guilty of two crimes: attempted murder (or voluntary manslaughter) of B and likewise of C? For that matter, if C is killed, is A guilty of the attempted murder of B and the murder of C? See People v. Scott, 927 P.2d 288 (Cal.1996), discussing the issue and concluding that there is no barrier to dual convictions. The court said:

> [D]efendants' exposure to a murder conviction based on a transferred intent theory of liability was proper regardless of the fact they were also charged with attempted murder of the intended victim. Contrary to what its name implies, the transferred intent doctrine does not refer to any actual intent that is "used up" once it has been employed to convict a defendant of a specific intent crime against an intended victim. Rather, the doctrine of transferred intent connotes a policy. As applied here, the transferred intent doctrine is but another way of saying that a defendant who shoots with an intent to kill but misses

and hits a bystander instead should be punished for a crime of the same seriousness as the one he tried to commit against his intended victim.

Id. at 289. Does that dispose of the problem?

The Model Penal Code takes care of such cases in its provisions on causation, § 2.03(2)(a), p. 325 below.

DEGREES OF MURDER

If the circumstances of an intentional (criminal) homicide do not "reduce" the crime from murder to manslaughter, are there nevertheless variables that the law should recognize in a general way? If so, what are they? What principles or policies make them relevant?

---

64.   The Pennsylvania formula. In the United States, the crime of murder, already distinguished from manslaughter by the common law, has been further separated into degrees, usually first degree and second degree. This formula is derived from a statute enacted in 1794 by the Pennsylvania Assembly as a measure toward the abolition of the death penalty.[44] The statute did away with the death penalty for all crimes except murder in the first degree. The reason for dividing murder into degrees was that "the several offences, which are included under the general denomination of murder, differ so greatly from each other in the degree of their atrociousness, that it is unjust to involve them in the same punishment." Act of April 22, 1794, § 2, 15 Statutes at Large of Pennsylvania from 1682 to 1801 ch. 1777, at 174, 175 (1911). In the preamble to the statute the legislators said: "[T]he design of punishment is to prevent the commission of crimes, and to repair the injury that hath been done thereby to society or the individual, and it hath been found by experience, that these objects are better obtained by moderate but certain penalties, than by severe and excessive punishments. And . . . it is the duty of every government to endeavor to reform, rather than exterminate offenders, and the punishment of death ought never to be inflicted where it is not absolutely necessary to the public safety." Id. at 174. The statute provided "that all murder which shall be perpetrated by means of poison, or by lying in wait, or by any other kind of willful, deliberate or premeditated killing, or which shall be committed in the perpetration, or attempt to perpetrate, any arson, rape, robbery or burglary, shall be deemed murder of the first degree; and

---

44. On capital punishment generally, see pp. 334–62 below.

all other kinds of murder shall be deemed murder in the second degree,'' § 2, id. at 175.

The original intention was probably that the penalty of death be imposed only for killing that was fully deliberate and premeditated, as the specific references to poisoning and lying in wait suggest if they are regarded simply as examples of the kind of killing that the legislators had in mind. Sometimes, however, in keeping with decisions requiring little deliberation or premeditation, poisoning and lying in wait have been treated as sui generis. Compare Sparf v. United States, 156 U.S. 51, 60 (1895) (''deliberate premeditation and design . . . implied from external circumstances capable of proof, such as lying in wait''), with State v. Johnson, 344 S.E.2d 775 (N.C.1986) (murder by poisoning or lying in wait does not require proof of premeditation), and People v. Ruiz, 749 P.2d 854 (Cal.1988) (lying in wait; same). The Pennsylvania formula, with local variations, was widely adopted in other jurisdictions.

———

People v. Caruso
246 N.Y. 437, 159 N.E. 390 (1927)

■ ANDREWS, J. This judgment must be reversed.

In reviewing <u>convictions for murder in the first degree</u>, the Court of Appeals has broad powers. It is to see that justice is done both to the accused and to the state. If guilt is clear, errors or instances of unfair conduct by the prosecutor may sometimes be ignored. The greater the doubt of guilt, however, the more likely are errors to affect the substantial rights of the accused. The more likely are appeals to sympathy or passion or prejudice to influence the jury. It is our duty, not only to weigh the evidence, but to grant a new trial, if we believe justice requires such a course.

[margin note: Ethnicity & social class is important in th[is] case.]

Francesco Caruso, an <u>illiterate Italian, 35 years old,</u> came to this <u>country about 1911. He worked as a laborer, and in the early part of 1927 was living with his wife and six small children in an apartment in Brooklyn.</u> On Friday, February 11th, one of these children, a boy of six, was ill with a sore throat. That day and the next he treated the boy with remedies bought at a drug store. The child grew worse, and at 10 o'clock of the night of the 12th he sent for a Dr. Pendola, who had been recommended to him, but with whom he was not acquainted.

What followed depends upon a statement made by Caruso and upon his testimony on the stand. Any proper inferences may be drawn therefrom. The belief that what he said was false, however, or any reasoning based upon his failure to call friendly witnesses, will not supply the want of affirmative testimony of the facts necessary to constitute the crime. Those facts, if they exist, must be inferred from his own admissions.

Some time between 10:30 and 11 in the evening Dr. Pendola arrived. The child had diphtheria. Caruso was sent out to buy some antitoxin, and, when he returned, the doctor administered it. He then gave Caruso another prescription with instructions as to its use, and left promising to return in the morning.

Caruso watched the child all night, giving remedies every half hour. "About 4 o'clock in the morning," he testified, "my child was standing up to the bed, and asked me to, he says, 'Papa' he said, 'I am dying.' I say that time, I said, 'You don't die.' I said, 'I will help you every time.' The same time that child he will be crazy—look like crazy, that time—don't want to stay any more inside. All I can do, I keep my child in my arms, and I held him in my arms from 4 o'clock until 8 o'clock in the morning. After 8 o'clock in the morning the poor child getting worse—the poor child in the morning he was"—(slight interruption in the testimony while the defendant apparently stops to overcome his emotion). "The poor child that time, and he was asking me, 'Papa,' he said, 'I want to go and sleep.' So I said, 'All right, Giovie, I will put you in the sleep.' I take my Giovie, and I put him in the bed, and he started to sleep, to wait until the doctor came, and the doctor he never came. I waited from 10 o'clock, the doctor he never came."

Then, after trying in vain to get in touch with the doctor, he sent for an ambulance from a drug store.

"When I go home I seen my child is got up to the bed that time, and he says to me, 'Papa, I want to come with you.' I take my child again up in my arms, and I make him look to the backyard to the window. He looked around the yard about a couple of minutes, and after, when he looked around, he says to me, 'Papa, I want to go to sleep again.' I said, 'All right, Giovie, I will put you in the sleep.' I put my child on the bed. About a few seconds my child is on the bed, my child says to me, he says, 'Papa, I want to go to the toilet.' I said, 'All right, Giovie, I will take you to the toilet.' So I was trying to pick up the child, and make him go to the toilet, when I held that child I felt that leg—that child started to shake up in my arms. My wife know about better than me—I cannot see good myself in the face, so she tell what kind of shakes he do, and she has told me, she says, 'Listen, Frank, why, the child has died already.' I said, 'All right, you don't cry. No harm, because you make the child scared.' That time I go right away and put the child on the bed. When I put the child, before I put my hand to the pillow, my child said to me, 'Goodbye, Papa, I am going already.' So that time I put my hands to my head—I said, 'That child is dead. I don't know what I am going to do myself now.' That time I never said nothing, because I said, 'Jesus, my child is dead now. Nobody will get their hands on my child.' "

About 12 o'clock Dr. Pendola arrived. The child had been dead for some time. He was told, and then Caruso says the doctor laughed, and he "lost his head." This seems incredible. Yet Caruso apparently believed it, for his testimony on the stand is a repetition of the same charge made in his statement that same night, before it is likely that a man of Caruso's mentality would be preparing a false defense. The probability is there was, from one cause or another, some twitching of the facial muscles that might be mistaken for a smile.

Besides the delay of the doctor and the smile was another circumstance, which, if true, would exasperate Caruso. He says, and again this appears in the statement as well as in his testimony on the trial, that, when he was buying the antitoxin, the druggist told him that the dose was too large for a child of the age of his son. This he told the doctor. The latter was indignant, and paid no heed to the warning. The druggist denied any such conversation, and apparently the dose was proper. But it seems probable that something occurred that left on Caruso's mind the impression that the death of his child was caused by malpractice. At least, immediately after the death, he told an ambulance surgeon that Dr. Pendola had killed his child by an injection, and also complained of his delay in not coming that morning. And within a short time he made the same charge to others.

Then followed some talk. Caruso accused the doctor of killing his child. The doctor denied it. Caruso attacked him in anger, choked him until he fell to the floor, then went to a closet ten or twelve feet away, took a knife, and stabbed him twice in the throat, so killing him. Caruso then took his family to the janitor's apartment downstairs, and himself went to his brother's house on Staten Island, where he was arrested that night. He made no attempt whatever to conceal the facts of the homicide, and his departure cannot fairly be viewed as a flight, indicating consciousness of guilt.

The case for the people was simple. Formal identification of the dead body was required. That Caruso committed a homicide, neither excusable nor justifiable, was abundantly shown by his own statement, and, indeed, was not denied. The real issue was as to state of mind of the defendant, whether he formed the intent to kill Dr. Pendola, and, if so, whether the killing was the result of premeditation and deliberation. What Caruso in fact believed and thought, what he had in mind at the time of the homicide, is the issue—not whether his beliefs were justified. And the jury, horrified at the conceded brutality of his acts, are still to decide this issue in a judicial temper. Appeals to sympathy or prejudice can but be harmful.

Mrs. Pendola, the widow of the deceased, was a young woman, placed upon the stand by the state. The right to use her as a witness for a proper purpose is not questioned, notwithstanding the natural sympathy her presence would arouse. But she knew nothing of the circumstances of the crime. She might have been asked as to the identity of the deceased, although he could be identified by others. She might give any other material evidence, notwithstanding any influence her presence might have upon the jury. Mrs. Pendola was not called for any such purpose. She was allowed to say she had been married for 18 months; that she had one child, 6 months old; that her husband was a medical graduate; she explained why his call on Caruso was delayed on Sunday, the 13th; she gave conversations with the doctor when he received the telephone call from Caruso Saturday night, and again after his return; she told how he sat on his baby's crib and sang her to sleep. All this had no materiality upon the issues before the jury. The object of the state is clear. Although, doubtless, the result of "well intentioned though misguided zeal," it was an "unseemly and unsafe" appeal to prejudice. Nor here can we overlook it as probably unheeded. And the object of the prosecution is emphasized by questions, ruled out it is true, as to whether the defendant was a citizen, or had applied for naturalization. They were so plainly incompetent, it cannot be believed they were asked in good faith.

Testimony was given by an expert that the treatment of the child was correct, and the doses of antitoxin not excessive. The belief of Caruso as to these facts was the question, not whether his belief was mistaken. Nor did this testimony tend to corroborate the denial of the druggist that he had ever told Caruso that the dose was too large. . . .

But, passing the two questions already discussed, which would under the circumstances of this case require a reversal, there is also a fundamental reason requiring a new trial. Conviction here of murder in the first degree is not justified by the weight of the evidence. The jury might find that the intent to kill existed. While in his testimony on the stand Caruso denies such an intent, and says that in his rage he did not know what he was doing, yet in his statement he expressly admits his intent to kill, and the inference that the intent existed might also be drawn from the two wounds in the neck inflicted with a large knife.

But was there premeditation and deliberation? This seems to have been the question which troubled the jury. They considered their verdict for six hours—twice returning for definitions of homicide and of deliberation and premeditation. Time to deliberate and premeditate there clearly was. Caruso might have done so. In fact, however, did he?

Until the Saturday evening Caruso had never met Dr. Pendola. Nothing occurred at that interview that furnished any motive for murder. Then came nervous strain and anxiety culminating in grief, deep and genuine, for the death of his child. Brooding over his loss, blaming the doctor for his delay in making the promised visit, believing he had killed the boy by his treatment, the doctor finally enters. And, when told of the child's death he appears to laugh. This, added to his supposed injuries, would fully account for the gust of anger that Caruso says he felt. Then came the struggle and the homicide.

As has been said, Caruso had the time to deliberate, to make a choice whether to kill or not to kill—to overcome hesitation and doubt—to form a definite purpose. And, where sufficient time exists, very often the circumstances surrounding the homicide justify—indeed require—the necessary inference. Not here, however. No plan to kill is shown, no intention of violence when the doctor arrived—only grief and resentment. Not until the supposed laugh did the assault begin. "If the defendant inflicted the wound in a sudden transport of passion, excited by what the deceased then said and by the preceding events which, for the time, disturbed her reasoning faculties and deprived her of the capacity to reflect, or while under the influence of some sudden and uncontrollable emotion excited by the final culmination of her misfortunes, as indicated by the train of events which have been related, the act did not constitute murder in the first degree. Deliberation and premeditation imply the capacity at the time to think and reflect, sufficient volition to make a choice, and by the use of these powers to refrain from doing a wrongful act." People v. Barberi, 149 N.Y. 256. When the supposed laugh came, there was apparent cause for excitement and anger. There was enough to indicate hot blood and unreflecting action. There was immediate provocation. . . . The attack seems to have been the instant effect of impulse. Nor does the fact that the stabbing followed the beginning of the attack by some time affect this conclusion. It was all one transaction under the peculiar facts of this case. If the assault was not deliberated or premeditated, then neither was the infliction of the fatal wound.

With due consideration of all the facts presented there is insufficient evidence to justify a conviction of murder in the first degree. Doubtless, on this record the defendant might be convicted of some crime, either murder in the second degree, or, if his testimony on the stand is accepted, manslaughter in the first degree. Either verdict might be sustained on the facts. Not the one actually rendered.

. . . .

———

65. Is it likely, on the facts given in the opinion, that the court would have reversed Caruso's conviction if he had been a native-born high school teacher? Does the court's rejection of the verdict of the jury, which was able to observe Caruso as a witness and at the trial generally, substitute the court's evaluation of Caruso as a member of a class for the jury's evaluation of him as an individual? In view of the court's own apparent attitude, how weighty is its condemnation of "appeals to sympathy or passion or prejudice"?

In that connection, may the fact that Sacco and Vanzetti were executed in Massachusetts on August 22, 1927, have some significance? The opinion of the Court of Appeals in People v. Caruso was announced on November 22, 1927.

For a more recent case in which, in a factual context somewhat akin to that of *Caruso*, the defendant presented a defense to a charge of first-degree murder very similar to that which the court accepted in *Caruso*, see Commonwealth v. Carroll, 194 A.2d 911 (Pa.1963). In *Carroll*, the court concluded that the prosecution's evidence was "without the slightest doubt sufficient in law to prove first degree."

66. Would the court's judgment have been the same if the evidence showed that after his child's death Caruso went out and bought the knife with which he later killed the doctor? If not, is the factual difference between the two cases sufficient to justify the substantial difference in the punishments for first and second degree murder (the former then being a capital offense in New York)? If it is, on what principle(s)?

67.   Caruso's second trial began on January 30, 1928, sixty-nine days after the Court of Appeals reversed the conviction at the first trial. On the second day of trial, over the prosecutor's objection, Caruso pleaded guilty to manslaughter in the first degree, the maximum penalty for which was 20 years' imprisonment. He was sentenced to five to ten years' imprisonment plus five to ten years' imprisonment for committing a felony armed with a dangerous weapon. See People v. Caruso, 164 N.E. 106 (N.Y.1928). He was released on parole in 1934, after serving about half of his maximum sentence after allowances. L. Hall & S. Glueck, Criminal Law 55 n.8 (2d ed. 1958).

68.   In State v. Forrest, 362 S.E.2d 252 (N.C.1987), the defendant shot and killed his father, who was in the hospital. Hospital authorities had classified his father as terminally ill and directed that extraordinary measures not be used to prolong his life. During a visit by the defendant, his father began to cough and emitted "a gurgling and rattling noise." After telling his father that he loved him, the defendant took a pistol from his pocket and shot his father four times. After the shooting, the defendant said that he had killed his father to end his father's suffering. "I promised my dad," he said, "I wouldn't let him suffer." The court rejected the defendant's argument that "his extreme distress over his father's suffering was adequate provocation . . . to negate the malice required for a murder conviction." Rather, the court said, "irrefutable proof of premeditation and deliberation is clearly present." Id. at 256. A jury having found the defendant guilty of first-degree murder, he was given the mandatory sentence of life imprisonment. Under the Model Penal Code formulation, p. 89 above, would the defendant have been entitled to an instruction on manslaughter?

69.   The courts have used a variety of formulas to explain to juries what they should look for to determine whether the defendant acted with premeditation and deliberation. In the search for "objective," or at least observable, determinants, they have often focused on some time element; but how much time is required and even what period of time is being measured is not always clear. Courts have said that premeditation and deliberation may require only "a brief moment of thought," Government of the Virgin Islands v. Lake, 362 F.2d 770, 776 (3d Cir.1966); it may be "a matter of seconds," State v. Stewart, 198 N.E.2d 439, 443 (Ohio 1964).

Others have approved the view expressed in Bullock v. United States, 122 F.2d 213–14 (D.C.Cir.1941): "To speak of premeditation and deliberation which are instantaneous, or which take no appreciable time, is a contradiction in terms. It . . . destroys the statutory distinction between first and second degree murder." The court split the difference in People v. Bender, 163 P.2d 8, 19 (Cal.1945): "[T]he instruction that there need be 'no appreciable space of time between the intention to kill and the act of killing . . .' is abstractly a correct statement of the law. It will be properly understood (at least upon *deliberation*) by those learned in the law as referring only to the interval between the fully formulated intent and its execution, *and as necessarily presupposing that true deliberation and premeditation characterized the process of, and preceded ultimate, formulation of such intent.*"

In Hemphill v. United States, 402 F.2d 187 (D.C.Cir.1968), the court of appeals emphatically rejected the passage of time as a sufficient indication of the defendant's state of mind: "[T]he jury may not find premeditation solely from the fact that defendant had time to premeditate." Id. at 189. "Premeditation and deliberation are facts, susceptible of proof like any other facts in a criminal trial. The jury is not supposed to be rendering a moral judgment of culpability based on whether it likes the defendant, or is horrified by the brutality of his killing. Whatever the difficulties of proving states of mind, and whatever the wisdom of distinguishing degrees of murder on that ground, the law now puts the burden of proving premeditation and deliberation on the prosecutor, and moreover requires that his evidence do so beyond reasonable doubt." Id. at 191.

70. "In homespun terminology, intentional murder is in the first degree if committed in cold blood, and is murder in the second degree if committed on impulse or in the sudden heat of passion. These are the archetypes, that clarify by contrast. The real facts may be hard to classify and may lie between the poles. A sudden passion, like lust, rage, or jealousy, may spawn an impulsive intent yet persist long enough and in such a way as to permit that intent to become the subject of a further reflection and weighing of consequences and hence to take on the character of a murder executed without compunction and 'in cold blood.' The term 'in cold blood' does not necessarily mean the assassin lying in wait. . . . Thus the common understanding might find both passion and cold blood in the husband who surprises his wife in adultery, leaves the house to buy a gun at a sporting goods store, and returns for a deadly sequel. The analysis of the jury would be illuminated, however, if it is first advised that a typical case of first degree is the murder in cold blood; that murder committed on impulse or in sudden passion is murder in the second degree; and then instructed that a homicide conceived in passion constitutes murder in the first degree only if the jury is convinced beyond a reasonable doubt that there was an appreciable time after the design was conceived and that in this interval there was a further thought, and a turning over in the mind—

and not a mere persistence of the initial impulse of passion." Austin v. United States, 382 F.2d 129, 137 (D.C.Cir.1967).

"[I]t underscores the difference between the statutory degrees of murder to emphasize that premeditation and deliberation must be given independent meaning in a prosecution for first-degree murder. The ordinary meaning of the terms will suffice. To premeditate is to think about beforehand; to deliberate is to measure and evaluate the major facets of a choice or problem. As a number of courts have pointed out, premeditation and deliberation characterize a thought process undisturbed by hot blood. While the minimum time necessary to exercise this process is incapable of exact determination, the interval between initial thought and ultimate action should be long enough to afford a reasonable man time to subject the nature of his response to a 'second look.' " People v. Morrin, 187 N.W.2d 434, 439 (Mich.Ct.App.1971).

Do metaphors like "cold blood" and "sudden heat" convey the distinction between first and second degree murder better than explanations like that of the California court in *Bender*, p. 117 note 69, above? If so, do they do well enough to sustain the distinction as a basis for differentiating intentional homicides?

71.

The type of evidence which this court has found sufficient to sustain a finding of premeditation and deliberation falls into three basic categories: (1) facts about how and what defendant did *prior* to the actual killing which show that the defendant was engaged in activity directed toward, and explicable as intended to result in, the killing—what may be characterized as "planning" activity; (2) facts about the defendant's *prior* relationship and/or conduct with the victim from which the jury could reasonably infer a "motive" to kill the victim, which inference of motive, together with facts of type (1) or (3), would in turn support an inference that the killing was the result of "a pre-existing reflection" and "careful thought and weighing of considerations" rather than "mere unconsidered or rash impulse hastily executed" (People v. Thomas, 25 Cal.2d 880, at pp. 898, 900, 901); (3) facts about the nature of the killing from which the jury could infer that the *manner* of killing was so particular and exacting that the defendant must have intentionally killed according to a "preconceived design" to take his victim's life in a particular way for a "reason" which the jury can reasonably infer from facts of type (1) or (2).

Analysis of the cases will show that this court sustains verdicts of first degree murder typically when there is evidence of all three types and otherwise requires at least extremely strong evidence of (1) or evidence of (2) in conjunction with either (1) or (3).

People v. Anderson, 447 P.2d 942, 949 (Cal.1968). Subsequently, the court observed that in *Anderson*, it had attempted "to do no more than catalog common factors that had occurred in prior cases," and that the factors mentioned in *Anderson*, "while helpful for purposes of review, are not a sine qua non to finding first degree premeditated murder, nor are they exclusive." People v. Perez, 831 P.2d 1159, 1163 (Cal.1992).

In State v. Bingham, 719 P.2d 109 (Wash.1986), the defendant strangled his victim. An expert witness for the defense testified that the defendant would have had to maintain substantial continuous pressure with his hands on the victim's windpipe for three to five minutes to cause her death. The court held that the mere passage of time while a killing is carried out is not enough to support a finding of premeditation. Additional evidence of premeditation, such as motive, acquisition of a weapon, or planning related to the killing is required. The court said: "[T]o allow a finding of premeditation only because the act takes an appreciable amount of time obliterates the distinction between first and second degree murder. Having the opportunity to deliberate is not evidence the defendant did deliberate, which is necessary for a finding of premeditation. Otherwise, any form of killing which took more than a moment could result in a finding of premeditation, without some additional evidence showing reflection." Id. at 113. Compare State v. Ollens, 733 P.2d 984 (Wash.1987) (*Bingham* distinguished; multiple stab wounds indicative of premeditation). See also Midgett v. State, 729 S.W.2d 410 (Ark.1987) (evidence that defendant brutally beat his young son repeatedly over a substantial period insufficient to show premeditation and deliberation). (Shortly after the decision in *Midgett*, the Arkansas legislature amended the definition of first-degree murder to include "knowingly causing the death of a person age fourteen or younger under circumstances manifesting cruel and malicious indifference to the value of human life," evidently intending to bring a case like *Midgett* within the category of first-degree murder without proof of premeditation and deliberation. See Davis v. State, 925 S.W.2d 768 (Ark.1996).)

72. "When a legal distinction is determined, as no one doubts that it may be, between night and day, childhood and maturity, or any other extremes, a point has to be fixed or a line has to be drawn, or gradually picked out by successive decisions, to mark where the change takes place. Looked at by itself without regard to the necessity behind it the line or point seems arbitrary. It might as well or nearly as well be a little more to one side or the other. But when it is seen that a line or point there must be, and that there is no mathematical or logical way of fixing it precisely, the decision of the legislature must be accepted unless we can say that it is very wide of any reasonable mark." Louisville Gas & Electric Co. v. Coleman, 277 U.S. 32, 41 (1928) (Holmes, J., dissenting).

Justice Cardozo believed that the distinction between first and second degree murder "merely . . . offered to the jury a privilege to find the lesser degree when the suddenness of the intent, the vehemence of the passion, seems to call irresistibly for the exercise of mercy." "What Medicine Can

Cardozo thinks that jury shou decide on the own.

Do for Law," in B. Cardozo, Law and Literature 70, 99–100 (1931). Is it desirable that the jury have such a privilege? If so, should it be recognized explicitly?

73. "[T]he law is clear that where a deadly weapon is used in a homicide there is a presumption of second degree murder and the defendant has the burden of proving that it was justified and the state has the burden of proving that such killing was deliberate and premeditated and raising it to a first degree murder, all of which are jury questions." State v. Hamric, 151 S.E.2d 252, 262–63 (W.Va.1966).

If the "presumption" to which the court refers is a presumption of fact, that is, that a jury *may* infer malice aforethought as a matter of fact from the use of a deadly weapon, the court's statement is acceptable. On the other hand, see Caldwell v. Bell, 288 F.3d 838 (6th Cir.2002), stating that a jury instruction that "[w]hen the defendant is shown to have used a deadly weapon and death is clearly shown to have resulted from its use, it is a presumption of law that the killing was done maliciously, that is, with the malice necessary to support a conviction of murder in the second degree," violates the constitutional requirement that every element of a criminal offense be proved beyond a reasonable doubt. (See Mullaney v. Wilbur, p. 99 above.) A presumption of law has the effect that the proved fact establishes the presumed fact; a presumption of fact merely allows the jury in its own judgment to make an inference from one fact to another.

"There is no conflict between the legal principle that a *prima facie* case of first degree murder is established when the Commonwealth proves, as it has here, a mortal wound given with a deadly weapon in the previous possession of the slayer without any or upon very slight provocation . . . and that long established principle that every homicide is presumed to be murder in the second degree. . . . The first result, or presumption, follows upon proved facts; the second from incomplete proof of facts. A meets B on the street, pulls a pistol from his pocket and shoots and kills him for no apparent reason. When that is proved, a prima facie case of first degree murder is established, and A must offer evidence in explanation if he would escape the penalty. In another case, B is found dead on the street. It is proved that A killed him. On that evidence alone a presumption arises that A is guilty of murder in the second degree. To prove him guilty of murder in the first degree, the Commonwealth must go forward with evidence to show that A's action was wilful, deliberate and premeditated. To overcome the presumption, A must introduce evidence to lower the grade of the offense or show legal excuse for his act." Thomas v. Commonwealth, 41 S.E.2d 476, 479–80 (Va.1947). What assumptions must the court be making?

74. "Prior threats of an accused to do violence to the person eventually slain have consistently been held to be admissible in evidence as showing malice and criminal intent." People v. Slaughter, 194 N.E.2d 193, 195 (Ill.1963) ("I am going to take something and knock your brains out."). Accord, e.g., Rink v. United States, 388 A.2d 52 (D.C.1978). In People v. Holt, 153 P.2d 21, 39 (Cal.1944), the court said that the "very extravagance" of the defendant's threat to "'shoot [the victim's] God damn heart out and wipe it across his mouth,'" made it questionable "as proof of a deliberately conceived and premeditated intent."

Commonwealth v. Mazza

366 Mass. 30, 313 N.E.2d 875 (1974)

■ HENNESSEY, JUSTICE. The defendant was indicted for, and convicted of, murder in the first degree and robbery and brings these appeals. . . . He argues no assignments of error but urges only that we exercise our powers . . . and reduce the verdict to a lesser degree of guilt. The sole reason suggested for the invocation of such a procedure is alleged to be the defendant's mental retardation and consequent diminished criminal responsibility. We decline to disturb the verdict of the jury, which was fully warranted on the evidence.

The facts are as follows. On June 30, 1972, at approximately 11:30 A.M., the defendant asked Robert Anderson if he could use Anderson's apartment. That afternoon, Anderson, who had known the defendant for several months, gave the defendant permission to stay there. They then separated and did not spend the evening together. Robert Anderson spent the evening at the movies and the Novelty Bar, which he left at approximately 2 A.M. He then walked home to his apartment, arriving at approximately 2:45 A.M. When he entered the apartment, he went first to the refrigerator, and he then proceeded to his mother's bedroom. When he reached the room, he observed the defendant standing alone beside the dead body of a man. The dead man was lying face up and his pants pockets had been turned inside out. The defendant was wearing leather gloves. Anderson asked the defendant what had happened and was told that the defendant had "had a struggle." The defendant then stated that they should get the body out of the apartment immediately, and he began to tie up the dead man. He asked Anderson to help him and told Anderson not to mention what he had seen or he would be shot "or whatever." Despite Anderson's disagreement, the defendant said he would remove the body from the apartment on the following day, and he gave Anderson a watch, a ring, and a car key. These were shown later to be the property of the dead man. The body was then placed in a closet in the back hallway of the apartment. There was no lock on the closet door at that time. The defendant later bought a lock and installed it on the door.

There was evidence that the defendant used the dead man's credit cards to procure merchandise, and that he used the dead man's automobile. There was also evidence that the deceased had left a night club on the night of his death, accompanied by another man, whom the jury could find had an appearance consistent with that of the defendant. The victim died of strangulation.

The facts . . . were developed at a pre-trial hearing on the defendant's motion to suppress certain of his statements to police. At that hearing a Dr. Richard A. Pigott testified to the defendant's mental faculties. . . . Dr. Pigott testified that he had tested the defendant's "general mental ability or intelligence, and ability to understand verbal, auditory material, auditory comprehension." His overall I.Q. was seventy-seven; the nonverbal component was eighty-eight; and his verbal ability was in the high grade defective range. A test of auditory comprehension indicated an inability to understand material beyond the second-grade level. His handwriting demonstrated functional illiteracy.

An assistant superintendent of the Springfield schools then testified as to the defendant's educational background. After one year in an ordinary first-grade classroom, the defendant was transferred to an ungraded class for mentally handicapped children. Such classes are in two levels, educable and trainable, and the defendant was in the higher, educable classification. Later reports indicated that the defendant had no academic ability and that "[h]e is not vicious, but is a constant source of irritation to his teacher and classmates alike." The defendant left school at the minimum legal age of sixteen. His last report card rated him average on emotional stability.

No attempt was made to introduce any evidence as to the defendant's mental capacity at the time of the trial. It is conceded that the defendant is legally responsible. . . .

While G.L. c. 278, § 33E, gives us power on appeal broader than that of a trial judge on a motion for a new trial, to reduce verdicts or order new trials for any reason that justice may require . . . this power is to be used with restraint. . . . Heretofore, in acting under § 33E, we have not recognized any claim for relief resembling the defendant's argument in this case. . . .

The defendant here would in a sense have us use § 33E as a vehicle to promulgate the entirely new defense of diminished responsibility based on mental retardation. On the facts of this case, we decline to do so, although we do not state that the mental retardation of a defendant may not be a factor for consideration under § 33E in an appropriate case.

We adhere to the view . . . that there is no intermediate stage of partial criminal responsibility between insanity and ordinary responsibility as defined by statute. . . .

In the present case there was no evidence presented nor have we heard any argument that the defendant was incapable of the necessary intent for conviction of murder in the first degree, either premeditated or committed in the commission of a crime punishable by life imprisonment. On the contrary, there is considerable evidence in the record relative to disposing of the victim's body and the use of his personal property, particularly a car and some credit cards, to demonstrate that the defendant was capable of formulating and carrying out plans.

The record establishes, and the parties have agreed, that the defendant at the time of the crime had the "substantial capacity . . . to appreciate the criminality [wrongfulness] of his conduct . . . [and] to conform his conduct to the requirements of law." See Commonwealth v. McHoul, 352 Mass. 544, 547 (1967). We do not believe that one who has the capacity required by the test in the *McHoul* case should be relieved of any measure of criminal responsibility merely because his intellectual faculties are subnormal.

. . .

75.

The existence of general mental impairment, or partial insanity, is a scientifically established fact. There is no absolute or clear-cut dichotomous division of the inhabitants of this world into the sane and the insane. "Between the two extremes of 'sanity' and 'insanity' lies every shade of disordered or deficient mental condition, grading imperceptibly one into another." Weihofen, "Partial Insanity and Criminal Intent," 24 Ill. L. Rev. 505, 508.

More precisely, there are persons who, while not totally insane, possess such low mental powers as to be incapable of the deliberation and premeditation requisite to statutory first degree murder. Yet under the rule adopted by the court below, the jury must either condemn such persons to death on the false premise that they possess the mental requirements of a first degree murderer or free them completely from criminal responsibility and turn them loose among society. The jury is forbidden to find them guilty of a lesser degree of murder by reason of their generally weakened or disordered intellect.

Common sense and logic recoil at such a rule. And it is difficult to marshal support for it from civilized concepts of justice or from the necessity of protecting society. When a man's life or liberty is at stake he should be adjudged according to his personal culpability as well as by the objective seriousness of his crime. That elementary principle of justice is applied to those who kill while intoxicated or in the heat of passion; if such a condition destroys their deliberation and premeditation the jury may properly consider that fact and convict them of a lesser degree of murder. No different principle should be utilized in the case of those whose mental deficiency is of a more permanent character. Society, moreover, is ill-protected by a rule which encourages a jury to acquit a partially insane person with an appealing case simply because his mental defects cannot be considered in reducing the degree of guilt.

It is undeniably difficult . . . to determine with any high degree of certainty whether a defendant has a general mental impairment and whether such a disorder renders him incapable of the requisite deliberation and premeditation. The difficulty springs primarily from the present limited scope of medical and psychiatric knowledge of mental disease. But this knowledge is ever increasing. And juries constantly must judge the baffling psychological factors of deliberation and pre-meditation, Congress having entrusted the ascertainment of those factors to the good sense of juries. It seems senseless to shut the door on the assistance which medicine and psychiatry can give in regard to these matters, however inexact and incomplete that assistance may presently be. Precluding the consideration of mental deficiency only makes the jury's decision on deliberation and premeditation less intelligent and trustworthy.

Murphy, J., dissenting in Fisher v. United States, 328 U.S. 463, 490, 492–93 (1946), in which the Supreme Court upheld a lower court ruling that the defense of "diminished responsibility" was unavailable in the District of Columbia. (That ruling was overruled in United States v. Brawner, 471 F.2d 969 (D.C.Cir.1972). See p. 568 note 343 below.) Richard Wright wrote a fictionalized version of the *Fisher* case, called "The Man Who Killed a Shadow," in R. Wright, Eight Men 193 (1961).

———

People v. Wolff

61 Cal.2d 795, 394 P.2d 959 (1964)

■ SCHAUER, JUSTICE. Defendant appeals from a judgment imposing a sentence of life imprisonment (with recommendation that he be placed in a hospital for the criminally insane) after he pleaded not guilty by reason of insanity to a charge of murder, the jury found that he was legally sane at the time of the commission of the offense, and the court determined the killing to be murder in the first degree.

Defendant contends that the evidence is insufficient to support the verdict of sanity, that the court gave conflicting instructions on the presumptions of sanity and of the continuance of prior "permanent" insanity, and that his crime should have been determined to be second degree rather than first degree murder. Upon a comprehensive view of all the evidence we have concluded that the first two of these contentions are without merit, but that the judgment should be reduced to murder of the second degree.

Defendant, a fifteen year old boy at the time of the crime, was charged with the murder of his mother. The juvenile court found him to be "not a fit subject for consideration" under the Juvenile Court Law, and remanded him to the superior court for further proceedings in the criminal action. To the information accusing him of murder defendant entered the single plea of "not guilty by reason of insanity," thereby admitting commission of the basic act which, if not qualified under the special plea, constitutes the offense charged. . . . After considering reports of three alienists appointed to examine defendant . . . the court declared a doubt as to his mental capacity to stand trial. . . . At a hearing on that issue, however, the court found defendant to be "mentally ill but not to the degree that would preclude him from cooperation with his counsel in the preparation and presentation of his defense." The plea of not guilty by reason of insanity was then tried to a jury and resulted in a verdict that defendant was legally sane at the time of the commission of the jurisdictional act of killing. Defendant's motion for new trial on the ground of insufficiency of the evidence was heard and denied, and by stipulation the question of the degree of the crime was submitted to the court on the basis of the evidence introduced at the trial and the report of the probation officer. The court determined the crime to be murder in the first degree; sentenced defendant to life imprisonment; and to the judgment added, "Placement in hospital for criminally insane recommended."

. . .

In the case at bench there was evidence that in the year preceding the commission of the crime defendant "spent a lot of time thinking about sex." He made a list of the names and addresses of seven girls in his community whom he did not know personally but whom he planned to anesthetize by ether and then either rape or photograph nude. One night about three weeks before the murder he took a container of ether and attempted to enter the home of one of these girls through the chimney, but he became wedged in and had to be rescued. In the ensuing weeks defendant apparently deliberated on ways and means of accomplishing his objective and decided that he would have to bring the girls to his house to achieve his sexual purposes, and that it would therefore be necessary to get his mother (and possibly his brother) out of the way first.[45]

The attack on defendant's mother took place on Monday, May 15, 1961. On the preceding Friday or Saturday defendant obtained an axe handle from the family garage and hid it under the mattress of his bed. At about 10 p.m. on Sunday he took the axe handle from its hiding place and approached his mother from behind, raising the weapon to strike her. She sensed his presence and asked him what he was doing; he answered that it was "nothing," and returned to his room and hid the handle under his mattress again. The following morning defendant arose and put the customary signal (a magazine) in the front window to inform his father that he had not overslept. Defendant ate the breakfast that his mother prepared, then went to his room and obtained the axe handle from under the mattress. He returned to the kitchen, approached his mother from behind and struck her on the back of the head. She turned around screaming and he struck her several more blows. They fell to the floor, fighting. She called out her neighbor's name and defendant began choking her. She bit him on the hand and crawled away. He got up to turn off the water running in the sink, and she fled through the dining room. He gave chase, caught her in

---

45. Defendant lived with his mother and older brother since his parents were divorced some 13 years previously. However, his father remained on good terms with the family; he drove by their house each morning to ascertain that they had not overslept, and he often ate with them in the evening.

the front room, and choked her to death with his hands. Defendant then took off his shirt and hung it by the fire, washed the blood off his face and hands, read a few lines from a Bible or prayer book lying upon the dining room table, and walked down to the police station to turn himself in. Defendant told the desk officer, "I have something I wish to report. . . . I just killed my mother with an axe handle." The officer testified that defendant spoke in a quiet voice and that "His conversation was quite coherent in what he was saying and he answered everything I asked him right to a T."

Defendant's counsel repeatedly characterizes as "bizarre" defendant's plan to rape or photograph nude the seven girls on his list. Certainly in common parlance it may be termed "bizarre"; likewise to a mature person of good morals, it would appear highly unreasonable. But many a youth has committed—or planned—acts which were bizarre and unreasonable. This defendant was immature and lacked experience and judgment in sexual matters. But it does not follow therefrom that the jury were precluded as a matter of law from finding defendant *legally* sane at the time of the murder. From the evidence set forth hereinabove the jury could infer that defendant had a motive for his actions (gratification of his sexual desires),[46] that he planned the attack on his mother for some time (obtaining of the axe handle from the garage several days in advance; abortive attempt to strike his mother with it on the evening before the crime), that he knew that what he was doing was wrong (initial concealment of the handle underneath his mattress; excuse offered when his mother saw him with the weapon on the evening before the crime; renewed concealment of the handle under the mattress), that he persisted in the fatal attack (pursuit of his fleeing mother into the front room; actual infliction of death by strangling rather than bludgeoning), that he was conscious of having committed a crime (prompt surrender to the police), and that he was calm and coherent (testimony of desk officer and others). We need not determine whether such conduct would alone constitute substantial evidence from which the jury could find defendant legally sane at the time of the murder, for as will next be shown the record contains further evidence on this issue.

. . .

In the case at bench defendant was questioned by Officers Stenberg and Hamilton shortly after he came to the police station and voluntarily announced that he had just killed his mother. The interrogation was transcribed and shown to defendant; he changed the wording of a few of his answers, then affixed his signature and the date on each page. When asked

---

46. This does not mean, of course, that it was his *only* motive. At different times defendant offered as reasons for the murder the fact that his mother nagged him, that they constantly bickered, and that he was ashamed to bring friends home because his mother did not keep house well. However, the issue is not whether in the opinion of an appellate court such other reasons may some-how be deemed evidence of *in*sanity, but whether the record supports an inference that defendant had an actual—not just imagined or hallucinatory—motivating reason to commit these acts. As observed above, our inquiry must be to determine whether there is substantial evidence to support—not to undermine—the verdict of the jury.

by Officer Hamilton why he had turned himself in, defendant replied, "Well, for the act I had just committed." Defendant then related the events leading up to and culminating in the murder, describing his conduct in the detail set forth hereinabove. With respect to the issue of his state of mind at the time of the crime, the following language is both relevant and material: When asked how long he had thought of killing his mother, defendant replied, "I can't be clear on that. About a week ago, I would suppose, the very beginning of the thoughts. First I thought of giving her the ether. . . . Then Thursday and Friday I thought of it again. Q. Of killing your mother? A. Not of killing. Well, yes, I think so. Then Saturday and Sunday the same." After stating that he struck her the first blow on the back of the head, defendant was asked: "Q. Did you consider at the time that this one blow would render her unconscious, or kill her? A. I wasn't sure. I was hoping it would render her unconscious. Q. Was it your thought at this time to kill her? A. I am not sure of that. Probably kill her, I think." Defendant described the struggle in which he and his mother fell to the floor, and was asked: "Q. Then what happened. . . . A. She moved over by the stove, and she just laid still. She was breathing, breathing heavily. I said 'I shouldn't be doing this'—not those exact words, but something to that effect, and laid down beside her, because we were on the floor. Q. Were you tired? A. Yes." After defendant had choked her to death he said, "God loves you, He loves me, He loves my dad, and I love you and my dad. It is a circle, sort of, and it is horrible you have done all that good and then I come along and destroy it."

Detective Stenberg thereafter interrupted Officer Hamilton's interrogation, and asked the following questions: "Q. (Det. W. R. Stenberg) You knew the wrongfulness of killing your mother? A. I did. I was thinking of it. I was aware of it. Q. You were aware of the wrongfulness. Also had you thought what might happen to you? A. That is a question. No. Q. Your thought has been in your mind for three weeks of killing her? A. Yes, or of just knocking her out. Q. Well, didn't you feel you would be prosecuted for the wrongfulness of this act? A. I was aware of it, but not thinking of it." Officer Hamilton asked: "Q. Can you give a reason or purpose for this act of killing your mother? Have you thought out why you wanted to hurt her? A. There is a reason why we didn't get along. There is also the reason of sexual intercourse with one of these other girls, and I had to get her out of the way. Q. Did you think you had to get her out of the way permanently? A. I sort of figured it would have to be that way, but I am not quite sure."

Thus . . . Officer Stenberg's question ("You knew the wrongfulness of killing your mother?") related unequivocally to defendant's knowledge *at the time of the commission of the murder*; and defendant's equally unequivocal answer ("I did. I was thinking of it. I was aware of it.") related to the same period of time. This admission, coupled with defendant's uncontradicted course of conduct and other statements set forth hereinabove, constitutes substantial evidence from which the jury could find defendant legally sane at the time of the matricide.

It is contended that the foregoing evidence of defendant's conduct and declarations is equally consistent with the type of mental illness (i.e., a form of "schizophrenia") from which, according to the psychiatric witnesses, defendant is said to be suffering. But this consistency establishes only that defendant is suffering from the diagnosed mental illness—a point that the prosecution readily concedes; it does not compel the conclusion that on the very different issue of legal sanity the evidence is insufficient as a matter of law to support the verdict. To hold otherwise would be in effect to substitute a trial by "experts" for a trial by jury, for it would require that the jurors accept the psychiatric testimony as conclusive on an issue—the legal sanity of the defendant—which under our present law is exclusively within the province of the trier of fact to determine.

. . .

To the extent, moreover, that the psychiatric witnesses in the case at bench were asked their opinion as to defendant's legal sanity, a close examination of their responses discloses still further grounds in support of the verdict. The jury were entitled, of course, to consider on this issue the entire testimony of each such witness, including the reasons given for his conclusion that defendant was legally insane. Dr. Nielsen testified on direct examination that at the time of the murder defendant "knew right from wrong" but was "acting impulsively" and "didn't think it through"; that during the period of the final outburst "He knew what he was doing after all. He studied his mother to see whether she was dead and when she wasn't, he went ahead and finished it." On cross-examination Dr. Nielsen was asked whether defendant's compulsion to kill his mother resembled an "irresistible impulse"; he replied, "It was not resisted and it was an impulse." The doctor further agreed that defendant "was capable at the time, of knowing the difference between right and wrong, but that he didn't bother to think about it"; that defendant "could have and did appreciate what he did," and that "he knew what he did was wrong." The doctor testified that ordinarily a schizophrenic's description of his state of mind during an "outburst" is no more than his own interpretation or rationalization of what happened; but when asked whether a schizophrenic "know[s] in terms of right and wrong what he is doing" during an outburst, the doctor replied: "I don't want to answer that for every case but in this case, yes." Dr. Nielsen further stated that defendant "was hoping to escape by the plan that had been evolved by his father [i.e., by a successful plea of not guilty by reason of insanity] and he may have thought all the time that he could escape"; that while in custody defendant had been reading about schizophrenia in books that his father had furnished him on the subject.

The next psychiatric witness, Dr. Smith, testified that when defendant killed his mother "He was acting on an impulse"; that "his expressions of intention to go out and have intercourse and his intention to knock out his mother and the aunt, if she came, are evidence of his ability to think because of his ability to plan. Now beyond that point of having struck his mother, this is an impulsive schizophrenic piece of behavior which is entirely separated in my opinion from some planned piece of activity."

The final psychiatric witness, Dr. Skrdla, testified on direct examination that at the time of the killing defendant "knew that he had committed a wrong act, at least morally wrong, and possibly legally wrong, because, according to the story he gave me, he washed the blood from himself and changed his clothes, and, a few minutes after the murder, went to the police station to report it. This would indicate that he recognized that his act was wrong." On cross-examination Dr. Skrdla testified that when defendant killed his mother "he probably did know the difference between right and wrong" but that he was one of those schizophrenics who "because of their emotional problems, their own conflicts . . . are not able to prevent themselves from going ahead and acting on whatever ideas or compulsions they may have." The doctor agreed that the fact that defendant hid the axe handle under his mattress would indicate that "he didn't want to be caught with that axe handle before he was able to go ahead with the plan" and that "He had appreciation of the fact, perhaps, that it wasn't entirely right, however, he still planned to do it." Dr. Skrdla termed the killing "an automatic act," and explained that "once [defendant] attempted to get his mother out of the way . . . he went on as was described and couldn't stop until she was in fact dead."

. . .

The Degree of the Murder

From what has been said it follows that there was no substantial error in the trial on the issue raised by the plea of not guilty by reason of insanity and that the evidence adequately supports the jury's verdict. But another and more substantial problem remains to be considered: the contention that the evidence is insufficient to support the trial court's finding that the murder was of the first, rather than the second, degree. This problem, however, is by no means new to us. In dealing with it we recognize that every relevant and tenable presumption is to be indulged in favor of sustaining the judgment of the trial court; but when a proper case appears . . . we do not hesitate to modify the judgment to murder of the second degree and affirm it as modified.

. . .

[T]here has sometimes appeared to be a tendency to emasculate the distinction between the two degrees of murder. In [People v.] *Holt* [153 P.2d 21 (Cal.1944)] we declared firmly against any such emasculation: "Regardless of imperfection of academic concept either in the statutory law as enacted or in some of the decisions interpreting it, we are faced with the task of making practical application of that law to actual facts. In such application certain principles are entitled to recognition. Dividing intentional homicides into murder and voluntary manslaughter was a recognition of the infirmity of human nature. Again *dividing the offense of murder into two degrees is a further recognition* of that infirmity and *of difference in the quantum of personal turpitude of the offenders*. . . . The victim of manslaughter or second degree murder is just as dead as is the victim of first degree murder. The law has fixed standards by which such *personal depravity of the offender,* i.e., the character of the particular homicide, *is to be measured.* When the homicide is perpetrated by means of poison, or lying in wait, or torture, or in the perpetration of or attempt to perpetrate the enumerated felonies the standard is definite and no difficulty in fixing the degree ensues. But when it is claimed that the homicide is by 'any other kind of willful, deliberate, and premeditated killing' there is necessity for an appraisal which involves something more than the ascertainment of objective facts. This appraisal is primarily a jury [or trial court] function and within a wide field of discretion its determination is final. But as is true as to all factual issues resolved by a jury [or trial court], the evidence upon which the determination is made is subject to review on the question of its legal sufficiency to support the verdict. To the extent that the character of a particular homicide is established by the facts in evidence the jury is bound, as are we, to apply the standards fixed by law." (Italics added.)

. . .

[T]he more general words "or any other kind of willful, deliberate, and premeditated killing," following the specifically enumerated instances of killing which are expressly declared to constitute murder of the first degree, must be construed in the light of such specifically listed types and be held to include only killings of the same general kind or character as those specifically mentioned. By conjoining the words "willful, deliberate, and premeditated" in its definition and limitation of the character of killings falling within murder of the first degree the Legislature apparently emphasized its intention to require as an element of such crime substantially more reflection than may be involved in the mere formation of a specific intent to kill. . . .

. . . Neither the statute nor the court undertakes to measure in units of time the length of the period during which the thought must be pondered before it can ripen into an intent which is truly deliberate and premeditated. The time would vary with different individuals and under differing circumstances. The true test is not the duration of time as much as it is the *extent of the reflection.* [People v. Thomas, 156 P.2d 7, 18 (1945)] (Italics added.) In the case now at bench, in the light of defendant's youth and undisputed mental illness, all as shown under the California M'Naughton rule on the trial of the plea of not guilty by reason of insanity, and properly considered by the trial judge in the proceeding to determine the degree of the offense, the true test must include consideration of the somewhat limited extent to which this defendant could *maturely and meaningfully reflect* upon the gravity of his contemplated act. . . .

. . .

Certainly in the case now at bench the defendant had ample *time* for any normal person to maturely and appreciatively reflect upon his contemplated act and to arrive at a cold, deliberated and premeditated conclusion. He did this in a sense—and apparently to the full extent of which he was capable. But, indisputably on the record, this defendant was not and is not a fully normal or mature, mentally well person. He knew the difference between right and wrong; he knew that the intended act was wrong and nevertheless carried it out. But the extent of his understanding, reflection upon it and its consequences, with realization of the enormity of the evil, appears to have been materially—as relevant to appraising the quantum of his moral turpitude and depravity—vague and detached. We think that our analysis in *Holt* of the minimum essential elements of first degree murder, especially in respect to the quantum of reflection, comprehension, *and turpitude of the offender*, fits precisely this case: that the use by the Legislature of "wilful, deliberate, and premeditated" in conjunction indicates its intent to require as an essential element of first degree murder (of that category) substantially more reflection; i.e., more understanding and comprehension of the character of the act than the mere amount of thought necessary to form the intention to kill. . . .

Analysis of Holt Case... Elements of first degree murder
. reflection
. comprehension
. turpitude of the offender

. . .

Upon the facts, upon the law, and for all of the reasons hereinabove stated we are satisfied that the evidence fails to support the finding that the murder by this defendant, in the circumstances of his undisputed mental illness, was of the first degree, but that it amply sustains conviction of second degree murder.

The fact that we reduce the degree of the penal judgment from first to second degree murder is not to be understood as suggesting that this defendant's confinement should be in an institution maintaining any lower degree of security than for persons convicted of murder of the first degree. To the contrary we approve of the trial court's recommendation that defendant be placed in a hospital for the criminally insane of a high security character, such as the California Medical Facility at Vacaville where he is presently confined.

. . .

---

76. Notice the court's recommendation about disposition in the last paragraph of *Wolff*. What should the state do about a defendant who is found to be less responsible criminally than the rest of the population but who is not insane? The maximum penalty for murder in the second degree in California was imprisonment for life. Cal. Penal Code § 190. Wolff was 18 years old when the court announced its decision. He was sentenced to imprisonment for an indeterminate period of five years to life. Six years later, in 1970, he was released on parole, which expired in 1976.

77. The California court went further in People v. Conley, 411 P.2d 911 (Cal.1966), in which it held that a defendant's capacity for reflection might be so diminished temporarily (as by intoxication) or permanently (as by disease or defect short of insanity) that even if the act of killing were willful, deliberate, and premeditated, it was committed without malice aforethought, the killing therefore being not murder but manslaughter. Although in *Wolff* the court emphasized the element of the defendant's "moral turpitude and depravity," it indicated in *Conley* that it was not distinguishing murder from manslaughter simply on that basis: "one who commits euthanasia bears no ill will toward his victim and believes his act is morally justified, but he nonetheless acts with malice if he is able to comprehend that society prohibits his act regardless of his personal belief." 411 P.2d at 918.[47] See p. 134 note 78, below.

Other courts have reached results looking in the same direction as the California court. In State v. Gramenz, 126 N.W.2d 285, 290 (Iowa 1964), for example, the court held that evidence of the defendant's mental condition not amounting to insanity was admissible on the issue of "willfulness, deliberation and premeditation," but not on "the elements of malice aforethought and general criminal intent." In State v. Barney, 244 N.W.2d 316 (Iowa 1976) (assault with intent to commit murder), the court said that "evidence of diminished responsibility should be admissible as a defense in any crime which requires proof of a specific intent as an element." See Veverka v. Cash, 318 N.W.2d 447 (Iowa 1982); State v. Beach, 699 P.2d 115 (N.M.1985) (diminished capacity defense available "only for willful and deliberate murder and those crimes which include an element to do a further act or achieve a further consequence"). See also Commonwealth v. Walzack, 360 A.2d 914, 916 (Pa.1976), in which the court held that evidence of mental incapacity was admissible to show that the defendant "did not possess sufficient mental capacity to form the specific intent required for a conviction of murder of the first degree." The defendant had undergone a lobotomy. The court said: "It is inconsistent with fundamental principles of American jurisprudence to preclude an accused from offering relevant and competent evidence to dispute the charge against him. This, of course, includes any of the elements that comprise the charge." Id. at 921. To the same effect is State v. Christensen, 628 P.2d 580 (Ariz.1981), in which the defendant sought to introduce expert psychiatric testimony of a "character trait"—that he "had difficulty dealing with stress and in stressful situations his actions were more reflexive than reflective"—to show a lack of premeditation, an element of first-degree murder. Id. at 582. The court held that the evidence should have been admitted. For a more skeptical attitude toward evidence of "personality traits," see United States v. Kepreos, 759 F.2d 961 (1st Cir.1985). See also Taylor v. State, 452 So.2d 441 (Miss.1984) (evidence of "emotional background" not admissible to negate malice aforethought; other cases cited and discussed).

47. Compare People v. Bassett, 443 P.2d 777, 793–94 (Cal.1968), a case resembling *Wolff*, in which the court said that in *Wolff* it had made clear that the test of premeditation "is not simply an adequate time to deliberate, or a manifest intent to kill, or even an abstract appearance of 'rationality' in the defendant's planning, but rather the depth of his appreciation of the 'enormity of the evil' he proposes to commit."

Concluding that the defense of diminished responsibility should not be allowed, the District of Columbia Court of Appeals observed:

> The concept of mens rea involves what is ultimately the fiction of determining the actual thoughts or mental processes of the accused. . . . It is obvious that a certain resolution of this issue is beyond the ken of scientist and laymen alike. Only by inference can the existence of intent—or the differentiation between its forms, such as general or specific—be determined. . . . The law presumes that all individuals are capable of the mental processes which bear the jurisprudential label "mens rea"; that is, the law presumes sanity. Moreover, for the sake of administrative efficiency and in recognition of fundamental principles of egalitarian fairness, our legal system further presumes that each person is equally capable of the same forms and degrees of intent. . . . The concept of insanity is simply a device the law employs to define the outer limits of that segment of the general population to whom these presumptions concerning the capacity for criminal intent shall not be applied. The line between the sane and the insane for the purposes of criminal adjudication is not drawn because for one group the actual existence of the necessary mental state (or lack thereof) can be determined with any greater certainty, but rather because those whom the law declares insane are demonstrably so aberrational in their psychiatric characteristics that we choose to make the assumption that they are incapable of possessing the specified state of mind. Within the range of individuals who are not "insane," the law does not recognize the readily demonstrable fact that as between individual criminal defendants the nature and development of their mental capabilities may vary greatly. . . . By contradicting the presumptions inherent in the doctrine of mens rea, the theory of diminished capacity inevitably opens the door to variable or sliding scales of criminal responsibility. . . . We should not lightly undertake such a revolutionary change in our criminal justice system.

Bethea v. United States, 365 A.2d 64, 87–88 (D.C.1976).

See generally United States v. Cameron, 907 F.2d 1051 (11th Cir. 1990), discussing the various judicial uses of the terms "diminished responsibility" and "diminished capacity." The court carefully distinguishes their use to refer to evidence that contradicts an element of the offense ("psychiatric evidence to negate specific intent") and their use to refer to an affirmative defense. The court concludes that the 1984 federal statute making insanity an affirmative defense and eliminating other affirmative defenses based on mental disease or defect, see p. 575 below, did not preclude the introduction of the former kind of evidence. The opinion cites the opinions of other courts of appeals to the same effect. See also Humanik v. Beyer, 871 F.2d 432 (3d Cir.1989), making the same distinction and holding the New Jersey statute, under which the defendant had the burden of proof to show the *existence* of a mental disease or defect that might have affected an element of the offense, unconstitutional under *Winship* (see Mullaney v. Wilbur, p. 99 above).

78. After a period in which there was great interest in questions about a defendant's mental capacity, either with reference to a distinct general defense of diminished responsibility or diminished capacity or with reference to specific elements of the crime charged, there has been a clear trend back to the all-or-nothing approach of the insanity defense. See generally Muench v. Israel, 715 F.2d 1124, 1144–45 (7th Cir.1983), holding that "a state is not constitutionally compelled to recognize the doctrine of diminished capacity and hence a state may exclude expert testimony offered for the purpose of establishing that a criminal defendant lacked the capacity to form a specific intent." One reason for the decline of interest in diminished capacity may have been the widespread adoption in the 1960s and 1970s of the Model Penal Code's broadened standard of insanity. See, e.g., State v. Baker, 691 P.2d 1166 (Haw.1984). Since then, there has been a drift toward a narrower standard, without, however, much sign of a resurgence of the defense of diminished capacity. See p. 575 note 347, below.

In California, where the courts seemed to have gone furthest in recognizing the relevance of a diminished mental capacity, see *Wolff* and *Conley*, pp. 124, 131 above, the legislature pointedly turned in the other direction. Evidently responding to *Wolff*, it added to the statutory definition of first-degree murder the following: "To prove the killing was 'deliberate and premeditated,' it shall not be necessary to prove the defendant maturely and meaningfully reflected upon the gravity of his or her act." Cal. Penal Code § 189.[48] The legislature also enacted a provision that declared more generally: "The defense of diminished capacity is hereby abolished." Cal. Penal Code § 25(a). Evidently taking no chances, the legislature provided elsewhere: "As a matter of public policy there shall be no defense of diminished capacity, diminished responsibility, or irresistible impulse in a criminal action or juvenile adjudication hearing." Cal. Penal Code § 28(b). And further: "Evidence of mental disease, mental defect, or mental disorder shall not be admitted to show or negate the capacity to form any mental state, including, but not limited to, purpose, intent, knowledge, premeditation, deliberation, or malice aforethought, with which the accused committed the act. Evidence of mental disease, mental defect, or mental disorder is admissible solely on the issue of whether or not the accused actually formed a required specific intent, premeditated, deliberated, or harbored malice aforethought, when a specific intent crime is charged." Cal. Penal Code § 28(a). Another section provides that an expert testifying about the defendant's mental condition "shall not testify as to whether the defendant had or did not have the required mental states, which include, but are not limited to, purpose, intent, knowledge, or malice aforethought, for the crime charged. The question as to whether the defendant had or did not have the required mental states shall be decided by the trier of fact."

48. For good measure, the legislature added to the provision defining malice: "When it is shown that the killing resulted from the intentional doing of an act with express or implied malice as defined above, no other mental state need be shown to establish the mental state of malice aforethought. Neither an awareness of the obligation to act within the general body of laws regulating society nor acting despite such awareness is included within the definition of malice." Cal. Penal Code § 188.

Cal. Penal Code § 29. Evidence of diminished capacity is admissible with respect to sentencing or other disposition. Cal. Penal Code § 25(c). See generally People v. Saille, 820 P.2d 588 (Cal.1991).

In *Johnson*, above, the court observed that rejection of the defense of diminished capacity with respect to guilt does not mean "that evidence of a defendant's mental abnormality which does not establish his insanity has been totally precluded from the consideration of those operating the machinery of our criminal justice system. Such evidence typically constitutes part of the range of data upon which the trial judge, following establishment of guilt, focuses attention when sentencing the individual accused. Such use of this information squares with practice prevailing in our jurisprudence of permitting the judge wide latitude in making individualized sentencing decisions after consideration of information both in aggravation and mitigation of penalty. . . . Consequently, although the diminished capacity defense has not been written into our laws defining criminal guilt, evidence of a defendant's mental abnormality which does not establish his insanity can be considered at sentencing." Such consideration, the court said, was particularly appropriate in cases involving a possibility of capital punishment; and the legislature had expressly provided that a defendant's impaired mental capacity was a mitigating circumstance to be taken into account by the sentencing body. 439 A.2d at 555–56.

If evidence of diminished capacity may be considered at sentencing, the effect of its exclusion from consideration with respect to guilt depends on differences between the trier of fact and the sentencing authority, as affected by the different procedures, as well as the range of discretion allowed to the sentencing authority. Assuming that the range of discretion allowed, how, if at all, should evidence of the mental capacities of Mazza and Wolff have affected their sentences?

79.

It is undisputed that . . . fourteen year old Mary Alice Taylor shot and killed Mrs. Maple Markham. The story of Mary Taylor's life was put before the jury in detail, and is encompassed by the record here. Only a part of that story will be repeated in this opinion.

Mary, an unwed teenaged mother, arrived in Greenwood, Mississippi, with her infant son on October 15, 1980. As she was unable to properly care for the child, the Leflore County Court, acting *ex parte*, and without notice to the appellant, temporarily placed the child in the custody of the Leflore County Welfare Department. On December 21, 1980, Mrs. Maple Markham came to the lodgings of Mary Taylor and took the child from her custody. So began the relationship between these two that has led us to this place.

The baby was placed in a foster home, but Mary Taylor did have visitations with the baby which were arranged for her by Mrs. Markham, as the case worker assigned to the case. These visits were terminated on February 24, 1981, when the County Court made permanent the original temporary order of removal. After that Mary continued to ask Markham to let her visit her baby son, even after March, when Mary learned that she was again pregnant. These visitation requests were denied by Mrs. Markham, and the relationship between the two women seriously deteriorated.

Mary Taylor made her last effort to talk Mrs. Markham into letting her visit her child on the day of July 19, 1981. Mary went to Markham's office and stayed for over three hours, seeking a visit with her first born. Her efforts were fruitless. Finally, Markham offered to drive Mary home. While in the automobile, Markham told Mary that not only could she not visit her child, but that as soon as the baby Mary was then carrying was born, that baby, too, would be removed from Mary's custody. At this point, Mary Taylor took a pistol from her purse and shot Mrs. Markham to death.

Taylor v. State, 452 So.2d 441, 443 (Miss.1984).

Assuming that the defenses of infancy (see pp. 616–19 below) and insanity are not available, do the facts of the *Taylor* case set forth above differentiate the defendant's crime from the "standard" case of murder sufficiently to call for a different verdict? If so, is the defense of provocation as defined by the Model Penal Code, p. 89 note 56, above, or the defense of diminished capacity the more appropriate basis of differentiation? Or is it enough that the particular facts be taken into account at sentencing?

80. What rationale supports the conclusion that a homicide committed on the highest moral grounds (whether rightly or wrongly) to terminate another person's pain and suffering may display malice aforethought, but a deliberate, planned killing for unworthy motives by a person not insane may not? Is a mistake of moral judgment—if it can confidently be pronounced a mistake and not simply another view—less a circumstance of mitigation than a deficiency of intellectual or emotional capacity? See, e.g., State v. Forrest, p. 116 note 68, above; People v. Roberts, 178 N.W. 690 (Mich.1920), p. 380 below.

81. Although the Pennsylvania formula persists in the laws of many jurisdictions, it has recently lost ground. The Illinois Criminal Code, for example, defines murder, so far as relevant here, as killing intentionally or knowingly, without mention of premeditation or deliberation. Ill. Rev. Stat. ch. 38, ¶ 9–1. The special significance of premeditation and deliberation is eliminated also, e.g., in the codes of New York, Penal Law §§ 125.25, 125.27, and Wisconsin, Stat. § 940.01, both of which make an intention to kill determinative, and in the Model Penal Code, which refers to killing "purposely or knowingly," § 210.2(1)(a).

82. Look again at the question at the beginning of this section, p. 110 above. Was the Pennsylvania Assembly wrong in trying to draw lines at all or only in the line that it drew (if that)?

If you conclude that there are no variables that should be the basis of advance categorization, what variables ought to be taken into account in particular cases? The Reporters of the Model Penal Code concluded that aside from the question of capital punishment, there is no further useful categorization within the category of murder. 1 MPC Commentaries Part II (comment to § 210.2). In an alternative provision on capital punishment, the code specifies aggravating and mitigating circumstances of a homicide which should be taken into account on the matter of penalty and provides that capital punishment may not be imposed unless some aggravating and no mitigating circumstance is present.

Most jurisdictions that have retained capital punishment have enacted similar provisions. The federal statute, 18 U.S.C. § 3592, is representative:

(a) Mitigating factors. In determining whether a sentence of death is to be imposed on a defendant, the finder of fact shall consider any mitigating factor, including the following:

(1) Impaired capacity. The defendant's capacity to appreciate the wrongfulness of the defendant's conduct or to conform conduct to the requirements of law was significantly impaired, regardless of whether the capacity was so impaired as to constitute a defense to the charge.

(2) Duress. The defendant was under unusual and substantial duress, regardless of whether the duress was of such a degree as to constitute a defense to the charge.

(3) Minor participation. . . .

(4) Equally culpable defendants. Another defendant or defendants, equally culpable in the crime, will not be punished by death.

(5) No prior criminal record. . . .

(6) The defendant committed the offense under severe mental or emotional disturbance.

(7) Victim's consent. The victim consented to the criminal conduct that resulted in the victim's death.

(8) Other factors. Other factors in the defendant's background, record, or character or any other circumstance of the offense that mitigates against imposition of the death sentence.

(b) . . .

(c) Aggravating factors for homicide. In determining whether a sentence of death is justified . . . the jury, or if there is no jury, the court, shall consider each of the following aggravating factors for which notice has been given and determine which, if any, exist:

(1) Death during commission of another crime. . . .

(2) Previous conviction of violent felony involving firearm. . . .

(3) Previous conviction of offense for which a sentence of death or life imprisonment was authorized. . . .

(4) Previous conviction of other serious offenses. The defendant has previously been convicted of 2 or more Federal or State offenses, punishable by a term of imprisonment of more than 1 year, committed on different occasions, involving the infliction of, or attempted infliction of, serious bodily injury or death upon another person.

(5) Grave risk of death to additional persons. . . .

(6) Heinous, cruel, or depraved manner of committing offense. . . .

(7) Procurement of offense by payment. . . .

(8) Pecuniary gain. . . .

(9) Substantial planning and premeditation. . . .

(10) Conviction for two felony drug offenses. . . .

(11) Vulnerability of victim. The victim was particularly vulnerable due to old age, youth, or infirmity. . . .

(12) Conviction for serious Federal drug offenses. . . .

(13) Continuing criminal enterprise involving drug sales to minors. . . .

(14) High public officials. The defendant committed the offense against the President . . . the Vice President . . . [a foreign head of state or certain other domestic and foreign officials].

(15) Prior conviction of sexual assault or child molestation. . . .

83. We may regard it as an accident of legal history that the separation between murder and voluntary manslaughter was marked by the use of two different terms altogether and the separation between first and second degree murder by use of the same term and two "degrees." The Pennsylvania Assembly, in a more creative mood, might have used two different words to define the two distinct offenses. Some modern codifications have retained the substantive distinction among the categories of intentional homicide, without using the traditional rubrics. Reconsider the defendants: Girouard, Bedder, Alexander, Caruso, and Wolff. Consider also the case of Dr. R. Bernard Finch, who was convicted with an accomplice, who was said to be his lover, of murdering his wife in 1959. Mrs. Finch was killed by blows that fractured her skull and a gunshot in the back. Dr. Finch and his accomplice were sentenced to life in prison. Their prison terms began in 1961. She was paroled in 1969, when she was 32 years old; he was paroled in 1971 when he was 53 or 54. See The New York Times,

August 27, 1972, at 37.[49] And consider the case of Lester Zygmaniak, 23 years old, who shot and killed his 26-year-old brother. His brother was paralyzed from the neck downward, as the result of a motorcycle accident several days earlier. He had apparently begged Zygmaniak to kill him. Zygmaniak performed the killing in front of other persons, patients and employees, in the hospital. According to the newspaper report, before he shot he said, "Close your eyes now, I'm going to shoot you." Zygmaniak was charged with murder. He was tried and found not guilty. See The New York Times, June 23, 1973, at 35; Nov. 6, 1973, at 1.[50]

Each of these defendants committed an intentional killing. Girouard, Bedder, Alexander, Caruso, Wolff, and Finch were imprisoned for different periods and then released. Holmes, see p. 76 note 39 above, was executed. Zygmaniak was not convicted of homicide at all and not imprisoned. Do the results reveal a consistent basis for distinguishing among intentional homicides? Does such basis, if there is one, conform to your own assessment of the defendant's individual desert in each case? Or are the results idiosyncratic outcomes of unique facts, which different persons inevitably perceive differently?[51]

IS AN INTENTION TO KILL ESSENTIAL TO MURDER?

Whatever your conclusion about the desirability of establishing categories within the area of conduct marked by an intention to kill, what do you think of equating that intention with other intentions in cases where conduct causes a death? When we are typing homicides, should we regard intent to kill as unique? Or are there other intentions which the criminal

49. Finch was later granted a license to practice medicine again in Missouri. The Boston Globe, Nov. 13, 1974, at 2.

50. Cf. State v. Forrest, 362 S.E.2d 252 (1987), p. 116 note 68 above.

51. The penalties fixed by the legislatures for the types of homicide vary widely. The common penalty for the most serious category of homicide, usually first degree murder, is life imprisonment; if capital punishment is retained, the penalty of death may also be authorized. The penalty for second degree murder is generally imprisonment for a maximum term of life or a large number (20–30) of years; the minimum term is generally ten years or less. Manslaughter is punished typically by imprisonment for not more than ten or twenty years and not less than five years or as little as two years or one year; in some states there is no minimum term of imprisonment. If involuntary manslaughter (see below pp. 251–305), is treated separately, the term of imprisonment is usually short, the maximum being five years or less.

Because the court usually has broad discretion over the sentence, the legislative formulas are at best an imprecise indication of the sentence imposed in a particular case. In addition, except in rare cases where release before the end of the term is prohibited, the availability of parole and "good time" allowances usually means that actual time in prison is much less than the term of the sentence.

law should treat as the equivalent of an intention to kill if an act to carry out the intention causes someone's death?

Suppose, for example, a person intends to beat someone "within an inch of his life" but not to go that last inch.

Suppose the person does not intend to injure anyone but her act is one that she could not but know gravely endangers life other than her own.

Suppose the person does not intend to injure anyone but his act is a serious crime, like arson or robbery.

In all of these cases, the courts have said that the defendant acts with malice aforethought (unless some exculpatory or mitigating factor is present) and, therefore, that the homicide is murder.

INTENTION TO INJURE

Consider the following cases:

(i) "[Wellar and] Margaret Campbell . . . had lived together for several months, and on the occasion of her death she had been out on an errand of her own in the neighborhood, and on coming back into the house entered the front door of the bar-room, and fell, or was knocked down upon the floor. While on the floor there was evidence tending to show that Wellar ordered her to get up, and kicked her, and that he drew her from the bar-room through the dining-room into a bedroom, where he left her, and where she afterwards died. The injury of which she died was inflicted on her left temple. . . . It was claimed by the prosecution to have been inflicted by a blow when she first came in, and if not, then by a blow or kick afterwards." Wellar v. People, 30 Mich. 16, 17 (1874).

(ii) "For a number of years . . . [the defendant] had been having illicit relations with the deceased, which he determined to end; she came to his office the evening of January 19, 1926, and asked him for money; they quarreled, and he took her by the throat—in his words 'to give her a scare.' She screamed, whereupon he stuffed handkerchiefs into her mouth and continued to choke her, until she was dead." Commonwealth v. Marshall, 135 A. 301, 303 (Pa.1926).

In both cases, the defendant claimed that he did not intend to kill the victim. In both, the court sustained the verdict of murder on the basis that the defendant, having had at least an intention grievously to injure, had acted with malice aforethought. Can the conduct of the defendants in these cases be distinguished significantly from the conduct of Girouard or Caruso? Is the distinction, if there is one, well described as a difference in the defendant's intention? On what basis would such a difference be established?

———

84. Applying the usual (rebuttable) presumption that a man intends the likely consequences of his conduct, courts have stated that the use of a deadly weapon—or any weapon—in a deadly manner is a fact from which malice may be inferred. See, e.g., Hardy v. State, 251 S.E.2d 289 (Ga.1978); Commonwealth v. Boyd, 334 A.2d 610 (Pa.1975). Where death has resulted from a blow or blows of the fist, some courts have and others have not been willing to sustain a conviction of murder, depending on the circumstances. See, e.g., Commonwealth v. Dorazio, 74 A.2d 125 (Pa.1950) (defendant a professional prizefighter; conviction affirmed), with which compare State v. Basting, 572 N.W.2d 281 (Minn.1997), holding that, in the circumstances of the case—a brief encounter, in which the defendant struck the victim twice and then left the scene—a professional boxer's fist was not a deadly weapon. See also People v. Aguilar, 945 P.2d 1204 (Cal.1997), holding that a reference to a "deadly weapon" in a statute defining the crime of assault with a deadly weapon did not include the use of hands or feet but referred to use of a weapon other than one's own body. The court did not say whether the shoes on a person's foot would satisfy the statutory requirement.

In a number of cases, courts have sustained a conviction for attempted murder when a defendant infected with the AIDS virus assaulted or engaged in unprotected sex with another person in a manner that exposed the person to a risk of infection and there were accompanying words or conduct manifesting an intent to transmit the disease. E.g., State v. Hinkhouse, 912 P.2d 921 (Or.Ct.App.1996) (unprotected sex); State v. Caine, 652 So.2d 611 (La.Ct.App.1995) (assault). In Smallwood v. State, 680 A.2d 512 (Md.Ct.App.1996), however, the court reversed the conviction of a defendant who, knowing that he was HIV-positive, raped several women without protection. His actions, the court said, "are wholly explained by an intent to commit rape" and do not "provide evidence that he also had an intent to kill." Id. at 516.

For a careful, thorough discussion of the difference between intention grievously to injure, on one hand, and other states of mind like foresight of a risk of serious injury, intention to expose to a risk, and so forth, see Hyam v. Director of Public Prosecutions, [1975] App. Cas. 55 (H.L.). The issue is discussed further in Regina v. Cunningham, [1982] App. Cas. 566 (H.L.); R. v. Moloney, [1985] App. Cas. 905 (H.L.); and Regina v. Hancock [1986] App. Cas. 455, 467 (H.L.).

85. If an intention grievously to injure is treated as the equivalent of an intention to kill in the law of homicide, the jury is relieved of the burden to decide a difficult question of fact in cases where an intention to kill is not evident from the nature of the act itself (as it would be, for example, if the act were shooting a person through the heart). Does that consideration coupled with the facts (1) that death has resulted from the defendant's acts; (2) that the defendant's intention was at best very bad; and (3) that if the issue is at all in doubt from the nature of the act, the defendant will predictably assert that he had the lesser intention and there will seldom be evidence to refute that assertion directly, help to explain this category of malice aforethought?

86.   The Model Penal Code omits reference to intention to injure in its definition of criminal homicide. The commentary points out that such intent is relevant in determining whether there was the extreme recklessness or recklessness that suffices for convictions respectively of murder (see below) and (involuntary) manslaughter (see pp. 251–305 below). "In the rare case of purposeful infliction of serious injury not involving recklessness with respect to death, the actor should be prosecuted for some version of aggravated assault or, perhaps, for negligent homicide." 1 MPC Commentaries Part II, 29 (comment to § 210.2). Although intention grievously to injure remains a type of malice aforethought in a number of states, recent statutory revisions have generally followed the lead of the Code.

EXTREME RECKLESSNESS

The New York Times

Monday, August 19, 1968.

Rider Slain As Bullet Rips Into L.I.R.R. Train A Second Passenger Wounded—Youth Seized In Queens

By Maurice Carroll

A bullet ripped through the side of a Long Island Rail Road train as it rolled through Queens toward Pennsylvania Station early yesterday morning, killing one passenger and wounding another.

Within a half hour, after the shooting at 4:38 A.M., a pink-cheeked 16-year-old boy [Whitmore] who liked to dress up like a fireman was seized by railroad policemen near the bridge where rifle bullets had hurtled through the darkness toward two passing trains.

The fatal shot tore through the elbow of one man, then struck the second in the neck. It was fired from a sandy, weed-covered embankment just east of the 43d Street trestle in Sunnyside across from a huge white-on-black Urban Coalition sign that said "Give a Damn."

———

Assuming that Whitmore was simply "taking some potshots" at the train and that no defense like infancy[52] or insanity is available to him, what crime has he committed?

———

People v. Poplis

30 N.Y.2d 85, 281 N.E.2d 167 (1972)

■ BERGAN, JUDGE. Defendant has been convicted of murder under new Penal Law, Consol. Laws, c. 40, section 125.25 (subd. 2). In relevant text this provides: "A person is guilty of murder" when "[u]nder circumstances evincing a depraved indifference to human life, he recklessly engages in conduct which creates a grave risk of death to another person, and thereby causes the death of another person."

Penal code Law, Consol. Law, c.40 § 125.25

The proof abundantly establishes that the death of Roxanne Felumero, the three-and-a-half-year-old child of defendant's wife, was caused by repeated physical beatings by defendant between March 16 and March 21, 1969 when the child died.

The beatings were brutal, callous and inhuman. The medical proof is that the resulting injuries produced death. The beating of the child by defendant was established by several witnesses and especially by Marie Poplis, defendant's wife and the mother of the child, who described the repeated physical violence of defendant to the child and ultimately her death.

The argument of appellant is not that the proof would not sustain a finding of physical brutality by him resulting in death, but rather that the acts as alleged "do not fall within the murder statute." It is suggested there is no substantial difference in the definitions of murder under section 125.25 (subd. 2) and manslaughter second degree under section 125.15 (subd. 1). The latter provision states a person is guilty of manslaughter when "[h]e recklessly . . . causes the death of another person."

A person who, with a "depraved indifference to human life," recklessly engages in conduct which "creates a grave risk of death to another person" resulting in death, also by included definition "recklessly causes" the death. But the murder prescription requires more than recklessly causing death which could happen, for example, from gross carelessness in motor vehicle operation.

---

52. At that time available in New York only to a person under the age of 16. New York has since provided that in cases of murder of this type and some other serious crimes the defense of infancy is available only to persons under the age of 13. N.Y. Penal Law § 30.00.

The murder definition requires conduct with "depraved indifference" to "human life," plus recklessness. This is conduct of graver culpability, and it is the kind which has been rather well understood at common law to involve something more serious than mere recklessness alone which has had an incidental tragic result. The continued brutality toward a child, found by the jury in this case, fits within the accepted understanding of the kind of recklessness involving "a depraved indifference to human life."

The predecessor to section 125.25 was former Penal Law section 1044 (subd. 2). This was very similar in effect, but somewhat different in text. It prescribed an act "imminently dangerous to others, and evincing a depraved mind, regardless of human life." This is just about another way of saying "depraved indifference to human life" but the new text eliminates the psychiatrically complicating term "evincing a depraved mind" and is a distinct improvement.

The court had the former definition for consideration in People v. Jernatowski, 238 N.Y. 188 [1924] where the act charged was recklessly shooting a gun into a house, killing one of the occupants. Chief Judge Hiscock, on analysis of the problem raised by "depraved mind, regardless of human life," reached this conclusion (p. 192): "So in this case, when the defendant fired two or more shots into the house where he knew there were human beings, he committed an act which the jury certainly could say was imminently dangerous, and which evinced a wicked and depraved mind, regardless of human life, and which amply supplied the evidence of malice and felonious intent which were charged in the indictment, and proof of which was necessary to establish the crime of murder in the first degree."

. . .

. . . The new Penal Law provision is analyzed in the Practice Commentary by Denzer and McQuillan (McKinney's Cons. Laws of N.Y., Book 39, Penal Law, pp. 235–236) which notes that both the former provision and the present one embrace "extremely dangerous and fatal conduct performed without specific homicidal intent but with a depraved kind of wantonness." The statute is sufficiently definite and the kind of conduct described is sufficiently laid out to sustain a valid penal sanction. The evidence here supports the conviction.

———

87. Other cases illustrative of this category of murder are the following:

[S]ometime between 7:30 and 8:00 P.M. on July 7, 1981, defendant drove a car, owned by Americo Junco, out of a gas station located on the west side of 10th Avenue at 45th Street in Manhattan and entered 10th Avenue at a speed of approximately 40 miles an hour. He then accelerated across 10th Avenue, struck and careened off a parked car and continued traveling north, weaving from lane to lane. As he did so, he struck the left side of a moving vehicle, accelerated to over 50 miles an hour, and mounted the curb of the sidewalk adjacent to a parking lot entrance south of the southwest corner of 46th Street. He then drove the car along the sidewalk at a high rate of speed and struck a boy riding his bicycle, Daniel Calibar, throwing him completely across 46th Street. An occupant of the car testified that at that point he told defendant to apply the brakes, but defendant responded: "No I cannot brake, I cannot put the brakes on any longer. I have killed a person already."

Defendant then accelerated his speed further, crossed 46th Street and mounted the opposite sidewalk where several people were standing. He drove up the block on the sidewalk, striking another child riding a bicycle, Rene Mercado, near the corner of 47th Street, and dragging his body approximately 80 feet. Junco's vehicle then crossed 47th Street and mounted the curb on the northwest corner. He again sped along the sidewalk at over 50 miles an hour nearly striking several people standing along 48th Street until defendant braked for the first time and the car came to rest. After the car stopped, defendant attempted to escape but he was apprehended and arrested.

People v. Gomez, 478 N.E.2d 759, 760–61 (N.Y.1985).

The shootings occurred about 12:30 A.M. on January 15, 1977 in a crowded barroom in downtown Rochester. The evidence established that defendant and a friend, Duval, had been drinking heavily that day celebrating the fact that Duval, through an administrative mixup, would not have to spend the weekend in jail. Sometime between 7:00 P.M. and 8:00 P.M., the two men left home for the bar. Defendant took a loaded pistol with him and shortly after they arrived at the bar, he produced it when he got into an argument with another patron over money owed him. Apparently the dispute ended without incident and defendant continued his drinking. After midnight another argument developed, this time between Duval and Willie Mitchell. Defendant took out the gun again, shot at Mitchell but mistakenly injured Lawrence Evans who was trying to stop the fight. He then stepped forward and shot Mitchell in the stomach from close range. At that, the 40 or 50 patrons in the bar started for the doors. Some of the bystanders tried to remove Mitchell to a hospital and while they were doing so, the decedent, Marvin Lindsey, walked by defendant. Lindsey was apparently a friend or acquaintance of defendant although that was the first time he had seen him that night. For no explained reason, defendant turned and fired his gun killing Lindsey.

[D]efendant's counsel elicited evidence during the prosecution's case of defendant's considerable drinking that evening. . . .

. . .

[In the bar, defendant] said that he was "going to kill somebody tonight," or similar words, several times, and he had brought the gun out in the bar once before during the evening only to be told to put it away.

People v. Register, 457 N.E.2d 704, 705–706 (N.Y.1983).

88. As the illustrations in note 87 suggest, cases that fall within this category of murder commonly involve the use of a manifestly dangerous instrumentality in a manifestly dangerous way, like Whitmore's shooting at the passing train. See, in addition to *Jernatowski*, cited in *Poplis*, King v. State, 505 So.2d 403 (Ala.Crim.App.1987) (firing at moving vehicle manifested " 'don't give a damn attitude,' " displaying "extreme indifference to human life"); State v. Ibn Omar-Muhammad, 694 P.2d 922 (N.M.1985) (driving car at high speed directly at persons, through roadblock, etc., in attempt to escape law officers); Commonwealth v. Coleman, 318 A.2d 716 (Pa.1974) ("malice in the sense of a wicked disposition" shown by firing revolver on public bus); Banks v. State, 211 S.W. 217 (Tex.Crim.App.1919) (firing pistol into a moving train; "heart regardless of social duty and fatally bent on mischief"). "It is not necessary to show that [the defendant] formed an intent to kill any particular person since there can be no question but that the natural tendency of this act [firing a shotgun into a group of men] would be to destroy another's life. In a situation such as this the criminal intent to murder may be implied from the character of the act." People v. Gonzales, 239 N.E.2d 783, 789 (Ill.1968). In Commonwealth v. Malone, 47 A.2d 445 (Pa.1946), the defendant, aged 17, placed a gun against the side of the decedent, aged 13, and pulled the trigger three times, in a game of Russian roulette; he thought that he had so placed the bullet that the gun would not fire. He was wrong. The court affirmed his conviction of murder. See also Commonwealth v. Ashburn, 331 A.2d 167 (Pa.1975).

Poplis is illustrative of another group of cases in this category. E.g., People v. Burden, 140 Cal.Rptr. 282 (Ct.App.1977) (defendant's failure to feed infant with knowledge that infant was starving to death was sufficient to show an "abandoned and malignant heart"); Robinson v. State, 517 A.2d 94 (Md.1986) (shooting victim with intent to disable); State v. Crocker, 435 A.2d 58 (Me.1981) (brutality); Commonwealth v. Matthews, 389 A.2d 71 (Pa.1978) (repeated use of excessive force against child manifested "extreme indifference to value of human life"); State v. Nicholson, 585 P.2d 60 (Utah 1978) (neglect). But cf. People v. Northrup, 442 N.Y.S.2d 658 (App.Div.1981) (failure to get help for infant; *not* murder).

Courts have sometimes construed statutes referring to "extreme indifference to human life" not to cover a case like *Poplis*, in which the conduct causing death is directed at a specific person. They have reasoned that other statutes referring to intention to kill (or seriously to injure) cover such cases and that the former statute requires an indifference to human life *generally*. See Northington v. State, 413 So.2d 1169 (Ala.Crim.App. 1981); State v. Berge, 607 P.2d 1247 (Wash.Ct.App.1980). The issue is discussed in United States v. Houser, 130 F.3d 867 (9th Cir.1997), which upholds the inclusion of conduct directed at a specific person within the category of extreme recklessness.

89. In *Register*, note 87 above, the court rejected the argument that the defendant's intoxication might be considered as evidence that his conduct did not satisfy the statutory requirement of "circumstances evincing a depraved indifference to human life." It said that the requirement did not refer to a state of mind that could be contradicted by evidence of intoxication, but was "a definition of the factual setting in which the risk-creating conduct must occur" and referred only to "objective circumstances." It added: "In utilitarian terms, the risk of excessive drinking should be added to and not subtracted from the risks created by the conduct of the drunken defendant for there is no social or penological purpose to be served by a rule that permits one who voluntarily drinks to be exonerated from failing to foresee the results of his conduct if he is successful at getting drunk." 457 N.E.2d at 707, 709. The significance of intoxication aside, can the court's description of this element of "depraved mind murder" be taken entirely at face value? Must not the "factual setting" somehow be manifest to someone in the defendant's situation in order to evince anything at all about his attitude?

A dissenting judge observed: "Under the majority's rule . . . a person who possessed only a reckless state of mind when he caused the death of another could be convicted of depraved mind murder . . . and sentenced to a term of 15 years to life imprisonment simply because objective circumstances surrounding the killing presented a 'grave risk' of death even though the actor, due to intoxication, was unaware of those circumstances and could not appreciate the risks. The majority would also hold that another person who is fully aware of a 'substantial and unjustifiable risk' and consciously disregards that risk can only be found guilty of manslaughter in the second degree and sentenced to as little as one and one-half years in jail. . . . While there may be a technical distinction between a 'grave' risk and a 'substantial' one, the only real difference is about 15 years in prison. . . . To accept this distinction as justification for the disparate penalties which the respective crimes carry defies basic principles of fairness and logic. I simply cannot agree that the Legislature intended that convictions for murder as opposed to manslaughter would turn upon the nature of the objective surrounding circumstances regardless of whether or not the accused was aware of those circumstances or could appreciate the consequences of his conduct." Id. at 712.

90. The question whether drunk driving can satisfy the requirement of extreme indifference to the value of life, however it is expressed, has troubled the courts. Stating (apparently contrary to the New York court's statement in *Register*, note 89 above) that this category of murder was distinguished from manslaughter by the defendant's actual appreciation of the risk, "i.e., a *subjective* standard," the Supreme Court of California held that a person whose drunk driving caused the death of two people could be prosecuted for murder.

> [W]e believe that there exists a rational ground for concluding that defendant's conduct was sufficiently wanton to hold him on a second degree murder charge. The facts upon which we base this conclusion are as follows: Defendant had consumed enough alcohol to raise his blood alcohol content to a level which would support a finding that he was legally intoxicated. He had driven his car to the establishment where he had been drinking, and he must have known that he would have to drive it later. It also may be presumed that defendant was aware of the hazards of driving while intoxicated. . . . "One who wilfully consumes alcoholic beverages to the point of intoxication, knowing that he thereafter must operate a motor vehicle, thereby combining sharply impaired physical and mental faculties with a vehicle capable of great force and speed, reasonably may be held to exhibit a conscious disregard of the safety of others." Defendant drove at highly excessive speeds through city streets, an act presenting a great risk of harm or death. Defendant nearly collided with a vehicle after running a red light; he avoided the accident only by skidding to a stop. He thereafter resumed his excessive speed before colliding with the victims' car, and then belatedly again attempted to brake his car before the collision (as evidenced by the extensive skid marks before and after impact) suggesting an actual awareness of the great risk of harm which he had created. In combination, these facts reasonably and readily support a conclusion that defendant acted wantonly and with a conscious disregard for human life.
>
> We do not suggest that the foregoing facts conclusively demonstrate implied malice, or that the evidence necessarily is sufficient to convict defendant of second degree murder. On the contrary, it may be difficult for the prosecution to carry its burden of establishing implied malice to the moral certainty necessary for a conviction. Moreover, we neither contemplate nor encourage the routine charging of second degree murder in vehicular homicide cases. We merely determine that the evidence before us is sufficient to uphold the second degree murder counts in the information, and to permit the prosecution to prove, if it can, the elements of second degree murder.

People v. Watson, 637 P.2d 279, 283, 285–86 (Cal.1981).

So also, in United States v. Fleming, 739 F.2d 945 (4th Cir.1984), the defendant, while drunk, drove at a speed of about 70–80 miles per hour, far above the limit, and crossed into the lanes for the opposite direction to avoid traffic congestion in the correct lanes. He crashed into a car and someone was killed. Upholding his conviction for murder, the court said: "In the vast majority of vehicular homicides, the accused has not exhibited such wanton and reckless disregard for human life as to indicate the presence of malice on his part. In the present case, however, the facts show a deviation from established standards of regard for life and the safety of others that is markedly different in degree from that found in most vehicular homicides. In the average drunk driving homicide, there is no proof that the driver has acted while intoxicated with the purpose of wantonly and intentionally putting the lives of others in danger. Rather, his driving abilities were so impaired that he recklessly put others in danger simply by being on the road and attempting to do the things that any driver would do. In the present case, however, danger did not arise only by defendant's determining to drive while drunk. Rather, in addition to being intoxicated while driving, defendant drove in a manner that could be taken to indicate depraved disregard of human life, *particularly* in light of the fact that *because he was drunk* his reckless behavior was all the more dangerous." Id. at 948.

Disagreeing with the courts above, the Supreme Court of Virginia held that although the defendant "was intoxicated and guilty of an appalling degree of reckless driving" and caused the death of three people, there was not evidence to support a conviction of murder. Essex v. Commonwealth, 322 S.E.2d 216, 222 (Va.1984). His intoxication, the court said, was a factor that supports a conviction for involuntary manslaughter and might also warrant a more severe penalty if he were convicted of that offense. One might be guilty of murder if he set out to get drunk with the purpose of driving out of control so as to endanger life. See also Langford v. State, 354 So.2d 313 (Ala.1977).

See p. 268 note 142 below.

91.   The Supreme Court of California has disapproved instructions to the jury that use the phrase "abandoned and malignant heart" to define malice aforethought, even though the phrase is used in the statutory definition of murder. Cal. Penal Code § 188. "The instruction phrased in the latter terms adds nothing to the jury's understanding of implied malice; its obscure metaphor invites confusion and unguided speculation. . . . [It] could lead the jury to equate the malignant heart with an evil disposition or a despicable character; the jury then, in a close case, may convict because it believes the defendant a 'bad man.' " People v. Phillips, 414 P.2d 353, 363 (Cal.1966). The phrase "wicked and malignant heart" is used to characterize first-degree murder by an act greatly dangerous to others, "indicating a depraved mind without regard for human life," in State v. Hernandez, 873 P.2d 243 (N.M.1994). Compare State v. Weso, 210 N.W.2d 442, 445 (Wis. 1973), in which, in describing this category of murder, the court said: "A depraved mind is one having an inherent deficiency of moral sense and rectitude. Otherwise it would not prompt an act which in its nature is imminently dangerous to the safety of another. The element of the disregard for life likewise calls for a state of mind which has no regard for the moral or social duties of a human being."

92.   The Model Penal Code § 210.2(1)(b) provides that criminal homicide is murder if "it is committed recklessly under circumstances manifesting extreme indifference to the value of human life." The comment states:

[T]here is a kind of reckless homicide that cannot fairly be distinguished in grading terms from homicides committed purposely or knowingly. . . .

. . . Ordinary recklessness . . . is made sufficient for a conviction for manslaughter. . . . In a prosecution for murder, however, the Code calls for the further judgment whether the actor's conscious disregard of the risk, under the circumstances, manifests extreme indifference to the value of human life. The significance of purpose or knowledge as a standard of culpability is that, cases of provocation or other mitigation apart, purposeful or knowing homicide demonstrates precisely such indifference to the value of human life. Whether recklessness is so extreme that it demonstrates similar indifference is not a question, it is submitted, that can be further clarified. It must be left directly to the trier of fact under instructions which make it clear that recklessness that can fairly be assimilated to purpose or knowledge should be treated as murder and that less extreme recklessness should be punished as manslaughter.

1 MPC Commentaries Part II, 21–22 (comment to § 210.2).

The difference between evidence that will support a finding of intent to cause grievous bodily harm (or death) and that which will support a finding of extreme indifference to the value of human life may not be very great. A man's intention is displayed (ordinarily) by his conduct, and the consequences of conduct (ordinarily) define it (to a large extent); which is to say, in more common legal language, that in the absence of evidence to the contrary a man is presumed to intend the natural and probable consequences of his acts. The main difference is likely to be that an actual intention to kill or injure is harder to establish in circumstances in which the killer has not singled out a particular victim.

FELONY MURDER

Suppose the defendant's purposeful conduct manifests disregard of some value other than human life or safety, say, the peaceful possession of property or the integrity of the person. Are there intentions that are "just as bad" as an intention to kill or to injure seriously? Are there other kinds of intention that, within the framework of the criminal law, are the equivalent of homicidal intent, so that if death results from conduct accompanied by such intent it should be regarded as murder?

The robbery was planned by appellant who invited his co-defendant, a boy of 18, to take part. The place robbed was a gasoline filling station near the city of Sheridan. Shores, the man in charge of the station, was held up at the point of a revolver in the hand of appellant. While appellant was taking money from a money drawer with his left hand, holding the gun in his right, Shores bravely tried to take the revolver. In the struggle, the revolver, still in appellant's hand, was discharged three times, wounding Shores in the arm and body and causing his death.

State v. Best, 12 P.2d 1110, 1111 (Wyo.1932). If the appellant's claim "that the revolver was fired accidentally and solely as the result of the struggle for its possession," id., is believed, is he nevertheless guilty of murder? If so, on what theory?

The well-established answer is that the appellant is guilty of "felony murder." "The felony murder rule as it was formulated in England was a doctrine of constructive malice. To make out a case of murder it was necessary only to establish that the defendant had committed a homicide while engaged in the commission of a felony. No other evidence had to be introduced to prove the essential element of malice aforethought." Commonwealth v. Balliro, 209 N.E.2d 308, 312 (Mass.1965). See State v. Valeriano, 468 A.2d 936 (Conn.1983), holding that it was immaterial in a prosecution for felony murder arising out of a homicide in the course of arson that the defendant had made a substantial effort to ensure that no one would be in the building at the time of the fire; the "mens rea" requirement is fully satisfied by the intention to commit the underlying felony. Cf. People v. Burns, 686 P.2d 1360, 1362 (Colo.Ct.App.1983): "The felony murder statute requires only that the death of a person result in furtherance of the commission of a felony. Thus, the affirmative defense of self-defense may properly be raised only as it pertains to the underlying felony, and not to the resulting death." See also State v. Lea, 485 S.E.2d 874, 879 (N.C.App.1997), holding, in accord with the prevailing rule, "that a charge of 'attempted felony murder' is a logical impossibility in that it would require the defendant to intend what is by definition an unintentional result."

What of Best's co-defendant? If he was engaged in robbing the filling station at the time Shores was shot but was not at all involved in the struggle between Best and Shores, should he also be guilty of murder? If so, on what theory?

———

United States v. Heinlein

490 F.2d 725 (D.C.Cir.1973)

■ McGOWAN, CIRCUIT JUDGE. Appellants were charged with felony-murder . . . murder in the second degree . . . rape while armed . . . and rape . . . . They were convicted of felony-murder, and of the lesser included offense of assault with intent to commit rape while armed. When the jury was unable to agree as to punishment on the felony-murder count, the District Court sentenced appellant Heinlein to death, and both of the Walker brothers to prison sentences of twenty years to life. On the assault offense, each of the three appellants received a sentence of fifteen years to life. The death sentence for Heinlein has been invalidated . . . with the effect that Heinlein stands before us in respect of his felony-murder conviction as one under a life sentence.

All of the participants in the events giving rise to these appeals appear to have lived in the nether world of chronic alcoholism, and the events themselves are of a singularly squalid nature. Because of this, as well as the difficulties of reconstructing—through the imperfect instrument of a chronic alcoholic—what happened in this instance in that confused and cloudy environment, this was obviously a difficult and distasteful case to try, both for judge and jury.

We have, accordingly, examined the record in this case with special care. We have concluded that, with the exception of what we believe to have been a misconception by the court of the law of felony-murder in its application to accomplices, appellants had a fair trial, and that no unacceptable risk of a miscarriage of justice resides in affirming Heinlein's convictions on both counts, and the convictions of the Walker brothers for assault with intent to commit rape while armed. The convictions of the latter for felony-murder are reversed.

I

Appellants chose not to testify at trial. Accordingly, the only purportedly eyewitness version of the events in question was given by Mr. James Harding, a chronic alcoholic. On the morning of April 13, 1968, so Harding testified, he and Marie McQueen, the murder victim, were released after overnight incarceration for drunkenness. After buying some wine, they met Bernard Heinlein and the Walker brothers, David and Frank, on the street. The five of them then went to an apartment occupied by the Walkers to drink the wine. Heinlein told McQueen that he wanted to have sexual relations with her, and the Walkers both voiced support of this proposal. When McQueen refused, the three appellants seized her, held her down, and began to remove her clothing. During the struggle, McQueen slapped Heinlein in the face. His response was to take a knife from his pocket and stab her, inflicting what proved to be a fatal wound. McQueen was then carried down into the basement by her assailants, and Harding last saw her lying on the floor there, apparently just barely alive.

. . .

Appellants Frank and David Walker seek reversal of their felony-murder convictions on the ground that the jury was improperly instructed. Their counsel unsuccessfully requested use of the felony-murder instruction on accomplices contained in the Junior Bar Association Criminal Jury Instructions.[53] The words in that instruction which appellants regard as of

_____

53. This Junior Bar Instruction (No. 84) . . . is as follows:

. . .

[Instruction When There Are Multiple Defendants—If two or more persons, acting

critical importance are contained in the phrase "in the course of the felony and in furtherance of the common purpose to commit the felony." These words are, in their submission, to be compared with the qualifying phrases in the instruction as given, namely, "in the course of," and "as a part of" the rape or attempted rape, and "within the scope of the rape which one or more of the defendants undertook to commit."

It may be true, as appellants assert, that the words "in furtherance of the common purpose" in the requested instruction would have focused the jury's attention more directly on the causational element of felony-murder than did the instruction given by the District Court. Those words emphasized that the slaying must be causally related to the objects of the felony, whereas under the latter mere coincidence of time and place between the felony and the murder might be thought to suffice. To that extent, the Junior Bar instruction conforms more nearly to the requirements of our statute as it has been interpreted in respect of accomplices, and is therefore preferable to the instruction given.

It may also be true, however, that the verbal differences between these two formulations, in terms of practical impact upon the jury, are not very great. A slaying which may be said to have occurred "within the scope of" a particular felony might also be regarded as "in furtherance of the common purpose to commit the felony." Under either instruction defense counsel could presumably argue to the jury that the slaying was so unrelated to the object of the felony as to be beyond its scope, in the one case, or not in

together, are perpetrating or attempting to perpetrate [one of the enumerated felonies] and one of them, *in the course of the felony and in furtherance of the common purpose to commit the felony*, kills a human being, both the person who committed the killing and the person who aided and abetted him in the felony are guilty of murder in the first degree.] [Emphasis supplied].

The instruction given by the court was in this form:

. . .

If two or more persons acting together and jointly are perpetrating a rape or attempting to perpetrate a rape, and one or more of them *in the course of the rape or attempted rape*, kills another person, then all of the persons involved in the rape or attempted rape are guilty of murder in the first degree.

If one person is perpetrating or attempting to perpetrate a rape and one or more other persons aids and abets him in so doing, and the first of these persons *in the course of the rape or attempted rape, as a part of the rape or attempted rape*, kills a human being,

then the person or persons who aided him in the rape or attempted rape and the person who committed the killing are all guilty of murder in the first degree.

Under the circumstances of this case the elements of the offense of murder in the first degree which the Government must establish beyond a reasonable doubt as to the first count are as follows:

One, that the defendants were in the District of Columbia jointly perpetrating or attempting to perpetrate a rape or that one of the defendants was perpetrating or attempting to perpetrate a rape and the other defendants aided and abetted him in so doing.

Two, that in the course of so doing one of the defendants killed the deceased, Marie McQueen.

Three, that the victim, Marie McQueen, died as a result of a wound or wounds inflicted by one or more of the defendants.

Four, *that the killing was within the scope of the rape or attempted rape which one or more of the defendants undertook to commit.* (Emphasis supplied).

furtherance of the common purpose to commit it, in the other. On our facts, the argument would be that Heinlein's stabbing of McQueen was an unexpected response to his being slapped in the face and was independent of any common purpose to rape. Indeed, any sudden killing of McQueen by one of the appellants could be regarded as frustrating and defeating that common purpose, and therefore alien to it.

If such argument had been permitted in this case, the differences between the two instructions might not be such as to compel reversal. The District Court, however, appears to have construed the statutory definition of felony-murder to preclude such a defense, and to have restricted argument to the jury accordingly. . . .

. . .

[T]he trial judge foreclosed counsel from arguing to the jury matters not going to intent as such, but which do relate to a concept which may, without significant alteration of meaning, be variously phrased as either (1) the scope of the felony which the participants undertook to commit, or (2) the furtherance of the common purpose which the participants entertained in embarking upon it.

We deal with the crime of felony-murder as it is defined in our statute.[54] Our central task is, thus, one of statutory interpretation. It would perhaps be possible to read the relevant statute as contemplating only a coincidence in point of time and place between the commission of the felony and the occurrence of the slaying. This is what the trial judge did, but this does not, however, seem to be what the formulators of jury instructions in this jurisdiction have done. Both the Junior Bar Instruction refused by the trial judge, and the one given by him, include phrases which seem to look beyond this concept of mere coincidence.

If these inclusions reflect a proper interpretation of the statute, then the trial judge erred in ruling that, on the evidence adduced, the slaying was clearly within the scope of the felony of rape which the defendants undertook to commit. By so doing, he prevented defense counsel from suggesting to the jurors that the evidence warranted a finding by them that, insofar as the Walker brothers were concerned, the scope of the common undertaking had been exceeded. They would, of course, not have been obliged to make that finding, but it would appear to have been open to them even under the terms of the court's instruction as given.

The D.C. felony-murder statute is addressed in terms only to the person who kills while perpetrating a felony. Accomplices, like the Walker brothers, are exposed to first degree murder accountability by reason of the

---

54. In pertinent part 22 D.C. Code § 2401 provides:

Whoever . . . in perpetrating or attempting to perpetrate any offense punishable by imprisonment in the penitentiary . . . kills another . . . is guilty of murder in the first degree.

Although this provision applies only to the person who actually does the killing, its scope is extended to accomplices by the aiding and abetting statute, 22 D.C. Code § 105.

aiding and abetting statute. It is true that that exposure does not depend upon proof of an intent to kill on the part of the accomplice; that intent is supplied by the fact of participation in the felony giving rise to the killing. But, certainly as to accomplices, the matter does not end there. The common law concepts of causation and vicarious responsibility are operative. The accomplice who aids and abets the commission of a felony is legally responsible as a principal for all acts of the other person which are in furtherance of the common design or plan to commit the felony, or are the natural and probable consequence of acts done in the perpetration of the felony.

It was upon these terms that the common law encompassed the imposition of liability for first degree murder upon one who neither killed nor had any intent to kill, but only took part knowingly in the commission of a felony. . . .

Under the common law concept it seems clear that there was room for jury issues relating to whether the slaying occurred within the scope of the felony which the parties undertook to commit, or in furtherance of their common plan or purpose to commit it. The Supreme Court of Oregon recently pointed to what appears to have been the common law concept. Quoting with approval Wharton's Criminal Law & Procedure, Vol. I, at 544, the court stated the rule in these terms:

> Something more than a mere coincidence of time and place between the wrongful act and the death is necessary. It must appear that there was such actual legal relation between the killing and the crime committed or attempted that the killing can be said to have occurred as a part of the perpetration of the crime, or in furtherance of an attempt or purpose to commit it. State v. Schwensen, 237 Or. 506 (1964).

It does not appear to be true, as some have supposed, that the current felony-murder statutes embody a legislative purpose to deter the commission of felonies to the point of embracing the coincidence rationale. As the New York Court of Appeals commented in People v. Wood, 8 N.Y.2d 48, 51–52 (1960):

> [A] felony murder embraces not any killing incidentally coincident with the felony . . . but only those committed by one of the criminals in the attempted execution of the unlawful end. Although the homicide itself need not be within the common design . . . the *act* which results in death must be in furtherance of the unlawful purpose. . . .

> In other words, in order for a felon to be guilty of the homicide, the act (as in agency) must be "either actually or constructively his, and it cannot be his act in either sense unless committed by his own hand or by someone acting in concert with him or in furtherance of a common object or purpose." . . . Where, however, the felon kills someone during the felony, but in a separate and distinct act and to satisfy his own end, his accomplice in the felony is not guilty of murder in the first degree. . . . If the lethal *act* is in furtherance of their common purpose, the accomplice is guilty even though there was an

express agreement not to kill, and even if he actually attempts to prevent the homicide. . . .

There is no basis for believing that the D.C. felony-murder statute goes beyond its common law origins and is thereby different from others in effect around the country. . . .

Thus it would seem that the felony-murder instruction which has been used in this jurisdiction, as well as the one proposed for use by the Junior Bar Association, reflect an understanding that the statute embraces occasions when the jury may properly be urged to find that the homicidal act fell outside the scope of the felonious crime which the parties undertook to commit. It was error for the trial court to forbid counsel to argue this to the jury; and the felony-murder convictions of the Walker brothers must be reversed.

. . .

———

93. Assuming that it makes sense to hold both defendants liable for murder if one of them *intentionally* kills the victim of a robbery that they jointly commit, does it equally make sense to hold both liable if the killing is entirely accidental?[55] If the killing is accidental, is there any more reason to hold the felon who kills liable for murder than to hold his accomplice(s) liable? Consider People v. Stamp, below.

———

People v. Stamp

2 Cal.App.3d 203, 82 Cal.Rptr. 598 (1969)

■ COBEY, ASSOCIATE JUSTICE. These are appeals by Jonathan Earl Stamp, Michael John Koory and Billy Dean Lehman, following jury verdicts of guilty of robbery and murder, both in the first degree. Each man was given a life sentence on the murder charge together with the time prescribed by law on the robbery count.

Defendants appeal their conviction of the murder of Carl Honeyman who, suffering from a heart disease, died between 15 and 20 minutes after Koory and Stamp held up his business, the General Amusement Company, on October 26, 1965, at 10:45 a.m. Lehman, the driver of the getaway car, was apprehended a few minutes after the robbery; several weeks later Stamp was arrested in Ohio and Koory in Nebraska.

. . .

---

55. Compare State v. Bilal, 776 P.2d 153 (Wash.Ct.App.1989), holding that a statute providing an enhanced sentence for the robber and any accomplices, if a robbery is committed with a deadly weapon, is applicable to an accomplice without proof that he knew that the other robber was armed.

On this appeal appellants primarily rely upon their position that the felony-murder doctrine should not have been applied in this case due to the unforeseeability of Honeyman's death.

appellants argument

THE FACTS

Defendants Koory and Stamp, armed with a gun and a blackjack, entered the rear of the building housing the offices of General Amusement Company, ordered the employees they found there to go to the front of the premises, where the two secretaries were working. Stamp, the one with the gun, then went into the office of Carl Honeyman, the owner and manager. Thereupon Honeyman, looking very frightened and pale, emerged from the office in a "kind of hurry." He was apparently propelled by Stamp who had hold of him by an elbow.

The robbery victims were required to lie down on the floor while the robbers took the money and fled out the back door. As the robbers, who had been on the premises 10 to 15 minutes, were leaving, they told the victims to remain on the floor for five minutes so that no one would "get hurt."

Honeyman, who had been lying next to the counter, had to use it to steady himself in getting up off the floor. Still pale, he was short of breath, sucking air, and pounding and rubbing his chest. As he walked down the hall, in an unsteady manner, still breathing hard and rubbing his chest, he said he was having trouble "keeping the pounding down inside" and that his heart was "pumping too fast for him." A few minutes later, although still looking very upset, shaking, wiping his forehead and rubbing his chest, he was able to walk in a steady manner into an employee's office. When the police arrived, almost immediately thereafter, he told them he was not feeling very well and that he had a pain in his chest. About two minutes later, which was 15 to 20 minutes after the robbery had occurred, he collapsed on the floor. At 11:25 he was pronounced dead on arrival at the hospital. The coroner's report listed the immediate cause of death as heart attack.

The employees noted that during the hours before the robbery Honeyman had appeared to be in normal health and good spirits. The victim was an obese, sixty-year-old man, with a history of heart disease, who was under a great deal of pressure due to the intensely competitive nature of his business. Additionally, he did not take good care of his heart.

Health Condiction of the victim

Three doctors, including the autopsy surgeon, Honeyman's physician, and a professor of cardiology from U.C.L.A., testified that although Honeyman had an advanced case of atherosclerosis, a progressive and ultimately fatal disease, there must have been some immediate upset to his system which precipitated the attack. It was their conclusion in response to a hypothetical question that but for the robbery there would have been no fatal seizure at that time. The fright induced by the robbery was too much of a shock to Honeyman's system. There was opposing expert testimony to the effect that it could not be said with reasonable medical certainty that fright could ever be fatal.

SUFFICIENCY OF THE EVIDENCE RE CAUSATION

Appellants' contention that the evidence was insufficient to prove that the robbery factually caused Honeyman's death is without merit. . . . A review of the facts as outlined above shows that there was substantial evidence of the robbery itself, that appellants were the robbers, and that but for the robbery the victim would not have experienced the fright which brought on the fatal heart attack.

APPLICATION OF THE FELONY–MURDER RULE

Appellants' contention that the felony-murder rule is inapplicable to the facts of this case is also without merit. Under the felony-murder rule of *Rule* section 189 of the Penal Code, a killing committed in either the perpetration of or an attempt to perpetrate robbery is murder of the first degree. This is true whether the killing is willful, deliberate and premeditated, or merely accidental or unintentional, and whether or not the killing is planned as a part of the commission of the robbery. . . . People v. Washington, 62 Cal. 2d 777, 783,[56] merely limits the rule to situations where the killing was committed by the felon or his accomplice acting in furtherance of their common design. . . .

The doctrine presumes malice aforethought on the basis of the commission of a felony inherently dangerous to human life. . . . This rule is a rule of substantive law in California and not merely an evidentiary shortcut to finding malice as it withdraws from the jury the requirement that they find either express malice or the implied malice which is manifested in an intent to kill. . . . Under this rule no intentional act is necessary other than the attempt to or the actual commission of the robbery itself. When a robber enters a place with a deadly weapon with the intent to commit robbery, malice is shown by the nature of the crime. . . .

There is no requirement that the killing occur, "while committing" or "while engaged in" the felony, or that the killing be "a part of" the felony, other than that the few acts be a part of one continuous transaction. . . . Thus the homicide need not have been committed "to perpetrate" the felony. There need be no technical inquiry as to whether there has been a completion or abandonment of or desistence from the robbery before the homicide itself was completed. . . .

The doctrine is not limited to those deaths which are foreseeable. . . . Rather a felon is held strictly liable for *all* killings committed by him or his accomplices in the course of the felony. . . . As long as the homicide is the direct causal result of the robbery the felony-murder rule applies whether or not the death was a natural or probable consequence of the robbery. So long as a victim's predisposing physical condition, regardless of its cause, is not the *only* substantial factor bringing about his death, that condition, and the robber's ignorance of it, in no way destroys the robber's criminal responsibility for the death. . . . So long as life is shortened as a result of

[56] See p. 168 below.

the felonious act, it does not matter that the victim might have died soon anyway. . . . In this respect, the robber takes his victim as he finds him.

. . .

The judgment is affirmed.

————

Cases like *Stamp*, in which the victim of a robbery or burglary subsequently dies of a heart attack, are not uncommon. Courts have generally upheld a conviction of murder. E.g., State v. Reardon, 486 A.2d 112 (Me.1984); Stewart v. State, 500 A.2d 676 (Md.Ct.Spec.App.1985) ("death by fright"); State v. Dixon, 387 N.W.2d 682 (Neb.1986); Matter of Anthony M., 471 N.E.2d 447 (N.Y.1984).

Do these cases clearly satisfy the requirement stated in *Heinlein*, p. 151 above, that the death be within the scope of the felony?

94. Often enough, the circumstances are more complicated.

We have considered the case in which one of the robbers accidentally kills the victim of the robbery. Suppose a policeman performing his duty accidentally kills the victim of the robbery;

or a bystander;

or (accidentally or, using necessary deadly force to prevent a felony, deliberately) one of the robbers?

Should the robbers (or the one remaining alive) be guilty of murder (or any other degree of criminal homicide)? Why (not)?

Suppose the victim of the intended robbery, in an effort to prevent the robbery, accidentally kills a bystander;

or (accidentally or, using necessary deadly force to prevent a felony, deliberately) one of the robbers?

Murder by the robber(s)? Criminal homicide?

Suppose one of the robbers accidentally shoots himself?

Is the remaining robber a murderer?

Commonwealth ex rel. Smith v. Myers

438 Pa. 218, 261 A.2d 550 (1970)

■ O'BRIEN, JUSTICE. This is an appeal from the order of the Court of Common Pleas of Philadelphia County, denying James Smith's petition for a writ of habeas corpus. The facts upon which the convictions of appellant and his co-felons, Almeida and Hough, rest are well known to this Court and to the federal courts. In addition to vexing the courts, these cases have perplexed a generation of law students, both within and without the Commonwealth, and along with their progeny, have spawned reams of critical commentary.

procedural Hist.

Facts

Briefly, the facts of the crime are these. On January 30, 1947, Smith, along with Edward Hough and David Almeida, engaged in an armed robbery of a supermarket in the City of Philadelphia. An off-duty policeman, who happened to be in the area, was shot and killed while attempting to thwart the escape of the felons. Although the evidence as to who fired the fatal shot was conflicting in appellant's 1948 trial, the court charged the jury that it was irrelevant who fired the fatal bullet:

> Even if you should find from the evidence that Ingling was killed by a bullet from the gun of one of the policemen, that policeman having shot at the felons in an attempt to prevent the robbery or the escape of the robbers, or to protect Ingling, the felons would be guilty of murder, or if they did that in returning the fire of the felons that was directed toward them.

To this part of the charge appellant took a specific exception.

The jury convicted Smith of first degree murder, with punishment fixed at life imprisonment. . . .

On February 4, 1966, appellant filed the present petition for a writ of habeas corpus. In his petition appellant raised the following contentions: . . . that he was denied his constitutional right to a fair trial by reason of the trial judge's charge to the jury, quoted above, which was allegedly inconsistent with the rule later announced by this Court in Commonwealth v. Redline, 391 Pa. 486, 137 A.2d 472 (1958).

appellant's argument.

We reverse, grant the writ, allow an appeal nunc pro tunc, and grant a new trial. . . .

. . .

Appellant urges that he was denied due process by virtue of the trial court's charge that it was irrelevant who fired the fatal bullet. Such a charge was consistent . . . with the holding shortly thereafter in the appeal of appellant's co-felon, David Almeida, in Commonwealth v. Almeida, 362

Pa. 596 (1949). In the latter case, by a stretch of the felony-murder rule, we held that Almeida could indeed be found guilty of murder even though the fatal bullet was fired by another officer acting in opposition to the felony.

Rule → We adopted a proximate cause theory of murder: "[H]e whose felonious act is the *proximate* cause of another's death is *criminally* responsible for that death and must answer to society for it exactly as he who is *negligently* the *proximate cause* of another's death is civilly responsible for that death and must answer in damages for it." *Almeida*, 362 Pa. at page 603 (emphasis in original). We thus affirmed Almeida's conviction, stating at page 607: "The felonious acts of the robbers in firing shots at the policeman, well knowing that their fire would be returned, as it should have been, was [sic] the proximate cause of Officer Ingling's death."

The proximate cause theory was taken a millimeter further by this Court in Commonwealth v. Thomas, 382 Pa. 639 (1955). In that case the victim of an armed robbery shot and killed one of the felons, Jackson; the other felon, Thomas, was convicted of the murder.

Thomas was repudiated by this Court in Commonwealth v. Redline, 391 Pa. 486 (1958). The facts there were virtually identical to those of *Thomas*; a policeman shot one fleeing felon and the other was convicted of murder. In a famous opinion by the late Chief Justice Charles Alvin Jones, this Court interred *Thomas* and dealt a fatal blow to *Almeida*. At the outset of this Court's opinion in *Redline*, we stated: "The decision in the Almeida case was a radical departure from common law criminal jurisprudence." The thorough documentation which followed in this lengthy opinion proved beyond a shadow of a doubt that *Almeida* and *Thomas* constituted aberrations in the annals of Anglo-American adjudicature.

. . . *Redline* reaffirmed that the distinguishing criterion of murder is malice. The common law felony-murder rule is a means of imputing malice where it may not exist expressly. Under this rule, the malice necessary to make a killing, even an accidental one, murder, is constructively inferred from the malice incident to the perpetration of the initial felony.

The common law felony-murder rule as thus explicated has been subjected to some harsh criticism, most of it thoroughly warranted. . . .

. . .

In fact, not only is the felony-murder rule non-essential, but it is very doubtful that it has the deterrent effect its proponents assert. . . . Justice Oliver Wendell Holmes, in The Common Law, argued that the wise policy is not to punish the fortuity, but rather to impose severe penalties on those types of criminal activity which experience has demonstrated carry a high degree of risk to human life. In this respect, we note the recent amendment to the Penal Code, providing for increased penalties when certain crimes are committed with firearms.

We have gone into this lengthy discussion of the felony-murder rule not for the purpose of hereby abolishing it. That is hardly necessary in the instant case. But we do want to make clear how shaky are the basic premises on which it rests. With so weak a foundation, it behooves us not to extend it further and indeed, to restrain it within the bounds it has always known. As stated above, *Redline*, 391 Pa. at page 495 et seq., demolished the extension to the felony-murder rule made in *Almeida*: "In adjudging a felony-murder, it is to be remembered at all times that the thing which is imputed to a felon for a killing incidental to his felony is *malice* and *not the act of killing*. . . . 'The malice of the *initial* offense attaches to whatever else the *criminal* may do in connection therewith.' . . . And so, until the decision of this court in Commonwealth v. Almeida, supra, in 1949, the rule which was uniformly followed, whether by express statement or by implication, was that in order to convict for felony-murder, *the killing must have been done by the defendant or by an* — Rule *accomplice or confederate or by one acting in furtherance of the felonious undertaking . . . .*"

. . .

. . . [In *Redline*], we distinguished the *express* malice cases. These included the so-called "shield" cases, where a felon used the interposition of the body of an innocent person to escape harm in flight from the scene of the crime. . . . These cases were not based on the felony-murder rule and imputed malice, but on the express malice found in the use of an innocent person as a shield or breastwork against hostile bullets. . . .

. . . *Redline* . . . rejected the proximate cause tort analogy which *Almeida* found so appealing. . . .[57]

. . .

Such an approach has met with approval from the commentators: "It seems preferable, however, to impose liability only for homicides resulting from acts done in furtherance of the felony. A closer causal connection between the felony and the killing than the proximate-cause theory normally applicable to tort cases should be required because of the extreme penalty attaching to a conviction for felony murder and the difference between the underlying rationales of criminal and tort law. The former is intended to impose punishment in appropriate cases while the latter is primarily concerned with who shall bear the burden of a loss. Requiring this closer causal connection, although it precludes the imputation of the act of killing under the felony-murder rule, would not relieve a felon from responsibility for homicides committed by a cofelon since one member of a conspiracy is responsible for the acts of his coconspirators committed in furtherance of the object of the conspiracy."[58]

After this review of *Redline*, the uninitiated might be surprised to learn that *Redline* did not specifically overrule *Almeida*. This Court did overrule *Thomas*, holding that no conviction was possible for a *justifiable* homicide, where a policeman shot a felon, but "distinguished" *Almeida* on the ground that the homicide there, where an innocent third party was killed by a policeman, was only *excusable*. . . .

[57] See p. 318 note 188 below.

58. [Case Note,] 71 Harv. L. Rev. 1565 [1958].

. . .

The "distinction" *Redline* half-heartedly tries to draw has not escaped criticism from the commentators. While the result reached in *Redline* and most of its reasoning have met with almost unanimous approval, the *deus ex machina* ending has been condemned. One learned journal has commented:

> It seems, however, that *Almeida* cannot validly be distinguished from [*Redline*]. The probability that a felon will be killed seems at least as great as the probability that the victim will be an innocent bystander. Any distinction based on the fact that the killing of a felon by a policeman is sanctioned by the law and therefore justifiable, while the killing of an innocent bystander is merely excusable, seems unwarranted. No criminal sanctions now attach to either in other areas of criminal law, and any distinction here would seem anomalous. Indeed, to make the result hinge on the character of the victim is, in many instances, to make it hinge on the marksmanship of resisters. Any attempt to distinguish between the cases on the theory that the cofelon assumes the risk of being killed would also be improper since this tort doctrine has no place in the criminal law in which the wrong to be redressed is a public one—a killing with the victim's consent is nevertheless murder. It is very doubtful that public desire for vengeance should alone justify a conviction of felony murder for the death of an innocent bystander when no criminal responsibility will attach for the death of a cofelon.[59]

Redline concluded, at page 510, in this manner: "The limitation which we thus place on the decision in the *Almeida* case renders unnecessary any present reconsideration of the extended holding of that case. It will be time enough for action in such regard if and when a conviction for murder based on facts similar to those presented by the *Almeida* case (both as to the performer of the lethal act and the status of its victim) should again come before this court." The time is now. The facts are not merely similar to those of *Almeida*; they are identical, Smith and Almeida being co-felons. The case law of centuries and the force of reason, both dealt with in great detail in *Redline* and above, require us to overrule *Almeida*.

. . .

———

95. In Campbell v. State, 444 A.2d 1034, 1040–41 (Md.1982), after reviewing extensively cases in which, in the course of a felony, a person is killed by someone other than the felon, the court concluded: "The present trend has been for courts to employ the agency theory and to limit criminal culpability under the felony-murder doctrine to lethal acts committed by the felons themselves or their accomplices, and not to employ the proximate cause theory to extend criminal culpability for lethal acts of nonfel-

---

59. 71 Harv. L. Rev. *op. cit.* 1566. . . .

ons." Following the trend, the court limited felony murder to acts of a felon or an accomplice in furtherance of a common design. To the same effect, see, e.g., Hill v. State, 295 S.E.2d 518 (Ga.1982) (police officer killed bystander); State v. Branson, 487 N.W.2d 880 (Minn.1992) (member of rival gang killed bystander). In People v. Hernandez, 624 N.E.2d 661, 665 (N.Y.1993), however, upholding the defendant's conviction for felony murder based on a police officer's killing of another officer, the court observed that application of a proximate cause theory is "consistent with fundamental principles of criminal law."

Ought it make a difference if the person killed is a cofelon? In State v. Sophophone, 19 P.3d 70, 76 (Kan.2001), construing a statute that used the usual formula of a killing "committed in the commission of a felony," the court rejected liability for felony murder and observed that "to impute the act of killing to [the defendant] when the act was the lawful and courageous one of a law enforcement officer acting in the line of his duties is contrary to the strict construction we are required to give criminal statutes." See State v. Bonner, 411 S.E.2d 598 (N.C.1992) (security guard killed cofelon). In Wooden v. Commonwealth, 284 S.E.2d 811 (Va.1981), the court concluded that a felon may not be convicted of felony murder for the death of a cofelon killed by the victim. Liability is upheld in similar circumstances in State v. Baker, 607 S.W.2d 153, 156 (Mo.1980), and State v. Canola, 343 A.2d 110 (N.J.Super.Ct.App.Div.1975).

In several cases, a felon acting together with others to commit arson has been killed in the fire. Courts have generally upheld the liability of the surviving cofelons for felony murder. E.g., State v. Hoang, 755 P.2d 7 (Kan.1988); People v. Djordjevic, 584 N.W.2d 610 (Mich.App.1998) ("natural tendency" of defendants' acts was death or great bodily harm).

Is application of the felony murder rule in these cases significantly different from its application in a case like *Stamp*, p. 156 above?

96.

The factual situation which resulted in the trial of the defendants occurred on the evening of April 2, 1970, at which time seventeen policemen from the police force of the city of Joliet were participating in a surveillance of a building known as the Illinois Wine and Liquor Warehouse. Among the officers involved in the surveillance was Sergeant James Cronk, who shortly before 10:15 P.M. noticed Robert Bruce Papes and the defendant Anthony Rock pass by the warehouse several times in a Cadillac automobile. Later several officers saw a Chevrolet automobile enter an alley south of the warehouse and stop at a side door of the building. Several people left the automobile and disappeared from sight into the doorway. The driver of this vehicle, who was Papes, walked a short distance, made a surveillance of the area, returned to the automobile and then drove out of the sight of the officers. After several minutes Papes was again seen walking in the alley and after once more looking over the area he again disappeared from the sight of the police officers when he went to the location of the side doorway of the warehouse. It was within a matter of a few seconds of Papes' disappearance that Sergeant Cronk saw three individuals exit from the side doorway of the warehouse, at which time he signaled the officers to close in from various directions towards a concrete parking lot which was to the rear and west of the warehouse.

Papes and the defendants Rock and Hickman upon seeing the officers approaching them proceeded to run. Papes ran in a southwesterly direction and the defendants Rock and Hickman in a northwesterly direction towards some bushes located at the northwest corner of the parking lot. Papes was apprehended when a Sergeant Erwin pointed a shotgun at him. Papes submitted to an arrest and upon his person was found a loaded pistol and additional cartridges. As the defendant Rock was running he was carrying a small object in his hand. The defendant Hickman was carrying an attache case as he was fleeing.

The defendants Rock and Hickman ran through the bushes while in the meantime Sergeant Cronk ran to the rear of the warehouse where he noticed two people running in a northwesterly direction. Sergeant Cronk yelled "halt—police" several times but his commands were ignored. He lost sight of the two fleeing individuals but within seconds thereafter saw a man carrying a handgun running towards the bushes at the northwest corner of the parking lot. Sergeant Cronk, believing that this approaching individual was one of the burglars of the Illinois Wine and Liquor Warehouse, and referring to the handgun, ordered the person to "drop it." When there was no compliance to this warning Sergeant Cronk fired his shotgun at the individual, who was later discovered to be Detective William Loscheider of the Joliet police force. Loscheider was killed by this shot from his fellow officer's gun.

Approximately one-half hour later the defendants Rock and Hickman were arrested as they were walking on a street approximately two and a half blocks from the warehouse. Neither of the defendants had a weapon on his person.

People v. Hickman, 297 N.E.2d 582, 583 (Ill.Ct.App.1973).

Applying a statute which provided that one "who kills an individual without lawful justification commits murder if, in performing the acts which cause the death . . . he is attempting or committing a forcible felony other than voluntary manslaughter," Ill. Rev. Stat. ch. 38, para. 9–1(a)(3) (since amended), the court upheld the defendants' convictions of murder.

The court distinguished a prior case in which the defendant's conviction of murder for the death of his cofelon, killed by a bystander, was reversed. In that case, it said, "the victim was not free from culpability but was in fact an individual who was attempting to commit a felony. We do not hold that the character of the victim is controlling merely because he was a felon, nor do we indulge in the fanciful theory that the victim being a felon assumed the risk and thereby constructively consented to his death, but we do hold that he assisted in setting in motion a chain of events which was the proximate cause of his death and therefore in the criminal law as in the civil law there is no redress for the victim." 297 N.E.2d at 586. It concluded: "There should be no doubt about the 'justice' of holding a felon guilty of murder who engages in a robbery followed by an attempted escape and thereby inevitably calls into action defensive forces against him, the activity of which results in the death of an innocent human being." Id.

Observing that the defendants' attempt to escape "invited retaliation, opposition and pursuit," the Supreme Court of Illinois affirmed. 319 N.E.2d 511, 513 (Ill.1974). In United States ex rel. Rock v. Pinkey, 430 F.Supp. 176 (N.D.Ill.1977), the district court rejected the claim that the application of the felony murder rule in the circumstances of *Hickman* was so arbitrary and irrational that the murder conviction was violative of due process.

In People v. Graham, 477 N.E.2d 1342 (Ill.Ct.App.1985), the court applied *Hickman* to a felon's accidental killing of a cofelon during the course of a felony. It said: "Our examination of *Hickman* reveals no indication of an intent to render the felony-murder rule inapplicable where the deceased was not an innocent party to the forcible felony. Indeed, *Hickman* focused on the character of the killer, not the victim." 477 N.E.2d at 1347.

———

Taylor v. Superior Court of Alameda County
3 Cal.3d 578, 477 P.2d 131 (1970)

■ BURKE, JUSTICE. Petitioner and his codefendant Daniels were charged by information with the murder of John H. Smith, robbery, assault with a deadly weapon against Linda West, and assault with a deadly weapon against Jack West. The superior court denied petitioner's motion to set aside the information as to the murder count . . . and we issued an alternative writ of prohibition.

At the preliminary hearing, the following facts were adduced regarding the murder count: On the evening of January 12, 1969, two men attempted to rob Jax Liquor Store which was operated by Mrs. Linda Lee West and her husband Jack. Mrs. West testified that James Daniels entered the store first and asked Mr. West, who was behind the counter, for a package of cigarettes. While Mr. West was getting the cigarettes, John Smith entered the store and approached the counter. Mrs. West, who was on a ladder at the time the two men entered the store, then heard her husband say something about money. Turning her attention to the counter, she heard Daniels repeatedly saying, "Put the money in the bag," and observed her husband complying with the order.

While Mr. West was putting the money from the register in the bag, Daniels repeatedly referred to the fact that he and Smith were armed.

According to Mrs. West, Daniels "chattered insanely" during this time, telling Mr. West "Put the money in the bag. Put the money in the bag. Put the money in the bag. Don't move or I'll blow your head off. He's got a gun. He's got a gun. Don't move or we'll have an execution right here. Get down on the floor. I said on your stomach, on your stomach." Throughout this period, Smith's gun was pointed at Mr. West. Mrs. West testified that Smith looked "intent" and "apprehensive" as if "waiting for something big to happen." She indicated that Smith's apparent apprehension and nervousness was manifested by the way he was staring at Mr. West.

While Daniels was forcing Mr. West to the floor, Mrs. West drew a pistol from under her clothing and fired at Smith, who was standing closest to her. Smith was struck on the right side of the chest. Mrs. West fired four more shots in rapid succession, and observed "sparks" coming from Smith's gun, which was pointed in her direction. A bullet hole was subsequently discovered in the wall behind the place Mrs. West had been standing, approximately eight or nine feet above the floor. During this period, Mr. West had seized a pistol and fired two shots at Smith. Mrs. West's last shot was fired at Daniels as he was going out of the door. He "lurched violently and almost went down, [but] picked himself up and kept going." Smith died as the result of multiple gunshot wounds.

The evidence at the preliminary examination indicated that petitioner was waiting outside the liquor store in a getaway car. He was apprehended later and connected with the crime through bills in his possession and through the automobile which was seen by a witness leaving the scene of the robbery.

. . . [A]n information must be set aside if the defendant has been committed without "reasonable or probable cause." . . .

The information herein charged petitioner with the crime of murder. . . . Petitioner correctly contends that he cannot be convicted under the felony-murder doctrine, since "When a killing is not committed by a robber or by his accomplice but by his victim, malice aforethought is not attributable to the robber, for the killing is not committed by him in the perpetration or attempt to perpetrate robbery." (People v. Washington, [62 Cal. 2d 777] at p. 781.) However, apart from the felony-murder doctrine, petitioner could be found guilty of murder on a theory of vicarious liability.

As stated in People v. Gilbert, 63 Cal. 2d 690, 704–705, . . . "When the defendant or his accomplice, with a conscious disregard for life, intentionally commits an act that is likely to cause death, and his victim or a police officer kills in reasonable response to such act, the defendant is guilty of murder. In such a case, the killing is attributable, not merely to the commission of a felony, but to the intentional act of the defendant or his accomplice committed with conscious disregard for life. . . . Thus, the victim's self-defensive killing or the police officer's killing in the performance of his duty cannot be considered an independent intervening cause for which the defendant is not liable, for it is a reasonable response to the dilemma thrust upon the victim or the policeman by the intentional act of the defendant or his accomplice. . . ."

Therefore, if petitioner were an accomplice to the robbery, he would be vicariously responsible[60] for any killing attributable to the intentional acts of his associates committed with conscious disregard for life, and likely to result in death. We must determine whether the committing magistrate had any rational ground for believing that Smith's death was attributable to intentional acts of Smith and Daniels meeting those criteria.

Petitioner relies upon the following language in *Washington*, wherein defendant's accomplice merely pointed a gun at the robbery victim who, without further provocation, shot and killed him: "In every robbery there is a possibility that the victim will resist and kill. The robber has little control over such a killing once the robbery is undertaken as this case demonstrates. To impose an additional penalty for the killing would discriminate between robbers, *not on the basis of any difference in their own conduct*, but solely on the basis of the response by others that the robber's conduct happened to induce." (62 Cal. 2d at p. 781, italics added.)

As indicated by the italicized words in the foregoing quotation, the central inquiry in determining criminal liability for a killing committed by a resisting victim or police officer is whether the *conduct* of a defendant or his accomplices was sufficiently provocative of lethal resistance to support a finding of implied malice. If the trier of fact concludes that under the particular circumstances of the instant case Smith's death proximately resulted from acts of petitioner's accomplices done with conscious disregard for human life, the natural consequences of which were dangerous to life, then petitioner may be convicted of first degree murder.

For example, we pointed out in *Washington* that "Defendants who initiate gun battles may also be found guilty of murder if their victims resist and kill. Under such circumstances, 'the defendant for a base, antisocial motive and with wanton disregard for human life, does an act that involves a high degree of probability that it will result in death' [citation], and it is unnecessary to imply malice by invoking the felony-murder doctrine." (62 Cal. 2d at p. 782.)

Petitioner contends that since neither Daniels nor Smith fired the first shot, they did not "initiate" the gun battle which led to Smith's death. However, depending upon the circumstances, a gun battle can be initiated by acts of provocation falling short of firing the first shot. Thus, in People v. Reed, 270 Cal. App. 2d 37, defendant resisted the officers' commands to "put up your hands," and pointed his gun toward the officers and toward the kidnap-robbery victim. The officers commenced firing, wounding defendant and killing the victim. Although defendant did not fire a single shot, his murder conviction was upheld on the theory that his "aggressive actions" were sufficient evidence of implied malice, and that "under these

---

60. "Under the rules defining principals and criminal conspiracies, the defendant may be guilty of murder for a killing attributable to the act of his accomplice. To be so guilty, however, the accomplice must cause the death of another human being by an act committed in furtherance of the common design." (People v. Gilbert, supra, 63 Cal. 2d 690, 705.) Petitioner does not dispute that the conduct of his confederates set forth above was in furtherance of the robbery.

circumstances it may be said that defendant initiated the gunplay . . . ." (270 Cal. App. 2d at pp. 45–46.)

Similarly, in Brooks v. Superior Court, 239 Cal. App. 2d 538, petitioner had directed "opprobrious language" to the arresting officer and had grasped the officer's shotgun. The officer, being startled and thinking that petitioner was trying to disarm him, yanked backwards and fired the gun, mortally wounding a fellow officer. In upholding an indictment for murder, the court concluded that under the circumstances, the petitioner's act of reaching for and grasping the officer's shotgun was "fraught with grave and inherent danger to human life," and therefore sufficient to raise an inference of malice. (239 Cal. App. 2d at p. 540.)

In the instant case, the evidence at the preliminary hearing set forth above discloses acts of provocation on the part of Daniels and Smith from which the trier of fact could infer malice, including Daniels' coercive conduct toward Mr. West and his repeated threats of "execution," and Smith's intent and nervous apprehension as he held Mr. West at gunpoint. The foregoing conduct was sufficiently provocative of lethal resistance to lead a man of ordinary caution and prudence to conclude that Daniels and Smith "initiated" the gun battle, or that such conduct was done with conscious disregard for human life and with natural consequences dangerous to life.[61] Accordingly, we conclude that the evidence supported the magistrate's finding that reasonable and probable cause existed to charge petitioner with first degree murder.

. . .

■ PETERS, JUSTICE (dissenting).

I dissent.

In holding that petitioner can be convicted of murder of John H. Smith, the majority repudiate this court's holdings in People v. Washington, 62 Cal. 2d 777, 779–783, and People v. Gilbert, 63 Cal. 2d 690, 703–705, that robbers cannot be convicted of murder for a killing by a victim unless the robbers commit malicious acts, in addition to the acts constituting the underlying felony, which demonstrate culpability beyond that of other robbers. The majority . . . purport to distinguish *Washington* from the instant case, resulting in the absurd distinction that robbers who point guns at their victims without articulating the obvious threat inherent in

---

61. Petitioner contends that we should ignore evidence regarding Smith's conduct, on the theory that Smith could not have been held responsible for his own death. We rejected a similar contention in *Washington*, stating that "A distinction based on the person killed, however, would make the defendant's criminal liability turn upon the marksmanship of victims and policemen. A rule of law cannot reasonably be based on such a fortuitous circumstance. The basic issue therefore is whether a robber can be convicted of mur-

der for the killing of *any* person by another who is resisting the robbery." (62 Cal. 2d at p. 780, italics added.) Therefore, the trier of fact may find that Smith set into motion, through the intentional commission of acts constituting implied malice and in furtherance of the robbery, a gun battle resulting in his own death. Since petitioner may be held vicariously responsible for *any* killing legally attributable to his accomplices, he may be charged with Smith's death.

. . .

such action cannot be convicted of murder for a killing committed by the victims, whereas robbers who point guns at their victims and articulate their threat can be convicted of murder in the same situation. To hold, as do the majority, that petitioner can be convicted of murder for acts which constitute a first degree robbery solely because the victims killed one of the robbers is in effect to reinstate the felony-murder rule in cases where the victim resists and kills.

. . .

In *Washington* the decedent-accomplice pointed a gun directly at the victim. If this court was of the opinion that a defendant in such a situation could properly be convicted of murder for the killing committed by the victim, it would have so stated and would have held that Washington could be so convicted of murder. Instead, it held that Washington could not be convicted of murder and mentioned only one case where defendants could properly be convicted of murder for a killing committed by the victim: the case where the defendants initiate the gun battle. Therefore, *Washington* stands for the proposition that the act of pointing a gun at the victim, unlike the act of initiating a gun battle, is *not* an act done " 'with wanton disregard for human life,' " involving " 'a high degree of probability that it will result in death' " from which malice can be implied. (See id.)

. . .

In *Washington*, a gun was pointed at the victim by a robber appearing suddenly in the victim's office; in the instant case, a gun was pointed at one of the victims and threatening language was used. The majority are making the incredible statement that because the robber in *Washington* did not articulate his obvious threat—because, in the majority's words, he "merely" pointed a gun at the victim—it cannot be said that he committed an act with conscious disregard for life and likely to result in death, whereas if he articulated his threat—as did the robbers in the instant case—his act could be found to have met such criteria.

To me, it is too obvious to dispute that inherent in the brandishing of a gun in a robbery is the conditional threat of the robber that he will use the gun if his demands are not complied with. The fact that the robber makes his threat express does not serve to distinguish *Washington*. It is unreasonable to assume that, just because the robber in *Washington* did not articulate his threat, the victim in that case had less reason to fear for his safety or, as the majority assert, less "provocation" for shooting the robber than did the victims in the instant case. It is absurd to suggest that the robber's acts in *Washington* were, as a matter of law, not "sufficiently provocative of lethal resistance to support a finding of implied malice," whereas the robbers' acts in the instant case could be so considered.

In sum, the articulation of threats does not without more show that the robber's acts were done " 'with wanton disregard for human life,' " involving " 'a high degree of probability that it will result in death' " from which malice can be implied. . . . The difference between an implied and an express threat furnishes no significant basis for discrimination between robbers. To permit additional punishment for a homicide committed by the victim on the basis of the articulation of the threats would deter robbery "haphazardly at best."

. . .

Not only is the majority's holding contrary to the holdings and language of *Washington* and *Gilbert*, it is also contrary to the fundamental rationale of those cases—that the culpability of criminal defendants should be determined by their own acts, not by the fortuitous acts of their victims which are beyond the defendants' control and thus logically irrelevant to the defendants' culpability. In rejecting the contention that a purpose of the felony-murder rule is to prevent the commission of robberies, this court in *Washington* reasoned that whether robbers can be convicted of murder should not depend on the uncontrollable responses of their victims. "In every robbery there is a possibility that the victim will resist and kill. The robber has little control over such a killing once the robbery is undertaken as this case demonstrates. To impose an additional penalty for the killing would discriminate between robbers, not on the basis of any difference in their own conduct, but solely on the basis of the response by others that the robber's conduct happened to induce. An additional penalty for a homicide committed by the victim would deter robbery haphazardly at best. To 'prevent stealing [the law] would do better to hang one thief in every thousand by lot.' (Holmes, The Common Law, p. 58.)" (62 Cal. 2d at p. 781.)

In the instant case as in *Washington*, the robbers committed acts constituting a first degree robbery; they committed no additional acts—such as initiating a gun battle—that would reflect a culpability beyond that of any other first degree robbers and that would justify the additional charge of murder. As *Washington* stated, "[i]n every robbery there is a possibility that the victim will resist and kill," and robbers cannot be charged with murder for a killing by a victim unless they commit acts *in addition to those constituting a robbery* upon which additional acts a murder charge can be based. Any murder instruction in the instant case would be based solely on acts constituting first degree robbery. To convert such acts—i.e., to convert a first degree robbery—into murder solely because the victim killed one of the robbers is in effect to reinstitute the felony-murder doctrine in such a situation—contrary to the basic *Washington* holding that a defendant cannot be convicted of murder simply because he and his accomplices committed a felony in which a death resulted. In the instant case as in *Washington*, to impose an additional penalty on the defendant, not because of any independently malicious act (such as initiating a gun battle) by him or his accomplices, but because of the uncontrollable act of the victim who resists and kills is to "deter robbery haphazardly at best."

In conclusion, the majority have rejected the *Washington* holding that robbers can be convicted of murder for a killing by a victim only if the robbers commit malicious acts, in addition to the acts which constitute the underlying felony, which demonstrate culpability beyond that of other robbers. By purporting to distinguish *Washington* from the instant case, the majority have set forth a new, wholly irrational, rule: if robbers point guns at their victims without articulating the obvious threat inherent in such action they cannot be convicted of murder for a killing committed by the victims, whereas if they articulate their threat they can be convicted of murder in the same situation. As we have seen, the majority's purported distinction of *Washington* makes absolutely no sense. In my opinion, it simply demonstrates a desire on the part of the majority to overrule *Washington sub silentio*.

. . .

It is absurd to suggest—as does the Attorney General—that to hold that petitioner is not chargeable with murder would be "to condemn the victims for not standing idly and waiting for some further action by the robbers. . . ." I am not "condemning" the victims in any way; I am adhering to the fundamental principle that the culpability of criminal defendants should be determined by their own acts—not by the fortuitous acts of their victims which are beyond the defendants' control and thus logically irrelevant to the defendants' culpability.

. . .

———

97. Taylor was subsequently convicted of murder. In the meantime, his accomplice Daniels was tried separately and convicted of robbery but acquitted of murder. On appeal, the court reversed Taylor's conviction. Since he had been driving the getaway car and was not involved in the events inside the store, his liability for murder could only be predicated on vicarious liability for the acts of an accomplice that supplied malice aforethought. That finding having been rejected by the verdict in Daniels's trial, collateral estoppel was a bar to Taylor's conviction. People v. Taylor, 527 P.2d 622 (Cal.1974).

In People v. Antick, 539 P.2d 43 (Cal.1975), the defendant's accomplice initiated a gun battle in which the accomplice himself was killed by a policeman. The court held that, while the accomplice's acts supplied the necessary malice, the defendant was not liable for murder because the accomplice's acts had not resulted in the death of *another* human being; since the accomplice himself could not be guilty of murder for his own death, neither could the defendant be vicariously guilty of murder for it. (The court explained that to the extent that its opinion in the first *Taylor* case, p. 167 above, suggested that Taylor's liability for murder could be based on acts of Smith as well as acts of Daniels and not on the latter alone, it was too broad and was, to that extent, overruled.) See also Jackson v. State, 589 P.2d 1052 (N.M.1979), adopting the "best-reasoned view" that "the felony-murder doctrine should not be expanded to cover the situation where the victim of the crime kills a perpetrator."

98. Limitation of felony murder. The fictions—are they "fictions"?—on which the felony murder rule rests can be extended very far; at their farthest reach they would make a felon liable as a murderer for any death that would not have occurred but for the commission of the felony. At one time most felonies were punishable, though not always punished, with death,[62] so it may have seemed not to matter so much whether a felon was held liable also for a related accidental homicide. (For the same reason, though, one may wonder why it was thought important that the felon be held liable for homicide.) The application of the rule has more importance if, as in modern codes, the deliberate taking of life is a more serious crime than almost all others. While courts have from time to time extended the rule very far, some limitations have developed which are generally accepted.

One common limitation is that the felony must be of a kind involving violence or danger to life. In People v. Phillips, 414 P.2d 353 (Cal.1966), another aspect of which is discussed on p. 149 above, the state charged that the defendant, who was a chiropractor, told the parents of a young girl that he could cure her of a dangerous cancer. Acting on this representation, the parents did not have a necessary operation performed; instead, they submitted the girl to the defendant's treatment. The girl's death from the cancer was hastened by the lack of proper treatment. If the state's charges were true, the defendant had committed the felony of grand theft. The court held that an instruction on felony murder should not have been given. Even if in this case the defendant's crime had endangered life, grand theft was not a felony inherently dangerous to life, and the felony murder doctrine had no application. Following this reasoning in People v. Satchell, 489 P.2d 1361, 1369 (Cal.1971) (underlying felony, previously convicted felon's possession of a concealable firearm, not inherently dangerous), the California court emphasized that "in determining whether a felony is inherently dangerous for purposes of the felony-murder rule we assess that felony *in the abstract*. . . . We do *not* look to the specific facts of the case before us . . . ." In People v. Burroughs, 678 P.2d 894, 897–98 (Cal.1984) (felonious unlicensed practice of medicine), a case similar to *Phillips*, above, the court observed: "This form of analysis is compelled because there is a killing in every case where the rule might potentially be applied. If in such circumstances a court were to examine the particular facts of the case prior to establishing whether the underlying felony is inherently dangerous, the court might well be led to conclude the rule applicable despite any unfairness which might redound to the defendant by so broad an application: the existence of the dead victim might appear to lead inexorably to the conclusion that the underlying felony is exceptionally hazardous. We continue to resist such unjustifiable bootstrapping."

Adhering to the rule that the felony underlying a conviction of felony murder must be one that, considered abstractly and without regard to the

---

62. Petty larceny and mayhem were felonies not punishable with death. See generally 1 Stephen, History 457–92.

particular circumstances, is inherently dangerous to life, the Supreme Court of Kansas rejected a charge of felony murder against a prison inmate who stabbed and killed another inmate. The underlying felony was possession of a weapon inside a prison. The court said:

> Reduced to its essence, the argument is that it is proper to infer the existence of the requisite mental elements required in first-degree murder because of the accused's status as a prisoner or because of the accused's presence within the confines of the penal institutions. In the present case the State is requesting a rule which would operate to make every homicide committed by a prisoner possessing contraband murder in the first degree. To state that a person's status is the controlling factor ignores the fact that homicides 'behind the walls' are as capable of occurring by accident, in self-defense or heat of passion, or without the requisite mental state, as are homicides occurring among the free population. We do not agree with the State's position. Even assuming the accused's status as an inmate is a relevant consideration, it would be unreasonable and overbroad to adopt a rule imputing the malice, premeditation and deliberation necessary for first-degree murder every time an inmate violates the rules against possession of contraband. If these mental elements exist in a particular case, it imposes no undue burden on the State to prove them, and the fiction of felony murder is unnecessary for conviction. If these mental elements do not exist, it would be a travesty to elevate an accidental killing, or a killing in self-defense, into first-degree murder through the felony murder doctrine, thereby foreclosing an accused's ability to plead the traditional defenses and virtually insuring conviction of a crime the accused simply did not commit.

State v. Brantley, 691 P.2d 26, 29 (Kan.1984). Cf. Commonwealth v. Matchett, 436 N.E.2d 400, 410 (Mass.1982): "[W]hen a death results from the perpetration or attempted perpetration of the statutory felony of extortion, there can be no conviction of felony-murder in the second degree unless the jury find that the extortion involved circumstances demonstrating the defendant's conscious disregard of the risk to human life. The crime of extortion may be committed in a way not inherently dangerous to human life." See also State v. Noren, 371 N.W.2d 381 (Wis.Ct.App.1985) (construing statute that requires that death be a "natural and probable consequence" of the commission of a felony).

Contrary to the cases above, see People v. Golson, 207 N.E.2d 68, 73 (Ill.1965) (underlying felony, theft from the mails by stealth, "violent" in the circumstances), stating that the test "is not whether the felony is normally classified as non-violent, but . . . whether, under the facts of a particular case, it is contemplated that violence might be necessary." A requirement that the underlying felony be inherently dangerous to life is rejected in State v. Chambers, 524 S.W.2d 826 (Mo.1975), the felony there being theft of a motor vehicle; the court observed, however, that the element of dangerousness, or reckless disregard for life, was satisfied by the act of towing a vehicle on a highway at night without lights, after drinking.

Can a conviction for felony murder be predicated on a felony that requires only reckless rather than intentional conduct? Does such a conviction violate "fundamental principles of justice"? See Bethea v. Scully, 834 F.2d 257 (2d Cir.1987) (felony murder predicated on felony of reckless arson; conviction affirmed).

Courts are divided on the question whether someone who sells or administers drugs to another person can be guilty of felony murder if ingestion of the drugs causes the person's death. Not only the qualification of the felony murder rule but also the characterization of the felony has been at issue. See, e.g., Sheriff, Clark County v. Morris, 659 P.2d 852 (Nev.1983) (felony must be inherently dangerous viewed abstractly; sale and involvement in, or presence during, ingestion of drugs may be sufficient); Heacock v. Commonwealth, 323 S.E.2d 90 (Va.1984) (felony murder statute does not require that felony be foreseeably dangerous to life; in any case, supplying and administering injection of cocaine is inherently dangerous). In State v. Randolph, 676 S.W.2d 943 (Tenn.1984), after reviewing cases in other jurisdictions, the court concluded that although there was abundant evidence of the dangerousness of using heroin, "an isolated sale of a controlled substance to a stranger" was not a felony to which the felony murder rule was applicable; but in the particular circumstances of the case, it was possible that the defendants "acted with such conscious indifference to the consequences of their highly unlawful activities as to evince malice" (apparently not as a matter of felony murder). The court added: "Although an issue of causation will be presented whether the charge be murder or manslaughter, we are of the opinion that the act of the customer in injecting himself is not necessarily so unexpected, unforeseeable or remote as to insulate the seller from criminal responsibility as a matter of law." Id. at 947, 948.

In many states, the approach that limits felony murder to inherently dangerous felonies is adopted in part by statutes that provide that homicides committed in the perpetration of the most serious felonies (usually arson, rape, robbery, and burglary; sometimes also larceny, kidnapping, mayhem, and sodomy) are murder in the first degree, and homicides committed in the perpetration of other felonies are murder in the second degree. A similar rationale underlies some older holdings that the felony must have been a felony at common law, e.g., State v. Burrell, 199 A. 18 (N.J.1938), or must be *malum in se*, e.g., People v. Pavlic, 199 N.W. 373 (Mich.1924) (sale of liquor, felonious by statute).

Another method of limiting the rule has been narrowly to confine the period during which, for purposes of the rule, the felony is in progress. E.g., State v. Diebold, 277 P. 394 (Wash.1929). Recent cases, however, have held that the felony murder doctrine continues to be applicable while the felons are attempting to escape from the scene of the crime. E.g., People v. Salas, 500 P.2d 7 (Cal.1972); Whitman v. People, 420 P.2d 416 (Colo.1966); People v. Johnson, 302 N.E.2d 20 (Ill.1973). Compare Commonwealth v. Barkley, 484 A.2d 189 (Pa.Super.Ct.1984) (robber's attempt to elude apprehension by police a day after robbery, after having split proceeds with companion, spent time at home, gone jogging, and committed another unrelated robbery, was not a "renewed flight" bringing homicide within commission of robbery for purpose of felony murder rule).

Construing a statutory provision that the felony murder rule applies to a killing committed in "immediate flight" from a felony, the New York Court of Appeals concluded that the issue should ordinarily be left to the jury. "The jury should be instructed to give consideration to whether the homicide and the felony occurred at the same location or, if not, to the distance separating the two locations. Weight may also be placed on whether there is an interval of time between the commission of the felony and the commission of the homicide. The jury may properly consider such additional factors as whether the culprits had possession of the fruits of criminal activity, whether the police, watchmen or concerned citizens were in close pursuit, and whether the criminal had reached a place of temporary safety. These factors are not exclusive; others may be appropriate in differing factual settings. If anything, past history demonstrates the fruitlessness of attempting to apply rigid rules to virtually limitless factual variations. No single factor is necessarily controlling; it is the combination of several factors that leads to a justifiable inference." People v. Gladman, 359 N.E.2d 420, 424 (N.Y.1976).

The felony murder rule has commonly been declared inapplicable if the underlying felony is not "independent of the homicide and of the assault merged therein," People v. Moran, 158 N.E. 35, 36 (N.Y.1927), lest every felonious homicide (e.g., voluntary manslaughter) become a case of felony murder. See, e.g., People v. Smith, 678 P.2d 886 (Cal.1984) (beating of child); Sullinger v. State, 675 P.2d 472 (Okla.Crim.App.1984) (aggravated assault and battery).

The merger rule is rejected in a few states. E.g., Mapps v. State, 520 So.2d 92 (Fla.Dist.Ct.App.1988) (aggravated child abuse); State v. Cromey, 348 N.W.2d 759 (Minn.1984) (beating of child). Cf. People v. Hansen, 885 P.2d 1022 (Cal.1994) (death resulting from felony of discharging firearm at inhabited dwelling not merged). In Baker v. State, 225 S.E.2d 269 (Ga. 1976), the court concluded that the requirement was not applicable and affirmed a conviction of murder based on an unintentional killing that resulted from a felonious assault on the victim. The court acknowledged that its holding might allow the state "to bootstrap practically all killings with dangerous weapons into murder simply by showing that the assault out of which the death arose was a felony," id. at 271, but thought that result was required by the statutory homicide provisions, which appeared to provide no other category of intentional or unintentional homicide that fit the case. For an unusual situation involving the requirement of independence, see People v. Carlson, 112 Cal.Rptr. 321 (Ct.App.1974). There the defendant was convicted of the voluntary manslaughter of his wife; the court said that that felony should not be used as the basis of a charge of felony murder for the death of the fetus that his wife was then carrying (see p. 14 note 12 above).[63]

Should the merger doctrine be applied to a homicide committed in the course of a burglary (defined as a forcible entry to commit a felony) if the felony in question is an assault on the person killed? Most courts have concluded that the merger doctrine is not applicable. E.g., United States v. Loonsfoot, 905 F.2d 116 (6th Cir.1990), State v. Lucas, 794 P.2d 1353 (Ariz.App.1990); Commonwealth v. Claudio, 634 N.E.2d 902 (Mass.1994). To the contrary, holding that the merger doctrine does apply, see Sellers v. State, 749 S.W.2d 669 (Ark.1988); People v. Wilson, 462 P.2d 22 (Cal.1969).

99. Abolition of felony murder. The history and current status of the doctrine of felony murder is reviewed thoroughly in People v. Aaron, 299 N.W.2d 304 (Mich.1980). The Supreme Court of Michigan concluded that the felony murder rule should be abolished.

> We believe that it is no longer acceptable to equate the intent to commit a felony with the intent to kill, intent to do great bodily harm, or wanton and willful disregard of the likelihood that the natural tendency of a person's behavior is to cause death or great bodily harm. . . .

> Accordingly, we hold today that malice is the intention to kill, the intention to do great bodily harm, or the wanton and willful disregard of the likelihood that the natural tendency of defendant's behavior is to cause death or great bodily harm. We further hold that malice is an essential element of any murder, as that term is judicially defined, whether the murder occurs in the course of a felony or otherwise. The facts and circumstances involved in the perpetration of a felony may evidence an intent to kill, an intent to cause great bodily harm, or a wanton and willful disregard of the likelihood that the natural tendency of defendant's behavior is to cause death or great bodily harm; however, the conclusion must be left to the jury to infer from all the evidence. . . .

> . . . From a practical standpoint, the abolition of the category of malice arising from the intent to commit the underlying felony should have little effect on the result of the majority of cases. In many cases where felony murder has been applied, the use of the doctrine was unnecessary because the other types of malice could have been inferred from the evidence.

299 N.W.2d at 326–27.

63. Can a person be convicted of felony murder if a prosecution for the underlying felony is barred by the statute of limitations? See People v. Lilliock, 71 Cal.Rptr. 434, 441–42 (Ct.App.1968). Or if he has been acquitted of the underlying felony? See People v. Murray, 459 N.Y.S.2d 810 (App.Div.1983) (yes; "completion of the underlying felony is not an essential element of felony murder").

See State v. Doucette, 470 A.2d 676 (Vt.1983), interpreting the Vermont statute, which refers to "murders" rather than "killings" in the course of designated felonies, to reach the result of the court in *Aaron*; a distinct category of felony murder was held not to be included within the meaning of "malice aforethought." The Supreme Court of California has expressed its agreement generally with the reasoning of the Michigan court in *Aaron* that the felony murder rule is an anachronism that might well be discarded, but concluded that the rule had been enacted by statute in California and could not be abolished judicially. People v. Dillon, 668 P.2d 697 (Cal.1983). The rule has been abolished legislatively in a few states. E.g., Haw. Rev. Stat. § 707.701; Ky. Rev. Stat. Ann. § 507.020.

In *Dillon*, above, the defendant was a 17-year-old high school student at the time of the crime. He was convicted of first-degree murder, the statutory penalty for which was death (precluded because of his age) or life imprisonment with or without possibility of parole. He was sentenced to life imprisonment with possibility of parole, for which he would be eligible under current regulations after a minimum of 14 years' imprisonment. The court said:

> It follows from the foregoing analysis [of the felony murder statute] that the two kinds of first degree murder in this state differ in a fundamental respect: in the case of deliberate and premeditated murder with malice aforethought, the defendant's state of mind with respect to the homicide is all-important and must be proved beyond a reasonable doubt; in the case of first degree felony murder it is entirely irrelevant and need not be proved at all. From this profound legal difference flows an equally significant factual distinction, to wit, that first degree felony murder encompasses a far wider range of individual culpability than deliberate and premeditated murder. It includes not only the latter, but also a variety of unintended homicides resulting from reckless behavior, or ordinary negligence, or pure accident; it embraces both calculated conduct and acts committed in panic or rage, or under the dominion of mental illness, drugs, or alcohol; and it condemns alike consequences that are highly probable, conceivably possible, or wholly unforeseeable.
>
> . . .
>
> Because of his minority no greater punishment could have been inflicted on defendant if he had committed the most aggravated form of homicide known to our law—a carefully planned murder executed in cold blood after a calm and mature deliberation. Yet despite the prosecutor's earnest endeavor throughout the trial to prove a case of premeditated first degree murder, the triers of fact squarely rejected that view of the evidence: as the jurors' communications to the judge made plain, if it had not been for the felony-murder rule they would have returned a verdict of a lesser degree of homicide than first degree murder. Moreover, after hearing all the testimony and diligently evaluating defendant's history and character, both the judge and the jury manifestly believed that a sentence of life imprisonment as a first

degree murderer was excessive in relation to defendant's true culpability: . . . they made strenuous but vain efforts to avoid imposing that punishment.

668 P.2d at 719, 726. Concluding that the sentence of life imprisonment violated the state constitutional provision against cruel and unusual punishments, the court modified the judgment to a conviction of murder in the second degree, which made him eligible for commitment to the Youth Authority.

The Model Penal Code § 210.2 abandons the felony murder rule but provides that the recklessness and extreme indifference which characterize a homicide as murder are presumed "if the actor is engaged or is an accomplice in the commission of, or an attempt to commit, or flight after committing or attempting to commit robbery, rape or deviate sexual intercourse by force or threat of force, arson, burglary, kidnapping or felonious escape." Justifying abandonment of the common law rule, the Reporters of the Code said: "[T]here is no basis in experience for thinking that homicides *which the evidence makes accidental* occur with disproportionate frequency in connection with specified felonies." 1 MPC Commentaries Part II, 38 (comment to § 210.2). Explaining the Code's provision, they said: "[I]t remains indefensible in principle to use the sanctions that the law employs to deal with murder unless there is at least a finding that the actor's conduct manifested an extreme indifference to the value of human life. The fact that the actor was engaged in a crime of the kind that is included in the usual first-degree felony-murder enumeration or was an accomplice in such crime . . . will frequently justify such a finding. Indeed, the probability that such a finding will be justified seems high enough to warrant the presumption of extreme indifference. . . . But liability depends, as plainly it should, upon the crucial finding. The result may not differ often under such a formulation from that which would be reached under some form of the felony-murder rule. But what is more important is that a conviction on this basis rests solidly upon principle." Id. at 38–39.

The revisers of the New York Penal Law reached similar conclusions but devised a different statutory formula:

§ 125.25 Murder in the second degree

A person is guilty of murder in the second degree when:

    . . .

    3. Acting either alone or with one or more other persons, he commits or attempts to commit robbery, burglary, kidnapping, arson, rape in the first degree, sodomy in the first degree, sexual abuse in the first degree, aggravated sexual abuse, escape in the first degree, or escape in the second degree, and, in the course of and in furtherance of such crime or of immediate flight therefrom, he, or another participant, if there be any, causes the death of a person other than one of the participants, except that in any prosecution under this subdivision, in which the defendant was not the only participant in the underlying crime, it is an affirmative defense that the defendant:

(a) Did not commit the homicidal act or in any way solicit, request, command, importune, cause or aid the commission thereof; and

(b) Was not armed with a deadly weapon, or any instrument, article or substance readily capable of causing death or serious physical injury and of a sort not ordinarily carried in public places by law-abiding persons; and

(c) Had no reasonable ground to believe that any other participant was armed with such a weapon, instrument, article or substance; and

(d) Had no reasonable ground to believe that any other participant intended to engage in conduct likely to result in death or serious physical injury. (McKinney 1998)

———

§ 125.25
NY Penal
Law

The New York Times

Sunday, November 7, 1971.

Investment Banker Slain in Cross Fire Between Police and Two Robbery Suspects on Fifth Avenue

By PAUL L. MONTGOMERY

A 33-year-old investment banker was shot to death near 40th Street and Fifth Avenue late Friday night when he was caught in a cross fire between the police and a pair of robbery suspects.

The two suspects were discovered by the police in Brooklyn yesterday morning. One was found dead on a street in East Flatbush, apparently dumped from a car. The other, who had a bullet wound in his shoulder, was delivered to Coney Island Hospital by several men who immediately fled.

The victim in the holdup, Mario Sereni of 420 East 72d Street, had been a guest at the Engineers Club, which is at 32 West 40th Street, when there was a robbery attempt. He was killed on the street when two policemen who happened to be in the building shot it out with the robbers. The police of the 17th Precinct station on East 51st Street said tests had not yet been completed to determine who fired the fatal shots.

According to the police, the holdup at the club, which is across from Bryant Park, occurred about 11:30 P.M. Two men held the club bellman at gunpoint and rifled the cash register. There had been another holdup at the club about four months ago in which $1,000 was taken.

While the holdup was going on, two policemen, Ralph Hayes and Joseph Nuovo, emerged from the club men's room and spotted the robbers. A chase ensued, and the robbers ran into the street. There were several bullet holes in the glass-paneled entrance to the club.

According to the police, about 12 shots were exchanged between the policemen and the fleeing suspects. Mr. Sereni, who was leaving the club, was shot several times in the chest.

The robbers got away in a light yellow 1966 Buick, apparently driven by a third man. When they were found later, they had mud on their clothing, leading the police to theorize that they had fallen in the street construction on 40th Street before getting away.

The first suspect, Ralph Ronga, 32 years old, of 65-10 Bay Parkway in Bensonhurst, was found lying face down on the curb in front of 6828 Avenue L in East Flatbush. He was dead of a chest wound. His police record included three burglary arrests: he had served time in Sing Sing for robbery.

The other suspect, Nicholas Rao, 36, of 447 East 46th Street, Brooklyn, turned up at Coney Island Hospital with a bullet wound in his shoulder and neck. The people who brought him fled before they could be questioned. Mr. Rao, who had no police record, was listed as in serious condition.

Witnesses connected the two men with the Manhattan shoot out.

Which of the approaches to the problem of deaths resulting from the commission of a felony discussed in the preceding pages responds most fully and effectively to the death of Mario Sereni?

100.

On the evening of December 30, 1970, respondent and his code-fendant encountered a thoroughly intoxicated man named Stafford in a bar in Rochester, N.Y. After observing Stafford display at least two $100 bills, they decided to rob him, and agreed to drive him to a nearby town. While in the car, respondent slapped Stafford several times, took his money, and, in a search for concealed funds, forced Stafford to lower his trousers and remove his boots. They then abandoned him on an unlighted, rural road, still in a state of partial undress, and without his coat or his glasses. The temperature was near zero, visibility was obscured by blowing snow, and snow banks flanked the roadway. The time was between 9:30 and 9:40 p.m.

At about 10 p.m., while helplessly seated in a traffic lane about a quarter mile from the nearest lighted building, Stafford was struck by a speeding pickup truck. The driver testified that while he was traveling 50 miles per hour in a 40–mile zone, the first of two approaching cars flashed its lights—presumably as a warning which he did not understand. Immediately after the cars passed, the driver saw Stafford sitting in the road with his hands in the air. The driver neither swerved nor braked his vehicle before it hit Stafford. Stafford was pronounced dead upon arrival at the local hospital.

Henderson v. Kibbe, 431 U.S. 145, 147 (1977).

Can the defendants be convicted of murder? If so, on what theory, or theories?

———

101. Resistance to a lawful arrest. Traditionally included among the categories of conduct that, if death results, constitutes murder is resistance to a lawful arrest. E.g., 3 Stephen, History 22. If the import of this principle is that an attempt to make a lawful arrest does not constitute provocation that will reduce an intentional killing to manslaughter, it accurately reflects the decisions, and its rationale is apparent if not ineluctable: "If the agent of the law is to be encouraged in his duty to arrest the defendant, the law cannot at the same time give indulgence to him who willfully chooses to be unlawful to the extent of deadly resistance." Dickey, "Culpable Homicides in Resisting Arrest," 18 Corn. L. Q. 373, 374 (1933). The rule has frequently been stated more broadly: that resistance to a lawful arrest itself constitutes malice aforethought whether or not there was an intention to kill, so that a wholly accidental killing that results from resistance is murder. E.g., 3 Stephen, History 22. The cases do not generally support such a rule. See, e.g., State v. Weisengoff, 101 S.E. 450 (W.Va.1919). It has been said, however, that "a much less degree of violence may be sufficient to justify a verdict of guilty of murder in the case of a police officer who is killed in the execution of his duty, in arresting a person or detaining a person in custody, so long as the arrest is lawful, than would suffice in the case of another person." R. v. Appleby, 28 Crim.

App. 1, 5 (1940). Compare People v. Arnett, 214 N.W. 231 (Mich.1927), in which the court affirmed a conviction of murder in reliance on a statute that made it a felony to restrict or obstruct lawful arrest.

Suppose the arrest is unlawful. Under the common law, it was permissible to resist an unlawful arrest by opposing force with force. See John Bad Elk v. United States, 177 U.S. 529 (1900); cf. United States v. Di Re, 332 U.S. 581 (1948). The trend of the law is currently to the contrary. The Model Penal Code 3.04(2)(a)(i), see p. 235 below, and statutes in some states require submission to an illegal arrest if the person being arrested knows that the person making the arrest is a police officer. See p. 196 note 115 below.

---

102. At the outset of this section, p. 69 above, "malice aforethought" was said to refer collectively to all the states of mind that mark a homicide as murder. We are now able to catalogue those states of mind. Malice aforethought includes, first and most obviously,

> (1) an intention to kill.

If there is an intention to kill, malice aforethought may nevertheless be "negatived" by the doctrine of adequate provocation, which reduces an intentional killing from murder to voluntary manslaughter.

Other kinds of malice aforethought are:

> (2) an intention grievously to injure;
>
> (3) extreme recklessness;
>
> (4) accompanying commission of a felony; and
>
> (5) in theory, according to the traditional rule, but probably not in practice, resistance to a lawful arrest.

Keep in mind that malice aforethought is not something in addition to any of these elements. More particularly, none of them requires proof of malice (e.g. *Zygmaniak*, p. 139) or forethought (e.g. *Alexander*, p. 92). For clarity's sake, we should probably do better never to refer to malice aforethought at all.

---

4. JUSTIFICATION AND EXCUSE

The unique value of human life is the dominant theme of the law of homicide. The highest penalties are now reserved almost exclusively for those who unambiguously display disregard of that value. Severe penalties are imposed on persons whose conduct destroys life, although the same conduct would have gone largely or wholly unpunished but for the fact of death, often a fortuity from the point of view of the actor. With almost no exception, the value of life so far exceeds all other values that the particular value of the particular life taken is of no significance.

Nevertheless, it is not always a crime to kill someone intentionally. When society imposes the penalty of death for criminal conduct, it utilizes considerable resources to take the life of a person who is a member of the community and who is specified (by pronouncement of the sentence of death) in advance. Killing the enemy in battle during a war is another example of deliberate homicide that society officially approves.[64] But for society's acceptance of some value or complex of values that is thought to prevail over the value of the life or lives taken, each of these kinds of killing would fit neatly into a category of criminal homicide. An execution is unequivocally deliberate and premeditated. Acts of killing in war may be deliberate and premeditated; many acts in war display "extreme indifference" to the value of some human lives.[65]

A justification for the taking of life may be that on balance life will be preserved. Such justification, if it is offered in defense of a *type* of killing, is likely to depend on a large, complicated set of uncertain observations and judgments. For example, there is widespread disbelief on both factual and analytic grounds that the threat of capital punishment deters people from committing murder more than some other penalty would.[66] The judgment that killing is necessary to preserve life may be made more easily for a particular case if a life is clearly endangered and a life must be threatened if the danger is to be avoided. Even then one may ask whether approval of the conduct that saves life will serve the goal of preserving life in the long run.[67]

64. When an enemy is killed in war, membership of the killer and the killed in a common community is at best uncertain, and the killer does not ordinarily know the personal identity of the killed. What relevance have these features of the situation? Are they present equally or to a lesser degree in some of the other situations involving homicide that we have considered?

65. Whether or not one approves of capital punishment or killing in war, it is not possible, except in extraordinary circumstances in which the legal validity of the order to kill is called into question, to assign legal guilt; in a significant sense, the acts that cause death do not "belong" to the individuals who perform them. (The bearing of this conclusion on the *moral blameworthiness* of the individuals who perform the acts depends on complex judgments about the role of an individual as a member of a society.) The primary attack on such killing is directed at those who have made the judgment for the

community that the killing is justified, not at those who kill. The movement to abolish capital punishment is directed at the legislature, not the hangman. Pacifists generally protest against a war, not against the soldiers who fight it. (There are, of course, significant differences, besides the ones mentioned here, between the roles of hangman and soldier. Many, probably most, men who do not resist military service in wartime would decline to be the public executioner.)

66. See, e.g., T. Sellin, The Death Penalty 19–34 (1959).

67. A purpose to save life is an incomplete justification for the taking of life if the number of lives saved and taken is the same and remote effects are unknown or ignored. Even if a saving of lives on balance could be demonstrated, the problem of justification would not obviously be solved. The Model Penal Code § 3.02, p. 242 below, allows a defense based on the choice of a lesser evil.

Are there situations in which some value justifies the taking of life even though no life is threatened?

DEFENSE OF SELF

Commonwealth v. Kendrick
351 Mass. 203, 218 N.E.2d 408 (1966)

■ KIRK, JUSTICE.

The defendant was convicted of murder in the second degree on an indictment which charged him with the murder of Thomas D. Giangreco at Barnstable on September 20, 1964. . . .

. . .

Of the three assignments of error which have been argued, the principal one relates to the judge's ruling that a verdict of manslaughter could not be returned by the jury, and to his refusal to instruct the jury on the law of homicide as it pertains to manslaughter. The issue presented is whether, on the evidence, the jury were precluded as matter of law from finding the defendant guilty of manslaughter. The principles of law are settled and well understood. The application of them, however, sometimes requires, as here, consideration in detail of the evidence bearing on the issue. . . . Most of the evidence now to be stated originated with the defendant, either as statements to the police or as testimony by him at the trial.

Facts   The defendant was forty-four years of age, married, and the father of three children. He was employed as a rural mail carrier in Dennisport on Cape Cod. With his family he lived in Dennisport as the terms of his employment required. Commencing in May, 1963, an amorous relationship developed between the defendant and Mrs. Giangreco, who lived with her husband, the deceased, in Centerville. The defendant had known Mrs. Giangreco since she was three or four years old; or at least since grammar school. During the spring of 1963 he visited her daily, usually in the morning, after her husband had gone to work. On these occasions he did not park his car in front of the Giangreco house, but in a road or driveway near by. Together, they took frequent rides in her husband's car. The defendant was admittedly the father of a child born to Mrs. Giangreco in June, 1964.

The comment states that in such a situation all lives must be assumed to be of equal value, and "the numerical preponderance in the lives saved compared to those sacrificed surely should establish legal justification for the act." 2 MPC Commentaries Part I, 15.

Not all moral systems would approve without further explanation the deliberate killing of a wholly innocent person in order to preserve the lives of two or twenty or even two hundred innocent persons.

The deceased, Thomas Giangreco, was sixty years old. He owned and operated on a seasonal basis, a small restaurant in Hyannisport. The defendant and the deceased had known one another since 1956. They had played golf together but were not close friends. The intimacy between the defendant and Mrs. Giangreco was known to the defendant's wife, and to many people in the community. The deceased did not suspect the infidelity of his wife, if indeed he ever suspected it, until two weeks before his death. If he had then suspected it, he gave no indication of it to the defendant when they once met in the interval. There had never been an argument between the defendant and the deceased. The defendant had never talked with the deceased about his relations with Mrs. Giangreco or about the baby.

For about a year prior to the fatal event the defendant had planned to get a divorce. He hoped that the deceased would permit Mrs. Giangreco to get a divorce so that he and Mrs. Giangreco could marry. As a step in the execution of the plan, the defendant on September 13, 1964, hired a cottage in Dennisport where Mrs. Giangreco and the baby were to live. During the following week, he stocked the cottage with food. On Sunday morning, September 20, 1964, he took Mrs. Giangreco and the baby, and many personal effects, including the crib, to the Dennisport cottage. In the cupboard were placed three cups, bearing the names Charles, Ruth, and Robert, the names, respectively, of the defendant, Mrs. Giangreco and the infant. Following a tour of the Cape, including a stop where the two adults played miniature golf, the party returned in the early evening to Centerville where the defendant dropped off Mrs. Giangreco and the baby at their residence. The defendant left for Hyannis. It was the defendant's purpose to go back to Centerville later in the evening and discuss with Giangreco in the presence of Mrs. Giangreco the prospect of the latter getting a divorce. He did go back and he drove past the Giangreco house several times wondering just how he would "break the news" to Tom. He was attired then, as he had been all day, in Bermuda shorts, a shirt, and rubber soled canvas shoes.

About 8:45 P.M. the defendant parked his motor vehicle at a place nearby, and took from it and put in his pocket or belt a German army knife and scabbard which he had brought home from Germany as a souvenir of his service in World War II as an infantry platoon sergeant. The blade of the knife, of Solingen steel, was seven and one-half inches long and, at the hilt, almost an inch wide. It had one keen edge and came to a point at the tip of the blade. The handle was slotted to make the weapon adaptable for use as a short bayonet. The defendant used his motor vehicle in his duties as a rural mail carrier. The car had a folding sign on the top identifying its use. The knife, as the Commonwealth conceded, had always been kept in the defendant's car and was used by the defendant to cut bundles of mail. The defendant took the knife with him as he went to the Giangreco house because he thought there might be trouble with Tom when he brought up the subject of Tom's wife and the baby, and because he wanted to protect Mrs. Giangreco and the baby if Tom "got mad." He had seen Tom "get mad" with people on other occasions. Tom had "quite a temper."

The defendant went to the front door of the Giangreco dwelling. Although darkness had descended, the area in front of the house was sufficiently lighted by a nearby street light to permit recognition of persons. The front door is in a recessed area or alcove. The defendant knocked at the door and waited for an answer. When no answer came, he walked along the front of the house and looked in the windows. Through one window he saw the deceased, seated at the kitchen table, wearing a bathrobe and working on some papers. The defendant leaned over the bushes near the house, tapped on the window, and called out loudly, "Tom, will you let me in?" While the defendant was leaning forward, the light from the kitchen fell on his face. Tom looked directly at him, got up from the table and went into the living room. The defendant returned to the front door which was locked, and faced it, expecting the deceased to open it. He knew that the door opened inward. He soon heard footsteps behind him. He turned in the alcove and saw Tom with a fireplace poker in his right hand and a flashlight in his left hand. While the defendant was still in the alcove, Tom raised the poker and struck the defendant on the shoulder. The defendant said, "What's the matter with you, Tom?" The deceased answered, "I will show you what's the matter with me," and struck at him again with the poker. The defendant partly deflected the blow with his left arm, but he was hit on the nose. The defendant tried to hold off the deceased with his fists; he tried to grapple with him with his hands and could not; he then pulled his knife and said, "[S]tay away from me." The deceased advanced again, and the next thing the defendant knew, the deceased was on the ground. He could not recall stabbing the deceased, or the number of times he stabbed him.

[handwritten margin note: victim actually attacked the Δ.]

Giangreco was dead upon the arrival of the police in response to a telephone call at 9:01 P.M. from Mrs. Giangreco who reported that there had been a fight outside her house. The deceased was lying near some bushes along the foundation of the house at a point at least fifteen feet from the front door area. A fireplace poker protruded from under his right arm. A flashlight was five feet away from the body. The cause of death was stab wounds in the neck and chest. Some of the wounds were three inches deep and were obviously inflicted with plunging force rather than as slashes with the edge of the blade. There was a complete severance of the left vertebral artery. The deceased's left hand was cut. There were also some relatively superficial wounds and abrasions on his body.

The defendant had left the scene immediately. He threw away the knife and scabbard, which were later recovered with his help. He went to the Dennisport cottage where he washed and attempted to dress his "wounds." He then went to a public telephone and called the Giangreco house. A police officer answered. The defendant asked for Tom and was told that Tom was busy. The defendant then returned to his own home where at 12:50 A.M. on September 21, 1964, the police, who in the interim, had questioned two other rural mail carriers, interviewed him. The defendant told the police that he had played golf with a friend on September 20. In response to an inquiry whether the injuries to his face were caused by having been hit with a club, he explained that his face had been scratched by the bushes while playing golf. A telephone call by the police, made in the defendant's presence, to the man with whom he said he had played golf, disclosed that the man had been out of the State on September 20. At this point, the defendant was told by the police that he was suspected of a serious crime, that he did not have to answer any questions, but that if he did answer, the answers could be used against him, and that if he wanted a lawyer he could get one. The defendant replied that he did not need a lawyer, that he had done nothing wrong. He then gave the narrative as heretofore stated. At 2:45 A.M. the defendant told his lawyer that he had been in a fight, that the fellow had died, and that he was going to plead self-defence.

A physician who examined the defendant on September 22 reported that he had four "skin wounds" on his lips and cheek, a swelling over the bridge of his nose, a "wound" back of the shoulder blade and a sixteenth of an inch "wound" or "hole" on his left thigh.

The poker found at the scene was, according to police testimony, part of the Giangreco fireplace set. It was a heavy forged steel poker, twenty-five inches long, with a crescent-shaped hook two inches from the end of the shaft. Obviously, and as the police testified, it was a "dangerous weapon."

The record gives no indication of the size, strength and agility of the deceased as compared to the defendant whom the jury observed. The defendant testified on both direct and cross-examination that he had engaged in knife fighting while on night patrols into the German lines during the war.

We now turn to the charge. In so far as the indictment charged murder in the first degree, the judge eliminated the element of deliberately premed-itated malice aforethought as well as the element of the commission or attempted commission of a crime punishable with death or life imprison-ment. . . . He left the element of extreme atrocity or cruelty to the determination of the jury. The judge instructed the jury on the law pertaining to self-defence. He then told the jury, however, that there was "no evidence to warrant a verdict of manslaughter in this case."

Prefatory to our discussion of this ruling, it should be said that there was ample evidence to support the verdict returned by the jury. Accordingly, we direct our attention to the correctness of the judge's decision to withdraw the issue of manslaughter from the consideration of the jury. The number and nature of the wounds inflicted on Giangreco establish that the killing was intentional. When the killing is caused by the intentional use of a deadly weapon, there arises the presumption of malice aforethought, as that term has long been understood and applied in this Common-wealth. . . . The circumstances which attended the killing may, however, be shown to rebut the presumption of malice. This may be done by a showing that the homicide was committed in self-defence and was therefore excusable, or by a showing of circumstances which although they would not excuse or justify the act would mitigate the crime from murder to man-slaughter. It is the last proposition which primarily concerns us.

Hovering over the case are the admitted facts that the defendant armed himself with a deadly weapon and went, unbidden, to the deceased's house for the purpose of discussing with him a subject which the defendant knew would arouse Giangreco's strongest emotions and might produce violence. On the other hand, there is the countervailing circumstance, if the jury believed the defendant, that the confrontation and the mortal affray occurred before the defendant had an opportunity to mention the subject which he feared would provoke Giangreco to anger. Another circumstance which the jury could find was that a meeting of the two men in the Giangreco household was planned by the defendant but was neither sought nor expected by the deceased. They could find, however, that the actual place of the confrontation was a surprise to both. Giangreco had last seen the defendant, if indeed he had recognized him, at the kitchen window. He had no reason to suppose that the defendant had a knife in his pocket or belt. The defendant, on his part, expected Giangreco to meet him by opening the front door, unarmed. Instead, it could be found, Giangreco armed himself with the poker, left the house by the back door, and came around the end of the house to the front lawn. On the defendant's version, the clash in the recessed area of the front door could be found to have been a sudden combat in which the deceased was initially the aggressor. . . . If the deceased initiated the assault with the poker while the defendant was cornered in the areaway of the door so that the defendant in fact feared and reasonably feared that he was in danger of being killed or suffering grievous bodily harm at the hands of Giangreco, he had the right to use whatever means were reasonably necessary to avert the threatened harm.

. . . "In order to create a right to defend oneself with a dangerous weapon likely to cause serious injury or death, it must appear that the person using the weapon had a reasonable apprehension of great bodily harm and a reasonable belief that no other means would suffice to prevent such harm." Commonwealth v. Houston, 332 Mass. 687. . . . If the jury found that the circumstances immediately preceding and attending the killing created in the defendant the right to use the deadly weapon to defend himself against Giangreco, the homicide was excusable and the defendant was entitled to a verdict of not guilty. In substance the judge so instructed the jury. His instructions were correct as far as they went. The jury, however, should have been instructed further, upon the assumption that the deceased was the original assailant, that if the use of the knife by the defendant as a means of averting harm to himself was unreasonable and clearly excessive in light of the existing circumstances, they could conclude that the defendant himself became the attacker and, since death resulted from his use of excessive force, he would be guilty of manslaughter. "Ordinarily the question how far a party may properly go in self-defense is a question for the jury, not to be judged of very nicely, but with due regard to the infirmity of human impulses and passions." Monize v. Begaso, 190 Mass. 87, 89, quoted in Commonwealth v. Houston, 332 Mass. 687, 690. The judge's charge left it to the jury to accept wholly or to reject wholly self-defence as an excuse for the killing. We think that the legal consequence of using manifestly disproportionate violence in the supposed exercise of the right of self-defence should likewise have been made known to the jury.

In passing upon the reasonableness of the force used by the defendant, again on the hypothesis that he was acting in self-defence, the jury should consider evidence of the relative physical capabilities of the combatants, the characteristics of the weapons used, and the availability of maneuver room in, or means of escape from, the doorway area. In addition, the distance from the doorway to the spot where the deceased's body was found could be a significant factor in determining who was doing the attacking when the deceased was felled.

Indeed, the place where the body was found might well be of significance in determining whether the defendant had the right of self-defence at all. If in fact the confrontation and fight took place on the front lawn where the body was found, the right of self-defence might not be available to the defendant, since it might then appear that the defendant had a clear field to escape before delivering the lethal blows. The right of self-defence does not accrue to a person until he has availed all proper means to avoid physical combat. . . . The right of self-defence arises from necessity, and ends when the necessity ends.

The issue of manslaughter was also open for consideration by the jury on other grounds if the evidence is viewed, as the jury could view it, in another aspect. If the jury should find that the encounter did take place on the front lawn rather than at the doorway and that the deceased struck the first blow which roused the defendant to the heat of passion and that, while thus stirred to anger, he retaliated "with a weapon likely to endanger life, and death ensues, it is regarded as done through heat of blood or violence of anger, and not through malice," with the result that the homicide is unlawful but, the element of malice being missing, the crime is mitigated from murder to manslaughter. . . .

Our conclusion is that the issue of manslaughter should not have been foreclosed and that there was error in not giving to the jury instructions relating to that offence. *Holding in favor of △*

. . .

---

103. What is the justification for allowing a person who reasonably believes that she is in danger of being killed or seriously injured by the act of another to take the life of her aggressor? Suppose the person who is killed was not an aggressor. Suppose, for example, that a person reasonably believes that she is in danger of being killed or seriously injured by a mad bull that is charging at her. May she protect her own life by using the body of another person as a shield? May one survivor of a shipwreck throw another survivor off a log which will support the weight of only one of them?

104.   Does anything turn on the motives of the aggressor? Or on the intended victim's own degree of fault? Suppose the intended victim has done the aggressor a great wrong for which the law provides no redress, as some might describe the facts in *Kendrick*, above. May the intended victim nevertheless preserve his life by taking his aggressor's life? Suppose the "aggressor" is unaware, reasonably or unreasonably, that his conduct endangers the life of someone else. If a bird watcher, watching in the forest, looks up and sees a hunter, evidently mistaking the bird watcher for a deer, about to shoot him, may he shoot the hunter if that is the only way to save himself? Does it matter whether it is hunting season?

105.   Is it a desirable development of the law that defense of self be allowed on a broadened scale?

"There does exist . . . gentlemen, a law which is a law not of the statute-book, but of nature; a law which we possess not by instruction, tradition, or reading, but which we have caught, imbibed, and sucked in at Nature's own breast; a law which comes to us not by education but by constitution, not by training but by intuition—the law, I mean, that, should our life have fallen into any snare, into the violence and the weapons of robbers or foes, every method of winning a way to safety would be morally justifiable. When arms speak, the laws are silent; they bid none to await their word, since he who chooses to await it must pay an undeserved penalty ere he can exact a deserved one." Cicero, Pro T. Annio Milone [On Behalf of Milo] in The Speeches (N.H. Watts, trans.) 17 (1931). The speech was prepared in 52 B.C.

In an ungoverned society the savage law of the jungle prevails. The fundamental instinct of the creatures of such a society is one of self-preservation, which causes the wreaking of unregulated violence on one whose actions are felt to endanger the security of another. When government becomes invested in a single person or authority, rules are straightway laid down for the discipline of those governed. Obedience to those rules is a condition precedent to the very life of the ruling body.

The first business of a ruler is the elimination of all forms of self-help; this is responsible for the strict liability of earliest law. As the power of the ruler becomes more firmly established the need for these strict rules diminishes, and in rare cases a man's efforts on his own behalf are regarded as being justified. Any such exceptions to the general principle that self-help is illegal are, however, severely restricted by the prerequisites of necessity and public policy. They emerge only as the products of a firmly entrenched system of law which has attained a high standard of efficiency and functional precision.

Brown, "Self-Defence in Homicide From Strict Liability to Complete Exculpation," 1958 Crim. L. Rev. 583.

106. How closely should the law scrutinize a judgment that life must be taken to save life? If it reasonably appears to a person that his life is in danger, "he may safely act upon appearances," Shorter v. People, 2 N.Y. 193, 197 (1849), and will not be criminally liable if it turns out that the appearances were false and he was in no danger at all.

107. How imminent must the danger be? In Reece v. State, 683 S.W.2d 873 (Tex.Ct.App.1984), the victim assaulted the defendant and said that he was going to get a gun and "waste him." The court held that the defense of self-defense was not available, because there was no immediate need to use deadly force. See also State v. Schroeder, 261 N.W.2d 759 (Neb.1978) (prison inmate killed sleeping cell-mate who before going to bed had threatened to assault him sexually that night; self-defense not available). The Model Penal Code § 3.04(1) requires that a person believe that the use of force is "immediately necessary" to protect himself on the present occasion.

Suppose the defendant reasonably fears that once he is immediately threatened, he will no longer be in a position to defend himself. If he acts sooner, does he respond to an "imminent" danger? Compare People v. Humphrey, p. 206 below.

108. Distinguishing Patterson v. New York, p. 106 above, and holding that if the issue of self-defense is presented, the prosecution has the burden of proving the absence of self-defense beyond a reasonable doubt, the

Supreme Court of Washington observed that in a prosecution for murder, the unlawfulness of the killing "including the absence of self-defense—is an essential ingredient of the crime charged. Since proof of self-defense negates the element of intent in first degree murder, requiring an accused to prove self-defense places on him or her the burden of proving absence of an unlawful criminal intent." State v. McCullum, 656 P.2d 1064, 1072 (Wash. 1983). In a majority of states, the law is the same. But see Martin v. Ohio, 480 U.S. 228 (1987) (5–4), p. 108 above. *Martin* is discussed and applied in Smart v. Leeke, 873 F.2d 1558 (4th Cir.1989).

109.   Past acts and threats of the victim are relevant to the defendant's claim of self-defense "to show the circumstances confronting the defendant, the extent of his apparent danger, and the motive by which he was influenced"; the defendant should be given "substantial latitude" to introduce such evidence. People v. Hoddenbach, 452 N.E.2d 32, 35 (Ill.Ct. App.1983). See People v. Torres, 474 N.E.2d 1305 (Ill.Ct.App.1985) (testimony of victim's statements about his gang affiliation and gang-related activities should have been admitted).

110.

A youth, approximately fourteen years of age, entered a news shop where the defendant, a young adult, was present and performing certain tasks as a friend of the proprietor. An altercation ensued in the course of which the child and the adult struggled. Glasses being worn by the defendant allegedly were knocked from his face and the youth's nose was bloodied. He went home, and complained to his seventeen year old brother who, in the company of another brother and a friend, one James Hargrove (the deceased), returned with him to the news shop to ascertain the cause of the altercation. Being forewarned of their return, defendant had taken a pistol from beneath a counter and placed it in the waistband of his trousers, where it was concealed by his shirt.

The group of four entered and confronted the defendant. An argument between the elder brother and defendant developed which was quieted when Hargrove suggested that the best way to settle the dispute was for the youth to "take out a warrant," whereupon they left the store. Very shortly thereafter, the elder brother re-entered, his testimony being that he had to obtain change for his bus fare. It is uncontroverted that while the defendant had his back turned, the elder brother struck him on the shoulder with a belt, the buckle of which left a discernible mark upon the flesh. Upon trial, defendant testified as follows: "[I] knew [I] was being attacked by them. And so when he hit me, I just drawed the gun and turned around and fired."

When the shot was fired, the victim and the brothers were fleeing from the premises. Hargrove suffered a wound in his right chest into the abdomen and expired during surgery less than eight hours later as a consequence thereof.

The accused relied upon self-defense as justification for the homicide, and testified that when he fired the weapon he was in fear of his life or bodily harm.

State v. Clifton, 290 N.E.2d 921, 921–22 (Ohio Ct.App.1972).

If the defendant's testimony about his state of mind when he fired is believed, what result?

111. Does Justice Holmes's observation that "detached reflection cannot be demanded in the presence of an uplifted knife," Brown v. United States, 256 U.S. 335, 343 (1921), provide a full answer to the problem of cases like *Clifton*, note 110 above? (If so, what of the person attacked by a bull or the survivor of a shipwreck who sees a means to safety that imperils someone else?)

112. To whom must the danger be apparent? To what extent should the defendant's particular "physical and mental equipment," United States v. King, 34 F. 302, 309 (C.C.E.D.N.Y.1888), be considered in determining what "the apparent danger" was? Suppose the defendant spoke English badly and mistook mild threats accompanied by menacing gestures for an announcement that he was about to be killed. Cf. State v. Kuehn, 53 N.W. 721 (Mich.1892). Compare State v. Bess, 247 A.2d 669 (N.J.1968) (defendant emotionally unstable under pressure). Should physical or other idiosyncrasies have more bearing on the excuse of self-defense than on the mitigating effect of provocation?

113. How should we measure the seriousness of a danger of physical harm? May a pianist or a surgeon take life to avoid an injury to his hands that (perhaps unknown to his aggressor) will disable him professionally but not otherwise be "serious"? Should we distinguish in this respect between reasonable idiosyncratic fears or susceptibilities and morbid idiosyncratic fears having no special basis?

114. In *Kendrick*, above, the court states that if the defendant used means to defend himself that were "unreasonable and clearly excessive in light of the existing circumstances," he would be guilty of (voluntary) manslaughter. More generally, a person's honest belief that he is in danger of death or serious injury may fail to excuse him for killing his supposed or actual aggressor, because the belief or conduct pursuant to the belief is unreasonable. In such circumstances, which are often described as "imperfect self-defense," what crime has he committed? How do you explain that result? See, e.g., State v. Faulkner, 483 A.2d 759 (Md.1984); Commonwealth v. Galloway, 485 A.2d 776 (Pa.Super.Ct.1984).

Construing the state statute, which explicitly limited the defense of self-defense to conduct based on reasonable belief, the New Jersey court rejected a distinct defense of imperfect self-defense. It added, however, "that in many cases the issues of the reasonableness of the defendant's conduct presented to the jury in defense of the substantive crimes charged will have relevance to the essential elements of the homicidal act: whether it was the actor's conscious object to inflict deadly force, whether death was almost certain to follow, or whether the act was done recklessly or with reasonable provocation." State v. Bowens, 532 A.2d 215, 221 (N.J.1987). See also Sanchez v. People, 470 P.2d 857 (Colo.1970) (defendant, who stabbed victim in heart, was entitled to an instruction on involuntary manslaughter, on theory that he acted in self-defense, only to protect himself and without intention to kill); State v. Hughes, 721 P.2d 902 (Wash.1986) (rejecting imperfect self-defense but noting that one who uses deadly force in self-defense, in disregard of risk of serious harm to victim, may be convicted of manslaughter instead of murder).

Suppose a person uses nondeadly force in legitimate self-defense and his aggressor dies as a result of the blow. See State v. Drew, 344 N.W.2d 923 (Neb.1984) (gun discharged, killing victim, when defendant attempted to hit him with gun; no crime if death resulted from accident in course of proper self-defense).

115.   Abandoning a rule that was adopted in 1865, the Supreme Judicial Court of Massachusetts held that "in the absence of excessive or unnecessary force by an arresting officer, a person may not use force to resist an arrest by one who he knows or has good reason to believe is an authorized police officer, engaged in the performance of his duties, regardless of whether the arrest was unlawful in the circumstances." Commonwealth v. Moreira, 447 N.E.2d 1224, 1227 (Mass.1983). The court noted that its new rule was "the modern view," adopted in a majority of states by legislative enactment or judicial decision. "In this era of constantly expanding legal protection of the rights of the accused in criminal proceedings, an arrestee may be reasonably required to submit to a possibly unlawful arrest and to take recourse in the legal processes available to restore his liberty. . . . An arrestee has the benefit of liberal bail laws, appointed counsel, the right to remain silent and to cut off questioning, speedy arraignment, and speedy trial. . . . As a result of these rights and procedural safeguards, the need for the common law rule disappears—self-help by an arrestee has become anachronistic." Id.

The court added: "Our conclusion does not apply to cases in which the police officer uses excessive force in his attempt to subdue the arrestee. In such a situation, the disposition of the case depends on the application of the rules pertaining to self-defense. Thus, we conclude that where the officer uses excessive or unnecessary force to subdue the arrestee, regardless of whether the arrest is lawful or unlawful, the arrestee may defend himself by employing such force as reasonably appears to be necessary. . . . Moreover, once the arrestee knows or reasonably should know that if he desists from using force in self-defense, the officer will cease using force, the arrestee must desist. Otherwise, he will forfeit his defense. . . .

"The questions whether the officer used excessive force and whether the arrestee used reasonable force to resist the excessive force are questions of fact to be resolved by the jury on proper instruction by the trial judge. Application of this rule will not require that the arrestee act in a manner commensurate with such action as would follow detached and reasoned reflection. . . . Some recognition must be given to the frailty of human nature. The rule merely requires the finder of fact to determine whether the arrestee's conduct was reasonable in light of all the circumstances." Id. at 1228.

State v. Valentine, 935 P.2d 1294 (Wash.1997), is to the same effect. Observing that the rule allowing resistance to an unlawful arrest had developed at a time when the conditions in prison were horrible and "imprisonment until the next term of court was often equivalent to a death sentence," id. at 1300, the court said that the rule was inapt in current circumstances. "[I]f the rule were . . . that a person being unlawfully arrested may always resist such an arrest with force, we would be inviting anarchy. While we do not . . . condone the unlawful use of state force, we can take note of the fact that in the often heated confrontation between a police officer and an arrestee, the lawfulness of the arrest may be debatable. To endorse resistance by persons who are being arrested by an officer of the law, based simply on the arrested person's belief that the arrest is unlawful, is to encourage violence that could, and most likely would, result in harm to the arresting officer, the defendant, or both. In our opinion, the better place to address the question of the lawfulness of an arrest that does not pose harm to the arrested person is in court and not on the street." Id. at 1304.

Although the conditions of jails now are not as bad as former conditions in English prisons described by the court, they are typically far from benign. Persons held pending a court hearing may be confined in a cell with other detainees. There have been cases of appalling abuse occurring overnight or even within a few hours. The clear trend of the law is, however, to require submission to a police officer who attempts to make an arrest, lawful or not, without excessive force.

Retreat.

116. "Indeed, the tendency of the American mind seems to be very strongly against the enforcement of any rule which requires a person to flee

when assailed, to avoid chastisement or even to save human life . . . ."
Runyan v. State, 57 Ind. 80, 84 (1877), quoted in Beard v. United States,
158 U.S. 550, 561–62 (1895).

The question whether one who is neither the aggressor nor a party
to a mutual combat must retreat has divided the authorities. Self-
defense is measured against necessity. . . . From that premise one
could readily say there was no necessity to kill in self-defense if the use
of deadly force could have been avoided by retreat. The critics of the
retreat rule do not quarrel with the theoretical validity of this conclusion, but rather condemn it as unrealistic. The law of course should not
denounce conduct as criminal when it accords with the behavior of
reasonable men. Upon this level, the advocates of no-retreat say the
manly thing is to hold one's ground, and hence society should not
demand what smacks of cowardice. Adherents of the retreat rule reply
it is better that the assailed shall retreat than that the life of another
be needlessly spent. They add that not only do right-thinking men
agree, but further a rule so requiring may well induce others to adhere
to that worthy standard of behavior. There is much dispute as to which
view commands the support of ancient precedents, a question we think
it would be profitless to explore.

Other jurisdictions are closely divided upon the retreat doctrine. It
is said that the preponderant view rejects it. . . . The Model Penal
Code embraces the retreat rule while acknowledging that on numerical
balance a majority of the precedents oppose it. Model Penal Code
§ 3.04, comment 3, at p. 24 (Tent. Draft No. 8, 1958).

We are not persuaded to depart from the principle of retreat. We
think it salutary if reasonably limited. Much of the criticism goes not
to its inherent validity but rather to unwarranted applications of the
rule. For example, it is correctly observed that one can hardly retreat
from a rifle shot at close range. But if the weapon were a knife, a lead
of a city block might well be enough. Again the rule cannot be stated
badly, with indifference to the excitement of the occasion. . . . Such
considerations, however, do not demand that a man should have the
absolute right to stand his ground and kill in any and all situations.
Rather they call for a fair and guarded statement of appropriate
principles.

. . .

We believe the following principles are sound:

1.   The issue of retreat arises only if the defendant resorted to a
deadly force. It is deadly force which is not justifiable when an
opportunity to retreat is at hand. Model Penal Code § 3.04(2)(b)(iii).
As defined in § 3.12(2) a deadly force means "force which the actor
uses with the purpose of causing or which he knows to create a
substantial risk of causing death or serious bodily harm."

Hence it is not the nature of the force defended against which
raises the issue of retreat, but rather the nature of the force which the

accused employed in his defense. If he does not resort to a deadly force, one who is assailed may hold his ground whether the attack upon him be of a deadly or some lesser character. Although it might be argued that a safe retreat should be taken if thereby the use of *any* force could be avoided, yet, as the comment in the Model Penal Code observes (at p. 23), "The logic of this position never has been accepted when moderate force is used in self-defense; here all agree that the actor may stand his ground and estimate necessity upon that basis." . . .[68]

2. What constitutes an opportunity to retreat which will defeat the right of self-defense? As § 3.04(2)(b)(iii) of the Model Penal Code states, deadly force is not justifiable "if the actor *knows* that he can avoid the necessity of using such force *with complete safety* by retreating. . . ." We emphasize "knows" and "with complete safety." One who is wrongfully attacked need not risk injury by retreating, even though he could escape with something less than serious bodily injury. It would be unreal to require nice calculations as to the amount of hurt, or to ask him to endure any at all. And the issue is not whether in retrospect it can be found the defendant could have retreated unharmed. Rather the question is whether he knew the opportunity was there, and of course in that inquiry the total circumstances including the attendant excitement must be considered. . . .

State v. Abbott, 174 A.2d 881, 884–86 (N.J.1961).

On the existence of a duty to retreat only if the actor is aware that there is a safe avenue of retreat, see Commonwealth v. Palmer, 359 A.2d 375 (Pa.1976).

117. Is "the tendency of the American mind," *Runyan*, note 116 above, whatever that is, today as it was described by the Supreme Court of Indiana in 1887? What evidence can you point to, either way? If so, should the Model Penal Code have incorporated the retreat rule? Why (not)? In Brown v. United States, 256 U.S. 335, 343 (1921), Justice Holmes observed: "Rationally the failure to retreat is a circumstance to be considered with all the others in order to determine whether the defendant went farther than he was justified in doing; not a categorical proof of guilt."

[68] See, e.g., State v. Evenson, 97 N.W. 979, 980 (Iowa 1904): "[The principle] that one may not, under the plea of self-defense, justify the taking of human life, if it reasonably appears that the same could have been avoided by making use of an avenue of escape open to him . . . has no application to a case where . . . one is wrongfully assaulted, and repels force by the use of like force. In the one case the law regards the liberty of the citizen to come and go as he pleases without molestation, save at the hands of the law, as the thing paramount. In the other case the law regards the temporary deprivation of the exercise of personal liberty on the part of one citizen as of less importance than is the life of another citizen, and this even though the latter is for the moment engaged in making an unlawful assault upon the former. Hence the injunction that a person assaulted must retreat, if he can do so in reasonable safety, before resorting to the extreme measure of taking the life of his assailant."

118. Even in jurisdictions that require a person who can safely retreat to do so before endangering life to protect his own, the duty to retreat does not arise in some situations. "It is not now and never has been the law that a man assailed in his own dwelling is bound to retreat. If assailed there, he may stand his ground, and resist the attack. He is under no duty to take to the fields and the highways, a fugitive from his own home. . . . Flight is for sanctuary and shelter, and shelter, if not sanctuary, is in the home." People v. Tomlins, 107 N.E. 496, 497 (N.Y.1914). Accord, e.g., Gainer v. State, 391 A.2d 856 (Md.Ct.Spec.App.1978).

On what should the existence of a duty to retreat depend?

> The right of the person attacked to be where he is?
>
> The right of the attacker to be where she is?
>
> Ownership of the place where the attack occurs?
>
> The nature of the place where the attack occurs?
>
> The reason why either the person attacked or the attacker is at the place where the attack occurs?

If the desirability of safe retreat before the use of deadly force is accepted in general, what additional features of a situation overcome the value of human life to which the retreat rule gives recognition?

A majority of jurisdictions have given primary significance to the relation of the person attacked to the place of the assault. There is a tendency to enlarge the exception to the duty to retreat to include not only the home but any premises where the person attacked is lawfully present. In People v. White, 484 N.Y.S.2d 994 (Sup.Ct.1984), for example, the court construed a statutory exception to the duty to retreat for a person "in his own dwelling" to include all persons having a right to be in the dwelling. To hold otherwise, the court said, "would saddle nonresident family members, household employees, babysitters, social guests and others, who have a right to be in a dwelling with an obligation to retreat before defending themselves with deadly and unreasonable [sic] force. Such a result seems unreasonable. This court cannot believe that the Legislature meant to revert back to the 'castle doctrine' exception, and ignore the realities of modern-day living mores and customs, expressed in more enlightened judicial interpretations, which seem to represent the majority view that one who is assaulted in a place where he has a right to be is under no duty to retreat." Id. at 996. See also Barton v. State, 420 A.2d 1009, 1012 (Md.Ct.Spec.App.1980), holding that the exception to the duty to retreat is available to a temporary resident who is a member of the household when the attack occurs, "especially . . . with respect to . . . [someone] who was a mere guest and not himself a member of the household." Also, State v. Laverty, 495 A.2d 831 (Me.1985), holding that a person in his own dwelling has no duty to retreat even if his assailant is a co-dweller. But see People v. Fisher, 420 N.W.2d 858 (Mich.Ct.App.1988), holding the home exception to the retreat rule not applicable where the defendant had an ownership interest in the premises but had not resided there for eight months.

Looking more toward the assailant's relation to the place of the assault, the Supreme Court of Connecticut construed a statutory exception similar to that in *White*, above, *not* to apply if the dwelling is also that of the assailant. State v. Shaw, 441 A.2d 561 (Conn.1981) (tenant defending against co-occupant landlord). Acknowledging that it was in the minority, the court said: "This rule is in line with a policy favoring human life over the burden of retreating from the home, and the usual self-defense principles would still apply to allow defense at the wall or where retreat is impossible. In the great majority of homicides the killer and the victim are relatives or close acquaintances. . . . We cannot conclude that the Connecticut legislature intended to sanction the reenactment of the climactic scene from 'High Noon' in the familial kitchens of this state." Id. at 566. See Cooper v. United States, 512 A.2d 1002 (D.C.1986), reviewing cases and concluding that there is a duty to retreat from one's home before responding to a co-occupant assailant with deadly force. Accord State v. Quarles, 504 A.2d 473 (R.I.1986).

The variety of situations that may arise is large. Consider the following cases:

(i) The defendant and the deceased were playing cards in a room at the local Elks' Club, of which the defendant but not the deceased was a member. It was not known how the deceased happened to be at the club. Defending himself from an attack with a chair, the defendant shot and killed the deceased. Was he under an obligation to retreat before shooting if he could have done so? See State v. Marlowe, 112 S.E. 921 (S.C.1922).

(ii) The defendant, who was in his car on a public highway, and the deceased were involved in an argument. The deceased jumped on the running board of the car and assaulted the defendant. The defendant shot and killed the deceased. Was he under an obligation to retreat before shooting if he could have done so? See State v. Johnson, 274 N.W. 41 (Iowa 1937); State v. Borwick, 187 N.W. 460 (Iowa 1922); State v. McGee, 193 S.E. 303 (S.C.1937). Suppose the encounter occurred while both were standing on a public highway. See State v. Marish, 200 N.W. 5 (Iowa 1924). Suppose both were in the defendant's car when the quarrel started, and the deceased then jumped out of the car and pulled the defendant out also. After some fighting on the ground, the defendant shot and killed the deceased. See State v. Sedig, 16 N.W.2d 247 (Iowa 1944).

(iii) The deceased was a patron at a bar owned and operated by the defendant. Following an argument, the defendant ordered the deceased out of the tavern. The deceased assaulted the defendant, and the defendant knocked him down, causing his death. Was the defendant under an obligation to retreat before swinging (assuming the blow to have been deadly force) if he could have done so? See State v. Baratta, 49 N.W.2d 866 (Iowa 1951); State v. Turner, 79 P.2d 46 (Utah 1938) (defendant's restaurant). Suppose the defendant was not the owner of the premises but a hired bartender. See Wilson v. State, 69 Ga. 224 (1882). Suppose both the defendant and the deceased were employees on the premises where the homicide occurred. See State v. Gordon, 122 S.E. 501 (S.C.1924). Suppose the defendant worked on the premises but at the time of the homicide was not engaged in his employment or supposed to be. See State v. Davis, 51 S.E.2d 86 (S.C.1948). Does it make any difference if the business carried on by the defendant at his place of business is unlawful? See Hill v. State, 69 So. 941 (Ala.1915) (unlawful distillery); State v. Sorrentino, 224 P. 420 (Wyo.1924) (same).

The Model Penal Code § 3.04(2)(b)(ii), which requires retreat generally if it can be accomplished "with complete safety," does not require retreat from one's dwelling or place of work unless the actor "was the initial aggressor or is assailed in his place of work by another person whose place of work the actor knows it to be," § 3.04(2)(b)(ii)(1). The comment observes: "Because the sentimental factors relevant to dwellings may not apply to one's place of work, it can be argued that this extension is inappropriate; but it was concluded that the practical considerations concerning the two locations were far too similar to sustain a distinction." 2 MPC Commentaries Part I, 56. What practical considerations are involved? What difference does it make whether the actor's assailant works at the same place? See generally Commonwealth v. Johnston, 263 A.2d 376 (Pa.1970), applying the Model Penal Code rule.

(iv) The defendant had "for some time" lived with the deceased and their respective parents in a house the rent for which the deceased paid. When the deceased attacked the defendant, was the defendant under an obligation to retreat, if he could have done so, before responding with deadly force? See State v. Phillips, 187 A. 721 (Del.1936); People v. Tomlins, p. 200 above. Suppose the two are husband and wife who both live in the home in which the homicide occurs. See People v. Lenkevich, 229

N.W.2d 298 (Mich.1975); State v. Pontery, 117 A.2d 473 (N.J.1955); cf. Collier v. State, 328 So.2d 626 (Ala.Crim.App.1975). Compare State v. Lamb, 366 A.2d 981 (N.J.1976) (victim was estranged husband of defendant; killing occurred in apartment occupied by defendant).

(v) The deceased was the defendant's lover and was accustomed to sleeping at her house. On the night of the homicide they had been drinking elsewhere and returned together to her house. About half an hour later, following a quarrel, he attacked her. She stabbed and killed him. Was she under an obligation to retreat before stabbing if she could have done so? See State v. Grierson, 69 A.2d 851 (N.H.1949); cf. Jackson v. State, 357 A.2d 845 (Md.Ct.Spec.App.1976).

119. The majority rule, stated in *Tomlins*, and reflected in the provisions of the Model Penal Code § 3.04(2)(b)(ii)(1), note 118 above, is rejected in Commonwealth v. Shaffer, 326 N.E.2d 880 (Mass.1975). In that case,

> [t]he defendant, who was separated from her husband and in the process of being divorced, resided with her two children in a one-story ranch house in Sharon. The victim, to whom the defendant was engaged, had lived in the house since 1971. The defendant had received several severe beatings at the hands of the victim, and on at least one occasion he had threatened to kill her and the children when asked to leave the defendant's home. Although the defendant loved the victim, she feared for herself and the children, and had persuaded him to seek psychiatric help.
>
> On the morning of the homicide, the defendant was having breakfast with the victim when an argument ensued. At one point, the victim rose, saying, "Never mind. I'll take care of you right now." The defendant threw a cup of tea at him and ran downstairs to the basement playroom, where the children were having breakfast and watching television.
>
> Shortly thereafter, the victim opened the door at the top of the basement stairs and said, "If you don't come up these stairs, I'll come down and kill you and the kids." She started to telephone the police, but hung up the telephone when the victim said he would leave the house. Instead, he returned to the top of the stairs, at which time the defendant took a .22 caliber rifle from a rack on the wall and loaded it. She again started to telephone the police when the victim started down the stairs. She fired a fatal shot. More than five minutes elapsed from the time the defendant went to the basement until the shooting took place.

Id. at 882–83.

The court held that its own "long-established rule" was applicable: "[T]he right to use deadly force by way of self-defense is not available to one threatened until he has availed himself of all reasonable and proper means in the circumstance[s] to avoid combat." That rule, the court said, "has equal application to one assaulted in his own home." While "the fact that one is threatened in his own home or in a place where he has exclusive right to be is one of the more important factors" bearing on the duty to retreat and should be "stressed to the jury," that fact does not confer an "unlimited right to react with deadly force without any attempt to retreat."

Among the circumstances that might have led the jury to conclude that the defendant was not in imminent serious danger from the deceased, the court noted the following:

> There was no evidence that he had a dangerous weapon at any time. He was only two or three steps from the top of the stairway when he was shot. The defendant had ample opportunity to call the police. She could have left the basement with her children. A period of five minutes had elapsed from the time the defendant first went down to the basement until the shooting occurred. The defendant did not warn the victim that she would shoot if he continued his descent down the stairway. There was evidence from the defendant's husband that she had considerable experience in the use of that rifle. One shot was sufficient to kill the victim.

Id. at 884.

The decision in *Shaffer* prompted much discussion and widespread criticism from persons who asserted that the defendant was a battered woman, see People v. Humphrey, p. 206 below. In 1981, the Massachusetts legislature enacted a statute providing that an occupant of a dwelling has no duty to retreat before using force in self-defense or defense of another person lawfully in the dwelling against someone who is unlawfully in the dwelling. Mass. Gen. L. ch. 278, § 8A. The statute was evidently a reaction to *Shaffer* and changed the law in some respects. See Commonwealth v. Gregory, 461 N.E.2d 831 (Mass.App.Ct.1984). Would the statute have helped the defendant in *Shaffer*?

120. In situations in which there is no duty to retreat generally, the defendant's conduct may oblige him to retreat before using deadly force to defend himself. In State v. Flory, 276 P. 458 (Wyo.1929), the defendant went to his father-in-law's house armed with a gun and accused his father-in-law of having raped the defendant's wife. He claimed that he killed his father-in-law in self-defense. The court held that, having provoked the encounter with his father-in-law, the defendant was under an "absolute duty to retreat" before defending himself: "[T]o go into another man's house with a deadly weapon under circumstances of ill-temper and for altercation is in nearly all cases in itself an ominous sign of dangerous trouble ahead, and for us to hold that under the evidence in this case the defendant had a right to stand his ground would be but to indulge and humor the weakness of human nature and invite and encourage murder and disaster." Id. at 463.

Courts have generally held that someone who precipitates a violent confrontation with another person is obliged to retreat, if he can do so safely, before using deadly force to defend himself, even if he did not explicitly threaten the other person. E.g., Atkins v. State, 339 S.E.2d 782 (Ga.Ct.App.1986); State v. Harris, 717 S.W.2d 233 (Mo.Ct.App.1986); State v. Hall, 366 S.E.2d 527 (N.C.Ct.App.1988).

What other conduct of the defendant short of a physical assault should deprive him of a right to stand his ground and repel a deadly assault with deadly force?

(i) If the defendant's verbal abuse of the deceased prompts a deadly assault, must he retreat before responding with deadly force? See, e.g., LaPierre v. State, 734 P.2d 997, 1001 n.3 (Alaska Ct.App.1987), holding that the defendant's sexual remarks and "momentary touching" of victim did not make him the initial aggressor. Is it of any significance that the deceased would (not) have been able to assert that the verbal abuse—"mere words"—constituted provocation for his assault on the defendant?

(ii) On adulterous conduct as affecting the right of self-defense against an enraged spouse, see generally Barger v. State, 202 A.2d 344 (Md.1964).

(iii) Suppose a would-be robber enters a store and, pointing a gun at the storekeeper, demands his money. The storekeeper attacks the robber, who abandons his purpose and attempts to leave. If the storekeeper fails to perceive that the robber has changed his mind and presses the attack, is the robber permitted to defend himself with deadly force if that is the only way he can save his own life? If not, what crime does he commit if he kills the storekeeper? People v. Sullivan, 177 N.E. 733 (Ill.1931); State v. Bradley, 521 A.2d 289 (Me.1987).

121. In what circumstances should a person who physically assaults another person and finds himself the target of a defensive assault be able to exercise his right to self-defense? "A man who is the instigator of an encounter that ultimately proves fatal may claim self-defense if, prior to the fatal blow, he attempts in good faith to disengage himself from the altercation and communicates his desire to do so to his opponent." United States v. Grover, 485 F.2d 1039, 1042 (D.C.Cir.1973). To the same effect, see State v. Graham, 195 N.W.2d 442, 444 (Minn.1972): "[A]n aggressor who has withdrawn from the conflict may assert the defense of self-defense. The deceased attacker, however, must know or have reasonable grounds to know that the former aggressor has withdrawn. A past aggressor must clearly evince his desire to make a good-faith withdrawal from the conflict." Also, State v. Ehlers, 685 S.W.2d 942 (Mo.Ct.App.1985) ("withdrawal . . . coupled with effective communication of that fact to the other person").[69]

---

69. It is sometimes said that the initial aggressor's right to defend himself does not revive unless his intention to withdraw is in fact perceived by his opponent. E.g., State v.

If a person who assaults another person with nondeadly force is met by a deadly defensive assault and, there being no opportunity to "disengage himself," he uses deadly force in necessary self-defense, should he be liable for homicide? If so, what category of homicide? In a swift and uninterrupted encounter of that sort, the survivor may, of course, have difficulty convincing the jury that his original intention was nondeadly.

People v. Humphrey

13 Cal.4th 1073, 56 Cal.Rptr.2d 142, 921 P.2d 1 (1996)

■ CHIN, JUSTICE.

The Legislature has decreed that, when relevant, expert testimony regarding "battered women's syndrome" is generally admissible in a criminal action. . . . We must determine the purposes for which a jury may consider this evidence when offered to support a claim of self-defense to a murder charge.

The trial court instructed that the jury could consider the evidence in deciding whether the defendant actually believed it was necessary to kill in self-defense, but not in deciding whether that belief was reasonable. The instruction was erroneous. Because evidence of battered women's syndrome may help the jury understand the circumstances in which the defendant found herself at the time of the killing, it is relevant to the reasonableness of her belief. Moreover, because defendant testified, the evidence was relevant to her credibility. The trial court should have allowed the jury to consider this testimony in deciding the reasonableness as well as the existence of defendant's belief that killing was necessary.

Finding the error prejudicial, we reverse the judgment of the Court of Appeal.

I. THE FACTS

A. Prosecution Evidence

During the evening of March 28, 1992, defendant shot and killed Albert Hampton in their Fresno home. Officer Reagan was the first on the scene. A neighbor told Reagan that the couple in the house had been arguing all day. Defendant soon came outside appearing upset and with her hands raised as if surrendering. She told Officer Reagan, "I shot him. That's right, I shot him. I just couldn't take him beating on me no more." She led the officer into the house, showed him a .357 magnum revolver on

---

Huemphreus, 270 N.W.2d 457 (Iowa 1978); State v. Mayberry, 226 S.W.2d 725 (Mo. 1950). If the latter is killed, a conclusion about what he perceived is likely to differ little from a conclusion about what he "must have" perceived, which will usually be based on what the defendant did to communicate his intention.

a table, and said, "There's the gun." Hampton was on the kitchen floor, wounded but alive.

A short time later, defendant told Officer Reagan, "He deserved it. I just couldn't take it anymore. I told him to stop beating on me." "He was beating on me, so I shot him. I told him I'd shoot him if he ever beat on me again." A paramedic heard her say that she wanted to teach Hampton "a lesson." Defendant told another officer at the scene, Officer Terry, "I'm fed up. Yeah, I shot him. I'm tired of him hitting me. He said, 'You're not going to do nothing about it.' I showed him, didn't I? I shot him good. He won't hit anybody else again. Hit me again; I shoot him again. I don't care if I go to jail. Push come to shove, I guess people gave it to him, and, kept hitting me. I warned him. I warned him not to hit me. He wouldn't listen."

Officer Terry took defendant to the police station, where she told the following story. The day before the shooting, Hampton had been drinking. He hit defendant while they were driving home in their truck and continued hitting her when they arrived. He told her, "I'll kill you," and shot at her. The bullet went through a bedroom window and struck a tree outside. The day of the shooting, Hampton "got drunk," swore at her, and started hitting her again. He walked into the kitchen. Defendant saw the gun in the living room and picked it up. Her jaw hurt, and she was in pain. She pointed the gun at Hampton and said, "You're not going to hit me anymore." Hampton said, "What are you doing?" Believing that Hampton was about to pick something up to hit her with, she shot him. She then put the gun down and went outside to wait for the police. [*she felt threatened.*]

Hampton later died of a gunshot wound to his chest. The neighbor who spoke with Officer Reagan testified that shortly before the shooting, she heard defendant, but not Hampton, shouting. The evening before, the neighbor had heard a gunshot. Defendant's blood contained no drugs but had a blood-alcohol level of .17 percent. Hampton's blood contained no drugs or alcohol.

B. Defense Evidence

Defendant claimed she shot Hampton in self-defense. To support the claim, the defense presented first expert testimony and then nonexpert testimony, including that of defendant herself.

1. Expert Testimony

Dr. Lee Bowker testified as an expert on battered women's syndrome. The syndrome, he testified, "is not just a psychological construction, but it's a term for a wide variety of controlling mechanisms that the man or it can be a woman, but in general for this syndrome it's a man, uses against the woman, and for the effect that those control mechanisms have."

Dr. Bowker had studied about 1,000 battered women and found them often inaccurately portrayed "as cardboard figures, paper-thin punching bags who merely absorb the violence but didn't do anything about it." He found that battered women often employ strategies to stop the beatings, including hiding, running away, counter-violence, seeking the help of friends and family, going to a shelter, and contacting police. Nevertheless, many battered women remain in the relationship because of lack of self-confidence, inadequate police response, and a fear (often justified) of reprisals by the batterer. "The battering man will make the battered woman depend on him and generally succeed at least for a time." A battered woman often feels responsible for the abusive relationship, and "she just can't figure out a way to please him better so he'll stop beating her." In sum, "It really is the physical control of the woman through economics and through relative social isolation combined with the psychological techniques that make her so dependent."

Many battered women go from one abusive relationship to another and seek a strong man to protect them from the previous abuser. "[W]ith each successful victimization, the person becomes less able to avoid the next one." The violence can gradually escalate, as the batterer keeps control using ever more severe actions, including rape, torture, violence against the woman's loved ones or pets, and death threats. Battered women sense this escalation. In Dr. Bowker's "experience with battered women who kill in self-defense their abusers, it's always related to their perceived change of what's going on in a relationship. They become very sensitive to what sets off batterers. They watch for this stuff very carefully. [¶] . . . Anybody who is abused over a period of time becomes sensitive to the abuser's behavior and when she sees a change acceleration begin in that behavior, it tells them something is going to happen . . . ."

Dr. Bowker interviewed defendant for a full day. He believed she suffered not only from battered women's syndrome, but also from being the child of an alcoholic and an incest victim. He testified that all three of defendant's partners before Hampton were abusive and significantly older than she.

Dr. Bowker described defendant's relationship with Hampton. Hampton was a 49-year-old man who weighed almost twice as much as defendant. The two had a battering relationship that Dr. Bowker characterized as a "traditional cycle of violence." The cycle included phases of tension building, violence, and then forgiveness-seeking in which Hampton would promise not to batter defendant any more and she would believe him. During this period, there would be occasional good times. For example, defendant told Dr. Bowker that Hampton would give her a rose. "That's one of the things that hooks people in. Intermittent reinforcement is the key." But after a while, the violence would begin again. The violence would recur because "basically . . . the woman doesn't perfectly obey. That's the bottom line." For example, defendant would talk to another man, or fail to clean house "just so."

The situation worsened over time, especially when Hampton got off parole shortly before his death. He became more physically and emotionally abusive, repeatedly threatened defendant's life, and even shot at her the night before his death. Hampton often allowed defendant to go out, but she was afraid to flee because she felt he would find her as he had in the past. "He enforced her belief that she can never escape him." Dr. Bowker testified that unless her injuries were so severe that "something absolutely had to be treated," he would not expect her to seek medical treatment. "That's the pattern of her life. . . ."

Dr. Bowker believed defendant's description of her experiences. In his opinion, she suffered from battered women's syndrome in "about as extreme a pattern as you could find."

2. Nonexpert Testimony

Defendant confirmed many of the details of her life and relationship with Hampton underlying Dr. Bowker's opinion. She testified that her father forcefully molested her from the time she was seven years old until she was fifteen. She described her relationship with another abusive man as being like "Nightmare on Elm Street." Regarding Hampton, she testified that they often argued and that he beat her regularly. Both were heavy drinkers. Hampton once threw a can of beer at her face, breaking her nose. Her dental plates hurt because Hampton hit her so often. He often kicked her, but usually hit her in the back of the head because, he told her, it "won't leave bruises." Hampton sometimes threatened to kill her, and often said she "would live to regret it." Matters got worse towards the end.

Continuous Pattern of abusive behavior

The evening before the shooting, March 27, 1992, Hampton arrived home "very drunk." He yelled at her and called her names. At one point when she was standing by the bedroom window, he fired his .357 Magnum revolver at her. She testified, "He didn't miss me by much either." She was "real scared."

The next day, the two drove into the mountains. They argued, and Hampton continually hit her. While returning, he said that their location would be a good place to kill her because "they wouldn't find [her] for a while." She took it as a joke, although she feared him. When they returned, the argument continued. He hit her again, then entered the kitchen. He threatened, "This time, bitch, when I shoot at you, I won't miss." He came from the kitchen and reached for the gun on the living room table. She grabbed it first, pointed at him, and told him "that he wasn't going to hit [her]." She backed Hampton into the kitchen. He reached for her hand and she shot him. She believed he was reaching for the gun and was going to shoot her.

Several other witnesses testified about defendant's relationship with Hampton, his abusive conduct in general, and his physical abuse of, and threats to, defendant in particular. This testimony generally corroborated defendant's. A neighbor testified that the night before the shooting, she heard a gunshot. The next morning, defendant told the neighbor that Hampton had shot at her, and that she was afraid of him. After the shooting, investigators found a bullet hole through the frame of the bedroom window and a bullet embedded in a tree in line with the window. Another neighbor testified that shortly before hearing the shot that killed Hampton, she heard defendant say, "Stop it, Albert. Stop it."

C.   Procedural History

Defendant was charged with murder with personal use of a firearm. At the end of the prosecution's case-in-chief, the court granted defendant's motion under Penal Code section 1118.1 for acquittal of first degree murder.

The court instructed the jury on second degree murder and both voluntary and involuntary manslaughter. It also instructed on self-defense, explaining that an actual and reasonable belief that the killing was necessary was a complete defense; an actual but unreasonable belief was a defense to murder, but not to voluntary manslaughter. In determining reasonableness, the jury was to consider what "would appear to be necessary to a reasonable person in a similar situation and with similar knowledge."

self-defense

The court also instructed:

> Evidence regarding Battered Women's Syndrome has been introduced in this case. Such evidence, if believed, may be considered by you only for the purpose of determining whether or not the defendant held the necessary subjective honest [belief] which is a requirement for both perfect and imperfect self-defense. However, that same evidence regarding Battered Women's Syndrome may not be considered or used by you in evaluating the objective reasonableness requirement for perfect self-defense.
>
> . . .
>
> Battered Women's Syndrome seeks to describe and explain common reactions of women to that experience. Thus, you may consider the evidence concerning the syndrome and its effects only for the limited purpose of showing, if it does show, that the defendant's reactions, as demonstrated by the evidence, are not inconsistent with her having been physically abused or the beliefs, perceptions, or behavior of victims of domestic violence.

During deliberations, the jury asked for and received clarification of the terms "subjectively honest and objectively reasonable." It found defendant guilty of voluntary manslaughter with personal use of a firearm. The court sentenced defendant to prison for eight years, consisting of the lower term of three years for manslaughter, plus the upper term of five years for firearm use. The Court of Appeal remanded for resentencing on the use enhancement, but otherwise affirmed the judgment.

We granted defendant's petition for review.

II.   DISCUSSION

A.   Background

. . . Evidence Code section 1107, subdivision (a), makes admissible in a criminal action expert testimony regarding "battered women's syndrome, including the physical, emotional, or mental effects upon the beliefs, perceptions, or behavior of victims of domestic violence . . . ." Under subdivision (b) of that section, the foundation for admission is sufficient "if the proponent of the evidence establishes its relevance and the proper qualifications of the expert witness." Defendant presented the evidence to support her claim of self-defense. It is undisputed that she established the proper qualifications of the expert witness. The only issue is to what extent defendant established its "relevancy." To resolve this question we must examine California law regarding self-defense.

For killing to be in self-defense, the defendant must actually and reasonably believe in the need to defend. . . . If the belief subjectively exists but is objectively unreasonable, there is "imperfect self-defense," i.e., "the defendant is deemed to have acted without malice and cannot be convicted of murder," but can be convicted of manslaughter. (In re Christian S. (1994) 7 Cal. 4th 768, 783.) To constitute "perfect self-defense," i.e., to exonerate the person completely, the belief must also be objectively reasonable. . . . As the Legislature has stated, "[T]he circumstances must be sufficient to excite the fears of a reasonable person . . . ." (Pen. Code § 197, subds. 2, 3.) Moreover, for either perfect or imperfect self-defense, the fear must be of imminent harm. "Fear of future harm—no matter how great the fear and no matter how great the likelihood of the harm—will not suffice. The defendant's fear must be of *imminent* danger to life or great bodily injury." (In re Christian S., supra, 7 Cal. 4th at p. 783, italics in original.)

[margin note: definition & Requirement for self-defense]

Although the belief in the need to defend must be objectively reasonable, a jury must consider what "would appear to be necessary to a reasonable person in a similar situation and with similar knowledge. . . ." (CALJIC No. 5.50.) It judges reasonableness "from the point of view of a reasonable person in the position of defendant. . . ." (People v. McGee (1947) 31 Cal. 2d 229, 238.) To do this, it must consider all the " ' "facts and circumstances . . . in determining whether the defendant acted in a manner in which *a reasonable man* would act in protecting his own life or bodily safety." ' " (People v. Moore (1954) 43 Cal. 2d 517, 528, italics in original.) As we stated long ago, ". . . a defendant is entitled to have a jury take into consideration all the elements in the case which might be expected to operate on his mind . . . ." (People v. Smith (1907) 151 Cal. 619, 628.)

. . .

. . . Although the ultimate test of reasonableness is objective, in determining whether a reasonable person in defendant's position would have believed in the need to defend, the jury must consider all of the relevant circumstances in which defendant found herself.

With these principles in mind, we now consider the relevance of evidence of battered women's syndrome to the elements of self-defense.

B.   Battered Women's Syndrome[70]

Battered women's syndrome "has been defined as 'a series of common characteristics that appear in women who are abused physically and psychologically over an extended period of time by the dominant male figure in their lives.' " (State v. Kelly (1984) 97 N.J. 178, 193.) . . .

'issue'

The trial court allowed the jury to consider the battered women's syndrome evidence in deciding whether defendant actually believed she needed to kill in self-defense. The question here is whether the evidence was also relevant on the reasonableness of that belief. . . .

. . .

The Attorney General argues . . . that evidence of battered women's syndrome is irrelevant to reasonableness. We disagree. . . . [T]he jury, in determining objective reasonableness, must view the situation from the *defendant's perspective*. Here, for example, Dr. Bowker testified that the violence can escalate and that a battered woman can become increasingly sensitive to the abuser's behavior, testimony relevant to determining whether defendant reasonably believed when she fired the gun that this time the threat to her life was imminent. Indeed, the prosecutor argued that, "from an objective, reasonable man's standard, there was no reason for her to go get that gun. This threat that she says he made was like so many threats before. There was no reason for her to react that way." Dr. Bowker's testimony supplied a response that the jury might not otherwise receive. As violence increases over time, and threats gain credibility, a battered person might become sensitized and thus able reasonably to discern when danger is real and when it is not. "[T]he expert's testimony might also enable the jury to find that the battered [woman] . . . is particularly able to predict accurately the likely extent of violence in any attack on her. That conclusion could significantly affect the jury's evaluation of the *reasonableness* of defendant's fear for her life." (State v. Kelly (1984) 97 N.J. 178, italics added, fn. omitted.)

The Attorney General concedes that Hampton's behavior towards defendant, including prior threats and violence, was relevant to reasonableness . . . but distinguishes between evidence of this *behavior*—which the trial court fully admitted—and *expert testimony* about its effects on defendant. The distinction is untenable. "To effectively present the situation as perceived by the defendant, and the reasonableness of her fear, the defense

---

70. We use the term "battered women's syndrome" because Evidence Code section 1107 and the cases use that term. We note, however, that according to amici curiae California Alliance Against Domestic Violence et al., ". . . the preferred term among many experts today is 'expert testimony on battering and its effects' or 'expert testimony on battered women's experiences.' Domestic violence experts have critiqued the phrase 'battered women's syndrome' because (1) it implies that there is one syndrome which all battered women develop, (2) it has pathological connotations which suggest that battered women suffer from some sort of sickness, (3) expert testimony on domestic violence refers to more than women's psychological reactions to violence, (4) it focuses attention on the battered woman rather than on the batterer's coercive and controlling behavior and (5) it creates an image of battered women as suffering victims rather than as active survivors." (Fns. omitted.)

has the option to explain her feelings to enable the jury to overcome stereotyped impressions about women who remain in abusive relationships. It is appropriate that the jury be given a professional explanation of the battering syndrome and its effects on the woman through the use of expert testimony . . . ." (State v. Allery (1984) 101 Wash. 2d 591.)

The Attorney General also argues that allowing consideration of this testimony would result in an undesirable "battle of the experts" and raises the specter of other battles of experts regarding other syndromes. The Legislature, however, has decided that, if relevant, expert evidence on battered women's syndrome is admissible. . . . We have found it relevant; it is therefore admissible. We express no opinion on the admissibility of expert testimony regarding other possible syndromes in support of a claim of self-defense . . . .

Contrary to the Attorney General's argument, we are not changing the standard from objective to subjective, or replacing the reasonable "person" standard with a reasonable "battered woman" standard. Our decision would not, in another context, compel adoption of a " 'reasonable gang member' standard." . . . The jury must consider defendant's situation and knowledge, which makes the evidence relevant, but the ultimate question is whether a reasonable *person*, not a reasonable battered woman, would believe in the need to kill to prevent imminent harm. Moreover, it is the *jury*, not the expert, that determines whether defendant's belief and, ultimately, her actions, were objectively reasonable.

Battered women's syndrome evidence was also relevant to defendant's credibility. . . . For example, in urging the jury not to believe defendant's testimony that Hampton shot at her the night before the killing, the prosecutor argued that "if this defendant truly believed that [Hampton] had shot at her, on that night, I mean she would have left. . . . [¶] If she really believed that he had tried to shoot her, she would not have stayed." Dr. Bowker's testimony " 'would help dispel the ordinary lay person's perception that a woman in a battering relationship is free to leave at any time. The expert evidence would counter any "common sense" conclusions by the jury that if the beatings were really that bad the women would have left her husband much earlier. Popular misconceptions about battered women would be put to rest . . . .' " (People v. Day, 2 Cal. App. 4th [405] at p. 417 [(1992)], quoting State v. Hodges (1986) 239 Kan. 63.) "[I]f the jury had understood [defendant's] conduct in light of [battered women's syndrome] evidence, then the jury may well have concluded her version of the events was sufficiently credible to warrant an acquittal on the facts as she related them." (People v. Day, supra, 2 Cal. App. 4th at p. 415).

. . .

We do not hold that Dr. Bowker's entire testimony was relevant to both prongs of perfect self-defense. Just as many types of evidence may be relevant to some disputed issues but not all, some of the expert evidence was no doubt relevant only to the subjective existence of defendant's belief. Evidence merely showing that a person's use of deadly force is scientifically explainable or empirically common does not, in itself, show it was objectively reasonable. To dispel any possible confusion, it might be appropriate for the court, on request, to clarify that, in assessing reasonableness, the question is whether a reasonable person in the defendant's circumstances would have perceived a threat of imminent injury or death, and not whether killing the abuser was reasonable in the sense of being an understandable response to ongoing abuse; and that, therefore, in making that assessment, the jury may not consider evidence merely showing that an abused person's use of force against the abuser is understandable.

We also emphasize that, as with any evidence, the jury may give this testimony whatever weight it deems appropriate in light of the evidence as a whole. The ultimate judgment of reasonableness is solely for the jury. We simply hold that evidence of battered woman's syndrome is generally *relevant* to the reasonableness, as well as the subjective existence, of defendant's belief in the need to defend, and, to the extent it is relevant, the jury may *consider* it in deciding both questions. . . .

. . .

———

122. After a period of some uncertainty about the scientific validity of the so-called battered women's syndrome, testimony about a defendant's abuse by the victim of a homicide as well as expert testimony about the syndrome are now generally admissible. Such testimony may be relevant both to the defendant's belief that she had to use deadly force to defend herself and to the reasonableness of her belief, although, as the court stated in *Humphrey*, "the ultimate test of reasonableness is objective," p. 211. For other representative cases, see People v. Christel, 537 N.W.2d 194 (Mich. 1995); State v. Kelly, 478 A.2d 364 (N.J.1984). See also State v. Mott, 931 P.2d 1046 (Ariz.1997), holding that expert testimony about battered women's syndrome is not admissible to support a defense of diminished capacity. The defendant in *Mott* was convicted of child abuse and first-degree murder, arising out of her failure to protect her child from injury or to secure medical attention for injuries to the child by the defendant's boyfriend. In a number of jurisdictions, as in California, the admissibility of such evidence has been mandated by statute.

The scientific status of the syndrome as a genuine syndrome and its effect on the capacity of a woman accurately to perceive and to respond to an abusive situation are controversial. It has also been suggested that incautious application of the syndrome, even if it exonerates or mitigates a defendant's culpability, preserves the stereotype of women in earlier criminal law as less competent and, therefore, less responsible than men. Such controversies may not engage what is probably the strongest ground of support for the syndrome's admissibility: the unquestioned phenomenon of widespread domestic violence by men against women. In this context as in some others, see *Alexander*, p. 92 above, and the comments following, one might ask whether the criminal law transforms a *social* factor that might help to explain and perhaps mitigate a homicide into an *individual* one.

Are there reasons why the incidence of domestic violence should be taken into account but the racially charged and violent atmosphere surrounding the events in *Alexander* should not?

123. The requirement that the danger be imminent has often troubled the courts in the context of a claim that the defendant is a battered woman. In State v. Norman, 378 S.E.2d 8 (N.C.1989), for example, the defendant, who had been subjected to extreme, persistent abuse by her husband, shot him while he was asleep. Declining to modify the requirement that the danger be imminent, the court said, "[S]tretching the law of self-defense to fit the facts of this case would require changing the 'imminent death or great bodily harm' requirement to something substantially more indefinite than previously required and would weaken our assurances that justification for the taking of human life remains firmly rooted in real or apparent necessity. . . . [To relax the requirement] would tend to categorically legalize the opportune killing of abusive husbands by their wives solely on the basis of the wives' testimony concerning their subjective speculation as to the probability of future felonious assaults by their husbands. Homicidal self-help would then become a lawful solution, and perhaps the easiest and most effective solution, to this problem." Id. at 15.

A dissenting judge observed that the evidence "revealed no letup of tension or fear, no moment in which the defendant felt released from impending serious harm, even while the defendant slept. . . . Where the defendant is a battered wife, there is no analogue to the victim-turned-aggressor, who . . . turns the tables on the decedent in a fresh confrontation. Where the defendant is a battered wife, the affray out of which the killing arises can be a continuing assault. There was evidence before the jury that it had not been defendant but her husband who had initiated 'the affray,' which the jury could have regarded as lasting twenty years, three days, or any number of hours preceding his death. And there was evidence from which the jury could infer that in defendant's mind the affray reached beyond the moment at which her husband fell asleep. Like the ongoing threats of death or great bodily harm, which she might reasonably have perceived as imminent, her husband continued to be the aggressor and she the victim." Id. at 18, 21.

To the same effect, in a case also involving extreme, persistent abuse of the defendant by her husband, see State v. Stewart, 763 P.2d 572 (Kan. 1988). In *Stewart*, a dissenting judge observed:

> It is a jury question to determine if the battered woman who kills her husband as he sleeps fears he will find and kill her if she leaves, as is usually claimed. Under such circumstances the battered woman is not under actual physical attack when she kills but such attack is imminent, and as a result she believes her life is in imminent danger. She may kill during the tension-building stage when the abuse is apparently not as severe as it sometimes has been, but nevertheless has escalated so that she is afraid the acute stage to come will be fatal

to her. She only acts on such fear if she has some survival instinct remaining after the husband-induced "learned helplessness." . . . The jury . . . needs to know about the nature of the cumulative terror under which a battered woman exists and that a batterer's threats and brutality can make life-threatening danger imminent to the victim of that brutality even though, at the moment, the batterer is passive. Where a person believes she must kill or be killed, and there is the slightest basis in fact for this belief, it is a question for the jury as to whether the danger was imminent.

Id. at 582–83, 595.

Also, see People v. Yaklich, 833 P.2d 758 (Colo.Ct.App.1991), reviewing cases construing the requirement of imminent danger in the context of a battered woman defense and concluding that an instruction on self defense is not available when the defendant, who claims that she is a battered woman, hires a third person to kill the alleged batterer.

In State v. Hundley, 693 P.2d 475 (Kan.1985), however, which the court described as "a textbook case of the battered wife," id. at 478, the court held that it was reversible error to instruct the jury that self-defense must be a response to reasonable belief that it is necessary to defend oneself against *"immediate* use of unlawful force," rather than *"imminent* use."* It said:

Under the facts of this case, after ten years of abuse, Betty finally became so desperate in her terror of Carl she fled. Her escape was to no avail; he followed her. Her fear was justified. He broke through the locked door of her motel room and started his abuse again. Carl's threat was no less life-threatening with him sitting in the motel room tauntingly playing with his beer bottle than if he were advancing toward her. The objective test is how a reasonably prudent battered wife would perceive Carl's demeanor. Expert testimony is admissible to prove the nature and effect of wife-beating just as it is admissible to prove the standard mental state of hostages, prisoners of war, and others under long-term life-threatening conditions. Thus, we can see the use of the word "immediate" in the instruction on self-defense places undue emphasis on the immediate action of the deceased, and obliterates the nature of the buildup of terror and fear which had been systematically created over a long period of time. "Imminent" describes the situation more accurately.

Id. at 479.

A dissenting judge observed: "There were only two persons in the motel room. One admits killing the other. The only version of what transpired is that of the defendant herein. Taking this as true, the deceased told the defendant to leave the premises, giving her money to buy cigarettes. The deceased then sat on the bed in his shorts, not even looking in defendant's direction. The defendant reached for her purse by the door, took a gun therefrom and fired five shots at the deceased. The parties were in a motel room in a busy part of the city of Topeka in the early evening hours. They were not in some remote area where help would be difficult to obtain. At the very least, defendant would have had a five minute head start on the defendant had she failed to return with the cigarettes. I fail to see how, in this factual situation, it could be reversible error to use 'immediate' rather than 'imminent' in the self-defense instruction as it would not have altered the outcome." Id. at 481.

124. See Jahnke v. State, 682 P.2d 991 (Wyo.1984), a case of patricide in which the teenage defendant introduced evidence of persistent abuse by his father. The court held that it was not an abuse of discretion to exclude psychiatric testimony about a "battered child" syndrome, which the defendant sought to introduce to support his claim of self-defense. In the course of a lengthy opinion, the court observed:

> It is clear that self-defense is circumscribed by circumstances involving a confrontation, usually encompassing some overt act or acts by the deceased, which would induce a reasonable person to fear that his life was in danger or that at least he was threatened with great bodily harm.
>
> . . . Although many people, and the public media, seem to be prepared to espouse the notion that a victim of abuse is entitled to kill the abuser that special justification defense is antithetical to the mores of modern civilized society. It is difficult enough to justify capital punishment as an appropriate response of society to criminal acts even after the circumstances have been carefully evaluated by a number of people. To permit capital punishment to be imposed upon the subjective conclusion of the individual that prior acts and conduct of the deceased justified the killing would amount to a leap into the abyss of anarchy.

Id. at 997.

In Werner v. State, 711 S.W.2d 639 (Tex.Crim.App.1986), the defendant was convicted of murder. He argued on appeal that the trial court improperly excluded evidence of the "Holocaust syndrome," which, he asserted, was relevant to his claim of self-defense. Members of the defendant's family had been in concentration camps, where some had died. His father and grandmother, who were survivors, often told him stories about the concentration camps. According to the excluded expert testimony, the Holocaust syndrome, manifest in the children of survivors of concentration camps, is a perception that one must defend himself if his life is threatened and should not retreat. The conviction was affirmed.

See also State v. Hampton, 558 N.W.2d 884 (Wis.App.1996), in which the defendant sought to introduce evidence of his "psycho-social" history as a defense to a charge of intentional homicide by a dangerous weapon. The defendant shot the victim twice in the head at point-blank range. They were both 15 years old. The defense argued that the defendant's history, filled with violence and threats of violence by others toward him or observed by him, affected his perception of the need to defend himself in the circumstances of the killing. The court upheld exclusion of such evidence as irrelevant.

DEFENSE OF OTHERS

Commonwealth v. Martin

369 Mass. 640, 341 N.E.2d 885 (1976)

■ KAPLAN, J. The defendant Daniel R. Martin appeals . . . from his multiple convictions . . . arising from a clash between inmates and guards at Massachusetts Correctional Institution at Concord on October 15, 1972. The issue on appeal is whether the trial judge committed error in failing to instruct the jury with respect to the defendant's claimed justification or defense, namely, that the acts of which he was accused were part of an attempt on his part to come to the aid of a fellow inmate and friend, Gene Tremblay (tried and convicted together with the defendant), who was being unlawfully beaten by prison guards. . . .

1. We sketch very briefly the facts as they appeared at trial. The prosecution was of course intent to show that the defendant's acts were simply aggressive attacks on the correction officers in a prison brawl, while the defendant strove to prove that he acted honestly and reasonably upon observing the inmate Tremblay being beaten by the officers.

According to the prosecution's case, a struggle erupted between two correction officers and two inmates as the inmates were being escorted from a second-floor segregation unit down to a first-floor area for showers and exercise. One of the inmates, Tremblay, fought with an officer near the stairwell and the officer fell or was shoved down the stairs, with Tremblay following him down. The fallen officer yelled to officers on the first floor for help, and one of them, John Quealey, restrained Tremblay, while others went to summon aid. Officer Quealey held Tremblay by the hair while pushing him toward and into an open cell on the first floor. According to the prosecution's proof, Tremblay was held in the cell but not beaten; no clubs or other weapons were used by the officers in the affray although it appeared that clubs were kept in a nearby desk.

Meantime the second inmate involved in the fight on the second floor had taken the cell keys from the other officer and released other inmates of the segregation unit. Several of the inmates, including the defendant, ran down the stairs and met officers who had arrived to give help. In the melee, Officer Quealey was stabbed a number of times in the chest and once on the arm. Officer Quealey testified that as he was struggling with an inmate, he saw the defendant strike at him three times, and he saw a knife in the defendant's hand as the defendant stepped back. Other officers testified that they saw an attack by the defendant on Officer Quealey, or saw the defendant with a knife immediately after the attack (the testimony was not entirely consistent). There was further testimony that the defendant struck Frederick Taylor, a correction officer, with his fist and threatened him with a knife, saying "Back off, or I will give it to you, too."

The defendant took the stand to give his version of the facts. He was corroborated in part by the codefendant Tremblay. Because the defendant's view was obstructed by a partition between the rows of cells on either side of the second floor, he had not been able to see the fight there and did not know who had started it. When his cell was opened, he walked to the end of the partition but, seeing blood on the floor and hearing sounds of a struggle on the stairs, he started back to his cell. He then heard Tremblay calling for help and surmised that Tremblay was in grave danger. The defendant raced down the stairs and saw Officer Quealey and two other officers striking Tremblay with clubs and a metal mop handle as he lay on the floor of an open cell. Tremblay had his arms over his head and was trying to fend off the blows. He was yelling for help. The defendant struck several officers, including Officers Quealey and Taylor, with his fists in his effort to pull the officers off Tremblay. The defendant denied that he had a knife at this time; he did not stab Officer Quealey or threaten Officer Taylor with a knife. He testified that he first saw the knife on the floor where another inmate had dropped it after the stabbing of Officer Quealey.

The violence ended when assistant deputy superintendent Nicholas Genakos ordered the officers to withdraw while he and Jon Cooke, a social worker, negotiated with the inmates. During the negotiation Cooke saw the defendant with a knife and, when Genakos asked for it, the defendant said, "We'll see how this goes." The defendant testified that he made the statement and that he did have a knife, but only for a short interval when Cooke saw it. A search by the State police after the inmates had returned peaceably to their cells failed to turn up a knife.

The evidence on the part of the defendant, summarized above, was sufficient to lay a basis for a charge to the jury on the justification claimed by him (see point 3 below). It is of course immaterial that the triers might very well, in the end, lend no credence whatever to the defendant's version of the facts. . . .

2.   The judge instructed the jury with respect to self-defense and even related these instructions to the question whether the defendant was privileged to use a dangerous weapon to protect himself from attack by Officer Quealey. But he gave the jury no instructions on the subject of the privileged use of force to protect another. This failure seems to have been due to the judge's belief that the claimed justification was not recognized in the law of Massachusetts.

The defendant made due request in writing for jury instructions on the subject. His request was submitted the day before the judge charged the jury. The main requested instruction (No. 9) was a quotation from the relevant statute law of Illinois as reproduced in the case of People v. Johnson, 4 Ill. App. 3d 249, 251 (1972): "A person is justified in the use of force against another when and to the extent that he reasonably believes that such conduct is necessary to defend himself or another against such other's imminent use of unlawful force . . . ." Smith–Hurd Ill. Ann. Stat. c. 38, § 7–1 (1972). . . .

. . .

3. We hold that a justification corresponding roughly to that quoted from the Illinois statute is recognized by the law of the Commonwealth. . . .

. . .

[I]t is hardly conceivable that the law of the Commonwealth, or, indeed, of any jurisdiction, should mark as criminal those who intervene forcibly to protect others; for the law to do so would aggravate the fears which lead to the alienation of people from one another, an alienation symbolized for our time by the notorious Genovese incident.[71] To the fear of "involvement" and of injury to oneself if one answered a call for help would be added the fear of possible criminal prosecution.

It becomes necessary to sketch the conditions justifying the use of intervening protective force. The essence is this: An actor is justified in using force against another to protect a third person when (a) a reasonable person in the actor's position would believe his intervention to be necessary for the protection of the third person, and (b) in the circumstances as that reasonable person would believe them to be, the third person would be justified in using such force to protect himself. The reasonableness of the belief may depend in part on the relationships among the persons involved (a matter to which we return below). The actor's justification is lost if he uses excessive force, e.g., aggressive or deadly force unwarranted for the protective purpose.

Of course, the subject cannot be exhausted in a paragraph. Without subscribing in advance to all the relevant provisions of the Model Penal Code of the American Law Institute, we recommend it for study.[72] Accelerated by that Code, the trend, which is exemplified by legislation adopted in many States, has been to interweave closely the justification of defense of a third person with self-defense; to eliminate some earlier authority restricting the justification of third-person defense to situations where the third person is seen retrospectively to have been entitled to use force in his own defense (regardless of the belief, which might be mistaken, of the "reasonable person" at the time); and to remove earlier artificial or factitious restrictions of the justification, e.g., restrictions to protection of spouse, child, parent, master, or servant.

. . .

. . . [T]he justification of defense of a third person does not necessarily stop short at the prison gates. But the fact that an episode occurs in prison may have considerable significance. So the question of the reasonableness

[71] See p. 295 below.   [72] See p. 235 below.

of a belief that an inmate would be justified in using force against a prison guard, thus justifying intervening protective force, is conditioned by the fact that the guard, by the nature of his job, is himself privileged to apply force to inmates when necessary to preserve order in the institution. Therefore the guard's mere taking an inmate into custody or holding him in custody would not be a proper occasion for intervening force. This may have an important bearing on the present case in the event of retrial.

. . .

125. As the court observed in *Martin*, the law in a number of states, by statute or judicial decision, formerly restricted the right to use deadly force in defense of others to those within a narrow circle, typically including close relations and servant or master. See, e.g., Blankenship v. State, 719 P.2d 829 (Okla.Crim.App.1986) (defense of another limited by statute to spouse, parent, child, master, mistress, or servant). Recent statutory formulations have eliminated such restrictions.

What reason might there be for restricting the circle of those whom one can defend, when it is necessary, with deadly force?

126. Should the right to defend oneself and the right to defend another, whether a close relation or not, stand on the same footing? Someone who acts to defend himself knows what he is doing, at least to the extent of knowing that he is not the aggressor.

> [T]he defendant was walking . . . toward his home . . . and . . . he heard noises as of an altercation, and upon coming nearer he saw his brother, John Maine . . . engaged in a fight with two other persons, one the deceased, James Murphy, and the other Frank Bower. The defendant had but one hand, his right arm having been amputated at the wrist several years before. He instantly . . . went to help his brother, calling out to his brother's assailants to let him alone or they would get cut or stabbed. He drew out his pocket or jack-knife, having a single blade two and a quarter inches long, opened it with his teeth, and rushing into the fight, engaged with Murphy, and in the contest struck him a single blow with his knife; the blade reached his heart and caused his death a few minutes later. The defense was justifiable homicide in that the defendant had reasonable ground to apprehend a design on the part of Murphy to do some great personal injury to his brother, and that there was imminent danger of such design being accomplished. . . . The fight between John Maine and the deceased and Bowers was active for a minute before the defendant came up and discovered that his brother was engaged in it.

People v. Maine, 59 N.E. 696 (N.Y.1901). The prosecutor offered evidence of John Maine's conduct before the defendant came on the scene, which tended to show that John Maine was the aggressor. Should the evidence have been admitted?

The New York Court of Appeals thought not. "Of course the acts and conduct of the defendant must be judged solely with reference to the situation as it was when he first and afterwards saw it." Id. at 696.

Some courts have reached the contrary conclusion and have held that a defendant who goes to the aid of another stands fully in the latter's shoes, by which reasoning the defendant's criminal liability would have been the same as John Maine's, had the latter killed Murphy. E.g., State v. Barnes, 675 S.W.2d 195, 196 (Tenn.Crim.App.1984): "[A] person interfering in a dispute, affray, or fight on behalf of another simply steps into the latter's shoes. He may lawfully do in another's defense only what that person could have done, and no more. He stands on the same plane, is entitled to the same rights, and is subject to the same conditions, limitations, and responsibilities as the person defended. And his act must receive the same construction as the act of the person defended would receive if the killing had been committed by that person. Thus, a person is not entitled to the plea of defense of another unless a plea of self-defense would have been available to the person on whose behalf he intervened. In other words, a person can do whatever the person for whom he intervened could have done in his own self-defense."

There is reason to suspect that the "other person's shoes" metaphor may have confused the issue so far as the defender's belief is concerned. See, for example, State v. Saunders, 330 S.E.2d 674 (W.Va.1985), in which the court, expressing agreement with *Barnes*, above, said: "One simply steps into the shoes of the victim and is able to do only as much as the victim himself would lawfully be permitted to do," id. at 677, and then went on to hold that an instruction referring to the *defendant's* belief in the necessity to use force should have been given. (Might one say that the defender stands in the other person's shoes, but does not wear the other person's hat? Still a bad metaphor, no doubt, but at least it directs attention to the defender's head and not her feet.)

As indicated in *Martin*, above, most recent authority, including the Model Penal Code § 3.05, p. 238 below, and other statutory formulations, have allowed one to go to the aid of a third person if the actor reasonably believes such aid is necessary in the third person's defense. E.g., State v. Fair, 211 A.2d 359, 367–68 (N.J.1965):

> There are . . . two approaches as to the scope of the right of one person to intervene in defense of another. One is that the fault of the defended party is imputed to the one who intervenes on his behalf, while the other is that the intervening party is bound only by his own intent. The former, commonly referred to as the *"alter ego"* rule, emphasizes that the right of one person to defend another is co-extensive with the right of the other to defend himself. The latter, categorized as the "objective test" theory, proceeds on the thesis that one who intervenes in a struggle under a reasonable but mistaken

belief that he is protecting another who he assumes is being unlawfully assaulted is thereby exonerated from criminal liability. . . .

New Jersey has aligned itself with the latter view; the test of whether a party may intervene in defense of a third person being determined by the subjective intent of the intervenor, subject only to the qualification that a jury objectively find that he reasonably arrived at the conclusion that the apparent victim was in peril, and that the force he used was necessary. Thus, the so-called "reasonable mistake of fact" doctrine is given its due, both as to the amount of force and the initial lawfulness of the intervention, and precludes criminal liability even though it later appears that the person in whose behalf he intervened was in fact the aggressor or that no defensive measures on his part were actually necessary. . . .

The defense is founded upon, and strengthened by, persuasive policy considerations. Not only is it just that one should not be convicted of a crime if he selflessly attempts to protect the victim of an apparently unjustified assault, but how else can we encourage bystanders to go to the aid of another who is being subjected to an assault?

See State v. Penn, 568 P.2d 797, 799 (Wash.1977): "We are aware this approach may cause an innocent person who is striking in self-defense, to be harmed with impunity merely because appearances were against him. However, we consider this to be a lesser evil than allowing an innocent defender who is acting under a mistake of fact to be convicted of a serious crime."

DEFENSE OF PROPERTY

How should the law reconcile the propositions (a) that persons are strongly attached to their property and regard it as natural for someone to resist with all the force that is necessary an effort to dispossess him of what is his, and (b) that no property right is superior to the value of human life? Even though the law does not in general allow a person to endanger life to protect property, are there circumstances in which an exception should be made?

Crawford v. State

231 Md. 354, 190 A.2d 538 (1963)

■ BRUNE, CHIEF JUDGE. The defendant-appellant, Crawford, was tried in the Criminal Court of Baltimore before the court, sitting without a jury, on a charge of murder, was convicted of manslaughter and was sentenced to eight years' imprisonment. His defense was that he was defending himself and his home against an attack by the decedent Bobbie Ferrell, who was seeking to force his way into the appellant's home to beat and rob him. He admitted having fired the fatal shot, but claimed that he intended only to shoot the intruder in the hand and that shooting him in the head was accidental. The trial judge believed at least most of the essentials of the defendant's statements, but found that he had used excessive force in resisting the intrusion and for that reason found him guilty of manslaughter. The defendant appeals.

The appellant was a forty-two year old man who had suffered from ulcers and nervous disorders, and was on relief for disability. He lived in a first floor front room at 16 North Pearl Street, in Baltimore, and for a week or two before the shooting had shared his quarters with a man named William Robinson. No one else lived in the building. There was a front outside door which opened into a vestibule, and there was an inner door between the vestibule and a long hallway. This inner door could be secured by a spring lock, which seems to have been the only lock protecting the appellant's room. One of four panes of glass in the upper portion of this door had been broken and had been replaced by a piece of masonite nailed to the inside of the door. The appellant's room opened off the hallway just inside this inner door.

The deceased, Bobbie Ferrell, his brother Lee, and one Harold Austin (known as "Slim"), and probably others, had been in the habit of "hanging around" the appellant's room or the front of the house where he lived. Bobbie Ferrell, according to the death certificate, was twenty-three years old and the other two named above were near his age. The exact state of relations between these boys and the appellant, Crawford, is by no means clear. It seems that they had gone into Crawford's room pretty much whenever they pleased and that if they had ever been welcome, they no longer were so on March 12, 1962, the day when the shooting here involved occurred. On that very day Crawford had complained about them to the police and the police had visited his home at some time during the morning, but found none of the boys there at the time.

The appellant stated that Bobbie Ferrell and Austin had come to his room shortly after the police left, that Ferrell accused the appellant of being a "police snitcher," that Ferrell hit him in the face and charged him with trying to get Ferrell locked up for stealing, that Ferrell asked him for money and Ferrell and Austin left when the appellant said that he had none, but would have some later in the day.

That day the appellant was to receive his welfare check by mail. He stated that in order to keep it away from Ferrell and Austin, he went out on the street and met the postman about a block from his home, got his welfare check, cashed it at a nearby bar, and left $45.00 of the proceeds with a neighbor for safekeeping. He then met the police officers who had visited his home earlier that day and told them that the boys had come to his home and demanded money. They told him to call the police if the boys returned.

When he met the officers the appellant was on his way to a pawnshop. There he redeemed a shotgun which he had pawned about a year before, and he took it home "to keep it there to scare them away." According to the appellant, Ferrell and Austin soon came back to his room and Ferrell picked up the shotgun from a bed, looked for shells, and said that if he found them he would use the gun. He did not find any; but again according to the appellant, Austin, with a knife in his hand, threw an arm around the appellant's neck, and Austin and Ferrell proceeded to rifle the appellant's pockets and took about $7.00 from him. The appellant's testimony is confirmed to some extent by Robinson, who was present at the time of this visit, but Robinson's testimony is somewhat confused. A third man, identified only by the name Thomas, was reportedly present at this second visit of Ferrell and Austin and later (at the time of the shooting), but he did not testify. Robinson confirmed the appellant's statements that Ferrell and Austin had visited the appellant's room before the appellant got his check and redeemed the gun. He also confirmed Crawford's statement that they returned after Crawford had cashed his check and brought back the gun and that they demanded money.

There are some differences between the appellant's testimony and Robinson's as to what was said at the time of Ferrell's and Austin's visits, and Robinson states (the appellant does not) that Lee Ferrell was also present. Robinson confirms the appellant's statements that Ferrell demanded money and said that they were coming back to get it, and he indicates that they knew that the appellant had received or was to receive his relief check that day. Robinson's testimony does not confirm (and Austin's testimony contradicts) the appellant's testimony that Ferrell and Austin robbed him at knife point. (Austin, at the time of Crawford's trial, was held on a charge of assault with intent to rob Crawford. We are not informed of the outcome of that case.) Robinson did, however, state that Ferrell's parting remark, after the appellant had told him and Austin to leave, was "We're going out, but you better damn sight have the money when we get back."

The appellant testified that Ferrell and Austin soon returned, Ferrell going to the front door and Austin to the rear door of the house. He said (partly in a statement made to the police shortly after his arrest, which was admitted in evidence without objection, and which he largely reaffirmed in his testimony) that he called to Robinson and Thomas to get the police but that they and he would not go out of the house for fear that they would be "jumped" by Ferrell or Austin. He testified that Ferrell entered the vestibule and was trying to get through the inner door, which the appellant had locked with the spring lock after Ferrell and Austin had left. The appellant picked up his gun and loaded it and went into the front hall just inside this inner door. He could see Ferrell. Ferrell, finding the inner door locked, kicked at the bottom of it and said to appellant, "I'm coming in to kick your ass." Appellant, holding the door with his feet, warned Ferrell to stay out and told him that he had the gun, but (according to the appellant) Ferrell said he did not care about the gun. Ferrell then knocked loose the piece of masonite and reached inside to unlock the door, and as he did so, appellant backed away from the door and fired the gun killing Ferrell who was hit in the side of the face with the shotgun blast. The appellant said he backed away from the door because he "was scared" and Ferrell "was coming right in on me." He said he did not "aim for the head," that instead he fired at Ferrell's hand but the gun jerked up as he fired. He said that he did intend "for the gun to go off because the boys made me angry and I was scared they was coming in and hurt me."

Robinson confirmed most of the essentials of the appellant's account of what happened immediately before and just after the shooting. He said that he heard Crawford warn Ferrell not to come in and that if he did Crawford would shoot. Robinson made contradictory statements as to whether he had or had not heard anything said by Ferrell just before the shooting. His final testimony on this point was in accord with what he had said in a statement made to the police a few hours after the shooting (which was admitted by stipulation) that he heard Ferrell say: "I'm coming in here anyhow."

A police officer confirmed the appellant's statement that he had complained to the police earlier in the day about some boys bothering him in his home. He also confirmed the fact that the piece of masonite on the door had been knocked loose so that a man could get his hand in.

The trial court's comments at the end of the trial indicated that he accepted and believed these material parts of appellant's story: (1) that Ferrell had been in the appellant's room demanding and taking money; (2) that Ferrell had warned that he would be back; (3) that at the time of the shooting Ferrell was unlawfully forcing or attempting to force his way into the appellant's home; (4) that the appellant did not deliberately fire at Ferrell's head. In addition, the court thought reasonable the appellant's explanation for not going outside to summon police help. But the court then found that "the defendant went further than the situation required," and entered a verdict of not guilty of murder but guilty of manslaughter.

. . . Most American jurisdictions in which the question has been decided have taken the view that if an assault on a dwelling and an attempted forcible entry are made under circumstances which would create a reasonable apprehension that it is the design of the assailant *to commit a felony* or to inflict on the inhabitants injury which may result in loss of life or great bodily harm, and that the danger that the design will be carried into effect is imminent, a lawful occupant of the dwelling may prevent the entry even by the taking of the intruder's life. . . .

. . .

There is also a generally accepted rule, which we think is correct, that a man faced with the danger of an attack upon his dwelling need not retreat from his home to escape the danger, but instead may stand his ground and, if necessary to repel the attack, may kill the attacker. . . .

It also seems appropriate to note at this point that one not seeking a fight may arm himself in anticipation of a violent attack. . . . Here we think that the appellant did have reason to anticipate such an attack.

Authorities elsewhere have recognized, correctly we think, that the rules regarding the defense of one's person and the rules regarding the defense of one's habitation are generally similar. . . . We have had occasion in recent years to consider several cases involving the right to defend one's person and we think that the rules recognized in such cases, other than (as already noted) the duty to retreat, are generally applicable in cases where one is defending his own home against attack to prevent a felony or great bodily injury to an occupant. . . .

The most difficult problem in this case is whether the force used by the appellant in resisting the intrusion was excessive. The authorities generally seem to agree that the force used must not be excessive. . . .

. . .

The material parts of the defendant's statements which the trial court accepted as true, which we have set forth above, and his acceptance of the appellant's explanation as to why he did not seek help from the police at the time of the attack lead us to conclude that the trial court was clearly in error in finding that the appellant used excessive force. One conclusion which the trial judge did not state, but which we think is a proper and, indeed, inescapable one to be drawn from the testimony which he did believe, is that Ferrell's purpose in seeking to break into the appellant's residence was to beat him and rob him. Robbery is a felony.

The appellant was in his home, and as we have already held, was under no duty to retreat therefrom. We might add that retreat seemed impossible with Ferrell at one door and Austin at the other. He defended his home first by locking the door, by warning the deceased to stay out, then by holding the door against the deceased, and finally, when it became apparent that the deceased would be able to force his way in, by backing away from the door and firing his shotgun at the deceased's hand. The trial court believed appellant when he said he did not fire at the deceased's head, and believed that the appellant's statement that the gun jerked up when fired was reasonable. . . . We do not believe that the circumstances in this case show the use of unnecessary force by appellant, a man of 42 years of age with a history of illness and unable to work, in resisting the attack being actively made by a 23 year old man with the cooperation of a youthful partner, when these two had previously had no apparent difficulty in overcoming appellant. . . . [I]mportant characteristics of the attack were that it was on the appellant's home and that its object was to beat and rob him. . . . [T]he appellant had the burden of proving by a preponderance of the evidence that he acted reasonably in defense of his habitation against forcible entry. We think that he met this burden.

. . .

127. Defense of habitation. As the opinion in *Crawford* indicates, the right to use deadly force in defense of one's habitation seldom arises in circumstances that do not also create a right to act in defense of oneself or others. In Semayne's Case, 5 Coke 91a, 91b, 77 Eng. Rep. 194, 195 (K.B.1604), which is regarded as the source of the proposition that "the house of everyone is to him as his castle," the court referred to a householder's (or his servants') killing would-be thieves "in defense *of himself* and his house" [emphasis added].

Similarly, in People v. Hubbard, 220 P. 315, 319 (Cal.Dist.Ct.App. 1923), the court said: "While one may use force if necessary to remove an intruder who refuses to leave after being requested to depart, it must not be assumed that he may intentionally kill another solely in defense of habitation. No person may intentionally kill merely because he cannot otherwise effect his object, although the object sought to be effected is right. He can kill intentionally only in defense of life or person, or to prevent a felony. . . . But a person assailed in his own house is not bound to retreat from the house to avoid violence, even though a retreat may safely be made. And, if the intruder resist his ejection and assaults the lawful occupant, the latter need not retreat, but, in protecting his person, he may, if necessary, intentionally take the intruder's life if he has reason to believe and does believe that his own life is in danger or that he is in danger of receiving great bodily harm."

If the right to defend one's habitation against intruders is so restricted, its significance as a distinct defense is generally that it may allow the use of deadly force somewhat sooner—to prevent entry—than would some other defense. A man against whom one would be entitled to use deadly force after entry if he persisted in his apparent intention can be prevented, with whatever force is necessary, from entering at all. E.g., State v. Ivicsics, 604 S.W.2d 773, 777 (Mo.Ct.App.1980) (the defense of habitation is "nothing more than accelerated self defense, and the difference between the two defenses is a function of time and space").

The defense has occasionally been given distinct significance; the use of deadly force has been allowed to resist an entry by someone who does not appear to intend some act that itself could be resisted by deadly force. In People v. Eatman, 91 N.E.2d 387, 390 (Ill.1950), the Supreme Court of Illinois held that one could use deadly force to prevent the entry of a person who intended to commit only a simple assault not involving danger of serious injury: "We think it may be safely laid down to be the law of this State that a man's habitation is one place where he may rest secure in the knowledge that he will not be disturbed by persons coming within, without proper invitation or warrant, and that he may use all of the force apparently necessary to repel any invasion of his home." In People v. Stombaugh, 284 N.E.2d 640 (Ill.1972), the court said that the defense was available not only to prevent entry but to terminate an entry: the right to use force "does not cease once the intruder has crossed the threshold into a person's dwelling." See Ill. Rev. Stat. para. 38, § 7–2. The defense is not available, however, unless the entry was unlawful; deadly force may not be used to eject someone who has entered lawfully and is not making an attack on the dwelling. People v. Ellis, 437 N.E.2d 409 (Ill.Ct.App.1982).

128.   Prevention of felony. The right to defend one's property other than a dwelling is bound up with the right, at one time the duty, to prevent the commission of a felony with whatever force is necessary.[73] The well-established rule that one could use deadly force to prevent the commission of a felony enabled one in most circumstances to protect his property from being taken or destroyed. See State v. Moore, 31 Conn. 479 (1863). The reasonable connection between the use of deadly force to prevent a felony and the use of deadly force to protect one's property was broken not only by elimination of the death penalty for crimes involving only property, notably larceny, but still more by the increase in the number of statutory felonies which neither endangered life nor were punishable by death.

In Storey v. State, 71 Ala. 329, 338–41 (1882), the court said:

The question is . . . presented, as to the circumstances under which one can kill in order to prevent the perpetration of a larceny which is made a felony by statute. . . .

We find it often stated, in general terms, both by text writers and in many well considered cases, that one may, as Mr. Bishop expressed it, "oppose another who is attempting to perpetrate *any felony*, to the extinguishment, if need be, of the felon's existence."—1 Bish. Cr. Law, §§ 849–50. . . .

After a careful consideration of the subject we are fully persuaded that the rule, as thus stated, is neither sound in principle, nor is it supported by the weight of modern authority. The safer view is that taken by Mr. Wharton, that the rule *does not authorize the killing of persons attempting* SECRET *felonies, not accompanied by* FORCE—Whart. on Hom. § 539. . . .

. . . It is true the rule has been extended to statutory felonies, as well as felonies at common law, which is doubtless the correct doctrine, but the cases adjudged have been open crimes committed by force, and not those of a secret nature. . . .

. . .

. . . Where opportunity is afforded to secure the punishment of the offender by due course of law, the case must be an urgent one which excuses a killing to prevent any felony, much less one not of a forcible or atrocious nature. . . . It is everywhere settled that the law

---

73. Prevention of a felony may, of course, also involve defense of self or others. In some such cases, it may provide a justification otherwise lacking for the use of force. See, for example, Commonwealth v. Jackson, 355 A.2d 572 (Pa.1976), in which prevention of a felony was allowed as a defense but, because the relationship between the defendant and the person whom she aided was only that of aunt and niece, defense of others was not.

will not justify a homicide which is perpetrated in resisting a mere civil trespass upon one's premises or property, unaccompanied by force, or felonious intent. . . . The reason is that the preservation of human life is of more importance than the protection of property. The law may afford ample indemnity for the loss of the one, while it utterly fails to do so for the other.

The rule we have above declared is the safer one, because it better comports with the public tranquility and the peace of society. The establishment of any other would lead to disorderly breaches of the peace of an aggravated nature, and therefore tend greatly to cheapen human life. This is especially true in view of our legislative policy which has recently brought many crimes, formerly classed and punished as petit larcenies within the class of statutory felonies. It seems settled that no distinction can be made between statutory and common law felonies, whatever may be the acknowledged extent of the rule. . . . The stealing of a hog, a sheep, or a goat is, under our statute, a felony, without regard to the pecuniary value of the animal. So would be the larceny of a single ear of corn, which is "a part of any outstanding crop."—Code, § 4358; Acts 1880–81, p. 47. It would be shocking to the good order of government to have it proclaimed, with the sanction of the courts, that one may, in the broad daylight, commit a willful homicide in order to prevent the larceny of an ear of corn. . . .[74]

129. Prevention of escape. The common law permitted the use of deadly force not only to prevent the commission of a felony but also to prevent the felon's escape. As codified in many states, this rule is typically unlimited with respect to the nature of the felony but is sometimes limited by a requirement that a felony actually have been committed, reasonable mistake being no defense.

A private person in fresh pursuit of one who has committed a felony may arrest without a warrant. . . . And in Pennsylvania we have always followed the common law rule that if the felon flees and his arrest cannot be effected without killing him, the killing is justified. . . . We hasten to note that before the use of deadly force is justified the private person must be in fresh pursuit of the felon and also must give notice of his purpose to arrest for the felony if the attending circumstances are themselves insufficient to warn the felon of the intention of the pursuing party to arrest him.

The common law principle that a killing necessary to prevent the escape of a felon is justifiable developed at a time when the distinction

---

74. But cf. Slack v. State, 149 S.W. 107, 108 (Tex.Crim.App.1912), in which, relying on a statute, the court said that the defendant was justified in shooting the deceased if he "was stealing corn in the night-time and was leaving the premises [a field] with the corn in his possession."

between felony and misdemeanor was very different than it is today. Statutory expansion of the class of felonies has made the common law rule manifestly inadequate for modern law. Hence, the need for a change or limitation in the rule is indicated. We therefore hold that from this date forward the use of deadly force by a private person in order to prevent the escape of one who has committed a felony or has joined or assisted in the commission of a felony is justified only if the felony committed is treason, murder, voluntary manslaughter, mayhem, arson, robbery, common law rape, common law burglary, kidnapping, assault with intent to murder, rape or rob, or a felony which normally causes or threatens death or great bodily harm. We also note that for the use of deadly force to be justified it remains absolutely essential, as before, that one of the enumerated felonies has been committed and that the person against whom the force is used is the one who committed it or joined or assisted in committing it. . . . If the private citizen acts on suspicion that such a felony has been committed, he acts at his own peril. For the homicide to be justifiable, it must be established that his suspicion was correct.

Commonwealth v. Chermansky, 242 A.2d 237, 239–40 (Pa.1968). See also Commonwealth v. Klein, 363 N.E.2d 1313 (Mass.1977), adopting the rules of the Model Penal Code § 3.07, p. 239 below.

The use of deadly force to prevent the escape of a felon is restricted on constitutional grounds along the lines of *Chermansky*, without resort to the act-at-your-peril rule, in Tennessee v. Garner, 471 U.S. 1 (1985), in which the Court held that a police officer can use deadly force "to prevent the escape of an apparently unarmed suspected felon . . . [only if] it is necessary to prevent the escape and the officer has probable cause to believe that the suspect poses a significant threat of death or serious physical injury to the officer or others." Id. at 3.

The Wall Street Journal

Friday, October 29, 1971.

There Is This Store in Queens That's Not the Best Place To Rob

FELIX TORO, A GROCER, DEFENDS HIS PROFITS BY KILLING THREE, WOUNDING FOUR IN 11 MONTHS

By STANLEY PENN

Staff Reporter of THE WALL STREET JOURNAL.

NEW YORK—For five years or so, Felix Toro worked as a private detective or a cop. In all that time, he never shot another man. Then, about a year ago, Mr. Toro entered a new field. He opened a small grocery store.

Since then, he has killed three men and wounded four.

Since Thanksgiving of last year, Mr. Toro, a thin, wiry 35-year-old Puerto Rican, has owned and operated the Quasar Delicatessen, a small neighborhood grocery store in a mixed Puerto Rican-and-white section of the borough of Queens. In those 11 months, Mr. Toro has learned what it's like to own something in New York City. He has also become a bit of a legend among crime-conscious New Yorkers.

Eight times bandits, alone or in groups, have walked into Mr. Toro's little store and attempted hold-ups. Seven of the 15 bandits involved in the various robbery attempts have left the store dead or wounded. None of the bandits has successfully left the store with any of Mr. Toro's money. And he intends to keep it that way.

"It seems so easy to them," says the tense grocer with the long sideburns and the Fu Manchu mustache. "They think they just pull a gun and rob me. Well, I'm not gonna let them. I work too hard for my money."

"The Shooter"

A police spokesman, who calls Mr. Toro's shooting record "incredible," says he does not know of any cop in all of New York City who has gunned down as many bandits in a year as Felix Toro has. "I recall one top policeman who may have killed three or four in his whole career," he says. Somewhat in awe, the neighborhood police have dubbed Mr. Toro "the shooter."

Mr. Toro says he has received over 1,500 letters from admirers since he started killing the gunmen who try to rob him. His latest exploit, the gunning to death of a 23-year-old heroin addict and father of three who tried to rob the store last Monday afternoon, seems certain to bring more fan mail. "They say I have a lot of courage and that we need more people in this city like me," he says. As he chats with a visitor, Mr. Toro opens an envelope and takes out a dollar bill some admirer has sent in.

Felix Toro never dreamed he would wind up as a gun-slinging grocer. He saved his money for years. He invested $14,000 in equipment for his store. He spent more for inventory. "I wanted to make a living. Who expected all this?" he asks, waving at the glass door of his beer compartment, shattered by a bullet, and at a bullet hole in the store ceiling.

That's not to say Mr. Toro was naive. He knew robbers are a busy bunch in New York City. Police say the city had 74,102 robberies last year, or about 203 every day. This year, the average is up to 242 per day.

Merry Christmas

So cautious Felix Toro kept a .38 caliber revolver in his store from the first day he opened for business. One month later, on Christmas Day, was the first time he reached for it. "A man and a woman come in and tell me to open the register. 'Only when I need to,' I say. Then this girl went for her handbag. I moved one step and grabbed my gun. They saw my movement and didn't try anything. They left. They went down the block and robbed somebody else."

A few weeks after that, Mr. Toro killed his first stickup men. Three gunmen walked in, and one of them began beating a customer with the butt of his gun. Enraged, Mr. Toro snatched up his own gun and opened fire. He killed two of the men and wounded the third.

Four days ago, the stickup man actually managed to leave the store with $30 or so. Mr. Toro was in the basement when the robber pulled a gun on Ruben Morales, the 15-year-old clerk on duty behind the counter. Ruben says the robber told him to get Mr. Toro from the basement and to hand over the money. He did both. As the robber left, Mr. Toro grabbed his own pistol, leapt over the counter and gave chase down Jamaica Avenue.

"I said to stop and drop the money," Mr. Toro recounts. "Instead he pulled a gun out of a bag. I shot him in the shoulder. Then we began to struggle. He kept fighting with me and pointing the gun at me." Mr. Toro shot the man several times in the head. Police later discovered the stickup man's gun was a toy pistol.

Felix Toro first came to New York from Puerto Rico in 1953. He worked at a variety of odd jobs, went back to Puerto Rico in 1964 where he worked for a while as an undercover man for the Puerto Rican police department and returned to New York in 1966 to work as a private investigator. He did that for four years before turning to shopkeeping. He still does private-eye work, part-time.

The attempted thefts have put great strain on Mr. Toro. Warily, he eyes everyone who comes in—especially at night, when his is one of the few stores open in the neighborhood. By now, he says, he can almost sense when somebody is going to try to pull a heist. They ask odd questions, he says. "'How's business?' they ask. 'Who's the boss?' 'How late you stay open?' Or they'll pick up a little bag of cake. It's marked 12 cents on it. They see it's marked 12 cents. Then they ask, 'How much is this cake?' You know they got other things on their mind."

Each time Mr. Toro wounds or kills a thief, he must make appearances in court or at the district attorney's office to describe the circumstances that led to the shooting. But he doesn't seem worried that he will ever be held liable or that his registered gun might be taken from him. "If they ever take the gun, I'd have to close the store. They'd take every nickel."

But he does worry, constantly, that some vengeful relative of a wounded or dead stickup man will walk into his store someday and try to blow his brains out. In fact, he suspects that a relative or friend of the dope addict he killed earlier this week showed up at his store on Tuesday night. "It was the first time he'd been in," Mr. Toro says with suspicion. "He looks around, picks up something, then looks around some more. I think, 'This guy, maybe he's a relative.' Then he buys four bags of potatoes. That's too many potatoes to buy. I watch him, and I got my gun in my pocket." But the man walked out with his potatoes.

Also because he fears revenge seekers, Mr. Toro has an unlisted telephone number and does not like to reveal where he lives. He is unhappy about a newspaper report earlier this week that said he lives above his store. He does not, and he fears the people who do live **above the store might be mistaken for him by some vengeance-minded visitor.**

Police say Mr. Toro's section of Queens is a high-crime area. A contractor who has offices on the same block as the grocer says he keeps his front doors locked all day. "Everybody has been robbed on this block at least once," he says. "It makes me very uneasy." Mr. Toro says his wife wants him to quit and get out. But, he says, "It's not that easy. You can't just pick up and go."

Of course, Ruben Morales, the teen-age clerk at the Quasar Delicatessen, could pick up and go if he wished. Ruben, working behind the counter, is, so to speak, in the line *of* fire. Does that thought ever worry him?

"Not when Toro is around," he says. [120]

[120] The facts of the killing on October 25, 1971, were presented to a grand jury which declined to charge Felix Toro with any crime. His license to possess a gun was later revoked following his arrest on a drug charge.

MODEL PENAL CODE §§ 3.04–.11

Section 3.04. Use of Force in Self-Protection.

(1) Use of Force Justifiable for Protection of the Person. Subject to the provisions of this Section and of Section 3.09, the use of force upon or toward another person is justifiable when the actor believes that such force is immediately necessary for the purpose of protecting himself against the use of unlawful force by such other person on the present occasion.

(2) Limitations on Justifying Necessity for Use of Force.

(a) The use of force is not justifiable under this Section:

(i) to resist an arrest which the actor knows is being made by a peace officer, although the arrest is unlawful; or

(ii) to resist force used by the occupier or possessor of property or by another person on his behalf, where the actor knows that the person using the force is doing so under a claim of right to protect the property, except that this limitation shall not apply if:

(1) the actor is a public officer acting in the performance of his duties or a person lawfully assisting him therein or a person making or assisting in a lawful arrest; or

(2) the actor has been unlawfully dispossessed of the property and is making a re-entry or recaption justified by Section 3.06; or

(3) the actor believes that such force is necessary to protect himself against death or serious bodily harm.

(b) The use of deadly force is not justifiable under this Section unless the actor believes that such force is necessary to protect himself against death, serious bodily harm, kidnapping or sexual intercourse compelled by force or threat; nor is it justifiable if:

(i) the actor, with the purpose of causing death or serious bodily harm, provoked the use of force against himself in the same encounter; or

(ii) the actor knows that he can avoid the necessity of using such force with complete safety by retreating or by surrendering possession of a thing to a person asserting a claim of right thereto or by complying with a demand that he abstain from any action which he has no duty to take, except that:

(1) the actor is not obliged to retreat from his dwelling or place of work, unless he was the initial aggressor or is assailed in his place of work by another person whose place of work the actor knows it to be; and

(2) a public officer justified in using force in the performance of his duties or a person justified in using force in his assistance or a person justified in using force in making an arrest or preventing an escape is not obliged to desist from efforts to perform such duty, effect such arrest or prevent such escape because of resis-

tance or threatened resistance by or on behalf of the person against whom such action is directed.

(c) Except as required by paragraphs (a) and (b) of this Subsection, a person employing protective force may estimate the necessity thereof under the circumstances as he believes them to be when the force is used, without retreating, surrendering possession, doing any other act which he has no legal duty to do or abstaining from any lawful action.

(3) Use of Confinement as Protective Force. The justification afforded by this Section extends to the use of confinement as protective force only if the actor takes all reasonable measures to terminate the confinement as soon as he knows that he safely can, unless the person confined has been arrested on a charge of crime.

Section 3.05. Use of Force for the Protection of Other Persons.

(1) Subject to the provisions of this Section and of Section 3.09, the use of force upon or toward the person of another is justifiable to protect a third person when:

(a) the actor would be justified under Section 3.04 in using such force to protect himself against the injury he believes to be threatened to the person whom he seeks to protect; and

(b) under the circumstances as the actor believes them to be, the person whom he seeks to protect would be justified in using such protective force; and

(c) the actor believes that his intervention is necessary for the protection of such other person.

(2) Notwithstanding Subsection (1) of this Section:

(a) when the actor would be obliged under Section 3.04 to retreat, to surrender the possession of a thing or to comply with a demand before using force in self-protection, he is not obliged to do so before using force for the protection of another person, unless he knows that he can thereby secure the complete safety of such other person; and

(b) when the person whom the actor seeks to protect would be obliged under Section 3.04 to retreat, to surrender the possession of a thing or to comply with a demand if he knew that he could obtain complete safety by so doing, the actor is obliged to try to cause him to do so before using force in his protection if the actor knows that he can obtain complete safety in that way; and

(c) neither the actor nor the person whom he seeks to protect is obliged to retreat when in the other's dwelling or place of work to any greater extent than in his own.

Section 3.06. Use of Force for the Protection of Property.

(1) Use of Force Justifiable for Protection of Property. Subject to the provisions of this Section and of Section 3.09, the use of force upon or

toward the person of another is justifiable when the actor believes that such force is immediately necessary:

(a) to prevent or terminate an unlawful entry or other trespass upon land or a trespass against or the unlawful carrying away of tangible, movable property, provided that such land or movable property is, or is believed by the actor to be, in his possession or in the possession of another person for whose protection he acts; or

(b) to effect an entry or re-entry upon land or to retake tangible movable property, provided that the actor believes that he or the person by whose authority he acts or a person from whom he or such other person derives title was unlawfully dispossessed of such land or movable property and is entitled to possession, and provided, further, that:

(i) the force is used immediately or on fresh pursuit after such dispossession; or

(ii) the actor believes that the person against whom he uses force has no claim of right to the possession of the property and, in the case of land, the circumstances, as the actor believes them to be, are of such urgency that it would be an exceptional hardship to postpone the entry or re-entry until a court order is obtained.

(2) Meaning of Possession. For the purposes of Subsection (1) of this Section:

(a) a person who has parted with the custody of property to another who refuses to restore it to him is no longer in possession, unless the property is movable and was and still is located on land in his possession;

(b) a person who has been dispossessed of land does not regain possession thereof merely by setting foot thereon;

(c) a person who has a license to use or occupy real property is deemed to be in possession thereof except against the licensor acting under claim of right.

(3) Limitations on Justifiable Use of Force.

(a) Request to Desist. The use of force is justifiable under this Section only if the actor first requests the person against whom such force is used to desist from his interference with the property, unless the actor believes that:

(i) such request would be useless; or

(ii) it would be dangerous to himself or another person to make the request; or

(iii) substantial harm will be done to the physical condition of the property which is sought to be protected before the request can effectively be made.

(b) Exclusion of Trespasser. The use of force to prevent or terminate a trespass is not justifiable under this Section if the actor knows that the exclusion of the trespasser will expose him to substantial danger of serious bodily harm.

(c) Resistance of Lawful Re-entry or Recaption. The use of force to prevent an entry or re-entry upon land or the recaption of movable property is not justifiable under this Section, although the actor believes that such re-entry or recaption is unlawful, if:

    (i) the re-entry or recaption is made by or on behalf of a person who was actually dispossessed of the property; and

    (ii) it is otherwise justifiable under paragraph (1)(b) of this Section.

(d) Use of Deadly Force. The use of deadly force is not justifiable under this Section unless the actor believes that:

    (i) the person against whom the force is used is attempting to dispossess him of his dwelling otherwise than under a claim of right to its possession; or

    (ii) the person against whom the force is used is attempting to commit or consummate arson, burglary, robbery or other felonious theft or property destruction and either:

        (1) has employed or threatened deadly force against or in the presence of the actor; or

        (2) the use of force other than deadly force to prevent the commission or the consummation of the crime would expose the actor or another in his presence to substantial danger of serious bodily harm.

(4) Use of Confinement as Protective Force. The justification afforded by this Section extends to the use of confinement as protective force only if the actor takes all reasonable measures to terminate the confinement as soon as he knows that he can do so with safety to the property, unless the person confined has been arrested on a charge of crime.

(5) Use of Device to Protect Property. The justification afforded by this Section extends to the use of a device for the purpose of protecting property only if:

(a) the device is not designed to cause or known to create a substantial risk of causing death or serious bodily harm; and

(b) the use of the particular device to protect the property from entry or trespass is reasonable under the circumstances, as the actor believes them to be; and

(c) the device is one customarily used for such a purpose or reasonable care is taken to make known to probable intruders the fact that it is used.

(6) Use of Force to Pass Wrongful Obstructor. The use of force to pass a person whom the actor believes to be purposely or knowingly and unjustifiably obstructing the actor from going to a place to which he may lawfully go is justifiable, provided that:

(a) the actor believes that the person against whom he uses force has no claim of right to obstruct the actor; and

(b) the actor is not being obstructed from entry or movement on land which he knows to be in the possession or custody of the person obstructing him, or in the possession or custody of another person by whose authority the obstructor acts, unless the circumstances, as the actor believes them to be, are of such urgency that it would not be reasonable to postpone the entry or movement on such land until a court order is obtained; and

(c) the force used is not greater than would be justifiable if the person obstructing the actor were using force against him to prevent his passage.

Section 3.07. Use of Force in Law Enforcement.

(1) Use of Force Justifiable to Effect an Arrest. Subject to the provisions of this Section and of Section 3.09, the use of force upon or toward the person of another is justifiable when the actor is making or assisting in making an arrest and the actor believes that such force is immediately necessary to effect a lawful arrest.

(2) Limitations on the Use of Force.

(a) The use of force is not justifiable under this Section unless:

(i) the actor makes known the purpose of the arrest or believes that it is otherwise known by or cannot reasonably be made known to the person to be arrested; and

(ii) when the arrest is made under a warrant, the warrant is valid or believed by the actor to be valid.

(b) The use of deadly force is not justifiable under this Section unless:

(i) the arrest is for a felony; and

(ii) the person effecting the arrest is authorized to act as a peace officer or is assisting a person whom he believes to be authorized to act as a peace officer; and

(iii) the actor believes that the force employed creates no substantial risk of injury to innocent persons; and

(iv) the actor believes that:

(1) the crime for which the arrest is made involved conduct including the use or threatened use of deadly force; or

(2) there is a substantial risk that the person to be arrested will cause death or serious bodily harm if his apprehension is delayed.

(3) Use of Force to Prevent Escape from Custody. The use of force to prevent the escape of an arrested person from custody is justifiable when the force could justifiably have been employed to effect the arrest under which the person is in custody, except that a guard or other person authorized to act as a peace officer is justified in using any force, including deadly force, which he believes to be immediately necessary to prevent the escape of a person from a jail, prison, or other institution for the detention of persons charged with or convicted of a crime.

(4) Use of Force by Private Person Assisting an Unlawful Arrest.

(a) A private person who is summoned by a peace officer to assist in effecting an unlawful arrest, is justified in using any force which he would be justified in using if the arrest were lawful, provided that he does not believe the arrest is unlawful.

(b) A private person who assists another private person in effecting an unlawful arrest, or who, not being summoned, assists a peace officer in effecting an unlawful arrest, is justified in using any force which he would be justified in using if the arrest were lawful, provided that (i) he believes the arrest is lawful, and (ii) the arrest would be lawful if the facts were as he believes them to be.

(5) Use of Force to Prevent Suicide or the Commission of a Crime.

(a) The use of force upon or toward the person of another is justifiable when the actor believes that such force is immediately necessary to prevent such other person from committing suicide, inflicting serious bodily harm upon himself, committing or consummating the commission of a crime involving or threatening bodily harm, damage to or loss of property or a breach of the peace, except that:

(i) any limitations imposed by the other provisions of this Article on the justifiable use of force in self-protection, for the protection of others, the protection of property, the effectuation of an arrest or the prevention of an escape from custody shall apply notwithstanding the criminality of the conduct against which such force is used; and

(ii) the use of deadly force is not in any event justifiable under this Subsection unless:

(1) the actor believes that there is a substantial risk that the person whom he seeks to prevent from committing a crime will cause death or serious bodily harm to another unless the commission or the consummation of the crime is prevented and that the use of such force presents no substantial risk of injury to innocent persons; or

(2) the actor believes that the use of such force is necessary to suppress a riot or mutiny after the rioters or mutineers have been ordered to disperse and warned, in any particular manner that the law may require, that such force will be used if they do not obey.

(b) The justification afforded by this Subsection extends to the use of confinement as preventive force only if the actor takes all reasonable measures to terminate the confinement as soon as he knows that he safely can, unless the person confined has been arrested on a charge of crime.

Section 3.08. Use of Force by Persons with Special Responsibility for Care, Discipline or Safety of Others.

. . .

Section 3.09. Mistake of Law as to Unlawfulness of Force or Legality of Arrest; Reckless or Negligent Use of Otherwise Justifiable Force; Reckless or Negligent Injury or Risk of Injury to Innocent Persons.

(1) The justification afforded by Sections 3.04 to 3.07, inclusive, is unavailable when:

(a) the actor's belief in the unlawfulness of the force or conduct against which he employs protective force or his belief in the lawfulness of an arrest which he endeavors to effect by force is erroneous; and

(b) his error is due to ignorance or mistake as to the provisions of the Code, any other provision of the criminal law or the law governing the legality of an arrest or search.

(2) When the actor believes that the use of force upon or toward the person of another is necessary for any of the purposes for which such belief would establish a justification under Sections 3.03 to 3.08 but the actor is reckless or negligent in having such belief or in acquiring or failing to acquire any knowledge or belief which is material to the justifiability of his use of force, the justification afforded by those Sections is unavailable in a prosecution for an offense for which recklessness or negligence, as the case may be, suffices to establish culpability.

(3) When the actor is justified under Sections 3.03 to 3.08 in using force upon or toward the person of another but he recklessly or negligently injures or creates a risk of injury to innocent persons, the justification afforded by those Sections is unavailable in a prosecution for such recklessness or negligence towards innocent persons.

. . .

Section 3.11. Definitions.

In this Article, unless a different meaning plainly is required:

(1) "unlawful force" means force, including confinement, which is employed without the consent of the person against whom it is directed and the employment of which constitutes an offense or actionable tort or would constitute such offense or tort except for a defense (such as the absence of intent, negligence, or mental capacity; duress; youth; or diplomatic status) not amounting to a privilege to use the force. Assent constitutes consent, within the meaning of this Section, whether or not it otherwise is legally effective, except assent to the infliction of death or serious bodily harm;

(2) "deadly force" means force which the actor uses with the purpose of causing or which he knows to create a substantial risk of causing death or serious bodily harm. Purposely firing a firearm in the direction of another person or at a vehicle in which another person is believed to be constitutes deadly force. A threat to cause death or serious bodily harm, by the production of a weapon or otherwise, so

long as the actor's purpose is limited to creating an apprehension that he will use deadly force if necessary, does not constitute deadly force;

(3) "dwelling" means any building or structure, though movable or temporary, or a portion thereof, which is for the time being the actor's home or place of lodging.

DURESS AND NECESSITY

MODEL PENAL CODE

Section 2.09. Duress.

(1) It is an affirmative defense that the actor engaged in the conduct charged to constitute an offense because he was coerced to do so by the use of, or a threat to use, unlawful force against his person or the person of another, which a person of reasonable firmness in his situation would have been unable to resist.

(2) The defense provided by this Section is unavailable if the actor recklessly placed himself in a situation in which it was probable that he would be subjected to duress. The defense is also unavailable if he was negligent in placing himself in such a situation, whenever negligence suffices to establish culpability for the offense charged.

(3) It is not a defense that a woman acted on the command of her husband, unless she acted under such coercion as would establish a defense under this Section. [The presumption that a woman, acting in the presence of her husband, is coerced is abolished.]

(4) When the conduct of the actor would otherwise be justifiable under Section 3.02, this Section does not preclude such defense.

Section 3.02. Justification Generally: Choice of Evils.

(1) Conduct which the actor believes to be necessary to avoid a harm or evil to himself or to another is justifiable, provided that:

(a) the harm or evil sought to be avoided by such conduct is greater than that sought to be prevented by the law defining the offense charged; and

(b) neither the Code nor other law defining the offense provides exceptions or defenses dealing with the specific situation involved; and

(c) a legislative purpose to exclude the justification claimed does not otherwise plainly appear.

(2) When the actor was reckless or negligent in bringing about the situation requiring a choice of harms or evils or in appraising the necessity for his conduct, the justification afforded by this Section is unavailable in a prosecution for any offense for which recklessness or negligence, as the case may be, suffices to establish culpability.

---

130. The Model Penal Code rejects the traditional rule that the defenses of duress and necessity ("choice of evils") is not available for the crime of murder, which some statutory formulations extended to other very serious crimes as well. Notwithstanding the Code, recent statutory revisions have generally excluded murder and sometimes other offenses against the person and other felonies from the defense of duress. 1 MPC Commentaries Part I, 381 & n.54. See United States v. LaFleur, 971 F.2d 200 (9th Cir.1991). In *LaFleur*, the court also rejected duress as a mitigating factor that might reduce an intentional killing from murder to voluntary manslaughter. Necessity, on the other hand, has been allowed more broadly, as in the Code. 2 MPC Commentaries Part I, 18.

Should duress be allowed as a defense to a charge of murder? If not, should it be allowed in mitigation, perhaps to reduce the crime to voluntary manslaughter or, if the crime were unchanged, to reduce the punishment, as Stephen thought (2 Stephen, History 108)?

The English courts reconsidered the defense of duress in a series of much-discussed cases. First, in D.P.P. v. Lynch, [1975] App. Cas. 653 (H.L. (N.I.)), it was concluded that duress is a defense to a charge of murder as an aider and abettor. Two years later, it was concluded that duress is not a defense to a charge of murder as a principal, i.e., someone who did the actual killing. Abbott v. The Queen, [1977] App. Cas. 755 (P.C.). Finally, the contradictory positions in *Lynch* and *Abbott* having been strongly criticized, it was decided to return to the traditional rule and reject the defense of duress in all cases of murder. Reg. v. Howe [1987] 1 App. Cas. 417 (H.L. (E.)).

In *Howe*, Lord Hailsham said:

[W]hile there can never be a direct correspondence between law and morality, an attempt to divorce the two entirely is, and has always proved to be, doomed to failure, and, in the present case, the overriding objects of the criminal law must be to protect innocent lives and to set a standard of conduct which ordinary men and women are expected to observe if they are to avoid criminal responsibility.

. . .

In general, I must say that I do not at all accept in relation to the defence of murder it is either good morals, good policy or good law to suggest . . . that the ordinary man of reasonable fortitude is not to be supposed to be capable of heroism if he is asked to take an innocent life rather than sacrifice his own. Doubtless in actual practice many will succumb to temptation. . . . But many will not, and I do not believe that as a "concession to human frailty" the former should be exempt from liability to criminal sanctions if they do. I have known in my own lifetime of too many acts of heroism by ordinary human beings of no more than ordinary fortitude to regard a law as either "just or humane" which withdraws the protection of the criminal law from the innocent victim and casts the cloak of its protection upon the coward and the poltroon in the name of a "concession to human frailty."

I must not, however, underestimate the force of the arguments on the other side, advanced as they have been with such force and such persuasiveness by some of the most eminent legal minds, judicial and academic, in the country.

First, amongst these is, perhaps, the argument from logic and consistency. A long line of cases, it is said, carefully researched and closely analysed, establish duress as an available defence in a wide range of crimes, some at least, like wounding with intent to commit grievous bodily harm, carrying the heaviest penalties commensurate with their gravity. . . .

. . . Consistency and logic, though inherently desirable, are not always prime characteristics of a penal code based like the common law on custom and precedent. Law so based is not an exact science. All the same, I feel I am required to give some answer to the question posed. If duress is available as a defence to some crimes of the most grave why, it may legitimately be asked, stop at murder, whether as accessory or principal and whether in the second or the first degree? But surely I am entitled . . . to believe that some degree of proportionality between the threat and the offence must, at least to some extent, be a prerequisite of the defence under existing law. Few would resist threats to the life of a loved one if the alternative were driving across the red lights or in excess of 70 m.p.h. on the motorway. But . . . it would take rather more than the threat of a slap on the wrist or even moderate pain or injury to discharge the evidential burden even in the case of a fairly serious assault. In such a case the "concession to human frailty" is no more than to say that in such circumstances a reasonable man of average courage is entitled to embrace as a matter of choice the alternative which a reasonable man could regard as the lesser of two evils. Other considerations necessarily arise where the choice is between the threat of death or a fortiori of serious injury and deliberately taking an innocent life. In such a case a reasonable man might reflect that one innocent human life is at least as valuable as his own or that of his loved one. In such a case a man cannot claim that he is choosing the lesser of two evils. Instead he is embracing the cognate but morally disreputable principle that the end justifies the means.

. . .

Far less convincing than the argument based on consistency is the belief which appears in some of the judgments that the law must "move with the times" in order to keep pace with the immense political and social changes since what are alleged to have been the bad old days of Blackstone and Hale. . . . The argument is based on the false assumption that violence to innocent victims is now less prevalent than in the days of Hale or Blackstone. But I doubt whether this is so. We live in the age of the holocaust of the Jews, of international terrorism on the scale of massacre, of the explosion of aircraft in mid air, and murder sometimes at least as obscene as anything experienced in Blackstone's day. . . . [W]ithin weeks of hearing this appeal a man was convicted at the Central Criminal Court of sending his pregnant mistress on board an international aircraft at Heathrow, with her suitcase packed with a bomb and with the deliberate intention of sending the 250 occupants, crew, passengers, mistress and all to a horrible death in mid air. . . . [H]ad the attempt succeeded, the miscreant who did this would have been free to escape scot free had he been in a position to discharge the evidential burden on duress and had the prosecution . . . been unable to exclude beyond reasonable doubt the possibility of his uncorroborated word being true. I must also point out in this context that known terrorists are more and not less vulnerable to threats than the ordinary man and that a plea of duress in such a case may be all the more plausible on that account. . . . The question is not one of the reliability of juries. It is one of principle. Should the offence of duress be available in principle in such a case . . .? The point which I am at the moment concerned to make is that it is not clear to me that the observations of Blackstone and Hale, and almost every respectable authority, academic or judicial, prior to *Lynch* are necessarily to be regarded in this present age as obsolescent or inhumane or unjust owing to some supposed improvement in the respect for innocent human life since their time which unfortunately I am too blind to be able for myself to perceive. Still less am I able to see that a law which denies such a defence in such a case must be condemned as lacking in justice or humanity rather than as respectable in its concern for the sanctity of innocent lives. I must add that, at least in my view, if *Abbott* were wrongly decided some hundreds who suffered the death penalty at Nuremberg for murders were surely the victims of judicial murder at the hands of their conquerors. . . . Social change is not always for the better and it ill becomes those of us who have participated in the cruel events of the 20th century to condemn as out of date those who wrote in defence of innocent lives in the 18th century.

During the course of argument it was suggested that there was available to the House some sort of half way house between allowing these appeals and dismissing them. The argument ran that we might treat duress in murder as analogous to provocation, or perhaps diminished responsibility, and say that, in indictments for murder, duress might reduce the crime to one of manslaughter. I find myself quite unable to accept this. The cases show that duress, if available and made out, entitles the accused to a clean acquittal, without, it has been said, the "stigma" of a conviction. Whatever other merits it may have, at least the suggestion makes nonsense of any pretence of logic or consistency in the criminal law. It is also contrary to principle. Unlike the doctrine of provocation, which is based on emotional loss of control, the defence of duress, as I have already shown, is put forward as a "concession to human frailty" whereby a conscious decision, it may be coolly undertaken, to sacrifice an innocent human life is made as an evil lesser than a wrong which might otherwise be suffered by the accused or his loved ones at the hands of a wrong doer. The defence of diminished responsibility . . . has a conceptual basis . . . which is totally distinct from that of duress if duress be properly analysed and understood. Provocation . . . is a concession to human frailty due to the extent that even a reasonable man may, under sufficient provocation temporarily lose his self control towards the person who has provoked him enough. Duress, as I have already pointed out, is a concession to human frailty in that it allows a reasonable man to make a conscious choice between the reality of the immediate threat and what he may reasonably regard as the lesser of two evils. Diminished responsibility . . . depends on abnormality of mind impairing mental responsibility. It may overlap duress or even necessity. But it is not what we are discussing in the instant appeal.

[1987] 1 App. Cas. at 430–35.

Lord Hailsham referred in the remarks above to the defendants at Nuremberg. Elsewhere, he observed further that the defense of "superior orders" had been rejected at Nuremberg. " 'Superior orders,' " he said, "is not identical with 'duress,' but in the circumstances of the Nazi regime, the difference must often have been negligible." Id. at 427.

See generally State v. Toscano, 378 A.2d 755 (N.J.1977), adopting the Model Penal Code's formulation of the defense of duress for crimes other than murder. See also United States v. Contento-Pachon, 723 F.2d 691 (9th Cir.1984) (defense of duress available to person prosecuted for illegal importation of narcotics, who claimed that he and his family were threatened with death or injury if he refused). Compare United States v. Jennell, 749 F.2d 1302 (9th Cir.1984) (drug offenses; *Contento-Pachon* distinguished). In Jefferson v. State, 484 N.E.2d 22 (Ind.1985), relying on a statute providing that the defense of duress is not available for an "offense against the person," the court held that it is not available for the crime of robbery.

131. The defense of necessity was raised and rejected in The Queen v. Dudley and Stephens, [1881–85] All E.R. 61 (Q.B. 1884), a case of murder and cannibalism the facts of which are set forth below, p. 382. In *Dudley and Stephens*, the court said:

[T]he temptation to the act which existed here was not what the law has ever called necessity. Nor is this to be regretted. Though law and morality are not the same, and many things may be immoral which are not necessarily illegal, yet the absolute divorce of law from morality would be of fatal consequence; and such divorce would follow if the temptation to murder in this case were to be held by law an absolute defence of it. It is not so. To preserve one's life is generally speaking a duty, but it may be the plainest and the highest duty to sacrifice it. War is full of instances in which it is a man's duty not to live, but to die. The duty, in case of shipwreck, of a captain to his crew, of the crew to the passengers, of soldiers to women and children . . . these duties impose on men the moral necessity, not of the preservation, but of the sacrifice of their lives for others, from which in no country, least of all, it is to be hoped, in England, will men ever shrink, as indeed, they have not shrunk. It is not correct, therefore, to say that there is any absolute or unqualified necessity to preserve one's life. . . . It is not needful to point out the awful danger of admitting the principle which has been contended for. Who is to be the judge of this sort of necessity? By what measure is the comparative value of lives to be measured? Is it to be strength, or intellect, or what? It is plain that the principle leaves to him who is to profit by it to determine the necessity which will justify him in deliberately taking another's life to save his own. In this case the weakest, the youngest, the most unresisting, was chosen. Was it more necessary to kill him than one of the grown men? The answer must be "No"—

"So spake the Fiend, and with necessity,
The tyrant's plea, excused his devilish deeds."

It is not suggested that in this particular case the deeds were "devilish," but it is quite plain that such a principle once admitted might be made the legal cloak for unbridled passion and atrocious crime. . . .

It must not be supposed that in refusing to admit temptation to be an excuse for crime it is forgotten how terrible the temptation was; how awful the suffering; how hard in such trials to keep the judgment straight and the conduct pure. We are often compelled to set up standards we cannot reach ourselves, and to lay down rules which we could not ourselves satisfy. But a man has no right to declare temptation to be an excuse, though he might himself have yielded to it, nor allow compassion for the criminal to change or weaken in any manner the legal definition of the crime.

[1881–85] All E.R. at 67–68.

132. In People v. Pena, 197 Cal.Rptr. 264 (Super.1983), the defendant followed a police car in which, late at night, an officer had placed the defendant's girlfriend, ostensibly to drive her home. The defendant was prosecuted for drunk driving. Observing that the defense of "duress" (used here interchangeably with necessity) is available with respect to any crime except one that involves taking the life of an innocent person, the court held that the defense might be available to the defendant if he followed the police car because he feared for his friend's physical safety. (In a subsequent case, the court described the *Pena* court's construction of the necessity defense as "excessively expansive." People v. Garziano, 281 Cal.Rptr. 307, 308 (Ct.App.1991).) The defense of necessity to a charge of driving without a license was allowed in State v. Cole, 403 S.E.2d 117 (S.C.1991), in which the defendant was apprehended after driving his pregnant wife to the hospital for treatment.

133. The defense of duress or necessity, based on threats of abuse or injury or on general prison conditions, has been used as a defense to the charge of escape from prison. Courts have been reluctant to allow such a defense, which, it is feared, would be available to a great many prisoners who could persuasively argue that they were subjected to unhealthy, dangerous, and abusive conditions. (For a chilling description of the perils to which prisoners are subjected, see McGill v. Duckworth, 944 F.2d 344 (7th Cir.1991), in which the court rejected an inmate's claim for damages against prison personnel on either Eighth Amendment or negligence grounds; the inmate had been raped in the shower by an inmate, while three other inmates stood guard outside. The first sentence of the opinion is: "Prisons are dangerous places." Id. at 345.) Some courts have allowed the defense to be raised but have defined it narrowly. In People v. Lovercamp, 118 Cal.Rptr. 110, 115 (Ct.App.1974), for example, the court said that there was a limited defense of necessity in escape cases, which was available if: "(1) The prisoner is faced with a specific threat of death, forcible sexual attack or substantial bodily injury in the immediate future; (2) there is no time for a complaint to the authorities or there exists a history of futile complaints which make any result from such complaints illusory; (3) there is not time or opportunity to resort to the courts; (4) there is no evidence of force or violence used towards prison personnel or other 'innocent' persons in the escape; and (5) the prisoner immediately reports to the proper authorities when he has attained a position of safety from the immediate threat." In People v. Unger, 362 N.E.2d 319 (Ill.1977), the court referred to the conditions specified in *Lovercamp* as relevant to the defendant's claim of necessity but said that they were not each individually essential to such a claim.

Construing the federal escape statute, 18 U.S.C. § 751(a), the Supreme Court has held "that, in order to be entitled to an instruction on duress or necessity as a defense to the crime charged, an escapee must first offer evidence justifying his continued absence from custody as well as his initial departure, and that an indispensable element of such an offer is testimony of a bona fide effort to surrender or return to custody as soon as the claimed duress or necessity had lost its coercive force." United States v. Bailey, 444 U.S. 394, 412–13 (1980) (6–2). The Court observed that the defense was not available unless there was no "reasonable, legal alternative" to the otherwise criminal conduct, id. at 410, and that without an indication of an effort to return to custody that requirement was not satisfied. In a dissenting opinion, Justice Blackmun said: "If departure was justified . . . it seems too much to demand that respondents, in order to preserve their legal defenses, return forthwith to the hell that obviously exceeds the normal deprivations of prison life and that compelled their leaving in the first instance." Id. at 419, 419–20.

———

For the most famous American case of necessity involving the taking of innocent lives, see United States v. Holmes, 26 F. Cas. 360 (C.C.E.D.Pa. 1842) (No. 15,383) p. 370 below.

———

The New York Times
Thursday, March 17, 1966

Ashau Team Shot 7 On Its Own Side

U.S. SAYS THEY INTERFERED WITH EVACUATION COPTERS

WASHINGTON, March 16—Defense Department officials confirmed today that some South Vietnamese troops had been shot by their American and Vietnamese comrades when they overloaded evacuation helicopters after the outpost at Ashau had been overrun by enemy forces last week.

The officials said that seven South Vietnamese soldiers had been killed by co-defenders of the post as a "last-ditch resort" to permit evacuation of the wounded. The Vietnamese had overloaded the helicopters so that they could not take off and disregarded orders to get off.

. . .

On the basis of information supplied by the United States Military Command in Saigon, defense officials reported that on the first day of evacuation, which was supposed to have been reserved for removal of the wounded, some "able-bodied" members of the defense group rushed onto the helicopters before the wounded could be taken aboard.

As a result the helicopters became so overloaded, it was reported, that they could not take off. The American Special Forces and the Nung [Vietnamese] troops then had to forcefully remove some of the militiamen.

According to the report, about seven militiamen who were clinging to the helicopters were killed. It was not clear from the report whether the shots were fired by Americans or the Nung forces.

The extreme measure apparently had a disciplinary effect, for on the second day the evacuation was reported to have proceeded smoothly, with the operations kept under control by the Nung forces.

But on the third and final day of the evacuation, the militiamen were reported to have "panicked" again. Although there were sufficient helicopters to remove all the survivors, fighting broke out within the defense group for places in the aircraft. During the fighting, one militiaman threw a grenade, wounding several of his comrades.

. . .

134. In State v. Dorsey, 395 A.2d 855 (N.H.1978), the defendant participated in a mass occupation of the construction site of the Seabrook Nuclear Power Plant. He was prosecuted for criminal trespass. At trial, he sought to introduce evidence of the danger of nuclear power in order to establish a defense of necessity or "choice of evils." The court held that the defense was not available.

> The common-law defense dealt with imminent dangers from obvious and generally recognized harms. It did not deal with non-imminent or debatable harms; nor did it deal with activities that the legislative branch of government had expressly sanctioned and found not to be harms. . . . To allow nuclear power plants to be considered a danger or harm within the meaning of that defense either at common law or under the statute would require lay jurors to determine in individual cases matters of State and national policy in a very technical field. Competing factions would produce extensive expert testimony on the danger or lack of danger of nuclear power plants, and jurors in each case would then be asked to decide issues already determined by the legislature. The competing harms statute is intended to deal only with harms that are readily apparent and recognizable to the average juror.

> Defendant and others who oppose nuclear power have other lawful means of protesting nuclear power; therefore, they are not justified in breaking the law. . . . The act of criminal trespass was a deliberate and calculated choice and not an act that was urgently necessary to avoid a clear and imminent danger. The matter of the Seabrook Nuclear Power Plant has been before the regulatory agencies and the courts of both the United States and this State with a full opportunity for the opponents of nuclear power plant construction to be heard. Opponents still have the right to try to induce the people's representatives in Congress and the legislature to change the statutes. The fact that their efforts so far have failed does not make a case of necessity.

Id. at 857.

See In re Weller, 210 Cal.Rptr. 130, 133 (Ct.App.1985) (anti-nuclear protesters convicted of trespass; defense of necessity not available): "Unless the laws are held unconstitutional, those challenging or defying them must be prepared to bear the short-term consequences of their actions in the hope that society will benefit and that historians will look charitably upon them." Accord United States v. Dorrell, 758 F.2d 427 (9th Cir.1985). The defendant, who had entered a military base with the intention of damaging missiles, was convicted of unlawfully entering the base and willfully damaging government property. The court held that the trial court properly rejected his offer of proof of a necessity defense because it did not establish the lack of available alternative means to change government policy or avert the risk of nuclear war and did not establish that he believed reasonably that his actions would achieve those ends. With respect to the availability of alternatives, the court said:

> Admittedly, Dorrell's offer of proof details his participation in a variety of protest activities and asserts that his political efforts were unavail-

ing in preventing the development of the MX missile. In this respect Dorrell differs little from many whose passionate beliefs are rejected by the will of the majority legitimately expressed. Moreover, it may be he understates the effectiveness of the political process in this particular instance. To accept Dorrell's position would amount to recognizing that an individual may assert a defense to criminal charges whenever he or she disagrees with a result reached by the political process. While the policy underlying the necessity defense is the promotion of greater values at the expense of lesser values . . . it does not follow that the law should excuse criminal activity intended to express the protestor's disagreement with positions reached by the lawmaking branches of the government. To do otherwise would deprive the protest of the validation of its sincerity that lawful punishment provides, force the courts to choose among causes they should make legitimate by extending the defense of necessity, and transgress the principle of separation of powers.

Id. at 432. In United States v. Schoon, 971 F.2d 193 (9th Cir.1991) (obstruction of IRS office to protest U.S. policy in El Salvador), the court said that the necessity defense is never available for activities of indirect civil disobedience involving violation of a law that is not itself the object of protest. See also United States v. Montgomery, 772 F.2d 733 (11th Cir. 1985) (defense of justification under international law similarly unavailable); Commonwealth v. Capitolo, 498 A.2d 806 (Pa.1985); State v. Champa, 494 A.2d 102 (R.I.1985).

5. UNINTENTIONAL INJURY

Brat, ten years old, is taken for a stroll near a pond in a park by Char, his governess. Brat splashes water on Albert, a man of 22, who has never seen Brat before. Albert has just been fired from his job without cause by Pres, his boss. Irritated by Brat's rudeness, Albert pushes him into the pond. As Albert knows, the pond is ordinarily only about one foot deep; but unknown to Albert, Ground, the caretaker of the park, has let holes develop in the bottom of the pond and, at the point where Brat falls in, the water is well over his head. Brat cannot swim. Char is an excellent swimmer and can easily rescue Brat. She, however, is engaged in conversation with Walt, a personal friend, and does nothing except wave to Brat and encourage him to kick his legs harder. Walt is also an excellent swimmer. He goes over to the edge of the pond and reaches out for Brat, but Brat is too far from the edge and Walt returns to his conversation with Char. Brat drowns. Albert, who has kept walking, doesn't learn that the pond was deeper than he thought and that Brat has drowned until he reads about it in the newspaper the next day.

Who killed Brat?

Whom, if anyone, should we blame for Brat's death?

If anyone is to blame for Brat's death, should that person be held criminally liable for homicide?

What is the relationship among the preceding three questions?

Before we make a moral or legal judgment about an event, we have to know what happened—who did what to whom. If A intends to do X to B (or we reason "as if" that were so without regard to the facts), tries to do so, and X happens to B, the connection between the actor, his act, and the result is usually supplied by his intention, and we can readily say, "A did X to B." Suppose, however, that no one intends that X happen to B. How do we decide whether to say, "X happened to B" or to say, "A [or some other person(s) out of all the persons in the world] did X to B"? Did Brat just happen to die or did someone or several persons kill him?

———

Bell v. Commonwealth

170 Va. 597, 195 S.E. 675 (1938)

■ SPRATLEY, JUSTICE. This case presents the question of the degree of negligence required to convict one of involuntary manslaughter where the homicide is alleged to have been caused by the negligent operation of an automobile.

issue —

Gordon A. Bell, the plaintiff in error, who will be hereinafter referred to as the defendant, was indicted for manslaughter. The indictment was in the short or statutory form, Code 1936, § 4865, and charged the defendant "did on February 1, 1937, in said county of Arlington, Virginia, feloniously kill and slay one, Jessie Cooley, against the peace and dignity of the Commonwealth."

Upon his arraignment, he entered a plea of not guilty, and moved the court to require the Commonwealth to furnish him with a bill of particulars, which motion the court granted.

facts

The bill of particulars sets out the following specifications: "That at the time and place laid in the indictment now pending against the said Gordon A. Bell, he did operate a motor vehicle recklessly and unlawfully, in that he then and there operated the said motor vehicle at a rate of speed in excess of a lawful rate of speed; that he drove the said motor vehicle upon the left of the center of the street or highway; that he operated said motor vehicle, without any headlights, or with headlights which failed to comply with the requirements of the law of Virginia; that he failed to have the said motor vehicle under proper control or to keep a proper lookout for the safety of other persons using the said highway; that he drove the said motor vehicle at a speed that was greater than reasonable and proper, having due regard to the traffic, surface and width of the highway, and other conditions existing at the said time and place, and at such a speed as to endanger the life of persons on the said highway; and that while so unlawfully operating the said motor vehicle, it struck and injured the person of one Jessie Cooley, from which injuries she died."

Upon motion of the defendant for further and more definite specifications, the Commonwealth amended its bill of particulars by further setting forth the place where the crime was alleged to have been committed, and the direction in which the defendant was driving. The trial court refused to grant a motion for a more definite bill. To this refusal, the defendant excepted, and this exception constitutes one of his assignments of error.

The case then proceeded to trial, and a jury, upon the evidence and instructions given by the court, found the defendant guilty of involuntary manslaughter, and fixed his punishment at two and one-half years in the penitentiary.

. . .

To sustain a charge of involuntary manslaughter, the Commonwealth presented the following evidence:

On the night of February 1, 1937, there was a benefit card party at the community house in Clarendon, a thickly settled community, attended by quite a number of people. The community house is located on the east side of North Irving street, near the intersection of that street with North Wilson and North Washington boulevards. North Irving street is 25 feet wide, and runs north and south. North Wilson boulevard runs northeast and southwest, and North Washington boulevard runs northwest and southeast. The lot on which the community house is located is in a long city block, extending 525 feet southerly from the above-described intersection to North Tenth street, another intersecting street. On the east side of North Irving street a sidewalk extends from the north end of the block about 118 feet to a point in front of the community house. Beyond this, going south on the same street, there is no sidewalk, but there is a ditch or gutter marking a division line between the street and the adjoining property.

On the day in question, it had been raining, and the ground to the east of the street was muddy. There were automobiles parked on both sides of the street, and extending on the east side thereof to the community house, leaving a space in the center of the street 13 feet wide for traffic. The street was unlighted between the intersections.

A few minutes before 12 o'clock on that night, the card party ended, and the participants left, some going to their parked automobiles to return home. Among those so leaving were the now deceased, Mrs. Cooley, and three companions, Mrs. Grace Dagger, Mrs. Bertha Warner, and Mrs. Lillian Johnson. These four women came out of the community house, and stepped immediately into North Irving street, turned left, and began walking southerly, two abreast, down the left-hand or east side of the street. The two couples were five or six feet apart, and the two ladies on the inside walked as close as possible to the parked cars, with Mrs. Dagger on the outside of the front couple and Mrs. Cooley on the outside of the rear couple. The two women in each pair walked closely together, their elbows within touch. While so walking, and when they had reached a distance about 200 feet from the community house, Mrs. Cooley and Mrs. Dagger, the outside women of both pairs, were struck from the rear and knocked down by the defendant's automobile, which was being operated to the left of the center of the street. Neither of the three surviving women heard any warning signal, nor saw any lights on the automobile, or any reflection therefrom on the street. They say that the road was entirely dark at the point of the collision. Mrs. Warner, who was the companion on the left of Mrs. Cooley, says she received her first impression of the approach of the car when she turned her head to speak to Mrs. Cooley, and that the car struck the latter at that moment.

Two other witnesses, Mrs. Julia Thomas and Elmer Jacobs, testified that they, too, had left the card party at its conclusion, and after getting to the end of the sidewalk on the east side of North Irving street, in front of the community house, they started directly and immediately across that street to the west side thereof. When they reached the center of the street,

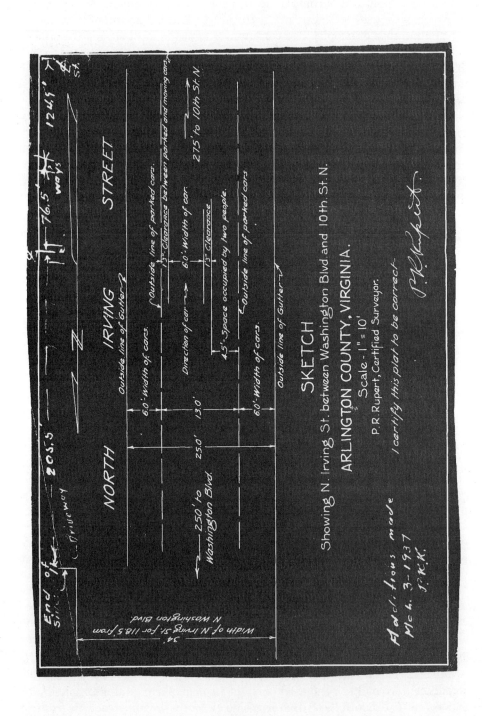

SKETCH

Showing N. Irving St. between Washington Blvd and 10th. St. N.

ARLINGTON COUNTY, VIRGINIA.

Scale - 1" = 10'

P.R. Rupert, Certified Surveyor.

I certify this plat to be correct -

Addi. tions made
Mc 4. 3-1937
J.P.K.K.

they noticed an automobile coming from their right without lights, and they safely hurried across. They estimated that the automobile was then running at a speed of from 18 to 20 miles per hour. They turned to watch it pass, and Mrs. Thomas called out to the driver, "Where are your lights?" She received no answer, and the car continued its course. While they were speaking to each other about the car being without lights, and within "a few seconds," they heard a crash ahead of them. The crash appeared to be at a distance variously estimated by them at from 60 to 100 feet away. If they were at a point directly opposite the community house, the actual distance, as shown by a survey, to the place of the accident would be 205 feet. These two witnesses proceeded to the place of the crash, and there saw Mrs. Cooley and Mrs. Dagger lying on the street and the defendant's car stopped close thereby.

A police officer soon came up, and, taking charge of the situation, found that the lights on the defendant's car were out and could not be turned on. He also found its left front headlight lamp had been tilted upward, but was not broken.

All of the above witnesses agree that the defendant wore a sweater or lumber jacket, which inclosed his right arm in the body of the jacket rather than in the right sleeve, and that it was fastened so that only the right hand was exposed to the wrist below the lower part of the jacket. It further appeared that the defendant had injured his right arm in a fall some two weeks before the occurrence.

Mrs. Cooley and Mrs. Dagger were taken to a hospital, and after securing medical services, were allowed to return to their respective homes; it being thought that they had received only superficial injuries. Shortly after returning home, Mrs. Cooley became ill, sank into a coma, and died about 4:30 a.m. The autopsy disclosed a ruptured artery in the tissue surrounding the brain and a blood clot producing pressure on the brain.

At the conclusion of the Commonwealth's evidence, the court overruled the motion of the defendant to strike the evidence.

The defendant showed in the evidence that he was the owner of a model 1934 Ford coupe, which was being driven by him that night. He was accompanied by Mrs. Eva Wright, with whom he boarded, and whom he was returning home from a moving picture performance attended by her. His automobile had been regularly inspected under the laws in this state as late as November, 1936, at which time his headlights had been found to need adjustment, and had been adjusted.

He stated that about 8 o'clock that night, and again at 10 o'clock, he had operated his automobile along North Irving street, past the point of the accident in proceeding twice to Clarendon, and that at both times his headlights were burning properly. Prior to leaving North Wilson boulevard, where he had taken up Mrs. Wright for the fatal trip, and immediately prior to entering North Irving street, on this trip, both he and Mrs. Wright and two other witnesses testified that the headlights of his car were burning brightly. He says that he first saw Mr. Jacobs and Mrs. Thomas in the street in front of him about 3 feet from the parked cars on his right side, at which time he was running between 15 and 18 miles an hour, and that he swerved his car to his left to avoid striking them, and continued at a speed of 12 to 15 miles an hour; that before he could get back to the right side of the center of the road he saw immediately in front of him two women, who had apparently stepped out from between the automobiles parked on the street; that while he did not have an opportunity to change the direction of his car, he did attempt to stop it; that before he could do this, he struck one of the women, who was apparently knocked against the other woman; that he stopped his car immediately; and then noticed the lights on the machine were out, and could not be switched on, although he got a slight flash from trying to switch them on. He had not used the car for the prior two weeks, because of tire trouble. He claimed that his right arm was free, and was not inclosed within the body of his jacket, as the jacket was thrown over his shoulders, and not fastened; and that he was driving with both hands. He also stated that Jacobs and Mrs. Thomas were some distance below the community house, as opposed to their statement that they were almost directly in front thereof, and that he did not hear Mrs. Thomas call out to him about the lack of lights.

Mrs. Eva Wright, the passenger in the defendant's car, stated that the lights were burning when they entered the car to return home, and were burning as they proceeded along North Irving street, until the time of the accident. She testified that the two women, who were struck down, walked out from between the cars parked on the street, into the side of the car driven by the defendant, and she was certain that they were not walking south on the street. She did not, however, see Mrs. Thomas or Mr. Jacobs, nor did she observe the defendant swing or swerve his car to the left side of the road.

An automobile mechanic, who examined the defendant's car some days after the collision, said that when he began work on it the headlight bulbs had already been replaced, but would not burn; that he found the light fuse burned out, an exposed wire, and a loose connection in the light wiring system. He said that while it did not always occur that both fuse and light bulbs would burn out at the same time, it had been known to occur; the fuse being for the protection of the light bulbs.

Upon the completion of all of the evidence, the defendant again moved the court to strike out the Commonwealth's evidence as insufficient to sustain a conviction, and assigned as grounds therefor the following: (1) That the conduct of the defendant did not amount to gross and culpable negligence; (2) that the evidence did not show that the defendant had knowledge that his automobile was without lights, if, in fact, it was prior to the accident without lights; and (3) that the evidence of the Commonwealth showed that the defendant was driving his car at a proper and lawful rate of speed, and was forced to operate it on the left side of the center of the road because persons were unlawfully using the highway. The court over-ruled the motion.

. . .

The first assignment of error relates to the refusal of the court to require the Commonwealth, in its bill of particulars, to specify with greater particularity the elements of the offense alleged, and to designate the specific charge upon which the Commonwealth intended to prosecute. The defendant contends that since the various acts of negligence allege separate criminal offenses, they should have been alleged in separate counts or paragraphs, and that the Commonwealth should have been required to designate which charge it would rely upon.

. . .

The answer to the defendant's contention is clear. The defendant here was not being tried for violation of the motor vehicle laws. In the instant case, the indictment contained only one count, and that was for manslaughter. A conviction was sought only on that count for involuntary manslaughter. The bill of particulars objected to was not a count or several counts. It was a statement of the several acts of negligence alleged to have existed in creating the offense. It recited an accumulation of negligent acts, each based, more or less, on the other, or proceeding one upon the other, to show an attitude of indifference to consequences, or a reckless, wanton, and callous disregard of the rules of safety.

In determining whether or not one is guilty of gross and culpable negligence, it is important to consider the cumulative effect of a series of — *Rule* connected, or independent negligent acts, out of which arise the injuries, as showing the attitude of the offender. All of the immediate acts and actions of the offender presenting a causal relation to the injury and a part of the res gestae are pertinent to the inquiry. A disregard of all or of several simple and primary rules of conduct prescribed by law for the benefit of society becomes the more aggravated as the disregard increases in extent. If each of the violations of law alleged in the bill of particulars followed immediately one upon the other, and contributed or concurred in producing the injury, each would be a factor in determining the degree and character of negligence committed. The bill of particulars, therefore, only sets out the means whereby the alleged offense of involuntary manslaughter was committed, and the constituent elements of the gross and culpable negligence relied on. In this respect, it gave notice to the defendant of the charge he would be required to meet and defend.

. . .

The three assignments of error, which relate to the refusal of the court to strike the evidence of the Commonwealth, and to set aside the verdict of the jury as contrary to the law and the evidence, present the question as to whether the verdict is supported by the law and the evidence.

In some states it is held that the breach of a statute is negligence per se, and that if there is a causal connection between the disregard of the statute and the injury inflicted, and such negligence is the proximate cause of the injury, it is sufficient to constitute manslaughter. . . .   *torts statute/ negligence RuL*

This court, in the absence of statute, has defined involuntary manslaughter in substantially the terms uniformly adopted in this country. In

Mundy v. Commonwealth, 144 Va. 609, Judge Chichester approves the following definition: "Involuntary manslaughter is the killing of one accidentally, contrary to the intention of the parties, in the prosecution of some unlawful, but not felonious, act; or in the improper performance of a lawful act." . . .

Mr. Chief Justice Prentis, in Goodman v. Commonwealth, 153 Va. 943, after discussing the application of this definition to a homicide committed in the operation of a motor vehicle, says:

"The precise grade of such a homicide, whether murder or manslaughter, depends upon the facts of the particular case. One, however, who accidentally kills another, even though he may be chargeable with some actionable negligence, is not guilty of a crime, unless his negligence is so gross and culpable as to indicate a callous disregard of human life and of the probable consequences of his act. The crime is imputed because of the recklessness, and, where there is no recklessness, there is no crime."

The courts and the authorities agree, in the absence of statutory regulations, that a higher degree of negligence is required to establish criminal negligence than to establish liability in a civil action. The negligence required in a criminal proceeding must be more than the lack of ordinary care and precaution. It must be something more than mere inadvertence or misadventure. It is a recklessness or indifference incompatible with a proper regard for human life. It must be shown that a homicide was not improbable under all of the facts existing at the time, and that the knowledge of such facts should have had an influence on the conduct of the offender. . . .

It is most difficult to define and to determine "gross and culpable negligence" in brief terms applicable to every situation. No completely satisfactory definition covering every situation has yet been given. The definitions given are restricted almost invariably to the facts of the particular case. The term "gross and culpable negligence" is descriptive of conduct. The very nature of the word "gross" indicates that it is more than mere or ordinary negligence; it is an aggravated or increased negligence. It is such negligence as may be often best evidenced by a series of acts of commission or omission indicating a state of mind or lack of thought of the offender. The commissions or omissions may be dependent, independent, interdependent, or cumulative, provided there is some causal relation to the state of the mind, or to the acts of the offender, with the offense charged. The word "culpable," in popular use and acceptation, means deserving of blame or censure. "Gross negligence" is culpable or criminal when accompanied by acts of commission or omission of a wanton or willful nature, showing a reckless or indifferent disregard of the rights of others, under circumstances reasonably calculated to produce injury, or which make it not improbable that injury will be occasioned, and the offender knows, or is charged with the knowledge of, the probable result of his acts.

When we reach the question, whether or not the evidence of the Commonwealth is sufficient to justify a verdict of involuntary manslaughter, we must consider that evidence in the light most favorable to the

Commonwealth, since the jury's verdict is final as to the conflicts arising in the testimony.

The evidence shows that the defendant, at the time of and immediately before the accident, was driving his car without lights, or without proper lights, on the left-hand side of a dark street, with a partially-disabled right arm confined closely to his side. The parking of other cars on both sides of the street, the presence of other persons on the street and in the vicinity when the card party was breaking up, were circumstances bringing home to him knowledge that he might expect people to be on the street. The width of the driveway was narrowed to 13 feet, but was otherwise unobstructed. The circumstances made the situation exceptionally risky and dangerous, and pointed to the constant risk and danger of any person using the narrow driveway, presenting a need for the exercise of great care in the operation of an automobile. In this narrow space, four women, two abreast, had walked for a distance of 200 feet on their left side of the street, and for at least the greater portion of that distance the defendant had proceeded in the same direction, and, if his lights had been burning properly, he could and should have seen them.

The defendant contends that the evidence did not show that he knew his lights were not burning. It is impossible for us to believe that a normal man can drive a motor vehicle under the conditions herein recited, and not observe the lights of his car go out, if he pays the slightest attention to the operation of his car. If he was looking where he was going on this street, on this dark night, he was bound to have seen the change made from burning bright headlights to the absence of lights. That he struck the two women on the outside of the pairs, and did not see their two companions, further shows a lack of proper lights. That the women did not immediately walk out from between the parked cars into the side of his car, is corroborated not only by their evidence, but by the tilted condition of his left front headlight, and by the position in which the injured women were found lying in the street. The condition of the headlight after the mishap, and the condition of the wires of the lighting system on the car, do not controvert the evidence that the lights were not burning as the car proceeded along North Irving street.

A common knowledge of the added hazards upon the public highways, through the increased use thereof by motor vehicles, makes it highly necessary that the simplest of safeguards provided by law for the protection of the public should be observed and followed.

There was a disregard both of the positive rules of law and of the ordinary rules of safety. The injuries inflicted upon the deceased were not improbable, and might have been reasonably anticipated under the circumstances existing at the time. The knowledge of these surrounding circumstances should have reasonably influenced the conduct of the defendant. There was ample evidence to justify the jury in believing that the defendant was guilty of such a callous indifference or disregard of the rules of law and safety, and of the rights of others, as was incompatible with a proper regard for human life, and amounted to gross, wanton, and culpable misconduct.

Another assignment of error relates to the giving of instruction No. 1 at the instance of the Commonwealth. This instruction simply defines, according to the provisions of the State Motor Vehicle Code . . . certain acts as constituting reckless driving, and recites the legal requirement for lights on automobiles. It does not undertake to define manslaughter, or to say that the defendant was guilty of involuntary manslaughter, or of reckless driving. It merely tells the jury that for the protection of the public, certain acts in driving a motor vehicle are made unlawful. It does not state that the defendant was guilty of any such unlawful acts, or deny to him the right to justify or defend any alleged violation.

There were other instructions given, which defined involuntary manslaughter, and repeatedly told the jury that the defendant could not be convicted of such an offense unless he were guilty of gross, wanton, and culpable negligence. Whether the defendant was guilty of several cumulative acts of negligence bearing a causal relation to the injury inflicted is material on the question of gross and culpable negligence. The violation of a positive law, or the commission of an act expressly prohibited, is prima facie unlawful, but this does not prohibit the defendant from showing a provocation or emergency which produced such act, if either a provocation or emergency existed. Such proof is a matter of defense.

. . . Instruction F was properly refused by the trial court. That instruction undertook to tell the jury that the defendant was not guilty, if the deceased was guilty of contributory negligence. All of the authorities agree that contributory negligence has no place in a case of involuntary manslaughter. This case is one of the state against the defendant, and not one of a party seeking damages in a civil action. The conduct of the decedent may have a material bearing on the degree of the defendant's guilt, but if the criminal negligence of the latter is found to be the cause of the death, the defendant is criminally responsible, whether the decedent's failure to use due care contributed to the injury or not.

Evidence of the conduct of the deceased, so far as it was material and affected the actions of the defendant, was admitted in evidence; and the jury, in another instruction, was correctly told the effect of such conduct, if proved.

. . . In the instant case, instructions, given at the request of the defendant, presented to the jury the theory of the defense, that the injuries were caused by reason of an emergency not created by him. These instructions also correctly directed the jury to consider whether or not the homicide was caused by misadventure, unavoidable accident, or by some supervening cause, for which the defendant was not responsible.

. . .

The judgment of the trial court is affirmed.[75]

---

[75] Partly because of the difficulty of obtaining a conviction for manslaughter in a case involving a death caused by the careless operation of an automobile, many states have

135. On what basis does the law hold someone like Bell, who had no intention of causing anyone's death, liable for manslaughter? Suppose Mrs. Cooley had recovered at the hospital. Of what crime, if any, would Bell then have been guilty? Since Bell's conduct is the same in both cases, should his criminal liability also be the same? Or does the fact that Mrs. Cooley died make all the difference?

136. Courts in other jurisdictions have agreed with the court in *Bell* that the high degree of negligence that constitutes criminal negligence is "most difficult to define." See, e.g., People v. Haney, 284 N.E.2d 564 (N.Y.1972). Compare the explanation of the term "wanton or reckless conduct" in Commonwealth v. Welansky, 55 N.E.2d 902, 909–12 (Mass. 1944). The Model Penal Code § 2.02(2)(c)–(d) uses the terms "recklessly" and "negligently":

> Recklessly.
>
> A person acts recklessly with respect to a material element of an offense when he consciously disregards a substantial and unjustifiable risk that the material element exists or will result from his conduct. The risk must be of such a nature and degree that, considering the nature and purpose of the actor's conduct and the circumstances known to him, its disregard involves a gross deviation from the standard of conduct that a law-abiding person would observe in the actor's situation.
>
> Negligently.
>
> A person acts negligently with respect to a material element of an offense when he should be aware of a substantial and unjustifiable risk that the material element exists or will result from his conduct. The risk must be of such a nature and degree that the actor's failure to perceive it, considering the nature and purpose of his conduct and the circumstances known to him, involves a gross deviation from the standard of care that a reasonable person would observe in the actor's situation.[76]

enacted special statutes covering deaths so caused, which impose a lesser penalty than that imposed for manslaughter. E.g., Cal. Penal Code §§ 192, 193. Courts have held that only "ordinary" negligence is required to establish criminal liability under such a statute. E.g., People v. Pociask, 96 P.2d 788 (Cal.1939).

[76] The problem of defining the degree of negligence necessary for criminal liability has arisen mostly in cases of involuntary manslaughter, and the requirement of a higher degree of negligence than that necessary for civil liability is well established for that crime. It is questionable whether there is such a requirement generally for crimes involving negligence. In the federal courts it has been established that ordinary negligence suffices for criminal liability under 18 U.S.C. § 1115, which makes it a felony for ship's officers to cause a death by misconduct or neglect. E.g., United States v. Abbott, 89 F.2d 166 (2d Cir.1937). See generally United States v. Meckling, 141 F.Supp. 608, 620 n. 27 (D.Md.1956). Compare United States v. LaBrecque, 419 F.Supp. 430 (D.N.J.1976).

For a case in which the Virginia court (citing *Bell*) found that the defendant's conduct in driving an automobile was negligent but not so grossly negligent as to warrant a verdict of involuntary manslaughter, see Tubman v. Commonwealth, 348 S.E.2d 871 (Va.Ct.App.1986). The court distinguished "ordinary or simple" negligence, "gross" negligence, and "willful, wanton, and reckless" negligence, and gave examples. (For purposes of involuntary manslaughter, the latter two categories are evidently equivalent.)

In People v. Hall, 999 P.2d 207 (Colo.2000), the court sustained a charge of reckless manslaughter against a ski racer who collided fatally with another skier on the slope. The evidence indicated that the defendant was an experienced skier and was skiing straight down the mountain, out of control and at an excessive speed. The statute provided that a person is liable for reckless manslaughter only if his conduct created a "substantial and unjustifiable risk" of death. The court said:

> Whether a risk is substantial must be determined by assessing both the likelihood that harm will occur and the magnitude of the harm should it occur. We hold that whether a risk is unjustifiable must be determined by assessing the nature and purpose of the actor's conduct relative to how substantial the risk is. Finally, in order for conduct to be reckless, the risk must be of such a nature that its disregard constitutes a gross deviation from the standard of care that a reasonable person would exercise.

Id. at 217. The court added that "[a] risk may be substantial even if the chance that the harm will occur is well below fifty percent." Id.

Construing the federal statute, 18 U.S.C. § 1112, that defines involuntary manslaughter, inter alia, as homicide "in the commission . . . without due caution and circumspection, of a lawful act which might produce death," in United States v. Keith, 605 F.2d 462, 463 (9th Cir.1979), the court said that two essential elements of the offense "are that: (1) the defendant committed with gross negligence the action causing death; and (2) the defendant had actual knowledge that his conduct was a threat to the lives of others, or had knowledge of such circumstances as would have made reasonably foreseeable to him the peril to which his acts might subject others."

137. Suppose Smith is aware that a proposed course of action would create a great and obvious risk of serious injury to others and, disregarding the risk, goes ahead anyway. Jones, on the other hand, engages in the same conduct but, because he is distracted or drunk or simply thoughtless, is oblivious to the risk. Can a useful distinction be drawn between the conduct of Smith and Jones? Is one more culpable than the other? See Regina v. Caldwell, [1982] App. Cas. 341, holding, over a dissent, that the conduct of Smith and of Jones alike satisfy a requirement of recklessness. *Caldwell* is followed in Regina v. Lawrence, [1982] App. Cas. 510.

138. In United States v. Escamilla, 467 F.2d 341, 343 (4th Cir.1972), the defendant was convicted of involuntary manslaughter for a killing that occurred on T–3, "an island of glacial ice . . . which meanders slowly about the general area of the Arctic Ocean." The defendant and the decedent were members of a research team stationed on the island during the summer months "when it is virtually impossible to remove any wrongdoer from the ice." Id. at 343–44. The killing arose out of circumstances that led the defendant to arm himself against a third member of the team who had previously attacked the defendant and others. Holding that the trial court should have given the defendant's requested instruction that the jury should consider the special situation on T–3, the court of appeals said:

> Gross negligence or even simple negligence is to be determined by all of the facts and circumstances surrounding an act which is asserted to be either. It would seem plain that what is negligent or grossly negligent conduct in the Eastern District of Virginia may not be negligent or grossly negligent on T–3 when it is remembered that T–3 has no governing authority, no police force, is relatively inaccessible from the rest of the world, lacks medical facilities and the dwellings thereon lack locks—in short, that absent self-restraint on the part of those stationed on T–3 and effectiveness of the group leader, T–3 is a place where no recognized means of law enforcement exist and each man must look to himself for the immediate enforcement of his rights. Certainly, all of these factors are ones which should be considered by a jury given the problem of determining whether defendant was grossly negligent. This is not to say that the standards of civilized conduct and the law of the United States do not prevail even on T–3, but those standards and that law admit of consideration of the circumstances surrounding alleged involuntary manslaughter both in the continental United States and on T–3.

Id. at 347–48.

139. Contributory negligence. The rule is as stated in *Bell*, p. 262 above. "While it is true that in a criminal prosecution for negligent homicide the contributory negligence of the deceased is not a defense . . . the trier of fact may still consider the decedent's conduct when determining whether the defendant's act was criminally negligent. . . . In the instant case [involving an automobile collision at an intersection], the decedent's conduct may be relevant because her failure to yield the right of way could relieve the defendant of criminal responsibility. For example, the defendant might prove that he expected the victim to yield and, therefore, did not slow down as he approached the intersection. The jury might therefore conclude that the defendant's failure to slow down was not criminal negligence, i.e., 'a gross deviation from the standard of care that a responsible person would observe in the situation.' " State v. Shumway, 672 P.2d 929, 932 (Ariz.1983).

140.

To hold a defendant criminally responsible for a homicide, the defendant's act must have been a proximate cause of the death. . . . [M]ere proof of a negligent act does not establish its causal relation to the injury. Further, evidence of causal relation is not necessarily proof of proximate cause.

So familiar is the definition of proximate cause that it can be stated, without citation, as a cause: (1) which, in a natural and continuous sequence and unbroken by any new and independent cause, produces an injury; (2) without which the injury would not have occurred; and (3) from which a person of ordinary prudence could have reasonably foreseen that such a result, or some similar injurious result, was probable under the facts as they existed.

State v. Hall, 299 S.E.2d 680, 683 (N.C.Ct.App.1983).

In Commonwealth v. Colvin, 489 A.2d 1378, 1379–80 (Pa.Super. Ct.1985), the defendant threw a stone through a window of the Adams' residence. The stone broke the window and caused minor damage. A week later, after 1:00 a.m., the defendant threw a stone at the side of the house. Mr. and Mrs. Adams were asleep. Their son Frederick heard the noise and ran up the stairs screaming. He met his father in the hall and told him that someone had thrown a stone at the house. Then his mother came into the hall. He told her what had happened. "Upon hearing this news, she collapsed and died." A doctor testified that Mrs. Adams had "died of fright or some other intense emotion, whether it was fright or fear or just excitement, some intense emotional state 'was the cause of death.'"

The court held that the defendant could not be convicted of involuntary manslaughter, defined by statute as causing the death of another person "as a direct result of the doing of an unlawful act in a reckless or grossly negligent manner, or the doing of a lawful act in a reckless or grossly negligent manner." Although the defendant was guilty of criminal mischief, the death was not a "direct result." "[T]he noise caused by the stone was not heard by the decedent. The stone caused property damage and the noise frightened Frederick Adams, and there the direct causal relationship ends." Id. at 1379–80.

141. Misdemeanor-manslaughter. As the court in *Bell* indicates, p. 259 above, in some jurisdictions the rule is said to be that any homicide which results from the commission of an unlawful act (not a felony) is manslaughter. See, e.g., Stanley v. Turner, 6 F.3d 399 (6th Cir.1993) (construing Ohio statute); State v. Hupf, 101 A.2d 355 (Del.1953). Even when the so-called "misdemeanor-manslaughter rule" is thus broadly stated, however, ordinarily more is required for its application than conjunction of an unlawful act and a death. If Bell had been driving a car with inoperative headlights in full daylight and without any other fault ran down Mrs. Cooley, it is unlikely that any court would find him guilty of manslaughter. In *Hupf*, the court observed: "The doctrine of proximate cause is an important limitation on the common-law rule that a homicide occurring in the commission of an unlawful act is manslaughter. The mere violation of the statute is not enough; the violation must be the proximate cause of the death, and that causal connection must affirmatively appear. The unlawful act must be 'something more than a factor which might be denominated more properly as an attendant condition than a cause of the death.'" Id. at 360. So, for example, in State v. Hall, 299 S.E.2d 680 (N.C.Ct.App.1983), the defendant, who was hunting deer, shot and killed another hunter. He was convicted of involuntary manslaughter. Holding that evidence that the defendant did not have a hunting license should not have been admitted, the court said: "Whether the defendant had a hunting license on the day in question was irrelevant to the question whether his conduct was criminally negligent. The violation of a statute is pertinent when, and only when, that statute is designed for the protection of human life or limb and there is evidence tending to show that a violation thereof proximately caused the death." Id. at 685.

Some courts have explicitly limited the misdemeanor-manslaughter rule to situations in which the violation of law is one that endangers life and the conduct that constitutes the violation can be described as grossly negligent. E.g., State v. Strobel, 304 P.2d 606 (Mont.1956). "[A]n unlawful act causing the death of another cannot, simply because it is an unlawful act, render a manslaughter verdict inevitable. For such a verdict inexorably to follow, the unlawful act must be such as all sober and reasonable people would inevitably recognise must subject the other person to, at least, the risk of some harm resulting therefrom, albeit not serious harm." Regina v. Church, [1966] 1 Q.B. 59, 70 (Crim. App. 1965). See United States v. Walker, 380 A.2d 1388 (D.C.1977) (carrying pistol without a license; manslaughter charge sustained). As in *Bell*, if a statute prescribes a standard of care its violation may be strong evidence of negligence.

Reviewing its holding in *Bell* and other cases, the Virginia court subsequently declared:

> In the operation of motor vehicles violation of a safety statute amounting to mere negligence proximately causing an accidental death is not sufficient to support a conviction of involuntary manslaughter. Likewise, the improper performance of a lawful act proximately causing an accidental killing is also insufficient unless that improper performance constitutes criminal negligence.

> We conclude that involuntary manslaughter arising from the operation of a motor vehicle should be predicated solely upon criminal negligence proximately causing death. Accordingly, we define involuntary manslaughter in the operation of a motor vehicle as the accidental killing which, although unintended, is the proximate result of negligence so gross, wanton, and culpable as to show a reckless disregard of human life.

King v. Commonwealth, 231 S.E.2d 312, 316 (Va.1977).

limitation on misdemeanor

The rule has also been limited in some jurisdictions by a requirement that the offense be *malum in se*, "one which is naturally evil as adjudged by the sense of a civilized community," and not merely *malum prohibitum*, "wrong only because made so by statute," State v. Horton, 51 S.E. 945, 946 (N.C.1905). See generally Bartlett v. State, 569 P.2d 1235 (Wyo.1977).

For a general discussion, see Commonwealth v. Catalina, 556 N.E.2d 973 (Mass.1990), rejecting "unlawful-act manslaughter," except when the defendant engages in wanton or reckless conduct or is guilty of a battery.

142. Drunk driving. The connection that must be established between drunk driving and a death for the driver to be liable for homicide has divided the courts. Some courts have required that a causal connection be established between the driver's state of intoxication and the homicide.

See People v. Bennett, 819 P.2d 849 (Cal.1991) (where statute specifies gross negligence and driving while intoxicated as distinct elements of offense, latter alone is insufficient to establish former but may be considered as aspect of defendant's conduct bearing on gross negligence). In State v. Wong, 486 A.2d 262 (N.H.1984), the court said that under the statute defining negligent homicide, driving while intoxicated was negligence per se, and a person proved to have been driving while intoxicated could not defend by showing that he had driven with due care. The court evidently required, however, that a causal connection be established between driving *while intoxicated* and the homicide. It must be proved "that 'as a consequence' of the defendant's being under the influence of intoxicating liquor at the time of the collision, he caused the victim's death." Id. at 269.

How would the causal connection, as understood by the court, be established without proof of negligence, which the court seemed to say was unnecessary?

Other courts have held that if a defendant is proved to have been driving while intoxicated, the causal connection need only be between his driving and the homicide. In State v. Caibaiosai, 363 N.W.2d 574 (Wis. 1985), the court agreed with the reasoning of the New Hampshire court in *Wong* about culpability but not causation. It said:

> The legislature has determined that combining the operation of a motor vehicle with being in an intoxicated state is conduct which is *malum prohibitum* and is pervasively antisocial. Since the conduct is considered inherently evil, it conceptually cannot be divided into portions which are bad and portions which are not bad. Section 346.63, Stats., entitled "Operating under the influence of intoxicants" is violated by a person who, one, operates a motor vehicle, and two, is at the time under the influence of an intoxicant. The commission of the offense does not require any erratic or negligent driving. Because driving under the influence of an intoxicant is *malum prohibitum* it is impossible to separate the intoxication from the driving or the driving from the intoxication. The result is the potentially lethal and illegal combination of driving while intoxicated.

Section 940.09, Stats., requires that the prosecution prove and the jury find beyond a reasonable doubt a causal connection between the defendant's unlawful conduct, operation of a motor vehicle while intoxicated, and the victim's death. The statute does not include as an element of the crime a direct causal connection between the fact of defendant's intoxication, conceptualized as an isolated act, and the victim's death. Under this statute there is an inherently dangerous activity in which it is reasonably foreseeable that driving while intoxicated may result in the death of an individual. The legislature has determined this activity so inherently dangerous that proof of it need not require causal connection between the defendant's intoxication and the death.

363 N.W.2d at 577–78. To the same effect, see People v. Garner, 781 P.2d 87 (Colo.1989).

In 1988, Larry Mahoney, who was drunk and driving his pickup truck on the wrong side of an interstate highway, crashed into a church school bus. Twenty-four children and three adults were killed, the worst drunk-driving accident in the nation's history. Twelve other persons were badly burned. Mahoney had a prior conviction for drunk driving. He was indicted for murder. Contesting the indictment—"It's a terrible mistake he made . . . But that boy ain't no murderer"—people in the small town where he lived rallied to his support. The jury acquitted him of murder and convicted him of manslaughter. It recommended that he be sentenced to 16 years' imprisonment, which recommendation the judge accepted. Mahoney was eligible for parole after about seven and a half years in prison. The New York Times, Aug. 5, 1988, at 14; Feb. 24, 1990, at 9.

143. (i) A car which the defendant was driving collided with a telephone pole, and a person was killed. The collision was not due to any negligence of the defendant. He had obtained a driving license in the past but had failed to renew it on time, and at the time of the accident was driving without a license, a misdemeanor.

[handwritten margin note: Not enough of a causal connection]

(ii) The defendant sold moonshine whiskey to a person who became drunk and, after spending the night in the open, died of acute alcoholism and exposure. Sale of the whiskey was a felony.

[handwritten margin note: — there is cause in fact & Proximate cause]

(iii) Upon being told by the deceased that he intended to break off their engagement, the defendant took a pistol and tried to shoot herself. The deceased struggled with her to prevent her from committing suicide. The pistol, which was in the defendant's hand, was accidentally discharged and the deceased was killed. There was no criminal penalty for attempted suicide or suicide.

[handwritten margin note: the Ct. says suicide is morally wrong, not a crime. misdemeanor – manslaughter]

Should the defendant in any of these cases be liable for manslaughter? See (i) Commonwealth v. Williams, 1 A.2d 812 (Pa.Super.Ct.1938); (ii) People v. Pavlic, 199 N.W. 373 (Mich.1924); (iii) Commonwealth v. Mink, 123 Mass. 422 (1877).

Suppose a person picks up a woman's unattended pocketbook while she is standing across the street and starts to walk off with it. If she pursues him, trips, and dies from her injuries, is he guilty of manslaughter? See People v. Burroughs, 678 P.2d 894, 902 n.11 (Cal.1984).

144. Liability for negligence, even great negligence, is not characteristic of the criminal law, which generally requires more serious fault. Statutes, however, commonly proscribe specific conduct which would ordinarily be described as negligent or reckless. Many rules of the road, for the violation of which minor penalties are imposed, are in this category. Statutes in many states deal in this way with the danger of fires. The California Health and Safety Code, for example, makes it a misdemeanor for a person to allow a fire kindled by him to escape from his control or spread to anyone else's lands "without using every reasonable and proper precaution to prevent the fire from escaping" (§ 13000); "through careless or negligent action" to throw or place a burning substance or other substance which might cause a fire in a place where it might do so (§ 13001); to throw such a substance from a vehicle (§ 13002), etc. See the Model Penal Code § 220.1(2)–(3) (recklessly burning or exploding; failure to control or report dangerous fire). A great many other specific negligent or reckless acts are proscribed by legislation. Unlike the crime of negligent homicide, violations of such statutes are complete even if no harm occurs; but the penalty for violation of the statutes is typically not great.

Should the criminal law generally proscribe negligent conduct that endangers an interest worthy of protection? Compare the Model Penal Code § 211.2: "Recklessly Endangering Another Person. A person commits a misdemeanor if he recklessly engages in conduct which places or may place another person in danger of death or serious bodily injury. Recklessness and danger shall be presumed where a person knowingly points a firearm at or in the direction of another, whether or not the actor believed the firearm to be loaded." See also, in addition to the provisions dealing with fires and explosions, above, the Model Penal Code § 220.2(2)–(3) (recklessly risking or failing to prevent catastrophe). If any interests at all should be protected generally by the criminal law against negligent or reckless conduct, are there some interests that should be protected by the criminal law against intentional conduct but not negligent conduct? Why (not)?

Maryland v. Chapman

101 F.Supp. 335 (D.Md.1951)

■ CHESNUT, DISTRICT JUDGE. These three cases, by agreement tried concurrently, present a very unusual set of facts resulting in the unintentional death of two small children and one adult who were occupants of a house in a settlement known as Morningside, just north of the United States Air

Force Base known as Andrews Field, situated in Prince George's County, Maryland, about four miles distant from the District of Columbia Line. The deaths of these three persons resulted from the abandonment of a B–25 type of aircraft belonging to the United States Government and stationed at Andrews Field. The pilot of the plane was Captain Paul V. Chapman, a regular officer of the United States Air Force and an experienced pilot with prior service of about 1,700 hours of flying time and who had been for some years past actively engaged as an officer of the Air Force. The Grand Jury of Prince George's County indicted Captain Chapman in the three separate cases for manslaughter. Under the applicable federal statute[77] the cases were removed to this court for trial, on the ground that the acts performed by the defendant were in the course of his official duties as a federal officer. There has been no question raised as to the propriety of this removal of the cases. They have been tried without a jury by the request of the defendant, concurred in by counsel for both parties.

In a removal case of this nature the substantive law of the State of Maryland must be applied by the court. . . . There is practically no controversy as to any of the facts. The question in the case is whether the facts establish a case of manslaughter.

Andrews Field was established by the United States during the last war, after condemnation of the land in Prince George's County. Since then, and possibly as a result of activities at the Air Base, a considerable residential settlement has grown up just north of the Field, consisting of nearly 400 separate houses with a population of about 1,800.

The B–25 involved in this case had been stationed at Andrews Field for a year or more prior to the occurrence of the events on April 8, 1951, which are the subject of this case. It was a bomber type of plane which had recently been in use for continued training flights by officers of the Army, mostly stationed in the Pentagon Building in or near Washington, D.C. The day before April 8, 1951, a mechanical defect had been noticed with respect to the operation of the landing gear of this plane. The landing gear consisted of two wheels at the rear of the plane and one front wheel, constituting what is called a tricycle formation arrangement. As is well known, as soon as the airplane takes off and is airborne, these wheels are retracted upwards into the body of the plane and when the plane alights they are released to form a cushion for the landing. They are actuated by cylinders which are operated with hydraulic fluid. A mechanic repaired the landing gear equipment on Saturday, April 7, and in accordance with usual

[77] 28 U.S.C. § 1442: "(a) A civil action or criminal prosecution commenced in a State court against any of the following persons may be removed by them to the district court of the United States for the district and division embracing the place wherein it is pending: (1) Any officer of the United States or any agency thereof, or person acting under him, for any act under color of such office or on account of any right, title or authority claimed under any Act of Congress for the apprehension or punishment of criminals or the collection of the revenue . . . ."

practice before it was released for general flight it was necessary to ascertain by a test flight if it was in operating condition. Such a test flight for this plane was authorized in writing on April 8. Capt. Sander, an experienced pilot with 2,000 hours of flying time, was directed to make the test flight. The regulations provided that he be accompanied by a co-pilot and an engineer. On request, Capt. Chapman, who was available at the time, was asked to and agreed to make the test flight for this particular plane and two other planes which were to be tested.

On inspecting the B–25 prior to the test flight some further difficulty was noticed with respect to the operation of the landing gear. A mechanic was called to make the necessary adjustment and in the meantime Sander and Chapman and the engineer tested and found satisfactory another plane. On returning to the B–25, inspection indicated that the adjustment had been satisfactorily made. They immediately proceeded to test it. Capt. Sander suggested to Capt. Chapman that as the latter was in a measure voluntarily assuming extra duty he might prefer to act as pilot and get the credit for additional flying time, and Chapman so agreed and did act as pilot on the test flight. Almost immediately after the plane was airborne it was noticed that the landing gear did not properly retract and release. This fact was at once communicated by radio-telephone to the officer on duty in the Control Tower at the Field. He advised trying various customary procedures to overcome the difficulty. These were unsuccessful and later the Control Tower advised the plane to try so-called "violent" maneuvers, which also proved unsuccessful, but resulted in shaking down the left wheel to the landing position but causing it to be locked in that position so that it could not be again retracted; while the right wheel was only half released and could not be either retracted or fully lowered; nor could the front wheel be released. This condition of the two rear wheels was observed by the pilot and co-pilot on their respective sides of the plane. They concluded that the trouble was with loss or non-functioning of hydraulic fluid. The Control Tower then ordered another plane to attempt to lower a can of needed hydraulic fluid. This very difficult maneuver was unsuccessful because the rope first used was too short. The second attempt with a longer rope was later tried also unsuccessfully.

The test flight had begun at 11 A.M., and these various maneuvers had occupied several hours. In the meantime the plane had been flown over and several miles away from the Field. Chapman and Sander discussed various possibilities which the situation presented. They were in almost constant radio contact with the Tower. The latter suggested that a crash landing might be possible but both Chapman and Sander concluded on their best judgment, with their immediate knowledge of the condition of the landing gear, that this would be very hazardous. The Tower's suggestion that a crash landing might be feasible was apparently based on the supposition that the pilots were provided with shoulder harnesses, which however, they did not have. Both pilots testified that in the condition of the landing gear a crash landing would be extremely dangerous to all three occupants of the plane and likely fatal to one or more of them.

Information that a plane in the air was in serious trouble soon became known to other superior officers of the Air Force at Andrews Field and six of them assembled in the Tower and after consultation directed replies and advice to be given from time to time to the plane. It is recognized that the ultimate responsibility for final action rests with the pilot of the plane, but advice from the Tower is naturally carefully heeded and considered by the pilot.

At 3:45 P.M., the plane was near Annapolis, about 30 miles from Andrews Field, and the gas supply was running low. The pilots had lost nearly all hope of repairing the landing gear and decided to return to the Field for further instructions. On nearing the Field and coming into radio contact with the Tower the recorded messages between the Tower and the plane were as follows: The plane said: "We are five miles north of ADW (Andrews Field), 2300 feet, we are now attempting to force some gasoline into the hydraulic system in a final effort to get this gear down. We plan to abandon the aircraft, request you figure out a proper heading so that we will miss the populated area."

Tower—"ADW tower advises that after you make a final attempt to use the gasoline fly over ADW field on a heading of 120 degrees and have the co-pilot and engineer bail out."

Plane to Tower—"Repeat."

Tower—"Fly over ADW field on a heading of 120 degrees, have the co-pilot and engineer bail out."

Plane—"I understand we are to take a heading of 120 (garbled) is that roger?"

Tower—"Negative, 395, what we would like to have you do is fly directly over the ADW field and on the first pass have the co-pilot and engineer bail out. The pilot will take the airplane around and come in on a heading of 120 degrees, trim the airplane and the pilot will bail out on the second pass on a heading of 120 degrees over Andrews."

The two pilots concurred in and acted on this advice. None of the three occupants of the plane had ever previously attempted a parachute landing but the parachutes were, in accordance with regulations, attached to their bodies. Chapman, the pilot, did as he was advised. The co-pilot and engineer bailed out of the plane and after the pilot performed the circling motions as advised, he also abandoned the plane. All three landed safely with only minor injuries.

The standard operations procedure at Andrews Field provided that if it became necessary to abandon a plane in the Washington area, the pilot should first set the plane on a compass course of 140 degrees which, counting the north as zero, would tend to continue the flight of the airplane in a generally southeasterly direction over a sparsely populated area. When, in accordance with the above recited communications between the plane and the Tower the Tower advised that in this particular instance when the plane was abandoned it should be set on a course of 120 degrees, the expectation was that it would in its continued flight proceed in a generally southeasterly direction toward the Chesapeake Bay which was about 15 miles away and which would be reached in normal flight in about 7 or 8 minutes. Simultaneously the Tower gave orders to two jet planes to follow the abandoned B–25, and when it reached over the Chesapeake Bay, as expected, to shoot it down.

There was a reasonable expectation on the part not only of the pilot and co-pilot of the B–25, but also by the superior Air Force officers stationed in the Control Tower (many of whom testified as witnesses in this case to that effect) that the plane would so continue on its charted course. This expectation was based on their prior experience with B–25's which they, or some of them, had personally piloted for some minutes at a time without the pilot touching the instruments at all after setting the course. The unexpected development in this case was that after the pilot had set the course and carried out other instructions from the Tower and abandoned the plane, the latter after proceeding only a very short distance on the course set, began to swerve or circle to the left and finally came to the ground about 200 feet from the house which was finally struck with great force and set on fire and apparently completely destroyed, with the lives of the three occupants. This erratic course of the plane was unexpected and is entirely unexplained.

More specifically I find with respect to the facts—

1. The judgment of the pilots that a crash landing would be extremely dangerous if not fatal to all three occupants of the plane was well founded and highly probably correct. And this also seems to have been the judgment of the six officers in the Tower after learning the full conditions and exhausting the possibility of repairing the landing gear. The great danger in a crash landing with the landing gear in its condition was that on landing the airplane would "cartwheel" and probably turn over and catch on fire. It would not have been reasonably possible for the co-pilot and engineer to bail out leaving the pilot alone to attempt a crash landing in view of the numerous things that would have to be done by him alone at that time. A crash landing in the Chesapeake Bay with all three occupants of the plane was likewise rejected because the plane was not equipped with water life-saving devices of any kind, and from experience the pilots thought that impact with the water would probably cartwheel the plane and cause their drowning.

2. It is not contended by the State that the defendant had any intention to kill or harm any of the three decedents or any other persons. In the emergency situation which developed in the plane during the five hours that it was in the air, and in the difficult alternatives which had developed and were carefully considered by the pilots, it is not surprising that in their final action they elected to abide by the advice of the Control Tower as to the time for and the method of abandoning the plane.

The most serious contention of the State is that the pilot himself should not have abandoned the plane over Andrews Field but, after the co-pilot and engineer had left the plane over the Andrews Field, the defendant as pilot should have kept on in the plane and abandoned it only after it was safely away from the populated area of Morningside. At least with regard to future action, the contention is certainly a reasonable one in the interest of the safety of the citizens of Prince George's County. And it is to be noted that the standard operations procedure (S.O.P.) has been amended since this occurrence, and doubtless in the light of the experience gained thereby, so that there is added to the procedure, in the case of an abandonment of an airplane in or around Andrews Field, the following:

"To proceed toward the Atlantic Ocean area and abandon the aircraft at such altitude and attitude as to preclude return trip to populated area."

It appears from these facts that at the time the airplane was abandoned by the defendant as pilot, the situation that existed was (1) a crash landing would certainly imperil the life of the defendant; (2) it was therefore imperative that the defendant should abandon the plane by the only means available to him, a very risky one at that, of landing by parachute; (3) that every possible effort had been made to avoid this ultimate situation; (4) that in abandoning the plane the pilot, in addition to his own judgment, and that of his copilot, thought it necessary to do so; (5) that this judgment was confirmed by the advice, if not instruction, of the six superior officers in the Control Tower; (6) that it was the reasonable expectation of all of them that the plane would continue on its southeasterly course for at least some miles into the sparsely occupied territory where it was highly improbable that any one's life or property would be endangered.

Counsel for the State does not seriously dispute these facts but maintains that there was at the moment of final abandonment no immediate urgency or necessity for the plane to be abandoned by the pilot over Andrews Field which was in proximity to the populated area north and that therefore the pilot should have known or realized that it was dangerous to human life to abandon the plane at that time and place. This is the real question in the case. On the other hand, hindsight is proverbially better than foresight. It was said during the trial that there was no prior instance on record where an airplane abandoned by the pilot had resulted in serious danger to life of persons on the ground. As a result of the experience in this case the standard operations procedure has been further amended as above stated for further future safety. Should it be held in this case that the defendant should have reasonably anticipated the probability that the plane would circle and swerve, as it did, back into an area almost directly opposite to the course on which it was set when the pilot abandoned it? The burden of establishing an affirmative answer to this question beyond a reasonable doubt is on the prosecution. After careful consideration, I have concluded that it has not been so established.

. . .

In the instant case it is conceded that the defendant had no intention to kill or harm anyone. Obviously, therefore, the case if one of manslaughter at all, is one of involuntary manslaughter.

. . .

Again it is to be importantly noted that in considering the subject of what constitutes negligence, we must distinguish between its application in cases involving civil liability and those, as in this one, involving alleged criminal liability. We are not dealing here with a civil case and it is therefore quite unnecessary to determine whether the injuries caused by the abandonment of this plane constituted a civil liability of any one. In my view the law is reasonably clear that a charge of manslaughter by negligence is not made out by proof of ordinary simple negligence that would constitute civil liability. In other words, the amount or degree or character of the negligence to be proven in a criminal case is *gross* negligence, to be determined on the consideration of all the facts of the particular case, and the existence of such gross negligence must be shown beyond a reasonable doubt. If the resultant deaths were merely accidental or the result of a misadventure or due to simple negligence, or an honest error of judgment in performing a lawful act, the existence of gross negligence should not be found.

In a succinct and well prepared brief counsel for the State has aptly expressed the matter in saying that the question is whether the conduct of the defendant, considering all the factors of the case, was such that it amounted to a "wanton or reckless disregard for human life." On the facts I conclude that the defendant's action was neither wanton nor reckless, and because the State has not established beyond a reasonable doubt that it was, the verdict must accordingly be Not Guilty. The clerk is therefore instructed to enter that judgment.

---

145. Was the risk of injury to life or property created by Chapman greater or less than the risk created by Bell?

Was Chapman's conduct more or less deterrable by criminal law than Bell's conduct?

146. Would Chapman have been guilty of manslaughter:

(i) if it were somewhat less likely that he would be killed by a crash landing?

(ii) if it were somewhat more likely that someone's life or property would be endangered if he abandoned the plane?

(iii) if it were somewhat less likely that he would fall safely to the ground with the aid of a parachute if he abandoned the plane?

147. Consider all the circumstances, including the preparations for the flight and the efforts to retract the landing gear upward while the airplane was in flight. Even if, as the court found, the decision to abandon the airplane was not reckless at the time it was made, might one conclude that it was reckless to postpone the decision until it was too late to do anything else? (Whether, in the circumstances, Chapman himself or some other person(s) should be accountable is a separate question.) Incidentally, the court states that it was the "reasonable expectation" of all the officers in the control tower that the airplane "would . . . continue . . . on course," p. 275. According to well-known principles of aerodynamics, if the left wheel was shaken down lower than the right wheel, unless the pilot had trimmed the airplane to compensate, it was predictable that the airplane would swerve to the left; and if, as is likely, he had trimmed the airplane, its course after he abandoned it would have been unpredictable. Someone who piloted a B–25 has observed about the facts of the case: "Basically, the pilot probably set it up as best he could, but he should have had nothing more than a forlorn hope that the airplane would keep going in that general direction for a few minutes. Foolish hope, in my opinion."

148. Could Chapman have been found criminally liable for the deaths without some other persons involved in the incident also being found criminally liable (whether or not they were prosecuted)? If not, which other persons? If so, why?

149. What is the significance of the amendment of the standard operations procedure after the accident?

150. Feinberg owned a cigar store on skid row in Philadelphia. He sold residents of the area cans of Sterno which, as he knew, they diluted and drank. The wood alcohol content of the Sterno was about 4%. In December 1963 Feinberg purchased cases of Sterno for industrial use, the wood alcohol content of which was 54%. Unlike the cans he had purchased earlier the cans of the new Sterno were marked with the words "Danger. Poison," and a skull and crossbones. In one week in December, starting two days after Feinberg bought the new cans of Sterno, 31 persons in the area died from alcohol poisoning. Feinberg returned the unsold cans. He was aware of the warning on the cans and gave no warning to purchasers. Assuming that some of the deaths could be traced to drinking the new Sterno, did he commit any form of criminal homicide? See Commonwealth v. Feinberg, 253 A.2d 636 (Pa.1969).

Gian-Cursio v. State

180 So.2d 396 (Fla.Dist.Ct.App.1965)

■ CARROLL, JUDGE. The appellants, who are chiropractic physicians, were informed against in Dade County, charged with manslaughter by having

(victim)

caused the death of one Roger Mozian through culpable negligence. The defendants were tried together and convicted. Dr. Gian-Cursio was sentenced to confinement for a period of five years, and sentence was suspended as to Dr. Epstein. Motions for new trial filed by defendants were denied, and they appealed. The two appeals were consolidated for presentation in this court.

Procedural History

Appellants contend the evidence was insufficient to support the verdicts and judgments of conviction. . . .

appellants' argument

The record discloses that one Roger Mozian died of pulmonary tuberculosis in May of 1963. His disease had been diagnosed in 1951 by Dr. Matis, a New York medical doctor in whose charge he remained for some ten years, during which his tuberculosis continued dormant or arrested. An X-ray examination of Mozian by Dr. Matis in January of 1962 showed his disease had become active. Dr. Matis recommended hospitalization and drug treatment, which Mozian refused. Mozian went under the care of Dr. Gian-Cursio, a licensed chiropractic physician in the State of New York, who practiced Natural Hygiene. Dr. Gian-Cursio was advised that Mozian was suffering from tuberculosis. His treatment of the patient was without drugs and by a vegetarian diet, interspersed with fasting periods. Evidence was in conflict as to length of fasting. There was testimony that on occasion the fasting continued 14 days. Dr. Epstein was a licensed chiropractic physician of Florida. Acting with Dr. Gian-Cursio and under his direction, Dr. Epstein operated a home or establishment for patients in Dade County, Florida. Beginning in the winter of 1962, on the advice of Dr. Gian-Cursio, Mozian went there and was treated by the appellant doctors, in the manner stated above. Eventually, in May of 1963 he was hospitalized, where through other doctors he was given drugs and other approved treatment for the disease but within a matter of days he died, on May 16, 1963. There was testimony that the treatment given Mozian was not approved medical treatment for one with active tuberculosis, and that had he been treated by approved medical methods and given available drugs his disease could have been arrested or controlled. From the evidence the jury could, and no doubt did conclude that the treatment afforded by the appellants advanced rather than retarded the patient's tuberculosis infection and caused his death, and that their method of treatment of this tuberculosis patient amounted to culpable negligence as it has been defined in the decisions of the Supreme Court of this State. In State v. Heines, 144 Fla. 272, 197 So. 787, 788, the Florida Supreme Court reversed an order quashing a manslaughter information which charged a chiropractic physician with causing the death of a patient who suffered from diabetes, by culpable negligence through treatment which included taking him off insulin. . . . [T]he Florida Supreme Court said:

Facts

Example Case

> We need add little more to what has been written in the three cases cited to show how one who is proven to have offended as detailed in the information has violated the law against manslaughter. If a person undertakes to cure those who search for health and who are, because of their plight, more or less susceptible of following the advice

of any one who claims the knowledge and means to heal, he cannot escape the consequence of his gross ignorance of accepted and established remedies and methods for the treatment of diseases from which he knows his patients suffer and if his wrongful acts, positive or negative, reach the degree of grossness he will be answerable to the State.

In the earlier case of Hampton v. State, [39 So. 421,] the Florida Court went into the matter at greater length, and what they held there is applicable to the situation presented by this record. In that case the Court said (39 So. at 424):

> We do not agree with this contention of the able counsel for the defendant. The law seems to be fairly well settled, both in England and America, that where the death of a person results from the criminal negligence of the medical practitioner in the treatment of the case the latter is guilty of manslaughter, and that this criminal liability is not dependent on whether or not the party undertaking the treatment of the case is a duly licensed practitioner, or merely assumes to act as such, acted with good intent in administering the treatment, and did so with the expectation that the result would prove beneficial, and that the real question upon which the criminal liability depends in such cases is whether there was criminal negligence; that criminal negligence is largely a matter of degree, incapable of precise definition, and whether or not it exists to such a degree as to involve criminal liability is to be determined by the jury; that criminal negligence exists where the physician or surgeon, or person assuming to act as such, exhibits gross lack of competency, or gross inattention, or criminal indifference to the patient's safety, and that this may arise from his gross ignorance of the science of medicine or surgery and of the effect of the remedies employed, through his gross negligence in the application and selection of remedies and his lack of proper skill in the use of instruments, or through his failure to give proper instructions to the patient as to the use of the medicines; that where the person treating the case does nothing that a skillful person might not do, and death results merely from an error of judgment on his part, or an inadvertent mistake, he is not criminally liable. [. . .]

We reject as unsound the arguments of appellants that because their treatment conformed to generally accepted practice of drugless healers and was rendered in good faith in an effort to help Mozian, it was proper and could not be found to constitute criminal negligence. That, and appellants' further argument that their treatment of Mozian could not have been tested through testimony of medical doctors, is answered adversely to appellants by Hampton v. State, supra. In Hampton it was held to be immaterial "whether or not the party undertaking the treatment of the case is a duly licensed practitioner, or merely assumes to act as such, acted with good intent in administering the treatment, and did so with the expectation that the results would prove beneficial." Additionally, appellants argue that proximate cause was not established. The issue of proxi-

appellants' argument

mate cause was one for the jury, and the record furnished substantial evidence upon which that issue was submitted for jury determination.

Under the applicable law as enunciated in the cited Florida cases, the trial court was eminently correct in denying defendants' motions for directed verdict and in submitting the issue of their alleged culpable negligence to the jury. . . .

---

151. Should it be relevant to the defendants' liability for manslaughter whether or not they "acted with good intent in administering the treatment, and did so with the expectation that the results would prove beneficial," *Gian-Cursio*, above?

152.

Lee Swatsenbarg had been diagnosed by the family physician as suffering from terminal leukemia. Unable to accept impending death, the 24-year-old Swatsenbarg unsuccessfully sought treatment from a variety of traditional medical sources. He and his wife then began to participate in Bible study, hoping that through faith Lee might be cured. Finally, on the advice of a mutual acquaintance who had heard of defendant's ostensible successes in healing others, Lee turned to defendant for treatment.

During the first meeting between Lee and defendant, the latter described his method of curing cancer. This method included consumption of a unique "lemonade," exposure to colored lights, and a brand of vigorous massage administered by defendant. Defendant remarked that he had successfully treated "thousands" of people, including a number of physicians. He suggested the Swatsenbargs purchase a copy of his book, *Healing for the Age of Enlightenment*. If after reading the book Lee wished to begin defendant's unorthodox treatment, defendant would commence caring for Lee immediately. During the 30 days designated for the treatment, Lee would have to avoid contact with his physician.

Lee read the book, submitted to the conditions delineated by defendant, and placed himself under defendant's care. Defendant instructed Lee to drink the lemonade, salt water, and herb tea, but consume nothing more for the ensuing 30 days. At defendant's behest, the Swatsenbargs bought a lamp equipped with some colored plastic sheets, to bathe Lee in various tints of light. Defendant also agreed to massage Lee from time to time, for an additional fee per session.

Rather than improve, within two weeks Lee's condition began rapidly to deteriorate. He developed a fever, and was growing progressively weaker. Defendant counseled Lee that all was proceeding according to plan, and convinced the young man to postpone a bone marrow test urged by his doctor.

During the next week Lee became increasingly ill. He was experiencing severe pain in several areas, including his abdomen, and vomiting frequently. Defendant administered "deep" abdominal massages on two successive days, each time telling Lee he would soon recuperate.

Lee did not recover as defendant expected, however, and the patient began to suffer from convulsions and excruciating pain. He vomited with increasing frequency. Despite defendant's constant attempts at reassurance, the Swatsenbargs began to panic when Lee convulsed for a third time after the latest abdominal massage. Three and a half weeks into the treatment, the couple spent the night at defendant's house, where Lee died of a massive hemorrhage of the mesentary in the abdomen. The evidence presented at trial strongly suggested the hemorrhage was the direct result of the massages performed by defendant.

People v. Burroughs, 678 P.2d 894, 896 (Cal.1984).

The court reversed the defendant's conviction for felony murder, but held that he could be convicted of involuntary manslaughter, defined as a homicide caused by an "act . . . without due caution and circumspection." It said: "[T]here was substantial testimony that a reasonably prudent physician would have known that administering 'deep abdominal massage' to a leukemia victim such as Swatsenbarg would render the likelihood of hemorrhage very high. Burroughs' treatment of Swatsenbarg, given defendant's apparent indifference to, or lack of awareness of this common medical knowledge, is at the core of activity performed 'without due caution and circumspection.' " Id. at 901 n.9.

Does the *Burroughs* case differ significantly from *Gian-Cursio*? If so, how?

153. In Commonwealth v. Pierce, 138 Mass. 165 (1884), the defendant, who practiced as a physician, treated a patient by having her wrapped in flannels soaked in kerosene, as a result of which she died. He was convicted of manslaughter. Affirming the conviction, Justice Holmes said for the court:

So far as civil liability is concerned, at least, it is very clear that what we have called the external standard would be applied, and that, if a man's conduct is such as would be reckless in a man of ordinary prudence, it is reckless in him. Unless he can bring himself within some broadly defined exception to general rules, the law deliberately leaves his idiosyncrasies out of account, and peremptorily assumes that he has as much capacity to judge and to foresee consequences as a man of ordinary prudence would have in the same situation. . . .

If this is the rule adopted in regard to the redistribution of losses, which sound policy allows to rest where they fall in the absence of a clear reason to the contrary, there would seem to be at least equal reason for adopting it in the criminal law, which has for its immediate object and task to establish a general standard, or at least general negative limits, of conduct for the community, in the interest of the safety of all.

. . .

If a physician is not less liable for reckless conduct than other people, it is clear, in the light of admitted principle and the later Massachusetts cases, that the recklessness of the criminal no less than that of the civil law must be tested by what we have called an external standard. In dealing with a man who has no special training, the question whether his act would be reckless in a man of ordinary prudence is evidently equivalent to an inquiry into the degree of danger which common experience shows to attend the act under the circumstances known to the actor. The only difference is, that the latter inquiry is still more obviously external to the estimate formed by the actor personally than the former. But it is familiar law that an act causing death may be murder, manslaughter, or misadventure, according to the degree of danger attending it. If the danger is very great, as in the case of an assault with a weapon found by the jury to be deadly, or an assault with hands and feet upon a woman known to be exhausted by illness, it is murder. . . .

The very meaning of the fiction of implied malice in such cases at common law was, that a man might have to answer with his life for consequences which he neither intended nor foresaw. To say that he was presumed to have intended them is merely to adopt another fiction, and to disguise the truth. The truth was, that his failure or inability to predict them was immaterial, if, under the circumstances known to him, the court or jury, as the case might be, thought them obvious.

As implied malice signifies the highest degree of danger, and makes the act murder; so, if the danger is less, but still not so remote that it can be disregarded, the act will be called reckless, and will be manslaughter, as in the case of an ordinary assault with feet and hands, or a weapon not deadly, upon a well person. . . .

If the principle which has thus been established both for murder and manslaughter is adhered to, the defendant's intention to produce the opposite result from that which came to pass leaves him in the same position with regard to the present charge that he would have been in if he had had no intention at all in the matter. We think that the principle must be adhered to where, as here, the assumption to act as a physician was uncalled for by any sudden emergency, and no exceptional circumstances are shown; and that we cannot recognize a privilege to do acts manifestly endangering human life, on the ground of good intentions alone.

We have implied, however, in what we have said, and it is undoubtedly true, as a general proposition, that a man's liability for his acts is determined by their tendency under the circumstances known to him, and not by their tendency under all the circumstances actually affecting the result, whether known or unknown. And it may be asked why the dangerous character of kerosene . . . is not one of the circumstances the defendant's knowledge or ignorance of which might have a most important bearing on his guilt or innocence.

But knowledge of the dangerous character of a thing is only the equivalent of foresight of the way in which it will act. We admit that, if the thing is generally supposed to be universally harmless, and only a specialist would foresee that in a given case it would do damage, a person who did not foresee it, and who had no warning, would not be held liable for the harm. If men were held answerable for everything they did which was dangerous in fact, they would be held for all their acts from which harm in fact ensued. The use of the thing must be dangerous according to common experience, at least to the extent that there is a manifest and appreciable chance of harm from what is done, in view either of the actor's knowledge or of his conscious ignorance. And therefore, again, if the danger is due to the specific tendencies of the individual thing, and is not characteristic of the class to which it belongs, which seems to have been the view of the common law with regard to bulls, for instance, a person to be made liable must have notice of some past experience, or, as is commonly said, "of the quality of his beast." 1 Hale P.C. 430. But if the dangers are characteristic of the class according to common experience, then he who uses an article of the class upon another cannot escape on the ground that he had less than the common experience. Common experience is necessary to the man of ordinary prudence, and a man who assumes to act as the defendant did must have it at his peril. When the jury are asked whether a stick of a certain size was a deadly weapon, they are not asked further whether the defendant knew that it was so. It is enough that he used and saw it such as it was. . . . So here. The defendant knew that he was using kerosene. The jury have found that it was applied as the result of foolhardy presumption or gross negligence, and that is enough. . . . Indeed, if the defendant had known the fatal tendency of the prescription, he would have been perilously near the line of murder. . . . It will not be necessary to invoke the authority of those exceptional decisions in which it has been held, with regard to knowledge of the circumstances, as distinguished from foresight of the consequences of an act, that, when certain of the circumstances were known, the party was bound at his peril to inquire as to the others, although not of a nature to be necessarily inferred from what were known. . . .

138 Mass. at 176–80.

154. Both of the defendants in *Gian-Cursio* were licensed chiropractors, Dr. Gian-Cursio by New York and Dr. Epstein by Florida, in which state they were convicted of manslaughter. What were they licensed to do? What did they do "wrong"? Were the States of New York and Florida primarily responsible for Mozian's death?[78]

155. So long as his refusal to be treated himself did not endanger the health of others (by contagion, etc.) couldn't Mozian have declined any treatment at all?[79] Should that have a bearing on the liability of the defendants in *Gian-Cursio*?

156. The usual rule is that it is not a defense to a criminal charge that the victim consented to the performance of the criminal act on him. E.g., State v. Brown, 364 A.2d 27, 31–32 (N.J.Super.Ct.Law Div.1976) (assault and battery): "To allow an otherwise criminal act to go unpunished because of the victim's consent would not only threaten the security of our society but also might tend to detract from the force of the moral principles underlying the criminal law." (The consent of the participants in recognized sports such as football and boxing is a defense to a charge of assault and battery based on the ordinary physical contact and blows incurred in such sports.)

Is that rule a sufficient explanation of Gian-Cursio's liability despite Mozian's (apparently) voluntary submission to his treatment?

157. In *Chapman*, p. 270 above, should the defendant (or his employer, the United States) be liable civilly for the wrongful death of the persons killed in the crash? In *Gian-Cursio*, should the defendants be liable civilly for the wrongful death of Mozian? Why (not)?

---

78. Both states had extensive legislation regulating the practice of chiropractic. Fla. Stat. ch. 460; N.Y. Educ. Law art. 132. In Florida a licensed chiropractor was authorized to "examine, analyze and diagnose the human living body and its diseases," and to treat the human body by manipulation and dietary and hygienic methods; he was expressly prohibited from prescribing or administering medicine or drugs or performing surgery. Fla. Stat. § 460.11(2).

79. On the right to die rather than submit to medical treatment, see In re Estate of Brooks, 205 N.E.2d 435 (Ill.1965) (competent adult may not be compelled to submit to medical treatment contrary to religious beliefs); Lane v. Candura, 376 N.E.2d 1232 (Mass.App.Ct.1978) (competent adult may not be compelled to submit to medical treatment); Application of Lydia E. Hall Hospital, 455 N.Y.S.2d 706 (Sup.Ct.1982) (life-sustaining treatment of terminally ill, comatose patient stopped, in accordance with patient's previously expressed wish); Matter of the Welfare of Colyer, 660 P.2d 738 (Wash.1983) (order on application of guardian, for removal of life-support systems from incompetent patient in chronic vegetative state affirmed). But cf. In re Caulk, 480 A.2d 93 (N.H.1984) (healthy prison inmate, who has no expectation of being released, has no right to die by refusing to eat).

FAILURE TO ACT

———

People v. Beardsley

150 Mich. 206, 113 N.W. 1128 (1907)

■ McALVAY, C.J. Respondent was convicted of manslaughter before the circuit court for Oakland county, and was sentenced to the state prison at Jackson for a minimum term of one year and a maximum term not to exceed five years.   *proc. History*

He was a married man living at Pontiac, and at the time the facts herein narrated occurred he was working as a bartender and clerk at the Columbia Hotel. He lived with his wife in Pontiac, occupying two rooms on the ground floor of a house. Other rooms were rented to tenants, as was also one living room in the basement. His wife being temporarily absent from the city, respondent arranged with a woman named Blanche Burns, who at the time was working at another hotel, to go to his apartments with him. He had been acquainted with her for some time. They knew each other's habits and character. They had drunk liquor together, and had on two occasions been in Detroit and spent the night together in houses of assignation. On the evening of Saturday, March 18, 1905, he met her at the place where she worked, and they went together to his place of residence. They at once began to drink, and continued to drink steadily, and remained together, day and night, from that time until the afternoon of the Monday following, except when respondent went to his work on Sunday afternoon. There was liquor at these rooms, and when it was all used they were served with bottles of whisky and beer by a young man who worked at the Columbia Hotel, and who also attended respondent's fires at the house. He was the only person who saw them in the house during the time they were there together. Respondent gave orders for liquor by telephone. On Monday afternoon, about 1 o'clock, the young man went to the house to see if anything was wanted. At this time he heard respondent say they must fix up the rooms, and the woman must not be found there by his wife, who was likely to return at any time. During this visit to the house the woman sent the young man to a drug store to purchase, with money she gave him, camphor and morphine tablets. He procured both articles. There were six grains of morphine in quarter-grain tablets. She concealed the morphine from respondent's notice, and was discovered putting something into her mouth by him and the young man as they were returning from the other room after taking a drink of beer. She in fact was taking morphine. Respondent struck the box from her hand. Some of the tablets fell on the floor, and of these respondent crushed several with his foot. She picked up and swallowed two of them, and the young man put two of them in the spittoon. Altogether it is probable she took from three to four grains of morphine. The young man went away soon after this. Respondent called him by telephone about an hour later, and after he came to the house requested him to take the woman into the room in the basement which was occupied by a Mr. Skoba. She was in a stupor, and did not rouse when spoken to. Respondent was too intoxicated to be of any assistance, and the young man proceeded to take her downstairs. While doing this, Skoba arrived, and together they put her in his room on the bed. Respondent requested Skoba to look after her, and let her out the back way when she waked up. Between 9 and 10 o'clock in the evening, Skoba became alarmed at her condition. He at once called the city marshal and a doctor. An examination by them disclosed that she was dead..

Many errors are assigned by respondent, who asks to have his conviction set aside. The principal assignments of error are based upon the charge of the court and refusal to give certain requests to charge, and are upon the theory that under the undisputed evidence in the case, as claimed by the people and detailed by the people's witnesses, the respondent should have been acquitted and discharged. In the brief of the prosecutor, his position is stated as follows: "It is the theory of the prosecution that the facts and circumstances attending the death of Blanche Burns in the house of respondent were such as to lay upon him a duty to care for her, and the duty to take steps for her protection, the failure to take which was sufficient to constitute such an omission as would render him legally responsible for her death. . . . There is no claim on the part of the people that the respondent was in any way an active agent in bringing about the death of Blanche Burns, but simply that he owed her a duty which he failed to perform, and that in consequence of such failure on his part she came to her death." Upon this theory a conviction was asked and secured.

The law recognizes that under some circumstances the omission of a duty owed by one individual to another, where such omission results in the death of the one to whom the duty is owing, will make the other chargeable with manslaughter. . . . This rule of law is always based upon the proposition that the duty neglected must be a legal duty, and not a mere moral obligation. It must be a duty imposed by law or by contract, and the omission to perform the duty must be the immediate and direct cause of death. . . .

Although the literature upon the subject is quite meagre and the cases few, nevertheless the authorities are in harmony as to the relationship which must exist between the parties to create the duty, the omission of which establishes legal responsibility. One authority has briefly and correctly stated the rule, which the prosecution claims should be applied to the case at bar, as follows: "If a person who sustains to another the legal relation of protector, as husband to wife, parent to child, master to seaman, etc., knowing such person to be in peril, willfully and negligently fails to make such reasonable and proper efforts to rescue him as he might have done, without jeopardizing his own life, or the lives of others, he is guilty of manslaughter at least, if by reason of his omission of duty the dependent person dies." "So one who from domestic relationship, public duty, voluntary choice, or otherwise, has the custody and care of a human being, helpless either from imprisonment, infancy, sickness, age, imbecility, or other incapacity of mind or body is bound to execute the charge with proper

Rule

diligence, and will be held guilty of manslaughter, if by culpable negligence he lets the helpless creature die." 21 Am. & Eng. Enc. of Law (2d Ed.) p. 192, notes and cases cited.

. . .

. . . In a federal case tried in California before Mr. Justice Field, of the United States Supreme Court, where the master of a vessel was charged with murder in omitting any effort to rescue a sailor who had fallen overboard, the learned justice, in charging the jury, said: "There may be in the omission to do a particular act under some circumstances, as well as in the commission of an act, such a degree of criminality as to render the offender liable to indictment for manslaughter. . . . In the first place, the duty omitted must be a plain duty. . . . In the second place, it must be one which the party is bound to perform by law, or by contract, and not one the performance of which depends simply upon his humanity, or his sense of justice and propriety." United States v. Knowles, 4 Sawy. (U.S.) 517, Fed. Cas. No. 15,540.

. . .

. . . Seeking for a proper determination of the case at bar by the application of the legal principles involved, we must eliminate from the case all consideration of mere moral obligation, and discover whether respondent was under a legal duty towards Blanche Burns at the time of her death, knowing her to be in peril of her life, which required him to make all reasonable and proper effort to save her, the omission to perform which duty would make him responsible for her death. This is the important and determining question in this case. If we hold that such legal duty rested upon respondent, it must arise by implication from the facts and circumstances already recited. The record in this case discloses that the deceased was a woman past 30 years of age. She had been twice married. She was accustomed to visiting saloons and to the use of intoxicants. She previously had made assignations with this man in Detroit at least twice. There is no evidence or claim from this record that any duress, fraud, or deceit had been practiced upon her. On the contrary, it appears that she went upon this carouse with respondent voluntarily, and so continued to remain with him. Her entire conduct indicates that she had ample experience in such affairs.

It is urged by the prosecutor that the respondent "stood towards this woman for the time being in the place of her natural guardian and protector, and as such owed her a clear legal duty which he completely failed to perform." The cases cited and digested establish that no such legal duty is created based upon a mere moral obligation. The fact that this woman was in his house created no such legal duty as exists in law and is due from a husband towards his wife, as seems to be intimated by the prosecutor's brief. Such an inference would be very repugnant to our moral sense. Respondent had assumed either in fact or by implication no care or control over his companion. Had this been a case where two men under like circumstances had voluntarily gone on a debauch together, and one had attempted suicide, no one would claim that this doctrine of legal duty could be invoked to hold the other criminally responsible for omitting to make effort to rescue his companion. How can the fact that in this case one of the parties was a woman change the principle of law applicable to it? Deriving and applying the law in this case from the principle of decided cases, we do not find that such legal duty as is contended for existed in fact or by implication on the part of respondent towards the deceased, the omission of which involved criminal liability. We find no more apt words to apply to this case than those used by Mr. Justice Field, in United States v. Knowles, supra: "In the absence of such obligations, it is undoubtedly the moral duty of every person to extend to others assistance when in danger . . . and, if such efforts should be omitted by any one when they could be made without imperiling his own life, he would by his conduct draw upon himself the just censure and reproach of good men; but this is the only punishment to which he would be subjected by society."

. . .

Holding   The conviction is set aside, and respondent is ordered discharged.

———

158.   How does the problem of homicidal failure to act differ from the problem of homicidal negligent action? Is the relevant difference only that where there is a negligent act, the act focuses our attention on the actor and provides a link between the death and a particular individual, whereas when an omission is asserted as the basis of culpability the link must be sought elsewhere?

Consider the following two statements:

(i) If A had not accidentally left the motor of the car running, B would not have died.

(ii) If anyone had turned off the motor, B would not have died.

159.   "The idea of killing by an omission implies, in the first place, the presence of an opportunity of doing the act the omission of which causes death. It would be extravagant to say that a man who having food in London omits to give it to a person starving to death in China has killed the man in China by omitting to feed him; but it would be natural to say that a nurse who being supplied with food for a sick person under her care omits to give it, and thereby causes the sick person's death, has killed that person. Whether a person, who being able to save the life of another without inconvenience or risk refuses to do so, even in order that he may die, can be said to have killed him is a question of words, and also a question of degree. A man who caused another to be drowned by refusing to hold out his hand to save him probably would in common language be said to have killed him, and many similar cases might be put, but the limit of responsibility is soon reached. It would hardly be said that a rich man who allowed a poor man to die rather than give, say £ 5, which the rich man would not miss, in order to save his life, had killed him, and though it might be cowardly not to run some degree of risk for the purpose of saving the life of another, the omission to do it could hardly be described as homicide. A number of people who stand round a shallow pond in which a child is drowning, and let it drown without taking the trouble to ascertain the depth of the pond, are no doubt, shameful cowards, but they can hardly be said to have killed the child." 3 Stephen, History 9–10.

160. "There are at least four situations in which the failure to act may constitute breach of a legal duty [sustaining liability for homicide if death results]. One can be held criminally liable: first, where a statute imposes a duty to care for another; second, where one stands in a certain status relationship to another; third, where one has assumed a contractual duty to care for another; and fourth, where one has voluntarily assumed the care of another and so secluded the helpless person as to prevent others from rendering aid." Jones v. United States, 308 F.2d 307, 310 (D.C.Cir. 1962).

[handwritten margin note: 4 sources / Statute / Status / contract / Voluntarily]

161. The duty to care for another based on a relationship with the other person is well settled when the person needing care is a child and the person under a duty is the parent. There are a number of cases in which a parent has been found guilty of homicide (involuntary manslaughter or murder, see note 168 below) for failure to give ordinary care to a small child. E.g., Nozza v. State, 288 So.2d 560 (Fla.Dist.Ct.App.1974); McMichael v. State, 471 N.E.2d 726 (Ind.Ct.App.1984); People v. Sealy, 356 N.W.2d 614 (Mich.Ct.App.1984). Cf. State v. Walden, 293 S.E.2d 780 (N.C.1982) (parent who failed to intervene to prevent assault on child liable as aider and abettor to assault). Children are not generally held to have a duty to an infirm parent based simply on the relationship. See generally People v. Heitzman, 886 P.2d 1229, 1231 (Cal.1994), limiting a statute imposing criminal liability for permitting the abuse of a dependent or elder adult to a person "who, under existing tort principles, has a duty to control the conduct of the individual who is directly causing or inflicting abuse." The court held that the defendant, not having such a duty, was not liable for her brother's abusive and ultimately fatal failure of care of her father, of which she was aware.

It is commonly assumed that a duty is owed by one spouse to another; but cases are few. See Commonwealth v. Konz, 450 A.2d 638 (Pa.1982), concluding that while both spouses are competent, there is no duty of care that would give rise to criminal liability for a failure to act, but that there might be a duty when one spouse is "unwillingly rendered incompetent to evaluate the need for aid, or helpless to obtain it." The court said: "Spouses . . . do not generally suffer the same incapacity as do children with respect to the ability to comprehend their states of health and obtain medical assistance. We reject, therefore, the holding of the Superior Court that the marital relationship gives rise to an unrestricted duty for one spouse to summon medical aid whenever the other is in a serious or immediate need of medical attention. Recognition of such a duty would place lay persons in peril of criminal prosecution while compelling them to medically diagnose the seriousness of their spouses' illnesses and injuries. In addition, it would impose an obligation for a spouse to take action at a time when the stricken individual competently chooses *not* to receive assistance. The marital relationship gives rise to an expectation of reliance between spouses, and to a belief that one's spouse should be trusted to respect, rather than ignore, one's expressed preferences. That expectation would be frustrated by imposition of a broad duty to seek aid, since one's spouse would then be forced to ignore the expectation that the preference to forego assistance will be honored." Id. at 642. See People v. Robbins, 443 N.Y.S.2d 1016 (App.Div.1981). Cf. *Flayhart*, note 164 below (brother and sister-in-law of decedent).

    162.   The defendants were charged with involuntary manslaughter for failing to provide necessary medical attention for their 17-month-old child. The child had an abscessed tooth, which caused an infection in his mouth and cheeks that eventually became gangrenous. This condition accompanied by malnutrition, because he was unable to eat, led to pneumonia, from which he died. There was medical testimony that the infection had lasted for about two weeks and that the odor associated with gangrene would have been present for about ten days before the child died, but that if medical care had not been obtained until the week before the child died, it would have been too late to save his life. The defendant husband, who was the child's stepfather, was a laborer. He had a sixth-grade education. The defendant wife had an eleventh-grade education. There was another child.

    "The testimony concerning the child's apparent condition during the critical period is not crystal clear, but is sufficient to warrant the following statement of the matter. The defendant husband testified that he noticed the baby was sick about 2 weeks before the baby died. The defendant wife testified that she noticed the baby was ill about a week and a half or 2 weeks before the baby died. The evidence showed that in the critical period the baby was fussy; that he could not keep his food down; and that a cheek started swelling up. The swelling went up and down, but did not disappear. In that same period, the cheek turned 'a bluish color like.' The defendants, not realizing that the baby was as ill as it was or that the baby was in danger of dying, attempted to provide some relief to the baby by giving the baby aspirin during the critical period and continued to do so until the night before the baby died. The defendants thought the swelling would go down and were waiting for it to do so; and defendant husband testified, that from what he had heard, neither doctors nor dentists pull out a tooth 'when it's all swollen up like that.' There was an additional explanation for not calling a doctor given by each defendant. Defendant husband testified that 'the way the cheek looked . . . and that stuff on his hair, they would think we were neglecting him and take him away from us and not give him back.' Defendant wife testified that the defendants were 'waiting for the swelling to go down,' and also that they were afraid to take the child to a doctor for fear that the doctor would report them to the welfare department, who, in turn, would take the child away. 'It's just that I was so scared of losing him.' They testified that they had heard that the defendant husband's cousin lost a child that way. The evidence showed that the defendants did not understand the significance or seriousness of the baby's symptoms. However, there is no evidence that the defendants were physically or financially unable to obtain a doctor, or that they did not know an available doctor, or that the symptoms did not continue to be a matter of concern during the critical period. Indeed, the evidence shows that in April 1968 defendant husband had taken the child to a doctor for medical attention." State v. Williams, 484 P.2d 1167, 1174 (Wash.Ct.App.1971).

What result? If the defendants are guilty, what would be an appropriate sentence?

163. In *Beardsley*, the court states that failure to perform a contractual obligation the performance of which would have prevented a death is manslaughter. Although this is generally said to be the rule, it is difficult to find cases in which liability for manslaughter was based on a contractual obligation and nothing more.

Liability for murder based on a failure to perform a contractual duty to provide food and medical care was upheld in Commonwealth v. Pestinikas, 617 A.2d 1339 (Pa.Super.1992). The defendants had agreed to provide a home and care for the elderly victim, who died from starvation and dehydration. They secluded him from others who were interested in his welfare and before his death, over a period of many months, regularly withdrew sums from his bank account equal to and, later, far exceeding the amount that he had agreed to pay them. See also People v. Montecino, 152 P.2d 5 (Cal.Ct.App.1944) (nurse liable for failure to care for patient); Davis v. Commonwealth, 335 S.E.2d 375 (Va.1985) (child liable for failure to take care of senile parent; implied contract). In some cases the courts have reasoned, not quite explicitly, that a contractual obligation arising out of a private contract gave rise to a duty to the public generally for whose benefit the contract was made, and that failure to perform that duty was the basis for liability. See State v. Irvine, 52 So. 567 (La.1910); State v. Harrison, 152 A. 867 (N.J.Sup.Ct.1931).

It is clear, isn't it, that by itself the duty to perform a contractual obligation is an inadequate basis for criminal liability for manslaughter? Suppose that in *Montecino*, above, the defendant had quit her job in breach of contract in order to take a better paying job elsewhere but had given her employer ten days notice. If her employer did nothing in those ten days or for thirty days thereafter to find another nurse and died from lack of care, should the defendant be liable for manslaughter? On the other hand, can a railroad gate tender avoid liability for manslaughter by shouting, "I quit.

Sue me for breach of contract," if, knowing that a train is due, he leaves the gate unattended and walks off for a beer?

164. For an example of liability for manslaughter arising out of a voluntary assumption of duty, see Regina v. Stone, [1977] 2 W.L.R. 169 (Crim. App.). There, the victim, who was an eccentric woman in her fifties, came to live with her brother and his mistress, the two defendants. The victim remained in her room and did not take care of herself. Over a period of months her condition deteriorated. The defendants made some ineffectual efforts to take care of her. Both were found to have been grossly negligent in failing to perform the duty of care that they had undertaken, and were convicted of manslaughter. Cf. State v. Brown, 631 P.2d 129 (Ariz.Ct.App.1981) (defendant kept helpless person as lodger after court ordered that she no longer do so).

See People v. Flayhart, 523 N.Y.S.2d 225, 226 (App.Div.1988), in which the decedent, a retarded adult, lived with the defendants, his brother and sister-in-law. Without specifying the basis on which the defendants had a duty to act, the court referred to their "incredible neglect of one entirely dependent on others for his care and support," and affirmed their convictions of criminally negligent homicide. See also People v. Oliver, 258 Cal.Rptr. 138, 144 (Ct.App.1989), a case somewhat resembling *Beardsley*, in which, upholding a conviction for involuntary manslaughter, the court noted that the defendant had taken the deceased "from a public place where others might have taken care to prevent him from injuring himself, to a private place—her home—where she alone could provide such care," and in so doing "to a certain, if limited extent . . . took charge of a person unable to prevent harm to himself."

165. "The decedent's girlfriend visited the apartment of the decedent Thomas Brown on the evening of March 20, 1979. Brown was lying on the floor breathing erratically; his lips were turning blue. The defendant informed her that Brown 'had done some Dilaudid.' The girlfriend could not wake Brown up, and she, the defendant and a third person moved him to his bed. After the third person left, she became concerned about Brown's condition and called her brother, a technician at a hospital. Following that conversation, she started to call an ambulance, but the defendant 'bodily shoved [her] away from the phone, took it from [her],' and threatened to kill her if she attempted to obtain help. He stated that 'he didn't want any police or anything because he had a long narcotics record and he had drugs on him and a syringe and he didn't want anyone around him.' The defendant also stated that he would watch the decedent and take care of him. Brown's girlfriend left. When she returned the next morning, she found Brown dead. The medical examiner testified that the cause of death was 'abuse of alcohol and Dilaudid,' and another medical expert testified that Brown could have 'been saved' had he obtained medical help earlier." Commonwealth v. Marcelli, 441 N.E.2d 270, 270–71 (Mass.Ct.App.1982).

The court affirmed the defendant's conviction of involuntary manslaughter. "While the law does not, except in special circumstances, impose a duty on bystanders to take action to preserve the life of another . . . here the defendant by his conduct increased the danger of harm to Brown. Although medical assistance was urgently needed, he bodily prevented the decedent's girlfriend from procuring aid and threatened to kill her if she persisted in that endeavor. We have no doubt that such conduct is wanton and reckless . . . ." Id. at 271.

166. What is the explanation of criminal liability for unintended deaths resulting from a failure to act? Is the accepted rule, that in the absence of an express statutory provision there is liability only if "a duty to perform the omitted act is otherwise imposed by law," Model Penal Code § 2.01(3)(b), congruent with the explanation? Or does it go too far in some cases and not far enough in others?

167. Consider the following cases:

(i) A shoots B in necessary self-defense. The wound is not mortal, but B is unable to do anything to treat the wound and is too weak to go for medical assistance. A perceives B's condition but does nothing. B dies. (See State ex rel. Kuntz v. Montana Thirteenth Judicial District Court, 995 P.2d 951 (Mont.2000); King v. Commonwealth, 148 S.W.2d 1044 (Ky.1941).)

(ii) A shoots B accidentally while they are hunting. A sees that B is unable to help himself but in his anxiety to get another shot at the deer that he missed leaves him lying in the woods for several hours. B dies. (Cf. Jones v. State, 43 N.E.2d 1017 (Ind.1942).) See N.H. Rev. Stat. Ann. § 207.38, providing that "[a]ny person who shall have shot and wounded or killed a human being shall forthwith render necessary assistance to the injured person and report immediately to the nearest conservation officer or law enforcement officer," and that the knowing failure to do so is a felony.

(iii) A shoots B accidentally while they are hunting. C, another member of the hunting party, knows that B has been shot and is unable to help himself and knows also that A is unaware that B has been shot. Unwilling to have A get ahead of him in the hunt, C rushes off after a deer and doesn't help B or get other help for him for several hours. B dies.

(iv) A is hunting and comes across B, a stranger, lying in the woods. B has evidently been attacked by a bear and is bleeding profusely. A perceives that B may die if unaided. Anxious to add a trophy to his collection (and, perhaps, to stop the bear from hurting others) A rushes off to see if he can shoot the bear. B dies.

(v) A invites B to his home to discuss a business transaction. Late in the evening B indicates that he feels ill and asks if he can stay the night. A refuses the request but helps B to prepare for the journey home. B falls to the ground on the way home and dies of exposure during the night. (Cf. Depue v. Flateau, 111 N.W. 1 (Minn.1907).)

Should A be criminally liable for B's death in any of these cases?

168. An omission to perform an act that one has a duty to perform, with the intention that the person to whom the duty is owed die, is murder if that is the result. E.g., People v. Burden, 140 Cal.Rptr. 282 (Ct.App. 1977); State v. Evangelista, 353 S.E.2d 375 (N.C.1987). If Beardsley had perceived Burns's condition and had given her no assistance because he thought it prudent for himself, in the circumstances, to let her die, would he have been guilty of any form of criminal homicide? Should he have been?

The New York Times
Friday, March 27, 1964.

37 Who Saw Murder Didn't Call The Police

By Martin Gansberg

. . .

Twenty-eight-year-old Catherine Genovese, who was called Kitty by almost everyone in the neighborhood, was returning home from her job as manager of a bar in Hollis. She parked her red Fiat in a lot adjacent to the Kew Gardens Long Island Rail Road Station, facing Mowbray Place. Like many residents of the neighborhood, she had parked there day after day since her arrival from Connecticut a year ago, although the railroad frowns on the practice.

She turned off the lights of her car, locked the door and started to walk the 100 feet to the entrance of her apartment at 82–70 Austin Street, which is in a Tudor building, with stores on the first floor and apartments on the second.

The entrance to the apartment is in the rear of the building because the front is rented to retail stores. At night the quiet neighborhood is shrouded in the slumbering darkness that marks most residential areas.

Miss Genovese noticed a man at the far end of the lot, near a seven-story apartment house at 82–40 Austin Street. She halted. Then, nervously, she headed up Austin Street toward Lefferts Boulevard, where there is a call box to the 102d Police Precinct in nearby Richmond Hill.

'He Stabbed Me!'

She got as far as a street light in front of a bookstore before the man grabbed her. She screamed. Lights went on in the 10-story apartment house at 82–67 Austin Street, which faces the bookstore. Windows slid open and voices punctured the early-morning stillness.

Miss Genovese screamed: "Oh, my God, he stabbed me! Please help me! Please help me!"

From one of the upper windows in the apartment house, a man called down: "Let that girl alone!"

The assailant looked up at him, shrugged and walked down Austin Street toward a white sedan parked a short distance away. Miss Genovese struggled to her feet.

Lights went out. The killer returned to Miss Genovese, now trying to make her way around the side of the building by the parking lot to get to her apartment. The assailant stabbed her again.

"I'm dying!" she shrieked. "I'm dying!"

A City Bus Passed

Windows were opened again and lights went on in many apartments. The assailant got into his car and drove away. Miss Genovese staggered to her feet. A city bus, Q–10, the Lefferts Boulevard line to Kennedy International Airport, passed. It was 3:35 A.M.

The assailant returned. By then, Miss Genovese had crawled to the back of the building, where the freshly painted brown doors to the apartment house held out hope of safety. The killer tried the first door; she wasn't there. At the second door, 82–62 Austin Street, he saw her slumped on the floor at the foot of the stairs. He stabbed her a third time —fatally.

It was 3:50 by the time the police received their first call, from a man who was a neighbor of Miss Genovese. In two minutes they were at the scene.

. . .

. . .

Aside from the man who called the police after Genovese had been stabbed a third time, there were 37 or 38 respectable, middle-class persons who witnessed the stabbing from their homes but did nothing. Should any of the silent witnesses to her death have been liable for manslaughter or any other crime? *No; can not be held liable for a moral duty. witnesses had no legal duty to act*

The New York Times

Saturday, March 28, 1964.

Editorial

What Kind Of People Are We?

Seldom has The Times published a more horrifying story than its account of how 38 respectable, law-abiding, middle-class Queens citizens watched a killer stalk his young woman victim in a parking lot in Kew Gardens over a half-hour period, without one of them making a call to the Police Department that might have saved her life. They would not have been exposed to any danger themselves; a simple telephone call in the privacy of their own homes was all that was needed. How incredible it is that such motivations as "I didn't want to get involved" deterred them from this act of simple humanity. Does residence in a great city destroy all sense of personal responsibility for one's neighbors? Who can explain such shocking indifference on the part of a cross section of our fellow New Yorkers? We regretfully admit that we do not know the answers.

On June 11, 1964, Winston Moseley was found guilty of first degree murder in the slaying of Catherine Genovese. On June 15, 1964, a jury recommended the death penalty. When this was announced there were applause "and a few cheers" in the courtroom. The New York Times, June 16, 1964, at 1.

Moseley was sentenced to death. Because of error in the sentencing proceedings, his sentence was subsequently changed to life imprisonment. People v. Moseley, 228 N.E.2d 765 (N.Y.1967). While he was in prison, he completed a college program with the help of a state tuition grant. In 1977, he received a degree in sociology from Niagara College. The New York Times, April 10, 1977, at 30. In an article on the "op-ed" page of The New York Times, on April 16, 1977, at 25, Moseley wrote that "the man who killed Kitty Genovese in Queens in 1964 is no more" and that he was "a man who wants to be an asset to society, not a liability to it."

In 1995, Mosley, then 61 years old, made a motion for a new trial on the ground that he had had ineffective assistance of counsel, because his trial lawyer had once in the past represented Genovese when she was arrested for a minor gambling offense. The motion was denied. The New York Times, July 25, 1995, at B1; Nov. 14, 1995, at B4.

169. Jeremy Strohmeyer, then an 18-year-old high school student, was charged with sexually molesting and murdering Sherrice Iverson, who was seven years old, in 1997. His encounter with Iverson occurred at a hotel near Las Vegas. He was with a friend, David Cash. According to the evidence, Sherrice's father had left her and her 14-year-old brother alone in an arcade of the hotel while he gambled at the hotel casino. Strohmeyer evidently played hide and seek with Iverson in the arcade and then either lured or followed her into a women's bathroom, where he molested and strangled her in one of the stalls. Cash saw Strohmeyer follow Iverson into the bathroom. He entered and saw Strohmeyer assaulting Iverson. He left the bathroom and did nothing. Later Strohmeyer told Cash that he had murdered the girl.

Strohmeyer pleaded guilty to murder and was sentenced to life imprisonment without parole. Cash was excoriated in the press and criticized by fellow students at the University of California at Berkeley. He was not charged with any crime.

In both California (where Strohmeyer, Cash, and Iverson had lived) and Nevada, legislation was subsequently enacted making it a criminal offense not to report certain crimes against children. Cal. Penal Code § 152.3(a) (West 2003); Nev. Rev. Stat. § 202.882 (2002). Prosecutors and defense attorneys alike opposed the legislation, which, they feared, might lead to inappropriate prosecutions and impede prosecution of the principal offender. Los Angeles Times, June 4, 1997, at A1; Aug. 15, 1997, at A3; The Boston Globe, Aug. 7, 1998, at A1; June 20, 1999, at A3.

----

170. In most European countries, some of the people who witnessed Genovese's death might have been criminally liable for their failure to act. Statutes commonly make it an offense punishable by fine and/or imprisonment knowingly to fail to give aid to a person in serious danger, sometimes limited to danger of death, if aid could be given without danger to oneself or others.

171. Reconsider the problem of homicide (or injury) arising out of the defense of another person, discussed on pp. 218–23 above, in light of the Genovese case and the issues it raises.

THE SHERIDAN CASE

Early in the morning on March 18, 1967, Lisa Sheridan, a five-year-old girl, died at her home in Harwichport, Massachusetts, where she lived with her mother and older brother.

About three weeks earlier there had been a school holiday and she and her brother went on an expedition with their mother. Lisa complained that she felt ill; they returned home immediately and Lisa went to bed. She had a high fever and coughed a lot for the first day. The fever then subsided; the cough lasted for a few days more and then stopped. Lisa remained listless. She showed no pain and no symptoms, apart from listlessness, of illness.

Mrs. Sheridan was a member of the Christian Science Church, which she had joined three years earlier. After her daughter became ill, Mrs. Sheridan called a practitioner, a member of the church, who prayed with her and advised her of the passages to be read from church writings. About three days before Lisa died, Mrs. Sheridan contacted another church practitioner because she was concerned about Lisa's failure to recover. Mrs. Sheridan was head teacher at a local nursery school. She was 31 years old, and divorced.

The First Amendment to the Constitution of the United States provides: "Congress shall make no law respecting an establishment of religion, or prohibiting the free exercise thereof. . . ."

Article II of the Declaration of Rights of the Constitution of Massachusetts provides: "[N]o subject shall be hurt, molested, or restrained, in his person, liberty, or estate, for worshipping God in the manner and season most agreeable to the dictates of his own conscience; or for his religious profession or sentiments; provided he doth not disturb the public peace, or obstruct others in their religious worship."

A Massachusetts statute provided: "[A]ny parent of a minor child . . . who wilfully fails to provide necessary and proper physical, educational or moral care and guidance, or who permits said child to grow up under conditions or circumstances damaging to the child's sound character development, or who fails to provide proper attention for said child, shall be punished by a fine of not more than five hundred dollars or by imprisonment for not more than two years, or both." Mass. Gen. L. ch. 273, § 1. The provision requiring a parent to provide "proper physical care" was originally enacted in 1909. 1909 Mass. Acts 180.

On April 5, 1967, a grand jury returned an indictment against Mrs. Sheridan. The indictment charged that she "being under the legal duty, and being of sufficient ability to provide Lisa Gray Sheridan, who was her daughter, with sufficient medical care for sustenance and maintenance, did neglect and refuse so to do; by reason whereof said Lisa Gray Sheridan being unable to provide sufficient medical care for herself, became and was mortally sick and died."[80]

Charges

On April 18, 1967, Mrs. Sheridan made an affidavit in which she stated:

> Since 1963 I have constantly adhered to the teachings of Christian Science with respect to healing physical illness through spiritual

---

80. Record, Commonwealth v. Sheridan, No. 26307 (Barnstable Cy. Super. Ct.).

means, that is, through a systematic and concentrated reliance on prayer and the ordering of life conformably to Christian teaching, consistently and conscientiously carried out. I am personally convinced of the efficacy of this method both by personal experience, observation of others, and verified official reports of other Christian Scientists.

The Christian Science Church has approximately 3300 churches around the world, of which approximately 2412 are in the United States, and 75, including the Mother Church, are in Massachusetts.[81] It is one of the generally recognized forms of healing in the community. I felt justified therefore in relying on it.

Prior to March, 1967, I had relied on the teachings and practice of Christian Science in the healing of illness affecting my children, which was successful. Lisa attended Christian Science Sunday School and was acquainted with Christian Science healings and believed in them.

At no time up until the filing of this indictment has any public official advised, suggested or ordered that I secure a physician for my children or that the law required me to secure a physician for them.

Total and absolute faith and reliance in God is the heart of the Christian Science faith and essential to Christian Science healing. The use of medical aids is inconsistent with this total commitment. It follows therefore that the Christian Science method of healing can not effectively be used simultaneously with medical science.

I was not aware, nor was I advised by any person during Lisa's illness that she was in serious danger of death as a result of her illness, and I was convinced that she would recover. I provided her with food, and clothing and constant personal attention during her illness and sought and received assistance from Christian Science Practitioners.[82]

The trial of Mrs. Sheridan for manslaughter began on November 6, 1967, in the Superior Court of Barnstable County. In his opening statement the district attorney explained the Commonwealth's case: Mrs. Sheridan was aware that her child was ill; she had a legal duty to call for medical assistance and was able to do so; she did not do so; "and that failure and negligence resulted in the death of the child and is why she stands charged by the Commonwealth here today."[83]

[margin note: Commonwealth's argument]

The Commonwealth presented its case. The first witness was a police sergeant summoned to the Sheridan home after Lisa died. He testified that Lisa's room was "an ordinary child's bedroom,"[84] clean and neat. The pathologist who performed the autopsy testified that the cause of death was empyema, a complication of pneumonia, which arose out of a streptococcal sore throat. He testified that "in all probability either no treatment or

[margin note: cause of death]

---

[81] A witness testified at the trial that there are about 3400 churches in the world, about 2400 in the United States, and eighty-two in Massachusetts. Transcript at 205.

[82] Record. The affidavit was made in support of a motion to dismiss the indictment, which was denied.

83. Transcript at 38.

84. Id. at 44.

inadequate treatment had been rendered to this girl"[85] and that "she would not have died if she had been treated by acceptable medical standards."[86] She had "nine chances in ten"[87] of recovering, he said, if she had been treated early in her illness. On cross-examination he said that after the first four or five days the chances of recovery steadily decreased.

In his opening statement defense counsel said he would offer testimony that it could not be certain that Lisa would not have died even if a doctor had been called; that Christian Science had been practiced in the community for a hundred years and was recognized by government agencies; that "responsible, reasonable people throughout the world"[88] relied on Christian Science for healing; and that such reliance was "within that broad embrace of reasonable disagreement, reasonable disagreement between reasonable men."[89] Mrs. Sheridan would testify, he said, that "she did not avoid calling a doctor because of a lack of sense of duty"[90] but because "she chooses her way as a better way, more reliable way of dealing with illness . . . [a way] which she believes in her heart and her mind is the best way for her child."[91]

Among the witnesses for the defense was the editor-in-chief of the Christian Science Monitor, a past president of the Christian Science Church. He was past president and member of the board of directors of the United States Chamber of Commerce, former member of the United States delegation to the United Nations, and trustee of several colleges and a university. He said that healing through prayer "is the central basic element in the Christian Science teaching and doctrine" and that "the Christian Scientist tries to rely exclusively on spiritual, prayerful methods of healing."[92] He testified that it was his practice to rely on Christian Science without medical aid in treating his own and his children's and grandchildren's illnesses. Other witnesses testified to the same effect.

The Director of the Massachusetts Division of Child Guardianship testified that he knew of no case in which the state took custody of a child of Christian Scientist parents because the child was not receiving proper medical care.

Proof was offered that the Christian Science practice had been recognized by state and federal law in a variety of ways. Under state law, for example, religious objection was a basis for exemption from requirements that a child be immunized against various diseases.[93] There was also an offer of proof that children in families which practiced Christian Science were as healthy as other children.[94]

85. Id. at 80.
86. Id. at 82.
87. Id. at 85.
88. Id. at 164.
89. Id. at 165.
90. Id. at 166.
91. Id. at 167.

92. Id. at 208.

93. Mass. Gen. L. ch. 76, § 15. Some of the evidence was excluded on the ground that it was too far afield from the main inquiry and was therefore irrelevant.

94. The evidence was excluded as irrelevant.

Mrs. Sheridan testified. She told the circumstances of Lisa's illness and explained her belief in Christian Science.

At the close of all the evidence, defense counsel made a motion for a directed verdict.

Should the motion be granted?

The motion was denied.

Defense counsel requested that the jury be given the following instructions:

No. 5 "Proper physical care for a sick child means adherence to any accepted healing system recognized in the community, including those specifically recognized by statute such as osteopathy and chiropractic, as well as Christian Science."

No. 6 "If you find that the defendant conscientiously cared for her child according to accepted practices of Christian Science, and you find that Christian Science is accepted in the community as a healing system, then you must find the defendant not guilty."

No. 7 "Even if you find that Christian Science is not accepted as a healing system in the community, but also find that it is a recognized religion, and that it is an essential and fundamental part of the religious worship and practice of the Christian Science Church to rely on the teachings of Christian Science exclusively in the healing of the sick, and you further find that the defendant followed these teachings, then you must find her not guilty."

No. 11 "If you find that reasonable and responsible people in the community rely on Christian Science in the case of illness in their families, and the defendant sincerely and conscientiously did the same, then you must find the defendant not guilty."[95]

Would you, as the trial judge, have given those instructions?

All of the instructions listed were denied.[96]

The jury retired to consider its verdict at 10:59 a.m.

---

95. Transcript at 401–405.

96. Other requested instructions concerned the defendant's right to the free exercise of religious belief under the First and Fourteenth Amendments to the Constitution of the United States and the Declaration of Rights of the Constitution of Massachusetts. Borrowing language from Prince v. Massachusetts, 321 U.S. 158, 166 (1944), the trial judge instructed the jury: "Acting to guard the general interest in youth's well-being, the state with the sovereign power of guardianship over minors may restrict the parent's control. Its authority is not nullified merely because the parent grounds his claim to control the child's course of conduct in religion or conscience. The right to practice religion freely does not include liberty to expose the community or the child to communicable disease or the latter to ill health or to death. The state has a wide range of power for limiting parental freedom and authority in things affecting the child's welfare, and this includes matters of conscience and religious conviction." Transcript at 399.

How would you, as a juror, have voted?

The jury returned with a verdict at 3:50 p.m. Mrs. Sheridan was found guilty.

The penalty for manslaughter was "imprisonment in the state prison for not more than 20 years or a fine of not more than $1000 and imprisonment in jail for not more than two and one half years." Mass. Gen. L. ch. 265, § 13.

What sentence would you, as trial judge, have imposed?

Mrs. Sheridan was placed on probation for five years without imposition of sentence.[97]

———

172. Although such prosecutions were formerly very rare, more recently there have been a number of cases in which parents who practiced Christian Science were convicted of manslaughter or reckless endangerment for the death of a child who was not given conventional medical treatment. E.g., Walker v. Superior Court, 222 Cal.Rptr. 87 (Ct.App.1986) (involuntary manslaughter under the same statute applied in *Chavez*, p. 1 above). The sentence in such cases has typically not been imprisonment. Cases are described in an article, "Death and Faith, Law and Christian Science," The New York Times, Aug. 6, 1990, at A1.

For a full account of the *Sheridan* case, see L. Damore, The "Crime" of Dorothy Sheridan (1978).

173. The New York Times, September 12, 1984, at A26, reported that Kathleen and David Bergmann, a couple in Indiana, "who prayed, fasted and quoted Scripture over their dying infant daughter without calling a doctor" had been convicted of reckless homicide and child neglect. Their daughter was nine months old. She died of bacterial meningitis. There was testimony that she had been ill for 11 days, with fever, listlessness, and other symptoms before she died. The prosecution offered evidence to show that her illness was an easily curable respiratory infection, which developed into pneumonia because it was not treated.

The Bergmanns were members of the fundamentalist Faith Assembly sect. Mrs. Bergmann said at the trial: "I didn't kill my daughter. I gave her to the Lord to heal. When you're a Christian, you believe to the end." "I rebuked the fever. I quoted Scripture to her and I told her God was faithful. Satan is the author of sickness." "I never in my wildest imagination thought my daughter was going to die of meningitis. I didn't think it was serious. If I had, I probably would have prayed in that direction." Mr.

97. At the request of the defendant, the trial judge reported the case for review by the Supreme Judicial Court. The report was subsequently discharged by consent of the parties.

Bergmann said: "I can't see anywhere that we truly neglected our child." "We live the word of God. We were by her side every day. We did all we could by the word of God." He said that he had fasted for four days. Id.

An article in the Chicago Tribune, October 30, 1984, at 4, later reported that the Bergmanns were sentenced to ten years' imprisonment for child neglect and five years' imprisonment for reckless homicide, the sentences to be served concurrently. At the time they were sentenced, they had a daughter of preschool age and were expecting another child in two weeks. Another couple who were members of the Faith Assembly had recently been convicted of homicide for the death of their 26-day-old son, who died of pneumonia, and sentenced to five years' imprisonment.

The Tribune article reported also that the leader of the Faith Assembly had been indicted "on three felony charges related to the death of a fifteen-year-old girl from an untreated illness." About a year earlier, an article in The New York Times, November 7, 1983, at D14, had reported allegations that "dozens" of members of the Faith Assembly had died from untreated illnesses. The article gave a reported account of the Faith Assembly, according to which its members were based in a "tiny community" in northern Indiana and "shun smoking, drinking, drugs, abortion and the theater." Their leader demanded also that they give up insurance policies, refuse all immunizations and medication, remove seat belts from cars, destroy credit cards, and never borrow money, "the idea being that 'God will protect.'"

It is not unusual in cases of this kind for defendants who belong to a religious group less established than the Christian Science Church to receive a prison sentence. See, e.g., The New York Times, June 11, 1997, at 23 (Faith Tabernacle Congregation).

Can the *Sheridan* case be distinguished from the case of the Bergmanns? Does the size of the religious community or its acceptance into the "mainstream" of American life or the role of its members in the larger community make a difference? Why (not)?

174. In 1971, the Massachusetts legislature added the following sentence to Mass. Gen. L. ch. 273, § 1, p. 298 above: "A child shall not be deemed to be neglected or lack proper physical care for the sole reason that he is being provided remedial treatment by spiritual means alone in accordance with the tenets and practice of a recognized church or religious denomination by a duly accredited practitioner thereof." Had that provision been in effect when Lisa Sheridan died, would Mrs. Sheridan have been criminally liable for the death? *Yes*

Twenty-three years after the *Sheridan* case, a Massachusetts couple who were Christian Scientists were convicted of manslaughter for the death of their son, who was two years old. The defendants relied on prayer to heal their son of a bowel obstruction. Over the objection of the defense, the trial judge declined to refer to the 1971 amendment to the law, above; he evidently concluded that it had no application in a case of serious illness

leading to death. The defendants were sentenced to probation. The probation order required them to provide regular pediatric care for their other
children. The conviction was subsequently reversed, because the appellate
court concluded that the defendants should have been allowed to assert the
defense of mistake of law in reliance on an opinion of the Commonwealth's
Attorney General, issued in 1975. The court said that the Attorney General's opinion might reasonably have been understood to indicate that the
1971 amendment was a defense to a charge of manslaughter. The court
went on to say, however, that the statute was not a defense to a prosecution for homicide. Commonwealth v. Twitchell, 617 N.E.2d 609 (Mass.
1993).

175. Should it have made a difference in the *Sheridan* case if the
failure to provide medical treatment caused a disabling deformity rather
than death?[98] In In re Seiferth, 127 N.E.2d 820 (N.Y.1955), the Court of
Appeals upheld an order dismissing a petition that a 14-year-old boy be
required to submit to surgery to repair a cleft palate and harelip. Such
operations are common and the risks of death negligible; the longer surgery
is delayed the less favorable the result is likely to be for physical and
psychological reasons. The boy's father declined to consent to the operation
because he believed in letting " 'the forces of the universe work on the
body,' " Id. at 822. The boy agreed with the father, who had "inculcated a
distrust and dread of surgery in the boy since childhood." Id. In In re
Tuttendario, 21 Pa. D. 561 (1912), the court declined to order an operation
to cure a seven year old boy of rickets without which operation he would be
crippled and unable to make a living in "anything that requires standing or
walking." Id. at 561. The operation was not a dangerous one. The parents,
who had lost seven children out of ten born to them, refused to permit the
operation. So also, in In re Green, 292 A.2d 387 (Pa.1972), the court said
that where the child's life is not in peril, the state may not override
parents' religious belief in opposition to a medical procedure; but the court
added that the wishes of the child, in this case 16 years old, should be
consulted. See generally In the Matter of Appeal in Cochise County Juvenile Action, 650 P.2d 467 (Ariz.Ct.App.1981) (court has power to order
medical care and treatment even when child's life not endangered), vacated, 650 P.2d 459 (1982). In some cases an operation has been ordered. E.g.,
In re Vasko, 263 N.Y.S. 552 (App.Div.1933). See Matter of Gregory S, 380
N.Y.S.2d 620 (Fam.Ct.1976).

176. "In the area of negligent harms, especially in involuntary manslaughter by very ignorant parents, by persons whose religious faiths bar

98. Model Penal Code § 230.4. "Endangering Welfare of Children. A parent, guardian, or other person supervising the welfare
of a child under 18 commits a misdemeanor if
he knowingly endangers the child's welfare
by violating a duty of care, protection or
support." Had Lisa Sheridan not died, could
Mrs. Sheridan have been convicted of violating such a provision?

the summoning of medical aid, and by primitive persons who for some reason find themselves subjected to the law of a culture that is totally different from their own,[99] it should be recognized that the criminal law remains a crude instrumentality, that we simply have not reached the point of treating such persons as morally innocent agents of social harm." Hall, "Interrelationships of Criminal Law and Torts" 43 Colum. L. Rev. 753, 967, 981 (1943).

6. CAUSATION

If anything but for which an event would not have happened is a cause of the event, there are any number of "causes" of every event. When we select a cause as *the* cause, the selection is based on some principle that reflects our interests. By making the selection we focus our attention on some aspect of the situation, usually one that we think is (most) under our control, so that we can ensure or prevent its repetition. When someone drops a cup and it breaks, for example, we are more likely to say, "You should be more careful," than to say, "I wish the floor were not so hard"; if an infant drops the cup we are very likely to say, "We'll have to get him an unbreakable plastic cup," instead of, "He really must not drop things." As a crude and preliminary approximation of ordinary speech, it is probably accurate to say that we distinguish the cause of an event from the (necessary) conditions of an event according to our interests, which usually but not always means that we single out as the "cause" some element of the situation that we can control and describe as "conditions" the other necessary elements. Some necessary conditions are taken so much for granted that unless some curious feature of the situation focuses our attention on them, we don't even mention them as conditions. Without some frame of reference the question, "What is (are) the cause(s) of X?" is as meaningless as the question, "What are all the conditions but for which X would not have occurred?" Ordinarily the frame of reference is clear and is supplied by common sense.

Not only do our causal descriptions reflect our interests. They also are particularizations of some general theory of order to which we (tacitly and ordinarily unreflectively) subscribe. To say that a cup broke because it was dropped is, after all, to suggest (if not to assert) a good deal about the way cups (or glass objects, or objects) behave when they are set loose in the air and when they come into sudden contact with a hard surface.

In a great many situations with which the criminal law is concerned the problem of causation does not arise. It ordinarily does not arise when the defendant intended by his conduct to produce the harm that occurs.

[99] See Regina v. Machekequonabe, 28 Ont. R. 309 (1897).

(Why not?) When the problem does arise, common sense providing no answer, the way to proceed may not be obvious. How helpful is it to ask, without elaboration, "Who caused Brat's death?" p. 251 above. Consider whether the rules about causation and the applications of the rules discussed in the materials following, which are ostensibly matters of fact, do not implicate unexpressed normative judgments.

———

Fine v. State

193 Tenn. 422, 246 S.W.2d 70 (1952)

■ NEIL, CHIEF JUSTICE. The plaintiff in error, who will be later referred to as the defendant, was convicted in the criminal court of Knox County of voluntary manslaughter and sentenced to the penitentiary for not less than two (2) and not more than ten (10) years.

Facts

While numerous assignments of error are assigned to the action of the trial court in refusing to grant the defendant a new trial we think the determinative question is whether or not the deceased died as the result of a criminal agency or from natural causes. The defendant, Fine, and the deceased, Hodges, were residents of Jefferson County and lived upon adjoining farms. They were interested in buying and selling livestock and had come to the Knoxville Stock Yards on the day of the alleged homicide. The two men had previously engaged in a dispute about a line fence, but this difference was not of a serious nature. A witness for the State, one James Bailey, testified that the defendant had made the remark, "I'll get mine if I have to beat the devil out of him (referring to the deceased) and throw him in the creek." The defendant evidently was referring to the fact that the deceased owed him a few dollars for repairing the line fence.

There is little, if any, conflict in the evidence upon which the State relies to support the conviction of the defendant. A fair statement of the facts appears in the State's brief, as follows:

Events leading to death

"Witnesses introduced on behalf of the State testified that within ten to thirty minutes after Hodges' arrival at the stockyards they saw him and Plaintiff in Error together outside the calf barn. Plaintiff in Error was seen to place his hand on deceased's shoulder and shake him. He then placed one or both hands about Hodges' throat and choked him. Plaintiff in Error turned him loose within a matter of seconds and deceased slumped to the ground near, if not against, the side of the calf barn. . . .

"Deceased was taken immediately to a Knoxville hospital and transferred that same afternoon to St. Mary's Hospital, also in Knoxville. He stayed at St. Mary's about two weeks and never regained consciousness while there. He was then taken to Milligan Clinic in Jefferson City where he stayed another two weeks, never regaining consciousness there. From Milligan Clinic he was taken to his home where he died on February 17, 1950. He remained paralyzed from the time of the assault until his death.

His wife seemed to think that after he was taken to his home he was conscious part of the time. After his death she refused to give permission to perform an autopsy."

Dr. Herbert Acuff, a State's witness, saw the deceased at St. Mary's Hospital on the afternoon following the alleged assault. He gave it as his opinion that Hodges had suffered a ruptured blood vessel in the brain which had paralyzed his right side. The blood pressure of the deceased was found to be 220 over 120, which according to Dr. Acuff, was "alarmingly high," and *"excitement of any kind or nature* will accelerate that pressure, and of course the acceleration of the pressure forcing into the little blood vessels in the brain." (Emphasis supplied.)

testimony: possible cause of death

"Q. State whether or not in your opinion the increase in blood pressure caused the cerebral hemorrhage at that time, while he was being choked. A. Well, from some cause or other the pressure increased; because he had an alarmingly high pressure, and if he was already carrying all the column the pressure could stand, and then he was beaten, or any excitement, or what not, would normally cause a hemorrhage.

"Q. Would you or would you not, then, Doctor, say that this assault on the body of Mr. Hodges in the condition he was in either directly or indirectly caused this cerebral hemorrhage with the resulting death? A. I wouldn't want to say that that alone did it, because the man had the high pressure he did.

"Q. Yes, I understand. A. I mean . . .

"Q. But was it a contributing factor or not? A. I can truthfully say that it was a contributing factor."

It definitely appears that this expert medical witness, in response to a hypothetical question, was rather hesitant in expressing the opinion that the act of the defendant in "choking the deceased" was the "effective agency" in causing his death. He would go no further than to say that in his opinion "it was a contributing factor." This opinion was later modified. He gave the following testimony on cross-examination:

"A. Well, the blood pressure for a man of his age should have been around 150 over around 80 to a hundred. (Mr. Hodges was about 75). So the 220 was an inordinately high pressure.

"Q. He had how much above the normal pressure? A. At least 70 or 80 above. And in addition to that a man at that age has hardening of the arteries, and any pressure or any sudden stroke or anything of that character would break the artery and cause it to rupture. And so for that reason I think that this sudden increase in the pressure for whatever cause was responsible for the split in the vessel.

. . .

"Q. Is that a highly dangerous condition? A. Yes.

"Q. Would a person of that age with that blood pressure be liable to have a stroke without anybody even touching them? A. Yes, he could have.

"Q. Could he have it while he was in bed? A. He could have."

The defendant testified he had known the deceased for about five years and they had always been on friendly terms; that when they met at the stockyards they talked briefly about the repairs to a line fence; that in the course of the conversation Hodges became very angry when the defendant suggested that deceased owed him "about $5.00," saying, "You are a damned liar, it ain't that much." The defendant further testified that deceased "had a wild, angry look on his face, one he had never seen before." He thought deceased was about to attack him and he "grabbed him by the shirt collar" as deceased ran his hand in his pocket. When asked how long he held Hodges, he stated, "I turned him loose just as I took a breath; it was over just in a second"; that he staggered back about three or four steps against the seed house and slumped over on his left side. The testimony of the defendant was corroborated by several eyewitnesses.

While there is testimony to the effect that there were fingerprints and scratches on deceased's neck, the hospital records fail to confirm these facts. Dr. Frank L. Milligan, a qualified medical expert, testified that it would be very difficult to ascertain without an autopsy, if the hemorrhage was due to a ruptured blood vessel or tumor. The hospital records also showed that the deceased suffered a cardiac condition in August, 1949, when he had a temporary partial paralysis of the left arm. In answering the same hypothetical question which had been propounded to Dr. Acuff, Dr. Milligan testified as follows: "We see patients who have cerebral hemorrhage under every kind of a condition you want to mention, some asleep, some at work, some having their dinner, and what not. There is no way to tell when you are going to have a heart attack or cerebral accident."

The death certificate shows that death was primarily pulmonary infection, commonly known as pneumonia, secondary cause was cerebral hemorrhage, and his paralysis was the secondary cause.

In the light of the proven facts, including that of the medical experts bearing upon the cause of death, it cannot be said with any degree of certainty that the deceased died as the result of any criminal agency. The conclusion reached by the jury, of necessity, had to be based upon an inference upon an inference and upon a third inference which could not be thought of otherwise than a fantastic speculation. "To sustain a conviction, proof of the criminal agency is as indispensable as the proof of death." Wharton's Criminal Evidence, Vol. 2, § 872, page 1506. Moreover it is settled law in all jurisdictions that criminal agency must be shown beyond a reasonable doubt; it cannot rest upon conjecture or speculation.

. . .

[T]he death of Mr. Hodges was neither accidental nor intentional; nor can it be said that the defendant, by word or act, caused his death, which occurred two months and seventeen days after he is said to have had a brain hemorrhage. It is settled law in all homicide cases that the collateral crime, i.e. the alleged unlawful act antedating death, must be so integrated with and related to the homicide that it can be said to have proximately caused or contributed to it. The related occurrences in the instant case, which immediately preceded the sudden paralysis of the deceased, were so remote in causal effect that his death can only be thought of as a fortuitous circumstance.

The facts disclosed in this record are wholly insufficient to establish criminal liability. . . .

––––––––

177. Would the Tennessee court have substituted its finding for the verdict of the jury:

(i) if Hodges had died on the way to the hospital instead of two and a half months later?

(ii) if Hodges had not had very high blood pressure?

(iii) if Hodges had been not about 75 but about 35 years old?

(iv) if instead of grabbing Hodges around the neck the defendant had knocked him out?

178. According to the state's and the defendant's evidence, Hodges slumped to the ground immediately after he was grabbed by the defendant. He was taken directly to the hospital and, if he ever regained consciousness again at all before his death, it was not for a significant period. Why is it that these facts do not even *permit* the jury to conclude that Fine's assault caused Hodges's death?

179. With *Fine*, compare State v. Chavers, 294 So.2d 489 (La.1974). In that case, the defendant struck Johnston on the jaw; Johnston, who had a severe heart condition, died of a heart attack precipitated by the blow. The conviction of manslaughter was affirmed. Another such case, in which the victim of a robbery suffered from heart disease and died in the hospital five days after being robbed, is Commonwealth v. Cotton, 487 A.2d 830 (Pa.Super.Ct.1984). See also Adams v. State, 310 So.2d 782 (Fla.Dist.Ct. App.1975), in which the defendants snatched the purse of an elderly woman who fell and broke her hip; during an operation on the fracture four days later, she died from a cardiac arrest. The defendants' conviction of murder was affirmed.

180. State v. Frazier, 98 S.W.2d 707 (Mo.1936). The defendant struck the deceased, who was a hemophiliac, once on the jaw with his fist. The blow caused a slight laceration on the inside of the deceased's mouth, which, according to medical testimony, resulted in hemorrhage from which the deceased died ten days after the assault. The defendant was convicted of manslaughter. His conviction was affirmed on appeal.

Remembering the appellant was convicted of manslaughter, two questions remain: (1) was it an adequate defense that the appellant did not know the deceased was a hemophiliac, and struck only one moderate blow with his fist, which ordinarily would not have been dangerous to life; (2) is he to be excused because the blow producing the hemorrhage would not have resulted fatally if deceased had not been a hemophiliac? Both these questions must be answered in the negative. Section 3988, Revised Statutes 1929 (Mo. Stat. Ann., p. 2793), provides that "every killing of a human being by the act, procurement or culpable negligence of another, not herein declared to be murder or excusable or justifiable homicide, shall be deemed manslaughter." If one commits an unlawful assault and battery upon another without malice and death results, the assailant is guilty of manslaughter although death was not intended and the assault was not of a character likely to result fatally. . . .

[handwritten margin note: Rule for manslaughter]

Neither is it an excuse that appellant did not know the deceased was a hemophiliac, and that death would not have resulted but for that affliction. On this point 13 Ruling Case Law, section 55, page 750, says: "The law declares that one who inflicts an injury on another and thereby accelerates his death shall be held criminally responsible therefor, although death would not have resulted from the injury but for the diseased or wounded condition of the person so injured." And the doctrine is more fully set out in 29 Corpus Juris, section 57, page 1082, as follows: "If the deceased was in feeble health and died from the combined effects of the injury and of his disease, or if the injury accelerated the death from the disease, he who inflicted the injury is liable, although the injury alone would not have been fatal. The same rule applies, although the disease itself would probably have been fatal, if the injury accelerated death. It is immaterial that defendant did not know that the deceased was in the feeble condition which facilitated the killing, or that he did not reasonably anticipate that his act would cause death." . . .

Id. at 713.

In People v. Brackett, 510 N.E.2d 877 (Ill.1987), the defendant raped and beat an 85-year-old woman. She was hospitalized and then transferred to a nursing home. Although her injuries were healing, she became depressed and refused to eat. She died about a month after she was attacked. The immediate cause of death was asphyxiation resulting from food in her trachea. Expert testimony described her depression as not uncommon when an elderly person suffers a trauma and is removed from her home. Affirming the conviction of murder, the court observed: "[W]e believe this is precisely the kind of case where the defendant takes his victim as he finds him. . . . There are many cases in this State where the victim's existing health condition contributed to the victim's death. However, so long as the defendant's acts contribute to the death there is still sufficient proof of causation, despite the preexisting health condition. . . . It appears to this court that a person's advanced age is as significant a part of his existing health condition as diabetes or hardening of the arteries." Id. at 881–82. See People v. Caldwell, 692 N.E.2d 448 (Ill.App.1998), in which the victim of the defendant's assault indicated to an attending physician that she wanted life supports to be removed; they were removed, and she died a few minutes later. The defendant's conviction of involuntary manslaughter was affirmed.

Why should Frazier and Brackett but not Fine be guilty of homicide?

181. The penalty for manslaughter in Missouri was imprisonment in the penitentiary for not less than two nor more than ten years or in the county jail for not less than six months, or a fine of not less than $500, or a fine of not less than $100 and imprisonment in jail for not less than three months. Mo. Rev. Stat. § 559.140 (since transferred to § 565.031). The penalty for a "common assault" was imprisonment in the county jail for not more than six months or a fine of not more than $100, or both. Mo. Rev. Stat. § 559.220 (since amended, see § 565.070). Frazier's sentence was six months in the county jail and a fine of $400.

182. Suppose the defendant has assaulted someone and inflicted injuries from which the injured person will in all likelihood recover. While he is recovering, however, he contracts a disease from which he dies. If there is medical testimony that the disease was unrelated to the injuries (1) except that if the person had not been in a weakened condition from them he probably would not have contracted the disease, or (2) except that if the person had not been in a weakened condition he probably would have recovered from the disease, may the jury find the defendant guilty of homicide? Why (not)? See Livingston v. Commonwealth, 55 Va. (14 Gratt.) 592 (1857).

183. The decedent, who was then 70 years old, was diagnosed as having stomach cancer. He began chemotherapy treatment, to which he responded well. He continued to live an active life and was treated as an outpatient. About six months later, he was shot. He was hospitalized and underwent surgery. As a result, it was necessary to postpone chemotherapy for about two weeks. During that period, the cancer developed rapidly. He remained in the hospital and died about two months later. The death certificate listed the primary cause of death as tumor cachexia, a terminal form of cancer. Matter of Estate of Eliasen, 668 P.2d 110 (Idaho 1983).

Is the person who fired the shot liable for homicide? Why (not)?

184. The defendant stabbed the victim, LaBere, in the course of a robbery. LaBere drove himself to the police station and reported the incident. He was taken to the hospital for treatment. Although LaBere was alert and conscious, an exploratory laparotomy was performed to see whether any vital organ had been injured. Because he was extremely obese and had circulatory problems, the laparotomy was a "high risk procedure." It showed no injury to vital organs but also showed a serious heart condition. Two weeks later, LaBere died. The cause of death was a blood clot, which did not originate from the site of the stabbing wound. The blood clot was partly a product of Mr. LaBere's obesity and his post-operative immobility. Had he not undergone a laparotomy he probably would have survived. Pittman v. State, 528 N.E.2d 67 (Ind.1988).

Is the defendant liable for LaBere's death? Why (not)?

Is your answer in this case entirely consistent with your answer in *Eliasen*, note 183 above? If so, on what basis? If not, how do you account for the inconsistency?

United States v. Hamilton

182 F.Supp. 548 (D.D.C.1960)

■ HOLTZOFF, DISTRICT JUDGE. This is a trial on a charge of murder in the second degree. The trial is before the Court without a jury, as the defendant has waived his right to trial by jury.

The indictment avers that on or about December 2, 1959, within the District of Columbia, Benjamin E. Hamilton, with malice aforethought, murdered John W. Slye by means of striking him with his fists and stamping and kicking him with his shod feet. Specifically, the charge is that on the evening of December 2, 1959, the defendant and the deceased were in a fight on Lamont Street near Georgia Avenue in the City of Washington; that the deceased was knocked down in the course of the fight, and that then the defendant jumped on his face and kicked his face, inflicting wounds of which the deceased later died. The defense is that the wounds inflicted by the defendant on the deceased were not the cause of death.

The evidence in this case establishes the following salient facts. On the afternoon and evening of December 2, 1959, a number of men had gathered in a poolroom on Georgia Avenue near Lamont Street for the purpose of recreation. The defendant and the deceased were in that group. They played several games of pool. They imbibed intoxicating beverages in the rear of the establishment, and they also carried on desultory conversations. There was an exchange of banter between the deceased and the defendant, which developed into an argument, and finally into an acrimonious quarrel. The subject matter of the argument must have been trivial and inconsequential, because the defendant, although he narrated with a great degree of particularity the events of that evening, does not remember what the discussion was about. Both the deceased and the defendant were asked by the person in charge of the poolroom to leave, because it was undesirable that a fight should develop inside. Accordingly, both of them went outside and a fight started on Lamont Street. In the course of the fight, the deceased was knocked down by the defendant. While he was lying on the ground, the defendant apparently exploded in a fit of ungovernable rage and jumped on the face of the deceased and kicked him in the head as well.

[handwritten margin note: fight]

The deceased was taken to the District of Columbia General Hospital, arriving there at 11:30 p.m. No useful purpose would be served by recounting the gory and harrowing details concerning the nature of the injuries sustained by the deceased to his face and head. Suffice it to say that he apparently was in a semi-comatose condition. He was violent and in shock. Blood was coming from his face.

[handwritten margin note: victims condition @ the hospital]

Promptly upon arrival at the hospital, the deceased came into the competent hands of the Chief Resident of the Neurological Service, who impressed the Court as a completely dedicated and entirely devoted physician. He did everything possible that could be done for his patient. A blood transfusion was given to the deceased, his airways were cleansed, and tubes inserted into his nasal passages and trachea in order to maintain the breathing process. In view of the fact that he was violent, it was necessary to restrain the patient by fastening leather handcuffs on him. The doctor saw the patient several times during the night. In addition, the registered nurse in charge of the ward in which the deceased was placed saw him at least every half hour or every thirty-five minutes. The deceased was in a room with only one other patient. A licensed practical nurse was constantly in attendance in that room. It is obvious that the patient received incessant and continuous care and treatment at the hands of both the medical and nursing staff of the hospital.

[handwritten margin note: victim recieve good care @ the hospital]

During the night it became desirable to change the bed clothes of the deceased, because they had become bloody. To accomplish this result, it was necessary to remove the restraints from the patient. They were not put back, because by that time, the patient was no longer violent and was resting better than when he arrived. About 6:30 in the morning, the patient had a convulsion, and immediately thereafter, he himself, with his own hands, pulled out the tubes. At 7:30 a.m., the patient died.

[handwritten margin note: immediate actions by victim's death]

The Deputy Coroner, who performed the autopsy and who himself is an experienced physician, found the cause of death to be asphyxiation due to aspiration or inhalation of blood caused by severe injuries to the face, including multiple fractures of the nasal bones. The attending physician testified that the cause of death was asphyxia. In other words, the two physicians agree as to the cause of death. It should be said at this point that the purpose of the tubes was to assist in keeping the airways clear in order that the patient might breathe normally. It is claimed by able counsel for the defendant that the immediate cause of death was the fact that the patient pulled out the tubes, and that, therefore, he brought about his own death. This contention requires a consideration of the applicable principles of law.

[handwritten margin note: cause of death. asphyxia]

Law

It is well established that if a person strikes another and inflicts a blow that may not be mortal in and of itself but thereby starts a chain of causation that leads to death, he is guilty of homicide. This is true even if the deceased contributes to his own death or hastens it by failing to take proper treatment.

The principles of the common law on this subject are summarized in Hale's Pleas of the Crown, Volume 1, p. 427, in a passage that has been frequently quoted. He says:

> If a man give another a stroke, which it may be, is not in itself so mortal, but that with good care he might be cured, yet if he die of this wound within a year and a day, it is homicide or murder, as the case is, and so it hath been always ruled.

And, again, Hale says:

> But if a man receives a wound, which is not in itself mortal, but either for want of helpful applications, or neglect thereof, it turns to a gangrene, or a fever, and that gangrene or fever be the immediate cause of his death, yet, this is murder or manslaughter in him that gave the stroke or wound, for that wound, tho it were not the immediate cause of his death, yet, if it were the mediate cause thereof, and the fever or gangrene was the immediate cause of his death, yet the wound was the cause of the gangrene or fever, and so consequently is *causa causati*.

Judicial decisions applying this doctrine are too numerous to require a review. Suffice it to say that these principles have been adopted and applied in the District of Columbia, in Hopkins v. United States, 4 App. D.C. 430, 439. In that case, the defendant had struck the deceased. Several weeks later the deceased died, and the autopsy showed that the death was caused by the blow that had been inflicted by the defendant. It was argued that the defendant was not guilty of homicide, because the deceased had neglected to take medical treatment after he was struck and that his failure to do so either caused or contributed to bringing about his death. This contention was overruled, and it was held that the mere fact that the deceased had neglected to procure proper treatment for the effects of the blow or wound did not relieve the defendant of his responsibility for the homicide.

Hawkins' Pleas of the Crown, Volume 1, Chapter 31, Section 10, summarizes this principle very succinctly. He says:

> But if a person hurt by another, die thereof within a year and a day, it is no excuse for the other that he might have recovered, if he had not neglected to take care of himself.

It is urged by defense counsel, however, that this case should not be governed by the principles just discussed, because, in this instance, the deceased was not guilty merely of neglect, but took affirmative action which contributed to his death, namely, pulling out the tubes. The evidence is far from clear whether the action of the deceased in pulling out the tubes was a reflex action, or whether he was then only semi-conscious, or whether it was a conscious, deliberate act on his part. It is not necessary, however, to resolve this question of fact, because even if the act of the deceased in pulling out the tubes was conscious and deliberate, it would not help the defendant. First, there is not sufficient evidence to justify a finding that if the tubes had remained in the trachea and nasal passages of the deceased, he would have continued to live. Second, and quite irrespective of that consideration, even if it were to be assumed, *arguendo*, that the deceased might have lived if he had not pulled out the tubes, this circumstance would not have any effect on the liability and responsibility of the defendant for the death of the deceased.

In People v. Lewis, 124 Cal. 551, 559, the facts were as follows. The defendant inflicted a gunshot wound on the deceased. This wound was mortal. The deceased, however, procured a knife and cut his throat, and thereby brought about his death sooner than would have been the case if it had resulted from the original wound. The defendant was convicted of manslaughter, and the conviction was affirmed by the highest court of California.

An even more extreme case is Stephenson v. State, 205 Ind. 141, 183. There the defendant attempted to rape the deceased, and seriously, but not mortally, wounded her. She took poison and died as a result of the poisoning. The defendant was convicted of murder in the second degree, and the Supreme Court of Indiana affirmed the conviction. As against the argument in behalf of the defendant that there was no homicide, since the deceased took her own life by committing suicide, the Court held that the jury was justified in finding that the defendant by his acts or conduct rendered the deceased distracted and mentally irresponsible and that her taking poison was a natural and probable consequence of the unlawful and criminal treatment that the defendant had inflicted on the deceased.

Here the question before the Court is whether the defendant should be deemed guilty of homicide or guilty merely of assault with a dangerous weapon. As has been indicated by the Supreme Court, assault is a lesser included offense in an indictment for murder, Logan v. United States, 144 U.S. 263, 307. Further, the Court of Appeals for this Circuit has held that shoes on feet are dangerous weapons, at least when they inflict serious injuries. . . . The Court is of the opinion, however, that the injuries inflicted on the deceased by the defendant were the cause of death in the light of the principles of law heretofore discussed, and that, therefore, the defendant should be adjudged guilty of homicide.

. . . [100]

---

[100] Concluding that there was an absence of malice aforethought, the court found Hamilton guilty of manslaughter. The opinion does not indicate whether the verdict was voluntary manslaughter or involuntary manslaughter.

185. Would Hamilton have been guilty of criminal homicide:

(i) if it were established that prompt action by hospital personnel after it was discovered that Slye had removed the tubes would have saved his life?

(ii) if it were established that it was a clearly negligent departure from normal practice not to replace the leather handcuffs after the bed clothes were changed?

(iii) if by chance, a nurse in attendance on Slye were his old enemy and, intending that he die, she deliberately failed to replace the handcuffs?

(iv) if by chance, a doctor in attendance on Slye were his old enemy and, intending that he die, he deliberately failed to take prompt action after he learned that the tubes were removed?

(v) if the other patient in the hospital room were an old enemy of Slye and during the night he obtained a gun and shot Slye, who died instantly?

Hamilton, we may assume, was nowhere near the hospital when any of these hypothetical events occurred. Can his punishment, then, be made dependent on distinctions among them? Can his punishment be made dependent on what actually occurred—Slye's removal of the tubes—if Slye would not otherwise have died?

See (i) People v. McGee, 187 P.2d 706, 714–15 (Cal.1947); Wright v. State, 374 A.2d 824 (Del.1977); (ii) Kusmider v. State, 688 P.2d 957 (Alaska Ct.App.1984) (decedent removed breathing tubes in throat; assailant liable for death even if paramedics were negligent in failing to restrain decedent); People v. Robinson, 331 N.W.2d 226 (Mich.1983) (testimony that failure to amputate limb of victim was "grossly erroneous treatment" was admissible to prove that defendant's shooting of victim was not cause of death); People v. Stewart, 358 N.E.2d 487 (N.Y.1976) (cardiac arrest in course of incidental surgical procedure; conviction of manslaughter reversed); (iii)–(iv) Smith v. State, 8 S.W. 941 (Ark.1888); (v) People v. Elder, 59 N.W. 237 (Mich.1894); Wilson v. State, 24 S.W. 409 (Tex.Crim.App.1893).

On intervening causes, see generally McKinnon v. United States, 550 A.2d 915 (D.C.1988), in which the defendant stabbed the victim, who died six weeks later from a rare form of hepatitis, most likely resulting from the treatment of her wounds. There was expert testimony that the risk of hepatitis was small. Affirming the conviction of homicide, the court said that a defendant can be held criminally liable for "all harms that are reasonably foreseeable consequences of his or her actions." 550 A.2d at 918. Although the risk of hepatitis was small, it was not unforeseeable.

186.   The *Stephenson* case, the facts of which are described in *Hamilton*, p. 315 above, is often cited. Another similar, although somewhat less extreme case is State v. Govan, 744 P.2d 712 (Ariz.Ct.App.1987). In *Govan* the defendant shot a woman with whom he had been living. As a result, she was paralyzed from the neck down. He was charged with aggravated assault. He subsequently married the woman, and the charge was dismissed. The woman was a quadriplegic and needed constant care. More than four years later, she contracted pneumonia and died. The defendant was prosecuted for murder and convicted of manslaughter. (Notice the absence of a year-and-a-day rule.) On appeal, the defendant argued that the victim, who did not seek medical attention for two weeks after she knew she was ill, "simply gave up her will to live, and this broke the chain of causation between the shooting and the death." Upholding the conviction, the court said: "Although a victim may break the chain of causation by voluntarily doing harm to himself, this should not be so when an individual causes the victim to commit suicide or lose the will to live because of extreme pain from wounds inflicted by the appellant, or when the wound has rendered the victim irresponsible. . . . The impact of quadriplegia on a person's physical and mental well-being may be equated with the effects of extreme pain. . . . The appellant's conduct could be regarded as a proximate cause of the victim's death, and he would still be criminally liable for it." Id. at 717. Would, or should, it have made a difference if the defendant had been convicted of the original charge of aggravated assault?

187.   The defendant was charged with vehicular homicide. The car that he was driving collided with another car, a passenger in which was injured. The passenger, who was a member of the Jehovah's Witnesses, was in need of a blood transfusion, which she refused. She died two days after the accident. Neither the attending physician nor the coroner was able to say whether she would have survived had she had a blood transfusion. The conviction of homicide was affirmed. State v. Baker, 720 So.2d 767 (La.App. 1998). A similar case, in which there was medical testimony that the victim probably would have lived if she had received a transfusion, is reported in the Los Angeles Times, March 13, 1999, at B5.

Does the result in *Baker* follow from *Frazier*, note 180 above? Or from the first of Hale's rules in *Hamilton*, p. 312 above? Does the fact that the victim in *Baker* refused treatment make a difference?

188. "A fundamental principle of criminal law is that a person is held responsible for all consequences proximately caused by his criminal conduct. The concept of proximate cause incorporates the notion that an accused may be charged with a criminal offense even though his acts were not the immediate cause of the victim's death or injury. . . . In many situations giving rise to criminal liability, the death or injury is not directly caused by the acts of the defendant but rather results from intervening forces or events, such as negligent medical treatment, escape attempts, or the negligent or intentional acts of a third party. Where such intervening events are foreseeable and naturally result from a perpetrator's criminal conduct, the law considers the chain of legal causation unbroken and holds the perpetrator criminally responsible for the resulting harm. . . . This principle applies even where the direct cause of death is a force set in motion by the victim himself. For example, if a person acting on a well grounded and reasonable fear of death or bodily injury induced by an accused's threats or actual assaults, dies in an attempt to extricate himself from the danger, the accused bears criminal liability for the death." United States v. Guillette, 547 F.2d 743, 749 (2d Cir.1976). In *Guillette*, the victim was killed by an explosion when he opened the front door of his house and touched off a booby trap. The defendants claimed that the victim had set the trap himself as a defense against them and others who were looking for him, and had detonated it accidentally. The court said that even if that were true, the defendants "would still be considered in the chain of legal causation if the immediate cause of death—setting a bomb as a booby trap—was a foreseeable protective reaction to their criminal efforts to locate . . . him. . . ." Id.

The concept of proximate cause is discussed and applied in State v. Wassil, 658 A.2d 548 (Conn.1995), in which the court upheld the defendant's conviction for involuntary manslaughter, based on his supplying drugs to the victim. The defendant argued that the victim's act of injecting the drugs into himself, from which he died, was an intervening cause that relieved the defendant of responsibility. The court concluded that despite the victim's act, supplying the drugs was the proximate cause of the death.

189. Commonwealth v. Root, 170 A.2d 310, 311–12 (Pa.1961):

While precedent is to be found for application of the tort law concept of "proximate cause" in fixing responsibility for criminal homicide, the want of any rational basis for its use in determining criminal liability can no longer be properly disregarded. When proximate cause was first borrowed from the field of tort law and applied to homicide prosecutions in Pennsylvania, the concept connoted a much more direct causal relation in producing the alleged culpable result than it does today. Proximate cause, as an essential element of a tort founded in negligence, has undergone in recent times, and is still undergoing, a marked extension. More specifically, this area of civil law has been progressively liberalized in favor of claims for damages for personal injuries to which careless conduct of others can in some way be associated. To persist in applying the tort liability concept of proximate cause to prosecutions for criminal homicide after the marked expansion of *civil* liability of defendants in tort actions for negligence would be to extend possible *criminal* liability to persons chargeable with unlawful or reckless conduct in circumstances not generally considered to present the likelihood of a resultant death.

. . .

Legal theory which makes guilt or innocence of criminal homicide depend upon such accidental and fortuitous circumstances as are now embraced by modern tort law's encompassing concept of proximate cause is too harsh to be just.

The *Root* case involved a prosecution for involuntary manslaughter, the death occurring in an automobile race between the defendant and the decedent; there was no evidence that the defendant intended any harm to the decedent. For another such case also reaching the conclusion that the survivor should not be liable for manslaughter, see State v. Petersen, 526 P.2d 1008 (Or.1974), reversing 522 P.2d 912 (Or.Ct.App.1974).

To the contrary, however, see State v. McFadden, 320 N.W.2d 608 (Iowa 1982). Considering cases of drag racing in other jurisdictions, the Iowa court expressly disagreed with *Root*. It said: "[D]efendant has suggested no specific policy differences, nor can we think of any, that would justify a different standard of proximate causation under our involuntary manslaughter statute than under our tort law. . . . Proximate cause is based on the concept of foreseeability. We believe the foreseeability requirement, coupled with the requirement of recklessness . . . will prevent the possibility of harsh or unjust results in involuntary manslaughter cases. We disagree with the *Root* court's apparent opinion that drag racing on a public street is 'not generally considered to present the likelihood of a resultant death.' " 320 N.W.2d at 613.

Is the *Root* court's rejection of "proximate cause" as a basis for criminal liability equally applicable in a case where the defendant intentionally injures the deceased and death results from an unintended series of consequent events? See Commonwealth v. Cheeks, 223 A.2d 291, 294 (Pa.1966), in which the Pennsylvania court said: "[O]ne charged with homicide cannot escape liability merely because the blow he inflicted is not mortal or the immediate cause of death. If his blow is the legal cause, i.e., if it started a chain of causation which led to the death, he is guilty of homicide."

190. "In cases of homicide, it is rarely necessary to give the jury any direction on causation as such. Of course, a necessary ingredient of the crimes of murder and manslaughter is that the accused has by his act caused the victim's death. But how the victim came by his death is usually not in dispute. What is in dispute is more likely to be some other matter: for example, the identity of the person who committed the act which indisputably caused the victim's death; or whether the accused had the necessary intent; or whether the accused acted in self-defence, or was provoked. Even where it is necessary to direct the jury's minds to the question of causation, it is usually enough to direct them simply that in law the accused's act need not be the sole cause, or even the main cause, of the victim's death, it being enough that his act contributed significantly to that result. It is right to observe in passing, however, that even this simple direction is a direction of law relating to causation, on the basis of which the jury are bound to act in concluding whether the prosecution has established, as a matter of fact, that the accused's act did in this sense cause the victim's death. Occasionally, however, a specific issue of causation may arise. One such case is where, although an act of the accused constitutes a *causa sine qua non* of (or necessary condition for) the death of the victim, nevertheless the intervention of a third person may be regarded as the sole cause of the victim's death, thereby relieving the accused of criminal responsibility. Such intervention, if it has such an effect, has often been described by lawyers as a *novus actus interveniens*. We are aware that this time-honoured Latin term has been the subject of criticism. We are also aware that attempts have been made to translate it into English; though no simple translation has proved satisfactory, really because the Latin term has become a term of art which conveys to lawyers the crucial feature that there has not merely been an intervening act of another person, but that that act was so independent of the act of the accused that it should be regarded in law as the cause of the victim's death, to the exclusion of the act of the accused." Regina v. Pagett, 76 Crim.App. 279, 288 (1983).

What factors are relevant to the determination whether an intervening act of another person is "so independent of the act of the accused that it should be regarded in law as the cause of the victim's death"?

191.

Defendant and his accomplice were observed leaving the scene of a robbery at 12 Kensington Oval in a red Dodge van. Information concerning the incident, including the description of the getaway van was related to police. Officer Pagano received this information while on patrol with Sgt. Eric Halbekath in New Rochelle and shortly thereafter observed a van fitting this description heading toward the southbound entrance ramp of Interstate 95. The van failed to pull over, entered the highway and a high-speed chase ensued with speeds approaching 90 MPH or more.

Defendant eluded his pursuers by blocking, weaving and speeding. Clearly, defendant's manifest intent was to put as much distance as possible between himself and the police car.

Two witnesses also traveling southbound observed a portion of the chase. Each observed the vehicles pass out of sight because of their speed and the fact that the interstate gradually began to curve to the right. At a point within the curve, just inside the Bronx, the witnesses observed a large cloud of dust rise up. Traversing this distance, which took upwards of ten seconds and ¼ to ½ mile, the witnesses came upon the accident involving the police car and an abandoned truck illegally parked on the right-hand shoulder of the roadway. Police Officer Pagano was killed and Sgt. Halbekath was seriously injured.

People v. Flores, 476 N.Y.S.2d 478, 479–80 (Sup.Ct.1984).

Is the defendant criminally liable for the officer's death?

Concluding that he was not, the court said:

. . . [T]o establish legally sufficient trial evidence, the People must show that a defendant committed some act which is a proximate cause of death (irrespective of his intent) and upon evaluating that act it must be said that death was a reasonably foreseeable and nonaccidental consequence.

. . .

Taking the evidence in its best light to the People . . . we find that the defendant eluded his pursuers solely by means of defensive tactics, i.e., blocking, weaving and speeding. Accordingly, no affirmative acts on defendant's part can be said to be a "sufficiently direct cause" of the accident being mindful that there was no contact between vehicles.

In addition, there are a number of factors which may be considered as interrupting or superseding the chain of events which defendant set in motion. Among these factors are the condition of the roadway, the condition of the police vehicle and the reasonableness of the pursuit. We consider the reasonableness of pursuit highly significant in light of the Vehicle and Traffic Law Section 1104.

That statute, *inter alia*, provides that a driver of an emergency vehicle, when involved in an emergency operation (such as hot pursuit) may "exceed the maximum speed limits so long as he does not endanger life or property." Further, the statute admonishes emergency drivers that they will not be relieved "from the duty to drive with due regard for the safety of all persons, nor shall [this statute] protect the driver from the consequences of his reckless disregard for the safety of others."

Testimony of the expert witness for the People in accident reconstruction, Officer Stephen Coulon, established that in the few seconds before the accident, the police officer never applied his brakes. The vehicle bounced off the center divider yawing and skidding sideways diagonally to the right and striking the abandoned truck on the right shoulder. The precise position of the truck at that point was not foreseeable and was a cause of great damage.

As to the condition of the vehicle and the road surface, the People's expert witness testified that the police vehicle had a partially bald left front tire and the road surface had a "drag factor" of slightly less than average. Since the road surface was dry on the date of the accident, both of these conditions, in the opinion of the expert, had little or no effect on the accident. However, Officer Coulon conceded the tire was below required State standards and maintenance records for the police vehicle reflected a recent complaint the car pulled to the left. This was allegedly corrected.

On these facts, taken in the light most favorable to the People, we hold that *prima facie* proof with respect to *causation* by the defendant has not been established.

476 N.Y.S.2d at 480–81.

Do you agree? *Flores* is criticized in People v. Matos, 568 N.Y.S.2d 683 (Sup.Ct.1991).

With *Flores*, compare People v. Rakusz, 484 N.Y.S.2d 784, 786 (Sup.Ct. 1985): "Police Officer Hipple attempted to arrest defendant as a coconspirator in a drug bust. When the officer announced that defendant was under arrest, defendant ran. Hipple pursued, grabbed defendant and struggled with him. During the struggle defendant reached into his jacket pocket. Hipple pulled defendant's arm out of the pocket. Thinking that defendant had a gun, Hipple put his own hand into defendant's jacket pocket cutting himself on a serrated kitchen knife resting there."

The defendant was prosecuted for causing physical injury to a police officer with intent to prevent him from performing his lawful duty. Concluding that he was liable, the court said: "Defendant, during his resistance, attempted to place his hand in his pocket. I conclude that it was foreseeable that Officer Hipple would try to prevent him from extracting a weapon from that pocket. Among the foreseeable ways in which Officer Hipple would bend his efforts was that the officer would place his own hand in the pocket during the struggle. Therefore, it cannot be said that Officer Hipple's intervening conduct, instigated as it was by defendant's action, was the sole cause of his injury so as to relieve defendant of criminal responsibility." Id. at 787.

192.   The appellant was convicted of criminally negligent homicide for the death of a 15-year-old boy, who shot himself in the side of the head in the following circumstances: "The victim had been present when the appellant and his brother played Russian Roulette with a loaded gun some time during the week prior to the victim's death. The appellant and the victim had played Russian Roulette on the day of the victim's death. It is unclear whether the gun was loaded or not during this time but there was some evidence that it was not. After the two finished playing the game, the appellant put the gun away. Later, the victim was seen alone holding a gun and spinning the chamber. A few minutes later, a noise which sounded like a gunshot was heard." Lewis v. State, 474 So.2d 766, 770 (Ala.Crim.App. 1985).

Assuming that there is evidence sufficient to establish that the victim would not have shot himself if the appellant had not previously played Russian Roulette with him, should the conviction be affirmed? Is it significant that the appellant had put the gun away and was not in the room when the victim resumed playing Russian Roulette and shot himself? Would it matter if the victim had not shot himself until several weeks later?

193.

On April 19, 1980, Roosevelt Batiste and Reginald Holmes were both in Oscar Bardell's bar. Batiste's two stepdaughters told him that Reginald Holmes, "Scalp," had been annoying them. Batiste attempted to remonstrate with Holmes and Holmes slung a bar stool at him. Batiste was standing near the center of the bar and Holmes was close to the telephone by the back wall. According to the photographs, Batiste was to the left of Holmes. Batiste said Holmes reached in his pocket. Thinking Holmes was armed with a knife, Batiste pulled his gun and started shooting. Batiste fired five times and hit Holmes three times. One shot hit the music box and another injured a bystander, Freddie Cook. Holmes staggered toward Batiste and grabbed him in a bear hug. Batiste's stepson, LeRoy Bolden, seized Holmes around the neck with his left arm. Bolden hit Holmes with a gun and it fired up in the air. Bolden then shot Holmes in the forehead at close range.

Dr. Richard Tracy, a specialist in forensic medicine, testified that Holmes received four separate wounds. Two of the bullets entered the body from left to right. One of these passed through both lungs and the heart, then struck a rib and turned backwards. The second went through the abdomen. Another bullet entered the head at close range from right to left, the opposite direction from the two through the body. This bullet also had a slight angle from back to front. There was also a superficial bullet wound in the arm. Either one of two wounds, that in the head or that in the chest, would have caused Holmes' death. (Tr. 64) Both should have caused an immediate collapse. The chest wound was fatal and the head wound was "immediately fatal." (Tr. 60) The chances of surviving the shot in the abdomen would have been small. Holmes was living when all the wounds were inflicted.

The evidence establishes that the two body wounds, the one in the abdomen and the one in the chest, were fired by defendant Batiste from his position to the left of Holmes. The shot to the head was fired by Bolden. Either the chest wound or the head wound and possibly the abdominal wound would have caused the victim's death.

State v. Batiste, 410 So.2d 1055, 1056 (La.1982).

Who is criminally liable for Holmes's death?

Concluding that both Batiste and Bolden could be liable, the court said: "Separate fatal wounds inflicted in one encounter by two individuals make each guilty of homicide." "Bolden accelerated Holmes' death, but Batiste had independently fired a fatal shot." Id. at 1057, 1058.

Suppose that Holmes had been taken to the hospital after Batiste shot him, and, a day later, while he was in critical condition in the emergency room, Bolden had entered and shot him in the head, immediately killing him. What result?

See also Henderson v. State, 65 So. 721 (Ala.Ct.App.1914); People v. Lewis, 57 P. 470 (Cal.1899); Bennett v. Commonwealth, 150 S.W. 806 (Ky.1912); Wilson v. State, 24 S.W. 409 (Tex.Crim.App.1893).

The defendant in Nguyen v. Lindsey, 232 F.3d 1236 (9th Cir.2000) was convicted of murder. The victim was an innocent bystander hit by a bullet during a gun battle between the defendant's gang and another gang. During the trial, evidence was introduced that a member of the defendant's gang had fired first, and the prosecutor referred to that evidence in his closing argument. At a prior trial, a member of the rival gang had been convicted of the murder of the same victim. In that trial, evidence was introduced that the defendant had fired the first shot, and the prosecutor so argued. The theory of the prosecution in both cases was that in a case of voluntary mutual combat, it makes no difference who had fired first. The court held that there was no prosecutorial misconduct and that the rights of the defendant in the second trial were not violated. See, to the same effect, People v. Russell, 693 N.E.2d 193 (N.Y.1998).

A more extreme case is reported in The New York Times, Sept. 7, 2002, at A12. In the first trial, the defendant, a 40-year-old man, was prosecuted for the murder of the father of two teenage boys. At the end of the trial, the jury's verdict was sealed. The same prosecutor then prosecuted the two boys, who had previously been indicted for their father's murder. Following their conviction, the prosecutor announced that the jury had acquitted the defendant in the prior case. Part of an explanation for the unusual situation is that the boys had first confessed to the crime and later recanted and accused the man, with whom one of them had been sexually involved. There were indications that the prosecutor did not present the case against the man as forcefully as he might have done. He acknowledged that the case against the man was not very strong. The judge who tried both cases subsequently vacated the conviction of the boys, on the basis that the prosecutor's successive prosecutions of the man and the two boys denied them due process of law. The New York Times, Oct. 18, 2002, at A1. (The boys later pleaded guilty to a lesser degree of murder. The New York Times, Nov. 15, 2002, at A1.)

194. The Model Penal Code § 2.03 provides:

(1) Conduct is the cause of a result when:

(a) it is an antecedent but for which the result in question would not have occurred; and

(b) the relationship between the conduct and result satisfies any additional causal requirements imposed by the Code or by the law defining the offense.

(2) When purposely or knowingly causing a particular result is an element of an offense, the element is not established if the actual result is not within the purpose or the contemplation of the actor unless:

(a) the actual result differs from that designed or contemplated, as the case may be, only in the respect that a different person or different property is injured or affected or that the injury or harm designed or contemplated would have been more serious or more extensive than that caused; or

(b) the actual result involves the same kind of injury or harm as that designed or contemplated and is not too remote or accidental in its occurrence to have a [just] bearing on the actor's liability or on the gravity of his offense.

(3) When recklessly or negligently causing a particular result is an element of an offense, the element is not established if the actual result is not within the risk of which the actor is aware or, in the case of negligence, of which he should be aware unless:

(a) the actual result differs from the probable result only in the respect that a different person or different property is injured or affected or that the probable injury or harm would have been more serious or more extensive than that caused; or

(b) the actual result involves the same kind of injury or harm as the probable result and is not too remote or accidental in its occurrence to have a [just] bearing on the actor's liability or on the gravity of his offense.

(4) When causing a particular result is a material element of an offense for which absolute liability is imposed by law, the element is not established unless the actual result is a probable consequence of the actor's conduct.

195. To what extent is the limited utility of causation as a concept for the analysis of problems of criminal liability a reflection of:

(i) uncertainty about what interests us in a situation (i.e., uncertainty about what aspects of the situation, if any, we can and should try to control by criminal law);

(ii) the variety of purposes served by criminal law;

(iii) failure to develop adequate theories of criminal liability;

(iv) the primitive—fully basic—content of the concept of causation generally?

---

7. PUNISHMENT

The cases that we have considered to develop the distinctions among various categories of homicide may sometimes seem like exercises in abstract logic—and somewhat arbitrary at that. In all of them, however, the outcome is a matter of the greatest consequence for the defendant. Most often in homicide cases, the consequence of conviction is imprisonment, for many years in the most serious cases or even for life. Imprisonment typically means not only loss of liberty but also subjection to a bleak existence and, all too often, victimization by other prisoners. In a small number of cases, the outcome is literally a matter of life or death.

Although a community may impose on some of its members other burdens that are equally harsh simply in terms of their effect on one's life—e.g., military service in time of war—the harms imposed as the result of a criminal conviction are peculiarly in need of justification. For, in the first instance at least, they are imposed not because of some sought-after benefit to the community but simply because of the harm previously done by the criminal, that is, the commission of a crime. For aught that appears, the imprisonment of Chavez or Caruso, for example, did not on balance benefit the community but injured it, because her child or his other children were deprived of a parent, with all that that may imply. (To be sure, an estimate of the likely consequences for the community of conviction and punishment in a particular case is exceedingly complex and conjectural at best.) If we do not pause in each case to ask "What good will it do?" we must, all the more insistently, ask what justifies the rule under which the case falls. The summary answer is that the harm to the defendant and even, if it occurs, the incidental harm to the community are justified as the defendant's punishment for his crime. But that only raises the more general question: What is the justification of punishment?

What *is* the justification of punishment? Suppose someone—the always available "visitor from another planet"—asked you why Caruso—or Chavez or Girouard or Bell or any of the others—was sent to prison. The most likely reply is a reference to his crime: "Well, he killed Dr. Pendola" or, more formally, "He committed first-degree manslaughter." Suppose the conversation then continued:

"Yes, but why do you do something so unpleasant to him?"

"To punish him."

"But why? Wouldn't it be better to spend your resources on helping Dr. Pendola's widow?"

"What about Caruso?"

"What about him?"

"He can't get away unpunished."

"Why not? That is what I don't understand. Explain punishment to me."

How would you respond?

There are two general approaches to a response. The first is that punishment is *retribution* for the wrong done by the criminal; it is retro- spective, a requirement of justice justified directly and completely by the past conduct of the person punished. That view of punishment is associated most strongly with Immanuel Kant, who urged that punishment "must in all cases be imposed on . . . [a person] only on the ground that he has committed a crime." I. Kant, The Metaphysical Elements of Justice 100 (J. Ladd trans., 1965) (first published in German in 1797). Not only does retribution justify punishment; it prohibits a relaxation of punishment in order to accomplish some social good: "The law concerning punishment is a categorical imperative, and woe to him who rummages around in the winding paths of a theory of happiness looking for some advantage to be gained by releasing the criminal from punishment or by reducing the amount of it . . . ." Id.

The second view is the one to which Kant scornfully referred as "the winding paths of a theory of happiness": that punishment is justified by its *utility*, the good that it does, not necessarily for the criminal himself but for the community. "[T]o suppose that infliction of retributive suffering suf- fices, without reference to concrete consequences, is to leave untouched old causes of criminality and to create new ones by fostering revenge and brutality. . . . No amount of guilt on the part of the evil-doer absolves us from responsibility for the consequences upon him and others of our way of treating him, or from our continuing responsibility for the conditions under which persons develop perverse habits." J. Dewey, Human Nature and Conduct 20–21 (Modern Library ed. 1957).

Both positions, the retributive and the utilitarian, have had distin- guished supporters. With Kant, for example, Hegel argued that it is "superficial" to regard punishment as itself an evil; rather, it is the righting of a wrong, annulment of "an infringement of the right as right." So understood, "punishment is regarded as containing the criminal's right and hence by being punished he is honoured as a rational being. He does not receive this due of honour unless the concept and measure of his punishment are derived from his own act. Still less does he receive it if he is treated either as a harmful animal who has to be made harmless, or with a view to deterring and reforming him." G. Hegel, Philosophy of Right 70– 71 (T. Knox trans., 1942) (first published in German in 1821). Echoing Hegel's last point, Mabbott has argued: "[T]he essential point about retributive punishment is that it treats the criminal as a man. . . . Retribution is the agent's own act. The law can *threaten*; but there is only one thing that can justify a punishment and that is something the legislator cannot bring about, namely, a free choice by the subject. . . . To be punished for reform reasons is to be treated like a dog. A sane adult demands to be held responsible for his actions. He rejects as an intolerable insult the well-meaning exculpations of the sympathetic scientist, whether presented on social or psychological grounds. Retributive punishment closes the account, reformative punishment opens it." Mabbott, "Freewill and Punishment," in Contemporary British Philosophy (3d Series) 289, 303 (H. Lewis ed., 1956).

Bentham, the unswerving British utilitarian, agreed, of course, with Dewey's position. "[A]ll punishment is mischief: all punishment in itself is evil. Upon the principle of utility, if it ought at all to be admitted, it ought only to be admitted in as far as it promises to exclude some greater evil." J. Bentham, An Introduction to the Principles of Morals and Legislation 170 (1907 ed.) (first published in 1789). Holmes, who subscribed generally to the utilitarian justifications for punishment, especially its preventive function, said of the retributive argument: "There remains to be mentioned the affirmative argument in favor of the theory of retribution, to the effect that the fitness of punishment following wrong-doing is axiomatic, and is instinctively recognized by unperverted minds. I think that it will be seen, on self-inspection, that this feeling of fitness is absolute and unconditional only in the case of our neighbors. It does not seem to me that any one who has satisfied himself that an act of his was wrong, and that he will never do it again, would feel the least need or propriety, as between himself and an earthly punishing power alone, of his being made to suffer for what he had done, although, when third persons were introduced, he might, as a philosopher, admit the necessity of hurting him to frighten others. But when our neighbors do wrong, we sometimes feel the fitness of making them smart for it, whether they have repented or not. The feeling of fitness seems to me to be only vengeance in disguise . . . ." O. Holmes, The Common Law 39 (M. Howe ed., 1963) (first published in 1881). To the argument that punishment for utilitarian reasons treats a person "as a thing," Holmes replied, "If a man lives in society, he is liable to find himself so treated." Id. at 38.

Despite the suggestions in the preceding quotations that one or the other of the two general theories of punishment is not only wrong but absolutely, unequivocally, and unqualifiedly wrong, recent efforts to explain and justify punishment have quite commonly incorporated something of both. Wholly to ignore the retributive aspect, it is said, leads too easily to "punishing" the innocent, provided only that it is proved to be beneficial in the circumstances. In any case, it regards punishment for crime as the equivalent of conscription or taxation or any other forward-looking social policy, contrary to what we know, or at any rate feel, intuitively to be a difference between them. Wholly to ignore the utilitarian aspect, it is said, is not, as Hegel said, to annul a wrong, but to compound it. Especially in view of individuals' widely varying attributes and circumstances, it is simply impossible to know what justice requires in any particular case.

The composite theories that are offered, however, are unconvincing. It may be suggested, for example, that retribution alone ought to determine *whether* a person may be punished but that utilitarian considerations ought to determine the *extent* of punishment. H. Packer, The Limits of the Criminal Sanction 35–70 (1968). Or it may be suggested that utilitarian considerations ought to determine what conduct is criminal and how it is punished generally but that retribution ought to determine the application and extent of punishment in a particular case. E.g., Greenawalt, "Punishment," in 4 Encyclopedia of Crime and Justice 1336 (1983); H.L.A. Hart, Punishment and Responsibility 18–22 (1968). The former approach seems to regard punishment from a retributive perspective as indivisible, as if individual desert were a kind of sluice gate, which is either fully closed or fully open. But we all know that pain can be greater or less; it makes no sense to expend so much effort distinguishing, say, between first-degree murder and involuntary manslaughter only to conclude that the distinction need have no effect on punishment, provided only that the defendant deserves to be punished at all. The latter approach purports to avoid the useless infliction of punishment by adopting utilitarian rules and to acknowledge retribution by restricting the rules' application to cases in which punishment is deserved. But the apparent separation of rules and their application is illusory. For it is the rules that determine who is guilty and who, therefore, is punished. If it were the case that punishment of someone in Caruso's situation were useless or worse than useless, ought the rule to declare such conduct by a person in that situation noncriminal or, at any rate, not punishable? On the other hand, if it were decided that it would be socially useful to punish some group of persons for certain conduct, ought the rule to provide that they are guilty of a crime if they engage in the conduct, without regard to their individual desert? (Consider the verdict of "guilty but mentally ill," discussed below, p. 576.) If the rule does so provide, what room is there for consideration of desert in a particular case? This approach evidently intends that utilitarian considerations govern only the *kinds of conduct* that are criminal and not the exculpatory (or inculpatory) effect of the actor's individual circumstances. But it is evident from the homicide cases that the latter are highly significant in the formulation of the rules themselves.

It is striking that for all the disagreement and uncertainty about theories of punishment, there is ordinarily remarkable convergence about punishment in particular cases. There is disagreement about how punitive the criminal law should be in general—i.e., longer or shorter sentences—or about particular kinds of punishment, most notably capital punishment, but for the most part there is agreement about who ought to be punished and about relative punishments for different crimes. That agreement lends point to Greenawalt's observation: "Theories of justification are often built with existing practices in mind and do not usually stray too far from the reflective moral views of ordinary citizens. The fact that sharply divergent philosophical theories can have closely similar implications across a broad range of actual practices is less a startling coincidence than a product of the existential basis on which those theories are constructed." 4 Encyclopedia of Crime and Justice, at 1345.

———

196. Passing for the moment the question of how punitive the criminal law ought to be in general and the question whether a criminal's individual circumstances not directly related to the crime ought to have a bearing on the punishment—see the presentence reports, pp. 721–39 below—rank the cases below in the order of appropriate severity of punishment for the convicted defendant:

Chavez (p. 1)

Girouard (p. 72)

Bedder (p. 83)

Alexander (p. 92)

Caruso (p. 111)

Mazza (p. 121)

Zygmaniak (p. 139)

Poplis (p. 143)

Stamp (p. 156)

Humphrey (p. 206)

Bell (p. 254)

Feinberg (p. 277)

Beardsley (p. 285)

Sheridan (p. 297)

Hamilton (p. 312)

How closely does your ranking track the actual pattern of the law?

Looking ahead a little, where in the previous ranking would you place a case of joyriding (p. 416); theft of $10,000 (see p. 430); robbery (p. 452); *Rusk* (p. 465), in which the defendant was convicted of raping a woman whom he had met at a bar earlier that night; attempted murder; and conspiracy to murder?

Can you articulate the retributive and/or utilitarian considerations that guide your ranking? To what extent are they consistent or not consistent? Do you apply the same considerations in every case, or do they vary from one case to another?

Insofar as your ranking is guided by retributive considerations, on what are your judgments about individual desert based? How firm are they? (Do you think that anyone who disagrees with you on that score is simply mistaken?)

Insofar as your ranking is guided by utilitarian considerations, what functions do you believe that punishment serves? Do the functions of punishment vary according to the crime? The defendant? The nature and length of the punishment?

———

The most obvious function of punishment is the prevention of crime. Writing in 1881, Holmes observed that "probably most English-speaking lawyers would accept the preventive theory without hesitation." The Common Law 37. That is no less likely to be true today. In one respect, the preventive theory is unassailable. Imprisonment prevents for the time being commission of the same or another crime by the same defendant—except, it should be recalled, within the prison, where violence among prisoners is altogether common. More controversial, although on the whole accepted, is the function of general prevention: the impact of criminal law and the threat of punishment to deter persons who might otherwise commit crimes. How such prevention works is much studied. The threat of punishment may simply alter a person's calculation of risks, costs, and benefits. Such calculations aside, the law's prohibition may create or reinforce moral restraints on the conduct. Still more diffusely, the criminal law and punishment may substantiate a sense of justice and moral order, without which moral restraints are weakened. For an influential discussion, see Andenaes, "General Prevention—Illusion or Reality," 43 J. Crim. L. C. & P. S. 176 (1952).

Another function that punishment is thought to serve is satisfaction of a deeply felt human need for requital of wrongdoing or, simply, vengeance. That is not what Hegel had in mind when he spoke of annulling a wrong, above; but it is a close psychological specification of his abstract formula. Stephen observed: "The doctrine that hatred and vengeance are wicked in themselves appears to me to contradict plain facts, and to be unsupported by any argument deserving of attention. . . . The unqualified manner in which they have been denounced is in itself a proof that they are deeply rooted in human nature. No doubt they are peculiarly liable to abuse, and in some states of society are commonly in excess of what is desirable, and so require restraint rather than excitement, but unqualified denunciations of them are as ill-judged as unqualified denunciations of sexual passion. The forms in which deliberate anger and righteous disapprobation are expressed, and the execution of criminal justice is the most emphatic of such forms, stand to the one set of passions in the same relation in which marriage stands to the other." 2 Stephen, History 82. And Newman: "To reduce the collective feeling and demand for justice in humanity to an animal impulse for vindictiveness and vengeance would be oversimplifying things. The failure of the state to satisfy this collective feeling leads to widespread fear and insecurity. . . . If the state fails, therefore, to repress lawless, individual action, the citizens may rightly claim that they have been released from the social contract, and that each is again free to do as he pleases. Hence the criminality increases as a result of the state's failure to do proportional justice. It is for these reasons that aversion to crime and to the criminal who personifies it is unavoidable; unless the social group maintains its reprobation of crime it cannot remain intact." Newman, "Punishment and the Breakdown of the Legal Order: The Experience in East Pakistan," in C. Friedrich, ed., Responsibility (3 Nomos) 128, 135–36 (1960).

Punishment has also been justified as an effort to reform or rehabilitate the wrongdoer, which may be thought to be good in itself. (Hence the term "penitentiary" for a place of imprisonment.) See the judge's statement to the defendant, before sentencing him to life imprisonment, in State v. Thompson, Wright 617 (Ohio 1834). Or it may be sought for its social benefit. "The best thought in what was once called the penal field and is now significantly called the correctional field is directed toward developing institutional plants, personnel and programs that will accomplish the rehabilitation of as many offenders as possible and will enable those who cannot be released to adjust as well as possible to the restricted life of the prison." American Correctional Association, Manual of Correctional Standards 8 (3d ed. 1966). A related but rather different argument is that punishment satisfies the criminal's own need to be punished, for relief from his own sense of guilt. See J. Flugel, Man, Morals, and Society 143–46 (1945).

––––––––

197. Reconsider the cases of homicide on the list in note 196 above. In all of them the preventive function of criminal law was evidently inoperative. In which of them is the preventive function likely to have an effect on the incidence of that type of crime or of crimes generally, even if it did not on the particular defendant? In which of them is the specific function of preventing the defendant from repeating his crime a relevant consideration?

In which of the cases is the function of satisfying the community's demand for retribution (whether or not the demand can be justified) a relevant consideration?

In which of the cases is the function of reform or rehabilitation a relevant consideration?

How much do your answers to the preceding questions affect your conclusion about the appropriateness of punishment, or the appropriate punishment, in each case?

––––––––

The Model Penal Code's statement of its purposes largely adopts a utilitarian rationale for punishment and incorporates in general terms most of the functional arguments above. The retributive justification is not excluded entirely; but it is mentioned, one may believe, rather diffidently.

MODEL PENAL CODE

Section 1.02. Purposes; Principles of Construction.

(1) The general purposes of the provisions governing the definition of offenses are:

(a) to forbid and prevent conduct that unjustifiably and inexcusably inflicts or threatens substantial harm to individual or public interests;

(b) to subject to public control persons whose conduct indicates that they are disposed to commit crimes;

(c) to safeguard conduct that is without fault from condemnation as criminal;

(d) to give fair warning of the nature of the conduct declared to constitute an offense;

(e) to differentiate on reasonable grounds between serious and minor offenses.

(2) The general purposes of the provisions governing the sentencing and treatment of offenders are:

(a) to prevent the commission of offenses;

(b) to promote the correction and rehabilitation of offenders;

(c) to safeguard offenders against excessive, disproportionate or arbitrary punishment;

(d) to give fair warning of the nature of the sentences that may be imposed on conviction of an offense;

(e) to differentiate among offenders with a view to a just individualization in their treatment;

. . .

Most observers would probably conclude that none of the justifications of punishment, except the preventive function, can be regarded as beyond controversy. In the 1960s, retribution was given little weight, at least theoretically, and the main emphasis was on reform and rehabilitation. So, the American Correctional Association could assert that whatever validity retribution may have "is so far out-weighed by the merits of the philosophy of rehabilitation that the latter should take unquestioned precedence in current penal thought." Manual of Correctional Standards, at 7–8. In recent years, the number of persons in prison has risen dramatically, and the situation is almost precisely the reverse. Skepticism about the possibility of rehabilitation is pervasive, and the argument that a criminal deserves to be punished and it is right to punish him is heard often and is widely accepted. Even the preventive function is not free from controversy, except to the extent that it depends simply on "locking him up."

The nature and, to a very limited extent, the amount of punishment is subject to the provision of the Eighth Amendment that "cruel and unusual punishments" shall not be inflicted. On the application of the Cruel and Unusual Punishments Clause, see pp. 715–17 below.

————

198. "On the whole, the problem of imprisonment and in general of punishing those who violate the law is one of the most disheartening ones that face modern civilization. It represents the breakdown of human intelligence, as well as good will. It shows perhaps the ugliest phase of our human nature." Cohen, "Moral Aspects of the Criminal Law," 49 Yale L. J. 987, 1025 (1940).

Is that so? On what view of punishment is Cohen's harsh judgment most likely based? Might it be argued that if our practices of punishment show a "phase of our human nature" it is beside the point to describe it as ugly? How much, in the end, do our theories determine our practices, and how much do our practices determine our theories?

Judges newly appointed to the trial bench commonly report that none of their responsibilities is so daunting and none weighs so heavily on them as sentencing a convicted criminal. Judge Learned Hand is said to have observed, "Here I am an old man in a long nightgown making muffled noises at people who may be no worse than I am."

————

CAPITAL PUNISHMENT

————

Capital punishment is reserved all but exclusively for intentional killing in circumstances of unusual cruelty or coldbloodedness. In Coker v. Georgia, 433 U.S. 584 (1977), four Justices expressed the view that capital punishment for rape violates the Cruel and Unusual Punishments Clause. Nineteen years later, the Supreme Court of Louisiana upheld the constitutionality of capital punishment for the rape of a child under the age of 12, in State v. Wilson, 685 So.2d 1063 (La.1996). It noted that it was the only state that had such a provision. The Supreme Court of the United States denied a petition for certiorari; three Justices took the unusual step of noting that such a denial does not constitute a ruling on the merits. Bethley v. Louisiana, 520 U.S. 1259 (1997). In Enmund v. Florida, 458 U.S. 782, 797 (1982) (5–4), the Court held that the Clause did not permit capital punishment for a person convicted of felony murder who did not himself "kill, attempt to kill, or intend that a killing take place or that lethal force will be employed." Subsequently, in Tison v. Arizona, 481 U.S. 137, 149 (1987) (5–4), *Enmund* was restricted to a felon who is a "minor actor . . . not on the scene, who neither intended to kill nor was found to have had any culpable mental state." The Cruel and Unusual Punishments Clause does not prohibit capital punishment for a defendant convicted of felony murder who does not himself kill or intend to kill but whose participation in the felony "is major and whose mental state is one of reckless indifference to the value of human life." Id. at 152. Although the constitutional issue remains in doubt, as a practical matter capital punishment is imposed extremely rarely for anything except an intentional killing, either because the statute restricts it or because the prosecutor does not seek it or the judge or jury does not impose it for anything less.

Capital punishment has been abolished altogether in most countries, by law or effectively in practice. A considerable number of other countries retain it only in exceptional circumstances, like wartime. Most of the countries of western Europe and Latin America are in one or the other of those groups. Some other countries retain capital punishment in law but have not executed anyone for ten years or more. In the United States, capital punishment is retained in federal law and in the laws of 38 states; there is no provision for capital punishment in 12 states and the District of Columbia. In all of the states that retain capital punishment, the statutory provisions have been revised and reenacted since 1972. Although a movement for abolition of capital punishment remains strong, only two Justices (Brennan and Marshall), neither of them now on the Court, have expressed the view that the Constitution does not permit capital punishment in any circumstances. See the concurring opinions of Justice Brennan and Justice Marshall in Furman v. Georgia, 408 U.S. 238, 257, 314 (1972), and their dissenting opinions in Gregg v. Georgia, 428 U.S. 153, 227, 231 (1976).[101]

Between 1930 and 1968, 3,859 persons were executed in the United States. From 1968, the first such year on record, to 1977, there were no executions in the United States. Starting in 1977, the number of executions rose erratically to a high in 1999. The number of executions for the most recent years is:

1995 – 56

1996 – 45

101. In 2002, two federal district judges held that the Federal Death Penalty Act was unconstitutional. United States v. Quinones, 205 F.Supp.2d 256 (S.D.N.Y.2002) (Rakoff, J.) (in light of "unacceptably high rate" of convictions of innocent persons for capital crimes and delayed or fortuitous circumstances in which their innocence is detected, execution of sentence of death is denial of due process). United States v. Fell, 217 F.Supp.2d 469 (D.Vt.2002) (Sessions, J.) (relaxed evidentiary standards at hearing to determine eligibility for capital punishment violate Fifth Amendment's Due Process Clause and Sixth Amendment rights to confrontation and cross-examination). The decision in *Quinones* was reversed on appeal. The court of appeals declared that decisions of the Supreme Court foreclosed the arguments on which the district court had relied. 313 F.3d 49 (2d Cir.2002). An appeal of *Fell* was pending in early 2003.

1997 – 71

1998 – 68

1999 – 98

2000 – 85

2001 – 66

2002 – 71

From 1977 through 2002, 820 persons have been executed, of whom ten were women. 57% were identified as white, 35% as black, and 7% as Hispanic. (Statistics, Death Penalty Information Center.)

The predominant method of execution is lethal injection, which is used in all but two of the states having the death penalty. Nine states authorize electrocution, two of them exclusively. A few states authorize the use of other methods in addition to lethal injection: lethal gas, hanging, or a firing squad. If more than one method is authorized, the choice is generally made by the condemned person. All but two of the executions in 2002 were by lethal injection, the remaining two by electrocution.

From 1977 to the end of 2001, 3697 persons were sentenced to death, of whom 497 (11%) were executed. At the end of 2001, 3581 persons were under sentence of death, of whom 51 were women. 55% were identified as white, 42.9% as black, and among those whose ethnicity was known, 11% as Hispanic. 35% were between the ages of 30 and 39, and 67% between the ages of 25 and 44. The youngest person sentenced to death was 19, the oldest 86. At the time of arrest for a capital offense, about 50% were between the ages of 20 and 29 and 13.7% were younger. The median time in prison since the imposition of a death sentence was seven years and four months. In 2001, 155 persons, all men, were sentenced to death, the smallest number since 1973. Nineteen persons under sentence of death died, 17 from natural causes and two by suicide. (Statistics, Department of Justice Bureau of Justice Statistics.)

199. How do you explain the exceptional position of the United States in comparison with most, if not all, of the countries with which it is usually aligned? The five countries that have employed capital punishment in the recent past are (in descending order of number executed): China, the Republic of Congo, Iran, Saudi Arabia, and the United States. Professor Carol Steiker has argued that a significant element of the explanation may be the Supreme Court's decision in Furman v. Georgia, 408 U.S. 238 (1972) (per curiam), which had the effect of invalidating the provisions for capital punishment in federal law and the law of all the states that retained it. When, four years later, the Court (with a different membership) upheld the constitutionality of Georgia's revised provision for capital punishment in Gregg v. Georgia, 428 U.S. 153 (1976) (5–4), it had the effect in subsequent decades of validating capital punishment not merely as a constitutional matter but much more generally as a matter of human rights or, simply, morality. In effect, she argues, the constitutional debate displaced the moral debate that led to the abolition of capital punishment in Europe and elsewhere during the same period. Steiker, Capital Punishment and American Exceptionalism, 81 Ore. L. Rev. 97 (2002).

200. With the exception of Missouri, all ten of the states having the most executions from 1977 through 2002 are in the south: Texas executed 289 persons, Virginia 87, Missouri 59, Oklahoma 55, Florida 54, Georgia 31, South Carolina 28, Louisiana 27, Alabama 25, Arkansas 24, and North Carolina 23. Arizona executed 22 persons. The number then drops sharply to Delaware with 13.

Figures for the number of persons under sentence of death are comparable. More than half are held in southern states, although California, which has executed few people, has the largest number, followed by Texas, Florida, North Carolina, and Alabama. (Statistics, Department of Justice Bureau of Justice Statistics.)

How do you explain the clear geographic pattern of executions and sentences in the United States?

In a large number of cases since 1972, the Supreme Court has struggled with conflicting demands that the imposition of capital punishment be principled and not arbitrary or capricious, and that it reflect particular aggravating or mitigating circumstances of the crime and the individual defendant. See, for example, Gregg v. Georgia, 428 U.S. 153 (1976) (5–4) (statute providing for consideration of aggravating and mitigating factors upheld); Woodson v. North Carolina, 428 U.S. 280 (1976) (5–4) (mandatory death penalty allowing no room for consideration of special factors invalid); Lockett v. Ohio, 438 U.S. 586 (1978) (statute restricting consideration of mitigating factors invalid). For other related cases, see, e.g., Mills v. Maryland, 486 U.S. 367 (1988) (5–4); Penry v. Lynaugh, 492 U.S. 302 (1989) (5–4); Blystone v. Pennsylvania, 494 U.S. 299 (1990) (5–4); Walton v. Arizona, 497 U.S. 639 (1990) (5–4). The frequency with which the Court has decided by a 5–4 vote emphasizes the difficulty of reconciling the quest for consistency, on one hand, and attention to the individual case, on the other, in the context of a punishment that is regarded as extraordinary and of overwhelming import for the person punished and for the community as a whole.

The Constitution does not prohibit capital punishment for a crime committed at the age of 17 or 16. Stanford v. Kentucky, 492 U.S. 361 (1989) (5–4). In Thompson v. Oklahoma, 487 U.S. 815 (1988) (5–4), four Justices concluded that the Constitution prohibits capital punishment for a crime committed by a person who was less than 16 years old. (Without deciding the general issue, a fifth Justice concurred in the judgment vacating the sentence in that case, on the ground that the state legislature had not specifically addressed the question, because the statute specified no minimum age.)

The current division of opinion in the United States about capital punishment is reflected in the opinions of the Justices in Atkins v. Virginia, 536 U.S. 304 (2002) (6–3), which follows.

Atkins v. Virginia

536 U.S. 304, 122 S.Ct. 2242 (2002)

■ JUSTICE STEVENS delivered the opinion of the Court.

Those mentally retarded persons who meet the law's requirement for criminal responsibility should be tried and punished when they commit crimes. Because of their disabilities in areas of reasoning, judgment, and control of their impulses, however, they do not act with the level of moral culpability that characterizes the most serious adult criminal conduct. Moreover, their impairments can jeopardize the reliability and fairness of capital proceedings against mentally retarded defendants. Presumably for these reasons, in the 13 years since we decided Penry v. Lynaugh, 492 U.S. 302 (1989), the American public, legislators, scholars, and judges have deliberated over the question whether the death penalty should even be imposed on a mentally retarded criminal. The consensus reflected in those deliberations informs our answer to the question presented by this case: whether such executions are "cruel and unusual punishments" prohibited by the Eighth Amendment to the Federal Constitution.

I

Petitioner, Daryl Renard Atkins, was convicted of abduction, armed robbery, and capital murder, and sentenced to death. At approximately midnight on August 16, 1996, Atkins and William Jones, armed with a semiautomatic handgun, abducted Eric Nesbitt, robbed him of the money on his person, drove him to an automated teller machine in his pickup truck where cameras recorded their withdrawal of additional cash, then took him to an isolated location where he was shot eight times and killed.

Jones and Atkins both testified in the guilt phase of Atkins' trial. Each confirmed most of the details in the other's account of the incident, with the important exception that each stated that the other had actually shot and killed Nesbitt. Jones' testimony, which was both more coherent and credible than Atkins', was obviously credited by the jury and was sufficient to establish Atkins' guilt. At the penalty phase of the trial, the State introduced victim impact evidence and proved two aggravating circumstances: future dangerousness and "vileness of the offense." To prove future dangerousness, the State relied on Atkins' prior felony convictions as well as the testimony of four victims of earlier robberies and assaults. To prove the second aggravator, the prosecution relied upon the trial record, including pictures of the deceased's body and the autopsy report.

In the penalty phase, the defense relied on one witness, Dr. Evan Nelson, a forensic psychologist who had evaluated Atkins before trial and concluded that he was "mildly mentally retarded." His conclusion was based on interviews with people who knew Atkins, a review of school and court records, and the administration of a standard intelligence test which indicated that Atkins had a full scale IQ of 59.

The jury sentenced Atkins to death, but the Virginia Supreme Court ordered a second sentencing hearing because the trial court had used a misleading verdict form. . . . At the resentencing, Dr. Nelson again testified. The State presented an expert rebuttal witness, Dr. Stanton Samenow, who expressed the opinion that Atkins was not mentally retarded, but rather was of "average intelligence, at least," and diagnosable as having antisocial personality disorder. App. 476. The jury again sentenced Atkins to death.

The Supreme Court of Virginia affirmed the imposition of the death penalty. . . . Atkins did not argue before the Virginia Supreme Court that his sentence was disproportionate to penalties imposed for similar crimes in Virginia, but he did contend "that he is mentally retarded and thus cannot be sentenced to death." [260 Va. 375], at 386. The majority of the state court rejected this contention, relying on our holding in *Penry*. 260 Va., at 387. The Court was "not willing to commute Atkins' sentence of death to life imprisonment merely because of his IQ score." Id., at 390.

Justice Hassell and Justice Koontz dissented. They rejected Dr. Samenow's opinion that Atkins possesses average intelligence as "incredulous as a matter of law," and concluded that "the imposition of the sentence of death upon a criminal defendant who has the mental age of a child between the ages of 9 and 12 is excessive." Id., at 394, 395–396. In their opinion, "it is indefensible to conclude that individuals who are mentally retarded are not to some degree less culpable for their criminal acts. By definition, such individuals have substantial limitations not shared by the general population. A moral and civilized society diminishes itself if its system of justice does not afford recognition and consideration of those limitations in a meaningful way." Id., at 397.

Because of the gravity of the concerns expressed by the dissenters, and in light of the dramatic shift in the state legislative landscape that has occurred in the past 13 years, we granted certiorari to revisit the issue that we first addressed in the *Penry* case. . . .

II

The Eighth Amendment succinctly prohibits "excessive" sanctions. It provides: "Excessive bail shall not be required, nor excessive fines imposed, nor cruel and unusual punishments inflicted." In Weems v. United States, 217 U.S. 349 (1910), we held that a punishment of 12 years jailed in irons at hard and painful labor was excessive. We explained "that it is a precept of justice that punishment for crime should be graduated and proportioned to the offense." Id., at 367. We have repeatedly applied this proportionality precept in later cases interpreting the Eighth Amendment. . . .

A claim that punishment is excessive is judged not by the standards that prevailed in 1685 when Lord Jeffreys presided over the "Bloody Assizes" or when the Bill of Rights was adopted, but rather by those that currently prevail. As Chief Justice Warren explained in his opinion in Trop v. Dulles, 356 U.S. 86 (1958): "The basic concept underlying the Eighth Amendment is nothing less than the dignity of man. . . . The Amendment must draw its meaning from the evolving standards of decency that mark the progress of a maturing society." Id., at 100–101.

Proportionality review under those evolving standards should be informed by " 'objective factors to the maximum possible extent,' " see *Harmelin* [v. Michigan], 501 U.S. [957 (1991)], at 1000 (quoting Rummel v. Estelle, 445 U.S. 263, 274–275 (1980)). We have pinpointed that the "clearest and most reliable objective evidence of contemporary values is the legislation enacted by the country's legislatures." *Penry*, 492 U.S., at 331. Relying in part on such legislative evidence, we have held that death is an impermissibly excessive punishment for the rape of an adult woman, Coker v. Georgia, 433 U.S. 584, 593–596 (1977), or for a defendant who neither took life, attempted to take life, nor intended to take life, Enmund v. Florida, 458 U.S. 782, 789–793 (1982). In *Coker*, we focused primarily on the then-recent legislation that had been enacted in response to our decision 10 years earlier in Furman v. Georgia, 408 U.S. 238 (1972) (per curiam), to support the conclusion that the "current judgment," though "not wholly unanimous," weighed very heavily on the side of rejecting capital punishment as a "suitable penalty for raping an adult woman." *Coker*, 433 U.S., at 596. The "current legislative judgment" relevant to our decision in *Enmund* was less clear than in *Coker* but "nevertheless weigh[ed] on the side of rejecting capital punishment for the crime at issue." *Enmund*, 458 U.S., at 793.

We also acknowledged in *Coker* that the objective evidence, though of great importance, did not "wholly determine" the controversy, "for the Constitution contemplates that in the end our own judgment will be brought to bear on the question of the acceptability of the death penalty under the Eighth Amendment." 433 U.S., at 597. . . . Thus, in cases involving a consensus, our own judgment is "brought to bear," *Coker*, 433 U.S., at 597, by asking whether there is reason to disagree with the judgment reached by the citizenry and its legislators.

Guided by our approach in these cases, we shall first review the judgment of legislatures that have addressed the suitability of imposing the death penalty on the mentally retarded and then consider reasons for agreeing or disagreeing with their judgment.

III

The parties have not called our attention to any state legislative consideration of the suitability of imposing the death penalty on mentally retarded offenders prior to 1986. In that year, the public reaction to the execution of a mentally retarded murderer in Georgia apparently led to the enactment of the first state statute prohibiting such executions. In 1988, when Congress enacted legislation reinstating the federal death penalty, it expressly provided that a "sentence of death shall not be carried out upon a person who is mentally retarded." In 1989, Maryland enacted a similar prohibition. It was in that year that we decided *Penry*, and concluded that those two state enactments, "even when added to the 14 States that have rejected capital punishment completely, do not provide sufficient evidence at present of a national consensus." 492 U.S., at 334.

Much has changed since then. Responding to the national attention received by the Bowden execution and our decision in *Penry*, state legislatures across the country began to address the issue. In 1990 Kentucky and Tennessee enacted statutes similar to those in Georgia and Maryland, as did New Mexico in 1991, and Arkansas, Colorado, Washington, Indiana, and Kansas in 1993 and 1994. In 1995, when New York reinstated its death penalty, it emulated the Federal Government by expressly exempting the mentally retarded. Nebraska followed suit in 1998. There appear to have been no similar enactments during the next two years, but in 2000 and 2001 six more states—South Dakota, Arizona, Connecticut, Florida, Missouri, and North Carolina—joined the procession. The Texas Legislature unanimously adopted a similar bill, and bills have passed at least one house in other States, including Virginia and Nevada.

It is not so much the number of these States that is significant, but the consistency of the direction of change. Given the well-known fact that anticrime legislation is far more popular than legislation providing protections for persons guilty of violent crime, the large number of States prohibiting the execution of mentally retarded persons (and the complete absence of States passing legislation reinstating the power to conduct such executions) provides powerful evidence that today our society views mentally retarded offenders as categorically less culpable than the average criminal. The evidence carries even greater force when it is noted that the legislatures that have addressed the issue have voted overwhelmingly in favor of the prohibition. Moreover, even in those States that allow the execution of mentally retarded offenders, the practice is uncommon. Some States, for example New Hampshire and New Jersey, continue to authorize executions, but none have been carried out in decades. Thus there is little need to pursue legislation barring the execution of the mentally retarded in those States. And it appears that even among those States that regularly execute offenders and that have no prohibition with regard to the mentally retarded, only five have executed offenders possessing a known IQ less than 70 since we decided *Penry*. The practice, therefore, has become truly unusual, and it is fair to say that a national consensus has developed against it.[102]

---

102. Additional evidence makes it clear that this legislative judgment reflects a much broader social and professional consensus. For example, several organizations with germane expertise have adopted official positions opposing the imposition of the death penalty

To the extent there is serious disagreement about the execution of mentally retarded offenders, it is in determining which offenders are in fact retarded. In this case, for instance, the Commonwealth of Virginia disputes that Atkins suffers from mental retardation. Not all people who claim to be mentally retarded will be so impaired as to fall within the range of mentally retarded offenders about whom there is a national consensus. As was our approach in Ford v. Wainwright, with regard to insanity, "we leave to the State[s] the task of developing appropriate ways to enforce the constitutional restriction upon its execution of sentences." 477 U.S. 399, 405, 416–417 (1986).

IV

This consensus unquestionably reflects widespread judgment about the relative culpability of mentally retarded offenders, and the relationship between mental retardation and the penological purposes served by the death penalty. Additionally, it suggests that some characteristics of mental retardation undermine the strength of the procedural protections that our capital jurisprudence steadfastly guards.

As discussed above, clinical definitions of mental retardation require not only sub-average intellectual functioning, but also significant limitations in adaptive skills such as communication, self-care, and self-direction that became manifest before age 18. Mentally retarded persons frequently know the difference between right and wrong and are competent to stand trial. Because of their impairments, however, by definition they have diminished capacities to understand and process information, to communicate, to abstract from mistakes and learn from experience, to engage in logical reasoning, to control impulses, and to understand the reactions of others. There is no evidence that they are more likely to engage in criminal conduct than others, but there is abundant evidence that they often act on impulse rather than pursuant to a premeditated plan, and that in group settings they are followers rather than leaders. Their deficiencies do not warrant an exemption from criminal sanctions, but they do diminish their personal culpability.

In light of these deficiencies, our death penalty jurisprudence provides two reasons consistent with the legislative consensus that the mentally retarded should be categorically excluded from execution. First, there is a

upon a mentally retarded offender. See Brief for American Psychological Association et al. as Amici Curiae; Brief for AAMR et al. at Amici Curiae. In addition, representatives of widely diverse religious communities in the United States, reflecting Christian, Jewish, Muslim, and Buddhist traditions, have filed an amicus curiae brief explaining that even though their views about the death penalty differ, they all "share a conviction that the execution of persons with mental retardation cannot be morally justified." . . . Moreover, within the world community, the imposition of the death penalty for crimes committed by mentally retarded offenders is overwhelmingly disapproved. . . . Finally, polling data shows a widespread consensus among Americans, even those who support the death penalty, that executing the mentally retarded is wrong. . . . Although these factors are by no means dispositive, their consistency with the legislative evidence lends further support to our conclusion that there is a consensus among those who have addressed the issue. . . .

serious question as to whether either justification that we have recognized as a basis for the death penalty applies to mentally retarded offenders. Gregg. v. Georgia, 428 U.S. 153, 183 (1976), identified "retribution and deterrence of capital crimes by prospective offenders" as the social purposes served by the death penalty. Unless the imposition of the death penalty on a mentally retarded person "measurably contributes to one or both of these goals, it 'is nothing more than the purposeless and needless imposition of pain and suffering,' and hence an unconstitutional punishment." Enmund, 458 U.S., at 798.

With respect to retribution—the interest in seeing that the offender gets his "just deserts"—the severity of the appropriate punishment necessarily depends on the culpability of the offender. Since *Gregg*, our jurisprudence has consistently confined the imposition of the death penalty to a narrow category of the most serious crimes. For example, in Godfrey v. Georgia, 446 U.S. 420 (1980), we set aside a death sentence because the petitioner's crimes did not reflect "a consciousness materially more 'depraved' than that of any person guilty of murder." Id. at 433. If the culpability of the average murderer is insufficient to justify the most extreme sanction available to the State, the lesser culpability of the mentally retarded offender surely does not merit that form of retribution. Thus, pursuant to our narrowing jurisprudence, which seeks to ensure that only the most deserving of execution are put to death, an exclusion for the mentally retarded is appropriate.

With respect to deterrence—the interest in preventing capital crimes by prospective offenders—"it seems likely that 'capital punishment can serve as a deterrent only when murder is the result of premeditation and deliberation,'" *Enmund*, 458 U.S., at 799. Exempting the mentally retarded from that punishment will not affect the "cold calculus that precedes the decision" of other potential murderers. *Gregg*, 428 U.S., at 186. Indeed, that sort of calculus is at the opposite end of the spectrum from behavior of mentally retarded offenders. The theory of deterrence in capital sentencing is predicated upon the notion that the increased severity of the punishment will inhibit criminal actors from carrying out murderous conduct. Yet it is the same cognitive and behavioral impairments that make these defendants less morally culpable—for example, the diminished ability to understand and process information, to learn from experience, to engage in logical reasoning, or to control impulses—that also make it less likely that they can process the information of the possibility of execution as a penalty and, as a result, control their conduct based upon that information. Nor will exempting the mentally retarded from execution lessen the deterrent effect of the death penalty with respect to offenders who are not mentally retarded. Such individuals are unprotected by the exemption and will continue to face the threat of execution. Thus, executing the mentally retarded will not measurably further the goal of deterrence.

The reduced capacity of mentally retarded offenders provides a second justification for a categorical rule making such offenders ineligible for the death penalty. The risk "that the death penalty will be imposed in spite of factors which may call for a less severe penalty," Lockett v. Ohio, 438 U.S. 586, 605 (1978), is enhanced, not only by the possibility of false confessions, but also by the lesser ability of mentally retarded defendants to make a persuasive showing of mitigation in the face of prosecutorial evidence of one or more aggravating factors. Mentally retarded defendants may be less able to give meaningful assistance to their counsel and are typically poor witnesses, and their demeanor may create an unwarranted impression of lack of remorse for their crimes. . . . [M]oreover, reliance on mental retardation as a mitigating factor can be a two-edged sword that may enhance the likelihood that the aggravating factor of future dangerousness will be found by the jury. . . . Mentally retarded defendants in the aggregate face a special risk of wrongful execution.

Our independent evaluation of the issue reveals no reason to disagree with the judgment of "the legislatures that have recently addressed the matter" and concluded that death is not a suitable punishment for a mentally retarded criminal. We are not persuaded that the execution of mentally retarded criminals will measurably advance the deterrent or the retributive purpose of the death penalty. Construing and applying the Eighth Amendment in the light of our "evolving standards of decency," we therefore conclude that such punishment is excessive and that the Constitution "places a substantive restriction on the State's power to take the life" of a mentally retarded offender. *Ford*, 477 U.S., at 405.

■ Chief Justice Rehnquist, with whom Justice Scalia and Justice Thomas join, dissenting.

The question presented by this case is whether a national consensus deprives Virginia of the constitutional power to impose the death penalty on capital murder defendants like petitioner, i.e., those defendants who indisputably are competent to stand trial, aware of the punishment they are about to suffer and why, and whose mental retardation has been found an insufficiently compelling reason to lessen their individual responsibility for the crime. The Court pronounces the punishment cruel and unusual primarily because 18 States recently have passed laws limiting the death eligibility of certain defendants based on mental retardation alone, despite the fact that the laws of 19 other states besides Virginia continue to leave the question of proper punishment to the individuated consideration of sentencing judges or juries familiar with the particular offender and his or her crime. . . .

. . . [T]he Court's assessment of the current legislative judgment regarding the execution of defendants like petitioner more resembles a post hoc rationalization for the majority's subjectively preferred result rather than any objective effort to ascertain the content of an evolving standard of decency. I write separately . . . to call attention to the defects in the Court's decision to place weight on foreign laws, the views of professional and religious organizations, and opinion polls in reaching its conclusion. . . . The Court's suggestion that these sources are relevant to the constitutional question finds little support in our precedents and, in my view, is antithetical to considerations of federalism, which instruct that any "permanent prohibition upon all units of democratic government must [be apparent] in the operative acts (laws and the application of laws) that the people have approved." Stanford v. Kentucky, 492 U.S. 361, 377 (1989) (plurality opinion). The Court's uncritical acceptance of the opinion poll data brought to our attention, moreover, warrants additional comment, because we lack sufficient information to conclude that the surveys were conducted in accordance with generally accepted scientific principles or are capable of supporting valid empirical inferences about the issue before us.

In making determinations about whether a punishment is "cruel and unusual" under the evolving standards of decency embraced by the Eighth Amendment, we have emphasized that legislation is the "clearest and most reliable objective evidence of contemporary values." Penry v. Lynaugh, 492 U.S. 302, 331 (1989). . . . The reason we ascribe primacy to legislative enactments follows from the constitutional role legislatures play in expressing policy of a State. . . . And because the specifications of punishments are "peculiarly questions of legislative policy," Gore v. United States, 357 U.S. 386, 393 (1958), our cases have cautioned against using " 'the aegis of the Cruel and Unusual Punishment Clause' " to cut off the normal democratic processes, Gregg [v. Georgia, 428 U.S. 153 (1976)], at 176 (quoting Powell v. Texas, 392 U.S. 514, 533 (1968) (plurality opinion)).

Our opinions have also recognized that data concerning the actions of sentencing juries, though entitled to less weight than legislative judgments, " 'is a significant and reliable index of contemporary values,' " Coker v. Georgia, 433 U.S. 584, 596 (1977) (plurality opinion) (quoting Gregg, supra, at 181), because of the jury's intimate involvement in the case and its function of " 'maintain[ing] a link between contemporary community values and the penal system,' " Gregg, supra, at 181 (quoting Witherspoon v. Illinois, 391 U.S. 510, 519, n.15 (1968)). . . .

In my view, these two sources—the work product of legislatures and sentencing jury determinations—ought to be the sole indicators by which courts ascertain the contemporary American conceptions of decency for purposes of the Eighth Amendment. They are the only objective indicia of contemporary values firmly supported by our precedents. More importantly, however, they can be reconciled with the undeniable precepts that the democratic branches of government and individual sentencing juries are, by design, better suited than courts to evaluating and giving effect to the complex societal and moral considerations that inform the selection of publicly acceptable criminal punishments.

In reaching its conclusion today, the Court does not take notice of the fact that neither petitioner nor his amici have adduced any comprehensive statistics that would conclusively prove (or disprove) whether juries routinely consider death a disproportionate punishment for mentally retarded offenders like petitioner. Instead, it adverts to the fact that other countries have disapproved imposition of the death penalty for crimes committed by mentally retarded offenders. . . . I fail to see, however, how the views of other countries regarding the punishment of their citizens provide any support for the Court's ultimate determination. While it is true that some of our prior opinions have looked to "the climate of international opinion," *Coker,* supra, at 596, n.10, to reinforce a conclusion regarding evolving standards of decency . . . we have since explicitly rejected the idea that the sentencing practices of other countries could "serve to establish the first Eighth Amendment prerequisite, that [a] practice is accepted among our people." *Stanford,* supra, at 369, n.1. . . .

Stanford's reasoning makes perfectly good sense, and the Court offers no basis to question it. For if it is evidence of a *national* consensus for which we are looking, then the viewpoints of other countries simply are not relevant. . . .

To further buttress its appraisal of contemporary societal values, the Court marshals public opinion polls results and evidence that several professional organizations and religious groups have adopted official positions opposing the imposition of the death penalty upon mentally retarded offenders. . . . In my view, none should be accorded any weight on the Eighth Amendment scale when the elected representatives of a State's populace have not deemed them persuasive enough to prompt legislative action. . . . For the Court to rely on such data today serves only to illustrate its willingness to proscribe by judicial fiat—at the behest of private organizations speaking only for themselves—a punishment about which no across-the-board consensus has developed through the workings of normal democratic processes in the laboratories of the States.

Even if I were to accept the legitimacy of the Court's decision to reach beyond the product of legislatures and practices of sentencing juries to discern a national standard of decency, I would take issue with the blind-faith credence it accords the opinion polls brought to our attention. An extensive body of social science literature describes how methodological and other errors can affect the reliability and validity of estimates about the opinions and attitudes of a population derived from various sampling techniques. Everything from variations in the survey methodology, such as the choice of the target population, the sampling design used, the questions asked, and the statistical analyses used to interpret the data can skew the results. . . .

The Federal Judicial Center's Reference Manual on Scientific Evidence 221–271 (1994) and its Manual for Complex Litigation § 21.493 pp. 101–103 (3d ed. 1995), offer helpful suggestions to judges called upon to assess the weight and admissibility of survey evidence on a factual issue before a court. Looking at the polling data . . . in light of these factors, one cannot help but observe how unlikely it is that the data could support a valid inference about the question presented by this case. For example, the questions reported to have been asked in the various polls do not appear designed to gauge whether the respondents might find the death penalty an acceptable punishment for mentally retarded offenders in rare cases. Most are categorical (e.g., "Do you think that persons convicted of murder who are mentally retarded should or should not receive the death penalty?"), and, as such, would not elicit whether the respondent might agree or disagree that all mentally retarded people by definition can never act with the level of culpability associated with the death penalty, regardless of the severity of their impairment or the individual circumstances of their crime. Second, none of the 27 polls cited disclose the targeted survey population or the sampling techniques used by those who conducted the research. Thus, even if one accepts that the survey instruments were adequately designed to address a relevant question, it is impossible to know whether the sample was representative enough to tell us anything about the opinions of the citizens of a particular State or the American public at large. Finally, the information provided to us does not indicate why a particular survey was conducted or, in a few cases, by whom, factors which also can bear on the objectivity of the results. In order to be credited here, such surveys should be offered as evidence at trial, where their sponsors can be examined and cross-examined about these matters.

* * *

There are strong reasons for limiting our inquiry into what constitutes an evolving standard of decency under the Eighth Amendment to the laws passed by legislatures and the practices of sentencing juries in America. Here, the Court goes beyond these well-established objective indicators of contemporary values. It finds "further support to [its] conclusion" that a national consensus has developed against imposing the death penalty on all mentally retarded defendants in international opinion, the views of professional and religious organizations, and opinion polls not demonstrated to be reliable. Ante, at ___, n.[102]. Believing this view to be seriously mistaken, I dissent.

[Appendix omitted.]

■ JUSTICE SCALIA, with whom THE CHIEF JUSTICE and JUSTICE THOMAS join, dissenting.

Today's decision is the pinnacle of our Eighth Amendment death-is-different jurisprudence. Not only does it, like all of that jurisprudence, find no support in the text or history of the Eighth Amendment; it does not even have support in current social attitudes regarding the conditions that render an otherwise just death penalty inappropriate. Seldom has an opinion of this Court rested so obviously upon nothing but the personal views of its members.

I

I begin with a brief restatement of facts that are abridged by the Court but important to understand this case. After spending the day drinking alcohol and smoking marijuana, petitioner Daryl Renard Atkins and a partner in crime drove to a convenience store, intending to rob a customer. Their victim was Eric Nesbitt, an airman from Langley Air Force Base, whom they abducted, drove to a nearby automated teller machine, and forced to withdraw $200. They then drove him to a deserted area, ignoring his pleas to leave him unharmed. According to the co-conspirator, whose testimony the jury evidently credited, Atkins ordered Nesbitt out of the vehicle and, after he had taken only a few steps shot him one, two, three, four, five, six, seven, eight times in the thorax, chest, abdomen, arms, and legs.

The jury convicted Atkins of capital murder. At resentencing (the Virginia Supreme Court affirmed his conviction but remanded for resentencing because the trial court had used an improper verdict form) . . . the jury heard extensive evidence of petitioner's alleged mental retardation. A psychologist testified that petitioner was mildly mentally retarded with an IQ of 59, that he was a "slow learne[r]," App. 444, who showed a "lack of success in pretty much every domain of his life," id., at 442, and that he had an "impaired" capacity to appreciate the criminality of his conduct and to conform his conduct to the law, id., at 453. Petitioner's family members offered additional evidence in support of his mental retardation claim (e.g., that petitioner is a "follower," id., at 421). The State contested the evidence of retardation and presented testimony of a psychologist who found "absolutely no evidence other than the IQ score . . . indicating that [petitioner] was in the least bit mentally retarded" and concluded that petitioner was "of average intelligence, at least." Id., at 476.

The jury also heard testimony about petitioner's 16 prior felony convictions for robbery, attempted robbery, abduction, use of a firearm, and maiming. . . . The victims of these offenses provided graphic depictions of petitioner's violent tendencies: He hit one over the head with a beer bottle . . .; he slapped a gun across another victim's face, clubbed her in the head with it, knocked her to the ground, and then helped her up, only to shoot her in the stomach . . . . The jury sentenced petitioner to death. The Supreme Court of Virginia affirmed petitioner's sentence.

II

As the foregoing history demonstrates, petitioner's mental retardation was a *central issue* at sentencing. The jury concluded, however, that his alleged retardation was not a compelling reason to exempt him from the death penalty in light of the brutality of his crime and his long demonstrated propensity for violence. "In upsetting this particularized judgment on the basis of a constitutional absolute," the Court concludes that no one who is even slightly mentally retarded can have sufficient "moral responsibility to be subjected to capital punishment for any crime. As a sociological and moral conclusion that is implausible; and it is doubly implausible as an interpretation of the United States Constitution." Thompson v. Oklahoma, 487 U.S. 815, 863–864 (1988) (Scalia, J., dissenting).

Under our Eighth Amendment jurisprudence, a punishment is "cruel and unusual" if it falls within one of two categories: "those modes or acts of punishment that had been considered cruel and unusual at the time that the Bill of Rights was adopted," Ford v. Wainwright, 477 U.S. 399, 405 (1986), and modes of punishment that are inconsistent with modern "standards of decency," as evinced by objective indicia, the most important of which is "legislation enacted by the country's legislatures," Penry v. Lynaugh, 492 U.S. 302, 330–331 (1989).

The Court makes no pretense that execution of the mildly mentally retarded would have been considered "cruel and unusual" in 1791. Only the *severely* or *profoundly* mentally retarded, commonly known as "idiots," enjoyed any special status under the law at that time. They, like lunatics, suffered a "deficiency in will" rendering them unable to tell right from wrong. . . . Due to their incompetence, idiots were "excuse[d] from the guilt, and of course from the punishment, of any criminal action committed under such deprivation of the senses." 4 [W.] Blackstone [Commentaries on the Laws of England (1769)] 25 . . . . Instead, they were often committed to civil confinement or made wards of the State, thereby preventing them from "go[ing] loose, to the terror of the king's subjects." 4 Blackstone 25 . . . . Mentally retarded offenders with less severe impairments—those who were not "idiots"—suffered criminal prosecution and punishment, including capital punishment. . . .

The Court is left to argue, therefore, that execution of the mildly retarded is inconsistent with the "evolving standards of decency that mark the progress of a maturing society." Trop v. Dulles, 356 U.S. 86, 101 (1958) (plurality opinion) (Warren, C.J.). Before today, our opinions consistently emphasized that Eighth Amendment judgments regarding the existence of social "standards" "should be informed by objective factors to the maximum possible extent" and "should not be, or appear to be, merely the subjective views of individual Justices." Coker v. Georgia, 433 U.S. 584, 592 (1977) (plurality opinion) . . . . "First" among these objective factors are the "statutes passed by society's elected representatives," Stanford v. Kentucky, 492 U.S. 361, 370 (1989); because it "will rarely if ever be the case that the Members of this Court will have a better sense of the evolution in views of the American people than do their elected representatives," *Thompson*, supra, at 865 (Scalia, J., dissenting).

The Court pays lip service to these precedents as it miraculously extracts a "national consensus" forbidding execution of the mentally retarded, ante, at ___, from the fact that 18 states—less than *half* (47%) of the 38 States that permit capital punishment (for whom the issue exists)—have very recently enacted legislation barring execution of the mentally retarded. Even that 47% figure is a distorted one. If one is to say, as the Court does today, that *all* executions of the mentally retarded are so morally repugnant as to violate our national "standards of decency," surely the "consensus" it points to must be one that has set its righteous face against *all* such executions. Not 18 States but only seven—18% of death penalty jurisdictions—have legislation of that scope. Eleven of those that the court counts enacted statutes prohibiting execution of mentally retarded defendants *convicted after, or convicted of crimes committed after, the effective date* of the legislation; those already on death row, or consigned there before the statute's effective date, or even (in those States using the date of the crime as the criterion of retroactivity) tried in the future for murders committed many years ago, could be put to death. That is not a statement of absolute moral repugnance, but one of current preference between two tolerable approaches. Two of these States permit execution of the mentally retarded in other situations as well: Kansas apparently permits execution of all except the *severely* mentally retarded; New York permits execution of the mentally retarded who commit murder in a correctional facility. . . .

But let us accept, for the sake of argument, the Court's faulty count. That bare number of States alone—*18*—should be enough to convince any reasonable person that no "national consensus" exists. How is it possible that agreement among 47% of the death penalty jurisdictions amounts to "consensus"? Our prior cases have generally required a much higher degree of agreement before finding a punishment cruel and unusual on "evolving standards" grounds. . . . What the Court calls evidence of "consensus" in the present case (a fudged 47%) more closely resembles evidence that we found *inadequate* to establish consensus in earlier cases. Tison v. Arizona, 481 U.S. 137, 154, 158 (1987), upheld a state law authorizing capital punishment for major participation in a felony with reckless indifference to life where only 11 of the 37 death penalty States (30%) prohibited such punishment. *Stanford*, supra, at 372, upheld a state law permitting execution of defendants who committed a capital crime at age 16 where only 15 of the 36 death penalty States (42%) prohibited death for such offenders.

Moreover, a major factor that the Court entirely disregards is that the legislation of all 18 States it relies on is still in its infancy. The oldest of the statutes is only 14 years old; five were enacted last year; over half were enacted within the past eight years. Few, if any, of the States have had sufficient experience with these laws to know whether they are sensible in the long term. It is "myopic to base sweeping constitutional principles upon the narrow experience of [a few] years." *Coker*, 433 U.S., at 614 (Burger, C.J., dissenting) . . . .

The Court attempts to bolster its embarrassingly feeble evidence of "consensus" with the following: "It is not so much the number of these States that is significant, but the *consistency* of the direction of change." Ante, at ___ (emphasis added). But in what *other* direction *could we possibly* see change? Given that 14 years ago *all* the death penalty statutes included the mentally retarded, *any* change (except precipitate undoing of what had just been done) was *bound to be* in the one direction the Court finds significant enough to overcome the lack of real consensus. That is to say, to be accurate the Court's "*consistency*-of-the-direction-of-change" point should be recast into the following unimpressive observation: "No State has yet undone its exemption of the mentally retarded, one for as long as 14 whole years." In any event, reliance upon "trends," even those of much longer duration than a mere 14 years, is a perilous basis for constitutional adjudication . . . .

The Court's thrashing about for evidence of "consensus" includes reliance upon the *margins* by which state legislatures have enacted bans on execution of the retarded. Ante, at ___. Presumably, in applying our Eighth Amendment "evolving-standards-of-decency" jurisprudence, we will henceforth weigh not only how many States have agreed, but how many States have agreed *by how much*. Of course if the percentage of legislators voting for the bill is significant, surely the number of people *represented* by the legislators voting for the bill is also significant: the fact that 49% of the legislators in a State with a population of 60 million voted *against* the bill should be more impressive than the fact that 90% of the legislators in a State with a population of 2 million voted *for* it. (By the way, the population of the death penalty States that exclude the mentally retarded is only 44% of the population of all death penalty States . . . .) This is quite absurd. What we have looked for in the past to "evolve" the Eighth Amendment is a consensus of the same sort as the consensus that *adopted* the Eighth Amendment: a consensus of the sovereign States that form the Union, not a nose count of Americans for and against.

Even less compelling (if possible) is the Court's argument, ante at ___, that evidence of "national consensus" is to be found in the infrequency with which persons are executed in the United States that do not bar their execution. To begin with, what the Court takes as true is in fact quite doubtful. It is not at all clear that the execution of the mentally retarded is "uncommon," ibid. . . . *If*, however, execution of the mentally retarded *is* "uncommon"; and if it is not a sufficient explanation of this that the retarded comprise a tiny fraction of society (1% to 3%) . . . then surely the explanation is that mental retardation is a constitutionally mandated mitigating factor at sentencing. . . . For that reason, even if there were uniform national sentiment in *favor* of executing the retarded in appropriate cases, one would still expect execution of the mentally retarded to be "uncommon." . . .

But the Prize for the Court's Most Feeble Effort to fabricate "national consensus" must go to its appeal (deservedly relegated to a footnote) to the views of assorted professional and religious organizations, members of the so-called "world community," and respondents to opinion polls. Ante, at ___, n.[102]. I agree with the Chief Justice, ante, at ___ (dissenting opinion), that the views of professional and religious organizations and the results of opinion polls are irrelevant. Equally irrelevant are the practices of the "world community," whose notions of justice are (thankfully) not always those of our people. "We just never forget that it is a Constitution for the United States of America that we are expounding. . . . [W]here there is not first a settled consensus among our own people, the views of other nations, however enlightened the Justices of this Court may think them to be, cannot be imposed upon Americans through the Constitution." *Thompson*, 487 U.S., at 868–869, n.4 (Scalia, J., dissenting).

III

Beyond the empty talk of a "national consensus," the Court gives us a brief glimpse of that really underlies today's decision: pretension to a power confined *neither* by the moral sentiments originally enshrined in the Eighth Amendment (its original meaning) *nor even* by the current moral sentiments of the American people. " '[T]he Constitution,' the Court says, 'contemplates that in the end *our own judgment* will be brought to bear on the question of the acceptability of the death penalty under the Eighth

Amendment.' " Ante, at ___ (quoting *Coker*, 433 U.S., at 597) (emphasis added). (The unexpressed reason for this unexpressed "contemplation" of the Constitution is presumably that really good lawyers have moral sentiments superior to those of the common herd, whether in 1791 or today.) The arrogance of this assumption of power takes one's breath away. And it explains, of course, why the Court can be so cavalier about the evidence of consensus. It is just a game, after all. "[I]n the end," it is the *feelings* and *intuition* of a majority of the Justices that count—"the perceptions of decency, or of penology, or of mercy, entertained . . . by a majority of the small and unrepresentative segment of our society that sits on this Court." *Thompson*, supra, at 873 (Scalia, J., dissenting).

The genuinely operative portion of the opinion, then, is the Court's statement of the reasons why it agrees with the contrived consensus it has found, that the "diminished capacities" of the mentally retarded render the death penalty excessive. Ante, at ___. The Court's analysis rests on two fundamental assumptions: (1) that the Eighth Amendment prohibits excessive punishments, and (2) that sentencing juries or judges are unable to account properly for the "diminished capacities" of the retarded. The first assumption is wrong . . . . The Eighth Amendment is addressed to always-and-everywhere "cruel" punishments, such as the rack and the thumbscrew. But where the punishment is in itself permissible, "[t]he Eighth Amendment is not a ratchet, whereby a temporary consensus on leniency for a particular crime fixes a permanent constitutional maximum, disabling the States from giving effect to altered beliefs and responding to changed social conditions." [Harmelin v. Michigan, 501 U.S. 957 (1991) (opinion of Scalia, J.)], at 990. The second assumption—inability of judges to take proper account of mental retardation—is not only unsubstantiated, but contradicts the immemorial belief, here and in England, that they play an *indispensable* role in such matters . . . .

Proceeding from these faulty assumptions, the Court gives two reasons why the death penalty is an excessive punishment for all mentally retarded offenders. First, the "diminished capacities" of the mentally retarded raise a "serious question" whether their execution contributes to the "social purposes" of the death penalty, viz., retribution and deterrence. Ante, at ___. (The Court conveniently ignores a third "social purpose" of the death penalty—"incapacitation of dangerous criminals and the consequent prevention of crimes that they may otherwise commit in the future," Gregg v. Georgia, 428 U.S. 153, 183, n.28 (1976) (joint opinion of Stewart, Powell, and Stevens, JJ.). But never mind; its discussion of even the other two does not bear analysis.) Retribution is not advanced, the argument goes, because the mentally retarded are *no more culpable* than the average murderer, whom we have already held lacks sufficient culpability to warrant the death penalty . . . . Who says so? Is there an established correlation between mental acuity and the ability to conform one's conduct to the law in such a rudimentary matter as murder? Are the mentally retarded really more disposed (and hence more likely) to commit willfully cruel and serious crime than others? In my experience, the opposite is true: being childlike generally suggests innocence rather than brutality.

Assuming, however, that there is a direct connection between diminished intelligence and the inability to refrain from murder, what scientific analysis can possibly show that a mildly retarded individual who commits an exquisite torture-killing is "no more culpable" than the "average" murderer in a holdup-gone-wrong or a domestic dispute? Or a moderately retarded individual who commits a series of 20 exquisite torture-killings? Surely culpability, and deservedness of the most severe retribution, depends not merely (if at all) upon the mental capacity of the criminal (above the level where he is able to distinguish right from wrong) but also upon the depravity of the crime—which is precisely why this sort of question has traditionally been thought answerable not by a categorical rule of the sort the Court today imposes upon all trials, but rather by the sentencer's weighing of the circumstances (both degree of retardation and depravity of crime) in the particular case. The fact that juries continue to sentence mentally retarded offenders to death for extreme crimes shows that society's moral outrage sometimes demands execution of retarded offenders. By what principle of law, science, or logic can the Court pronounce that this is wrong? There is none. Once the Court admits (as it does) that mental retardation does not render the offender morally *blameless*, ante at ___, there is no basis for saying that the death penalty is *never* appropriate retribution, no matter *how* heinous the crime. As long as a mentally retarded offender knows "the difference between right and wrong," ante at ___, only the sentencer can assess whether his retardation reduces his culpability enough to exempt him from the death penalty for the particular murder in question.

As for the other social purpose of the death penalty that the Court discusses, deterrence: That is not advanced, the Court tells us, because the mentally retarded are "less likely" than their non-retarded counterparts to "process the information and the possibility of execution as a penalty and . . . control their conduct based upon that information." Ante, at ___. Of course this leads to the same conclusion discussed earlier—that the mentally retarded (because they are less deterred) are more likely to kill—which neither I nor the society at large believes. In any event, even the Court does not say that *all* mentally retarded individuals cannot "process the information of the possibility of execution as a penalty and . . . control their conduct based upon that information"; it merely asserts that they are "less likely" to be able to do so. But surely the deterrent effect of a penalty is adequately vindicated if it successfully deters many, but not all, of the target class. Virginia's death penalty, for example, does not fail of its deterrent effect simply because *some* criminals are unaware that Virginia *has* the death penalty. In other words, the supposed fact that *some* regarded criminals cannot fully appreciate the death penalty has nothing to do with the deterrence rationale, but is simply an echo of the arguments denying a retribution rationale, discussed and rejected above. I am not sure that a murderer is somehow less blameworthy if (though he knew his act was wrong) he did not fully appreciate that he could die for it; but if so, we should treat a mentally retarded murderer the way we treat an offender who may be "less likely" to respond to the death penalty because he was abused as a child. We do not hold him immune from capital punishment, but require his background to be considered by the sentencer as a mitigating factor. . . .

The Court throws one last factor into its grab bag of reasons why execution of the retarded is "excessive" in all cases: Mentally retarded offenders "face a special risk of wrongful execution" because they are less able "to make a persuasive showing of mitigation," "to give meaningful assistance to their counsel," and to be effective witnesses. Ante, at ___. "Special risk" is pretty flabby language (even flabbier than "less likely")— and I suppose a similar "special risk" could be said to exist for just plain stupid people, inarticulate people, even ugly people. If this unsupported claim has any substance to it (which I doubt) it might support a due process claim in all criminal prosecutions of the mentally retarded; but it is hard to see how it has anything to do with an *Eighth Amendment* claim that execution of the mentally retarded is cruel and unusual. We have never before held it to be cruel and unusual punishment to impose a sentence in violation of some *other* constitutional imperative.

* * *

Today's opinion adds one more to the long list of substantive and procedural requirements impeding imposition of the death penalty imposed under this Court's assumed power to invent a death-is-different jurisprudence. None of those requirements existed when the Eighth Amendment was adopted, and some of them were not even supported by current moral consensus. . . . There is something to be said for popular abolition of the death penalty; there is nothing to be said for its incremental abolition by this Court.

This newest invention promises to be more effective than any of the others in turning the process of capital trial into a game. One need only read the definitions of mental retardation adopted by the American Association of Mental Retardation and the American Psychiatric Association . . . to realize that the symptoms of this condition can readily be feigned. And whereas the capital defendant who feigns insanity risks commitment to a mental institution until he can be cured (and then tried and executed) . . . the capital defendant who feigns mental retardation risks nothing at all. The mere pendency of the present case has brought us petitions by death row inmates claiming for the first time, after multiple habeas petitions, that they are retarded. . . .

Perhaps these practical difficulties will not be experienced by the minority of capital-punishment States that have very recently changed mental retardation from a mitigating factor (to be accepted or rejected by the sentencer) to an absolute immunity. Time will tell—and the brief time in place (an average of 6.8 years) is surely not enough. But if the practical difficulties do not appear, and if the other States share the Court's perceived moral consensus that *all* mental retardation renders the death penalty inappropriate for *all* crimes, then that majority will presumably follow suit. But there is no justification for this Court's pushing them into the experiment—and turning the experiment into a permanent practice—on constitutional pretext. . . .

———

201. The effort to find a principled ground of distinction between crimes that merit capital punishment and crimes that do not goes back, as we have seen, to the Pennsylvania statute of 1794, p. 110 above. The direction of the effort has, however, changed considerably. Whereas formerly it was thought that specific aggravating circumstances, like the "willful, deliberate, and premeditated" formula, would identify a category of capital cases, it is now thought that no specific circumstance is conclusive and that all the aggravating and mitigating circumstances in each case should be considered together as the basis for a judgment applicable uniquely to that case. The change was prompted by the Model Penal Code's adoption of the latter approach, in the context of considerable controversy whether capital punishment should not be abolished altogether. Look again at the list of aggravating and mitigating circumstances in the federal statute, pp. 137–38 above. If capital punishment is retained, does the list include all the factors to which you would specifically direct the attention of the sentencing authority?

202. The uneven course of the Supreme Court's decisions about capital punishment strongly suggests, as indeed some of the holdings indicate, that capital punishment cannot well be considered abstractly. Test your own position on the question whether capital punishment should ever be permitted against the following four cases.

Would you authorize capital punishment in any of these cases? If so, would you vote to impose it?

If not, what sentence would you impose? Is there any case in which you would authorize capital punishment?

Is there other information that you want to have in any of these cases before deciding whether capital punishment is appropriate?

If you would impose capital punishment, can you explain your conclusion on a basis that satisfies the search for principled, consistent results?

(i)

"[O]n September 4, 1977 . . . petitioner and his coindictee, Thomas Stevens, both privates [at Fort Stewart, Georgia], were drinking at a club on the post. They talked on the telephone with Private James Botsford, who had just arrived at the Savannah Airport, and agreed to pick him up and bring him back to the base. They stole a butcher knife and a sharpening tool from the mess hall and called a cab that was being driven by Roger Honeycutt, a soldier who worked part-time for a taxi company. On the way to the airport, petitioner held the knife and Stevens held the sharpening tool against Honeycutt. They forced him to stop the automobile, robbed him of $16, and placed him in the backseat. Petitioner took over the driving. Stevens then ordered Honeycutt to undress, threw each article of his clothing out of the car window after searching it, blindfolded him, and tied his hands behind his back. As petitioner drove, Stevens climbed into the backseat with Honeycutt, where he compelled Honeycutt to commit oral sodomy on him and anally sodomized him. After stopping the car a second time, petitioner and Stevens placed their victim, nude, blindfolded, and hands tied behind his back, in the trunk of the cab. They then proceeded to pick up Botsford at the airport. During the ride back to Fort Stewart, they told Botsford that they had stolen the cab and confirmed their story by conversing with Honeycutt in the trunk. In exchange for Botsford's promise not to notify the authorities, they promised that they would not harm Honeycutt after leaving Botsford at the base.

"Ultimately, however, petitioner and Stevens drove to a pond in Wayne County where they had gone swimming in the past. They removed the cab's citizen-band radio and, while Stevens was hiding the radio in the bushes, petitioner opened the trunk and asked Honeycutt if he was all right. He answered affirmatively. Petitioner then closed the trunk, started the automobile, and put it in gear, getting out before it entered the water. Honeycutt drowned." Burger v. Kemp, 483 U.S. 776, 778–79 (1987).

Burger and Stevens were both convicted of murder. "[A]t the time the crime was committed Burger was seventeen; Stevens was twenty. Burger has an I.Q. of 82 and possible brain damage. Stevens appeared to be the leader in their relationship; Burger the follower. Stevens planned and initiated the robbery of the victim; Burger followed his instructions. Stevens actually committed the robbery; Stevens made the victim undress; Stevens forced the victim to perform oral sodomy on Stevens; Stevens anally sodomized the victim; Stevens tied the victim up and forced him to get in the trunk of the cab. Stevens told Burger they would have to kill him; Burger said he didn't want to kill him. Stevens told Burger they would have to get rid of the cab by driving it into the pond; Stevens ordered Burger to drive the cab with the victim locked in the trunk into the pond. Burger drove the cab and the victim into the pond.

. . .

". . . Burger's parents had been married when his mother was fourteen and his father was sixteen. His parents divorced when he was a child. Neither parent wanted Burger and his childhood was spent shuffled between the two. His father threw him out of the house; his mother sent him back to live with his father. Burger's mother remarried. Burger's stepfather beat Burger, and beat Burger's mother in his presence; Burger's stepfather involved him in drugs and alcohol when he was eleven years old. Burger's mother and stepfather moved from Indiana to Florida. Burger was sent to live with his father. Burger's father beat him and refused to have anything to do with him. Burger ran away and hitchhiked to Florida to live with his mother, selling his shoes to buy food along the way. When Burger arrived barefoot in Florida his stepfather told him he could not stay with them. Burger's mother told the juvenile authorities that she didn't want him, and to send him back to his father in Indiana. When Burger arrived in Indiana, his father locked him out of the house. Burger was taken in by a neighbor, as he had nowhere else to go." Burger v. Zant, 718 F.2d 979, 989, 993 (11th Cir.1983) (dissenting opinion).

(ii)

"In the early hours of May 11, 1978, a young man was abducted at gunpoint from a Homewood gasoline station where he was employed and which was robbed and looted. His fiancee, visiting him at his job, was also abducted. The two young people were taken some five miles away to an abandoned apartment, part of a housing complex where Paula [Gray] and her family and Dennis Williams and his family lived as close neighbors. In the abandoned apartment, while Paula held a lighter for the men to see, the young woman was raped by Williams, Rainge, Adams, and Jimmerson; Williams then shot the young woman to death. The young man was next taken to a nearby field, with Paula in attendance. Williams shot the young man twice in the head and handed his gun to Rainge who shot the young man in the back. Williams and Paula went to a creek close at hand where Williams threw away the gun which had been used. Williams at this point told Paula not to tell the police what she had seen or he would kill her and her family." United States ex rel. Gray v. Director, Department of Corrections, State of Illinois, 721 F.2d 586, 587–88 (7th Cir.1983).

Williams was 21 when the crimes were committed. He had been convicted of theft and arson in 1976. The other defendants, except Gray, were over 18 at the time of the crimes. Gray was about one month short of her eighteenth birthday. All the defendants lived in a depressed, impoverished community. Gray's IQ was under 70, which classified her as mentally retarded. (An attorney in the prosecutor's office expressed the view that Gray was a reasonably intelligent, alert person; the IQ test, he thought, was culturally biased and unrelated to her intellectual ability.) Gray had a twin sister. They and some younger children were raised by their mother. The family was indigent and was supported by public aid. Gray had no criminal record.

(iii)

". . . Mrs. Linda Goldstone, on March 30, 1978, was employed at Northwestern Memorial Hospital in Chicago as an instructor in the Lamaze method of childbirth. On that evening, as she was alighting from her car in the vicinity of the hospital, she was approached by the defendant and robbed at gunpoint. He made her undress from the waist down. He then forced her into his car and, it appears, took her to a shop owned by his father. There he bound her hands and feet.

"He then forced her into the trunk of his car. With Mrs. Goldstone in the trunk, the defendant picked up his sister at work and drove her home. He then drove the victim to a motel, forced her inside and raped her.

"On the next day, with Mrs. Goldstone bound and locked in the trunk of the car, the defendant appeared at a suburban court where charges of aggravated kidnaping, rape, and armed robbery were pending against him. The case was continued, and the defendant then drove to visit a friend, Nettie Jones, at her apartment. While he was there, people of the area heard cries for help coming from the trunk of his auto. Someone notified the police of the incident. The defendant drove away from a crowd that had gathered and proceeded to a tavern where he visited other friends.

"Early that evening, the defendant checked into another motel. He forced Mrs. Goldstone into the motel and again raped her. Later, he forced her back into the trunk and picked up his niece at a friend's house and drove the niece home. As he had done the day before, he drove his sister home from work and spent the evening visiting various taverns with friends.

"In the meantime, police were searching for the defendant's car. The victim's husband, Dr. James Goldstone, a physician, after learning that his wife had not appeared for class that evening, notified the police of her absence. The victim's car was found by Northwestern University security officers. Early the following morning, Dr. Goldstone received a phone call from his wife in which she told him that she would be home soon. He heard a voice in the background say, 'Shut up bitch, tell him you'll be home in about an hour.' The victim asked Dr. Goldstone if he had called the police, and he told her to tell the man whose voice he had heard that he had not informed the police.

"Officers investigating the incident at Jones' apartment obtained the license number of the car and learned that the defendant had visited Jones. The police searched the area for the auto without success and periodically watched the defendant's home, but the car was not located.

"On April 1, at 6 a.m., the defendant released the victim from the trunk of the auto. He gave her $1.25 and instructed her to take a bus home and not to call the police. He then drove off. The victim, ignoring his instructions, ran to the porch of a nearby house for help. The person who came to the door refused to allow her to enter, but he did call the police. The defendant, who had only driven around the block to see whether his instructions would be obeyed, returned and ordered the victim off the porch. He then took her to an abandoned garage and killed her, shooting her in the chest and head. There was medical evidence that the victim had been beaten once or more during her captivity." People v. Williams, 454 N.E.2d 220, 224–25 (Ill.1983).

Williams's father was an ordained minister and owned and operated a small manufacturing business, which employed six persons. Williams did not graduate from high school. He had a child when he was fourteen years old. He had joined the National Guard and while in the Guard, received a high school equivalency certificate. He was given a general discharge from the Guard because he failed to appear as required. At one time, he had been an active church member and was assistant director of the young adults choir. When he was arrested for the crimes against Goldstone, he was married and had four children, one of whom was the child of his wife. He was unemployed and was not living with his wife or supporting his children. He was in good health and had no history of mental or emotional conditions.

A law student who represented Williams in court on the charges pending against him (while Goldstone was locked in the trunk) described him then as "articulate, well-dressed, calm and quite normal." Id. at 240.

(iv)

"Shortly before these crimes, Fountain and Silverstein, both of whom were already serving life sentences for murder, had together murdered an inmate in the Control Unit of Marion, and had again been sentenced to life imprisonment. . . . After that, Silverstein killed another inmate, pleaded guilty to that murder, and received his third life sentence. At this point Fountain and Silverstein had each killed three people. (For one of these killings, however, Fountain had been convicted only of voluntary manslaughter. And Silverstein's first murder conviction was reversed for trial error, and a new trial ordered, after the trial in this case.) The prison authorities—belatedly, and as it turned out ineffectually—decided to take additional security measures. Three guards would escort Fountain and Silverstein (separately), handcuffed, every time they left their cells to go to or from the recreation room, the law library, or the shower. (Prisoners in Marion's Control Unit are confined, one to a cell, for all but an hour or an hour and a half a day, and are fed in their cells.) But the guards would not be armed; nowadays guards do not carry weapons in the presence of prisoners, who might seize the weapons.

"The two murders involved in these appeals took place on the same October day in 1983. In the morning, Silverstein, while being escorted from the shower to his cell, stopped next to Randy Gometz's cell; and while two of the escorting officers were for some reason at a distance from him, reached his handcuffed hands into the cell. The third officer, who was closer to him, heard the click of the handcuffs being released and saw Gometz raise his shirt to reveal a home-made knife ('shank')—which had been fashioned from the iron leg of a bed—protruding from his waistband. Silverstein drew the knife and attacked one of the guards, Clutts, stabbing him 29 times and killing him. While pacing the corridor after the killing, Silverstein explained that 'this is no cop thing. This is a personal thing between me and Clutts. The man disrespected me and I had to get him for it.' Having gotten this off his chest he returned to his cell.

"Fountain was less discriminating. While being escorted that evening back to his cell from the recreation room, he stopped alongside the cell of another inmate . . . and reached his handcuffed hands into the cell, and when he brought them out he was out of the handcuffs and holding a shank. He attacked all three guards, killing one (Hoffman) with multiple stab wounds (some inflicted after the guard had already fallen), injuring another gravely (Ditterline, who survived but is permanently disabled), and inflicting lesser though still serious injuries on the third (Powles). After the wounded guards had been dragged to safety by other guards, Fountain threw up his arms in the boxer's gesture of victory, and laughing walked back to his cell." United States v. Fountain, 768 F.2d 790, 793 (7th Cir.1985). Both Fountain and Silverstein testified that the killing had been in self-defense. Silverstein was a member of the governing board of the Aryan Brotherhood, a whites-only prison gang that extolled violence. Fountain was an "associate" of the Aryan Brotherhood. United States v. Silverstein, 732 F.2d 1338 (7th Cir.1984).

203. Both the defendants in case (i), two of the defendants (Williams and Jimmerson) in case (ii), and the defendant in case (iii) were sentenced to death. The defendants in case (iv) were sentenced to life imprisonment, the federal statute not then authorizing capital punishment for their crimes (since changed, 18 U.S.C. § 1118(a)). After further judicial proceedings, the defendants in case (i) were put to death in 1993, and the defendant in case (iii) was put to death in 1995. As to case (ii), see note 204 below.

It has been argued against capital punishment that in the United States, it has been used, deliberately or not, in a racially biased way, black persons being sentenced to death disproportionately often. It has also been alleged that capital punishment is imposed more often if the victim is white than if the victim is black. Both of the defendants in case (i) were white; the victim also was white. All of the defendants in case (ii) were black; both victims were white. The defendant in case (iii) was black; the victim was white. (Both defendants in case (iv) were white.) For more general statistics, see page 336 above. Do those facts affect your view of the appropriate sentence in each case? If the races of the defendant and the victim are statistically significant, does that affect your view about the imposition of capital punishment generally?

In McCleskey v. Kemp, 481 U.S. 279 (1987) (5–4), the Court rejected a claim that the imposition of capital punishment was constitutionally invalid because racial considerations had entered into the decision whether it would be imposed. The defendant was black and was convicted of killing a white person during the course of a robbery. Under Georgia law, a jury recommended that he be sentenced to death following a sentencing hearing, and the judge accepted the jury's recommendation. The claim of racial discrimination was supported by extensive statistical studies of Georgia murder cases, which showed, *inter alia*, that black defendants who kill white victims have the greatest likelihood of being sentenced to death. According to one statistical model, defendants charged with killing white victims were 4.3 times as likely to be sentenced to death than defendants charged with killing black victims. The Court emphasized that there was no evidence other than the statistical studies that racial discrimination was a factor in this case. It observed that discretion is intended to and does play a large role in capital sentencing proceedings and that were the statistical evidence accepted as proof of racial discrimination in this case, comparable proof of statistical disparities related to any impermissible factor might likewise invalidate a death sentence. "At most," the Court said, "the . . . [statistical] study indicates a discrepancy that appears to correlate with race," but it "does not demonstrate a constitutionally significant risk of racial bias affecting the Georgia capital-sentencing process." Id. at 312, 313.

In 1994, Congress enacted a provision that was responsive to the concern about discrimination that was expressed in McCleskey v. Kemp. Before the jury returns a finding on the sentence in a capital case, "the court . . . shall instruct the jury that, in considering whether a sentence of death is justified, it shall not consider the race, color, religious beliefs, national origin, or sex of the defendant or of any victim and that the jury is not to recommend a sentence of death unless it has concluded that it would recommend a sentence of death for the crime in question no matter what the race, color, religious beliefs, national origin, or sex of the defendant or of any victim may be." When it returns its finding, the jury "shall also return to the court a certificate, signed by each juror, that consideration of the race, color, religious beliefs, national origin, or sex of the defendant or any victim was not involved in reaching his or her individual decision and that the individual juror would have made the same recommendation regarding a sentence for the crime in question no matter what the race, color, religious beliefs, national origin, or sex of the defendant or any victim may be." 18 U.S.C. § 3593(f).

For an extended discussion of sentence proportionality in capital cases, including discussion of racial sentencing disparity, see State v. Marshall, 613 A.2d 1059 (N.J.1992).

204. The facts about the crime stated in case (ii), note 202 above are quoted from an opinion of the United States Court of Appeals. In 1996, after 18 years in prison, all four defendants were released and all charges against them were dropped. Williams had spent most of that time on Death Row. Jimmerson had been on Death Row for 11 years. (Gray had served about nine years in prison.) DNA tests proved that semen found on the dead woman's body did not come from any of the men. A man in prison for the murder of another woman in 1990 confessed that he and his brother and others had committed the 1978 crime. The New York Times, June 15, 1996, at 6; July 3, 1996, at A14.

A lawyer who had represented the state in post-conviction proceedings observed after the defendants' release that he had believed that they were guilty, partly because he was convinced that the defendants' lawyer believed that they were guilty. He said that in his opinion the mistake was made because the police who investigated the case were not competent and that the crime occurred in the south suburbs of Chicago, which are notorious for "intolerable" police practices. Furthermore, because the victims of the crime were white, middle-class persons and the defendants were black, underclass persons, the defendants were at a disadvantage in the conflict of credibility. Mistakes of this kind, the lawyer said, are not so unusual in the state courts, because police work is less effective and because lawyers are often less competent than in federal court. For that reason, he said, although he is not opposed to capital punishment in all circumstances as a matter of philosophic principle, he is opposed to it as it is practiced in this country. The best argument for capital punishment, he said, is simply democracy: a majority of the people in the United States are in favor of capital punishment.

There are indications that popular sentiment favoring capital punishment has declined since 1999, notably the decrease in the number of executions annually since then. The most significant factor causing the decline is apparently the growing number of cases in which evidence (mostly DNA analysis) has shown conclusively that a person convicted and sentenced to death (and in a few cases executed) was not guilty. In 2000, cases of this kind prompted Governor Ryan of Illinois to declare a moratorium on executions until the convictions of persons sentenced to death were reviewed by a special panel. The review was completed in 2002. Early in 2003, days before he left office, Governor Ryan pardoned four persons who had been on death row and commuted the sentences of all the remaining persons on death row to life imprisonment or less. He observed: "Our capital system is haunted by the demon of error: error in determining guilt, and error in determining who among the guilty deserves to die." The governor-elect, who was scheduled to take office three days later, said that the mass commutation was "a big mistake." The New York Times, Jan. 11, 2003, at A13; Jan. 12, 2003, at 1, 22.

---

8. THE LIMITS OF CRIMINAL LAW

The Last Voyage of the *William Brown*
From A.W. Brian Simpson, Cannibalism and the Common Law 162–74 (1984).

. . . Built in New York in about 1826, the *William Brown*'s tonnage was just under 560. Her owner, Stephen Baldwin, sold her to Joseph P. Vogels on December 30, 1840. Having loaded a full general cargo, she left Liverpool for Philadelphia at 10:00 A.M. on March 13, 1841, an imprudent breach of maritime tradition, bound for her home port. Her first mate, Francis Rhodes, was aged 32 and an American from Kennebunk, Maine; her second mate was an Englishman, Walter Parker. The crew, including the officers, consisted of 17 men; typically, they were a mixed band: Charley Smith, aged 20, came from Sheerness, England; William Miller, aged 16, from Aalberg, Denmark; Isaac Freeman, aged 28, from Stockholm, Sweden; James Norton, aged 22, from Tipperary, Ireland. The crew also included two black Americans: Joseph Marshall, aged 37, the cook, from Beaufort, South Carolina; and Henry Murray, the steward, aged 22, from Georgetown, Maryland.

[The captain of the ship was George L. Harris, a Philadelphian, aged 44. "Alexander Williams, alias Alexander William Holmes," was an able seaman. Holmes was a Finn, born in Gothenburg and in 1842 aged 26.]

In addition to cargo, the *William Brown* carried 65 passengers. Most were Irish emigrants, but there were some Scots too, including the Edgar family from Lochmaben, comprising Mrs. Margaret Edgar; her three daughters; and a niece, Jean or Jane Johnstone Edgar, who was also a servant; all going to join Mr. Edgar and his brother, established as farmers in Germanstown, Pennsylvania. Among the Irish, there were unaccompanied men, such as John Welsh, all married, who were emigrating and leaving their wives behind, no doubt in the hope of bringing them over later; others were traveling to join families already in America. Bridget McGee, aged 19, from Drogheda, was to join her father, a livery stable keeper in Philadelphia; Biddy Nugent, aged 17, was traveling with her uncle, John Nugent, to join her mother, who ran a lodging house in the same city. Included were complete families: for example, the Leyden family of 16 people, driven by unknown necessity or inhumanity to leave Colonel Stewart's property in County Tyrone; and the Carrs (or Corrs), 11 in all: mother, father, five children, two nieces, and two nephews, all refugees from another landed estate in Tyrone. The Conlins, another family, numbered 15. Some passengers may have been reasonably affluent, like Mrs. Anderson and her five children on their way to join Mr. Anderson, a medical man in practice in Cincinnati. Most, however, would be poor or very poor victims of the grim conditions that existed in Ireland even before the years of the Great Hunger, though not so poor as those who emigrated by the cheaper route to Canada.

Initially the *William Brown* had a very rough passage, and conditions for the passengers were bad; one child died. But nothing exceptional occurred until Monday, April 19. That evening the ship was running before a south-southwesterly gale at between eight and 10 knots; John Stetson was at the wheel. The night was dark and foggy, and it was the second mate's watch, though Captain Harris himself was on deck. At about 9:45 P.M. she ran into a patch of ice and, in spite of Stetson's efforts, twice struck ice floes; her position at the time was at 43°30′ north and 49°39′ west, about 300 miles southeast of Cape Race, Newfoundland. The first impact was very violent; it flung Mary Carr, who was hanging a lamp at the time, over the provisions box in the steerage and even knocked Walter Parker, an experienced sailor, off his feet. The first mate and a sailor immediately inspected the damage, as did the captain, as the sails were clewed up and secured by gaskets. It was found that the bows had been stove in and water was pouring in. Sailing ships at this date did not possess collision bulkheads; and although the crew, aided by some of the passengers (like Ellen Black) exhausted themselves at the pumps, it was all to no avail. The ship was sinking. Julia McCadden spoke to the captain. She "asked him what he was going to do for them, who replied that he could do nothing, and that they must do the best they could for themselves." In panic passengers rushed on deck, leaving behind Isabella Edgar, too ill to climb the ladder out of the steerage. Most had gone to bed, and were barely clothed. They saw the sailors clearing away the boats, which were got overboard and brought alongside. This task took from 9:45 P.M. to about 10:20 P.M. There were two boats, a jolly boat rigged as a sailing cutter, and a shallower longboat propelled by oars. The jolly boat was between 19 and 20 feet long, the longboat 22½ and some six feet in beam.

Launching the boats was a complicated operation, involving cutting away part of the ship's rail; the jolly boat was lowered with four crew members in it and one of the emigrants, Eliza Lafferty. It must soon have become obvious that the two boats could not possibly hold all 83 persons on board. This was normal; the received wisdom was that it was wholly impracticable to carry an adequate complement of boats. With the fatalistic attitude adopted to shipwreck by sailors, nobody even tried; in consequence, when a passenger ship sank at sea, it was inevitable that some must be selected, either by circumstances or deliberate action, to die. Human nature being what it is, the crew usually took priority in survival; women and children (and for that matter, male passengers) normally came last. Nor was this necessarily unreasonable, for the management of small ships required experience, and their navigation required officers possessing instruments and the ability to use them. . . .

The jolly boat obviously offered the best hope, and at first all the officers and the majority of the crew got into it, together with the enterprising Eliza Lafferty. But then a rearrangement took place. The captain, the second mate Walter Parker, six sailors, and the favored Eliza stayed in the jolly boat; and John Smith, the ship's boy, was moved into it. Though potentially this action was of sinister implications, it must be said in fairness that the boat was otherwise provisioned. Mrs. Matilda Patrick, Eliza's sister, asked that she and her husband might join Eliza, but the captain refused. The first mate, Francis Rhodes, together with eight sailors and 33 passengers, moved to the longboat, presumably so that Rhodes could navigate and command it. He was given a chart, a compass, a quadrant and a watch, told by the captain that he was 200 miles from land, and given a course. This all indicated that Captain Harris did not propose to keep him company. The longboat, though little bigger than the jolly boat, was quite disproportionately crowded, having 41 or 42 on board.

The two boats were veered off on lines, leaving on board the *William Brown* some 30 or 31 passengers. The decision as to who should be left does not seem to have been taken in any systematic way. Bridget McGee, who had got into the longboat, was ordered out and back on the sinking ship by Holmes, but she refused; so, too, did Biddy Nugent. Julia McCadden was also ordered out of the longboat by one of the sailors, but she remained. Holmes in particular behaved kindly and very courageously, going back on board the sinking ship to rescue the sick Isabella Edgar, who called out, "I am coming, Mother, I am coming." Mrs. Edgar, together with her other two daughters, Susannah and Margaret, and her niece and servant girl Jane (or Jean) had managed to get into the longboat: the sick Isabella had not. Holmes brought her off the ship on his back, sliding down the falls of the ropes by which the longboat was lowered. One of her sisters in the longboat was crying out for her. He gave his coat to a passenger and was the last man to leave the sinking ship. Mrs. Anderson, left on board, offered Holmes as much as he could earn in a year to take her off, but he replied that money was no object; it was lives he wished to save. She and her children were left on board. After this, the boats were pushed off and held on long lines, and at some point Francis Rhodes called out, referring to those left on board, "Poor souls, you're only going down just before us." The abandoned shrieked in vain for rescue, and at about 11:20 P.M., the *William Brown* stood on her bows and sank; they were all drowned. There was a curious and eery silence just before she went. The line securing the longboat was cut only just in time to prevent its being sucked down in the vortex created by the sinking vessel.

In the process of embarkation, families had been split up. Thus, though Charles Conlin had got into the longboat, his 14 relatives all went down with the *William Brown*; Ann Bradley, who was saved, had a sister on board; and Owen Carr, aged 11 or 13, was separated from his parents and his five brothers and sisters. Later he deposed pathetically that "all his friends were lost in the ship."

The two boats remained moored together during the night. There is a conflict of description as to the state of the weather, but there was a squally north wind, and a heavy sea was running. It may also have been raining and hailing. The longboat leaked and had to be bailed continuously, the passengers taking their turns. They were quite inadequately clad, some half naked. The mate gave a coat to Mrs. Edgar (he had two), and other sailors gave spare clothing away. Jack Stetson gave young Owen Carr a pair of stockings; a sailor gave Jane Edgar a coat. Holmes cut up his oilcloth pants to cover Julia McCadden (also called Judy McAdden—there was considerable confusion over the correct form of names). At dawn, around 5:00 A.M., a conversation took place between Captain Harris and the first mate, Francis Rhodes. Rhodes took a gloomy view of the chances of survival of the longboat; it was, he said, "impossible for the boat to live." In his view, the longboat was grossly overcrowded; it had lost its rudder and was unmanageable. The gunwales were within five inches of the water. Later on the passengers, at least some of them, put forward a less pessimistic view, but the mate's opinion is to be preferred. The captain proposed to set out for Newfoundland: he is reported to have said, "His boat was light, and he will go." The mate replied, "I think you might keep company with us today." But the captain was unwilling to do this and knew that the mate and longboat could not follow him. The mate also told the captain that unless he took some of the passengers into the jolly boat, it would be necessary to cast lots and throw some overboard. The captain replied, "I know what you mean" or, according to another witness, "I know what you will have to do. Don't speak of that now. Let it be the last resort." Yet another version has it that Rhodes said, "Captain Harris, we will have to draw lots." He replied, "I know what you mean. I don't want to hear any more about it." The gist of the various accounts is the same— Captain Harris did not explicitly take any responsibility for what might have to be done. According to Julia McCadden, Rhodes had raised the question of drawing lots the evening before as well, with much the same result.

A list was made by the captain of those in the longboat—he missed one name—and then he sailed off; within 10 minutes he was out of sight in the mist. Later he admitted that he thought the longboat had no chance at all of reaching land, and the chance of being picked up he put at 1%. He knew that the longboat, in its overloaded condition, would not ride head to wind, the only safe attitude if the wind rose. After four hours' futile attempt to head for Newfoundland, the sailors consulted and then set off south; at Holmes's suggestion, the captain's idea of heading for land was not followed. The crew rowed in turns; their course would take them further and further away from land but into warmer water and across the shipping routes. The evidence suggests that in fact Rhodes was not a competent navigator, and he later admitted as much.

An attempt was made to rig a makeshift sail, but it was taken down because of the risk of a capsize. Under oars, and with the wind behind them, they appear to have made a good almost three miles an hour. It rained heavily all day, and that afternoon the wind rose again; at night they met ice. Persistent trouble appears to have been caused by a drainage plug in the bottom of the boat. During the first night it had come out and been lost; the leak was temporarily blocked with caps, and Holmes made a new plug with an axe. The boat continued to leak, and another larger hole, about eight by four inches, was discovered at some point in the day; there is considerable conflict of evidence as to how serious the leakage was, though one would expect a hole of this size to be very serious indeed if below or near the waterline. According to the mate's later account, "finding that the boat was literally surrounded by small and large masses of ice, and that the water was gaining upon her, I thought it improbable that she could hold out, unless relieved of some of her weight. I then consulted the sailors, and we were all of the opinion that it was necessary to throw overboard those who were nearly dead, until we had room enough to work the boat and take to our oars." And so, starting at about 10:00 on Thursday evening, when it was fairly dark, the sailors began to throw the passengers overboard. Fairly precise details of how this was done have survived, though there are inevitably discrepancies in detail.

After the discussion between the mate and the sailors, an interval occurred. Then the mate, who had been bailing, suddenly said, "This work [i.e., the bailing] won't do. Help me God. Men, go to work." This initially produced no reaction. The mate repeated the instruction: "Now you must go to work.'' He later denied that what he did was to issue an *order*, claiming that he merely pointed out the position they were all in: ''If they did not lighten her, they would all be lost, remarking at the same time that it was better that a few should be saved, than that all should perish, telling them also that they had as much to say in the business as he had . . . that he did not order the men to throw any overboard, but stated, that from the position in which they were, whatever was necessary to be done must be done immediately or that the boat would swamp. . . .'' According to a story that appeared later both in the American press and in the London *Times* on July 24, 1884, one of the sailors, John Messer, held out against killing without drawing lots, but the mate threatened to kill him for his intransigence. But this story was almost certainly fabricated.

It was later claimed that the choice of those to be thrown overboard was dictated simply by practicalities, those nearest to the sailors being selected, by chance predominantly men. But it seems fairly clear that the sailors deliberately decided to jettison the men, rather than the women, though the mate may not have been involved in this decision. Whether he gave what counted as an order or not, his remark could easily be interpreted as one, for he was in command, and the sailors had undertaken the captain's directive to obey him. Isaac Freeman, for example, thought an order was given. There were 16 adult men, and from what occurred it looks as if it was agreed that all were to go. Having initiated the proceedings, the mate himself took no further active part in the operation; the passengers were neither informed nor consulted. The sailors directly involved were Charley Smith, Alexander Williams (Alexander William Holmes), Joseph Stetson, and Henry Murray, the cook. Isaac Freeman also later admitted assisting. According to Stetson, the first attempt was abandoned because of resistance. The sailors then tried again, and the first man to go was Owen Riley, a married man whose wife lived in Philadelphia. He was told to stand up and must have known what was about to happen, as he asked Mr. Edgar to beg the sailors to preserve his life; he also called to Isabella Edgar and to Julia McCadden. She also realized what was happening, for she called out, ''Good God, are they going to drown the man?'' He was thrust overboard, soon followed by a Scotsman, James Todd. James MacAvoy was probably the next. He begged five minutes' grace to say his prayers and button his coat and, at the instance of Henry Murray, he was given it. He said ''Lord, be merciful to me, a sinner'' and may have thrown himself over. Soon after, Frank Askins was seized by Holmes. He appears to have been the only passenger to put up serious resistance; Holmes called for help. Askins said, ''I'll not go out, you know I wrought well all the time. I'll work like a man till morning, and do what I can to keep the boat clear of water; I have five sovereigns, and I'll give it for my life till morning, and when morning comes if God does not help us we will cast lots, and I'll go out like a man if it is my turn.'' Holmes replied to the effect that it was lives he was interested in, not money. Frank's two sisters, Ellen and Mary, then attempted to intercede; Mary, the younger, said that if her brother was to go she should go too; she was willing to die instead of him. Holmes and his assistants, having thrown Frank over, said that the sisters might as well go too. Mary may have gone voluntarily, unwilling to live now her brother was dead. Ellen, before she went, begged pathetically not to be thrown over, as she was practically naked. A cloak was thrown to her, though it was not her own. James Black was then seized: his wife Ellen offered to die with him. His own account reads, "He heard a mournful noise and found himself seized by one of the crew, who told him he must go overboard as it was necessary to lighten the boat . . . he asked him to let his wife go with him, when Mr. Rhodes called out, don't separate man and wife, they can't live long." He was spared, as was James Patrick for the same reason. During the night, another eight men were killed in the same way—George Duffy (who pleaded for his life as he had three children on shore, and because his niece, Bridget McGee, for whom he was responsible, was in the boat), Martin MacAvoy, Robert Hunter, Archibold Carr, John Wilson, John Welsh, and then James Smith. One called out "blood-an-ouns, let go of me and I'll go myself." The operation was still in progress as dawn broke the next day. Then it was the turn of Charles Conlin. He said, "Holmes, dear, you won't put me over." Holmes replied, "Charles, you must go." Mary Carr seized Holmes and pleaded for him, saying he was the last of a family of 15, but Holmes did not relent, and Charles Conlin was thrown into the icy waters of the North Atlantic.

Later, when it became fully light, two more men were found, apparently either hiding or hidden; they may have been in a dying condition, and Holmes later claimed one was actually dead. But according to Sarah Carr, the sailors "told the women not to hide them, as they would not leave a d . . . d soul of them in the boat." Holmes did not join in the last stages of what seems to have degenerated into a man-hunt. Hugh Keegan was thrown out by Joseph Stetson and John Nugent by Charley Smith. Nugent's niece, 17-year-old Biddy Nugent, heard him plead for his life and for him to be left to care for her orphaned self. As Nugent was thrown into the sea, the mate said, "Lord, cruel, cruel." One account suggests that one boy was thrown over but managed to cling under the bow and survive. This is improbable, but, if so, the boy could only have been Owen Carr, unless the reference is to one of those who died. Later a story circulated that those flung over clung to the sides of the longboat and their hands were cut off, but this story was denied and seems to have no foundation. In the conditions prevailing, they would in any event have rapidly lost consciousness.

The story told by the sailors was that all those jettisoned were nearly dead; although some of the passengers agreed with this, the probability is that this was not the case. The passengers were divided in their attitude as to what had been done—some at least said on Wednesday that the crew should be made to die the death they had given to the others. In particular, Bridget McGee repeatedly said that Holmes should be punished; her uncle had been killed before her eyes. Accounts of the whole incident give the impression that, although Francis Rhodes was nominally in charge and initiated the killings, Holmes was in reality the effective leader until after the three Askins had been killed; he then appears to have tried to stop the killings, but Stetson and Murray carried on. Charley Smith later claimed that the passengers, after praying, all accepted their fate voluntarily, but this is quite unconvincing.

It was now possible to deal properly with the persistent leakage of water into the boat, which became manageable; the sailors could row southward. But at about 6:00 in the morning, very shortly indeed after the last two passengers had been jettisoned, the longboat was sighted by Captain George T. Ball from an American ship, the *Crescent*; he was aloft, conning his ship through the ice. At some considerable risk, he picked them up at about 7:00 A.M.—an hour or so later rescue would not have been possible. Immediately afterward, the longboat itself was crushed by the ice. Thus, in the event, the sacrifice of the passengers had probably made no difference to the survival of the others. When the *Crescent* was sighted, Holmes, the grim realist, prevented the survivors from standing up, calling out: "Lie down, every soul of you, and lie still. If they make out so many of us on board, they will steer off another way, and pretend they have not seen us." He even pushed Mary Carr down when she tried to stand. Numerous contemporary tales confirm the potential realization of his fears. But Captain Ball lavished every kindness on the survivors, even burning his own longboat for fuel to warm them. Their condition by this time was very bad. Owen Carr had no recollection of the rescue at all; the others could not walk. The *Crescent* was herself trapped for some time in the ice after the rescue. Captain Ball took them to Le Havre; en route, on May 2, he met another American vessel, the *Ville de Lyons* (commanded by a Captain Stoddard), to which he transferred some of the survivors. He secured a statement from Francis Rhodes as to what had happened, and Rhodes and eight sailors signed it; this was probably entered in the ship's log. Two passengers, James Patrick and James Black, also signed. They had reason to be grateful—their wives and James Patrick's child had been saved; and apart from the boy Owen Carr, they were the only males spared. The other 15 did not sign; the women were either unwilling or were ignored.

The *Ville de Lyons* reached Le Havre on May 10 and the *Crescent* on May 12. . . .

. . .

. . . In Le Havre, a subscription . . . [was] raised, and the emigrants set out again for Philadelphia, where they arrived in July—Bridget McGee on July 13, the others perhaps on the same date. Francis Rhodes, Charley Smith, and William Miller also traveled to Philadelphia; what became of the other sailors, particularly Joseph Stetson and James Murray, does not appear. Fate had been kinder to them or most of them, than to those in the captain's jolly boat. Those who had sailed off with Captain Harris had been rescued after six days by a French fishing lugger, *La Mère de famille*, and landed at S. Pierre in Breton Island, but they were badly frostbitten and one subsequently died in the hospital. Captain Harris, Walter Parker, and Eliza Lafferty also eventually reached Philadelphia on the *Childe Harold*. There must have existed in the Irish community in Philadelphia bitter resentment against the sailors for what could be viewed as an outrage, in which a captain had deserted his passengers, and his crew then killed them. There were also hints of racial favoritism—survival of the Scots preferred over that of the Irish; traditional religious hostilities lie behind this suspicion. Of the survivors Bridget McGee, Julia McCadden, and Nancy Bradley all resented what had been done, though Julia, no doubt to get away from Le Havre, had exonerated the sailors in her statement there. How precisely it came about is obscure, but it must surely have been pressure from kinsfolk that led to the involvement of the district attorney, William M. Meredith, in the matter. In the end Holmes alone was arrested and eventually, on October 18, 1841, indicted before a grand jury on a number of charges of murder and one charge . . . of larceny. Perhaps it was larceny that put him in the hands of the authorities. Francis Rhodes, Joseph Stetson, and James Murray seem simply to have disappeared, as sailors did; they were never brought to trial. The captain had committed no offense known to the law.

The grand jury found two true bills for manslaughter only and threw out the others. On December 9, depositions were taken from Captain Harris and Walter Parker; eventually, after long delay, Holmes stood trial on one indictment only for the manslaughter of Francis Askins. The trial opened on Wednesday, April 13, 1842, before Chief Justice Baldwin and Justice Randall of the U.S. Circuit Court for the Eastern District of Pennsylvania, and it lasted until April 23. For the prosecution, evidence from the survivors was given by Bridget McGee, Mary Carr, Owen Carr, Ann Bradley, Julia McCadden, Sarah Carr, and Biddy Nugent—those to be expected to support the prosecution. The defense relied on depositions from Captain Harris and Walter Parker (by then at sea), the Edgar family, and Eliza Lafferty. Again the defense team selected itself.

Holmes was ably and indeed flamboyantly defended by David Paul Brown, assisted by Messrs Hazehurst and Armstrong; in court, reporting the proceedings, was the famous American law reporter, J.W. Wallace. . . .

. . .

United States v. Holmes

26 F. Cas. 360 (C.C.E.D.Pa.1842) (No. 15,383)

. . .

[From the Reporter's account of the case]

. . .

[T]he character of the prisoner stood forth, in many points, in manly and interesting relief. A Finn by birth, he had followed the sea from youth, and his frame and countenance would have made an artist's model for decision and strength. He had been the last man of the crew to leave the sinking ship. His efforts to save the passengers, at the time the ship struck, had been conspicuous, and, but that they were in discharge of duty, would have been called self-forgetful and most generous. As a sailor, his captain and the second mate testified that he had ever been obedient to orders, faithful to his duty, and efficient in the performance of it,—"remarkably so," said the second mate. "He was kind and obliging in every respect," said the captain, "to the passengers, to his shipmates, and to everybody. Never heard one speak against him. IIe was always obedient to officers. I never had a better man on board ship. He was a first-rate man." (Captain's deposition.) While on the longboat, in order to protect the women, he had parted with all his clothes, except his shirt and pantaloons; and his conduct and language to the women were kind. After Askin had been thrown out, some one asked if any more were to be thrown over. "No," said Holmes, "no more shall be thrown over. If any more are lost, we will all be lost together." Of both passengers and crew, he finally became the only one whose energies and whose hopes did not sink into prostration. He was the first to descry the vessel which took them up, and by his exertions the ship was made to see, and, finally, to save, them.

. . .

[Mr. Dallas, for the prosecution]

The prisoner is charged with "unlawful homicide," as distinguished from that sort which is malicious. His defence is that the homicide was necessary to self-preservation. First, then, we ask: Was the homicide thus necessary? That is to say, was the danger instant, overwhelming, leaving no choice of means, no moment for deliberation? For, unless the danger were of this sort, the prisoner, under any admission, had no right, without notice or consultation, or lot, to sacrifice the lives of 16 fellow beings. Peril, even extreme peril, is not enough to justify a sacrifice such as this was. Nor would even the certainty of death be enough, if death were yet prospective. It must be instant. The law regards every man's life as of equal value. It regards it, likewise, as of sacred value. Nor may any man take away his brother's life, but where the sacrifice is indispensable to save his own. (Mr. Dallas then examined the evidence, and contended that the danger was not so extreme as is requisite to justify homicide.) But it will be answered, that death being certain, there was no obligation to wait until the moment of death had arrived. Admitting, then, the fact that death was certain, and that the safety of some persons was to be promoted by an early sacrifice of the others, what law, we ask, gives a crew, in such a case, to be the arbiters of life and death, settling, for themselves, both the time and the extent of the necessity? No. We protest against giving to seamen the power thus to make jettison of human beings, as of so much cargo; of allowing sailors, for their own safety, to throw overboard, whenever they may like, whomsoever they may choose. If the mate and seamen believed that the ultimate safety of a portion was to be advanced by the sacrifice of another portion, it was the clear duty of that officer, and of the seamen, to give full notice to all on board. Common settlement would, then, have fixed the principle of sacrifice, and, the mode of selection involving all, a sacrifice of any would have been resorted to only in dire extremity. Thus far, the argument admits that, at sea, sailor and passenger stand upon the same base, and in equal relations. But we take, third, stronger ground. The seaman, we hold, is bound, beyond the passenger, to encounter the perils of the sea. To the last extremity, to death itself, must he protect the passenger. It is his duty. It is on account of these risks that he is paid. It is because the sailor is expected to expose himself to every danger, that, beyond all mankind, by every law, his wages are secured to him. . . .

[Mr. Armstrong, followed by Mr. Brown, for the defense]

[T]his case should be tried in a long-boat, sunk down to its very gunwale with 41 half naked, starved, and shivering wretches,—the boat leaking from below, filling from above, a hundred leagues from land, at midnight, surrounded by ice, unmanageable from its load, and subject to certain destruction from the change of the most changeful of the elements, the winds and the waves. To these super-add the horrours of famine and the recklessness of despair, madness, and all the prospects, past utterance, of this unutterable condition. Fairly to sit in judgment on the prisoner, we should, then, be actually translated to his situation. It was a conjuncture which no fancy can image. Terrour had assumed the throne of reason, and passion had become judgment. Are the United States to come here, now, a year after the events, when it is impossible to estimate the elements which combined to make the risk, or to say to what extent the jeopardy was imminent? Are they, with square, rule and compass, deliberately to measure this boat, in this room, to weigh these passengers, call in philosophers, discuss specific gravities, calculate by the tables of a life insurance company the chances of life, and because they, these judges, find that, by their calculation, this unfortunate boat's crew might have had the thousandth part of one poor chance of escape, to condemn this prisoner to chains and a dungeon, for what he did in the terrour and darkness of that dark and terrible night. Such a mode of testing men's acts and motives is monstrous. We contend, therefore, that what is honestly and reasonably believed to be certain death will justify self-defence to the degree requisite for excuse. According to Dr. Rutherford (Inst. Nat. Law, bk. 1, c. 16, § 5): "This law,"—i.e. the law of nature,—"cannot be supposed to oblige a man to expose his life to such dangers as may be guarded against, and to wait till the danger is just coming upon him, before it allows him to secure himself." In other words, he need not wait 'til the certainty of the danger has been proved, past doubt, by its result. Yet this is the doctrine of the prosecution. They ask us to wait until the boat has sunk. We may, then, make an effort to prevent her from sinking. They tell us to wait till all are drowned. We may, then, make endeavours to save a part. They command us to stand still till we are all lost past possibility of redemption, and then we may rescue as many as can be saved. Where the danger is instantaneous, the mind is too much disturbed, says Rutherford, in a passage hereafter cited, to deliberate upon the method of providing for one's own safety, with the least hurt to an aggressor. The same author then proceeds: "I see not, therefore, any want of benevolence which can be reasonably charged upon a man in these circumstances, if he takes the most obvious way of preserving himself, though perhaps some other method might have been found out, which would have preserved him as effectually, and have produced less hurt to the aggressor, if he had been calm enough, and had been allowed time enough to deliberate about it." Rutherf. Inst. Nat. Law, bk. 1, c. 16, § 5. . . .

Counsel say that lots are the law of the ocean. Lots, in cases of famine, where means of subsistence are wanting for all the crew, is what the history of maritime disaster records; but who has ever told of casting lots at midnight, in a sinking boat, in the midst of darkness, of rain, of terrour, and of confusion? To cast lots when all are going down, but to decide who shall be spared, to cast lots when the question is, whether any can be saved, is a plan easy to suggest, rather difficult to put in practice. The danger was instantaneous, a case, says Rutherford (Inst. Nat. Law, bk. 1, c. 16, § 5), when "the mind is too much disturbed to deliberate," and where, if it were "more calm," there is no time for deliberation. The sailors adopted the only principle of selection which was possible in an emergency like theirs,—a principle more humane than lots. Man and wife were not torn asunder, and the women were all preserved. Lots would have rendered impossible this clear dictate of humanity. But again: The crew either were in their ordinary and original state of subordination to their officers, or they were in a state of nature. If in the former state, they are excusable in law, for having obeyed the order of the mate,—an order twice imperatively given. Independent of the mate's general authority in the captain's absence, the captain had pointedly directed the crew to obey all the mate's orders as they would his, the captain's; and the crew had promised to do so. It imports not to declare that a crew is not bound to obey an unlawful order, for to say that this order was unlawful is to postulate what remains to be proved. Who is to judge of the unlawfulness? The circumstances were peculiar. The occasion was emergent, without precedent, or parallel. The lawfulness of the order is the very question which we are disputing; a question about which this whole community has been agitated, and is still divided; the discussion of which crowds this room with auditors past former example; a question which this court, with all its resources, is now engaged in considering, as such a question demands to be considered, most deliberately, most anxiously, most cautiously. It is no part of a sailor's duty to moralize and to speculate, in such a moment as this was, upon the orders of his superiour officers. . . . But if the whole company were reduced to a state of nature, then the sailors were bound to no duty, not mutual, to the passengers. The contract of the shipping articles had become dissolved by an unforeseen and overwhelming necessity. The sailor was no longer a sailor, but a drowning man. Having fairly done his duty to the last extremity, he was not to lose the rights of a human being, because he wore a roundabout instead of a frock coat. We do not seek authorities for such doctrine. The instinct of these men's hearts is our authority,—the best authority. Whoever opposes it must be wrong, for he opposes human nature. All the contemplated conditions, all the contemplated possibilities of the voyage, were ended. The parties, sailor and passenger, were in a new state. All persons on board the vessel became equal. All became their own lawgivers; for artificial distinctions cease to prevail when men are reduced to the equality of nature. Every man on board had a right to make law with his own right hand, and the law which did prevail on that awful night having been the law of necessity, and the law of nature too, it is the law which will be upheld by this court, to the liberation of this prisoner.

[Baldwin, Circuit Justice, charging the Jury]

. . . Where, indeed, a case does arise, embraced by this "law of necessity," the penal laws pass over such case in silence; for law is made to meet but the ordinary exigencies of life. But the case does not become "a case of necessity," unless all ordinary means of self preservation have been exhausted. The peril must be instant, overwhelming, leaving no alternative but to lose our own life, or to take the life of another person. An illustration of this principle occurs in the ordinary case of self-defense against lawless violence, aiming at the destruction of life, or designing to inflict grievous injury to the person; and within this range may fall the taking of life under other circumstances where the act is indispensably requisite to self-existence. For example, suppose that two persons who owe no duty to one another that is not mutual, should, by accident, not attributable to either, be placed in a situation where both cannot survive. Neither is bound to save the other's life by sacrificing his own, nor would either commit a crime in saving his own life in a struggle for the only means of safety. Of this description of cases are those which have been cited to you by counsel, from writers on natural law,—cases which we rather leave to your imagination than attempt minutely to describe. And I again state that when this great "law of necessity" does apply, and is not improperly exercised, the taking of life is devested of unlawfulness.

But in applying this law, we must look, not only to the jeopardy in which the parties are, but also to the relations in which they stand. The slayer must be under no obligation to make his own safety secondary to the safety of others. A familiar application of this principle presents itself in the obligations which rest upon the owners of stages, steamboats, and other vehicles of transportation. In consideration of the payment of fare, the owners of the vehicle are bound to transport the passengers to the place of contemplated destination. Having, in all emergencies, the conduct of the journey, and the control of the passengers, the owners rest under every obligation for care, skill, and general capacity; and if, from defect of any of these requisites, grievous injury is done to the passenger, the persons employed are liable. The passenger owes no duty but submission. He is under no obligation to protect and keep the conductor in safety, nor is the passenger bound to labour, except in cases of emergency, where his services are required by unanticipated and uncommon danger. Such, said the court, is the relation which exists on shipboard. The passenger stands in a position different from that of the officers and seamen. It is the sailor who must encounter the hardships and perils of the voyage. Nor can this relation be changed when the ship is lost by tempest or other danger of the sea, and all on board have betaken themselves, for safety, to the small boats; for imminence of danger can not absolve from duty. The sailor is bound, as before, to undergo whatever hazard is necessary to preserve the boat and the passengers. Should the emergency become so extreme as to call for the sacrifice of life, there can be no reason why the law does not still remain the same. The passenger, not being bound either to labour or to incur the risk of life, cannot be bound to sacrifice his existence to preserve the sailor's. The captain, indeed, and a sufficient number of seamen to navigate the boat, must be preserved; for, except these abide in the ship, all will perish. But if there be more seamen than are necessary to manage the boat, the supernumerary sailors have no right, for their safety, to sacrifice the passengers. The sailors and passengers, in fact, cannot be regarded as in equal positions. The sailor (to use the language of a distinguished writer) owes more benevolence to another than to himself. He is bound to set a greater value on the life of others than on his own. And while we admit that sailor and sailor may lawfully struggle with each other for the plank which can save but one, we think that, if the passenger is on the plank, even "the law of necessity" justifies not the sailor who takes it from him. This rule may be deemed a harsh one towards the sailor, who may have thus far done his duty, but when the danger is so extreme, that the only hope is in sacrificing either a sailor or a passenger, any alternative is hard; and would it not be the hardest of any to sacrifice a passenger in order to save a supernumerary sailor?

But, in addition, if the source of the danger have been obvious, and destruction ascertained to be certainly about to arrive, though at a future time, there should be consultation, and some mode of selection fixed, by which those in equal relations may have equal chance for their life. By what mode, then, should selection be made? The question is not without difficulty; nor do we know of any rule prescribed, either by statute or by common law, or even by speculative writers on the law of nature. In fact, no rule of general application can be prescribed for contingencies which are wholly unforeseen. There is, however, one condition of extremity for which all writers have prescribed the same rule. When the ship is in no danger of sinking, but all sustenance is exhausted, and a sacrifice of one person is necessary to appease the hunger of others, the selection is by lot. This mode is resorted to as the fairest mode, and, in some sort, as an appeal to God, for selection of the victim. . . . For ourselves, we can conceive of no mode so consonant both to humanity and to justice; and the occasion, we think, must be peculiar which will dispense with its exercise. If, indeed, the peril be instant and overwhelming, leaving no chance of means, and no moment for deliberation, then, of course, there is no power to consult, to cast lots, or in any such way to decide; but even where the final disaster is thus sudden, if it have been foreseen as certainly about to arrive, if no new cause of danger have arisen to bring on the closing catastrophe, if time have existed to cast lots, and to select the victims, then, as we have said, sortition should be adopted. In no other than this or some like way are those having equal rights put upon an equal footing, and in no other way is it possible to guard against partiality and oppression, violence and conflict. What scene, indeed more horrible, can imagination draw than a struggle between sailor and sailor, passenger and passenger, or, it may be, a mixed affray, in which promiscuously, all destroy one another? This, too, in circumstances which have allowed time to decide, with justice, whose life should be calmly surrendered.

When the selection has been made by lots, the victim yields of course to his fate, or, if he resist, force may be employed to coerce submission. Whether or not "a case of necessity" has arisen, or whether the law under which death has been inflicted have been so exercised as to hold the executioner harmless, cannot depend on his own opinion; for no man may pass upon his own conduct, when it concerns the rights, and especially, when it affects the lives, of others. We have already stated to you that, by the law of the land, homicide is sometimes justifiable; and the law defines the occasions in which it is so. The transaction must, therefore, be justified to the law; and the person accused rests under obligation to satisfy those who judicially scrutinize his case that it really transcended ordinary rules. In fact, any other principle would be followed by pernicious results, and, moreover, would not be practicable in application. Opinion or belief may be assumed, whether it exist or not; and if this mere opinion of the sailors will justify them in making a sacrifice of the passengers, of course, the mere opinion of the passengers would, in turn, justify these in making a sacrifice of the sailors. The passengers may have confidence in their own capacity to manage and preserve the boat, or the effort of either sailors or passengers to save the boat, may be clearly unavailing; and what, then, in a struggle against force and numbers, becomes of the safety of the seamen? Hard as is a seaman's life, would it not become yet more perilous if the passengers, who may outnumber them tenfold, should be allowed to judge when the dangers of the sea will justify a sacrifice of life? We are, therefore, satisfied, that, in requiring proof, which shall be satisfactory to you, of the existence of the necessity, we are fixing the rule which is, not merely the only one which is practicable, but, moreover, the only one which will secure the safety of the sailors themselves.

The court said, briefly, that the principles which had been laid down by them, as applicable to the crew, applied to the mate likewise, and that his order (on which much stress had been laid), if an unlawful order, would be no justification to the seamen, for that even seamen are not justified, in law, by obedience to commands which are unlawful. The court added that the case was one which involved questions of gravest consideration, and, as the facts, in some sort, were without precedent, that the court preferred to state the law, in the shape of such general principles as would comprehend the case, under any view which the jury might take of the evidence.

[After deliberating for about 16 hours the jury found Holmes guilty of manslaughter and recommended him to the mercy of the court.

In favor of a new trial Mr. Brown argued that the jury should have been instructed that the persons in the long-boat were in a "state of nature, as distinguished from the social state."]

[The Court, denying a new trial]

. . . It is true, said the court, as is known by every one, that we do find in the text writers, and sometimes in judicial opinions, the phrases, "the law of nature," "the principles of natural right," and other expressions of a like signification; but, as applied to civilized men, nothing more can be meant by those expressions than that there are certain great and fundamental principles of justice which, in the constitution of nature, lie at the foundation and make part of all civil law, independently of express adoption or enactment. And to give to the expressions any other signification, to claim them as shewing an independent code, and one contrariant to those settled principles, which, however modified, make a part of civil law in all Christian nations, would be to make the writers who use the expressions lay down as rules of action, principles which, in their nature, admit of no practical ascertainment or application. The law of nature forms part of the municipal law; and, in a proper case (as of self-defence), homicide is justifiable, not because the municipal law is subverted by the law of nature, but because no rule of the municipal law makes homicide, in such cases, criminal. It is, said the court, the municipal or civil law, as thus comprehensive, as founded in moral and social justice,—the law of the land, in short, as existing and administered amongst us and all enlightened nations,—that regulates the social duties of men, the duties of man towards his neighbour, everywhere. Everywhere are civilized men under its protection; everywhere, subject to its authority. It is part of the universal law. We cannot escape it in a case where it is applicable; and if, for the decision of any question, the proper rule is to be found in the municipal law, no code can be referred to as annulling its authority. Varying however, or however modified, the laws of all civilized nations, and, indeed, the very nature of the social constitution, place sailors and passengers in different relations. And, without stopping to speculate upon over-nice questions not before us, or to involve ourselves in the labyrinth of ethical subtleties, we may safely say that the sailor's duty is the protection of the persons intrusted to his care, not their sacrifice,—a duty we must again declare our opinion, that rests on him in every emergency of his calling, and from which it would be senseless, indeed, to absolve him exactly at those times when the obligation is most needed.

. . .

[Sentence]

When the prisoner was brought up for sentence, the learned judge said to him, that many circumstances in the affair were of a character to commend him to regard, yet, that the case was one in which some punishment was demanded; that it was in the power of the court to inflict the penalty of an imprisonment for a term of three years, and a fine of $1,000, but, in view of all the circumstances, and especially as the prisoner had been already confined in gaol several months, that the court would make the punishment more lenient. The convict was then sentenced to undergo an imprisonment in the Eastern Penitentiary of Pennsylvania, (solitary confinement) at hard labour, for the term of six months, and to pay a fine of $20.

After giving the jury's verdict the foreman said that the jury unanimously recommended mercy. A petition to President Tyler for a pardon, in which the members of the jury joined, was denied because the judges who presided at the trial did not join in the petition. Holmes served his sentence of imprisonment; the fine was remitted. F. Hicks, Human Jettison 275–76 (1927); see A. Simpson, Cannibalism and the Common Law 177 (1984).

———

205. According to the reporter's account, Holmes was a model of the so-called "Handsome Sailor," see H. Melville, Billy Budd 1 (standard ed. 1963). Are his exemplary character and his exemplary conduct during the shipwreck relevant to the question of his guilt? Why (not)?

206. Assuming generally that the seaman is paid, as Mr. Dallas said, to protect the passengers "to the last extremity, to death itself," p. 372, does their obligation extend to the particular situation in which Holmes found himself?

207. Do you agree with Mr. Armstrong that the "clear dictate of humanity," p. 373, is not to separate husband and wife and is to spare women? If so, does that overcome the presumption in favor of lots? Does the law require a bachelor (or a misogynist) to sacrifice his principles (and his life) to womanhood?

208. How persuasive is the appeal to the seaman's duty to protect the passengers? If the law is so far overthrown, so irrelevant to the situation, that what would otherwise be murder is permitted, how relevant is a contractual obligation? Does the same necessity that excuses the killing not terminate the contract?

Is there a relevant difference between asking a seaman to risk his life in the performance of his regular duties—for example, by going out on deck in a violent storm—and imposing on him a duty to throw himself into the sea?

209. Before he left in the jollyboat, the captain advised the members of the crew in the longboat "to obey all the orders of the mate, as they would obey his, the captain's," 26 F. Cas. at 360. The crew acted under the direction of the mate when they threw the passengers overboard. Should

Holmes have been allowed the defense of "superior orders"?[103]

210. If the necessity of the situation is so great that killing is permitted, is the situation one in which the calm and reason required to cast lots and abide by the result can be demanded by the law?

211. Would any set of facts overcome the presumption in favor of lots? Suppose a passenger were

(i) dying

(ii) very old

(iii) very young

(iv) an escaped convict (condemned to death)

(v) an ex-convict

(vi) a believer in heaven

(vii) a public official (the President)

(viii) a great artist.

212. Do you agree with the court that "the very nature of the social constitution" places "sailors and passengers in different relations," p. 377, in the circumstances of this case? What is the "social constitution"? What binds Holmes to obey it?

213. Does the court truly acknowledge the force of the "law of nature," those "great and fundamental principles of justice which, in the constitution of nature, lie at the foundation and make part of all civil law, independently of express adoption or enactment," p. 377? What force did it have in this case? Did the court and Mr. Armstrong for the defense have in mind the same thing when they referred to natural law? Where would each of them look for an indication of the content of natural law?

---

103. "In a state of open and public war, where military law prevails, and the peaceful voice of municipal law is drowned in the din of arms, great indulgences must necessarily be extended to the acts of subordinate officers done in obedience to the orders of their superiors. But even there the order of a superior officer to take the life of a citizen . . . would not shield the inferior against a charge of murder . . . in the regular judicial tribunals of the country." United States v. Bright, 24 F. Cas. 1232, 1237–38 (C.C.D.Pa.1809) (No. 14,647).

214. Is there a sense of "law of nature" in which it is obviously incorrect that the law of nature obliged the sailors to sacrifice their lives for the passengers?

———

It is not asserted in *Holmes* or in *Roberts* and *Dudley & Stephens*, the two cases that follow, that the defendant was not generally responsible for his conduct. Since all three cases involved intentional homicide, there was no question that the law was competent to declare the conduct criminal in general. The possible defense in each case was, rather, that the circumstances in which the defendant acted put his conduct beyond the reach of the law. The Constitution imposes limitations on law, with respect both to the defendant's responsibility for conduct and to the nature of the conduct itself. See Part Five below.

———

People v. Roberts

211 Mich. 187, 178 N.W. 690 (1920)

The defendant pleaded guilty to the charge of murdering his wife by poison. Witnesses were then called to give testimony bearing on the degree of the crime.

. . .

[Cross-examination of Dr. Michael Bronstetter by Mr. Dusenberry, defense counsel.]

"Q. You had reference to a time you had seen Mrs. Roberts as a patient? A. Yes, sir.

"Q. When was that, Doctor? A. I could not say just when; . . . about three or four months before her death. I saw her at her home where they lived. She was a bed patient, or practically so at that time. She was in bed, and I believe she said she was unable to do any kind of work. Whether she could get up and around or not I don't know. Her body was considerably wasted. She showed evidence of a long drawn out sickness. She showed symptoms of a multiple sclerosis.

"Q. What is that? A. It is a disease of the central nervous system, affecting both the brain and cord. The causes of these patches in the brain and cord is unknown. This condition I found with this patient. She had the outward signs of multiple sclerosis, the rapid pulse, hesitating, singsong speech. And from these signs you diagnose the multiple sclerosis.

"Q. Was she practically helpless? A. I should say practically. Just how specifically I could not say.

"Q. Basing your answer upon your observation at that time, did you consider her a hopeless patient, or did you consider she might possibly recover? A. I considered her case as incurable."

. . .

Defendant, Roberts, then took the stand, and was interrogated by counsel as follows:

Examined by Mr. Dusenberry:

"Q. Your wife was sent to the hospital at Ann Arbor? A. I took her myself. She was there 30 days, I think. I did not stay there at Ann Arbor while she was there. I took her myself, and made three trips down to see her while she was there, and I brought her back myself. I paid the expenses incident to her going to the hospital and staying there the 30 days. It wasn't paid by the county. I paid it out of my own pocket."

Examined by Mr. McClintic [for the State]:

"Q. On May 23, 1919, Mr. Roberts, I understand you told me that you had mixed a quantity of paris green in a cup? A. Yes, sir.

"Q. At your wife's request, and placed that on a chair near her side? A. Yes, sir.

"Q. Is that right? A. Yes, sir.

"Q. You did that? A. Yes, sir.

"Q. And that she had requested you to do that, so she could drink it. Is that right? A. Yes, sir.

"Q. And that subsequently she did take that? A. Yes, sir.

"Q. And a few hours after that she died. Is that right? A. Yes, sir."

Examined by Mr. Dusenberry:

"Q. Had she ever tried to commit suicide before? A. Yes, sir.

"Q. When was that? A. Last summer.

"Q. What means did she try to use? A. Carbolic acid.

"Q. So that by her previous actions you knew that she was desirous of dying? A. Yes, sir."

The court, after having a private conference with defendant, proceeded to sentence him in the following language:

"After hearing your plea of guilty as charged in the information in this case to killing, and murdering your wife, Mr. Roberts, and after hearing the testimony and evidence introduced in court bearing upon the degree of the crime charged, the court hereby determines that you have committed murder in the first degree, and judgment will be rendered accordingly, by the order of the court. Under the finding of the court there is only one sentence that can be pronounced upon you, and that is the severer one, of course. The statute provides that, where murder shall be perpetrated by means of poison, that shall be murder in the first degree, and the punishment shall be confinement in the state's prison.

"It is beyond my comprehension how a human being of normal conditions at least, or apparent normal conditions, can commit such a crime as you have in this case, by placing poison within reach of your wife or giving it to your wife with the intention as you claim. It doesn't make any difference whether she had that intention or not of committing suicide. You are a principal, under the law of the state, to committing the crime of murder. It was, indeed, an inhuman and dastardly act. The sentence of the court is that you be confined to the state's prison, located at Marquette, for the period of your natural life, at hard labor, and in solitary confinement, in accordance with section 15192 of the Compiled Laws of 1915."

[The conviction was affirmed on appeal.]

----

215. Roberts was sentenced on July 12, 1919. He was 35 or 36 years old. He was received at the Marquette prison four days later. On December 19, 1920, his sentence was commuted to imprisonment for five years, so that his sentence was to expire on July 12, 1924. He was discharged from prison on October 23, 1923.

In People v. Kevorkian, 527 N.W.2d 714, 716 (Mich.1994), the court overruled *Roberts* "to the extent that the common-law definition of murder encompasses the act of intentionally providing the means by which a person commits suicide. Only where there is probable cause to believe that death was the direct and natural result of a defendant's act can the defendant be properly bound over on a charge of murder. Where a defendant merely is involved in the events leading up to the death, such as providing the means, the proper charge is assisting in a suicide . . . ." The court upheld the constitutionality of a statute making it a felony to assist a suicide. On the latter constitutional issue, see Washington v. Glucksberg, 521 U.S. 702 (1997); Vacco v. Quill, 521 U.S. 793 (1997).

THE OPEN BOAT

A case comparable in many respects to *Holmes* is The Queen v. Dudley & Stephens, 14 Q.B. 273 (1884). The private yacht *Mignonette* sailed from Southampton on May 19, 1884, bound for Sydney, Australia, where it was to be delivered to its owner. There were four persons aboard, all members of the crew: Dudley, the captain; Stephens, mate; Brooks, seaman; and Parker, a boy of about 17, cabin boy and apprentice seaman. The yacht went down in the South Atlantic and the men and the boy put off in a small dinghy. After 20 days in the boat, during which they had no fresh water except rain water and during the last eight of which they had no food, Dudley, with Stephens's assent, killed the boy. Brooks may have objected. Thereafter all three fed on the body of the boy for four days. On the fifth day they were rescued. According to the jury's special verdict, there was no likelihood that any of them would have survived unless one were killed and eaten, and it so appeared to the men. The defendants were convicted of murder, then a capital crime in England. Their sentences were commuted to six months' imprisonment.[104]

216. If Brooks objected to killing Parker, should he also have been prosecuted, since he ate of the boy's body? If not, should he have been denied any portion of the body? Suppose that before the boy was killed the defendants had acknowledged Brooks's objection to the killing but had said also that since he objected he could not claim a share of sustenance from the killing, which was the only way his objection would have had significance. Should Brooks have been allowed to starve to death even if there was clearly enough for all?

217. If Dudley and Stephens and the boy had agreed to draw lots fairly to see which one should be killed and Brooks had refused to accept the proposal, what should have been done?

(i) Should the three who agreed have drawn lots among themselves, killed the loser, and denied sustenance to Brooks, who would then, so far as the others could tell, die of starvation before rescue? If so, what of the justification for the killing, that it was necessary to preserve life?

(ii) Should the three who agreed have drawn lots, drawing one (fairly) also in the name of Brooks and killing him if the lot drawn for him was the losing one? If so, does he then not have the right to object to inclusion in the drawing (at least so long as he acknowledges that he will not be entitled to sustenance from the body of the loser)? By what authority is his objection overcome?

Suppose Dudley and Stephens announce that lots will be drawn (fairly) over the objection of the other two and that the loser will be killed and eaten. If they then conduct a fair drawing and the boy loses, is the boy's life forfeited? If so, by what authority is his objection to being included in the drawing overcome?

218. If the decision of three, or two, or one powerful enough to make his (their) decision effective does not overcome the objections of one, or

104. For a highly detailed account of the case and the factual background, see A.W. Brian Simpson, Cannibalism and the Common Law (1984). Simpson gives information about other similar disasters and observes that cannibalism *in extremis* was part of the custom of the sea: "[T]he popular literature, augmented by the unrecorded tales seamen told each other, ensured that there was general understanding of what had to be done on these occasions and that survivors who had followed the custom could have a certain professional pride in a job well done; there was nothing to hide." Id. at 144–45. Another book that tells in narrative form the story of the last voyage of the *Mignonette* and the trial that followed and also includes some pictures is Neil Hanson, The Custom of the Sea (1999).

two, or three, is it the case that there can be no lottery at all unless each truly consents; or is it the case that those who agree should conduct a lottery among themselves and deny sustenance even if they do not need the food for themselves to those who withheld consent, who must then surely die? If those who withhold consent are denied sustenance and, leaving enough for the others, they take it by force, are they murderers or merely thieves?

219. Does an individual in society ever have authority to object significantly to the jurisdiction of its criminal laws over him? Of any of its criminal laws? If not, why not? If so, what is the source and nature of the authority, and how does he exercise it? Who decides when an individual is in "the open boat"?

PART TWO

DEVELOPMENT OF THE LAW

In Part One the criminal law was presented largely as a body of formed principles that could be tested by setting them against one another and against policies of the criminal law, more general social policies, and individual and social values. Sometimes it was necessary to depart from this examination of the law as fixed at a moment in time and to regard it as a *process*, which was most fully understood by observing its changes. The distinctions between murder and voluntary manslaughter and between degrees of murder, for example, are best perceived in the context of their sources, now well in the past, and their probable modifications in the future.

Part Two explores the criminal law primarily as a social process: first, by observing the growth, maturation, and consolidation of the law relating to three forms of theft—larceny, embezzlement, and false pretenses; and second, by raising sets of questions about the ownership and acquisition of property that have persistently confronted the law and continue to do so. The development of the three historical forms illustrates the fundamental question that remains at the heart of the policies and practices on which a law of theft depends: How ought the law separate kinds of appropriation that are prohibited from those that are permitted or even encouraged? The materials in this Part are unified by the theme of "property" and its protection by criminal law.

So far as these materials permit, study the problems presented in the light of the historical and legal contexts in which they arose, or arise, or will arise. If the question is, "Is A guilty of theft?" look for your answer not in a code or book of reports—where, likely as not, you would not find it anyway—but in the sources out of which the law develops. Often, questions are asked and the response that has been given by a court, or the courts, or a code or commentator, provided immediately thereafter or in a footnote. Such responses do not necessarily provide answers to the questions asked.

Cautionary note: In the historical materials, a few cases and statutes are presented in considerable detail because from our current vantage they seem to be major landmarks. Whether they seemed to mark much of anything at the time they appeared is another question, as is the question whether they will seem to do so in the future. Cases or statutes may acquire reputations beyond their contemporary or historical importance for reasons as remote as inclusion in a book of cases or citation in a treatise and then, by later application, acquire importance to justify their reputation. The result may or may not be good law; it is certainly bad history.

---

1. BALES OF WOAD

1473. England, the thirteenth year in the reign of King Edward IV. The times were disorderly. Violence was commonplace, and property was insecure. An Italian diplomat stationed in England around 1500 wrote to his superiors that "there is no country in the world where there are so many thieves and robbers as in England."[1] "In the England of the later middle ages the preservation of public order was very often the biggest problem the king had to face. It was not just a police matter. At heart were the crucial issues of royal authority and the structure of the state, whether they were to survive in their existing forms or wither away." J. Bellamy, Crime and Public Order in England in the Later Middle Ages 1 (1973).

A foreign merchant, probably a Genoese or Venetian, entrusted some bales of goods to a carrier, who was to carry them to Southampton. The carrier broke open the bales and took the goods. He abandoned them somewhere in London, and they were recovered. The merchant sought the return of his goods. The Sheriff of London also claimed them. Property that was taken feloniously and later abandoned by the felon became *waif*, which belonged to the king or his delegate, the sheriff in this case since the goods were recovered in London.

The goods were woad, a blue dye used in the woolen industry. The production of and trade in wool and woolen goods was a major economic enterprise in England.[2] Even the king was a wool merchant. Earlier, most of the trading had been done by foreign merchants. By 1473 their dominance had declined, but foreign merchants were still a significant factor in English commerce and their interests could not lightly be set aside. The treatment of aliens was an important subject of international diplomacy. The merchant whose goods were taken, moreover, traveled with a covenant of safe conduct from the king.

The sheriff had no claim to the goods unless the carrier had committed larceny, the only felony at all related to the facts.[3] The law on larceny did

---

1. A Relation of the Island of England (Camden Society O.S. No. 37) 34 (trans. C. Sneyd 1847).

2. "[W]ool entered into every phase of English life in the middle ages. English economy, society and government reacted, each in its own way, to changes in the wool trade: its ebb and flow, its varying relations with the crown, and its continually changing organiza-

tion." E. Power, The Wool Trade in English Medieval History 19 (1941).

3. The other felonies were treason, murder (and manslaughter, when the two became separate), rape, robbery, burglary, arson, and mayhem. See generally 2 Stephen, History 192–94.

not support the sheriff. "Larceny is the treacherous taking of a corporeal movable thing of another, against the will of him to whom it belongs, by evil acquisition of possession or of the use. Taking, we say: for bailment or livery excludes larceny." The Mirror of Justices (7 Selden Society) 25 (W. Whittaker ed., 1895).[4] Some legal experts thought that if the owner of an object delivered it to another person for a very limited purpose and continued to exercise control over it, true possession remained in the owner, so that if the other person made off with it, it was larceny; such a case might be an innkeeper's delivery of a cup to a man when he served him a drink or a master's delivery of his goods to a servant.

How should the case be decided?

————

Anon. v. The Sheriff of London
(The Carrier's Case)

Y.B. Pasch. 13 Edw. 4 pl. 5 (1473), 64 Selden Society 30 (1945)[5]

Before the King's Council[6] in the Star Chamber the matter shown and debated was how a man had made a bargain with another to carry certain

---

4. The Mirror is a work of uncertain authorship and doubtful authority written around 1290. See F. Maitland's introduction to the Selden Society edition, id. at ix–lv. On this point, at any rate, its accuracy is accepted. See 3 Stephen, History 134–35. "[P]rimitive law in its weakness did not get much beyond an effort to prevent violence, and very naturally made a wrongful taking, a trespass, part of its definition of the crime." Holmes, "The Path of the Law," 10 Harv. L. Rev. 456, 470 (1897). " '[T]aking and carrying away' . . . had been from the first the very core of the English idea of theft. 'He stole, took and carried away': this is the charge made against the thief. The crime involves a violation of possession; it is an offence against a possessor and therefore can never be committed by a possessor." 2 F. Pollock & F. Maitland, The History of English Law 498 (2d ed. 1911).

5. The report of this case appears in the Year Book for 1473, the thirteenth year of the reign of Edward 4. "Pasch." indicates that the case was heard in the Easter (Paschal) Term.

The year books are the earliest English case reports. Cases in the earliest collections date from the second half of the thirteenth century; the series continues largely uninterrupted until 1535, when the series ends. Of unknown authorship, the year books were private compilations probably based on notes taken in open court by the compiler of the year book or others. The report of the Carrier's Case illustrates a feature of the year books: they were more concerned with the subtleties of pleading and the display of skill in oral argument than with the decision of a case and the reasoning on which the decision was based. At least in the earlier years, they were not intended to provide prior decisions on which courts or counsel could rely as precedents.

[6] The King's Council originated as a body of his personal advisers which met to consider political and administrative as well as judicial matters; there was at first no clear separation of the latter from other issues important to the Crown. Justices of both of the king's courts (King's Bench and Common Pleas) as well as serjeants (see n.7 below) and other legal experts might be summoned to consult with the council on legal matters. The council did not have a clearly defined jurisdiction. It acted in response to petitions for extraordinary relief; after taking the special action that was required, it often referred

bales of woad and other things to Southampton, and he took them and carried them to another place, and broke open the bales and took the goods contained in the same feloniously and converted them to his own use, and concealed them. And the case was whether this could be called felony or not.

Bryan [C.J.C.P.].[7] It seems not, for where they aver that the party has possession by bailment and lawful delivery, there cannot afterwards be said to be felony or trespass touching this; and there can be no felony except with violence and *vi et armis*. But such thing as he himself holds, he cannot take *vi et armis* nor against the peace; therefore it cannot be said to be felony or trespass, for there can be no action for these goods except action of detinue etc.

Huse. It is felony to claim the goods feloniously without cause from the party with intent to defraud him to whom the property belongs, *animo furandi*. And here, notwithstanding the bailment as above, the property remains in him who made the bailment etc. Hence he to whom they were given, can claim this property feloniously just as well as a stranger can; therefore it may well be felony.

The Chancellor. Felony is according to the intent, and the intent here may just as well be felony as if he had not possession.

Molyneux. To the same effect. A thing done lawfully may be said to be felony or trespass according to the intent and the circumstances, to wit, if he who committed the act does not carry out the purpose for which he took the goods. For instance, if a man distrains for damage feesant or rent in arrear, and then he sells the goods or slaughters the beasts, this is now tort, and yet at the start the taking was good. So it is here. So it is if a man comes to a tavern to drink, this is lawful, but if he took the drinking cup or committed other trespass, then everything is wrong. So although the taking was lawful, to carry *ut supra*, when he took the goods and carried them to another place *ut supra*, he did not carry out his purpose; so, by his action later, it may be said to be felony or trespass according to the intent etc.

a case to another court or to a special commission for decision. It "gave attention to anything that, because of the incompleteness of the law, required in whole or part exceptional treatment." I. Leadam & J. Baldwin, Select Cases Before the King's Council 1243–1482 (35 Selden Society) xxvi (1918). Among the reasons why the Carrier's Case might have reached the council are that the king's interests were affected; that the problems of an alien merchant, involving the treatment of foreigners, were a matter of diplomatic importance; and that an alien had no right to sue as a plaintiff in the king's courts. The Star Chamber, so named because there were stars on the ceiling, was a room in which the council often met. In the sixteenth century the "Star Chamber" became the name given

to a court for criminal cases on which members of the council sat.

[7] Bryan was Chief Justice of the Court of Common Pleas. Of the others whose views are given, Choke was a justice of the Court of Common Pleas; Needham and Laken were justices of the Court of King's Bench; Huse, Vavasour, and perhaps Molyneux were serjeants. *Serjeants* were a small, select group of lawyers with special duties and prerogatives from whose ranks the judges were selected. Huse and Vavasour later became judges. Serjeants might participate in discussions of the council on matters of law generally in the same manner as the judges. Their views are commonly reported in the year books with as much evidence of the reporter's interest as the views of judges.

Bryan [C.J.C.P.]. Where a man has done something of his own will it may be a lawful act in one case and not in another, according to his action afterwards, as in the cases that you have put. For his intent shall be judged by his action, but where I have goods by your bailment, this taking cannot afterwards become wrong because of anything etc.

Vavasour. Our case is better than a bailment, for here the goods were not delivered to him but someone made a bargain that he should carry the goods to Southampton *ut supra*. And then if he took them in order to carry them there, then he took them by warrant, and the case put now on the matter shown afterwards in evidence, proves that he took them as a felon and with other intent than to carry them *ut supra*, in which case he took them without warrant, and, because of that he did not carry out his purpose, thus it is felony.

Choke [J.C.P.]. It seems that where a man has goods in his possession by reason of a bailment, he cannot take them feloniously when he is in possession, but yet it seems that it is felony, for here the things which were in the bale were not given to him, but the bales as chose entire were delivered *ut supra* to carry etc. in which case if he had given away the bales or sold them, it would not be felony, but when he broke open and took out of it what was inside, he did this without warrant. Thus if a man is given a tun of wine to carry, if he sells the tun, it is not felony or trespass, but if he took out twenty pints it is felony, for the twenty pints were not given to him, and peradventure he had no knowledge of it at the time of the bailment. So it is if I give the key of my chamber to anyone, if he takes my goods in this chamber, it is felony for they were not given to him.

. . .

And the matter of felony was argued before the justices in the Exchequer Chamber.[8] And all except Needham held that where goods are given to a man he cannot take them feloniously. But *Needham* [J.K.B.] holds the contrary, for he can take them feloniously just as any other person can, and he says that it has been held that a man can take his own goods feloniously. For instance, if I give goods to a man to take care of, and I come secretly like a felon because I want to recover damages against him by a writ of detinue, and I take the goods secretly like a felon, it is felony. And it was held that where a man has possession and it is determined, it may be felony. For example, if I gave a man goods to carry to my house and he took

[8] All the justices of the king's courts assembled to hear cases in the Exchequer Chamber, which "embodied the most expert legal learning and opinion of the day on the common law of England." M. Hemmant, Select Cases in the Exchequer Chamber (51 Selden Society) xviii (1933). A case was referred to the Exchequer Chamber only if it was of special importance and difficulty. It was, strictly speaking, not a court but an assembly, which had no original jurisdiction and no formally established appellate jurisdiction, but all the other major courts referred their hardest cases to it. Cases referred to the assembly became known as Exchequer Chamber cases because the assembly met for a long period in a chamber in the Exchequer buildings; later cases that the assembly debated elsewhere were also called "Exchequer Chamber cases."

them there and then took them out of it, this is felony, for when they were in the house his possession is determined etc. But if a taverner serves a man with a drinking cup and he takes it away, this is felony, for he shall not have possession of this drinking cup, for it was put on the table to enable him to drink. And so it is in my house with my butler or my cellarer; they are only servants to do me service, if they carry off etc. it is felony, for they have not possession, but possession is always mine. It would be otherwise if they were given to the servants, peradventure then it may be that they are not felons etc.

Laken [J.K.B.]. There is a difference it seems between a bailment of goods and a bargain to take and to carry etc., for he has possession delivered to him by the bailment, but by the bargain he has no possession of them (the goods) recognised: until he takes them etc. the which things if he takes them to carry then it is lawful; but if he takes them with other intent than to carry them, so that he does not carry out the purpose, it seems that it shall quite well be said to be felony.

Bryan [C.J.C.P.]. A bargain to carry and a bailment seem to be all one, for in both cases he has authority from the party himself to whom the property belonged, thus it cannot be said to be felony. . . . And in this case the taking cannot be feloniously because the possession was lawful, hence the breaking open of the bale is not felony. . . .

And then the justices made report to the Chancellor that it was felony; yet the goods cannot be claimed as waif since it appears that he who sued here for the goods is an alien and the King has granted him safe and secure conduct, both for his goods and his person. And this is a covenant between the King and himself, hence if a felon takes them, it is not right that this alien shall incur loss or that he shall be put to sue the felon himself, but he shall sue to the King upon the covenant. And it seems that the King cannot have such goods as waif. And for the same reason he cannot grant them to any other person nor can anyone else claim them by prescription.

    . . .

---

220. The justices reported to the Chancellor that "it was felony"; yet all but Needham had held that a man cannot take goods feloniously if they are given to him. What line of reasoning had the justices apparently adopted? Is it sound?

221. Justice Choke compared delivery of the bales to delivery of the key to a room. If a person took the contents of the bales, it was as if he took the goods in the room. Since the latter taking was a felony so was the former. Is the analogy persuasive?

"NOTHING BUT WOAD, WOAD, WOAD!"

222. According to the reasoning of the justices, would the carrier have committed a felony if he had made off with the bales and abandoned them or sold them unopened? Can the distinction be maintained? Would the justices have maintained it if the facts had been as supposed?

223. The decision in the Carrier's Case gave the protection of the king's law to merchants who entrusted their goods to a carrier, and at the same time the merchant in the case recovered his goods. Stephen thought that "the decision was a compromise intended to propitiate the chancellor, and perhaps the king. This required a deviation from the common law, which was accordingly made, but was as slight as the judges could make it. They would have liked to hold that where the original taking was lawful no subsequent dealing with the property could be felonious. The chancellor, who seems to have had regard rather to the position of the owner of the goods than to the criminality of the carrier,[9] seems to have wished to make the matter turn upon the moral character of the act of misappropriation. The judges resorted to the expedient of treating the breaking bulk as a new taking. They thus preserved the common law definition of theft, but qualified it by an obscure distinction resting on no definite principle." 3 Stephen, History 139–40.

[9] In a portion of the report not duplicated here, the chancellor indicated his concern for the merchant whose goods were taken. 64 Selden Society at 32.

224. What *was* the principle established by the Carrier's Case? That if goods given to a man are packaged they are not given to him? Or that if a man is given possession of another man's goods for a particular purpose and does something with them that is inconsistent with the purpose for which they were given to him, his possession of the goods ends, so that by continuing to possess them he takes them? Or only that if a carrier breaks bulk and makes off with the goods, he commits a felony?

What difference does it make?

225. Could the court have reached the same result without resorting to Humpty Dumpty's doctrine: A word means just what we "choose it to mean—neither more nor less"; the question is "which is to be master—that's all." L. Carroll, Through the Looking Glass, ch. 6, at 117 (1902 ed.). Should the court have done so if it could? As Dumpty knew, when a word does "a lot of work" you have to "pay it extra." Id. at 119.

226. In 1821, the Maryland legislature enacted a statute requiring importers of foreign articles to obtain a license costing $50. The statute was challenged on the ground that it was in conflict with the provision of the Constitution art. I, § 10, that "no State shall, without the consent of the congress, lay any imposts or duties on imports or exports, except what may be absolutely necessary for executing its inspection laws." Chief Justice Marshall sought to accommodate the "constitutional prohibition on the States to lay a duty on imports" and "their acknowledged power to tax persons and property within their territory" by the "original package" doctrine: "[G]enerally, . . . when the importer has so acted upon the thing imported, that it has become incorporated and mixed up with the mass of property in the country, it has, perhaps, lost its distinctive character as an import, and has become subject to the taxing power of the State; but while remaining the property of the importer, in his warehouse, in the original form or package in which it was imported, a tax upon it is too plainly a duty on imports to escape the prohibition in the constitution." Brown v. Maryland, 25 U.S. (12 Wheat.) 419, 441–42 (1827). Is Marshall's use of "breaking bulk" to draw a line more acceptable than Choke's? If so, why?

For a recent case remarkably similar to the Carrier's Case, in which the court relied on the doctrine of breaking bulk, see United States v. Mafnas, 701 F.2d 83 (9th Cir.1983).

2. BAD AND FAITHLESS SERVANTS

The "inconvenient and indeed absurd consequences," as Stephen thought them,[10] of the rule that there was no theft unless there was a trespassory taking were partly allayed in the case of a thieving servant by the distinction between "possession" and a "charge."[11]

> For so long as he is in my house or with me, that which I have delivered to him is considered to be in my possession. Thus if my butler, who has my plate in his custody, flees this is felony. And the law is the same if he who has charge of my horse goes off with it. The reason is that the things continued, all the while, to be in my own possession. But if I deliver to my servant a horse to ride to market, and he flees with it there is no felony; for he comes by the horse lawfully, through delivery. Similarly if I give him a ring to take to London, or money to pay to someone or to buy something, and he flees with it; there is no felony. For it is out of my possession and he comes by it lawfully.

Y.B. Hil. 21 Hen. 7, pl. 21 (1506).

Any doubt about the validity of the distinction was resolved in 1529 by enactment of a statute that provided (with an exception for apprentices and persons under eighteen): "That all and singular such servants, to whom any . . . caskets, jewels, money, goods, or chattels, by his or their said masters or mistresses, shall from henceforth . . . be delivered to keep, that if any such servant or servants withdraw him or them from their said masters and mistresses, and go away with the said caskets, jewels, money, goods, or other chattels, or any part thereof, to the intent to steal the same, and defraud his or their said masters or mistresses thereof, contrary to the trust and confidence to him or them put by his or their said masters or mistresses, or else being in the service of his said masters or mistresses, without assent or commandment of his masters or mistresses, he imbezil the same caskets, jewels, money, goods, or chattels, or any part thereof, or otherwise convert the same to his own use, with like purpose to steal it, that if the said caskets, jewels, money, goods, or chattels, that any such servant shall so go away with, or which he shall imbezil with purpose to steal it, as is aforesaid, be of the value of xl. s. [40 shillings] or above, that then the same false, fraudulent, and untrue act or demeanour, from henceforth shall be deemed and adjudged felony; and he or they so offending, to be punished, as other felons be punished for felonies committed, by the course of the common law." 21 Hen. 8, ch. 7.

––––––––

10. 3 Stephen, History 151.

11. Needham made this distinction in the Carrier's Case, see p. 390 above, but it was not yet established in 1473. See Y.B. Mich. 3 Hen. 7 pl. 9 (1487).

227. Did a servant commit felony if he absconded with goods that a third person gave him to take to his master? Does it matter whether the delivery to the servant took place in his master's house or elsewhere? If you were a judge, how would you have ruled, before 1529? After 1529?[12]

---

3.   Embezzlement

By the eighteenth century, business and finance had so developed that there were many business relationships that, like the relationship between master and servant, required the parties to trust one another for some purposes. Certain breaches of the trust engendered by the necessities of business came particularly to public attention. Parliament responded. In 1742, it was made a capital offense for an officer or servant of the Bank of England to embezzle property belonging to the bank, 15 Geo. 2, ch. 13. In 1751, the same courtesy was extended to officers and servants of the South Sea Company, 24 Geo. 2, ch. 11, and in 1765, to officers and servants of the post office, 5 Geo. 3, ch. 25.

In 1799 Joseph Bazeley was employed as principal teller at the banking house of Esdaile and Hammett on Lombard Street. A grocer named William Gilbert sent his servant to the banking house to make a deposit of 137 pounds. Bazeley took the money and entered the deposit in Mr. Gilbert's bankbook. He placed 37 pounds in the appropriate receptacles and pocketed a hundred pound note. Later that day he used the note to pay a bill of the Ding Dong Mining Company, of which he was treasurer. (His annual salary, incidentally, was a hundred pounds.)

Bazeley was prosecuted for felony and found guilty by the jury. The question on appeal was "whether under the circumstances above stated, the taking of the Bank-note was in law a felonious taking, or only a [noncriminal] fraudulent breach of trust."

How would you have argued the case on each side?

How should the case be decided?

The King v. Bazeley

2 Leach 835, 168 Eng. Rep. 517 (Ex. Ch. 1799)

Const, *for the prisoner*, after remarking that the prosecutor[13] never had *actual possession* of the Bank-note, and defining the several offences of

---

12. The development of this aspect of the law of theft is traced by Holmes in Commonwealth v. Ryan, 30 N.E. 364 (Mass.1892).

13. The prosecutor was Esdaile and Hammett, Bazeley's former employer. The practice of relying on private prosecutors to

larceny, fraud, and *breach of trust, viz.* that LARCENY is the taking of valuable property from *the possession* of another *without his consent and against his will*. Secondly, That FRAUD consists in obtaining valuable property from the possession of another *with his consent and will,* by means of some artful device, against the subtilty of which common prudence and caution are not sufficient safeguards.[14] And, Thirdly, That BREACH of TRUST is the abuse or misusing of that property which the owner has, *without any fraudulent seducement*, and with his own *free will and consent*, put, or permitted to be put, either for particular or general purposes, into *the possession* of the trustee, proceeded to argue the case upon the following points.

FIRST, That the prosecutors cannot, in contemplation of law, be said to have had *a constructive possession* of this Bank-note, at the time the prisoner is charged with having tortiously converted it to his own use.

SECONDLY, That supposing the prosecutors to have had the possession of this note, the prisoner, under the circumstances of this case, cannot be said to have tortiously taken it from that possession with a felonious intention to steal it.

THIRDLY, That the relative situation of the prosecutors and the prisoner makes this transaction merely *a breach of trust*; and,

FOURTHLY, That this is not one of those *breaches of trust* which the Legislature has declared to be felony.

THE FIRST POINT, *viz.* That *the prosecutor* cannot, in contemplation of law, be said to have had a constructive possession of this Bank-note at the time *the prisoner* is charged with having tortiously converted it to his own use.—To constitute the crime of larceny, the property must be taken from *the possession* of the owner; this possession must be either actual or constructive; it is clear that the prosecutors had not, upon the present occasion, the *actual possession* of the Bank-note, and therefore the inquiry must be, whether they had the *constructive possession* of it? or, in other words, whether the possession of the servant was, under the circumstances of this case, the possession of the master. Property in possession is said by *Sir William Blackstone* to subsist only where a man hath both *the right to*, and also *the occupation of*, the property. The prosecutors in the present case had only a right or title to possess the note, and not the absolute or even qualified possession of it. It was never in their custody or under their controul. . . . Suppose the prisoner had not parted with the note, but had merely kept it in his own custody, and refused, on any pretence whatever, to deliver it over to his employers, they could only have recovered it by means of an action of trover or detinue, the first of which presupposes the person against whom it is brought, to have obtained possession of the property by lawful means, as by delivery, or finding; and the second, that the right of property only, and not the possession of it, either really or constructively, is in the person bringing it. The prisoner received this note

vindicate the state's interest is still common
in England.

14. See p. 400 below.

See p. 400 below.

by the permission and consent of the prosecutors, while it was passing from the possession of Mr. *Gilbert* to the possession of Messrs. *Esdaile's and Hammett's*; and not having reached its destined goal, but having been thus intercepted in its transitory state, it is clear that it never came to the *possession* of the prosecutors. It was delivered into the possession of the prisoner, upon an implied confidence on the part of the prosecutors, that he would deliver it over into their possession, but which, from the pressure of temporary circumstances, he neglected to do: at the time therefore of the supposed conversion of this note, it was in the legal possession of the prisoner. To divest the prisoner of this possession, it certainly was not necessary that he should have delivered this note into the hands of the prosecutors, or of any other of their servants personally; for if he had deposited it in the drawer kept for the reception of this species of property, it would have been a delivery of it into the possession of his masters; but he made no such deposit: and instead of determining in any way his own possession of it, he conveyed it immediately from the hand of Mr. *Gilbert's* clerk into his own pocket. Authorities are not wanting to support this position. . . .

SECONDLY, Supposing the prosecutor to have had *the possession* of this note, yet the prisoner, under the circumstances of this case, cannot be said to have tortiously taken it from that possession with a felonious intent to steal it. . . . In the present case there was no evidence whatever to shew that any such intention existed in his mind at the time the note came to his hands . . . . Besides, the prisoner had given a bond to account faithfully for the monies that should come to his hands; he was the agent of a trading company, and had the means of converting bills into cash, which would have enabled him, at the time, to repay to the prosecutor the 100*l.* which he *detained for his own use*; but if, at the very time he received the note, he had no intent to steal it, it is no felony; for *Sir Edward Coke*, and all the writers on Crown Law agree, that the intent to steal must be when the property comes to his hands or possession; and that if he have the possession of it once lawfully, though he hath the *animus furandi* afterwards, when he carrieth it away, it is no larceny.

BUT, THIRDLY, the situation which the prisoner held, and the capacity in which he acted in the banking-house of the prosecutors, make this transaction only *a breach of trust*. . . .

FOURTHLY. But *a breach of trust* is not, either by the Common Law or by Act of Parliament, in this case, felony. . . . [I]f there be such a consent of the owner of the property as argues *a trust* in the prisoner, and gives him a possession against all strangers, then his breaking that trust, or abusing that possession, though to the owner's utter deceit of all his interest in those goods, it will not be felony. . . . Taking it, therefore, as a settled point, that a *breach of trust* cannot, by the rules of the *common law*, be converted into a felonious taking, the next and last inquiry will be, in what cases the Legislature has made this particular breach of trust felony. There are only four statutes upon this subject, *viz.* the 21 Hen. VIII. c. 7, the 15 Geo. II. c. 13. s. 12, the 5 Geo. III. c. 35. s. 17, and 7 Geo. III. c. 50. The two last Acts relate entirely and exclusively to breaches of trust committed by servants employed in the business of *the Post-Offices*; and the second to breaches of trust committed by servants employed in the business of *the Bank of England*, and of course, cannot affect, in any manner whatever, the present case. Nor can the case of the prisoner be construed within the statute 21 Hen. VIII. c. 7 . . . for it has been determined upon this statute, that it is strictly confined to such goods as are *delivered* by the master to the servant to *keep*. But this Bank-note, as has been already shewn, was not in the possession of the master, and therefore it cannot have been *delivered* by him; it being impossible for a man to deliver, either by himself or his agent, a thing of which he is neither actually nor constructively possessed; but, even admitting that it had been in the master's possession, and delivered by him to the prisoner, it would not have been delivered to him *to keep*, but for the purpose of entering it faithfully in the book, and handing it over to the Bank-note cashier. The authorities, however, are still stronger upon this point of the case; for it is said by *Sir William Staund-ford*, *Sir Edward Coke*, *Hale*, and *Hawkins*, in their comments upon this statute, "that a receiver, who, having received his master's rents, runs away with them; or a servant, who, being entrusted to sell goods, & c. departs with the money; is not within the statute."[15] . . .

FIELDING, *for the Crown*, argued the case entirely on the question, Whether the prosecutors, *Esdaile* and *Hammett*, had such a constructive possession of the Bank-note as to render the taking of it by the prisoner felony? He insisted, that in the case of personal chattels, *the possession* in law follows the right of property; and, that as *Gilbert's* clerk did not deposit the notes with *Bazeley* as a matter of trust to him; for they were paid at the counter, and in the banking-house of the prosecutors, of which *Bazeley* was merely one of the organs; and, therefore, the payment to him was in effect a payment to them, and his receipt of them vested the property *eo instanter* in their hands, and gave them the legal *possession* of it. . . .

THE JUDGES, it is said, were of opinion that this Bank-note never was in the legal custody or possession of the prosecutors, Messrs. *Esdaile* and *Hammett*; but no opinion was ever publicly delivered; and the prisoner was included in the Secretary of State's letter as a proper object for a pardon.

———

228. In a note to the case the reporter states: "On consultation among the Judges, some doubt was at first entertained; but at last all assembled agreed that it was not felony, inasmuch as the note was never in the possession of the bankers, distinct from the possession of the prisoner: though it would have been otherwise if the prisoner had deposited it in the drawer, and had afterwards taken it." 168 Eng. Rep. at 523. Thus, by 1799, the answer to the question in note 227, p. 393 above, was clear: it was not larceny for a servant to make off with something given to him for delivery to his master. If the hundred pound note had passed into the bank's

15. 4 Bac. Abr. 590.

possession even for a moment and even if the "possession" were no more than placing it in a drawer set aside for that purpose, his subsequent removal of it would have been larceny. Would Humpty Dumpty have thought that the notion of "trespassory taking" had earned extra pay in such a case?

229. What was Fielding, for the Crown, saying when he urged that Esdaile and Hammett had "constructive possession" of the bank-note? Should the court have accepted his argument? Would it have been easier or harder for the court to do so if Parliament had not enacted the statutes mentioned by Const, for the defense?

———

Bazeley got in just under the wire (which, in fact, he helped to string up). Less than three months after his case was argued, Parliament, noting that there were doubts whether such conduct "amounts to Felony," enacted 39 Geo. 3, ch. 85 (1799), "an act to protect masters against embezzlements by their clerks or servants." The first general embezzlement statute, it applied to "any servant or clerk, or any person employed for the purpose in the capacity of a servant or clerk," and made it a felony punishable by transportation to embezzle goods or any valuables received or taken into possession in behalf of the employer.

As might have been expected the wire was not yet strung low enough. In 1812, the general embezzlement statute was found not to cover a stockbroker who diverted a client's funds to his own use, since he was neither a servant nor a clerk. The King v. Walsh, 168 Eng. Rep. 624 (1812). Parliament responded promptly with a statute covering persons acting as a banker, merchant, broker, attorney, or agent "of any description whatsoever." 52 Geo. 3, ch. 63 (1812).[16]

4. CHEATS AND FRAUDS

Not long after 1529, when Parliament attended to the problem of untrustworthy servants, it turned to artisans and merchants, whose low standard of commercial morality was too low even for that disorderly period.[17] The common law had already developed the crime of cheating, a

---

16. Coverage was still not complete. See 7 & 8 Geo. 4, ch. 29, § 51 (1827); 20 & 21 Vict., ch. 54 (1857).

17. "[I]f there was any way of evading the regulations and earning a dishonest penny, there were plenty of craftsmen ready to do so. Fraudulent weights and measures were

misdemeanor.[18] Generally it was cheating to deprive someone of his property by fraud involving the use of a token or device or practice which was directed at the public at large and against which prudence was no protection. "Simple" dishonesty in business was regarded as a risk of doing business, against which the criminal law could not or should not give protection.

The statute of 33 Hen. 8, ch. 1, enacted in 1541, "a bill against them that counterfeit letters or privy tokens to receive money or goods in other men's names," carried forward this distinction: "[B]e it ordained and enacted by authority of this present parliament, that if any person or persons . . . falsely and deceitfully obtain or get into his or their hands or possession, any money, goods, chattels, jewels, or other things of any other person or persons, by colour and means of any such false token or counterfeit letter made in any other man's name, as is aforesaid, that then every person and persons so offending, and being thereof lawfully convict . . . shall have and suffer such correction and punishment, by imprisonment of his body, setting upon the pillory, or otherwise by any corporal pain (except pains of death) as shall be unto him or them limited, adjudged or appointed by the person or persons before whom he shall be so convict of the said offenses, or of any of them." As at common law, the crime was a misdemeanor.

------

230. Was the distinction between "public" and "private" fraud, or fraud against which common prudence could or could not guard, which was made by the common law and confirmed by the statute, sound? Why (not)? Was the means of marking the distinction, the use of a "false token or counterfeit letter," sound?[19]

Two centuries later, in 1757, Parliament abandoned the distinction. The statute of 30 Geo. 2, ch. 24 made it a misdemeanor for any person "knowingly and designedly, by false pretense or pretenses . . . [to] obtain

---

constantly being seized by the authorities; cloth was so stretched that when it was wetted it would shrink and become useless, or it was so folded that defects were not visible; pots were made of such base metal that they melted as soon as they were put on the fire; and everything that could be adulterated was. It is quite a mistake to suppose that the medieval tradesman was an honest and innocent being whose descendants have been corrupted by the commercialism of our age." L. Salzman, English Life in the Middle Ages 241–42 (1926).

18. There were also many statutes prohibiting fraudulent practices in a particular industry. For example, in the woolen industry, 3 Hen. 8, ch. 6 (1511) (adding oil or water, etc., to wool cloth, or over-stretching it, etc.); 5 Hen. 8, ch. 4 (1513) (adding gum or oil to worsted to make it look like a better grade cloth); 34 & 35 Hen. 8, ch. 11 (1542–43) (making "Welsh friezes," a type of cloth, that are undersized or underweight).

19. For another way of marking the distinction, developed by the courts rather than the legislature, see p. 710 note 452 below.

from any person or persons, money, goods, wares or merchandizes, with intent to cheat or defraud any person or persons of the same."

The case of R. v. Wheatly, 97 Eng.Rep. 746 (1761), was decided four years later. Wheatly was charged in an indictment with having "falsely, fraudulently and deceitfully" sold and delivered to Richard Webb as 18 gallons of amber (a beer) what was really only 16 gallons, for which he received 15 shillings. He was convicted. Defense counsel made a motion in arrest of judgment on the ground that the facts charged showed only a breach of a civil contract. The prosecutor argued that the case involved "a *cheat*, a *public fraud*, in the course of his *trade*": "here is a *false pretence*, at the least: and it appeared upon the trial to be a very foul case." Id. at 747.

The defense prevailed. Lord Mansfield said: "And that the fact here charged should not be considered as an indictable offence, but left to a civil remedy by an action, is reasonable and right in the nature of the thing: because it is only an inconvenience and injury to a *private* person, arising from that private person's own negligence and *carelessness* in not measuring the liquor, upon receiving it, to see whether it held out the just measure or not.

"The offence that is indictable must be such a one as affects the PUBLIC. As if a man *uses false weights and measures*, and sells *by them* to all or to many of his customers, or uses them in the *general* course of his dealing: so, if a man defrauds another, under *false tokens*. For these are deceptions that *common* care and prudence are not sufficient to guard against. So, if there be a *conspiracy* to cheat: for *ordinary* care and caution is no guard against this.

"Those cases are much more than mere private injuries: they are *public offences*. But here, it is a mere *private* imposition or deception: no false weights or measures are used; no false tokens given; no conspiracy; only an imposition upon the person he was dealing with, in delivering him a less quantity instead of a greater which the other carelessly accepted. 'Tis only a non-performance of his contract: for which nonperformance, he may bring his action." Id. at 748. The other judges concurred.[20]

———

On July 2, 1779, Pear went to Samuel Finch's livery stable in London and hired a horse. Pear told Finch that he wanted to take the horse to Sutton and would return with it at about eight o'clock that evening. He said that he lived at No. 25 in King-street. Pear sold the horse on the same day to William Hollist in Smithfield Market. He had no lodgings at No. 25 in King-street.

He was indicted and tried for stealing the horse. Justice Ashhurst asked the jury to find specially whether Pear "meant *at the time of the hiring* to take such journey, but was *afterwards* tempted to sell the horse . . . [or] if . . . at the time of the hiring the journey was a mere pretence to get the horse into his possession, and he had no intention to take such journey but intended to sell the horse." The jury found that Pear "had hired the horse with a fraudulent view and intention of selling it immediately." The King v. Pear, 168 Eng. Rep. 208, 209 (Ex. Ch. 1779).

Justice Ashhurst referred to all the judges the question whether Pear's conversion of the horse was felonious. The loss of a horse was a serious matter. How should the judges have responded to the question?

A majority of the judges concluded that since Pear's original intention in hiring the horse was fraudulent, "the parting with the *property* had not changed the nature of the *possession*, but that it remained unaltered in the prosecutor at the time of the conversion; and that the prisoner was therefore guilty of felony." Id. at 209.

According to East, the case was considered by only eleven of the twelve judges, Justice Blackstone being absent on account of illness.[21] Of the eleven, ten judges thought that Pear's offense was a felony at common law:

[L]arceny was defined by Lord Coke to mean a felonious and fraudulent taking and carrying away of the goods of another. But it was settled by old authorities, that the taking need not be by force. If a carrier or porter received goods to carry from one place to another, and he opened the pack and sold them; that was felony: yet in that case there was no taking by force, but on a delivery by the owner. That the

---

20. There is no mention in the report of *Wheatly* of the statute enacted four years earlier.

21. East notes that Blackstone "always held that it was a felony." 2 E. East, Pleas of the Crown 686 n. b. (1803).

reason assigned for the determination in Kel. 82[22] was because the opening and disposing of them declared that his intent originally was not to take the goods upon the agreement and contract of the party, but only with a design of stealing them. So if A. cheapened goods of B.'s and B. delivered them to A. to look at, and A. ran away with them; this was felony by the apparent intent of A. T. Ray. 276. Kel. 82. So if a horse were upon sale, and the owner let the thief mount him in order to try him, and the thief rode away with him, it was felony. Kel. 82. So in the case of one Tunnard, tried at the O.B. in October Sessions 1729, who was indicted for stealing a brown mare of Henry Smith's, and upon the evidence it appeared, that Smith lived in the Isle of Ely, and lent Tunnard the mare to ride three miles; but he, instead of riding three miles only, rode her up to London and sold her: this was holden to be felony. And Lord C.J. Raymond, who tried the prisoner, left it to the jury to consider, Whether Tunnard rode away with her with an intent to steal her? and the jury found him guilty. That here the same directions were given to the jury by the learned Judge who tried the prisoner, and the jury had given the same verdict. That even in the case of burglary, which the law defined to be the breaking into a house in the night time with intent to commit felony, if a man procured the door of a house to be opened by fraud, and by that means entered into the house through the door-way without any actual breaking, it had been adjudged to be burglary. That in all these cases the intention was the thing chiefly regarded, and fraud supplied the place of force. That what was the intention was a fact, which in every case must be left upon the evidence to the sound judgment of a jury. And in this case the jury had found that at the time when the prisoner obtained the possession of the mare, he intended to steal her. That the obtaining the possession of the mare, and afterwards disposing of her in the manner stated, was in the construction of law such a taking as would have made the prisoner liable to an action of trespass at the suit of the owner, if he had not intended to steal her. For she was delivered to the prisoner for a special purpose only, viz. to go to Sutton, which he never intended to do, but immediately sold her.

2 E. East, Pleas of the Crown 687–88 (1803). The eleventh judge "held that this was not felony by the common law; because there was no actual taking of the mare by the prisoner." Id. at 687.

What of the statutes, 33 Hen. 8, ch. 1, and 30 Geo. 2, ch. 24? Seven of the ten judges who thought Pear's act was a felony at common law concluded that the statutes did not affect the result.

[T]he stat. of Hen. 8, was confined to the cases of obtaining goods *in other men's names, by false tokens or counterfeit letters,* made in any other man's name. The stat. of Geo. 2 extended that law to all cases where goods were obtained by *false pretences* of any kind. But both

---

[22] J. Kelyng, Pleas of the Crown, pub-   Chief Justice from 1665 to 1671.
lished in 1708. Sir John Kelyng was Lord

these statutes were confined to cases where credit was obtained in the name of a third person; and did not extend to cases where a man, on his own account, got goods with an intention to steal them. That besides, the seven Judges held that neither of those statutes were intended to mitigate the common law, or to make that a less offence which was a greater before. On the contrary, the Legislature, by those statutes, meant to inflict a severer punishment in the cases of fraud than the common law had done. That in many cases it was extremely difficult, and sometimes impossible to prove what the offender's original intention was. . . . That where an original felonious intent appeared, the statutes did not apply. Where no such intent appeared, if the means mentioned in the statutes were made use of, the Legislature had made the offender answerable criminally, who before by the common law of the land was only answerable civilly. That in the prisoner's case the intention was apparent, and the jury had rightly found that it was felonious. The crime then was felony, and of a nature which the statute law had made punishable with death.

Id. at 689.

Two of the remaining judges thought that since the two statutes "had made the offence of obtaining goods by false tokens or false pretences, punishable as a misdemeanor only; and the stat. 33. H. 8. had distinguished the case of obtaining goods by false tokens from the case of obtaining goods by stealth; they were bound by those statutes to say, that the prisoner's offence was not felony." Id. at 687.[23]

---

231. How do you explain the confusion among the judges? Was the majority's conclusion "a novelty, and an unwarranted modification of the

---

23. East's careful analysis of the judge's views breaks down at this point and leaves unexplained the views of one dissenting judge. He does say, as indicated above, that only one judge thought the offense was not a felony at common law and that the doubt of the dissenters was based chiefly on the statutes. Id. at 686.

law of larceny"?[24] Look back to the exchange between Molyneux for the Crown and Chief Justice Bryan and to the opinion of Justice Needham in the Carrier's Case.

232. Pear's Case is regarded as the source of the crime of larceny by trick, in which fraud replaces force as the "trespassory" element. Would it be more accurate to find the source of larceny by trick in the Carrier's Case? Look again at p. 392 note 224 above. Kelyng was not the only one who thought that the analytic significance of breaking bulk in the Carrier's Case was not, as Choke had argued, that the carrier thereby took the contents of the bales but that it showed that the carrier's "intent originally was not to take the goods upon the agreement and contract of the party, but only with a design of stealing them." Kel. 82 (1789 ed.).[25] That analysis, of course, left unsatisfied the element of *taking*—satisfied in Choke's argument on the shaky ground that the merchant had never given up possession of the *contents* of the bales to the carrier—which most authorities up to the time of Pear's Case satisfied by the argument that the carrier's deviation from the contract to carry "determined" the bailment so that possession was restored to the merchant and the carrier's misappropriation was a taking from the merchant's possession: "the privity of contract is determined by the act of breaking the package which makes him a trespasser," 2 E. East, Pleas of the Crown 697 (1803).[26]

24. Beale, "The Borderland of Larceny," 6 Harv. L. Rev. 244, 248 (1892).

25. Kelyng was unhappy about this analysis, since taking the whole seemed as good an indication of a prior intent to steal as taking a part: "But I marvel at the case put, 13 E. 4. 9. That if a carrier have a tun of wine delivered to him to carry to such a place, and he never carry it but sell it, all this is no felony; but if he draw part of it out above the value of twelve-pence, this is felony; I do not see why the disposing of the whole should not be felony also." Kel. 83 (1789 ed.).

26. Kelyng apparently limited that argument to a case in which a carrier carried out his bargain and brought the goods to the place appointed and thereafter took them. See Kel. 83 (1789 ed.). He does not explain whether and, if so, how he thinks the requirement of a taking would be satisfied in a case in which the goods are taken before the carriage is completed, evidently because he thought the Carrier's Case did not involve those facts. See id.

The ease with which the elements of taking and intent could be confused or con-

flated is suggested by Chisser's Case, 83 Eng. Rep. 142 (K.B. 1678), on which the judges relied in Pear's Case, see p. 402 above ("T. Ray 276"). The defendant was shown goods in a shop and ran off with them. The court said that it was felony: "He shall be said to have taken these goods *feleo* [sic] *animo*; for the act subsequent, *viz. His running away with them*, explains his intent precedent . . . ." 83 Eng. Rep. at 142. The element of taking in such a case was satisfied by the distinction between a charge and possession, according to which the goods remained in the possession of the shopkeeper while they were being shown to Chisser. That distinction was not easily applicable to Pear's Case, in which Pear had rented the horse to ride away. East noticed the point, as did some of the judges who considered Pear's Case, see 2 E. East, Pleas of the Crown 683–84 (1803). East says that some judges thought that the notion of a "charge" whereby the owner remained in possession of goods physically delivered to another in his presence was "too refined, as setting up a legal fiction against the fact, which ought never to be done in criminal cases." Id.

233. The Carrier's Case is regarded as the source of the doctrine of breaking bulk. But Choke's view, which made breaking bulk, as opposed to other ways of "determining the bailment" like selling the goods intact, particularly significant, was not applied before the nineteenth century,[27] before which time a view like that expressed by the Chancellor in the King's Council seems to have prevailed. At what point did the doctrine of breaking bulk become part of the law? When Choke, reasoning by a doubtful analogy to earlier cases, stated it? Or when, in the nineteenth century, judges relied on it?

234. Had Pear in fact committed two crimes, neither one very well established: larceny, according to the suggestions made in the Carrier's Case 300 years before; and false pretenses, according to the act of Parliament 22 years before? If so, the judges' confusion is understandable. Larceny of a horse was a capital felony. False pretenses was not.

235. How did the ten judges who thought, the statute aside, that Pear's offense was a felony reconcile the common law and the statute? How would you have reconciled them?

———

The view of the majority in Pear's Case that the statute of 30 Geo. 2, ch. 24, was "confined to cases where credit was obtained in the name of a third person," p. 403, may have been necessary to rationalize their decision, but it was not supported by anything in the statute. It did not prevail. Ten years later the judges of the King's Bench heard an appeal in the case of Young v. The King, 100 Eng. Rep. 475 (1789). Young and three other defendants were indicted for obtaining property by false pretenses in violation of the statute. According to the indictment the defendants obtained money from one Thomas by falsely pretending to have made bets about a race to be run on the following day and inducing Thomas to cover some of the bets. They were convicted and sentenced to be transported for seven years.

On appeal counsel for the defendants argued that their conduct did not constitute an offense under the statute, which, he said, did not cover cases "against which common caution may guard." The defendants' false pretense was "a bare naked lie, without any appearance of truth." Id. at 477. The argument was rejected.

"Lord Kenyon, Ch. J.— . . . said, undoubtedly this indictment, being founded on the statute of 30 Geo. 2, c. 24, is different from a common law

---

27. E.g., Rex v. Madox, Russ. & Ry. 92 (1805). Other cases are cited in F. Pollock & R. Wright, Possession in the Common Law 133 n.1 (1888). For an American case, see, e.g., Robinson v. State, 41 Tenn. (1 Cold.) 120 (1860).

indictment. When it passed, it was considered to extend to every case where a party had obtained money by falsely representing himself to be in a situation in which he was not, or any occurrence that had not happened, to which persons of ordinary caution might give credit. The statute of the 33 Hen. 8, cl. 1, requires a false seal, or token, to be used in order to bring the person imposed upon into confidence of the other; but that being found to be insufficient, the statute 30 Geo. 2, c. 24, introduced another offense, describing it in terms extremely general. It seems difficult to draw the line, and to say to what cases this statute shall extend; and therefore we must see whether each particular case, as it arises, comes within it. In the present case, four men came to the prosecutor representing a race as about to take place, that William Lewis should go a certain distance within a limited time; that they had betted upon the event, and they should probably win: he was perhaps too credulous, and gave confidence to them, and advanced his money; and afterwards the whole story proved to be an absolute fiction. Then the defendants, morally speaking, have been guilty of an offence. I admit that there are certain irregularities which are not the subject of criminal law. But when the criminal law happens to be auxiliary to the law of morality, I do not feel any inclination to explain it away. Now this offence is within the words of the Act; for the defendants have by false pretenses fraudulently contrived to obtain money from the prosecutor; and I see no reason why it should not be held to be within the meaning of the statute. . . .

"Ashhurst, J.— . . . Cases which happened before the passing of the 30 Geo. 2, c. 24, do not apply to this. For that statute created an offence which did not exist before, and I think it includes the present. The Legislature saw that all men were not equally prudent, and this statute was passed to protect the weaker part of mankind. The words of it are very general . . . ." Id. at 477–78. Justices Buller and Grose wrote opinions to the same effect.

Was Pear, then, guilty of false pretenses (as well as larceny, perhaps) after all? Apparently not. The rule was established that if the owner of goods was fraudulently induced to part not only with the possession of them but also with the property in them—if he intended to pass ownership when he delivered them to his defrauder—it was not larceny. For example, in The King v. Harvey, 168 Eng. Rep. 355 (Chelmsford Assizes 1787), the defendant purchased a horse for eight pounds and, after saying to the seller that he would return immediately and pay for the horse, rode off and never returned. The court said: "It is impossible by any construction whatever to make this case a felony. . . . [T]he delivery was unconditional, and the contract was completed. It was a sale; and the *property* as well as the *possession* was entirely parted with. The prisoner has defrauded the prosecutor of *the price* of the horse, but not of the horse itself; and the only remedy the prosecutor has is by action to recover the eight pounds . . . ." Id. at 335–36.[28] The rule that larceny was committed only if possession and

---

28. In his report of Pear's Case, East notes: "On the debate in this case Eyre B., adverting to these statutes [33 H. 8, cl. 1, and 30 Geo. 2, c. 24], said he doubted if there

not property was passed was accompanied by a somewhat different rule, that if only possession was passed, the statutory crime of false pretenses was not committed. Since Samuel Finch never intended that Pear should become the owner of his horse, Pear was not guilty of false pretenses.

———

236. The rule by which larceny and false pretenses are distinguished has been frequently applied in English and American cases but seldom explained. Is the hint of an explanation in *Harvey* p. 406, above, adequate? Or the following: "[I]f possession only of money or goods is given, and the property is not intended to pass, that may be larceny by a trick; the reason being that there is a taking of the chattel by the thief against the will of the owner; but if possession is given and it is intended by the owner that the property shall also pass, that is not larceny by a trick, but may be false pretenses, because in that case there is no taking, but a handing over of the chattel by the owner"? The Queen v. Russett, [1892] 2 Q.B. 312, 316.

237. Professor Beale argued that the "logical conclusion" of the decision in Pear's Case is that a contract fraudulent in its inception should equally be disregarded if it is intended that property as well as possession pass. "If fraud can supply the place of force, it must be as powerful in the one case as in the other." Beale, "The Borderland of Larceny," 6 Harv. L. Rev. 244, 253 (1892). Do the origins and development of the crimes of larceny and false pretenses provide an explanation hidden to logic for the distinction that the judges made between the two cases?

238. Does the distinction based on the owner's intention make more sense than the distinction suggested in Pear's Case based on the nature of the false pretense? Is it more in keeping with the statute, 30 Geo. 2, ch. 24?

239.

Although some legal scholars have treated larceny by trick as closely related functionally to false pretenses, or even as completely

were not a distinction in this respect between the owner's parting with the possession and with the property in the thing delivered. That where goods were delivered upon a false token, and the owner meant to part with the *property* absolutely and never expected to have the goods returned again, it might be difficult to reach the case otherwise than through the statutes; aliter, where he parted with the *possession* only; for there if the possession were obtained by fraud, and not taken according to the agreement; it was on the whole a taking against the will of the owner; and if done animo furandi, it was felony." 2 E. East Pleas of the Crown 689 n. a. (1803).

engulfing it, the offenses are respectively aimed at quite different acquisitive techniques. False pretenses is theft by deceit. The misappropriation it punishes must be effected by communication to the owner. Larceny by trick is theft by stealth. It punishes misappropriation effected by unauthorized disposition of the owner's property. The former focuses on defendant's behavior while face to face with the owner: did it amount to a false pretense? The focus of the latter is upon defendant's behavior behind the owner's back: did it amount to an unauthorized appropriation?

. . .

It should be apparent that deceit had little to do with the offensiveness of Pear's behavior. . . .

In contrast, the antisocial act defined by the crime of false pretenses consists entirely of deceit. It consists of so deceiving the owner of the property that he is induced to consent to the defendant's treating the property as his own. This being so, it is unnecessary as well as impossible for the defendant to subsequently misappropriate property which he has stolen by false pretenses. . . .

. . . This functional distinction between larceny and false pretenses suggests a simple test by which specific fact situations can be distributed between the two offenses. If the deceit be eliminated from the transaction by which the property initially came into the defendant's hands, would his subsequent behavior with respect to the property constitute a conversion? If so, the offense may be larceny by trick; it cannot be false pretenses. If not, the offense may be false pretenses; it cannot be larceny by trick.

Pearce, "Theft by False Promises," 101 U. Pa. L. Rev. 967, 987–89 (1953).

Is the distinction "functional"? Does it call attention to a factor of significance for the criminal law?

240. "If a person honestly receives the possession of the goods, chattels or money of another upon any trust, express or implied, and, after receiving them, fraudulently converts them to his own use, he may be guilty of the crime of embezzlement, but cannot be of that of larceny, except as embezzlement is by statute made larceny. If the possession of such property is obtained by fraud, and the owner of it intends to part with his title as well as his possession, the offence is that of obtaining property by false pretenses, provided the means by which they are acquired are such as, in law, are false pretenses. If the possession is fraudulently obtained, with intent on the part of the person obtaining it, at the time he receives it, to convert the same to his own use, and the person parting with it intends to part with his possession merely, and not with his title to the property, the offence is larceny." Commonwealth v. Barry, 124 Mass. 325, 327 (1878).

241. "Appellant [Polzin] was secretary-treasurer, managing officer, and owner of more than one-third of the capital stock, of Surety Finance Corporation, which was located in Port Angeles and was engaged in the business of lending money in moderate amounts. Appellant was also president of, and a large stockholder in, Clallam Adjustment Corporation, located in the same city and engaged in the business of collecting commercial accounts; appellant's wife was secretary and managing officer of the collection company.

"The capital stock of Clallam Adjustment Corporation was owned and held exclusively by appellant and members of his family and relatives; the capital stock of Surety Finance Corporation had a wider diversity of ownership. The two corporations had their offices in the same building, although on different floors, and, to all intents and purposes, the business of each was conducted as a family affair.

"Mamie E. Braseth, the complaining witness in the case, was employed as a telephone operator in Port Angeles. Upon a number of occasions, over a period of about three years, she had borrowed money from Surety Finance Corporation upon her personal notes, which, latterly, had been secured by the pledge of a diamond ring. In November, 1937, she owed the finance corporation a balance of ninety dollars upon her last note. She was also indebted, in varying amounts, to a number of creditors who were pressing her for payment.

"Desirous of obtaining a sum of money from which she could make partial payments to her various creditors and also realize a small amount of cash for herself, Mrs. Braseth called on appellant at the office of the finance corporation on November 24, 1937. After some discussion, it was agreed between her and appellant that the finance corporation would lend her two hundred dollars upon her note, payable in semi-monthly installments and secured by a pledge of the ring. It was further agreed that the proceeds of the loan should be applied, first, to the payment of the ninety dollars then owing to the finance corporation; second, to the payment of the expense of the immediate loan and interest on the note; third, to a cash payment of seven dollars to the borrower; and the balance to partial payments, but without discount, upon her indebtedness to five of her creditors, according to a schedule outlined by Mrs. Braseth. At the suggestion of appellant, it was agreed that it would be advisable that he, rather than she, should attend to the distribution of the money. The note was thereupon executed, and seven dollars in cash was immediately paid to Mrs. Braseth. An amount sufficient to pay the ninety dollars owing upon her former note and to satisfy the expense incident to the present loan was reserved by the finance corporation.

"Partial payments were made upon three of the accounts in the manner directed by Mrs. Braseth. The other two accounts, totalling $57.50, were handled in a manner contrary to her directions. Instead of paying those accounts directly, in full or in part, to the creditors, appellant, on November 24, 1937, and immediately following his transaction with Mrs. Braseth, executed and delivered to Clallam Adjustment Corporation the check of Surety Finance Corporation in the sum of fifty-seven dollars. The check showed upon its face, however, that it was for the two particular accounts against Mrs. Braseth.

"Shortly thereafter, appellant called on the two creditors whose accounts were covered by the check and solicited the collection of their accounts against Mrs. Braseth. He did not tell them that he then had the money to pay those accounts, nor did he advise them of Mrs. Braseth's direction that only partial payments were to be made and that there was to be no discount taken thereon. As a result of his solicitation, appellant obtained the two accounts for collection by Clallam Adjustment Corporation on the basis of a fee of one-third of the amount collected. Nothing, however, was paid to either of the two creditors prior to January 8, 1938.

"On or about that date Mrs. Braseth learned from the two creditors that nothing had been paid them. At the same time, she was also advised by them of their arrangement with appellant for the collection of the accounts on a fee basis. She thereupon made complaint to appellant regarding nonpayment, but made no specific complaint regarding the proposed collection charge. Appellant assured her that his former arrangement with her had been carried out as agreed, and that all her bills had been paid. On the same day, but after Mrs. Braseth had made complaint to him, appellant delivered to the two creditors checks of the Clallam Adjustment Corporation in the full amounts of their respective accounts, less the one-third collection fees. The checks were received and acknowledged by the two creditors as in full payment of their accounts against Mrs. Braseth, and no further demand has ever been made upon her by either of them. The collection charges retained by the Clallam Adjustment Corporation amounted to nineteen dollars." State v. Polzin, 85 P.2d 1057, 1058 (Wash. 1939).

You may assume that Polzin acted throughout in his individual capacity rather than as a representative of the two corporations in which he had an interest. By statute, larceny of not more than $25 is petty larceny; larceny of more than $25 is grand larceny.

What crime, if any, has Polzin committed?

242. Sentry, an armored courier service, had an arrangement with one of its client banks to pick up bulk amounts of cash at the bank's offices, "fine count" it, and deliver it for deposit in the bank's account at the Federal Reserve Bank. It was agreed that the delivery would be made within 72 hours after the pickup. Sentry was able to complete the fine count in about 24 hours. Instead of making an immediate delivery to the Federal Reserve Bank, without informing the bank Sentry arranged for the money to be deposited in its own account for 48 hours, after which the required delivery was made. Sentry earned interest on the money while it was deposited in its account.

Was Sentry guilty of any crime? See People v. Jennings, 504 N.E.2d 1079 (N.Y.1986).

243. Johnson presented four $20 and two $10 bills at the teller's window of a bank and asked for a hundred dollar bill. The teller gave him a hundred dollar bill, which Johnson palmed and replaced with a ten dollar bill. He showed the smaller bill to the teller and said she had made a mistake. She exchanged the bill for another hundred dollar bill. United States v. Johnson, 575 F.2d 678 (8th Cir.1978). At common law, what crime did Johnson commit?

244. Deposit slips for the deposit of receipts of the State Lottery Agency were mistakenly encoded with the number of Posner's checking account. Using those slips, bank employees deposited the amount of such receipts turned in to the bank by lottery agents, which deposits were credited to Posner's account. Over a period of 15 months, about $183,000 was mistakenly credited to Posner's account, of which he withdrew about $177,000. Posner knew that the funds he was withdrawing were not rightfully his. He was prosecuted under a statute that covered common-law larceny. United States v. Posner, 408 F.Supp. 1145 (D.Md.1976). What result?

The defendant opened a checking account at the Hibernia National Bank. He made no further deposits, and within two weeks the account was overdrawn. Because of a mistake in the operation of Hibernia's computer program, the bank honored the overdrawn check, only sending the defendant a notice of the overdraft. The defendant continued to write overdrawn checks, which the bank treated in the same way. Over the next six months, the defendant received 198 overdraft notices; the amount of the overdraft finally totaled almost $850,000. The notices stated the amount of the accumulated overdraft but did not explicitly demand repayment. No bank official authorized the overdrafts, which were handled automatically by the computer. The defendant was prosecuted for theft, which required proof of a nonconsensual taking. State v. Langford, 483 So.2d 979 (La.1986). What result?

245. The defendant deposited stolen checks in his own and his wife's accounts, with forged endorsements. He then withdrew the money. All these transactions were conducted at the bank with a teller who knew the checks were stolen and was paid for her cooperation. United States v. Guiffre, 576 F.2d 126 (7th Cir.1978). What crime, if any, did the defendant commit?

If a bank teller pretends to turn over money to a robber under threat but is in fact in a conspiracy with the apparent robber and turns over the money willingly, does the theft constitute larceny or embezzlement? See United States v. Bowser, 532 F.2d 1318 (9th Cir.1976). Cf. State v. Palumbo, 347 A.2d 535 (N.J.Super.Ct.App.Div.1975) (officer of company and another cooperate in theft of goods).

———

By the end of the nineteenth century the law of theft was "an enormous, lumbering, ramshackle machine . . . [with] a variety of attachments of whimsical aspect and mysterious purpose added at various times by maladroit journeymen." Elliott, "Ten Years of Larceny and Such 1954–63," 1964 Crim. L. Rev. 182. For the same reasons that led courts and the legislature to include novel situations in the prohibited area of theft, in some form or other, the differences among the various kinds of theft became less important than the common element of an involuntary loss of property to another without some socially prescribed justification. Not only did the differences become less important; they also became less apparent. As gaps were filled by a fiction here and statute there,[29] it became less easy

29. "[G]aps or crevices have separated particular crimes of this general class and guilty men have escaped through the breach- es. The books contain a surfeit of cases drawing fine distinctions between slightly different circumstances under which one

to "see light" between different kinds of theft; when a gap was closed there was bound to be an area in which it was not so easy to tell where one crime left off and another began. Since the intention was to leave no gap, one might suppose that the lack of clear separations was to be regretted only by legal scholars of a certain mental bent. But the law's fine distinctions are not so easily dismissed, and the courts of England and this country continued to make distinctions that only history could explain. Larceny remained in form a crime against possession. The fictions and analogies that developed (breaking bulk, fraud for force) were primarily intended to provide a substitute for the trespassory taking that characterizes the paradigm of larceny. False pretenses was no longer limited to the use of false tokens or other means of deceiving the public generally; an intent to deceive a particular individual simply by a false representation was sufficient. But its origin in the marketplace remained discernible in the requirement that the owner have intended to pass the "property" in his goods. Embezzlement included breaches of trust growing out of business relationships far removed from the direct relationship between a master and his household servant; the notion of "entrusting" remained, however attenuated the reasons for trust.[30]

5.   CONSOLIDATION

American courts adopted the common law of theft as it had developed in England, with like results.[31] The Supreme Judicial Court of Massachusetts, for example, found that the conviction for embezzlement of Martin O'Malley, already tried for larceny and acquitted because the trial judge thought his crime was embezzlement, see Commonwealth v. King, 88 N.E.

may obtain wrongful advantages from another's property." Morissette v. United States, 342 U.S. 246, 271 (1952).

30. "[T]he individual characteristic of the crime is the fiduciary relation of the defendant. Hence, the relation by virtue of which the defendant acquires possession of the property is a necessary element of the offense . . . ." Phelps v. State, 219 P. 589, 590 (Ariz.1923).

31. For another hundred years after it extended the law of embezzlement to cover cases like *Walsh*, p. 398 above, Parliament continued to patch up the law of theft. In 1916 it gave up the effort as a bad job and took a big but incomplete step toward statutory consolidation. Larceny Act, 6 & 7 Geo. 5,

ch. 50, § 1 (1916). In 1966 the Criminal Law Revision Committee recommended that Parliament enact "a new law of theft and related offences, based on a fundamental reconsideration of the principles underlying this branch of the law and embodied in a modern statute." Criminal Law Revision Committee, Eighth Report (Theft and Related Offences) (Cmnd. 2977) 7. In 1968 Parliament followed this recommendation. The Theft Act 1968, ch. 60, revised and simplified the law of theft. The act provides a "basic definition" of theft: "A person is guilty of theft if he dishonestly appropriates property belonging to another with the intention of permanently depriving the other of it; and 'thief' and 'steal' shall be construed accordingly." Theft Act 1968, ch. 60, § 1(1). See also Theft Act 1978, ch. 31.

454 (Mass.1909), had to be reversed because the crime proved against him was in fact larceny. Commonwealth v. O'Malley, 97 Mass. 584 (1867). Such "scandals in the administration of justice," id. at 458, were avoided afterward in Massachusetts by statutory consolidation of the types of theft. The Massachusetts statutes illustrate two methods of reform: by consolidation of the substantive crimes and by procedural devices.[32] See Commonwealth v. Corcoran, 204 N.E.2d 289 (Mass.1965). Even after statutory consolidation problems might remain. Despite consolidation of the types of theft into the single crime of "larceny," the New York Court of Appeals held that where the act charged was larceny and the act proved was false pretenses, the conviction could not be sustained since "the defendant was left uninformed of the real act committed by him and subject to the charge of larceny for an act which he did not perform." People v. Dumar, 13 N.E. 325, 329 (N.Y.1887). To the same effect, see State v. Smith, 98 P.2d 647 (Wash.1939). Compare State v. Talley, 466 A.2d 78 (N.J.1983), in which the defendant, who was prosecuted for robbery, defended on the ground that he had received the victims' money in a purported drug transaction. He gave them herbal tea instead of the drugs and, he said, they accused him of robbery in retaliation. The court concluded that if the facts were as he alleged, he could be convicted of theft by deception under the consolidation statute. In People v. Noblett, 155 N.E. 670, 671 (N.Y.1927), the Court of Appeals acknowledged that "narrow technical distinctions by which a wrongdoer may escape the consequences of a crime hinder the administration of justice"; but it said also that "it is the function of the Legislature to determine whether modern conditions dictate a wider definition of acts which should subject the wrongdoer to criminal responsibility" and proceeded to acquit the defendant on the basis of a distinction which, so the court seemed rightly to think, was narrow and technical.[33]

Similarly, in United States v. Sayklay, 542 F.2d 942 (5th Cir.1976), the court reversed the defendant's conviction for embezzlement. She was a bookkeeper in a bank and used her access to bank records and equipment to write and cash checks on other persons' accounts. The court said that

---

32. "Whoever steals, or with intent to defraud obtains by a false pretense, or whoever unlawfully, and with intent to steal or embezzle, converts, or secretes with intent to convert, the property of another as defined in this section, whether such property is or is not in his possession at the time of such conversion or secreting, shall be guilty of larceny . . . ." Mass. Gen. L. ch. 266, § 30(1).

"In an indictment for criminal dealing with personal property with intent to steal, an allegation that the defendant stole said property shall be sufficient; and such indictment may be supported by proof that the defendant committed larceny of the property, or embezzled it, or obtained it by false pretences." Mass. Gen. L. ch. 277, § 41.

For indications that the common law of theft has not been overcome even in federal law, which is entirely statutory, see, e.g., United States v. Hill, 835 F.2d 759 (10th Cir.1987), with which compare, e.g., United States v. Guiffre, 576 F.2d 126 (7th Cir. 1978). See also Bell v. United States, 462 U.S. 356 (1983) (construing 18 U.S.C. § 2113(b), Federal Bank Robbery Act) and United States v. Turley, 352 U.S. 407 (1957) (construing 18 U.S.C. § 2312, National Motor Vehicle Theft (Dyer) Act), holding respectively that a statutory reference to stealing encompasses false pretenses and embezzlement.

33. For the legislative solution in New York, see N.Y. Penal Law § 155.45.

although the evidence clearly showed a willful misapplication of bank funds, there was no embezzlement. "The essence of embezzlement lies in breach of a fiduciary relationship deriving from the entrustment of money. In this case the defendant's position at the bank aided her in her crime, but it did not place her in lawful possession of others' funds that she converted to her own use. This is a hard case, but the bad law (if such it be) was made when Congress chose to carry forward the technical and antediluvian elements by which the Supreme Court long ago distinguished embezzlement from similar crimes." Id. at 944. (Compare the attitude of the judges in the Carrier's Case or Pear's Case.)

The Model Penal Code provides an example of an effort to achieve full statutory consolidation. Section 223.1(1) provides: "Consolidation of Theft Offenses. Conduct denominated theft in this Article constitutes a single offense. An accusation of theft may be supported by evidence that it was committed in any manner that would be theft under this Article, notwithstanding the specification of a different manner in the indictment or information, subject only to the power of the Court to ensure fair trial by granting a continuance or other appropriate relief where the conduct of the defense would be prejudiced by lack of fair notice or by surprise." (The text of Article 223 of the Model Penal Code, covering Theft and Related Offenses, is set forth at pp. 457–62 below.)

The closing of the gaps that separated larceny, embezzlement, and false pretenses, and statutory consolidation of the crimes in many jurisdictions reflect a judgment that they have features in common that override their differences.[34] If one looks at the crimes at the points where they touch one another, the judgment can hardly be disputed. What difference does it make, after all, to someone who is cheated out of her property whether she intended that the property be only temporarily in the cheat's possession or that the cheat have it for good, in return for something else of comparable value? In both cases the elements of cheating and deprivation of property may seem easily to overshadow the difference in intention. So too, if a person rents a car and later, having decided to keep it, fails to return it to its owner; the intention to keep and the owner's loss may seem far more significant than the precise moment when the person decided to keep the car.[35]

If one looks at the paradigm cases, however, the differences appear to have more importance. A society in which one is not well protected even from the snatchpurse is different from a society in which one is so protected, even if there is not effective protection against deceptive trade

---

34. "The distinction [between larceny and embezzlement], now largely obsolete, did not ever correspond to any essential difference in the character of the acts or in their effect upon the victim. The crimes are one today in the common speech of men, as they are in moral quality." Van Vechten v. American Eagle Fire Ins. Co., 146 N.E. 432, 433 (N.Y.1925).

35. Compare Stegall v. Commonwealth, 160 S.E.2d 566 (Va.1968).

practices. Even the finer distinction between larceny by trick and false pretenses is not self-evidently pointless; someone who expects the return of the property with which she has parted, or who at least still believes that the property is hers, may react differently to its loss than she would to the loss of her part of a bargain by which she gave up that particular property for good. Similarly, the community may feel different moral sentiments about someone who initiates or engages in a transaction for the purpose of depriving another person of her property and someone who cannot resist the lure of property that he has come by honestly.

How should we determine whether these distinctions should be given effect in the criminal law? The recent view, perhaps influenced by cases in which a thief proved his innocence of the crime charged by proving that he had committed a different crime, is that the distinctions mentioned should not be included in the definitions of theft offenses. Rather, for the most part the law should separate criminal and noncriminal acquisitions of property and include the former in a general category of theft. If the legislative determination of sentences is very general and the actual sentence is determined by the particular facts of each case, such an approach has the virtue of simplifying prosecution, whether or not it ignores "real" differences in the nature of the crime. If, however, the legislature establishes the sentencing pattern more particularly, it will have to consider whether there are not variations in the criminal acquisition of property that ought to be reflected in the penalties. Even the Model Penal Code does not wholly avoid such categorization. The unlawful use of vehicles is defined separately from other unlawful acquisitions. See p. 462 below. The explanation for treating this crime separately is that it is concerned mainly with "the 'joyride,' i.e., the taking of another's automobile without his permission, not for the purpose of keeping it but merely to drive it briefly. The offense is typically committed by young people, and the car is often recovered undamaged. Such behavior would not amount to larceny, which, as traditionally defined, requires proof that the actor intended to deprive the owner permanently." 2 MPC Commentaries Part II, 271 (comment to § 223.9).

The reasons given for treating "joy-riding" separately and more leniently than other unlawful acquisitions reflect complex judgments about the nature of the conduct involved and the purposes of the criminal law. Whether or not such judgments are embodied in a penal code's provisions on theft, within the range of her discretion a judge will have to give attention to factors that she thinks relevant when she imposes punishment. Ought she to treat a taking by force more severely than a taking by trick, a breach of trust more severely than a fraud? Somewhere in the elaboration of the criminal law these questions have to be faced.

Not only the distinctions among types of theft give difficulty. The lines between criminal and noncriminal acquisitions of property are hard to see, as any number of sharp fellows in (and out of) prison can attest.

6. PROPERTY

246. For the purposes of the law of theft,[36] what is "property"? The Model Penal Code § 230.0(6) defines "property" as "anything of value." Is that satisfactory? Why (not)? What is meant by "anything of value"?

Would it be as good to define "property" as anything that is "capable of appropriation by another than the owner"[37] or, more simply, anything that can be owned?

247. Dogs. According to the common law, a person who took another person's dog committed no crime, dogs being "considered of so base a nature that no larceny can be committed of them."[38] Ownership of domestic animals for which more practical uses could be found was protected by the criminal law. In 1861 Parliament made it a crime to steal a dog,[39] but until 1968 dog-theft was treated in England as a minor offense.[40] Decisions in the United States have gone both ways, most of them adhering to the common law for a time and more recently, sometimes pursuant to a statute, changing it.[41]

36. "Theft" has no established meaning nor has one been assigned to it in these materials. It is used here and hereafter in this section to refer roughly to the group of activities involving the criminal appropriation of property that we all understand as theft.

37. United States v. Carlos, 21 Philippine 553, 560 (1911).

38. 2 E. East, Pleas of the Crown 614 (1803).

39. Larceny Act, 24 & 25 Vict. ch. 96, § 18 (1861).

40. See the Larceny Act of 1916, 6 & 7 Geo. 5, ch. 50, § 5, repealed and replaced by the Theft Act 1968, ch. 60.

41. New York's Court of Appeals, for example, incidentally calling to mind "the small spaniel that saved the life of William of Orange and thus probably changed the current of modern history . . . and the faithful St. Bernards, which after a storm has swept over the crests and side of the Alps, start out in search of lost travelers," concluded that a dog was "personal property" within the meaning of a statute defining the crime of petty larceny. Mullaly v. People, 86 N.Y. 365, 367 (1881). Compare the more judicious statement of the Supreme Court: "While the higher breeds rank among the noblest representatives of the animal kingdom, and are justly esteemed for their intelligence, sagacity, fidelity, watchfulness, affection, and, above all, for their natural companionship with man, others are afflicted with such serious infirmities of temper as to be little better than a public nuisance. All are more or less subject to attacks of hydrophobic madness." Sentell v. New Orleans & C. R.R., 166 U.S. 698, 701 (1897).

The wheel came full circle in Massachusetts in 1966, when dogs were excepted from the definition of "property" that is the subject of theft under the general larceny provision and theft of a dog was made the subject of a special provision, in order to increase the penalty for theft of a dog the value of which would have made the crime only petty larceny. 1966 Mass. Acts 153. Later, dogs were reincorporated within the general definition of property. Mass. Gen. L. ch. 266, § 30.

248. Is it theft to appropriate from another goods which he has no right to possess, such as contraband? What "property" interest is invaded or threatened by such a taking?[42]

Real property.

249. At one time, real property could not be the subject of theft, nor could goods attached to the land. The land itself not being movable, it was concluded that it could not be taken away, an element of larceny. Things attached to the property, easily detached though they might be, were regarded as part of it. East suggested that the reason for the rule that goods attached to the land could not be stolen was "that things annexed to the freehold, being usually more difficult to remove, are less liable to be

---

42. In this connection, consider the statement of the Supreme Court in *Sentell*, p. 417 n. 41 above, 166 U.S. at 701: "The very fact that they are without the protection of the criminal laws shows that property in dogs is of an imperfect or qualified nature . . . ."

The established rule is that illegality of possession does not affect the illegality of a taking from the possessor. See, e.g., United States v. Benson, 548 F.2d 42 (2d Cir.1977), rejecting the argument that the defendants could not be convicted of obtaining property by false pretenses because the jewels in question were not the property of the person defrauded, himself allegedly a jewel thief; People v. Dillon, 668 P.2d 697, 704 n.5 (Cal. 1983).

In Commonwealth v. Rourke, 64 Mass. (10 Cush.) 397, 401, 402 (1852), which involved the theft of money obtained from the unlawful sale of liquor, the court said: "Of the alternative moral and social evils, which is the greater,—to deprive property unlawfully acquired of all protection as such, and thus to discourage unlawful acquisition but encourage larceny; or to punish, and so discourage larceny, though at the possible risk of thus omitting so far forth to discourage unlawful acquisition? The balance of public policy, if we thus attempt to estimate the relative weight of alternative evils, requires, it seems to us, that the larceny should be punished. Each violation of law is to be dealt with by itself. The felonious taking has its appropriate and specific punishment; so also has the unlawful acquisition." The court relied also on cases involving an owner's theft of his property from a bailee or theft of property from a person who had himself acquired it by theft. Was such reliance justified?

Is there a relevant distinction between theft of receipts from the unlawful sale of liquor and theft of contraband liquor? See People v. Otis, 139 N.E. 562 (N.Y.1923), one of many cases involving theft of liquor unlawfully possessed during prohibition, in which the court said: "The possessor, not being able to make any legal use of it, it is said the liquor itself has no value. This is, however, to make the value of a chattel to its possessor the test as to whether it is the subject of larceny. Such is not the rule. . . . It is enough if the object taken has inherent value. . . . No one can doubt that whisky has such value. It may be sold by the government and the proceeds covered into the treasury. It may be sold by druggists. That it is held illegally is immaterial." What is "inherent value"? Compare People v. Walker, 90 P.2d 854, 855 (Cal.Dist.Ct.App.1939): "Although it may be illegal to own or possess slot machines there yet exist certain rights in the individual who may possess such a contraband article as against anyone other than the state. The owner at least has the privilege of destroying the machine, he also has the right to surrender it to the authorities. It is true his right to the possession of a slot machine is by law very limited, nevertheless he has certain claims and powers not possessed by any other which invests in him something real and tangible."

In Commonwealth v. Crow, 154 A. 283, 286 (Pa.1931), the court observed simply: "To establish the rule that the owner of liquor, illegally held, had no property right therein, would lead to a condition of terror and bloodshed among rival bootleggers far worse than we have known."

stolen; and therefore need not be secured by such severe laws as mere personal goods require."[43] That the roots of the rule were more conceptual than practical is suggested by a qualification: once goods attached to the realty "are severed from the freehold, either by the owner, or even by the thief himself, if there be an interval between his severing and taking them away, so that it cannot be considered as one continued act, it would then be felony to take them away."[44] As might be expected, such fine reasoning led to some curious results.[45]

250. In People v. Dillon, 668 P.2d 697 (Cal.1983), the defendant was prosecuted for felony murder. The underlying felony was attempted robbery. With some companions, he had tried to take marijuana from a marijuana farm. One argument for the defense was that a standing crop cannot be the subject of robbery.

> Defendant . . . contends that a standing crop of marijuana cannot in any event be the subject of robbery or attempted robbery because it is realty, not personalty. Although defendant's argument finds apparent support in the common law definition of property subject to larceny, we hold that robbery of a standing crop is punishable in California. We reach this conclusion both because the Legislature has said as much with regard to the lesser included offense of larceny, and because the common law rule to the contrary is a hypertechnical remnant of an archaic formalism that can no longer be seriously defended.

> The common law rule limiting larceny to the unlawful taking of personalty derived from the undeniable fact that realty, in the sense of land subject to description by metes and bounds, cannot be "carried away." . . . When restricted to land, the logic of the rule was unassailable. But for various reasons unrelated to the criminal law, "realty" was defined in due course to include many items that can be more or less readily detached and removed from the land. Unfortunately, the legal fiction that these objects are "immovable" has never hindered would-be thieves from moving most of them. Nevertheless, probably

---

43. 2 E. East, Pleas of the Crown 587 (1803).

44. Id.

45. See, e.g., State v. Collins, 199 S.E. 303 (S.C.1938). It was also the rule that deeds and other evidences of ownership in realty could not be the subject of theft because they too "savoured" of the realty or had no value "in themselves." 2 E. East, Pleas of the Crown 596 (1803). That rule was in time sometimes met by reasoning that a piece of paper had some "intrinsic value" of its own aside from its evidentiary import, so that theft of the paper was at least petty larceny. See Roberts v. State, 135 S.W. 144 (Tex.Crim.App.1911), in which the court said that the deed stolen by the defendant having no market value, the proper standard of value was the cost of replacing it. Compare Jolly v. United States, 170 U.S. 402, 406 (1898), in which the Supreme Court affirmed a conviction for theft of postage stamps partly on the basis that even while stamps are still in the possession of the Government they have "some intrinsic value . . . as representatives of a certain amount of cost of material and labor."

because larceny was a felony at common law and therefore a capital offense, judges resisted its application to those who had merely pilfered growing food or wood. Courts therefore clung to the artificial distinction between personal property and things that "savour of the realty" (4 Stephen, New Commentaries on the Laws of England (1st Am. ed. 1846) p. 155), and held that if the thief maintained possession continuously during severance and asportation, the property never became personalty in the possession of its owner and hence no larceny could occur. . . . Thus, in a perverse and unintended application of the work ethic, thieves industrious enough to harvest what they stole and to carry it away without pause were guilty at most of trespass, while those who tarried along the way, or enjoyed fruits gathered by the labor of others, faced the hangman's noose.

. . .

. . . In 1872 . . . [the Legislature] adopted a statute redefining detachable fixtures and crops as personalty subject to larceny, "in the same manner as if the thing had been severed by another person at some previous time." (Pen. Code, § 495) Contemporaneously, it enacted a statute dividing the crime of larcenous severance of realty into grand larceny, if the object of the theft is worth $50 or more, and petty larceny otherwise. . . . Defendant argues that because those statutes are explicitly directed at larceny only, they reveal a legislative intent to leave intact the common law rule as it applies to robbery.

To so argue is to presume the Legislature concluded that although the old rule was absurd as applied to thieves, it should nevertheless be maintained to exonerate robbers. We are given no reason to believe the Legislature intended to be more solicitous of the more violent criminal, nor can we conceive of any rational motivation it could have had for doing so. A more plausible interpretation is that the Legislature foresaw as likely only theft, and not robbery, of things attached to the land: it had little reason to expect that robbers would eschew bank vaults in favor of barnyards, or that farmers would patrol their fields so assiduously that covetous criminals would need to resort to robbery to achieve their ends. Had the Legislature anticipated in 1872 that the meteoric rise in popularity and hence in value of an illicit plant would lead to violent confrontations between black market cultivators and armed bandits, we have no doubt it would have explicitly applied the rule to robbery as well.

We recognize that it did not do so. But this circumstance does not compel us to conclude that the old rule as to larceny applies today to robbery. In fact, defendant offers no evidence that there ever existed at common law an explicit doctrine regarding robbery of crops, and we have been unable to find a single case in any jurisdiction raising that precise issue. . . .

Defendant points out that despite the lack of any express rule regarding robbery of crops or fixtures, it has always been understood that the law of robbery borrows its definition of subject property from

11

the law of larceny, because the former crime is distinguished from the latter only by the less circuitous means of its accomplishment. . . .

First, the rule requiring an interruption between severance and asportation has suffered such erosion and criticism during the past century that we no longer feel compelled to preserve it . . . particularly in an area of law not previously marred by its application. Many courts have found the doctrine at odds with reason and have therefore abolished it rather than await legislative intervention. . . . Of the courts that have hesitated to overrule the doctrine outright, many have found ways of limiting it; some redefine "fixtures" for this purpose to exclude items that the civil law includes in the term . . . while others effectively eliminate the requirement of a separation between severance and asportation by creative reconstruction of the facts to establish a sufficient temporal gap. . . .

Moreover, in England the rule has been continuously eroded by statute since 1601 (4 Blackstone, Commentaries 233–234), and in those few American jurisdictions in which courts have refrained from adopting the modern rule, lawmakers have often done so . . . . Hence despite the common law, "it is the generally accepted modern rule that he who by his wrongful act converts a fixture into personal property, and then with larcenous intent forthwith carries it away without the consent of the owner, may be rightfully convicted of larceny." (50 Am. Jur. 2d, Larceny, § 73, p. 245.)

Today, the old rule is less justifiable and more mischievous than ever. As the Maine court observed, "In a modern mobile society in which the attachment of all manner of valuable appliances and gadgets to the realty is commonplace, we see no occasion to attribute to the Legislature any intention to so narrowly circumscribe the meaning of the words 'goods or chattels' in our larceny statute as to make the stealing of chattels severed from realty an attractive and lucrative occupation." (State v. Day (Me. 1972) supra, 293 A.2d 331, 333.) We perceive no reason to reach a different conclusion regarding the words "goods" and "chattels" as they apply to robbery in our statute. (See Pen. Code, § 7, subd. (12).) . . . Because we find no reasoned support for the continued application of the common law rule, even in the narrow context in which it was traditionally invoked, we refrain from extending it to the crime of robbery.

. . .

For the reasons stated, we hold that a robbery . . . is committed when property affixed to realty is severed and taken therefrom in circumstances that would have subjected the perpetrator to liability for robbery if the property had been severed by another person at some previous time. Defendant was properly convicted of attempting to commit such a robbery.

668 P.2d at 704–708.

251. Should there be distinctions between real and personal property in the law of theft? If Smith secretly shifts the boundary markers between his own and neighbor Jones's land, thereby increasing his own and reducing Jones's holding, should he be guilty of theft?

252. Suppose Smith simply settles on a piece of unoccupied land which is owned by someone else. Has he committed theft? If so, does he continue to be a thief up to the time when, if his possession is not disturbed, he becomes the owner of the land by adverse possession? Suppose he occupies an empty house for a week or two and then departs. If he knows that the owner has been trying to rent the house, has he committed theft?

253. If Smith shoots a wild bird in Jones's forest and takes it away with him, is he a thief or only a poacher? Why? Suppose he plucks and removes a wild flower? Cf. United States v. Long Cove Seafood, Inc., 582 F.2d 159 (2d Cir.1978) (harvesting clams in violation of conservation laws not theft).

254. If Smith goes on Jones's land and removes a meteor which has fallen onto the land, is he a thief?[46]

---

46. See Goodard v. Winchell, 52 N.W. 1124 (Iowa 1892), holding that the owner of land onto which a meteorite fell was entitled to recover it from a finder. Compare State v. Burt, 64 N.C. 619 (1870) (finder of gold nugget does not commit larceny when he removes it from land of another).

Intangibles.

255. "It is obvious that it is physically impossible to misappropriate a right of action against the world at large, such as the copyright of a book or a patent to an invention, though it is possible to infringe and so to diminish or destroy its value. It is equally obvious that it is physically impossible to misappropriate a right of action against a particular person . . . [like] a debt, or a share in a partnership . . . ." 3 Stephen, History 125.

"Anyone who frees himself from the crudest materialism readily recognizes that as a legal term property denotes not material things but certain rights. . . . [T]he essence of private property is always the right to exclude others." M. Cohen, "Property and Sovereignty," 13 Corn. L. Q. 8, 11–12 (1927).[47]

Which is correct?

256. Should it make any difference in the law of theft whether the "property" taken is tangible or intangible? Why (not)?

257. In People v. Menagas, 11 N.E.2d 403 (Ill.1937), the defendant was prosecuted for the theft of electric current. His counsel argued that "as electrons are the only elements of electricity and electrical energy which are matter, and as none of the electrons were consumed but were returned to the generator, there was nothing charged to have been stolen by the defendant that could be made the subject of larceny." Id. at 405. What result?[48]

258. Does a person commit theft if he uses his employer's machinery and the labor of other employees to produce goods for sale without the consent of the owner and without intending to pay for the use?[49] Does it matter how the machinery is used by the owner or whether the machinery

---

47. "Property, a creation of law, does not arise from value, although exchangeable—a matter of fact. Many exchangeable values may be destroyed intentionally without compensation. Property depends upon exclusion by law from interference . . . ." International News Service v. Associated Press, 248 U.S. 215, 246 (1918) (Holmes, J., separate opinion).

48. The court concluded that electrical energy could be stolen: "It is a valuable commodity, bought and sold like other personal property. It may be transported from place to place. While it is intangible, it is no less personal property and is within the larceny

statute." 11 N.E.2d at 407. Other courts have reached the same result. "[I]n all the cases where the issue has in fact been directly confronted, the judicial answer has been uniform and unanimous: metered electricity, as well as natural gas, water in pipes, heat, power, and similar forms of 'intangible' energy, are of sufficient 'concreteness' to be the subject of larceny." People v. McLaughlin, 402 N.Y.S.2d 137, 139 (Sup.Ct.1978). In some states, the misappropriation of electrical energy has been made a crime by a special statute. E.g., Mass. Gen. L. ch. 164, § 127.

49. In People v. Ashworth, 222 N.Y.S. 24, 28 (App.Div.1927), the court concluded

is available for rental? (Incidentally, in a jurisdiction which preserves the distinction between larceny and false pretenses, which of the two is it, if it is theft at all?[50])

259. "Defendant was employed by the City of Indianapolis as a computer operator. The City leased computer services on a fixed charge or flat rate basis, hence the expense to it was not varied by the extent to which it was used. Defendant was provided with a terminal at his desk and was assigned a portion of the computer's information storage capacity, called a 'private library,' for his utilization in performing his duties. No other employees were authorized to use his terminal or his library.

"Defendant became involved in a private sales venture and began soliciting his coworkers and using a small portion of his assigned library to maintain records associated with the venture. He was reprimanded several times for selling his products in the office and on 'office time,' and he was eventually discharged for unsatisfactory job performance and for continuing his personal business activities during office hours.

"Defendant, at the time of his being hired by the City, received a handbook, as do all new employees, which discloses the general prohibition against the unauthorized use of city property. Other city employees sometimes used the computer for personal convenience or entertainment; and although Defendant's supervisor knew or suspected that Defendant was using the computer for his business records, he never investigated the matter or reprimanded Defendant in this regard, and such use of the computer was not cited as a basis for his discharge.

"Defendant, following his discharge, applied for and received unemployment compensation benefits, over the protest of the City. He requested a former fellow employee to obtain a 'print-out' of his business data and

---

that he does not; it said that a "mere property right," a right to use, "as distinguished from physical property" is not the subject of larceny. Responding to *Ashworth*, the legislature enacted a statute making it theft of services to divert labor of a person in the employ of another to one's own use. N.Y. Penal Law § 165.15(10) (McKinney 1999), p. 426 below. See United States v. Delano, 55 F.3d 720, 727–28 (2d Cir.1995).

In Lund v. Commonwealth, 232 S.E.2d 745 (Va.1977), referring to *Ashworth*, the court concluded that the unauthorized use of a computer was not larceny. The state legislature subsequently provided that "computer time or services or data processing services or information or data stored in connection therewith" is property that can be the subject of theft. Va. Code Ann. § 18.2–98.1.

50. Compare *Ashworth*, n. 49 above, 222 N.Y.S. at 27: "We must bear in mind, also, that asportation is an essential element of larceny. . . . It may be conceivable that, if these defendants stole the use of the spinning facilities of the A–O Company, they carried the 'use' away, or appreciably changed its location, although the work was all done on the premises of the A–O Company. But to conceive this requires a certain intellectual flexibility which is probably not possessed by the average person."

then to erase it from what had been his library. Instead, the 'print-out' was turned over to Defendant's former supervisor and became the basis for the criminal charges." State v. McGraw, 480 N.E.2d 552, 553–54 (Ind.1985).

The defendant was prosecuted under a statute providing: "A person who knowingly or intentionally exerts unauthorized control over property of another person with intent to deprive the other of any part of its value or use, commits theft . . . ." Assuming that the defendant's use of the computer was unauthorized and that it was "property" under the statute, what result?

The court concluded that the defendant's conduct did not violate the statute. It said: "Not only was there no evidence that the City was ever deprived of any part of the value or the use of the computer by reason of Defendant's conduct, the uncontradicted evidence was to the contrary. The computer was utilized for City business by means of terminals assigned to various employee-operators, including Defendant. The computer processed the data from the various terminals simultaneously, and the limit of its capacity was never reached or likely to have been. The computer service was leased to the City at a fixed charge, and the tapes or discs upon which the imparted data was stored were erasable and reusable. Defendant's unauthorized use cost the City nothing and did not interfere with its use by others. He extracted from the system only such information as he had previously put into it. He did not, for his own benefit, withdraw City data intended for its exclusive use or for sale. Thus, Defendant did not deprive the City of the 'use of computers and computer services' as the information alleged that he intended to do. We find no distinction between Defendant's use of the City's computer and the use, by a mechanic, of the employer's hammer or a stenographer's use of the employer's typewriter, for other than the employer's purposes. Under traditional concepts, the transgression is in the nature of a trespass, a civil matter—and a de minimis one, at that. Defendant has likened his conduct to the use of an employer's vacant bookshelf, for the temporary storage of one's personal items, and to the use of an employer's telephone facilities for toll-free calls. The analogies appear to us to be appropriate." 480 N.E.2d at 554. The court noted that the defendant might be convicted of conversion, a lesser offense, which does not contain a requirement of intent to deprive.

One judge, dissenting, said: "In the first place, intent is clearly shown in that Defendant used the City computer system for his personal business, well knowing that he was doing so and well knowing that it was unauthorized. . . . Time and use are at the very core of the value of a computer system. To say that only the information stored in the computer plus the tapes and discs and perhaps the machinery involved in the computer system, are the only elements that can be measured as the value or property feature of that system, is incorrect.

"I think it is irrelevant that the computer processed the data from various terminals simultaneously and the limit of its capacity was never reached by any or all of the stations, including the defendant's. It is also irrelevant that the computer service was leased to the City at a fixed charge and that the tapes or discs upon which the imparted data was stored were erasable and reusable. The fact is the City owned the computer system of all the stations including the defendant's. The time and use of that equipment at that station belonged to the City. Thus, when the defendant used the computer system, putting on data from his private business and taking it out on printouts, he was taking that which was property of the City and converting it to his own use, thereby depriving the City of its use and value." Id. at 555.

See United States v. Wilson, 636 F.2d 225 (8th Cir.1980) (defendant's use of secretary to type private business documents during time when there was no other work to be done was not conversion of government property, because there was not evidence of intent seriously to interfere with property rights of government as employer).

The New York Penal Law § 165.15(10) provides that a person is guilty of theft of services when: "Obtaining or having control over labor in the employ of another person, or of business, commercial or industrial equipment or facilities of another person, knowing that he is not entitled to the use thereof, and with intent to derive a commercial or other substantial benefit for himself or a third person, he uses or diverts to the use of himself or a third person such labor, equipment or facilities." Section 165.15(11) provides that a person is guilty of theft of services when: "With intent to avoid payment by himself or another person of the lawful charge for use of any computer or computer service which is provided for a charge or compensation he uses, causes to be used or attempts to use a computer or computer service and avoids or attempts to avoid payment therefor." (McKinney 1999.) Would the defendant in *McGraw* have been guilty under either of these provisions? Would the defendant in *Wilson* have been guilty under the former provision? If so, is that result desirable? How would the theft provisions of the Model Penal Code, pp. 457–62 below, deal with these cases?

260.   The Progressive Machinery Company had a special tool for making small hinges, which its president had developed at large expense over a two-year period. It was unpatented; its method of manufacture was held by the company as a trade secret. Two employees who had signed an agreement not to divulge the company's trade secrets were discharged. If they reveal how to make the hinge tool to one of the company's competitors for a price, have they committed theft? If a competitor bribes an employee still working at the company to reveal the secret, has the competitor or the employee committed theft? See Commonwealth v. Engleman, 142 N.E.2d 406 (Mass.1957).[51] See also United States v. DiGilio, 538 F.2d 972 (3d Cir.1976) (appropriation of information by unlawful copying of government

---

51. Looking to the statutory definition of theft, the court said no. The statute was later amended to include trade secrets. Mass. Gen. L. ch. 266, § 30.4.

records); United States v. Girard, 601 F.2d 69 (2d Cir.1979) (same; held within federal theft statute).

261. The defendant made phonorecords of unreleased Elvis Presley recordings from movie soundtracks, tapes of concerts and television shows, etc., in violation of the copyrights of owners of the materials. With some associates, he marketed the records and did a substantial business. He was prosecuted for shipments of the records under the National Stolen Property Act, which makes it criminal to transport interstate "any goods, wares, merchandise, securities or money . . . knowing the same to have been stolen, converted or taken by fraud." 18 U.S.C. § 2314.

The defendant argued that he was not guilty under the statute because the goods shipped were not "stolen, converted or taken by fraud." The government argued that they were, because the records "physically embodied performances of musical compositions that Dowling had no legal right to distribute," and "the unauthorized use of the musical compositions rendered the phonorecords 'stolen, converted or taken by fraud' within the meaning of the statute." Dowling v. United States, 473 U.S. 207, 214–15 (1985).

Concluding that the statute had not been violated, the Supreme Court said: "There is no dispute in this case that Dowling's unauthorized inclusion on his bootleg albums of performances of copyrighted compositions constituted infringement of those copyrights. It is less clear, however, that the taking that occurs when an infringer arrogates the use of another's protected work comfortably fits the terms associated with physical removal employed by § 2314. The infringer invades a statutorily defined province guaranteed to the copyright holder alone. But he does not assume physical control over the copyright; nor does he wholly deprive its owner of its use. While one may colloquially link infringement with some general notion of wrongful appropriation, infringement plainly implicates a more complex set of property interests than does run-of-the-mill theft, conversion, or fraud. As a result, it fits but awkwardly with the language Congress chose— 'stolen, converted or taken by fraud'—to describe the sorts of goods whose interstate shipment § 2314 makes criminal." 473 U.S. at 217–18. The Court noted also that there was no need to tie copyright provisions to interstate commerce, since Congress had authority to legislate directly in this area. Under the government's theory, the Court said, all kinds of misappropriation of intellectual property would become a kind of theft pursuant to the statute, if the idea were embodied in goods shipped interstate.

Justice Powell, dissenting, said: "[A]mong the rights a copyright owner enjoys is the right to publish, copy, and distribute the copyrighted work. Indeed, these rights define virtually the entire scope of an owner's rights in intangible property such as a copyright. Interference with these rights may be 'different' from the physical removal of tangible objects, but it is not clear why this difference matters under the terms of § 2314. The statute makes no distinction between tangible and intangible property. The basic goal of the National Stolen Property Act, thwarting the interstate transportation of misappropriated goods, is not served by the judicial imposition of this distinction. Although the rights of copyright owners in their property may be more limited than those of owners of other kinds of property, they are surely 'just as deserving of protection . . . .' United States v. Drum [733 F.2d 1503 (11th Cir.1984)], at 1506." 473 U.S. at 230–31.

The federal Copyright Law makes it a crime to infringe a copyright "wilfully . . . for purposes of commercial advantage or private financial gain." 17 U.S.C. § 506(a). The crime may be a misdemeanor or a felony according to its scope. For a second or subsequent offense, the penalty may be up to ten years in prison and a fine. 18 U.S.C. § 2319. Another similar provision covers the unauthorized transmission, fixation in sound recordings or music videos, and commerce in such recordings or videos, of live music performances. 18 U.S.C. § 2319A.

262. Is it theft to obtain a person's services without intending to pay for them?[52] Or to obtain the services of another person's employee with the same intent? If so, might the employee be liable for theft if he moonlighted on his employer's time?

Is it theft to "second act" a play, i.e. wait until the intermission and then slip into an empty seat? Or to slip into an empty seat at a movie theatre? Should it be? Is it relevant that there are many empty seats?

The New York Penal Law § 165.15(9) provides that a person is guilty of theft of services when: "With intent to avoid payment of the lawful charge for admission to any theatre or concert hall, or with intent to avoid payment of the lawful charge for admission to or use of a chair lift, gondola, rope-tow or similar mechanical device utilized in assisting skiers in transportation to a point of ski arrival or departure, he obtains or attempts to obtain such admission without payment of the lawful charge therefor."

How do the Model Penal Code's theft provisions, pp. 457–62 below, deal with these problems?

---

52. Yes. United States v. Croft, 750 F.2d 1354 (7th Cir.1984) (services of research assistant a "thing of value" under 18 U.S.C. § 641); State v. Ball, 75 So. 373, 374 (Miss. 1917) (professional services of a physician): "As the goods, wares, and merchandise of the storekeeper are his stock in trade, so are the services of the doctor, lawyer, or mechanic their stock in trade, and the one should not be deprived of his property by false pretenses any more than the other, as the mischief intended to be cured is the obtaining of the 'valuable thing' by one person from another by means of deceit and false representation."

No. State v. Smith, 197 So. 429, 431 (La.1940) (services of a housepainter): "The labor, or personal services, which defendant is charged with obtaining in this case did not constitute 'worldly goods or possessions,' or 'tangible things'; nor were such services an 'object of value' that a person may lawfully acquire and hold, or any valuable interest therein or thereto.'"

263. Is it theft to secure renewal of a loan by false representations? Or falsely to induce a person to become a guarantor of one's debt? Or falsely to induce a person to sign a lease as lessee? Or falsely to induce a person to assign part of his claim to damages as an accident victim in return for legal services to collect on the claim?[53]

264. Is plagiarism theft? Why (not)?

265. Is conduct that will support an action for alienation of affections a form of theft? If so, should it be punished as such?[54]

266. Does the inclusion of more items "of value" within the interests protected by the law of theft necessarily represent an advance in the law? If so, according to what assumptions? Does such a development tell you anything about a society?

267. Is it necessary to refer to basic notions about property generally in order to rationalize distinctions between what "can" and what "cannot" be the subject of theft? Even if we haven't the time or inclination to settle the question anew each time it is asked, can we disregard altogether the "thief's" argument that, given a set of assumptions that he happens to accept and that direct his conduct, his "title" to property is as good as the owner's[55] or the argument, again based on a set of articulable assumptions, that there is no ownership, and hence there can be no theft, of the "property" in question?

53. No, no, no, no. State v. Eicher, 140 So. 498 (La.1932) (renewal of loan); State v. Miller, 233 P.2d 786 (Or.1951) (guaranty); People v. Weisbard, 139 Misc. 385 (N.Y. City Magis.Ct.1931) (lease); State v. Picou, 107 So.2d 691 (La.1958) (claim).

54. Cf. C. von Furer-Haimendorf, Morals and Merit 27 (1967): among the Andamanese, a tribal society of semi-nomadic foodgatherers who live on the Andaman Islands in the Bay of Bengal, "adultery, apparently is considered as a kind of theft, but society does not assist the duped husband in punishing his rival."

55. Compare Johnson v. M'Intosh, 21 U.S. (8 Wheat.) 543, 584, 587 (1823): "[A]ll the nations of Europe, who have acquired territory on this continent, have asserted in themselves, and have recognized in others, the exclusive right of the discoverer to appropriate the lands occupied by the Indians. . . .

. . .

"The United States, then, have unequivocally acceded to that great and broad rule by which its civilized inhabitants now hold this country. They hold, and assert in themselves, the title by which it was acquired. They maintain, as all others have maintained, that discovery gave an exclusive right to extinguish the Indian title of occupancy, either by purchase or by conquest; and gave also a right to such a degree of sovereignty, as the circumstances of the people would allow them to exercise."

268. What answer should we make to the argument: "Property is theft"?[56]

---

7. VALUE

269. Should thefts be distinguished according to the value of the property taken? Why (not)?

———

After experimenting with such a distinction for at least 552 years, England abolished it in 1827. By the statute of 3 Edw. 1 (1275), larceny of property worth not more than twelve pence was petty larceny.[57] The statute of 24 & 25 Vict. ch. 96, § 2 (1827), however, provided that "Every larceny, whatever be the value of the property stolen, shall be deemed to be of the same nature, and shall be subject to the same incidents in all respects as grand larceny . . . ." The Criminal Law Revision Committee recommended in 1966 that this unitary treatment be preserved: "[A]lthough there is a case for specially high penalties for stealing large sums, we are not in favour of such a provision. Apart from the difficulty of laying down a satisfactory scale, the value of the property is only one of the possible aggravating features of theft, and it seems to us wrong to single this out. Besides, the property may be far more or less valuable than the thief imagined." Eighth Report (Theft and Related Offenses) 30–31 (Cmnd. 2977) (1966).

In the United States theft is typically divided into two classes according to the value of the property stolen. Petty larceny, most often defined as theft of property worth less than $50, is commonly a misdemeanor with a maximum penalty of imprisonment for not more than a year. There are many other classifications, including some with three classes. The Model Penal Code adopts a tripartite classification. In general, theft of property worth more than $500 is a felony (punishable by fine and/or imprisonment for not more than five years, § 6.06(3)); $50 or more, a misdemeanor (fine

---

56. "La propriété, c'est le vol." P.-J. Proudhon, Qu'est-ce que la Propriété? 14 (nouvelle éd. 1867).

57. Petty larceny remained a felony but was not punishable by death. The distinction was probably made even before the statute was enacted. See 3 Stephen, History 129.

One early explanation for fixing the line between grand and petty larceny at 12 pence is that in the time of Edward I 12 pence was about eight days' wages for a man who made a poor living, and that a man could survive without food for eight days but would die on the ninth, so that if more than 12 pence were taken the offense would involve the taking of life. Britton 47 n.2 (F. Nichols trans. 1901 ed.). Plucknett interprets Britton's explanation differently. T. Plucknett, Concise History of the Common Law 447 (5th ed. 1956).

and/or imprisonment for not more than one year, § 6.08); and less than $50, a petty misdemeanor (fine and/or imprisonment for not more than 30 days, § 6.08). § 223.1(2). (It should be noted that these classifications were adopted in 1962, when the Proposed Official Draft of the Code was promulgated. The amounts specified probably had different significance then than they do now.)

The usual rule is that the relevant value for classification of theft offenses is market value. "As a general rule, that value will be determined by market forces—the price at which the minds of a willing buyer and a willing seller would meet. . . . If no commercial market for particular contraband exists, value may be established by reference to a thieves' market." United States v. DiGilio, 538 F.2d 972, 979 (3d Cir.1976).

---

270. What bases are there for classifications of value? The commentary to the Model Penal Code states:

> Putting a ceiling on punishment of petty theft accords with the almost universal present practice and with popular feeling. The ordinary individual feels a lesser repugnance to the taking of smaller rather than larger amounts. Thus, the petty thief evinces a lesser departure from normal standards of respect for others' property; he is presumably not as hardened or dangerous. Shorter sentences should be sufficient to deter those who have not as much to gain. On the other hand, longer sentences are called for in the case of offenders who realize greater sums. Escalation of penalty according to amount stolen decreases the incentive for crime that greater profits might induce.

> [The Code] adopts a three-step classification on the ground that the attitudes that justify discrimination by amount probably recognize three groups of transactions: those involving really petty values, those at the opposite end of the scale relating to very substantial amounts, and a third group that falls between these two. There is a necessary measure of arbitrariness in selecting the dollar values to mark the different categories. . . .

> . . .

> In accepting a classification of theft by amount stolen, the Model Code does not purport to represent that amount is the only or even the most important measure of the anti-social tendencies of the particular thief's character.

2 MPC Commentaries Part II, 139–40, 147.[58]

---

58. Compare Stephen's statement objecting to the English unitary rule: "It is true that the value of a stolen article is no test of the moral guilt of the theft, but this is not the only matter to be considered in fixing maximum punishments. The temptation to steal is usually proportional to the amount to be gained by stealing. This temptation ought as far as possible to be counteracted by a corresponding increase in the punishment. When the property is specially valuable, it is usually guarded with special care, and the

271. What if the property is much more or much less valuable than the thief supposed? Should the would-be grand thief escape a heavy penalty on the ground that what he thought was a silk purse turned out to be a sow's ear? On the other hand, should a thief of more modest aspiration be heavily punished because the owner of a pocketbook which the thief casually lifts from a chair was foolish enough to be carrying $1000 in cash?[59]

272. Assuming that the value of the property taken is a relevant basis for distinguishing among thefts, why should the relevant value be market value? Suppose the property had great "sentimental" value for the owner.

273. The defendant was an automobile dealer. He sold a used car after turning the odometer back from over 82,000 miles to under 53,000 miles. He was prosecuted for theft by deception. The defendant sought to prove as a defense that the car was worth more than the buyer had paid for it. The evidence was excluded. The defendant was convicted and sentenced to two to four years' imprisonment and a fine. The court held that the defense should have been allowed. Acknowledging that the statute on its face did not appear to allow the defense, the court said: "[T]he potential penalty to the defendant is so severe when compared to the 'loss,' if any, sustained by the victim, that we decline to find the statutory offense of theft by deception applicable in situations where the 'victim' receives value in excess of the consideration paid, absent a clearer indication of legislative intent." State v. Kelly, 484 A.2d 1066, 1068 (N.H.1984). The court observed: "In the situation where property is exchanged between two willing parties, even if fraud is committed, the deceiving party can only intend to deprive the victim of the value of the victim's property that exceeds the

---

attempt to steal it is made by specially experienced and ingenious thieves, who usually conspire for the purpose. This, again, is a reason why such offences should be liable to be punished with special severity." 3 Stephen, History 168.

59. The Model Penal Code provides: "The amount involved in a theft shall be deemed to be the highest value, by any reasonable standard, of the property or services which the actor stole or attempted to steal." § 223.1(2)(b). The commentary makes plain that the ordinary defense of mistake of fact applies. On the other hand, a criminal's mistaken belief that the property is more valuable than it is makes him more culpable. The commentary observes: "The amount involved in a theft has criminological significance only if it corresponds with what the thief expected or hoped to get. To punish on the basis of actual harm rather than on the basis of foreseen or desired harm is to measure the extent of criminality by fortuity. It is the general premise of the Model Code that fortuity should be replaced as a measure of grading by an examination of the individual characteristics of the offender and by an evaluation of the culpability actually manifested by his conduct." 2 MPC Commentaries Part II, 146–47. The pattern of current law on this issue is unclear. Many states probably retain the view that the actual value of the property taken is controlling.

value of the property which the victim receives in the exchange." Id. at 1067.

The matter of statutory interpretation aside, is the court's reasoning sound? If the defendant in a case like *Kelly* were convicted and value were relevant to the category of the offense, how should it be determined?

8. INTENT

From the earliest days the law has counted as theft only takings accompanied by an intention to deprive the owner of his property.[60] Bracton tells us with some circularity that theft is a taking *"cum animo furandi,"* with intention to steal.[61] And the *Mirror*: "Larceny is the treacherous taking . . . . Treacherously, we say: because if the taker

60. The law does not require an intention to gain personally (often labeled *lucri causa*) from the theft. "The law evaluates the 'animus furandi' . . . [of larceny] in terms of the detriment projected to the legally protected interests of the owner rather than the benefits intended to accrue to the wrongdoer from his invasion of the rights of the owner."

State v. Gordon, 321 A.2d 352, 356 (Me. 1974). (For an old suggestion that there be such a requirement, see Rex v. Cabbage, Russ. & Ry. 292 (1815).)

61. 2 H. Bracton, On the Laws and Customs of England 425 (c. 1250) (S. Thorne trans., 1968).

believed the things to be his own, so that he could lawfully take them, in such a case he does not commit this sin. Nor does he where he takes another's goods believing that his taking them is agreeable to the owner. . . ."[62]

—

274. Consider the following cases: (i) Brown sees Jones's coat on a hanger in a restaurant. Deciding that it is just the thing to complete his fall outfit, Brown surreptitiously takes the coat from the hanger, places it over his arm, and starts to walk out. Jones sees Brown going out the door, chases him, and recovers the coat. (ii) Smith carelessly removes Jones's coat from a restaurant. Before Smith discovers his mistake, his wife gives the coat to a local church group, which sells it at a rummage sale.

Why should Brown be a thief and Smith not? Despite Brown's conduct, Jones has his coat. Smith, however, caused Jones's permanent loss of his coat.

275. O. Holmes, The Common Law 58–59 (M. Howe ed., 1963):

In larceny the consequences immediately flowing from the act are generally exhausted with little or no harm to the owner. Goods are removed from his possession by trespass, and that is all, when the crime is complete. But they must be permanently kept from him before the harm is one which the law seeks to prevent. A momentary loss of possession is not what has been guarded against with such severe penalties. What the law means to prevent is the loss of it wholly and forever, as is shown by the fact that it is not larceny to take for a temporary use without intending to deprive the owner of his property. If then the law punishes the mere act of taking, it punishes an act which will not of itself produce the evil effect sought to be prevented, and punishes it before that effect has in any way come to pass.

The reason is plain enough. The law cannot wait until the property has been used up or destroyed in other hands than the owner's, or until the owner has died, in order to make sure that the harm which it seeks to prevent has been done. And for the same reason it cannot confine itself to acts likely to do that harm. For the harm of permanent loss of property will not follow from the act of taking, but only from the series of acts which constitute removing and keeping the property after it has been taken. After these preliminaries, the bearing of intent upon the crime is easily seen.

---

62. The Mirror of Justices (7 Selden Society) 25 (W. Whittaker ed., 1895).

For a discussion of the requirement of criminal intent generally, in the context of a prosecution under the federal theft statute, 18 U.S.C. § 641, see Morissette v. United States, 342 U.S. 246 (1952).

. . .

There must be an intent to deprive such owner of his ownership therein, it is said. But why? Is it because the law is more anxious not to put a man in prison for stealing unless he is actually wicked, than it is not to hang him for killing another? That can hardly be. The true answer is, that the intent is an index to the external event which probably would have happened, and that, if the law is to punish at all, it must, in this case, go on probabilities, not on accomplished facts. The analogy to the manner of dealing with attempts is plain. Theft may be called an attempt to permanently deprive a man of his property, which is punished with the same severity whether successful or not. If theft can rightly be considered in this way, intent must play the same part as in other attempts. An act which does not fully accomplish the prohibited result may be made wrongful by evidence that but for some interference it would have been followed by other acts co-ordinated with it to produce that result. This can only be shown by showing intent. In theft the intent to deprive the owner of his property establishes that the thief would have retained, or would not have taken steps to restore, the stolen goods. Nor would it matter that the thief afterwards changed his mind and returned the goods. From the point of view of attempt, the crime was already complete when the property was carried off.

Is Holmes's explanation satisfactory?

276. The distinction that Holmes mentions between a temporary taking and a taking intended to be permanent may make all the difference, but it is not always easy to see. A person who takes another's property for "fun," or for revenge, or for a brief use, and intends promptly to return it may not be a thief.[63] Suppose, however, he takes property with the intention of claiming a reward for its return. Is he a thief?[64] Should it make any difference what he intends to do if the owner decides that he does not care enough about the property to give a reward for its return?

Suppose a person takes someone else's property without his consent and intends promptly to pay for it. Is he a thief?[65] Suppose he regards the

---

63. "[A]cts of taking money or small articles of property from associates in joke . . . are of almost daily occurrence. Such conduct is silly and frequently leads to altercation, but it falls far short of larceny, in the absence of all proof of secret action or of evidence tending clearly to show an intent to deprive the owner of his property." Devine v. People, 20 Hun. 98, 103 (N.Y.Sup.Ct.1880). See People v. Brown, 38 P. 518 (Cal.1894) (revenge); People v. Pastel, 138 N.E. 194 (Ill.1923) (joy-ride).

64. Yes. "It is not necessary to constitute larceny, that the property should be itself permanently appropriated. It is sufficient if the property be taken and carried away with the intent to appropriate any pecuniary right or interest therein, as where it is taken with the expectation of claiming a reward for its return." Slaughter v. State, 38 S.E. 854, 855 (Ga.1901). Accord, e.g., Commonwealth v. Mason, 105 Mass. 163 (1870); State v. Hauptmann, 180 A. 809, 819–20 (N.J.Ct.Err.& App.1935).

65. No, at least if the property is for

taking as a loan that he will repay as soon as he is able.[66]

277. What of the many cases in which there is neither an intention to keep nor an intention to return? If Brown, caught in a rainstorm on his way to an important appointment, takes an umbrella belonging to someone else and after the appointment abandons the umbrella far from the place from which he took it, has he committed theft? Can he defend on the ground that he had no intention of keeping the umbrella? Or that by some chance the umbrella was recovered by its owner? What about Brown's son, who sees a car parked on the street with the keys inside? If he takes the car for a "joy ride" and leaves it two miles from where he found it, has he committed theft? Can he defend on the ground that, so far as he thought about the matter at all, he hoped (and expected) that the owner would get his car back? Suppose he damages the car.[67]

278. Are cases involving a homicide caused by the actor's recklessness or extreme recklessness helpful here? Is it strictly accurate that there is no crime of negligent theft, however extreme the negligence?[68]

279.

Concretely illustrative of the point that a wrongdoer may intend to use wrongfully taken property "only temporarily" and yet, without contradiction, intend that the owner be deprived of his property permanently is the case of a defendant who proposes to use the

sale and repayment is (intended to be) truly prompt. E.g., Mason v. State, 32 Ark. 238 (1877) (property for sale taken on Saturday night; offer of payment on Monday morning); see State v. Savage, 186 A. 738 (Del.Ct.Gen. Sess.1936) (gasoline taken from unattended car). The Model Penal Code § 223.1(3)(c) provides that it is an affirmative defense that a person "took property exposed for sale, intending to purchase and pay for it promptly, or reasonably believing that the owner, if present, would have consented."

66. Yes. "The intention to take, and the intention at some future time to make restitution, may be two different operations of the mind, just as the taking of money at one time and the repayment of it at some subsequent period are two distinct transactions. But even if it can be supposed that these two purposes, having in view the accomplishment of objects entirely distinct from each other, may be so blended together, by being contemplated at one and the same moment, as to be absolutely insepara-

ble, still it is undeniable that the execution of them can be worked out only by successive acts, with some intervening space of time between them. The abstraction must necessarily precede the restitution. The first will be complete before there is a possibility of commencing the act by which it is to be followed . . . . The past is complete and unchangeable; and as to the future [the actor] is dependent upon the will of others and upon circumstances over which he cannot exercise an absolute control." Commonwealth v. Tuckerman, 76 Mass. (10 Gray) 173, 205–206 (1857).

67. In Saferite v. State, 93 P.2d 762 (Okla.Crim.App.1939), the court held that there was no larceny when the defendant wrecked a car while returning it to the place from which he had taken it. Compare State v. Ward, 10 P. 133 (Nev.1886).

68. "If a person take another's watch from his table, with no intent to return it,

property only for a short time and then to destroy it. At the opposite pole, and excluding (as a matter of law) specific intent to deprive permanently the owner of his property, is the case of a defendant who intends to make a temporary use of the property and then by his own act to return the property to its owner. Between these two extremes can lie various situations in which the legal characterization of the wrongdoer's intention, as assessed by the criterion of whether it is a specific intent to deprive permanently the owner of his property, will be more or less clear and raise legal problems of varying difficulty.

In these intermediate situations a general guiding principle may be developed through recognition that a "taking" of property is *by definition* "temporary" only if the possession, or control, effected by the taking is relinquished. Hence, measured by the correct criterion of the impact upon the interests of the owner, the wrongdoer's "animus furandi" is fully explored for its true legal significance only if the investigation of the wrongdoer's state of mind extends beyond his anticipated *retention* of possession and includes an inquiry into his contemplated manner of *relinquishing* possession, or control, of the property wrongfully taken.

On this approach, it has been held that when a defendant takes the tools of another person with intent to use them temporarily and then to leave them wherever it may be that he finishes with his work, the fact-finder is justified in the conclusion that defendant had specific intent to deprive the owner permanently of his property. . . .

but for the purpose of timing his walk to the station to catch a train, and when he reaches there leaves it on the seat, for the owner to get it back or lose it, as may happen. If a man take another's axe with no intent to return it, but to take it to the woods to cut trees, and after he has finished his work cast it in the bushes, at the owner's risk of losing it, such reckless conduct would be accounted criminal." State v. Davis, 38 N.J.L. 176, 179 (Sup.Ct.1875).

Similarly, it has been decided that a defendant who wrongfully takes the property of another intending to use it for a short time and then to relinquish possession, or control, in a manner leaving to chance whether the owner recovers his property is correctly held specifically to intend that the owner be deprived permanently of his property. . . .

The rationale underlying these decisions is that to negate, as a matter of law, the existence of specific intent to deprive permanently the owner of his property, a wrongful taker of the property of another must have in mind not only that his retention of possession, or control, will be "temporary" but also that when he will relinquish the possession, or control, he will do it in some manner (whatever, particularly, it will be) he regards as having affirmative tendency toward getting the property returned to its owner. In the absence of such thinking by the defendant, his state of mind is fairly characterized as *indifference* should the owner *never* recover his property; and such indifference by a wrongdoer who is the moving force separating an owner from his property is appropriately regarded as his "willingness" that the owner *never* regain his property. In this sense, the wrongdoer may appropriately be held to entertain specific intent that the deprivation to the owner be permanent.

State v. Gordon, 321 A.2d 352, 357–58 (Me.1974).

280. If Brown (p. 436 note 277 above), thinking about his appointment, had taken the umbrella without realizing that it was not his own and discovered only after the appointment that it did not belong to him, is he a thief if he abandons it? If he keeps it?[69] Suppose he knew when he took it that it was not his but intended to return it promptly; if after his appointment he decides not to bother to return the umbrella and abandons it, is he a thief?[70] If he keeps it?[71] Should it make any difference in such

---

69. No. People v. Miller, 11 P. 514 (Utah 1886).

70. Yes. Ruse v. Read, [1949] 1 K.B. 377 (defendant was drunk and "borrowed" a bicycle for about two hours; then, sober, became frightened and consigned the bicycle for delivery elsewhere without intending to pick it up).

71. Yes. State v. Coombs, 55 Me. 477 (1868) (defendant hired a horse and sleigh, intending to return them but intending to go further than agreed; then became drunk and sold them); see R. v. Kindon, 41 Crim.App. 208 (1957).

Explaining its holding in *Coombs*, the Maine court subsequently said: "The general rule has long been stated to be that to constitute larceny the intent to steal must exist at the time of the taking . . . . Maine is one of the jurisdictions that has recognized as an exception to this rule the principle that if property is taken from the owner against his will, by a trespass or fraud, a subsequently formed intent to deprive the owner permanently of his property will constitute larceny. . . . However, if . . . possession of the . . . [property] was originally obtained lawfully . . . a subsequently formed intent to deprive the owner permanently would not constitute larceny." State v. Boisvert, 236 A.2d 419 (Me.1967).

cases that the mistake is not his but someone else's? Suppose, for example, the person in charge of the cloak room gave him the umbrella by mistake.[72]

281. One commentator has said of the English cases of the kind involved in the preceding paragraph: "[T]he complexities of the law are now such as to be beyond the capabilities of the best bench of magistrates. Hence the practice in this sort of case of the court paying tribute to the manful way in which the justices have struggled with the subject, before going on to demonstrate that they reached the wrong answer anyway." Elliott, "Ten Years of Larceny and Such 1954–1963," 1964 Crim. L. Rev. 182, 187. Why do these cases give so much difficulty?

282. Why should the law of theft try to prevent only losses of property "wholly and forever," Holmes, p. 434 note 275 above? Suppose someone takes property, just when its owner is about to use it, with the intention of returning it soon and intact.

———

In none of the cases just considered would the person who took property (once she learned, if she didn't know from the start, that the property was not hers) claim that she was entitled to do so. The difficulty, if there is a difficulty, is to decide whether her intention in taking the property is in relevant respects sufficiently like the paradigm *animus furandi* to be regarded as such. Suppose a person takes property and claims that she *is* entitled to it, despite someone else's possession and apparently superior claim.

"Although an intent to steal may ordinarily be inferred when one person takes the property of another, particularly if he takes it by force, proof of the existence of a state of mind incompatible with an intent to steal precludes a finding of either theft or robbery. It has long been the rule in this state and generally throughout the country that a bona fide belief, even though mistakenly held, that one has a right or claim to the property

---

72. No crime. Moynes v. Cooper, [1956] 1 Q.B. 439 (defendant mistakenly given extra wages; discovered mistake later and kept extra amount). But see Russell v. Smith, [1958] 1 Q.B. 27 (1957). In The Queen v. Ashwell, 16 Q.B.D. 190 (1885), the defendant asked to borrow a shilling, and the lender mistakenly gave him a sovereign. The defendant discovered the mistake later and kept the money. The court split seven to seven, and the conviction of larceny was affirmed. See Rex v. Hudson, [1943] K.B. 458 (defendant kept funds mistakenly mailed to him).

"In cases where the owner mistakenly gives the taker more than the taker was due, if the taker discovers the error before he acquires lawful possession, it is his duty to disclose the error, and if he takes the excess with the intent of converting it to his own use and without disclosing the error, the taking is a constructive trespass and sufficient for larceny." United States v. Posner, 408 F.Supp. 1145, 1151 (D.Md.1976), the facts of which are described at p. 411 note 244 above.

negates felonious intent. . . . A belief that the property taken belongs to the taker . . . or that he had a right to retake goods sold . . . is sufficient to preclude felonious intent. Felonious intent exists only if the actor intends to take the property of another without believing in good faith that he has a right or claim to it." People v. Butler, 421 P.2d 703, 706 (Cal.1967). *Butler* is reconsidered in People v. Tufunga, 987 P.2d 168 (1999). The court limited the claim-of-right defense to cases in which the defendant believes in good faith that he owns the specific property that he takes by force; it held that the defense does not apply to a forcible taking "to satisfy, settle, or otherwise collect on a debt, liquidated or unliquidated." Id. at 181.

"B, a debtor, has in his pocket two five dollar bills. His title to each is perfect. He owes A five dollars. A has not now, and never had, any title or possession of either of the bills. A presents a pistol to B and says: 'Pay me the five dollars you owe me immediately, else I will kill you.' B, out of fear, hands him one of the five dollar bills." Butts v. Commonwealth, 133 S.E. 764, 768 (Va.1926). Does A's taking constitute theft?

The court said no. "Has not A, by trespass, taken the bill, with intent to deprive B permanently of his property? Undoubtedly, but with no dishonest or criminal intent . . . . He took an unlawful means of collecting his debt, and was guilty of an aggravated assault, but not of robbery . . . ."

Butts is rejected in most jurisdictions, which, as in *Tufunga*, above, do not apply the claim-of-right defense to collection of a debt. In Cates v. State, 320 A.2d 75, 79, 80–81 (Md.Ct.Spec.App.1974), for example, the court observed:

> The phrase *claim of right* and the phrase *honestly believes himself to be entitled*, when applied to an intentional taking of property, must be given a limited and not a broad interpretation. They must be taken to require a legally recognizable right which can be successfully asserted in our courts. The *intent to steal*, the element of larceny which makes it and robbery specific intent crimes, must be evaluated objectively and not subjectively, and within the framework of rights and obligations given and imposed by the law.
>
> . . .
>
> A number of our sister States have adopted the view that one may resort to "self-help" in order to recoup gambling losses, and some States go so far as to hold that a creditor may by force of arms recover from his debtor that owed to the creditor without transgressing the criminal law. We do not share those points of view. Imagine a situation, for example, where a finance company or bank is allowed to obtain payment from their debtor, not by judicial process, but by simply meeting the debtor on his payday when he exits his place of employment, and by the use of a weapon collecting the amount due from the debtor. We have no hesitancy in stating that in all probability debtors would commence carrying guns in order to resist their credi-

tors. If we were persuaded by the reasoning employed in some of the other States then it is conceivable that those persons who engage in illegal gambling would also carry weapons so that they could recover their losses. Needless to say such occurrences could easily lead to the revival of the "Wild West," with an Eastern flavor—and turn our streets into "shoot-outs at the OK Corral."

See People v. Moseley, 566 P.2d 331 (Colo.1977), reversing an earlier holding in agreement with *Butts* on the basis that the current statute did not include as an element of robbery a specific intent to deprive another of his property. The statute read: "A person who takes anything of value from the person or presence of another by the use of force, threats, or intimidation commits robbery." In State v. Martin, 516 P.2d 753 (Or.Ct.App. 1973), the court distinguished between reclaiming specific personal property wrongfully withheld by another person and taking money from a debtor in satisfaction of a debt; in the latter case, the court said, there was no defense to a charge of theft. To the same effect, see State v. Hicks, 683 P.2d 186 (Wash.1984).[73]

In Commonwealth v. Larmey, 438 N.E.2d 382 (Mass.Ct.App.1982), the three defendants, wielding a hatchet and a hammer, took money from the two victims. The defendants claimed that they had just seen two women being mugged and had offered the women assistance. After seeing that the women were not hurt, they went after the muggers. Seeing the two men and believing that they were the muggers, they forced the men to surrender the money because they believed it belonged to the women. They were arrested while they were on their way back to the women to give them the money. If the defendants' story is true, are they guilty of robbery? (Incidentally, suppose the defendants' story were true and they had brought the money back to the women. If the amount were less than had been taken from the women but they had other reason to doubt that the men from whom it was taken had been the muggers, would the women have committed a crime if they had simply expressed their gratitude to the defendants and accepted the money? If so, what?)

Suppose a "claim of right" is honest but unreasonable.[74] Or suppose that instead of openly taking what one believes is due, by force or

---

73. Compare cases in which a shopkeeper extracts from an actual or supposed shoplifter the amount which the shopkeeper believes is due him by threatening to prosecute the shoplifter. The courts have not agreed about the shopkeeper's liability for extortion in such cases, the results in which are likely to turn on the wording of the statute defining extortion and the presumed legislative purpose. Compare People v. Fichtner, 118 N.Y.S.2d 392 (App.Div.1952), affirmed without opinion, 114 N.E.2d 212 (N.Y. 1953) (defendant liable), with State v. Burns, 297 P. 212 (Wash.1931) (defendant not liable

if the demand is limited to the "exact amount" due).

74. If the defendant takes more than the amount that he claims is due him the defense is, of course, unavailable at least with regard to the excess. E.g., State v. Trujillo, 489 P.2d 977 (Or.Ct.App.1971); cf. People v. Williams, 302 P.2d 393, 395 (Cal.Dist.Ct.App. 1956) (sums "disproportionate" on their face to services rendered). Courts have pointed out that a claim was unliquidated or highly uncertain when they disallowed the claim as a defense. E.g., Thomas v. State, 148 So. 225 (Miss.1933) (uncertain claim to unliquidated

otherwise, he takes it by stealth; if he does not reveal the taking but intends thereafter to make no further claim for the amount he believed due him, is he guilty of theft?[75]

283.

In the afternoon of September 3, 1932, a large number of unemployed people, among whom were the appellants, gathered together and marched to the Red Cross commissary in the city of Anacortes. Their purpose was to make a demonstration in support of a demand for a greater allowance of flour than had theretofore been made by the relief committee. Not finding the chairman of the committee at the commissary, they dispatched a messenger for him. On being informed that the chairman could not leave his place of business, they then marched to his office.

. . . The chairman advised them that it was impossible to comply with the demand, whereupon someone asked if that was final. Being informed that it was, several persons in the crowd said, in substance: "Very well, we'll get it." Up to this point, the assemblage had been peaceable and lawful.

The crowd then left the chairman's office, and a large number of them (variously estimated from forty to seventy-five) proceeded to the Skaggs store, which they entered. Many of them helped themselves to groceries, which they took away without paying for them.

State v. Moe, 24 P.2d 638, 639 (Wash.1933).

At their trial for grand larceny and riot the appellants "offered to prove the conditions of poverty and want among the unemployed of Anacortes and Skagit county on and prior to September 3rd. This proof was offered for the purpose of showing a motive and justification for the raid on the Skaggs store, and to show that the raid was spontaneous and not premeditated." Id. at 639–40.

With respect to the charge of grand larceny, should the proof be received? Should a "claim of right" based on economic necessity be a defense to a charge of theft?[76]

damages for killing of defendant's dog); Tipton v. State, 212 P. 612 (Okla.Crim.App. 1923) (uncertain claim to unliquidated damages for assault on defendant's wife). See generally People v. Stewart, 544 P.2d 1317 (Cal.1976).

[75] It is safe to say at least that secrecy will not strengthen a defense based on a claim of right, although that may be more because secrecy casts doubt on the genuineness of the claim than because secrecy as such defeats the claim. See People v.

Williams, 302 P.2d 393, 395 (Cal.Dist.Ct.App. 1956); State v. Sawyer, 110 A. 461, 462 (Conn.1920); State v. Schmidt, 30 N.W.2d 473, 475 (Iowa 1948); cf. Commonwealth v. Peakes, 121 N.E. 420 (Mass.1919).

[76] The court said no. "Economic necessity has never been accepted as a defense to a criminal charge. The reason is that, were it ever countenanced, it would leave to the individual the right to take the law into his own hands. In larceny cases, economic necessity is frequently invoked in mitigation of

284. The Model Penal Code § 223.1(3) provides that "it is an affirmative defense to prosecution for theft that the actor . . . acted under an honest claim of right to the property or service involved or that he had a right to acquire or dispose of it as he did . . . ." Would the evidence offered by the defendants in *Moe*, note 283 above, be admissible to establish such a defense? Would it be admissible to establish the defense of choice of evils under the Model Penal Code, p. 243 above?

9. METHOD

The method that is used to separate a person from his property has been a matter of considerable importance in the law of theft. It could not well be otherwise in a community where there is little of value lying around unowned, whose members do not all have as much property as they want, and which values and largely depends on individual enterprise. We have already considered three acquisitive techniques that the law has long prohibited: taking, breaking trust, and cheating or defrauding. The prohibitions of each of these techniques do not stand on the same footing, nor is the prohibition of each of them obviously equally necessary.

The law very early recognized the need to give protection against outright taking. It is not quite true that the concept of property implies protection against taking—one might meaningfully talk of my property and your property even if we both were limited to what we could presently possess and defend against taking[77]—but ownership over (limited) time and despite (temporary) distance is surely close to the center of the concept.[78]

punishment, but has never been recognized as a defense." 24 P.2d at 640.

77. But see P. Fitzgerald, Criminal Law and Punishment 12 (1962): "Food could not be eaten, clothing worn, or implements used if the consumer, the wearer, and the user were constantly exposed to the possibility of loss of possession. Without some measure of guarantee of quiet enjoyment of such things life could not go on. . . . Moreover, because of the vital importance of possession and quiet enjoyment, any interference with these tends to result in violence and disorder. In our own society, where private acquisition and ownership of property is recognized and accepted as a basic institution, it is all the more necessary that rules of law should have been developed to protect people against deprivation, damage, or destruction of their property."

78. Compare H.L.A. Hart, The Concept of Law 192 (1961): "It is a merely contingent fact that human beings need food, clothes, and shelter; that these do not exist at hand in limitless abundance: but are scarce, have to be grown or won from nature, or have to be constructed by human toil. These facts alone make indispensable some minimal form of the institution of property (though not necessarily individual property), and the distinctive kind of rule which requires respect for it. The simplest forms of property are to be seen in rules excluding persons generally other than the 'owner' from entry, or the use of land, or from taking or using material things. If crops are to grow, land must be secure from indiscriminate entry, and food must, in the intervals between its growth or capture and consumption, be secure from being taken by others. At all times and places life itself

The law's early uncertainty whether and how far to protect a fool, or a worthier fellow, from being parted too easily from his gold suggests that protection generally against misplaced trust and fraud is not so near the center.

Readily as we take for granted that the law should protect us against taking, or faithlessness, or fraud, answers in particular cases are not nearly so obvious as comfortably vague generalities. Even the prohibition against taking, obvious as it is, can be called into question. If A can save his child only by taking, perhaps destroying, B's property—say, by using something of B's to smother a fire—should A not take it? Should he be criminally liable for doing so? Is it obvious even that he should be civilly liable to B for the cost of the property destroyed? Suppose A uses B's property to save the life of a stranger, endangered without fault of his own. Some, perhaps most, of the distinctions which the criminal law draws between lawful and criminal acquisitive techniques can be traced to theories about human society that are not nearly so obvious or universally accepted as the right to own some property. As the development of the basic forms of theft shows, the distinctions that we draw now are not ineluctable and should be questioned, as much to demonstrate that they are right as to discover if they are wrong.

———

285.   Wheeler owned some lots of land near the expensive home of Kitts. In order to induce Kitts to buy the lots, which Kitts did not want, Wheeler arranged to have building operations started on them and to have Kitts informed that the operations were the first steps in the construction of a soap factory. Whereupon Kitts bought the lots. People v. Wheeler, 62 N.E. 572 (N.Y.1902).[79]

Did Wheeler commit any crime?

Suppose that instead of responding as he did to the information that a soap factory was to be built, Kitts immediately puts his own property up for sale. If he fails to tell a purchaser that, as he believes, a soap factory is about to be built near the property, does he commit a crime? (Suppose the purchaser mentions to him in casual conversation that he is interested in Kitts's property because there is such a "fine, large residence" going up next door.)[80]

depends on these minimal forbearances. Again, in this respect, things might have been otherwise than they are. The human organism might have been constructed like plants, capable of extracting food from air, or what it needs might have grown without cultivation in limitless abundance."

79.   The scheme was considerably more complicated than this summary of the court of appeals' statement suggests. See People v. Wheeler, 73 N.Y.S. 130, 134–36 (App.Div. 1901).

80.   "[T]he maxim of *caveat emptor* . . . requiring the purchaser to take care of his own interests, has been found best adapted to the wants of trade in the business transactions of life." Barnard v. Kellogg, 77 U.S. (10 Wall.) 383, 388 (1870).

Suppose the purchaser, having done some investigating on his own, does not tell Kitts that in fact no soap factory will be built. If Kitts has said nothing to him, may the purchaser, without committing a crime, in turn keep silent and purchase at a low price, which he knows reflects Kitts's misinformation? (Suppose Kitts has told the purchaser that he is selling at a low price because a soap factory is to be built.)

Suppose the situations are reversed, and Wheeler wants Kitts's land which Kitts refuses to sell even at a "good price." If Wheeler then commences mock building operations on his land and thereby persuades Kitts to sell, does he commit a crime? Does it matter whether he gives Kitts a good price?

Suppose Wheeler, being a man of great wealth and very anxious to have Kitts's residence, in fact builds a soap factory after Kitts refuses to sell to him. After the factory has been in operation for one week, Kitts sells to Wheeler. Wheeler promptly converts the factory into a greenhouse at a considerable loss. Has Wheeler committed a crime? Would it be at all relevant that

(i) Wheeler was very wealthy indeed, and Kitts was not;

(ii) Kitts had put his heart and most of his savings into the residence that Wheeler wanted;

(iii) Wheeler was in fact not a man but the Wheeler Corporation, a very large company with assets in the hundreds of millions;

(iv) Wheeler had no desire for Kitts's property and built the soap factory because he disliked Kitts, or to display his power, or from "disinterested malevolence."[81]

286.   False pretenses. In the *Wheeler* case, the trial judge instructed the jury that the representations made to Kitts that Wheeler intended to build a soap factory on his lots were not false pretenses. The court of appeals agreed. 62 N.E. at 573. Both courts evidently relied on the rule, accepted in most jurisdictions, that a false statement that does not misrepresent an "existing fact," such as a prediction or statement of intention or promise to do something in the future, is not a false pretense.

> Not only is the rule deeply rooted in our law, but moreover, we think the reasons upon which it is founded are no less cogent today than they were when the early cases were decided under the English statute cited by Wharton[82]. . . . It is of course true that then, as now, the intention to commit certain crimes was ascertained by looking backward from the act and finding that the accused intended to do what he did do. However, where, as here, the act complained of—namely, failure to repay money or use it as specified at the time of borrowing— is as consonant with ordinary commercial default as with criminal conduct, the danger of applying this technique to prove the crime is quite apparent. Business affairs would be materially incumbered by the ever present threat that a debtor might be subjected to criminal penalties if the prosecutor and jury were of the view that at the time of borrowing he was mentally a cheat. The risk of prosecuting one who is guilty of nothing more than a failure or inability to pay his debts is a very real consideration. It is not enough to say that if innocent the accused would be found not guilty. The social stigma attaching to one accused of a crime as well as the burdens incident to the defense would, irrespective of the outcome, place a devastating weapon in the hands of a disgruntled or disappointed creditor.

81. American Bank & Trust Co. v. Federal Reserve Bank of Atlanta, 256 U.S. 350, 358 (1921). "[T]he principle that a man may use his own property according to his own needs and desires, while true in the abstract, is subject to many limitations in the concrete. Men cannot always, in civilized society, be allowed to use their own property as their interests or desires may dictate without reference to the fact that they have neighbors whose rights are as sacred as their own. The existence and well-being of society require that each and every person shall conduct himself consistently with the fact that he is a social and reasonable person. . . . [W]hen a man starts an opposition place of business, not for the sake of profit to himself, but regardless of loss to himself, and for the sole purpose of driving his competitor out of business, and with the intention of himself retiring upon the accomplishment of his malevolent purpose, he is guilty of a wanton wrong and an actionable tort." Tuttle v. Buck, 119 N.W. 946, 947, 948 (Minn.1909).

82. The statute is 30 Geo. 2, ch. 24, p. 399 above. For an argument that Wharton, who gave the rule its accepted form, see 2 F. Wharton, Criminal Law 1731–32 (12th ed. 1932), misapplied the English cases, see Pearce, "Theft by False Promises," 101 U. Pa. L. Rev. 967, 968–74 (1953).

. . .

If we were to accept the government's position the way would be open for every victim of a bad bargain to resort to criminal proceedings to even the score with a judgment proof adversary. No doubt in the development of our criminal law the zeal with which the innocent are protected has provided a measure of shelter for the guilty. However, we do not think it wise to increase the possibility of conviction by broadening the accepted theory of the weight to be attached to the mental attitude of the accused.

Chaplin v. United States, 157 F.2d 697, 698–99 (D.C.Cir.1946).

See also United States v. Rothhammer, 64 F.3d 554 (10th Cir.1995) (signing promissory note without intention to pay); State v. Neal, 680 S.W.2d 310 (Mo.Ct.App.1984) (defendant who received money from under-cover police agent by representing that he would return with cocaine and who did not return *not* proved to have committed theft by deceit).

After reviewing the cases, including *Chaplin*, the California Supreme Court concluded in People v. Ashley, 267 P.2d 271, 282 (Cal.1954), that the general rule should not be followed: "The problem of proving intent when the false pretense is a false promise is no more difficult than when the false pretense is a misrepresentation of existing fact, and the intent not to perform a promise is regularly proved in civil actions for deceit. Specific intent is also an essential element of many crimes. Moreover, in cases of obtaining property by false pretenses, it must be proved that any misrepresentations of fact alleged by the People were made knowingly and with intent to deceive. If such misrepresentations are made innocently or inadvertently, they can no more form the basis for a prosecution for obtaining property by false pretenses than can an innocent breach of contract. Whether the pretense is a false promise or a misrepresentation of fact, the defendant's intent must be proved in both instances by something more than mere proof of non-performance or actual falsity . . . ." Accord State v. West, 252 N.W.2d 457 (Iowa 1977); State v. Aurgemma, 358 A.2d 46 (R.I.1976). See People v. Kiperman, 138 Cal.Rptr. 271 (Ct.App.1977) (fraudulent guarantee of workmanship by appliance repair service; *Ashley* applied).

Did the false representation that Wheeler intended to build a soap factory present the problem that troubled the court in *Chaplin*?

The Supreme Court has rejected the accepted rule from the beginning in its construction of the federal mail fraud statute, now 18 U.S.C. § 1341, expressly including false promises. Durland v. United States, 161 U.S. 306 (1896). The rule has been rejected in some other jurisdictions by decision or statute, and in the Model Penal Code § 223.3(a). The Reporters for the code inquired in the states that have rejected the rule and found that the fears expressed in *Chaplin* have not been realized. 2 MPC Commentaries Part II, 189 (comment to § 223.3).

There are a few cases denying liability for a false representation about the law, on the ground that a man is presumed to know the law and that a man who does not is negligent. E.g., State v. Edwards, 227 N.W. 495 (Minn.1929). The Model Penal Code § 223.3(a) rejects this rule.

287. Puffing. How should the law draw the line between a false representation that may be the basis of criminal liability and "puffing," such as a representation that a used car is "as good as new" or that a soap will "clean like magic." Excessive praise of one's product may, of course, be controlled, like other conduct that is criminal or borders on the criminal, by other legal resources, such as an action for rescission of the contract or for damages. At what point, in what circumstances, does puffing so far violate accepted norms of conduct as to become criminal? The Model Penal Code § 223.3 excepts from the crime of theft by deception "puffing by statements unlikely to deceive ordinary persons in the group addressed." Is that a satisfactory basis of distinction? Why (not)? Isn't the point of making such statements to encourage or induce people to buy goods that they otherwise might not buy?

288. False advertising. Many states have enacted "printer's ink" statutes which prohibit false or misleading advertising. E.g., N.Y. Penal Law § 190.20: "A person is guilty of false advertising when, with intent to promote the sale or to increase the consumption of property or services, he makes or causes to be made a false or misleading statement in any advertisement . . . to the public or to a substantial number of persons; except that, in any prosecution under this section, it is an affirmative defense that the allegedly false or misleading statement was not knowingly or recklessly made or caused to be made."

If the makers of "My Secret" lipstick advertise their product with a photograph of a woman surrounded by admiring men and a woman buys the lipstick with that image in mind, have the makers violated the statute if no one asks her what her secret is? If a weakling faithfully follows a bodybuilding course advertised by pictures of heroic men and just as always has sand kicked in his face when he goes back on the beach, has the statute been violated? If not, is it because the "statements" were not express but implied? (Suppose the caption on the lipstick advertisement read: "What is her secret? My Secret.") Or because they were not (knowingly) false or misleading? Or because they weren't intended to promote sales? Or because no reasonable person could be expected to believe the statements? If the latter, why then are they made? Is the point that they are not expected to be believed but are designed only to associate the product with a favorable stimulus?[83] If so, is it clear that such efforts to encourage a purchase by

---

83. If so, one might ask why the lipstick advertisement shows a woman surrounded by admirers and the body-building advertisement a man flexing bulging biceps, rather than a lovely still life or mountain view. "A famous soap . . . made its reputation by advertising that it floated. Why should floating be a saponic virtue? Chemists

irrelevant mental associations should not be criminal? According to what assumptions?

289. Some courts have been receptive to the claim that a contract is "unconscionable" and should not be enforced. The Uniform Commercial Code § 2–302 provides explicitly that a court may refuse to enforce a contract or portion of a contract that it finds as a matter of law to have been unconscionable at the time it was made. See, e.g., Williams v. Walker–Thomas Furniture Co., 350 F.2d 445 (D.C.Cir.1965). If a court finds that a party to a contract, without explicit fraud, deliberately so played on the other person's ignorance, foolishness, need, or desire as to induce him to agree to an unconscionable contract and thereafter collected according to the contract's terms, is there a sufficient basis in those findings to warrant criminal prosecution? Why (not)?

Finding.

290. A boarded a trolley-car and sat down next to B. A was carrying a small package of money, about $1100, wrapped in plain, unmarked brown paper which he placed on the bench between himself and B. When he left the car, he inadvertently left the package on the bench. B picked it up and took it with her when she left the car. She put the package in her handbag and took it home with her where she opened it that evening and discovered its contents. She placed the money in a desk. That same day, from a newspaper account of the loss she learned A's name and address and that he had offered a reward for return of the package. The next day A, accompanied by a detective, visited B and inquired about the package. B denied having any knowledge of it.

Did B commit theft? If so, when? What form of theft was it at common law?[84]

Would B have committed theft if, as she claimed, she had picked up the package by mistake because she thought it was one of several similarly wrapped packages that she was carrying, and did not discover the mistake

have told me that it is not, but on the contrary a vice, and that good soaps ought not to float." M. Radin, The Lawful Pursuit of Gain 73 (1931).

84. "If the accused took up the package in question honestly believing that it had been lost by the owner, but took it, knowing or having the means of ascertaining the owner, with the felonious intent to convert it to her own use at all events and deprive the owner of it although he should thereafter be discovered, the taking was unlawful and she would be guilty of larceny." State v. Courtsol, 94 A. 973, 975 (Conn.1915). The court referred also to a distinction between "lost" and "mislaid" property on which courts relied in early cases to preserve the requirement of a trespass. Property was mislaid and not lost if it was left in a place and in circumstances making it likely that the owner would quickly return to recover it; mislaid property was regarded as in the "constructive" possession of its owner, so that its removal by a finder was a "taking." Id. at 975. See also Long v. State, 33 So.2d 382 (Ala.Ct.App.1948).

until she arrived at home several hours later (and thereafter acted as described above)? Why (not)?[85]

291. If B saw A leaving without his package and plainly understood that he did not intend to leave it behind, is she guilty of any crime if she watches him walk off and then walks off herself, leaving the package on the seat? Why (not)? Does it make any difference whether she knew the value of the package? Does it make any difference whether B knew who A was?

292. Should the law require a person who finds property that is plainly lost and not abandoned to take any steps to restore it to its owner? If so, should there be criminal penalties for failure to comply with such requirements? Does anything turn on the nature or value of the property? Or the place where it is found? Or the size and population of the community? Can such factors be treated generally by a requirement that "reasonable measures" be taken to restore the property to its owner? If the law does make such requirements, should a person be able to avoid them by leaving the property where it is found or promptly returning it to the place where it is found? Reconsider pp. 285–94 above.

293. "From 1957 until the date of his death on June 1, 1974, Pasquale Stellato resided with his wife in the home he had built at 173 Canton Street, West Haven. Approximately three years before his sudden death at the age of 84, Stellato conveyed the property to West Haven Gardens, but he and his wife continued to live there. His wife lived there after he died until August, 1974.

---

85. The cases, most of them not recent, are agreed that "there must be a felonious intent to steal at the time of the taking in order to constitute larceny; and a subsequently formed intent is not sufficient." Brewer v. State, 125 S.W. 127, 128 (Ark. 1910). See Williams v. State, 268 S.W.2d 670 (Tex.Crim.App.1954).

In Thompson v. Nixon, [1966] 1 Q.B. 103, 110 (1965), the court followed this rule on authority but said it was "not only odd but wrong that those who find goods and who, at the time of the finding, have honest intentions towards them cannot be held to have committed any crime at all if later they dishonestly appropriate those goods." This conclusion has been accepted in the Model Penal Code § 223.5, p. 460 below. The Code's provision makes irrelevant not only an inno-

cent but also a felonious intent at the time of taking. "The search for an initial fraudulent intent appears to be largely fictional, and in any event poses the wrong question. The realistic objective in this area is not to prevent initial appropriation but to compel subsequent acts to restore to the owner. The section therefore permits conviction even where the original taking was honest in the sense that the actor then intended to restore; if he subsequently changes his mind and determines to keep the property, he will then be guilty of theft. Similarly, the section bars conviction where the finder acts with reasonable promptness to restore the property, even though he may have entertained a purpose to deprive at the time he acquired the property or at some other time during his possession." 2 MPC Commentaries Part II, 228.

"On August 15, 1974 . . . [West Haven Gardens, of which Vitagliano was president] began demolition of Stellato's former residence in preparation for construction of an apartment house. Vitagliano, Simpson and another employee Jay Hickerson were present. The demolition process attracted the neighbors, Mr. and Mrs. Malenda, who lived across the street. They observed the bulldozer operated by Simpson as it destroyed the Stellato home and knocked down the cinder block walls of the foundation.

"As the bulldozer struck the foundation near the front porch, many rolls of money fell out of the cinder blocks. When he had finished demolishing the front porch, Simpson observed the money on the ground. He got off the bulldozer and called Vitagliano to see what he had discovered. The rolls of bills were wrapped in aluminum foil and rubber bands. Each roll was approximately three and one-half inches in diameter, about the diameter of a baseball. The collision of the bulldozer with the house had caused some of the rolls to come apart.

"Vitagliano, who had been sitting with Hickerson on the steps of an adjacent building, immediately came to the area where Simpson had discovered the money. Vitagliano got down on his hands and knees and

stuffed all the rolls and the remaining loose bills in his shirt. Simpson, who was within six to seven feet of Vitagliano at the time, observed him picking up bunches of bills. The Malendas, who were on friendly terms with Vitagliano, observed . . . [his] actions from a distance of thirty to forty feet away. Mr. Malenda observed Vitagliano pick up four or five secured rolls and the bills from one additional roll which had broken apart and stuff them in his shirt. Mrs. Malenda observed Vitagliano pick up between five and seven rolls and the bills from two or three additional rolls which had broken apart and stuff them in his shirt. Immediately after Vitagliano finished stuffing the money in his shirt, which created a huge bulge, the Malendas heard him tell one of his employees that the bills he found totaled $60,000 to $70,000.

"Simpson, who picked up $1000 in loose bills at random, found only bills of $100 denomination. All bills seen by Simpson, who had discovered the money, were located within a five foot radius and were in $100 denomination. Later that day Mr. Malenda found one $100 bill among the debris.

"As soon as Vitagliano finished stuffing the money into his shirt, his wife, accompanied by their two children aged two and four, arrived at the job site in her automobile. Vitagliano pulled the children from the car, left them with Hickerson and told his wife to drive him home. He was very nervous during the drive home. His wife was upset because he dragged the children out of the car. When she asked him what happened, he opened his shirt and she saw the money. When they arrived home, Vitagliano told his wife to remain in the car. He entered the house, put the money in a bag and hid it in the attic.

"His wife drove him back to the job site. Later that day Simpson gave Vitagliano $200 of the money he had found. That evening Vitagliano returned to the job site alone with the money and counted it in his trailer. He never, even as of the date of trial, told his wife how much money he had found. Nor did he ever return or offer to return any of the money found to the estate or the heirs of Pasquale Stellato." Grant v. West Haven Gardens Co., 435 A.2d 970, 971–72 (Conn.1980).

It was subsequently determined that the estate of Stellato was entitled to the money that Vitagliano had found. Was Vitagliano guilty of theft?

294. Aggravated theft. The common law and legislation typically have recognized robbery as a particularly serious method of unlawful acquisition, an "aggravated" theft, because it involves not only a criminal invasion of property rights but also (danger of) bodily harm. Robbery is larceny committed by taking property from a person by force or threat of force. So long as robbery and larceny were both punishable by death, the aggravating feature of robbery was not so significant, although there is a suggestion that very early, robbery, being direct and open, was more honorable than larceny.[86] Now, statutes generally prescribe greater penal-

---

86. Albeit, in the same period, more clearly a violation of the king's peace. See 2 F. Pollock & F. Maitland, History of English Law 493–95 (2d ed. 1911).

ties for robbery than larceny. Statutes in particular states may establish degrees of robbery according to factors such as the use of a dangerous weapon, actual harm to the victim, and the nature of the victim (banks being particularly vulnerable and therefore protected by heavier penalties).

Robbery is typically distinguished from the lesser crime of larceny from the person, a more serious crime than simple larceny. Larceny from the person does not involve the use of force or threat of force.[87] Thus, a pickpocket who is skilled enough to remove property without its owner's knowledge is guilty of larceny from the person. If the owner is alerted, however, and resists, the crime is robbery. Some states require that the property that is taken be physically attached to the person to constitute larceny from the person. In others, it is sufficient if property is taken from the immediate possession and control of a person, even if it is not physically attached to her. E.g., Commonwealth v. Shamberger, 788 A.2d 408 (Pa.Super.2001).

295. Should the false portrayal of oneself as a police officer, accompanied by a show of authority, be sufficient to satisfy the element of force in the crime of robbery?

On November 10, 1982, Thomas Roa was the manager of a store on St. Nicholas Avenue in Manhattan, which was a former beauty parlor. Some old wigs were still displayed in the window. In actuality, however, the location was now an illegal policy parlor—a numbers place—and had been for some time previously. At about 11:00 p.m. that evening, Roa was closing up shop for the night. A co-worker, Maria, was tallying up the evening's receipts. They both were in a locked area behind a glass partition.

Suddenly, three young men, later identified as the defendants herein, appeared in the public portion of the store. Defendant Silverman displayed a badge, which was hanging around his neck, said "police," and demanded entry to the private part of the location. No weapon was displayed or employed, however, by any defendant during the entire incident.

When Roa hesitated to obey Silverman's command, Maria pleaded to let the policemen in, and Roa opened the door to the inner sanctum. Silverman then placed his hand on Roa's chest, cursed, and said,

---

87. See Commonwealth v. Jones, 283 N.E.2d 840, 844–45 (Mass.1972), holding that the force applied in a purse-snatching "is sufficient to make the crime a robbery, even though the application of force may, in practice, be so quick as to deny the victim any opportunity to resist." The court noted that the rule in most jurisdictions is to the contrary: "snatching does not involve sufficient force to constitute robbery, unless the victim resists the taking or sustains physical injury, or unless the article taken is so attached to the victim's clothing as to afford resistance." Very slight force or injury to the victim may be sufficient to make a purse-snatching robbery. See, e.g., People v. Bowel, 488 N.E.2d 995 (Ill.1986); State v. Butler, 719 S.W.2d 35 (Mo.Ct.App.1986).

"Don't move; get against the wall." Roa complied and raised his hands. Maria was told to leave, and did.

Thereafter, while defendants Flynn and Coppola were searching the garbage cans and the refrigerator (fruitlessly, as it eventuated), Silverman confiscated a group of policy slips and over $400 in cash. All of the defendants then, nonchalantly, walked out of the establishment. At this point, Roa surmised that the three were not policemen, since they had not arrested him in the supposed "raid." He then quickly pursued them with a metal awning pole and was soon joined by a real policeman, who was passing by at the time.

About ten minutes later, after the defendants had disappeared following a four block chase, a shower of observable policy slips alerted what had now become a veritable army of policemen to make a roof-top apprehension of all three defendants. Additional policy slips and $463 in cash were found stashed in a skylight on the roof.

People v. Flynn, 475 N.Y.S.2d 334, 336–37 (Sup.Ct.1984).

The court concluded that the defendants were not guilty of robbery. "[I]t is clear that here the *modus operandi* of the thieves was not the use or threatened use of physical force at all, but a ruse that they were police officers. Until they departed the premises without making an arrest, they plainly acted not as robbers, but as law enforcement officials. Their masquerade had not been exposed or even questioned. The submission of the complainant Roa was not to physical force or to any immediate threat thereof, but merely to what was perceived by him to be police authority— the power of the badge. Indeed, the locked inner door was opened by Roa only when Maria urged him to obey a police order. Thereafter, the complainant's anxiety was not of bodily danger or of physical harm, but of a police search of his illegal premises and of a subsequent arrest for his unlawful activities." Id. at 338.

Extortion.

296. Another form of theft, closely related to robbery and sometimes described as "aggravated theft," is extortion,[88] a crime in every state. Instead of the violence characteristic of robbery, extortion involves threats of certain kinds: generally, threats of injury to the person or to property or reputation and threats to accuse of a crime. In a majority of states the crime is committed if the threats are made with the requisite intent, whether or not property is actually acquired thereby.[89]

---

88. The statutory crime is also commonly known as blackmail. There was a crime of extortion in the early common law but it was limited to unauthorized takings by public officials accomplished by threats under color of office. See, e.g., 1 E. East, Pleas of the Crown 382 (1803).

The Model Penal Code treats robbery in a separate article, Art. 222, but treats obtaining property by extortion as a form of theft, § 223.4, punishable like other forms of theft with one qualification about penalty, see § 223.1(2)(b).

89. If the crime is complete when the threats are made it resembles theft less than

297. Not all threats to do something harmful to another person can be made criminal. Suppose, for example, that Wheeler, p. 444 note 285, above, had intended to build a soap factory, and so advised Kitts. If Kitts had offered Wheeler an inducement to build elsewhere and Wheeler had accepted, would Wheeler have been guilty of extortion?[90] All bargaining situations have in them an element of matched "threats" to withhold what one has to offer, although, to be sure, a bargaining position takes on the color of a threat only when the other party's need for the particular bargain is (known to be) especially great.

How should the law distinguish between the criminal and non-criminal use of threats to obtain property? By specifying the nature of prohibited threats? The Model Penal Code § 223.4 specifies threats to:

(1) inflict bodily injury on anyone or commit any other criminal offense; or

(2) accuse anyone of a criminal offense; or

(3) expose any secret tending to subject any person to hatred, contempt or ridicule, or to impair his credit or business repute; or

(4) take or withhold action as an official, or cause an official to take or withhold action; or

(5) bring about or continue a strike, boycott or other collective unofficial action, if the property is not demanded or received for the benefit of the group in whose interest the actor purports to act; or

(6) testify or provide information or withhold testimony or information with respect to another's legal claim or defense; or

(7) inflict any other harm which would not benefit the actor.[91]

some other crimes. Counterfeiting, kidnapping, burglary, arson and forgery may also be committed to acquire someone else's property but are regarded as serious harms in themselves, whether or not that is the result. The fact that forgery is usually prosecuted along with "uttering"—passing—the forged instrument suggests an uncertain judgment that forgery by itself is no longer a very serious matter and should perhaps be assimilated to false pretenses or theft generally. See the comment to the Model Penal Code § 224.1, which treats forgery separately, 2 MPC Commentaries Part II, 282–85. The Model Penal Code treats the making of threats without obtaining property as a crime distinct from theft by extortion. §§ 211.3, 212.5.

90. "[T]he word 'threats' often is used as if, when it appeared that threats had been made, it appeared that unlawful conduct had begun. But it depends on what you threaten. As a general rule, even if subject to some exceptions, what you may do in a certain event you may threaten to do, that is, give warning of your intention to do in that event, and thus allow the other person the chance of avoiding the consequences." Vegelahn v. Guntner, 44 N.E. 1077, 1081 (Mass.1896) (Holmes, J., dissenting).

91. "It is an affirmative defense to prosecution based on paragraphs (2), (3) or (4) that the property obtained by threat of accusation, exposure, lawsuit or other invocation of official action was honestly claimed as restitution or indemnification for harm done in the circumstances to which such accusation, exposure, lawsuit or other official action relates, or as compensation for property or lawful services." Id.

Is subdivision (7) too broad? Does it clearly exclude the proprietor of the only garage in town who refuses to send a towing truck on a rainy night unless the stranded motorist agrees to pay far more than a reasonable price? If it does exclude such a case, what is the principle of exclusion? Is the principle sound? Should such a case be excluded?

If Wheeler, perceiving Kitts's delight in his residence, decides to build a soap factory on his lot nearest Kitts's lot, rather than on an equally desirable lot farther away, unless Kitts buys him off, does Wheeler commit extortion if he communicates his decision to Kitts and Kitts does buy him off? Why (not)?

298. Destruction of property. Is the criminal law's traditional distinction between depriving another person of his property by appropriating it to oneself and depriving him of his property by destroying it sound?[92] Should the crime of theft be distinguished from the crime of malicious mischief and related crimes involving harm to property? Why (not)?

299. Asportation. The requirement of "asportation," a carrying away, is usually stated as a distinct element of the crime of larceny.[93] Aside from the possibility of consuming property on the spot—which might be regarded as both carrying it away and destroying it, or neither, according to one's purpose[94]—there could be no taking without a carrying away, unless the property were destroyed on the spot. The requirement of asportation, as well as ensuring that the "taking" is complete, serves to distinguish theft from the destruction of property.[95]

Asportation does not require that goods be taken far. E.g., Caver v. State, 466 So.2d 190 (Ala.Crim.App.1985) (goods do not need to be removed from premises); State v. Moultrie, 322 S.E.2d 663 (1984) (same).

92. Model Penal Code § 220.3. "Criminal Mischief. (1) Offense Defined. A person is guilty of criminal mischief if he: (a) damages tangible property of another purposely, recklessly, or by negligence in the employment of fire, explosives, or other dangerous means listed in Section 220.2(1) [flood, avalanche, collapse of building, release of poison gas, radioactive material or other harmful or destructive force or substance, or by any other means of causing potentially widespread injury or damage]; or (b) purposely or recklessly tampers with tangible property of another so as to endanger person or property; or (c) purposely or recklessly causes another to suffer pecuniary loss by deception or threat."

93. E.g., People v. Johnson, 289 P.2d 90, 94 (Cal.Dist.Ct.App.1955); see State v. Patton, 271 S.W.2d 560 (Mo.1954).

94. If one's purpose were a larceny prosecution, it would surely be regarded as a "taking and carrying away," as indeed it would shortly become unless the man remained on the spot.

95. Lack of any requirement in larceny that the taking be *lucri causa*, for gain (see p. 433, n. 60 above) may give the element of asportation undue significance in a case where a person removes property from its place in order to destroy or damage it, and immediately does so. Cf. O. Holmes, The Common Law 59–60 (M. Howe ed., 1963).

"Where a larceny is committed by trespassory taking, a thief's responsibility for the crime is not diminished because his act of carrying away the loot (asportation) is frustrated at an early stage. Thus, a shoplifter who exercises dominion and control over the goods wholly inconsistent with the continued rights of the owner can be guilty of larceny even if apprehended before leaving the store . . . a car thief who starts the car can commit larceny before he actually drives the automobile away . . . and a pickpocket can be guilty of larceny even though his removal of the victim's possessions is interrupted before completion. . . . By the same token, one who learns of a larceny while it is in progress and assists its perpetrator cannot avoid accomplice liability merely because such participation occurs after the principal, for purposes of his own liability, has technically completed the crime." People v. Robinson, 459 N.E.2d 483, 484 (N.Y.1983).

In State v. Johnson, 558 N.W.2d 375 (Wis.1997), the defendant, armed with a gun, ordered the owner of a car to get out and himself got into the driver's seat. The car for some reason would not start, and it did not move. Reaffirming that asportation is an element of the crime of robbery, the court held that "a person may not be convicted of armed robbery when the property at issue is an automobile and the person does not move the automobile."

10. A CONSOLIDATED THEFT STATUTE

Many of the theft provisions of the Model Penal Code have been quoted or described above in connection with particular problems. The provisions are set forth here all together to provide an integrated example of the modern statutory law of theft.

————

Article 223. Theft and Related Offenses

Section 223.0. Definitions.

In this Article, unless a different meaning plainly is required:

(1) "deprive" means: (a) to withhold property of another permanently or for so extended a period as to appropriate a major portion of its economic value, or with intent to restore only upon payment of reward or other compensation; or (b) to dispose of the property so as to make it unlikely that the owner will recover it.

(2) "financial institution" means a bank, insurance company, credit union, building and loan association, investment trust or other

organization held out to the public as a place of deposit of funds or medium of savings or collective investment.

(3) "government" means the United States, any State, county, municipality, or other political unit, or any department, agency or subdivision of any of the foregoing, or any corporation or other association carrying out the functions of government.

(4) "movable property" means property the location of which can be changed, including things growing on, affixed to, or found in land, and documents although the rights represented thereby have no physical location. "Immovable property" is all other property.

(5) "obtain" means: (a) in relation to property, to bring about a transfer or purported transfer of a legal interest in the property, whether to the obtainer or another; or (b) in relation to labor or service, to secure performance thereof.

(6) "property" means anything of value, including real estate, tangible and intangible personal property, contract rights, choses-in-action and other interests in or claims to wealth, admission or transportation tickets, captured or domestic animals, food and drink, electric or other power.

(7) "property of another" includes property in which any person other than the actor has an interest which the actor is not privileged to infringe, regardless of the fact that the actor also has an interest in the property and regardless of the fact that the other person might be precluded from civil recovery because the property was used in an unlawful transaction or was subject to forfeiture as contraband. Property in possession of the actor shall not be deemed property of another who has only a security interest therein, even if legal title is in the creditor pursuant to a conditional sales contract or other security agreement.

Section 223.1. Consolidation of Theft Offenses; Grading; Provisions Applicable to Theft Generally.

(1) Consolidation of Theft Offenses. Conduct denominated theft in this Article constitutes a single offense. An accusation of theft may be supported by evidence that it was committed in any manner that would be theft under this Article, notwithstanding the specification of a different manner in the indictment or information, subject only to the power of the Court to ensure fair trial by granting a continuance or other appropriate relief where the conduct of the defense would be prejudiced by lack of fair notice or by surprise.

(2) Grading of Theft Offenses.

(a) Theft constitutes a felony of the third degree if the amount involved exceeds $500, or if the property stolen is a firearm, automobile, airplane, motorcycle, motorboat or other motor-propelled vehicle, or in the case of theft by receiving stolen property, if the receiver is in the business of buying or selling stolen property.

(b) Theft not within the preceding paragraph constitutes a misdemeanor, except that if the property was not taken from the person or by threat, or in breach of a fiduciary obligation, and the actor proves by a preponderance of the evidence that the amount involved was less than $50, the offense constitutes a petty misdemeanor.

(c) The amount involved in a theft shall be deemed to be the highest value, by any reasonable standard, of the property or services which the actor stole or attempted to steal. Amounts involved in thefts committed pursuant to one scheme or course of conduct, whether from the same person or several persons, may be aggregated in determining the grade of the offense.

(3) Claim of Right. It is an affirmative defense to prosecution for theft that the actor:

(a) was unaware that the property or service was that of another; or

(b) acted under an honest claim of right to the property or service involved or that he had a right to acquire or dispose of it as he did; or

(c) took property exposed for sale, intending to purchase and pay for it promptly, or reasonably believing that the owner, if present, would have consented.

(4) Theft from Spouse. It is no defense that theft was from the actor's spouse, except that misappropriation of household and personal effects, or other property normally accessible to both spouses, is theft only if it occurs after the parties have ceased living together.

Section 223.2. Theft by Unlawful Taking or Disposition.

(1) Movable Property. A person is guilty of theft if he unlawfully takes, or exercises unlawful control over, movable property of another with purpose to deprive him thereof.

(2) Immovable Property. A person is guilty of theft if he unlawfully transfers immovable property of another or any interest therein with purpose to benefit himself or another not entitled thereto.

Section 223.3. Theft by Deception.

A person is guilty of theft if he purposely obtains property of another by deception. A person deceives if he purposely:

(1) creates or reinforces a false impression, including false impressions as to law, value, intention or other state of mind; but deception as to a person's intention to perform a promise shall not be inferred from the fact alone that he did not subsequently perform the promise; or

(2) prevents another from acquiring information which would affect his judgment of a transaction; or

(3) fails to correct a false impression which the deceiver previously created or reinforced, or which the deceiver knows to be influencing

another to whom he stands in a fiduciary or confidential relationship; or

(4) fails to disclose a known lien, adverse claim or other legal impediment to the enjoyment of property which he transfers or encumbers in consideration for the property obtained, whether such impediment is or is not valid, or is or is not a matter of official record.

The term "deceive" does not, however, include falsity as to matters having no pecuniary significance, or puffing by statements unlikely to deceive ordinary persons in the group addressed.

Section 223.4. Theft by Extortion.

A person is guilty of theft if he purposely obtains property of another by threatening to:

(1) inflict bodily injury on anyone or commit any other criminal offense; or

(2) accuse anyone of a criminal offense; or

(3) expose any secret tending to subject any person to hatred, contempt or ridicule, or to impair his credit or business repute; or

(4) take or withhold action as an official, or cause an official to take or withhold action; or

(5) bring about or continue a strike, boycott or other collective unofficial action, if the property is not demanded or received for the benefit of the group in whose interest the actor purports to act; or

(6) testify or provide information or withhold testimony or information with respect to another's legal claim or defense; or

(7) inflict any other harm which would not benefit the actor.

It is an affirmative defense to prosecution based on paragraphs (2), (3), or (4) that the property obtained by threat of accusation, exposure, lawsuit or other invocation of official action was honestly claimed as restitution or indemnification for harm done in the circumstances to which such accusation, exposure, lawsuit or other official action relates, or as compensation for property or lawful services.

Section 223.5. Theft of Property Lost, Mislaid, or Delivered by Mistake.

A person who comes into control of property of another that he knows to have been lost, mislaid, or delivered under a mistake as to the nature or amount of the property or the identity of the recipient is guilty of theft if, with purpose to deprive the owner thereof, he fails to take reasonable measures to restore the property to a person entitled to have it.

Section 223.6. Receiving Stolen Property.

(1) Receiving. A person is guilty of theft if he purposely receives, retains, or disposes of movable property of another knowing that it has been stolen, or believing that it has probably been stolen, unless the

property is received, retained, or disposed with purpose to restore it to the owner. "Receiving" means acquiring possession, control or title, or lending on the security of the property.

(2) Presumption of Knowledge. The requisite knowledge or belief is presumed in the case of a dealer who:

(a) is found in possession or control of property stolen from two or more persons on separate occasions; or

(b) has received stolen property in another transaction within the year preceding the transaction charged; or

(c) being a dealer in property of the sort received, acquires it for a consideration which he knows is far below its reasonable value.

"Dealer" means a person in the business of buying or selling goods.

Section 223.7. Theft of Services.

(1) A person is guilty of theft if he purposely obtains services which he knows are available only for compensation, by deception or threat, or by false token or other means to avoid payment for the service. "Services" includes labor, professional service, transportation, telephone or other public service, accommodation in hotels, restaurants or elsewhere, admission to exhibitions, use of vehicles or other movable property. Where compensation for service is ordinarily paid immediately upon the rendering of such service, as in the case of hotels and restaurants, refusal to pay or absconding without payment or offer to pay gives rise to a presumption that the service was obtained by deception as to intention to pay.

(2) A person commits theft if, having control over the disposition of services of others, to which he is not entitled, he knowingly diverts such services to his own benefit or to the benefit of another not entitled thereto.

Section 223.8. Theft by Failure to Make Required Disposition of Funds Received.

A person who purposely obtains property upon agreement, or subject to a known legal obligation, to make specified payment or other disposition, whether from such property or its proceeds or from his own property to be reserved in equivalent amount, is guilty of theft if he deals with the property obtained as his own and fails to make the required payment or disposition. The foregoing applies notwithstanding that it may be impossible to identify particular property as belonging to the victim at the time of the actor's failure to make the required payment or disposition. An officer or employee of the government or of a financial institution is presumed: (i) to know any legal obligation relevant to his criminal liability under this Section, and (ii) to have dealt with the property as his own if he fails to pay or account upon lawful demand, or if an audit reveals a shortage or falsification of accounts.

Section 223.9. Unauthorized Use of Automobiles and Other Vehicles.

A person commits a misdemeanor if he operates another's automobile, airplane, motorcycle, motorboat, or other motor-propelled vehicle without consent of the owner. It is an affirmative defense to prosecution under this Section that the actor reasonably believed that the owner would have consented to the operation had he known of it.

———

300. Reconsider the development of the law of theft from the days when it was doubted whether the carrier had committed a crime when he made off with the merchant's goods. Is it surprising that the law has changed so much? Or so little?

301. How would you describe the process by which the law of theft developed? To what extent can new departures be located precisely in the course of development? What were the roles played by courts or individual judges, the legislature, and commentators? To what extent were changes in the law the product of a deliberate decision and to what extent were they made unwittingly? Are we less in need of legal fictions now than before?

302. The specific problems in the law of theft now are certainly not those that troubled the judges 500 years ago. Has the nature of the underlying issues changed? In what directions would you expect the law of theft to move in the next hundred years? Which issues will be settled? Which will emerge? Are there some forms of conduct now regarded as distinct from theft, fit for special legislation, which within that period we shall discover are enough like theft to be consolidated with it? What about false advertising? Some cases of price-fixing?

———

"The true grounds of decision are considerations of policy and of social advantage, and it is vain to suppose that solutions can be attained merely by logic and the general propositions of law which nobody disputes." Holmes, J., dissenting in Vegelahn v. Guntner, 44 N.E. 1077, 1080 (Mass. 1896).

PART THREE

LAW IN SOCIAL CONTEXT

Since around 1970, the crime of rape has possibly been the subject of more discussion and controversy than any other single crime. While public concern about "crime in the streets" and a loss of a sense of personal security increased generally, rape in particular has aroused attention and anger for reasons peculiar to it. Organized women's groups have claimed insistently that the law has shown little regard for the victim of a rape and too often responds to the injury to her as if it were inconsequential. Too often, they assert, rape is treated as a serious crime only if the woman suffers a substantial injury in addition to the sexual violation or if the latter injures some male interest in her sexual conduct. Official institutions responsible for enforcement of the law have been accused not only of minimizing the victim's injury but of explicitly or implicitly blaming her for it, as if the man who raped her was acting normally and would not have been in trouble had she not abnormally enticed or refused him. The public ordeal of making an accusation of rape, it is said, is so great that many victims prefer to remain silent. Even if an accusation is made, prosecutions are few, convictions fewer, and sentences light. These official responses to the crime are said to reflect the attitude of the male public generally. Sometimes it is added that the law and the official attitude toward rape make it difficult for many women to be certain that they have been the victim of a rape, when it is in fact the case.

The law has changed dramatically in response to these assertions—an indication that they are, or were, well founded. Not only the central definition of the crime itself, but, more sharply, many collateral aspects of the law have been revised in ways intended to give greater protection to the victim and increase the likelihood of prosecution, conviction, and punishment. It has become easier to talk openly about the danger of rape and to prepare women against becoming victims. Public and private support agencies, like rape-crisis centers, are much more available to victims.

Many people, especially active feminists and members of women's organizations, believe that the changes have for the most part been ineffective and that the law and related public institutions remain peculiarly indifferent to rape. They have argued that the problem of rape ought therefore to be regarded as a political rather than a legal matter. Other people believe that the law now comes as close as it can to a proper balance between deterrent potential on one hand and fairness and justice on the other. They assert that intractable features of the crime itself, such as the very nature of sexual relations and the nonpublic circumstances in which they usually occur, account for the limitations of the law's response. Some persons believe—although the belief is openly expressed less often than it used to be—that the problem of rape as a crime is exaggerated, that the law more or less accurately reflects correct social values, and that its enforcement is not much worse than enforcement of the criminal law generally.

The crime of rape affords an especially good opportunity to study the criminal law in its social context. Most students will themselves have had to consider social attitudes about sexual roles and relationships and to work out their own responses. Such attitudes are peculiarly relevant to the crime of rape, at least at present, because so many people believe that the prevailing attitudes are wrong and impose on and injure women generally, and many others believe that the prevailing attitudes are right or, in any event, "natural" and of themselves cause no injury. Nor does everyone agree about what the prevailing attitudes are.

Two general questions ought to be kept in mind as you read the materials in this section:

(1) No other crime that we have considered provides so obvious and automatic a distinction between criminal and victim. What is the significance of the fact that rape is largely (although not exclusively) a crime that is committed only by men and only against women?

(2) Most of the leading positions in the legal profession and in public office generally have in the past been held by men. Although that pattern is changing as an increasing number of women enter the profession, it has not disappeared. What is the significance of that fact—however one explains it—for the law of rape? How (if at all) ought the law take account of male domination of the profession, while it persists?

Consider in connection with those questions, the "general assumptions . . . that there are constant pressures for sexual gratification and experience among all males and that some aggression is an expected part of the male role in sexual encounters." M. Amir, Patterns in Forcible Rape 130 (1971). With that compare the observation of Brownmiller that rape "is nothing more or less than a conscious process of intimidation by which *all men* keep *all women* in a state of fear." S. Brownmiller, Against Our Will: Men, Women, and Rape 5 (1975).

————

303. "[R]ape is the most under-reported crime in the United States, with only a fraction of the cases reported to police. A major reason for this is the victim's fear about the treatment she will receive from the criminal justice system as her case proceeds to trial. Even when crimes are reported, only 5 percent result in apprehension of a suspect and in less than 3 percent is there an actual conviction. Rapists are largely indistinguishable from the rest of the population. The victim is generally aged 20 or younger, while the rapist's age is typically 30 or younger. Most attacks involve strangers or slight acquaintances. Most rapes take place in the victim's home or on the street. Severe force is used in 60 percent of the cases, while some degree of 'strong-arm' force is present in 75 percent of the incidents. Most physical injuries are minor, but the psychological effects on the victim may be extremely severe." Battelle Memorial Institute Law and Justice Study Center, Forcible Rape: Final Project Report ix (1978).

————

The statement of the Battelle Institute, note 303 above, that most rapes involve "strangers or slight acquaintances" depends a good deal on how rape is defined. Although the statement reflects accurately the actual pattern of the law, it has been suggested forcefully that rape includes, or ought to include, the many occasions when a woman engages unwillingly in sexual relations because she believes that it is "expected" of her or because her indication of unwillingness is not perceived or is misunderstood or ignored.

————

State v. Rusk

289 Md. 230, 424 A.2d 720 (1981)

■ MURPHY, C.J. delivered the opinion of the Court. . . .

Edward Rusk was found guilty by a jury in the Criminal Court of Baltimore (Karwacki, J. presiding) of second degree rape in violation of Maryland Code (1957, 1976 Repl. Vol., 1980 Cum. Supp.), Art. 27, § 463(a)(1), which provides in pertinent part:

A person is guilty of rape in the second degree if the person engages in vaginal intercourse with another person:

(1) By force or threat of force against the will and without the consent of the other person . . . .

On appeal, the Court of Special Appeals, sitting *en banc*, reversed the conviction; it concluded by an 8–5 majority that in view of the prevailing law as set forth in Hazel v. State, 221 Md. 464 (1960), insufficient evidence of Rusk's guilt had been adduced at the trial to permit the case to go to the jury. . . . We granted certiorari to consider whether the Court of Special Appeals properly applied the principles of *Hazel* in determining that insufficient evidence had been produced to support Rusk's conviction.

At the trial, the 21-year-old prosecuting witness, Pat, testified that on the evening of September 21, 1977, she attended a high school alumnae meeting where she met a girl friend, Terry. After the meeting, Terry and Pat agreed to drive in their respective cars to Fells Point to have a few drinks. On the way, Pat stopped to telephone her mother, who was baby sitting for Pat's two-year-old son; she told her mother that she was going with Terry to Fells Point and would not be late in arriving home.

The women arrived in Fells Point about 9:45 p.m. They went to a bar where each had one drink. After staying approximately one hour, Pat and Terry walked several blocks to a second bar, where each of them had another drink. After about thirty minutes, they walked two blocks to a third bar known as E.J. Buggs. The bar was crowded and a band was playing in the back. Pat ordered another drink and as she and Terry were leaning against the wall, Rusk approached and said "hello" to Terry. Terry, who was then conversing with another individual, momentarily interrupted her conversation and said "Hi, Eddie." Rusk then began talking with Pat and during their conversation both of them acknowledged being separated from their respective spouses and having a child. Pat told Rusk that she had to go home because it was a week-night and she had to wake up with her baby early in the morning.

Rusk asked Pat the direction in which she was driving and after she responded, Rusk requested a ride to his apartment. Although Pat did not know Rusk, she thought that Terry knew him. She thereafter agreed to give him a ride. Pat cautioned Rusk on the way to the car that " 'I'm just giving a ride home, you know, as a friend, not anything to be, you know, thought of other than a ride;' " and he said, " 'Oh, okay.' " They left the bar between 12:00 and 12:20 a.m.

Pat testified that on the way to Rusk's apartment, they continued the general conversation that they had started in the bar. After a twenty-minute drive, they arrived at Rusk's apartment in the 3100 block of Guilford Avenue. Pat testified that she was totally unfamiliar with the neighborhood. She parked the car at the curb on the opposite side of the street from Rusk's apartment but left the engine running. Rusk asked Pat to come in, but she refused. He invited her again, and she again declined. She told Rusk that she could not go into his apartment even if she wanted to because she was separated from her husband and a detective could be observing her movements. Pat said that Rusk was fully aware that she did not want to accompany him to his room. Notwithstanding her repeated refusals, Pat testified that Rusk reached over and turned off the ignition to her car and took her car keys. He got out of the car, walked over to her side, opened the door and said, " 'Now, will you come up?' " Pat explained her subsequent actions:

> "At that point, because I was scared, because he had my car keys. I didn't know what to do. I was someplace I didn't even know where I was. It was in the city. I didn't know whether to run. I really didn't think, at that point, what to do.
>
> "Now, I know that I should have blown the horn. I should have run. There were a million things I could have done. I was scared, at that point, and I didn't do any of them."

Pat testified that at this moment she feared that Rusk would rape her. She said: "[I]t was the way he looked at me, and said 'Come on up, come on up'; and when he took the keys, I knew that was wrong."

It was then about 1 a.m. Pat accompanied Rusk across the street into a totally dark house. She followed him up two flights of stairs. She neither saw nor heard anyone in the building. Once they ascended the stairs, Rusk unlocked the door to his one-room apartment, and turned on the light. According to Pat, he told her to sit down. She sat in a chair beside the bed. Rusk sat on the bed. After Rusk talked for a few minutes, he left the room for about one to five minutes. Pat remained seated in the chair. She made no noise and did not attempt to leave. She said that she did not notice a telephone in the room. When Rusk returned, he turned off the light and sat down on the bed. Pat asked if she could leave; she told him that she wanted to go home and "didn't want to come up." She said, " 'Now, [that] I came up, can I go?' " Rusk, who was still in possession of her car keys, said he wanted her to stay.

Rusk then asked Pat to get on the bed with him. He pulled her by the arms to the bed and began to undress her, removing her blouse and bra. He unzipped her slacks and she took them off after he told her to do so. Pat removed the rest of her clothing, and then removed Rusk's pants because "he asked me to do it." After they were both undressed Rusk started kissing Pat as she was lying on her back. Pat explained what happened next:

> "I was still begging him to please let, you know, let me leave. I said, 'you can get a lot of other girls down there, for what you want,' and he just kept saying, 'no'; and then I was really scared, because I can't describe, you know, what was said. It was more the look in his eyes; and I said, at that point—I didn't know what to say; and I said, 'If I do what you want, will you let me go without killing me?' Because I didn't know, at that point, what he was going to do; and I started to cry; and when I did, he put his hands on my throat, and started lightly to choke me; and I said, 'If I do what you want, will you let me go?' And he said, yes, and at that time, I proceeded to do what he wanted me to."

Pat testified that Rusk made her perform oral sex and then vaginal intercourse.

Immediately after the intercourse, Pat asked if she could leave. She testified that Rusk said, " 'Yes,' " after which she got up and got dressed and Rusk returned her car keys. She said that Rusk then "walked me to my car, and asked if he could see me again; and I said, 'Yes'; and he asked me for my telephone number; and I said, 'No, I'll see you down Fells Point sometime,' just so I could leave." Pat testified that she "had no intention of meeting him again." She asked him for directions out of the neighborhood and left.

On her way home, Pat stopped at a gas station, went to the ladies room, and then drove "pretty much straight home and pulled up and parked the car." At first she was not going to say anything about the incident. She explained her initial reaction not to report the incident: "I didn't want to go through what I'm going through now [at the trial]." As she sat in her car reflecting on the incident, Pat said she began to "wonder what would happen if I hadn't of done what he wanted me to do. So I thought the right thing to do was to go report it, and I went from there to Hillendale to find a police car." She reported the incident to the police at about 3:15 a.m. Subsequently, Pat took the police to Rusk's apartment, which she located without any great difficulty.

Pat's girlfriend Terry corroborated her testimony concerning the events which occurred up to the time that Pat left the bar with Rusk. Questioned about Pat's alcohol consumption, Terry said she was drinking screwdrivers that night but normally did not finish a drink. Terry testified about her acquaintanceship with Rusk: "I knew his face, and his first name, but I honestly couldn't tell you—apparently I ran into him sometime before. I couldn't tell you how I know him. I don't know him very well at all."

Officer Hammett of the Baltimore City Police Department acknowledged receiving Pat's rape complaint at 3:15 a.m. on September 22, 1977. He accompanied her to the 3100 block of Guilford Avenue where it took Pat several minutes to locate Rusk's apartment. Officer Hammett entered Rusk's multi-dwelling apartment house, which contained at least six apartments, and arrested Rusk in a room on the second floor.

Hammett testified that Pat was sober, and she was taken to City Hospital for an examination. The examination disclosed that seminal fluid and spermatozoa were detected in Pat's vagina, on her underpants, and on the bed sheets recovered from Rusk's bed.

At the close of the State's case-in-chief, Rusk moved for a judgment of acquittal. . . . [The motion was denied.]

Rusk and two of his friends, Michael Trimp and David Carroll, testified on his behalf. According to Trimp, they went in Carroll's car to Buggs' bar to dance, drink and "tr[y] to pick up some ladies." Rusk stayed at the bar, while the others went to get something to eat.

Trimp and Carroll next saw Rusk walking down the street arm-in-arm with a lady whom Trimp was unable to identify. Trimp asked Rusk if he needed a ride home. Rusk responded that the woman he was with was going to drive him home. Trimp testified that at about 2:00–2:30 a.m. he returned to the room he rented with Rusk on Guilford Avenue and found Rusk to be the only person present. Trimp said that as many as twelve people lived in the entire building and that the room he rented with Rusk was referred to as their "pit stop." Both Rusk and Trimp actually resided at places other than the Guilford Avenue room. Trimp testified that there was a telephone in the apartment.

Carroll's testimony corroborated Trimp's. He saw Rusk walking down the street arm-in-arm with a woman. He said "[s]he was kind of like, you know, snuggling up to him like. . . . She was hanging all over him then." Carroll was fairly certain that Pat was the woman who was with Rusk.

Rusk, the 31-year-old defendant, testified that he was in the Buggs Tavern for about thirty minutes when he noticed Pat standing at the bar. Rusk said: "She looked at me, and she smiled. I walked over and said, hi, and started talking to her." He did not remember either knowing or speaking to Terry. When Pat mentioned that she was about to leave, Rusk asked her if she wanted to go home with him. In response, Pat said that she would like to, but could not because she had her car. Rusk then suggested that they take her car. Pat agreed and they left the bar arm-in-arm.

Rusk testified that during the drive to her apartment, he discussed with Pat their similar marital situations and talked about their children. He said that Pat asked him if he was going to rape her. When he inquired why she was asking, Pat said that she had been raped once before. Rusk expressed his sympathy for her. Pat then asked him if he planned to beat her. He inquired why she was asking and Pat explained that her husband used to beat her. Rusk again expressed his sympathy. He testified that at no time did Pat express a fear that she was being followed by her separated husband.

According to Rusk, when they arrived in front of his apartment Pat parked the car and turned the engine off. They sat for several minutes "petting each other." Rusk denied switching off the ignition and removing the keys. He said that they walked to the apartment house and proceeded up the stairs to his room. Rusk testified that Pat came willingly to his room and that at no time did he make threatening facial expressions. Once inside his room, Rusk left Pat alone for several minutes while he used the bathroom down the hall. Upon his return, he switched the light on but immediately turned it off because Pat, who was seated in the dark in a chair next to the bed, complained it was too bright. Rusk said that he sat on the bed across from Pat and reached out

> "and started to put my arms around her, and started kissing her; and we fell back into the bed, and she—we were petting, kissing, and she stuck her hand down in my pants and started playing with me; and I undid her blouse, and took off her bra; and then I sat up and I said 'Let's take our clothes off'; and she said, 'Okay'; and I took my clothes off, and she took her clothes off; and then we proceeded to have intercourse."

Rusk explained that after the intercourse, Pat "got uptight."

> "Well, she started to cry. She said that—she said, 'You guys are all alike,' she says, 'just out for,' you know, 'one thing.'

> "She started talking about—I don't know, she was crying and all. I tried to calm her down and all; and I said, 'What's the matter?' And she said, that she just wanted to leave; and I said, 'Well, okay'; and she walked out to the car. I walked out to the car. She got in the car and left."

Rusk denied placing his hands on Pat's throat or attempting to strangle her. He also denied using force or threats of force to get Pat to have intercourse with him.

In reversing Rusk's second degree rape conviction, the Court of Special Appeals, quoting from *Hazel*, 221 Md. at 469, noted that:

> Force is an essential element of the crime [of rape] and to justify a conviction, the evidence must warrant a conclusion either that the victim resisted and her resistance was overcome by force or that she was prevented from resisting by threats to her safety.

Writing for the majority, Judge Thompson said:

> In all of the victim's testimony we have been unable to see any resistance on her part to the sex acts and certainly can we see no fear as would overcome her attempt to resist or escape as required by *Hazel*. Possession of the keys by the accused may have deterred her vehicular escape but hardly a departure seeking help in the rooming house or in the street. We must say that 'the way he looked' fails utterly to support the fear required by *Hazel*. 43 Md. App. at 480.

The Court of Special Appeals interpreted *Hazel* as requiring a showing of a reasonable apprehension of fear in instances where the prosecutrix did not resist. It concluded:

> we find the evidence legally insufficient to warrant a conclusion that appellant's words or actions created in the mind of the victim a reasonable fear that if she resisted, he would have harmed her, or that faced with such resistance, he would have used force to overcome it. The prosecutrix stated that she was afraid, and submitted because of 'the look in his eyes.' After both were undressed and in the bed, and she pleaded to him that she wanted to leave, he started to lightly choke her. At oral argument it was brought out that the 'lightly choking' could have been a heavy caress. We do not believe that 'lightly choking' along with all the facts and circumstances in the case, were sufficient to cause a reasonable fear which overcame her ability to resist. In the absence of any other evidence showing force used by appellant, we find that the evidence was insufficient to convict appellant of rape. Id. at 484.

In argument before us on the merits of the case, the parties agreed that the issue was whether, in light of the principles of *Hazel*, there was evidence before the jury legally sufficient to prove beyond a reasonable doubt that the intercourse was "[b]y force or threat of force against the will and without the consent" of the victim in violation of Art. 27, § 463(a)(1). Of course, due process requirements mandate that a criminal conviction not be obtained if the evidence does not reasonably support a finding of guilt beyond a reasonable doubt. . . . However, as the Supreme Court made clear in Jackson v. Virginia, 443 U.S. 307 (1979), the reviewing court does not ask itself whether *it* believes that the evidence established guilt beyond a reasonable doubt; rather, the applicable standard is "whether, after viewing the evidence in the light most favorable to the prosecution, *any* rational trier of fact could have found the essential elements of the crime beyond a reasonable doubt." 443 U.S. at 319 (emphasis in original).

The vaginal intercourse once being established, the remaining elements of rape in the second degree under § 463(a)(1) are, as in a prosecution for common law rape (1) force—actual or constructive, and (2) lack of consent. The terms in § 463(a)(1)—"force," "threat of force," "against the will" and "without the consent"—are not defined in the statute, but are to be afforded their "judicially determined meaning" as applied in cases involving common law rape. . . . In this regard, it is well settled that the terms "against the will" and "without the consent" are synonymous in the law of rape.

Hazel, which was decided in 1960, long before the enactment of § 463(a)(1), involved a prosecution for common law rape, there defined as "the act of a man having unlawful carnal knowledge of a female over the age of ten years by force without the consent and against the will of the victim." 221 Md. at 468–69. The evidence in that case disclosed that Hazel followed the prosecutrix into her home while she was unloading groceries from her car. He put his arm around her neck, said he had a gun, and threatened to shoot her baby if she moved. Although the prosecutrix never saw a gun, Hazel kept one hand in his pocket and repeatedly stated that he had a gun. He robbed the prosecutrix, tied her hands, gagged her, and took her into the cellar. The prosecutrix complied with Hazel's commands to lie on the floor and to raise her legs. Hazel proceeded to have intercourse with her while her hands were still tied. The victim testified that she did not struggle because she was afraid for her life. There was evidence that she told the police that Hazel did not use force at any time and was extremely gentle. Hazel claimed that the intercourse was consensual and that he never made any threats. The Court said that the issue before it was whether "the evidence was insufficient to sustain the conviction of rape because the conduct of the prosecutrix was such as to render her failure to resist consent in law." Id. at 468. It was in the context of this evidentiary background that the Court set forth the principles of law which controlled the disposition of the case. It recognized that force and lack of consent are distinct elements of the crime of rape. It said:

> Force is an essential element of the crime and to justify a conviction, the evidence must warrant a conclusion either that the victim resisted and her resistance was overcome by force or that she was prevented from resisting by threats to her safety. But no particular amount of force, either actual or constructive, is required to constitute rape. Necessarily that fact must depend upon the prevailing circumstances. As in this case force may exist without violence. If the acts and threats of the defendant were reasonably calculated to create in the mind of the victim—having regard to the circumstances in which she was placed—a real apprehension, due to fear, of imminent bodily harm, serious enough to impair or overcome her will to resist, then such acts and threats are the equivalent of force. Id. at 469.

As to the element of lack of consent, the Court said in *Hazel*:

[I]t is true, of course, that however reluctantly given, consent to the act at any time prior to penetration deprives the subsequent intercourse of its criminal character. There is, however, a wide difference between consent and a submission to the act. Consent may involve submission, but submission does not necessarily imply consent. Furthermore, submission to a compelling force, or as a result of being put in fear, is not consent. Id.

The Court noted that lack of consent is generally established through proof of resistance or by proof that the victim failed to resist because of fear. The degree of fear necessary to obviate the need to prove resistance, and thereby establish lack of consent, was defined in the following manner:

> The kind of fear which would render resistance by a woman unnecessary to support a conviction of rape includes, but is not necessarily limited to, a fear of death or serious bodily harm, or a fear so extreme as to preclude resistance, or a fear which would well nigh render her mind incapable of continuing to resist, or a fear that so overpowers her that she does not dare resist. Id. at 470.

Hazel thus made it clear that lack of consent could be established through proof that the victim submitted as a result of fear of imminent death or serious bodily harm. In addition, if the actions and conduct of the defendant were reasonably calculated to induce this fear in the victim's mind, then the element of force is present. *Hazel* recognized, therefore, that the same kind of evidence may be used in establishing both force and nonconsent, particularly when a threat rather than actual force is involved.

The Court noted in *Hazel* that the judges who heard the evidence, and who sat as the trier of fact in Hazel's non-jury case, had concluded that, in light of the defendant's acts of violence and threats of serious harm, there existed a genuine and continuing fear of such harm on the victim's part, so that the ensuing act of sexual intercourse under this fear " 'amounted to a felonious and forcible act of the defendant against the will and consent of the prosecuting witness.' " In finding the evidence sufficient to sustain the conviction, the Court observed that "[t]he issue of whether the intercourse was accomplished by force and against the will and consent of the victim was one of credibility, properly to be resolved by the trial court." 221 Md. at 470.

Hazel did not expressly determine whether the victim's fear must be "reasonable." Its only reference to reasonableness related to whether "the acts and threats of the defendant were reasonably calculated to create in the mind of the victim . . . a real apprehension, due to fear, of imminent bodily harm . . . ." 221 Md. at 469. Manifestly, the Court was there referring to the calculations of the accused, not to the fear of the victim. While *Hazel* made it clear that the victim's fear had to be genuine, it did not pass upon whether a real but unreasonable fear of imminent death or serious bodily harm would suffice. The vast majority of jurisdictions have required that the victim's fear be reasonably grounded in order to obviate the need for either proof of actual force on the part of the assailant or physical resistance on the part of the victim. We think that, generally, this is the correct standard.

As earlier indicated, the Court of Special Appeals held that a showing of a reasonable apprehension of fear was essential under *Hazel* to establish the elements of the offense where the victim did not resist. The Court did not believe, however, that the evidence was legally sufficient to demonstrate the existence of "a reasonable fear" which overcame Pat's ability to resist. In support of the Court's conclusion, Rusk maintains that the evidence showed that Pat voluntarily entered his apartment without being subjected to a "single threat nor a scintilla of force"; that she made no effort to run away nor did she scream for help; that she never exhibited a will to resist; and that her subjective reaction of fear to the situation in which she had voluntarily placed herself was unreasonable and exaggerated. Rusk claims that his acts were not reasonably calculated to overcome a will to resist; that Pat's verbal resistance was not resistance within the contemplation of *Hazel*; that his alleged menacing look did not constitute a threat of force; and that even had he pulled Pat to the bed, and lightly choked her, as she claimed, these actions, viewed in the context of the entire incident—no prior threats having been made—would be insufficient to constitute force or a threat of force or render the intercourse nonconsensual.

We think the reversal of Rusk's conviction by the Court of Special Appeals was in error for the fundamental reason so well expressed in the dissenting opinion by Judge Wilner when he observed that the majority had "trampled upon the first principle of appellate restraint . . . [because it had] substituted [its] own view of the evidence (and the inferences that may fairly be drawn from it) for that of the judge and jury . . . [and had thereby] improperly invaded the province allotted to those tribunals." 43 Md. App. at 484–85. In view of the evidence adduced at the trial, the reasonableness of Pat's apprehension of fear was plainly a question of fact for the jury to determine. . . . Applying the constitutional standard of review articulated in Jackson v. Virginia, supra, i.e.—whether after considering the evidence in the light most favorable to the prosecution, any rational trier of fact could have found the essential elements of the crime beyond a reasonable doubt—it is readily apparent to us that the trier of fact could rationally find that the elements of force and non-consent had been established and that Rusk was guilty of the offense beyond a reasonable doubt. Of course, it was for the jury to observe the witnesses and their demeanor, and to judge their credibility and weigh their testimony. Quite obviously, the jury disbelieved Rusk and believed Pat's testimony. From her testimony, the jury could have reasonably concluded that the taking of her car keys was intended by Rusk to immobilize her alone, late at night, in a neighborhood with which she was not familiar; that after Pat had repeatedly refused to enter his apartment, Rusk commanded in firm tones that she do so; that Pat was badly frightened and feared that Rusk intended to rape her; that unable to think clearly and believing that she had no other choice in the circumstances, Pat entered Rusk's apartment; that once inside Pat asked permission to leave but Rusk told her to stay; that he then pulled Pat by the arms to the bed and undressed her; that Pat was afraid that Rusk would kill her unless she submitted; that she began to cry and Rusk then put his hands on her throat and began " 'lightly to choke' " her; that Pat asked him if he would let her go without killing her if she complied with his demands; that Rusk gave an affirmative response, after which she finally submitted.

Just where persuasion ends and force begins in cases like the present is essentially a factual issue, to be resolved in light of the controlling legal precepts. That threats of force need not be made in any particular manner in order to put a person in fear of bodily harm is well established. . . . Indeed, conduct, rather than words, may convey the threat. . . . That a victim did not scream out for help or attempt to escape, while bearing on the question of consent, is unnecessary where she is restrained by fear of violence. . . .

Considering all of the evidence in the case, with particular focus upon the actual force applied by Rusk to Pat's neck, we conclude that the jury could rationally find that the essential elements of second degree rape had been established and that Rusk was guilty of that offense beyond a reasonable doubt.

Judgment of the Court of Special Appeals reversed. . . .

■ COLE, J., dissenting:

I agree with the Court of Special Appeals that the evidence adduced at the trial of Edward Salvatore Rusk was insufficient to convict him of rape. I, therefore, respectfully dissent.

The standard of appellate review in deciding a question of sufficiency, as the majority correctly notes, is "whether, after viewing the evidence in the light most favorable to the prosecution, *any* rational trier of fact could have found the essential elements of the crime beyond a reasonable doubt." Jackson v. Virginia, 443 U.S. 307, 319 (1979) (emphasis in original). . . . However, it is equally well settled that when one of the essential elements of a crime is not sustained by the evidence, the conviction of the defendant cannot stand as a matter of law.

The majority, in applying this standard, concludes that "[i]n view of the evidence adduced at the trial, the reasonableness of Pat's apprehension of fear was plainly a question of fact for the jury to determine." In so concluding, the majority has skipped over the crucial issue. It seems to me that whether the prosecutrix's fear is reasonable becomes a question only after the court determines that the defendant's conduct under the circumstances was reasonably calculated to give rise to a fear on her part to the extent that she was unable to resist. In other words, the fear must stem from his articulable conduct, and equally, if not more importantly, cannot be inconsistent with her own contemporaneous reaction to that conduct. The conduct of the defendant, in and of itself, must clearly indicate force or the threat of force such as to overpower the prosecutrix's ability to resist or will to resist. In my view, there is no evidence to support the majority's conclusion that the prosecutrix was forced to submit to sexual intercourse, certainly not fellatio.

This Court defined rape in Hazel v. State, 221 Md. 464, 468–69 (1960). . . .

To avoid any confusion about the substantive law to be applied, we . . . stated in *Hazel* that while

> [t]he authorities are by no means in accord as to what degree of resistance is necessary to establish the absence of consent . . . the generally accepted doctrine seems to be that a female—who was conscious and possessed of her natural, mental and physical powers when the attack took place—must have resisted to the extent of her ability at the time, unless it appears that she was overcome by numbers or so terrified by threats as to overcome her will to resist. [221 Md. at 469–70.]

. . .

. . . *Hazel* intended to require clear and cognizable evidence of force or the threat of force sufficient to overcome or prevent resistance by the female before there would arise a jury question of whether the prosecutrix had a reasonable apprehension of harm. The majority today departs from this requirement and places its imprimatur on the female's conclusory statements that she was in fear, as sufficient to support a conviction of rape.

It is significant to note that in each of the fourteen reported rape cases decided since *Hazel*, in which sufficiency of the evidence was the issue, the appellate courts of this State have adhered to the requirement that evidence of force or the threat of force overcoming or preventing resistance by the female must be demonstrated on the record to sustain a conviction. In two of those cases . . . the convictions were reversed by the Court of Special Appeals. . . .

. . .

Of the other twelve cases, four from this Court, not one contains the paucity of evidence regarding force or threat of force which exists in the case *sub judice*. . . .

. . .

In each of the above twelve cases there was either physical violence or specific threatening words or conduct which were calculated to create a very real and specific fear of *immediate* physical injury to the victim if she did not comply, coupled with the apparent power to execute those threats in the event of non-submission.

While courts no longer require a female to resist to the utmost or to resist where resistance would be foolhardy, they do require her acquiescence in the act of intercourse to stem from fear generated by something of substance. She may not simply say, "I was really scared," and thereby transform consent or mere unwillingness into submission by force. These words do not transform a seducer into a rapist. She must follow the natural instinct of every proud female to resist, by more than mere words, the violation of her person by a stranger or an unwelcomed friend. She must make it plain that she regards such sexual acts as abhorrent and repugnant to her natural sense of pride. She must resist unless the defendant has objectively manifested his intent to use physical force to accomplish his purpose. The law regards rape as a crime of violence. The majority today attenuates this proposition. It declares the innocence of an at best distraught young woman. It does not demonstrate the defendant's guilt of the crime of rape.

My examination of the evidence in a light most favorable to the State reveals no conduct by the defendant reasonably calculated to cause the prosecutrix to be so fearful that she should fail to resist and thus, the element of force is lacking in the State's proof.

Here we have a full grown married woman who meets the defendant in a bar under friendly circumstances. They drink and talk together. She agrees to give him a ride home in her car. When they arrive at his house, located in an area with which she was unfamiliar but which was certainly not isolated, he invites her to come up to his apartment and she refuses. According to her testimony he takes her keys, walks around to her side of the car, and says "Now will you come up?" She answers, "yes." The majority suggests that "from her testimony the jury could have reasonably concluded that the taking of her keys was intended by Rusk to immobilize her alone, late at night, in a neighborhood with which she was unfamiliar . . . ." But on what facts does the majority so conclude? There is no evidence descriptive of the tone of his voice; her testimony indicates only the bare statement quoted above. How can the majority extract from this conduct a threat reasonably calculated to create a fear of imminent bodily harm? There was no weapon, no threat to inflict physical injury.

She also testified that she was afraid of "the way he looked," and afraid of his statement, "come on up, come on up." But what can the majority conclude from this statement coupled with a "look" that remained undescribed? There is no evidence whatsoever to suggest that this was anything other than a pattern of conduct consistent with the ordinary seduction of a female acquaintance who at first suggests her disinclination.

After reaching the room she described what occurred as follows:

> I was still begging him to please let, you know, let me leave. I said, "you can get a lot of other girls down there, for what you want," and he just kept saying, "no," and then I was really scared, because I can't describe, you know, what was said. It was more the look in his eyes; and I said, at that point—I didn't know what to say; and I said, "If I do what you want, will you let me go without killing me?" Because I didn't know, at that point, what he was going to do; and I started to cry; and when I did, he put his hands on my throat and started lightly to choke me; and I said "If I do what you want, will you let me go?" And he said, yes, and at that time, I proceeded to do what he wanted me to.

The majority relies on the trial court's statement that the defendant responded affirmatively to her question "If I do what you want, will you let me go without killing me?" The majority further suggests that the jury could infer the defendant's affirmative response. The facts belie such inference since by the prosecutrix's own testimony the defendant made *no* response. *He said nothing!*

She then testified that she started to cry and he "started lightly to choke" her, whatever that means. Obviously, the choking was not of any persuasive significance. During this "choking" she was able to talk. She said "If I do what you want will you let me go?" It was at this point that the defendant said yes.

I find it incredible for the majority to conclude that on these facts, without more, a woman was *forced* to commit oral sex upon the defendant and then to engage in vaginal intercourse. In the absence of any verbal threat to do her grievous bodily harm or the display of any weapon and threat to use it, I find it difficult to understand how a victim could participate in these sexual activities and not be willing.

What was the nature and extent of her fear anyhow? She herself testified she was "fearful that maybe I had someone following me." She was afraid because she didn't know him and she was afraid he was going to "rape" her. But there are no acts or conduct on the part of the defendant to suggest that these fears were created by the defendant or that he made any objective, identifiable threats to her which would give rise to this woman's failure to flee, summon help, scream, or make physical resistance.

As the defendant well knew, this was not a child. This was a married woman with children, a woman familiar with the social setting in which these two actors met. It was an ordinary city street, not an isolated spot. He had not forced his way into her car; he had not taken advantage of a difference in years or any state of intoxication or mental or physical incapacity on her part. He did not grapple with her. She got out of the car, *walked with him* across the street and *followed* him up the stairs to his room. She certainly had to realize that they were not going upstairs to play *Scrabble.*

Once in the room she waited while he went to the bathroom where he stayed for five minutes. In his absence, the room was lighted but she did not seek a means of escape. She did not even "try the door" to determine if it was locked. She waited.

Upon his return, he turned off the lights and pulled her on the bed. There is no suggestion or inference to be drawn from her testimony that he yanked her on the bed or in any manner physically abused her by this conduct. As a matter of fact there is no suggestion by her that he bruised or hurt her in any manner, or that the "choking" was intended to be disabling.

He then proceeded to unbutton her blouse and her bra. He did not rip her clothes off or use any greater force than was necessary to unfasten her garments. He did not even complete this procedure but requested that she do it, which she did "because he asked me to." However, she not only removed her clothing but took his clothes off, too.

Then for a while they lay together on the bed kissing, though she says she did not return his kisses. However, without protest she then proceeded to perform oral sex and later submitted to vaginal intercourse. After these activities were completed, she asked to leave. They dressed and he walked her to her car and asked to see her again. She indicated that perhaps they might meet at Fells Point. He gave her directions home and returned to his apartment where the police found him later that morning.

The record does not disclose the basis for this young woman's misgivings about her experience with the defendant. The only substantive fear she had was that she would be late arriving home. The objective facts make it inherently improbable that the defendant's conduct generated any fear for her physical well-being.

In my judgment the State failed to prove the essential element of force beyond a reasonable doubt and, therefore, the judgment of conviction should be reversed.

     . . .

———

304. As indicated in the first paragraph of the court's opinion, Rusk's conviction of rape was first reversed by the Court of Special Appeals sitting en banc, by a vote of 8–5. The decision of the court to reinstate the conviction was by a vote of 4–3. Aside from the judge who presided at the trial, therefore, of the judges who heard the case on appeal, 11 voted to reverse the conviction for insufficiency of the evidence and nine voted to affirm the conviction. All of the judges on the Court of Special Appeals and all but one of the judges on the Court of Appeals were men. The female judge on the Court of Appeals voted with the majority to affirm the conviction.

305. Rusk was convicted of assault and rape. He did not appeal from the conviction for assault, which was affirmed. The incongruity of an affirmance of the conviction for assault coupled with reversal of the conviction for rape was noted in the dissenting opinion of the Court of Special Appeals. Rusk v. State, 406 A.2d 624, 636 n.17 (Md.Ct. Spec.App.1979).

Rusk was sentenced to concurrent terms of ten years' imprisonment for rape and five years' imprisonment for assault. He began service of his sentence on March 2, 1981, six weeks after affirmance of his conviction by the Court of Appeals. At a parole hearing in September 1983, parole was denied. He was released from prison in April 1986. After his release, he moved to Florida and, so far as is known, has not been in further trouble with the law.

306. The Court of Special Appeals reversed Rusk's conviction because it concluded that, viewing the evidence "in the light most favorable to the prosecution," 406 A.2d 624, 625 (Md.Ct.Spec.App.1979), there was insufficient evidence to show that Pat's fear that Rusk would use force if she resisted was reasonable. Its assessment of the evidence is quoted in the majority opinion in *Rusk*, p. 470 above.

Four months after the decision in *Rusk*, the Court of Special Appeals decided Offutt v. State, 410 A.2d 611 (Md.Ct.Spec.App.1980). In *Offutt*, the defendant was convicted of assault with intent to rob. He went up to a clerk at the cash register of a toy store and handed her a note saying "give me call [sic] your money." The clerk testified, " 'He had his hand in his pocket and he—like he had a gun and I guess he wanted me to believe he had a gun and he said, "Do you want to die?" ' ' " She said to him, "This is a joke or something." The man replied that it was a joke. He started to buy a toy, but the clerk asked him to leave and he left. The encounter evidently lasted for a minute or less. Id. at 613. One issue on appeal, as in *Rusk*, was whether the victim had a reasonable fear that force would be used. Writing for the court, Judge Thompson, the same judge who wrote that court's opinion in *Rusk*, said: "The testimony that the appellant put his hand in his pocket and 'pointed it up to me and said "Do you want to die?" ' is sufficient for the finder of the facts to conclude that the victim . . . was reasonably in fear that force would be used against her." Id. at 614.

Are the conclusions of the Court of Special Appeals in *Rusk* and *Offutt* consistent? Many commentators have observed that the force or threat of force that will easily support a conviction for robbery may not be enough to support a conviction for rape. Is there any basis for such a distinction?

307. The statute under which Rusk was convicted defines rape as intercourse "by force or threat of force against the will and without the consent of the other person," p. 465 above. The phrases "against the will" and "without the consent," the court says, are synonymous, p. 471 above. The court also discusses resistance by the victim as evidence of, or the equivalent of, the requirements that intercourse be by force and without consent.

The ambiguity, or duplication, of these elements in the Maryland statute furnishes support for the observation in the commentary to the Model Penal Code that "the primary problem in determining how the elements of rape should be stated concerns the method by which the imposition by the male or the lack of consent by the female should be described." 1 MPC Commentaries Part II, 279 (comment to Art. 213).

Many older cases required that a woman resist "to the utmost," meaning that she had to manifest her lack of consent constantly and unambiguously by struggling until she is forcibly overcome. E.g., Brown v. State, 106 N.W. 536 (Wis.1906). Modern legislation and cases do not generally require resistance as an element of rape distinct from compulsion by the assailant and nonconsent of the victim. "The degree of resistance, if any, employed by a rape victim is material only in that it may evidence that the submission was or was not compelled. Circumstances . . . that render resistance impossible or unreasonable, render issues of resistance moot. In other words, that the submission was compelled may be shown by evidence other than acts of resistance." Woodson v. State, 483 N.E.2d 62, 64 (Ind.1985). It is accepted that a failure actively to resist may be the product of fear, or caution, or simply the desire to end what seems unavoidable as quickly as possible. Consent (and its counterpart, compulsion) referring imprecisely to a concurrence of behavior and attitude, however, the extent and quality of resistance may figure largely in the determination that the woman did or did not in fact consent.

The phrase "force or threat of force" in the Maryland statute evidently refers to the conduct of the alleged rapist, Rusk. The other two phrases "against the will" and "without the consent" refer to the alleged victim, Pat. Is the statute ambiguous in this respect? Or are these two distinct elements of the crime?

MPC

The Model Penal Code provides that a man commits rape if he "compels . . . [a woman] to submit by force or by threat of death, serious bodily injury, extreme pain or kidnapping, to be inflicted on anyone." § 213.1(1)(a). (The lesser offense of gross sexual imposition is committed if a man compels a woman to submit "by any threat that would prevent resistance by a woman of ordinary resolution." § 213.1(2)(a). See p. 508 below.)

The commentary states:

The law of rape protects the female's freedom of choice and punishes unwanted and coerced intimacy. The male who imposes upon the female by force or compulsion obviously violates these interests. . . .

. . . If the law regards the female as competent to consent and if she does so, intercourse is not rape. It may be fornication, which has always been treated as a minor offense and is virtually never enforced, or it may be incest, an offense that is rather narrowly addressed to sexual relations between close relatives. But it is not and cannot be rape, for the law of rape is concerned with imposition by the actor under circumstances where there is an actual failure of consent or where the law is prepared to characterize an actual consent as incompetent.

. . .

There are a number of problems that arise if too much emphasis is placed upon the non-consent of the victim as opposed to the over-reaching of the actor. In the first place, overemphasis on non-consent tends to obscure differences among the various circumstances covered by the law of rape. An exclusive focus on non-consent would collect under one label the wholly uninvited and forceful attack by a total stranger, the excessive zeal of a sometime boyfriend, and the clever seducer who dupes his victim into believing that they are husband and wife. In the words of one commentator, such an approach would compress into a single statute a diversity of conduct ranging from "brutal attacks . . . to half won arguments . . . in parked cars."[1]

Many older statutes failed to recognize this point and hence did not make provision for grading differentials within the law of rape. Such statutes generally assigned to every case within their coverage the same draconian penalties deemed appropriate for the most violent and shocking version of the offense. The result under such an approach is that some offenders are subjected to punishment more drastic than any rational grading scheme would allow, while others are windfall beneficiaries of the reluctance of jurors to condemn every offender to possible death or life imprisonment.

A second way in which overemphasis on non-consent can be troublesome relates to problems of proof. Evidentiary considerations aside, consent appears to be a conceptually simple issue. Either the female assented to intercourse, or she did not. Searching for consent in a particular case, however, may reveal depths of ambiguity and contradiction that are scarcely suspected when the question is put in the abstract. Often the woman's attitude may be deeply ambivalent. She may not want intercourse, may fear it, or may desire it but feel compelled to say "no." Her confusion at the time of the act may later resolve into non-consent. Some have expressed the fear that a woman who subconsciously wanted to have sexual intercourse will later feel guilty and "cry rape." It seems plain, on the other hand, that a barrage of conflicting emotions at the time of the assault does not necessarily imply the victim's consent, although it may lead to misperception by the actor. Further ambiguity may be introduced by the fact that the woman may appear to consent because she is frozen by fear and panic, or because she quite rationally decides to "consent" rather than risk being killed or injured.

The point, in any event, is that inquiry into the victim's subjective state of mind and the attacker's perceptions of her state of mind often will not yield a clear answer. The deceptively simple notion of consent may obscure a tangled mesh of psychological complexity, ambiguous communication, and unconscious restructuring of the event by the participants. Courts have not been oblivious to this difficulty, but in attempting to resolve it they have often placed disproportionate emphasis upon objective manifestations of non-consent by the woman. It seems plain that some courts have gone too far in this direction, although it is equally plain that one can go too far in the opposite direction.

What is required is that a balanced inquiry be made into the factors that indicate imposition by the male as well as those that indicate non-consent by the victim. It is appropriate in this effort to focus primarily upon the conduct of the male, particularly in the more serious forms of the offense, and to seek objective verification in the

---

1. Comment, Forcible and Statutory Rape: An Exploration of the Operation and Objectives of the Consent Standard, 62 Yale L.J. 55, 56 (1952).

actor's conduct of the overreaching and imposition that is the major characteristic of the offense in its most serious form. At the same time, however, the possibility of consent by the victim, even in the face of conduct that may give some evidence of overreaching, cannot be ignored. As intractable as the imposition–consent issue necessarily will be, it cannot be avoided.

1 MPC Commentaries Part II, 301–303.

308.

(i)

facts

"Complainant testified that on the afternoon of July 1, 1980, she rode her bicycle to Horstman's Point which overlooks the Carbondale City Reservoir in Carbondale. While complainant was standing alone at Horstman's Point, defendant approached her and initiated and engaged in a conversation with her. Although complainant did not know defendant, she responded to his conversation which was general in nature.

"Complainant started to walk away from the lake in the direction of her bicycle which was at the top of the hill. While she walked up the hill, defendant continued talking as he walked alongside of her. Complainant testified that when she got on her bicycle defendant placed his hand on her shoulder. At this time, complainant stated, 'No, I have to go now,' to which defendant responded, 'This will only take a minute. My girlfriend doesn't meet my needs.' Defendant also told her that 'I don't want to hurt you.'

"According to complainant, defendant then lifted her off the ground and carried her into a wooded area adjacent to the reservoir. Upon entering the woods, defendant placed complainant on the ground and told her to put her head on his backpack. Defendant then told her to take her pants down which she did part way. Defendant pulled her pants completely off and placed them underneath her. He then proceeded to pull up complainant's tank top shirt and began kissing her breasts and vaginal area. After he finished kissing complainant, defendant sat up and unzipped his pants and complainant performed an act of fellatio upon him.

"At the completion of this second act, defendant gave complainant an article of clothing to wipe her mouth. Complainant then dressed and defendant picked her up again and carried her back to her bicycle. Defendant testified that complainant asked him, 'Is that all?' to which he answered, 'Yes.' "

[The complainant got on her bicycle and left. She reported the incident immediately. About seven months later, she saw the defendant and identified him as her assailant.]

π's argument

". . . Defendant admits that he performed the acts upon which the deviate sex charges are based. He contends, however, that the acts complained of were performed without force or threat of force." People v.

Warren, 446 N.E.2d 591, 592 (Ill.Ct.App.1983). The complainant was 32 years old. The defendant was 30 years old. What result?

The court reversed the conviction.

"In the present case, the State contends that defendant coerced complainant into engaging in deviate sexual acts by threatening to use physical force. The State maintains that this threat was conveyed by defendant's statement that, 'I don't want to hurt you,' the implication being that he would hurt her if she did not comply. Although this interpretation has some merit, we do not believe that it is the most reasonable conclusion drawn from the facts. Defendant did not make the above statement while brandishing a weapon or applying physical force, a circumstance which would support the State's construction. Instead, we find that the record is devoid of any attendant circumstances which suggest that complainant was compelled to submit to defendant.

"In addition, the State argues that the threat of force was conveyed by the disparity of size and strength between the parties. The record shows that at the time of the incident complainant was 5'2" tall weighing 100 to 105 pounds, whereas defendant was 6'3" and 185 pounds. The State further maintains that the seclusion of the woods contributed to this threat of force. Although it is proper to consider such factors in weighing the evidence, we do not believe that the evidence taken as a whole supports the State's conclusion. Aside from picking up complainant and carrying her into and out of the woods, defendant did not employ his superior size and strength. Furthermore, complainant did not attempt to flee or in any meaningful way resist the sexual advances of defendant.

"Much of the State's case rests upon its contention that complainant's absence of effort in thwarting defendant's advances was motivated by her overwhelming fear. In support of this position, the State offers complainant's statement that she did not attempt to flee because, 'it was in the middle of the woods and I didn't feel like I could get away from him and I thought he'd kill me.' Moreover, complainant stated that she did not yell or scream because the people she had seen in the area were too far away and that under the circumstances she felt that 'screaming . . . would be bad for me.'

"Despite professing fear for her safety, complainant concedes that defendant did not strike her or threaten to strike her or use a weapon. When defendant picked up complainant and carried her into the wooded area, she did not protest but merely stated, 'I can walk.' Although she maintained that she stiffened up to make it harder for him to carry her, defendant did not recall any resistance. At no time did complainant tell defendant to leave her alone or put her down. Furthermore, complainant did not object when defendant instructed her to take off her pants, but instead she complied with his request by pulling down her pants part way.

. . .

"In the case before us, defendant maintains that once complainant became aware that defendant intended to engage in sexual relations it was incumbent upon her to resist. This resistance would have the effect of giving defendant notice that his acts were being performed without her consent. It is well settled that if complainant had the use of her faculties and physical powers, the evidence must show such resistance as will demonstrate that the act was against her will. If the circumstances show resistance to be futile or life endangering or if the complainant is overcome by superior strength or paralyzed by fear, useless or foolhardy acts of resistance are not required. . . . We cannot say that any of the above factors are present here. Complainant's failure to resist when it was within her power to do so conveys the impression of consent regardless of her mental state, amounts to consent and removes from the act performed an essential element of the crime. . . . We do not mean to suggest, however, that the complainant did in fact consent; however, she must communicate in some objective manner her lack of consent." 446 N.E.2d at 593–94.

Is the court's conclusion sound? If not, what is its error? Compare State v. Lima, 643 P.2d 536 (Haw.1982) (conviction of rape affirmed).

(ii)

"The State's evidence tended to show that at the time the incident occurred the defendant and the prosecuting witness in this case, Cottie Brown, had been involved for approximately six months in a consensual sexual relationship. During the six months the two had conflicts at times and Brown would leave the apartment she shared with the defendant to stay with her mother. She testified that she would return to the defendant and the apartment they shared when he called to tell her to return. Brown testified that she and the defendant had sexual relations throughout their relationship. Although she sometimes enjoyed their sexual relations, she often had sex with the defendant just to accommodate him. On those occasions, she would stand still and remain entirely passive while the defendant undressed her and had intercourse with her.

"Brown testified that at times their consensual sexual relations involved some violence. The defendant had struck her several times throughout the relationship when she refused to give him money or refused to do what he wanted. Around May 15, 1981, the defendant struck her after asking her for money that she refused to give him. Brown left the apartment she shared with the defendant and moved in with her mother. She did not have intercourse with the defendant after May 15 until the alleged rape on June 15. After Brown left the defendant, he called her several times and visited her at Durham Technical Institute where she was enrolled in classes. When he visited her they talked about their relationship. Brown testified that she did not tell him she wanted to break off their relationship because she was afraid he would be angry.

"On June 15, 1981, Brown arrived at Durham Technical Institute by taxicab to find the defendant standing close to the school door. The defendant blocked her path as she walked toward the door and asked her where she had moved. Brown refused to tell him, and the defendant grabbed her arm, saying that she was going with him. Brown testified that it would have taken some effort to pull away. The two walked toward the parking lot and Brown told the defendant she would walk with him if he let her go. The defendant then released her. She testified that she did not run away from him because she was afraid of him. She stated that other students were nearby.

"Brown stated that she and the defendant then began a casually paced walk in the neighborhood around the school. They walked, sometimes side by side, sometimes with Brown slightly behind the defendant. As they walked they talked about their relationship. Brown said the defendant did not hold her or help her along in any way as they walked. The defendant talked about Brown's 'dogging' him and making him seem a fool and about Brown's mother's interference in the relationship. When the defendant and Brown left the parking lot, the defendant threatened to 'fix' her face so that her mother could see he was not playing. While they were walking out of the parking lot, Brown told the defendant she wanted to go to class. He replied that she was going to miss class that day.

"The two continued to walk away from the school. Brown testified that the defendant continually talked about their relationship as they walked, but that she paid little attention to what he said because she was preoccupied with her own thoughts. They passed several people. They walked along several streets and went down a path close to a wooded area where they stopped to talk. The defendant asked again where Brown had moved. She asked him whether he would let her go if she told him her address. The defendant then asked whether the relationship was over and Brown told him it was. He then said that since everyone could see her but him he had a right to make love to her again. Brown said nothing.

"The two turned around at that point and began walking towards a street they had walked down previously. Changing directions, they walked in the same fashion they had walked before—side by side with Brown sometimes slightly behind. The defendant did not hold or touch Brown as they walked. Brown testified that the defendant did not say where they were going but that, when he said he wanted to make love, she knew he was going to the house of a friend. She said they had gone to the house on prior occasions to have sex. The defendant and Brown passed the same group of men they had passed previously. Brown did not ask for assistance because some of the men were friends of the defendant, and she assumed they would not help. The defendant and Brown continued to walk to the house of one of the defendant's friends, Lawrence Taylor.

"When they entered the house, Taylor was inside. Brown sat in the living room while the defendant and Taylor went to the back of the house and talked. When asked why she did not try to leave when the defendant and Taylor were in the back of the house, Brown replied, 'It was nowhere to go. I don't know. I just didn't.' The defendant returned to the living room area and turned on the television. He attempted to fix a broken fan. Brown asked Taylor for a cigarette, and he gave her one.

"The defendant began talking to Brown about another man she had been seeing. By that time Taylor had gone out of the room and perhaps the house. The defendant asked if Brown was 'ready.' The evidence tended to show that she told him 'no, that I wasn't going to bed with him.' She testified that she did not want to have sex with the defendant and did not consent to do so at any time on June 15.

"After Brown finished her cigarette, the defendant began kissing her neck. He pulled her up from the chair in which she had been sitting and started undressing her. He noticed that she was having her menstrual period, and she sat down pulling her pants back up. The defendant again took off her pants and blouse. He told her to lay down on a bed which was in the living room. She complied and the defendant pushed apart her legs and had sexual intercourse with her. Brown testified that she did not try to push him away. She cried during the intercourse. Afterwards they talked. The defendant told her he wanted to make sure she was not lying about where she lived and that he would not let her up unless she told him.

"After they dressed they talked again about the man Brown had been seeing. They left the house and went to the defendant's mother's house. After talking with the defendant's mother, Brown took a bus home. She talked with her mother about taking out a complaint against the defendant but did not tell her mother she and the defendant had had sex. Brown made a complaint to the police the same day.

"The defendant continued to call Brown after June 15, but she refused to see him. One evening he called from a telephone booth and told her he had to talk. When he got to her apartment he threatened to kick her door down and Brown let him inside. Once inside he said he had intended merely to talk to her but that he wanted to make love again after seeing her. Brown said she sat and looked at him, and that he began kissing her. She pulled away and he picked her up and carried her to the bedroom. He performed oral sex on her and she testified that she did not try to fight him off because she found she enjoyed it. The two stayed together until morning and had sexual intercourse several times that night. Brown did not disclose the incident to the police immediately because she said she was embarrassed.

. . .

"[T]he defendant contends that there was no substantial evidence that the sexual intercourse between Brown and him was by force and against her will." State v. Alston, 312 S.E.2d 470, 471–75 (N.C.1984). What result?

Holding   The court reversed the conviction. It concluded that there was substantial evidence that the intercourse was against Brown's will but not that it was by force. "As we have stated, actual physical force need not be shown in order to establish force sufficient to constitute an element of the crime of rape. Threats of serious bodily harm which reasonably induce fear thereof are sufficient. . . . In the present case there was no substantial evidence of either actual or constructive force.

"The evidence in the present case tended to show that, shortly after the defendant met Brown at the school, they walked out of the parking lot with the defendant in front. He stopped and told Brown he was going to 'fix' her face so that her mother could see he was not 'playing.' This threat by the defendant and his act of grabbing Brown by the arm at the school, although they may have induced fear, appeared to have been unrelated to the act of sexual intercourse between Brown and the defendant. More important, the record is devoid of evidence that Brown was in any way intimidated into having sexual intercourse with the defendant by that threat or any other act of the defendant on June 15. Brown said she did not pay a lot of attention to what the defendant said because she was thinking about other things. She specifically stated that her fear of the defendant was based on an experience with him prior to June 15 and that on June 15 he did not hold her down or threaten her with what would happen if she refused to submit to him. The State failed to offer substantial evidence of force used or threatened by the defendant on June 15 which related to his desire to have sexual intercourse on that date and was sufficient to overcome the will of the victim.

State failed to offer evidence.

"We note that the absence of an explicit threat is not determinative in considering whether there was sufficient force in whatever form to overcome the will of the victim. It is enough if the totality of the circumstances gives rise to a reasonable inference that the unspoken purpose of the threat was to force the victim to submit to unwanted sexual intercourse. . . . The evidence introduced in the present case, however, gave rise to no such inference. Under the peculiar facts of this case, there was no substantial evidence that threats or force by the defendant on June 15 were sufficiently related to sexual conduct to cause Brown to believe that she had to submit to sexual intercourse with him or suffer harm. Although Brown's general fear of the defendant may have been justified by his conduct on prior occasions, absent evidence that the defendant used force or threats to overcome the will of the victim *to resist the sexual intercourse alleged to have been rape,* such general fear was not sufficient to show that the defendant used the force required to support a conviction of rape." 312 S.E.2d at 476.

Is the court's conclusion sound? If not, what is its error? (The court later expressed misgivings about its ruling in *Alston* and limited its reasoning about the victim's "general fear" to the "peculiar facts" of that case. State v. Etheridge, 352 S.E.2d 673, 681 (N.C.1987).) See also Richards v. State, 475 So.2d 893 (Ala.Crim.App.1985) (defendant's physical acts in sexual encounter with stepdaughter sufficient to show forcible compulsion); Commonwealth v. Mlinarich, 498 A.2d 395 (Pa.Super.Ct.1985) (threat to send 14-year-old girl to juvenile detention home was not "forcible compulsion"); Commonwealth v. Biggs, 467 A.2d 31 (Pa.Super.Ct.1983) (defendant's statements to 17–year-old daughter that Bible required her to submit and threat to humiliate her did not constitute force); State v. St. Amant, 536 A.2d 897, 900 (R.I.1988) (exercise of parental authority by stepfather, head of household, satisfied requirement of "force or coercion"). See also Commonwealth v. Caracciola, 569 N.E.2d 774, 779 (Mass.1991) (defendant's posing as police officer and threatening to arrest victim satisfied requirement that victim submit "by force and against her will").

(iii)

"Tommy Cloninger and Fred Hartshorn were well acquainted with one another before the night of 20 August 1981. Earlier that day Mr. Hartshorn invited Tommy to assist him in mowing the lawn of a husband and wife named Thorpe. After the work was finished, Fred and Tommy chatted with the Thorpes until about midnight and, according to Tommy, drank wine and smoked marijuana. Thereafter they both accepted the Thorpes' offer to stay the night. They settled down next to one another with sleeping bags on the floor. From this point the parties' accounts of what subsequently occurred vary dramatically.

"The appellant and Mrs. Thorpe (who testified on his behalf) insist that nothing unseemly took place that night. Mrs. Thorpe was adamant that she and her husband would have heard any unusual nocturnal activity in the adjacent room where the appellant and Tommy were asleep. She explained that her bed was but nine feet from where the two grass cutters lay and that no door separated the two rooms to muffle extraneous noise.

"Tommy had a rather different version of the night's events. He related how he settled down next to the appellant on his sleeping bag and began to doze. A few moments later Mr. Hartshorn reached over, unzipped Tommy's trousers and began to fondle him. Tommy, this time, was able to persuade the appellant to stop. By his own testimony Tommy decided not to dwell on the event and tried to sleep. In this, however, he was unsuccessful. Tommy maintains that suddenly Fred Hartshorn accosted him and pulled his trousers down to his ankles. The appellant then wrapped his legs around him and held him tightly in his arms. Despite his 'pretty loud' protestations Tommy insists that the appellant sodomized him. Tommy asserts that he did not appeal for help from the Thorpes because they 'were more *his* friends than mine.' After the appellant had his way with Tommy, both of them went to sleep. Tommy testified that he was awakened, a third time, a few hours later by the appellant who again was stroking him. But this time, when Tommy asked him to stop, the appellant complied.

"Tommy testified that he did not leave the Thorpes after the sexual assault because he was intoxicated with wine and marijuana and because his house was over a mile distant. He also claimed that the defendant probably would have prevented his leaving." State v. Hartshorn, 332 S.E.2d 574, 575 (W.Va.1985). The defendant was convicted of first-degree sexual assault. He argued on appeal that there was insufficient evidence of "forcible compulsion," as required by the statute. "Forcible compulsion" is defined as "(a) Physical force that overcomes such earnest resistance as might reasonably be expected under the circumstances; or (b) Threat or intimidation expressed or implied, placing a person in fear of immediate death or bodily injury to himself or another person or in fear that he or another person will be kidnapped." What result?

The court reversed the conviction. "There is no evidence that the appellant threatened or otherwise intimidated Tommy. He did not hit him or even attempt to do so. None of the appellant's actions constituted forcible compulsion to overcome such 'earnest resistance as might reasonably be expected under the circumstances.' Tommy admitted that he did not cry out to the Thorpes who were asleep in the next room or make any concerted effort to escape the appellant. On cross-examination he first mentioned that he attempted to strike Mr. Hartshorn with his elbows but offered no other evidence of serious resistance.

"This Court understands that the victim of a sodomy assault may be so petrified by his attacker that he is struck dumb with terror during a sexual assault and therefore meekly submits. However, in this case Tommy, by his own admission, did not plead with the appellant or attempt to offer him any serious resistance. He did not try to escape from the appellant.

"Furthermore he was clearly a 'voluntary social companion' of the appellant . . . who had offered to help with the yard work and spend the night next to him thereafter. In these circumstances the Court cannot believe that Tommy offered the degree of 'earnest resistance' to the sexual assault against him . . . necessary to sustain a conviction for sexual assault in the first degree. Indeed, Tommy does not claim to have been afraid of the appellant at all." Id. at 577.

Holding

Is the court's conclusion sound? If not, what is its error? Compare McQueen v. State, 423 So.2d 800 (Miss.1982) (conviction of rape reversed).

309. State of New Jersey in the Interest of M.T.S., 609 A.2d 1266 (N.J.1992). The defendant, a juvenile, was charged with conduct that, if committed by an adult, would constitute second-degree sexual assault, defined by statute as an act of sexual penetration using physical force or coercion. According to the defendant, he penetrated the complainant, who was 15, after they had undressed and were in bed kissing and touching one another; after a few moments, she pushed him off, and he complied immediately. The act of intercourse, he testified, was entirely consensual. According to the complainant, she was asleep alone in bed and woke up to find her underpants and shorts removed and the defendant on top of her with his penis inside her. She immediately told him to get off, and he complied.

The defendant argued on appeal that the element of physical force was not present. Sustaining the judgment of delinquency, the court concluded that the statute required no physical force beyond the act of penetration itself. It said:

The understanding of sexual assault as a criminal battery, albeit one with especially serious consequences, follows necessarily from the Legislature's decision to eliminate nonconsent and resistance from the substantive definition of the offense. Under the new law [adopted in 1979], the victim no longer is required to resist and therefore need not have said or done anything in order for the sexual penetration to be unlawful. The alleged victim is not put on trial, and his or her responsive or defensive behavior is rendered immaterial. We are thus satisfied that an interpretation of the statutory crime of sexual assault to require physical force in addition to that entailed in an act of involuntary or unwanted sexual penetration would be fundamentally inconsistent with the legislative purpose to eliminate any consideration of whether the victim resisted or expressed nonconsent.

We note that the contrary interpretation of force—that the element of force need be extrinsic to the sexual act—would not only reintroduce a resistance requirement into the sexual assault law, but also would immunize many acts of criminal sexual contact short of penetration. The characteristics that make a sexual contact unlawful are the same as those that make a sexual penetration unlawful. An actor is guilty of criminal sexual contact if he or she commits an act of sexual contact with another using "physical force" or "coercion." . . . That the Legislature would have wanted to decriminalize unauthorized sexual intrusions on the bodily integrity of a victim by requiring a showing of force in addition to that entailed in the sexual contact itself is hardly possible.

Because the statute eschews any reference to the victim's will or resistance, the standard defining the role of force in sexual penetration must prevent the possibility that the establishment of the crime will turn on the alleged victim's state of mind or responsive behavior. We conclude, therefore, that any act of sexual penetration engaged in by the defendant without the affirmative and freely-given permission of the victim to the specific act of penetration constitutes the offense of sexual assault. Therefore, physical force in excess of that inherent in the act of sexual penetration is not required for such penetration to be unlawful. The definition of "physical force" is satisfied . . . if the defendant applies any amount of force against another person in the absence of what a reasonable person would believe to be affirmative and freely-given permission to the act of sexual penetration.

[P]ermission to engage in sexual penetration must be affirmative and it must be given freely, but that permission may be inferred either from acts or statements reasonably viewed in light of the surrounding circumstances. . . . Persons need not, of course, expressly announce their consent to engage in intercourse for there to be affirmative permission. Permission to engage in an act of sexual penetration can be and indeed often is indicated through physical actions rather than words. Permission is demonstrated when the evidence, in whatever form, is sufficient to demonstrate that a reasonable person would have believed that the alleged victim had affirmatively and freely given authorization to the act.

. . .

In a case such as this one, in which the State does not allege violence or force extrinsic to the act of penetration, the factfinder must decide whether the defendant's act of penetration was undertaken in circumstances that led the defendant reasonably to believe that the alleged victim had freely given affirmative permission to the specific act of sexual penetration. Such permission can be indicated either through words or through actions that, when viewed in the light of all the surrounding circumstances, would demonstrate to a reasonable person affirmative and freely-given authorization for the specific act of sexual penetration.

In applying that standard to the facts in these cases, the focus of attention must be on the nature of the defendant's actions. The role of the factfinder is not to decide whether reasonable people may engage in acts of penetration without the permission of others. The Legislature answered that question when it enacted the reformed sexual assault statute: reasonable people do not engage in acts of penetration without permission, and it is unlawful to do so. The role of the factfinder is to decide not whether engaging in an act of penetration without permission of another person is reasonable, but only whether the defendant's belief that the alleged victim had freely given affirmative permission was reasonable.

Role of factfinder (jury)

In these cases neither the alleged victim's subjective state of mind nor the reasonableness of the alleged victim's actions can be deemed relevant to the offense. The alleged victim may be questioned about what he or she did or said only to determine whether the defendant was reasonable in believing that affirmative permission had been freely given. To repeat, the law places no burden on the alleged victim to have expressed nonconsent or to have denied permission, and no inquiry is made into what he or she thought or desired or why he or she did not resist or protest.

In short, in order to convict under the sexual assault statute in cases such as these, the State must prove beyond a reasonable doubt that there was sexual penetration and that it was accomplished without the affirmative and freely-given permission of the alleged victim. As we have indicated, such proof can be based on evidence of conduct or words in light of surrounding circumstances and must demonstrate beyond a reasonable doubt that a reasonable person would not have believed that there was affirmative and freely-given permission. If there is evidence to suggest that the defendant reasonably believed that such permission had been given, the State must demonstrate either that defendant did not actually believe that affirmative permission had been freely-given or that such a belief was unreasonable under all of the circumstances. Thus, the State bears the burden of proof throughout the case.

609 A.2d at 1276–79.

Responding to the argument that its construction of the statute made the reference to "physical force" redundant or inadvertent, the court said that the reference qualified "the nature and character of the 'sexual penetration' " as "unauthorized sexual penetration." Id. at 1277.

The circumstances of the incident, as described by the complainant, are bound to be unusual. In view of the court's statement that permission need not be express and can be inferred from the alleged victim's actions and the surrounding circumstances, does the court's ruling fully accomplish its intention not to let the crime depend on the victim's "responsive behavior"? Could, or should, it have gone further?

See Commonwealth v. Berkowitz, 641 A.2d 1161 (Pa.1994), distinguishing "forcible compulsion" as an element of rape from absence of consent as an element of the crime of indecent assault. See also People v. Iniguez, 872 P.2d 1183 (Cal.1994), holding that the definition of rape as an act of sexual intercourse "accomplished against a person's will by means of fear of immediate and unlawful bodily injury" was satisfied without any show of resistance by the victim.

Commonwealth v. Sherry

386 Mass. 682, 437 N.E.2d 224 (1982)

■ LIACOS, J. Each defendant was indicted on three charges of aggravated rape (G.L. c. 265, § 22) and one charge of kidnapping (G.L. c. 265, § 26). A jury acquitted the defendants of kidnapping and convicted them of so much of each of the remaining three indictments as charged the lesser included offense of rape without aggravation. Each defendant was sentenced on each conviction to be imprisoned at the Massachusetts Correctional Institution, Walpole, for a term of not more than five years nor less than three years. Six months of the sentence was to be served, with the balance of the sentence to be suspended. On completion of the sentence served, each defendant was to be placed on probation for the term of one year. The sentences on the second and third convictions of each defendant were to be served concurrently with the first sentence. The trial judge ordered a stay of execution of sentence, pending appeal. The defendants appeal from their convictions and from the denial of their posttrial motions to set aside the verdicts and to enter findings of not guilty. . . . We transferred the appeals here on our own motion. We now affirm each of the defendants' convictions on one charge of rape and vacate each defendant's convictions on the other two charges of rape.

. . .

There was evidence of the following facts. The victim, a registered nurse, and the defendants, all doctors, were employed at the same hospital in Boston. The defendant Sherry, whom the victim knew professionally, with another doctor was a host at a party in Boston for some of the hospital staff on the evening of September 5, 1980. The victim was not acquainted with the defendants Hussain and Lefkowitz prior to this evening.

According to the victim's testimony, she had a conversation with Hussain at the party, during which he made sexual advances toward her. Later in the evening, Hussain and Sherry pushed her and Lefkowitz into a bathroom together, shut the door, and turned off the light. They did not open the door until Lefkowitz asked them to leave her in peace.[2] At various times, the victim had danced with both Hussain and Sherry.

Some time later, as the victim was walking from one room to the next, Hussain and Sherry grabbed her by the arms and pulled her out of the apartment as Lefkowitz said, "We're going to go up to Rockport." The victim verbally protested but did not physically resist the men because she said she thought that they were just "horsing around" and that they would eventually leave her alone.[3] She further testified that, once outside, Hussain carried her over his shoulder to Sherry's car and held her in the front seat as the four drove to Rockport. En route, she engaged in superficial conversation with the defendants. She testified that she was not in fear at this time. When they arrived at Lefkowitz's home in Rockport, she asked to be taken home. Instead, Hussain carried her into the house.

Once in the house, the victim and two of the men smoked some marihuana, and all of them toured the house. Lefkowitz invited them into a bedroom to view an antique bureau, and, once inside, the three men began to disrobe. The victim was frightened. She verbally protested, but the three men proceeded to undress her and maneuver her onto the bed. One of the defendants attempted to have the victim perform fellatio while another attempted intercourse. She told them to stop. At the suggestion of one of the defendants, two of the defendants left the room temporarily. Each defendant separately had intercourse with the victim in the bedroom. The victim testified that she felt physically numbed and could not fight; she felt humiliated and disgusted. After this sequence of events, the victim claimed that she was further sexually harassed and forced to take a bath.

Some time later, Lefkowitz told the victim that they were returning to Boston because Hussain was on call at the hospital. On their way back, the group stopped to view a beach, to eat breakfast, and to get gasoline. The victim was taken back to where she had left her car the prior evening, and she then drove herself to an apartment that she was sharing with another woman.

The defendants testified to a similar sequence of events, although the details of the episode varied significantly. According to their testimony, Lefkowitz invited Sherry to accompany him from the party to a home that his parents owned in Rockport. The victim was present when this invitation was extended and inquired as to whether she could go along. As the three were leaving, Sherry extended an invitation to Hussain. At no time on the way out of the apartment, in the elevator, lobby, or parking lot did the victim indicate her unwillingness to accompany the defendants.

Upon arrival in Rockport, the victim wandered into the bedroom where she inquired about the antique bureau. She sat down on the bed and kicked

2. The victim testified that after this incident she complained to a Dr. Sheskey about the defendant Hussain's behavior. Dr. Sheskey corroborated this testimony.

3. The victim testified that she was not physically restrained as they rode down an elevator with an unknown fifth person, or as they walked through the lobby of the apartment building where other persons were present.

off her shoes, whereupon Sherry entered the room, dressed only in his underwear. Sherry helped the victim get undressed, and she proceeded to have intercourse with all three men separately and in turn. Each defendant testified that the victim consented to the acts of intercourse.

Motions for a required finding of not guilty. At the close of the Commonwealth's case, the defendants moved for a required finding of not guilty on each of the indictments. . . . The defendants argued that there was no evidence of force or threat of bodily injury, a required element of the crime of rape. The defendants also argued that aggravating circumstances, i.e., kidnapping or rape by joint enterprise, had not been proved. The judge denied their motions.

The defendants contend that, at the close of the Commonwealth's case . . . the evidence was insufficient to persuade a rational trier of fact of each of the elements of the crime charged beyond a reasonable doubt. . . . The defendants may prevail on this claim of error only if we are convinced that no "rational trier of fact could have found the essential elements of [rape] beyond a reasonable doubt." Commonwealth v. Latimore, 378 Mass. 671, 677 (1979), quoting from Jackson v. Virginia, 443 U.S. 307, 319 (1979).

The essence of the crime of rape, whether aggravated or unaggravated, is sexual intercourse with another compelled by force and against the victim's will or compelled by threat of bodily injury. . . . At the close of the Commonwealth's case, the evidence viewed in the light most favorable to the Commonwealth established the following. The victim was forcibly taken from a party by the three defendants and told that she would accompany them to Rockport. Despite her verbal protestations, the victim was carried into an automobile and restrained from leaving until the automobile was well on its way. Notwithstanding her requests to be allowed to go home, the victim was carried again and taken into a house. The three defendants undressed and began to undress the victim and to sexually attack her in unison over her verbal protestations. Once they had overpowered her, each in turn had intercourse with her while the others waited nearby in another room.

The evidence was sufficient to permit the jury to find that the defendants had sexual intercourse with the victim by force and against her will. The victim is not required to use physical force to resist; any resistance is enough when it demonstrates that her lack of consent is "honest and real." Commonwealth v. McDonald, 110 Mass. 405, 406 (1872). The jury could well consider the entire sequence of events and acts of all three defendants as it affected the victim's ability to resist. . . . There was no error in the denial of the defendants' motions.

. . .

Evidence of fresh complaint. The defendants contend that the judge erred in admitting testimony indicating that the victim made a fresh complaint of the rape to several persons. The defendants do not dispute the general principle that "testimony reporting statements made by the victim shortly after [a rape] are universally admitted to corroborate the victim's testimony." Commonwealth v. Bailey, 370 Mass. 388, 392 (1976). Rather, the defendants argue, in substance, that the victim's delay in making the statements disqualifies the complaints as being admissible, particularly in light of opportunities she may have had to complain while still in the company of the defendants.

The evidence of fresh complaint that was admitted was as follows. The victim's roommate testified that the victim related the facts of the rape to her in their apartment in the early hours of the morning following the incident. Another friend of the victim testified that the victim told her about the rape over the telephone at approximately 9 A.M. on the same morning. The police officer who spoke with the victim the day following the incident testified as to what the victim told him about the rape, and a hospital report reciting the events that occurred was also admitted in evidence.

Although the judge made no explicit preliminary findings whether the statements were sufficiently prompt to constitute fresh complaint . . . the record indicates that the judge looked at all the circumstances of the case and concluded that on these particular facts the victim's complaints were reasonably prompt. The judge instructed the jury that they could reject the proffered evidence as being corroborative of the victim's testimony if they did not find that the complaints were made "reasonably promptly." See Commonwealth v. McGrath, 364 Mass. 243, 250 (1973).

We cannot say that the judge abused his discretion. There is no rule that requires a victim to complain of a rape to strangers in an unfamiliar place while still in the company of the alleged rapist. The actions of the victim were reasonable in the particular circumstances of the case. . . . The victim first reported the rape to her friend and roommate within a few hours after being dropped off by the defendants. There was no error.

Exclusion of victim's prior out-of-court statements. Defense counsel sought a pretrial ruling regarding the admissibility of two out-of-court statements of the victim. A voir dire was conducted, during which one Cheryl Rowley testified that the victim had made statements at a rape crisis seminar. Rowley testified that the victim stated at the seminar "that she had been raped in the past, and that she had had a couple of occasions where she was almost raped. And she told us about different ways that she got out of being raped—the times that she did." Rowley testified further that "[t]he one that I remembered the most was that she had been taken to a sand pit by some man, and he was attempting to rape her, and she said that she got out of it by what she said, 'Jerking the guy off.' " The trial judge ruled that this evidence would not be admitted.

. . . There was no error. There was no showing that the statements were false or even an exaggeration of the truth. . . . Without evidence of falsity, the statements become irrelevant to any issue in the case, including the credibility of the complainant. . . .

. . .

Jury charge on unaggravated rape. The defendants contend that the judge erred in charging the jury that they could find the defendants guilty of unaggravated rape. The defendants objected to the charge, arguing that the Commonwealth's theory throughout the case was an aggravated rape by joint enterprise or kidnapping. The judge, however, stated that the jury could find the defendants guilty of unaggravated rape if there was insufficient evidence of the aggravating factors, viz., kidnapping or joint enterprise, but that rape was otherwise proved. . . .

. . .

. . . On the state of the evidence, the jury were warranted in concluding that the victim did not consent to intercourse with any of the defendants. The jury could have accepted or rejected the evidence that the defendants were engaged in a joint enterprise, or raped the victim in the course of a kidnapping. The charge properly put the factual issues raised by the evidence to the jury. This was not error.

Instructions to the jury. The defendants next contend that because the judge failed to give two instructions exactly as requested, the judge's jury charge, considered as a whole, was inadequate and the cause of prejudicial error. . . .

. . .

To the extent the defendants, at least as to the first requested instruction, appear to have been seeking to raise a defense of good faith mistake on the issue of consent, the defendants' requested instruction would have required the jury to "find beyond a reasonable doubt that the accused had *actual knowledge* of [the victim's] lack of consent" (emphasis added). The defendants, on appeal, argue that mistake of fact negating criminal intent is a defense to the crime of rape. The defense of mistake of fact, however, requires that the accused act in good faith and with reasonableness. . . . Whether a reasonable good faith mistake of fact as to the fact of consent is a defense to the crime of rape has never, to our knowledge, been decided in this Commonwealth. We need not reach the issue whether a reasonable and honest mistake to the fact of consent would be a defense, for even if we assume it to be so, the defendants did not request a jury instruction based on a reasonable good faith mistake of fact. We are aware of no American court of last resort that recognizes mistake of fact, without consideration of its reasonableness, as a defense; nor do the defendants cite such authority. There was no error.

. . .

. . . There was no evidence of three separate rapes by each defendant which would warrant a conviction on all three indictments. . . .

Although affirmance of all of the convictions would have no practical effect on the terms of incarceration, since the multiple sentences were imposed concurrently, we believe that justice requires that the convictions on two of the indictments as to each defendant be set aside. . . .

———

310. In *Sherry*, since it was reviewing the sufficiency of the evidence to sustain a conviction, the court summarized the evidence from the point of view of the prosecution. As the opinion indicates briefly, the defendants testified that the victim's conduct led them to believe that she was accompanying them willingly. The victim testified that when she asked one of the defendants why they were doing what they did, he replied, "Stop playing games." One possible interpretation of the testimony of the victim and the defendants alike is that they mistook her genuine protests for "playing games." A mistake of that kind is the more plausible if one takes into account the "general assumption" that "some aggression is an expected part of the male role in sexual encounters," see p. 464 above. Expected by whom? If the man assumes that he is "supposed" to prevail on the woman and that she is "supposed" to "resist" whether she is willing or not, and the woman in fact is simply resisting or is simply taking the man's apparent aggression at face value, what should be the result?

Is it enough to say that the man has made an honest mistake? Or is it enough to say that in such a situation the man acts at his peril (rather than the woman's peril) and should pay the penalty of his mistake (rather than the woman)?

If, as elsewhere in the criminal law, the law should require that the mistake be not only genuine but also reasonable, what in this context are the bounds of reason? If, as some have suggested, men and women in general have distinctly different and evolving perspectives of the male and female sexual roles, from which perspective ought the reasonableness of the defendant's mistake be evaluated?

The Massachusetts court left the question of mistake open in *Sherry*, saying only that if such a defense were available at all it includes only mistakes that are in good faith and reasonable, p. 496 above. Subsequently it held that an honest and reasonable mistake about the victim's consent is not a defense. Commonwealth v. Ascolillo, 541 N.E.2d 570 (Mass.1989); see Commonwealth v. Simcock, 575 N.E.2d 1137 (Mass.Ct.App.1991). The defense of reasonable mistake is rejected also in State v. Cantrell, 673 P.2d 1147 (Kan.1983); State v. Reed, 479 A.2d 1291 (Me.1984). In many other jurisdictions, it is accepted. E.g., People v. Mayberry, 542 P.2d 1337 (Cal.1975). In *Cantrell*, the court said that rape is not a "specific intent" crime and, therefore, does not require more than an intention to engage in sexual intercourse with the victim; it is her state of mind, not the defendant's, that is controlling. 673 P.2d at 1154. In *Mayberry*, the court said: "If a defendant entertains a reasonable and bona fide belief that a prosecutrix voluntarily consented to accompany him and to engage in sexual intercourse, it is apparent he does not possess the wrongful intent that is a prerequisite . . . to a conviction . . . ." 542 P.2d at 1345. Is either statement sufficient?

311. For a lengthy discussion of the question whether a man can be convicted of rape if he honestly but unreasonably and inaccurately believes that the woman consents to have sexual relations, see Regina v. Morgan, [1976] App. Cas. 182 (H.L.). A majority of the Court concluded that an honest albeit unreasonable belief was a defense. Parliament later enacted legislation providing that a man can be convicted of rape if the woman does not in fact consent and the man knows she does not or is "reckless as to whether she consents." Sexual Offenses (Amendment) Act, 1976, ch. 92, § 1(1).[4]

312. In cases like *Rusk* and *Sherry*, the official and unofficial reaction (including that of jurors) is often that the woman "asked for it." "Why else would Pat have given a casual acquaintance a lift home late at night? Why was she in a bar unattended in the first place?" "Why was the nurse horsing around with those doctors that way at the party?" Although it is agreed abstractly that the woman's general morality and behavior are not in issue, concretely the pattern of prosecution and conviction suggests otherwise. Women have charged that when the law of rape gives effect to such reactions directly or indirectly, explicitly or implicitly, it constitutes an infringement on the liberty of women to behave as they choose not only with respect to sexual conduct but much more generally. The stereotypes that distinguish the "virtuous" woman, who may be a victim of rape, from the "nonvirtuous" woman, who is presumed not to be a victim, are said to impose on women a model of conventional respectability, both to avoid the danger of rape and, secondly, to make a prosecution possible if they are raped. Rapists themselves point to factors like a woman's dress or manner, her presence in a "male" preserve, hitchhiking, and drinking alone in public as increasing the danger of being raped. Prosecution and conviction of a rapist may be tied to other aspects of the woman's life as well. For example, a married woman is generally regarded as a more credible victim than a single woman.

These phenomena were graphically illustrated by a Florida case in 1989. The complaining witness, a 22-year-old woman, had been wearing a lace miniskirt without underwear. According to her testimony, the defendant abducted her from the parking lot of a restaurant and raped her repeatedly during a five-hour drive; she escaped 120 miles from where she was abducted. Defense counsel told the jury that she had agreed to have sex in exchange for drugs and money but had changed her mind. The jury of three men and three women found the defendant not guilty. After the verdict, the jury foreman said: "We felt she asked for it the way she was dressed." "The way she was dressed with that skirt, you could see everything she had. She was advertising for sex." A woman juror said: "She was obviously dressed for a good time, but we felt she may have bitten off more than she could chew." The defendant was facing other rape and assault charges elsewhere. The Boston Globe, Oct. 6, 1989, at 12.

---

4. The statutory provision was not inconsistent with *Morgan*, several of the opinions in that case having distinguished an unreasonable belief from recklessness.

Consider the following comment:

Although many men who rape may suffer serious psychological distur-
bances, there is no reason to assume that their attitudes regarding
women, sex and violence are significantly different from other males in
the population. The offenders interviewed at Atascadero[5] believed
that the prevention or avoidance of rape was the responsibility of the
female. When asked specifically how such acts could be prevented, the
rapists sounded very much like crime prevention officers. Women were
advised not to go out alone . . . not to hitchhike . . . to learn self-
defense . . . to buy a dog . . . to carry weapons . . . to dress conserva-
tively . . . and not to drink alone. . . .

These findings, and this advice, will depress or enrage many
women for they represent a gross impingement on their basic free-
doms. However, the findings and advice should come as no surprise for
they reflect, in part, the male attitudes toward women that have been
so completely condemned by feminist writers. . . .

Battelle Memorial Institute Law and Justice Study Center, Forcible Rape:
Final Project Report 13 (1978).

If the analysis of the Battelle Institute is correct, how should the law
respond?

313. The manner in which the law defines the conduct that constitutes rape is not unrelated to the question whether a defense of mistake
ought to be allowed.

The circumstances of most serious crimes ordinarily leave no doubt
that the criminal's act was not wanted by the victim. The act of sexual
intercourse is one that we presume, but for the facts that make it a rape, is
wanted by both persons. And, in general, the community does not want to
inhibit voluntary sexual relations. If a requirement that the attacker use
force or the victim resist is substantial, the likelihood that there will be a
mistake about consent is diminished. If consent is the critical issue, the
possibility of a mistake may be large. Women have argued forcefully that
the only way fully to protect a woman's choice is not to accept a defense of
mistake based on belief, however honest, that "no" means "yes." That,
they assert, is the least that the law should provide, since it is frequently
the case that social mores and attitudes lead women to acquiesce without
genuine willingness and that "yes" in fact means "no."

In *Rusk* and *Sherry*, taking into account that the testimony of the
defendant(s) and the victim was given months after the event in the
context of a criminal prosecution, might one conclude that the descriptions
of the incident in each case are not so different after all? Aside from the
question whether any of the participants lied about or misremembered the

[5] Atascadero State Hospital, a maximum security mental institution for the
treatment of sex offenders in California. Fifty
rapists were interviewed.

events, may it not be the case that neither conclusion, "she was willing" or "she was not willing," is fully accurate? "Willing" or "not willing" when, and about what? In what sense: pleased, acquiescent, reluctant, opposed?

Would it be preferable to give less weight to the elements of force and resistance, thereby bringing within the definition of rape a broader range of intercourse without consent, but make the defense of mistake more available (e.g. by lowering somewhat the requirement that the mistake be reasonable)? Or would it be preferable to include a requirement of substantial force and/or resistance, thereby excluding cases in which the woman does not manifest her lack of consent clearly, and narrow or eliminate the defense of mistake?

Elsewhere in the criminal law, doubts about guilt are resolved in favor of the accused, our assumption being that we should risk not convicting the guilty rather than risk convicting the innocent. Ought the same principle apply here? If so, how ought the law take account of the ambiguity inherent in some rape situations, lest too many of the guilty not be convicted and the crime generally go unpunished? If the principle ought to be relaxed here, how ought the law guard against convicting the innocent? Can the principle be articulated more precisely for this crime in particular?

314. Grading. The common law made no distinctions within the crime of rape. In the 1940s, legislatures started to classify the crime according to the seriousness of the actual conduct. One of the clear trends of the current law is to introduce two or more categories of the offense, which may all be called rape or be designated by different names. Many observers have called for such distinctions because a uniform crime, often carrying the most severe penalty,[6] is thought not to reflect substantial differences in culpability. One may, for example, contrast a brutal assault on a stranger in an alleyway with the would-be seduction of a friend. The grading of rape may also reflect unwillingness to risk imposition of the most serious penalties unless there is uncontrovertible proof that the offense was committed. The commentary to the Model Penal Code observes: "In some measure the grading determinations of Section 213.1 reflect an inevitable and irreducible unease about the substantive standards of liability employed in the law of rape. Rape is the only major assaultive offense in which the offender engages in physical conduct that in other contexts may be desirable to the victim. The law of rape faces the task of predicating felony sanctions on definitions of proscribed conduct that, in some circumstances, closely parallels socially acceptable behavior. . . . [I]t is no simple matter to differentiate by generalized statement conduct that should be punished from actions that are beyond the proper reach of the penal law. The wrong involved in rape is simply too grave to

---

6. In Coker v. Georgia, 433 U.S. 584 (1977), four Justices declared that a sentence of death for the crime of rape violated the Eighth Amendment's prohibition of cruel and unusual punishment. See pp. 715–16 below.

allow retreat from this difficulty, but candid recognition of the problems confronted in defining the offense requires a healthy sense of caution in assigning sanctions." 1 MPC Commentaries Part II, 355–56 (comment to § 213.1). Grading of rape offenses has also been supported as the only way to obtain a verdict of guilty for offenses that do not arouse the jury's sympathy for the victim.

On the other hand, it has been argued that distinguishing among rapes diminishes or even trivializes the seriousness of the wrong to the victim in even the least violent cases. Many persons, including some women's groups, have argued forcefully that the crime of rape itself should be treated uniformly whatever the circumstances and that additional crimes, such as assault, should be added to reflect distinct harms to the victim. Consider in this connection the following comment:

> The myth of "real rape" is fostered by sensational newspaper accounts of rapes which are especially brutal—particularly those involving children—and, as it turns out, these rapes are usually perpetrated by men suffering from a diagnosable mental illness. But it is time to recognize that these rapes should neither be the standard against which all reported rapes are judged, nor set apart as qualitatively different from "everyday rape." It may in fact be the case that the most violent and "abnormal" rapes are simply the extreme product of a society which refuses to take rape seriously. When rape results in the victim's death or near-death, we are prepared to condemn it and to find labels which justify severe punishment of the offender. Our failure to take rape seriously at an earlier stage, or to find new labels for the offender, may contribute to the ultimate consequence of the most violent cases. "Everyday rape" should not be dismissed because it fails to exhibit the extreme brutality of those rape-murders which we attribute to the "criminally insane." In allowing rapes of this type to function as the standard of comparison, we simply obscure the real motivation for all rape, the social conditions which explain it, and the true similarities between all cases of rape.

L. Clark & D. Lewis, Rape: The Price of Coercive Sexuality 145–46 (1977).

The most elaborate grading provisions in the criminal law are those for the law of homicide. The many distinctions drawn there are perhaps explained by the fact that the central element of homicide is not the actor's conduct but its consequence, the death of another person. But for that unifying element, we should probably separate the conduct that constitutes homicide into distinct crimes, which would accomplish grading of the conduct in another way.

Are there similar reasons for grading the crime of rape? Is there a sense in which one might say that, like homicide, the core of the crime is not the actor's conduct but its consequence? Whichever it is, ought the criminal law in principle identify alike all the conduct that constitutes rape, leaving any differences to individual sentencing decisions? If not, what are the crucial differences that ought to be recognized in the law? Are there practical considerations arising out of the methods of enforcing the law that make grading of rape offenses desirable or undesirable?

315.   The defendants in *Sherry* were sentenced to three to five years in prison, which was reduced to six months in prison and one year of probation. If they were in fact guilty of rape, as the court concluded, is the sentence appropriate? After the sentencing, some of the jurors said publicly that they had been confused about the crime of rape, especially the requirement that the victim be "compelled by force," and that although they had expected the defendants to be punished, they did not expect the punishment to be for rape.

Is the difference between the sentence in *Rusk*, see p. 478 note 305 above, and the sentences in *Sherry* justified?

316.   The law has long included within rape sexual relations not involving compulsion in circumstances in which the woman is deemed incapable of consent. See, e.g., the Model Penal Code §§ 213.1(1)(b)–(d), (2)(b)–(c), p. 508 below. Such circumstances typically include deliberate conduct by the man, such as deception or the administration of intoxicants, as well as factors like the woman's youth or mental incapacity that make her consent ineffective.

The Model Penal Code places cases in which the victim has been stupefied by the man or is unconscious or below the age of ten in the category of those that are punished most severely. Cases of mental disease or defect and cases of deception, including the somewhat common case involving a doctor and his patient, are placed in a lesser category. Differentiation of this kind is typical of recent formulations.

The most significant of these cases are those involving a girl who is deemed too young to consent, the crime commonly known as "statutory rape." Recent legislation has raised the age of consent from ten, the age at common law, to ages ranging up to 16 or, rarely, 17 or 18. In many jurisdictions, the seriousness of the offense depends on the victim's age. The question of reasonable mistake about the victim's age is discussed below, pp. 627–29. The Model Penal Code allows no defense if the victim is below the age of ten; if she is older than ten, the crime then being not rape but corruption of minors, § 213.3, "it is a defense for the actor to prove by a preponderance of the evidence that he reasonably believed the child to be above the critical age." § 213.6(1). While the traditional rule that allowed no defense of mistake is followed in some jurisdictions, a majority now allow the defense at least for categories above the very young age that defines the most serious offense.

Ought the law distinguish between rape as a crime involving compulsion and as a crime involving no compulsion but unawareness or ineffective consent? If so, is a distinction of "degree" and punishment sufficient? Or ought the names of the offenses be different?

See generally State v. Bartlett, 830 P.2d 823 (Ariz.1992), holding that a 40-year sentence without possibility of parole was grossly disproportionate to the crime of consensual sexual intercourse with two girls six months under the ages of 15, the age of valid consent. The sentences finally imposed were concurrent sentences of five and a quarter years and seven years.

317. Husband and wife. The common-law rule provided that it was not rape if a man had forcible sexual relations with a woman who was his wife. Hale's justification for the rule, to which it is commonly traced, was that "the wife hath given up herself in this kind unto her husband, which she cannot retract." 1 M. Hale, History of the Pleas of the Crown 628 (1800 ed.)[7]

The "spousal exclusion" has been attacked strongly in recent years. A small number of states have eliminated it by legislation or judicial decision. E.g., Warren v. State, 336 S.E.2d 221 (Ga.1985). Most have retained it, commonly with an exception for couples living apart pursuant to a court order or separation agreement. In People v. Liberta, 474 N.E.2d 567 (N.Y.1984), concluding that a statutory spousal exclusion was unconstitutional, the New York Court of Appeals said:

> We find that there is no rational basis for distinguishing between marital rape and nonmarital rape. The various rationales which have been asserted in defense of the exemption are either based upon archaic notions about the consent and property rights incident to marriage or are simply unable to withstand even the slightest scrutiny. We therefore declare the marital exemption for rape in the New York statute to be unconstitutional.
>
> Lord Hale's notion of an irrevocable implied consent by a married woman to sexual intercourse has been cited most frequently in support of the marital exemption. . . . Any argument based on a supposed consent, however, is untenable. Rape is not simply a sexual act to which one party does not consent. Rather, it is a degrading, violent act which violates the bodily integrity of the victim and frequently causes severe, long-lasting physical and psychic harm. . . . To ever imply consent to such an act is irrational and absurd. Other than in the context of rape statutes, marriage has never been viewed as giving a husband the right to coerced intercourse on demand. . . . Certainly, then, a marriage license should not be viewed as a license for a husband to forcibly rape his wife with impunity. A married woman has the same right to control her own body as does an unmarried wom-

---

7. Sir Matthew Hale was Chief Justice of the Court of King's Bench from 1671 to 1676. His treatise, found among his papers after his death in 1676, was published in 1736.

an. . . . If a husband feels "aggrieved" by his wife's refusal to engage in sexual intercourse, he should seek relief in the courts governing domestic relations, not in "violent or forceful self-help" (State v. Smith, 85 N.J. 193, 206).

The other traditional justifications for the marital exemption were the common-law doctrines that a woman was the property of her husband and that the legal existence of the woman was "incorporated and consolidated into that of the husband" (1 Blackstone's Commentaries [1966 ed], p. 430. . .). Both these doctrines, of course, have long been rejected in this State. Indeed, "[n]owhere in the common-law world—[or] in any modern society—is a woman regarded as chattel or demeaned by denial of a separate legal identity and the dignity associated with recognition as a whole human being" (Trammel v. United States, 445 U.S. 40, 52).

Because the traditional justifications for the marital exemption no longer have any validity, other arguments have been advanced in its defense. The first of these recent rationales, which is stressed by the People in this case, is that the marital exemption protects against governmental intrusion into marital privacy and promotes reconciliation of the spouses, and thus that elimination of the exemption would be disruptive to marriages. While protecting marital privacy and encouraging reconciliation are legitimate State interests, there is no rational relation between allowing a husband to forcibly rape his wife and these interests. The marital exemption simply does not further marital privacy because this right of privacy protects consensual acts, not violent sexual assaults. . . . Just as a husband cannot invoke a right of marital privacy to escape liability for beating his wife, he cannot justifiably rape his wife under the guise of a right to privacy.

Similarly, it is not tenable to argue that elimination of the marital exemption would disrupt marriages because it would discourage reconciliation. Clearly, it is the violent act of rape and not the subsequent attempt of the wife to seek protection through the criminal justice system which "disrupts" a marriage. . . . Moreover, if the marriage has already reached the point where intercourse is accomplished by violent assault it is doubtful that there is anything left to reconcile. . . . This, of course, is particularly true if the wife is willing to bring criminal charges against her husband which could result in a lengthy jail sentence.

Another rationale sometimes advanced in support of the marital exemption is that marital rape would be a difficult crime to prove. A related argument is that allowing such prosecutions could lead to fabricated complaints by "vindictive" wives. The difficulty of proof argument is based on the problem of showing lack of consent. Proving lack of consent, however, is often the most difficult part of any rape prosecution, particularly where the rapist and the victim had a prior relationship. . . . Similarly, the possibility that married women will fabricate complaints would seem to be no greater than the possibility of unmarried women doing so. . . . The criminal justice system, with all of its built-in safeguards, is presumed to be capable of handling any false complaints. Indeed, if the possibility of fabricated complaints were a basis for not criminalizing behavior which would otherwise be sanctioned, virtually all crimes other than homicides would go unpunished.

The final argument in defense of the marital exemption is that marital rape is not as serious an offense as other rape and is thus adequately dealt with by the possibility of prosecution under criminal statutes, such as assault statutes, which provide for less severe punishment. The fact that rape statutes exist, however, is a recognition that the harm caused by a forcible rape is different, and more severe, than the harm caused by an ordinary assault. . . . "Short of homicide, [rape] is the 'ultimate violation of self' " (Coker v. Georgia, 433 U.S. 584, 597 [citation omitted]). Under the Penal Law, assault is generally a misdemeanor unless either the victim suffers "serious physical injury" or a deadly weapon or dangerous instrument is used (Penal Law, §§ 120.00, 120.05, 120.10). Thus, if the defendant had been living with Denise [his wife] at the time he forcibly raped and sodomized her he probably could not have been charged with a felony, let alone a felony with punishment equal to that for rape in the first degree.

Moreover, there is no evidence to support the argument that marital rape has less severe consequences than other rape. On the contrary, numerous studies have shown that marital rape is frequently quite violent and generally has *more* severe, traumatic effects on the victim than other rape. . . .

. . . Justice Holmes wrote: "It is revolting to have no better reason for a rule of law than that so it was laid down in the time of Henry IV. It is still more revolting if the grounds upon which it was laid down have vanished long since, and the rule simply persists from blind imitation of the past" (Holmes, "The Path of the Law," 10 Harv. L. Rev. 457, 469). This statement is an apt characterization of the marital exemption; it lacks a rational basis, and therefore violates the equal protection clauses of both the Federal and State Constitutions (US Const, 14th Amdt, § 1; NY Const, art I, § 11).

474 N.E.2d at 573–75.

The commentary to the Model Penal Code, which retains the spousal exclusion, observes:

First, marriage or equivalent relationship, while not amounting to a legal waiver of the woman's right to say "no," does imply a kind of generalized consent that distinguishes some versions of the crime of rape from parallel behavior by a husband. The relationship itself creates a presumption of consent, valid until revoked. At a minimum, therefore, husbands must be exempt from those categories of liability based not on force or coercion but on a presumed incapacity of the woman to consent. For example, a man who has intercourse with his unconscious wife should scarcely be condemned to felony liability on the ground that the woman in such circumstances is incapable of consenting to sex with her own husband, at least unless there are aggravating circumstances. The same holds true for intercourse with a wife who for some reason other than unconsciousness is not aware that a sexual act is committed upon her. Plainly there must also be some form of spousal exclusion applicable to the crime of statutory rape. Given the age limit for effective consent to sexual relations set in some states, the possibility of marriage exists, and without a spousal exclusion every act of sex between the husband and wife would be a literal violation of the statute.

The major context of which those who would abandon the spousal exclusion are thinking, however, is the situation of rape by force or threat. The problem with abandoning the immunity in many such situations is that the law of rape, if applied to spouses, would thrust the prospect of criminal sanctions into the ongoing process of adjustment in the marital relationship. Section 213.1, for example, defines as gross sexual imposition intercourse coerced "by any threat that would prevent resistance by a woman of ordinary resolution." It may well be that a woman of ordinary resolution would be prevented from resisting by her husband's threat to expose a secret to her mother, for example. Behavior of this sort within the marital relationship is no doubt unattractive, but it is a risky business for the law to intervene by threatening criminal sanctions. Retaining the spousal exclusion avoids this unwarranted intrusion of the penal law into the life of the family.

Finally, there is the case of intercourse coerced by force or threat of physical harm. Here the law already authorizes a penalty for assault. If the actor causes serious bodily injury, the punishment is quite severe. The issue is whether the still more drastic sanctions of rape should apply. The answer depends on whether the injury caused by forcible intercourse by a husband is equivalent to that inflicted by someone else. The gravity of the crime of forcible rape derives not merely from its violent character but also from its achievement of a particularly degrading kind of unwanted intimacy. Where the attacker stands in an ongoing relation of sexual intimacy, that evil, as distinct from the force used to compel submission, may well be thought qualitatively different. The character of the voluntary association of husband and wife, in other words, may be thought to affect the nature of the harm involved in unwanted intercourse. That, in any event, is the conclusion long endorsed by the law of rape and carried forward in the Model Code provision.

1 MPC Commentaries Part II, 344–46 (comment to § 213.1).

The authors of the commentary evidently felt some uncertainty about the continued vitality of the spousal exclusion. The final sentence suggests that they may have been accepting it more than approving it. Do the arguments for the exclusion made in the commentary have weight? Or are they, as the New York Court of Appeals suggests, the same old arguments in modern dress?

If there ought to be any exclusion of this kind, can it be based simply on the marriage relationship? Suppose two persons who are still married are living apart without mutual affection or in open hostility? Is an exception when a married couple is living separately pursuant to a court order or a formal agreement sufficient?[8] On the other hand, if there ought to be an exemption, ought the marriage relationship be essential? Suppose a couple has lived together more or less harmoniously without being married. (The Model Penal Code provides that the spousal exclusion applies "to persons living as man and wife regardless of the legal status of their relationship" and does not extend to "spouses living apart under a decree of judicial separation." § 213.6(2).)

318. Is there any reason why the law should restrict rape to an act by a man against a woman? That is unquestionably the most common kind of sexual aggression and is the subject of most of the current concern. Male or female homosexual rape is not unknown, however. In most prisons it is common, certainly more common than the incidence of rape in the general population. Rape of a male by a female may also occur.

Although the law prohibits homosexual rape by that or another name, as a practical matter it disregards all but the most horrifying occurrences within prisons. Does that have any bearing on the other problems in this section?

A large majority of states have adopted legislation making rape a gender-neutral crime. The Model Penal Code preserves the traditional rule that rape is a crime committed only by a male against a female. Expressing some doubt about the matter, the commentary concludes that the advantage of gender neutrality "seems primarily to be symbolic" and that the seriousness of rape of a female by a male ordinarily is greater than other rape. 1 MPC Commentaries Part II, 337–39 (comment to § 213.1).

MODEL PENAL CODE

§ 213.0 Definitions

In this Article, unless a different meaning plainly is required:

(1) the definitions given in Section 210.0 ["human being," "bodily injury," etc.] apply;

8. Cf. Kizer v. Commonwealth, 321 S.E.2d 291 (Va.1984), reversing the defendant's conviction for rape of his wife because she had failed to make clear that the marriage was *de facto* ended; the spousal exception, therefore, remained applicable.

(2) "Sexual intercourse" includes intercourse per os or per anum, with some penetration however slight; emission is not required;

(3) "Deviate sexual intercourse" means sexual intercourse per os or per anum between human beings who are not husband and wife, and any form of sexual intercourse with an animal.

§ 213.1 Rape and Related Offenses

(1) Rape. A male who has sexual intercourse with a female not his wife is guilty of rape if:

(a) he compels her to submit by force or by threat of imminent death, serious bodily injury, extreme pain or kidnapping, to be inflicted on anyone; or

(b) he has substantially impaired her power to appraise or control her conduct by administering or employing without her knowledge drugs, intoxicants or other means for the purpose of preventing resistance; or

(c) the female is unconscious; or

(d) the female is less than 10 years old.

Rape is a felony of the second degree unless (i) in the course thereof the actor inflicts serious bodily injury upon anyone, or (ii) the victim was not a voluntary social companion of the actor upon the occasion of the crime and had not previously permitted him sexual liberties, in which cases the offense is a felony of the first degree.

(2) Gross Sexual Imposition. A male who has sexual intercourse with a female not his wife commits a felony of the third degree if:

(a) he compels her to submit by any threat that would prevent resistance by a woman of ordinary resolution; or

(b) he knows that she suffers from a mental disease or defect which renders her incapable of appraising the nature of her conduct; or

(c) he knows that she is unaware that a sexual act is being committed upon her or that she submits because she mistakenly supposes that he is her husband.

§ 213.2 Deviate Sexual Intercourse by Force or Imposition

(1) By Force or Its Equivalent. A person who engages in deviate sexual intercourse with another person, or who causes another to engage in deviate sexual intercourse, commits a felony of the second degree if:

(a) he compels the other person to participate by force or by threat of imminent death, serious bodily injury, extreme pain or kidnapping, to be inflicted on anyone; or

(b) he has substantially impaired the other person's power to appraise or control his conduct, by administering or employing without the knowledge of the other person drugs, intoxicants or other means for the purpose of preventing resistance; or

(c) the other person is unconscious; or

(d) the other person is less than 10 years old.

(2) By Other Imposition. A person who engages in deviate sexual intercourse with another person, or who causes another to engage in deviate sexual intercourse, commits a felony of the third degree if:

(a) he compels the other person to participate by any threat that would prevent resistance by a person of ordinary resolution; or

(b) he knows that the other person suffers from a mental disease or defect which renders him incapable of appraising the nature of his conduct; or

(c) he knows that the other person submits because he is unaware that a sexual act is being committed upon him.[9]

---

319. The Model Penal Code is less favorable to the victim of a rape than much subsequent legislation. See, for example, the materials below on evidentiary rules. At the time the Code's provisions were drafted, there were no women on the council of the American Law Institute. Nor were there any women among the reporters, associate reporters, and special consultants for the Code. Three of the 11 research associates were women. One of the 40 members of the Criminal Law Advisory Committee was a woman. One commentator has observed: "Whether the Model Penal Code is a repressive document with regard to the treatment of women who are victims of sex offenses because the American Law Institute was a very conservative organization, or whether the Code took its particularly unsympathetic stance because of the period in which it was drafted, is now impossible to determine. Most of the research and drafting were accomplished in the 1950s, when there was little awareness of the legal inequities facing women in the criminal court or elsewhere." Bienen, "Rape I," 3 Women's Rights L. Rep. 53 (1976). At the time when the Code's provisions were adopted, they may not have seemed so conservative. Most of the legislation more favorable to rape victims was enacted later, after the women's rights movement had gained greatly in strength.

TRIAL ISSUES

---

320. Corroboration. In addition to the problems raised above about how the law ought to draw the line between rape or nonconsensual sexual

[9] Other sections of the Model Penal Code cover Corruption of Minors and Seduction (§ 213.3), Sexual Assault (§ 213.4), and Indecent Exposure (§ 213.5). Section 213.6 contains additional provisions generally applicable to Article 213. See p. 510 below.

relations generally and noncriminal sexual relations, rape has been thought to raise special problems of proof. The general requirement that guilt be proved beyond a reasonable doubt was in the past commonly supplemented by a specific requirement that an accusation of rape be corroborated. A variety of reasons were given for the requirement. Women were said sometimes to have motives to lie about sexual relations that were consensual: to avoid blame or unwanted consequences, like pregnancy; to reduce their own shame; or to get "revenge." Some women (or women generally) were said to fantasize about being raped, which fantasies sometimes became false beliefs in the fact. Racial or other factors in some cases were thought so likely to sway the jury to sympathize with the supposed victim that corroboration was peculiarly necessary to safeguard the accused. Or simply, as Hale had said, rape "is an accusation easily to be made and hard to be proved, and harder to be defended by the party accused, tho never so innocent."[10] 1 M. Hale, History of the Pleas of the Crown 634 (1800 ed.).

Women's organizations point out that the rate of convictions for rape hardly supports Hale's fear. They attack the requirement of corroboration as only a manifestation of male chauvinism and an insult to women. The requirement in all criminal cases that guilt be proved beyond a reasonable doubt is enough, they argue, to require corroboration if the victim's testimony is not strong. By the 1970s, the special requirement of corroboration in rape was generally eliminated. The requirement was retained in the Model Penal Code in the following form: "No person shall be convicted of any felony under this Article upon the uncorroborated testimony of the alleged victim. Corroboration may be circumstantial." § 213.6(5). The comment, after rejecting specific arguments for the requirement like those above, observes that its purpose is simply to ensure that the case against the defendant is proved. The comment does not explain why a special provision is needed for rape and concludes rather lamely: "That the existence of a rule of corroboration may not make much difference lends as much support to retention as it does to repeal." 1 MPC Commentaries Part II, 429 (comment to § 213.6).

The Model Penal Code § 213.6 also provides: "In any prosecution before a jury for an offense under this Article, the jury shall be instructed to evaluate the testimony of a victim or complaining witness with special care in view of the emotional involvement of the witness and the difficulty of determining the truth with respect to alleged sexual activities carried out in private."[11] This cautious nod in Hale's direction is consistent with an

---

10. Hale, also the source of the spousal exclusion that benefited men who sexually assaulted their wives, see p. 503 above, is said to have been a misogynist. See Bienen, "Rape III—National Developments in Rape Reform Legislation," 6 Women's Rights L. Rep. 184 n.78 (1980).

11. Still another provision of the Model Penal Code provides: "Prompt Complaint. No prosecution may be instituted or maintained under this Article unless the alleged offense was brought to the notice of public authority within [3] months of its occurrence or, where the alleged victim was less than 16 years old

instruction that used to be given regularly in rape cases and was required in many jurisdictions. The older instruction followed Hale's language, quoted above, more closely. The requirement that such an instruction be given has generally been eliminated, and in many jurisdictions the instruction has been prohibited, by statute or judicial decision. See People v. Gammage, 828 P.2d 682 (Cal.1992), holding that in addition to a general instruction in all appropriate cases that "before finding any fact to be proved solely by the testimony of . . . a single witness, you should carefully review all of the testimony upon which proof of such fact depends," it is proper to instruct a jury in a case involving a sex offense that it is not necessary that the testimony of the complaining witness be corroborated by other evidence.

321. Prior Sexual Conduct. In the past, evidence concerning prior sexual conduct of the rape victim was regularly admitted at trial. One basis for admission was an application of the rule of evidence for criminal cases generally that a witness's testimony can be impeached by evidence that raises questions about the witness's credibility. Such evidence typically consists of proof that the witness has a reputation for bad character or has been convicted of crimes involving moral turpitude. See Federal Rules of Evidence 608, 609. In a prosecution for rape the victim almost inevitably must testify. Courts have frequently allowed evidence of her sexual conduct in the past, or her reputation for such conduct, to be introduced as part of the effort to impeach her testimony. Another basis for admission was that the victim's claim that she had not consented to have sexual relations with the defendant was contradicted directly by evidence that she was sexually promiscuous in the past, generally or with the defendant in particular. Even if evidence were only admitted for purposes of impeaching the victim's credibility, there was some (most people thought a strong) likelihood that the jury would make the theoretically impermissible inference from prior conduct to present similar conduct. (The need to keep a jury from learning about a defendant's prior convictions for similar conduct is often given as the reason why defendant did not testify.) Whatever the basis for admission of evidence of the victim's conduct, there was a possibility that the jury would "punish" her for what it considered immoral behavior in the past by acquitting the defendant.

The attitude of the courts admitting such evidence is stated in somewhat extreme terms in a frequently quoted passage from the opinion in People v. Abbot, 19 Wend. 192 (N.Y.1838):

or otherwise incompetent to make complaint, within [3] months after a parent, guardian or other competent person specifically interested in the victim learns of the offense." § 213.6(4). This provision, which was an innovation, has been followed in a small number of jurisdictions. Its purpose is to limit the opportunity for a vindictive prosecution or blackmail. 1 MPC Commentaries Part II, 421 (comment to § 213.6). See the discussion in *Sherry*, p. 492 above, where the issue is not whether a "fresh complaint" is necessary for a prosecution but whether evidence that the victim made a prompt complaint is admissible as corroboration of her testimony.

[A]re we to be told that previous prostitution shall not make one among those circumstances which raise a doubt of assent? That the triers should be advised to make no distinction in their minds between the virgin and a tenant of the stew? Between one who would prefer death to pollution, and another who, incited by lust and lucre, daily offers her person to the indiscriminate embraces of the other sex? . . .

On a question of scienter you may show other acts, as in passing counterfeit money or bills. Why? Because in the practised vender of bad coin or bad bills we more readily infer a guilty knowledge than in the novice. . . . And will you not more readily infer assent in the practised Messalina, in loose attire, than in the reserved and virtuous Lucretia? Both knowledge and assent are affections of the mind, and the mode of proving both, rests on the same principle in the philosophy of evidence.

. . . It seems, in the first place, to be perfectly agreed that you may prove the prosecutrix to be in fact (not merely by general reputation, but in fact) a common prostitute. . . . It has been repeatedly adjudged that, in the same view, you may also show a previous voluntary connection between the prosecutrix and the prisoner. . . . Why is this? Because there is not so much probability that a common prostitute or the prisoner's concubine would withhold her assent, as one less depraved; and may I not ask, does not the same probable distinction arise between one who has already submitted herself to the lewd embraces of another, and the coy and modest female, severely chaste and instinctively shuddering at the thought of impurity? Shall I be answered that both are equally under the protection of the law? That I admit, and so are the common prostitute and the concubine. If either have in truth been feloniously ravished, the punishment is the same, but the proof is quite different. It requires that stronger evidence be added to the oath of the prosecutrix, in one case than in the other. Shall I be answered that an isolated instance of criminal connection does not make a common prostitute? I answer yes: it only makes a prostitute, and I admit introduces a circumstance into the case of less moment; but the question is not whether it be of more or less persuasive force, it is one of competency; in other words, whether it be of any force at all.

[N]o court can overrule the law of human nature, which declares that one who has already started on the road of prostitution, would be less reluctant to pursue her way, than another who yet remains at her home of innocence and looks upon such a career with horror. . . .

Id. at 195–96.

In recent years, the admissibility of evidence about the victim's sexual history has been sharply restricted. "Shield laws" protective of the woman's privacy have been enacted in every state. Generally, the effect of the laws and judicial decisions has been to eliminate the earlier presumption that such evidence is admissible and to substitute a presumption that it is not admissible except in special circumstances and/or unless its specific relevance is shown. Rule 412 of the Federal Rules of Evidence, adopted in 1978 and substantially revised in 1994, is representative:

———

Rule 412. Sex Offense Cases; Relevance of Alleged Victim's Past Sexual Behavior or Alleged Sexual Predisposition.

(a) Evidence generally inadmissible.—The following evidence is not admissible in any civil or criminal proceeding involving alleged sexual misconduct except as provided in subdivisions (b) and (c):

(1) Evidence offered to prove that any alleged victim engaged in other sexual behavior.

(2) Evidence to prove any alleged victim's sexual predisposition.

(b) Exceptions.—

(1) In a criminal case, the following evidence is admissible, if otherwise admissible under these rules:

(A) evidence of specific instances of sexual behavior by the alleged victim offered to prove that a person other than the accused was the source of semen, injury or other physical evidence;

(B) evidence of specific instances of sexual behavior by the alleged victim with respect to the person accused of the sexual misconduct offered by the accused to prove consent or by the prosecution; and

(C) evidence the exclusion of which would violate the constitutional rights of the defendant.

(2) In a civil case, evidence offered to prove the sexual behavior or sexual predisposition of any alleged victim is admissible if it is otherwise admissible under these rules and its probative value substantially outweighs the danger of harm to any victim and of unfair prejudice to any party. Evidence of an alleged victim's reputation is admissible only if it has been placed in controversy by the alleged victim.

(c) Procedure to determine admissibility.—

(1) A party intending to offer evidence under subdivision (b) must—

(A) file a written motion at least 14 days before the trial specifically describing the article and stating the purpose for which it is offered unless the court, for good cause requires a different time for filing or permits filing during trial; and

(B) serve the motion on all parties and notify the alleged victim or, when appropriate, the alleged victim's guardian or representative.

(2) Before admitting evidence under this rule the court must conduct a hearing in camera and afford the victim and parties a right to attend and be heard. The motion, related papers, and the record of the hearing must be sealed and remain under seal unless the court orders otherwise.

People v. Williams
416 Mich. 25, 330 N.W.2d 823 (1982)

■ WILLIAMS, J.

Defendants in this case have called into question the constitutionality of Michigan's "rape shield" law, which is set forth in the margin below. MCL 750.520j; MSA 28.788(10) (also referred to hereinafter as § 520j).[12] All four defendants herein were prosecuted on charges of first-degree criminal sexual conduct; all four defendants asserted at trial that the complainant had consented to the various acts of sexual intercourse with them as a group. In support of this defense the defendants sought to present evidence that the complainant had had prior sexual relations with one of them and that she had practiced prostitution in the past. The trial judge, however, precluded the admission of such evidence based on the defendants' failure to timely comply with the "rape shield" law's notice provision. Thus it is the defendants' contention to us on appeal that the "rape shield" law, at least as applied to the facts of this case, violates the defendants' right of effective cross-examination protected by the confrontation clause of the Sixth Amendment.

Under the facts of this case we believe the trial judge reached the proper result in foreclosing inquiry, either through cross-examination of

---

12. The "rape shield" law was enacted as part of this state's modernization of its sexual assault laws. See 1974 PA 266, effective November 1, 1974, MCL 750.520a et seq.; MSA 28.788(1) et seq.

MCL 750.520j; MSA 28.788(10), in particular, provides:

"Evidence of specific instances of the victim's sexual conduct, opinion evidence of the victim's sexual conduct, and reputation evidence of the victim's sexual conduct shall not be admitted under sections 520b to 520g unless and only to the extent that the judge finds that the following proposed evidence is material to a fact at issue in the case and that its inflammatory or prejudicial nature does not outweigh its probative value:

"(a) Evidence of the victim's past sexual conduct with the actor.

"(b) Evidence of specific instances of sexual activity showing the source or origin of semen, pregnancy, or disease.

"(2) If the defendant proposes to offer evidence described in subsection (1)(a) or (b), the defendant within 10 days after the arraignment on the information shall file a written motion and offer of proof. The court may order an in camera hearing to determine whether the proposed evidence is admissible under subsection (1). If new information is discovered during the course of the trial that may make the evidence described in subsection (1)(a) or (b) admissible, the judge may order an in camera hearing to determine whether the proposed evidence is admissible under subsection (1)."

the complainant or the presentation of direct testimony, into any alleged past sexual relations of one of the defendants with the complainant or into alleged specific instances of, or reputation for, prostitution on the part of the complainant. . . . [W]e find that the evidence sought to be admitted was irrelevant in the context of this particular case to the asserted defense of consent. As such, it was properly excluded. . . .

Reasoning

I. Facts

Complainant testified at trial that she met defendant Williams shortly after midnight on October 19, 1977, in the Moon Glow Lounge in the City of Detroit. According to complainant, she had a casual acquaintanceship with defendant Williams, both having lived in the same neighborhood and the complainant having had Williams' sister babysit for her daughter. After a short period of small talk in the bar during which complainant declined defendant Williams' offer to "go out and have some fun," defendant Williams grabbed one of complainant's arms, telling her to come with him, defendant Anderson grabbed the other arm, and then in the company of the other two defendants, one of whom she had observed with a knife in the bar, she was ushered from the bar. Once outside the bar, according to the complainant, she was ordered into a car and then, accompanied by all four defendants, driven to defendant Respress' house. It was here, pursuant to defendant Williams' instruction that complainant do as she was told if she didn't want to get hurt, that the defendants engaged in the various sexual acts of which they were convicted.

complainant's story

Defendant Williams was the only one of the four accused to take the stand. He testified that while in the Moon Glow bar he asked complainant if she wanted to have sexual intercourse with him. After giving an affirmative response the complainant voluntarily accompanied all four defendants to defendant Respress' house. Once inside, defendant Williams, at the request of defendants Respress and Anderson, asked complainant if she would have intercourse with all four defendants. According to defendant Williams, complainant "said it was okay, that she'd done it before." Thereafter complainant willingly engaged in sexual intercourse with all four defendants.

Δ's story

. . . In discussing preliminary matters prior to jury selection, the prosecutor informed the court that defense counsel had informed him of its [sic] intention to offer evidence of prior sexual relations between the complainant and one defendant. Counsel for defendant Williams acknowledged his intent to cross-examine the complainant about prior sexual activity with defendant Williams and to offer evidence on complainant's alleged past prostitution. . . .

. . .

Prior to cross-examination of the complainant, counsel for defendant Williams and the prosecutor again argued to the trial court about the scope of cross-examination of the complainant. This argument was fueled by the fact that defense counsel had obtained a temporary "rap sheet" on the complainant indicating that she had been charged with accosting and soliciting within six days of the crimes for which the defendants were on trial. . . .

Proc. History Following their jury trial, defendants Williams, Anderson, and Johnson were each convicted, under separate counts, of first-degree criminal sexual conduct. . . . Defendant Respress was convicted of two counts of first-degree criminal sexual conduct.

A divided Court of Appeals reversed and remanded for a new trial. . . .

We granted leave to appeal and directed the parties to include among the issues to be briefed whether application of § 520j violated defendants' Sixth Amendment rights to confrontation and cross-examination. . . .

II. Discussion

Δ's argument Defendants assert on appeal to us that their Sixth Amendment rights to confrontation and cross-examination were violated by the trial court's preclusion of any inquiry into alleged prior sexual relations between defendant Williams and the complainant[13] and the alleged reputation of the complainant as a prostitute. This evidence, defendants argue, is relevant to their defense of consent and the closely related issue of complainant's credibility.

. . .

A. *Prior Sexual Relations Between One of Four Defendants and the Complainant*

1. *Consent*

Defendants assert that the trial court denied their rights of confrontation and cross-examination by excluding evidence of prior sexual relations between defendant Williams and the complainant. Such an assertion must rest on the premise that such evidence is probative of their claim that the complainant consented to have group sexual relations with all four of them, one after the other, with defendant Williams constantly present and the other defendants intermittently so.

We are unable to agree with defendants' premise. There seems to be little, if any, logic to the proposition that because the complainant might have voluntarily consented to sexual intercourse with defendant Williams in the past, in what we must assume in the absence of evidence to the contrary to have been an encounter between just the two of them, she would more probably have consented in this case to intercourse with not only defendant Williams again, but also group intercourse with three other men in his company. . . .

---

13. Although § 520j(1)(a) speaks in terms of past sexual conduct between only the victim and actor, defendants Anderson, Johnson, and Respress insist that they are entitled to benefit from the introduction of evidence of past sexual relations between de-fendant Williams and the complainant. They point out that all four defendants have asserted the defense of consent and that the prosecutor opposed, and the trial court denied, their motions for separate trial.

We feel the fact of sexual intercourse between a complainant and a defendant alone should not, without more, serve as substantive evidence that the complainant would consent to any type of group sexual encounter. In short, the facts of this record present us with little or no logical relevance between the excluded prior sexual acts evidence and the issue of consent respecting either defendant Williams alone or the other three defendants collectively.

2. *Credibility*

In their briefs some of the defendants also seem to be arguing to us that the excluded prior sexual act evidence should have been admitted on the issue of the complainant's credibility. It is unclear, however, whether or not the defendants mean simply that the prior sexual act evidence is relevant insofar as it tends to prove consent, thus tending to impugn the complainant's account of forced sexual intercourse. In such an event it is the complainant's veracity as to the particular instance in issue which is more properly being challenged than her overall credibility as a witness, although the distinction is admittedly fine. If this is the substance of the defendants' assertion that the prior sexual relations of defendant Williams with the complainant are relevant to complainant's credibility, we have held to the contrary in our immediately preceding discussion.

On the other hand, if the defendants are asserting that the prior sexual activity of the complainant with defendant Williams is admissible to impeach the complainant's general credibility as a witness, we likewise find no merit in such an argument. While it is true that prior sexual act conduct was used in the past by some courts to attack the credibility of a complaining witness in forcible sexual assault cases . . . the notion that unchaste women are especially prone to lying has become as antiquated and as fatuous as the belief that simply because a woman has consented to intercourse with a third party on another occasion, she probably consented to intercourse with the defendant. As the North Carolina Supreme Court has observed in discussing the subject of impeachment of credibility through sexual history evidence:

"Common sense dictates the unreasonableness of this attitude. If sexual experiences outside marriage render one woman less truthful than her virgin sister, then sexual experience outside marriage would be an issue at any trial where a woman was a witness. This is plainly not the case. A woman, just as a man, 'may be intemperate, incontinent, profane and addicted to many other vices that ruin the reputation, and yet retain a scrupulous regard for the truth . . . .' Gilchrist v. McKee, 4 Watts 380, 386 (Pa.1835), quoted in Commonwealth v. Crider, 240 Pa. Super. 403, 406 (1976)." State v. Fortney, 301 N.C. 31, 40 (1980).

It is enough therefore to dispose of this matter that we point to MRE 608 and its limitation on evidence seeking to impeach a witness's credibility to character and conduct evidence bearing solely on the witness's truthfulness. . . .

B. Evidence of Prostitution

1. Consent

Defendants also maintain that the trial court denied their Sixth Amendment rights by foreclosing inquiry into evidence of the complainant's prostitution. Defendants' argument in this regard is basically that evidence of complainant's prostitution is supportive of defendants' account of their group sexual encounters as consensual, although there is little or no evidence they were undertaken for pay.

Again, defendants do not clearly state exactly why they consider such evidence probative of consent. It seems that part of the claimed relevance is based on the defendants' belief that the complainant, to quote defendant Williams' brief, "in furtherance of this pattern of prostitution, willingly engaged in sexual relations with him [defendant Williams] in the past, and on the night in question." However, the record is virtually devoid of any suggestion that the complainant was engaging in sexual intercourse with the four defendants on the night in question for money. Defendant Williams, the only defendant to testify, stated on direct examination that while in the Moon Glow bar he simply asked the complainant to have sex with him. . . . There is not the slightest hint here in defendant Williams' version of the events that the complainant expected financial recompense for any sexual services. Nor is any such expectation present in defendant Williams' account on direct examination of his solicitation of the complainant to have intercourse with the other defendants. . . . In fact, according to defendant Williams, the only talk of money between the complainant and any of the defendants occurred *after* the acts of sexual intercourse which form the subject matter of this case, as defendants Anderson and Williams were letting her out of the car after having taken her back to the City of Detroit. According to defendant Williams, as the complainant was leaving the car she asked for $15 or $20. However, defendant Williams admitted, on cross-examination, that that was the first time complainant had asked for any money. . . .

It is evident that defendants did not seek to establish at trial that the complainant consented to sexual intercourse with all four defendants as an act of prostitution. Thus we need not decide whether upon a proper record supporting the defense of financially induced consent, a trial court could constitutionally exclude evidence of prior or past prostitution based on § 520j(2).

Defendants' argument that evidence of prostitution has probative value on the issue of consent depends on whether the bare fact that a complainant has engaged in intercourse for money has any tendency to make it more probable that such a complainant would consent to intercourse without financial arrangements. We believe that any proffered evidence of complainant's reputation for, or specific acts of, prostitution, on the record made below, was not sufficiently probative to have been admitted. Other courts have been faced with this same type of issue and have held as we do now. . . .

. . .

In fact, if anything, evidence that a complainant was a prostitute would seem more probative of the fact that she would be reluctant to provide sexual services to four men gratis. Accordingly, we find no denial of defendants' right of confrontation and cross-examination in foreclosing this proposed inquiry into irrelevant evidence.

2. *Credibility*

Finally, defendants assert that the trial court denied their constitutional right to confront the complainant by not permitting them to impeach her credibility through evidence of her prostitution. This claim is of minimal merit and need not detain us long.

Initially, we note that even had the complainant been convicted of the charge of accosting and soliciting at the time this case went to trial—of which there is no record support—defendants could not have impeached her credibility due to this fact alone under MRE 609 since accosting and soliciting is a misdemeanor, MCL 750.448; MSA 28.703, and it cannot seriously be contended that accosting and soliciting involves "theft, dishonesty or false statement." See Committee Note on MRE 609.

As to defendants' endeavor to impeach the complainant's credibility through her alleged reputation as a prostitute, we stress again this Court's requirement that the impeaching evidence be related to the character trait of truthfulness or untruthfulness. As with prior sexual conduct evidence, we see no logical relation between a complainant's reputation for prostitution and the character trait of truthfulness or untruthfulness. The law should not recognize any necessary connection between a witness's veracity and her sexual immorality. . . .

The defendants were not denied any right of confrontation in being foreclosed from attempting to impeach the credibility of the complainant due to her specific acts of, or reputation for, prostitution.

III. Conclusion

In our opinion it would have been error under the facts of this case for the trial court to have admitted evidence that one of four defendants had past sexual relations with the complainant, and that the complainant was a prostitute. This is not to say, however, that evidence of a complainant's prior sexual behavior with a sole defendant or even one of several defendants, or her reputation as a prostitute can never be relevant to an issue presented at trial. Our decision today rests solely on the irrelevance in this particular case of the proffered evidence to the asserted defense of consent and to impeachment of the complainant's credibility. It is, therefore, unnecessary to address ourselves to constitutional questions which may arise in the future by the application of this state's "rape shield" law to different circumstances of enhanced probative value. Accordingly, we reverse the judgment of the Court of Appeals and reinstate defendants' convictions.

. . .

■ LEVIN, J [dissenting].

I

. . . A judge cannot exercise the discretion confided to him by Rule 403 to exclude relevant evidence on the grounds of prejudice, confusion, or waste of time, without conducting an evidentiary hearing focused on that question. No such hearing was held in this case.

. . .

The evidence of Williams' past sexual contact with the complainant and tending to show that she was a prostitute is relevant for reasons set forth below. If the probative value of such evidence outweighs the potential for prejudice, the evidence was admissible under the Rules of Evidence without regard to the rape shield statute.

. . .

III

The evidence of prior sexual contact between complainant and defendant Williams and evidence concerning her reputation as a prostitute is here relevant.

definition of relevant evidence

MRE 401 defines "relevant evidence" as: "evidence having any tendency to make the existence of any fact that is of consequence to the determination of the action more probable or less probable than it would be without the evidence."

Some jurors would find it difficult to believe that a woman would agree to sexual intercourse with a man who approached her in a bar. Most jurors would find it incredible that a woman would agree to intercourse with four men in succession. Such behavior is likely to be considered most unusual and unlikely to occur voluntarily.

Juror's believing the probability of the events

Jurors might thus find Williams' story more probable if it is shown that complainant previously had intercourse with him. Likewise jurors might regard it more believable that a woman would consent to sexual acts with four men in succession, if they heard evidence that complainant has had sexual intercourse with a number of men in succession on a professional basis.

To be sure, a woman's willingness to have sexual intercourse with one man on one or more occasions does not prove or even make it probable that she will consent to intercourse with that man and three others on some later occasion. Nor, I agree, does evidence that a woman is a prostitute establish or make it probable that she would be willing to have sexual intercourse without compensation with four men.[14] But evidence need not

---

14. Clearly, a defendant should not be permitted to impeach a complainant's credibility by showing she was a prostitute. That a woman is a prostitute has nothing to do with her credibility. Witnesses lie because they are under pressure and not because of their past histories.

make a conclusion probable in order to be relevant; it must only make the conclusion more probable than it would have been without the evidence.[15]

IV

Because the trial judge did not hold an *in camera* hearing or allow defense counsel to make an offer of proof, the judge had no opportunity to determine whether the danger of prejudice substantially outweighed the probative value of the proposed evidence. MRE 403. Accordingly, I would affirm the decision of the Court of Appeals and remand for a new trial.

———

322. The court in *Williams*, above, refers to the Confrontation Clause of the Sixth Amendment, which provides that a criminal defendant has a right "to be confronted with the witnesses against him." That provision protects the right to cross-examine witnesses for the prosecution. For example, in Davis v. Alaska, 415 U.S. 308 (1974), the Supreme Court held that a state could not foreclose cross-examination of a witness with respect to his prior criminal conduct, pursuant to a state law protecting the secrecy of juvenile records. The Court said: "The State's policy interest in protecting the confidentiality of a juvenile offender's record cannot require yielding of so vital a constitutional right as the effective cross-examination for bias of an adverse witness. The State could have protected the witness from exposure of his juvenile adjudication in these circumstances by refraining from using him to make out its case; the State cannot, consistent with right of confrontation, require the petitioner to bear the full burden of vindicating the State's interest in the secrecy of juvenile criminal records." Id. at 320.

In *Williams*, the prosecution did not have the option, suggested by the Court in *Davis*, of not using the victim of the alleged rape as a witness. Did the court reach an appropriate resolution of the competing interests of the victim and the defendants?

323. Like Federal Rule 412, other shield laws generally contain exceptions allowing the introduction of evidence of the victim's prior sexual conduct if it bears directly on the facts of the case, e.g., to explain the presence of semen in her body. Evidence of past promiscuity or prostitution is generally not admitted pursuant to such an exception; but it may be admitted if it is specifically relevant. For a lengthy discussion, see People v. Sandoval, 552 N.E.2d 726 (Ill.1990) (evidence of complainant's specific

---

15. The question is not whether it is probable that a woman who consented in the past would consent again, but whether defendant's story is more probable if complainant has consented in the past than it would be if she has not consented in the past. Similarly, the question is not whether it is probable that a prostitute would consent to sexual intercourse with four men in succession, but whether it is more probable that a prostitute would do this than a woman who is not a prostitute.

sexual acts with another man, which contradicted her testimony that she had not engaged in such acts, properly excluded). Other cases considering the application of shield laws include Thomas v. State, 471 N.E.2d 677 (Ind.1984) (evidence of sexual conduct with another person, to explain presence of semen; exclusion upheld, because slight probative value outweighed by prejudice to victim); Testerman v. State, 486 A.2d 233 (Md.Ct. Spec.App.1985) (evidence of long-term prior sexual relationship with defendant; exclusion held improper); Commonwealth v. Joyce, 415 N.E.2d 181 (Mass.1981) (evidence of prior charges of prostitution, to show motive to fabricate; exclusion held improper); People v. Hackett, 365 N.W.2d 120 (Mich.1984) (evidence of prior sexual acts with others, to show consent; exclusion upheld); State v. Jalo, 557 P.2d 1359 (Or.Ct.App.1976) (evidence of prior sexual conduct with another person, to show motive to fabricate; exclusion held improper); Commonwealth v. Spiewak, 617 A.2d 696 (Pa. 1992) (evidence of prior inconsistent testimony concerning prior sexual act; exclusion held improper); Commonwealth v. Majorana, 470 A.2d 80 (Pa. 1983) (evidence of recent prior act with defendant, to explain presence of semen; exclusion held improper); Holloway v. State, 751 S.W.2d 866 (Tex. Crim.App.1988) (evidence of prostitution to show consent; exclusion upheld).

Should rape shield laws extend to questioning by the defense about whether the victim of the alleged rape had in the past made a false accusation of rape? If such questioning is permitted, what should be the limits of such questioning if, say, answers to the questions reveal that the prior incident involved sexual conduct? See, e.g., State v. Boggs, 588 N.E.2d 813 (Ohio 1992) (evidence of prior false accusation admissible unless sexual activity evidence of which is excluded by shield law actually occurred; other cases cited).

In Tanford & Bocchino, "Rape Victim Shield Laws and the Sixth Amendment," 128 U. Pa. L. Rev. 544 (1980), the authors conclude that some of the current rape shield laws violate the defendant's right to defend himself. "An analysis of laws affecting criminal defendants must be approached not from the standpoint of the victim, but from the standpoint of the accused. Whatever indignities are suffered by the complaining witness in any criminal trial, they do not compare with those a convicted defendant must suffer. There is no more serious undertaking of the state than accusing a person of a crime, with the concomitant threat of loss of liberty or life." Id. at 545. They offer as an example of a valid shield law, the Texas statute:

> "(a) Evidence of specific instances of the victim's sexual conduct, opinion evidence of the victim's sexual conduct, and reputation evidence of the victim's sexual conduct may be admitted . . . only if, and only to the extent that, the judge finds that the evidence is material to a fact at issue in the case and that its inflammatory or prejudicial nature does not outweigh its probative value.
>
> (b) If the defendant proposes to ask any question concerning specific instances, opinion evidence, or reputation evidence of the

victim's sexual conduct, either by direct examination or cross-examination of any witness, the defendant must inform the court out of the hearing of the jury prior to asking any such question. After this notice, the court shall conduct an in camera hearing . . . to determine whether the proposed evidence is admissible under Subsection (a) of this section . . . ." Tex. Penal Code Ann. § 22.065 (Vernon Supp. 1985), since repealed.

Tanford & Bocchino, above, at 590.

The Model Penal Code does not contain a shield law. The commentary states that the question whether evidence of the victim's prior sexual conduct is admissible in a prosecution for rape is "essentially an evidentiary one and not a question of substantive law," and for this reason is not addressed by the Code. 1 MPC Commentaries Part II, 348 (comment to § 213.1). However, the Code makes rape a more serious offense if "the victim was not a voluntary social companion of the actor upon the occasion of the crime and had not previously permitted him sexual liberties." § 213.1. The commentary observes: "Even where past experience with the accused is not explicitly incorporated as a substantive standard of liability or grading, admission of such evidence is justified as relevant to the question of imposition or consent. It simply ignores reality to suggest that past practice with the accused is not relevant to the issue of consent on a given occasion, though it is equally a distortion to regard proof of such experience as dispositive." 1 MPC Commentaries Part II, 350 (comment to § 213.1). The commentary takes a more restrictive view of evidence of general sexual history or reputation. Id. at 350–53.

324. As part of the Violent Crime Control and Law Enforcement Act of 1994, 108 Stat. 1796, 2135, Congress enacted Federal Rule of Evidence 413, which provided in part: "(a) In a criminal case in which the defendant is accused of an offense of sexual assault, evidence of the defendant's commission of another offense or offenses of sexual assault is admissible, and may be considered for its bearing on any matter to which it is relevant." The Act provided that the Judicial Conference should report its views about Rule 413 (and other amendments to the Rules of Evidence) to Congress within 150 days. The Judicial Conference strongly opposed the rule. The report noted that all the members of its Committees that studied the rule, which included judges, practicing lawyers, and academicians, opposed it except the representatives of the Department of Justice. It observed that evidence of prior criminal conduct was already admissible in certain circumstances and said that the new rule was "not supported by empirical evidence, [and] could diminish significantly the protections that have safeguarded persons accused in criminal cases . . . against undue prejudice. The protections form a fundamental part of American jurisprudence and have evolved under long-standing rules and case law. A significant concern . . . was the danger of convicting a criminal defendant for past, as opposed to charged, behavior or for being a bad person." Congress did not follow the Judicial Conference's recommendation, and the Rule became effective in 1995.

The provision of Rule 413 contrasts sharply with the policy of rape shield laws. Is there a reasoned justification for treating the past conduct of the victim and the defendant so differently?

325. It is widely believed that one reason why victims of rape so often do not report the crime is that they do not want to subject themselves to the further ordeal of investigation by police, and later, cross-examination as a witness at trial. Defense counsel have been excoriated for conducting such questioning. If the rules of evidence permit defense counsel to inquire into the victim's sexual history, does he have any independent obligation to consider its effect on the victim? Should he try to restrict the impact of the evidence to issues to which it is relevant? How should defense counsel resolve the competing interests of the defendant and the victim?

326. The changes in the evidentiary rules described above affect the trial of rape cases. Most cases, like criminal cases generally, do not go to trial but are resolved by a plea-bargain. Therefore, it has been argued, the changes are much less significant than they may appear. Effective reform requires not only that irrelevant evidence be kept from the jury but also that it not be considered by those who make the critical plea and sentencing decisions. Police, prosecutors, and judges alike generally rely on a few crude indicators of guilt, among which the most common are evidence of violence, physical injury to the victim, and the absence of a prior sexual relationship between the victim and her assailant.

After several decades of legislative and judicial reform, the trends in the law of rape are reasonably clear. They include definition of the offense in terms of objective circumstances, especially the offender's conduct, rather than the victim's state of mind; greater protection of the victim, including especially modification of evidentiary rules; assimilation of various kinds of sexual assault, including homosexual rape and rape of a male by a female; elimination or qualification of the spousal exclusion; grading of offenses; and reduction of penalties. All of these changes (except, in some views, the latter two) are intended to strengthen the law and increase its deterrent and punitive effects.

The only way to be certain of the success or lack of success of these measures is to observe the incidence of the offense and the effectiveness of the law's response in actual cases. Information of that kind is difficult to obtain and difficult to interpret. There has been an increase in the number of reported rapes, for example. Does that mark a significant achievement?

Does it mean that women generally are in a stronger position and that the number of unreported rapes has declined?[16] Or do the vast majority of rapes, especially those not involving an attack by a stranger, remain unreported, as before? If there is more effective prosecution of the most serious cases, are those more than isolated instances? What bearing have such prosecutions on the range of cases in which the injury to the woman is less palpable? Beyond all the legislative activity, how much have social attitudes to the stereotypical sexual roles of men and women changed with respect to a woman's freedom fully to decide for herself?

What is the role of the criminal law anyway?

> The substantive criminal law cannot temper public fear generated by the sensational press or by the racial overtones that some would attribute to the crime of rape. It can exert little influence on whether the victim chooses to report the offense or whether the police choose to credit the victim's account. There are also many factors associated with arrest and conviction that are beyond the remedial powers of substantive criminal legislation. There is a danger, moreover, that public apprehension will lead to an overreaction in legislative halls. It is, after all, both politically rewarding and relatively easy to take a public stand by passing a law against plainly offensive and unpopular conduct. Although the point is valid with respect to any crime, it deserves special emphasis here that definition of the crime of rape calls for a balanced judgment on the many difficult issues that must be resolved.

1 MPC Commentaries Part II, 286 (comment to § 213.1).

> Reforms in the area of rape speak to more than the criminal justice system, even though rape, by whatever name, is a crime. Because in the past rape served to express more than the society's declaration of an illegal act, reforms in the area of sex offenses will continue to be a vehicle for women to insist that their autonomy must be protected by the agents of social control. In the coming decade, legislative reforms in the area of rape will continue to mirror and to measure the ongoing transformation of the status of American women.

Bienen, "Rape III—National Developments in Rape Reform Legislation," 6 Women's Rights L. Rep. 170 (1981).

---

16. An increase in reported rapes might also mean that the number of rapes has increased. There is not persuasive evidence that is the case.

*

PART FOUR

ACTOR AND ACT

So far we have considered general problems of criminal law in the context of particular crimes: first, crimes involving security of the person, more particularly, homicide; second, crimes involving the security of property, more particularly, theft; and third, another crime involving security of the person, rape. We turn now to some aspects of the "general part" of criminal law. The issues that we shall consider are treated generally because they may arise in connection with any crime, or at least a great many very different crimes, and can be discussed largely without regard to the elements of specific crimes.

In this Part we shall not deal with all the subjects that have been treated generally in cases or codes or by commentators. The nature of an "act," for example, has been extensively treated elsewhere as a general problem of the criminal law.[1] It is given no explicit attention here because the level of abstraction at which one considers the concept of an "act" seems too abstract to be useful for our present purposes; but we have considered the issue concretely in a variety of contexts.

The subjects with which we shall deal present some of the most basic and persistent problems of the criminal law. As before, it would be a mistake to regard the particular topics that furnish headings for subdivisions as your only concern. It may be less important that you know the precise formulation of various tests of insanity or all the intricate rules governing conspiratorial liability than that you see both as manifesting the tension in the criminal law between attention to the harm done and attention to the person who has done harm, the same tension that we considered earlier in a number of different settings. That tension is exacerbated if the harm is very great and the person who has done harm has an especially strong claim to exculpation based on his peculiar condition. It is exacerbated if his culpability is great but he has (as yet) done no serious harm.

---

1. See, e.g., Model Penal Code § 2.01.

1. INSANITY

327. "[I]t is remarkable how it has always been taken for granted that, *if* the presence of incapacitating mental illness can be established, then there can be no question of the law taking its [punitive] course. Dispute turns only on the terms in which mental incapacity should in this context be defined, never on the question whether the sick should be exempted from the penalty imposed upon the healthy. The principle that any illness which causes misconduct also excuses that misconduct is certainly deep-seated in contemporary notions of responsibility, at least as these are applied in practice." B. Wootton, Social Science and Social Pathology 208 (1959).

On what premises, if any, does the proposition that "mental incapacity" excuses from the penalties of the criminal law depend? Is the proposition an axiom of any system of *criminal* law? Or is it a postulate that can meaningfully and usefully be questioned?

Either way, does (must) incapacity excuse from liability for all crimes, if it excuses from any? Or does something depend on the nature of the crime in question? Does something depend on the penalties for crime generally or for particular crimes?

What does "incapacity" mean? In the dispute about "the terms in which mental incapacity . . . should be defined," is there any minimum content that the concept of incapacity must have if the proposition that incapacity excuses is to be meaningful? Might the nature and/or degree of mental incapacity that excuses vary according to the nature of the crime in question?

328. "Cruelty, ignorance, prejudice, and the like, are freely ascribed to the law and to those who administer it, on the grounds that it is said not to keep pace with the discoveries of science and to deny facts medically ascertained. The heat and vehemence with which such charges are made makes a perfectly impartial discussion of the whole matter difficult. . . . The interest and possibly the importance of the task is, however, upon a par with its difficulty . . . ." 2 Stephen, History 124–25.

———

The Times (London)

Saturday, January 21, 1843.

Attempt To Assassinate Mr. Edward Drummond, Sir R. Peel's Private Secretary

Yesterday afternoon a most determined attempt was made to assassinate Mr. Drummond, the private secretary of Sir Robert Peel, in the open street, and in the broad face of day. The motives of the assassin are at present involved in mystery, not the slightest clue being yet obtained to the cause that could have impelled him to the commission of so aggravated a crime. But, whatever may have been the reasons influencing his mind, it will be seen, from the subjoined account, that his purpose was carried out with the most cold-blooded determination, though, fortunately, no fatal results are at present expected to accrue from the wound which he succeeded in inflicting on his intended victim:—

It appears, from information on which perfect reliance may be placed, that Mr. Drummond left Downing street at about half-past 3 o'clock in the afternoon of yesterday, in company with the Earl of Haddington. They proceeded together as far as the Admiralty, where Mr. Drummond left the Earl of Haddington, and went to the banking-house of his brother of the same name, at Charing-cross. On his return therefrom, and when he had proceeded as far as the space between the Admiralty and the Horse Guards, he was shot at by a man who approached him from behind. The assassin walked close up to Mr. Drummond, and, showing a determination not to fail in the perpetration of the foul deed which he contemplated, actually put the muzzle of the pistol into the back of the unsuspecting gentleman. He then fired. Immediately after the pistol was discharged, a policeman, who had witnessed the act, rushed up, and seized the criminal. In the meantime he had returned the pistol with which he had shot Mr. Drummond to his breast, and had drawn out another loaded pistol from the same place, and was in the act of pointing it at Mr. Drummond, when the policeman seized him and pinioned his arms from behind. The pistol was discharged, but the aim of the assassin being thus diverted, the contents did not touch Mr. Drummond, nor was any other person injured by them.

. . .

The assassin, on being secured by the policeman, was conveyed to Garciner's-lane police-station, where he gave his name as M'Naughten. He refused to give his place of residence, but it is supposed that he is either a Scotchman or a native of the north of Ireland, who had been located at Glasgow.   . . .

Nothing transpired that could with certainty lead to a knowledge of the motives which induced the prisoner to commit this dreadful act. It does not appear that he had had any previous correspondence with Mr. Drummond, or that he had preferred any claim or complaint to the Treasury, or was a disappointed applicant for office. His demeanour throughout was cool and collected, nor did there appear any evidence of insanity.

The policeman who apprehended him heard him say, on his being arrested, "He" or "she" (the policeman is uncertain which) "shall not disturb my mind any longer."

It is stated that the prisoner had been seen loitering about the public offices for some days previously.   . . .

In answer to inquiries made at the residence of Mr. Drummond, in Grosvenor-Street, we were informed that he was still doing well—that no immediate danger was anticipated.   . . .

. . . .

The Times (London)

Monday, January 23, 1843.

The Attempt To Assassinate Mr. Edward Drummond

It having become generally known that the person charged with attempting the life of Mr. Edward Drummond would be examined at Bow-street on Saturday morning, the court, as soon as the doors were thrown open, was densely thronged by persons anxious to hear the proceedings.

Shortly before 10 o'clock the prisoner was brought to the court from the station-house, in a cab, accompanied by two inspectors of the A division of police.

. . .

It having been arranged that Mr. Hall should hear the case, that gentleman took his seat upon the bench at half-past 10 o'clock. . . .

The prisoner . . . is a young man, rather above the middle height, having the appearance of a mechanic, and was respectably dressed in a black coat and waistcoat and drab trousers. He is rather thin, has a good colour, and his countenance betokened nothing ferocious or determined.

The clerk.—What is your name, prisoner!

The prisoner replied in a very broad Scotch accent, "Daniel M'Naughten."

. . .

Mr. Hall addressing the prisoner, said, I am about to remand you for a fortnight, and if you wish to say anything in answer to the charge, I am ready to hear you. You are not compelled to say anything unless you think proper. But it is my duty to tell you, that if you do say anything, it will be taken down in writing and made use of, if necessary, hereafter. Now, having given you that caution, do you wish to say anything?

Prisoner.—I am much obliged to you, Sir, but I shall say nothing at present.

The clerk.—Then you are remanded for a fortnight.

The prisoner immediately left the dock, and was removed to one of the cells attached to the court, but had not been there more than a minute or two, when he sent a message to the magistrate intimating that he wished to say something: he was accordingly again placed at the bar.

Mr. Hall.—I understand you wish to say something: if so, I am ready to hear you.

The prisoner, after a slight pause, said—The Tories in my native city have compelled me to do this; they follow and persecute me wherever I go, and have entirely destroyed my peace of mind. They followed me to France, into Scotland, and all over England: in fact they follow me wherever I go: I can get no rest for them night or day. I cannot sleep at nights, in consequence of the course they pursue towards me. I believe they have driven me into a consumption. I am sure I shall never be the man I formerly was. I used to have good health and strength, but I have not now. They have accused me of crimes of which I am not guilty: they have every thing in their power to harass and persecute me, in fact they wish to murder me. It can be proved by evidence—that's all I wish to say at present.

The clerk.—Is that all you wish to say?

Prisoner (hesitatingly.)—I can only say they have completely disordered my mind, and I am not capable of doing anything, compared to what I was. I am a very different man to what I was before they commenced this system of persecution.

The clerk.—Do you wish to say anything more?

Prisoner.—Oh! yes, I wish to know whether I am to be kept in that place (pointing towards the cell) for a fortnight? If so, I am sure I shall not live.

The clerk.—Oh, no, you will be taken to a proper place of confinement, where you will be taken care of till you are brought here again.

Prisoner.—Oh, very well, then I have nothing more to say.

Mr. Hall.—Have you any objection to sign the statement you have made?

Prisoner.—No, I have no objection.

The statement having been read over to the prisoner, it was handed to him in the dock, when he immediately signed it.

He was then removed from the bar.

. . .

STATE OF MR. DRUMMOND'S HEALTH

It is with extreme regret we have to announce that a very unfavorable change in Mr. Drummond's symptoms took place on Saturday morning. . . .

. . .

Sir Robert and Lady Peel frequently call to make inquiries respecting the state of Mr. Drummond's health, as do many of the nobility and gentry at present in town.

. . .

The Times (London)

Wednesday, January 25, 1843.

The Prisoner M'Naughten

The few facts which have transpired since our last, in reference to this lamentable event, have rather been of a nature to excite, than to satisfy, the natural desire for information upon the subject. . . .

. . .

These facts, meager as they are, would seem to warrant the conclusion, that whatever of eccentricity there may have been in the man's behaviour, there has been so much of "method" in it—such symptoms of foresight, prudence, deliberation, and design, that it can hardly have been the conduct of a madman : and it is certainly evident that his condition was the reverse of uncomfortable, so far as pecuniary matters were concerned.

But the moment we attempt to divine any imaginable motive for an act so deadly as that which he committed, all appears wrapt in impenetrable darkness. We understand that no inquiries can lead to the discovery of any communication, or attempt at communication, on his part, with the Cabinet or the Privy Council, so as to have brought him in contact with the unfortunate gentleman under circumstances at all calculated, or likely, to create any ill-feeling towards him. No clue had been discovered of any inducement, no trace found of any instigators, to the dreadful deed. . . .

The Times (London)

Thursday, January 26, 1843.

Death of Mr. Drummond

It has now become our very painful duty to announce that Mr. Edward Drummond died yesterday morning about half-past 10 o'clock.

.   .   .

Shortly before 8 o'clock a messenger from the Queen called to make inquiries, and returned with the intelligence of the hopeless situation in which the deceased then was to Windsor. Immediately after the unfortunate gentleman breathed his last another messenger was despatched to convey the melancholy tidings to Her Majesty.   .   .   .

THE ASSASSIN M'NAUGHTEN

(From the *Glasgow Chronicle* of Monday.)

From inquiry, we have found that M'Naughten is an illegitimate son of Mr. M'Naughten, formerly turner in this city, who still lives, but who, having quarrelled with his son some considerable time ago, has had no communication with him.   .   .   .

It appears that M'Naughten, upwards of two years ago, showed symptoms of mental aberration. To the landlady with whom he at that time lived he had repeatedly expressed his opinion that there were devils in human shape seeking his life; and one day he showed her a pair of pistols, and declared his determination to use them against his tormentors. About a year ago it is also reported that he applied to the police here for protection against Tory persecutors, who sought his life. We have seen a letter addressed to the prisoner from Mr. A. Johnston, M. P., in answer to some communication of M'Naughten, in which that gentleman expressed his belief that the writer was not of sane mind. These, and a number of concurrent circumstances, we think sufficiently attest the state of mind under which M'Naughten made the rash and violent attempt upon the life of Mr. Drummond.

.   .   .

The Times (London)

Friday, January 27, 1843.

The Assassin M'Naughten

(From the *Glasgow Constitutional.*)

.   .   .

.   .   . [W]e learn that about the end of May, or beginning of June, M'Naughten did call at   .   .   . [the] residence [of Sir James Campbell, the Lord Provost] in Bath-street. There

.   .   . [the Lord Provost] had some conversation in the hall with McNaughten, who is described by the Lord Provost as a jolly-looking man, and as speaking very coolly, although evidently labouring under some hallucination of mind. He told the Provost with great earnestness that he had been incessantly watched and dogged by certain parties who had an illwill at him. He said they had forced him from his home by their spiteful machinations, and the very night before they had obliged him to fly to the fields in the suburbs for refuge. Sir James Campbell asked the name of the complainer, which he gave, as also the name of his father, and afterwards reasoned with him as to the folly of his notions. Sir James likewise inquired, pretty broadly, whether he had ever been treated as if it had been suspected there was anything wrong with his (M'Naughten's) intellects, and being replied to in the negative, seriously advised him to consult his relations or some medical man as to the state of his health. At this visit he talked neither of religion nor politics; but just shook his head, and said that "he could not get rid of them at all." Immediately after this the Lord Provost sent for his father to converse with him on the subject; but it would appear now, that although the man called, he did not find his Lordship within, and the matter was forgotten . . . .

Because of Drummond's death, the final examination of M'Naughten was moved forward from February 6 to January 28, so that he could be tried at the next Central Criminal Court sessions. At the conclusion of the examination, M'Naughten was committed to Newgate, to be tried for wilful murder. The Times (London), Jan. 30, 1843, at 5.

The Times (London)

Thursday, February 3, 1843.

The Assassin M'Naughten

CENTRAL CRIMINAL COURT, FEB. 2.

(*Before Lord* ABINGER *and Mr. Justice* MAULE.)

At the sitting of the Court the prisoner, Daniel M'Naughten, was placed at the bar, charged with the wilful murder of Mr. Edward Drummond.

The prisoner, upon his name being called, immediately walked with a firm step to the front of the dock. He appeared perfectly calm and collected; he looked extremely well; and his general appearance was very little altered from what it was when under examination at Bow-street; but, if anything, he looked rather paler.

The Attorney-General, Mr. Adolphus, and Mr. Waddington appeared on behalf of the Crown; and Mr. Clarkson for the prisoner.

.   .   .

Mr. Straight, the deputy clerk of arraigns, then read the indictment, which was of very considerable length. It alleged that the prisoner, "on the 20th of January, at the parish of St. Martin-in-the-Fields, did feloniously assault Mr. Edward Drummond with a certain pistol, which he then and there held in his right hand, loaded with gunpowder and a leaden bullet, and which he of his malice aforethought discharged at and against the said Edward Drummond, thereby giving him a certain mortal wound, in and upon the left side of the back of the said Edward Drummond, a little below the bladebone of his left shoulder, of the breadth of half an inch and of the depth of 12 inches, and of which wound the said Edward Drummond did languish until the 25th of January, and languishing did live, on which 25th of January he, of the said mortal wound so given in manner aforesaid by him, the said Daniel M'Naughten, died; and that he did wilfully kill and murder the said Edward Drummond."

Mr. Straight.—How say you, prisoner, are you guilty of the charge or not guilty?

The prisoner, who kept his eyes steadily fixed towards the bench, made no reply to the question.

Mr. Straight again asked him whether he was guilty or not guilty?

Mr. Cope, the governor of the prison, here asked the prisoner whether he had heard the question?

Mr. Straight.—Prisoner, you must answer the question, whether you are guilty or not?

The prisoner, after again hesitating for some time, said, "I was driven to desperation by persecution."

Lord Abinger.—Will you answer the question? You must say either guilty or not guilty.

Prisoner, after another pause, "I am guilty of firing."

Lord Abinger.—By that do you mean to say you are not guilty of the remainder of the charge, that is, of intending to murder Mr. Drummond?

Prisoner.—Yes.

Lord Abinger.—That certainly amounts to a plea of "Not guilty;" therefore, such a plea must be recorded.

.   .   .

The Queen v. M'Naughton

4 State Trials (N.S.) 847 (1892)
Central Criminal Court, Old Bailey; Friday, March 3, 1843

["This day having been appointed for the trial of the assassin Daniel M'Naughton, every avenue leading to the court was at an early hour thronged to excess by numbers of well-dressed persons of both sexes, anxious to hear a case, the excitement of which has not been surpassed by any of the extraordinary events of a similar character which have taken place during the last quarter of a century.

.   .   .

"At 10 o'clock precisely Lord Chief Justice Tindal, Mr. Justice Williams, and Mr. Justice Coleridge took their seats upon the bench.

"The prisoner, Daniel M'Naughton, was immediately placed at the bar. He walked to the front of the dock with a firm step, though it was evident he was much excited; he was dressed, apparently, in the same clothes as when under examination at Bow-street, and appeared to have altered very little, if any, in his general appearance.

"The Solicitor-General, Mr. Waddington, and Mr. Russell Gurney, appeared on behalf of the prosecution; Mr. Cockburn, Queen's counsel, with Mr. Clarkson, Mr. Bodkin, and Mr. Monteith were retained to defend the prisoner.

"Mr. Clark, the clerk of the Court, then read over the indictment. . . .

"To this indictment the prisoner firmly replied *Not Guilty*.

"He was then charged upon the coroner's inquisition with the same offence, to which he also pleaded *Not Guilty*.

"A chair was then placed in the dock for the prisoner, upon which he immediately sat down, and throwing his head back appeared to be asleep; he remained in the same situation during the whole of the Solicitor-General's opening address, but when the witnesses were under examination he appeared to be listening attentively to what they said." The Times (London), March 4, 1843, at 5.]

Opening Speech for the Crown.

The *Solicitor General*: May it please you, my Lord, Gentlemen of the jury. . . .

. . .

. . . You will be satisfied, from the facts of the case, from the threats used by the prisoner before he committed his crime, and his declarations afterwards, that it was not the life of Mr. *Drummond* that he sought. You will be satisfied that it was the life of Sir *Robert Peel* that he desired to take, and that it was his life that he believed he was destroying when he discharged the fatal pistol against the person of Mr. *Drummond*.

Gentlemen, the nature of his crime is not altered by this circumstance, but it affords a reason for it. I need not tell you that he is guilty of murder, although he might have mistaken the person against whom he discharged the pistol. Of the guilt of the prisoner—of the fact of his having deprived Mr. *Drummond* of life—it is impossible I can suggest a doubt; it is impossible that any doubt can be suggested that the crime was committed, and that that crime was murder. But I cannot conceal from you, because I know, from applications which have been made to this Court, and the depositions which have been made on behalf of the prisoner, that it is intended to rest the defence on the plea that he was insane at the time he committed the crime; and, gentlemen, it will be your painful duty—for painful it must be—to decide whether he was in that degree of insanity at the time he committed that crime which would render him not a responsible agent, and not answerable to the laws of his country for the offence of which he has been guilty. This defence is a difficult one at all times; for while, on the one hand, everyone must be anxious that an unconscious being should not suffer, yet, on the other hand, the public safety requires that this defence should not be too readily listened to; and, above all, the public safety requires that the atrocious nature of the act itself, and the circumstances under which it was committed, should not form any ingredient in that defence. There are few crimes that are committed, and, above all, crimes of an atrocious nature like this, that are not committed by persons labouring under some morbid affection of the mind; and it is difficult for well-regulated minds to understand the motives which lead to such offences in the absence of that morbid affection of the mind. . . .

But I know that in this case the defence on the part of the prisoner will not rest upon this, but that evidence will be offered to show that the prisoner was not in a sane state of mind at the time he committed the crime; and knowing that, I feel that I ought, in this stage of the case, to refer to some authorities, and state my view of the principles of the English law. . . . The whole question will turn upon this: if you believe the prisoner at the bar at the time he committed this act was not a responsible agent; if you believe that when he fired the pistol he was incapable of distinguishing between right and wrong; if you believe that he was under the influence and control of some disease of the mind which prevented him from being conscious that he was committing a crime; if you believe that he did not know he was violating the law both of God and man: then, undoubtedly, he is entitled to your acquittal. But it is my duty, subject to the correction of my Lord and to the observations of my learned friend, to tell you that nothing short of that will excuse him upon the principle of the English law. To excuse him it will not be sufficient that he laboured under partial insanity upon some subjects—that he had a morbid delusion of mind upon some subjects, which could not exist in a wholly sane person; that is not enough, if he had that degree of intellect which enabled him to know and distinguish between right and wrong, if he knew what would be the effects of his crime, and consciously committed it, and if with that consciousness he wilfully committed it. . . .

. . .

[Evidence for the Crown omitted.]

Speech for the Defence.

Cockburn: May it please your Lordships, Gentlemen of the Jury,—I rise to address you on behalf of the unfortunate prisoner at the bar, who stands charged with the awful crime of murder, under a feeling of anxiety so intense—of responsibility so overwhelming, that I feel almost borne down by the weight of my solemn and difficult task. . . .

Gentlemen, my learned friend the *Solicitor General*, in stating this case to you, anticipated, with his usual acuteness and accuracy, the nature of the defence which would be set up. The defence upon which I shall rely will turn, not upon the denial of the act with which the prisoner is charged, but upon the state of his mind at the time he committed the act. There is no doubt, gentlemen, that, according to the law of England, insanity absolves a man from responsibility and from the legal consequences which would otherwise attach to the violation of the law. And in this respect, indeed, the law of England goes no further than the law of every other civilised community on the face of the earth. It goes no further than what reason strictly prescribes; and, if it be not too presumptuous to scan the judgments of a higher tribunal, it may not be too much to believe and hope that Providence, when in its inscrutable wisdom and its unfathomable councils, it thinks fit to lay upon a human being the heaviest and most appalling of all calamities to which, in this world of trial and suffering, human nature can be subjected—the deprivation of that reason, which is man's only light and guide in the intricate and slippery paths of life—will absolve him from his responsibility to the laws of God as well as to those of man. The law, then, takes cognisance of that disease which obscures the intellect and poisons the very sources of thought and feeling in the human being—which deprives man of reason, and converts him into the similitude of the lower animal—which bears down all the motives which usually stand as barriers around his conduct, and bring him within the operation of the Divine and human law—leaving the unhappy sufferer to the wild impulses which his frantic imagination engenders, and which urge him on with ungovernable fury to the commission of acts which his better reason, when yet unclouded, would have abhorred. The law, therefore, holds that a human being in such a state is exempt from legal responsibility and legal punishment; to hold otherwise would be to violate every principle of justice and humanity. The principle of the English law, therefore, as a general proposition, admits of no doubt whatsoever. But, at the same time, it would be idle to contend that, in the practical application of this great principle, difficulties do not occur. . . .

. . . That which you have to determine is, whether the prisoner at the bar is guilty of the crime of wilful murder. Now, by "wilful" must be understood, not the mere will that makes a man raise his hand against another; not a blind instinct that leads to the commission of an irrational act, because the brute creation, the beasts of the field, have, in that sense, a will; but by will, with reference to human action, must be understood the necessary moral sense that guides and directs the volition, acting on it through the medium of reason. I quite agree with my learned friend, that it is a question—being, namely, whether this moral sense exists or not—of fact rather than of law. At the same time, whatever light legal authorities may afford on the one hand or philosophy and science on the other, we ought to avail ourselves of either with grateful alacrity. This being premised, I will now take the liberty of making a few general observations upon what appears to me to be the true view of the nature of this disease with reference to the application of the important principle of criminal responsibility. To the most superficial observer who has contemplated the mind of man, it must be perfectly obvious that the functions of the mind are of a twofold nature—those of the intellect or faculty of thought alone—such as perception, judgment, reasoning—and again, those of the moral faculties— the sentiments, affections, propensities, and passions, which it has pleased Heaven, for its own wise purposes, to implant in the nature of man. . . . By any one of the legion of casualties by which the material organisation may be affected, any one or all of these various faculties of the mind may be disordered,—the perception, the judgment, the reason, the sentiments, the affections, the propensities, the passions—any one or all may become subject to insanity; and the mistake existing in ancient times, which the light of modern science has dispelled, lay in supposing that in order that a man should be mad—incapable of judging between right and wrong, or of exercising that self-control and dominion, without which the knowledge of right and wrong would become vague and useless—it was necessary that he should exhibit those symptoms which would amount to total prostration of the intellect; whereas modern science has incontrovertibly established that any one of these intellectual and moral functions of the mind may be subject to separate disease, and thereby man may be rendered the victim of the most fearful delusions, the slave of uncontrollable impulses impelling or rather compelling him to the commission of acts such as that which has given rise to the case now under your consideration. This is the view of the subject on which all scientific authorities are agreed—a view not only entertained by medical, but also by legal authorities. . . .

. . . The question is not here, as my learned friend would have you think, whether this individual knew that he was killing another when he raised his hand to destroy him, although he might be under a delusion, but whether under that delusion of mind he did an act which he would not have done under any other circumstances, save under the impulse of the delusion which he could not control, and out of which delusion alone the act itself arose. . . .

. . .

. . . I am bound to show that the prisoner was acting under a delusion, and that the act sprung out of that delusion, and I will show it. I will show it by evidence irresistibly strong; and when I have done so, I shall be entitled to your verdict. On the other hand, my learned friend the *Solicitor General* told you yesterday that in the case before you the prisoner had some rationality, because in the ordinary relations of life he had manifested ordinary sagacity, and that on this account you must come to the conclusion that he was not insane on any point, and that the act with which he now stands charged was not the result of delusion. I had thought that the many occasions upon which this matter had been discussed would have rendered such a doctrine as obsolete and exploded in a court of law as it is everywhere else. . . .

. . . You will see that all the evidence of my learned friend the *Solicitor General* relates to the ordinary relations of a man's life. That does not effect the real question. It may be that this man understood the nature of right and wrong on general subjects—it may be that he was competent to manage his own affairs, that he could fulfil his part in the different relations of life, that he was capable of transacting all ordinary business. I grant it. But admitting all this, it does not follow that he was not subject to delusion, and insane. . . . My learned friend has also remarked upon the silent design and contrivance which the prisoner manifested upon the occasion in question, as well as upon his rationality in the ordinary transactions of life. But my friend forgets that it is an established fact in the history of this disease, perhaps one of its most striking phenomena, that a man may be mad, may be under the influence of a wild and insane delusion,—one who, all barriers of self-control being broken down, is driven by frenzied impulse into crime, and yet, in carrying out the fell purposes which a diseased mind has suggested, may show all the skill, subtlety, and cunning, which the most intelligent and sane would have exhibited. . . . What then, gentlemen, is the result of these observations? What is the practical conclusion of these investigations of modern science upon the subject of insanity? It is simply this: that a man, though his mind may be sane upon other points, may, by the effect of mental disease, be rendered wholly incompetent to see some one or more of the relations of subsisting things around him in their true light, and though possessed of moral perception and control in general, may become the creature and the victim of some impulse so irresistibly strong as to annihilate all possibility of self dominion or resistance in the particular instance; and this being so, it follows, that if, under such an impulse, a man commits an act which the law denounces and visits with punishment, he cannot be made subject to such punishment, because he is not under the restraint of those motives which could alone create human responsibility. If, then, you shall find in this case that the moral sense was impaired, that this act was the result of a morbid delusion, and necessarily connects itself with that delusion; if I can establish such a case by evidence, so as to bring myself within the interpretation which the highest authorities have said is the true principle of law as they have laid it down for the guidance of courts of law and juries in inquiries of this kind, I shall feel perfectly confident that your verdict must be in favour of the prisoner at the bar.

. . .

. . . Gentlemen, the life of the prisoner is in your hands; it is for you to say whether you will visit one on whom God has been pleased to bring the heaviest of all human calamities—the most painful, the most appalling of all mortal ills—with the consequences of an act which most undoubtedly, but for this calamity, never would have been committed. It is for you to say whether you will consign a fellow being under such circumstances to a painful and ignominious death. May God protect both you and him from the consequences of erring reason and mistaken judgment! In conclusion, let me remind you, that though you do not punish the prisoner for an offence committed at a time when he was unconscious of wrong you have, on the other hand, the power of causing him to be placed in an asylum provided by the mercy of the law, where he will be protected from the consequences of his own delusions, and society will be secured from the danger of his acts. With these observations I trust the case in your hands, with the full conviction that justice will be upheld in the verdict to which you shall come.

[Evidence for the defense.]

. . .

Dr. *E.T. Monro.*—Examined by *Cockburn.*

I have devoted much attention to the subject of insanity, and have an experience of thirty years. I was requested by the friends of the prisoner to visit him in Newgate. I was accompanied by Sir *A. Morrison*, Mr. *M'Clure*, and other professional gentlemen.

You met on that occasion some medical gentlemen, who were deputed on the part of the Crown to visit the prisoner?—I met Dr. *Sutherland*, jun., and Dr. *Bright.*

I believe you all saw the prisoner together?—Yes, we saw and examined the prisoner together.

How was the examination conducted?—We all asked the prisoner questions in turn.

Did you make at the time any note of the examination?—No; but I made some notes afterwards.

When did that examination take place?—On the 18th of February.

What did the prisoner say in answer to the questions put to him?—With the permission of the Court, I will state the substance of what he stated. In reply to the questions put to him, the prisoner said he was persecuted by a system or crew at Glasgow, Edinburgh, Liverpool, London, and Boulogne. That this crew preceded or followed him wherever he went; that he had no peace of mind, and he was sure it would kill him; that it was grinding of the mind. I asked him if he had availed himself of medical advice? He replied, that physicians could be of no service to him, for if he took a ton of drugs it would be of no service to him; that in Glasgow he observed people in the streets pointing at him, and speaking of him. They said that is the man, he is a murderer and the worst of characters. That everything was done to associate his name with the direst of crimes. He was tossed like a cork on the sea, and that wherever he went, in town or country, on sea or shore, he was perpetually watched and followed. At Edinburgh he saw a man on horseback watching him. That another person there nodded to him, and exclaimed, "That's he"; that he had applied to the authorities of Glasgow for protection and relief. His complaints had been sneered and scouted at by Sheriff *Bell*, who had it in his power to put a stop to the persecution if he had liked. If he had had a pistol in his possession, he would have shot Sheriff *Bell* dead as he sat in the court-house; that Mr. *Salmond*, the procurator-fiscal, Mr. Sheriff *Bell*, Sheriff *Alison*, and Sir *R. Peel* might have put a stop to this system of persecution if they would; that on coming out of the court-house he had seen a man frowning at him, with a bundle of straw under his arm; that he knew well enough what was meant; that everything was done by signs; that he was represented to be under a delusion; that the straw denoted that he should lie upon straw in an asylum; that whilst on board the steamboat on his way from Glasgow to Liverpool, he was watched, eyed, and examined closely by persons coming near him; that they had followed him to Boulogne on two occasions; they would never allow him to learn French, and wanted to murder him—he was afraid of going out after dark, for fear of assassination—that individuals were made to appear before him, like those he had seen at Glasgow. He mentioned having applied to Mr. *A. Johnston*, M.P. for Kilmarnock, for protection; Mr. *Johnston* had told him that he (the prisoner) was labouring under a delusion, but that he was sure he was not. That he had seen paragraphs in the *Times* newspaper containing allusions which he was satisfied were directed at him; he had seen articles also in the *Glasgow Herald*, beastly and atrocious, insinuating things untrue and insufferable of him; that on one or two occasions something pernicious had been put into his food; that he had studied anatomy to obtain peace of mind, but he had not found it. That he imagined the person at whom he fired at Charing Cross to be one of the crew—a part of the system that was destroying his health.

When you referred to the person whom he had fired at at Charing Cross, how did you put your question?—I cannot recollect the exact question. I have no doubt I asked him who he thought the person was.

State, Dr. *Monro*, as correctly as you can, what the prisoner said on this point?—He observed that when he saw the person at Charing Cross at whom he fired, every feeling of suffering which he had endured for months and years rose up at once in his mind, and that he conceived that he should obtain peace by killing him.

I believe all the medical men heard the questions put to him and the answers?—Yes. Drs. *Bright* and *Sutherland* were present. I do not know if they saw the prisoner yesterday.

Do you think that your knowledge of insanity enables you to judge between the conduct of a man who feigns a delusion and one who feels it?—I do, certainly.

Do you consider, Dr. *Monro*, that the delusions were real or assumed?—I am quite satisfied that they were real. I have not a shadow of a doubt on the point.

Supposing you had heard nothing of the examination which took place in Newgate, but only the evidence which has been adduced in court for the last two days, would you then say that the prisoner was labouring under a delusion?—Most certainly. The act with which he is charged, coupled with the history of his past life, leaves not the remotest doubt on my mind of the presence of insanity sufficient to deprive the prisoner of all self-control. I consider the act of the prisoner in killing Mr. *Drummond* to have been committed whilst under a delusion; the act itself I look upon as the crowning act of the whole matter—as the climax—as a carrying out of the pre-existing idea which had haunted him for years.

Is it consistent with the pathology of insanity, that a partial delusion may exist, depriving the person of all self-control, whilst the other faculties may be sound?—Certainly; monomania may exist with general sanity. I have frequently known a person insane upon one point exhibit great cleverness upon all others not immediately associated with his delusions. I have seen clever artists, arithmeticians, and architects, whose mind was disordered on one point. An insane person may commit an act similar to the one with which the prisoner is charged, and yet be aware of the consequences of such an act. The evidence which I have heard in Court has not induced me to alter my opinion of the case. Lunatics often manifest a high degree of cleverness and ingenuity, and exhibit occasionally great cunning in escaping from the consequences of such acts. I see a number of such cases every day.

Cross-examined by the Solicitor General.

. . .

I should like you to acquaint the Court with the exact form of the question you put to him which had a reference to his firing the pistol at Mr. *Drummond*, at Charing Cross?—I did not take any notes at the time.

Did you ask him if he knew whom he fired at?—I am not quite certain. I think I asked the prisoner whom he fired at.

Did anyone present ask the prisoner if he knew that it was Sir *Robert Peel* he shot at?—I think he was asked the question more than once. He hesitated and paused, and at length said he was not sure whether it was Sir *Robert Peel* or not. This was asked in my presence.

Please to refer to your notes, and tell me whether he did not say that if he thought it was not Sir *Robert Peel,* he would not have fired at all?—I have no notes to that effect. The notes that I have with me were made at home, and not at the time of the examination.

Did he not say he would not have fired if he had known that it was not Sir *Robert Peel*?—No, I think he did not. On this point he observed that the person at whom he fired gave him as he passed a scowling look. At that moment all the feelings of months and years rushed into his mind, and he thought that he could only obtain peace by shooting him. He stated this in answer to my questions. I avoided all leading questions. There was much repetition in the questions put to him. The gentlemen from Scotland also examined him.

What was the form of the question which related to his firing at Sir *Robert Peel*?—I think the question was, "Did you know whom you were firing at?" In reply he observed, "He was one of the crew that had been following him."

. . .

I wish to know whether your skill would enable you to ascertain the nature of the delusion under which the prisoner was labouring without seeing the depositions taken in his case?—Certainly. I have formed my opinion from an examination of the prisoner personally, in conjunction with the depositions.

Is it not necessary to examine the bodily symptoms in these cases; for instance, the pulse?—Yes, sometimes. I did not feel his pulse, neither did I lay much stress upon the appearance of his eye.

Do you always assume that the party tells you what is passing in his mind?—Not always.

What do you mean by insanity? Do you consider a person labouring under a morbid delusion of unsound mind?—I do.

Do you think insanity may exist without any morbid delusion?—Yes; a person may be imbecile; but there is generally some morbid delusion; there are various shades of insanity. A person may be of unsound mind, and yet be able to manage the usual affairs of life.

May insanity exist with a moral perception of right and wrong?—Yes; it is very common.

A person may have a delusion and know murder to be a crime?—If there existed antecedent symptoms I should consider the murder to be an overt act, the crowning piece of his insanity. But if he had stolen a 10*l.* note it would not have tallied with his delusion.

But suppose he had stolen the note from one of his persecutors?—

(Dr. *Monro's* answer was not heard owing to the laughter which followed the *Solicitor General's* observation.)

A delusion like *M'Naughton's* would carry him quite away. I think a person may be of unsound mind, labour under a morbid delusion, and yet know right from wrong.

Have you heard of what is called moral insanity? Have you read the works of M. *Marc?*—I understand what monomania means. It is attended by an irresistible propensity to thieve or burn, without being the result of particular motives.

Re-examined by *Cockburn.*

You said, Dr. *Monro*, that a person might labour under a particular form of insanity without having his moral perceptions deranged. For illustration—a man may fancy his legs made of glass. There is nothing in that which could affect his moral feelings?—Certainly not.

You have not the slightest doubt that *M'Naughton's* moral perceptions were impaired?—No.

[Additional witnesses testified for the defense to the same effect.]

. . .

Tindal, C.J.: Mr. *Solicitor General*, are you prepared, on the part of the Crown, with any evidence to combat this testimony of the medical witnesses who now have been examined, because we think, if you have not, we must be under the necessity of stopping the case? Is there any medical evidence on the other side?

Solicitor General: No, my Lord.

Tindal, C.J.: We feel the evidence . . . to be very strong, and sufficient to induce my learned brother and myself to stop the case.

Solicitor General: Gentlemen of the jury, after the intimation I have received from the Bench I feel that I should not be properly discharging my duty to the Crown and to the public if I asked you to give your verdict in this case against the prisoner. The Lord Chief Justice has intimated to me the very strong opinion entertained by himself and the other learned judges who have presided here to-day, that the evidence on the part of the defendant, and more particularly the evidence of the medical witnesses, is sufficient to show that this unfortunate man at the time he committed the act was labouring under insanity; and, of course, if he were so, he would be entitled to his acquittal. I was anxious, however, to say, on the part of the Crown, that they have had no object whatever but the attainment of public justice, and I believe I am right in saying that, on the part of the prosecution, every facility has been given to the defence. There is no wish, there can be no wish on the part of the public prosecutor, but that the ends of public justice shall be attained; and, certainly, when in the streets of this metropolis a crime of this sort was committed, it was incumbent on those who have the care of the public peace and safety to have the case properly investigated. The safety of the lives and persons of all of us requires that there should be such an investigation. On the part of the Crown I felt it my duty to lay before you the evidence we possessed of the conduct of this young man. I cannot agree with the observations my learned friend has made on the doctrines and authorities that have been laid down in this case, because I think those doctrines and authorities are correct law; our object being to ascertain whether at the time the prisoner committed the crime he was at that time to be regarded as a responsible agent, or whether all control of himself was taken away? The Lord Chief Justice I understand, means to submit that question to you. I cannot press for a verdict against the prisoner. The learned judge will submit the case to you, and then it will be for you to come to your decision.

TINDAL, C.J.: Gentlemen of the jury, in this important case which has excited very great anxiety during the two preceding days, the point I shall have to submit to you is whether on the whole of the evidence you have heard, you are satisfied that at the time the act was committed, for the commission of which the prisoner now stands charged, he had that competent use of his understanding as that he knew that he was doing, by the very act itself, a wicked and a wrong thing. If he was not sensible at the time he committed that act, that it was a violation of the law of God or of man, undoubtedly he was not responsible for that act, or liable to any punishment whatever flowing from that act. Gentlemen, that is the precise point which I shall feel it my duty to leave to you. I have undoubtedly been very much struck, and so have my learned brethren, by the evidence we have heard during the evening from the medical persons who have been examined as to the state of the mind of the unhappy prisoner, for unhappy I must call him in reference to his state of mind. Now, gentlemen, I can go through the whole of the evidence, and particularly call back your attention to that part of it to which I at first adverted, but I cannot help remarking, in common with my learned brethren, that the whole of the medical evidence is on one side, and that there is no part of it which leaves any doubt on the mind. It seems almost unnecessary that I should go through the evidence. I am, however, in your hands; but if on balancing the evidence in your minds you think the prisoner capable of distinguishing between right and wrong, then he was a responsible agent and liable to all the penalties the law imposes. If not so, and if in your judgment the subject should appear involved in very great difficulty, then you will probably not take upon yourselves to find the prisoner guilty. If that is your opinion then you will acquit the prisoner. If you think you ought to hear the evidence more fully, in that case I will state it to you, and leave the case in your hands. Probably, however, sufficient has now been laid before you, and you will say whether you want any further information.

Foreman of the Jury: We require no more, my Lord.

TINDAL, C.J.: If you find the prisoner not guilty, say on the ground of insanity, in which case proper care will be taken of him.

Foreman: We find the prisoner not guilty, on the ground of insanity.

The clerk of the arraigns, by order of the Court, directed the gaoler to keep the prisoner in safe custody till Her Majesty's pleasure be known.

The prisoner was then removed, and the jury were discharged.

On Wednesday, the 15th of March, the prisoner was removed by Mr. *Cope*, the governor of Newgate, to Bethlem Hospital, St. George's in the Fields, under an order from the Right Hon. Sir *James Graham*, Her Majesty's Secretary of State for the Home Department.

———

329. The Queen was not amused. On March 12, 1843, she wrote to Peel: "The law may be perfect, but how is it that whenever a case for its application arises, it proves to be of no avail. We have seen the trials of Oxford[2] and MacNaghten conducted by the ablest lawyers of the day . . . and *they allow* and *advise* the Jury to pronounce the verdict of *Not Guilty* on account of *Insanity*,—whilst *everybody* is morally *convinced* that both malefactors were perfectly conscious and aware of what they did!" 1 The Letters of Queen Victoria 587 (A. Benson & Esher eds. 1907).

2. In 1840 Edward Oxford was accused of having fired a pistol at the Queen with intent to kill her. At his trial for treason he was found not guilty because he was insane. Regina v. Oxford, 173 Eng. Rep. 941 (Cent. Crim. Ct. 1840).

330. M'Naughten was confined in Bethlem Hospital. An entry for March 21, 1854, in the records of the hospital states: "He is a man of so retiring a disposition and so averse to conversation or notice that it is very difficult even for his Attendant to glean from him any information as to his state of mind or the character of his delusions, but one point has been made out, that he imagines he is the subject of annoyance from some real or fancied beings; but more than this is not known for he studiously avoids entering into the subject with anyone. If a stranger walks through the Gallery he at once hides in the Water Closet or in a Bedroom and at other times he chooses some darkish corner where he reads or knits."

In 1864, Broadmoor Institution for the criminally insane was opened, and M'Naughten was transferred to it on March 26 of that year. A record entry for March 28 states: "A native of Glasgow, an intelligent man, states that he must have done something very bad or they would not have sent him to Bethlem; gives distinctly the Sentence of the Chief Justice 'Acquitted on the ground of Insanity to be confined during "Her Majesty's Pleasure" ' when asked whether he now thinks that he must have been out of his mind, he replies, 'Such was the Verdict, the opinion of the "Jury after hearing the evidence." ' " His health was not good by this time. There is a final entry in his record for May 3, 1865: "Gradually sank and died at 1.10 a.m."

M'Naghten's[3] Case

10 Cl. & F. 200, 8 Eng. Rep. 718 (H.L. 1843)

This verdict [of not guilty, on the ground of insanity], and the question of the nature and extent of the unsoundness of mind which would excuse the commission of a felony of this sort, having been made the subject of debate in the House of Lords, it was determined to take the opinion of the Judges on the law governing such cases. . . .

. . .

Lord Chief Justice *Tindal*:[4]

. . .

[3] This (apparent mis)spelling has become common usage. See United States v. Freeman, 357 F.2d 606, 608 n.2 (2d Cir. 1966). The reports in The (London) Times used the spellings "M'Naughten" and "M'Naughton"; the report of the case in 4 State Trials 847 (n.s. 1892) uses "M'Naughton."

For an exchange between Justice Frankfurter and The Times on the subject—in which the Justice asked "to what extent is a lunatic's spelling even of his own name to be deemed an authority"—see Note, "The Real Mhicneachdain," 74 L. Q. Rev. 321 (1958), which contains a variorum including, as in the title of the note, "the original Gaelic." See also a note of the editors of the Weekly Law Reports, [1957] 1 W.L.R. 122, stating that "M'Naughten" "was and is the correct standard spelling." But see Note, "The Real McNaughton," 74 L. Q. Rev. 1 (1958). Walker uses the common spelling, which, he says, "has the distinction of being the only one that cannot be reconciled with the man's own signature." N. Walker, Crime and Insanity in England 102 n.1 (1968). Extending the suggestion of Justice Frankfurter, I have used "M'Naughten" when referring to the man but have not allowed his possibly lunatic spelling to govern the name of the test, for which I have adopted the now familiar "M'Naghten."

[4] All the judges except Justice Maule, who gave his opinion separately, concurred in the opinion.

The first question proposed by your Lordships is this: "What is the law respecting alleged crimes committed by persons afflicted with insane delusion in respect of one or more particular subjects or persons: as, for instance, where at the time of the commission of the alleged crime the accused knew he was acting contrary to law, but did the act complained of with a view, under the influence of insane delusion, of redressing or revenging some supposed grievance or injury, or of producing some supposed public benefit?"

In answer to which question, assuming that your Lordships' inquiries are confined to those persons who labour under such partial delusions only, and are not in other respects insane, we are of opinion that, notwithstanding the party accused did the act complained of with a view, under the influence of insane delusion, of redressing or revenging some supposed grievance or injury, or of producing some public benefit, he is nevertheless punishable according to the nature of the crime committed, if he knew at the time of committing such crime that he was acting contrary to law; by which expression we understand your Lordships to mean the law of the land.

Your Lordships are pleased to inquire of us, secondly, "What are the proper questions to be submitted to the jury, where a person alleged to be afflicted with insane delusion respecting one or more particular subjects or persons, is charged with the commission of a crime (murder, for example), and insanity is set up as a defence?" And, thirdly, "In what terms ought the question to be left to the jury as to the prisoner's state of mind at the time when the act was committed?" And as these two questions appear to us to be more conveniently answered together, we have to submit our opinion to be, that the jurors ought to be told in all cases that every man is to be presumed to be sane, and to possess a sufficient degree of reason to be responsible for his crimes, until the contrary be proved to their satisfaction; and that to establish a defence on the ground of insanity, it must be clearly proved that, at the time of the committing of the act, the party accused was labouring under such a defect of reason, from disease of the mind, as not to know the nature and quality of the act he was doing; or, if he did know it, that he did not know he was doing what was wrong. The mode of putting the latter part of the question to the jury on these occasions has generally been, whether the accused at the time of doing the act knew the difference between right and wrong: which mode, though rarely, if ever, leading to any mistake with the jury, is not, as we conceive, so accurate when put generally and in the abstract, as when put with reference to the party's knowledge of right and wrong in respect to the very act with which he is charged. If the question were to be put as to the knowledge of the accused solely and exclusively with reference to the law of the land, it might tend to confound the jury, by inducing them to believe that an actual knowledge of the law of the land was essential in order to lead to a conviction; whereas the law is administered upon the principle that every one must be taken conclusively to know it, without proof that he does know it. If the accused was conscious that the act was one which he ought not to do, and if that act was at the same time contrary to the law of the land, he is punishable; and the usual course therefore has been to leave the question to the jury, whether the party accused had a sufficient degree of reason to know that he was doing an act that was wrong: and this course we think is correct, accompanied with such observations and explanations as the circumstances of each particular case may require.

The fourth question which your Lordships have proposed to us is this:—"If a person under an insane delusion as to existing facts, commits an offence in consequence thereof, is he thereby excused?" To which question the answer must of course depend on the nature of the delusion: but, making the same assumption as we did before, namely, that he labours under such partial delusion only, and is not in other respects insane, we think he must be considered in the same situation as to responsibility as if the facts with respect to which the delusion exists were real. For example, if under the influence of his delusion he supposes another man to be in the act of attempting to take away his life, and he kills that man, as he supposes, in self-defence, he would be exempt from punishment. If his delusion was that the deceased had inflicted a serious injury to his character and fortune, and he killed him in revenge for such supposed injury, he would be liable to punishment.

The question lastly proposed by your Lordships is:—"Can a medical man conversant with the disease of insanity, who never saw the prisoner previously to the trial, but who was present during the whole trial and the examination of all the witnesses, be asked his opinion as to the state of the prisoner's mind at the time of the commission of the alleged crime, or his opinion whether the prisoner was conscious at the time of doing the act that he was acting contrary to law, or whether he was labouring under any and what delusion at the time?" In answer thereto, we state to your Lordships, that we think the medical man, under the circumstances supposed, cannot in strictness be asked his opinion in the terms above stated, because each of those questions involves the determination of the truth of the facts deposed to, which it is for the jury to decide, and the questions are not mere questions upon a matter of science, in which case such evidence is admissible. But where the facts are admitted or not disputed, and the question becomes substantially one of science only, it may be convenient to allow the question to be put in that general form, though the same cannot be insisted on as a matter of right.

. . .

———

331. The London Times approved the rules—the M'Naghten rules, as they came to be called—but observed with some justice that it was difficult to reconcile them with "what took place at the late unfortunate trial." "[S]urely it ought to have been left to the jury to determine from the facts of the case whether M'Naughten's delusion, proved by the doctors, was or was not such as to render him incapable of telling right from wrong when he shot Mr. Drummond. . . . The fact of his madness or delusion is one thing, but its effect upon his moral perception is quite another; and the importance of keeping the questions distinct is now clear from the answers of the Judges." The Times (London), June 21, 1843, at 5.

332. Antecedents. The judges' answers to the second and third questions—that the defense of insanity depended on proof that, "at the time of the committing of the act, the party accused was labouring under such a defect of reason, from disease of mind, as not to know the nature and quality of the act he was doing; or, if he did know it, that he did not know he was doing what was wrong"—gave the common law for the first time what could be called an established test of insanity for criminal cases.

That a man might be mad and on that account not criminally responsible was well understood. Probably even before the Norman Conquest a madman who committed a crime was treated leniently, despite the otherwise strict liability imposed by the law. By the thirteenth century, the practice was apparently to have the facts of the case determined by the regular system of prosecution and then to resort to the king's mercy as a basis for the indefinite detention of the mad felon in place of his execution. "This state of affairs represented a compromise between a legal system founded on strict liability and the ecclesiastical insistence on the importance of *mens rea*. On the one hand the harm done must be acknowledged by the legal process; on the other hand the legal process could not be carried to its grim conclusion if the harm was unintentional. So there must be interference with the due process of law by the one person who could properly interfere—the king."[5]

By the sixteenth century, it had become proper to acquit a madman rather than simply to remit the penalty for his crime,[6] but there was not an established test of madness for criminal cases. In 1582 Lambard wrote in his manual for justices of the peace: "If a mad man, or a natural foole, or a Lunatike in the time of his lunacie, or a childe that apparently hath no knowledge of good nor evill, doe kill a man, this is no felonie: for that they cannot be said to have any understanding will . . . ."[7] Hale, whose treatise on the criminal law gives the only extended treatment of the subject of insanity before the nineteenth century, also closely relates the defenses of infancy and insanity.[8] As a test of "ideocy," he says that Fitzherbert's tests for civil matters, that an idiot is one "who knows not to tell 20s. nor knows who is his father or mother, nor knows his own age; but if he knows letters,

---

5. N. Walker, Crime and Insanity in England 24 (1968). See 2 Stephen, History 151.

6. Walker, above, at 25–26.

7. W. Lambard, Eirenarcha 218. In another such manual first published in 1618, Dalton wrote: "[I]f one that is '*Non compos mentis*,' or an Ideot, kill a man, this is no felonie; for they have no knowledge of good and evil, nor can have a felonious intent, nor

a will or mind to do harme." M. Dalton, The Countrey Justice 215 (1618).

8. See 1 M. Hale, History of the Pleas of the Crown 14–37 (1800 ed.). In the thirteenth century, Bracton made the same connection between infancy and insanity. 2 H. Bracton, On the Laws and Customs of England 384 (S. Thorne trans., 1968).

or can read by the instruction of another, than he is no ideot," may provide "evidences yet they are too narrow, and conclude not always; for *ideocy or not* is a question of fact triable by jury, and sometimes by inspection."[9] Of insanity he says that the line between perfect insanity, which exculpates, and partial insanity, which does not, is "very difficult to define . . . [and] must rest upon circumstances duly to be weighed and considered both by the judge and jury"; the "best measure" that he can suggest is that "such a person as labouring under melancholy distempers hath yet ordinarily as great understanding, as ordinarily a child of fourteen years hath, is such a person as may be guilty of treason or felony."[10]

The "use of understanding"[11] was for Hale the touchstone of the defenses he was discussing. "Man is naturally endowed with these two great faculties, understanding and liberty of will, and therefore is a subject properly capable of a law properly so called, and consequently obnoxious to guilt and punishment for the violation of that law, which in respect of these two great faculties he hath a capacity to obey: The consent of the will is that, which renders human actions either commendable or culpable; as where there is no law, there is no transgression, so regularly, where there is no will to commit an offense, there can be no transgression, or just reason to incur the penalty or sanction of that law instituted for the punishment of crimes or offenses. And because the liberty or choice of the will presupposeth an act of the understanding to know the thing or action chosen by the will, it follows that, where there is a total defect of the understanding, there is no free act of the will in the choice of things or actions."[12]

In 1724 Edward Arnold was tried for shooting at and wounding Lord Onslow. A large number of witnesses testified that he was mad. Mr. Justice Tracy charged the jury: "When a man is guilty of a great offence, it must be very plain and clear, before a man is allowed such an exemption [from punishment]; therefore it is not every kind of frantic humour or something unaccountable in a man's actions, that points him out to be such a madman as is to be exempted from punishment: it must be a man that is totally deprived of his understanding and memory, and doth not know what he is doing, no more than an infant, than a brute, or a wild beast . . . ."[13] Thirty-six years after Arnold's trial, Earl Ferrers was tried for murder in the House of Lords. Summing up, the Solicitor General relied heavily on Hale's analysis and told the lords: "If there be a total permanent want of reason, it will acquit the prisoner. If there be a total temporary want of it, when the offence was committed, it will acquit the prisoner: but if there be

---

9. Hale, above, at 29. Fitzherbert's test is in A. Fitzherbert, La Novel Natura Brevium 233B (1537).

10. Hale, n.8 above, at 30. Hale's best was not nearly good enough for Stephen, who observed: "Surely no two states of mind can be more unlike than that of a healthy boy of fourteen, and that of a man 'labouring under melancholy distempers.' The one is healthy immaturity, the other diseased maturity, and between these there is no sort of resemblance." 2 Stephen, History 150–51.

11. Hale, n.8 above, at 34.

12. Id. at 14.

13. Rex v. Arnold (Kingston upon Thames Assizes 1724), 16 State Trials 695, 764–65 (1812).

only a partial degree of insanity, mixed with a partial degree of reason; not a full and complete use of reason, but . . . a competent use of it, sufficient to have restrained those passions, which produced the crime; if there be thought and design; a faculty to distinguish the nature of actions; to discern the difference between moral good and evil; then, upon the fact of the offence proved the judgment of the law must take place."[14]

On May 15, 1800, James Hadfield fired a shot at King George III as the King was entering the royal box of the Theatre Royal in Drury Lane. Hadfield was tried for high treason. He had been a soldier and had suffered head wounds. His counsel, Thomas Erskine, who later became Lord Chancellor, said in his opening statement that he would prove that Hadfield believed he had been commanded by God to sacrifice himself for the salvation of the world and, rather than commit suicide, intended to commit a crime that would secure his execution. On such a theory Hadfield plainly knew what he was doing when he shot at the king and that it was criminal; he counted on being hanged for his act. Erskine argued that the requirement "that to protect a man from *criminal responsibility*, there must be a TOTAL *deprivation of memory and understanding*" could not be taken literally; "if it was meant, that, to protect a man from punishment, he must be in such a state of prostrated intellect, as not to know his name, nor his condition, nor his relation towards others—that if a husband, he should not know he was married; or, if a father, could not remember that he had children; nor know the road to his house, nor his property in it—then no such madness ever existed in the world. It is IDIOCY alone which places a man in this helpless condition . . . ."[15] There were other cases in which a man might not lack all power to reason or understanding of what he did but be in the thrall of an insane delusion; "a delusive image, the inseparable companion of real insanity, is thrust upon the subjugated understanding, incapable of resistance, because unconscious of attack." Delusion, he said, "where there is no frenzy or raving madness, is the true character of insanity." Hadfield would be entitled to an acquittal if the jury were convinced "not only that the unhappy prisoner was a lunatic, within [Erskine's] definition of lunacy, but that the act in question was the IMMEDIATE, UNQUALIFIED OFFSPRING OF THE DISEASE." A person should be acquitted only if his "whole reasoning and corresponding conduct, though governed by the ordinary dictates of reason, proceed upon something which has no foundation or existence."[16]

Before Erskine finished presenting his case, the Attorney General and the court agreed that the trial should be stopped. The jury was invited to, and did, return a verdict that Hadfield was "Not Guilty; he being under the influence of Insanity at the time the act was committed."[17] The court and counsel agreed that Hadfield must be confined, and he was temporarily remanded to Newgate jail, where he had been confined before the trial,

14. Rex v. Ferrers (H.L. 1760), 19 State Trials 886, 947–48 (1813).

15. Rex v. Hadfield (K.B.1800), 27 State Trials 1281, 1312 (1820).

16. Id. at 1314–15.

17. Id. at 1356.

until a more permanent confinement could be arranged. Parliament acted promptly. A month later, it passed an act "for the safe custody of insane persons charged with offenses," which provided that when a person charged with "treason, murder, or felony" was acquitted because he was insane at the time of the commission of the offense, the jury should return a special verdict so declaring, and that the court should then order the person "kept in strict custody . . . until his Majesty's pleasure shall be known; and it shall thereupon be lawful for his Majesty to give such order for the safe custody of such person, during his pleasure, in such place and such manner as to his Majesty shall seem fit." 40 Geo. 3, ch. 94 (1800). Hadfield in mind, a clause was included making the new provisions for custody applicable to persons already acquitted because of insanity and currently detained.

All this "law" on the subject of insanity as a criminal defense was prominent at M'Naughten's trial. The Solicitor General argued that the kind of "morbid delusion" on which Erskine relied to save Hadfield should not save M'Naughten if, despite the delusion, "he had that degree of intellect which enabled him to know and distinguish between right and wrong, if he knew what would be the effects of his crime, and consciously committed it, and if with that consciousness he wilfully committed it," p. 536 above.[18] Cockburn, of course, relied heavily on "that eminent man, Lord *Erskine*,"[19] and quoted extensively from Erskine's argument in behalf of Hadfield.[20]

333. Did the M'Naghten rules satisfactorily integrate the law's uncertain understanding of the defense of insanity generally and the more particular application of the defense urged by Erskine? Was it a sound approach to integration to borrow the notion of being able generally to

---

18. Erskine's success in the trial of Hadfield did not establish the correctness of his argument. See, for example, Lord Mansfield's charge to the jury in the trial of Bellingham in 1812, reported in 1 G. Collinson, The Law Concerning Idiots, Lunatics and Other Persons Non Compotes Mentis 636, 669–74 (1812). (The full charge is printed also in N. Walker, Crime and Insanity in England 270 (1968).) On the other hand, Hadfield was not the first madman who was treated with less severity than the strictly stated tests required. See Walker, at 12, 63–65.

The slowness of the law to establish a test of insanity has been attributed to the lack of cases in which the defense of insanity was presented. A single judge was unlikely to see more than one or two such cases himself; and the number of reported cases remained very small until the nineteenth century. Law which relied on cases for its development was thus unlikely to develop. See Walker, above, at 6–13. Another suggested explanation for the law's slow progress is that except in cases of treason (e.g., *Hadfield*) defendants were not allowed to have counsel to speak for them. "[T]he officers of government have always been at liberty to put their own construction on the law, and urge it on the jury as the only correct one, without fear of being contradicted or gainsaid." I. Ray, Medical Jurisprudence of Insanity 23 n.1 (5th ed. 1871).

19. 4 State Trials (n.s.) at 889.

20. Id. at 879–81, 889.

distinguish right from wrong and apply it, to quite different effect, to an appreciation of the wrongfulness of a particular act?

334.   After the judges announced their answers to the lords, the Lord Chancellor and others expressed "thanks to the Judges, for the attention and learning with which they have answered the questions now put to them."[21] At a meeting of the Association of Medical Officers of Hospitals and Asylums for the Insane on July 14, 1864, however, Dr. Harrington Tuke moved and the assembly adopted a resolution: "That so much of the legal test of the mental condition of an alleged criminal lunatic as renders him a responsible agent, because he knows the difference between right and wrong, is inconsistent with the fact well known to every member of this meeting, that the power of distinguishing between right and wrong exists very frequently among those who are undoubtedly insane, and is often associated with dangerous and uncontrollable delusions."[22] Stephen was the most eminent, and the most persistent, critic of the test. "[If the answers to the questions were meant to be exhaustive] they certainly imply that the effect of insanity (if any) upon the emotions and the will is not to be taken into account in deciding whether an act done by an insane man did or did not amount to an offence, but they do not explicitly assert this, and the proposition that the effect of disease upon the emotions and the will can never under any circumstances affect the criminality of the acts of persons so afflicted is so surprising, and would, if strictly enforced, have such monstrous consequences, that something more than an implied assertion of it seems necessary before it is admitted to be part of the law of England."[23]

335.   Reception in the United States.   The easy reception of the M'Naghten rules into the laws of the states suggests that, as in England, there was no well-developed test of insanity.[24] By 1858, Circuit Justice

21.   8 Eng. Rep. at 724.

22.   Royal Commission on Capital Punishment, Report (Cmd. 8932) 398 (1953).

23.   2 Stephen, History 159. Stephen thought that the judges' answers could be interpreted to make them acceptable. "[E]ven if the answers given by the judges in McNaghten's case are regarded as a binding declaration of the law of England [on which point Stephen had some 'speculative' doubt, see id. at 154], that law, as it stands, is, that a man who by reason of mental disease is prevented from controlling his own conduct is not responsible for what he does. I also think that the existence of any insane delusion, impulse, or other state which is com-

monly produced by madness, is a fact relevant to the question whether or not he can control his conduct, and as such may be proved and ought to be left to the jury." Id. at 167–68.

24.   As in England before 1800, there were probably not enough reported cases to require (or permit) the law to develop. "Criminal trials, in which insanity was pleaded in defense, have been generally so little known beyond the place of their occurrence, that it is difficult to ascertain on what particular principles of the common law the decisions of American courts have been founded, though from all that can be gathered, it appears that their practise, like that of the

Clifford was able to observe: "All of the well-considered cases since 1843, in both countries, are founded upon the doctrine laid down by the fourteen judges, in the opinion delivered in the house of lords at that time." United States v. Holmes, 26 F. Cas. 349, 358 (C.C.D.Me.) (No. 15,382).

336. Irresistible impulse. In a Massachusetts murder case in 1844, Chief Justice Shaw based his instruction to the jury about insanity partly on the M'Naghten rules. He said also: "If then it is proved, to the satisfaction of the jury, that the mind of the accused was in a diseased and unsound state, the question will be, whether the disease existed to so high a degree, that for the time being it overwhelmed the reason, conscience, and judgment, and whether the prisoner, in committing the homicide, acted from an irresistible and uncontrollable impulse: if so, then the act was not the act of a voluntary agent, but the involuntary act of the body, without the concurrence of a mind directing it." Commonwealth v. Rogers, 48 Mass. (7 Met.) 500, 502 (1844). The proposition that a defendant was not criminally responsible if he acted "from an irresistible and uncontrollable impulse" was accepted, though not always unequivocally, by other courts as well.[25] In a leading case, after reviewing a large number of early decisions, the Supreme Court of Alabama asked itself "whether an old rule of legal responsibility shall be adhered to, based on theories of physicians promulgated a hundred years ago, which refuse to recognize any evidence of insanity, except the single test of mental capacity to distinguish right and wrong—or whether the courts will recognize as a possible fact, if capable of proof by clear and satisfactory testimony, the doctrine, now alleged by those of the medical profession who have made insanity a special subject of investigation, that the old test is wrong, and that there is no single test by which the existence of the disease, to that degree which exempts from punishment, can in every case be infallibly detected." Parsons v. State, 2 So. 854, 858 (Ala.1887). The court rejected the M'Naghten test and concluded that the proper test should be:

1. Was the defendant at the time of the commission of the alleged crime, as matter of fact, afflicted with a *disease of the mind*, so as to be either idiotic, or otherwise insane?

2. If such be the case, did he know right from wrong as applied to the particular act in question? If he did not have such knowledge, he is not legally responsible.

3. If he did have such knowledge, he may nevertheless not be legally responsible if the two following conditions concur:

British, has been diverse and fluctuating." I. Ray, Medical Jurisprudence of Insanity 57 (5th ed. 1871).

25. E.g., State v. Johnson, 40 Conn. 136, 139, 142 (1873); Hopps v. People, 31 Ill. 385, 391–92 (1863); Stevens v. State, 31 Ind. 485 (1869); State v. Felter, 25 Iowa 67, 83–84 (1868); Commonwealth v. Mosler, 4 Pa. 264, 266–67 (1846).

(1.) If, by reason of the duress of such mental disease, he had so far lost the *power to choose* between the right and wrong, and to avoid doing the act in question, as that his free agency was at the time destroyed.

(2.) And if, at the same time, the alleged crime was so connected with such mental disease, in the relation of cause and effect, as to have been the product of it *solely*.

Id. at 866–67.

337.   In the years after 1843, American courts employed the M'Naghten test with or without the addition of "irresistible impulse." When the latter phrase is used, it is not always easy to tell whether reference to "irresistible impulse" or a comparable phrase is meant as an addition to or explanation of the M'Naghten test, or is merely insignificant verbiage. Sometimes a court that followed, or at least appeared to have followed, one formulation later decided, or appeared to decide, to follow another. Despite considerable controversy over the two formulations, there were not two distinct, well-defined tests. Rather, there was a collection of more or less closely related phrases, woven into jury instructions and appellate opinions, used in one jurisdiction or another. Even if a court opted firmly to restrict the test of insanity to the M'Naghten test or to supplement that test with the irresistible impulse test, it is not clear that the choice had a significant impact on the outcome of many cases.[26]

338.   Criticism. Criticism of the M'Naghten test has been persistent. Psychiatric fact and theory have given some of the arguments against the test a more solid foundation, but the major objection is the one stated more than a hundred years ago in Dr. Tuke's resolution, p. 554 above.

"In our view the test of criminal responsibility contained in the M'Naughten Rules cannot be defended in the light of modern medical knowledge and modern penal views. It is well established that there are offenders who know what they are doing and know that it is wrong (whether 'wrong' is taken to mean legally or morally wrong), but are nevertheless so gravely affected by mental disease that they ought not to be held responsible for their actions. It would be impossible to apply modern methods of care and treatment in mental hospitals, and at the same time to maintain order and discipline, if the great majority of the patients, even among the grossly insane, did not know what is forbidden by the rules and that, if they break them, they are liable to forfeit some privilege. Examination of a number of individual cases in which a verdict of guilty but insane

---

26. For the rules in the states, before the developments of the 1950s and thereafter, see 2 MPC Commentaries Part I, 165–68 (comment to § 4.01); H. Weihofen, Mental Disorder as a Criminal Defense 129–73 (1954). Before the 1950s about two-thirds of the states followed the M'Naghten test, about one-third the combined test.

was returned, and rightly returned, has convinced us that there are few indeed where the accused can truly be said not to have known that his act was wrong." Royal Commission on Capital Punishment, Report (Cmd. 8932) 103 (1953).

The extensive use of psychiatrists as expert witnesses, a novelty at M'Naughten's trial, is now common, and has produced another ground of criticism:

[P]resent day knowledge of mental life limits the psychiatrist in the following respects:

1. He cannot fit any scientifically validated entity of psychopathology into present legal formulae of insanity. He cannot determine by scientific method the existence of "knowledge" as implied in the legal tests, excepting in cases of disturbed consciousness or profound mental deficit.

2. He cannot testify in any manner in terms of moral judgment. . . .

3. He cannot within the framework of present court requirements determine degrees of legal responsibility calibrated to medical degrees of psychopathology. . . .

Group for the Advancement of Psychiatry, Report No. 26, "Criminal Responsibility and Psychiatric Expert Testimony," 6 (1954).[27]

There was also criticism of another kind: "[T]he mental competency of recidivists should be questioned by realistic means at the earliest possible stage. So long as the courts judge criminal responsibility by the test of knowledge of right and wrong, psychotics who have served prison terms or

---

27. But cf. Guttmacher, "The Psychiatrist as an Expert Witness," 22 U. Chi. L. Rev. 325, 329 (1955): "[M]ost psychiatrists who have had courtroom experience feel that they have been as greatly hampered from giving honest and effective assistance to the court by the methods and rules of legal procedure as they have been by working in the *M'Naghten* strait jacket. Doubtless, the adversary method of trial has proved through the centuries to be an effective way of presenting factual evidence, but it seems to this author a far less satisfactory method for the presentation of opinion testimony. This is particularly true in the field of psychiatry, where one is in large measure dealing with complex concepts and imponderable entities. The same criticism may be made in regard to the insistence on 'yes or no' answers. Psychiatrists share the opposition of most other expert witnesses to the hypothetical question as a means of ascertaining truth. Psychiatrists are in general agreement that the only congenial way in which to appear as an expert witness in a criminal proceeding is as the neutral representative of the court. More than twenty per cent of psychiatrists, and among them are many of the ablest members of the profession, refuse all employment as a partisan witness."

Professor Goldstein also notes "the abrasive effect of the adversary process" in this context. A. Goldstein, The Insanity Defense 58 (1967). He suggests that there is nothing in the nature of the M'Naghten test or generally in its interpretation by the courts that limits the psychiatrist's ability to testify in his own terms or defense counsel's ability to present fully the defendant's mental state. Rather, it is defense counsel's and the psychiatrist's assumptions about the nature of the test that lead them to confine the evidence more narrowly than they would wish. He adds, however, that our preconceptions may be such that the words of the test lend themselves to a restrictive interpretation. Id. at 53–66. He makes a similar analysis of the irresistible impulse test. Id. at 70–75.

are granted probation are released to commit increasingly serious crimes, repeating crime and incarceration and release until murder is committed. Instead of being treated as are ordinary criminals, they should be confined to institutions for the insane at the first offense and not be released until or unless cured." J. Biggs, The Guilty Mind 144–45 (1955).[28]

Disregard of the strict terms of the test in practice in order to overcome its limitations led people to describe it as a "sham" that the law should correct.[29]

The "irresistible impulse" test was also the subject of criticism. Courts expressed doubt whether there was any such thing,[30] or at least whether its existence could be proved.[31] They suggested that to allow the defense might "make an impulse irresistible, which before was not."[32] Those more sympa-

---

28. Judge Biggs expressed this view also in United States v. Currens, 290 F.2d 751, 767 (3d Cir.1961). "To the extent that these individuals ['who can distinguish between good and evil but who cannot control their behavior'] continue to be released from prison because of the narrow scope of *M'Naghten*, that test poses a serious danger to society's welfare." United States v. Freeman, 357 F.2d 606, 618 (2d Cir.1966).

29. Royal Commission on Capital Punishment, Report (Cmd. 8932) 102 (1953) (remarks of Justice Frankfurter); H. Weihofen, The Urge to Punish 53–54 (1956).

30. E.g., Cunningham v. State, 56 Miss. 269, 279 (1879); State v. Maish, 185 P.2d 486, 490–91 (Wash.1947). "[G]iven the premise of an integrated personality, the concept of 'irresistible impulse'—of will totally separated from reason and emotion—is untenable." Hall, "Psychiatry and Criminal Responsibility," 65 Yale L.J. 761, 775 (1956).

31. E.g., State v. Cumberworth, 43 N.E.2d 510, 512–13 (Ohio Ct.App.1942); State v. Bundy, 24 S.C. 439, 445 (1886). "Why has the law refused to accept uncontrollable impulse as an excuse? The reason is an entirely practical one—difficulty of proof. In fact it is impossible at present to distinguish between an uncontrollable impulse and an uncontrolled one." A. Goodhart, Essays in Jurisprudence and the Common Law 47 (1931). "The concept of an irresistible impulse is well-defined only in a central area where certain impulses are irresistible to all people. . . . [W]hen we enter the territory of impulses that are resisted by some and not by others, and we should decide whether an urge that Tom could safely check was unconquerable for Dick, we are on shaky ground. There are no criteria for this decision."

Waelder, "Psychiatry and the Problem of Criminal Responsibility," 101 U. Pa. L. Rev. 378, 383 (1952).

Compare Cressey, "The Differential Association Theory and Compulsive Crimes," 45 J. Crim. L. C. & P. S. 29, 35–36 (1954): "In most cases now labeled 'kleptomania,' 'pyromania,' etc. . . . the actors appear to be motivated in the same way that other criminals are motivated. Consequently they are, in the terminology of the criminal law, 'responsible.' They select secluded places in which to perpetrate their acts, plan their activities in advance, realize that they will be arrested if detected, and do many other things indicative that there is a conscious normative referent in their behavior. . . .

". . . Casual observation indicates, at least, that the application of the 'compulsive crime' label often accompanies the inability of either the subject or the examiner to account for the behavior in question *in terms of motives which are current, popular, and sanctioned in a particular culture or among the members of a particular group within a culture.* For example, one criterion, usually overlooked, for designating behavior 'kleptomania' rather than 'theft' is apparent lack of economic need for the item on the part of the person exhibiting the behavior. . . . [T]he probability that the term 'kleptomania' will be applied to a destitute shoplifter is much lower than the probability that it will be applied to a wealthy person performing the same kind of acts. . . . An interesting but erroneous assumption in such logic is that the behavior of normal persons committing property crimes is explainable in terms of economic need."

32. People v. Hubert, 51 P. 329, 331 (Cal.1897). Compare The King v. Creighton,

thetic to the substance of the test were nevertheless critical of its formulation, which carried "the misleading implication that a crime impulsively committed must have been perpetrated in a sudden and explosive fit. . . . [I]t excludes the far more numerous instances of crimes committed after excessive brooding and melancholy by one who is unable to resist sustained psychic compulsion or to make any real attempt to control his conduct."[33]

339. Defense.

[B]oth its strength and its weakness are derived from its distinctively intellectualist nature: *intellectual* understanding of the nature of one's actions, and *intellectual* grasp of the accepted meaning of right and wrong are the McNaghten criteria of responsibility.

The strength of this intellectualism lies, first and foremost, in the fact that, by virtue of its very narrowness, it provides a safe and commonsensical definition of the *minimum* group about whose inclusion in the category of irresponsibles there can be no dispute. It may be, and indeed it is, much criticised as being unduly *ex*clusive: but no-one could suggest that it *in*cludes any who ought to be counted as sane. So long as any concept of responsibility survives at all, the man who literally does not know what he is doing, or who literally does not know what are the everyday moral judgments of his own community—the man, in fact, who would have committed his crime "with a policeman at his elbow"—such a man must surely have the strongest claim to rank as mad to the point of irresponsibility.

In the second place, the intellectualist quality of the McNaghten formula makes it, at least by comparison with suggested alternatives . . . a model of clarity and precision—in spite of the clouds of legal argument in which its interpretation has from time to time been enveloped. . . .[34]

---

14 Can.Cr.Cas. 349, 350 (Owen Sound Assizes 1908): " 'If you cannot resist an impulse in any other way, we will hang a rope in front of your eyes, and perhaps that will help.' "

33. United States v. Freeman, 357 F.2d 606, 620–21 (2d Cir.1966). See generally Royal Commission on Capital Punishment, Report (Cmd. 8932) 109–10 (1953).

[34] The two main ambiguities are those surrounding the words "know" and "wrong." See Sauer v. United States, 241 F.2d 640, 649 (9th Cir.1957). The former ambiguity, which was at the heart of Stephen's approach to the M'Naghten test, is closely connected with the "irresistible impulse" test; an expansive conception of "knowledge" in this context would deny that there is knowledge where there is not normal emotional appreciation of it.

Compare Hall, "Psychiatry and Criminal Responsibility," 65 Yale L.J. 761, 780–81 (1956). That conduct may be "wrong" morally or legally (or, of course, both) has frequently been pointed out, but the issue has not often troubled the courts. In People v. Schmidt, 110 N.E. 945 (N.Y.1915), the court held that in some circumstances, at least, lack of knowledge that conduct was morally wrong was sufficient for the defense. In England, it was settled in 1952 that "wrong" meant only "contrary to law." Regina v. Windle, [1952] 2 Q.B. 826 (Crim.App.). The scarcity of opinions on either point indicates that neither ambiguity much troubled the courts, which were content, if not indeed anxious, to leave blanks in the test of insanity to be filled by

. . .

Most important of all the merits of the McNaghten formula, however, is the fact that a defence of intellectual insufficiency can be tested by criteria external to the actions which it is invoked to excuse. The proof that a man is deluded or lacks understanding lies, not in the fact that he commits a crime, so much as in his behavior before and afterwards, or even in his capacity to understand things that have nothing to do with his offence. He is deemed to be mad, not because of the crime which he has committed, but because of his inability to appreciate such facts as that he is not the King of Siam and that the trees in his garden are not a horde of parachutists. And, since his insanity is thus inferred from aspects of his behavior other than his actual offence, there is comparatively little risk of becoming entangled in the circular argument that the offender "must have been mad to do such a thing."

B. Wootton, Social Science and Social Pathology 229, 231 (1959).

So long as we have two processes which may be employed to deal custodially with anti-social conduct, one criminal and the other civil, the test for their application must be the existence or non-existence of blameworthiness in a personal sense. . . . Our social order accepts a postulate, held in varying degrees by most citizens and buttressed by religious tenet, that every man is endowed with the capacity to choose a correct course of behavior so long as he is able to detect it. In separating the sick from the bad, we start with the indisputable ability of man to adhere to the right. Upon that assumption, *M'Naghten* is unassailable. . . .

. . . Man may one day obtain a better glimpse of himself, but until a basis for personal blameworthiness can be scientifically demonstrated, I would not tinker with the existing law of criminal accountability.

State v. Lucas, 152 A.2d 50, 75 (N.J.1959) (Weintraub, C.J., concurring).

340. One of the authorities on whom Cockburn relied to establish that M'Naghten was insane was an American, Dr. Isaac Ray, whose

the jury's common sense. See *Sauer*, above, 241 F.2d at 649.

See generally State v. Crenshaw, 659 P.2d 488 (Wash.1983), holding that "wrong" means wrong legally, but allowing a "narrow exception" for someone who "performs a criminal act, knowing it is morally and legally wrong, but believing, because of a mental defect, that the act is ordained by God." The court said that it would be "unrealistic" to hold such a person responsible, since "her free will has been subsumed by her belief in the deific decree." Id. at 494. The exception allowed in *Crenshaw* is applied in State v. Cameron, 674 P.2d 650 (Wash.1983). In People v. Serravo, 823 P.2d 128, 138 (Colo.1992), the court reviewed the issue generally and concluded that a statutory right-wrong test referred to "existing societal standards of morality rather than . . . a defendant's personal and subjective understanding of the legality or illegality of the act in question." The court said also that a defendant laboring under a "deific decree" delusion could be found insane.

Treatise on the Medical Jurisprudence of Insanity was published in 1838 and became one of the standard texts. On his own side of the Atlantic, Ray's work convinced Justice Doe of the Supreme Judicial Court of New Hampshire that there was no single test of insanity, which, like other diseases, "is never established by a single diagnostic symptom, but by the whole body of symptoms, no particular one of which is present in every case."[35] Through Doe's efforts, in 1871 New Hampshire became the first state to reject the M'Naghten test in all its forms. In State v. Jones, 50 N.H. 369, 398 (1871), the court held that a defendant was "not guilty by reason of insanity" if his crime "was the offspring or product of mental disease in the defendant." Such an instruction fully covered "the only general, universal element of law involved in the inquiry"; any further instruction could not be given as a rule of law because "for ought we can know" it might be false in fact. Id.[36]

New Hampshire stood alone for 83 years.

Durham v. United States

341. In 1954, the United States Court of Appeals for the District of Columbia Circuit adopted a test of insanity modeled on the New Hampshire test, in Durham v. United States, 214 F.2d 862 (D.C.Cir.1954). The opinion by Judge Bazelon, which attracted great attention, declared:

> The fundamental objection to the right-wrong test . . . is not that criminal irresponsibility is made to rest upon an inadequate, invalid or indeterminable symptom or manifestation, but that it is made to rest upon *any* particular symptom. In attempting to define insanity in terms of a symptom, the courts have assumed an impossible role, not merely one for which they have no special competence. . . . In this field of law as in others, the fact finder should be free to consider all information advanced by relevant scientific disciplines.
>
> . . .
>
> We find that as an exclusive criterion the right-wrong test is inadequate in that (a) it does not take sufficient account of psychic realities and scientific knowledge, and (b) it is based upon one symptom and so cannot validly be applied in all circumstances. We find that the "irresistible impulse" test is also inadequate in that it gives no recognition to mental illness characterized by brooding and reflection and so relegates acts caused by such illness to the application of the inadequate right-wrong test. We conclude that a broader test should be adopted.

35. I. Ray, Medical Jurisprudence of Insanity 39 (5th ed. 1871). In the trial of M'Naughten, Cockburn, for the defense, relied heavily on Ray's treatise, which he described as "perhaps the most scientific treatise that the age has produced upon the subject of insanity in relation to jurisprudence." The Queen v. M'Naughton, 4 State Trials (N.S.) 847, 878 (1892).

36. This conclusion was foreshadowed by the court's opinion in State v. Pike, 49 N.H. 399, 407–408 (1870).

The rule we now hold must be applied on the retrial of this case and in future cases is not unlike that followed by the New Hampshire court since 1870.[37] It is simply that an accused is not criminally responsible if his unlawful act was the product of mental disease or mental defect.

We use "disease" in the sense of a condition which is considered capable of either improving or deteriorating. We use "defect" in the sense of a condition which is not considered capable of either improving or deteriorating and which may be either congenital, or the result of injury, or the residual effect of a physical or mental disease.

Whenever there is "some evidence" that the accused suffered from a diseased or defective mental condition at the time the unlawful act was committed, the trial court must provide the jury with guides for determining whether the accused can be held criminally responsible. We do not, and indeed could not, formulate an instruction which would be either appropriate or binding in all cases. But under the rule now announced, any instruction should in some way convey to the jury the sense and substance of the following: If you the jury believe beyond a reasonable doubt that the accused was not suffering from a diseased or defective mental condition at the time he committed the criminal act charged, you may find him guilty. If you believe he was suffering from a diseased or defective mental condition when he committed the act, but believe beyond a reasonable doubt that the act was not the product of such mental abnormality, you may find him guilty. Unless you believe beyond a reasonable doubt either that he was not suffering from a diseased or defective mental condition, or that the act was not the product of such abnormality, you must find the accused not guilty by reason of insanity. Thus your task would not be completed upon finding, if you did find, that the accused suffered from a mental disease or defect. He would still be responsible for his unlawful act if there was no causal connection between such mental abnormality and the act. These questions must be determined by you from the facts which you find to be fairly deducible from the testimony and the evidence in this case.

The questions of fact under the test we now lay down are as capable of determination by the jury as, for example, the questions juries must determine upon a claim of total disability under a policy of insurance where the state of medical knowledge concerning the disease involved, and its effects, is obscure or in conflict. In such cases, the jury is not required to depend on arbitrarily selected "symptoms, phases or manifestations"[38] of the disease as criteria for determining the ultimate questions of fact upon which the claim depends. Similarly, upon a claim of criminal irresponsibility, the jury will not be required to rely on such symptoms as criteria for determining the ultimate

---

37. State v. Pike, 1870, 49 N.H. 399.   **38.** State v. Jones, 1871, 50 N.H. 369, 398.

question of fact upon which such claim depends. Testimony as to such "symptoms, phases or manifestations," along with other relevant evidence, will go to the jury upon the ultimate questions of fact which it alone can finally determine. Whatever the state of psychiatry, the psychiatrist will be permitted to carry out his principal court function which, as we noted in Holloway v. U.S., "is to inform the jury of the character of [the accused's] mental disease [or defect]."[39] The jury's range of inquiry will not be limited to, but may include, for example, whether an accused, who suffered from a mental disease or defect did not know the difference between right and wrong, acted under the compulsion of an irresistible impulse, or had "been deprived of or lost the power of his will."[40] . . .

Finally, in leaving the determination of the ultimate question of fact to the jury, we permit it to perform its traditional function which, as we said in Holloway, is to apply "our inherited ideas of moral responsibility to individuals prosecuted for crime."[41] . . . Juries will continue to make moral judgments, still operating under the fundamental precept that "Our collective conscience does not allow punishment where it cannot impose blame."[42] But in making such judgments, they will be guided by wider horizons of knowledge concerning mental life. The question will be simply whether the accused acted because of a mental disorder, and not whether he displayed particular symptoms which medical science has long recognized do not necessarily, or even typically, accompany even the most serious mental disorder.

The legal and moral traditions of the western world require that those who, of their own free will and with evil intent (sometimes called *mens rea*), commit acts which violate the law, shall be criminally responsible for those acts. Our traditions also require that where such acts stem from and are the product of a mental disease or defect as those terms are used herein, moral blame shall not attach, and hence there will not be criminal responsibility. The rule we state in this opinion is designed to meet these requirements.

214 F.2d at 872–76.

342. The "Durham rule," as it quickly came to be called, generated a great deal of heat and, in the end, light. The court of appeals developed the implications of the rule in a series of opinions.

In Carter v. United States, 252 F.2d 608, 616–17 (D.C.Cir.1957), the court said that an act was the "product" of mental disease or defect in the required sense if the facts justified the conclusion that the defendant would not have committed the act but for the disease or defect; it was not

39. 1945, 80 U.S. App. D.C. 3, 5, 148 F.2d 665, 667.

40. State v. White [270 P.2d 727, 730 (N.M.1954)].

41. 80 U.S. App. D.C. at page 5, 148 F.2d at page 667.

42. 80 U.S. App. D.C. at pages 4–5, 148 F.2d at pages 666–667.

necessary that the act be an "immediate issue" of the disease as it had been in Hadfield's case. "To the precise logician deduction of the foregoing inference involves a tacit assumption that if the disease had not existed the person would have been a law-abiding citizen. This latter is not necessarily factually true and can rarely, if ever, be proved, but in the ordinary conduct of these cases we make that tacit assumption. For ordinary purposes we make no mention of this logician's nicety." Id. at 617.

Judge (later Chief Justice) Burger, who was not a member of the panel that decided *Durham*, criticized the new test at length in Blocker v. United States, 288 F.2d 853 (D.C.Cir.1961) (concurring in the result). He noted that the terms "mental disease" and "mental defect" had not been defined and argued that they "mean in any given case whatever the expert witnesses say they mean." Id. at 859. Observing that psychiatrists were not agreed about the meaning of such terms or even about whether there was a definable condition of "mental disease," he argued that "no rule of law can possibly be sound or workable which is dependent upon the terms of another discipline whose members are in profound disagreement about what those terms mean." Id. at 860.

Apart from all other objections the product aspect of Durham is a fallacy in this: assuming arguendo that a criminal act can be the "product" of a "mental disease" that fact should not per se excuse the defendant; it should exculpate only if the condition described as a "mental disease" affected him so substantially that he could not appreciate the nature of the illegal act or could not control his conduct.

. . .

No test for criminal responsibility can be adequate if it does not place squarely before the jury the elements of cognition and capacity to control behavior. It is not enough for judges to say this is the *basis* or the "basic postulate"; it literally must be the "yardstick" the jury is *instructed* to apply. . . .

. . .

The inquiry of the law, whether as to a will, a contract, or a crime should be concerned with and directed to determining whether the act and its consequences were understood and appreciated by the one who performed it and whether it was a manifestation of will or choice. The fact that psychiatrists think of this in terms of behavior controls while lawyers may think of it in terms of will and choice is not particularly important. A jury which hears a psychiatrist testify that an accused suffered from some medically recognized abnormality which destroyed his capacity to control and regulate behavior generally can translate testimony about behavior controls and draw the inference that the accused lacked capacity to exercise his will and make and control a choice between doing or not doing the act charged.

. . .

The proposals we now make would, presumably, satisfy psychiatrists who believe that experts should give medical testimony and jurors apply legal standards to that testimony.

. . . The standards we propose for consideration are not at all intended to reduce the scope of the psychiatrist's contribution but, if anything, to enlarge it as to describing all the dimensions of the defendant's capacity, his competence and ability to control and regulate conduct and behavior.

Id. at 862, 867, 868.[43]

In McDonald v. United States, 312 F.2d 847, 850–51 (D.C.Cir.1962), a *per curiam* opinion for the court sitting en banc gave the Durham rule a new character:

Our eight-year experience under *Durham* suggests a *judicial* definition, however broad and general, of what is included in the terms "disease" and "defect." In *Durham*, rather than define either term, we simply sought to distinguish disease from defect. Our purpose now is to make it very clear that neither the court nor the jury is bound by *ad hoc* definitions or conclusions as to what experts state is a disease or defect. What psychiatrists may consider a "mental disease or defect" for clinical purposes, where their concern is treatment, may or may not be the same as mental disease or defect for the jury's purpose in determining criminal responsibility. Consequently, for that purpose the jury should be told that a mental disease or defect includes any abnormal condition of the mind which substantially affects mental or emotional processes and substantially impairs behavior controls.[44]

We emphasize that, since the question of whether the defendant has a disease or defect is ultimately for the triers of fact, obviously its resolution cannot be controlled by expert opinion. The jury must determine for itself, from all the testimony, lay and expert, whether the nature and degree of the disability are sufficient to establish a mental disease or defect as we have now defined those terms. What we have said, however, should in no way be construed to limit the latitude of expert testimony. . . .

In Washington v. United States, 390 F.2d 444, 446, 452–57 (D.C.Cir. 1967), Judge Bazelon, who wrote the *Durham* opinion, said:

We intended [in *Durham*] to widen the range of expert testimony in order to enable the jury "to consider all information advanced by relevant scientific disciplines" [p. 561 above].

---

43. Judge Burger continued the attack on the *Durham* rule in another noteworthy dissenting opinion in Campbell v. United States, 307 F.2d 597, 603 (D.C.Cir.1962).

44. The court of appeals thus arrived at about the same understanding of the "product" test that the New Hampshire court had: "If the defendant had an insane impulse to kill his wife, which he could not control, then mental disease produced the act. If he could have controlled it, then his will must have assented to the act, and it was not caused by disease, but by the concurrence of his will, and was therefore crime." State v. Jones, 50 N.H. 369, 399 (1871).

This purpose was not fully achieved, largely because many people thought *Durham* was only an attempt to identify a clearly defined category of persons—those classified as mentally ill by the medical profession—and excuse them from criminal responsibility. In fact, the medical profession has no such clearly defined category, and the classifications it has developed for purposes of treatment, commitment, etc., may be inappropriate for assessing responsibility in criminal cases. Since these classifications were familiar, however, many psychiatrists understandably used them in court despite their unsuitability. And some psychiatrists, perhaps unwittingly, permitted their own notions about blame to determine whether the term mental illness should be limited to psychoses, should include serious behavior disorders, or should include virtually all mental abnormalities. To ensure that the views of the experts would not bind the fact-finder, we decided to give mental illness a legal definition independent of its medical meaning. We announced in McDonald v. United States that mental illness "includes any abnormal condition of the mind which substantially affects mental or emotional processes and which substantially impairs behavior control." We recognized that there may be many reasons why a person's ability to control is impaired. His mental or emotional processes may have been adversely affected by his genetic structure, his physical condition, his family, educational or cultural backgrounds. Thus we called upon the jury to "consider testimony concerning the development, adaptation and functioning of these processes and controls."

. . .

. . . We clearly separated the legal and moral question of culpability from the medical-clinical concept of illness. We hoped thereby to separate the roles of the psychiatrist and the jury, with the former stating medical-clinical facts and opinions and the latter making the judgments required by the legal and moral standard. Also, we hoped that the expert's conclusion would not be so heavily weighted in the jury's minds if we made plain that the expert and the jury had different judgments to make.

Even after *McDonald*, though, we allowed the experts to state whether they thought the defendant had a mental disease or defect. We assumed that the expert could separate the medical judgments which he was supposed to make from the legal and moral judgments which he was not supposed to make. It has become abundantly apparent that this theory has not worked out. Too often conclusory labels—both medical and legal—have substituted, albeit unwittingly, for the facts and analysis which underlie them. . . . Also, testimony in terms of "mental disease or defect" seems to leave the psychiatrist too free to testify according to his judgment about the defendant's criminal responsibility.

This kind of testimony does not give the jury a satisfactory basis for determining criminal responsibility. A proper adjudication requires that the jury be fully informed about the defendant's mental and emotional processes and, insofar as it affects these processes, his social situation. Of course, we cannot hope to obtain *all* the relevant information about a defendant. We cannot explore in full the effects of his genetic structure, his family relationships, his upbringing in slum or suburb. But within the limits imposed by the courtroom context and the level of scientific knowledge we should provide the jury with as much of this information as is reasonably available. We are not excused from doing what we can do simply because there are things we cannot do.

With the relevant information about defendant, and guided by the legal principles enunciated by the court, the jury must decide, in effect, whether or not the defendant is blameworthy. Undoubtedly, the decision is often painfully difficult, and perhaps its very difficulty accounts for the readiness with which we have encouraged the expert to decide the question. But our society has chosen not to give this decision to psychiatrists or to any other professional elite but rather to twelve lay representatives of the community. The choice was not made on a naive assumption that all jurors would be fully capable of dealing with these difficult questions or with the underlying information. Nonetheless, this decision, along with many equally difficult ones in other areas, ranging from negligence to antitrust, was given to a jury. As long as this is our system, we should try to make it work.

The trial judge should limit the psychiatrists' use of medical labels—schizophrenia, neurosis, etc. It would be undesirable, as well as difficult, to eliminate completely all medical labels, since they sometimes provide a convenient and meaningful method of communication. But the trial judge should ensure that their meaning is explained to the jury and, as much as possible, that they are explained in a way which relates their meaning to the defendant.

The problem with labels, such as, "product" and "mental disease or defect," is even more difficult. Because these labels are employed in the legal test for responsibility, there is a danger that the psychiatric witness will view them as a legal-moral rather than a medical matter. There are two possible solutions. We could simply prohibit testimony in terms of "product" and "mental disease or defect." Or we could clearly instruct the expert to stick to medical judgments and leave legal-moral judgments to the jury.

A strong minority of this court has consistently advocated that psychiatrists be prohibited from testifying whether the alleged offense was the "product" of mental illness, since this is part of the ultimate issue to be decided by the jury. We now adopt that view. The term "product" has no clinical significance for psychiatrists. Thus there is no justification for permitting psychiatrists to testify on the ultimate issue. Psychiatrists should explain how defendant's disease or defect relates to his alleged offense, that is, how the development, adaptation and functioning of defendant's behavioral processes may have influenced his conduct. But psychiatrists should not speak directly in terms of "product," or even "result" or "cause."

It can be argued that psychiatrists should also be prohibited from testifying whether the defendant suffered from a "mental disease or defect," since this too is part of the ultimate issue. But unlike the term "product," the term "mental disease or defect" may have some clinical significance to the psychiatrist. Moreover, prohibition of testimony about "mental disease or defect" would not be a panacea. Other words and other concepts may similarly be transformed into labels. For example, in *McDonald* we spoke about "abnormal" conditions of the mind, about impairment of mental and emotional processes, and about control mechanisms. . . .

At least for now, rather than prohibit testimony on "mental disease or defect," we shall try to help the psychiatrists understand their role in court, and thus eliminate a fundamental cause of unsatisfactory expert testimony. A copy of the explanatory instruction to psychiatrists which we have set out in the Appendix[45] should accompany all orders requiring mental examinations so that the psychiatrists will be advised of the kind of information they are expected to provide. To ensure that counsel and the jury are also so advised, the trial judge should give the explanatory instruction in open court to the first psychiatric witness immediately after he is qualified as an expert. It need not be repeated to later witnesses. Some of it will be repeated in the court's instruction to the jury at the end of the trial, but we think the jury should hear it in full and *before* the testimony.

343. Not only in its own house did the *Durham* decision provoke comment. The announcement after so long a time of a "new" definition of criminal insanity prompted a flood of literature on the insanity defense and a major judicial reappraisal of the established doctrine. Approval of the abandonment of the M'Naghten test and the effort to develop a better test was usually accompanied, however, by the conclusion that the Durham rule in its original form was unsatisfactory, as the court that originated it found also. In the years after *Durham*, no other federal or state court and only one state legislature (and that only temporarily)[46] adopted the rule. Finally, in 1972, the Court of Appeals for the D.C. Circuit itself abandoned the Durham rule in favor of the Model Penal Code test, below, in United States v. Brawner, 471 F.2d 969 (1972), in which the history of the Durham rule is reviewed.

[45] The instruction explains to psychiatrists their role as expert witnesses and relieves them of some of the burdens of the adversary system, including in particular the need to give "yes or no" answers. 390 F.2d at 457–58. See p. 557 above.

46. Maine, which had adopted the Durham rule in 1963, abandoned it and adopted the test of the Model Penal Code, below, in 1976. Me. Rev. Stat. Ann., tit. 17–A § 58.

The achievement of *Durham* was not that it recalled to mind New Hampshire's old instruction on insanity, but "that it inspired re-examination throughout the country of the responsibility question, and that, together with the subsequent opinions, it furnished an impetus to long-overdue reform of the procedures for dealing with the insanity issue in criminal cases."[47]

MODEL PENAL CODE

Section 4.01. Mental Disease or Defect Excluding Responsibility

(1) A person is not responsible for criminal conduct if at the time of such conduct as a result of mental disease or defect he lacks substantial capacity either to appreciate the criminality [wrongfulness] of his conduct or to conform his conduct to the requirements of law.

(2) As used in this Article, the terms "mental disease or defect" do not include an abnormality manifested only by repeated criminal or otherwise anti-social conduct.

Comment
(2 MPC Commentaries Part I, 164–75)

1. *General.* No problem in the drafting of a penal code presents greater intrinsic difficulty than that of determining when individuals whose conduct would otherwise be criminal ought to be exculpated on the ground that they were suffering from mental disease or defect when they acted as they did. The problem is the drawing of a line between the use of public agencies and force (1) to condemn the offender by conviction, with resulting sanctions in which the ingredient of reprobation is present no matter how constructive one may seek to make the sentence and the process of correction, and (2) modes of disposition in which the condemnatory element is absent, even though restraint may be involved. When the sentence may be capital there is, of course, a starker contrast between the punitive reaction and a reaction of the second kind. Stating the matter differently, the problem is to etch a decent working line between the areas assigned to the authorities responsible for public health and those responsible for the correction of offenders. It is important to maintain this separation, not least in order to control the stigma involved in a hospital commitment.

When the Institute approved this section of the Code, the appropriateness of some defense based on irresponsibility caused by mental disease or defect was not doubted. It seemed clear that the culpability requirements, formulated with reference to competent individuals, call for adaptation with reference to the disordered or defective psyche. In our legal system, as

---

47. Krash, "The Durham Rule and Judicial Administration of the Insanity Defense in the District of Columbia," 70 Yale L.J. 905, 952 (1961).

in others, this adaptation is achieved by an independent criterion of criminal responsibility as affected by mental disease or defect. Attention was focused on the most desirable formulation of that criterion. Since the adoption of the Code, the movement to "abolish the insanity defense" has gained some momentum. That challenge to the Code formulation is considered later in this Comment.

2. *Prior Law.* When work upon the Model Penal Code began, the "insanity defense" in a substantial majority of American jurisdictions was based on adherence to the M'Naghten rule. . . .

As far as its principle extends, the M'Naghten rule is right. Those who are irresponsible under the test are plainly beyond the reach of the restraining influence of the law, and their condemnation would be both futile and unjust. A deranged person who believes he is squeezing lemons when he chokes his wife, or who kills in supposed self-defense on the basis of a delusion that another is attempting to kill him, is plainly beyond the deterrent influence of the law; he needs restraint but condemnation is meaningless and ineffective. Moreover, the category defined by the rule is so extreme that to the ordinary person the exculpation of those it encompasses bespeaks no weakness in the law. He does not identify such persons with himself; they are a world apart.

The question remains, however, whether the M'Naghten rule goes far enough to draw a fair and workable distinction. In two respects, this question must be answered in the negative. The M'Naghten test addresses itself to the actor's "knowledge," which can naturally be understood as referring to a simple awareness by the actor of his wrongdoing such as would be manifested by a verbal acknowledgment on his part of the forbidden nature of his conduct. One shortcoming of this criterion is that it authorizes a finding of responsibility in a case in which the actor is not seriously deluded concerning his conduct or its consequences, but in which the actor's appreciation of the wrongfulness of his conduct is a largely detached or abstract awareness that does not penetrate to the affective level. Insofar as a formulation centering on "knowledge" does not readily lend itself to application to emotional abnormalities, the M'Naghten test appears less than optimal as a standard of responsibility in cases involving affective disorder.

A second and more pervasive difficulty with the M'Naghten standard appears in cases in which the defendant's disorder prevents his awareness of the wrongfulness of his conduct from restraining his action. Stated otherwise, these are cases in which mental disease or defect destroys or overrides the defendant's power of self-control. Stephen and others have attempted to bring such cases within the scope of the standard by urging that the knowledge test requires also a capacity on the part of the defendant to function in the light of his knowledge. This conception has been rejected by some courts, though it has also been common to allow psychiatrists to testify in broad terms about a defendant's mental condition and to leave to the jury the decision how to interpret the word "know." However, even when the import of the M'Naghten standard is left open in practice, the very language of the test discourages juries from paying attention to noncognitive impairments and leads psychiatrists to believe that much that they consider relevant to a defendant's responsibility or lack of it is considered irrelevant by the law.

Responding to the M'Naghten formulation's inadequacy in connection with claims that emphasize a defendant's volitional incapacity rather than his inability to understand, a minority of jurisdictions at the time of work on the Model Code had explicitly supplemented the M'Naghten rule by what was commonly called the "irresistible impulse" test. Notwithstanding the general use of this nomenclature in referring to this supplementary standard, the "irresistible impulse" wording was only one of various formulations, and other formulations spoke more broadly of the defendant's self-control or capacity for choice. Furthermore, despite the over-tones of the term "impulse," there was generally no explicit requirement of sudden, spontaneous action as distinguished from insane propulsions that are accompanied by brooding or reflection.

3. *Model Code Formulation.* The Model Code formulation is based on the view that a sense of understanding broader than mere cognition, and a reference to volitional incapacity should be achieved directly in the formulation of the defense, rather than left to mitigation in the application of M'Naghten. The resulting standard relieves the defendant of responsibility under two circumstances: (1) when, as a result of mental disease or defect, the defendant lacked substantial capacity to appreciate the criminality [wrongfulness] of his conduct; (2) when, as a result of mental disease or defect, the defendant lacked substantial capacity to conform his conduct to the requirements of law.

The use of "appreciate" rather than "know" conveys a broader sense of understanding than simple cognition. The proposal as originally approved in 1955 was cast in terms of a person's lack of capacity to appreciate the "criminality" of his conduct, but the Institute accepted "wrongfulness" as an appropriate substitute for "criminality" in the Proposed Final Draft. Appreciating "wrongfulness" may be taken to mean appreciating that the community regards the behavior as wrongful.[48] Given the seriousness of most crimes for which the defense of insanity is interposed, a defendant who appreciates society's moral disapproval of his conduct will almost always assume that the conduct is criminal, and vice versa. The difference in wording is likely to matter significantly only in two situations.

First, where the wrongfulness standard is taken to refer to the actor's own moral perception, then differing results are conceivable under the two

48. In State v. Wilson, 700 A.2d 633 (Conn.1997), the defendant killed someone whom he delusionally believed was destroying his life. Construing a statute that used the Model Penal Code test with the word "wrongfulness," the court said that "a defendant may establish that he lacked substantial capacity to appreciate the 'wrongfulness' of his conduct if he can prove that, at the time, as a result of mental disease or defect, he substantially misperceived reality and harbored a delusional belief that society, under the circumstances as the defendant honestly but mistakenly understood them, would not have morally condemned his actions." Id. at 740.

formulations in a case in which the defendant thinks that an act he knows to be legally prohibited is commanded by God or otherwise morally justified. However, even in such a case, a defendant in a jurisdiction having the criminality formulation could probably argue that his capacity to appreciate the criminality of his conduct was insubstantial or that he lacked substantial capacity to conform his conduct to legal requirements.

The second conceivable situation is where the actor possesses a sense of right and wrong with respect to his actions, but, as a result of mental defect, is incapable of grasping the concepts of governmental prohibition and officially imposed sanctions which are implicit in the notion of criminality. However, in such a case as well, a defendant in a jurisdiction with the wrongfulness formulation might argue that, for purposes of determining criminal responsibility, his capacity for appreciating the wrongfulness of his conduct was insubstantial, or that, in light of his inability to understand what the law is, he was incapable of conforming his conduct to its requirements. Hence, notwithstanding the theoretical distinction between the two formulations, it is doubtful whether the actual result in many cases would turn on which is used.

The part of the Model Code test relating to volition is cast in terms of capacity to conform one's conduct to the requirements of the law. Application of the principle calls for a distinction, inevitable for a standard addressed to impairment of volition, between incapacity and mere indisposition. In drawing this distinction, the Model Code formulation effects a substantial improvement over pre-existing standards.

In contrast to the M'Naghten and "irresistible impulse" criteria, the Model Code formulation reflects the judgment that no test is workable that calls for complete impairment of ability to know or to control. The extremity of these conceptions had posed the largest difficulty for the administration of the old standards. Disorientation, psychiatrists indicated, might be extreme and still might not be total; what clinical experience revealed was closer to a graded scale with marks along the way. Hence, an examiner confronting a person who had performed a seemingly purposive act might helpfully address himself to the extent of awareness, understanding and control. If, on the other hand, he had to speak to utter incapacity vel non under the M'Naghten test, his relevant testimony would be narrowly limited to the question of whether the defendant suffered from delusional psychosis, where the act would not be criminal if the facts were as the defendant deludedly supposed them to be. A test requiring an utter incapacity for self-control imposes a comparably unrealistic restriction on the scope of the relevant inquiry. To meet these difficulties, it was thought that the criterion should ask if the defendant, as a result of mental disease or defect, was deprived of "substantial capacity" to appreciate the criminality (or wrongfulness) of his conduct or to conform his conduct to the requirements of law, meaning by "substantial" a capacity of some appreciable magnitude when measured by the standard of humanity in general, as opposed to the reduction of capacity to the vagrant and trivial dimensions characteristic of the most severe afflictions of the mind.

The adoption of the standard of substantial capacity may well be the Code's most significant alteration of the prevailing tests. It was recognized, of course, that "substantial" is an open-ended concept, but its quantitative connotation was believed to be sufficiently precise for purposes of practical administration. The law is full of instances in which courts and juries are explicitly authorized to confront an issue of degree. Such an approach was deemed to be no less essential and appropriate in dealing with this issue than in dealing with the questions of recklessness and negligence.

The Model Code rejected the formulation which was warmly supported by psychiatrists at the time and had been adopted by the Court of Appeals for the District of Columbia in Durham v. United States, 214 F.2d 862 (D.C.Cir.1954). Under the Durham rule (since repudiated in the District of Columbia and repealed in Maine, where it had been enacted) "an accused is not criminally responsible if his unlawful conduct was the product of mental disease or defect." The difficulty with this formulation inheres in the ambiguity of "product." One possibility would be to understand "product" as meaning that the crime would not have been committed but for the presence of the mental disease or defect. But this interpretation is too broad—in many such instances, the defendant clearly should be held responsible. Discounting the but-for construction, the only remaining possibility is to interpret the standard in terms of the type of factors referred to in the Model Code formulation—the defendant's crime is a "product" of mental illness in the sense that as a result of mental illness he lacks the capacity for understanding or control in relation to the offense. Even on this reading, however, an ambiguity remains, for the standard might be understood as calling for complete incapacity in these areas, or only substantial incapacity. Whichever of these causal concepts is intended by the word "product," the formulation ought to set it forth. The alternative is to allow the applicable standard to be determined on a case by case basis according to the fortuities of interpretation by the jury.

The Model Code also rejected the proposal of the majority of the Royal Commission on Capital Punishment, namely, "to leave the jury to determine whether at the time of the act the accused was suffering from disease of the mind (or mental deficiency) to such a degree that he ought not to be held responsible."[49] The Commission's standard appropriately recognizes gradations of degree in mental diseases or defects but fails to focus the attention of the trier of fact on the specific manifestations and effects of mental disease or defect that are relevant to the justice of conviction and punishment.

4. *Repeated Criminal Behavior Not by Itself a Mental Disease or Defect.* The Model Code does not attempt to define "mental disease or defect"; but Subsection (2) of 4.01 does include a cautionary limitation, namely, that the terms, as used in Article 4, "do not include abnormality manifested only by repeated criminal or otherwise antisocial conduct."

49. Royal Comm'n on Capital Punishment 1949–1953, Report, Cmd. No. 8932, para. 333, at 116 (1953).

Some critics have regarded this as a presumptuous legal intervention in the realm of psychiatric theory but there are conceptions of psychopathy and sociopathy as forms of mental illness that were thought to warrant caution of this kind. Subsection (2) addresses itself to an issue of legal policy that cannot sensibly be resolved as a question of fact or medical terminology. Apart from this qualification, the Code pursues the only course that was deemed feasible. It treats the question of disease as one of fact, to be determined by the court or jury on the evidence presented in the cases that arise. As medical understanding may develop in such areas, for example, as brain chemistry, it can thus have its proper impact on the application of the law.

---

344. In the years after its promulgation in 1962, the Model Penal Code's formulation of the insanity defense was widely approved. By 1972, it had been adopted by all but one of the United States Courts of Appeals.[50] The District of Columbia Circuit replaced the Durham test, as modified, see pp. 563–68 above, with the Model Penal Code, in United States v. Brawner, 471 F.2d 969 (D.C.Cir.1972) (cases in other circuits cited). A large number of states also adopted the Code test, by statute or by judicial decision. See 1 MPC Commentaries Part I, 175–76. Among the jurisdictions that followed the Code, the most common variation is substitution of the word "wrongfulness" for "criminality" (an alternative contained in the Code). See id. at 178–79. The proviso in subsection (2) of the Code test has generally been accepted. A few states (and two federal courts of appeals) rejected it. Id. at 177. See People v. Fields, 673 P.2d 680, 705–708 (Cal.1983) (proviso accepted); United States v. Smith, 404 F.2d 720, 727 n.8 (6th Cir.1968) (proviso rejected); Wade v. United States, 426 F.2d 64, 73 (9th Cir.1970) (same).

345. The Code test has been criticized as merely a "refurbishing" of the M'Naghten and irresistible impulse tests, which rests "on the same outdated psychological assumption that 'mind' is divisible into neatly separate functions, each operating independently of the other; that a person may have will power without understanding, or understanding without will power." H. Weihofen, The Urge to Punish 99–100 (1956).[51]

50. The exception was the First Circuit, which indicated that in an appropriate case, it too was likely to adopt the Code test. Amador Beltran v. United States, 302 F.2d 48 (1st Cir.1962).

51. Weihofen notes that the psychiatrists on the advisory committee for the Code preferred the "product" test and concludes that the Code test failed to "bridge the gap that now exists between legal and psychiatric thinking." Id. at 100. Compare the observations of Wertham, himself a psychiatrist, who criticizes the psychiatric authorities on whom Judge Bazelon relied in Durham and states that only if psychiatrists overcome their "psychoauthoritarianism will psychiatry find its proper place in the courtroom and play, as it should, a strong but subordinate role."

Does the substance of the Code test differ very much from the M'Naghten and irresistible impulse tests? If not, is it nevertheless an improvement over them?

346. What is the significance of the requirement that the defendant's incapacity be the "result of mental disease or defect"? There is a comparable requirement in the M'Naghten test. Would omission of the phrase substantially increase the number of persons who would be able to assert the insanity defense successfully? If not, would it be just as well to omit the phrase? If so, what is the explanation for limiting the group by the phrase?[52]

347. Before the end of the 1970s, when the Model Penal Code test had achieved its maximum impact, some states had expressly rejected it in favor of the M'Naghten test. E.g., State v. Smith, 574 P.2d 548 (Kan.1977). For a summary of the law in the states as of that time, see 1 MPC Commentaries Part I, 175–80; *Smith*, 574 P.2d at 550–52; State v. Johnson, 399 A.2d 469 (R.I.1979).

In the 1980s there was a noticeable shift away from the Model Penal Code and back to *M'Naghten*. California, which had adopted the Code test in 1978, People v. Drew, 583 P.2d 1318, restored the M'Naghten test by a voter initiative measure in 1982. Cal. Penal Code § 25(b). See People v. Skinner, 704 P.2d 752 (Cal.1985). In 1984, Congress enacted legislation restoring the M'Naghten test in the federal courts and giving it somewhat stricter form, as follows: "It is an affirmative defense to a prosecution under any Federal statute that, at the time of the commission of the acts constituting the offense, the defendant, as a result of a severe mental

---

"Psychoauthoritarianism and the Law," 22 U. Chi. L. Rev. 336, 338 (1955).

52. See generally Salzman v. United States, 405 F.2d 358, 364 (D.C.Cir.1968) (Wright, J., concurring) (alcoholism).

How should the criminal law dispose of a person who commits a clearly antisocial act, homicide perhaps, in a state of (some degree of) unconsciousness? See, e.g., People v. Wu, 286 Cal.Rptr. 868 (Ct.App.1991) (fugue state of unconsciousness); People v. Freeman, 142 P.2d 435 (Cal.Dist.Ct.App.1943) (epileptic unconsciousness); People v. Grant, 360 N.E.2d 809 (Ill.Ct.App.1977), rev'd, 377 N.E.2d 4 (Ill. 1978) (psychomotor epilepsy); Fain v. Commonwealth, 78 Ky. 183 (1879) (somnambulism); Bratty v. Attorney General, [1961] 3 W.L.R. 965 (N. Ire.) (automatism). Should cases of this kind be treated as cases of

insanity? Why (not)? See State v. Caddell, 215 S.E.2d 348, 363 (N.C.1975): "[U]nconsciousness, or automatism, is a complete defense to a criminal charge, separate and apart from the defense of insanity; . . . it is an affirmative defense; and . . . the burden rests upon the defendant to establish this defense, unless it arises out of the State's own evidence, to the satisfaction of the jury." Accord Polston v. State, 685 P.2d 1 (Wyo. 1984). The Model Penal Code § 2.01(1) provides that a person is not guilty of an offense "unless his liability is based on conduct which includes a voluntary act or the omission to perform an act of which he is physically capable." Suppose a person whose conduct is excused on the basis of § 2.01(1) commits a second "clearly antisocial act" while unconscious.

disease or defect, was unable to appreciate the nature and quality or the wrongfulness of his acts. Mental disease or defect does not otherwise constitute a defense." 18 U.S.C. § 20(a). (The statute also provides that the defendant has the burden of proving the defense of insanity "by clear and convincing evidence." § 20(b). See p. 582 note 353 below.)

Also in 1984, the American Bar Association endorsed a similar insanity test, which likewise eliminates the volitional aspect of the Model Penal Code test. ABA Standards for Criminal Justice 7–6.1. Emphasizing the conclusion that the volitional element of the insanity defense is largely responsible for mistakes, the ABA standards provide that in jurisdictions that have an exclusively cognitive test, like its own, the prosecution should have the burden of disproving insanity beyond a reasonable doubt; but that in jurisdictions retaining the Model Penal Code test, the defendant should have the burden of proving insanity by a preponderance of the evidence. Standard 7–6.9. See also United States v. Lyons, 731 F.2d 243 (5th Cir.1984), in which the court concluded that it had been mistaken to adopt the Model Penal Code test in 1969. For a sharp response to that conclusion, see the dissenting opinion of Judge Rubin, 739 F.2d at 994.

348. There is evidently a strong reaction against too easy availability of the insanity defense, which many persons thought was the result of changes in the law prompted by the *Durham* decision and the Model Penal Code. In that connection, reconsider the defense of the M'Naghten test, p. 559 note 339 above. Consider also Stone's comment, p. 610 note 372 below.

349. Partly in response to persistent calls for "abolition" of the insanity defense, some states have enacted legislation providing for a special verdict of "guilty but mentally ill" in addition to the insanity defense. See, e.g., Taylor v. State, 440 N.E.2d 1109 (Ind.1982); People v. Ramsey, 375 N.W.2d 297 (Mich.1985), upholding such statutes. Idaho, Kansas, Montana, and Utah have abolished the traditional insanity defense altogether. In all those states, evidence, including evidence of insanity, may be introduced insofar as it has a bearing on a state of mind that is an element of the offense charged. The Utah statute, for example, provides: "It is a defense to a prosecution under any statute or ordinance that the defendant, as a result of mental illness, lacked the mental state required as an element of the offence charged. Mental illness is not otherwise a defense." Utah Code Ann. § 76–2–305(1). In Finger v. State, 27 P.3d 66 (Nev.2001), the court struck down similar legislation, which, it said, was a denial of due process because it denied the defendant an opportunity to prove that he was unaware of the wrongfulness of his conduct, historically an element of most crimes.

MODEL PENAL CODE
COMMENT TO § 4.01

(2 MPC Commentaries Part I, 181–86)

[Another portion of the comment to § 4.01, explaining and defending the Code's provision appears at p. 569 above.]

Were the insanity defense eliminated, a person suffering from a mental disease would be excused if, and only if, he lacked the state of mind required as an element of the offense charged. Under the Model Code, evidence of mental illness, like any other evidence, may negate the existence of the mental element required for commission of the offense. One who appropriates another's property believing it to be his own is not a thief, whether the erroneous belief involves a simple error (two umbrellas look alike) or is a symptom of delusional psychosis. Abolition proposals would excuse the actor in this situation, but they would not excuse an actor who met the basic culpability requirements. Thus, the defendant in the famous *M'Naghten* case, who was apparently a paranoid schizophrenic and who killed the private secretary to the Prime Minister (meaning to kill the Prime Minister) because he believed he was being persecuted, would be held liable for murder because he plainly did intend to kill, whether or not he was able to understand the wrongfulness of his conduct.

A variety of reasons for abolition have been advanced from quite different ideological perspectives. Though it oversimplifies matters somewhat, it clarifies understanding to distinguish two basic positions in favor of abolition. The first position is perhaps epitomized by President Nixon's support of abolition, which he said was "the most significant feature" of the codification of general defenses in the Administration's proposed criminal code and was designed to curb "unconscionable abuse" of the insanity defense which had taken place under prior standards.[53] This position does not challenge the traditional assumption that an important function of the system of criminal justice is to label serious wrongdoers as blameworthy; it asserts that the insanity defense is a device by which too many wrongdoers are escaping punishment. Although fear of rising crime rates and unfocused distaste for "permissiveness" toward criminals may assure this position some popular backing, it has little empirical support. The insanity defense is in fact infrequently invoked and then only for very serious crimes. When it has been invoked, jurors have not shown themselves ready to accept attenuated claims. Those who do successfully claim the defense are often committed for long periods of time. Unfounded fears of "abuse" are hardly a sufficient reason for abolishing a defense that has properly come to be viewed as fundamental.

The other attack on the insanity defense is more complex and it goes to the roots of the criminal law. It shares with the first position a skepticism

53. State of the Union Message on Law Enforcement and Drug Abuse Prevention, in Pub. Papers 192, 195 (March 14, 1973).

that distinctions can sensibly be made between those who are responsible and those who are not. Critics taking this view cite the rarity of the employment of the defense as evidence that most mentally ill defendants are being convicted despite the availability of the defense. They doubt that the stigma of those convicted and subsequently treated as mentally disturbed is any worse than the stigma of those who commit criminal acts and are committed to high security institutions for the mentally ill without undergoing trial or after being acquitted on grounds of insanity. They argue that there is little basis for withholding condemnation of those whose mental illness causes them to act criminally when those whose deprived economic and social background causes them to act criminally are condemned. They regard the adversarial debate over the responsibility of particular defendants as wasteful, confusing for the jury, and possibly harmful for those defendants who are mentally disturbed. They think psychiatric diagnosis should be employed primarily after conviction to determine what sort of correctional treatment is appropriate instead of prior to conviction to determine criminal responsibility. Ideally, in the view of some of these critics, criminal convictions generally should not be regarded as stigmatizing, but as determinants of dangerousness to which the community must respond.

When properly understood, this attack is a challenge to the basic notion that a criminal conviction properly reflects moral condemnation by the community of the act performed. Yet those who advance the attack do not provide persuasive reasons for believing it would benefit society if the association between moral wrongdoing and criminal conviction were dissipated. Nor do they give reasons for supposing that the association will be dissipated in the near future. Yet they propose labeling as criminal many persons whom society at large would clearly not regard as morally blameworthy and whose mental condition might be fully exposed at a trial in which psychiatric evidence was introduced to establish the absence of the required state of mind for the most serious offenses.

The inappropriateness of this approach is most obvious if one considers crimes for which negligence suffices for culpability, a problem characteristically ignored by those who propose abolition. Since negligence is determined by largely objective criteria, a highly deranged person could be guilty of negligent homicide in the absence of an insanity defense. Suppose a psychotic kills in the deluded belief that he is imminently threatened and must act in self-defense. In many jurisdictions an unreasonable belief in justification supports no exculpation at all and under the Model Code it consistently supports exculpation only for crimes with a higher level of culpability than negligence. A similar problem can arise, so long as the mentally ill person perceives a risk of harm, when recklessness is deemed to be sufficient culpability for an offense, since the justifiability of risk creation is determined generally by objective standards.

Abolition of a special defense for mental irresponsibility would also make guilty of the most serious crimes all those who acted purposefully but did not appreciate that their acts were wrong or who had gravely impaired volitional capacities. The critics are right that decisions about responsibility are often extraordinarily difficult, but they are wrong to reject the attempt to make a distinction that human experience teaches us is basic, and they are wrong to accept the consequence that those who are clearly not responsible should be categorized in the same way as those who clearly are. Yet this is precisely the effect that abolition of a separate insanity defense would have, if abolition did not indirectly affect definitions of "act" and culpability.

It seems likely that judges and juries faced with the prospect of convicting obviously irresponsible actors would take refuge in requiring that actions or omissions be "voluntary" in more than the minimal sense demanded by the Model Code and in requiring that purpose and knowledge reflect deeper understanding than the definitions in the Code's culpability section prescribe. The battle over responsibility would then be fought not over a relatively straightforward formulation of mental incapacity, but over uncertain and confusing definitions of act and purposiveness that would inevitably be rendered less clear even for ordinary cases. If the intent of abolition were largely frustrated in this way, the effects might be less ominous but the price in confusion would be great. If the intent of abolition were carried out to the letter, the premise that only responsible actors should be convicted of crime would be sacrificed. Whether or not elimination of the insanity defense is unconstitutional, as the state courts considering the question have held,[54] rejection of the premise that only those who are responsible should be treated as criminal would constitute abandonment of a deservedly fundamental value in the system of criminal justice and would represent a seriously retrogressive step in the development of the criminal law.

———

350.

Today the great weight of legal authority clearly supports the view that evidence of mere narcotics addiction, standing alone and without other physiological or psychological involvement, raises no issue of such a mental defect or disease as can serve as a basis for the insanity defense. . . .

There are a number of reasons why. In the first place, there is an element of reasoned choice when an addict knowingly acquires and uses drugs; he could instead have participated in an addiction treatment program. . . . A person is not to be excused for offending "simply because he wanted to very, very badly." *Bailey* [v. United States], 386 F.2d [1 (5th Cir.1967)] at 4. Second, since the defense of insanity is "essentially an acknowledgement on the part of society that because of mental disease or defect certain classes of wrongdoers are

54. Cases cited for the proposition that abolition of the insanity defense is unconstitutional are State v. Lange, 123 So. 639 (La. 1929); Sinclair v. State, 132 So. 581 (Miss. 1931); State v. Strasburg, 110 P. 1020 (Wash. 1910). See p. 576 note 349 above.

not properly the subjects of criminal punishment," [United States v.] *Freeman*, 357 F.2d [606 (2d Cir.1966)] at 625, it seems anomalous to immunize narcotics addicts from other criminal sanctions when Congress had decreed severe penalties for mere possession and sale of narcotics. In addition, Congress has dealt with the problem of responsibility of narcotics addicts for their crimes by providing for civil commitment and treatment of addicts in lieu of prosecution or sentencing. . . .

Finally, what definition of "mental disease or defect" is to be employed by courts enforcing the criminal law is, in the final analysis, a question of legal, moral and policy—not of medical—judgment. Among the most basic purposes of the criminal law is that of preventing a person from injuring others or, perhaps to a lesser degree, himself. This purpose and others appropriate to law enforcement are not necessarily served by an uncritical application of definitions developed with medical considerations of diagnosis and treatment foremost in mind. . . . Indeed, it would be coincidental indeed should concepts deriving from such disparate sources correspond closely, one to the other. Thus it is, for example, that the law has not greatly concerned itself with medical opinion about such mental states as accompany the commission of crimes of passion or of those done while voluntarily intoxicated; whatever that opinion may be, policy considerations have been thought to forbid its cutting much of a figure in court.

. . .

Although mere narcotics addiction is not itself to be acknowledged as a mental disease or defect, evidence of narcotics addiction has been received by some courts as evidence of such an underlying condition. Green v. United States, 383 F.2d 199, 201 (D.C.Cir.1967). . . . In addition, if addiction has caused actual physical damage to the structures of a defendant's body, evidence of that addiction has been admitted to show any mental defect resulting from that damage. . . .

We view the reasoning of such rulings as *Green* with profound misgivings. To us it seems to rest on the proposition that, assuming drug addiction itself is neither a mental disease nor a defect, yet the two are often to be found in association, so that an addicted person is more likely to suffer from some mental disorder than is one who is not addicted. By a parity of reasoning, since combat veterans as a group are self-evidently more likely to have suffered the loss of a physical member than is the populace at large, evidence of whether a party is a combat veteran should be received on the issue whether he has lost a leg. Or, to take a less extreme example, since because of light skin pigmentation persons of Scandinavian ancestry are more subject to skin cancer than are others, the family tree of a suitor should be received in evidence when his skin cancer is at legal issue. The flaw in both illustrations seems evident: where evidence bearing directly on a legal question is available, that involving tangential matters, even though perhaps logically relevant in theory, is of small practical value.

Our review of numerous records over the course of years has revealed no dearth of experts ready and willing to testify squarely on the issue of insanity in criminal trials: direct evidence on the issue seems all but too readily available. Since this is so, receiving evidence of drug addiction in addition seems to us an exercise seldom likely to prove more probative than prejudicial in practice. . . .

Nor do we see how matters are clarified by reference to the condition of addiction as one involving "psychological damage" to the addict, e.g., Brinkley v. United States, [498 F.2d 505 (8th Cir.1974)]. As nearly as we can determine, the psychological condition so described is simply one of drug addiction to one degree or another, a condition that we have already declined to view as a mental disease or defect for legal purposes. An actual drug-induced or drug-aggravated psychosis, or physical damage to the brain or nervous system would, however, be another matter.

We do not doubt that actual physical damage to the brain itself falls within the ambit of "mental disease or defect." To refuse to recognize that a congenital microcephalic, or one who has suffered, say, extensive brain damage from a gunshot wound or other physical trauma, may be thereby rendered unable to appreciate the character of his conduct as wrongful would be presumptuous. Here, within the limits of appropriate legal and policy considerations, the medical model must have its day. The same is true of the question whether such organic brain pathology or psychosis can be caused by drugs.

United States v. Lyons, 731 F.2d 243, 245–47 (5th Cir.1984). See Robinson v. California, 370 U.S. 660 (1962), p. 742 below; Powell v. Texas, 392 U.S. 514 (1968), p. 744 below.

See United States v. Moore, 486 F.2d 1139 (D.C.Cir.1973) (narcotics addiction not a defense to prosecution for possession of heroin); cf. United States v. Davis, 772 F.2d 1339 (7th Cir.1985) (prosecution for theft offense; evidence of compulsive gambling to establish (MPC) insanity defense properly excluded); United States v. Gould, 741 F.2d 45 (4th Cir.1984) (same); United States v. Torniero, 735 F.2d 725 (2d Cir.1984) (same); United States v. Lewellyn, 723 F.2d 615 (8th Cir.1983) (same). In *Davis*, the court said: "[I]t does not seem to us enough to show that gambling is compulsive (the result of an irresistible impulse), money is necessary for gambling and therefore the stealing of money is equally 'compulsive.' The stealing may follow as a matter of logic or means-end reasoning but this in itself should not necessarily result in a psychiatric characterization of the act of stealing as 'compulsive.'" 772 F.2d at 1347.

351. Diminished responsibility. Reconsider pp. 124–35 above. After considering the nature of the insanity defense, do you find more or less reason to allow evidence of a person's mental condition to have a bearing on the question whether he had the mental state required for a particular crime? See generally State v. Humanik, 489 A.2d 691 (N.J.Super. Ct.App.Div.1985) comparing the defense of diminished responsibility and the defense of insanity. In State v. Wood, 686 P.2d 128 (Kan.1984), the court rejected the defense of diminished capacity as inconsistent with the defense of insanity as formulated in the M'Naghten test.

352. It is commonly provided that a defendant who intends to rely on the insanity defense shall give notice before trial, see, e.g., Fed. R. Crim. P. 12.2, and that upon such notice the court may order that the defendant be given a psychiatric examination and committed for a limited period for that purpose. E.g., 18 U.S.C. §§ 4242, 4247 (commitment for not more than 45 days, with extension of 30 days for good cause). Questions have arisen concerning the admissibility of psychiatric testimony based on the court-ordered examination. In general, it has been held that if the defendant asserts the insanity defense at trial, neither the Fifth Amendment privilege against compelled self-incrimination nor any other constitutional provision inhibits the admission of such testimony on the issue of insanity. The testimony is generally not admissible on any other issue, such as whether the defendant committed the act charged, by statute or rule, see Fed. R. Crim. P. 12.2(c), or on constitutional grounds, e.g., Gibson v. Zahradnick, 581 F.2d 75, 78 (4th Cir.1978). See generally United States v. Byers, 740 F.2d 1104 (D.C.Cir.1984).[55]

353. Burden of proof. In the absence of evidence to the contrary a defendant is presumed to be sane, and the prosecution need not offer proof on that issue. "It is an essential element of any crime that at the time of the commission of the crime, the defendant be sane. . . . Although that be an essential element, it is not put in issue in the vast majority of criminal cases. . . . Thus . . . in order to present a complete case, the government need not introduce evidence showing the sanity of a defendant until and unless the defendant shall have made an issue of that subject." United States v. Manetta, 551 F.2d 1352, 1357 (5th Cir.1977). If sufficient evidence of insanity is presented to raise the issue, about half the states require the prosecution to prove beyond a reasonable doubt that the defendant is not insane; the remainder place on the defendant the burden of proving insanity by a preponderance of the evidence.

In the wake of the *Hinckley* verdict, see p. 610 note 372 below, the trend of the law after 1982 has been toward shifting the burden of proof to make it more difficult for the defendant to be acquitted. In the federal

55. If a defendant does not claim that he is not competent to stand trial or assert the defense of insanity and introduces no psychiatric testimony on the issue of sanity at trial, testimony based on a court-ordered psychiatric examination is not admissible at trial over his objection. It is admissible only at a hearing to determine competence to stand trial. Estelle v. Smith, 451 U.S. 454 (1981).

courts, for example, the prosecution had been required to prove beyond a reasonable doubt that the defendant was sane at the time of the crime. In 1984, Congress enacted legislation requiring the defendant to prove his insanity "by clear and convincing evidence." 18 U.S.C. § 17(b).

Those jurisdictions which take the view that the prosecution has the burden of proving the sanity of the accused assert that the fundamental rule of law requiring the State to prove the guilt of a defendant beyond a reasonable doubt should logically extend to the issue of criminal responsibility. The reasoning is that since the basic elements of a criminal offense (except those which are *malum prohibitum*) are the act itself and the *mens rea* or intent to commit it, it is necessary, in order to prove the intent, to show that the perpetrator was capable of forming the requisite intent. In other words, it must be shown that the perpetrator was sane or else he could not have had the intent to commit the offense charged. These jurisdictions hold that proving the sanity of the defendant, once it has been brought into issue, is an essential element of the offense; and that since the State has the burden of proving all the elements thereof, it must necessarily have the burden of producing evidence and the burden of persuasion on the issue of insanity, despite the fact that, at the outset, the presumption of sanity places the initial burden of producing evidence on the defendant. But once the presumption has been rebutted it disappears as a rule of law and has no probative value as evidence. . . . When this takes place, the burden of producing evidence as well as persuading the trier of facts falls upon the State and it must then prove sanity beyond a reasonable doubt as it must do in proving all other elements of the crime.

The opposing view, which places the burden of proof on the defendant, treats the issue of criminal responsibility as an affirmative defense to be established by the defendant, rather than as an element of the criminal offense to be proved as a part of the State's case. The courts adhering to this view assert that although *mens rea* cannot exist without sanity, it is a preexisting fact inferable from general experience that the vast majority of men are rational beings; that, accordingly, the presumption of sanity is an inference of fact from which the trier of facts can draw conclusions of fact, rather than a legal presumption, and operates to place the entire burden of proof (i.e., the burden of producing evidence and the burden of persuasion) on the defendant; and that the burden prevails until the defendant has shown the trier of facts by a preponderance of all the evidence, taking into account the presumption of sanity, that the defendant is insane.

Bradford v. State, 200 A.2d 150, 154 (Md.1964). See generally People v. Duckett, 209 Cal.Rptr. 96 (Ct.App.1984) (jury's conclusion that defendant was legally sane not supported by evidence; defendant had burden of proving insanity).

The Supreme Court in 1952 upheld a state statute requiring a defendant to establish the defense of insanity beyond a reasonable doubt. Leland

v. Oregon, 343 U.S. 790.[56] The ruling in *Leland* was not affected by the holding in Mullaney v. Wilbur, 421 U.S. 684 (1975), p. 99 above. See Rivera v. Delaware, 429 U.S. 877 (1976), dismissing for want of a substantial federal question a challenge to a state statute requiring the defendant to prove the defense of insanity by a preponderance of the evidence; Patterson v. New York, 432 U.S. 197, 204–205 (1977). In Jones v. United States, 463 U.S. 354, 368 n.17 (1983), the Court, citing *Leland*, said: "A defendant could be required to prove his insanity by a higher standard than a preponderance of the evidence."

354.   "However much you charge a jury as to the M'Naghten Rules or any other test, the question they would put to themselves when they retire is—'Is this man mad or is he not?' " Royal Commission on Capital Punishment, Report (Cmd. 8932) 113 (1953) (testimony of Lord Cooper).[57]

355.   Many cases in which the defendant is charged with a serious crime and his sanity is in question do not reach the jury at all. It is the law everywhere that an accused may not be brought to trial if he lacks "the capacity to make a rational defense. . . . He should be capable of understanding the nature and object of the proceedings against him, his own condition in reference to such proceedings, and have sufficient mind to

56.   Oregon subsequently provided by statute that the defendant need establish his insanity by a preponderance of the evidence only. Or. Rev. Stat. §§ 161.305, 161.055(2).

57.   The number of acquittals by reason of insanity in the United States District Court for the District of Columbia increased markedly after announcement of the *Durham* decision. In fiscal 1954 three defendants were so acquitted. In fiscal 1961 and 1962 there were 66 such acquittals. After the *McDonald* decision (see p. 565 above) in 1962 the number fell again, to a low of 23 in fiscal 1964 and 26 in fiscal 1966. (The ratio of acquittals to trials changed correspondingly.) President's Commission on Crime in the District of Columbia, Report 535 (1966). While the changes in the test of insanity may have had something to do with the changes in the number of acquittals, a more likely explanation for the temporary increase, at least, is the heightened awareness of the insanity defense engendered by *Durham* and succeeding cases. A change in the test of insanity may, of course, have an impact in ways other than the number of acquittals, such as its effect on determinations of competency to stand trial,

see note 355, or more generally, on "tactical" decisions of the prosecutor and defense counsel before or during trial. One study of the impact of the changes in the definition of the insanity defense in the District of Columbia concluded that although the form and manner of disposition of cases was affected, the actual results for the defendants changed little. The author concludes: "Absent changes in the criminal system reaching far beyond the test for criminal responsibility the insanity defense cannot be tightened more than the participants (prosecutors, defendants, and possibly psychiatrists) are willing to see done. In the other direction what appears on its face to be a broadening of the defense beyond the limits found tolerable by prosecutors is unlikely to be successful (absent other, heroic measures)." Becker, "Durham Revisited," 3 Psychiatric Annals 12, 53 (Sept. 1973). In United States v. Brawner, 471 F.2d 969, 989 (D.C.Cir.1972), see p. 568 note 343 above, the court observed that its abandonment of the Durham rule was not intended to modify the number and percentage of insanity acquittals, nor did it believe that such a change could be forecast.

conduct his defense in a rational and reasonable manner, although upon other subjects his mind may be unsound or deranged." People v. Burson, 143 N.E.2d 239, 244 (Ill.1957). See Drope v. Missouri, 420 U.S. 162 (1975); Dusky v. United States, 362 U.S. 402 (1960). The federal provision is 18 U.S.C. § 4241. In Cooper v. Oklahoma, 517 U.S. 348 (1996), the Court reviewed the issue of competence to stand trial and held that, although a defendant may be required to prove by a preponderance of the evidence that he is not competent to stand trial, Medina v. California, 505 U.S. 437 (1992) (7–2), it is a violation of due process to impose a higher burden of proof ("clear and convincing evidence") that would permit a defendant to be tried "even though it is more likely than not that he is incompetent." 517 U.S. at 350. Wallace v. Kemp, 757 F.2d 1102 (11th Cir.1985) (evidence insufficient to sustain finding that defendant was competent to stand trial).

Despite the difference between insanity at the time an offense was committed and incompetence to stand trial, prosecutors and defense counsel alike have often been willing to avoid trial altogether rather than undergo the costs of a trial and risk an unfavorable verdict.

> [T]he defense of insanity can be raised only very late in the time sequence of the criminal process, that is, at the time of trial. Relatively few defendants (5%–15%) even reach the trial stage. Most cases are finished at the pre-trial stages, when the charges are dismissed or, more frequently, when the defendant pleads guilty. Furthermore, the defense of insanity requires expert psychiatric testimony, an expensive commodity; hence the defense is out of reach for indigent defendants, who make up the bulk of persons charged with crime. Another decisive factor is the inflexible "either-or" characteristic of the defense that limits the discretion of the lawyers by taking the disposition of the case, for all practical purposes, out of their hands. The most important reason [why use of the insanity defense has not increased with our increasing awareness of mental illness], however, is that officials discovered an alternative by which they could usually accomplish the same objectives as they could by a defense of insanity.

> Finding the defense of insanity impracticable, time-consuming, expensive, and largely irrelevant to the concerns of appropriate disposition, officials turned to the ancient procedures for determining the defendant's competence to stand trial: a requirement that the accused understand the charges against him and be able, with the help of counsel, to make his defense. The competency machinery was available in every conceivable type of case; it was relatively easy to invoke, providing expert yet inexpensive psychiatric evaluation; it was procedurally ambiguous enough to embrace conflicting and competing motivations and, most important, flexible enough to permit a rich exercise of discretion. This complicated yet flexible machinery has now become the dominant force in the actual processing of persons perceived as mentally disabled by officials administering the criminal law. The result, in brief, is that most mentally disabled persons (as well as most persons not mentally disabled) find their case is determined at the pre-

trial stage rather than at the trial stage when the defense of insanity can be raised.

> [M]ost cases are processed by administrative machinery invoked when the issue of competency to stand trial is raised rather than by the trial machinery when the defense of insanity is raised.

Matthews, "Mental Illness and the Criminal Law: Is Community Mental Health an Answer?" (Research Contribution of the American Bar Foundation No. 2), 2–3 (1967).

356. Should the standard of competence to plead guilty be different from the standard of competence to stand trial? Resolving a conflict among the courts of appeals, some of which had held that the standard of competence to plead guilty should be higher, the Supreme Court held that the standard of competence to plead guilty as well as competence to waive the right to counsel is the same as the standard of competence to stand trial. Godinez v. Moran, 509 U.S. 389 (1993). In that case, the defendant had been charged with three counts of capital murder, in the course of which he had also tried to commit suicide. He pleaded not guilty. Following a psychiatric examination, he was found competent to stand trial. Three months later, he told the court that he wanted to waive his right to counsel and to plead guilty, in order to avoid presentation of any evidence in mitigation of the sentence. After questioning the defendant, the court accepted his waiver of counsel and the guilty plea. Thereafter, he was sentenced to death. The sentence was later changed to life imprisonment without possibility of parole.

In 2002, the Supreme Court granted a writ of certiorari to consider whether the administration of anti-psychotic medication against a person's will, to render him competent to stand trial for nonviolent offenses, violated his rights under the First, Fifth, and Sixth Amendments. Sell v. United States, ___ U.S. ___, 123 S.Ct. 512 (2002).

357. The administrative procedures described above for commitment of persons not competent to stand trial continue to be used frequently as a substitute for trial of the issue of insanity. The utility of such procedures as effectively a final disposition of the criminal proceedings has been limited by the holding in Jackson v. Indiana, immediately below, and similar cases, at least where there is someone or some agency to ensure that a person who has been committed is not forgotten and abandoned.[58]

---

58. A brief commitment for a determination of competency may function in cases of relatively less serious crimes as an alternative to prosecution and punishment; following the determination that the defendant is competent to stand trial, the prosecution may be dropped. See, e.g., Geller & Lister, "The Process of Criminal Commitment for Pretrial Psychiatric Examination: An Evaluation," 135 Am. J. Psychiatry (No. 1) 53 (1978).

Jackson v. Indiana

406 U.S. 715, 92 S.Ct. 1845, 32 L.Ed.2d 435 (1972)

■ MR. JUSTICE BLACKMUN delivered the opinion of the Court.

We are here concerned with the constitutionality of certain aspects of Indiana's system for pretrial commitment of one accused of crime.

Petitioner, Theon Jackson, is a mentally defective deaf mute with a mental level of a pre-school child. He cannot read, write, or otherwise communicate except through limited sign language. In May 1968, at age 27, he was charged in the Criminal Court of Marion County, Indiana, with separate robberies of two women. The offenses were alleged to have occurred the preceding July. The first involved property (a purse and its contents) of the value of four dollars. The second concerned five dollars in money. The record sheds no light on these charges since, upon receipt of not-guilty pleas from Jackson, the trial court set in motion the Indiana procedures for determining his competency to stand trial. . . .

As the statute requires, the court appointed two psychiatrists to examine Jackson. A competency hearing was subsequently held at which petitioner was represented by counsel. The court received the examining doctors' joint written report and oral testimony from them and from a deaf-school interpreter through whom they had attempted to communicate with petitioner. The report concluded that Jackson's almost nonexistent communication skill, together with his lack of hearing and his mental deficiency, left him unable to understand the nature of the charges against him or to participate in his defense. One doctor testified that it was extremely unlikely that petitioner could ever learn to read or write and questioned whether petitioner even had the ability to develop any proficiency in sign language. He believed that the interpreter had not been able to communicate with petitioner to any great extent and testified that petitioner's "prognosis appears rather dim." The other doctor testified that even if Jackson were not a deaf mute, he would be incompetent to stand trial, and doubted whether petitioner had sufficient intelligence ever to develop the necessary communication skills. The interpreter testified that Indiana had no facilities that could help someone as badly off as Jackson to learn minimal communication skills.

On this evidence, the trial court found that Jackson "lack[ed] comprehension sufficient to make his defense," § 9–1706a, and ordered him committed to the Indiana Department of Mental Health until such time as that Department should certify to the court that "the defendant is sane."

Petitioner's counsel then filed a motion for a new trial, contending that there was no evidence that Jackson was "insane," or that he would ever attain a status which the court might regard as "sane" in the sense of competency to stand trial. Counsel argued that Jackson's commitment under these circumstances amounted to a "life sentence" without his ever having been convicted of a crime, and that the commitment therefore deprived Jackson of his Fourteenth Amendment rights to due process and equal protection, and constituted cruel and unusual punishment under the Eighth Amendment made applicable to the States through the Fourteenth. The trial court denied the motion. On appeal the Supreme Court of Indiana affirmed, with one judge dissenting. . . . Rehearing was denied, with two judges dissenting. We granted certiorari. . . .

For the reasons set forth below, we conclude that, on the record before us, Indiana cannot constitutionally commit the petitioner for an indefinite period simply on account of his incompetency to stand trial on the charges filed against him. Accordingly, we reverse.

I

INDIANA COMMITMENT PROCEDURES

Section 9–1706a contains both the procedural and substantive requirements for pretrial commitment of incompetent criminal defendants in Indiana. If at any time before submission of the case to the court or jury the trial judge has "reasonable ground" to believe the defendant "to be insane," he must appoint two examining physicians and schedule a competency hearing. The hearing is to the court alone, without a jury. The examining physicians' testimony and "other evidence" may be adduced on the issue of incompetency. If the court finds the defendant "has not comprehension sufficient to understand the proceedings and make his defense," trial is delayed or continued and the defendant is remanded to the state department of mental health to be confined in an "appropriate psychiatric institution." The section further provides that "[w]henever the defendant shall become sane" the superintendent of the institution shall certify that fact to the court, and the court shall order him brought on to trial. The court may also make such an order *sua sponte*. There is no statutory provision for periodic review of the defendant's condition by either the court or mental health authorities. Section 9–1706a by its terms does not accord the defendant any right to counsel at the competency hearing or otherwise describe the nature of the hearing; but Jackson was represented by counsel who cross-examined the testifying doctors carefully and called witnesses on behalf of the petitioner-defendant.

Petitioner's central contention is that the State, in seeking in effect to commit him to a mental institution indefinitely, should have been required to invoke the standards and procedures of Ind. Ann. Stat. § 22–1907, now Ind. Code 16–15–1–3 (1971), governing commitment of "feeble-minded" persons. . . .

. . .

II

EQUAL PROTECTION

Because the evidence established little likelihood of improvement in petitioner's condition, he argues that commitment under § 9–1706a in his case amounted to a commitment for life. This deprived him of equal protection, he contends, because, absent the criminal charges pending against him, the State would have had to proceed under other statutes generally applicable to all other citizens: either the commitment procedures for feeble-minded persons, or those for mentally ill persons. He argues that under these other statutes (1) the decision whether to commit would have been made according to a different standard, (2) if commitment were warranted, applicable standards for release would have been more lenient, (3) if committed under § 22–1907, he could have been assigned to a special institution affording appropriate care, and (4) he would then have been entitled to certain privileges not now available to him.

In Baxstrom v. Herold, 383 U.S. 107 (1966), the Court held that a state prisoner civilly committed at the end of his prison sentence on the finding of a surrogate was denied equal protection when he was deprived of a jury trial that the State made generally available to all other persons civilly committed. Rejecting the State's argument that Baxstrom's conviction and sentence constituted adequate justification for the difference in procedures, the Court said that "there is no conceivable basis for distinguishing the commitment of a person who is nearing the end of a penal term from all other civil commitments." 383 U.S., at 111–112. . . . The Court also held that Baxstrom was denied equal protection by commitment to an institution maintained by the state corrections department for "dangerously mentally ill" persons, without a judicial determination of his "dangerous propensities" afforded all others so committed.

If criminal conviction and imposition of sentence are insufficient to justify less procedural and substantive protection against indefinite commitment than that generally available to all others, the mere filing of criminal charges surely cannot suffice. . . .

Respondent argues, however, that because the record fails to establish affirmatively that Jackson will never improve, his commitment "until sane" is not really an indeterminate one. It is only temporary, pending possible change in his condition. Thus, presumably, it cannot be judged against commitments under other state statutes that are truly indeterminate. The State relies on the lack of "exactitude" with which psychiatry can predict the future course of mental illness. . . .

Were the State's factual premise that Jackson's commitment is only temporary a valid one, this might well be a different case. But the record does not support that premise. . . . There is nothing in the record that even points to any possibility that Jackson's present condition can be remedied at any future time.

. . .

We note also that neither the Indiana statute nor state practice makes the likelihood of the defendant's improvement a relevant factor. The State did not seek to make any such showing, and the record clearly establishes that the chances of Jackson's ever meeting the competency standards of § 9–1706a are at best minimal, if not nonexistent. The record also rebuts any contention that the commitment could contribute to Jackson's improvement. Jackson's § 9–1706a commitment is permanent in practical effect.

We therefore must turn to the question whether, because of the pendency of the criminal charges that triggered the State's invocation of § 9–1706a, Jackson was deprived of substantial rights to which he would have been entitled under either of the other two state commitment statutes. *Baxstrom* held that the State cannot withhold from a few the procedural protections or the substantive requirements for commitment that are available to all others. In this case commitment procedures under all three statutes appear substantially similar: notice, examination by two doctors, and a full judicial hearing at which the individual is represented by counsel and can cross-examine witnesses and introduce evidence. Under each of the three statutes, the commitment determination is made by the court alone, and appellate review is available.

In contrast, however, what the State must show to commit a defendant under § 9–1706a, and the circumstances under which an individual so committed may be released, are substantially different from the standards under the other two statutes.

Under § 9–1706a, the State needed to show only Jackson's inability to stand trial. We are unable to say that, on the record before us, Indiana could have civilly committed him as mentally ill under § 22–1209 or committed him as feeble-minded under § 22–1907. The former requires at least (1) a showing of mental illness and (2) a showing that the individual is in need of "care, treatment, training or detention." § 22–1201(1). Whether Jackson's mental deficiency would meet the first test is unclear; neither examining physician addressed himself to this. Furthermore, it is problematical whether commitment for "treatment" or "training" would be appropriate since the record establishes that none is available for Jackson's condition at any state institution. The record also fails to establish that Jackson is in need of custodial care or "detention." He has been employed at times, and there is no evidence that the care he long received at home has become inadequate. The statute appears to require an independent showing of dangerousness ("requires . . . detention in the interest of the welfare of such person or . . . others . . ."). Insofar as it may require such a showing, the pending criminal charges are insufficient to establish it, and no other supporting evidence was introduced. For the same reasons, we cannot say that this record would support a feeble-mindedness commitment under § 22–1907 on the ground that Jackson is "unable properly to care for [himself]." § 22–1801.

More important, an individual committed as feeble-minded is eligible for release when his condition "justifies it," § 22–1814, and an individual civilly committed as mentally ill when the "superintendent or administrator shall discharge such person, *or* [when] cured of such illness." § 22–1223 (emphasis supplied). Thus, in either case release is appropriate when the individual no longer requires the custodial care or treatment or detention that occasioned the commitment, or when the department of mental health believes release would be in his best interests. The evidence available concerning Jackson's past employment and home care strongly suggests that under these standards he might be eligible for release at almost any time, even if he did not improve. On the other hand, by the terms of his present § 9–1706a commitment, he will not be entitled to release at all, absent an unlikely substantial change for the better in his condition.

Baxstrom did not deal with the standard for release, but its rationale is applicable here. The harm to the individual is just as great if the State, without reasonable justification, can apply standards making his commitment a permanent one when standards generally applicable to all others afford him a substantial opportunity for early release.

As we noted above, we cannot conclude that pending criminal charges provide a greater justification for different treatment than conviction and sentence. Consequently, we hold that by subjecting Jackson to a more lenient commitment standard and to a more stringent standard of release than those generally applicable to all others not charged with offenses, and by thus condemning him in effect to permanent institutionalization without the showing required for commitment or the opportunity for release afforded by § 22–1209 or § 22–1907, Indiana deprived petitioner of equal protection of the laws under the Fourteenth Amendment.

III

DUE PROCESS

For reasons closely related to those discussed in Part II above, we also hold that Indiana's indefinite commitment of a criminal defendant solely on account of his incompetency to stand trial does not square with the Fourteenth Amendment's guarantee of due process.

. . .

The States have traditionally exercised broad power to commit persons found to be mentally ill. The substantive limitations on the exercise of this power and the procedures for invoking it vary drastically among the States. The particular fashion in which the power is exercised—for instance, through various forms of civil commitment, defective delinquency laws, sexual psychopath laws, commitment of persons acquitted by reason of insanity—reflects different combinations of distinct bases for commitment sought to be vindicated. The bases that have been articulated include dangerousness to self, dangerousness to others, and the need for care or treatment or training. Considering the number of persons affected, it is perhaps remarkable that the substantive constitutional limitations on this power have not been more frequently litigated.

We need not address these broad questions here. It is clear that Jackson's commitment rests on proceedings that did not purport to bring into play, indeed did not even consider relevant, *any* of the articulated bases for exercise of Indiana's power of indefinite commitment. The state statutes contain at least two alternative methods for invoking this power. But Jackson was not afforded any "formal commitment proceedings addressed to [his] ability to function in society,"[59] or to society's interest in his restraint, or to the State's ability to aid him in attaining competency through custodial care or compulsory treatment, the ostensible purpose of the commitment. At the least, due process requires that the nature and duration of commitment bear some reasonable relation to the purpose for which the individual is committed.

We hold, consequently, that a person charged by a State with a criminal offense who is committed solely on account of his incapacity to proceed to trial cannot be held more than the reasonable period of time necessary to determine whether there is a substantial probability that he will attain that capacity in the foreseeable future. If it is determined that this is not the case, then the State must either institute the customary civil commitment proceeding that would be required to commit indefinitely any other citizen, or release the defendant. Furthermore, even if it is determined that the defendant probably soon will be able to stand trial, his continued commitment must be justified by progress toward that goal. In light of differing state facilities and procedures and a lack of evidence in this record, we do not think it appropriate for us to attempt to prescribe arbitrary time limits. We note, however, that petitioner Jackson has now been confined for three and one-half years on a record that sufficiently establishes the lack of a substantial probability that he will ever be able to participate fully in a trial.

. . .

Reversed and remanded.

---

358.   In McNeil v. Director, Patuxent Institution, 407 U.S. 245 (1972), the petitioner was convicted of assault and sentenced to prison for five years. Instead of committing him to prison, the court referred him to the state institution for defective delinquents, for an examination to determine whether he should be committed to the institution for an indefinite term. After the term of his sentence had expired, he remained at the institution "for examination," the determination whether he should be committed never having been made. The state claimed that the petitioner's refusal to cooperate prevented them from completing the examination. Relying on Jackson v. Indiana, above, the Court ordered that he be released. "A confinement that is in fact indeterminate cannot rest on procedures designed to authorize a brief period of observation." Id. at 249.

See People v. Lang, 391 N.E.2d 350 (Ill.1979) (illiterate deaf mute charged with murder; involuntary commitment dependent on findings of dangerousness and continued incompetence held proper); see also Humphrey v. Cady, 405 U.S. 504 (1972) (applying Baxstrom v. Herold, p. 589 above).

---

59. In re Harmon, 425 F.2d 916, 918 (C.A.1 1970).

359. The courts are agreed that a defendant's amnesia affecting his memory of the period when the crime was committed is not by itself sufficient to prevent his trial. E.g., United States v. Mota, 598 F.2d 995 (5th Cir.1979); Morrow v. State, 443 A.2d 108 (Md.1982). See Commonwealth v. Hubbard, 355 N.E.2d 469 (Mass.1976) (amnesia does not affect validity of guilty plea). Although courts have occasionally intimated that amnesia should be disregarded altogether, see, e.g., Fajeriak v. State, 520 P.2d 795 (Alaska 1974), it is generally the rule that "a defendant's amnesia is a factor to be considered in dealing with the fundamental question whether the defendant can receive a fair trial," which is to be decided on a "case by case basis," Commonwealth v. Lombardi, 393 N.E.2d 346, 348–49 (Mass.1979).

"[I]n determining competency when amnesia concerning the circumstances of the crime is the fact, a court should consider the extent to which the amnesia affects the accused's ability to consult with his lawyer; the extent to which the amnesia affects the defendant's ability to testify on his own behalf; the extent to which the evidence in the suit could be extrinsically reconstructed in view of the defendant's amnesia including evidence relating to the crime itself, as well as any reasonably possible alibi; the extent to which the State assisted the accused and his counsel in that reconstruction; the strength of the prosecution's case; that is, whether it is such as to negate all reasonable hypotheses of innocence; and [on a post-trial review of competence] any other facts and circumstances which would indicate whether the defendant had a fair trial." State v. Wynn, 490 A.2d 605, 608 (Del.Super.Ct.1985).

The cases which have decided that amnesia *per se* does not establish lack of competence for trial have proceeded on two distinct theories. One is that, while amnesia may be relevant as a symptom evidencing a present infirmity in the defendant's reasoning capacity, if the defendant has the present ability to understand the proceedings against him, to communicate with his lawyer and generally to conduct his defense in a rational manner, memory or the want thereof is irrelevant to the issue of competence. . . . The second line of cases proceeds on the theory that lack of memory is relevant to the question of whether the defendant can meaningfully consult with his lawyer and that, while a showing of amnesia is not alone enough, a conviction of an amnesiac cannot stand unless it appears that he was not substantially prejudiced by his impairment. . . .

. . .

The amnesiac's plight is not unique. We know, for example, that the memory of any defendant "fades" to some degree. The innocent defendant who is arrested several months after the alleged crime and cannot recall where he was on the night in question is not in a dissimilar circumstance. Moreover, we know that defendants may be deprived of direct knowledge of crucial events by circumstances other than loss of memory. "The plight of an amnesiac differs very little from an accused who was home alone, asleep in bed at the time of the crime.''[60] Most importantly, we know that the defendant's recollection is only one of many sources of evidence which may permit the reconstruction of a past event and that extrinsic evidence far more valuable to the defense than the defendant's own testimony may be lost by reason of death, destruction or other fortuity prior to trial.

United States ex rel. Parson v. Anderson, 354 F.Supp. 1060, 1071–72 (D.Del.1972), aff'd, 481 F.2d 94 (3d Cir.1973).

Compare State v. McClendon, 437 P.2d 421, 423 (Ariz.1968): "[I]t is a reproach to justice to try a man suffering from amnesia of an uncertain type and extent when it appears that reasonable continuance of the trial may provide the time needed to effectuate a limited or full recovery from the amnesic state . . . ."

360. Following an established rule of the common law, the Supreme Court has held that the Eighth Amendment's Cruel and Unusual Punishments Clause prohibits execution of a person who is insane. Ford v. Wainwright, 477 U.S. 399 (1986). In *Ford*, the Court also considered the procedures that a state is required to follow to determine whether a condemned prisoner is sane, if that question is raised. In Penry v. Lynaugh, 492 U.S. 302 (1989), however, the Court held that the Constitution does not prohibit execution of a person who is mentally retarded, whose claim that he was not competent to stand trial and defense of insanity had been rejected. The defendant in *Penry* had the mental capacity of a seven-year-old.

"NOT GUILTY BY REASON OF INSANITY"

Jones v. United States

463 U.S. 354, 103 S.Ct. 3043, 77 L.Ed.2d 694 (1983)

■ JUSTICE POWELL delivered the opinion of the Court.

The question presented is whether petitioner, who was committed to a mental hospital upon being acquitted of a criminal offense by reason of insanity, must be released because he has been hospitalized for a period longer than he might have served in prison had he been convicted.

I

In the District of Columbia a criminal defendant may be acquitted by reason of insanity if his insanity is "affirmatively established by a prepon-

---

60. "Amnesia: A Case Study in the Limits of Particular Justice," 71 Yale L.J. 109, 128 (1961).

derance of the evidence." D.C. Code § 24–301(j) (1981).[61] If he successfully invokes the insanity defense, he is committed to a mental hospital. § 24–301(d)(1). The statute provides several ways of obtaining release. Within 50 days of commitment the acquittee is entitled to a judicial hearing to determine his eligibility for release, at which he has the burden of proving by a preponderance of the evidence that he is no longer mentally ill or dangerous. § 24–301(d)(2). If he fails to meet this burden at the 50-day hearing, the committed acquittee subsequently may be released, with court approval, upon certification of his recovery by the hospital chief of service. § 24–301(e). Alternatively, the acquittee is entitled to a judicial hearing every six months at which he may establish by a preponderance of the evidence that he is entitled to release. § 24–301(k).

Independent of its provision for the commitment of insanity acquittees, the District of Columbia also has adopted a civil-commitment procedure, under which an individual may be committed upon clear and convincing proof by the Government that he is mentally ill and likely to injure himself or others. § 21–545(b). The individual may demand a jury in the civil-commitment proceeding. § 21–544. Once committed, a patient may be released at any time upon certification of recovery by the hospital chief of service. §§ 21–546, 21–548. Alternatively, the patient is entitled after the first 90 days, and subsequently at 6-month intervals, to request a judicial hearing at which he may gain his release by proving by a preponderance of the evidence that he is no longer mentally ill or dangerous. §§ 21–546, 21–547. . . .

II

On September 19, 1975, petitioner was arrested for attempting to steal a jacket from a department store. The next day he was arraigned in the District of Columbia Superior Court on a charge of attempted petit larceny, a misdemeanor punishable by a maximum prison sentence of one year. §§ 22–103, 22–2202. The court ordered petitioner committed to St. Elizabeths, a public hospital for the mentally ill, for a determination of his competency to stand trial. On March 1, 1976, a hospital psychologist submitted a report to the court stating that petitioner was competent to stand trial, that petitioner suffered from "Schizophrenia, paranoid type," and that petitioner's alleged offense was "the product of his mental disease." Record 51. The court ruled that petitioner was competent to stand trial. Petitioner subsequently decided to plead not guilty by reason of insanity. The Government did not contest the plea, and it entered into a stipulation of facts with petitioner. On March 12, 1976, the Superior Court found petitioner not guilty by reason of insanity and committed him to St. Elizabeths pursuant to § 24–301(d)(1).

[61] This provision for the District of Columbia was not affected by the enactment in 1984 of a higher burden of proof for federal crimes, see p. 575 above.

On May 25, 1976, the court held the 50-day hearing required by § 24–301(d)(2)(A). A psychologist from St. Elizabeths testified on behalf of the Government that, in the opinion of the staff, petitioner continued to suffer from paranoid schizophrenia and that "because his illness is still quite active, he is still a danger to himself and to others." Tr. 9. Petitioner's counsel conducted a brief cross-examination, and presented no evidence. The court then found that "the defendant-patient is mentally ill and as a result of his mental illness, at this time, he constitutes a danger to himself or others." Id., at 13. Petitioner was returned to St. Elizabeths. Petitioner obtained new counsel and, following some procedural confusion, a second release hearing was held on February 22, 1977. By that date petitioner had been hospitalized for more than one year, the maximum period he could have spent in prison if he had been convicted. On that basis he demanded that he be released unconditionally or recommitted pursuant to the civil-commitment standards in § 21–545(b), including a jury trial and proof by clear and convincing evidence of his mental illness and dangerousness. The Superior Court denied petitioner's request for a civil-commitment hearing, reaffirmed the findings made at the May 25, 1976, hearing, and continued petitioner's commitment to St. Elizabeths.

Petitioner appealed to the District of Columbia Court of Appeals. . . . [T]he court heard the case en banc and affirmed the judgment of the Superior Court. 432 A.2d 364 (1981). The Court of Appeals rejected the argument "that the length of the prison sentence [petitioner] might have received determines when he is entitled to release or civil commitment under Title 24 of the D.C. Code." Id., at 368. It then held that the various statutory differences between civil commitment and commitment of insanity acquittees were justified under the equal protection component of the Fifth Amendment. . . .

We granted certiorari . . . and now affirm.

III

It is clear that "commitment for any purpose constitutes a significant deprivation of liberty that requires due process protection." Addington v. Texas, 441 U.S. 418, 425 (1979). Therefore, a State must have "a constitutionally adequate purpose for the confinement." O'Connor v. Donaldson, 422 U.S. 563, 574 (1975). Congress has determined that a criminal defendant found not guilty by reason of insanity in the District of Columbia should be committed indefinitely to a mental institution for treatment and the protection of society. . . . Petitioner does not contest the Government's authority to commit a mentally ill and dangerous person indefinitely to a mental institution, but rather contends that "the petitioner's trial was not a constitutionally adequate hearing to justify an indefinite commitment." Brief for Petitioner 14.

Petitioner's argument rests principally on Addington v. Texas, supra, in which the Court held that the Due Process Clause requires the State in a civil-commitment proceeding to demonstrate by clear and convincing evidence that the individual is mentally ill and dangerous. . . . Petitioner contends that these due process standards were not met in his case because the judgment of not guilty by reason of insanity did not constitute a finding of present mental illness and dangerousness and because it was established only by a preponderance of the evidence. Petitioner then concludes that the Government's only conceivably legitimate justification for automatic commitment is to ensure that insanity acquittees do not escape confinement entirely, and that this interest can justify commitment at most for a period equal to the maximum prison sentence the acquittee could have received if convicted. Because petitioner has been hospitalized for longer than the one year he might have served in prison, he asserts that he should be released unconditionally or recommitted under the District's civil-commitment procedures.

A

We turn first to the question whether the finding of insanity at the criminal trial is sufficiently probative of mental illness and dangerousness to justify commitment. A verdict of not guilty by reason of insanity establishes two facts: (i) the defendant committed an act that constitutes a criminal offense, and (ii) he committed the act because of mental illness. Congress has determined that these findings constitute an adequate basis for hospitalizing the acquittee as a dangerous and mentally ill person. . . . We cannot say that it was unreasonable and therefore unconstitutional for Congress to make this determination.

The fact that a person has been found, beyond a reasonable doubt, to have committed a criminal act certainly indicates dangerousness. . . . Indeed, this concrete evidence generally may be at least as persuasive as any predictions about dangerousness that might be made in a civil-commitment proceeding. We do not agree with petitioner's suggestion that the requisite dangerousness is not established by proof that a person committed a nonviolent crime against property. This Court never has held that "violence," however that term might be defined, is a prerequisite for a constitutional commitment.[62]

Nor can we say that it was unreasonable for Congress to determine that the insanity acquittal supports an inference of continuing mental illness. It comports with common sense to conclude that someone whose mental illness was sufficient to lead him to commit a criminal act is likely to remain ill and in need of treatment. The precise evidentiary force of the insanity acquittal, of course, may vary from case to case, but the Due

---

62. . . . The relative "dangerousness" of a particular individual, of course, should be a consideration at the release hearings. In this context, it is noteworthy that petitioner's continuing commitment may well rest in significant part on evidence independent of his acquittal by reason of insanity of the crime of attempted larceny. In December 1976 a medical officer at St. Elizabeths reported that petitioner "has a history of attempted suicide." Record 87. In addition, petitioner at one point was transferred to the civil division of the hospital, but was transferred back to the forensic division because of disruptive behavior. . . . The Government also advises that after petitioner was released unconditionally following the second panel decision below, he had to be recommitted on an emergency civil basis two weeks later for conduct unrelated to the original commitment. . . .

Process Clause does not require Congress to make classifications that fit every individual with the same degree of relevance. . . . Because a hearing is provided within 50 days of the commitment, there is assurance that every acquittee has prompt opportunity to obtain release if he has recovered.

Petitioner also argues that, whatever the evidentiary value of the insanity acquittal, the Government lacks a legitimate reason for committing insanity acquittees automatically because it can introduce the insanity acquittal as evidence in a subsequent civil proceeding. This argument fails to consider the Government's strong interest in avoiding the need to conduct a *de novo* commitment hearing following every insanity acquittal—a hearing at which a jury trial may be demanded . . . and at which the Government bears the burden of proof by clear and convincing evidence. Instead of focusing on the critical question whether the acquittee has recovered, the new proceeding likely would have to relitigate much of the criminal trial. These problems accent the Government's important interest in automatic commitment. . . . We therefore conclude that a finding of not guilty by reason of insanity is a sufficient foundation for commitment of an insanity acquittee for the purposes of treatment and the protection of society.

B

Petitioner next contends that his indefinite commitment is unconstitutional because the proof of his insanity was based only on a preponderance of the evidence, as compared to *Addington*'s civil-commitment requirement of proof by clear and convincing evidence. In equating these situations, petitioner ignores important differences between the class of potential civil-commitment candidates and the class of insanity acquittees that justify differing standards of proof. The *Addington* Court expressed particular concern that members of the public could be confined on the basis of "some abnormal behavior which might be perceived by some as symptomatic of a mental or emotional disorder, but which is in fact within a range of conduct that is generally acceptable." 441 U.S., at 426–427. . . . In view of this concern, the Court deemed it inappropriate to ask the individual "to share equally with society the risk of error." *Addington*, 441 U.S., at 427. But since automatic commitment under § 24–301(d)(1) follows only if the *acquittee himself* advances insanity as a defense and proves that his criminal act was a product of his mental illness, there is good reason for diminished concern as to the risk of error. More important, the proof that he committed a criminal act as a result of mental illness eliminates the risk that he is being committed for mere "idiosyncratic behavior," *Addington*, 441 U.S., at 427. A criminal act by definition is not "within a range of conduct that is generally acceptable." Id., at 426–427.

We therefore conclude that concerns critical to our decision in *Addington* are diminished or absent in the case of insanity acquittees. Accordingly, there is no reason for adopting the same standard of proof in both cases. . . . The preponderance of the evidence standard comports with due process for commitment of insanity acquittees.

C

The remaining question is whether petitioner nonetheless is entitled to his release because he has been hospitalized for a period longer than he could have been incarcerated if convicted. The Due Process Clause "requires that the nature and duration of commitment bear some reasonable relation to the purpose for which the individual is committed." Jackson v. Indiana, 406 U.S. 715, 738 (1972). The purpose of commitment following an insanity acquittal, like that of civil commitment, is to treat the individual's mental illness and protect him and society from his potential dangerousness. The committed acquittee is entitled to release when he has recovered his sanity or is no longer dangerous. . . . And because it is impossible to predict how long it will take for any given individual to recover—or indeed whether he ever will recover—Congress has chosen, as it has with respect to civil commitment, to leave the length of commitment indeterminate, subject to periodic review of the patient's suitability for release.

In light of the congressional purposes underlying commitment of insanity acquittees, we think petitioner clearly errs in contending that an acquittee's hypothetical maximum sentence provides the constitutional limit for his commitment. A particular sentence of incarceration is chosen to reflect society's view of the proper response to commission of a particular criminal offense, based on a variety of considerations such as retribution, deterrence, and rehabilitation. . . . The State may punish a person convicted of a crime even if satisfied that he is unlikely to commit further crimes.

Different considerations underlie commitment of an insanity acquittee. As he was not convicted, he may not be punished. His confinement rests on his continuing illness and dangerousness. Thus, under the District of Columbia statute, no matter how serious the act committed by the acquittee, he may be released within 50 days of his acquittal if he has recovered. In contrast, one who committed a less serious act may be confined for a longer period if he remains ill and dangerous. There simply is no necessary correlation between severity of the offense and length of time necessary for recovery. The length of the acquittee's hypothetical criminal sentence therefore is irrelevant to the purposes of his commitment.[63]

---

63. . . .

The inherent fallacy of relying on a criminal sanction to determine the length of a therapeutic confinement is manifested by petitioner's failure to suggest any clear guidelines for deciding when a patient must be released. For example, he does not suggest whether the Due Process Clause would require States to limit commitment of insanity acquittees to maximum sentences or minimum sentences. Nor does he explain what should be done in the case of indeterminate sentencing or suggest whether account would have to be taken of the availability of release time or the possibility of parole. And petitioner avoids entirely the important question how his theory would apply to those persons who committed especially serious criminal acts. Petitioner thus would leave the States to speculate how they may deal constitutionally with acquittees who might have received life

IV

We hold that when a criminal defendant establishes by a preponderance of the evidence that he is not guilty of a crime by reason of insanity, the Constitution permits the Government, on the basis of the insanity judgment, to confine him to a mental institution until such time as he has regained his sanity or is no longer a danger to himself or society. This holding accords with the widely and reasonably held view that insanity acquittees constitute a special class that should be treated differently from other candidates for commitment. We have observed before that "[w]hen Congress undertakes to act in areas fraught with medical and scientific uncertainties, legislative options must be especially broad and courts should be cautious not to rewrite legislation. . . ." Marshall v. United States, 414 U.S., at 427. This admonition has particular force in the context of legislative efforts to deal with the special problems raised by the insanity defense.

. . . [64]

---

361. Before *Jones* was decided, some courts had held that no substantial difference in the procedures and standards for commitment of persons acquitted by reason of insanity and persons civilly committed is permissible. E.g. State v. Clemons, 515 P.2d 324 (Ariz.1973); People v. McQuillan, 221 N.W.2d 569 (Mich.1974). More commonly, the insanity acquittal has been thought to justify differences not only in the procedures for commitment but also for release. E.g., In re Franklin, 496 P.2d 465 (Cal.1972); Chase v. Kearns, 278 A.2d 132 (Me.1971); Alter v. Morris, 536 P.2d 630 (Wash.1975). See also Lublin v. Central Islip Psychiatric Center, 372 N.E.2d 307 (N.Y.1977). For a thorough discussion of the issues, see the opinions of the district court and court of appeals in Benham v. Edwards, 501 F.Supp. 1050 (N.D.Ga.1980) (considering constitutionality of Georgia commitment and release provisions), affirmed, 678 F.2d 511 (5th Cir.1982), vacated and remanded for further consideration in light of Jones v. United States sub nom. Ledbetter v. Benham, 463 U.S. 1222 (1983).

362. Relying on *Jones*, in Stoneberg v. State, 681 P.2d 994 (Idaho 1984), the court upheld the indefinite commitment of a person charged with disturbing the peace, a misdemeanor subject to a maximum penalty of six months imprisonment, who was acquitted by reason of insanity; evidently insanity had been raised by the defense in the criminal proceeding.

imprisonment, life imprisonment without possibility of parole, or the death penalty.

[64] Justice Brennan wrote a dissenting opinion, which Justice Marshall and Justice Blackmun joined. Justice Stevens also wrote a dissenting opinion.

In State v. Lafferty, 472 A.2d 1275 (Conn.1984), the defendant was charged with embezzlement and acquitted on the ground of insanity. The amount involved was $309,000, which he had taken from his employer. The insanity defense was that he was a pathological or compulsive gambler. The trial court found that he was likely, as a result of his compulsion, to commit crimes against property in the future and that he posed a danger to the property of others. A state statute provided for commitment in such cases if the person's release would constitute a "danger to himself or others." Believing that the statute did not extend to dangers to property, the court refused to commit the defendant. On appeal, the Supreme Court of Connecticut held that the defendant should have been committed. The term "danger" in its ordinary usage, the court said, clearly includes "a danger to property, such as the financial loss of over $300,000 in this case." "The predatory tendencies of a potential embezzler seriously endanger the public at large." Id. at 1277, 1278.

363. In *Jones*, the Court said that a person who has been found not guilty by reason of insanity can be confined in a mental institution "until such time as he has regained his sanity or is no longer a danger to himself or society," p. 600. The conditions requiring release are stated in the alternative. Suppose he has regained his sanity but it is not clear that he is not dangerous. In Foucha v. Louisiana, 504 U.S. 71 (1992) (5–4), the Court considered a Louisiana statutory procedure by which after commitment such a person may continue to be confined unless he proves that he is no longer dangerous, whether or not he has regained his sanity. The defendant had been charged with aggravated burglary and illegal discharge of a firearm and was committed on a finding of not guilty by reason of insanity. More than three years later, a panel of doctors concluded that there was no evidence of continued mental illness and recommended his discharge. There was, however, medical testimony that he had "an antisocial personality, a condition that is not a mental disease and that is untreatable," id. at 75; and the doctors declined to certify that he was no longer dangerous. On that basis, he was recommitted to a mental institution.

The Court held that the Louisiana procedure was a violation of both the Due Process Clause and the Equal Protection Clause. With respect to the former, the Court said: "[T]he State asserts that because Foucha once committed a criminal act and now has an antisocial personality that sometimes leads to aggressive conduct, a disorder for which there is no effective treatment, he may be held indefinitely. This rationale would permit the State to hold indefinitely any other insanity acquittee not mentally ill who could be shown to have a personality disorder that may lead to criminal conduct. The same would be true of any convicted criminal, even though he has completed his prison term. It would also be only a step away from substituting confinements for dangerousness for our present system which, with only narrow exceptions and aside from permissible confinements for mental illness, incarcerates only those who are proved beyond reasonable doubt to have violated a criminal law." Id. at 82–83.

With respect to equal protection, Justice White, for four Justices, said:

Jones established that insanity acquittees may be treated differently in some respects from those persons subject to civil commitment, but Foucha, who is not now thought to be insane, can no longer be so classified. The State nonetheless insists on holding him indefinitely because he at one time committed a criminal act and does not now prove he is not dangerous. Louisiana law, however, does not provide for similar confinement for other classes of persons who have committed criminal acts and who cannot later prove they would not be dangerous. Criminals who have completed their prison terms, or are about to do so, are an obvious and large category of such persons. Many of them will likely suffer from the same sort of personality disorder that Foucha exhibits. However, state law does not allow for their continuing confinement based merely on dangerousness. Instead, the State controls the behavior of these similarly situated citizens by relying on other means, such as punishment, deterrence, and supervised release. Freedom from physical restraint being a fundamental right, the State must have a particularly convincing reason, which it has not put forward, for such discrimination against insanity acquittees who are no longer mentally ill.

Furthermore, in civil commitment proceedings the State must establish the grounds of insanity and dangerousness permitting confinement by clear and convincing evidence. . . . Similarly, the State must establish insanity and dangerousness by clear and convincing evidence in order to confine an insane convict beyond his criminal sentence, when the basis for his original confinement no longer exists. . . . However, the State now claims that it may continue to confine Foucha, who is not now considered to be mentally ill, solely because he is deemed dangerous, but without assuming the burden of proving even this ground for confinement by clear and convincing evidence. The court below gave no convincing reason why the procedural safeguards against unwarranted confinement which are guaranteed to insane persons and those who have been convicted may be denied to a sane acquittee, and the State has done no better in this Court.

Id. at 85–86.

364. The states have various provisions for the disposition of a defendant found not guilty by reason of insanity. It is commonly provided that the defendant be committed for observation and examination for a limited period, such as 60 days, after which he must be released or committed civilly. The procedures for civil commitment may be modified in certain respects. Automatic indefinite commitment subject to periodic review, the constitutionality of which is upheld in *Jones*, above, is authorized by the Model Penal Code § 4.08(1) and the laws of some states. The comment to the Code provision says that automatic commitment "not only provides the public with the maximum immediate protection, but may also work to the advantage of mentally diseased or defective defendants by making the defense of irresponsibility more acceptable to the public and to the jury." 2 MPC Commentaries Part I, 256. The comment continues:

There are substantial arguments both for and against mandatory commitment. Against, it may be said that mental disease at the time of the crime does not necessarily establish mental disease at the time of the acquittal. A person who was not responsible at the time he did what would otherwise have been a criminal act may have recovered and no longer require commitment. Mandatory commitment precludes his establishing such a recovery before he is placed in an institution. Apart from the possibility of a change in his condition, his acquittal on grounds of insanity may, in jurisdictions requiring the prosecution to establish sanity beyond a reasonable doubt, mean only that the jury doubts his sanity, not that it thinks it probable that he is insane. It can be argued that it is unfair to commit him unless it is at least probable that he is suffering from mental disease or defect, especially if the jury verdict does not even clearly establish that he performed the acts for which he is prosecuted.

However, it may also be argued that the distinction between the standards of criminal proof and civil commitment is one of the stronger arguments for mandatory commitment. In the vast majority of cases in which the defense of irresponsibility is invoked, it is undisputed that the defendant performed the acts for which he is prosecuted. Consider a case in which those acts reveal him to be highly dangerous, for example, because he has committed a brutal homicide. If the defendant does not persuade the jury that he was probably insane, but raises a reasonable doubt on that score, he will be acquitted. Under the circumstances it is most questionable whether the defendant, without showing any change in his condition since commission of the criminal acts, should be able to avoid commitment under civil standards on the ground that he is probably sane. It may be doubted whether in actuality such defendants will avoid commitment, regardless of whether it is mandatory and regardless of technical burdens of proof, but mandatory commitment is a straightforward protection of society's interests in such cases. As the example illustrates, it may be viewed as a way of rendering acceptable the placement of the burden of proof in the criminal case on the prosecution. . . .

The possibility that the defendant may have recovered his sanity since the time of the crime is more troublesome in respect to mandatory commitment. This section does provide that the defendant himself may have his application for release considered after six months and the Commissioner of Mental Hygiene may recommend release even more quickly. Given the seriousness of most crimes for which the claim of irresponsibility caused by mental disease is made, society's interest in protection from dangerous persons, and the difficulty of making precise assessments of changes in a person's mental condition, these provisions may provide as much protection of the defendant's interest as is warranted.

Id. at 257–58. Before the decision in *Jones*, several courts had held that automatic indefinite commitment was not constitutional. E.g., People v. McQuillan, 221 N.W.2d 569 (Mich.1974); State ex rel. Kovach v. Schubert, 219 N.W.2d 341 (Wis.1974).

The difference between mandatory and discretionary commitment is greater in principle than in practical effect; in either case, a defendant acquitted of a serious crime because he was insane is likely to be committed.

Provisions for release also vary. A majority of states require that release be by court order; some states require that the prosecutor be notified of proceedings that may lead to release. Some states require the concurrence of hospital authorities for the defendant to be released; and in some, the hospital can itself release a committed person. The Model Penal Code § 4.08(3) makes release conditional on a finding that a person can be released "without danger to himself or others," a provision that has also been enacted in a number of states. The decision in *Foucha*, p. 601 note 363 above, appears to declare such a provision unconstitutional. The Commentary to the Code (which was written before *Foucha*) noted that there were constitutional doubts about continued confinement based on dangerousness alone. It observed: "In virtually all actual cases the questions of dangerousness and continued mental disease are likely to be closely linked and it probably makes much less difference in practice than in theory whether the criterion for release is 'lack of dangerousness' or 'sanity' or a combination of the two." 2 MPC Commentaries Part I, 260 (comment to § 4.08). (*Foucha* was, in fact, a rather special case. His original commitment was evidently due to a drug-induced psychosis, which disappeared when the use of the drug was stopped. *Foucha*, 504 U.S. at 75.)

Federal law enacted in 1984 provides that a person found not guilty by reason of insanity be committed for examination and that a hearing be conducted within 40 days. At the hearing, if the offense involved "bodily injury" or "serious damage to the property" of another person or a "substantial risk of such injury or damage," the person "has the burden of proving by clear and convincing evidence that his release would not create a substantial risk of bodily injury to another person or serious damage of property of another due to a present mental disease or defect." For other offenses, the person has the burden of proof "by a preponderance of the evidence." At any subsequent hearing, the same proof must be established for the person to be discharged. 18 U.S.C. § 4243.

One way of reducing the obstacles facing a defendant who is committed following an insanity acquittal is to allow conditional release, which may not only allow him to leave the hospital but also help him to establish that he ought to be discharged. See generally State v. Carter, 316 A.2d 449 (N.J.1974).

365. Statutory provisions for commitment of persons acquitted by reason of insanity were held to apply to the defendant, who was mentally retarded rather than suffering from a mental disease, in United States v. Jackson, 553 F.2d 109 (D.C.Cir.1976). Legislative history, the court concluded, indicated an intention to distinguish all persons acquitted by reason of insanity from all other persons, even though civilly committed mentally retarded persons were treated differently. "Retarded individuals who are acquitted by reason of insanity are not merely retarded individuals. Acquittal of a retarded individual by reason of insanity requires proof by a preponderance of the evidence not only of retardation but proof as well of a causal connection between the retardation and the individual's lack of behavior controls. . . . It is this evidence, together with evidence of the acquittee's criminal conduct and consequent dangerousness, that provides a rational basis for treating him differently from civilly committed retarded or mentally ill persons." Id. at 120.

366. After the decision in Baxstrom v. Herold, 383 U.S. 107 (1966), discussed in *Jackson*, p. 589 above, New York State was required to release or recommit a large number of previously imprisoned persons who were being detained on grounds of mental illness in prison-like facilities. In United States ex rel. Schuster v. Herold, 410 F.2d 1071 (2d Cir.1969), another case involving New York's procedures for committing prisoners found to be insane, the court observed:

> Most judicial reform is accompanied by cries of horror and dismay that the action by the court has surely carried society over the brink and into the abyss of administrative chaos. Certainly this was true of *Baxstrom*. When § 384[65] was invalidated, the New York authorities decided to transfer all patients confined in Dannemora or Matteawan pursuant to that provision—a total of 992 inmates—to civil hospitals. This transfer was designated by them as "Operation Baxstrom." When this decision was announced, some segments of the community were anxious and outraged. Involved labor unions demanded special pay and training for working with the Operation Baxstrom transferees because they were presumptively "dangerous." Residents in the neighborhoods of civil mental hospitals protested the presence of "criminal lunatics" in their midst. Yet in only one year the protests evaporated. The transfer has been an astounding success. Of these nearly 1000 ex-prisoners whom the appropriate state authorities had prior to *Baxstrom* determined to be too dangerous to be placed in a civil hospital,

[65] Providing for civil commitment of prisoners at the end of their sentence without the safeguards available for civil commitment generally.

176 have been fully discharged—147 to their home communities and the rest to other hospitals; 454 others have elected to remain in civil mental hospitals on voluntary or informal status; and only seven have had to be returned to Matteawan after a judicial determination that they were dangerous. . . .

What could explain this massive misplacement of people in Matteawan and Dannemora—places which are more restrictive prisons than hospitals? The New York Bar Report indicated it was "another instance of institutionalized expectations putting blinders on our perceptions." [Special Committee on the Study of Commitment Procedures and the Law Relating to Incompetents of the Ass'n of the Bar of the City of New York, Mental Illness, Due Process, and the Criminal Defendant (1968)] at 227. The very fact that these men were in Dannemora may have induced the circular reasoning which impelled the New York authorities to the conclusion that they were "dangerous."

410 F.2d at 1085–86.

Compare the observations of Stone, p. 610 note 372 below.

367. Can a person who does not assert the defense of insanity but over his protest is found not guilty by reason of insanity be committed without resort to civil commitment proceedings? In Lynch v. Overholser, 369 U.S. 705, 711 (1962), the Supreme Court suggested that there were "not insubstantial constitutional doubts" whether commitment pursuant to a mandatory commitment statute in such a case would not be a denial of liberty without due process of law. See United States v. Marble, 940 F.2d 1543, 1547 (D.C.Cir.1991), in which the court declared that "a district court must allow a defendant to accept responsibility for a crime committed when he may have been suffering from a mental disease."

368. In Donaldson v. O'Connor, 493 F.2d 507 (5th Cir.1974), a case of involuntary civil commitment, the court of appeals held that there was a constitutional right to treatment in such cases. On review, the Supreme Court concluded that it need not decide "whether mentally ill persons dangerous to themselves or to others have a right to treatment upon compulsory confinement by the State, or whether the State may compulsorily confine a nondangerous, mentally ill individual for the purpose of treatment." The jury having found that Donaldson "was neither dangerous to himself nor dangerous to others, and also [having] found that, if mentally ill, Donaldson had not received treatment," the Court concluded that his continued confinement violated his constitutional right to liberty. "[A] state cannot constitutionally confine without more a nondangerous individual who is capable of surviving safely in freedom by himself or with the help of willing and responsible family members or friends." O'Connor v. Donaldson, 422 U.S. 563, 573, 576 (1975).

The constitutional rights of a person involuntarily civilly committed to a state institution for the mentally retarded are considered in Youngberg v. Romeo, 457 U.S. 307 (1982). Such a person, the Court said, has a protected interest in liberty that encompasses reasonably safe conditions of confinement, freedom from unreasonable bodily restraints, and minimally adequate training reasonably required by the foregoing. See also e.g., In the Interest of Goodwin, 366 N.W.2d 809 (N.D.1985); In re W.H., 481 A.2d 22 (Vt.1984) (limited commitment for examination), holding that the state is required to pursue less restrictive measures consistent with the necessary custody and treatment of a civilly committed person.

369. Could a state conclude (1) that a defendant charged with a serious crime is not guilty by reason of insanity and (2) that there is no known method of treatment that gives reasonable promise of success, and therefore that he shall be confined in nontherapeutic conditions permanently (or until, without treatment, his mental disorder disappears)?[66]

If so, could a state arrive at the same result if the second proposition were that there is no known method of treatment that gives reasonable promise of success *within the limits of the resources allocated to treatment of the criminally insane*?

If not, what should the state do with a defendant to whom both propositions are applicable?

If the answer to the second question is "No," what principle requires that a state allocate its resources in favor of the criminally insane?

370. Sexual offender statutes. In Kansas v. Hendricks, 521 U.S. 346 (1997) (5–4), the Court upheld a civil commitment under the Sexually Violent Predator Act, enacted by Kansas in 1994. The statute provided for commitment of persons who, due to a "mental abnormality" or "personality disorder," are likely to commit "predatory acts of sexual violence." The

---

66. See, for example, the recommendation of Waelder, a psychoanalyst, that the law adopt a "trifocal formulation," pursuant to which "the court, after determining the facts of the case, would proceed to the consideration of the way in which the offender should best be dealt with from the point of view of the merits of the case, the requirements of public morality and public safety and the chances of the offender's rehabilitation; and would dispose of each case by punishment, custody or treatment, or by a combination of these, or by release, as seems best fitted to the total situation." Waelder, "Psychiatry and the Problem of Criminal Responsibility," 101 U. Pa. L. Rev. 378, 389 (1952). The disposition of a person who is dangerous, deterrable, and treatable, would be punishment and treatment; that of a person who is dangerous, deterrable, and not treatable would be punishment; that of a person who is dangerous, not deterrable, and treatable would be preventive custody and treatment, etc. A person who is dangerous and not deterrable or treatable would be held in preventive custody. Id. at 390.

commitment continues "until such time as the person's mental abnormality or personality disorder has so changed that the person is safe to be at large." Kan. Stat. Ann. § 59–29a01 et seq. Hendricks, the first person committed under the statute, had been convicted in 1984 of taking "indecent liberties" with two adolescent boys. After serving ten years in prison, shortly before he was to be released the state initiated proceedings for his commitment under the statute. Hendricks had a history of convictions involving sexual abuse of children and repeated incarcerations going back to 1955. At the commitment hearing, he acknowledged his pedophilia, which he said he was not sure he could control. A jury found that beyond a reasonable doubt he was a sexually violent predator within the meaning of the statute.

The Court said that although "a finding of dangerousness, standing alone, is ordinarily not a sufficient ground upon which to justify indefinite involuntary commitment," the requirement of a finding of future dangerousness linked to a "mental abnormality" or "personality disorder" sufficiently narrowed "the class of persons eligible for confinement to those who are unable to control their dangerousness." 521 U.S. at 513. The Court rejected Hendricks's claim that the statute was criminal in nature and that his commitment constituted punishment, so that constitutional requirements applicable to criminal proceedings applied, notwithstanding the state court's possible finding that treatment was not possible for this class of persons and, alternatively, that there was no treatment available when Hendricks's crime was committed. It said: "Where the State has 'disavowed any punitive intent'; limited confinement to a small segment of particularly dangerous individuals; provided strict procedural safeguards; directed that confined persons be segregated from the general prison population and afforded the same status as others who have been civilly committed; recommended treatment if such is possible; and permitted immediate release upon a showing that the individual is no longer dangerous or mentally impaired, we cannot say that it acted with punitive intent. We therefore hold that the Act does not establish criminal proceedings and that involuntary confinement pursuant to the Act is not punitive." Id. at 519.

In a dissenting opinion, Justice Breyer observed that statutes in 16 states besides Kansas provide for civil commitment of sexually dangerous persons, all but one of which were less punitive in effect than the Kansas statute. His opinion provides a summary discussion of those provisions and citations to the statutes. Id. at 522.

Elaborating its holding in *Hendricks*, in Kansas v. Crane, 534 U.S. 407 (2002) (7–2), the Court said that the civil commitment of a dangerous sexual offender required not merely a finding that the person committed is likely to commit further crimes of sexual violence but "proof of serious difficulty in controlling behavior." Id. at 413. Such proof, the Court said, "must be sufficient to distinguish the dangerous sexual offender whose serious mental illness, abnormality, or disorder subjects him to civil commitment from the dangerous but typical recidivist convicted in an ordinary criminal case." Id. See Seling v. Young, 531 U.S. 250 (2001) (8–1), in which, considering a Washington statute for civil commitment of "sexually violent predators," similar to that involved in *Hendricks*, the Court said that once it has been concluded that a statute is civil in nature, it may not be attacked as punitive, and therefore subject to the requirements for criminal statutes, *as applied* to a particular person.

It is not uncommon for state statutes to provide extremely long prison sentences for persons convicted of sexual offenses, even relatively minor ones, especially if a child is involved. How significant is the difference between civil commitment and imprisonment in theory? How significant is it likely to be in practice?

––––

371. "The dissatisfaction of psychiatrists and social workers brought into contact with the criminal law is . . . a by-product of an issue which cannot be adequately represented as a mere discrepancy between eighteenth century legal-psychological dogma and modern conceptions of psychology and psychiatry. Those who appear to have assumed that it could be, have proceeded upon a curiously superficial understanding of the meaning and function of the legal formulae of responsibility and of intent, motive, deliberation, premeditation, wilfulness, heat of passion, adequate provocation, and the like, inherited though they are from the Common Law of a more primitive day. For the law is not, and never was, designed as a treatise on psychology or any one of the social sciences. Its formulae, while couched in terms of outmoded psychological concepts, reflect an underlying social policy with respect to the disposition of offenders and the degree of collective responsibility toward the underprivileged and maladjusted which American communities are accustomed to assume, and which appears to be by no means as outmoded as the concepts in which it is expressed.

"One must, therefore, venture beyond the realm of medical science and of psychology and seek sanctions or justifications which they cannot supply, in an effort to determine not merely what can be done with a given offender as a practical matter of the moment but even what should be done with him under more satisfactory hypothetical conditions. The psychiatrist may be able to describe a given offender. He may shed considerable light on the factors which conditioned his development and present state. It is within his province to indicate to what extent the offender may prove amenable to treatment, and to what kind of treatment. For the offender is a human being—and therefore like and in the same sense as other human beings, a problem for the psychiatrist. But there existing science stops. What varieties of personality the community shall take the trouble to maintain even though they have demonstrated their inability to get along with the group, what individuals it shall undertake to rehabilitate at public expense, what forms of treatment shall be made available, what types of special environment shall be created for the purpose, and how any given program shall be set up, are primarily questions of social values and of politics very much akin to such major issues of recent years as those raised by unemployment and the care of the aged.

. . .

". . . The healthy penal adjustment—unless indeed, our culture can still afford the privileges of infancy—would . . . consist in professing policies looking toward the rehabilitation of offenders, and employing such professed policies as a premise, only to the extent to which we may be willing at the same time to assume collective responsibility for the welfare of that whole segment of human subnormality, wreckage and underprivilege, which we experience as crime or delinquency. Let us make no mistake about this. Given such cultures as we know, the welfare in question would have to include material as well as spiritual elements. Any very extensive program of rehabilitation would require an assumption of responsibility of a degree to which our communities are unaccustomed. For the strains and conditions which account for the deviational personalities and behavior in question run the whole gamut of human inequality and need. The criminal or delinquent, viewed as a subject for treatment, does not differ as greatly in his processing needs from representatives of the other categories of social maladjustment and inequality as we have liked to believe. Nor would it be easy to justify a rehabilitory policy toward criminals more generous than whatever may be the prevailing policy with respect to the other classes of unfortunates at any given time . . . ." Dession, "Psychiatry and the Conditioning of Criminal Justice," 47 Yale L.J. 319, 331–32, 339–40 (1938).

372. Commenting on the wave of criticism of the insanity defense following the insanity acquittal in 1982 of John Hinckley for the attempted assassination of President Reagan, Alan Stone, a psychiatrist and Professor of Law and Psychiatry at Harvard Law School, observed:

[T]he [insanity] defense and the Hinckley verdict have become a symbol to the public of the failures of our criminal justice system, particularly a symbol of the courts' inability to deter crime and to exact retribution. The symbol, however, does not reflect reality. No one seriously believes that abolishing the insanity defense would deter crime, and if the goal is retribution, the obstacle is not the rare successful insanity defense but a mountain of other problems. Politicians who seek to abolish the insanity defense as if it were the mountain are dealing in rhetoric rather than reality.

Even if political attacks on the insanity defense are misguided, what should the lawyer concerned about civil rights and civil liberties think about the insanity defense and the Hinckley verdict? . . . Is the insanity defense a civilized standard of justice? What is the civil libertarian's answer to this question?

Civil libertarians exhibit embarrassing inconsistency in their approaches to these questions. During the past twenty years, in an effort to reform mental health law, civil libertarians have attacked the role of psychiatry in the courts, emphasizing the unreliability of psychiatric testimony, the fallibility of psychiatric predictions of future dangerousness, and the arbitrariness of psychiatric diagnoses. Wherever and whenever mental health law or the courts relied on psychiatric expertise, civil libertarians argued that there were violations of civil rights, civil liberties, and the rule of law. . . . These civil libertarian views have strongly influenced judicial opinions and legislative reform over the past two decades. It must, therefore, be awkward for the civil libertarian to turn around and urge the criminal law to retain the insanity defense when that defense relies on psychiatric testimony and diagnosis as the basis for determining criminal responsibility. If psychiatrists are incompetent to diagnose mental illness, if mental illness is a suspect classification, and if psychiatric testimony lacks credibility, how can a civil libertarian embrace the insanity defense?

. . .

If defending the insanity defense presents troubling inconsistencies to civil libertarians, they seem to be consistent on the crucial practical issue—disposition of those found not guilty by reason of insanity. Disposition of such persons involves statutory provisions similar to those for civil commitment, where many hard-fought civil libertarian struggles were litigated, lobbied, and won. The struggles produced state legislative provisions such as procedural safeguards, proof beyond a reasonable doubt, objective behavioral standards, the least restrictive alternative, and the right of a committed patient to refuse drug treatment. When Representative John Conyers' Subcommittee on Criminal Justice considered new legislation responsive to public indignation in the wake of the Hinckley verdict, its legislative provisions for the disposition of persons found not guilty by reason of insanity contained all of the civil libertarian reforms fashioned over the past twenty years.[67] Ironically, these provisions would have made it more difficult for the state to confine, and for psychiatrists to treat, persons like Hinckley who commit violent crimes but are found not guilty by reason of insanity. The A.B.A., in its proposed Criminal Justice Mental Health Standards published after the Hinckley verdict, adopted the same civil libertarian line.[68]

Whatever moral and legal questions are raised by the insanity defense, public protection requires that the question of disposition of acquittees be faced squarely. Under the civil libertarian approach, a mentally ill person who kills, rapes, or maims, and is found not guilty by reason of insanity, is allowed a few weeks later to stand before the law with the same legal status, the same due process safeguards, and

67. Insanity Defense in Federal Courts, 1982: Hearings on H.R. 6783 and Related Bills Before the Subcomm. on Criminal Justice of the House Comm. on the Judiciary, 97th Cong. 2d Sess. (1982).

68. Criminal Justice Mental Health Standards, Part VII (First Tentative Draft 1983).

the same substantive standards as a mentally ill person who harms no one. . . . The past act of violence may be relevant—it may even justify a few weeks of initial confinement under psychiatric observation—but it does not dispose of the question of whether the person continues to be committable. This and other decisions in other jurisdictions have made the fiction of "temporary insanity" a reality of the criminal justice system in the second half of the twentieth century. The impact of similar reforms and some tragic recidivism by insanity acquittees led the Michigan legislature to introduce into American law the guilty but mentally ill verdict.

Such reforms in rules governing the disposition of insanity acquittees force us to consider whether the insanity defense is a "civilized standard" with which we can live. Prior to the enactment of these civil libertarian reforms, the insanity acquittee's fate was little better than if he or she had been convicted; a life sentence in a mental hospital for the criminally insane might or might not have been preferable to a life sentence in a prison. With the reforms in place, however, the insanity defense was no longer a bad deal for the defendant, and it no longer guaranteed protection of the public. For the first time in modern civilization, the "civilized standard" had real bite.

. . .

The most important problem for society is not harmless people like Jones,[69] who are "diverted" or "dumped" by the criminal justice system into the mental health system. The greatest issue centers on people who, like John Hinckley, have been found not responsible for violent crimes. The public has a legitimate concern about whether Hinckley would commit new acts of violence if released. This concern threatens the "civilized standard" and can be allayed only by abolishing the insanity defense or by rejecting the civil libertarian reforms in rules governing the disposition of insanity acquittees.

Psychiatrists and civil libertarians agree that no valid basis exists for making individualized predictions about the likelihood of future violence by insanity acquittees. This view is now so widely accepted that the A.B.A.'s proposed Criminal Justice Mental Health Standards provide: "An expert opinion stating a conclusion that a particular person will or will not engage in dangerous behavior in the future should not be admissible in any criminal proceedings or in any special commitment hearing involving a person found not responsible under the criminal law."[70] This standard is fully justified by the empirical literature on "expert clinical" predictions of future dangerousness. Some judges want to deny this reality; Justice White, for example, when informed by an amicus brief of the American Psychiatric Association that psychiatrists were unable to predict future violence, respond-

69. The defendant in Jones v. United States, p. 594 above.

70. Criminal Justice Mental Health Standards, supra, Standard 7–3.9.

ed tartly that the Court was being asked to "disinvent the wheel."[71] Justice White's wheel, however, has yet to be invented. Rather, prodded by attacks from civil libertarians . . . psychiatrists have confessed that their *imaginary* wheel of expert clinical prediction of future dangerousness does not exist.

The best statistical predictor of future conduct is past conduct, and repeated acts of past violence do provide actuarial data with which statistical predictions about future violence can be made. These statistical probabilities, however, are not improved by clinical assessments of the personality or character of the particular individual. Furthermore, these statistical generalizations offer little help with individuals such as Hinckley, for whom there has been one dramatic episode of violence and no prior history of violent acts. The painful reality is that no good empirical answer exists to the public's most reasonable concern: Would Hinckley be likely to kill again if released? These problems of prediction make it as difficult to justify the continuing confinement of John Hinckley as it is to justify his release. The Supreme Court in deciding *Jones* [v. United States, 463 U.S. 354 (1983)] did not face up to this problem, but the lower standard of proof for indefinite commitment which it articulated in *Jones* will surely be relevant to any future consideration of this issue.

The proposed A.B.A. standards, in contrast, follow the civil libertarian line. In addition to the general commitment proceedings, the A.B.A. standards provide for special commitment proceedings. Under these procedures, the acquittee may be confined only if he or she "(i) is currently mentally ill . . . and, as a result, (ii) poses a substantial threat of serious bodily harm to others."[72] The commentary suggests that this standard is to be interpreted narrowly, as "a substantial threat of harm in a reasonably short period of time."[73] This standard is more stringent than is generally required for civil commitment of persons who have harmed no one, and it creates more barriers to commitment than some states' current criminal mental health statutes. Given the impossibility of predicting future violence, it is unclear how judges and juries can make these determinations for individuals such as John Hinckley. Such a standard is even more difficult to prove once a person has "adjusted" to an institution. Furthermore, the state bears the difficult burden of proving this standard by clear and convincing evidence, both for initial and continued confinement.[74]

The A.B.A. standards, therefore, provide for special commitment of insanity acquittees of violent crimes, but make it very difficult to commit and continue to confine anyone under this procedure. If these standards were applied honestly, John Hinckley and almost everyone else now confined as not guilty by reason of insanity would fail to meet

---

71. Barefoot v. Estelle, 463 U.S. 880, 896 (1983).

72. Criminal Justice Mental Health Standards, supra, Standard 7–7.4(b).

73. Id., Standard 7–7.4(b), commentary at 321.

74. Id., Standards 7–7.4(b), 7–7.8.

the criteria for special commitment. Courts would then have to fall back on general civil commitment procedures which are biased in favor of release. Since the A.B.A. standards were inspired by civil libertarian arguments, will civil libertarians rush to assist John Hinckley in obtaining his liberty? If they were to succeed, would this be a triumph for justice?

If it is true that no one can say with any degree of certainty that Hinckley will or will not be dangerous, what standard should the law require for continuing confinement? The endless debate over the insanity defense obscures the legal, moral, and practical problems of this dilemma. John Hinckley is entitled by law to force a judge to confront this dilemma every six months. He is entitled to a zealous advocate who will counsel him to stop making veiled threats against Jodie Foster and to keep out of trouble in the hospital if he wants to be released; a zealous advocate who can marshall the evidence of the fallibility of all predictions of future violent behavior; a zealous advocate who will question the reliability and validity of psychiatric testimony that Hinckley is currently mentally ill; and a zealous advocate who will point out that persons with similar serious mental illnesses are treated and discharged by psychiatrists in days or weeks. Given the empirical problems of prediction of future violence, what credible evidence could the state offer that Hinckley continues to be dangerous? If a judge or jury, hearing the available arguments, continued to confine Hinckley, it would become clear that the only thing standing in the way of John Hinckley's release is the potential outrage of the public. . . .

Should public outrage and judicial discretion be the hidden justifications for continuing confinement? Civil libertarians have never accepted public outrage as a reason to abandon zealous advocacy of civil rights. The civil libertarian view of the rule of law in the mental health law context emphasizes the objective behavioral standard of dangerousness, even though common sense and empirical evidence tell us that the standard is unworkable when it involves predictions of future behavior.

Congress, in the Insanity Defense Reform Act of 1984, solved this dilemma and rejected the above scenario by going even further than the Supreme Court's *Jones* decision. The act requires defendants like Hinckley to assume "the burden of proving by clear and convincing evidence that his release would not create a substantial risk of bodily injury to another person or serious damage of property . . . ."[75] This law turns the civil libertarian mental health law reforms of the past twenty years on their head. The civil libertarians had argued that dangerousness to others was the sole constitutional justification for civil commitment. They had also correctly argued that psychiatrists could not predict dangerousness. Furthermore, they urged that the

---

[75] 18 U.S.C. § 4243.

state should have the burden of proving beyond a reasonable doubt what was in fact unprovable. This stacked the deck against confinement. As to insanity acquittees, Congress has now stacked the deck the other way. The insanity acquittee has the burden of proving, by clear and convincing evidence, the unprovable—that he is no longer dangerous.

Civil libertarians will, no doubt, challenge this new provision. Is it enough, however, for civil libertarians to take the view that as long as there is an insanity defense they will insist on laws and safeguards that, if honestly enforced, strongly favor the early release of insanity acquittees? This has been their position, and I understand their arguments; but many of us who understand them will wonder about the vision of justice which compels this result.

Stone, "The Insanity Defense and the Civil Libertarian" (Book Review of L. Caplan, The Insanity Defense and the Trial of John W. Hinckley, Jr., 1984), 20 Harv. C.R.–C.L. L. Rev. 525, 527–36 (1985).

373. " 'Insanity,' however formulated, has been considered a defense. An evaluation of such a defense rests on first identifying a need for an exception to criminal liability. Unless a conflict can be discovered between some basic objective of the criminal law and its application to an 'insane' person, there can be no purpose for 'insanity' as a defense. Until a purpose is uncovered, debates about the appropriateness of any insanity-defense formula as well as efforts to evaluate various formulae with respect to the present state of psychiatric knowledge are destined to continue to be frustrating and fruitless." Goldstein & Katz, "Abolish the 'Insanity Defense'—Why Not?" 72 Yale L.J. 853, 854–55 (1963).

Is a "basic objective of the criminal law" undermined if it is applied to an insane person?

"[T]he [insanity] defense is not to absolve of criminal responsibility 'sick' persons who would otherwise be subject to criminal sanction. Rather, its real function is to authorize the state to hold those 'who must be found not to possess the guilty mind *mens rea*,' even though the criminal law demands that no person be held criminally responsible if doubt is cast on any material element of the offense charged. . . .

"[T]he insanity defense is not designed, as is the defense of self-defense, to define an exception to criminal liability, but rather to define for sanction an exception from among those who would be free of liability. . . . So conceived, the problem really facing the criminal process has been how to obtain authority to sanction the 'insane' who would be excluded from liability by an overall application of the general principles of the criminal law." Goldstein & Katz, above, at 864–65.

Does the history of the insanity defense sustain this analysis?

374. How much has the operation of the insanity defense in Anglo-American criminal law changed in the past thousand years?

---

2. INFANCY

Recall Hale's suggestion that the "best measure" of criminal responsibility when sanity is at issue is that a person is responsible if he has "as great understanding, as ordinarily a child of fourteen years hath," p. 551 above. Hale's test reflected the common law rule that a child of 14 was held criminally responsible as an adult. A child below the age of seven was not criminally responsible. From ages 7 to 14 he was presumed to be irresponsible, but his criminal capacity could be established by showing that he understood what he was doing.[76] See generally Little v. State, 554 S.W.2d 312, 321 (Ark.1977) (first-degree murder conviction of thirteen-year-old child affirmed; strength of presumption of incapacity "varies with the actual age of the child and decreases as the upper limit is reached").

The common law rules have not been changed in most of the states. In a few, the minimum age of responsibility has been raised and/or the maximum age of presumptive irresponsibility lowered. The rules have been markedly affected, however, by the enactment of statutes creating special juvenile courts that have jurisdiction over some or all offenses by juveniles. Compare Gammons v. Berlat, 696 P.2d 700 (Ariz.1985) (statutory presumption not applicable in juvenile proceedings); In the Interest of G.T., 597 A.2d 638 (Pa.Super.1991) (same), with State v. Q.D., 685 P.2d 557 (Wash. 1984) (statutory presumption applied). The relationship between the jurisdiction of the juvenile court and that of the criminal courts varies; it commonly depends on the age of the offender and the nature of the offense, more serious offenses being more likely to be tried in the criminal courts. The jurisdiction of the juvenile court may be exclusive or concurrent with the jurisdiction of the criminal courts. In no state is the juvenile court entirely without jurisdiction over persons below 16. Its jurisdiction ends in a few states at 16 and in some others at 17. In a large majority of states, jurisdiction ends at 18. For a tabular presentation, see 2 MPC Commentaries Part I, 284–92 (comment to § 4.10).

---

76. Under very early law, children, like the insane, were found guilty of the offense and then granted a pardon. See Kean, "The History of the Criminal Liability of Children," 53 L.Q. Rev. 364 (1937). By Hale's time certainly, and probably by the fifteenth century, children were no longer prosecuted, so a pardon was unnecessary. 1 M. Hale, History of the Pleas of the Crown 28 (1800 ed.); see Kean, above, at 366.

Before the seventeenth century there were no official records by which age could be proved. The age of a young defendant was determined by producing him in court for "inspection."

375. How should the age below which a person is not criminally responsible for any conduct be determined? Stephen thought that a child below 12 should not be held responsible. "Legal punishment at such an early age can rarely, if ever, be required for the protection of society. The punishment of a child of immature age can hardly fail to do harm to the offender to an extent altogether out of proportion to any good which it can possibly do to any one." 2 Stephen, History 98. Contrast the views of Oliphant, J., dissenting in State v. Monahan, 104 A.2d 21, 36 (N.J.1954), from a ruling that, pursuant to a statute, the juvenile court had exclusive jurisdiction over a boy charged with first degree murder committed when he was 15 years old: "I cannot comprehend the reasoning that suggests that marauding gangs of little hoodlums armed with guns, knives, switch knives or other lethal weapons are to be considered as a matter of law incapable of committing the crime of murder. Infants under the age of 21 years, according to statistics, perpetrate a high percentage of the heinous crimes committed throughout the country . . . ."

In cases of the kind suggested by Judge Oliphant, where very young persons engage in organized criminal activity for gain, should their age be a basis for treating them differently from older offenders? If it should, is the reason for treating them differently that they are less responsible for their conduct, in the sense required by the criminal law, than adult offenders?

There is typically a period above some age but below the age of adulthood when the juvenile court has authority to waive its jurisdiction and remit the person to be tried as an adult in the criminal courts. See 2 MPC Commentaries Part I, 271–72, 276–79 (comment to § 4.10). The seriousness of the offense is likely to be a significant factor in the determination that juvenile court jurisdiction should be waived. See id. In State in the Interest of C.A.H. & B.A.R., 446 A.2d 93 (N.J.1982), for example, the court concluded that the juvenile court incorrectly retained jurisdiction over two juveniles, aged 17 and 16 at the time of their offenses, who committed robbery and murder. The court said that "in the context of a waiver determination, the demands for deterrence are strengthened in direct proportion to the gravity and harmfulness of the offense and the deliberateness of the offender." Id. at 99. See generally Kent v. United States, 383 U.S. 541 (1966) (constitutional procedural guarantees, including the right to counsel, apply to a juvenile court hearing to determine whether to waive jurisdiction).

376. How should the age above which a person is held criminally responsible as an adult be determined? Should the common law's period of years during which responsibility is in doubt be retained? If so, what kind of evidence should be regarded as establishing responsibility?

377. "[D]ifficult considerations arise over arguments based upon children's knowledge of right and wrong. This conception is singularly difficult to apply when dealing with children, because we have always to think in terms of the child in his environment, including the climate of opinion in the family and group, as well as the physical surroundings. Differing environments may lead to wide variations in the age at which a child comes to this knowledge, so that any rule depending on a fixed age cannot have a sure foundation. Further, the environmental factors may be pulling in different directions. A child of, say, eleven, may know quite well that stealing is wrong, and yet follow the behaviour of a group. It is, of course, common to find that a child is under stress from two opposing sets of value judgments. The standards of school teaching can be accepted intellectually, and to some extent emotionally, and yet at the same time group standards may control the behaviour. The fact that the child 'knows right from wrong' does not mean that we should regard it as a personal responsibility equivalent to similar knowledge in an adult. A child's conception of right and wrong is, however, of vital importance in dealing with cases. In other words, we can properly use arguments of 'knowing right and wrong' to help us deal with a child long before that child is sufficiently independent of its surroundings to be saddled with a permanent personal responsibility." Committee on Children and Young Persons, Report (Cmnd. 1191) 31 (1960).

378.

One reason for the failure of the juvenile courts has been the community's continuing unwillingness to provide the resources—the people and facilities and concern—necessary to permit them to realize their potential and prevent them from taking on some of the undesirable features typical of lower criminal courts in this country. In few jurisdictions, for example, does the juvenile court judgeship enjoy high status in the eyes of the bar, and while there are many juvenile court judges of outstanding ability and devotion, many are not. One crucial presupposition of the juvenile court philosophy—a mature and sophisticated judge, wise and well-versed in law and the science of human behavior—has proved in fact too often unattainable. A recent study of juvenile court judges . . . revealed that half had not received undergraduate degrees; a fifth had received no college education at all; a fifth were not members of the bar. Almost three-quarters devote less than a quarter of their time to juvenile and family matters, and judicial hearings often are little more than attenuated interviews of 10 or 15 minutes' duration. . . .

Other resources are equally lacking. The survey of juvenile court judges reveals the scarcity of psychologists and psychiatrists—over half a century after the juvenile court movement set out to achieve the coordinated application of the behavioral and social sciences to the misbehaving child. Where clinics exist, their waiting lists usually are months long and frequently they provide no treatment but only diagnosis. And treatment, even when prescribed, is often impossible to carry out because of the unavailability of adequate individual and family casework, foster home placement, treatment in youth institutions. . . .

The dispositional alternatives available even to the better endowed juvenile courts fall far short of the richness and the relevance to individual needs envisioned by the court's founders. In most places, indeed, the only alternatives are release outright, probation, and institutionalization. Probation means minimal supervision at best. A large percentage of juvenile courts have no probation services at all, and in those that do, caseloads typically are so high that counseling and supervision take the form of occasional phone calls and perfunctory visits instead of the careful, individualized service that was intended. Institutionalization too often means storage—isolation from the outside world—in an overcrowded, understaffed, high-security institution with little education, little vocational training, little counseling or job placement or other guidance upon release. Programs are subordinated to everyday control and maintenance.

President's Commission on Law Enforcement and Administration of Justice, Task Force Report: Juvenile Delinquency and Youth Crime 7–8 (1967). See generally In re Gault, 387 U.S. 1 (1967). One commentator has observed that the effect of *Gault*, which imposed formal requirements on juvenile proceedings to protect the juvenile's rights, has been that "juvenile courts now converge procedurally and substantively with adult criminal courts." Feld, "The Transformation of the Juvenile Court," 75 Minn. L. Rev. 691, 691–92 (1991).

379. Should a person who commits a serious offense as a juvenile and is held in a juvenile institution automatically be released (subject to the possibility of civil commitment proceedings) when he reaches the age at which he is regarded by the criminal law as an adult? On what basis can his custody be continued? Compare the case of a defendant who successfully asserts the defense of insanity and immediately claims that he is not presently insane.

380. Recall the argument, p. 615 note 373 above, that the insanity "defense" is a means of bridging the gap between basic principles of the criminal law and our desire for protection against a dangerous person. Can the same argument be made about the defense of infancy?

381. The defense of infancy is sometimes available in a case in which the defendant plainly has a degree of comprehension of his conduct that would preclude any defense based on lack of responsibility or diminished responsibility were he an adult. In this respect, is the law inconsistent?

3. INTOXICATION

Every jurisdiction in this country recognizes the general principle that voluntary intoxication is not any excuse for crime. This is in accord with the common-law rule dating back to the sixteenth century which allowed no concession to a defendant because of his intoxication. However, by the early nineteenth century, the English courts began to fashion a doctrine to mitigate the harshness and rigidity of the traditional rule. The doctrine, which has come to be known as the exculpatory rule, was stated by Judge Stephen as follows: "[A]lthough you cannot take drunkenness as any excuse for crime, yet when the crime is such that the intention of the party committing it is one of its constituent elements, you may look at the fact that a man was in drink in considering whether he formed the intention necessary to constitute the crime."[77]

It is said that the theory behind this exculpatory doctrine is that it does not hold that drunkenness will excuse crime; rather, it inquires whether the very crime which the law defines has in fact been committed. Almost every state, by statute or by common law, has adopted the exculpatory rule.

The applicability of the exculpatory rule rests entirely on the determination whether the offense involved is categorized as a general- or specific-intent crime. . . . Thus, if a crime is determined to require only a general intent, the defendant's voluntary intoxication during the commission of an offense may not be asserted as a defense to the existence of the mental element of that crime.

The general intent–specific intent dichotomy arose as a compromise between the perceived need to afford some relief to the intoxicated offender whose moral culpability was considered less than that of a sober person who committed the same offense and the view that a person who voluntarily becomes drunk and commits a crime should not escape the consequences. Although the rule seems logical on the surface, it has proven to be far from logical in application. While specific intent can easily be defined as "a particular criminal intent beyond the act done"[78] (whereas general intent is the intent simply to do the physical act), the ease of stating the definition belies the difficulty of applying it in practice. In order to appreciate the problem, one need only note the divergence of opinion among the jurisdictions as

77. Regina v. Doherty, 16 Cox.Crim.C. 306, 308 (N.P.1887).

78. People v. Depew, 183 N.W. 750 (Mich.1921).

to which crimes require a specific intent and, therefore, to which crimes the exculpatory rule applies.

People v. Langworthy, 331 N.W.2d 171, 172–74 (Mich.1982).[79]

The subject of voluntary intoxication as a defense to crimes *not* requiring proof of a specific intent, in this case assault, is discussed at length in Director of Public Prosecutions v. Majewski, [1977] App. Cas. 443 (H.L.) (holding that the defense is not available).

In People v. Hood, 462 P.2d 370, 377–79 (Cal.1969), discussing the distinction between general and specific intent in a case of assault with a deadly weapon on a police officer, the court said

> Specific and general intent have been notoriously difficult terms to define and apply, and a number of textwriters recommend that they be abandoned altogether. . . . Too often the characterization of a particular crime as one of specific or general intent is determined solely by the presence or absence of words describing psychological phenomena— "intent" or "malice," for example—in the statutory language of defining the crime. When the definition of a crime consists of only the description of a particular act, without reference to intent to do a further act or achieve a future consequence, we ask whether the defendant intended to do the proscribed act. This intention is deemed to be a general criminal intent. When the definition refers to defendant's intent to do some further act or achieve some additional consequence, the crime is deemed to be one of specific intent. There is no real difference, however, only a linguistic one, between an intent to do an act already performed and an intent to do that same act in the future. . . .
>
> Even if we assume that the presence or absence of words clearly denoting mental activity is a valid criterion for determining the significance of intoxication, our present problem is not resolved. . . .
>
> . . . Even if assault requires an intent to commit a battery on the victim, it does not follow that the crime is one in which evidence of intoxication ought to be considered in determining whether the defendant had that intent. It is true that in most cases specific intent has come to mean an intention to do a future act or achieve a particular result, and that assault is appropriately characterized as a specific intent crime under this definition. An assault, however, is equally well characterized as a general intent crime under the definition of general intent as an intent merely to do a violent act. Therefore, whatever reality the distinction between specific and general intent may have in other contexts, the difference is chimerical in the case of assault with a deadly weapon or simple assault. Since the definitions of both specific intent and general intent cover the requisite intent to commit a

79. The rule applies also to voluntary intoxication from substances other than alcohol, such as narcotics. See, e.g., Pierce v. Turner, 276 F.Supp. 289 (D.Utah 1967), affirmed 402 F.2d 109 (10th Cir.1968) (glue-sniffing); State v. Bellue, 194 S.E.2d 193 (S.C. 1973).

battery, the decision whether or not to give effect to evidence of intoxication must rest on other considerations.

A compelling consideration is the effect of alcohol on human behavior. A significant effect of alcohol is to distort judgment and relax the controls on aggressive and anti-social impulses. . . . Alcohol apparently has less effect on the ability to engage in simple goal-directed behavior, although it may impair the efficiency of that behavior. In other words, a drunk man is capable of forming an intent to do something simple, such as strike another, unless he is so drunk that he has reached the stage of unconsciousness. What he is not as capable as a sober man of doing is exercising judgment about the social consequences of his acts or controlling his impulses toward anti-social acts. He is more likely to act rashly and impulsively and to be susceptible to passion and anger. It would therefore be anomalous to allow evidence of intoxication to relieve a man of responsibility for the crimes of assault with a deadly weapon or simple assault, which are so frequently committed in just such a manner. . . .

Those crimes that have traditionally been characterized as crimes of specific intent are not affected by our holding here. The difference in mental activity between formulating an intent to commit a battery and formulating an intent to commit a battery for the purpose of raping or killing may be slight, but it is sufficient to justify drawing a line between them and considering evidence of intoxication in the one case and disregarding it in the other. Accordingly, on retrial the court should not instruct the jury to consider evidence of defendant's intoxication in determining whether he committed assault with a deadly weapon on a peace officer or any of the lesser assaults included therein.[80]

See People v. Rocha, 479 P.2d 372 (Cal.1971) (following *Hood*). Compare State v. D'Amico, 385 A.2d 1082 (Vt.1978), holding that voluntary intoxication may be a defense to the crime of aggravated assault, in this case an attempt to cause bodily injury.

---

80. When *Hood* was decided, the California Penal Code § 22 provided: "No act committed by a person while in a state of voluntary intoxication is less criminal by reason of his having been in such condition. But whenever the actual existence of any particular purpose, motive, or intent is a necessary element to constitute any particular species or degree of crime, the jury may take into consideration the fact that the accused was intoxicated at the time, in determining the purpose, motive, or intent with which he committed the act." Since then, the statute has been twice amended. The Code now provides that evidence of voluntary intoxication "shall not be admitted to negate the capacity to form any mental states for the crimes charged, including, but not limited to, purpose, intent, knowledge, premeditation, deliberation, or malice aforethought, with which the accused committed the act" and that such evidence "is admissible solely on the issue of whether or not the defendant actually formed a required specific intent, or, when charged with murder, whether the defendant premeditated, deliberated, or harbored express malice aforethought." Cal. Pen. Code § 22(a)–(b). See People v. Mendoza, 58 Cal. Rptr.2d 498 (Ct.App.1996) (holding (2–1) that § 22, since amended, did not allow voluntary intoxication as a defense to aiding and abetting murder).

In United States v. Nix, 501 F.2d 516 (7th Cir.1974), the defendant was prosecuted for attempting to escape from prison, 18 U.S.C. § 751. He argued that since every crime of attempt requires a specific intent, he should have been allowed to defend on the ground of voluntary intoxication. The court said:

> Under the traditional analysis, specific intent is indeed required for attempted escape. We could end the inquiry here and remand this case because the instruction given erroneously states the law. Simplistic as the traditional analysis is, however, it does not further a logical resolution of the problem. This is true for several reasons.
>
> Implicit in Nix' argument is an acknowledgement that escape is a general-intent crime. Nix would say that, by choosing to charge him with *attempted* escape, the prosecutor injected the element of specific intent into the case. Therefore intoxication would be relevant in his case. . . .
>
> The trouble with this approach is the impossibility of drawing a line between escape and attempted escape. . . . Any escapee brought to trial was ultimately unsuccessful. . . . We believe the distinction between the two crimes is too flimsy to support a rule of law that would attach great importance to the prosecutor's choice between a charge of escape and one of attempted escape.
>
> This deficiency in the traditional analysis might be overcome by labeling both crimes as general-intent crimes . . . or as specific-intent crimes. . . . These labels are "often used in the cases but seldom defined." United States v. Williams, 332 F.Supp. 1, 3 (D.Md.1971). They were developed, at least with regard to intoxication, primarily to allow drunkenness as a defense to first-degree murder but not to lesser degrees of homicide. The attempt to apply the terms to nonviolent crimes such as escape has produced confused reasoning and disparate results. "Categorizing all crimes as either having 'general' or 'specific' intent seems too mechanical and often forecloses evaluation by the court of the important consideration involved, i.e., what elements are involved in the crime and whether the prosecution has satisfactorily established them." "Intoxication as a Criminal Defense," 55 Colum. L. Rev. 1210, 1217 (1955).
>
> Whenever intoxication (or coercion or mistake) is raised as a mitigating factor, use of the "specific" and "general" intent labels interferes with the crucial analysis a court should make in escape cases: what constitutes the "escape" element of the crime?
>
> Most courts, confronted with evidence that a defendant could not or did not form an intent to leave and not to return, have held such an intent essential to proof of the crime of escape. . . .
>
> . . .
>
> These cases lead us to a definition of escape as a voluntary departure from custody with an intent to avoid confinement. Whatever label is placed on this intent, a defendant under § 751 is entitled to an

instruction that includes this mental component as an element of the crime which the government must prove. If the defendant offers evidence that he was intoxicated at the time of the offense, the jury must be instructed to consider whether he was so intoxicated he could not form an intent to escape. The instructions in this case withdrew the mental element from the jury's consideration. In overruling Nix' objections to the two instructions quoted earlier, the district court erred.

501 F.2d at 518–20.

The relevance of voluntary intoxication to a specific state of mind as an element of an offense is restricted in some jurisdictions, by statute or by judicial decision. See, e.g., Commonwealth v. Bridge, 435 A.2d 151 (Pa. 1981) (voluntary intoxication not relevant to defendant's state of mind in prosecution for voluntary manslaughter); Griggs v. Commonwealth, 255 S.E.2d 475 (Va.1979) (voluntary intoxication relevant only to negate deliberation and premeditation of first-degree murder). See also State v. Stasio, 396 A.2d 1129 (N.J.1979), generally in accord with *Griggs*. In State v. Vaughn, 232 S.E.2d 328, 330–31 (S.C.1977) (burglary, assault with intent to ravish), the court evidently rejected the defense of voluntary intoxication altogether: "We adopt the rule that voluntary intoxication, where it has not produced permanent insanity, is never an excuse for or a defense to crime, regardless of whether the intent involved be general or specific. Reason requires that a man who voluntarily renders himself intoxicated be no less responsible for his acts while in such condition. To grant immunity for crimes committed while the perpetrator is in such a voluntary state would not only mean that many offenders would go unpunished but would also transgress the principle of personal accountability which is the bedrock of all law."

See State v. Ramos, 648 P.2d 119 (Ariz.1982), upholding the constitutionality of a statute making voluntary intoxication irrelevant except to disprove "the actual existence of the culpable mental state" of doing an act "intentionally" or with a specific intent. The defendant had contended that the statute was unconstitutional because it excluded consideration of intoxication in determining whether a person had acted "knowingly." But see Terry v. State, 465 N.E.2d 1085 (Ind.1984), in which the court held that a legislative provision restricting the defense of voluntary intoxication to specific intent crimes was unconstitutional. It said: "Any factor which serves as a denial of the existence of *mens rea* must be considered by a trier of fact before a guilty finding is entered." It added, however: "The potential of this defense of voluntary intoxication should not be confused with the reality of the situation. It is difficult to envision a finding of not guilty by reason of intoxication when the acts committed require a significant degree of physical or intellectual skills. As a general proposition, a defendant should not be relieved of responsibility when he was able to devise a plan, operate equipment, instruct the behavior of others or carry out acts requiring physical skill." Id. at 1088.

382. Courts generally have rejected voluntary intoxication as a defense to a charge of murder based on extreme recklessness. E.g., United States v. Fleming, 739 F.2d 945 (4th Cir.1984); Neitzel v. State, 655 P.2d 325 (Alaska Ct.App.1982); People v. Register, 457 N.E.2d 704 (N.Y.1983). It is the rule in most states that voluntary intoxication is not a defense to any crime for which only recklessness is required. The Model Penal Code so provides. § 2.08(2). In some states, however, statutory provisions explicitly or implicitly make voluntary intoxication relevant to the issue of recklessness. See 1 MPC Commentaries Part I, 358–59 & n.29.

383. There is a recognized exception to the rule that intoxication is not a defense that applies if a person becomes intoxicated *involuntarily*—because he is coerced or tricked into taking the intoxicating substance or is not aware that it is intoxicating—and loses the capacity to appreciate or control his conduct to such an extent that he is, in effect, "temporarily insane." E.g., City of Minneapolis v. Altimus, 238 N.W.2d 851 (Minn.1976). See Model Penal Code § 2.08(4). Cases in which the defense of involuntary intoxication has been accepted are rare.

Chronic alcoholism generally is not accepted as the basis for a claim that intoxication is involuntary. E.g., Shurbet v. State, 652 S.W.2d 425 (Tex.Ct.App.1982); see United States v. Poolaw, 588 F.2d 103 (5th Cir. 1979) (chronic alcoholism not a mental disease for purpose of insanity defense). On the relation of chronic alcoholism to criminal responsibility generally, see Powell v. Texas, 392 U.S. 514 (1968), p. 744 below.

If a defendant is so intoxicated that he is not able to act volitionally at all, his bodily movements do not constitute a crime. See State v. Smith, 296 S.E.2d 315 (N.C.Ct.App.1982) (unconsciousness or automatism due to intoxication is a "complete defense"). But see State v. Kolisnitschenko, 267 N.W.2d 321 (Wis.1978) (temporary psychosis resulting from interaction between voluntary intoxication and underlying mental disorder not a defense).

384. Corrivau went to a saloon in which Alain worked as a barkeeper. He had a few drinks. He argued with Alain and challenged him to fight; peace was restored. Corrivau became drunk. He spilled a drink on the bar and broke a glass. Alain threw him out of the bar. Corrivau threatened Alain, went across the street, obtained his gun and loaded it, and went back to the saloon. He made further threats, which a bystander reported to Alain, who came "out of the . . . door of the saloon, and walked rapidly towards [Corrivau], with his coat off and his hands at his sides. He was not armed, and there was nothing in his hands. When he was within about six feet of [Corrivau], the latter saw him, and said, 'There he is now,' raised his gun, and fired, striking the deceased in the abdomen, from the effect of which he died shortly before midnight." State v. Corrivau, 100 N.W. 638, 639 (Minn.1904).

What crime did Corrivau commit? How should the fact of his drunkenness affect the element of premeditation in first-degree murder, the element of provocation in voluntary manslaughter, or the defense of self-defense? With *Corrivau*, compare Commonwealth v. Lehman, 164 A. 526, 530 (Pa.1932). What disposition should be made of Corrivau's case? Why?

385. Consider the following cases:

(i) A, who suffers from a mental disease, because of which she fancies that she is persecuted, sees one of her supposed persecutors and shoots him.

(ii) B, who is 14 years old, is robbing a store and shoots the storekeeper to stop him from running out into the street.

(iii) C, who has been drinking at a bar all day and is very drunk, shoots a man who laughs when C offers to fight anyone in the bar.

Is there an overriding principle or set of principles according to which the law consistently determines the criminal responsibility of A, B, and C for their acts?

Are there any generally accepted principles of the criminal law according to which the law's determinations of the criminal responsibility of A, B, and C for their acts are inconsistent?

In each case, to what extent does the opportunity for treatment rather than punishment affect the offender's criminal responsibility?

4.   MISTAKE

FACT

We have already considered some cases in which a person makes a mistake of fact and causes or threatens to cause harm to someone else that the law tries to prevent. A believes that B is reaching for his gun and is about to shoot her, and uses deadly force against B; B was reaching for his handkerchief. C goes to the aid of her brother D, who is in a fight with E; it turns out that E was defending himself against an unjustified attack by D.

Q leaves the restaurant with an umbrella that she believes to be hers; when she opens it two weeks later, she sees R's name clearly marked on the inside.

In each such case, the apparent wrongdoer asks that her criminal responsibility be determined according to what seemed to her to be the facts. Her claim is not that no harm was done[81] but that she "didn't mean to" do the harm.[82] The criminal law, she asserts, should be concerned with knaves and not fools; still less should it be concerned with a person whose mistake was reasonable. In what situations should her argument be accepted or rejected?

---

386. What is the relevance in this context of the difference between A who uses deadly force in the reasonable but mistaken belief that it is necessary to defend himself against an aggressor, and Z who uses deadly force in the *un*reasonable, mistaken belief that it is necessary to defend himself against an aggressor? As we have seen, A is guiltless; Z commits some form of criminal homicide.

For no obvious reason, in a majority of jurisdictions the crime of bigamy has been held to be committed even though a husband or wife honestly and reasonably believes that he or she is no longer married; while acknowledging that the legislature certainly could make guilty intent an element of the offense, more often than not the courts have concluded that the omission of such a requirement from the statute defining the offense manifests a legislative determination that there be no such requirement.[83]

---

81. With respect to R's missing umbrella, see Holmes's analysis, p. 434 note 275 above.

82. "A relation between some mental element and punishment for a harmful act is almost as instinctive as the child's familiar exculpatory 'But I didn't mean to'. . . ." Morissette v. United States, 342 U.S. 246, 250–51 (1952).

83. MIKADO. . . . I forget the punishment for compassing the death of the Heir Apparent.

KO–KO.

POOH–BAH. Punishment. (*They drop down on their knees again.*)

PITTI–SING.

MIKADO. Yes. Something lingering, with boiling oil in it, I fancy. Something of that sort. I think boiling oil occurs in it, but I'm not sure. I know it's something humorous, but lingering, with either boiling oil or melted lead. Come, come, don't fret—I'm not a bit angry.

KO–KO. (*In abject terror*). If your Majesty will accept our assurance, we had no idea—

MIKADO. Of course you hadn't. That's the pathetic part of it. Unfortunately, the fool of an act says "compassing the death of the Heir Apparent." There's not a word about a mistake, or not knowing, or having no notion. There should be, of course, but there isn't. That's the slovenly way in which these acts are drawn. However, cheer up, it'll be all right. I'll have it altered next session.

KO–KO. What's the good of that?

MIKADO. Now let's see—will after luncheon suit you? Can you wait till then?

W.S. Gilbert, The Mikado, act 2 (first performed on March 14, 1885), at 96–97 (1911 ed.).

See, e.g., Braun v. State, 185 A.2d 905 (Md.1962) (sentence of five years' imprisonment); State v. De Meo, 118 A.2d 1 (N.J.1955). For a statement of the minority view, see People v. Vogel, 299 P.2d 850 (Cal.1956). See also State v. Audette, 70 A. 833, 834 (Vt.1908), holding that a man who innocently marries a married woman who represented herself as single is not guilty of adultery, because "the Legislature cannot have intended that one so defrauded should incur the penalty of adultery, although squarely within the terms of the statute."

Another crime which has generally been thus severely defined by the courts is "statutory" rape, sexual intercourse with a girl (or sometimes, more recently, a boy) under some specified age before which her consent is irrelevant. See, e.g., Commonwealth v. Moore, 269 N.E.2d 636 (Mass.1971); People v. Doyle, 167 N.W.2d 907 (Mich.Ct.App.1969) (same rule applied to "indecent liberties"). In Garnett v. State, 632 A.2d 797 (Md.Ct.App.1993), the court upheld the conviction for statutory rape of a mildly retarded 20-year-old man who had intercourse with a 13-year-old girl. The trial court excluded evidence that the girl and her friends had told the defendant that she was 16 years old, in which case he would have not violated the statute. Referring to its holding in *Vogel*, above, the Supreme Court of California again departed from the rule, in People v. Hernandez, 393 P.2d 673, 676 (Cal.1964), saying in part: "[The rule], rather than purporting to eliminate intent as an element of the crime, holds that the wrongdoer must assume the risk; that, subjectively, when the act is committed, he consciously intends to proceed regardless of the age of the female and the consequences of his act, and that the circumstances involving the female, whether she be a day or a decade less than the statutory age, are irrelevant. There can be no dispute that a criminal intent exists when the perpetrator proceeds with utter disregard of, or in the lack of grounds for, a belief that the female has reached the age of consent. But if he participates in a mutual act of sexual intercourse, believing his partner to be beyond the age of consent, with reasonable grounds for such belief, where is his criminal intent? In such circumstances he has not consciously taken any risk. Instead he has subjectively eliminated the risk by satisfying himself on reasonable evidence that the crime cannot be committed. If it occurs that he has been misled, we cannot realistically conclude that for such reason alone the intent with which he undertook the act suddenly becomes more heinous." Accord State v. Guest, 583 P.2d 836 (Alaska 1978); State v. Elton, 680 P.2d 727 (Utah 1984). See also People v. Mayberry, 542 P.2d 1337 (Cal.1975). *Hernandez* is rejected in People v. Cash, 351 N.W.2d 822 (Mich.1984). See also State v. Stiffler, 788 P.2d 220 (Idaho 1990) (crime of statutory rape, sexual intercourse with a woman under 18, is a crime of general intent; reasonable mistake about age not a defense).

In United States v. Brooks, 841 F.2d 268 (9th Cir.1988), the court held that the federal statutory rape provision, 18 U.S.C. § 2032, does not allow a defense of reasonable mistake of fact. In United States v. United States District Court for the Central District of California, 858 F.2d 534 (9th Cir.1988), however, the court said that the First Amendment requires that the defense be available in a prosecution for a violation of 18 U.S.C. § 2251(a), prohibiting employment of a person under 18 to engage in sexually explicit conduct for filming or photography. In order to establish the defense, the court said, the defendant must show "by clear and convincing evidence, that he did not know, and could not reasonably have learned, that the actor or actress was under 18 years of age." Id. at 543.

Hernandez was not applied to the crime of lewd or lascivious conduct with a child under the age of 14. People v. Olsen, 685 P.2d 52 (Cal.1984) (sexual intercourse with 13-year-old girl who looked 16 or 17). Similarly, the Alaska court did not apply *Guest*, above, to the crime of inducing a person under the age of 16 to engage in prostitution. Bell v. State, 668 P.2d 829 (Alaska Ct.App.1983). In Commonwealth v. Dunne, 474 N.E.2d 538 (Mass.1985), the court held that knowledge of the age of the victim is not an element of the crime of assault with intent to commit statutory rape, as it is not for the crime of statutory rape itself. Cf., e.g., United States v. Kairouz, 751 F.2d 467 (1st Cir.1985), holding that in a prosecution for importing a controlled substance, it is no defense that the defendant mistakenly thought he was carrying one controlled substance (cocaine) rather than another (heroin).

---

387. Is there more justification for rejecting a reasonable mistake about the girl's age as a defense to a charge of statutory rape than there is for rejecting a reasonable mistake about one's marital status as a defense to a charge of bigamy? Why (not)? Is it relevant that the maximum penalty for statutory rape is typically much more severe than the penalty for bigamy? If so, which way does the difference in penalties point? What is the relevance of society's attitudes respectively to remarriage after the death of or divorce from a spouse and to extramarital sexual relations with a person above the age of statutory rape?

388. Does the age below which the girl's consent is immaterial to the offense of statutory rape have a bearing on the question whether a mistake about her age should be a defense?

389. In United States v. Jewell, 532 F.2d 697 (9th Cir.1976), the defendant was prosecuted for "knowingly or intentionally" importing a controlled substance and possessing a controlled substance with intent to distribute it. He had driven a car across the border from Mexico to the United States, in a secret compartment of which a large quantity of marijuana was hidden. He testified that he did not know that the marijuana was there. After instructing the jury that an act is done "knowingly" if done "voluntarily and intentionally and not because of mistake or accident or other innocent reason," the trial judge instructed: "The Government can complete their burden of proof by proving, beyond a reasonable doubt, that if the defendant was not actually aware that there was marijuana in the vehicle he was driving when he entered the United States his ignorance in that regard was solely and entirely a result of his having made a conscious purpose to disregard the nature of that which was in the vehicle, with a conscious purpose to avoid learning the truth." Id. at 699 n.3, 700.

Citing extensive authority, the court sustained the instruction. It said:

It is worth emphasizing that the required state of mind differs from positive knowledge only so far as necessary to encompass a calculated effort to avoid the sanctions of the statute while violating its substance. "A court can properly find wilful blindness only where it can almost be said that the defendant actually knew." . . .

No legitimate interest of an accused is prejudiced by such a standard, and society's interest in a system of criminal law that is enforceable and that imposes sanctions upon all who are equally culpable requires it.

Id. at 704. Accord United States v. Caminos, 770 F.2d 361 (3d Cir.1985) (importing narcotics); United States v. McAllister, 747 F.2d 1273 (9th Cir.1984) (transportation of illegal aliens); United States v. Aleman, 728 F.2d 492 (11th Cir.1984) (importing narcotics).

The comment to the Model Penal Code § 2.02(7) states that this problem of wilful ignorance is taken care of by the provision that "knowledge" of a fact, as an element of an offense, is established "if a person is aware of a high probability of its existence, unless he actually believes that it does not exist." 1 MPC Commentaries Part I, 248.

The courts' treatment of mistake as it affects culpability for various crimes shows that there is not a distinct doctrine about "mistake of fact" in the criminal law. Whether mistake excuses, and if so whether it need be a reasonable mistake, depends in each case on the elements of the crime and the nature of the mistake. A man who carries off someone else's umbrella believing that it is his own or that the owner wishes him to have it does not commit theft because the intention that is an element of the crime of theft is absent. Mistaken belief that the owner is wealthy and can afford a dozen umbrellas does not provide a defense to a charge of theft; nor does mistaken belief that one is shooting at a man rather than a woman provide a defense to a charge of criminal homicide. There is no reason why such mistakes should provide a defense, since they are irrelevant to the offenses charged; they have no greater significance than mistaken belief that the day is Tuesday and not Wednesday.

LAW

"[E]very one must feel that ignorance of the law could never be admitted as an excuse . . . ." O. Holmes, The Common Law 41 (M. Howe ed. 1963). "It is no doubt true that there are many cases in which the criminal could not have known that he was breaking the law, but to admit the excuse at all would be to encourage ignorance where the law-maker has determined to make men know and obey, and justice to the individual is rightly outweighed by the larger interests on the other side of the scales." Id. See generally People v. Marrero, 507 N.E.2d 1068 (N.Y.1987).

Law pervasively affects our way of looking at matters "of fact" about ourselves and our affairs. Whether a particular matter is a matter of fact or of law is not always clear. In *De Meo*, p. 628 above, the defendant believed that he was not presently married and was free to remarry, because he had obtained a "Mexican mail order divorce" from his former wife. The divorce was invalid in New Jersey. Was his belief mistaken in fact or in law? If a woman mistakenly takes an umbrella because she believes that it is hers, the mistake would ordinarily be regarded as one of fact. Suppose she believes that the umbrella is hers because she mistakenly believes that an invalid contract for the sale of the umbrella to her is valid. See, e.g., United States v. Anton, 683 F.2d 1011, 1017–18 (7th Cir.1982) (construing 8 U.S.C. § 1326, illegal reentry of deported alien).

If, as in the last example, existence of the mistake establishes that an element—intent to steal—of the offense in question is lacking, the offense has not been committed, however one characterizes the mistake. The law has not (in this context) "determined to make men know and obey" the law of contracts under pain of the penalties for theft.[84]

---

84. "Whenever a special mental condition constitutes a part of the offence charged, and such condition depends on the question whether or not the culprit had certain knowledge with respect to matters of law, in every such case it has been declared that the subject of the existence of such knowledge is open to inquiry, as a fact to be found by the jury. This doctrine has often been applied to the offence of larceny. The criminal intent, which is an essential part of that crime, involves a knowledge that the property taken belongs to another; but even when all the facts are known to the accused, and so the right to the property is a mere question of law, still he will make good his defence if he can show, in a satisfactory manner, that being under a misapprehension as to his legal rights, he honestly believed the articles in question to be his own." State v. Cutter, 36 N.J.L. 125, 127 (Sup.Ct.1873). See also cases in which courts have held that reliance on the advice of counsel that conduct is lawful may help to establish that willfulness, an element of the offense charged, was absent. E.g., United States v. Phillips, 217 F.2d 435 (7th Cir.1954) (willful evasion of income tax); cf. United States v. Painter, 314 F.2d 939, 943 (4th Cir.1963).

Holmes had in mind cases in which, although a person knows what she is doing and characterizes her conduct accurately, she does not know that it is criminal. Is it true that everyone feels that she should not be excused? Or do we need to know more about the case? Consider the following:

(i) The defendant was captain of a ship. He quarreled with the captain of another ship at sea; after returning to his own ship he had three guns loaded with grapeshot fired at the second ship. While he was at sea, before the shooting, the law was changed to provide that all offenses committed on the high seas should be tried and punished as if committed on land; previously, only certain offenses at sea not including the defendant's had been so tried and punished. The defendant had no way of knowing about the change in the law. Rex v. Bailey, 168 Eng. Rep. 651 (1800). Should the defendant be prosecuted for willful and malicious shooting, pursuant to the new act?

(ii) The defendant had been convicted of forgery, a felony. She lived in Los Angeles and failed to comply with an ordinance requiring persons who had been convicted of a felony to register with the police and imposing a criminal penalty for noncompliance. She had no knowledge of the ordinance nor was it shown that there was any likelihood that she would have such knowledge. Lambert v. California, 355 U.S. 225 (1957). Did she commit a crime? Does it matter what the penalty for a violation of the ordinance is?

(iii) The defendant had been married in Delaware. He obtained a divorce decree in Arkansas and later remarried in Delaware. Before obtaining the divorce, he consulted a Delaware lawyer, who advised him that he could obtain a valid divorce in Arkansas with less embarrassment to his children and at less expense than he could in Delaware. Before remarrying he consulted the same lawyer, who advised him that he was free to remarry. The minister who performed the marriage ceremony also consulted the lawyer and was given the same advice. Long v. State, 65 A.2d 489 (Del.1949). If the Arkansas divorce was invalid in Delaware, did the defendant commit bigamy?

(iv) The defendant had a permanent place of business in Providence, Rhode Island, and in December opened a store temporarily in Woonsocket, Rhode Island. A statute required an "itinerant vender" to obtain a selling license. The defendant offered to deposit the amount required for the license and was advised by the state treasurer that the statute did not apply to him because he had a permanent place of business in the state. It was later decided that the statute applied to temporary businesses like the defendant's Woonsocket store. State v. Foster, 46 A. 833 (R.I.1900). Did he commit a crime?

(v) In 1902 and again in 1906, the Supreme Court of Iowa declared that state statutes prohibiting sales of liquor were unconstitutional because they violated the interstate commerce clause of the Federal Constitution. In 1908 the defendant made sales of liquor. In 1909 the Iowa court overruled its earlier decisions and held that the statute was constitutional. State v. O'Neil, 126 N.W. 454 (Iowa 1910). Did the defendant commit a crime?

(vi) The defendant was convicted of fishing without a permit. In post-conviction proceedings, the trial court declared the statute requiring a permit unconstitutional and set aside the conviction. The state appealed to the court of appeals, which certified the case to the supreme court. While the case was pending, the defendant was observed fishing by a state officer. The defendant admitted that he had no permit; the officer did not arrest him or try to stop him from fishing. A few days later, the state filed a request for a stay of the trial court's ruling; it alleged that because the defendant was continuing to fish without a permit, the stay was necessary to avoid "irreparable harm." The stay was granted. On the following day, the defendant was arrested for fishing without a permit on that day and on the earlier day. About two weeks later, the supreme court reversed the trial court and upheld the statute. The defendant's lawyer had advised him that he risked further prosecution by fishing while the case was on appeal but had said also that he was optimistic that the trial court's ruling would be upheld. Ostrosky v. Alaska, 913 F.2d 590 (9th Cir.1990). Did the defendant commit a crime on either day, or both?

(vii) A state statute proscribed the installation of gambling devices in a shop. The municipal court of Des Moines ruled that a gum-vending machine was not a gambling device. The distributors of the machine obtained a certified copy of the court decree and letters from the county attorney's office and the mayor stating that the machine was not a gambling device. They showed the documents to the defendant, who agreed to place a machine in his restaurant in the city. The municipal court and the county attorney's office (a representative of which later prosecuted the defendant) and the mayor turned out to be wrong. State v. Striggles, 210 N.W. 137 (Iowa 1926). Did the defendant commit a crime?

(viii) The defendant was a minister. He placed a sign at the entrance to his home, which said "Rev. W.F. Hopkins" and another sign along a highway which said "W.F. Hopkins, Notary Public, Information." A statute prohibited signs intended to aid in the solicitation or performance of marriages. Before erecting his signs, the defendant obtained an opinion of the State's Attorney that the signs did not violate the statute. The defendant performed a very large share of the marriages in the county. The State's Attorney was wrong. Hopkins v. State, 69 A.2d 456 (Md.1949). Did the defendant commit a crime?

(ix) Congress enacted a statute prohibiting anyone from doing business as a pawnbroker and charging more than six per cent interest in the District of Columbia without a license. "The defendant had been in business as a pawnbroker in Washington; but, anticipating the enactment of the . . . law, removed his headquarters to a place in Virginia at the other end of a bridge leading from the city. He continued to use his former building as a storehouse for his pledges, but posted notices on his office there that no applications for loans would be received or examination of pledges made there. He did, however, maintain a free automobile service from there to Virginia and offered to intending borrowers the choice of calling upon him in person or sending their application and security by a dime messenger service not belonging to him, but established in his

Washington building. If the loan was made, in the latter case the money and pawn ticket were brought back and handed to the borrower in Washington. When a loan was paid off, the borrower received a redemption certificate, presented it in Washington and got back his pledge." There was a steady stream of business through the Washington office. Horning v. District of Columbia, 254 U.S. 135, 136 (1920). As the defendant's course of conduct made plain, he did not intend to break the law. In fact, however, his conduct was within the statutory prohibition. Did he commit a crime?

In which of the cases does Holmes's argument against allowing the defendant's ignorance of the law to be an excuse apply?

In *Long*, case (iii) above, the court held that the defendant was not liable for bigamy. It conceded that Holmes's argument applied if (1) the defendant were unaware that his conduct was criminal because he did not know that the conduct in general was proscribed or (2) if he knew of the general proscription but concluded that it did not apply to him.

> But it seems . . . significantly different to disallow mistake of law where . . . together with the circumstances of the second classification, it appears that before engaging in the conduct, the defendant made a bona fide, diligent effort, adopting a course and resorting to sources and means at least as appropriate as any afforded under our legal system, to ascertain and abide by the law, and where he acted in good faith reliance upon the results of such effort. It is inherent in the way our legal system functions that the criminal law consequences of any particular contemplated conduct cannot be determined in advance with certainty. Not until after the event, by final court decision, may the consequences be definitely ascertained. Prior to the event, the ultimate that can be ascertained about the legal consequences consists of predictions of varying degrees of probability of eventuation. Hence, in the sense in which we are concerned with the expression, a "mistake of law" of the second or third classification refers to the failure of predictions of legal consequences to come to pass. No matter how logical, plausible and persuasive may be the bases for a prediction (assumptions, abstract legal rules, reasoning, etc.) a mistake of law arises if the prediction does not eventuate; and there is no mistake of law if the prediction eventuates.

> . . .

> Any deterrent effects upon the administration of the criminal law which might result from allowing a mistake of the third classification as a defense seem greatly outweighed by considerations which favor allowing it. To hold a person punishable as a criminal transgressor where the conditions of the third classification are present would be palpably unjust and arbitrary. Most of the important reasons which support the prohibition of ex post facto legislation are opposed to such a holding. It is difficult to conceive what more could be reasonably expected of a "model citizen" than that he guide his conduct by "the law" ascertained in good faith, not merely by efforts which might seem adequate to a person in his situation, but by efforts as well designed to

accomplish ascertainment as any available under our system. We are not impressed with the suggestion that a mistake under such circumstances should aid the defendant only in inducing more lenient punishment by a court, or executive clemency after conviction. The circumstances seem so directly related to the defendant's behavior upon which the criminal charge is based as to constitute an integral part of that behavior, for purposes of evaluating it. No excuse appears for dealing with it piecemeal. We think such circumstances should entitle a defendant to full exoneration as a matter of right, rather than to something less, as a matter of grace. Unless there be aspects of the particular crime involved which give rise to considerations impelling a contrary holding,—some special, cogent reasons why "justice to the individual is rightly outweighed by the larger interests on the other side of the scales"—a mistake of the third classification should be recognized as a defense.

65 A.2d at 497–98.[85]

---

390. Should Long have been found guilty if he had not consulted a lawyer before he remarried and had relied on the advice he received before he obtained a divorce? Suppose he had consulted only an Arkansas lawyer? Or only the minister who married him the second time? Suppose the lawyer whom he consulted was his brother, whose practice was largely tax cases. Suppose Long had limited funds and consulted a legal aid agency or a student group at a local law school.

391. Which other defendants in cases (i)–(ix) above should be exonerated under the reasoning of *Long*?

392. Should the defendant in *Ostrosky*, case (vi) above, benefit from the trial court's ruling that the statute was unconstitutional, if he fished after the ruling was stayed? If he was unaware of the stay, is he in a different position from any other defendant who is ignorant of the law?

For the most part, the courts have not accepted a mistake of law as a defense. In a few extreme cases like *Long*, *Lambert* (ii),[86] and *O'Neil* (v), the

85. Compare Staley v. State, 131 N.W. 1028, 1029 (Neb.1911), in which, holding the defendant liable, the court observed: "[The defendant] knew it was at least doubtful whether the [first] marriage was void. Otherwise he would not have asked the advice of counsel."

86. In *Lambert* the Supreme Court held, 5–4, that the defendant's conviction violated the Due Process Clause of the Four-

defense has been allowed. The Model Penal Code § 2.04(3)(b) codifies these special results and provides specific exceptions to the general rule: "A belief that conduct does not legally constitute an offense is a defense to a prosecution for that offense based upon such conduct when . . . [the actor] acts in reasonable reliance upon an official statement of the law, afterward determined to be invalid or erroneous, contained in (i) a statute or other enactment; (ii) a judicial decision, opinion or judgment; (iii) an administrative order or grant of permission; or (iv) an official interpretation of the public officer or body charged by law with responsibility for the interpretation, administration or enforcement of the law defining the offense." A defense based on this provision must be established by a preponderance of the evidence. § 2.04(4).

---

393. In which of cases (i)–(ix) above would the Model Penal Code's provision allow a defense?

The Code's provision appears to provide that the defense of mistake of law will be allowed only if the defendant relied on certain kinds of "official statement of the law." There is little reason to prefer one kind of official statement to another, however, and in fact almost any statement that is at all official is included in one of the Code's four categories. For example, the Code does not follow the ruling of the Supreme Court of Iowa in *Striggles* (vii) that a defendant might rely on its own decisions but not those of the municipal court. Compare United States v. Achter, 52 F.3d 753 (8th Cir.1995) (reliance on representations of state or local officials about federal firearms law not justified, since federal government not bound by erroneous interpretation of nonfederal officials); State v. Black, 380 N.E.2d 1261 (Ind.Ct.App.1978) (reliance on trial court's ruling that ordinance is

teenth Amendment. In dissent, Justice Frankfurter predicted that the decision would "turn out to be an isolated deviation from the strong current of precedents—a derelict on the waters of the law." 355 U.S. at 232. Compare Reyes v. United States, 258 F.2d 774 (9th Cir.1958); United States v. Juzwiak, 258 F.2d 844 (2d Cir.1958), both involving the failure of narcotics offenders to register as such before leaving the United States, as required by 18 U.S.C. § 1407. In United States v. Hutzell, 217 F.3d 966 (8th Cir.2000), the court held, over a lengthy dissent, that *Lambert* was not applicable to the crime of possessing a firearm after having been convicted of a misdemeanor crime of domestic violence, 18 U.S.C. § 922(g)(9). It approved the district court's conclusion that

"an individual's domestic violence conviction should itself put that person on notice that subsequent possession of a gun might well be subject to regulation." 217 F.3d at 968. See also United States v. Freed, 401 U.S. 601 (1971), distinguishing *Lambert* and holding that specific intent or knowledge was not essential to the crime of unregistered possession of firearms, 26 U.S.C. § 5861(d) (1982). "This is a regulatory measure in the interest of the public safety, which may well be premised on the theory that one would hardly be surprised to learn that possession of hand grenades is not an innocent act." 401 U.S. at 609. To the same effect, see United States v. International Minerals and Chemical Corp., 402 U.S. 558 (1971) (shipment of dangerous acids).

unconstitutional is justified if no appeal is pending and time for appeal has elapsed); State v. V.F.W. Post No. 3722, 527 P.2d 1020 (Kan.1974) (reliance on lower state court not allowed as defense). The Code's specification of the kinds of information on which the defense of mistake of law can be based is evidently intended to reject such a defense based simply on legal counsel's advice in a close case that conduct is lawful. It is not intended that a man who deliberately engages in conduct at the limits of what the law allows be able to defend himself against a criminal charge on the ground that his lawyer told him he could "get away with it."[87]

Does the Code accomplish its purpose? An "official statement of the law," however clearly stated, usually has to be applied by analogy to facts not precisely like those before the official body that made the statement. Advice of counsel will ordinarily be the source from which a person learns of a statute or decision or other official statement, and of the statement's bearing on his proposed course of conduct. Few persons can be expected to ask their lawyer to explain the basis of his advice, and few of those who do can be expected to evaluate it more than superficially. Indeed, a person who consults counsel and relies on his advice is probably acting more reasonably in most cases than a person (other than a lawyer, perhaps) who makes his own decision. Where counsel is consulted, may the effect of the Code's provision be to make the availability of the defense depend not on the actor's culpability but on the quality of his lawyer's judgment?[88]

In *Twitchell*, p. 304 note 174 above, should it make a difference whether the defendants read and interpreted the Attorney General's opinion themselves or relied on the interpretation of a Christian Science practitioner or an interpretation contained in a Christian Science journal?

Would it be preferable to limit the defense to cases like *Foster* (iv), *Striggles* (vi), and *Hopkins* (vii), in which the defendant has obtained an advisory opinion from an appropriate official that covers the particular facts of his case? If so, what of the defendant in *Long*?

---

394.   In Cheek v. United States, 498 U.S. 192 (1991), the Court held that a good-faith, albeit mistaken and unreasonable, belief that an act is lawful is a defense, if willfulness is an element of the offense. The defendant had failed to file income tax returns for a number of years and claimed that he had done so in reliance on his own study and the advice of a group that asserted that the tax laws were being unconstitutionally

---

87. "It may be assumed that [the defendant] intended not to break the law but only to get as near to the line as he could, which he had a right to do, but if the conduct described crossed the line, the fact that he desired to keep within it will not help him. It means only that he misconceived the law." Horning v. District of Columbia, 254 U.S. 135, 137 (1920), p. 634 above.

88. Would it be tolerable to allow the defendant's criminal liability to turn on a jury's or even a judge's determination that the "official statement of the law" on which the defendant (and, presumably, his lawyer) relied did or did not apply sufficiently clearly to the defendant's case?

enforced. The Court said that it was error to instruct the jury to disregard evidence of his belief "that, within the meaning of the tax laws, he was not a person required to file a return or to pay income taxes and that wages are not taxable income, as incredible as such misunderstandings of and beliefs about the law might be. Of course, the more unreasonable the asserted beliefs or misunderstandings are, the more likely the jury will consider them to be nothing more than simple disagreement with known legal duties imposed by the tax laws and will find that the Government has carried its burden of proving knowledge." Id. at 203–204. The Court added that claims that the tax laws are unconstitutional "are submissions of another order," id. at 205, a good faith belief in which would not preclude a finding of willfulness.

395. Should we distinguish between the person who tries conscientiously to conform his conduct to the law and the person who deliberately extends his conduct as far as the law allows? If they both have taken reasonable steps to learn what the law requires and are mistaken, should we treat them alike despite their rather different attitudes toward the law?

396. Is it so clear, as Holmes argued, that in every case when a man unwittingly breaks the law there are "larger interests" requiring that he be held guilty despite the demand of "justice to the individual"? In some cases are there larger interests which come out on the same side as justice? Is it relevant to consider:

(i) whether it is very important that no one engage in the prohibited conduct even once;

(ii) whether it is very important that people engage (if they choose) in conduct that is not prohibited but is similar to conduct that is prohibited;

(iii) whether the law can be made more clear;

(iv) whether the law can be made more widely known to people who are likely to disobey;

(v) whether the prohibited conduct is of a kind in which people who might rely on the defense of mistake of law are likely to engage?

LIABILITY WITHOUT FAULT

If a man engages in prohibited conduct because of a mistake that is not at all due to his own fault, is it ever the case that he should be found guilty of a crime because there are larger interests that override the demand of justice to the individual? The Supreme Court, with Holmes, has concluded that the legislature may so decide.[89]

"[T]hat category of offenses that dispense with a *mens rea* requirement," the Supreme Court has said, "embody the social judgment that it is fair to punish one who intentionally engages in conduct that creates a risk to others, even though no risk is intended or the actor, through no fault of his own, is completely unaware of the existence of any risk." United States v. Feola, 420 U.S. 671, 690–91 (1975). "Hardship there doubtless may be" under legislation that "dispenses with the conventional requirement for criminal conduct—awareness of some wrongdoing. In the interest of the larger good it puts the burden of acting at hazard upon a person otherwise innocent but standing in responsible relation to a public danger." United States v. Dotterweich, 320 U.S. 277, 281, 284 (1943) (shipping adulterated or misbranded drugs in interstate commerce). Similarly, in United States v. Balint, 258 U.S. 250, 254 (1922), the Court held that an innocent seller of narcotic drugs in violation of statutory requirements could be subjected to criminal penalties: "Congress weighed the possible injustice of subjecting an innocent seller to a penalty against the evil of exposing innocent purchasers to danger from the drug, and concluded that the latter was the result preferably to be avoided."[90]

The Supreme Court applied *Dotterweich* to the prosecution of the president of a large interstate retail food chain having "approximately 36,000 employees, 874 retail outlets, 12 general warehouses, and four special warehouses," in United States v. Park, 421 U.S. 658, 660 (1975) (6–3). The defendant (as well as the corporation of which he was president) was charged with allowing food held for sale after being shipped in interstate commerce to be exposed to contamination by rodents. The defendant acknowledged his general supervisory responsibility for the company's operations, and stated that he delegated responsibility for sanitary food storage to "dependable subordinates" and believed he had done all that he could have done. The Court said:

> *Dotterweich* and the cases which have followed reveal that in providing sanctions which reach and touch the individuals who execute the corporate mission—and this is by no means necessarily confined to a single corporate agent or employee—the Act imposes not only a positive duty to seek out and remedy violations when they occur but also, and primarily, a duty to implement measures that will insure that

89. "The power of the legislature to declare an offense, and to exclude the elements of knowledge and due diligence from any inquiry as to its commission, cannot, we think, be questioned." Chicago, B. & Q. R. Co. v. United States, 220 U.S. 559, 578 (1911). See Smith v. California, 361 U.S. 147, 150 (1959), suggesting that this power has limitations, evidenced by *Lambert*, p. 636 n.86 above. What limitations does *Lambert* establish?

90. See, e.g., People v. Dillard, 201 Cal. Rptr. 136 (Ct.App.1984) (misdemeanor of carrying loaded firearm in public place is a public-welfare, regulatory offense not requiring knowledge that firearm is loaded). For additional cases in which defendants were found criminally liable without fault, see 1 MPC Commentaries Part I, 284–91 (comment to § 2.05).

violations will not occur. The requirements of foresight and vigilance imposed on responsible corporate agents are beyond question demanding and perhaps onerous, but they are no more stringent than the public has a right to expect of those who voluntarily assume positions of authority in business enterprises whose services and products affect the health and well-being of the public that supports them. . . .

The Act does not, as we observed in *Dotterweich*, make criminal liability turn on "awareness of some wrongdoing" or "conscious fraud." The duty imposed by Congress on responsible corporate agents is, we emphasize, one that requires the highest standard of foresight and vigilance, but the Act, in its criminal aspect, does not require that which is objectively impossible. The theory upon which responsible corporate agents are held criminally accountable for "causing" violations of the Act permits a claim that a defendant was "powerless" to prevent or correct the violation to "be raised defensively at a trial on the merits." United States v. Wiesenfeld Warehouse Co., 376 U.S. 86, 91 (1964). If such a claim is made, the defendant has the burden of coming forward with evidence, but this does not alter the Government's ultimate burden of proving beyond a reasonable doubt the defendant's guilt, including his power, in light of the duty imposed by the Act, to prevent or correct the prohibited condition. Congress has seen fit to enforce the accountability of responsible corporate agents dealing with products which may affect the health of consumers by penal sanctions cast in rigorous terms, and the obligation of the courts is to give them effect so long as they do not violate the Constitution.

. . . The concept of a "responsible relationship" to, or a "responsible share" in, a violation of the Act indeed imports some measure of blameworthiness; but it is equally clear that the Government establishes a prima facie case when it introduces evidence sufficient to warrant a finding by the trier of the facts that the defendant had, by reason of his position in the corporation, responsibility and authority either to prevent in the first instance, or promptly to correct, the violation complained of, and that he failed to do so. The failure thus to fulfill the duty imposed by the interaction of the corporate agent's authority and the statute furnishes a sufficient causal link. The considerations which prompted the imposition of this duty, and the scope of the duty, provide the measure of culpability.

421 U.S. at 672–74.

In Liparota v. United States, 471 U.S. 419 (1985), the Court concluded that there is a requirement of *mens rea* in the crime of food stamp fraud under 7 U.S.C. § 2024(b), which provides that "whoever knowingly uses, transfers, acquires, alters, or possesses coupons or authorization cards in any manner not authorized by . . . [the statute] or the regulations" is guilty of an offense. The government contended that it had to prove only that the defendant committed the acts knowingly and that they were in fact unauthorized. The defendant argued that it had to prove that he committed the acts knowing that they were unauthorized. Acknowledging that Congress could have enacted a statute as the government claimed, the Court concluded that it had not done so in this case. To hold otherwise, it said, would make criminal "a broad range of apparently innocent conduct." Furthermore, in this case, unlike other cases involving "public welfare" offenses (e.g., *Dotterweich*, *Balint*, above) the conduct in question is not such "that a reasonable person should know is subject to stringent public regulation and may seriously threaten the community's health or safety." Id. at 426–27, 433.

See United States v. Johnson & Towers, Inc., 741 F.2d 662 (3d Cir.1984), involving the crime of disposal of hazardous wastes without a permit, in violation of the Resource Conservation and Recovery Act, 42 U.S.C. § 6928(d). The court held that knowledge of the requirement of a permit is an element of the offense, but that it may be appropriate, according to the evidence, to infer knowledge from the fact that a person holds a responsible corporate position. See also United States v. Anton, 683 F.2d 1011 (7th Cir.1982) (illegal reentry of deported alien; reasonable belief that reentry was lawful is a defense). But see Pena-Cabanillas v. United States, 394 F.2d 785 (9th Cir.1968).

––––––––

397. In Morissette v. United States, 342 U.S. 246, 253–56 (1952), Justice Jackson, for the Court, discussed crimes of this kind:

> The industrial revolution multiplied the number of workmen exposed to injury from increasingly powerful and complex mechanisms, driven by freshly discovered sources of energy, requiring higher precautions by employers. Traffic of velocities, volumes and varieties unheard of came to subject the wayfarer to intolerable casualty risks if owners and drivers were not to observe new cares and uniformities of conduct. Congestion of cities and crowding of quarters called for health and welfare regulations undreamed of in simpler times. Wide distribution of goods became an instrument of wide distribution of harm when those who dispersed food, drink, drugs, and even securities, did not comply with reasonable standards of quality, integrity, disclosure and care. Such dangers have engendered increasingly numerous and detailed regulations which heighten the duties of those in control of particular industries, trades, properties or activities that affect public health, safety or welfare.

> While many of these duties are sanctioned by a more strict civil liability, lawmakers, whether wisely or not, have sought to make such regulations more effective by invoking criminal sanctions to be applied by the familiar technique of criminal prosecutions and convictions. This has confronted the courts with a multitude of prosecutions, based on statutes or administrative regulations, for what have been aptly called "public welfare offenses." These cases do not fit neatly into any of such accepted classifications of common-law offenses, such as those against the state, the person, property, or public morals. Many of these

offenses are not in the nature of positive aggressions or invasions, with which the common law so often dealt, but are in the nature of neglect where the law requires care, or inaction where it imposes a duty. Many violations of such regulations result in no direct or immediate injury to person or property but merely create the danger or probability of it which the law seeks to minimize. While such offenses do not threaten the security of the state in the manner of treason, they may be regarded as offenses against its authority, for their occurrence impairs the efficiency of controls deemed essential to the social order as presently constituted. In this respect, whatever the intent of the violator, the injury is the same, and the consequences are injurious or not according to fortuity. Hence, legislation applicable to such offenses, as a matter of policy, does not specify intent as a necessary element. The accused, if he does not will the violation, usually is in a position to prevent it with no more care than society might reasonably expect and no more exertion than it might reasonably exact from one who assumed his responsibilities. Also, penalties commonly are relatively small, and conviction does no grave damage to an offender's reputation. Under such considerations, courts have turned to construing statutes and regulations which make no mention of intent as dispensing with it and holding that the guilty act alone makes out the crime. This has not, however, been without expressions of misgiving.[91]

Is Justice Jackson's distinction between the nature of crimes that do and those that do not require culpability persuasive? Is his explanation why some crimes need not require culpability?

398. In United States v. Wulff, 758 F.2d 1121, 1122 (6th Cir.1985), the court held that the provisions of the Migratory Bird Treaty Act that make it a felony to sell a migratory bird part, without any element of scienter, 16 U.S.C. § 707(b)(2), are unconstitutional: "[T]he crime is not one known to the common law, and . . . the felony provision is severe and would result in irreparable damage to one's reputation." See also State v. Guminga, 395 N.W.2d 344 (Minn.1986), holding that a state statute imposing vicarious criminal liability on an employer whose employee serves intoxicating liquor to a minor was unconstitutional under the state constitution. The court noted that the statute "does not distinguish between an employer who vigorously lectures his employees and one who does not," and said: "[I]n Minnesota, no one can be convicted of a crime punishable by

---

91. For one such expression of misgiving, see United States v. United States Gypsum Co., 438 U.S. 422 (1978), in which the Court held that intent is an element of a criminal antitrust offense. The Court observed that "intent generally remains an indispensable element of a criminal offense."

"While strict-liability offenses are not unknown to the criminal law and do not invariably offend constitutional requirements . . . the limited circumstances in which Congress has created and this Court has recognized such offenses . . . attest to their generally disfavored status." Id. at 437–38.

imprisonment for an act he did not commit, did not have knowledge of, or give expressed or implied consent to the commission thereof." Id. at 348–49. But see Stepniewski v. Gagnon, 732 F.2d 567 (7th Cir.1984), upholding a Wisconsin statute and regulations that made certain home improvement trade practices criminal without proof of intent or negligence. Compare Commonwealth v. Heck, 491 A.2d 212 (Pa.Super.Ct.1985), holding a vehicular homicide statute that required only ordinary negligence for a violation unconstitutional under the state constitution. The court noted that the crime, a misdemeanor, carried a maximum penalty of imprisonment for five years and imposed an "onerous moral stigma" on someone convicted under it.

————

The imposition of criminal liability without fault has been sharply criticized. There is neither a "moral justification . . . [nor] indeed, even a rational, amoral justification" "for condemning and punishing a human being as a criminal when he has done nothing which is blameworthy." Hart, "The Aims of the Criminal Law," 23 Law & Contemp. Prob. 401, 422 (1958). "In its conventional and traditional applications, a criminal conviction carries with it an ineradicable connotation of moral condemnation and personal guilt. Society makes an essentially parasitic, and hence illegitimate, use of this instrument when it uses it as a means of deterrence (or compulsion) of conduct which is morally neutral." Id. at 424. "To make a practice of branding people as criminals who are without moral fault tends to weaken respect for the law and the social condemnation of those who break it." G. Williams, Criminal Law 259 (2d ed. 1961). "The whole problem . . . arises from using the criminal process for a purpose for which it is not suited." Id. at 264. "Inasmuch as strict liability means that regardless of lack of intent, recklessness, negligence, the use of superior knowledge and skill, etc., penal liability must nonetheless be imposed, it is impossible to defend strict liability in terms of or by reference to the only criteria that are available to evaluate the influence of legal controls on human conduct." J. Hall, General Principles of Criminal Law 348 (2d ed. 1947).

"The liabilities involved are indefensible, unless reduced to terms that insulate conviction from the type of moral condemnation that is and ought to be implicit when a sentence of probation or imprisonment may be imposed. It has been argued, and the argument undoubtedly will be repeated, that strict liability is necessary for enforcement in a number of the areas where it obtains. But if practical enforcement precludes litigation of the culpability of alleged deviation from legal requirements, the enforcers cannot rightly demand the use of penal sanctions for the purpose. Crime does and should mean condemnation and no court should have to pass that judgment unless it can declare that the defendant's act was culpable. This is too fundamental to be compromised. The law goes far enough if it permits the imposition of a monetary penalty in cases where strict liability has been imposed." MPC Commentaries Part I, 283 (comment to § 2.05).

----

399. The Model Penal Code provides that culpability is an element of all offenses except "violations," §§ 2.02(1), 2.05(1)(a), which are not crimes and do not "give rise to any disability or legal disadvantage based on conviction of a criminal offense," § 1.04(5). The maximum penalty for a violation is a fine of not more than $500, § 6.03(4). Is this a satisfactory resolution of the problem of "strict liability"? What reasons are there for imposing fines for noncriminal "violations"?

400. Is the operation of the criminal law governed by common principles when the defendant commits a prohibited act and asserts that he is not criminally liable because of (i) insanity, (ii) infancy, (iii) intoxication, or (iv) mistake? If not, is the application of different principles justified by differences in the nature of the defenses?

----

401. So far in this Part, we have considered situations in which the defendant has unquestionably done harm that the law would like to prevent—no one claims that Drummond's death was not a bad thing[92]— and claims exoneration because he was not responsible for the harm in the sense or to the extent required by the criminal law. We are asked to focus our attention on the person and, so far as the criminal law is concerned, to disregard the harm. What if the situation is the converse: no prohibited harm is done, but the actor has unquestionably intended to do a prohibited act? What should be the role of the criminal law?

A is sitting alone in his library. He is brooding. On the previous day B, an acquaintance, beat him at a game of chess and before a group of onlookers said, "Ha, A, you are a toad at the game of chess. I knew I would beat you." A concludes that B has done him a great wrong. He decides to kill B.

Has A committed any crime?

He goes to his desk and writes down an elaborate plan to shoot B later that day.

Has he committed any (additional) crime?

---

[92]. Queen Victoria is said to have believed, however, that had M'Naghten succeeded in shooting Peel his death would not have been an *unmitigated* misfortune. See Hollis, "Essence of Parliament," 231 Punch 627 (Nov. 21, 1956) (report of debate on capital punishment).

A calls C, who has also been insulted by B, and discusses the plan with him. A and C agree to execute the plan together. They arrange to meet later that day and go to B's house, where they expect to find B.

Has A committed any (additional) crime?

C goes to the gun store and, in accordance with the A–C plan, purchases bullets for A's gun.

Has A committed any (additional) crime?

A and C meet and go to B's home. A is carrying his gun, now loaded with the bullets purchased by C. B is not there. A and C wait on the street.

Has A committed any (additional) crime?

A sees D, yet another of B's victims, and, without mentioning his arrangements with C, suggests to D that it would be better for all if B were dead. He points out that B is in excellent health and asks D whether he will not dispose of B for the betterment of all. D temporizes.

Has A committed any (additional) crime?

A sees the figure of a man in a window of B's house. Concluding that it is B, A fires. He hits the shop dummy that B has set in the window to play a trick on his wife. The dummy topples over. B is still at his office.

Has A committed any (additional) crime?

B comes home. A shoots him.

(A has committed an additional crime.)

5. ATTEMPTS

402. "A discussion of the law of criminal attempts usually commences with the statement that the problems involved are intricate and difficult to solve and that the cases are hopelessly confused." Arnold, "Criminal Attempts—The Rise and Fall of an Abstraction," 40 Yale L.J. 53 (1930). "[W]hen solution seems just within reach, it eludes the zealous pursuer, leaving him to despair ever of enjoying the sweet fruit of discovery." Hall, "Criminal Attempt—A Study of Foundations of Criminal Liability," 49 Yale L.J. 789 (1940).

———

People v. Rizzo

246 N.Y. 334, 158 N.E. 888 (1927)

■ CRANE, J. The police of the city of New York did excellent work in this case by preventing the commission of a serious crime. It is a great satisfaction to realize that we have such wide-awake guardians of our peace. Whether or not the steps which the defendant had taken up to the time of his arrest amounted to the commission of a crime, as defined by our law, is, however, another matter. He has been convicted of an attempt to commit the crime of robbery in the first degree, and sentenced to state's prison. There is no doubt that he had the intention to commit robbery, if he got the chance. An examination, however, of the facts is necessary to determine whether his acts were in preparation to commit the crime if the opportunity offered, or constituted a crime in itself, known to our law as an attempt to commit robbery in the first degree. Charles Rizzo, the defendant, appellant, with three others, Anthony J. Dorio, Thomas Milo, and John Thomasello, on January 14th planned to rob one Charles Rao of a pay roll valued at about $1,200 which he was to carry from the bank for the United Lathing Company. These defendants, two of whom had firearms, started out in an automobile, looking for Rao or the man who had the pay roll on that day. Rizzo claimed to be able to identify the man, and was to point him out to the others, who were to do the actual holding up. The four rode about in their car looking for Rao. They went to the bank from which he was supposed to get the money and to various buildings being constructed by the United Lathing Company. At last they came to One Hundred and

Eightieth street and Morris Park avenue. By this time they were watched and followed by two police officers. As Rizzo jumped out of the car and ran into the building, all four were arrested. The defendant was taken out from the building in which he was hiding. Neither Rao nor a man named Previti, who was also supposed to carry a pay roll, were at the place at the time of the arrest. The defendants had not found or seen the man they intended to rob. No person with a pay roll was at any of the places where they had stopped, and no one had been pointed out or identified by Rizzo. The four men intended to rob the pay roll man, whoever he was. They were looking for him, but they had not seen or discovered him up to the time they were arrested.

Does this constitute the crime of an attempt to commit robbery in the first degree? The Penal Law, § 2, prescribes:

> An act, done with intent to commit a crime, and tending but failing to effect its commission, is "an attempt to commit that crime."

The word "tending" is very indefinite. It is perfectly evident that there will arise differences of opinion as to whether an act in a given case is one *tending* to commit a crime. "Tending" means to exert activity in a particular direction. Any act in preparation to commit a crime may be said to have a tendency towards its accomplishment. The procuring of the automobile, searching the streets looking for the desired victim, were in reality acts tending toward the commission of the proposed crime. The law, however, has recognized that many acts in the way of preparation are too remote to constitute the crime of attempt. The line has been drawn between those acts which are remote and those which are proximate and near to the consummation. The law must be practical, and therefore considers those acts only as tending to the commission of the crime which are so near to its accomplishment that in all reasonable probability the crime itself would have been committed, but for timely interference. The cases which have been before the courts express this idea in different language, but the idea remains the same. The act or acts must come or advance very near to the accomplishment of the intended crime. . . .

The method of committing or attempting crime varies in each case, so that the difficulty, if any, is not with this rule of law regarding an attempt, which is well understood, but with its application to the facts. As I have said before, minds differ over proximity and the nearness of the approach. . . .

How shall we apply this rule of immediate nearness to this case? The defendants were looking for the pay roll man to rob him of his money. This is the charge in the indictment. Robbery is defined in section 2120 of the Penal Law as "the unlawful taking of personal property from the person or in the presence of another, against his will, by means of force, or violence, or fear of injury, immediate or future, to his person"; and it is made robbery in the first degree by section 2124 when committed by a person aided by accomplices actually present. To constitute the crime of robbery, the money must have been taken from Rao by means of force or violence, or through fear. The crime of attempt to commit robbery was committed, if these defendants did an act tending to the commission of this robbery. Did the acts above described come dangerously near to the taking of Rao's property? Did the acts come so near the commission of robbery that there was reasonable likelihood of its accomplishment but for the interference? Rao was not found; the defendants were still looking for him; no attempt to rob him could be made, at least until he came in sight; he was not in the building at One Hundred and Eightieth street and Morris Park avenue. There was no man there with the pay roll for the United Lathing Company whom these defendants could rob. Apparently no money had been drawn from the bank for the pay roll by anybody at the time of the arrest. In a word, these defendants had planned to commit a crime, and were looking around the city for an opportunity to commit it, but the opportunity fortunately never came. Men would not be guilty of an attempt at burglary if they had planned to break into a building and were arrested while they were hunting about the streets for the building not knowing where it was. Neither would a man be guilty of an attempt to commit murder if he armed himself and started out to find the person whom he had planned to kill but could not find him. So here these defendants were not guilty of an attempt to commit robbery in the first degree when they had not found or reached the presence of the person they intended to rob. . . .

For these reasons, the judgment of conviction of this defendant appellant must be reversed and a new trial granted.

. . .

———

403. Suppose that sometime before January 14, Rizzo had decided to commit the payroll robbery by himself[93] and that his intention was discovered before he had taken any steps to carry out the robbery. What reasons are there for holding him criminally liable at that point? What reasons are there for not holding him criminally liable?

404. Suppose that on January 13, Rizzo, still planning to act alone, had purchased a mask and a satchel to use in the holdup, had filled his car with gasoline, and had retired early to be ready to carry out his plan the next day. Is there significantly greater reason to hold him criminally liable than there was before he took those steps? Suppose he had also purchased a gun and loaded it.

405. All courts agree that the formation of an intention to commit a crime unaccompanied by the commission of any act toward its accomplishment does not constitute a crime. On what principles, of the criminal law or otherwise, is this conclusion based?[94]

406. A great many acts entirely innocent in themselves may be necessary steps toward the commission of a crime. Along the continuum from intent alone to a completed crime, how should the law distinguish between acts that are only "preparation," for which there is no criminal liability, and acts that constitute an attempt, for which there is criminal liability? Which of the following factors are significant?

(i) The nature of the intended crime.

"Since the extent to which criminal law may justifiably encroach upon and restrict the freedom and liberties of the individual varies directly with the extent to which social and public interests are endangered, it follows that the more serious the crime attempted or the greater the menace to the social security from similar efforts on the part of the defendant or others, the further back in the series of acts leading up to the consummated crime should the criminal law reach in holding the defendant guilty for an attempt." Sayre, "Criminal Attempts," 41 Harv. L. Rev. 821, 845 (1928).

In Commonwealth v. Kennedy, 48 N.E. 770 (Mass.1897), the defendant was charged with an attempt to murder Learoyd "by placing a quantity of

---

93. The relevance of the concerted action of the four robbers is considered in the materials on conspiracy, pp. 668–706 below. None of the other three appealed from his conviction. The court recommended that the district attorney call the matter to the attention of the governor, presumably for him to consider granting them a pardon. 158 N.E. at 890.

94. "We assume that the Legislature may fix the beginning of the crime at a point earlier than attempt, and identify it with the initial stages of combination or incitement or preparation." People v. Werblow, 148 N.E. 786, 789 (N.Y.1925).

deadly poison, known as 'rough on rats,' known to the defendant to be a deadly poison, upon, and causing it to adhere to the under side of the crossbar of a cup of Learoyd's, known as a mustache cup, the cup being then empty, with the intent that Learoyd should thereafter use the cup for drinking while the poison was there, and should swallow the poison.''

Writing for the court, Holmes said, ''Any unlawful application of poison is an evil which threatens death, according to common apprehension, and the gravity of the crime, the uncertainty of the result, and the seriousness of the apprehension, coupled with the great harm likely to result from poison even if not enough to kill, would warrant holding the liability for an attempt to begin at a point more remote from the possibility of accomplishing what is expected than might be the case with lighter crimes.'' Id. at 771. See People v. Townes, 474 N.E.2d 1334 (Ill.App.Ct. 1985) (defendant forced victim to stand in tub of water and dropped operating small electrical appliance into it; conviction of attempted murder sustained).

(ii) The nature of the act.

''[D]espite certainty as to criminal intention, the defendant must nonetheless be acquitted if he has not committed a substantial harm.'' Hall, ''Criminal Attempt—A Study of Foundations of Criminal Liability,'' 49 Yale L.J. 789, 825 (1940).

(iii) The manifestation of criminal intent.

''[T]he defendant's acts, taken as a whole, must strongly corroborate the required culpability; they must not be equivocal.'' United States v. McDowell, 705 F.2d 426, 428 (11th Cir.1983) (attempted possession of narcotics with intent to distribute). ''[T]he test to be applied is whether there is substantial evidence to support a finding that appellant committed some act which unequivocally manifested an existing intention to go forward to completion of the crime thus initiated." People v. Lyles, 319 P.2d 745, 747 (Cal.Ct.App.1957) (attempted burglary). There must be "an unequivocal overt act" toward commission of the crime. Gargan v. State, 436 P.2d 968, 971 (Alaska 1968) (attempted larceny).[95] "Whenever the design of a person to commit a crime is clearly shown, slight acts done in furtherance thereof will constitute an attempt." People v. Downer, 372 P.2d 107, 110–11 (Cal.1962) (attempted incest). See also People v. Bracey, 360 N.E.2d 1094 (N.Y.1977).

(iv) How much has been done.

"[A]ll that need be shown in a charge of attempt is the intent to commit a specific offense and an overt act constituting a substantial step toward commission of the crime." People v. Watson, 221 N.E.2d 645, 649 (Ill.1966) (attempted forgery). "[R]emote preparatory acts not reasonably in the chain of causation do not make out a case of attempt." Huggins v. State, 142 So.2d 915, 917 (Ala.Ct.App.1962) (attempt to have carnal knowledge). See United States v. Bilderbeck, 163 F.3d 971 (6th Cir.1999) (attempt to possess drugs); United States v. Rovetuso, 768 F.2d 809 (7th Cir.1985) (attempt to interfere with witness, 18 U.S.C. § 1512); United States v. Ivic, 700 F.2d 51 (2d Cir.1983) (attempted bombing); People v. Terrell, 459 N.E.2d 1337 (Ill.1984) (attempted armed robbery). The "substantial step" test is adopted and cases and statutes adopting it elsewhere are collected in Young v. State, 493 A.2d 352 (Md.1985). See the Model Penal Code formulation, p. 656 below, linking (iii) and (iv): "substantial step . . . strongly corroborative of the actor's criminal purpose."

In United States v. Joyce, 693 F.2d 838 (8th Cir.1982), the defendant flew to another city, where by prearrangement he met someone in order to purchase cocaine. He went to a hotel room with the apparent seller (an undercover agent), agreed on a price, and asked to see the cocaine. The seller gave him a wrapped package, which he immediately returned, saying that he could not see the cocaine. The package was partially unwrapped and passed back and forth. The defendant never showed his money and finally declared that he would not make the purchase. When he left, he was arrested and found to have more money than the agreed price on his person. Applying the Model Penal Code's provision, the court held that the evidence that the defendant had committed a "substantial step" toward possession of cocaine was clearly insufficient. *Joyce* is disapproved in United States v. McDowell, 705 F.2d 426 (11th Cir.1983), and distinguished in United States v. Rivera-Sola, 713 F.2d 866 (1st Cir.1983).

---

95. For an extreme version of the requirement that the act be "unequivocal," see Campbell v. Ward, [1955] N.Z.L.R. 471, 476 (1955): "[A]n overt act, no matter how proximate it may be, and even if it be the last step requiring to be taken in the commission of the crime, frustrated only by miscalculation or circumstances beyond the control of the actor, cannot be an attempt unless the act is in itself sufficient evidence of the intent to commit the particular crime" Cf. People v. Bowen, 158 N.W.2d 794, 801 (Mich.Ct.App. 1968) (the act "must manifest, or be symbolic of, the crime"); People v. Coleman, 86 N.W.2d 281, 285 (Mich.1957) (the defendant must have "gone beyond acts of an ambiguous nature").

(v) How much remains to be done.

"Acts in furtherance of a criminal project do not reach the stage of an attempt, unless they carry the project forward within dangerous proximity to the criminal end to be attained." People v. Werblow, 148 N.E. 786, 789 (N.Y.1925). "The crux of the determination of whether the acts are sufficient to constitute an attempt really is whether, when given the specific intent to commit an offense, the acts taken in furtherance thereof are such that there is a dangerous proximity to success in carrying out the intent." People v. Paluch, 222 N.E.2d 508, 510 (Ill.App.Ct.1966) (attempt to practice barbering without a license). "An overt act need not be the ultimate step toward the consummation of the design; it is sufficient if it is the first or some subsequent act directed towards that end after the preparations are made." People v. Fulton, 10 Cal.Rptr. 319, 325 (Cal.Dist. Ct.App.1961) (attempted theft). "Where the carrying out of an attempt to commit a crime is dependent upon and subservient to the conduct of some third person and that third person [not having agreed to the plan] . . . has the opportunity to frustrate the commission of the crime by refusing to accept the benefits of the plan, there can be no crime committed." State v. Block, 62 S.W.2d 428, 431 (Mo.1933) (attempted false pretenses). "Until defendant was armed with the alleged weapon, it was impossible for him to commit, or to take any step toward the commission of, the alleged offense." State v. Wood, 103 N.W. 25, 26 (S.D.1905) (attempted assault with a dangerous weapon).

(vi) Likelihood that the crime will be committed.

"[T]o constitute an attempt the acts of the defendant must go so far that they would result in the accomplishment of the crime unless frustrated by extraneous circumstances." State v. Judge, 131 N.W.2d 573, 575 (S.D. 1964) (attempted escape). "[T]he preparation must be such that, if not extraneously interrupted, it would be likely to end in the consummation of the crime intended." State v. Woodmansee, 205 A.2d 407, 410 (Vt.1964) (attempted arson).

(vii) Opportunity to desist.

"A neat doctrine by which to test when a person, intending to commit a crime which he fails to carry out, has 'attempted' to commit it, would be that he has done all that it is within his power to do, but has been prevented by intervention from outside; in short, that he has passed beyond any *locus poenitentiae.* Apparently that was the original notion, and may still be law in England; but it is certainly not now generally the law in the United States, for there are many decisions which hold that the accused has passed beyond 'preparation,' although he has been interrupted before he has taken the last of his intended steps." United States v. Coplon, 185 F.2d 629, 633 (2d Cir.1950) (attempt to deliver "defense information," 18 U.S.C. § 794). "[T]he defendant's conduct must pass that point where most men, holding such an intention as the defendant holds, would think better of their conduct and desist." Skilton, "The Requisite Act in a Criminal Attempt," 3 U. Pitt. L. Rev. 308, 309–10 (1937).

(viii) Proximity in time and space.

The overt acts "must be something more than mere preparation, remote from the time and place of the intended crime; but if they are not thus remote, and are done with the specific intent to commit the crimes, and directly tend in some substantial degree to accomplish it, they are sufficient to warrant a conviction." State v. Dumas, 136 N.W. 311, 314 (Minn.1912) (attempted arson). "The proximity of the overt acts to or their remoteness from the place where the substantive offense is to be committed enters largely into the question of whether the actual transaction has been commenced or not." People v. Lanzit, 233 P. 816, 819 (Cal.Dist.Ct.App. 1924) (attempted murder).

To what extent do the formulations suggested in (i)–(viii) differ in substance? Under which of them, if any, would Rizzo have been guilty?

For a review and discussion of the various formulations, which concludes that there is "fundamental agreement about what conduct will constitute a criminal attempt," see United States v. Mandujano, 499 F.2d 370, 376 (5th Cir.1974). *Mandujano*, which has been widely cited, substantially adopts the Model Penal Code formulation, p. 656 below. See also, applying the Model Penal Code, United States v. Dworken, 855 F.2d 12 (1st Cir.1988) (attempt to possess marijuana).

407.

Rodney Campbell, a convicted bank robber, agreed to cooperate with the F.B.I. on January 12, 1976 in return for a grant of immunity from prosecution for four armed bank robberies in which he admittedly participated between June and September, 1975. Arrangements were made for Campbell to use an undercover Government vehicle, provided with a tape recorder and monitoring equipment, to assist the authorities in apprehending some of his former accomplices. Campbell consented to the tape recording of all conversations taking place in his car.

After reestablishing contact with individuals named Larry Peterson, Willie Young, and appellant Johnny Sellers, Campbell transported the men in his specially equipped vehicle as they reconnoitered several banks in Queens, New York. The group began actual preparations for a robbery on Wednesday, January 21, by stealing ski masks from a department store. Later that day Peterson and Young appropriated surgical gloves from a hospital while Sellers, a recent patient, engaged several nurses in conversation. Finally, Peterson purchased a hacksaw and roofing nails which, he told Campbell, he needed to "fix" a shotgun.

On January 22, Sellers, Peterson, Young and Campbell perfected their plan to rob a branch of the First National City Bank in Whitestone, Queens. Peterson, formerly a factory worker in the neighborhood, advised the group that on Fridays (in this instance, January 23) large amounts of money would be on hand to accommodate industrial employees in cashing their salary checks. Young entered the bank on Thursday afternoon to examine its internal physical structure and reported to his colleagues that the tellers' counters were of average height and security was thin. The participants agreed to recruit appellant Clarence Stallworth to drive the getaway car.

On Friday morning Stallworth joined Young and Sellers, to whom he handed a .38 calibre revolver, and assumed the role of driver. Peterson met his comrades, gave them a sawed-off shotgun and distributed other paraphernalia required for the crime. En route to the bank in Whitestone the occupants of the Government-owned automobile covered their fingers with band-aids, their hands with surgical gloves and donned the ski masks. They prepared to destroy the vehicle after the robbery by stuffing gasoline-soaked newspapers under the seats.

The target bank was located in a small shopping center. As the car entered the parking lot, Sellers alighted and strolled past the bank several times, peering inside at each opportunity, as his accomplices circled the shopping center. At approximately 11 A.M., Stallworth stopped the vehicle directly in front of the bank. Sellers, who had stationed himself at an adjacent liquor store, started to approach the bank. Simultaneously, Campbell said, "let's go," and the occupants of the car reached for the doors. At this point, F.B.I. agents and New York City policemen, who had saturated the area as a result of intelligence acquired through the would-be robbers' monitored conversations, arrested the men without incident.

Appellants contend that their conduct, while admittedly sufficient to sustain a conspiracy conviction, punishable by a maximum of five years incarceration, will not support a judgment of attempted bank robbery, carrying a potential twenty-year prison term. They argue that their activities did not transcend a hypothetical fixed point on a spectrum of conduct culminating in the substantive offense of bank robbery.

United States v. Stallworth, 543 F.2d 1038, 1039–40 (2d Cir.1976). What result? If the defendants can be convicted of attempted bank robbery, how much sooner could they have been arrested and still be guilty of that crime? If they cannot be convicted of the attempt, how much longer must the police have waited before making the arrest for such a conviction to be valid?

In United States v. Prichard, 781 F.2d 179 (10th Cir.1986), the defendant was convicted of attempted bank robbery. Part of the plan was to hold the family of the bank manager hostage. On the night before the intended robbery, he was arrested as he was driving to the bank manager's house, evidently to watch the house. Summarizing the evidence, the court said: "Prichard spent two weeks observing the bank; he prepared a sketch of the bank; he had his supposed accomplice find out the bank manager's address and case the bank manager's home; he followed a different bank employee home who also was involved in opening the bank; he assembled the instruments necessary to commit the crime; and, finally, he went to the bank manager's house on the night of the arrest." Id. at 182. The court concluded that the defendant's conduct strongly corroborated his intent to rob the bank and affirmed the conviction. A conviction of attempted bank robbery was affirmed also in United States v. McFadden, 739 F.2d 149 (4th Cir.1984); United States v. Jackson, 560 F.2d 112 (2d Cir.1977).

In United States v. Harper, 33 F.3d 1143 (9th Cir.1994), police found the defendants sitting in a car parked in the lot of a bank after 10:00 p.m. Two loaded handguns were found hidden near the car, evidently placed there by the defendants. In the car were a roll of duct tape, a stun gun, and a pair of surgical gloves. One of the defendants was carrying another pair of surgical gloves and ammunition like that in one of the handguns. Earlier that night, one of the defendants had used an automatic teller machine to request a withdrawal but had not removed the cash from the cash drawer, thereby creating a "bill trap" that shut the machine down and led to service technicians being sent to repair the machine. The defendants' convictions for attempted bank robbery were reversed on appeal. The court said: "There is . . . a substantial difference between causing a bill trap, which will result in the appearance of potential victims, and moving toward such victims with gun and mask. . . . Making an appointment with a potential victim is not of itself such a commitment to an intended crime as to constitute an attempt, even though it may make a later attempt possible." Id. at 1148. (The defendants' convictions for conspiracy to rob the bank were affirmed.) A conviction of attempted bank robbery was reversed also in United States v. Still, 850 F.2d 607 (9th Cir.1988) (defendant arrested in van containing means for robbery, parked 200 feet away from bank); United States v. Buffington, 815 F.2d 1292 (9th Cir.1987) (defendant arrested in car in parking lot, not within 50 yards of bank).

MODEL PENAL CODE § 5.01. CRIMINAL ATTEMPT

(1) Definition of Attempt. A person is guilty of an attempt to commit a crime if, acting with the kind of culpability otherwise required for commission of the crime, he:

(a) purposely engages in conduct which would constitute the crime if the attendant circumstances were as he believes them to be; or

(b) when causing a particular result is an element of the crime, does or omits to do anything with the purpose of causing or with the belief that it will cause such result without further conduct on his part; or

(c) purposely does or omits to do anything which, under the circumstances as he believes them to be, is an act or omission constituting a substantial step in a course of conduct planned to culminate in his commission of the crime.

(2) Conduct Which May Be Held Substantial Step Under Subsection (1)(c). Conduct shall not be held to constitute a substantial step under

Subsection (1)(c) of this Section unless it is strongly corroborative of the actor's criminal purpose. Without negativing the sufficiency of other conduct, the following, if strongly corroborative of the actor's criminal purpose, shall not be held insufficient as a matter of law:

(a) lying in wait, searching for or following the contemplated victim of the crime;

(b) enticing or seeking to entice the contemplated victim of the crime to go to the place contemplated for its commission;

(c) reconnoitering the place contemplated for the commission of the crime;

(d) unlawful entry of a structure, vehicle or enclosure in which it is contemplated that the crime will be committed;

(e) possession of materials to be employed in the commission of the crime, which are specially designed for such unlawful use or which can serve no lawful purpose of the actor under the circumstances;

(f) possession, collection or fabrication of materials to be employed in the commission of the crime, at or near the place contemplated for its commission, where such possession, collection or fabrication serves no lawful purpose of the actor under the circumstances;

(g) soliciting an innocent agent to engage in conduct constituting an element of the crime.

————

408. Do provisions making an attempt to commit a crime itself criminal perform a function that would not be adequately served by more specific provisions proscribing particular conduct accompanied by a specific intent? Reconsider the crime of larceny and Holmes' analysis of it, p. 434 note 275 above. Consider such crimes as the possession of burglary tools, e.g., N.Y. Penal Law § 140.35, and "attempt to manufacture intoxicating liquor . . . by assembling the necessary apparatus for the purpose of manufacturing intoxicating liquor as prohibited by law," Tenn. Code Ann. § 39–2523 (deemed to be crime of unlawful manufacture).

————

IMPOSSIBILITY

————

If a person who intends to commit a crime carries out his plans and commits it, there is little point in mentioning that he attempted to commit it. Ordinarily we talk about "trying" to do something when the effort failed or is (or was) in doubt. The conduct that constitutes an attempt being something less than the conduct that constitutes the completed crime, the occurrence of an attempt leaves open the possibility that the intended crime will not be completed. It cannot be, therefore, that if an attempt to commit a crime fails, for that reason it does not constitute a criminal attempt.[96] Suppose, however, that it is obvious that there is no likelihood that the attempt will succeed.

"Obvious" to whom?

(1) Not to the actor. Unless he thinks he *might* succeed in doing X, he cannot be said to *intend* by his conduct to do X. And an intent to commit the crime in question is an element of a criminal attempt.

(2) Not to an *omniscient* observer, to whom it would be plain that every attempt that does in fact fail would fail.

It is somewhere along here, commonly considered under the rubric of "impossibility," that the "zealous pursuer," p. 647 note 402 above, ordinarily confronts despair.

(i)

People v. Siu, 271 P.2d 575, 575–76 (Cal.Dist.Ct.App.1954):

Jacob E. Siu, defendant in this case, was a sheriff's deputy in Los Angeles county assigned as bailiff to one of the criminal courts. He proposed to a fellow deputy, who was in the sheriff's narcotics detail, that that deputy supply him with narcotics for sale. Defendant said, "Do you have any connections for narcotics? I want something big. I have a connection that could handle any big quantity we could get."

The sheriff's narcotics deputy reported the conversation to his superiors, and was instructed to go along with defendant. So the next time he saw defendant he said to him, "Were you serious about what we were talking about the other day?" Defendant said, "Yes, I would like a large supply of heroin."

After that, the two men had several conversations, arranging for a delivery to defendant. Finally the narcotics deputy told defendant that he "had the stuff." They agreed to meet at defendant's home, where he had an office in which he conducted an insurance business on the side. Defendant said he would put the narcotics in his office safe.

The narcotics deputy met defendant outside his home, and delivered to him a package containing white powder. Defendant put the package into his trousers pocket. Then they went inside to the office.

---

96. An attempt to commit the crime charged is generally regarded as a "lesser included offense" within the crime charged. E.g., Fed. R. Crim. P. 31(c): "Conviction of Less Offense. The defendant may be found guilty of an offense necessarily included in the offense charged or of an attempt to commit either the offense charged or an offense necessarily included therein if the attempt is an offense."

Proof that a crime has been carried out generally does not prevent a conviction of an attempt to commit it, although occasionally a court has held to the contrary. A defendant may not, however, be convicted of a crime and an attempt to commit it, both based on the same transaction. See United States v. York, 578 F.2d 1036 (5th Cir.1978) (cases cited).

When defendant opened his safe to put the package into it, the narcotics deputy arrested him.

But the package did not contain heroin, nor any other narcotic. It had talcum powder in it.

The possession of heroin was unlawful. Siu was indicted for an attempt to possess narcotics unlawfully. What result? Why?

(ii)

State v. Guffey, 262 S.W.2d 152, 153–54 (Mo.Ct.App.1953):

Conservation agents . . . had procured the hide of a 2½ year old doe. . . . They had taken it to a taxidermist, who soaked it to soften it, stuffed it with excelsior and boards, inserted rods in the legs so it would stand upright and used the doe's skull in the head part of the hide so it would hold its former shape. For eyes, which had not been preserved, two small circular pieces of scotchlight reflector tape of a "white to amber color," had been placed over the eyeless sockets.

. . . The dummy was placed in a field. . . . The eight Conservation agents, fully armed, then concealed themselves in the brush on the south side of the road opposite the dummy and awaited the arrival of some citizen who might come that way, see the tempting bait and with visions of odoriferous venison cooking in pot or pan, decide not to wait until the 4th of December [when hunting season opened] to replenish his larder. . . .

. . .

[T]he State's evidence indicated that defendant Hoss, to use a colloquial expression, had shot the "stuffing" out of the dummy deer. . . . There was no evidence of a real live deer being anywhere in the vicinity.

There was abundant evidence that Hoss (and Guffey, who was with him) thought he was shooting at a real deer. They were charged with attempting to hunt deer out of hunting season. What result? Why?[97]

---

409. Clearly it is not a sufficient answer in each case that (i) Siu could not be convicted of possessing heroin, (ii) Hoss could not be convicted of hunting a deer out of season. Is it a sufficient answer that, in addition, (i) Siu could not be convicted of possessing talcum powder, and (ii) Hoss could not be convicted of hunting a dummy out of season, since there were no such crimes? Why (not)?

---

410. How do the actual cases differ from the following: (i) Siu arranges to purchase heroin from a "real" narcotics peddler who is a thief to boot and, following his usual practice, delivers talcum to Siu instead of heroin[98]; (ii) Hoss sees a real deer, but the sights on his gun are askew and, as anyone who knew anything about guns could have told him before he shot, he hadn't one chance in a thousand of hitting the deer? In these cases, are Siu and Hoss guilty of attempts?

Cases of this kind, involving circumstances in which it is appropriate to say not only that the attempt *did* not succeed but also that it *could* not succeed, are commonly discussed under the rubric of "impossibility." The cases fall more or less readily into two categories: those in which the actor's own steps toward the commission of the intended crime are bound to be ineffective, as if he attempts to commit murder by firing an unloaded gun or by conjuring; and those in which circumstances other than the actor's conduct are bound to make his efforts ineffective, as if he attempts to commit murder by firing a loaded gun at what turns out to be a dummy. In all such cases, there is

1) an intention to commit a crime; and
2) an effort to commit the intended crime; but

97. The court's conclusion in *Guffey* that the defendant was not guilty of an attempt was superseded by legislation like that of the Model Penal code, § 5.01(1)(a), p. 656 above. Mo. Stat., tit 38, § 564.011 (1995).

98. E.g., United States v. Pennell, 737 F.2d 521 (6th Cir.1984). In United States v. Oviedo, 525 F.2d 881 (5th Cir.1976), the defendant agreed to sell a pound of heroin to an undercover agent. He delivered a substance to the agent, who performed a field test on it with a positive result, and was arrested. An additional quantity of the same substance was found in a hiding place in his residence. The substance turned out not to be heroin but was something else, the possession of which was not unlawful. He was prosecuted for an attempt to distribute heroin. At trial, he testified that he had known that the substance was not heroin and was trying to "rip off" the agent. Can Oviedo be convicted of the attempt if the jury concludes that he believed the substance to be heroin? See, e.g., United States v. Hough, 561 F.2d 594 (5th Cir.1977); State v. Lopez, 669 P.2d 1086 (N.M.1983). Can he be convicted if the jury concludes that his testimony was truthful?

3) the effort is bound to fail.

How should such cases be decided? Since the rules governing attempts generally, as we have seen, require only (1) the intention, and (2) an effort sufficiently advanced to go beyond preparation, and since most attempts are crimes that failed, why be concerned about (3)? Why should criminal liability depend at all on the obviousness of failure? (The question, "Obvious to whom?" is still unanswered.) Is the conjurer, then, who does nothing but mumble hopefully fatal incantations over a cauldron guilty of attempted murder? Is he guilty of the same crime as the man who fires a gun into his enemy's bed just after his enemy has gone into another room or the man who fires a rifle with bad sights? If not, why not?

The problem of "impossibility" can be reformulated: For a criminal attempt, must there be, in addition to the criminal intent and the effort to carry it out, some (substantial) possibility of success? If one refers to the cases distinguishing preparation from attempt, it seems that the answer should be yes. If preparatory acts which *are* adapted to commission of the crime and make its commission more likely do not constitute an attempt, how can any acts that have no effect on the likelihood that the crime will be committed—since the crime is bound to fail—constitute an attempt?

Notice that in both *Siu* and *Guffey* the defendant's attempt—if it was an attempt—was prompted by deception of law officers who set up a situation to catch a criminal, a common characteristic of cases involving "impossibility"; in other such situations, a would-be thief tries to obtain property by false pretenses from someone who is not deceived and has already notified the police, e.g., Commonwealth v. Johnson, 167 A. 344 (Pa.1933) (intended victim a detective); see Harwei, Inc. v. State, 459 N.E.2d 52 (Ind.Ct.App.1984) (theft by deception; victim a police agent); an extortionist tries to obtain property by threats from someone who is unafraid and has told the police, e.g., People v. Camodeca, 338 P.2d 903 (Cal.1959); a fence receives "stolen" property from a thief, who has been caught and is working with the police with the consent of the owner of the property, e.g., People v. Rojas, 358 P.2d 921 (Cal.1961). See United States v. Farner, 251 F.3d 510 (5th Cir.2001) (enticing minor to commit criminal sexual activity; intended victim a federal agent), criticizing the factual/legal impossibility distinction. The frequency with which such cases arise in the law of attempts helps to identify one of the central difficulties of the problem of impossibility. People do not "try" to do what they know they cannot do. And "possibility" in its usual sense refers to what ordinary (reasonable) people with ordinary information can tell about the likely course of events. Ordinarily, therefore, in the absence of a situation structured to make look possible what is in fact impossible, or an odd actor like the conjurer in a contemporary community, we should have no difficulty in ignoring the fact that if we (or the defendant) had known all the facts in advance we could have predicted failure.[99] And the courts, for the most part, have so held. It is no less an attempt to commit larceny, or robbery, or

---

99. If the information and understanding of ordinary people about the relevant facts change, we might want to place in the impossibility category an attempt about

burglary that there is no property to be taken, as, for example, when a pickpocket reaches into an empty pocket, e.g., People v. Moran, 25 N.E. 412 (N.Y.1890); no less an attempt to commit murder that the victim is not where the actor (reasonably) expects him to be, e.g., State v. Mitchell, 71 S.W. 175 (Mo.1902), or that the means used could not actually kill, State v. Smith, 621 A.2d 493 (N.J.Super.Ct.1993) (HIV-positive inmate who bit corrections officer liable for attempted murder, even if bite could not transmit virus); no less an attempt to commit abortion that the woman is not pregnant, e.g., People v. Huff, 171 N.E. 261 (Ill.1930). On the defense of impossibility to a charge of attempted murder of a person (possibly) already dead, see People v. Dlugash, 363 N.E.2d 1155 (N.Y.1977).[100]

What then shall we say of the cases in which because of some deception (whether or not involving official action) or because the defendant lacks the awareness of ordinary men that an effort of the kind he is making is bound to fail, the ordinarily inconsistent statements (1) "He is trying to do X," and (2) "It is impossible that he will do X," are both true?

What is the purpose of making attempts criminal? What are the purposes properly to be served by criminal law?

Discussions of "impossibility" frequently distinguish between "factual impossibility" and "legal impossibility." For example:

> Generally speaking factual impossibility is said to occur when extraneous circumstances unknown to the actor or beyond his control prevent consummation of the intended crime. The classic example is the man who puts his hand in the coat pocket of another with the intent to steal his wallet and finds the pocket empty. . . . Generally, the cases which have imposed criminal liability for attempt where factual circumstances precluded commission of the intended crime have emphasized, as a primary requisite, proof of an intent to commit a specific crime.
>
> Legal impossibility is said to occur where the intended acts, even if completed, would not amount to a crime. Thus, legal impossibility would apply to those circumstances where (1) the motive, desire and expectation is to perform an act in violation of the law; (2) there is intention to perform a physical act; (3) there is a performance of the intended physical act; and (4) the consequence resulting from the intended act does not amount to a crime.

United States v. Berrigan, 482 F.2d 171, 188 (3d Cir.1973).

In *Berrigan*, the defendants were prosecuted for violations of 18 U.S.C. § 1791, which (supplemented by federal regulations, 28 C.F.R. § 6.1) makes it a crime to attempt to send letters into and out of a federal

---

which we formerly would have said only that it failed; or conceivably, if common information and understanding decrease, the reverse. Similarly, an attempted crime which to most people simply failed might be one that was impossible from the start to persons who have special knowledge.

100. Cf. People v. Rollins, 695 N.E.2d 61 (Ill.App.Div.1998), in which the defendant, convicted of murdering the victim by drowning her, argued that he was entitled to a mistake of fact defense, because when he threw her into the water he believed that she was already dead from the beating he had inflicted. The argument was rejected.

penitentiary "without the knowledge and consent of the warden." It was undisputed that, unknown to the defendants, the warden was aware that letters were being smuggled. The court concluded that this was a case of legal impossibility, and it reversed the convictions. "What the government did not prove—and could not prove because it was a legal impossibility— was the 'external, objective situation which the substantive law may require to be present,' to-wit, absence of knowledge and consent of the warden. Thus, the government failed to prove the *'Circumstances or attendant circumstances'* vital to the offense. Without such proof, the *Consequence* or Result did not constitute an offense that violated the federal statute." 482 F.2d at 189. (The quoted and italicized words are taken from Enker "Impossibility in Criminal Attempts—Legality and the Legal Process," 53 Minn. L. Rev. 665 (1969).) "We distinguish between the defense of factual impossibility, which is not involved here . . . and legal impossibility, which is. Even were we to concede that factual impossibility of success may not prevent an attempt, there can be no crime of attempt where there is a legal impossibility to commit a crime. Simply stated, attempting to do that which is not a crime is not attempting to commit a crime. Congress has not yet enacted a law that provides that intent plus act plus conduct constitutes the offense of attempt irrespective of legal impossibility. Until such time as such legislative changes in the law take place this court will not fashion a new non-statutory law of criminal attempt." 482 F.2d at 190.

Is it any easier to describe the warden's knowledge or its consequence as a "legal" impossibility than a "factual" impossibility? What difference does the label make in any event? Labels aside, are the court's analysis and result convincing? Compare United States v. Heng Awkak Roman, 356 F.Supp. 434 (S.D.N.Y.), aff'd, 484 F.2d 1271 (2d Cir.1973), and United States v. Oviedo, 525 F.2d 881 (5th Cir.1976), the facts of which are set out at p. 660, n.98 above. In *Oviedo*, the court observed that "a strict application of the *Berrigan* approach would eliminate any distinction between factual and legal impossibility, and such impossibility would *always* be a valid defense, since the 'intended' physical acts are never criminal." 525 F.2d at 884. See also United States v. Quijada, 588 F.2d 1253, 1255 (9th Cir.1978), in which, following the Model Penal Code and the preferred rule, the court said that "generally a defendant should be treated in accordance with the facts as he supposed them to be." In United States v. Everett, 700 F.2d 900 (3d Cir.1983), the reasoning in *Berrigan* is limited to the statute there in question; without quite saying so, the court cast considerable doubt on the reasoning in *Berrigan* generally. In United States v. Hsu, 155 F.3d 189 (3d Cir.1998), the court again questioned the viability of *Berrigan* and held that it was not a defense to a charge of attempted theft of trade secrets. The court observed that it was the only federal circuit that recognized the defense of impossibility any longer. Id. at 199–200.

———

411. People v. Jaffe, 78 N.E. 169 (N.Y.1906). The defendant was convicted of an attempt to commit a violation of § 550 of the Penal Code, which made it criminal to receive "stolen property . . . knowing the same to have been stolen." He had an arrangement with an employee of a dry goods firm that he would purchase goods that the employee stole from the firm. The employee was found out after he had stolen a roll of cloth but before he delivered it to the defendant. His employers cooperated with the police and allowed the employee to deliver the roll of cloth to the defendant, who paid the employee about half its value. When he took the roll of cloth the defendant believed that it was stolen property. The Court of Appeals held that the defendant was not guilty of an attempt. "The crucial distinction between the case before us and the pickpocket cases, and others involving the same principle, lies not in the possibility or impossibility of the commission of the crime, but in the fact that, in the present case, the act, which it was doubtless the intent of the defendant to commit would not have been a crime if it had been consummated. If he had actually paid for the goods which he desired to buy and received them into his possession, he would have committed no offense under section 550 of the Penal Code, because the very definition in that section of the offense of criminally receiving property makes it an essential element of the crime that the accused shall have known the property to have been stolen or wrongfully appropriated in such a manner as to constitute larceny. This knowledge being a material ingredient of the offense it is manifest that it cannot exist unless the property has in fact been stolen or larcenously appropriated. No man can know that to be so which is not so in truth and in fact. He may believe it to be so but belief is not enough under this statute. In the present case it appeared, not only by the proof, but by the express concession of the prosecuting officer, that the goods which the defendant intended to purchase had lost their character as stolen goods at the time of the proposed transaction. Hence, no matter what was the motive of the defendant, and no matter what he supposed, he could do no act which was intrinsically adapted to the then present successful perpetration of the crime denounced by this section of the Penal Code, because neither he nor any one in the world could know that the property was stolen property inasmuch as it was not, in fact, stolen property. In the pickpocket cases the immediate act which the defendant had in contemplation was an act which, if it could have been carried out, would have been criminal, whereas in the present case the immediate act which the defendant had in contemplation (to wit, the purchase of the goods which were brought to his place for sale) could not have been criminal under the statute even if the purchase had been completed, because the goods had not, in fact, been stolen, but were, at the time when they were offered to him, in the custody and under the control of the true owners.

"If all which an accused person intends to do would, if done, constitute no crime, it cannot be a crime to attempt to do with the same purpose a part of the thing intended." 78 N.E. at 169–70.[101]

The result in *Jaffe* has been regularly criticized and was rejected in People v. Rojas, 358 P.2d 921, 924 (Cal.1961). "[T]he criminality of the attempt is not destroyed by the fact that the goods, having been recovered

---

101. Compare, e.g., United States v. Monasterski, 567 F.2d 677 (6th Cir.1977), applying the usual rule that one cannot be convicted of possessing stolen goods knowing

by the commendably alert and efficient action of the Los Angeles police, had, unknown to defendants, lost their 'stolen' status. . . . In our opinion the consequences of intent and acts such as those of defendants here should be more serious than pleased amazement that because of the timeliness of the police the projected criminality was not merely detected but also wiped out." Accord, e.g., State v. Logan, 656 P.2d 777, 780 (Kan.1983), holding that the defense of legal impossibility had been eliminated by statute and observing: "The overwhelming trend in recent years has been the abolition of legal impossibility as a defense." Also, Commonwealth v. Henley, 474 A.2d 1115 (Pa.1984) (Pennsylvania statute; same).

(i) Should someone who, like Jaffe, purchases goods that the seller lawfully has in his possession be guilty of a crime if he incorrectly believes that the goods are stolen?

(ii) Was the decision in *Jaffe* correct?

(iii) If the answers to (i) and (ii) are "yes," how would you draft legislation to create criminal liability for someone like Jaffe?

(a) The Model Penal Code § 5.01(1)(a), p. 656 above, provides that a person is guilty of an attempt if, the other requirements being present, he engages in conduct "which would constitute the crime if the attendant circumstances were as he believes them to be . . . ."

(b) The New York Penal Law now provides for receiving stolen property as the crime of "criminal possession of stolen property," which is not committed unless a person "knowingly possesses stolen property." §§ 165.40–.50. Section 110.10 of the Penal Law provides: "If the conduct in which a person engages otherwise constitutes an attempt to commit a crime pursuant to section 110.00 [the general attempt section], it is no defense to a prosecution for such attempt that the crime charged to have been attempted was, under the attendant circumstances, factually or legally impossible of commission, if such crime could have been committed had the attendant circumstances been as such person believed them to be." Is that a good solution to the problem in *Jaffe*?

(c) Model Penal Code § 223.6(1). "Receiving. A person is guilty of theft if he receives, retains, or disposes of movable property of another knowing that it has been stolen, or believing that it has probably been stolen, unless the property is received, retained, or disposed with purpose to restore it to the owner." See, e.g., People v. Holloway, 568 P.2d 29 (Colo.1977), applying a similar statute.

412. Suppose Brown, more than a little absent-minded, has forgotten that he brought his own umbrella to the restaurant. Thinking it belongs to someone else, he takes and carries away his own umbrella with the intention of depriving the owner permanently of his property. Has he

them to have been stolen if before they were delivered to him the goods had been recovered by the owner and had lost their character as "stolen goods."

committed theft? The answer must be that he has not. However immoral his conduct may be, an element of larceny is taking and carrying away the property *of another*. Has he committed attempted theft? Suppose there were ten umbrellas in the rack from which he drew his own. (1) Might the attempt have been complete *before* he drew out his own? (2) If not, what, if anything, does the taking of his own umbrella add to his conduct for purposes of the crime of attempt? (3) Would it be desirable to have a statute providing that anyone who takes and carries away his own property believing that it is not his own and intending to deprive the supposed owner of his property commits a crime?[102]

413. If A, incorrectly believing that X is a crime, intends to do X, tries to do X, and does X, has he committed a crime? No one has had difficulty concluding that he has not. The commission of a lawful act, which is precisely the act intended, does not become a crime just because it is accompanied by a general willingness to break the law.

414. Renunciation. If the defendant's conduct constitutes an attempt to commit a crime, should it be a defense to the charge of attempt that he abandoned his criminal purpose before the crime was accomplished? The Model Penal Code § 5.01(4) provides that it is an affirmative defense that the defendant "abandoned his effort to commit a crime or otherwise prevented its commission, under circumstances manifesting a complete and voluntary renunciation of his criminal purpose." The code provides further that a renunciation is not voluntary if it is motivated by an increased danger of being caught or increased likelihood of failure, and is not complete if the intended crime is merely put off or modified in some respect. Id. See United States v. McDowell, 705 F.2d 426 (11th Cir.1983), petition for rehearing denied, 714 F.2d 106 (11th Cir.1983). In some of the jurisdictions that have considered the question, the defense has not been allowed. E.g., Wiley v. State, 207 A.2d 478 (Md.1965); Howard v. Commonwealth, 148 S.E.2d 800 (Va.1966). Suppose the defendant abandons his intention only in response to his intended victim's pleas. Compare Ross v. State, 601 So.2d 872 (Miss.1992) (abandonment defense to attempted rape

102. "Academic controversy has raged over the problem whether there could be a conviction for attempted larceny in the case where X, intending to steal Y's umbrella, takes his own in mistake for that of Y. To this there is no authoritative answer. The problem might be approached in the following way. If X, through mistake of law, thinks that a certain object, e.g. a corpse, is capable of being stolen, and if he makes off with it, then his mistake of law is irrelevant. He must be judged by what the law is, not by what he thinks it is; and since the law does not in fact prohibit the act which he intends to perform and does perform, he should not be guilty of either stealing or attempted stealing. But if his mistake is one of fact, e.g., he thinks that the umbrella belonging to him belongs to Y, then he should be judged according to what he thinks the circumstances are. Accordingly he should be guilty of attempted stealing, since the law prohibits the act intended." P. Fitzgerald, Criminal Law and Punishment 101 (1962). Do you agree? Why (not)?

accepted), with People v. McNeal, 393 N.W.2d 907 (Mich.Ct.App.1986) (abandonment defense to attempted criminal sexual conduct not accepted).

415. Some conduct that is accompanied by a culpable state of mind other than a criminal intent, such as recklessness, is a particular crime only if harm results. If no harm results, should such conduct be treated as an attempt to commit the crime?

In Thacker v. Commonwealth, 114 S.E. 504 (Va.1922), the defendant, who was drunk, was walking along the road with two companions. They entered a tent by the roadside and spoke to one of the occupants, who was lying in bed with her baby. After the men were back on the road, the defendant said he was going to shoot out the light of a lamp that was near the bed and fired three shots at the lamp. One bullet narrowly missed the woman and the baby. The defendant did not know the woman, and testified that he was simply shooting at the lamp, which he would not have done if he were sober.

What crime would he have committed if he had killed the woman or the baby? Having missed them both, was he guilty of an attempt? If he should be held guilty of crime, is it necessary to find him guilty of an attempt? Consider the Model Penal Code § 211.2: "Recklessly Endangering Another Person. A person commits a misdemeanor if he recklessly engages in conduct which places or may place another person in danger of death or serious bodily injury. Recklessness and danger shall be presumed where a person knowingly points a firearm at or in the direction of another, whether or not the actor believed the firearm to be loaded."

In State v. Johnson, 707 P.2d 1174, 1177 (N.M.Ct.App.1985), the court held that there is no crime of "attempted depraved mind murder," which would require that the defendant "intended to commit an unintended killing, a logical impossibility." The defendant had thrown a fire bomb into a mobile home when he knew the occupants were present. No one was killed. On such facts, the court said, the appropriate charge was attempted deliberate murder. But see People v. Castro, 657 P.2d 932 (Colo.1983) (attempted extreme-indifference murder a possible crime); People v. Thomas, 729 P.2d 972 (Colo.1986) (attempted reckless manslaughter). See also Charlton v. Wainwright, 588 F.2d 162 (5th Cir.1979) (attempted manslaughter by culpable negligence, involving "quasi-intentional" behavior). But see Taylor v. State, 444 So.2d 931 (Fla.1983), disapproving the reasoning in *Charlton* and restricting attempted manslaughter to cases in which, if death had resulted, the crime would have constituted *voluntary* manslaughter.

416. "It is the function of the law of criminal attempt to permit the courts to adjust the penalty in cases where the conduct falls short of a completed crime. . . . [T]he entire law of criminal attempt . . . admittedly is vague in that each case must be decided upon its own facts in determining whether the defendant's conduct has proceeded far enough toward the consummation of the crime to warrant punishment." State v. Wilson, 346 P.2d 115, 122–23 (Or.1959) (attempted assault). "The Law of Criminal Attempts and the Statutes making attempts generally punishable give the courts a power to extend the policy or limits of any particular criminal prohibition to cover (a) conduct which is not within the definition laid down by that rule but which in its tendencies is within its policy; or (b) conduct which is not sufficiently serious to make a court willing to apply the penalty provided in the particular rule invoked, but which it nevertheless feels should not go unpunished. We cannot go further than this without having the particular rule invoked before us." Arnold, "Criminal Attempts—The Rise and Fall of an Abstraction," 40 Yale L.J. 53, 76 (1930).

417. In view of the court's conclusion in *Rizzo*, had the police really done "excellent work," p. 647? Suppose Rizzo had been acting alone and was unarmed. What should the police have done when he jumped out of his car and ran into the building?

418. Criminal Solicitation. In a minority of states, by statute or common law, solicitation of crime, sometimes limited to serious crimes, is an offense whether or not the solicitation and accompanying conduct amounts to an attempt to commit the crime. The Model Penal Code § 5.02(1) provides: "A person is guilty of solicitation to commit a crime if with the purpose of promoting or facilitating its commission he commands, encourages or requests another person to engage in specific conduct which would constitute such crime or an attempt to commit such crime or which would establish his complicity in its commission or attempted commission." See generally United States v. Rovetuso, 768 F.2d 809, 822–23 (7th Cir. 1985) (solicitation as element of attempt).

419. What connections are there between the law's treatment of prohibited conduct that is accompanied by insanity, intoxication, infancy, or mistake, and conduct that is not otherwise prohibited but is prompted by an intention to engage in prohibited conduct?

6. CONSPIRACY

420. "For two or more to confederate and combine together to commit or cause to be committed a breach of the criminal laws is an offense of the gravest character, sometimes quite outweighing, in injury to the public, the mere commission of the contemplated crime. It involves deliberate plotting to subvert the laws, educating and preparing the conspirators for further and habitual criminal practices. And it is characterized by secrecy, rendering it difficult of detection, requiring more time for its discovery, and adding to the importance of punishing it when discovered." United States v. Rabinowich, 238 U.S. 78, 88 (1915).

"A conspiracy is constituted by an agreement. . . . [It] is a partnership in criminal purposes." United States v. Kissel, 218 U.S. 601, 608 (1910). "The gist of the offense is . . . the unlawful combination . . . ." Bannon v. United States, 156 U.S. 464, 468 (1895).

421. "The modern crime of conspiracy is so vague that it almost defies definition. Despite certain elementary and essential elements, it also, chameleon-like, takes on a special coloration from each of the many independent offenses on which it may be overlaid. It is always 'predominantly mental in composition' because it consists primarily of a meeting of minds and an intent." Krulewitch v. United States, 336 U.S. 440, 446–48 (1949) (Jackson, J., concurring).

422. Aiding and abetting. Liability as a conspirator is distinct from liability as an accomplice or "aider and abettor" of a crime committed by another person. Title 18 U.S.C. § 2(a), for example, provides: "Whoever commits an offense against the United States or aids, abets, counsels, commands, induces or procures its commission, is punishable as a principal." The development of the common law and the enactment of 18 U.S.C. § 2 are briefly traced in Standefer v. United States, 447 U.S. 10, 15–20 (1980), in which the Supreme Court held that a person may be convicted of aiding and abetting even though the named principal has previously been acquitted. The common law made distinctions among the parties to a felony as principal in the first or second degree, accessory before the fact, and accessory after the fact. There were not similar distinctions made with respect to misdemeanors; principals and accessories before the fact were alike treated as principals, and accessories after the fact were not included. Nor were there distinctions with respect to treason, all parties being equally guilty as principals. See 2 Stephen, History 229–40. Statutes have generally combined all the categories except accessory after the fact and treated persons within them alike as principals, as in the federal statute.[103]

---

103. The separate category of accessory after the fact typically covers those who assist a criminal after the crime is completed, usually to help him avoid detection or escape. See, e.g., 18 U.S.C. § 3: "Whoever, knowing that an offense against the United States has been committed, receives, relieves, comforts or assists the offender in order to hinder or prevent his apprehension, trial or punishment, is an accessory after the fact." A conviction under the statute is affirmed in United States v. Harris, 104 F.3d 1465 (5th Cir.

"Aiding, abetting, and counseling are not terms which presuppose the existence of an agreement. Those terms have a broader application, making the defendant a principal when he consciously shares in a criminal act, regardless of the existence of a conspiracy." Pereira v. United States, 347 U.S. 1, 11 (1954). To be liable as an aider and abettor one must have a "specific intent" or "purposive attitude" to aid commission of the crime. "The crime of aiding and abetting . . . occurs when an individual *associates* himself with a criminal venture, *participates* in it as in something he wishes to bring about, and seeks by his actions to make it succeed." United States v. Eddy, 597 F.2d 430 (5th Cir.1979). One who is merely present at the scene of the crime when it is committed and acquiesces in its commission without participating in any way is not liable as an aider and abettor. E.g., United States v. Hill, 464 F.2d 1287 (8th Cir.1972). "[M]ere knowledge that a crime is to be committed, even when coupled with subsequent concealment of the completed crime, does not make one guilty as an accessory before the fact or as a principal to the crime about which he has knowledge." Commonwealth v. Perry, 256 N.E.2d 745, 747 (Mass.1970).

"[E]ven without prior agreement, arrangement or understanding, a bystander to a robbery could be guilty of aiding and abetting its commission if he came to the aid of a robber and knowingly assisted him in perpetrating the crime. But regardless of the modus operandi and with or without a conspiracy or agreement to commit the crime and whether present or away from the scene of it, there is no aiding and abetting unless one 'in some sort associate himself with the venture, that he participate in it as in something that he wishes to bring about, that he seek by his action to make it succeed.' Nye & Nissen v. United States, 336 U.S. 613 (1949) [quoting from United States v. Peoni, 100 F.2d 401, 402 (2d Cir.1938)]." State v. Gladstone, 474 P.2d 274, 277–78 (Wash.1970). See United States v. Peichev, 500 F.2d 917 (9th Cir.1974).

As in cases of conspiracy, see pp. 672–83 below, it may be difficult to distinguish mere performance of an ordinarily lawful act accompanied by

1997). The maximum penalty under § 3 is one half the maximum penalty for the principal. More recent statutory formulations refer expressly to obstruction of justice or concealing or aiding a fugitive, and so forth. E.g., Ill. Rev. Stat., ch. 38, paras. 31–4, 31–5.

A related crime is "misprision of felony," which in its pure form was committed simply by failing to report a known felon. To the extent that misprision goes beyond liability as an accessory after the fact, it has for practical purposes been eliminated as a crime. See, e.g., Pope v. State, 396 A.2d 1054, 1068–78 (Md.1979). See generally United States v. Davila, 698 F.2d 715 (5th Cir.1983), upholding a conviction under 18 U.S.C. § 4, which provides that whoever having knowledge of the commission of a felony "conceals

and does not as soon as possible make known the same to some judge" or other authority commits a felony punishable by up to three years' imprisonment. "[M]ere failure to report a felony is not sufficient. Violation of the misprision statute additionally requires some positive act designed to conceal from authorities that a felony has been committed." Id. at 717. Cf. United States v. Jennings, 603 F.2d 650 (7th Cir.1979), holding that the defendants' prosecution for misprision violated their constitutional privilege against compulsory self-incrimination, because their reporting of the felony in question would have rendered them subject to prosecution themselves. Accord United States v. King, 402 F.2d 694 (9th Cir.1968).

knowledge that it will aid commission of a crime, like a sale of some item to be used in the crime, from aiding and abetting. The prevailing view is that there must be more than knowledge of the intended illegal purpose. For one to be liable as an aider and abettor, it is necessary that in some way he make the purpose his own. "All the words used—even the most colorless, 'abet'—carry an implication of purposive attitude toward it." United States v. Peoni, 100 F.2d 401, 402 (2d Cir.1938). For the contrary view, that selling with knowledge of the illegal purpose is sufficient for aiding and abetting, see Backun v. United States, 112 F.2d 635 (4th Cir.1940).

The drafters of the Model Penal Code originally proposed that a person be liable as an accomplice not only if he gives aid with the purpose of facilitating the crime but also if "acting with knowledge that such other person was committing or had the purpose of committing the crime, he knowingly, substantially facilitated its commission," Tent. Draft No. 1, § 2.04(3)(b) (1953), see 1 MPC Commentaries Part I, 315 n.47 (comment to § 2.06). The provision finally adopted, however, provides for liability as an accomplice only if one has "the purpose of promoting or facilitating the commission of the offense." § 2.06(3)(a).

The issue was whether knowingly facilitating the commission of a crime ought to be sufficient for complicity, absent a true purpose to advance the criminal end. The problem, to be sure, is narrow in its focus: often, if not usually, aid rendered with guilty knowledge implies purpose since it has no other motivation. But there are many and important cases where this is the central question in determining liability. A lessor rents with knowledge that the premises will be used to establish a bordello. A vendor sells with knowledge that the subject of the sale will be used in the commission of a crime. A doctor counsels against an abortion during the third trimester but, at the patient's insistence, refers her to a competent abortionist. A utility provides telephone or telegraph service, knowing it is used for bookmaking. An employee puts through a shipment in the course of his employment though he knows the shipment is illegal. A farm boy clears the ground for setting up a still, knowing that the venture is illicit. Such cases can be multiplied indefinitely; they have given courts much difficulty when they have been brought, whether as prosecutions for conspiracy or for the substantive offense involved.

. . .

Though the Chief Reporter favored a formulation that would broaden liability beyond merely purposive conduct, the Institute rejected that position, principally on the argument that the need for stating a general principle in this section pointed toward a narrow formulation in order not to include situations where liability was inappropriate. Many recent revisions and proposals reflect a similar judgment about accomplice liability. The possibility that a broadened liability should obtain in particular contexts is one that can be, and has been dealt with in the drafting of the substantive offenses themselves. . . . There is thus still room for the judgment that when the only interest of the actor is his wish to forego concern about the criminal purposes of others, though he knowingly facilitates in a substantial measure the achievement of such purposes, his interest is properly subordinated generally to the larger interest of preventing crime.

Some states have gone further . . . and have adopted general facilitation provisions. These extend accessorial liability to persons who engage in conduct with the awareness that it will aid others to commit serious crimes, but treat such facilitation as a less grave offense than the crimes that are aided. This approach may well constitute a sensible accommodation of the competing considerations advanced at the Institute meeting.

1 MPC Commentaries Part I, 315–19.

United States v. Falcone

109 F.2d 579 (2d Cir.), aff'd, 311 U.S. 205 (1940)

■ L. HAND, CIRCUIT JUDGE. These appeals are from convictions for a conspiracy to operate illicit stills. There were originally sixty-eight defendants, but the appeals before us concern only eight, which may be divided into two groups: one those of the appellants, Salvatore and Joseph Falcone, Alberico, John and Nicholas Nole; the other, of Grimaldi, Graniero and Soldano. Two other defendants, Milozzo and Melito, have withdrawn their appeals. The second group were actual distillers; the first supplied them and other distillers with sugar, yeast, and cans, out of which the alcohol was distilled, or in which it was sold. The evidence disclosed that in the year 1937 and 1938 within a radius of fifty miles from the City of Utica some twenty-two illicit stills had been set up, which were in each case to some extent operated after the same pattern; that is to say, real property was bought or leased, motor cars were registered, and applications for electric and water services were made, all in fictitious names; the equipment and materials were bought from the same persons; and the distillers frequented the same café or saloon, where they talked together. Grimaldi, Graniero and Soldano were all operators of one or more stills; the evidence of their guilt was ample. . . .

The case against Joseph Falcone was that during the year 1937 he sold sugar to a number of grocers in Utica, who in turn sold to the distillers. He was a jobber in Utica, and bought his supply from a New York firm of sugar brokers; between March first and September 14, 1937, he bought 8,600 bags of sugar of 100 pounds each, which he disposed of to three customers: Frank Bonomo & Company, Pauline Aiello, and Alberico and Funicello, all wholesale grocers in Utica. Some of the bags in which this sugar was delivered were later found at the stills, when these were raided by the officials; and Falcone was seen on one occasion assisting in delivering the sugar at Bonomo's warehouse, when a truckload arrived. His business in sugar was far greater while the stills were active than either before they were set up, or after they were seized, and we shall assume that the evidence was enough to charge him with notice that his customers were supplying the distillers. The evidence against Salvatore Falcone went no further than to show in various ways that he helped his brother in purchase of sugar during the period in question; there is really nothing to show that he knew its eventual destination. However, since in the view we take of the law he was equally innocent if he did, in disposing of his case we shall assume that he did know. Alberico was a member of the firm of Alberico and Funicello who, as we have just said, were buyers from Joseph Falcone. Alberico's purchases and sales of sugar also varied with the activity of the stills. In the first three months of 1937, when there were five or six of these operating in or about Utica, his purchases ran up to over a half-million pounds; after they had been raided in April, his business fell off to very little; when they became active again in September, his purchases rose again. A like correspondence, though less exact, was proved for the early part of the year 1938. A jury might also have taken the conversation which he had with one of the distillers, Morreale, as evidence of his knowledge of the kind of business that he was supplying. While the stills were active, Alberico also did a large business in five-gallon cans which he sold direct to the distillers. Many cans sold by him were found at the stills when they were raided. The evidence against Nicholas Nole consisted of his sales of yeast and cans to the distillers. The prosecution proved that in the spring of 1937 he had ordered and received shipments of imported yeast through a forwarding company of which he was the owner; and that in July and August of that year he bought of the Atlantic Yeast Company 8,300 pounds of yeast packed in wrappers, made expressly for the "Acme Yeast Company," a name under which he did business by virtue of a certificate, taken out for him by a cousin. Many of these wrappers were found at several of the stills. The case against John Nole depended upon the assistance which he gave his brother, Nicholas, and upon his being distributor for the National Grain Yeast Company for Utica during the years 1937 and 1938, a number of whose wrappers were found at the stills. Again we shall assume that the Noles knew that Nicholas's customers were illicit distillers.

In the light of all this, it is apparent that the first question is whether the seller of goods, in themselves innocent, becomes a conspirator with—or, what is in substance the same thing, an abettor of—the buyer because he knows that the buyer means to use the goods to commit a crime. . . . [I]n United States v. Peoni, 2 Cir., 100 F.2d 401 . . . we tried to trace down the doctrine as to abetting and conspiracy, as it exists in our criminal law, and concluded that the seller's knowledge was not alone enough. Civilly, a man's liability extends to any injuries which he should have apprehended to be likely to follow from his acts. If they do, he must excuse his conduct by showing that the interest which he was promoting outweighed the dangers which its protection imposed upon others; but in civil cases there has been a loss, and the only question is whether the law shall transfer it from the sufferer to another. There are indeed instances of criminal liability of the same kind, where the law imposes punishment merely because the accused did not forbear to do that from which the wrong was likely to follow; but in prosecutions for conspiracy or abetting, his attitude towards the forbidden undertaking must be more positive. It is not enough that he does not forego a normally lawful activity, of the fruits of which he knows that others will make an unlawful use; he must in some sense promote their venture himself, make it his own, have a stake in its outcome. The distinction is especially important today when so many prosecutors seek to sweep within the drag-net of conspiracy all those who have been associated in any degree whatever with the main offenders. That there are opportunities of great oppression in such a doctrine is very plain, and it is only by circumscribing the scope of such all comprehensive indictments that they can be avoided. We may agree that morally the defendants at bar should have refused to sell to illicit distillers; but, both morally and legally, to do so was toto coelo different from joining with them in running the stills. . . .

For these reasons the prosecution did not make out a case against either of the Falcones, Alberico, or John Nole; and this is especially true of Salvatore Falcone. As to Nicholas Nole the question is closer, for when he began to do business as the "Acme Yeast Company," he hid behind the name of a cousin, whom he caused to swear falsely that the affiant was to do the business. Yet it seems to us that this was as likely to have come from a belief that it was a crime to sell the yeast and the cans to distillers as from being in fact any further involved in their business. It showed a desire to escape detection, and that was evidence of a consciousness of guilt, but the consciousness may have as well arisen from a mistake of law as from a purpose to do what the law in fact forbade. We think therefore that even as to him no case was made out.

. . .

The convictions of Salvatore and Joseph Falcone, of Alberico and of Nicholas and John Nole are reversed. The convictions of Soldano, Grimaldi and Graniero are affirmed.

———

The government obtained review of the court of appeals' judgment reversing the convictions. In the Supreme Court, the government did not argue that the sales to the distillers were sufficient in themselves to constitute a conspiracy between buyer and seller. Rather it argued that by making sales to a distiller with knowledge of a conspiracy among the distillers, the sellers had made themselves parties to that conspiracy. The Supreme Court found that, even if the sellers knew of the intended illegal distilling, there was no evidence that they knew of a conspiracy among the distillers; and on that basis, the Court affirmed the judgment below. It said: "[O]ne who without more furnishes supplies to an illicit distiller is not guilty of conspiracy even though his sale may have furthered the object of a conspiracy to which the distiller was a party but of which the supplier had no knowledge." 311 U.S. 205, 210–11 (1940).

———

Direct Sales Co. v. United States
319 U.S. 703, 63 S.Ct. 1265, 87 L.Ed. 1674 (1943)

■ MR. JUSTICE RUTLEDGE delivered the opinion of the Court.

Petitioner, a corporation, was convicted of conspiracy to violate the Harrison Narcotic Act. It challenges the sufficiency of the evidence to sustain the conviction. Because of asserted conflict with United States v. Falcone, 311 U.S. 205, certiorari was granted.

Petitioner is a registered drug manufacturer and wholesaler. It conducts a nationwide mail-order business from Buffalo, New York. The evidence relates chiefly to its transactions with one Dr. John V. Tate and his dealings with others. He was a registered physician, practicing in Calhoun Falls, South Carolina, a community of about 2,000 persons. He dispensed illegally vast quantities of morphine sulphate purchased by mail from petitioner. The indictment charged petitioner, Dr. Tate, and three others, Black, Johnson and Foster, to and through whom Tate illegally distributed the drugs, with conspiring to violate §§ 1 and 2 of this Act,[104] over a period extending from 1933 to 1940. Foster was granted a severance, Black and Johnson pleaded guilty, and petitioner and Dr. Tate were convicted. Direct Sales alone appealed. The Circuit Court of Appeals affirmed. 131 F.2d 835.

The parties here are at odds concerning the effect of the *Falcone* decision as applied to the facts proved in this case. The salient facts are that Direct Sales sold morphine sulphate to Dr. Tate in such quantities, so frequently and over so long a period it must have known he could not dispense the amounts received in lawful practice and was therefore distributing the drug illegally. Not only so, but it actively stimulated Tate's purchases.

He was a small-town physician practicing in a rural section. All of his business with Direct Sales was done by mail. Through its catalogues petitioner first made contact with him prior to 1933. Originally he purchased a variety of pharmaceuticals. But gradually the character of his purchases narrowed, so that during the last two years of the period alleged for the conspiracy he ordered almost nothing but morphine sulphate. At all times during the period he purchased the major portion of his morphine sulphate from petitioner. The orders were made regularly on his official

104. The relevant portions of the Act restricted the sale of and other dealing in narcotic drugs; among the restrictions was a provision making it unlawful to sell the drugs except pursuant to the buyer's written order on an official form. As amended, 26 U.S.C. §§ 4704–05.

order forms. The testimony shows the average physician in the United States does not require more than 400 one-quarter grain tablets annually for legitimate use. Although Tate's initial purchases in 1933 were smaller, they gradually increased until, from November, 1937, to January, 1940, they amounted to 79,000 one-half grain tablets. In the last six months of 1939, petitioner's shipments to him averaged 5,000 to 6,000 half-grain tablets a month, enough as the Government points out to enable him to give 400 average doses every day.

These quantity sales were in line with the general mail-order character of petitioner's business. By printed catalogues circulated about three times a month, it solicits orders from retail druggists and physicians located for the most part in small towns throughout the country. Of annual sales of from $300,000 to $350,000 in the period 1936–1940, about fifteen per cent by revenue and two and a half per cent by volume were in narcotics. The mail-order plan enabled petitioner to sell at prices considerably lower than were charged by its larger competitors, who maintained sales forces and traveling representatives. By offering fifty per cent discounts on narcotics, it "pushed" quantity sales. Instead of listing narcotics, like morphine sulphate, in quantities not exceeding 100 tablets, as did many competitors, Direct Sales for some time listed them in 500, 1,000 and 5,000 tablet units. By this policy it attracted customers, including a disproportionately large group of physicians who had been convicted of violating the Harrison Act.

All this was not without warning, purpose or design. In 1936 the Bureau of Narcotics informed petitioner it was being used as a source of supply by convicted physicians. The same agent also warned that the average physician would order no more than 200 to 400 quarter-grain tablets annually and requested it to eliminate the listing of 5,000 lots. It did so, but continued the 1,000 and 500 lot listings at attractive discounts. It billed no more orders from Tate for more than 1,000 tablets, but continued to supply him for that amount at half-grain strength. On one occasion in 1939 he ordered on one form 1,000 half and 100 quarter grains. Petitioner sent him the 1,000 and advised him to reorder the 100 on a separate order form. It attached to this letter a sticker printed in red suggesting anticipation of future needs and taking advantage of discounts offered. Three days later Tate ordered 1,000 more tablets, which petitioner sent out. In 1940, at the Bureau's suggestion, Direct Sales eliminated its fifty and ten per cent discounts. But on doing so it translated its discount into its net price.

Tate distributed the drugs to and through addicts and purveyors, including Johnson, Black and Foster. Although he purchased from petitioner at less than two dollars, he sold at prices ranging from four to eight dollars per 100 half-grain tablets and purveyors from him charged addicts as much as $25 per hundred.

On this evidence, the Government insists the case is in different posture from that presented in United States v. Falcone. It urges that the effort there was to connect the respondents with a conspiracy between the distillers on the basis of the aiding and abetting statute. The attempt failed because the Court held the evidence did not establish the respondents knew of the distillers' conspiracy. There was no attempt to link the supplier and the distiller in a conspiracy *inter sese*. But in this case that type of problem is presented. Direct Sales was tried, and its conviction has been sustained, according to the claim, on the theory it could be convicted only if it were found that it and Tate conspired together to subvert the order form provisions of the Harrison Act. As the brief puts the Government's view, "Petitioner's guilt was not made to depend at all upon any guilt of Dr. Tate growing out of his relationship to defendants other than petitioner or upon whether these other defendants were linked with the Tate–Direct Sales conspiracy."

On the other hand, petitioner asserts this case falls squarely within the facts and the ruling in the *Falcone* case. It insists there is no more to show conspiracy between itself and Tate than there was to show conspiracy between the respondent sellers and the purchasing distillers there. At most, it urges, there were only legal sales by itself to Dr. Tate, accompanied by knowledge he was distributing goods illegally. But this, it contends, cannot amount to conspiracy on its part with him, since in the *Falcone* case the respondents sold to the distillers, knowing they would use the goods in illegal distillation.

Petitioner obviously misconstrues the effect of the *Falcone* decision in one respect. This is in regarding it as deciding that one who sells to another with knowledge that the buyer will use the article for an illegal purpose cannot, under any circumstances, be found guilty of conspiracy with the buyer to further his illegal end. The assumption seems to be that, under the ruling, so long as the seller does not know there is a conspiracy between the buyer and others, he cannot be guilty of conspiracy with the buyer, to further the latter's illegal and known intended use, by selling goods to him.

The *Falcone* case creates no such sweeping insulation for sellers to known illicit users. That decision comes down merely to this, that one does not become a party to a conspiracy by aiding and abetting it, through sales of supplies or otherwise, unless he knows of the conspiracy; and the inference of such knowledge cannot be drawn merely from knowledge the buyer will use the goods illegally. The Government did not contend, in those circumstances, as the opinion points out, that there was a conspiracy between the buyer and the seller alone. It conceded that on the evidence neither the act of supplying itself nor the other proof was of such a character as imported an agreement or concert of action between the buyer and the seller amounting to conspiracy. This was true, notwithstanding some of the respondents could be taken to know their customers would use the purchased goods in illegal distillation.

The scope of the concession must be measured in the light of the evidence with reference to which it was made. This related to both the volume of the sales and to casual and unexplained meetings of some of the respondents with others who were convicted as conspirators. The Court found this evidence too vague and uncertain to support a finding the respondents knew of the distillers' conspiracy, though not inadequate in some instances to sustain one that the seller knew the buyer would use the goods for illegal distilling. It must be taken also that the Government regarded the same evidence as insufficient to show the seller conspired directly with the buyer, by selling to him with knowledge of his intended illegal use.

Whether or not it was consistent in making this concession and in regarding the same evidence as sufficient to show that the sellers knew of and joined the buyers' distilling ring is not material. Nor need it be determined whether the Government conceded too much. We do not now undertake to say what the Court was not asked and therefore declined to say in the *Falcone* case, namely, that the evidence presented in that case was sufficient to sustain a finding of conspiracy between the seller and the buyer *inter sese*. For, regardless of that, the facts proved in this case show much more than the evidence did there.

The commodities sold there were articles of free commerce, sugar, cans, etc. They were not restricted as to sale by order form, registration, or other requirements. When they left the seller's stock and passed to the purchaser's hands, they were not in themselves restricted commodities, incapable of further legal use except by compliance with rigid regulations, such as apply to morphine sulphate. The difference is like that between toy pistols or hunting-rifles and machine guns. All articles of commerce may be put to illegal ends. But all do not have inherently the same susceptibility to harmful and illegal use. Nor, by the same token, do all embody the same capacity, from their very nature, for giving the seller notice the buyer will use them unlawfully. Gangsters, not hunters or small boys, comprise the normal private market for machine guns. So drug addicts furnish the normal outlet for morphine which gets outside the restricted channels of legitimate trade.

This difference is important for two purposes. One is for making certain that the seller knows the buyer's intended illegal use. The other is to show that by the sale he intends to further, promote and cooperate in it. This intent, when given effect by overt act, is the gist of conspiracy. While it is not identical with mere knowledge that another purposes unlawful action, it is not unrelated to such knowledge. Without the knowledge, the intent cannot exist. United States v. Falcone, supra. Furthermore, to establish the intent, the evidence of knowledge must be clear, not equivocal. Ibid. This, because charges of conspiracy are not to be made out by piling inference upon inference, thus fashioning what, in that case, was called a dragnet to draw in all substantive crimes.

The difference between sugar, cans, and other articles of normal trade, on the one hand, and narcotic drugs, machine guns and such restricted commodities, on the other, arising from the latters' inherent capacity for harm and from the very fact they are restricted, makes a difference in the quantity of proof required to show knowledge that the buyer will utilize the article unlawfully. Additional facts, such as quantity sales, high-pressure sales methods, abnormal increases in the size of the buyer's purchases, etc., which would be wholly innocuous or not more than ground for suspicion in relation to unrestricted goods, may furnish conclusive evidence, in respect to restricted articles, that the seller knows the buyer has an illegal object and enterprise. Knowledge, equivocal and uncertain as to one, becomes sure as to the other. So far as knowledge is the foundation of intent, the latter thereby also becomes the more secure.

The difference in the commodities has a further bearing upon the existence and the proof of intent. There may be circumstances in which the evidence of knowledge is clear, yet the further step of finding the required intent cannot be taken. Concededly, not every instance of sale of restricted goods, harmful as are opiates, in which the seller knows the buyer intends to use them unlawfully, will support a charge of conspiracy. But this is not to say that a seller of harmful restricted goods has license to sell in unlimited quantities, to stimulate such sales by all the high-pressure methods, legal if not always appropriate, in the sale of free commodities; and thereby bring about subversion of the order forms, which otherwise would protect him, and violation of the Act's other restrictions. Such a view would assume that the market for opiates may be developed as any other market. But that is not true. Mass advertising and bargain-counter discounts are not appropriate to commodities so surrounded with restrictions. They do not create new legal demand and new classes of legitimate patrons, as they do for sugar, tobacco and other free commodities. Beyond narrow limits, the normal legal market for opiates is not capable of being extended by such methods. The primary effect is rather to create black markets for dope and to increase illegal demand and consumption.

When the evidence discloses such a system, working in prolonged cooperation with a physician's unlawful purpose to supply him with his stock in trade for his illicit enterprise, there is no legal obstacle to finding that the supplier not only knows and acquiesces, but joins both mind and hand with him to make its accomplishment possible. The step from knowledge to intent and agreement may be taken. There is more than suspicion, more than knowledge, acquiescence, carelessness, indifference, lack of concern. There is informed and interested cooperation, stimulation, instigation. And there is also a "stake in the venture" which, even if it may not be essential, is not irrelevant to the question of conspiracy. Petitioner's stake here was in making the profits which it knew could come only from its encouragement of Tate's illicit operations. In such a posture the case does not fall doubtfully outside either the shadowy border between lawful cooperation and criminal association or the no less elusive line which separates conspiracy from overlapping forms of criminal cooperation.

Unless, therefore, petitioner has been exempted arbitrarily by the statute's terms, the evidence clearly was sufficient to sustain its conviction for conspiring with Tate. Its position here comes down ultimately to the view alluded to above that the statute has, in fact, thus immunized its action. In effect this means the only restriction imposed upon it, apart from other provisions not now material, such as those affecting registration, was the requirement it should receive from purchasing physicians a signed order form for each sale. That done, in its view, its full duty to the law was fulfilled, it acquired a complete immunity, and what the physician had done or might do with the drugs became of no further concern to itself. Such a view would legalize an express written agreement between a registered wholesaler and a physician for the former to supply him with all his requirements for drugs for both legal and illegal distribution, conditioned only upon his using the required order forms. The statute contains no such exemption in explicit terms. Nor was one implied.

This being true, it can make no difference the agreement was a tacit understanding, created by a long course of conduct and executed in the same way. Not the form or manner in which the understanding is made, but the fact of its existence and the further one of making it effective by overt conduct are the crucial matters. The proof, by the very nature of the crime, must be circumstantial and therefore inferential to an extent varying with the conditions under which the crime may be committed. But this does not mean either that the evidence may be equivocal or that petitioner is exempt from its effects when it is not so, merely because in the absence of excesses such as were committed and in other circumstances the order form would have given it protection. It follows the mere fact that none of petitioner's representatives ever met Dr. Tate face to face or held personal communion with him is immaterial. Conspiracies, in short, can be committed by mail and by mail-order houses. This is true, notwithstanding the overt acts consist solely of sales, which but for their volume, frequency and prolonged repetition, coupled with the seller's unlawful intent to further the buyer's project, would be wholly lawful transactions.

Accordingly, the judgment is

Affirmed.

---

423.   People v. Lauria, 59 Cal.Rptr. 628, 630 (Ct.App.1967):

In an investigation of call-girl activity the police focused their attention on three prostitutes actively plying their trade on call, each of whom was using Lauria's telephone answering service, presumably for business purposes.

On January 8, 1965, Stella Weeks, a policewoman, signed up for telephone service with Lauria's answering service. Mrs. Weeks, in the course of her conversation with Lauria's office manager, hinted broadly that she was a prostitute concerned with the secrecy of her activities and their concealment from the police. She was assured that the operation of the service was discreet and "about as safe as you can get." It was arranged that Mrs. Weeks need not leave her address with the answering service, but could pick up her calls and pay her bills in person.

On February 11, Mrs. Weeks talked to Lauria on the telephone and told him her business was modelling and she had been referred to the answering service by Terry, one of the three prostitutes under investigation. She complained that because of the operation of the service she had lost two valuable customers, referred to as tricks. Lauria defended his service and said that her friends had probably lied to her about having left calls for her. But he did not respond to Mrs. Weeks' hints that she needed customers in order to make money, other than to invite her to his house for a personal visit in order to get better acquainted. In the course of his talk he said "his business was taking messages."

On February 15, Mrs. Weeks talked on the telephone to Lauria's office manager and again complained of two lost calls, which she described as a $50 and a $100 trick. On investigation the office manager could find nothing wrong, but she said she would alert the switchboard operators about slip-ups on calls.

On April 1 Lauria and the three prostitutes were arrested. Lauria complained to the police that this attention was undeserved, stating that Hollywood Call Board had 60 to 70 prostitutes on its board while his own service had only 9 or 10, that he kept separate records for known or suspected prostitutes for the convenience of himself and the police. When asked if his records were available to police who might come to the office to investigate call girls, Lauria replied that they were whenever the police had a specific name. However, his service didn't "arbitrarily tell the police about prostitutes on our board. As long as they pay their bills we tolerate them." In a subsequent voluntary appearance before the Grand Jury Lauria testified he had always cooperated with the police. But he admitted he knew some of his customers were prostitutes, and he knew Terry was a prostitute because he had personally used her services, and he knew she was paying for 500 calls a month.

Lauria and the three prostitutes were indicted for conspiracy to commit prostitution. . . .

Was Lauria guilty of conspiracy? What is the relevance of the facts, separately or in combination, that:

(1) Lauria did not encourage or direct the prostitutes' business;

(2) he charged prostitutes the regular rates for the answering service;

(3) the answering service had legitimate uses as well as its use for furthering prostitution;

(4) there were not an unusually large number of prostitutes using Lauria's service;

(5) prostitution was a misdemeanor?

Is it of any significance that § 316 of the California Penal Code provides that it is a misdemeanor to let an apartment with knowledge that it will be used for prostitution? With *Lauria*, compare People v. Roy, 59 Cal.Rptr. 636 (Ct.App.1967).

424. In United States v. Morse, 851 F.2d 1317 (11th Cir.1988), the court upheld the defendant's convictions for conspiracy to possess marijuana with intent to distribute it and conspiracy to import marijuana. The basis of the conviction was the defendant's sale of an airplane to two marijuana smugglers. The court said that there were facts in addition to the sale that supported the conviction: that the airplane was without seats, which facilitated the transportation of cargo; that the defendant raised his price from $80,000 to $114,000, almost twice its market value; that the down payment was paid in cash in small denominations; and that there was no contract or receipt for the sale, which also was not reported to the FAA as required by law. Do those facts do more than prove knowledge of the purchasers' intended use? See generally United States v. Moran, 984 F.2d 1299 (1st Cir.1993).

425. "No one can join a conspiracy without knowledge of its existence—the gravamen is an *agreement* to commit an offense. . . . And even with knowledge that a conspiracy exists, one who allegedly 'joins' only by furnishing some peripheral services can hardly be deemed to have 'agreed' to conspire through his conduct unless he has the aim to forward or assist the conspiracy." United States v. Garcia-Torres, 280 F.3d 1 (1st Cir.2002).

"The agreement need not be explicit, but may be inferred from circumstantial evidence . . . and once the existence of a conspiracy is established, 'evidence establishing beyond a reasonable doubt a connection of a defendant with the conspiracy, even though the *connection is slight*, is sufficient to convict him with knowing participation in the conspiracy.' United States v. Dunn, 564 F.2d 348, 357 (9th Cir.1977) (emphasis in original). . . . On the other hand, there can be no conviction for guilt by association, and it is clear that mere association with members of a conspiracy, the existence of an opportunity to join a conspiracy, or simple knowledge, approval of, or acquiescence in the object or purpose of the conspiracy, without an intention and agreement to accomplish a specific illegal objective, is not sufficient to make one a conspirator. . . . While each of these circumstances may be a relevant factor to be considered in a given case where existence of an agreement is in issue, no mere suspicion or surmise is permitted to replace the essential analysis of the qualitative nature of the acts in question. . . . The line between conspiracy and an unexercised opportunity to join a conspiracy may be difficult to draw, but it must be drawn where the existence of an agreement is absent." United States v. Melchor-Lopez, 627 F.2d 886, 891 (9th Cir.1980).

426. In *Falcone*, the court noted that one of the defendants, Nicholas Nole, showed "a consciousness of guilt," p. 674 above, by attempting to conceal his identity as a seller of yeast and cans to the distributors but that this may have been from a mistaken belief that it was unlawful to make the sales rather than from guilty participation in the conspiracy. Even if the supposed mistake did not make the sales themselves unlawful, might it have a bearing on the existence of a conspiracy between him and the buyers?

427. Rather than prosecute the sellers in *Falcone*, would the Government have done better to recommend to Congress that it enact a statute making it unlawful to sell sugar, yeast, cans, etc., with knowledge that they will be used in an unlawful distilling operation?

In what circumstances, if any, ought knowledge of an intended unlawful use be enough to make the sale of an uncontrolled product unlawful?

428. In *Direct Sales*, the Court adverted to the possibility of liability as an aider and abettor to a conspiracy, see p. 677 above. In United States v. Galiffa, 734 F.2d 306 (7th Cir.1984), the court held that such liability was established by the performance of errands to further achievement of the object of the conspiracy with knowledge that there was a conspiracy. See also United States v. Kasvin, 757 F.2d 887 (7th Cir.1985), the dissenting opinion in which questions the extent of liability approved in *Galiffa*.

429. None of Direct Sales's representatives ever met Dr. Tate or "held personal communion with him"; the agreement was a "tacit understanding," p. 680 above. The conduct on which the Government relied to show such an understanding was apparently itself violative of the act which they were convicted of conspiring to violate. Should the Government have prosecuted Dr. Tate and Direct Sales for the violations and not for the conspiracy?

430. "A workable definition of conspiracy applicable equally in all cases and to all types of crime is a virtual impossibility. The courts have recognized this, in effect, by holding that persons can be involved in a conspiracy even though they do not know all other members of the conspiracy or participate in each phase. Recognition is thus given to reality, namely, that there must of necessity be a division of labor and function by those engaged in this business." United States v. Rich, 262 F.2d 415, 418 (2d Cir.1959).

> Agreement is the primary element of a conspiracy. The formalities of an agreement are not necessary and are usually lacking since the mark of a successful conspiracy is secrecy. "The agreement may be shown 'if there be concert of action, all the parties working together understandingly, with a single design for the accomplishment of a common purpose.' Fowler v. United States (C.C.A.9) 273 F. 15,

19." . . . While the parties to the agreement must know of each other's existence, they need not know each other's identity nor need there be direct contact. The agreement may continue for a long period of time and include the performance of many transactions. New parties may join the agreement at any time while others may terminate their relationship. The parties are not always identical, but this does not mean that there are separate conspiracies. . . .

The distinction must be made between separate conspiracies, where certain parties are common to all and one overall continuing conspiracy with various parties joining and terminating their relationship at different times. Various people knowingly joining together in furtherance of a common design or purpose constitute a single conspiracy. While the conspiracy may have a small group of core conspirators, other parties who knowingly participate with these core conspirators and others to achieve a common goal may be members of an overall conspiracy.

In essence, the question is what is the nature of the agreement. If there is one overall agreement among the various parties to perform different functions in order to carry out the objectives of the conspiracy, the agreement among all the parties constitutes a single conspiracy.

United States v. Varelli, 407 F.2d 735, 741–42 (7th Cir.1969).

Does it "recognize reality" to hold liable as conspirators persons who have never met one another? How far ought such liability be extended?

431. Brooks, a postal employee, made false entries in the Postal Service accounts-payable records and obtained a number of checks drawn on the United States and payable to persons having no claim to payment. He arranged with Rosenblatt to obtain payment on the checks, Rosenblatt being paid about ten per cent of their value for his service. Rosenblatt did not know the true nature of the checks; he believed that they were valid and that his services were wanted to help the payees evade taxes or conceal kickbacks on government contracts. The court held that there could be no conviction of conspiracy, there being no agreement on the "essential nature of the plan." Nor could the conspiracy be sustained as a conspiracy generally to defraud the United States without proof of agreement on the essential nature of the fraud. The court added that proof of agreement on the "details" of the criminal enterprise was not required. United States v. Rosenblatt, 554 F.2d 36 (2d Cir.1977).

432.

(i)

Simon Brown . . . was president of the Brownie Lumber Company. Having had experience in obtaining loans under the National

Housing Act, he undertook to act as broker in placing for others loans for modernization and renovation, charging a five per cent commission for his services. Brown knew, when he obtained the loans, that the proceeds were not to be used for the purposes stated in the applications.

In May, 1939, petitioner Lekacos told Brown that he wished to secure a loan in order to finance opening a law office, to say the least a hardly auspicious professional launching. Brown made out the application, as directed by Lekacos, to state that the purpose of the loan was to modernize a house belonging to the estate of Lekacos' father. Lekacos obtained the money. Later in the same year Lekacos secured another loan through Brown, the application being in the names of his brother and sister-in-law. Lekacos also received part of the proceeds of a loan for which one Gerakeris . . . had applied.

In June, 1939, Lekacos sent Brown an application for a loan signed by . . . Kotteakos. It contained false statements. Brown placed the loan, and Kotteakos thereafter sent Brown applications on behalf of other persons. The proceeds were received by Kotteakos and . . . Regenbogen, his partner. . . . Regenbogen, together with Kotteakos, had indorsed one of the applications. Kotteakos also sent to Brown an application for a loan in Regenbogen's name. This was for modernization of property not owned by Regenbogen. The latter, however, repaid the money in about three months after he received it.

Kotteakos v. United States, 328 U.S. 750, 753–54 (1946).

Brown made other fraudulent applications for loans under the National Housing Act on behalf of persons with whom Lekacos, Kotteakos, and Regenbogen had no connection. Were all of the people for whom Brown made such applications involved with him in a single conspiracy to defraud the Government?

(ii)

The evidence allowed the jury to find that there had existed over a substantial period of time a conspiracy embracing a great number of persons, whose object was to smuggle narcotics into the Port of New York and distribute them to addicts both in this city and in Texas and Louisiana. This required the cooperation of four groups of persons; the smugglers who imported the drugs; the middlemen who paid the smugglers and distributed to retailers; and two groups of retailers—one in New York and one in Texas and Louisiana—who supplied the addicts. The defendants assert that there were, therefore, at least three separate conspiracies; one between the smugglers and the middlemen, and one between the middlemen and each group of retailers. The evidence did not disclose any cooperation or communication between the smugglers and either group of retailers, or between the two groups of retailers themselves; however, the smugglers knew that the middlemen must sell to retailers, and the retailers knew that the middlemen must buy of importers of one sort or another. Thus the conspirators at one end of the chain knew that the unlawful business would not, and could not, stop with their buyers; and those at the other end knew that it had not begun with their sellers.

United States v. Bruno, 105 F.2d 921, 922 (2d Cir.), rev'd on other grounds, 308 U.S. 287 (1939).

How many conspiracies were there?

In *Kotteakos*, the Court held that the people for whom Brown made fraudulent applications could not all be drawn together into a single conspiracy. It quoted with approval the observation of the court of appeals, sub. nom. United States v. Lekacos, 151 F.2d 170, 173 (2d Cir.1945), that "thieves who dispose of their loot to a single receiver—a single 'fence'—do not by that fact alone become confederates: they may, but it takes more than knowledge that he is a 'fence' to make them such." 328 U.S. at 754–55.[105] See, to the same effect, United States v. Jackson, 696 F.2d 578 (8th Cir.1982) (arson).

In *Bruno*, the court of appeals held that there was a single conspiracy. "[A] jury might have found that all the accused were embarked upon a venture, in all parts of which each was a participant, and an abettor in the sense that the success of that part with which he was immediately concerned, was dependent upon the success of the whole. . . . It might still be argued that there were two conspiracies; one including the smugglers, the middlemen and the New York group, and the other, the smugglers, the middlemen and the Texas & Louisiana group, for there was apparently no privity between the two groups of retailers. That too would be fallacious. Clearly, quoad the smugglers, there was but one conspiracy, for it was of no moment to them whether the middlemen sold to one or more groups of retailers, provided they had a market somewhere. So too of any retailer; he knew that he was a necessary link in a scheme of distribution, and the others, whom he knew to be convenient to its execution, were as much parts of a single undertaking or enterprise as two salesmen in the same shop." 105 F.2d at 922–23.[106] See, discussing the problem of conspiracy

---

105. Discussing *Kotteakos* in another case, the Court said: "[N]o two of those agreements were tied together as stages in the formation of a larger all-inclusive combination, all directed to achieving a single unlawful end or result. On the contrary each separate agreement had its own distinct, illegal end. Each loan was an end in itself, separate from all others, although all were alike in having similar illegal objects. Except for Brown, the common figure, no conspirator was interested in whether any loan except his own went through. And none aided in any way, by agreement or otherwise, in procuring another's loan. The conspiracies therefore were distinct and disconnected, not parts of a larger general scheme, both in the phase of agreement with Brown and also in the ab-

sence of any aid given to others as well as in specific object and result. There was no drawing of all together in a single, over-all, comprehensive plan." Blumenthal v. United States, 332 U.S. 539, 558 (1947).

106. On the latter point, the court later expressed some doubt: "[I]t is not so clear why the New York and Texas groups of retailers were not in a 'spoke' relation with the smugglers and the middleman, so that there would be two conspiracies unless the evidence permitted the inference that each group of retailers must have known the operation to be so large as to require the other as an outlet." United States v. Borelli, 336 F.2d 376, 383 n.2 (2d Cir.1964).

related to drug transactions, United States v. Pressler, 256 F.3d 144 (3d Cir.2001).

Kotteakos and *Bruno* exemplify two structural types of conspiracy to which the courts frequently refer. The type suggested by *Kotteakos* (although found not to be present in that case) is a "wheel" or "spoke" conspiracy, in which a group of people are associated in a single enterprise primarily by their relationship to a common center. (In *Kotteakos*, as the Supreme Court put it, "the pattern was 'that of separate spokes meeting at a common center [Brown],' though we may add without the rim of the wheel to enclose the spokes," 328 U.S. at 755.[107]) See, e.g., United States v. Evans, 970 F.2d 663 (10th Cir.1992) (single narcotics conspiracy); United States v. Percival, 756 F.2d 600 (7th Cir.1985) (same). The conspiracy in *Bruno* was of the type described as a "chain," in which each conspirator is seen as a link taking part in one or more of a series of consecutive transactions comprising the conspiratorial venture. See United States v. Michelena-Orovio, 719 F.2d 738 (5th Cir.1983), holding that evidence sufficient to establish that a seaman on a ship transporting marijuana is guilty of a conspiracy to import may also be enough, in view of the quantity being transported, to establish participation in a conspiracy to distribute the marijuana. But see United States v. Manbeck, 744 F.2d 360, 388–90 (4th Cir.1984) (*Michelena-Orovio* criticized). Both metaphors, "wheel" and "chain," are intended to suggest the unity of a conspiracy the participants in which have not come together and explicitly entered into an agreement for collective action; if the conspirators do actually come together and agree, the metaphors are inapt (except perhaps with respect to the execution of the conspiratorial objective) and, in any event, have no significance.

United States v. Perez, 489 F.2d 51 (5th Cir.1973), involved an extensive scheme to stage fraudulent automobile accidents to create false personal injury claims. The scheme involved a number of persons, including the participants in the staged accidents and doctors and lawyers. Concluding that the evidence showed "one big, and hopefully profitable enterprise, which looked toward successful frequent but none-the-less discrete repetitions," id. at 64, the court expressed some impatience with the common metaphors: "As for us, the problem is difficult enough without trying to compress it into figurative analogies. Conspiracies are as complex as the versatility of human nature and federal protection against them is not to be measured by spokes, hubs, wheels, rims, chains, or any one or all of today's galaxy of mechanical, molecular or atomic forms." Id. at 59 n.11. See also United States v. Hutul, 416 F.2d 607 (7th Cir.1969), involving a similar scheme and the same outcome.

For a good discussion of conspiracy, including criticism of too ready application of the "wheel" and "chain" theories, in the context of a large

---

107. Even if each of the persons who obtained a loan through Brown were interested only in obtaining the loan to himself, if the success of any one of the applications depended on the success of all and all knew that they were "in it together" to that extent, this interdependency of the various agreements would have supplied a rim for the wheel. See, e.g., Rex v. Meyrick, 21 Crim.App. 94 (1929).

drug distribution network, see United States v. Townsend, 924 F.2d 1385 (7th Cir.1991).

433.   United States v. Borelli, 336 F.2d 376, 383–84 (2d Cir.1964): "[W]hatever the value of the chain concept where the problem is to trace a single operation from the start through its various phases to its successful conclusion, it becomes confusing when, over a long period of time, certain links continue to play the same role but with new counterparts, as where importers who regard their partnership as a single continuing one, having successfully distributed one cargo through X distributing organization, turn, years later, to moving another cargo obtained from a different source through Y. Thus, however reasonable the so-called presumption of continuity may be as to all the participants of a conspiracy which intends a single act, such as the robbing of a bank, or even as to the core of a conspiracy to import and resell narcotics, its force is diminished as to the outer links—buyers indifferent to their sources of supply and turning from one source to another, and suppliers equally indifferent to the identity of their customers.

"The basic difficulty arises in applying the seventeenth century notion of conspiracy, where the gravamen of the offense was the making of an *agreement* to commit a readily identifiable crime or series of crimes, such as murder or robbery, see Developments in the Law—Criminal Conspiracy, 72 Harv. L. Rev. 922, 923 (1959), to what in substance is the conduct of an illegal business over a period of years. There has been a tendency in such cases 'to deal with the crime of conspiracy as though it were a group [of men] rather than an act' of agreement. See 72 Harv. L. Rev. at 934. Although it is usual and often necessary in conspiracy cases for the agreement to be proved by inference from acts, the gist of the offense remains the agreement, and it is therefore essential to determine what kind of agreement or understanding existed as to each defendant. It is a great deal harder to tell just *what* agreement can reasonably be inferred from the purchase, even the repeated purchase, of contraband, than from the furnishing of dynamite to prospective bank robbers or the exchange of worthless property for securities to be subsequently distributed. Purchase or sale of contraband may, of course, warrant the inference of an agreement going well beyond the particular transaction. A seller of narcotics in bulk surely knows that the purchasers will undertake to resell the goods over an uncertain period of time, and the circumstances may also warrant the inference that a supplier or a purchaser indicated a willingness to repeat. But a sale or a purchase scarcely constitutes a sufficient basis for inferring agreement to cooperate with the opposite parties for whatever period they continue to deal in this type of contraband, unless some such understanding is evidenced by other conduct which accompanies or supplements the transaction."

434.   In 1970 Congress enacted provisions under the heading, Racketeer Influenced and Corrupt Organizations (RICO), 18 U.S.C. §§ 1961–

1968, as part of the Organized Crime Control Act of 1970, 84 Stat. 922. The purpose of the statute was to reach organized criminal activities as well as the infiltration by organized crime of otherwise legal businesses and commerce. Using interstate or foreign commerce as the basis of federal jurisdiction, RICO generally prohibits persons from acquiring an interest in or exercising any control over any "enterprise" engaged in or affecting such commerce by a "pattern of racketeering activity," or from using income of such activity to invest in an enterprise. Persons who are employed by or associated with an enterprise are prohibited from conducting its affairs by a pattern of racketeering activity. In addition to severe criminal penalties, including imprisonment for not more than 20 years and a fine, the statute provides for forfeiture of any interest or property acquired by a violation of the statute or with the proceeds of a violation. § 1963. The "interests" subject to forfeiture are construed broadly in Russello v. United States, 464 U.S. 16 (1983) (insurance proceeds derived from racketeering activities). One of its principal objectives, the Court said, was "to remove the profit from organized crime by separating the racketeer from his dishonest gains." Id. at 28. The statute provides also for an injured person to recover treble damages against anyone found in a private civil action to have violated RICO. § 1964.

An "enterprise" under the statute "includes any individual, partnership, corporation, association, or other legal entity, and any union or group of individuals associated in fact although not a legal entity." § 1961(4). "Racketeering activity" includes a broad range of offenses "chargeable under State law," including the major felonies ("murder, kidnapping, gambling, arson, robbery, extortion, dealing in obscene matter, or dealing in narcotic or other dangerous drugs") as well as a lengthy list of federal offenses commonly associated with organized crime (sports bribery, gambling, narcotics, extortion, etc.). § 1961(1). A "pattern of racketeering activity" consists of "at least two acts of racketeering activity" within a ten-year period.

In *Russello*, above, the Supreme Court indicated that the RICO statute should generally be given an expansive interpretation: "The legislative history clearly demonstrates that the RICO statute was intended to provide new weapons of unprecedented scope for an assault upon organized crime and its economic roots." 464 U.S. at 26. So, for example, it has been held that the acts "chargeable under State law" that establish a "pattern of racketeering activity" may include a substantive offense and a conspiracy to commit the offense, even though state law does not permit a conviction for both; or acts for which the defendants are no longer liable under state law, because the statute of limitations has run; or acts for which the defendants have been tried and acquitted in the state courts. The reference in the statute to state law only identifies the type of activity that is covered. E.g., United States v. Licavoli, 725 F.2d 1040 (6th Cir.1984).

The key provisions of the RICO statute have not been easy to construe. Part of the difficulty has been that, although the manifest purpose of the statute was to attack organized crime, its language reaches much further and, broadly construed, might sweep up a good deal of ordinary criminal activity adequately covered by other federal statutes or left to state laws. Because of the provision for treble damages, private persons have an incentive to cast crimes as violations of RICO. Acknowledging that organized crime was the primary target, the Court has nevertheless said that it is not the only target. "The occasion for Congress' action was the perceived need to combat organized crime. But Congress for cogent reasons chose to enact a more general statute, one which, although it had organized crime as its focus, was not limited in application to organized crime." H.J. Inc. v. Northwestern Bell Telephone Co., 492 U.S. 229, 248 (1989).

The Court has held that a statutory "enterprise" includes legal and illegal associations and is "an entity, for present purposes a group of persons associated together for a common purpose of engaging in a course of conduct. . . . [It] is proved by evidence of an ongoing organization, formal or informal, and by evidence that the various associates function as a continuing unit." United States v. Turkette, 452 U.S. 576, 583 (1981). See United States v. Porcelli, 865 F.2d 1352, 1362–64 (2d Cir.1989).

A "pattern of racketeering activity" requires continuity and relationship: at least two predicate offenses continuing over a period of time and having some "external organizing principle that renders them 'ordered' or 'arranged.' " H.J. Inc., 492 U.S. at 238.

"Continuity" is both a closed- and an open-ended concept, referring either to a closed period of repeated conduct, or to past conduct that by its nature projects into the future with a threat of repetition. . . . It is, in either case, centrally a temporal concept—and particularly so in the RICO context, where *what* must be continuous, RICO's predicate acts or offenses, and the *relationship* these predicates must bear one to another, are distinct requirements. A party alleging a RICO violation may demonstrate continuity over a closed period by proving a series of related predicates extending over a substantial period of time. Predicate acts extending over a few weeks or months and threatening no future criminal conduct do not satisfy this requirement: Congress was concerned in RICO with long-term criminal conduct. Often a RICO action will be brought before continuity can be established in this way. In such cases, liability depends on whether the *threat* of continuity is demonstrated. . . .

Whether the predicates proved establish a threat of continued racketeering activity depends on the specific facts of each case. Without making any claim to cover the field of possibilities—preferring to deal with this issue in the context of concrete factual situations presented for decision—we offer some examples of how this element might be satisfied. A RICO pattern may surely be established if the related predicates themselves involve a distinct threat of long-term racketeering activity, either implicit or explicit. Suppose a hoodlum were to sell "insurance" to a neighborhood's storekeepers to cover them against breakage of their windows, telling his victims he would be reappearing each month to collect the "premium" that would continue their "coverage." Though the number of related predicates involved may be small and they may occur close together in time, the racketeering acts themselves include a specific threat of repetition extending indefinitely into the future, and thus supply the requisite threat of continuity. In other cases, the threat of continuity may be established by showing that the predicate acts or offenses are part of an ongoing entity's regular way of doing business. Thus, the threat of continuity is sufficiently established where the predicates can be attributed to a defendant operating as part of a long-term association that exists for criminal purposes. Such associations include, but extend well beyond, those traditionally grouped under the phrase "organized crime." The continuity requirement is likewise satisfied where it is shown that the predicates are a regular way of conducting defendant's ongoing legitimate business (in the sense that it is not a business that exists for criminal purposes), or of conducting or participating in an ongoing and legitimate RICO "enterprise."

   The limits of the relationship and continuity concepts that combine to define a RICO pattern, and the precise methods by which relatedness and continuity or its threat may be proved, cannot be fixed in advance with such clarity that it will always be apparent whether in a particular case a "pattern of racketeering activity" exists. The development of these concepts must await future cases. . . .

Id. at 241–43. See Apparel Art International, Inc. v. Jacobson, 967 F.2d 720 (1st Cir.1992).

   The RICO statute provides that conspiracy to violate any of the substantive RICO offenses is itself a RICO offense, carrying the same heavy penalties and forfeiture provisions. 18 U.S.C. § 1962(d). The conspiracy provision has been used extensively.

[handwritten margin note: In NY you must have an overt act to sho[w] conspiracy]

435. "The act of agreeing with another to commit a crime . . . is concrete and unambiguous; it does not present the infinite degrees and variations possible in the general category of attempts. The danger that truly equivocal behavior may be misinterpreted as preparation to commit a crime is minimized; purpose must be relatively firm before the commitment involved in agreement is assumed." 2 MPC Commentaries Part I, 388 (comment to § 5.03).

   Does the foregoing material support that?

436. "[C]ollective criminal agreement—partnership in crime—presents a greater potential threat to the public than individual delicts. Concerted action both increases the likelihood that the criminal object will be successfully attained and decreases the probability that the individuals involved will depart from their path of criminality. Group association for criminal purposes often, if not normally, makes possible the attainment of ends more complex than those which one criminal could accomplish. Nor is the danger of a conspiratorial group limited to the particular end toward which it has embarked. Combination in crime makes more likely the commission of crimes unrelated to the original purpose for which the group was formed. In sum, the danger which a conspiracy generates is not confined to the substantive offense which is the immediate aim of the enterprise." Callanan v. United States, 364 U.S. 587, 593–94 (1961).

Is the argument that concerted action increases the danger to the public, or any other argument for making conspiracy a crime, sufficiently reflected in the courts' delineation of conspiratorial agreement? Should the courts (and the legislatures) be concerned not only with the question whether there *was* an agreement but also, if there was, with the *nature* of the agreement? Should we be content with the conclusion that agreement generally reinforces a criminal purpose or should we require as an element of conspiracy that aside from the agreement there was cooperation among the conspirators and mutual support for one another? Should the degree of organization among the conspirators make a difference? Should it constitute conspiracy for a group of people to work *openly* for a common purpose, e.g., to encourage others to defy an unpopular law? See, e.g., United States v. Spock, 416 F.2d 165 (1st Cir.1969) (conspiracy to hinder draft during war in Vietnam).

437. The Pinkerton rule. Most serious of the consequences that may depend on the extent of the conspiracy in which a particular defendant participated is his liability for substantive crimes committed by other conspirators. In Pinkerton v. United States, 328 U.S. 640 (1946), the Supreme Court held that all the participants in a conspiracy are liable as principals for the substantive crimes committed by each in furtherance of the conspiracy. Walter and Daniel Pinkerton were convicted of violations of the Internal Revenue Code involving unlawful dealings in whiskey, including one charge of conspiracy. There was no evidence that Daniel participated directly in the substantive offenses for which he was convicted, but there was evidence that Walter committed those offenses in furtherance of the conspiracy between them. The Court said that "a different case would arise if the substantive offense committed by one of the conspirators . . . did not fall within the scope of the unlawful project, or was merely a part of the ramifications of the plan which could not be reasonably foreseen as a necessary or natural consequence of the unlawful agreement." Id. at 647–48.

Justice Rutledge dissented:

Daniel has been held guilty of the substantive crimes committed only by Walter on proof that he did no more than conspire with him to commit offenses of the same general character. There was no evidence that he counseled, advised or had knowledge of those particular acts or offenses. There was, therefore, none that he aided, abetted or took part in them. There was only evidence sufficient to show that he had agreed with Walter at some past time to engage in such transactions general-ly. As to Daniel this was only evidence of conspiracy, not of substantive crime.

The court's theory seems to be that Daniel and Walter became general partners in crime by virtue of their agreement and because of that agreement without more on his part Daniel became criminally responsible as a principal for everything Walter did thereafter in the nature of a criminal offense of the general sort the agreement contem-plated, so long as there was not clear evidence that Daniel had withdrawn from or revoked the agreement. Whether or not his com-mitment to the penitentiary[108] had that effect, the result is a vicarious criminal responsibility as broad as, or broader than, the vicarious civil liability of a partner for acts done by a co-partner in the course of the firm's business.

Such analogies from private commercial law and the law of torts are dangerous, in my judgment, for transfer to the criminal field. . . . Guilt there with us remains personal, not vicarious, for the more serious offenses. It should be kept so. The effect of Daniel's conviction in this case, to repeat, is either to attribute to him Walter's guilt or to punish him twice for the same offense, namely, agreeing with Walter to engage in crime. Without the agreement Daniel was guilty of no crime on this record. With it and no more, so far as his own conduct is concerned, he was guilty of two.

Id. at 651, 652.

"[I]n a typical *Pinkerton* case, the court need not inquire into the individual culpability of a particular conspirator, so long as the substantive crime was a reasonably foreseeable consequence of the conspiracy." United States v. Alvarez, 755 F.2d 830, 849–50 (11th Cir.1985). Holding that *Pinkerton* applies to substantive crimes that were not originally intended as part of the conspiracy, the court added that its application in such cases is "within narrow confines"; because of "potential due process limitations" its application in such cases extends only to "conspirators who played more than a 'minor' role in the conspiracy, or who had actual knowledge of at least some of the circumstances and events culminating in the reasonably foreseeable but originally unintended substantive crime." Id. at 850, 851 n.27. See also United States v. Gironda, 758 F.2d 1201 (7th Cir.1985), applying *Pinkerton* to the carrying of a firearm by an accomplice during the commission of a felony. *Pinkerton* does not extend, however, to acts committed before a person has joined the conspiracy. United States v. Covelli, 738 F.2d 847 (7th Cir.1984).

The Pinkerton rule has been accepted in some but not all states. "[I]t is repugnant to our system of jurisprudence, where guilt is generally personal to the defendant . . . to impose punishment, not for the socially

[108] Daniel was in the penitentiary for other crimes when some of Walter's crimes were committed. 328 U.S. at 648.

harmful agreement to which the defendant is a party, but for substantive offenses in which he did not participate . . . ." People v. McGee, 399 N.E.2d 1177, 1182 (N.Y.1979). Accord Commonwealth v. Stasiun, 206 N.E.2d 672 (Mass.1965). The Model Penal Code rejects the rule. See 1 MPC Commentaries Part I, 308–309 (comment to § 2.06).

The extraordinary reach of the holding in *Pinkerton*, which the Supreme Court reaffirmed in Nye & Nissen v. United States, 336 U.S. 613, 618 (1949), is a marked extension of the readily acceptable proposition that participation in a conspiracy may be evidence, even very good evidence, of complicity as an aider and abettor in a substantive offense committed in furtherance of the conspiracy. See id. at 619. The "Pinkerton rule" also is easily confused with the evidentiary rule that statements made by any conspirator in furtherance of the conspiracy are admissible against all.[109]

438. The evidentiary significance of the extent of a conspiracy has been noted. More generally, a joint prosecution for conspiracy raises for the defendants all of the difficulties that attend joint trials. Ordinarily a defendant is entitled to be tried individually. It is common practice, however, for many defendants to be tried together if they are charged with the same crime or a connected series of crimes. E.g., Fed. R. Crim. P. 8(b), 12. At a joint trial each defendant and his counsel must accommodate their trial strategy to the strategies of the others, including possibly antagonistic defenses, e.g., United States v. Romanello, 726 F.2d 173 (5th Cir.1984) (conviction reversed); United States v. Micele, 327 F.2d 222 (7th Cir.1964) (cross-examination of prosecution witness that prejudices codefendant; conviction affirmed), or tactics, e.g., United States v. Kahn, 381 F.2d 824, 836–38 (7th Cir.1967) (codefendant pleaded guilty during trial; conviction affirmed). He may have to forego rights that he would have were he tried alone, e.g., United States v. Provenzano, 688 F.2d 194 (3d Cir.1982) (inability to call codefendant as witness; conviction affirmed), or have to share them with other defendants, see, e.g., Fed. R. Crim. P. 24(b) (peremptory challenges). He risks unintended harm from the poor strategy of other defendants and their counsel, and from the effect of being associated with the other defendants in front of the jury. The appearance of all the defendants and their counsel sitting together in the courtroom and engaging in whispered conversations or "huddles" to determine joint strategy may itself be suggestive of a conspiracy. See generally Krulewitch v. United States, 336 U.S. 440, 452–54 (1949) (Jackson, J., concurring). Provision is made for relief from "prejudicial joinder," see, e.g., Fed. R. Crim. P. 14, but once a trial is under way and still more after the defendants have been convicted and the case is on appeal, courts are reluctant to grant a severance and require that the trial of some or all of the defendants begin

---

109. This rule is an exception to the hearsay rule. See generally United States v. Lucido, 486 F.2d 868 (6th Cir.1973) (defendant acquitted on conspiracy charge entitled to new trial on substantive count because of admission of alleged co-conspirator's statements).

again; commonly they rely on the ability of juries to follow the instructions of the trial judge as protection against prejudice. See generally United States v. Jackson, 696 F.2d 578 (8th Cir.1982) (arson), in which the court held that the defendants were prejudiced by their joint trial for a single conspiracy when the evidence established at most that there were two distinct conspiracies, and reversed their convictions.

The justifications for joint trials are those of economy and efficiency. "Joint trials do conserve state funds, diminish inconvenience to witnesses and public authorities, and avoid delays in bringing those accused of crime to trial." Bruton v. United States, 391 U.S. 123, 134 (1968) (admission of codefendant's confession inculpating defendant denies defendant constitutional right to cross-examination and is prejudicial error despite cautionary instructions).

Conspiracy under common law — unlawful agreement

439. Overt act. Under the common law rule, the prohibited agreement is all that is required to constitute the crime of conspiracy. "[T]he unlawful agreement satisfies the definition of the crime . . . ." United States v. Kissel, 218 U.S. 601, 607 (1910). The federal conspiracy statute, 18 U.S.C. § 371, and the statutes of many of the states that have codified the crime of conspiracy provide that the statute is not violated unless one of the conspirators does an act in furtherance of the conspiratorial objective. The required "overt act" "may be that of only a single one of the conspirators and need not be itself a crime." Braverman v. United States, 317 U.S. 49, 53 (1942). It "may be merely a part of preliminary arrangements for commission of the ultimate crime." People v. Buono, 12 Cal.Rptr. 604, 615 (Dist.Ct.App.1961). "Any act," as many of the statutes put it, by any of the conspirators satisfies the requirement. "The function of the overt act in a conspiracy prosecution is simply to manifest 'that the conspiracy is at work,' Carlson v. United States, 187 F.2d 366, 370, and is neither a project still resting solely in the minds of the conspirators nor a fully completed operation no longer in existence." Yates v. United States, 354 U.S. 298, 334 (1957). Another suggested function of the requirement is that it is "a device for affording a *locus poenitentiae*." See *Braverman*, 317 U.S. at 53.

in NY there must be an overt act to show conspiracy [Penal Code 20.00]

Courts have debated whether an overt act, where it is required, is an element of the crime or only essential evidence of it, see id., and have sometimes given the time or place when an overt act was committed significance in determining when and where the conspiracy can be prosecuted, e.g., Grunewald v. United States, 353 U.S. 391, 396–97 (1957) (statute of limitations); Hyde v. United States, 225 U.S. 347 (1912) (venue). The requirement does not ordinarily have a significant effect on prosecutions for conspiracy.[110]

110. Indeed, in a number of states where an overt act is required generally, it is not required if the conspiratorial objective is a serious crime. The Model Penal Code § 5.03(5) is representative: "Overt Act. No person may be convicted of conspiracy to

Termination of a conspiracy

440. The extent of a conspiracy is defined not only by its "scope," the conspiratorial objective(s),[111] but also by its duration. Since the agreement constitutes the crime, a conspiracy ends when the agreement ends. When is that? In the absence of an express (effective) understanding among the conspirators that they are, or after a certain point will be, no longer bound by any agreement among them, what marks the termination of a conspiracy?

"[T]he unlawful agreement satisfies the definition of the crime, but it does not exhaust it. It also is true, of course, that the mere continuance of the result of a crime does not continue the crime. . . . But when the plot contemplates bringing to pass a continuous result that will not continue without the continuous co-operation of the conspirators to keep it up, and there is such continuous co-operation, it is a perversion of natural thought and of natural language to call such continuous co-operation a cinematographic series of distinct conspiracies, rather than to call it a single one. . . . A conspiracy is a partnership in criminal purposes. That as such it may have continuation in time is shown by the rule that an overt act of one partner may be the act of all without any new agreement specifically directed to that act." United States v. Kissel, 218 U.S. 601, 607–608 (1910).

"[T]he termination of the conspiracy need not coincide with the completion of the crime nor even with the arrest of a conspirator. . . . The time when a continuing conspiracy terminates depends upon the particular facts and purposes of such conspiracy. Completion of the object of the conspiracy completes the conspiracy. This varies with different offenses but a conspiracy to commit a crime of stealth for material gain usually has a minimum routine development from plan to commission to division of fruits, if any, among the conspirators." Cleaver v. United States, 238 F.2d 766, 769 (10th Cir.1956).

In Krulewitch v. United States, 336 U.S. 440, 443 (1949), the Government argued unsuccessfully that after the object of a conspiracy has been accomplished (or has finally failed of accomplishment) an "implicit subsidiary phase of the conspiracy . . . [having] concealment as its sole objective" continues. "[A] vital distinction must be made between acts of concealment done in furtherance of the *main* criminal objectives of the conspiracy, and acts of concealment done after these central objectives have been attained, for the purpose only of covering up after the crime." Grunewald v. United States, 353 U.S. 391, 405 (1957). See United States v. Freeman, 498 F.2d 569 (2d Cir.1974), holding that one who does no more than help to conceal

commit a crime, other than a felony of the first or second degree, unless an overt act in pursuance of such conspiracy is alleged and proved to have been done by him or by a person with whom he conspired."

111. An agreement to commit more than one crime is not more than one conspir-

acy. "Whether the object of a single agreement is to commit one or many crimes, it is in either case that agreement which constitutes the conspiracy which the statute punishes." Braverman v. United States, 317 U.S. 49, 53 (1942); see Model Penal Code § 5.03(3).

a conspiracy after it has failed to achieve its object is not liable as a conspirator in the main conspiracy.

In United States v. Jimenez Recio, ___ U.S. ___, 123 S.Ct. 819 (2003), police stopped a truck and seized a large quantity of drugs. With the help of the truck's drivers, they set up a sting operation. The truck was taken to the intended destination, and the drivers called a contact, who said that he would send someone for the truck. When the defendant and another person appeared, they were arrested. They argued that the conspiracy ended when the drugs were seized, because that frustrated the object of the conspiracy. Therefore, they argued, in order to convict them, the government had to prove that they had joined the conspiracy before the drugs were seized. The Court rejected that argument. It said that the agreement constitutes the crime of conspiracy, which poses a threat over and above the commission of the substantive offense that is the object of the conspiracy; the agreement makes it more likely that the conspirators will commit additional crimes. This threat continues while the agreement persists, even though the specific object of the conspiracy has been frustrated.

441. A, B, and C agree to rob a bank. They carry out the robbery successfully but discover afterwards that all of the bills are marked. Four months later they contact D, tell him how they acquired the bills, and collectively make an agreement with him that he will arrange to exchange the bills for unmarked ones in return for a share of the spoils. He makes the exchange three months later, and the unmarked bills are divided among the four men, who have no further contact with each other.

(i) Is D guilty of conspiracy to rob a bank? Why (not)?

(ii) If D is not guilty of conspiracy to rob a bank, is he guilty of any conspiracy?

(iii) Would your answer to (i) or (ii) be different if A, B, and C had consulted D before they robbed the bank and he had refused to participate in the robbery but had agreed to arrange for an exchange of any marked bills that they obtained?

See, e.g., Bollenbach v. United States, 326 U.S. 607, 611 (1946); United States v. Freeman, note 440 above; Cleaver v. United States, note 440 above; United States v. Zeuli, 137 F.2d 845 (2d Cir.1943). Compare Hudspeth v. McDonald, 120 F.2d 962 (10th Cir.1941).

442. A, B, and C agree to rob a bank. Is C guilty of conspiracy to rob a bank if:

(i) one day before the robbery is to take place, C catches cold and advises A and B that he will not be able to participate, and A and B carry out the robbery?

(ii) one day before the robbery is to take place, C realizes the error of his ways and advises A and B that he will not participate, and A and B carry out the robbery?

(iii) one day before the robbery is to take place, C realizes the error of his ways, advises A and B that he will not participate, and advises the police of their plan, so that the police arrest A and B as they are about to enter the bank to carry out the robbery?

In all three cases, C's initial agreement makes him liable for the crime of conspiracy, and the general rule is that no subsequent act has a bearing on his liability since the crime is already "complete." The Model Penal Code § 5.03(6) provides for a defense in case (iii): "Renunciation of Criminal Purpose. It is an affirmative defense that the actor, after conspiring to commit a crime, thwarted the success of the conspiracy, under circumstances manifesting a complete and voluntary renunciation of his criminal purpose."

443.   A, B, and C agree to rob a bank. Their plan is that A and B will carry out the actual holdup and that C will remain outside to drive the getaway car. As planned, C pulls up to the curb in front of the bank. A and B run into the bank. What is the effect on C's liability as a conspirator (for example, his liability for substantive crimes subsequently committed by A and B in the bank), if, at that point:

(i) he sees the error of his ways and drives off hastily?

(ii) he sees a policeman and drives off hastily?

(iii) a policeman sees him and arrests him?

See, e.g., People v. Nichols, 129 N.E. 883, 885–86 (N.Y.1921). Cf. Ferris v. United States, 40 F.2d 837, 839 (9th Cir.1930).

Suppose C's role was not to participate in the holdup at all but to have a getaway car ready at a point several miles from the bank. Several days before the robbery is to take place, C decides not to have anything to do with the bank robbery. What is the effect on his liability as a conspirator if:

(i) he says nothing to anyone and quietly packs his bags and departs for Florida a few minutes after A and B set off for the bank?

(ii) before the day on which the robbery is to take place, he tells A and B of his decision and departs for Florida (A and B then going forward with the robbery alone)?

(iii) on the day before the robbery is to take place, he places a note stating his decision where it is certain to be seen by A and B and departs for Florida, but A and B in their nervousness don't read the note and set out to commit the robbery, with the expectation that C will meet them at the appointed place?

Withdrawal from a conspiracy requires more than an uncommunicated decision not to abide by the agreement. "Mere cessation of activity is not

enough to start the running of the statute [of limitations]; there must also be affirmative action, either the making of a clean breast to the authorities . . . or communication of the abandonment in a manner reasonably calculated to reach co-conspirators." United States v. Borelli, 336 F.2d 376, 388 (2d Cir.1964). "Affirmative acts inconsistent with the object of the conspiracy and communicated in a manner reasonably calculated to reach co-conspirators have generally been regarded as sufficient to establish withdrawal or abandonment." United States v. United States Gypsum Co., 438 U.S. 422, 464–65 (1978). See United States v. Stouffer, 986 F.2d 916 (5th Cir.1993) (joint criminal enterprise, scheme to defraud). It has sometimes been held that there is no withdrawal unless the decision to withdraw has been "brought home to the other conspirators," People v. Drake, 310 P.2d 997, 1003 (Cal.Dist.Ct.App.1957). Compare Hyde v. United States, 225 U.S. 347, 369–70 (1912): "As he has started evil forces he must withdraw his support from them or incur the guilt of their continuance."[112]

"It is argued that . . . the requirement of showing affirmative action is too severe for cases where a defendant simply engaged in the supply, transportation, or purchase of contraband before the period of limitations and the only effects realistically continuing into the period were the profits the central core had realized and its hope of further assistance. We should be obliged to give most serious consideration to this argument if, as urged by the Government, mere proof of past dealings with the core sufficed to

112. The Model Penal Code § 5.03(7)(c) requires that the conspirator "advise" his conspirators of his decision and provides that the conspiracy also terminates as to him if "he informs the law enforcement authorities of the existence of the conspiracy and of his participation therein."

permit a jury to infer an agreement to participate in its continuing activities to the end of time. However, our conclusion, explained above [see p. 688 note 433 above], that so broad an inference is not allowable, deprives the argument of a good deal of its force. Since each defendant can be held only for that part of the conspiracy which he understood and assented to, and since the statute will begin to run for him when his own agreement terminates, it is neither unfair nor unreasonable to require affirmative demonstration that he was abrogating it at an earlier date." *Borelli*, 336 F.2d at 388–89. See United States v. Grimmett, 236 F.3d 452 (8th Cir. 2001), discussing the statement in *Borelli*, above, that in order to withdraw from a conspiracy, the conspirator must make "a clean breast to the authorities." The court concluded that that requirement does not mean that the conspirator must make a "full confession"; it is enough if the conspirator "severs all ties to the conspiracy and its fruits, *and* acts affirmatively to defeat the conspiracy by confessing to and cooperating with the authorities."

> Withdrawal marks a conspirator's disavowal or abandonment of the conspiratorial agreement. . . . By definition, after a defendant withdraws, he is no longer a member of the conspiracy and the later acts of the conspirators do not bind him. The defendant is still liable, however, for his previous agreement and for the previous acts of his co-conspirators in pursuit of the conspiracy. . . . Withdrawal is not, therefore, a complete defense to the crime of conspiracy. Withdrawal becomes a complete defense only when coupled with the defense of the statute of limitations. A defendant's withdrawal from the conspiracy starts the running of the statute of limitations as to him. If the indictment is filed more than five years after a defendant withdraws, the statute of limitations bars prosecution for his actual participation in the conspiracy. He cannot be held liable for acts or declarations committed in the five years preceding the indictment by other conspirators because his withdrawal ended his membership in the conspiracy. . . . It is thus only the interaction of the two defenses of withdrawal and the statute of limitations which shields the defendant from liability.

> Withdrawal, then, directly negates the element of membership in the conspiracy during the period of the statute of limitations. . . . [T]he government should disprove the defense of withdrawal beyond a reasonable doubt.

> The government, however, insists that Hyde v. United States, 225 U.S. 347 (1912), a long-established Supreme Court case, placed the burden of proving withdrawal on the defendant. Indeed, *Hyde* has often been cited for that proposition in the courts of appeals. Almost every case we researched holds that the burden is on the defendant to "prove" or "establish" withdrawal. . . .

> We have, however, reexamined *Hyde*. Our research convinces us that the cases, including our own, have misinterpreted *Hyde*. According

to our interpretation, *Hyde* placed only the burden of going forward on the defendant. . . .

. . .

As withdrawal negates the essential element of membership, it must be disproved beyond a reasonable doubt by the government. We therefore overrule those cases imposing the burden of proving withdrawal on the defendant. We hold today that the burden of going forward with evidence of withdrawal and with evidence that he withdrew prior to the statute of limitations remains on the defendant. However, once he advances sufficient evidence, the burden of persuasion is on the prosecution to disprove the defense of withdrawal beyond a reasonable doubt. As in the cases of other defenses, once the jury has been instructed on the withdrawal defense, the jury should be instructed that the government bears the burden of disproving withdrawal beyond a reasonable doubt.

United States v. Read, 658 F.2d 1225, 1232–33, 1236 (7th Cir.1981).

444. However attenuated the requirement of an agreement has become in some other respects, there is no agreement and hence no conspiracy unless there is more than one person involved. A hesitant lawbreaker who "promises himself" that "this time he'll do it" is not guilty of conspiracy. (In United States v. Dege, 364 U.S. 51 (1960), the Supreme Court discarded the rule of the common law that a husband and wife, being one, could not alone conspire with each other.) If all but one of the alleged conspirators is acquitted, it is commonly held that the one remaining may not be convicted. E.g., Commonwealth v. Campbell, 390 A.2d 761 (Pa.Super.Ct.1978), aff'd, 399 A.2d 130 (1979). That rule may not be applied, however, if the acquittal of the other alleged conspirator was at a separate trial. "A finding of not guilty at a criminal trial can result from any number of factors having nothing to do with the defendant's actual guilt. A not guilty verdict may result from an exclusionary rule of evidence, inadequate investigation or proof, the composition of the jury, or the defendant's own insanity. Moreover, the jury may assume the power to acquit out of compassion or prejudice, and the prosecution is then powerless to seek a judgment notwithstanding the verdict or a new trial on the ground that the verdict is against the weight of the evidence. . . . The injustice of an erroneous acquittal of a conspirator ought not to be compounded by a rule of law that requires the acquittal of his coconspirator. No doubt such inconsistency in verdicts is intellectually discomforting. Nevertheless, the public interest in securing just and accurate results in the criminal law leads us to conclude that the possibility of inconsistent verdicts should not bar the relitigation of an issue previously decided in favor of another defendant." Commonwealth v. Cerveny, 439 N.E.2d 754, 757 (Mass.1982). In the wake of decisions holding generally that inconsistency is not a basis for setting aside a verdict, the requirement of consistency in conspiracy cases has been rejected altogether in California and in a number of federal circuits. See People v. Palmer, 15 P.3d 234 (Cal.2001). Emphasizing "the time-honored rubric that a plea of guilty is a judicial admission of the truth of the factual allegations of the indictment," the court held that a conspirator who pleaded guilty was not entitled to withdraw his plea after the only other alleged conspirator was tried and acquitted, in United States v. Strother, 458 F.2d 424, 426 n.3 (5th Cir. 1972).

A person may be convicted of conspiring with "persons unknown," e.g., United States v. Lance, 536 F.2d 1065 (5th Cir.1976); with a person who is incapable of committing the offense that is the object of the conspiracy, e.g., Downs v. United States, 3 F.2d 855, 857 (3d Cir.1925) (participation of persons who are not government officers in conspiracy for government officers to receive bribe); or with a person who is immune to prosecution for the conspiracy, e.g., People v. Bryant, 100 N.E.2d 598 (Ill.1951) (grant of immunity in return for testimony). It has been held, however, that a person cannot be convicted of conspiracy with another person who is incapable of entering an agreement because of mental illness. United States v. Phillips, 630 F.2d 1138, 1146–47 (6th Cir.1980); Regle v. State, 264 A.2d 119 (Md.Ct.Spec.App.1970).

The Model Penal Code adopts a "unilateral" approach, according to which each actor's liability is determined by his own conduct (i.e. agreement) whether or not the person with whom he agreed, or intended to agree, is also liable. §§ 5.03, 5.04(1)(b). "Attention is directed . . . to each individual's culpability by framing the definition in terms of the conduct that suffices to establish the liability of any given actor, rather than the conduct of a group of which he is charged to be a part." 2 MPC Commentaries Part I, 398 (comment to § 5.03). That approach has been adopted in a considerable number of revised codes.

445. The defendant asked Zobel to help him kill the defendant's mother, for a price. Zobel informed the police and pretended to go along with the plan but at no time intended to do so. When he was prosecuted for conspiracy to murder, the defendant argued that there was no conspiracy since there was no true agreement. State v. St. Christopher, 232 N.W.2d 798 (Minn.1975). What result?

Following the approach taken by the Model Penal Code, the court in *St. Christopher* concluded that the defendant was guilty. Accord, e.g., Saienni v. State, 346 A.2d 152 (Del.1975); State v. Mace, 682 S.W.2d 163 (Mo.Ct.App.1984). The comment to the Model Penal Code says: "Under the unilateral approach of the Code, the culpable party's guilt would not be affected by the fact that the other party's agreement was feigned. He has conspired, within the meaning of the definition, in the belief that the other party was with him; apart from the issue of entrapment often presented in such cases, his culpability is not decreased by the other's secret intention. True, the project's chances of success have not been increased by the agreement; indeed, its doom may have been sealed by this turn of events.

But the major basis of conspiratorial liability, the unequivocal evidence of a firm purpose to commit a crime, remains the same." 2 MPC Commentaries Part I, 400 (comment to § 5.03).

The traditional rule in such cases, still widely followed, is that there is no conspiracy. E.g., People v. Foster, 457 N.E.2d 405 (Ill.1983); Delaney v. State, 51 S.W.2d 485 (Tenn.1932). Upholding the rule that there is no conspiracy when one of two supposed conspirators is a government agent who intends to frustrate commission of the crime ("the Sears rule"), the court in United States v. Escobar de Bright, 742 F.2d 1196 (9th Cir.1984) said:

> Strong considerations support the adoption of the Sears rule. A conspiracy is defined as an agreement between two or more people to commit an unlawful act . . . which arguably requires some form of a "meeting of minds," Krulewitch v. United States, 336 U.S. 440, 448 (1949) (Jackson, J., concurring). There is neither a true agreement nor a meeting of minds when an individual "conspires" to violate the law with only one other person and that person is a government agent. The principle was explained concisely . . . : "Since the act of agreeing is a group act, unless at least two people commit it, no one does. *When one of two persons merely pretends to agree, the other party, whatever he may believe, is in fact not conspiring with anyone.* Although he may possess the requisite criminal intent, there has been no criminal act." Developments in the Law—Criminal Conspiracy, 72 Harv. L. Rev. 920, 926 (1959) (emphasis added). . . . In short, the formal requirements of the crime of conspiracy have not been met unless an individual conspires with at least one bona fide co-conspirator.
>
> The rationale behind making conspiracy a crime also supports the Sears rule. Criminal conspiracy is an offense separate from the actual criminal act because of the perception "that collective action toward an antisocial end involves a greater risk to society than individual action toward the same end." [Id.]. . . . In part, this view is based on the perception that group activity increases the likelihood of success of the criminal act and of future criminal activity by members of the group, and is difficult for law enforcement officers to detect. . . .
>
> Such dangers, however, are non-existent when a person "conspires" only with a government agent. There is no continuing criminal enterprise and ordinarily no inculcation of criminal knowledge and practices. Preventive intervention by law enforcement officers also is not a significant problem in such circumstances. The agent, as part of the "conspiracy," is quite capable of monitoring the situation in order to prevent the completion of the contemplated criminal plan; in short, no cloak of secrecy surrounds any agreement to commit the criminal acts.
>
> Finally, the Sears rule responds to the same concern that underlies the entrapment defense: the legitimate law enforcement function of crime prevention "does not include the manufacturing of crime." Sherman v. United States, 356 U.S. 369, 372 (1958). . . . Allowing a

government agent to form a conspiracy with only one other party would create the potential for law enforcement officers to "manufacture" conspiracies when none would exist absent the government's presence.

742 F.2d at 1199–1200.

Would it be an appropriate resolution of cases like those discussed above to find the defendant guilty of an attempt to conspire? See State v. Kihnel, 488 So.2d 1238, 1244 (La.Ct.App.1986), in which, rejecting that approach, the court said:

> Attempt and conspiracy are both inchoate crimes. Just as there can be no attempt to commit an attempt, such as "attempted assault" . . . nor can there be an attempt to incite a felony . . . we conclude that under the bilateral formulation of conspiracy there can be no "attempted conspiracy."
>
> As part of the very foundation of criminal law, crimes include both a criminal act (or omission) and a criminal intent. . . . "Attempted conspiracy" suggests a crime formed only of criminal intent, as it is the agreement which constitutes the act.

446.   The Wharton rule. In an early Pennsylvania case, the court concluded that there could be no prosecution for conspiracy to commit adultery, than which, the court said, "nothing is more ridiculous." Shannon v. Commonwealth, 14 Pa. 226, 227 (1850). When the legislature had made adultery an offense, the court believed, it had not intended to make a prior agreement to commit adultery also criminal.[113] Without proposing to lay down "a rule for all cases," the court said that "where concert is a constituent part of the act to be done, as it is in fornication and adultery, a party acquitted of the major cannot be indicted of the minor." Id. at 227–28. From this limited source developed the "Wharton rule"[114] that "where it is impossible under any circumstances to commit the substantive offense without cooperative action, the preliminary agreement between the same parties to commit the offense is not an indictable conspiracy," Gebardi v. United States, 287 U.S. 112, 122 (1932). The rule has been accepted in American jurisdictions usually without discussion, as there was in *Shannon*, of legislative intent or the nature of the particular crime involved, except for the fact that agreement was necessary. There is no comparable rule in English law.

---

113.   The court noted that the male defendant in the case had already been acquitted of adultery. It said that it was "impossible to believe" that an unconsummated "adulterous enterprise" so injured society "as to admit of no propitiation for it but public castigation," and also noted "the danger from the uncertainty of the evidence" in such a case. 14 Pa. at 228.

114.   So named because Wharton formulated the principle as a general rule and is the usual authority for it. 2 F. Wharton, Criminal Law § 1604 (12th ed. 1932).

Is it an adequate explanation of the Wharton rule that "the gist of conspiracy is the enhanced danger to society from wrongful combination of purpose," People v. Comstock, 305 P.2d 228, 233 (Cal.Dist.Ct.App.1956), so that where agreement is an element of the offense itself, there is no basis for regarding it as a separate crime? That argument is now offered as the rationale not only of the rule but also of some limitations on the rule. The rule has been held inapplicable if more than the number necessary to accomplish the substantive offense are involved in the conspiracy to commit it, e.g., State v. Lennon, 70 A.2d 154 (N.J.1949), or if a statute establishing an offense provides that fewer than the number necessary to accomplish the offense are criminally liable for its commission, e.g., Vannata v. United States, 289 F. 424 (2d Cir.1923) (buyer and seller liable for conspiracy to sell whiskey without authority; buying not illegal).[115]

In Iannelli v. United States, 420 U.S. 770, 782 (1975), the Supreme Court discussed the Wharton rule at length and concluded that "it has current vitality only as a judicial presumption, to be applied in the absence of legislative intent to the contrary." The Court concluded that the rule was not applicable to 18 U.S.C. § 1955, proscribing an "illegal gambling business," defined as involving five or more persons. See Jeffers v. United States, 432 U.S. 137 (1977), discussing the application of *Iannelli* in another statutory context. Also, State v. Smith, 697 P.2d 512 (N.M.Ct.App. 1985) (harboring a felon; Wharton rule inapplicable).

The Wharton rule is rejected in the Model Penal Code. See 2 MPC Commentaries Part I, 482–84 (comment to § 5.04). A defendant may not, however, be convicted of both a substantive offense and a conspiracy to commit the offense, § 1.07(1)(b), nor is a conspiracy punishable more severely than the offense that is its object, § 5.05(1).[116]

115. Compare Ex parte O'Leary, 53 F.2d 956 (7th Cir.1931) (alternative holding) (giver and receiver of bribe both liable for conspiring to commit distinct statutory offenses of giving and receiving a bribe), with United States v. Sager, 49 F.2d 725 (2d Cir. 1931) (contra).

Related to the suggested rationale of the Wharton rule are decisions that a person cannot be convicted of a conspiracy to violate a statute if the statute manifests an affirmative legislative policy not to punish such a person for doing that which would be the basis of a charge of conspiracy. E.g., Gebardi v. United States, 287 U.S. 112 (1932).

116. The Wharton rule has both of these results in cases to which it applies. The desirability of limiting cumulative prosecutions and limiting the penalty that can be imposed for conspiracy, however, does not depend, as does the applicability of the Wharton rule, on the need for agreement for commission of the substantive offense; these results are, therefore, at most incidental benefits of the rule.

It was formerly held that a conspiracy to commit an offense was "merged" in the completed offense so that there could be no prosecution for the conspiracy. E.g., Commonwealth v. Kingsbury, 5 Mass. 106 (1809). This rule is no longer followed. See Callanan v. United States, 364 U.S. 587, 593 (1961), in which, relying on "the distinctiveness between a substantive offense and a conspiracy to commit it," the Court upheld consecutive sentences for conspiring to obstruct commerce by extortion and obstructing commerce by extortion, both made criminal by the same statute. Contra, e.g., State v. Hardison, 492 A.2d 1009 (N.J.1985), applying a

OBJECTIVES

Commonwealth v. Dyer

243 Mass. 472, 138 N.E. 296 (1923)

[The defendants were a large number of Boston dealers in fresh fish. They were indicted for conspiring to "create a monopoly in fresh fish, to fix, regulate, control, and to enhance exorbitantly and unreasonably the price of fresh fish, and thus to cheat and defraud the public." The period of the alleged conspiracy was during the years of World War I.]

The principles by which to determine the elements essential to conspiracy as a common law crime are settled in this Commonwealth. The subject was discussed at large by Chief Justice Shaw in Commonwealth v. Hunt, 4 Met. 111, where at page 123 it was said, "a conspiracy must be a combination of two or more persons, by some concerted action, to accomplish some criminal or unlawful purpose, or to accomplish some purpose, not in itself criminal or unlawful, by criminal or unlawful means. We use the terms criminal or unlawful, because it is manifest that many acts are unlawful, which are not punishable by indictment or other public prosecution; and yet there is no doubt, we think, that a combination by numbers to do them would be an unlawful conspiracy, and punishable by indictment. Of this character was a conspiracy to cheat by false pretences, without false tokens, when a cheat by false pretences only, by a single person, was not a punishable offence. . . . So a combination to destroy the reputation of an individual, by verbal calumny which is not indictable. So a conspiracy to

[handwritten margin note: definition of conspiracy]

state statute that, as in the Model Penal Code, preserves "merger" to the extent of a prohibition against convictions for *both* the underlying offense and a conspiracy to commit the offense. Statutory provisions in a number of other states are the same. For a suggestion of the dangers of successive prosecutions for the substantive offense and conspiracy to commit it, see State v. Chevencek, 23 A.2d 176 (N.J.Sup.Ct.1941), in which the defendants, who had been acquitted of rape, were subsequently indicted and convicted for conspiracy to commit fornication with the girl who was the complaining witness in the rape case. See also United States v. Boykins, 966 F.2d 1240 (8th Cir.1992), holding that it is permissible to convict and sentence a defendant for separate offenses of attempt and conspiracy based on the same course of conduct, under 21 U.S.C. § 846 (relating to drug offenses). Compare United States v. Touw, 769 F.2d 571 (9th Cir.1985) (separate charges of attempt and conspiracy for single act are permissible, but not multiple punishments).

In many states, the rule with respect to severity of the penalty for conspiracy is contrary to the Model Penal Code. E.g., Lane v. State, 288 N.E.2d 258, 260 (Ind.1972): "[A] conspiracy to commit a crime may properly be considered to be more serious than the commission of the contemplated crime." The defendant in *Lane* was sentenced to prison for two to fourteen years for conspiracy to commit second-degree burglary; the statutory penalty for the latter offense was two to five years imprisonment. The danger of excessive punishment for conspiracy is indicated also by State v. Coolidge, 171 A. 244 (Vt.1934), in which the court upheld convictions of common law conspiracy to defraud the state by falsely claiming a bounty for bobcats. A statute made it a misdemeanor punishable by a fine of not more than $20 to attempt to obtain such bounty by fraud; the sentences on the conspiracy convictions were four to five years and three to four years in a house of correction. See generally Clune v. United States, 159 U.S. 590, 594–95 (1895).

induce and persuade a young female, by false representations, to leave the protection of her parents' house, with a view to facilitate her prostitution. . . . But yet it is clear, that it is not every combination to do unlawful acts, to the prejudice of another by a concerted action, which is punishable as conspiracy . . . ."

. . .

The law has never declared otherwise than by the decision of specific cases as they arise the unlawful but not criminal acts which when made the object of co-operative design between two or more persons constitute criminal conspiracy. Manifestly the instances given by Chief Justice Shaw in 4 Met. at pages 123 and 124, were intended to be illustrative only and not exhaustive.

The great weight of authority in other jurisdictions is in harmony with the principle declared in Commonwealth v. Hunt, 4 Met. 111. That decision has been followed in many of the States of the Union. It is the consensus of opinion that conspiracy as a criminal offence is established when the object of the combination is either a crime, or if not a crime, is unlawful, or when the means contemplated are either criminal, or if not criminal, are illegal, provided that, where no crime is contemplated either as the end or the means, the illegal but non-criminal element involves prejudice to the general welfare or oppression of the individual of sufficient gravity to be injurious to the public interest. . . .

. . .

[T]he inquiry arises whether the illegal element in the monopoly here charged is of such nature as to render a combination for the purpose of establishing that monopoly a criminal conspiracy. By recurrence to the fundamental conception of conspiracy as a crime it is apparent that this monopoly involves prejudice to the general welfare of sufficient gravity to be injurious to the public interests. It seems to us manifest that a combination for the purpose of establishing a monopoly in an essential article of food and of raising excessively and unreasonably its price in time of war is highly inimical to the public welfare. The bald statement of the factors involved renders patent the harm to the public in manifold forms likely to ensue from such a monopoly. Enumeration of the general discontent, sufferings and other evils inevitable from the establishment of such a monopoly with such a purpose is not necessary to make plain its destructive and pernicious nature and its detriment to the public welfare. We are of opinion that a combination to create a monopoly for such a purpose and with such an intent is indictable as a conspiracy. This result follows from the considerations already stated and from the elements inherent in the situation.

. . .

447. Consider the examples of common law conspiracy mentioned by Chief Justice Shaw in *Hunt*, p. 706 above. If a group conspires to lure a girl from her parents' home "with a view to facilitate her prostitution," should its members be prosecuted for criminal conspiracy even if none of them would be criminally liable if he acted alone? If Polzin had a confederate in his effort to cheat Braseth, see p. 409 note 241 above, should they both have been criminally liable for common law conspiracy although Polzin acting alone committed no crime? If two persons agree to slander a third person and destroy his reputation, should both be prosecuted as criminals or should each be only civilly liable as would be the case if each acted independently? Or should the criminal law be amended to declare the conduct in each case, even by one person, criminal?

448. Assuming that the conduct of the defendants in *Dyer* was not criminal aside from the fact of their agreement, should they have been exempt from criminal liability and punishment if the commonwealth proved that they had agreed to fix prices of an essential commodity during wartime and thereby to realize "excessive and unreasonable" profits at the expense of the public?

Is it relevant, or controlling, that monopoly as such, with or without agreement, was unlawful in the sense that a contract that tended to create a monopoly was void?

449. In State v. Musser, 223 P.2d 193 (Utah 1950), the defendants were convicted of conspiracy to commit an act "injurious to public morals" in that they preached and practiced polygamy; the court reversed their convictions because the quoted statutory language was unconstitutionally vague and could not be narrowed by judicial construction. See also State v. Bowling, 427 P.2d 928 (Ariz.Ct.App.1967). But see People v. Sullivan, 248 P.2d 520 (Cal.Dist.Ct.App.1952); McKinnie v. State, 379 S.W.2d 214 (Tenn. 1964), rev'd on other grounds, 380 U.S. 449 (1965) (conspiracy "to commit any act injurious to public health, public morals, trade, or commerce"); see also Lorenson v. Superior Court, 216 P.2d 859 (Cal.1950).

The crime of conspiracy to corrupt public morals is extensively discussed in Shaw v. Director of Public Prosecutions, [1962] App.Cas. 220 (H.L.), involving publication of a prostitutes' business directory, and Knuller (Publishing, Printing and Promotions) Ltd. v. Director of Public Prosecutions, [1973] App.Cas. 435 (H.L.), involving a magazine that placed private advertisements for partners in homosexual activities. In both cases, convictions were sustained. In Reg. v. Kamara, [1974] App. Cas. 104 (H.L.), the defendants were convicted of conspiracy to commit a trespass, a noncriminal tort. They were students from Sierra Leone who entered the premises of that country's High Commissioner in London as a political protest. Their convictions also were affirmed. See the Report on Conspiracy and Criminal Law Reform (Law Com. No. 76) (1976), and the Criminal Law Act 1977, ch. 45, § 5(3), which continued in effect the common law crimes of agreement to engage in conduct that "tends to corrupt public morals or outrages public decency," even if the same conduct committed by a person acting alone would not be criminal.

Many prosecutions for criminal conspiracy were directed against the early efforts of labor to organize. E.g., State v. Glidden, 8 A. 890 (Conn. 1887). See generally R. Wright, Criminal Conspiracies and Agreements 43–62 (1873); Sayre, "Criminal Conspiracy," 35 Harv. L. Rev. 393 (1922).

450. Commonwealth v. Bessette, 217 N.E.2d 893, 897–98 (Mass. 1966).

The recent decisions undoubtedly have tended to apply the principles of criminal conspiracy primarily to group arrangements which have a criminal purpose or contemplate the use of criminal methods. Nevertheless, in view of the *Dyer* case [p. 706 above], we are not prepared to say that criminal conspiracy has been completely restricted to this extent. . . .

. . . [I]t is not now necessary to determine precisely when, in situations comparable to that presented in the *Dyer* case, joint action may create additional dangers and risks sufficient to make criminal as a conspiracy an agreement upon a plan for unlawful acts which would not be criminal when done by individuals separately. We think it plain, however, that the term "unlawful," as used in the criminal conspiracy cases (where neither a criminal object nor criminal means are in contemplation), is limited in any event to a narrow range of situations, (a) where there is strong probability (as in the monopolistic plans involved in the *Dyer* case) that the execution of the plan by group action will cause such significant harm to an individual or to the general public, as to be seriously contrary to the public interest, and (b) where the unlawfulness of objective or contemplated means is substantial and clear. There is sound reason for such limitation. As Perkins, Criminal Law, 544, points out, a more inclusive definition of "unlawful" might "be held void for vagueness under the Due Process Clause [of the Federal and Massachusetts Constitutions] unless what is . . . proscribed is spelled out with sufficient clearness to guide those who would be law-abiding and to advise defendants of the offense with which they are charged." Even as limited by this opinion, the rule of the *Dyer* case is necessarily indefinite and its application in a particular instance may present serious problems. This circumstance suggests strongly that certainty of statement of the criminal law would be greatly promoted by legislative definition of the types of unlawful, but not criminal, objectives and proposed means which may constitute elements of criminal conspiracy.[117]

117. The court suggests, 217 N.E.2d at 898, that an example of such "legislative definition" is the federal conspiracy statute, 18 U.S.C. § 371, which makes criminal a

For a case in which the Massachusetts court concluded that the object of a conspiracy did involve "great danger to the public interest," see Commonwealth v. Kelley, 260 N.E.2d 691 (Mass.1970) (use of public office for private profit).

451. Does the crime of criminal conspiracy limited to the "narrow range of situations" described in *Bessette* give the courts power to create new offenses? However you define the courts' power in such cases, is the need for it greater when concerted action is involved than when someone acts alone?

452. The crime of conspiracy at common law originated in the Ordinance of Conspirators, 33 Edw. 1, stat. 2, enacted in 1304, which prohibited agreements falsely to maintain indictments or pleas or to maintain vexatious suits. Until the seventeenth century the crime of conspiracy was limited to that offense. In the Poulterers' Case, 77 Eng. Rep. 813, which was decided in the Star Chamber in 1611 and involved a false accusation of robbery, it was held that the crime of conspiracy was committed even if the agreement were not carried into effect; the agreement itself constituted an offense "since there was a criminal intent manifested by an act done in furtherance of it, viz., by the agreement." R. Wright, Criminal Conspiracies and Agreements 7 (1873). From this conclusion developed the rule "that a combination to commit or to procure the commission of any crime was criminal and might be prosecuted as a conspiracy, although the crime might have nothing to do with the crime of conspiracy properly so called." Id.

In the seventeenth and eighteenth centuries the courts actively extended the criminal law. "It was a period when the courts were busy infusing morals into the law; and inevitably, as part of this process of infusion, there came to be a blurring of the line of distinction between law and morals, and a consequent confusion of the two." Sayre, "Criminal Conspiracy," 35 Harv. L. Rev. 393, 400 (1922). Toward the end of the seventeenth century the suggestion began to be made that an agreement to do a wrongful act might be criminal even if the act itself were not. In 1716 Hawkins published his Pleas of the Crown, in which he said that "there can be no doubt, but that all confederacies whatsoever, wrongfully to prejudice a third person, are highly criminal at common law." W. Hawkins, Pleas of the Crown 190 (1716). Unless by "wrongfully" Hawkins meant "criminal-

conspiracy "either to commit any offense against the United States, or to defraud the United States, or any agency thereof in any manner or for any purpose." That the important fact, however, is less the source—legislative or judicial—of the definition than its substance is indicated by one commentator's conclusion that conspiracy to defraud the United States is "a Kafkaesque crime, unknown and unknowable except in terms of the facts of each case—and even then, not until the verdict has been handed down." Goldstein, "Conspiracy to Defraud the United States," 68 Yale L.J. 405, 463 (1959).

ly," he had no case law to support his proposition. By the nineteenth century, however, the doctrine that an agreement to do an unlawful act—"unlawful" not necessarily meaning criminal—is itself criminal was accepted.[118] The doctrine developed first in the area of fraud. Even if the method used did not constitute the common law crime of cheating or violate the statute of 33 Hen. 8 against false tokens, see p. 399 above, a combination to defraud was regarded as bringing the case among those which the law should prohibit, because the combination, like the use of false weights or a false token, was something against which common prudence could not guard.[119]

453. The delimitation of conspiratorial objectives under current law typically reflects the development of conspiracy as a crime at common law. Where conspiracy has been made a statutory crime, the prohibited objectives are most often stated generally and/or by reference to the commission of a crime, interference with the administration of justice (e.g., false arrest or indictment, false maintenance of a suit), fraud, and acts injurious to the public welfare. In about a quarter of the states an agreement may be a criminal conspiracy only if it is an agreement to commit a crime (or, in some states, a felony). There are in addition many statutes making agreements for particular purposes criminal.[120]

The Model Penal Code § 5.03 limits the crime of conspiracy to agreements to commit a crime. "[T]here are some activities that should be criminal only if engaged in by a group, but they should be dealt with by special conspiracy provisions in the legislation governing the general class of conduct in question, and they should be no less precise than penal provisions generally in defining the conduct they prescribe." 2 MPC Commentaries Part I, 396 (comment to § 5.03).

454. "[W]hen two or more persons agree upon a course of conduct with the object of committing a criminal offence, but, unknown to them, it

---

118. "The truth of the matter is that judges found the Hawkins conception of criminal conspiracy entirely too convenient an instrument for enforcing their own individual notions of justice to be lightly discarded. It enabled judges to punish by criminal process such concerted conduct as seemed to them socially oppressive or undesirable, even though the actual deeds committed constituted of themselves no crime, either by statute or by common law. And in cases where the actual deeds were of doubtful criminality, it saved the judges from the often embarrassing necessity of having to spell out the crime." Sayre, "Criminal Conspiracy," 35 Harv. L. Rev. 393, 406 (1922).

119. See Rex v. Wheatly, p. 400 above.

120. E.g., Mass. Gen. L. ch. 93, §§ 4, 5, 6 (restraint of trade, monopolization).

Courts have commonly held that if persons agree to carry out an objective that is prohibited but is only "malum prohibitum," not wrongful in itself, they are not guilty of conspiracy unless they have some consciousness of wrongdoing, even if there is no such requirement for commission of the substantive offense. E.g., Commonwealth v. Benesch, 194 N.E. 905 (Mass.1935). Cf. United States v. Mack, 112 F.2d 290, 292 (2d Cir.1940).

is not possible to achieve their object by the course of conduct agreed upon, do they commit the crime of conspiracy?" Director of Public Prosecutions v. Nock, [1978] App. Cas. 979, 994. In *Nock*, the defendants agreed to extract cocaine from a quantity of a chemical substance in their possession. They made a variety of attempts to obtain cocaine from the substance, all of which were unsuccessful. After they had been arrested and the substance had been sent for chemical analysis, they learned to their surprise that the substance contained no cocaine and that there was no way to produce cocaine from it. What result?

With *Nock*, compare United States v. Waldron, 590 F.2d 33 (1st Cir.1979), in which the defendant was convicted of conspiring to transport stolen property having a value of at least $5000. He and others agreed to import valuable stolen paintings from Canada. The only painting actually transported turned out to be a forgery worth much less than $5000. The court observed that the conspiracy was far advanced and that there was abundant proof of overt acts, so that there was not "any danger of a trumped-up charge of conspiracy being successfully levied against persons for their mere wishful thinking." On that record, the court concluded, there was no reason "to back away from the principle that a culpable conspiracy may exist even though, because of the misapprehension of the conspirators as to certain facts, the substantive crime which is the object of the conspiracy may be impossible to commit." Id. at 34. To the same effect, see, e.g., United States v. Everett, 692 F.2d 596 (9th Cir.1982); United States v. Rose, 590 F.2d 232 (7th Cir.1978) ("stolen goods" not actually stolen because of government agent's participation in conspiracy). But cf. Ventimiglia v. United States, 242 F.2d 620 (4th Cir.1957).

455. A group of tenants have made representations to their landlord that their apartments are in disrepair and that maintenance of the building in its present condition violates provisions of the municipal housing code. The landlord has done nothing. Repeated complaints to the housing authority have had no effect. Because of the backlog of such complaints to the authority, if for no other reason, it is unlikely that it will act on the complaints soon. The tenants hold a meeting and agree that they will all withhold a portion of the monthly rent due until repairs are made. They understand that failure to pay the agreed rent constitutes a breach of their contract with the landlord; they assume that although the landlord would take action to evict one or two tenants who fail to pay the rent, he will not evict a large number of tenants at one time.

Are the tenants who participate in such a "rent strike" guilty of conspiracy? Should the criminal law intervene, by a general conspiracy prosecution or by prosecution under a narrowly drawn statute specifically prohibiting rent strikes, in a dispute of this kind? Cf. Roosevelt Hospital v. Orlansky, 400 N.Y.S.2d 663 (Sup.Ct.1977); Springfield, Bayside Corp. v. Hochman, 255 N.Y.S.2d 140 (Sup.Ct.1964).

456. Can the allied powers' prosecution of German nationals for war crimes during World War II be explained on a basis akin to the theory which produced the crime of conspiracy in the common law?

"The doctrine of common law conspiracy was conceived and nurtured to meet an urgent social necessity of the times. If a similar doctrine does not exist today in the international sphere, there is certainly a need for it to buttress the conviction of the war crime defendants who designed the serious crimes which were perpetrated against humanity and society. It is believed that if such a doctrine did exist it would form a valid answer to the critics of the Nuremberg trials; it is therefore conceivable that since a need exists, the world may see the development of a law of criminal conspiracy in international law, similar to that of common law conspiracy in Anglo-American jurisprudence." Pollack, "Common Law Conspiracy," 35 Geo. L.J. 328, 352 (1947).

*

PART FIVE

LIMITATIONS

In the preceding Parts, we have examined various aspects of the criminal law in the context of specific crimes or defenses to a criminal charge. Part Five reviews from a more general perspective some of the questions previously considered. First, it considers constitutional limitation of the punishment that can be imposed for a crime. And second, it considers constitutional limitation of the conduct that can be declared criminal. Another large array of constitutional limitations concerns the process by which the government investigates and prosecutes crime. Procedural requirements, contained in the Fourth, Fifth, Sixth, and Eighth Amendments and the Due Process Clause of the Fourteenth Amendment, are among the most familiar constitutional provisions: for example, the right to be free from unreasonable searches and seizures (Fourth), the privilege against compulsory self-incrimination (Fifth), and the right to a speedy and public trial (Sixth). These aspects of criminal process are usually considered apart from substantive criminal law and are not included here; but the actual impact of criminal law depends greatly on the process, as a matter of constitutional law and otherwise, by which it is applied. The deterrent effect of the law, for example, is not unaffected by the inordinate length of time that (notwithstanding the constitutional provision) usually elapses between the crime and detection of the criminal and the punishment. Finally, limitation of the conduct that can be declared criminal is enlarged from the constitutional framework to the fully open question considered above, in the context of homicide, at the end of Part One: What, so far as criminal law is concerned, are the proper bounds of the government's authority over the individual?

---

1. PUNISHMENT

The Eighth Amendment to the Constitution provides that "cruel and unusual punishments [shall not be] inflicted." Although the Cruel and Unusual Punishments Clause is applicable directly to the federal government and has been applied to the states through the Due Process Clause of the Fourteenth Amendment, it has had little effect on the punishments actually imposed. A few Justices of the Supreme Court have held the view that capital punishment is impermissible under the Clause; but that view has, for the present, at any rate, been rejected. See pp. 334–35 above. Capital punishment would surely be regarded as "cruel and unusual" if it were imposed for any but the most serious offenses. Whether capital punishment is permitted for any crime other than homicide is unclear; see Coker v. Georgia, 433 U.S. 584 (1977), in which four Justices who would not bar capital punishment altogether declared that it was prohibited for the crime of rape. Except in a very few states, capital punishment is restricted to the most serious category of homicide; so the constitutional issue is not likely to arise. By a close, shifting majority the Court has held that the Cruel and Unusual Punishments Clause does not prohibit the imposition of capital punishment for felony murder, even though the defendant did not himself kill or intend that anyone be killed. Tison v. Arizona, 481 U.S. 137 (1987) (5–4). See p. 335 above.

In a small number of instances, a sentence of imprisonment has been held invalid under the Cruel and Unusual Punishments Clause. See, e.g., Hart v. Coiner, 483 F.2d 136 (4th Cir.1973). In *Hart*, the defendant was convicted of perjury. He was sentenced to life imprisonment as a recidivist, the prior convictions being for writing a check for $50 on insufficient funds and interstate transportation of forged checks worth $140. The court concluded that "the recidivist mandatory life sentence *in this case* is so excessive and disproportionate to the underlying offenses as to constitute cruel and unusual punishment." Id. at 139.

The Supreme Court denied certiorari in *Hart*, sub nom. Coiner v. Hart, 415 U.S. 983 (1974). Subsequently, however, in Rummel v. Estelle, 445 U.S. 263 (1980) (5–4), the Court indicated its disapproval of the court of appeals' reasoning. The defendant in *Rummel* was convicted of obtaining $120.75 by false pretenses. Like Hart, he was sentenced to life imprisonment as a recidivist, the prior convictions being for fraudulent use of a credit card to obtain $80 worth of goods or services and passing a forged check for $28.36. The Court observed that "successful challenges to the proportionality of particular sentences have been exceedingly rare," id. at 272, one such being Weems v. United States, 217 U.S. 349 (1910), in which the defendant was sentenced in the Philippines to "*cadena temporal*," involving lengthy imprisonment in exceedingly harsh conditions, for the crime of falsifying a public record. The Court said that except with respect to a unique punishment like that in *Weems* or capital punishment, the length of a term of imprisonment for felonies "is purely a matter of legislative prerogative." 445 U.S. at 274. (Rummel was in fact released from prison within eight months of the Court's decision. Solem v. Helm, 463 U.S. 277, 297 n.25 (1983).) In Hutto v. Davis, 454 U.S. 370 (1982) (6–3), the Court held that consecutive sentences of twenty years' imprisonment on two counts of possession with intent to distribute and distribution of a small amount of marijuana did not violate the Eighth Amendment.

In Solem v. Helm, above, however, the Court held (5–4) that a sentence of life imprisonment without possibility of parole imposed for passing a bad check for $100, following convictions for six other nonviolent felonies, was a cruel and unusual punishment. Acknowledging "the broad authority that legislatures necessarily possess in determining the types and limits of punishments for crimes, as well as . . . the discretion that trial courts possess in sentencing convicted criminals," 463 U.S. at 290, the Court said, "[W]e hold as a matter of principle that a criminal sentence must be proportionate to the crime for which the defendant has been convicted." Id. An analysis of proportionality, the Court said, "should be guided by objective criteria, including (i) the gravity of the offense and the harshness of the penalty; (ii) the sentences imposed on other criminals in the same jurisdiction; and (iii) the sentence imposed for commission of the same crime in other jurisdictions." Id. at 292. Applying those factors, the Court concluded that Helm's sentence was "significantly disproportionate to his crime" and prohibited by the Eighth Amendment. Id. at 303. The Court purported to distinguish Rummel v. Estelle. Four dissenting Justices, however, asserted that the majority had overruled that case without saying so. In comparison with Helm, they said, Rummel "was a relatively 'model citizen.' " Id. at 304. The Court has upheld a mandatory sentence of life imprisonment without possibility of parole, for possession of more than 650 grams of cocaine. It rejected the defendant's arguments that the sentence was disproportionate to the crime and that aside from proportionality, a mandatory sentence of life imprisonment without consideration of possible mitigating factors was a cruel and unusual punishment. Harmelin v. Michigan, 501 U.S. 957 (1991) (5–4). A sentence of 25 years to life for the crime of petty theft, pursuant to the California "Three Strikes" (recidivist) statute has been found to violate the Eighth Amendment. Mayle v. Ylst, 283 F.3d 1019 (9th Cir.2002).

In view of the considerably inconsistent results in Rummel v. Estelle and Solem v. Helm, it is difficult to conclude that "proportionality analysis," as it is called, is as objective as the majority in the latter case suggested. Even if the factors to be considered are "objectively" determined, the weight and significance given them evidently is not. Since there was a 5–4 majority in both cases, the impact of proportionality analysis in future cases is difficult to predict.

———

457. Reconsider your ranking of homicides and the other crimes on p. 330 above. Without the benefit of actual comparative sentences, which the Court said was an important element of proportionality analysis, is there any ranking of the crimes on the list that you would regard as a violation of the Cruel and Unusual Punishments Clause on the basis of "the gravity of the offense and the harshness of the penalty" alone?

458. Rank the following crimes in the order of their "seriousness":

(i) Auto driver picked up for driving while drunk (policeman saw him weaving a little from side to side and stopped subject to investigate);

(ii) Father seriously beat four-year-old child;

(iii) Subject bought stolen property worth $1,000 knowing it was stolen;

(iv) Subject bribed a state's witness to the crime of a friend while the friend was on trial;

(v) Subject caught in stranger's home, attempting burglary;

(vi) Subject caught running away with wallet, containing $1000, taken from pocket of well-to-do man;

(vii) Subject deliberately cut telephone wires to neighbor's house;

(viii) Subject deliberately set fire to fur coat, worth $1000, of woman he hated;

(ix) Subject has married a second time while knowing that his first wife is alive and undivorced;

(x) Subject picked up carrying a pistol without a license;

(xi) Subject planned and deliberately assaulted with a knife a man he hated; victim was cut a little but not seriously;

(xii) Subject signed check for $1000 with another's name and cashed it;

(xiii) Subject visits friend in prison and brings him some narcotics, since friend is a drug addict.[1]

1. In an experiment conducted at the University of Minnesota in 1953, students ranked the 13 crimes (chosen because they had roughly the same penalties under the California Penal Code) in the following descending order of seriousness: (ii), (xi), (iv), (xiii), (ix), (xii), (vi), (viii), (v), (iii), (i), (x), (vii). See Rose & Prell, "Does the Punishment Fit the Crime? A Study in Social Valuation," 61 Am. J. Soc. 247 (1955).

The sociologists who conducted the experiment reported among their findings that:

"1. There is a significant discrepancy among the law, the application of the law, and popular judgment as to how the law should be applied in assigning punishments for thirteen selected minor felonies. For example, the crime of severe beating of a child by a father is regarded as much more serious, relatively speaking, by public opinion than it is by law. This is interpreted as a 'cultural lag' in the law as compared to popular conceptions of the rights of children.

"2. There is . . . a fairly consistent and stable hierarchy of the seriousness of crimes in the minds of most individuals. Yet, in our heterogenous society, the background characteristics of judges are related to the judg-ments they make in assigning punishments for various offenses, at least as far as sex, socioeconomic status, and size-of-community characteristics are concerned. . . . [T]here are certain specific relationships between an individual's personal characteristics and the punishments he would assign to offenders with similar or complementary characteristics. For example, persons from rural areas are inclined to assign harsher punishments for crimes which generally occur more frequently in urban areas, and they are especially inclined to deal harshly with those convicted of arson or of cutting electric or telephone lines—crimes which perhaps are of greater significance in rural areas than in urban ones.

"3. Punishments favored for criminals of different social classes and for the two sexes vary according to the crime and its cultural meaning in relation to class and sex. Our subjects were much more willing to be deliberately nonequalitarian in assignment of fines than in assignment of prison sentences and more deliberately nonequalitarian in punishing the upper-class offender than in punishing the middle-class, or lower-class, or women offenders." Id. at 257.

Having in mind the Supreme Court's holdings in Rummel v. Estelle and Solem v. Helm, above, would you conclude that a sentence of 20 years' imprisonment for any of the above offenses, by itself or by application of a recidivist statute, violated the Cruel and Unusual Punishments Clause? Ten years? Five?

———

There follow two presentence reports, preceded by a sentencing checklist. The reports are actual reports, only names having been changed. Using the sentencing checklist as a guide, fix the sentence in each case. (Assume that the sentence will specify actual time, if any, in prison and not be reduced by parole or a "good time" reduction.)

SENTENCING CHECKLIST

The Offense(s):
[ ] Nature of crime(s)
[ ] Mode of commission
[ ] Relation to organized crime
[ ] Threat or use of violence
[ ] Gravity of public injury
[ ] Defendant's role
[ ] Defendant's motivation
[ ] Other

Personal Characteristics:
[ ] Age
[ ] Intelligence
[ ] Education
[ ] Aptitudes
[ ] Leisure interests
[ ] Other

Personal History:
[ ] Family history
[ ] Social history
[ ] Marital history
[ ] Religious interests
[ ] Economic resources
[ ] Other

Special Considerations:
[ ] Motivation to reform
[ ] Capacity to reform
[ ] Dangerousness
[ ] Environmental factors
[ ] Community resources
[ ] Institutional resources
[ ] Other

Long Range Needs:
[ ] Counseling
[ ] Educational
[ ] Vocational training
[ ] Remedial medical care
[ ] Psychotherapy
[ ] Treatment for alcoholism
[ ] Treatment for drug addiction
[ ] Correction
[ ] Other

Employment History:
[ ] Vocational training
[ ] Vocational capabilities
[ ] Employment experience
[ ] Employment prospects
[ ] Other

Criminal History:
[ ] Criminal record
[ ] Extensiveness
[ ] Seriousness
[ ] Responses to past rehabilitative efforts
[ ] Other

Health:
[ ] Physical
[ ] Emotional stability
[ ] Mental normality
[ ] Alcoholic involvement
[ ] Narcotic involvement
[ ] Other

Diagnostic Needs:
[ ] Intelligence evaluation
[ ] Aptitude evaluation
[ ] Medical evaluation
[ ] Psychiatric/psychological evaluation
[ ] Sentencing policy information
[ ] Other

Attitudes:
[ ] Toward self
[ ] Toward offense(s)
[ ] Toward society
[ ] Toward present predicament
[ ] Toward the future
[ ] Other

Sentencing Objectives:
[ ] Community protection
[ ] Rehabilitation
[ ] Deterrence
[ ] Punishment
[ ] Other

**UNITED STATES DISTRICT COURT FOR THE
DISTRICT OF COLUMBIA**

PRESENTENCE REPORT

NAME
  REDDISH, Ernest

ADDRESS
  1000 Montgomery Street, S.E.
  Washington, D.C.

LEGAL RESIDENCE
  Same

AGE   25   DATE OF BIRTH   8-9-42

SEX   Male   RACE   Negro

CITIZENSHIP
  United States

EDUCATION
  11th grade (Claimed)

MARITAL STATUS
  Married

DEPENDENTS
  Five (Wife and four children)

SOC. SEC. NO.
  700-00-1111

FBI NO.
  000 000 Z

DETAINERS OR CHARGES PENDING:
  CC #500-67 Assault on Member of
  Police Force (Two)
  Carrying Dangerous Weapon (Gun)—
  Scheduled for trial week of 2-12-68.
  CC #00-68 Assault with Dangerous
  Weapon (Gun) (Two counts)—No
  trial date scheduled

CODEFENDANTS (*Disposition*)
  Scott A. Scarlet
  Albert Maroon
  Roy Ruby

DATE
  February, 16 1968

DOCKET NO.
  CC #000-67

OFFENSE
  Unauthorized Use of Vehicle
  (22 DCC 2204)
  Entering Back W/I to Commit
  Robbery; Bank Robbery (18 USC
  2113(a) Robbery (Holdup) (Violation
  22 DCC 2901)

PENALTY

PLEA

VERDICT
  1-29-68, Guilty, counts one to
  twelve, inclusive, Judge Solomon.

CUSTODY
  Arrested 11-22-66, released on $5,000
  bond 12-30-66; arrested 2-11-67, in CC
  #500-67, released on $2,000 bond on
  April 16, 1967; arrested on 11-18-67 in
  CC #00-68, released on $10,000 bond
  on 12-5-67.

ASST. U. S. ATTY.
  Victor Caputy

DEFENSE COUNSEL
  John T. Toomey

PENALTY:
  Count one: Fine of not more than
  $1,000 or not more than five years
  imprisonment, or both.
  Count two: Fine of not more than
  $5,000, or not more than twenty
  years imprisonment, or both.
  Counts three, five, seven, nine,
  eleven: Fine of not more than $5,000,
  or not more than twenty years
  imprisonment, as to each count.
  Counts four, six, eight, ten, twelve:
  Imprisonment for not less than six
  months, nor more than fifteen years.

I OFFENSE:

On January 29, 1968, at the conclusion of an eight day jury trial, before the Honorable Frank Solomon, defendant Reddish and codefendants Scott A. Scarlet, Albert Maroon, Jr. and Roy Ruby were found guilty of counts one to twelve, inclusive. Count one charges the four defendants with Unauthorized Use of an Automobile, on or about November 15, 1966, which belonged to Richard A. Thomas. Count two charges, on November 22, 1966, the entry of the Brookland Branch of The National Bank of Washington, FDIC insured, with intent to commit a robbery. Counts three, five, seven, nine, and eleven, cite the Federal charge of actual Bank Robbery of monies in the possession of said bank, in the aggregate total of $15,308.32; counts four, six, eight, ten, and twelve cite the D.C. Criminal Code charge of Robbery. Defendant Reddish was named in the thirteenth count of the indictment, charged with Carrying a Dangerous Weapon, pistol, however, this charge was dismissed during trial on the oral motion of the Government.

Official Version:

Your Honor undoubtedly remains familiar with the facts and testimony offered during the jury trial of this case. A brief review, however, is offered. Approximately only minutes to 9:55 a.m., November 22, 1966, three Negro male subjects, wearing masks over their faces, also armed with pistols, entered the Brookland Branch of The National Bank of Washington, D.C., 3006 12th Street, N.E. and announced a bank robbery: "All right folks, this is it, get on the floor!" Two of the subjects hurdled the counter in front of the teller cages and started grabbing all available monies from the respective teller cages. The aggregate sum of $15,308.02 was seized by subjects and placed in bank money bags. When an automobile horn sounded outside, more or less as a signal, the three original subjects then fled the bank and entered an awaiting 1965 Ford Mustang car, last seen to speed away on Perry Street, N.E. The bank manager and a teller pushed the alarm button; also, they and a private citizen outside of the bank managed to note the license number of the fleeing Mustang, which was later conveyed to responding police officers. The official time of the robbery was established as at 9:55 a.m.

Within minutes of the reported robbery cruising police officers spotted the aforementioned, aforedescribed Mustang car parked in the 1300 block of Perry Street, N.E., only a few blocks away from the scene of the bank robbery. A black, automatic loaded pistol, plus rolls of coins and paper money, were found and recovered from the aforementioned car. A quick canvass of nearby houses resulted in one witness telling the police officers that a small U–Haul truck had been parked in front of her residence at 1324 Perry Street since about 9:30 a.m.; also, the witness stated that she heard the same truck suddenly speed away at a high rate of speed, at about 10 a.m. A lookout was immediately broadcast for the U–Haul truck; several minutes later, the same truck was observed and stopped by police officers in the 1000 block of Kenilworth Avenue, N.E. After the police officers stopped the aforementioned truck, the driver, later identified as defendant Ernest Reddish, alighted from the driver's side of the truck. As he and the police officers approached one another, the latter observed a pistol handle protruding from subject's pants pocket; also, the officers glimpsed two subjects quickly looking out of the rear window of the truck and suddenly duck down. Defendant Reddish was immediately placed under arrest and a .38 caliber loaded pistol was seized from his pocket. Upon looking into the truck and observing three Negro subjects lying on the floor, the police officers immediately radioed for assistance, at the same time, ordered the three subjects not to move. Upon the arrival of police assistance, the three subjects were ordered from the truck and were immediately placed under arrest. A search of the truck resulted in the recovery of two cloth bank bags containing $14,911.00 in money, also, a (third) pistol, which one of the subjects had dropped as he emerged from the truck; further, a pair of sunglasses, silk handkerchiefs (used to cover their faces as masks) and four pairs of gloves were recovered, all or most of which had been used in the robbery. A personal search of codefendant Ruby's person resulted in the recovery of $320 in bills, which was identified as "bait" money taken during the robbery. A total of $15,297.00 in money was recovered, respectively, from the 1965 Mustang, the truck and from codefendant Ruby; $11.32 apparently was not recovered. After being arrested at 10:19 a.m. and charged with the instant bank robbery–holdup, the four defendants were transported to the Robbery Squad Office, where all four subjects denied the offense. In a subsequent lineup, the bank manager and other witnesses from inside the bank apparently could not be sure of any identification. On the other hand, a private citizen witness, who observed the robbery taking place as she entered the bank but managed to walk outside whereupon she observed the awaiting 1965 Mustang, parked in front of the bank and was able to look at the Negro driver behind the wheel, viewed the same lineup, and identified codefendant, Scott A. Scarlet, as the one she saw behind the wheel and who drove the other subjects away from the hold-up scene.

Intense investigation by both local police and FBI Agents resulted in the uncovering of the fact that the instant truck had been rented by one Alex Alexander, an uncle of defendant Reddish. He informed interrogating officers that he had rented the truck at the request of defendant Reddish and had turned same over to him; the latter had given him $25.00 with which to do so. Mr. Alexander also stated that the license tags found on the instant Mustang had come from a Dodge vehicle which had been given to Reddish and himself to repair and personally use. Alexander denied any knowledge of the intended use of the truck, or about the bank robbery. In subsequent contact with FBI Agents, he identified codefendant Maroon and defendant Reddish as close, long-term friends. As to the pieces of clothing recovered from the floor of the truck—a green raincoat, (2) black kerchiefs, (3) pillow cases, (4) multi-colored scarfs—most were identified by bank tellers—witnesses, as having been worn by the holdup subjects.

Your Honor is apprised of subsequent aggravating, additional information, that on February 11, 1967, while on bond in CC #000–67, the defendant was arrested in a new case charging assault on two police officers and Carrying a Dangerous Weapon, gun. The new case is represented in CC #500–67, which is scheduled for trial during the week of February 12, 1968. Also, while on bond in CC #000–67, and CC #500–67 the defendant was arrested on November 18, 1967 charged with two counts of Assault with a Dangerous Weapon, gun, now represented in CC #00–68, for which no trial date has been scheduled. Subject secured his release on bond ($10,000) in CC #00–68, on December 5, 1967.

II DEFENDANT'S VERSION OF OFFENSE:

In the writer's presentence interview with this defendant, he advised that he did not take the witness stand during his trial. He denied any knowledge of the bank robbery. He immediately elaborated that he was planning to move from his residence and was looking for a place to rent, also, a garage to rent to store excess furniture. He stated that he had been searching in the area of Rhode Island Avenue and Monroe Street, N.E., and eventually turned into an alley paralleling 13th and 12th Streets, N.E., off Newton Street, N.E. Here, he says he saw a mattress awaiting to be picked up by the trash people. It looked relatively in good condition, and he thought he would examine same closely. He says he left his parked truck, and, after looking at the mattress, picked it up and carried it back to the truck. When he threw the mattress in the back of the truck, he then claimed finding National Bank of Washington bank bags, containing a very large sum of money. After examining the money, also, noting that no one was around, he said he got "hungry" and took off, "asking no questions."

He then indicated coming upon codefendant Maroon, who was standing on a corner with Ruby and Scarlet. He stopped the truck and Maroon and the other two subjects entered the truck. He indicated only that this was on Kenilworth Avenue near the Benning Road viaduct. After pulling away from the curb, the police came up from behind him and pulled him over. "Only I knew what was up front (meaning the money bags)" . . . "I decided not to say anything to the police." He concluded his version by denying, again, having any knowledge of the bank robbery, or anything else as to how the money bags from the robbery got into his truck.

The defendant offered the foregoing in a very explicit matter-of-fact manner, without any overt concern for his predicament, or remorse for the case itself. What concern was expressed, and perhaps in a manner to entice some sympathy in his behalf, centered around frequent references made to his wife and children and their welfare. He impressed the writer as very sophisticated, also, adept at concealing inner feelings of hostility, particularly centered around the police.

III PRIOR RECORD:

3-11-58	Unauthorized Use of Vehicle	Probation, indefinite.

The defendant was apprehended while riding, with three other juveniles, in a stolen car. On March 21, 1958, Judge Wise of D.C. Juvenile Court placed him on indefinite probation supervision.

4-26-58	Unauthorized Use of Vehicle	Sentenced to National Training School for Boys.

Within five weeks after being placed on juvenile probation supervision in the above case, the defendant was arrested as the driver of a stolen car which had been rented by a doctor. Facts indicate he led the police on a high speed chase, which ended in a collision and more than $1,000 damages inflicted on the stolen automobile. On April 29, 1958, he was found involved in D.C. Juvenile Court, who immediately ordered him committed to the National Training School for Boys under a minority commitment. . . . The defendant made a satisfactory adjustment while at the National Training School and gained his release on parole on June 20, 1959.

11-7-59 (17)	Assault with Dangerous Weapon (Shod foot)	No disposition indicated.

The defendant was arrested with several other youths and charged with assaulting two young victims, one of whom the defendant kicked while lying on the ground. As a result of the arrest and circumstances surrounding same, the Youth Division of the U.S. Board of Parole issued a parole violation warrant, ordering his return to the National Training School.

11-30-59	Parole Violation Warrant	Returned to National Training School for Boys, effective 1-20.
4-8-60	Escape from National Training School	

Adult:

2-2-61	Affray	Consolidated records, Dept. of Prisons, Raleigh, N.C.	30 days jail
9-15-61	Assault with Dangerous Weapon	" "	Two years

Circumstances surrounding this arrest and two year sentence presently remain unknown. The FBI Report, however, indicated the defendant escaped on October 11, 1961, only to be recaptured on the following day, October 12, 1961.

10-25-62	Escape	Consolidated Records, Dept. of Prisons, Raleigh, N.C.	Three months added to the two year sentence.
5-23-66 Washington, D.C.	Carrying a Dangerous Weapon, Pistol		ISS, probation — one year

The arrest facts indicate a man entered a High's Dairy Store in northeast Washington, and announced a robbery by stating, "Give me all the money in your pocket," whereupon he displayed a pistol in his pants pocket. When a second female clerk suddenly emerged from the rear of the store, the man hastily said, "I'm only kidding, I'm not going to shoot you"; he then walked out of the store. The police responded to the scene, obtained a description of the suspect, and shortly afterward, came upon three young adults, including this defendant, one who [sic] matched the description of the suspect. All three suspects were searched. Police seized a loaded .38 caliber Empire State revolver, containing five rounds, from the person of defendant Reddish. A .38 caliber revolver was seized from a second subject—Lew E. Wood, who was identified as the suspect who had entered the High's Store and announced the robbery attempt. The third suspect—Pat A. Kidd, was identified as a strong suspect in a different robbery holdup violation. . . . After a presentence investigation the defendant was placed on probation, on August 18, 1967. The writer has reviewed the probation department file in D.C. Court of General Sessions; no indication was reflected in the file as to the issuance of a probation violation warrant in their case, based on the defendant's arrest and/or conviction in CC #000–67.

11-22-66	Bank Robbery (Holdup)	Instant Case CC #000–67
2-11-67	Assault on Police Officers (2) Carrying Dangerous Weapon, Gun	Indicted in CC # 500-67

As previously mentioned, while on bond in the instant case, on February 11, 1967, about 4:20 p.m., police officers observed the defendant in a 1966 Chevelle automobile with four other subjects. When the police officer (Moore) approached and asked the defendant for his operator's license, the police officer also observed one subject to push a paper bag under the car seat, but not before the officer had observed a pistol barrel protruding from the bag. When Officer Moore sought to obtain possession of the gun, defendant Reddish is said to have instigated an assault on the officer. When the officer's partner (Flynn) responded, a second occupant of the car, James Jamison, 21, intercepted and yoked Officer Flynn into unconsciousness. When Jamison continued to assault the unconscious officer, Officer Moore shot Jamison, necessitating his removal to a hospital. A third off-duty police officer assisted Officer Moore to subdue and maintain Reddish's arrest. Also, codefendant Maroon, who had been an original occupant of the car, stepped from the gathered crowd and began assaulting both police officers in an attempt to free this defendant Reddish. However, Maroon was subdued and his arrest also effected. Additional facts indicate that four guns (one an automatic pistol), two ski masks, gloves and clotheslines were seized as evidence from the aforementioned car. Reddish, Jamison and codefendant Maroon have been named in a three count indictment in CC #500–67, which is scheduled for trial during the week of February 21, 1968.

11-18-67 Assault with Dangerous   Indicted in
         Weapon, Gun   CC #00–68.

Arrest facts indicate the police responded to a report that Joseph and Jane Johnson, husband and wife, were shot in front of their home at 1000 Curry Avenue, S.E., by means of a gun held in the hands of this defendant. The defendant has now been indicted, however, a trial date has not been scheduled.

IV FAMILY HISTORY:

This defendant was born in Whiteville, Columbus County, North Carolina on August 9, 1942, and was brought to Washington, D.C., by his mother when approximately three or four years of age. He is the oldest of two boys of his natural parents, Ernest and Chellin, nee Redd, Reddish, who are respectively said to be about 50 and 45 years of age. The defendant has advised us he never knew his real father. However, after the birth of his younger brother, James, now 23, and serving in the Army in Vietnam, his mother "took to living in a common-law type marriage" with a Manuel Reddish, 52, whom he calls his stepfather, a chef cook, whom he understands to be his father's natural uncle. Subsequently, four children, two half-brothers and two half-sisters of the defendant, 18 to 13 years of age, resulted from the illicit relationship of the stepfather and mother. About five years ago, the defendant said his stepfather finally separated from his mother, due to the mother's problems with alcoholism. The stepfather now has custody of the four children. The defendant indicated the stepfather's address is known only as a corner house at 8th and W Streets, S.W., his mother is said to be "living with another man," somewhere in the vicinity of 3rd and F Streets, N.E.

The defendant described his early home life, aside from material needs and food being plentiful, as poor and an unhappy one. He indicated the family frequently moved from one place to another, hardly ever remained in one house for more than one year, and primarily due to his mother's alcoholism problem, wherein she mismanaged financial affairs to cater to her problem. The defendant also indicated his parents argued frequently and became embroiled in actual altercations. The defendant says his relationship with his mother was "only fair" whereas he denied having a satisfactory relationship with the stepfather. From this point, the defendant went on to discuss his past social-legal difficulties and ascribed same as due to the lack of a decent home, the lack of interest and failure to provide proper supervision by his parents, thus, the desire to escape from the "unpleasantness" of it all.

Past social, institutional records substantiate a very poor social-familial background, that the parents were seemingly concerned primarily with their own personal pursuits and were inadequate as stable, suitable parental figures. Several of the children have been known to local social-legal agencies; the defendant's half-brother, John Toney, 14, is presently a ward of the local welfare department's child-welfare division, confined at the Cedar Knoll Institution at the D.C. Children's Center.

The defendant has, more or less, been on his own since his initial commitment to the National Training School for Boys at fifteen years of age. While he appeared deliberately guarded about saying anything about leaving the District for North Carolina, or about his confinement period in North Carolina State Penal Institutions, he did claim he entered marriage in 1963 upon his return to the District, and has subsequently sought to live a relatively stable life.

V MARITAL HISTORY:

The defendant married Yvette May Oates, now 22, on September 28, 1963, in a religious ceremony in a private house in the District (verified). The defendant says he met his wife during the period after escaping from the National Training School and before "lighting out for North Carolina," by which time he had caused his future wife to conceive their first child. The two parties now have four children: Chalmers (DOB: 1–22–61); Wanda Pansy (DOB: 6–3–64); Ernest IV (DOB: 3–25–66) and Doretta (DOB: 5–13–67). The defendant professed having great interest in his wife and children and claims his prime concern is the life now centered around providing for his family as to a decent home, something which he missed in his own early background. His wife was interviewed, however, she was not able to talk freely, due to a dental infection. She did, however, profess love for the defendant, claims he is a good father and a good husband. The wife is not employed, nor expects to be. She says she will turn to public assistance should her husband be committed to jail in the instant case. Otherwise, during the writer's discussion of the offense with the defendant, the wife remained silent.

VI HOME AND NEIGHBORHOOD:

Since October 1967, the defendant and his wife and family have been living in a National Capitol Housing Authority row house, which contains three bedrooms, for which they are paying $52 per month rent. From January to October 1967, the family lived in a rented, small crowded one bedroom apartment on Dorchester Lane, S.E.; from December 5, 1964 to January 1967, the family occupied a basement apartment at 3192 Anacostia Avenue, S.E., from which they were evicted when the owner claimed he wanted the entire house for his own family. Prior thereto, it would appear the defendant and his family frequently moved about the southeast and northeast sections of the District, in unstable, crowded living situations, predominantly in lower class neighborhoods noted for high crime rates.

VII EDUCATION:

The defendant last attended Eliot Junior High School, where he was repeating the ninth grade before being committed to the National Training School for Boys. His public school record reflects poor grades, mostly D's and/or failing marks. It is interesting that at the National Training School, the defendant seemingly attended to his academic studies sufficient to have completed eleventh grade level courses. Intelligence examinations at the training school reflected an I.Q. of 83, considered low-average academic intelligence; one psychologist viewed the defendant as having the potential for above-average intellectual performance ability. At the National Training School, the defendant also received some vocational training in auto mechanics, in which field he was described as having favorable potentials. This defendant has impressed the writer as functioning on or about a tenth or eleventh grade social-intellectual level, yet to be highly sophisticated in criminal activities.

VIII RELIGION:

The defendant professes the Baptist faith, but admits he rarely attends church. His conscious concern towards religious values, as a way of life, appears very nil.

IX INTERESTS AND LEISURE TIME ACTIVITIES:

The defendant says his primary leisure time activities and interests center around boxing, swimming and auto drag racing.

X HEALTH:

This defendant stands 5'9", and says he weighs 200 pounds. He appears very dark brown skinned in complexion and evidences an old vertical scar on his left temple. He claims good physical health; he says he suffered a dislocated right hip while at the National Training School, which resulted in six months hospitalization, however, he denies any subsequent after effects. He describes himself as a social drinker, denies alcohol to be a problem.

During the presentence interview, the defendant was viewed as free from any signs of disturbing personality problems. He evidenced himself to be very fluent and tried to be very persuasive in relating his version of the offense. However, the greater impression is that of a young adult, who, though overtly appearing docile, is quite sophisticated in talking with people in authority. Past impressions of other professional workers and trained specialists describe this defendant as having an extensive suppressed feeling of hostility, particularly towards people in positions of authority. He has also been described as quick to react in antisocial, aggressive behavior. His amenability to personal counselling is questioned by this writer; his response to same would undoubtedly be superficial, without a sincere desire to emotionally integrate counselling.

XI EMPLOYMENT:

October 1967 to December 1967, three months: The defendant says he has been employed as a laborer for the General Construction Company, 1200 Congress Street, S.E. Verification was not made; it is interesting to note that the defendant was confined in the D.C. Jail from November 18, 1967 until December 5, 1967, as a consequence of his arrest in CC #00–68, on the foregoing date. Subsequent employment has been intermittent due to weather conditions.

May 1967 to October 1967, five months: The defendant worked at the Terry Auto Body Shop in the rear of 1450 R Street, N.W. under a work and training program funded through the D.C. Department of Public Welfare.

March 1964 to November 22, 1966, 32 months: The defendant worked as a truck-driver air-compressor operator for the Bell Air Compressor Rental Company. This company rented out air compressor trucks to construction contractors. His employment earnings varied between $75 to $100 per week, dependent upon the demand for such rental service.

September 1963 to December 1963, four months: Scott General Contractors employed the defendant as a laborer during the foregoing period until the job expired.

Verification of past employment was established at the three latter employers. The writer was advised that the defendant has the ability to be a satisfactory worker, though occasional absenteeism was noted. This writer is impressed with a fairly satisfactory employment record on the part of the defendant. The defendant also indicated he has augmented regular daytime employment, particularly wintertime employment when working conditions are limited, by working part-time and evening jobs, primarily those requiring a delivery truck-driver.

XII MILITARY SERVICE:

The defendant does not have active military service. He has registered with the Selective Service Board No. 24 in Whiteville, Columbus County, North Carolina (SS #00 00 00 000). He says his draft classification is 4–F, due to his criminal record.

XIII FINANCIAL CONDITION:

The defendant denies any assets. He says he possesses a 1965 Pontiac automobile, which he has a time payment contract on, with $1,000 outstanding. The instant car, according to the defendant, was to be surrendered during the week of February 5, 1968. The defendant denied any other outstanding obligations.

XIV EVALUATIVE SUMMARY:

This 25 year old married defendant stands convicted of multiple charges involving a holdup bank robbery, for which he faces sentencing along with three codefendants. Remorse for his actions and/or concern for his present predicament appears lacking. He has established a substantial criminal record, before and subsequent to the instant offense. Such a record portrays an individual who is completely defiant of the law and order and the well-being of others in society. In addition to the instant offense, he still faces trial on multiple charges of assaulting police officers and carrying dangerous weapons (guns); also, a second trial remains pending, which involves an assault with a dangerous weapon, again, a gun.

The defendant is the unfortunate product of parents who were ill-equipped and, least of all, personally-socially adequate for handling the responsibilities of such a role; whose home situation was deprived and least conducive to providing happiness, the proper preparations and motivations for eventually developing into a decent, meaningful member of society. The converse has been the reaction; negative inner feelings of hostility and antisocial, aggressive behavior have developed and long smoldered, finally erupting, within the past year, particularly into acts revealing the severe potential for violence.

The Court is dealing with a defendant who, overtly, appears docile and passive, yet who is now manifesting a manner of sophistication which was concealed or masked, a type of individual society needs least. His amenability for responding to corrective treatment techniques would seemingly offer a poor prognosis. If treatment is to have any potential, corrective measures would certainly have to be employed over a substantial duration in a controlled environmental situation.

Respectfully submitted,
Chief U.S. Probation Officer

By: _____
U.S. Probation Officer

———

**UNITED STATES DISTRICT COURT FOR THE
DISTRICT OF COLUMBIA**

PRESENTENCE REPORT

NAME
    BLAKE, Mary Ann

ADDRESS
    20 Cottage St.
    Barrington, New Jersey

LEGAL RESIDENCE
    Same

AGE   21   **DATE OF BIRTH**   6-12-46

SEX   Female   **RACE**   Caucasian

CITIZENSHIP
    United States

EDUCATION
    12th grade

MARITAL STATUS
    Single

DEPENDENTS
    None

SOC. SEC. NO.
    234 21 9290

FBI NO.
    111 211 D

DETAINERS OR CHARGES PENDING:
    Serving in Florida 7-24-67 Larceny
    6 to 8 months. Defendant to be
    returned to Florida upon disposition
    of instant Forgery case.

CODEFENDANTS (Disposition)

DATE
    October 18, 1967

DOCKET NO.
    CC #250-66

OFFENSE
    Count 1—Forgery
    (22 DCC 1401)

PLEA
    9-19-67 Guilty to Count 1

VERDICT

CUSTODY
    Arrested 8-19-61 & held until 10-
    26-66; released $100.00 personal
    recognizance until arrested 7-13-67
    in Florida

ASST. U. S. ATTY.
    Harold H. Titus

DEFENSE COUNSEL
    John H. Gullet

PENALTY:
    Count 1—Not less than one year
    nor more than ten years imprison-
    ment.

I OFFENSE:

Defendant was arraigned before Judge Solomon on October 26, 1966, at which time she pleaded not guilty to a six count Indictment which charged her with Forgery and Uttering, 22 DCC 1401.

On September 19, 1967 the defendant withdrew her plea of not guilty and pleaded guilty to Count 1, Forgery. Judge Solomon committed the defendant to the D.C. Jail.

The defendant was arrested for this offense on August 19, 1966 and was held in custody until October 28, 1966, at which time she was released on $100.00 personal recognizance. She was arrested in Miami, Florida on July 13, 1967, and had remained in custody within that state as a result of her being sentenced on July 24, 1967 to six to eight months for the offense of Larceny. It is our understanding that this defendant is to be returned to Florida upon disposition of the instant Forgery case in order to complete the sentence she is now serving in Florida.

Official Version:

According to the information obtained from the Questioned Document Laboratory examination, three checks were drawn on American Security Company and imprinted with National Life Insurance Company of America, 1200 Utah Avenue, N.W., the two makers' signatures appearing on each are genuine and only the endorsements are in question; the three checks referred to above are identified as follows:

Check #1500, dated 6–14–66, payable to Ira Moreland in the amount of $162.00 and endorsed Ira Moreland.

Check #2005, dated 8–11–66, payable to Myra Frank, in the amount of $147.04, endorsed Myra Frank. Also written above the endorsement is "GA 2000" "Cert #62222," appearing as part of the rubber stamp admonition thereon.

Check #2022, dated 8–11–66, payable to Bessie Mauer, in the amount of $308.10, endorsed Bessie Mauer. Also, written above the endorsement is "GA 2041" "Cert #62300," appearing as part of the rubber stamp admonition thereon.

The findings were that the writer was not Ira Moreland and the endorsement on Check #1500 is a forgery.

From specimens of her handwriting, Mary Ann Blake is identified as the person who wrote the endorsement on the three aforementioned checks.

II DEFENDANT'S VERSION OF OFFENSE:

Defendant was interviewed by the probation officer in the Cell Block of the United States District Courthouse on September 25, 1967.

She told us that she needed money to pay her rent on the apartment she shared with another girl. Since in the normal course of her job she typed out checks for her employer, the checks were accessible and she removed them from the normal distribution channels.

The defendant told the probation officer that the reason she took the second check approximately two months after the first, was due to the fact that her room mate had moved out of their apartment without proper notice and the landlord wanted payment, the defendant could not produce the money on her own at such short notice.

Regarding the third check, the defendant stated she wanted to leave this area, as at that time there had been no apparent repercussions from the first two checks she had taken. As a result of her attempting to cash the third check, she was detained at the bank. A member of her employer's firm was called to the bank and it became known that the defendant was not the person for whom the check had been intended.

The defendant told the probation officer that she had been at liberty while awaiting the disposition of this case and that she had received permission to reside in Florida until such time as her case in this Court was to be disposed of. Some time after arriving and living in Florida, the defendant found herself forced to move from her rented room and she was without funds. As a result, she was permitted to stay with another female acquaintance. She was notified the following day that her bed must be used by company which her benefactor was to receive the following day. With no funds, the defendant admitted that she stole some jewelry and had pawned it for $5.00. As a result, she was arrested on July 13, 1967 on a charge of Larceny and was presented before Court No. 2 in Miami, Florida. On July 20, 1967, she was sentenced to six to eight months in the Florida Correctional Center in Miami.

Our information is that this defendant is to be returned to Florida upon the disposition of this instant Forgery case. She is to serve the remaining portion of her term at Florida Correctional Center in Miami.

III PRIOR RECORD:

8-19-66	Washington, D.C.	Forgery & Uttering	9-19-67 pleaded guilty to Count 1 (instant case)
7-13-67	Miami, Florida	Larceny	7-20-67 6 to 8 mos.

IV FAMILY HISTORY:

The defendant was born in Chester, New Jersey, the second oldest of three children. When she was approximately two years old, the family moved to Philadelphia, Pennsylvania, remaining there for about one year and then moving to Barrington, New Jersey, where she had continued to reside with her family until she left home at eighteen years of age to enlist in the WAC. She remained in the military service for one and one-half years, being stationed at Fort Myer, Arlington, Va., and electing to remain in Washington, D.C. area until such time as she committed the instant offense.

She has an older sister who is married and has two children, graduated from Hampton College and has taught school for two years prior to her current pregnancy. She also has a younger brother. Her parents have always lived together and there have been no unusual circumstances other than an episode in which her father, who had held a steady position for a period of fifteen years, was allegedly involved in "taking some of the company's money," the defendant not knowing exactly what happened other than the fact that five years ago, her father was caused to seek another position and is currently a foreman with Froman Manufacturing Company, a subsidiary of Pennam Drugs, this company making a dye. Her mother has been employed fulltime as a department store saleslady for the past four years in the residence area.

During her formative years, the defendant claims to have had a normal childhood, her father apparently able to provide for the family until he was forced out of his position of long standing, at which time he was obliged to take a position with less remuneration and prestige.

Parents and Siblings:

Her father, Herman Blake, is 49 years of age and resides with his wife in a congenial manner in a home which they have been purchasing for the past ten years with an address of 20 Cottage Street, Barrington, New Jersey.

Her mother, Ann (Myer) Blake is 47 years old and she resides with her husband at the aforementioned address, employed fulltime as a department store saleslady.

Her older sister, Vera Pelham, is 26 years of age and is married and has two sons. She lives with her husband and family at 19 10th St., Seabrook, New Jersey.

Her younger brother, John Blake, is age 11 and he resides with his parents and is a normal, healthy student.

V MARITAL HISTORY:

The defendant claims to be presently engaged to a private in the U.S. Army for the past two years. She met him in January 1967, when he was temporarily stationed at Fort Belvoir, Virginia. His present address is with the 18th Airborne Corps, Fort Bragg, North Carolina. There is no certain date set for the marriage.

The defendant states that she has never given birth to any children.

VI HOME AND NEIGHBORHOOD:

Prior to entry into the service and subsequent residence in local Washington, D.C. apartments, the defendant resided with her parents in a home which her parents commenced to purchase ten years ago. It is located on the outskirts of the small town of Barrington, New Jersey, and is a one-story prefabricated frame ranch house. The residence consists of three bedrooms, a living room, bathroom and a kitchen. At the present time, the residence is occupied by her parents and a younger brother only. Prior to her arrest in Miami, Florida, she had a room at the Moors Hotel in Miami, where she resided from March 26, 1967 until June 30, 1967.

Prior to her discharge from the U.S. Army, she resided for a five month period in an apartment located at 22 Huntington, N.W., and for a two month period at an apartment at 35 Huntington Place, N.W., Washington, D.C.

She resided in Government quarters while stationed at Fort Myer, Va.

Prior to her entry into military service, the defendant resided with her parents at their present address for nearly eight years.

VII EDUCATION:

In June 1963, the defendant graduated from Merryman High School in Barrington, New Jersey, where she had attended from grade nine through grade twelve. She undertook a college preparatory course and finished number 48 out of a total senior enrollment of 265 pupils.

She commenced her formal education in kindergarten and continued through the eighth grade at Barrington Grammar School in Barrington, New Jersey.

As a result of her scholastic standing the defendant claimed she was accepted by both Ohio State and West Virginia University but had insufficient funds to attend either.

VIII RELIGION:

Defendant was born and brought up as a Presbyterian, attending with her family at the Barrington Presbyterian Church. As a youngster, she attended Sunday School, her parents attending church services at the same church. After completing Sunday School, she stated she attended regular church services only once or twice a month and of recent years, she attends only occasionally. Relative to her church attendance, for the last several years, she told the probation officer that if she does not like the service "I will go to another church."

IX INTERESTS AND LEISURE TIME ACTIVITIES:

Most of this defendant's constructive leisure time activities have been left behind at the residence of her parents. Prior to her completion of high school, she compiled a collection of sea shells, bells and miniature vases, but since entering the military service and thereafter she has been spending most of her spare time in no generally accepted constructive manner. She reads occasionally, usually selecting a paperback edition. She will also attend a movie occasionally and watch television theatrical productions.

X HEALTH:

Physical:

She has never been hospitalized for medical or surgical reasons other than a tonsillectomy when she was about nine years of age. She has never suffered a broken bone nor has she ever been knocked unconscious during her lifetime thus far.

Her smoking of cigarettes consists of approximately one to one and a half packages per day. She likes beer and mixed drinks and claims to drink socially only. She has never used drugs nor has she associated with any illegal drug users in the past.

Mental and Emotional:

According to this defendant, she has been interviewed by a psychiatrist only once. While a member of the WAC, her Commanding Officer required her to be examined by a psychiatrist before her case was presented before the Review Board.

To the probation officer, the defendant appeared to possess at least average intelligence. She volunteered much information as well as answering each question directed to her. She is a very tall girl, admitting to 175 lbs. but gives the observer the indication that she perhaps weighed more at one time in the past.

At the present time, she gives the indication that she is not quite sure what she will do with herself when next she is residing in the community.

She speaks about going back into some large city and obtaining employment in some office and then again, she believes she might go to Texas, where she would reside with her fiance's parents until he is discharged from the U.S. Army.

XI EMPLOYMENT:

After graduating from high school, the defendant enlisted in the WAC until she was discharged from the service on March 17, 1966.

Her first fulltime civilian employment was an office clerk's position with the National Life Insurance Company in Washington, D.C., where she was employed from May 16, 1966 until August 19, 1966, having been discharged as a result of the instant offense. This was a fulltime position for which she received $80.00 per week salary.

She told the probation officer that for a period of five or six weeks, commencing November 1966, she was employed by Putner Publishing Company for whom she sold encyclopedias from house-to-house, and admitted to making only one sale, and that, after her third week. The financial remuneration with this company consisted of commission only, that being $75.00 per set sold. The employer has informed us that the defendant worked for his concern from November 18, 1966 until February 13, 1967, that she "did not like the work," and terminated as she "ceased to produce sales." They would not consider reemploying her.

Although she told the probation officer that she commenced employment as a waitress during January 1967 at Place Vent, her employer informed us she left the same day she was hired, failing to report for work the following morning.

Defendant claims she went back to Barrington, New Jersey, during March 1967 and worked as a waitress using an assumed name. She was employed from April 12, 1967 until July 29, 1967 earning $45.00 per week, plus tips. The reason for termination was given as "Quit."

XII MILITARY SERVICE:

The defendant enlisted in the WAC on September 8, 1964. She received an Undesirable Discharge on March 17, 1966, as a result of a Board of Review which sat on February 17, 1966 and after being recommended by her Commanding Officer. This recommendation was made as she had received a Summary Court–Martial in September 1965, as a result of her theft from a room mate of $25.00. She was reduced in rank and given 45 days of extra duty, and prior to that occasion, she had written a bad check which she tendered to the Post Exchange. However, she made restitution on the bad check charge, but the Board of Review elected to separate the defendant from the military service with an Undesirable Discharge on March 17, 1966.

XIII FINANCIAL CONDITION:

Assets:

Defendant's total assets consist of an extremely limited amount of personal clothing.

Financial Obligations:

Her sole monetary obligations consist of her admittedly moral obligations to reimburse her former employer for the first two checks which she had cashed. The defendant claims she is willing to make restitution.

XIV EVALUATIVE SUMMARY:

Mary Ann Blake is a 21 year old, unmarried, Caucasian female who has pleaded guilty to Count 1 of an Indictment charging her with Forgery. She has admitted to the probation officer that she took a total of three checks, cashed two of them, and was refused payment on the third as she was attempting to cash that one. Her birthplace was Chester, New Jersey, the defendant being the second oldest of three children born to her parents. She appears to have had a normal childhood, indicating a congenial background with no material deprivations worthy of note. At age three, her family moved to Barrington, New Jersey, where she remained until she left home to enlist in the Women's Army Corps. After a year and a half of military service, she was given an Undesirable Discharge and the defendant elected to remain in the District of Columbia where she became employed as an office worker and shared an apartment with another young woman.

Since terminating employment with the insurance firm from whom she had taken the checks which are involved in this case, she has attempted to earn her livelihood by selling encyclopedias and working as a waitress.

She is a high school graduate, having taken a college preparatory course but finding her family unable to meet the financial requirements which would permit her to enter. As financial backing was not available, she turned to the military service.

Her inclination towards the type and nature of the instant offense began while she was on active duty in the military service as she has admitted to a theft from a WAC room mate and subsequently was punished under a Summary Court Martial Order. A worthless check presented to a Post Exchange some time later, resulted in a Board of Review recommendation that she receive an Undesirable Discharge.

While remaining in the community on personal bond in this instant case, she went to Florida and became involved in an admitted larceny of a necklace and ring from a room mate there. She is currently serving a six to eight month sentence awarded in Florida on July 24, 1967, the expiration date purported to be November 29, 1967.

At the present time, she alleges to be engaged to a nineteen year old PFC presently stationed at Fort Bragg, N.C., the defendant stating that there has been no date set as yet for their marriage. She feels that when she is next at liberty, she will either continue to live and work in Washington, D.C., or perhaps go to live with his parents in Texas, and work there, while waiting for her fiance to be discharged from the Army.

To the interviewing probation officer, the defendant appears to be unsure of her future at the present time. She feels that if she is given probation, she can start out anew, work and save, and thereby make restitution for the money she obtained when she took two of her employer's checks and cashed them.

She appeared to be very cooperative during her interview with the probation officer, and she volunteered much information, admitting her prior offenses without reservation.

Respectfully submitted,
Chief U.S. Probation Officer

By: _____
U.S. Probation Officer

2. CRIME

The principle that there is no crime without law—*nullum crimen sine lege*—is firmly established in American law. It is reflected in the constitutional provision forbidding Congress to pass an *ex post facto* law, U.S. Const. art. I, § 9, and in the doctrine that a statute that does not specify with sufficient clarity what conduct is criminal is "void for vagueness" under the Due Process Clause of the Fifth and Fourteenth Amendments. Such restrictions on legislative authority are not always easily applied. How does one distinguish, for example, between the permissible extension of an existing law to a somewhat novel set of facts and the creation of new law? (Had he been convicted, would Polzin (p. 409 note 241) or Wheeler (p. 444 note 285) have had a valid constitutional argument?)

In Lynce v. Mathis, 519 U.S. 433 (1997), the Court held that a Florida statute that cancelled a prisoner's early release credits that had already been awarded to him violated the Ex Post Facto Clause. The credits had been awarded pursuant to a statutory emergency provision intended to reduce prison overcrowding; credits became available when the prison population exceeded a specified level. Later, the legislature modified the plan and excluded prisoners serving sentences for certain crimes, including attempted murder, the crime for which the petitioner had been convicted. Having previously been given credits pursuant to the statute, the petitioner had been released. The state, construing the later statute to have cancelled the petitioner's credits retroactively, arrested him and returned him to prison.

The Court observed that "[t]he presumption against the retroactive application of new laws is an essential thread in the mantle of protection that the law affords the individual citizen," and that "[t]he specific prohibition on *ex post facto* laws is only one aspect of the broader constitutional protection against arbitrary changes in the law." 519 U.S. at 439, 440. "To fall within the *ex post facto* prohibition," the Court said, "a law must be retrospective—that is 'it must apply to events occurring before its enactment'—and it 'must disadvantage the offender affected by it,' [Weaver v. Graham, 450 U.S. 24 (1981)] at 29, by altering the definition of criminal conduct or increasing the punishment for the crime." Id. at 441. The Court concluded that the change in the early release provisions met those criteria, even though the purpose of the change was "administrative" and not to increase the petitioner's punishment.

For other cases interpreting the Ex Post Facto Clause, see Kansas v. Hendricks, 521 U.S. 346 (1997) (5–4) (Clause not violated by statute mandating civil commitment for sex offenders, because statute was not a penal statute), see p. 607 above; California Dept. of Corrections v. Morales,

514 U.S. 499 (1995) (7–2) (Clause not violated by reduction in frequency of parole hearings); Miller v. Florida, 482 U.S. 423 (1987) (Clause violated by revision of sentencing guidelines between offense and conviction); Weaver v. Graham, above (Clause violated by change in provision for "good time" reduction of sentence that had effect of increasing petitioner's time in prison). The Clause is discussed in the early civil case, Calder v. Bull, 3 U.S. (3 Dall.) 386 (1798). See also Rogers v. Tennessee, 532 U.S. 451 (2001) (5–4) (year-and-a-day rule), p. 50 above.

In Kolender v. Lawson, 461 U.S. 352, 357 (1983) (7–2), the Supreme Court said that "the void-for-vagueness doctrine requires that a penal statute define the criminal offense with sufficient definiteness that ordinary people can understand what conduct is prohibited and in a manner that does not encourage arbitrary and discriminatory enforcement." The California statute in question provided that a person "who loiters or wanders upon the streets or from place to place without apparent reason or business and who refuses to identify himself and to account for his presence when requested by any peace officer so to do, if the surrounding circumstances are such as to indicate to a reasonable man that the public safety demands such identification" is guilty of disorderly conduct, a misdemeanor. Cal. Penal Code § 647(e). As construed by the California courts, the statute required a person to give a "credible and reliable" identification in the circumstances when it applied. 461 U.S. at 353. Stating that the statute "contains no standard for determining what a suspect has to do" to satisfy this requirement and "vests virtually complete discretion in the hands of the police to determine whether the suspect has satisfied the statute," id. at 358, the Court concluded that the statute was void for vagueness. Applying *Kolender*, the Court struck down a Chicago ordinance that prohibited "criminal street gang members" from loitering with one another or with other persons in a public place. City of Chicago v. Morales, 527 U.S. 41 (1999) (6–3). Another (Florida) vagrancy law was declared void for vagueness in Papachristou v. City of Jacksonville, 405 U.S. 156 (1972). See Reno v. ACLU, 521 U.S. 844 (1997) (7–2), holding that a federal statute regulating the transmission of obscene or indecent material to minors over the Internet was unconstitutionally vague, in the specific context of the First Amendment's protection of freedom of speech. The Court did not reach the question whether the statute was void for vagueness under the Due Process Clause of the Fifth Amendment.

Related to the rule that criminal statutes must specify the prohibited conduct with sufficient definiteness is the doctrine that criminal statutes are to be construed strictly, that is, in a manner that defines the offense narrowly rather than broadly. E.g., United States v. Granderson, 511 U.S. 39, 54 (1994); United States v. Bass, 404 U.S. 336, 347–48 (1971). The doctrine has been rejected in some jurisdictions. E.g., N.Y. Penal Law § 5.00 (McKinney 1987): "The general rule that a penal statute is to be strictly construed does not apply to this chapter, but the provisions herein must be construed according to the fair import of their terms to promote justice and effect the objects of the law." See Model Penal Code § 1.02(3): "The provisions of the Code shall be construed according to the fair import of their terms but when the language is susceptible of differing constructions it shall be interpreted to further the general purposes stated in this Section and the special purposes of the particular provision involved . . . ." (Compare Model Penal Code § 1.02(1)(d), p. 333 above). Of course, whether a particular construction is "narrow" or not is itself a matter of interpretation. The most that can be said with assurance is that, like the doctrine of void-for-vagueness, the doctrine of strict construction emphasizes the importance of giving persons fair notice that conduct is prohibited.

---

459.   The Model Penal Code § 250.6 provides that a person commits a violation "if he loiters or prowls in a place, at a time, or in a manner not usual for law-abiding individuals under circumstances that warrant alarm for the safety of person or property in the vicinity." The balance of the provision gives a nonexclusive list of factors to be considered "in determining whether such alarm is warranted" (e.g., the person "refuses to identify himself") and provides that before making an arrest, an officer shall "afford the actor an opportunity to dispel any alarm which would otherwise be warranted, by requesting him to identify himself and explain his presence and conduct." It is provided also that no crime is committed if the person gives a true explanation that, if believed by the officer, would have dispelled any alarm.

Does the Model Penal Code's provision satisfy the constitutional requirement? Compare Watts v. State, 463 So.2d 205 (Fla.1985) (comparable Florida statute constitutional), with Fields v. City of Omaha, 810 F.2d 830 (8th Cir.1987) (comparable Nebraska statute not constitutional).

The importance that we attach to the requirement that crimes be specified in advance emphasizes our commitment to the proposition that crime is strictly a product of law. However else conduct may be judged for other purposes, whatever its other consequences, it is not criminal and not subject to legal punishment unless the law so declares.

Is even that enough? Is there any conduct that simply is beyond the legislative authority to declare specific conduct criminal? If so, what is the basis for such limitation?

In Robinson v. California, 370 U.S. 660 (1962), the Supreme Court held that a statute that made narcotics addiction a criminal offense was unconstitutional.

> It is unlikely that any State at this moment in history would attempt to make it a criminal offense for a person to be mentally ill, or a leper, or to be afflicted with a venereal disease. A State might determine that the general health and welfare require that the victims of these and other human afflictions be dealt with by compulsory treatment, involv-

ing quarantine, confinement, or sequestration. But, in the light of contemporary human knowledge, a law which made a criminal offense of such a disease would doubtless be universally thought to be an infliction of cruel and unusual punishment in violation of the Eighth and Fourteenth Amendments. . . .

We cannot but consider the statute before us as of the same category. In this Court counsel for the State recognized that narcotic addiction is an illness. Indeed, it is apparently an illness which may be contracted innocently or involuntarily. We hold that a state law which imprisons a person thus afflicted as a criminal, even though he has never touched any narcotic drug within the State or been guilty of any irregular behavior there, inflicts a cruel and unusual punishment in violation of the Fourteenth Amendment. To be sure, imprisonment for ninety days [the minimum sentence under the statute] is not, in the abstract, a punishment which is either cruel or unusual. But the question cannot be considered in the abstract. Even one day in prison would be a cruel and unusual punishment for the "crime" of having a common cold.

We are not unmindful that the vicious evils of the narcotics traffic have occasioned the grave concern of government. There are, as we have said, countless fronts on which those evils may be legitimately attacked.

Id. at 666–68.

Among the permissible methods by which a state could control the narcotics traffic, the Court included "criminal sanctions . . . against the unauthorized manufacture, prescription, sale, purchase, or possession of narcotics within its borders," "compulsory treatment for those addicted to narcotics" including "periods of involuntary confinement" and such measures as public health education. Id. at 664–65.

————

460. As the Court acknowledged, its conclusion in *Robinson* did not depend on a finding that the actual punishment imposed was "cruel or unusual"; it was the imposition of any punishment at all that the Court found impermissible. What is the basis of the Court's holding?

In a concurring opinion, Justice Douglas observed: "If addicts can be punished for their addiction, then the insane can also be punished for their insanity. . . . [T]he principle that would deny power to exact capital punishment for a petty crime would also deny power to punish a person by fine or imprisonment for being sick." Id. at 674, 676. Justice Harlan, also concurring, said: "Since addiction alone cannot reasonably be thought to amount to more than a compelling propensity to use narcotics, the effect of this instruction [that addiction without more was sufficient for a finding of guilt] was to authorize punishment for a bare desire to commit a criminal act." Id. at 678–79.

See State v. Akers, 400 A.2d 38 (N.H.1979), declaring unconstitutional a state statute making parents of minors criminally responsible for their children's offenses. The court said that "the net effect of the statute is to punish parenthood" and that "the status of parenthood cannot be made a crime." Id. at 40.

Powell v. Texas

392 U.S. 514, 88 S.Ct. 2145, 20 L.Ed.2d 1254 (1968)

[The appellant was convicted of being drunk in a public place and fined $50. At his trial, the court found that he was a chronic alcoholic, but ruled that chronic alcoholism was not a defense to the crime charged.]

■ MR. JUSTICE MARSHALL announced the judgment of the Court and delivered an opinion in which THE CHIEF JUSTICE, MR. JUSTICE BLACK and MR. JUSTICE HARLAN join.

. . .

Despite the comparatively primitive state of our knowledge on the subject, it cannot be denied that the destructive use of alcoholic beverages is one of our principal social and public health problems. The lowest current informed estimate places the number of "alcoholics" in America (definitional problems aside) at 4,000,000, and most authorities are inclined to put the figure considerably higher. The problem is compounded by the fact that a very large percentage of the alcoholics in this country are "invisible"—they possess the means to keep their drinking problems secret, and the traditionally uncharitable attitude of our society toward alcoholics causes many of them to refrain from seeking treatment from any source. Nor can it be gainsaid that the legislative response to this enormous problem has in general been inadequate.

There is as yet no known generally effective method for treating the vast number of alcoholics in our society. Some individual alcoholics have responded to particular forms of therapy with remissions of their symptomatic dependence upon the drug. But just as there is no agreement among doctors and social workers with respect to the causes of alcoholism, there is no consensus as to why particular treatments have been effective in particular cases and there is no generally agreed-upon approach to the problem of treatment on a large scale. Most psychiatrists are apparently of the opinion that alcoholism is far more difficult to treat than other forms of behavioral disorders, and some believe it is impossible to cure by means of psychotherapy; indeed, the medical profession as a whole, and psychiatrists in particular, have been severely criticised for the prevailing reluctance to undertake the treatment of drinking problems. Thus it is entirely possible that, even were the manpower and facilities available for a full-scale attack upon chronic alcoholism, we would find ourselves unable to help the vast bulk of our "visible"—let alone our "invisible"—alcoholic population.

However, facilities for the attempted treatment of indigent alcoholics are woefully lacking throughout the country. It would be tragic to return large numbers of helpless, sometimes dangerous and frequently unsanitary inebriates to the streets of our cities without even the opportunity to sober up adequately which a brief jail term provides. Presumably no State or city will tolerate such a state of affairs. Yet the medical profession cannot, and does not, tell us with any assurance that, even if the buildings, equipment and trained personnel were made available, it could provide anything more than slightly higher-class jails for our indigent habitual inebriates. Thus we run the grave risk that nothing will be accomplished beyond the hanging of a new sign—reading "hospital"—over one wing of the jailhouse.

One virtue of the criminal process is, at least, that the duration of penal incarceration typically has some outside statutory limit; this is universally true in the case of petty offenses, such as public drunkenness, where jail terms are quite short on the whole. "Therapeutic civil commitment" lacks this feature; one is typically committed until one is "cured." Thus, to do otherwise than affirm might subject indigent alcoholics to the risk that they may be locked up for an indefinite period of time under the same conditions as before, with no more hope than before of receiving effective treatment and no prospect of periodic "freedom."

Faced with this unpleasant reality, we are unable to assert that the use of the criminal process as a means of dealing with the public aspects of problem drinking can never be defended as rational. The picture of the penniless drunk propelled aimlessly and endlessly through the law's "revolving door" of arrest, incarceration, release and re-arrest is not a pretty one. But before we condemn the present practice across-the-board, perhaps we ought to be able to point to some clear promise of a better world for these unfortunate people. Unfortunately, no such promise has yet been forthcoming. If, in addition to the absence of a coherent approach to the problem of treatment, we consider the almost complete absence of facilities and manpower for the implementation of a rehabilitation program, it is difficult to say in the present context that the criminal process is utterly lacking in social value. This Court has never held that anything in the Constitution requires that penal sanctions be designed solely to achieve therapeutic or rehabilitative effects, and it can hardly be said with assurance that incarceration serves such purposes any better for the general run of criminals than it does for public drunks.

Ignorance likewise impedes our assessment of the deterrent effect of criminal sanctions for public drunkenness. The fact that a high percentage of American alcoholics conceal their drinking problems, not merely by avoiding public displays of intoxication but also by shunning all forms of treatment, is indicative that some powerful deterrent operates to inhibit the public revelation of the existence of alcoholism. Quite probably this deterrent effect can be largely attributed to the harsh moral attitude which our society has traditionally taken toward intoxication and the shame which we have associated with alcoholism. Criminal conviction represents the degrading public revelation of what Anglo-American society has long condemned as a moral defect, and the existence of criminal sanctions may serve to reinforce this cultural taboo, just as we presume they serve to reinforce other, stronger feelings against murder, rape, theft, and other forms of antisocial conduct.

Obviously, chronic alcoholics have not been deterred from drinking to excess by the existence of criminal sanctions against public drunkenness. But all those who violate penal laws of any kind are by definition unde-terred. The long-standing and still raging debate over the validity of the deterrence justification for penal sanctions has not reached any sufficiently clear conclusions to permit it to be said that such sanctions are ineffective in any particular context or for any particular group of people who are able to appreciate the consequences of their acts. . . .

. . .

On its face the present case does not fall within . . . [the *Robinson*] holding, since appellant was convicted, not for being a chronic alcoholic, but for being in public while drunk on a particular occasion. The State of Texas thus has not sought to punish a mere status, as California did in *Robinson*; nor has it attempted to regulate appellant's behavior in the privacy of his own home. Rather, it has imposed upon appellant a criminal sanction for public behavior which may create substantial health and safety hazards, both for appellant and for members of the general public, and which offends the moral and esthetic sensibilities of a large segment of the community. This seems a far cry from convicting one for being an addict, being a chronic alcoholic, being "mentally ill, or a leper . . . ." Id., at 666.

Robinson so viewed brings this Court but a very small way into the substantive criminal law. And unless *Robinson* is so viewed it is difficult to see any limiting principle that would serve to prevent this Court from becoming, under the aegis of the Cruel and Unusual Punishment Clause, the ultimate arbiter of the standards of criminal responsibility, in diverse areas of the criminal law, throughout the country.

. . . The entire thrust of *Robinson*'s interpretation of the Cruel and Unusual Punishment Clause is that criminal penalties may be inflicted only if the accused has committed some act, has engaged in some behavior, which society has an interest in preventing, or perhaps in historical common law terms, has committed some *actus reus*. It thus does not deal with the question of whether certain conduct cannot constitutionally be punished because it is, in some sense, "involuntary" or "occasioned by a compulsion."

. . .

Ultimately, then, the most troubling aspects of this case, were *Robinson* to be extended to meet it, would be the scope and content of what could only be a constitutional doctrine of criminal responsibility. . . . If Leroy Powell cannot be convicted of public intoxication, it is difficult to see how a State can convict an individual for murder, if that individual, while exhibit-ing normal behavior in all other respects, suffers from a "compulsion" to kill, which is an "exceedingly strong influence," but "not completely overpowering." . . .

. . .

Affirmed.

■ Mr. Justice Black, whom Mr. Justice Harlan joins, concurring.

. . .

Public drunkenness has been a crime throughout our history, and even before our history it was explicitly proscribed by a 1606 English statute, 4 Jac. 1, c. 5. It is today made an offense in every State in the Union. The number of police to be assigned to enforcing these laws and the amount of time they should spend in the effort would seem to me a question for each local community. Never, even by the wildest stretch of this Court's judicial review power, could it be thought that a State's criminal law could be struck down because the amount of time spent in enforcing it constituted, in some expert's opinion, a tremendous burden.

Jailing of chronic alcoholics is definitely defended as therapeutic, and the claims of therapeutic value are not insubstantial. As appellees note, the alcoholics are removed from the streets, where in their intoxicated state they may be in physical danger, and are given food, clothing, and shelter until they "sober up" and thus at least regain their ability to keep from being run over by automobiles in the street. Of course, this treatment may not be "therapeutic" in the sense of curing the underlying causes of their behavior, but it seems probable that the effect of jail on any criminal is seldom "therapeutic" in this sense, and in any case the medical authorities relied on so heavily by appellant themselves stress that no generally effective method of curing alcoholics has yet been discovered.

Apart from the value of jail as a form of treatment, jail serves other traditional functions of the criminal law. For one thing, it gets the alcoholics off the street, where they may cause harm in a number of ways to a number of people, and isolation of the dangerous has always been considered an important function of the criminal law. In addition, punishment of chronic alcoholics can serve several deterrent functions—it can give potential alcoholics an additional incentive to control their drinking, and it may, even in the case of the chronic alcoholic, strengthen his incentive to control the frequency and location of his drinking experiences.

These values served by criminal punishment assume even greater significance in light of the available alternatives for dealing with the problem of alcoholism. Civil commitment facilities may not be any better than the jails they would replace. In addition, compulsory commitment can hardly be considered a less severe penalty from the alcoholic's point of view. The commitment period will presumably be at least as long, and it might in fact be longer since commitment often lasts until the "sick" person is cured. And compulsory commitment would of course carry with it a social stigma little different in practice from that associated with drunkenness when it is labeled a "crime."

Even the medical authorities stress the need for continued experimentation with a variety of approaches. I cannot say that the States should be totally barred from one avenue of experimentation, the criminal process, in attempting to find a means to cope with this difficult social problem. . . .

. . . When we say that appellant's appearance in public is caused not by "his own" volition but rather by some other force, we are clearly thinking of a force that is nevertheless "his" except in some special sense. The accused undoubtedly commits the proscribed act and the only question is whether the act can be attributed to a part of "his" personality that should not be regarded as criminally responsible. Almost all of the traditional purposes of the criminal law can be significantly served by punishing the person who in fact committed the proscribed act, without regard to whether his action was "compelled" by some elusive "irresponsible" aspect of his personality. As I have already indicated, punishment of such a defendant can clearly be justified in terms of deterrence, isolation, and treatment. On the other hand, medical decisions concerning the use of a term such as "disease" or "volition," based as they are on the clinical problems of diagnosis and treatment, bear no necessary correspondence to the legal decision whether the overall objectives of the criminal law can be furthered by imposing punishment. For these reasons, much as I think that criminal sanctions should in many situations be applied only to those whose conduct is morally blameworthy . . . I cannot think the States should be held constitutionally required to make the inquiry as to what part of a defendant's personality is responsible for his actions and to excuse anyone whose action was, in some complex, psychological sense, the result of a "compulsion."

. . .

■ MR. JUSTICE WHITE, concurring in the result.

If it cannot be a crime to have an irresistible compulsion to use narcotics, Robinson v. California, 370 U.S. 660 (1962), I do not see how it can constitutionally be a crime to yield to such a compulsion. Punishing an addict for using drugs convicts for addiction under a different name. Distinguishing between the two crimes is like forbidding criminal conviction for being sick with flu or epilepsy but permitting punishment for running a fever or having a convulsion. Unless *Robinson* is to be abandoned, the use of narcotics by an addict must be beyond the reach of the criminal law. Similarly, the chronic alcoholic with an irresistible urge to consume alcohol should not be punishable for drinking or for being drunk.

. . .

. . . For the purposes of this case, it is necessary to say only that Powell showed nothing more than that he was to some degree compelled to drink and that he was drunk at the time of his arrest. He made no showing that he was unable to stay off the streets on the night in question.

. . .

■ MR. JUSTICE FORTAS, with whom MR. JUSTICE DOUGLAS, MR. JUSTICE BRENNAN, and MR. JUSTICE STEWART join, dissenting.

. . .

The sole question presented is whether a criminal penalty may be imposed upon a person suffering the disease of "chronic alcoholism" for a condition—being "in a state of intoxication" in public—which is a characteristic part of the pattern of his disease and which, the trial court found, was not the consequence of appellant's volition but of "a compulsion symptomatic of the disease of chronic alcoholism." We must consider whether the Eighth Amendment, made applicable to the States through the Fourteenth Amendment, prohibits the imposition of this penalty in these rather special circumstances as "cruel and unusual punishment." This case does not raise any question as to the right of the police to stop and detain those who are intoxicated in public, whether as a result of the disease or otherwise; or as to the State's power to commit chronic alcoholics for treatment. Nor does it concern the responsibility of an alcoholic for criminal *acts*. We deal here with the mere *condition* of being intoxicated in public.

. . .

Robinson stands upon a principle which, despite its subtlety, must be simply stated and respectfully applied because it is the foundation of individual liberty and the cornerstone of the relations between a civilized state and its citizens: Criminal penalties may not be inflicted upon a person for being in a condition he is powerless to change. In all probability, Robinson at some time before his conviction elected to take narcotics. But the crime as defined did not punish this conduct. The statute imposed a penalty for the offense of "addiction"—a condition which Robinson could not control. Once Robinson had become an addict, he was utterly powerless to avoid criminal guilt. He was powerless to choose not to violate the law.

In the present case, appellant is charged with a crime comprised of two elements—being intoxicated and being found in a public place while in that condition. The crime, so defined, differs from that in *Robinson*. The statute covers more than a mere status. But the essential constitutional defect here is the same as in *Robinson*, for in both cases the particular defendant was accused of being in a condition which he had no capacity to change or avoid. . . .

. . .

The findings in this case, read against the background of . . . medical and sociological data . . . compel the conclusion that the infliction upon appellant of a criminal penalty for being intoxicated in a public place would be "cruel and inhuman punishment" within the prohibition of the Eighth Amendment. This conclusion follows because appellant is a "chronic alcoholic" who, according to the trier of fact, cannot resist the "constant excessive consumption of alcohol" and "does not appear in public by his own volition but under a compulsion" which is part of his condition.

. . .

———

461. Although *Powell* is concerned with the constitutionality of a criminal charge, Justice Marshall's opinion begins with an appraisal of society's noncriminal responses to alcoholism. He declares that alcoholism is "one of our principal social and public health problems," for which "the legislative response . . . has in general been inadequate," p. 744. The Court, he says, is "faced with this unpleasant reality," p. 745, and he suggests that were it otherwise, the Court's decision might be different. What bearing does the absence of an effective noncriminal response to alcoholism have on the issue before the court, except, perhaps, to explain an evasion of the issue?

In his separate opinion, Justice Black also emphasizes the problem of alcoholism. He observes that jailing alcoholics serves a number of "traditional functions of the criminal law," p. 747, including prevention and deterrence. He concludes: "Almost all of the traditional purposes of the criminal law can be significantly served by punishing the person who in fact committed the proscribed act, without regard to whether his action was 'compelled' by some 'irresponsible' aspect of his personality," p. 748. Is that sufficient to dispose of Powell's argument? What function of the criminal law is at stake? Why does Black, as he says, "think that criminal sanctions should in many situations be applied only to those whose conduct is morally blameworthy," id.? Why does he (if he does) depart from that principle here?

462. Justice Marshall distinguishes *Robinson* on the basis that Powell's crime was not a "mere status," like Robinson's addiction, but was conduct, "public behavior" that created a risk of harm to the community, p. 746. He rejects an interpretation of *Robinson* to the effect that "conduct cannot constitutionally be punished because it is, in some sense, 'involuntary' or 'occasioned by a compulsion.' " Id. Is that satisfactory? Why is punishment for a status impermissible? According to Marshall's analysis, would it be constitutionally permissible under *Robinson* to punish a person for sneezing? Marshall says that the "thrust" of *Robinson* "is that criminal penalties may be inflicted only if the accused has committed some act, has engaged in some behavior," id. What in this context do the words "act" and "behavior" signify?

463. Justice White in his opinion states that if, under *Robinson*, "it cannot be a crime to have an irresistible compulsion," it cannot "constitutionally be a crime to yield to such a compulsion," p. 748. Does Marshall's opinion respond satisfactorily to that proposition? Does White's own argument that Powell "made no showing that he was unable to stay off the streets on the night in question," id., respond satisfactorily? (Would White uphold a law that made it a crime to sneeze in public?)

464. The four dissenting Justices concluded that the case could be decided on the basis of the principle established by *Robinson*: "Criminal penalties may not be inflicted upon a person for being in a condition he is powerless to change," p. 749. Does that principle dispose of this case? If so, having in mind Justice White's argument, how do you—how would the Justices—distinguish *Powell* from *Girouard*, p. 72 above, or *Wolff*, p. 124 above?

465. In State ex rel. Harper v. Zegeer, 296 S.E.2d 873 (W.Va.1982), the court held that, chronic alcoholism being a disease, criminal punishment of an alcoholic for being drunk in a public place violates the state constitution's prohibition against cruel and unusual punishment. The court observed that the state has a legitimate interest in keeping a chronic alcoholic who is drunk off the streets; but it said, the "drunk tanks" of the county jails, which are generally unfit for human habitation, cannot be used for that purpose. It indicated that criminal prosecution of an alcoholic for other crimes arising from intoxication is permissible. The opinion reviews at length decisions before and after *Powell* and legislative measures for the treatment of alcoholics. See also State v. Fearon, 166 N.W.2d 720 (Minn.1969). The West Virginia court noted that except for Minnesota, no other state had held that alcoholics could not be criminally punished for public intoxication.

See p. 579 note 350 above, for cases rejecting narcotics addiction and compulsive gambling as a defense to an accusation of crime for conduct allegedly caused thereby. For a lengthy, often illuminating discussion of narcotics addiction as a defense to prosecution for possession of heroin, see the opinions in United States v. Moore, 486 F.2d 1139 (D.C.Cir.1973) (defense not allowed).

———

As the Court recognized in *Powell*, the issue in that case and *Robinson* was not whether the legislature had authority to regulate and, if it could, prevent narcotics addiction or public drunkenness. No one doubts that it does. Rather, the issue was whether the defendant in each case was individually responsible for what the law had declared to be a crime. In *Robinson*, the Court found that the condition of being an addict was not something for which a person can be held criminally responsible, although he might be subjected involuntarily to various kinds of control or treatment. In *Powell*, the Court found that the defendant could be held criminally responsible for the conduct of being drunk in a public place, even though his condition of chronic alcoholism possibly had deprived him of the capacity to control his conduct in that respect. The dissenters in *Powell* argued not that Powell's conduct could not be made a crime but that in his case, because of his special circumstances, it was effectively his condition, not his conduct, that the law punished, and that as applied to him, therefore, the law was like the law declared invalid in *Robinson*.

Robinson and *Powell* focus our attention on the matter of criminal responsibility in general. If a person's responsibility for particular conduct is not in doubt, is there any limit on the legislature's authority to declare the conduct criminal? Is there any conduct that by its nature is excluded from the scope of the criminal law?

In Griswold v. Connecticut, 381 U.S. 479 (1965), the Supreme Court held that a statute forbidding the use of contraceptives was unconstitutional. The Court referred to specific constitutional guarantees of the right to privacy in other contexts, such as the protections against unreasonable searches and compelled self-incrimination. Observing that the statute operated "directly on an intimate relation of husband and wife," the Court said:

> The present case, then, concerns a relationship lying within the zone of privacy created by several fundamental constitutional guarantees. And it concerns a law which, in forbidding the *use* of contraceptives rather than regulating their manufacture or sale, seeks to achieve its goals by means having a maximum destructive impact upon that relationship. Such a law cannot stand in light of the familiar principles, so often applied by this Court, that a "governmental purpose to control or prevent activities constitutionally subject to state regulation may not be achieved by means which sweep unnecessarily broadly and thereby invade the area of protected freedoms." NAACP v. Alabama, 377 U.S. 288, 307. Would we allow the police to search the sacred precincts of marital bedrooms for telltale signs of the use of contraceptives? The very idea is repulsive to the notions of privacy surrounding the marriage relationship.
>
> We deal with a right of privacy older than the Bill of Rights—older than our political parties, older than our school system. Marriage is a coming together for better or for worse, hopefully enduring, and intimate to the degree of being sacred. It is an association that promotes a way of life, not causes; a harmony in living, not political faiths; a bilateral loyalty, not commercial or social projects. Yet it is an association for as noble a purpose as any involved in our prior decisions.

381 U.S. at 482, 485–86.

Justice Douglas, who wrote the opinion for the Court in *Griswold*, had expressed similar views in dissent, in Poe v. Ullman, 367 U.S. 497, 509 (1961), an earlier case challenging the Connecticut statute in which a majority of the Court declined to reach a decision on the merits. In that case, Justice Harlan, also dissenting, said:

> Precisely what is involved here is this: the State is asserting the right to enforce its moral judgment by intruding upon the most intimate details of the marital relation with the full power of the criminal law. Potentially, this could allow the deployment of all the incidental machinery of the criminal law, arrests, searches and sei-

zures; inevitably, it must mean at the very least the lodging of criminal charges, a public trial, and testimony as to the *corpus delicti*. Nor could any imaginable elaboration of presumptions, testimonial privileges, or other safeguards, alleviate the necessity for testimony as to the mode and manner of the married couples' sexual relations, or at least the opportunity for the accused to make denial of the charges. In sum, the statute allows the State to enquire into, prove and punish married people for the private use of their marital intimacy.

. . .

. . . The right of privacy most manifestly is not an absolute. Thus, I would not suggest that adultery, homosexuality, fornication and incest are immune from criminal enquiry, however privately practiced. So much has been explicitly recognized in acknowledging the State's rightful concern for its people's moral welfare. . . . But not to discriminate between what is involved in this case and either the traditional offenses against good morals or crimes which, though they may be committed anywhere, happen to have been committed or concealed in the home, would entirely misconceive the argument that is being made.

Adultery, homosexuality and the like are sexual intimacies which the State forbids altogether, but the intimacy of husband and wife is necessarily an essential and accepted feature of the institution of marriage, an institution which the State not only must allow, but which always and in every age it has fostered and protected. It is one thing when the State exerts its power either to forbid extramarital sexuality altogether, or to say who may marry, but it is quite another when, having acknowledged a marriage and the intimacies inherent in it, it undertakes to regulate by means of the criminal law the details of that intimacy.

In sum, even though the State has determined that the use of contraceptives is as iniquitous as any act of extra-marital sexual immorality, the intrusion of the whole machinery of the criminal law into the very heart of marital privacy, requiring husband and wife to render account before a criminal tribunal of their uses of that intimacy, is surely a very different thing indeed from punishing those who establish intimacies which the law has always forbidden and which can have no claim to social protection.

In my view the appellants have presented a very pressing claim for Constitutional protection. Such difficulty as the claim presents lies only in evaluating it against the State's countervailing contention that it be allowed to enforce, by whatever means it deems appropriate, its judgment of the immorality of the practice this law condemns.

367 U.S. at 522, 548, 552–54.

In Roe v. Wade, 410 U.S. 113 (1973), in which the Court upheld a woman's right to obtain an abortion, see p. 11 note 9 above, the Court said:

This right of privacy, whether it be founded in the Fourteenth Amendment's concept of personal liberty and restrictions upon state action, as we feel it is, or, as the District Court determined, in the Ninth Amendment's reservation of rights to the people, is broad enough to encompass a woman's decision whether or not to terminate her pregnancy. The detriment that the State would impose upon the pregnant woman by denying this choice altogether is apparent. Specific and direct harm medically diagnosable even in early pregnancy may be involved. Maternity, or additional offspring, may force upon the woman a distressful life and future. Psychological harm may be imminent. Mental and physical health may be taxed by child care. There is also the distress, for all concerned, associated with the unwanted child, and there is the problem of bringing a child into a family already unable, psychologically and otherwise, to care for it. In other cases, as in this one, the additional difficulties and continuing stigma of unwed motherhood may be involved. All these are factors the woman and her responsible physician necessarily will consider in consultation.

On the basis of elements such as these, appellant and some *amici* argue that the woman's right is absolute and that she is entitled to terminate her pregnancy at whatever time, in whatever way, and for whatever reason she alone chooses. With this we do not agree. Appellant's arguments that Texas either has no valid interest at all in regulating the abortion decision, or no interest strong enough to support any limitation upon the woman's sole determination, is unpersuasive. The Court's decisions recognizing a right of privacy also acknowledge that some state regulation in areas protected by that right is appropriate. As noted above, a State may properly assert important interests in safeguarding health, in maintaining medical standards, and in protecting potential life. At some point in pregnancy, these respective interests become sufficiently compelling to sustain regulation of the factors that govern the abortion decision. The privacy right involved, therefore, cannot be said to be absolute. In fact, it is not clear to us that the claim asserted by some *amici* that one has an unlimited right to do with one's body as one pleases bears a close relationship to the right of privacy previously articulated in the Court's decisions. The Court has refused to recognize an unlimited right of this kind in the past. Jacobson v. Massachusetts, 197 U.S. 11 (1905) (vaccination); Buck v. Bell, 274 U.S. 200 (1927) (sterilization).

We, therefore, conclude that the right of personal privacy includes the abortion decision, but that this right is not unqualified and must be considered against important state interests in regulation.

410 U.S. at 153–54.

The Court's holding is set forth at pp. 11–12 above.

See also Washington v. Glucksberg, 521 U.S. 702 (1997), holding that the liberty protected by the Due Process Clause does not include a right to physician-assisted suicide, and Cruzan v. Director, Missouri Dept. of Health, 497 U.S. 261 (1990) (5–4), recognizing a competent person's right to refuse "lifesaving hydration and nutrition," id. at 279, but upholding the state's authority to require clear and convincing evidence of an incompetent person's wishes, despite the decision of close family members that such treatment should be terminated.

Justice Harlan's statement in Poe v. Ullman, above, that "adultery, homosexuality, fornication and incest" are within the reach of the criminal law, as part of "the State's rightful concern for its people's moral welfare," accurately reflected the prevailing understanding at the time he wrote. In the years since, that view has been questioned.

Bowers v. Hardwick

478 U.S. 186, 106 S.Ct. 2841, 92 L.Ed.2d 140 (1986)

■ JUSTICE WHITE delivered the opinion of the Court.

In August 1982, respondent was charged with violating the Georgia statute criminalizing sodomy by committing that act with another adult male in the bedroom of respondent's home. After a preliminary hearing, the District Attorney decided not to present the matter to the grand jury unless further evidence developed.

Respondent then brought suit in the Federal District Court, challenging the constitutionality of the statute insofar as it criminalized consensual sodomy.[2] He asserted that he was a practicing homosexual, that the Georgia sodomy statute, as administered by the defendants, placed him in imminent danger of arrest, and that the statute for several reasons violates the Federal Constitution. The District Court granted the defendants' motion to dismiss for failure to state a claim. . . .

A divided panel of the Court of Appeals for the Eleventh Circuit reversed. 760 F.2d 1202 (1985). . . . [T]he court . . . [held] that the Georgia statute violated respondent's fundamental rights because his homosexual activity is a private and intimate association that is beyond the reach of state regulation by reason of the Ninth Amendment and the Due Process Clause of the Fourteenth Amendment. The case was remanded for trial, at which, to prevail, the State would have to prove that the statute is supported by a compelling interest and is the most narrowly drawn means of achieving that end.

Because other Courts of Appeals have arrived at judgments contrary to that of the Eleventh Circuit in this case, we granted the State's petition for certiorari questioning the holding that its sodomy statute violates the fundamental rights of homosexuals. We agree with the State that the Court of Appeals erred, and hence reverse its judgment.

---

2. . . .

The only claim properly before the Court . . . is Hardwick's challenge to the Georgia statute as applied to consensual ho- mosexual sodomy. We express no opinion on the constitutionality of the Georgia statute as applied to other acts of sodomy.

This case does not require a judgment on whether laws against sodomy between consenting adults in general, or between homosexuals in particular, are wise or desirable. It raises no question about the right or propriety of state legislative decisions to repeal their laws that criminalize homosexual sodomy, or of state court decisions invalidating those laws on state constitutional grounds. The issue presented is whether the Federal Constitution confers a fundamental right upon homosexuals to engage in sodomy and hence invalidates the laws of the many States that still make such conduct illegal and have done so for a very long time. The case also calls for some judgment about the limits of the Court's role in carrying out its constitutional mandate.

We first register our disagreement with the Court of Appeals and with respondent that the Court's prior cases have construed the Constitution to confer a right of privacy that extends to homosexual sodomy and for all intents and purposes have decided this case. The reach of this line of cases was sketched in Carey v. Population Services International, 431 U.S. 678, 685 (1977). Pierce v. Society of Sisters, 268 U.S. 510 (1925), and Meyer v. Nebraska, 262 U.S. 390 (1923), were described as dealing with child rearing and education; Prince v. Massachusetts, 321 U.S. 158 (1944), with family relationships; Skinner v. Oklahoma ex rel. Williamson, 316 U.S. 535 (1942), with procreation; Loving v. Virginia, 388 U.S. 1 (1967), with marriage; Griswold v. Connecticut, [381 U.S. 479 (1965)], and Eisenstadt v. Baird, [405 U.S. 438 (1972)], with contraception; and Roe v. Wade, 410 U.S. 113 (1973), with abortion. The latter three cases were interpreted as construing the Due Process Clause of the Fourteenth Amendment to confer a fundamental individual right to decide whether or not to beget or bear a child. . . .

Accepting the decisions in these cases and the above description of them, we think it evident that none of the rights announced in those cases bears any resemblance to the claimed constitutional right of homosexuals to engage in acts of sodomy that is asserted in this case. No connection between family, marriage, or procreation on the one hand and homosexual activity on the other has been demonstrated, either by the Court of Appeals or by respondent. Moreover, any claim that these cases nevertheless stand for the proposition that any kind of private sexual conduct between consenting adults is constitutionally insulated from state proscription is unsupportable. . . .

Precedent aside, however, respondent would have us announce, as the Court of Appeals did, a fundamental right to engage in homosexual sodomy. This we are quite unwilling to do. It is true that despite the language of the Due Process Clauses of the Fifth and Fourteenth Amendments, which appears to focus only on the processes by which life, liberty, or property is taken, the cases are legion in which those Clauses have been interpreted to have substantive content, subsuming rights that to a great extent are immune from federal or state regulation or proscription. Among such cases are those recognizing rights that have little or no textual support in the constitutional language. *Meyer*, *Prince*, and *Pierce* fall in this category, as do the privacy cases from *Griswold* to *Carey*.

Striving to assure itself and the public that announcing rights not readily identifiable in the Constitution's text involves much more than the imposition of the Justices' own choice of values on the States and the Federal Government, the Court has sought to identify the nature of the rights qualifying for heightened judicial protection. In Palko v. Connecticut, 302 U.S. 319, 325, 326 (1937), it was said that this category includes those fundamental liberties that are "implicit in the concept of ordered liberty," such that "neither liberty nor justice would exist if [they] were sacrificed." A different description of fundamental liberties appeared in Moore v. East Cleveland, 431 U.S. 494, 503 (1977) (opinion of Powell, J.), where they are characterized as those liberties that are "deeply rooted in this Nation's history and tradition." Id., at 503 (Powell, J.). . . .

It is obvious to us that neither of these formulations would extend a fundamental right to homosexuals to engage in acts of consensual sodomy. Proscriptions against that conduct have ancient roots. . . . Sodomy was a criminal offense at common law and was forbidden by the laws of the original 13 States when they ratified the Bill of Rights. In 1868, when the Fourteenth Amendment was ratified, all but 5 of the 37 States in the Union had criminal sodomy laws. In fact, until 1961, all 50 States outlawed sodomy, and today, 24 States and the District of Columbia continue to provide criminal penalties for sodomy performed in private and between consenting adults. . . . Against this background, to claim that a right to engage in such conduct is "deeply rooted in this Nation's history and tradition" or "implicit in the concept of ordered liberty" is, at best, facetious.

Nor are we inclined to take a more expansive view of our authority to discover new fundamental rights imbedded in the Due Process Clause. The Court is most vulnerable and comes nearest to illegitimacy when it deals with judge-made constitutional law having little or no cognizable roots in the language or design of the Constitution. That this is so was painfully demonstrated by the face-off between the Executive and the Court in the 1930s, which resulted in the repudiation of much of the substantive gloss that the Court had placed on the Due Process Clause of the Fifth and Fourteenth Amendments. There should be, therefore, great resistance to expand the substantive reach of those Clauses, particularly if it requires redefining the category of rights deemed to be fundamental. Otherwise, the Judiciary necessarily takes to itself further authority to govern the country without express constitutional authority. The claimed right pressed on us today falls far short of overcoming this resistance.

Respondent, however, asserts that the result should be different where the homosexual conduct occurs in the privacy of the home. He relies on Stanley v. Georgia, 394 U.S. 557 (1969), where the Court held that the First Amendment prevents conviction for possessing and reading obscene material in the privacy of his home. . . .

Stanley did protect conduct that would not have been protected outside the home, and it partially prevented the enforcement of state obscenity laws; but the decision was firmly grounded in the First Amendment. The right pressed upon us here has no similar support in the text of the Constitution, and it does not qualify for recognition under the prevailing principles for construing the Fourteenth Amendment. Its limits are also difficult to discern. Plainly enough, otherwise illegal conduct is not always immunized whenever it occurs in the home. Victimless crimes, such as the possession and use of illegal drugs, do not escape the law where they are committed at home. *Stanley* itself recognized that its holding offered no protection for the possession in the home of drugs, firearms, or stolen goods. . . . And if respondent's submission is limited to the voluntary sexual conduct between consenting adults, it would be difficult, except by fiat, to limit the claimed right to homosexual conduct while leaving exposed to prosecution adultery, incest, and other sexual crimes even though they are committed in the home. We are unwilling to start down that road.

Even if the conduct at issue here is not a fundamental right, respondent asserts that there must be a rational basis for the law and that there is none in this case other than the presumed belief of a majority of the electorate in Georgia that homosexual sodomy is immoral and unacceptable. This is said to be an inadequate rationale to support the law. The law, however, is constantly based on notions of morality, and if all laws representing essentially moral choices are to be invalidated under the Due Process Clause, the courts will be very busy indeed. Even respondent makes no such claim, but insists that majority sentiments about the morality of homosexuality should be declared inadequate. We do not agree, and are unpersuaded that the sodomy laws of some 25 States should be invalidated on this basis.

Accordingly, the judgment of the Court of Appeals is

Reversed.

■ JUSTICE BLACKMUN, with whom JUSTICE BRENNAN, JUSTICE MARSHALL, and JUSTICE STEVENS join, dissenting.

This case is no more about "a fundamental right to engage in homosexual sodomy," as the Court purports to declare, ante, at 191, than Stanley v. Georgia, 394 U.S. 557 (1969), was about a fundamental right to watch obscene movies, or Katz v. United States, 389 U.S. 347 (1967), was about a fundamental right to place interstate bets from a telephone booth. Rather, this case is about "the most comprehensive of rights and the right most valued by civilized men," namely, "the right to be let alone." Olmstead v. United States, 277 U.S. 438, 478 (1928) (Brandeis, J., dissenting).

The statute at issue, Ga. Code Ann. § 16–6–2 (1984), denies individuals the right to decide for themselves whether to engage in particular forms of private, consensual sexual activity. The Court concludes that § 16–6–2 is valid essentially because "the laws of . . . many States . . . still make such conduct illegal and have done so for a very long time." Ante, at 190. But the fact that the moral judgments expressed by statutes like § 16–6–2 may be "natural and familiar . . . ought not to conclude our judgment upon the question whether statutes embodying them conflict with the Constitution of the United States." Roe v. Wade, 410 U.S. 113, 117 (1973), quoting Lochner v. New York, 198 U.S. 45, 76 (1905) (Holmes, J., dissenting). Like Justice Holmes, I believe that "[i]t is revolting to have no better reason for a rule of law than that so it was laid down in the time of Henry IV. It is still more revolting if the grounds upon which it was laid down have vanished long since, and the rule simply persists from blind imitation of the past." Holmes, The Path of the Law, 10 Harv. L. Rev. 457, 469 (1897). I believe we must analyze respondent's claim in the light of the values that underlie the constitutional right to privacy. If that right means anything, it means that, before Georgia can prosecute its citizens for making choices about the most intimate aspects of their lives, it must do more than assert that the choice they have made is an " 'abominable crime not fit to be named among Christians.' " Herring v. State, 119 Ga. 709, 721 (1904).

I

In its haste to reverse the Court of Appeals and hold that the Constitution does not "confe[r] a fundamental right upon homosexuals to engage in sodomy," ante, at 190, the Court relegates the actual statute being challenged to a footnote and ignores the procedural posture of the case before it. A fair reading of the statute and of the complaint clearly reveals that the majority has distorted the question this case presents.

First, the Court's almost obsessive focus on homosexual activity is particularly hard to justify in light of the broad language Georgia has used. Unlike the Court, the Georgia Legislature has not proceeded on the assumption that homosexuals are so different from other citizens that their lives may be controlled in a way that would not be tolerated if it limited the choices of those other citizens. . . . Rather, Georgia has provided that "[a] person commits the offense of sodomy when he performs or submits to any sexual act involving the sex organs of one person and the mouth or anus of another." Ga. Code Ann. § 16–6–2(a) (1984). The sex or status of the persons who engage in the act is irrelevant as a matter of state law. In fact, to the extent I can discern a legislative purpose for Georgia's 1968 enactment of § 16–6–2, that purpose seems to have been to broaden the coverage of the law to reach heterosexual as well as homosexual activity. I therefore see no basis for the Court's decision to treat this case as an "as applied" challenge to § 16–6–2 . . . or for Georgia's attempt, both in its brief and at oral argument, to defend § 16–6–2 solely on the grounds that it prohibits homosexual activity. Michael Hardwick's standing may rest in significant part on Georgia's apparent willingness to enforce against homosexuals a law it seems not to have any desire to enforce against heterosexuals. . . . But his claim that § 16–6–2 involves an unconstitutional intrusion into his privacy and his right of intimate association does not depend in any way on his sexual orientation.

. . .

II

"Our cases long have recognized that the Constitution embodies a promise that a certain private sphere of individual liberty will be kept largely beyond the reach of government." Thornburgh v. American College of Obstetricians & Gynecologists, 476 U.S. 747, 772 (1986). In construing the right to privacy, the Court has proceeded along two somewhat distinct, albeit complementary, lines. First, it has recognized a privacy interest with reference to certain *decisions* that are properly for the individual to make. . . . Second, it has recognized a privacy interest with reference to certain *places* without regard for the particular activities in which the individuals who occupy them are engaged. . . . The case before us implicates both the decisional and the spatial aspects of the right to privacy.

A

The Court concludes today that none of our prior cases dealing with various decisions that individuals are entitled to make free of governmental interference "bears any resemblance to the claimed constitutional right of homosexuals to engage in acts of sodomy that is asserted in this case." Ante, at 190–191. While it is true that these cases may be characterized by their connection to protection of the family . . . the Court's conclusion that they extend no further than this boundary ignores the warning in Moore v. East Cleveland, 431 U.S. 494, 501 (1977) (plurality opinion), against "clos[ing] our eyes to the basic reasons why certain rights associated with the family have been accorded shelter under the Fourteenth Amendment's Due Process Clause." We protect those rights not because they contribute, in some direct and material way, to the general public welfare, but because they form so central a part of an individual's life. "[T]he concept of privacy embodies the 'moral fact that a person belongs to himself and not others nor to society as a whole.'" Thornburgh v. American College of Obstetricians & Gynecologists, 476 U.S., at 477, n.5 (Stevens, J., concurring), quoting Fried, Correspondence, 6 Phil. & Pub. Affairs 288–289 (1977). And so we protect the decision whether to marry precisely because marriage "is an association that promotes a way of life, not causes; a harmony in living, not political faiths; a bilateral loyalty, not commercial or social projects." Griswold v. Connecticut, 381 U.S. [479 (1965)], at 486. We protect the decision whether to have a child because parenthood alters so dramatically an individual's self-definition, not because of demographic considerations or the Bible's command to be fruitful and multiply. . . . And we protect the family because it contributes so powerfully to the happiness of individuals, not because of a preference for stereotypical households. . . . The Court recognized in *Roberts* [v. United States Jaycees], 468 U.S. [609 (1984)], at 619, that the "ability independently to define one's identity that is central to any concept of liberty" cannot truly be exercised in a vacuum; we all depend on the "emotional enrichment of close ties with others." Ibid.

Only the most willful blindness could obscure the fact that sexual intimacy is "a sensitive, key relationship of human existence, central to family life, community welfare, and the development of human personality," Paris Adult Theatre I v. Slaton, 413 U.S. 49, 63 (1973). . . . The fact that individuals define themselves in a significant way through their intimate sexual relationships with others suggests, in a Nation as diverse as ours, that there may be many "right" ways of conducting those relationships, and that much of the richness of a relationship will come from the freedom an individual has to *choose* the form and nature of these intensely personal bonds. . . .

In a variety of circumstances we have recognized that a necessary corollary of giving individuals freedom to choose how to conduct their lives is acceptance of the fact that different individuals will make different choices. For example, in holding that the clearly important state interest in public education should give way to a competing claim by the Amish to the effect that extended formal schooling threatened their way of life, the Court declared: "There can be no assumption that today's majority is 'right' and the Amish and others like them are 'wrong.' A way of life that is odd or even erratic but interferes with no rights or interests of others is not to be condemned because it is different." Wisconsin v. Yoder, 406 U.S. 205, 223–224 (1972). The Court claims that its decision today merely refuses to recognize a fundamental right to engage in homosexual sodomy; what the Court really has refused to recognize is the fundamental interest all individuals have in controlling the nature of their intimate associations with others.

B

The behavior for which Hardwick faces prosecution occurred in his own home, a place to which the Fourth Amendment attaches special significance. The Court's treatment of this aspect of the case is symptomatic of its overall refusal to consider the broad principles that have informed our treatment of privacy in specific cases. Just as the right to privacy is more than the mere aggregation of a number of entitlements to engage in specific behavior, so too, protecting the physical integrity of the home is more than merely a means of protecting specific activities that often take place there. Even when our understanding of the contours of the right to privacy depends on "reference to a 'place,'" Katz v. United States, 389 U.S., at 361 (Harlan, J., concurring), "the essence of a Fourth Amendment violation is 'not the breaking of [a person's] doors, and the rummaging of his drawers,' but rather is 'the invasion of his indefeasible right of personal security, personal liberty and private property.'" California v. Ciraolo, 476 U.S. 207, 226 (1986) (Powell, J., dissenting), quoting Boyd v. United States, 116 U.S. 616, 630 (1886).

The Court's interpretation of the pivotal case of Stanley v. Georgia, 394 U.S. 557 (1969), is entirely unconvincing. *Stanley* held that Georgia's undoubted power to punish the public distribution of constitutionally unprotected, obscene material did not permit the State to punish the private possession of such material. According to the majority here, *Stanley* relied entirely on the First Amendment, and thus, it is claimed, sheds no light on cases not involving printed materials. Ante, at 195. But that is not what *Stanley* said. Rather, the *Stanley* Court anchored its holding in the Fourth Amendment's special protection for the individual in his home. . . .

. . .

. . . *Stanley* rested as much on the Court's understanding of the Fourth Amendment as it did on the First. . . . "The right of the people to be secure in their . . . houses," expressly guaranteed by the Fourth Amendment, is perhaps the most "textual" of the various constitutional provisions that inform our understanding of the right to privacy, and thus I cannot agree with the Court's statement that "[t]he right pressed upon us here has no . . . support in the text of the Constitution," ante, at 195. Indeed, the right of an individual to conduct intimate relationships in the intimacy of his or her own home seems to me to be the heart of the Constitution's protection of privacy.

III

The Court's failure to comprehend the magnitude of the liberty interests at stake in this case leads it to slight the question whether petitioner, on behalf of the State, has justified Georgia's infringement on these interests. I believe that neither of the two general justifications for § 16–6–2 that petitioner has advanced warrants dismissing respondent's challenge for failure to state a claim.

First, petitioner asserts that the acts made criminal by the statute may have serious adverse consequences for "the general public health and welfare," such as spreading communicable diseases or fostering other criminal activity. Brief for Petitioner 37. Inasmuch as this case was dismissed by the District Court on the pleadings, it is not surprising that the record before us is barren of any evidence to support petitioner's claim. In light of the state of the record, I see no justification for the Court's attempt to equate the private, consensual sexual activity at issue here with the "possession in the home of drugs, firearms, or stolen goods," ante, at 195, to which *Stanley* refused to extend its protection. 394 U.S., at 568, n.11. None of the behavior so mentioned in *Stanley* can properly be viewed as "[v]ictimless," ante, at 195: drugs and weapons are inherently dangerous . . . and for property to be "stolen," someone must have been wrongfully deprived of it. Nothing in the record before the Court provides any justification for finding the activity forbidden by § 16–6–2 to be physically dangerous, either to the persons engaged in it or to others.[3]

---

3. Although I do not think it necessary to decide today issues that are not even remotely before us, it does seem to me that a court could find simple, analytically sound distinctions between certain private, consensual sexual conduct, on the one hand, and adultery and incest (the only two vaguely specific "sexual crimes" to which the majority points, ante, at 196), on the other. For example, marriage, in addition to its spiritual aspects, is a civil contract that entitles the contracting parties to a variety of governmentally provided benefits. A State might define the contractual commitment necessary to become eligible for these benefits to include a commitment of fidelity and then punish individuals for breaching that contract. Moreover, a State might conclude that adultery is likely to injure third persons, in particular, spouses and children of persons

The core of petitioner's defense of § 16–6–2, however, is that respondent and others who engage in the conduct prohibited by § 16–6–2 interfere with Georgia's exercise of the " 'right of the Nation and of the States to maintain a decent society,' " Paris Adult Theater I v. Slaton, 413 U.S., at 59–60, quoting Jacobellis v. Ohio, 378 U.S. 184, 199 (1964) (Warren, C.J., dissenting). Essentially, petitioner argues, and the Court agrees, that the fact that the acts described in § 16–6–2 "for hundreds of years, if not thousands, have been uniformly condemned as immoral" is a sufficient reason to permit a State to ban them today. Brief for Petitioner 19. . . .

I cannot agree that either the length of time a majority has held its convictions or the passions with which it defends them can withdraw legislation from this Court's scrutiny. . . . As Justice Jackson wrote so eloquently for the Court in West Virginia Board of Education v. Barnette, 319 U.S. 624, 641–642 (1943), "we apply the limitations of the Constitution with no fear that freedom to be intellectually and spiritually diverse or even contrary will disintegrate the social organization. . . . [F]reedom to differ is not limited to things that do not matter much. That would be a mere shadow of freedom. The test of its substance is the right to differ as to things that touch the heart of the existing order." . . . It is precisely because the issue raised by this case touches the heart of what makes individuals what they are that we should be especially sensitive to the rights of those whose choices upset the majority.

The assertion that "traditional Judeo-Christian values proscribe" the conduct involved, Brief for Petitioner 20, cannot provide an adequate justification for § 16–6–2. That certain, but by no means all, religious groups condemn the behavior at issue gives the State no license to impose their judgments on the entire citizenry. The legitimacy of secular legislation depends instead on whether the State can advance some justification for its law beyond its conformity to religious doctrine. . . . Thus, far from buttressing his case, petitioner's invocation of Leviticus, Romans, St. Thomas Aquinas, and sodomy's heretical status during the Middle Ages undermines his suggestion that § 16–6–2 represents a legitimate use of secular coercive power. A State can no more punish private behavior because of religious intolerance than it can punish such behavior because of racial animus. "The Constitution cannot control such prejudices, but neither can it tolerate them. Private biases may be outside the reach of the law, but the law cannot, directly or indirectly give them effect." Palmore v. Sidoti, 466 U.S. 429, 433 (1984). No matter how uncomfortable a certain group may make the majority of this Court, we have held that "[m]ere public intolerance or animosity cannot constitutionally justify the depriva-

---

who engage in extramarital affairs. With respect to incest, a court might well agree with respondent that the nature of familial relationships renders true consent to incestuous activity sufficiently problematical that a blanket prohibition of such activity is warranted. . . . Notably, the Court makes no effort to explain why it has chosen to group private, consensual homosexual activity with adultery and incest rather than with private, consensual heterosexual activity by unmarried persons or, indeed, with oral or anal sex within marriage.

tion of a person's physical liberty." O'Connor v. Donaldson, 422 U.S. 563, 575 (1975). . . .

Nor can § 16–6–2 be justified as a "morally neutral" exercise of Georgia's power to "protect the public environment," *Paris Adult Theatre I*, 413 U.S., at 68–69. Certainly, some private behavior can affect the fabric of society as a whole. Reasonable people may differ about whether particular sexual acts are moral or immoral, but "we have ample evidence for believing that people will not abandon morality, will not think any better of murder, cruelty and dishonesty, merely because some private sexual practice which they abominate is not punished by the law." H.L.A. Hart, Immorality and Treason, reprinted in The Law as Literature 220, 225 (L. Blom-Cooper ed. 1961). Petitioner and the Court fail to see the difference between laws that protect public sensibilities and those that enforce private morality. Statutes banning public sexual activity are entirely consistent with protecting the individual's liberty interest in decisions concerning sexual relations: the same recognition that those decisions are intensely private which justifies protecting them from governmental interference can justify protecting individuals from unwilling exposure to the sexual activities of others. But the mere fact that intimate behavior may be punished when it takes place in public cannot dictate how States can regulate intimate behavior that occurs in intimate places. . . .

This case involves no real interference with the rights of others, for the mere knowledge that other individuals do not adhere to one's value system cannot be a legally cognizable interest . . . let alone an interest that can justify invading the houses, hearts, and minds of citizens who choose to live their lives differently.

IV

It took but three years for the Court to see the error in its analysis in Minersville School District v. Gobitis, 310 U.S. 586 (1940), and to recognize that the threat to national cohesion posed by a refusal to salute the flag was vastly outweighed by the threat to those same values posed by compelling such a salute. See West Virginia Board of Education v. Barnette, 319 U.S. 624 (1943). I can only hope that here, too, the Court soon will reconsider its analysis and conclude that depriving individuals of the right to choose for themselves how to conduct their intimate relationships poses a far greater threat to the values most deeply rooted in our Nation's history than tolerance of nonconformity could ever do. Because I think the Court today betrays those values, I dissent.[4]

---

[4] Chief Justice Burger wrote a concurring opinion. Justice Powell also wrote a concurring opinion, in which he suggested strongly that if a person were sentenced to prison for a "single, private, consensual act of sodomy," 478 U.S. at 197, he would have a claim under the Eighth Amendment's Cruel and Unusual Punishments Clause. Justice Stevens wrote a dissenting opinion, which Justice Brennan and Justice Marshall joined.

466. How should we think about the issue in Bowers v. Hardwick? The majority says that the issue is "whether the Federal Constitution confers a fundamental right upon homosexuals to engage in sodomy," p. 756. The dissenting opinion dismisses the majority's statement summarily and says that the case is about " 'the right to be let alone,' " p. 758. It is difficult to disagree with the majority's conclusion that the right to which it refers cannot be found in the text of the Constitution. But then, neither can a right to use contraceptives. Is the disagreement about how to state the issue only rhetorical posturing? Or does it signal a matter of substance?

467. The majority goes out of its way to confine its ruling to homosexual sodomy, see p. 755 n.2, a step in its argument that the dissent sharply criticizes, see p. 759. Do you think the majority would have come out the same way if the defendant had been prosecuted for committing sodomy with a woman, or if the defendant had been a married man or woman and had been prosecuted for committing sodomy with his/her spouse? Consider in that connection Griswold v. Connecticut, p. 752 above. See State v. Chiaradio, 660 A.2d 276 (R.I.1995), holding that a state may constitutionally prosecute an unmarried heterosexual man who commits an act of cunnilingus. The defendants had performed cunnilingus on an exotic dancer at a bachelor party.

468. Responding to the argument that the only "rational basis" for the statute is "the presumed belief of a majority of the electorate in Georgia that homosexual sodomy is immoral and unacceptable," the majority says: "The law . . . is constantly based on notions of morality, and if all laws representing essentially moral choices are to be invalidated under the Due Process Clause, the courts will be very busy indeed," p. 758. Does the majority's response fairly reflect the argument it opposes? What is meant by the phrase "essentially moral choices"? On what basis did the respondent argue that "majority sentiments about the morality of homosexuality . . . [are] inadequate" to sustain the law, id.?

Would the central issue in Bowers v. Hardwick have been significantly different if the state had shown that there was a legislative judgment that consensual homosexual sodomy was dangerous to public health or safety and had presented evidence to substantiate that judgment? Evidently some such claim was made in the state's brief before the Court. See p. 762.

469. The Supreme Court of Kentucky has held that a state statute making it a misdemeanor to engage in "deviate sexual intercourse with another person of the same sex" violates the state constitution. Commonwealth v. Wasson, 842 S.W.2d 487, 488 (Ky.1992). In a lengthy opinion accompanied by two equally lengthy dissenting opinions, the court affirmed the judgment of a lower court that the statute violated constitutionally protected rights of privacy and equal protection of the laws.

With respect to the right to privacy, the court referred to earlier state cases invalidating the regulation of private drinking and smoking for the proposition that "immorality in private which does 'not operate to the detriment of others' is placed beyond the reach of state action by the guarantees of liberty in the Kentucky Constitution." It said also: "We view the United States Supreme Court decision in Bowers v. Hardwick . . . as a misdirected application of the theory of original intent. To illustrate: as a theory of majoritarian morality, miscegenation was an offense with ancient roots. It is highly unlikely that protecting the rights of persons of different races to copulate was one of the considerations behind the Fourteenth Amendment. Nevertheless, in Loving v. Virginia, 388 U.S. 1 (1967), the United States Supreme Court recognized that a contemporary, enlightened interpretation of the liberty interest involved in the sexual act made its punishment constitutionally impermissible." 842 S.W.2d at 496–97.

With respect to equal protection, the court said:

Certainly, the practice of deviate sexual intercourse violates traditional morality. But so does the same act between heterosexuals, which activity is decriminalized. Going one step further, all sexual activity between consenting adults outside of marriage violates our traditional morality. The issue here is not whether sexual activity traditionally viewed as immoral can be punished by society, but whether it can be punished solely on the basis of sexual preference.

. . .

The Commonwealth has tried hard to demonstrate a legitimate governmental interest justifying a distinction, but has failed. Many of the claimed justifications are simply outrageous: that "homosexuals are more promiscuous than heterosexuals . . . that homosexuals enjoy the company of children, and that homosexuals are more prone to engage in sex acts in public." The only proffered justification with superficial validity is that "infectious diseases are more readily transmitted by anal sodomy than by other forms of sexual copulation." But this statute is not limited to anal copulation, and this reasoning would apply to male-female anal intercourse the same as it applies to male-male intercourse. The growing number of females to whom AIDS (Acquired Immune Deficiency Syndrome) has been transmitted is stark evidence that AIDS is not only a male homosexual disease. The only medical evidence in the record before us rules out any distinction between male-male and male-female anal intercourse as a method of preventing AIDS. The act of sexual contact is not implicated, per se, whether the contact is homosexual or heterosexual. In any event, this statute was enacted in 1974 before the AIDS nightmare was upon us. It was 1982 or 1983 before AIDS was a recognized diagnostic entity.

In the final analysis we can attribute no legislative purpose to this statute except to single out homosexuals for different treatment for indulging their sexual preference by engaging in the same activity heterosexuals are now at liberty to perform. By 1974 there had already been a sea change in societal values insofar as attaching criminal penalties to extramarital sex. The question is whether a society that no longer criminalizes adultery, fornication, or deviate sexual intercourse between heterosexuals, has a rational basis to single out homosexual acts for different treatment. Is there a rational basis for declaring this one type of sexual immorality so destructive of family values as to merit criminal punishment whereas other acts of sexual immorality which were likewise forbidden by the same religious and traditional heritage of Western civilization are now decriminalized? If there is a rational basis for different treatment it has yet to be demonstrated in this case. We need not sympathize, agree with, or even understand the sexual preference of homosexuals in order to recognize their right to equal treatment before the bar of criminal justice.

842 S.W.2d at 499–501.

Laws prohibiting private sexual conduct between consenting adults (limited to homosexual conduct or applying to "deviate" homosexual or heterosexual conduct) have been declared unconstitutional in a number of states. Jegley v. Picado, 80 S.W.3d 332 (Ark.2002); Powell v. State, 510 S.E.2d 18 (Ga.1998); Gryczan v. State, 942 P.2d 112 (Mont.1997); People v. Onofre, 415 N.E.2d 936 (N.Y.1980); Commonwealth v. Bonadio, 415 A.2d 47 (Pa.1980); Campbell v. Sundquist, 926 S.W.2d 250 (Tenn.Ct.App.1996). A statute prohibiting "deviate sexual intercourse" with a person of the same sex is upheld in Lawrence v. State, 41 S.W.2d 349 (Tex.App.2001). The Supreme Court has granted a petition for certiorari. ___ U.S. ___, 123 S.Ct. 661 (2002). A decision is expected in June 2003. In a concurring opinion in *Jegley*, above, Justice Brown observed that in addition to Texas only two states, Kansas and Oklahoma, were reported still to make private homosexual conduct between adults criminal. 80 S.W.3d at 355.

Removed from the constitutional context, Bowers v. Hardwick as well as the cases that immediately precede it are about liberty, specifically the individual's right to choose and act for herself, without interference or restraint by the government. John Stuart Mill's essay On Liberty, if not the last word on the subject, is almost invariably the first word. Since it was written, few discussions of liberty have been able to avoid framing the issues as he did, whether to approve or disapprove his conclusions. Stephen's book Liberty, Equality, Fraternity was explicitly a response to Mill. Less timeless and now less well known than Mill's essay, it is nevertheless a powerful statement. Hart's book Law, Liberty and Morality, written almost a hundred years later, continues the debate between Mill and Stephen and adds to the arguments on Mill's side. The following are excerpts from all three works. The issues of Bowers v. Hardwick and the other cases are restated more generally, in nonconstitutional terms.

J.S. MILL, ON LIBERTY 95–100, 179–80, 183–89, 206–09
(EVERYMAN AMERICAN ED. 1951)[5]

J. STEPHEN, LIBERTY, EQUALITY, FRATERNITY
125–26, 130–49, 152–53, 158–60, 162–63 (1873)

H.L.A. HART, LAW, LIBERTY AND MORALITY
21–22, 36–38, 45–48, 69–77 (1963)

MILL

The object of this Essay is to assert one very simple principle, as entitled to govern absolutely the dealings of society with the individual in the way of compulsion and control, whether the means used be physical force in the form of legal penalties, or the moral coercion of public opinion. That principle is, that the sole end for which mankind are warranted, individually or collectively, in interfering with the liberty of action of any of their number, is self-protection. That the only purpose for which power can be rightfully exercised over any member of a civilised community, against his will, is to prevent harm to others. His own good, either physical or moral, is not a sufficient warrant. He cannot rightfully be compelled to do or forbear because it will be better for him to do so, because it will make him happier, because, in the opinions of others, to do so would be wise, or even right. These are good reasons for remonstrating with him, or reasoning with him, or persuading him, or entreating him, but not for compelling him, or visiting him with any evil in case he do otherwise. To justify that, the conduct from which it is desired to deter him must be calculated to produce evil to some one else. The only part of the conduct of any one, for which he is amendable to society, is that which concerns others. In the part which merely concerns himself, his independence is, of right, absolute. Over himself, over his own body and mind, the individual is sovereign.

It is, perhaps hardly necessary to say that this doctrine is meant to apply only to human beings in the maturity of their faculties. We are not speaking of children, or of young persons below the age which the law may fix as that of manhood or womanhood. Those who are still in a state to require being taken care of by others, must be protected against their own actions as well as against external injury. For the same reason, we may leave out of consideration those backward states of society in which the race itself may be considered as in its nonage. . . . Liberty, as a principle, has no application to any state of things anterior to the time when mankind have become capable of being improved by free and equal discussion. . . .

. . . If any one does an act hurtful to others, there is a prima facie *case for punishing him, by law, or, where legal penalties are not safely applicable, by general disapprobation. There are also many positive acts for the benefit of others, which he may rightfully be compelled to perform. . . . A person may cause evil to others not only by his actions but by his inaction, and in either case he is justly accountable to them for the injury. . . .*

---

5. First published in 1859.

But there is a sphere of action in which society, as distinguished from the individual, has, if any, only an indirect interest; comprehending all that portion of a person's life and conduct which affects only himself, or if it also affects others, only with their free, voluntary, and undeceived consent and participation. When I say only himself, I mean directly, and in the first instance; for whatever affects himself, may affect others through himself. . . . This, then, is the appropriate region of human liberty. It comprises, first, the inward domain of consciousness; demanding liberty of conscience in the most comprehensive sense; liberty of thought and feeling; absolute freedom of opinion and sentiment on all subjects, practical or speculative, scientific, moral, or theological. The liberty of expressing and publishing opinions may seem to fall under a different principle, since it belongs to that part of the conduct of an individual which concerns other people; but, being almost of as much importance as the liberty of thought itself, and resting in great part on the same reasons, is practically inseparable from it. Secondly, the principle requires liberty of tastes and pursuits; of framing the plan of our life to suit our own character; of doing as we like, subject to such consequences as may follow: without impediment from our fellow-creatures, so long as what we do does not harm them, even though they should think our conduct foolish, perverse, or wrong. Thirdly, from this liberty of each individual, follows the liberty, within the same limits, of combination among individuals; freedom to unite, for any purpose not involving harm to others: the persons combining being supposed to be of full age, and not forced or deceived.

No society in which these liberties are not, on the whole, respected, is free, whatever may be its form of government; and none is completely free in which they do not exist absolute and unqualified. The only freedom which deserves the name, is that of pursuing our own good in our own way, so long as we do not attempt to deprive others of theirs, or impede their efforts to obtain it. Each is the proper guardian of his own health, whether bodily, or mental and spiritual. Mankind are greater gainers by suffering each other to live as seems good to themselves, than by compelling each to live as seems good to the rest.

. . .

I do not mean that the feelings with which a person is regarded by others ought not to be in any way affected by his self-regarding qualities or deficiencies. This is neither possible nor desirable. . . . Though doing no wrong to any one, a person may so act as to compel us to judge him, and feel to him, as a fool, or as a being of an inferior order. . . . We have a right, also, in various ways, to act upon our unfavourable opinion of any one, not to the oppression of his individuality, but in the exercise of ours. We are not bound, for example, to seek his society; we have a right to avoid it. . . . We have a right, and it may be our duty, to caution others against him. . . . We may give others a preference over him in optional good offices. . . . In these various modes a person may suffer very severe penalties at the hands of others for faults which directly concern only himself; but he suffers these penalties only in so far as they are the natural, and, as it were, the spontaneous consequences of the faults themselves, not because they are purposely inflicted on him for the sake of punishment. . . .

    . . .

    . . . It is far otherwise if he has infringed the rules necessary for the protection of his fellow-creatures, individually or collectively. The evil consequences of his acts do not then fall on himself, but on others; and society, as the protector of all its members, must retaliate on him; must inflict pain on him for the express purpose of punishment, and must take care that it be sufficiently severe. In the one case, he is an offender at our bar, and we are called on not only to sit in judgment on him, but, in one shape or another, to execute our own sentence: in the other case, it is not our part to inflict any suffering on him, except what may incidentally follow from our using the same liberty in the regulation of our own affairs, which we allow to him in his.

    The distinction here pointed out between the part of a person's life which concerns only himself, and that which concerns others, many persons will refuse to admit. How (it may be asked) can any part of the conduct of a member of society be a matter of indifference to the other members? No person is an entirely isolated being; it is impossible for a person to do anything seriously or permanently hurtful to himself, without mischief reaching at least to his near connections, and often far beyond them. If he injures his property, he does harm to those who directly or indirectly derived support from it, and usually diminishes, by a greater or lesser amount, the general resources of the community. If he deteriorates his bodily or mental faculties, he not only brings evil upon all who depended on him for any portion of their happiness, but disqualifies himself for rendering the services which he owes to his fellow-creatures generally; perhaps becomes a burden on their affection or benevolence; and if such conduct were very frequent, hardly any offence that is committed would detract more from the general sum of good. Finally, if by his vices or follies a person does no direct harm to others, he is nevertheless (it may be said) injurious by his example; and ought to be compelled to control himself, for the sake of those whom the sight or knowledge of his conduct might corrupt or mislead.

    And even (it will be added) if the consequences of misconduct could be confined to the vicious or thoughtless individual, ought society to abandon to their own guidance those who are manifestly unfit for it? If protection against themselves is confessedly due to children and persons under age, is not society equally bound to afford it to persons of mature years who are equally incapable of self-government? If gambling, or drunkenness, or incontinence, or idleness, or uncleanliness, are as injurious to happiness, and as great a hindrance to improvement, as many or most of the acts prohibited by law, why (it may be asked) should not law, so far as is consistent with practicability and social convenience, endeavour to repress these also? And as a supplement to the unavoidable imperfections of law, ought not opinion at least to organise a powerful police against these vices, and visit rigidly with social penalties those who are known to practise them? There is no question here (it may be said) about restricting individuality, or impeding the trial of new and original experiments in living. The only things it is sought to prevent are things which have been tried and condemned from the beginning of the world until now; things which experience has shown not to be useful or suitable to any person's individuality. There must be some length of time and amount of experience after which a moral or prudential truth may be regarded as established: and it is merely desired to prevent generation after generation from falling over the same precipice which has been fatal to their predecessors.

I fully admit that the mischief which a person does to himself may seriously affect, both through their sympathies and their interests, those nearly connected with him and, in a minor degree, society at large. When, by conduct of this sort, a person is led to violate a distinct and assignable obligation to any other person or persons, the case is taken out of the self-regarding class, and becomes amenable to moral disapprobation in the proper sense of the term. If, for example, a man, through intemperance or extravagance, becomes unable to pay his debts, or, having undertaken the moral responsibility of a family, becomes from the same cause incapable of supporting or educating them, he is deservedly reprobated, and might be justly punished; but it is for the breach of duty to his family or creditors, not for the extravagance. . . . In like manner, when a person disables himself, by conduct purely self-regarding, from the performance of some definite duty incumbent on him to the public, he is guilty of a social offence. No person ought to be punished simply for being drunk; but a soldier or a policeman should be punished for being drunk on duty. Whenever, in short, there is a definite damage, or a definite risk of damage, either to an individual or to the public, the case is taken out of the province of liberty, and placed in that of morality or law.

But with regard to the merely contingent, or, as it may be called, constructive injury which a person causes to society, by conduct which neither violates any specific duty to the public, nor occasions perceptible hurt to any assignable individual except himself; the inconvenience is one which society can afford to bear, for the sake of the greater good of human freedom. If grown persons are to be punished for not taking proper care of themselves, I would rather it were for their own sake, than under pretence of preventing them from impairing their capacity of rendering to society benefits which society does not pretend it has a right to exact. But I cannot consent to argue the point as if society had no means of bringing its weaker members up to its ordinary standard of rational conduct, except waiting till they do something irrational, and then punishing them, legally or morally, for it. Society has had absolute power over them during all the early portion of their existence: it has had the whole period of childhood and nonage in which to try whether it could make them capable of rational conduct in life. . . . If society lets any considerable number of its members grow up mere children, incapable of being acted on by rational consideration of distant motives, society has itself to blame for the consequences. . . . Nor is there anything which tends more to discredit and frustrate the better means of influencing conduct than a resort to the worse. If there be among those whom it is attempted to coerce into prudence or temperance any of the material of which vigorous and independent characters are made, they will infallibly rebel against the yoke. . . .

But the strongest of all the arguments against the interference of the public with purely personal conduct is that, when it does interfere, the odds are that it interferes wrongly, and in the wrong place. On questions of social morality, of duty to others, the opinion of the public, that is, of an overruling majority, though often wrong, is likely to be still oftener right; because on such questions they are only required to judge of their own interests; of the manner in which some mode of conduct, if allowed to be practised, would effect themselves. But the opinion of a similar majority, imposed as a law on the minority, on questions of self-regarding conduct, is quite as likely to be wrong as right; for in these cases public opinion means, at the best, some people's opinion of what is good or bad for other people; while very often it does not even mean that; the public, with the most perfect indifference, passing over the pleasure or convenience of those whose conduct they censure, and considering only their own preference. There are many who consider as an injury to themselves any conduct which they have a distaste for, and resent it as an outrage to their feelings; as a religious bigot, when charged with disregarding the religious feelings of others, has been known to retort that they disregard his feelings, by persisting in their abominable worship or creed. But there is no parity between the feeling of a person for his own opinion, and the feeling of another who is offended at his holding it; no more than between the desire of a thief to take a purse, and the desire of the right owner to keep it. And a person's taste is as much his own peculiar concern as his opinion or his purse. . . .

STEPHEN

This is Mr. Mill's whole case, and it appears to me so weak that I fear that I may have misunderstood or understated it. If so, I have done so unconsciously. As it stands it seems to involve the following errors.

First, there is no principle on which the cases in which Mr. Mill admits the justice of legal punishment can be distinguished from those in which he denies it. The principle is that private vices which are injurious to others may justly be punished, if the injury be specific and the persons injured distinctly assignable, but not otherwise. If the question were as to the possibility in most cases of drawing an indictment against such persons I should agree with him. Criminal law is an extremely rough engine, and must be worked with great caution; but it is one thing to point out a practical difficulty which limits the application of a principle and quite another to refute the principle itself. Mr. Mill's proviso deserves attention in considering the question whether a given act should be punished by law, but he applies it to the moral coercion of public opinion, as well as to legal coercion, and to this the practical difficulty which he points out does not apply. . . .

Secondly, the arguments against legal interference in the cases not admitted to be properly subject to it are all open to obvious answers.

Mr. Mill says that if grown-up people are grossly vicious it is the fault of society, which therefore ought not to punish them.

This argument proves too much, for the same may be said with even greater force of gross crimes, and it is admitted that they may be punished.

It is illogical, for it does not follow that because society caused a fault it is not to punish it. A man who breaks his arm when he is drunk may have to have it cut off when he is sober.

It admits the whole principle of interference, for it assumes that the power of society over people in their minority is and ought to be absolute, and minority and majority are questions of degree, and the line which separates them is arbitrary.

Lastly, it proceeds upon an exaggerated estimate of the power of education. Society cannot make silk purses out of sows' ears, and there are plenty of ears in the world which no tanning can turn even into serviceable pigskin.

Mr. Mill's other arguments are, that compulsion in such cases will make people rebel, and, above all, that the moral persecutor himself may very probably be mistaken.

This is true and important, but it goes to show not that compulsion should not be used at all, but that its employment is a delicate operation.

. . .

. . . The restraints of criminal law in these days are few and most of them may be justified on any one of several grounds. Moreover, there are many reasons against extending the sphere of criminal law which are altogether independent of general considerations about liberty, as I shall show hereafter. Criminal law . . . though in many respects of great importance, can hardly be regarded as imposing any restraint on decent people which is ever felt as such. To the great mass of mankind a law forbidding robbery is no more felt as a restraint than the necessity of wearing clothes is felt as a restraint. The only restraints under which any one will admit that he frets are the restraints of public opinion, the "social intolerance" of which Mr. Mill gives such a striking account. . . . This, in a word, is the great engine by which the whole mass of beliefs, habits, and customs, which collectively constitute positive morality, are protected and sanctioned. The very object of the whole doctrine of liberty as stated by Mr. Mill is to lay down a principle which condemns all such interference with any experiments in living which particular people may choose to make. It is that or it is nothing, for the wit of man cannot frame any distinction between the cases in which moral and physical coercion respectively are justifiable except distinctions which arise out of the nature of criminal law and the difficulty of putting it into operation, and this is a small and technical matter. The result is that Mr. Mill's doctrine that nothing but self-defence can justify the imposition of restraint on a man's self-regarding vices by public opinion is not merely essential to the coherence of his theory, but is by far the most important part of it in practice.

HART

It is salutary to inquire precisely what it is that is *prima facie* objectionable in the legal enforcement of morality; for the idea of legal enforcement is in fact less simple than is often assumed. It has two different but related aspects. One is the actual punishment of the offender. This characteristically involves depriving him of liberty of movement or of property or of association with family or friends, or the infliction upon him of physical pain or even death. All these are things which are assumed to be wrong to inflict on others without special justification, and in fact they are so regarded by the law and morality of all developed societies. To put it as a lawyer would, these are things which, if they are not justified as sanctions, are delicts or wrongs.

The second aspect of legal enforcement bears on those who may never offend against the law, but are coerced into obedience by the threat of legal punishment. This, rather than physical restrictions, is what is normally meant in the discussion of political arrangements by restrictions on liberty. Such restrictions, it is to be noted, may be thought of as calling for justification for several quite distinct reasons. The unimpeded exercise by individuals of free choice may be held a value in itself with which it is *prima facie* wrong to interfere; or it may be thought valuable because it enables individuals to experiment—even with living—and to discover things valuable both to themselves and to others. But interference with individual liberty may be thought an evil requiring justification for simpler, utilitarian reasons; for it is itself the infliction of a special form of suffering—often very acute—on those whose desires are frustrated by the fear of punishment. This is of particular importance in the case of laws enforcing a sexual morality. They may create misery of a quite special degree. For both the difficulties involved in the repression of sexual impulses and the consequences of repression are quite different from those involved in the abstention from "ordinary" crime. Unlike sexual impulses, the impulse to steal or to wound or even kill is not, except in a minority of mentally abnormal cases, a recurrent and insistent part of daily life. Resistance to the temptation to commit these crimes is not often, as the suppression of sexual impulses generally is, something which affects the development or balance of the individual's emotional life, happiness, and personality.

MILL

The right inherent in society, to ward off crimes against itself by antecedent precautions, suggests the obvious limitations to the maxim, that purely self-regarding misconduct cannot properly be meddled with in the way of prevention or punishment. Drunkenness, for example, in ordinary cases, is not a fit subject for legislative interference; but I should deem it perfectly legitimate that a person, who had once been convicted of any act of violence to others under the influence of drink, should be placed under a special legal restriction, personal to himself; that if he were afterwards found drunk, he should be liable to a penalty, and that if when in that state he committed another offence, the punishment to which he would be liable for that other offence should be increased in severity. The making himself drunk, in a person whom drunkenness excites to do harm to others, is a crime against others. So, again, idleness, except in a person receiving support from the public, or except when it constitutes a breach of contract, cannot without tyranny be made a subject of legal punishment; but if, either from idleness or from any other avoidable cause, a man fails to perform his legal duties to others, as for instance to support his children, it is no tyranny to force him to fulfil that obligation, by compulsory labour, if no other means are available.

Again, there are many acts which, being directly injurious only to the agents themselves, ought not to be legally interdicted, but which, if done publicly, are a violation of good manners, and coming thus within the category of offences against others, may rightly be prohibited. Of this kind are offences against decency; on which it is unnecessary to dwell, the rather as they are only connected indirectly with our subject, the objection to publicity being equally strong in the case of many actions not in themselves condemnable, nor supposed to be so.

HART

It may no doubt be objected that too much has been made . . . of the distinction between what is done in public and what is done in private. For offence to feelings, it may be said, is given not only when immoral activities or their commercial preliminaries are thrust upon unwilling eyewitnesses, but also when those who strongly condemn certain sexual practices as immoral learn that others indulge in them in private. Because this is so, it is pointless to attend to the distinction between what is done privately and what is done in public; and if we do not attend to it, then the policies of punishing men for mere immorality and punishing them for conduct offensive to the feelings of others, though conceptually distinct, would not differ in practice. All conduct strongly condemned as immoral would then be punishable.

It is important not to confuse this argument with the thesis . . . that the preservation of an existing social morality is itself a value justifying the use of coercion. The present argument invokes in support of the legal enforcement of morality not the values of morality but Mill's own principle that coercion may be justifiably used to prevent harm to others. Various objections may be made to this use of the principle. It may be said that the distress occasioned by the bare thought that others are offending in private against morality cannot constitute "harm," except in a few neurotic or hypersensitive persons who are literally "made ill" by this thought. Others may admit that such distress is harm, even in the case of normal persons, but argue that it is too slight to outweigh the great misery caused by the legal enforcement of sexual morality.

Although these objections are not without force, they are of subsidiary importance. The fundamental objection surely is that a right to be protected from the distress which is inseparable from the bare knowledge that others are acting in ways you think wrong, cannot be acknowledged by anyone who recognises individual liberty as a value. For the extension of the utilitarian principle that coercion may be used to protect men from harm, so as to include their protection from this form of distress, cannot stop there. If distress incident to the belief that others are doing wrong is harm, so also is the distress incident to the belief that others are doing what you do not want them to do. To punish people for causing this form of distress would be tantamount to punishing them simply because others object to what they do; and the only liberty that could coexist with this extension of the utilitarian principle is liberty to do those things to which no one seriously objects. Such liberty plainly is quite nugatory. Recognition of individual liberty as a value involves, as a minimum, acceptance of the principle that the individual may do what he wants, even if others are distressed when they learn what it is that he does—unless, of course, there are other good grounds for forbidding it. No social order which accords to individual liberty any value could also accord the right to be protected from distress thus occasioned.

Protection from shock or offence to feelings caused by some public display is, as most legal systems recognise, another matter. The distinction may sometimes be a fine one. It is so, in those cases such as the desecration of venerated objects or ceremonies where there would be no shock or offence to feeling, if those on whom the public display is obtruded had not subscribed to certain religious or moral beliefs. Nonetheless the use of punishment to protect those made vulnerable to the public display by their own beliefs leaves the offender at liberty to do the same thing in private, if he can. It is not tantamount to punishing men simply because others object to what they do.

MILL

There is another question to which an answer must be found, consistent with the principles which have been laid down. In cases of personal conduct supposed to be blamable, but which respect for liberty precludes society from preventing or punishing, because the evil directly resulting falls wholly on the agent; what the agent is free to do, ought other persons to be equally free to counsel or instigate? This question is not free from difficulty. The case of a person who solicits another to do an act is not strictly a case of self-regarding conduct. To give advice or offer inducements to any one is a social act, and may, therefore, like actions in general which affect others, be supposed amenable to social control. But a little reflection corrects the first impression, by showing that if the case is not strictly within the definition of individual liberty, yet the reasons on which the principle of individual liberty is grounded are applicable to it. If people must be allowed, in whatever concerns only themselves, to act as seems best to themselves, at their own peril, they must equally be free to consult with one another about what is fit to be so done; to exchange opinions, and give and receive suggestions. Whatever it is permitted to do, it must be permitted to advise to do. The question is doubtful only when the instigator derives a personal benefit from his advice; when he makes it his occupation, for subsistence or pecuniary gain, to promote what society and the State consider to be an evil. Then, indeed, a new element of complication is introduced; namely, the existence of classes of persons with an interest opposed to what is considered as the public weal, and whose mode of living is grounded on the counteraction of it. Ought this to be interfered with, or not? Fornication, for example, must be tolerated, and so must gambling; but should a person be free to be a pimp, or to keep a gambling-house? The case is one of those which lie on the exact boundary line between two principles, and it is not at once apparent to which of the two it properly belongs. There are arguments on both sides. On the side of toleration it may be said that the fact of following anything as an occupation, and living or profiting by the practice of it, cannot make that criminal which would otherwise be admissible; that the act should either be consistently permitted or consistently prohibited; that if the principles which we have hitherto defended are true, society has no business, as society, to decide anything to be wrong which concerns only the individual; that it cannot go beyond dissuasion, and that one person should be as free to persuade as another to dissuade. In opposition to this it may be contended, that although the public, or the State, are not warranted in authoritatively deciding, for purposes of repression or punishment, that such or such conduct affecting only the interests of the individual is good or bad, they are fully justified in assuming, if they regard it as bad, that its being so or not is at least a disputable question: That, this being supposed, they cannot be acting wrongly in endeavouring to exclude the influence of solicitations which are not disinterested, of instigators who cannot possibly be impartial—who have a direct personal interest on one side, and that side the one which the State believes to be wrong, and who confessedly promote it for personal objects only. There can surely, it may be urged, be nothing lost, no sacrifice of good, by so ordering matters that persons shall make their election, either wisely or foolishly, on their own prompting, as free as possible from the arts of persons who stimulate their inclinations for interested purposes of their own. Thus (it may be said) though the statutes respecting unlawful games are utterly indefensible—though all persons should be free to gamble in their own or each other's houses, or in any place of meeting established by their own subscriptions, and open only to the members and their visitors—yet public gambling-houses should not be permitted. It is true that the prohibition is never effectual, and that, whatever amount of tyrannical power may be given to the police, gambling-houses can always be maintained under other pretences; but they may be compelled to conduct their operations with a certain degree of secrecy and mystery, so that nobody knows anything about them but those who seek them; and more than this society ought not to aim at. There is considerable force in these arguments. I will not venture to decide whether they are sufficient to justify the moral anomaly of punishing the accessory, when the principal is (and must be) allowed to go free; of fining or imprisoning the procurer, but not the fornicator—the gambling-house keeper, but not the gambler. . . .

STEPHEN

. . . How can the State or the public be competent to determine any question whatever if it is not competent to decide that gross vice is a bad thing? I do not think the State ought to stand bandying compliments with pimps. "Without offence to your better judgment, dear sir, and without presuming to set up my opinion against yours, I beg to observe that I am entitled for certain purposes to treat the question whether your views of life are right as one which admits of two opinions. I am far from expressing absolute condemnation of an experiment in living from which I dissent (I am sure that mere dissent will not offend a person of your liberality of sentiment), but still I am compelled to observe that you are not altogether unbiased by personal considerations in the choice of the course of life which you have adopted (no doubt for reasons which appear to you satisfactory, though they do not convince me). I venture, accordingly, though with the greatest deference, to call upon you not to exercise your profession; at least I am not indisposed to think that I may, upon full consideration, feel myself compelled to do so." My feeling is that if society gets its grip on the collar of such a fellow it should say to him, "You dirty rascal, it may be a question whether you should be suffered to remain in your native filth untouched, or whether my opinion about you should be printed by the lash on your bare back. That question will be determined without the smallest reference to your wishes or feelings; but as to the nature of my opinion about you, there can be no question at all."

Most people, I think, would feel that the latter form of address is at all events the more natural. . . .

. . .

I now pass to what I have myself to offer on the subject of the relation of morals to legislation, and the extent to which people may and ought to be made virtuous by Act of Parliament, or by "the moral coercion of public opinion."

I have no simple principle to assert on this matter. I do not believe that the question admits of any solution so short and precise as that which Mr. Mill supplies. I think, however, that the points relevant to its solution may be classified, and its discussion simplified . . . by considering whether the object for which the compulsion is employed is good? whether the compulsion employed is likely to be effective? and whether it will be effective at a reasonable expense?

The object is to make people better than they would be without compulsion. This statement is so very general that it can scarcely be understood without some preliminary observations as to the general position of morality in human affairs, and the manner in which it is produced and acted upon.

Men are so closely connected together that it is quite impossible to say how far the influence of acts apparently of the most personal character may extend. . . . The result is that we can assign no limits at all to the importance to each other of men's acts and thoughts. . . .

Besides this, we must recollect that the words virtue and vice, and their equivalents, have different meanings in different parts of the world and in different ages. . . . I agree with [Mr. Mill] in taking its tendency to produce happiness as the test of the moral quality of an action, but this is subject to several important qualifications, of which I may mention one by way of illustration. Different people form very different ideals of happiness. The ideals of different nations, ages, and classes differ as much as the ideals of different individuals. . . .

Not only are the varieties of morality innumerable, but some of them are conflicting with each other. . . .

[T]he intimate sympathy and innumerable bonds of all kinds by which men are united, and the differences of character and opinions by which they are distinguished, produce and must for ever produce continual struggles between them. . . . We are thus brought to the conclusion that in morals as well as in religion there is and must be war and conflict between men. The good man and the bad man, the men whose goodness and badness are of different patterns, are really opposed to each other. There is a real, essential, and eternal conflict between them.

At first sight it may appear as if this was a cynical paradox, but attention to another doctrine closely connected with it will show that it is far less formidable than it appears to be at first sight. The influences which tend to unite men and which give them an interest in each other's welfare are both more numerous and more powerful than those which throw them into collision. The effect of this is not to prevent collisions, but to surround them with acts of friendship and goodwill which confine them within limits and prevent people from going to extremities. . . . Complete moral tolerance is possible only when men have become completely indifferent to each other—that is to say, when society is at an end. If, on the other hand, every struggle is treated as a war of extermination, society will come to an end in a shorter and more exciting manner, but not more decisively.

A healthy state of things will be a compromise between the two. There are innumerable differences which obviously add to the interest of life, and without which it would be unendurably dull. Again, there are differences which can neither be left unsettled nor be settled without a struggle, and a real one, but in regard to which the struggle is rather between inconsistent forms of good than between good and evil. In cases of this sort no one need see an occasion for anything more than a good-tempered trial of strength and skill, except those narrow-minded fanatics whose minds are incapable of taking in more than one idea at a time, or of having a taste for more things than one, which one thing is generally a trifle. . . .

The real problem of liberty and tolerance is simply this: What is the object of contention worth? Is the case one—and no doubt such cases do occur—in which all must be done, dared, and endured that men can do, dare, or endure; or is it one in which we can honourably submit to defeat for the present subject to the chance of trying again? According to the answer given to this question the form of the struggle will range between internecine war and friendly argument.

These explanations enable me to restate without fear of misapprehension the object of morally intolerant legislation. It is to establish, to maintain, and to give power to that which the legislator regards as a good moral system or standard. For the reasons already assigned I think that this object is good if and in so far as the system so established and maintained is good. How far any particular system is good or not is a question which probably does not admit of any peremptory final decision; but I may observe that there are a considerable number of things which appear good and bad, though no doubt in different degrees, to all mankind. For the practical purpose of legislation refinements are of little importance. In any given age and nation virtue and vice have meanings which for that purpose are quite definite enough. . . . The result is that the object of promoting virtue and preventing vice must be admitted to be both a good one and one sufficiently intelligible for legislative purposes.

If this is so, the only remaining questions will be as to the efficiency of the means at the disposal of society for this purpose, and the cost of their application. Society has at its disposal two great instruments by which vice may be prevented and virtue promoted—namely law and public opinion; and law is either criminal or civil. The use of each of these instruments is subject to certain limits and conditions, and the wisdom of attempting to make men good either by Act of Parliament or by the action of public opinion depends entirely upon the degree in which those limits and conditions are recognized and acted upon.

First, I will take the case of criminal law. What are the conditions under which and the limitations within which it can be applied with success to the object of making men better? In considering this question it must be borne in mind that criminal law is at once by far the most powerful and by far the roughest engine which society can use for any purpose. Its power is shown by the fact that it can and does render crime exceedingly difficult and dangerous. Indeed, in civilized society it absolutely prevents avowed open crime committed with the strong hand, except in cases where crime rises to the magnitude of civil war. Its roughness hardly needs illustration. It strikes so hard that it can be enforced only on the gravest occasions, and with every sort of precaution against abuse or mistake. Before an act can be treated as a crime, it ought to be capable of distinct definition and of specific proof, and it ought also to be of such a nature that it is worth while to prevent it at the risk of inflicting great damage, direct and indirect, upon those who commit it. These conditions are seldom, if ever, fulfilled by mere vices. It would obviously be impossible to indict a man for ingratitude or perfidy. Such charges are too vague for specific discussion and distinct proof on the one side, and disproof on the other. Moreover, the expense of the investigations necessary for the legal punishment of such conduct would be enormous. It would be necessary to go into an infinite number of delicate and subtle inquiries which would tear off all privacy from the lives of a large number of persons. These considerations are, I think, conclusive reasons against treating vice in general as a crime.

The excessive harshness of criminal law is also a circumstance which very greatly narrows the range of its application. It is the *ratio ultima* of the majority against persons whom its application assumes to have renounced the common bonds which connect men together. When a man is subjected to legal punishment, society appeals directly and exclusively to his fears. It renounces the attempt to work upon his affections or feelings. In other words, it puts itself into distinct, harsh, and undisguised opposition to his wishes; and the effect of this will be to make him rebel against the law. The violence of the rebellion will be measured partly by the violence of the passion the indulgence of which is forbidden, and partly by the degree to which the law can count upon an ally in the man's own conscience. A law which enters into a direct contest with a fierce imperious passion, which the person who feels it does not admit to be bad, and which is not directly injurious to others, will generally do more harm than good; and this is perhaps the principal reason why it is impossible to legislate directly against unchastity, unless it takes forms which every one regards as monstrous and horrible. The subject is not one for detailed discussion, but any one who will follow out the reflections which this hint suggests will find that they supply a striking illustration of the limits which the harshness of criminal law imposes upon its range.

If we now look at the different acts which satisfy the conditions specified, it will, I think, be found that criminal law in this country actually is applied to the suppression of vice and so to the promotion of virtue to a very considerable extent; and this I say is right.

The punishment of common crimes, the gross forms of force and fraud, is no doubt ambiguous. It may be justified on the principle of self-protection, and, apart from any question as to their moral character. It is not, however, difficult to show that these acts have in fact been forbidden and subjected to punishment not only because they are dangerous to society, and so ought to be prevented, but also for the sake of gratifying the feeling of hatred—call it revenge, resentment, or what you will—which the contemplation of such conduct excites in healthily constituted minds. If this can be shown, it will follow that criminal law is in the nature of a persecution of the grosser forms of vice, and an emphatic assertion of the principle that the feeling of hatred and the desire of vengeance above-mentioned are important elements of human nature which ought in such cases to be satisfied in a regular public and legal manner.

The strongest of all proofs of this is to be found in the principles universally admitted and acted upon as regulating the amount of punishment. If vengeance affects, and ought to affect, the amount of punishment, every circumstance which aggravates or extenuates the wickedness of an act will operate in aggravation or diminution of punishment. If the object of legal punishment is simply the prevention of specific acts, this will not be the case. Circumstances which extenuate the wickedness of the crime will often operate in aggravation of punishment. If as I maintain, both objects must be kept in view, such circumstances will operate in different ways according to the nature of the case.

HART

Surely this argument is a *non sequitur* generated by Stephen's failure to see that the questions "What sort of conduct may justifiably be punished?" and "How severely should we punish different offenses?" are distinct and independent questions. There are many reasons why we might wish the legal gradation of the seriousness of crimes, expressed in its scale of punishments, not to conflict with common estimates of their comparative wickedness. One reason is that such a conflict is undesirable on simple utilitarian grounds: it might either confuse moral judgments or bring the law into disrepute, or both. Another reason is that principles of justice or fairness between different offenders require morally distinguishable offences to be treated differently and morally similar offences to be treated alike. These principles are still widely respected, although it is also true that there is a growing disinclination to insist on their application where this conflicts with the forward-looking aims of punishment, such as prevention or reform. But those who concede that we should attempt to adjust the severity of punishment to the moral gravity of offences are not thereby committed to the view that punishment merely for immorality is justified. For they can in perfect consistency insist on the one hand that the only justification for having a *system* of punishment is to prevent harm and only harmful conduct should be punished, and, on the other, agree that when the question of the *quantum* of punishment for such conduct is raised, we should defer to principles which make relative moral wickedness of different offenders a partial determinant of the severity of punishment.

It is in general true that we cannot infer from principles applied in deciding the severity of punishment what the aims of the system of punishment are or what sorts of conduct may justifiably be punished. For some of these principles, e.g., the exclusion of torture or cruel punishments, may represent other values with which we may wish to compromise, and our compromise with them may restrict the extent to which we pursue the main values which justify punishment. So if in the course of punishing only harmful activities we think it right (for either of the two reasons distinguished above) to mark moral differences between different offenders, this does not show that we must also think it right to punish activities which are not harmful. It only shows that, in the theory of punishment, what is in the end morally tolerable is apt to be more complex than our theories initially suggest. We cannot usually in social life pursue a single value or a single moral aim, untroubled by the need to compromise with others.

STEPHEN

Other illustrations of the fact that English criminal law does recognize morality are to be found in the fact that a considerable number of acts which need not be specified are treated as crimes merely because they are regarded as grossly immoral.

I have already shown in what manner Mr. Mill deals with these topics. It is, I venture to think, utterly unsatisfactory. The impression it makes upon me is that he feels that such acts ought to be punished, and that he is able to reconcile this with his fundamental principles only by subtleties quite unworthy of him. Admit the relation for which I am contending between law and morals, and all becomes perfectly clear. All the acts referred to are unquestionably wicked. Those who do them are ashamed of them. They are all capable of being clearly defined and specifically proved or disproved, and there can be no question at all that legal punishment reduces them to small dimensions, and forces the criminals to carry on their practices with the greatest secrecy and precaution. In other words, the object of their suppression is good, and the means adequate. In practice this is subject to highly important qualifications, of which I will only say here that those who have due regard to the incurable weaknesses of human nature will be

very careful how they inflict penalties upon mere vice, if even upon those who make a trade of promoting it, unless special circumstances call for their infliction. It is one thing however to tolerate vice so long as it is inoffensive, and quite another to give it a legal right not only to exist, but to assert itself in the face of the world as an "experiment in living" as good as another, and entitled to the same protection from law.

I now pass to the manner in which civil law may and does, and as I say properly, promote virtue and prevent vice. . . . It would . . . be easy to show that nearly every branch of civil law assumes the existence of a standard of moral good and evil which the public at large have an interest in maintaining, and in many cases enforcing—a proceeding which is diametrically opposed to Mr. Mill's fundamental principles.

. . .

The result of these observations is that both law and public opinion do in many cases exercise a powerful coercive influence on morals, for objects which are good in the sense explained above, and by means well calculated to attain those objects, to a greater or less extent at a not inadequate expense. If this is so, I say law and public opinion do well, and I do not see how either the premises or the conclusion are to be disproved.

Of course there are limits to the possibility of useful interference with morals, either by law or by public opinion; and it is of the highest practical importance that these limits should be carefully observed. The great leading principles on the subject are few and simple, though they cannot be stated with any great precision. It will be enough to mention the following:—

1.   Neither legislation nor public opinion ought to be meddlesome. A very large proportion of the matters upon which people wish to interfere with their neighbours are trumpery little things which are of no real importance at all. The busybody and world-betterer who will never let things alone, or trust people to take care of themselves, is a common and a contemptible character. The commonplaces directed against these small creatures are perfectly just, but to try to put them down by denying the connection between law and morals is like shutting all light and air out of a house in order to keep out gnats and blue-bottle flies.

2.   Both legislation and public opinion, but especially the latter, are apt to be most mischievous and cruelly unjust if they proceed upon imperfect evidence. To form and express strong opinions about the wickedness of a man whom you do not know, the immorality or impiety of a book you have not read, the merits of a question on which you are uninformed, is to run a great risk of inflicting a great wrong. It is hanging first and trying afterwards,

or more frequently not trying at all. This, however, is no argument against hanging after a fair trial.

3. Legislation ought in all cases to be graduated to the existing level of morals in the time and country in which it is employed. You cannot punish anything which public opinion, as expressed in the common practice of society, does not strenuously and unequivocally condemn. To try to do so is a sure way to produce gross hypocrisy and furious reaction. To be able to punish, a moral majority must be overwhelming. Law cannot be better than the nation in which it exists, though it may and can protect an acknowledged moral standard, and may gradually be increased in strictness as the standard rises. We punish, with the utmost severity, practices which in Greece and Rome went almost uncensured. It is possible that a time may come when it may appear natural and right to punish adultery, seduction, or possibly even fornication, but the prospect is, in the eyes of all reasonable people, indefinitely remote, and it may be doubted whether we are moving in that direction.

4. Legislation and public opinion ought in all cases whatever scrupulously to respect privacy. To define the province of privacy distinctly is impossible, but it can be described in general terms. All the more intimate and delicate relations of life are of such a nature that to submit them to unsympathetic observation, or to observation which is sympathetic in the wrong way, inflicts great pain, and may inflict lasting moral injury. Privacy may be violated not only by the intrusion of a stranger, but by compelling or persuading a person to direct too much attention to his own feelings and to attach too much importance to their analysis. The common usage of language affords a practical test which is almost perfect upon this subject. Conduct which can be described as indecent is always in one way or another a violation of privacy.

. . .

[T]here is a sphere, none the less real because it is impossible to define its limits, within which law and public opinion are intruders likely to do more harm than good. To try to regulate the internal affairs of a family, the relations of love or friendship, or many other things of the same sort, by law or by the coercion of public opinion is like trying to pull an eyelash out of a man's eye with a pair of tongs. They may put out the eye, but they will never get hold of the eyelash.

These, I think, are the principal forms in which society can and actually does promote virtue and restrain vice. It is impossible to form any estimate of the degree in which it succeeds in doing so, but it may perhaps be said that the principal importance of what is done in this direction by criminal law is that in extreme cases it brands gross acts of vice with the deepest mark of infamy which can be impressed upon them, and that in this manner it protects

the public and accepted standard of morals from being grossly and openly violated. In short, it affirms in a singularly emphatic manner a principle which is absolutely inconsistent with and contradictory to Mr. Mill's—the principle, namely, that there are acts of wickedness so gross and outrageous that, self-protection apart, they must be prevented as far as possible at any cost to the offender, and punished, if they occur, with exemplary severity.

HART

. . . Let us suppose, contrary to much evidence, that Stephen's picture of society and its moral mechanisms is a realistic one: that there really is a moral code in sexual matters supported by an overwhelming majority and that they are deeply disturbed when it is infringed even by adults in private; that the punishment of offenders really does sustain the sense that the conduct is immoral and without their punishment the prevalent morality would change in a permissive direction. The central question is: Can anything or nothing be said to support the claim that the prevention of this change and the maintenance of the moral *status quo* in a society's morality are values sufficient to offset the cost in human misery which legal enforcement entails? Is it simply a blank assertion, or does it rest on any critical principles connecting what is said to be of value here with other things of value?

Here certain discriminations are needed. There are three propositions concerning the value of preserving social morality which are in perennial danger of confusion. The first of these propositions is the truth that since all social moralities, whatever else they may contain, make provision in some degree for such universal values as individual freedom, safety of life, and protection from deliberately inflicted harm, there will always be much in social morality which is worth preserving even at the cost in terms of these same values which legal enforcement involves. It is perhaps misleading to say . . . that social morality, so far as it secures these things, is of value because they are required for the preservation of society; on the contrary, the preservation of any particular society is of value because among other things it secures for human beings some measure of these universal values. It is indeed arguable that a human society in which these values are not recognised at all in its morality is neither an empirical nor a logical possibility, and that even if it were, such a society could be of no practical value for human beings. In conceding this much, however, we must beware of . . . thinking of social morality as a seamless web and of all its provisions as necessary for the existence of the society whose morality it is. We should with Mill be alive to the truth that though these essential universal values must be secured, society can not only survive individual divergences in other fields from its prevalent morality, but profit from them.

Secondly, there is the truth, less familiar and less easy to state in precise terms, that the spirit or attitude of mind which characterises the practice of a social morality is something of very great value and indeed quite vital for men to foster and preserve in any society. For in the practice of any social morality there are necessarily involved what may be called *formal* values as distinct from the *material* values of its particular rules or content. In moral relationships with others the individual sees questions of conduct from an impersonal point of view and applies general rules impartially to himself and to others; he is made aware of and takes account of the wants, expectations, and reactions of others; he exerts self-discipline and control in adapting his conduct to a system of reciprocal claims. These are universal virtues and indeed constitute the specifically moral attitude to conduct. It is true that these virtues are learnt in conforming to the morality of some particular society, but their value is not derived from the fact that they are there accounted virtues. We have only to conduct the Hobbesian experiment of imagining these virtues totally absent to see that they are vital for the conduct of any cooperative form of human life and any successful personal life. No principles of critical morality which paid the least attention to the most elementary facts of human nature and the conditions in which human life has to be led could propose to dispense with them. Hence if by the preservation of morality is meant the preservation of the moral attitude to conduct and its formal values, it is certainly true that it is a value. But, though true, this is really irrelevant to the issue before us; for the preservation of morality in this sense is not identical with and does not require the preservation from change of a society's moral code as it is at any given moment of that society's existence; and *a fortiori* it does not require the legal enforcement of its rules. The moral attitude to conduct has often survived the criticism, the infringement, and the ultimate relaxation of specific moral institutions. The use of legal punishment to freeze into immobility the morality dominant at a particular time in a society's existence may possibly succeed, but even where it does it contributes nothing to the survival of the animating spirit and formal values of social morality and may do much to harm them.

From the preservation of morality in this sense which is so clearly a value we must, then, distinguish mere moral conservatism. This latter amounts to the proposition that the preservation from change of any existent rule of a social morality, whatever its content, is a value and justifies its legal enforcement. This proposition would be at least intelligible if we could ascribe to all social morality the status which theological systems or the doctrine of the Law of Nature ascribes to some fundamental principles. Then, at least, some general principle would have been adduced to support the claim that preservation of any rule of social morality was a value justifying its legal enforcement; something would have been said to indicate the source of this asserted value. The application of these general principles to the case in hand would then be something to be discussed and argued, and moral conservatism would then be a form of critical morality to be used in the criticism of social institutions. It would not then be—as it is when dissociated from all such general principles—a brute dogma, asserting that the preservation of any social morality necessarily outweighs its cost in human misery and deprivation of freedom. In this dogmatic form it in effect withdraws positive morality from the scope of any moral criticism.

No doubt a critical morality based on the theory that all social morality had the status of divine commands or of eternal truth discovered by reason would not for obvious reasons now seem plausible. It is perhaps least plausible in relation to sexual morals, determined as these so obviously are by variable tastes and conventions. Nonetheless, the attempt to defend the legal enforcement of morality on these lines would be something more than the simple unargued assertion that it was justified. . . .

However questionable this background of theory in any particular case may be, it is yet there for rational criticism, acceptance or rejection; it prevents the assertion of the value of social institutions being merely dogmatic. The assertion will stand or fall with the general theories deployed in its support. . . .

[The] distinction between the use of coercion to enforce morality and other methods which we in fact use to preserve it, such as argument, advice, and exhortation, is both very important and much neglected in discussions of the present topic. Stephen, in his arguments against Mill, seems most of the time to forget or to ignore these other methods and the great importance which Mill attached to them. For he frequently argues as if Mill's doctrine of liberty meant that men must never express any convictions concerning the conduct of their fellow citizens if that conduct is not harmful to others. It is true that Mill believed that "the state or the public" is not warranted *"for the purposes of repression or punishment"* in deciding that such conduct is good or bad. But it is not true that he thought that concerning such conduct or "the experiments in living" which it represents "no one else has anything to say to it." Nor did he think that society could "draw a line where education ends and perfect moral indifference begins." In making these ill-founded criticisms Stephen not only misunderstood and so misrepresented Mill, but he showed how narrowly he himself conceived of morality and the processes by which it is sustained. For Mill's concern throughout his essay is to restrict the use of coercion, not to promote moral indifference. It is true he includes in the coercion or "constraint" of which he disapproves not only legal enforcement of morality but also other peremptory forms of social pressure such as moral blame and demands for conformity. But it is a disastrous misunderstanding of morality to think that where we cannot use coercion in its support we must be silent and indifferent. . . . Mill takes great pains to show the other resources which we have and should use. . . . Discussion, advice, argument—all these, since they leave the individual "the final judge," may according to Mill be used in a society where freedom is properly respected. We may even "obtrude" on another "considerations to aid his judgment and exhortations to strengthen his will." We may in extreme cases "warn" him of our adverse judgment or feelings of distaste and contempt. We may avoid his company and caution others against it. Many might think that Mill here comes perilously near to sanctioning coercion even though he regards these things as "strictly inseparable from the unfavourable judgments of others" and never to be inflicted for the sake of punishment. But if he erred in that direction, it is certainly clear that he recognized the important truth that in morality we are not forced to choose between deliberate coercion and indifference.

BIBLIOGRAPHY

This bibliography provides some references for further study. It is not comprehensive. Materials were included or not according to their probable usefulness, based on general availability, currency, and treatment of the topic(s) with which they deal. They are keyed to the pages or sections of the book to which they seemed most relevant. Often a particular book or article deals with several aspects of a problem or with several problems treated separately in this book; it will frequently be useful to examine not only the materials listed for a particular topic but also those listed for closely related topics. For economy of space, except for works that may be regarded as classics, most references more than ten years old have been omitted. Materials cited in the main body of the book are generally not cited in the bibliography.

General

The Model Penal Code, prepared by The American Law Institute, provides an excellent model of American law, as its name suggests. The Commentaries analyze the law and give summaries of the law then in effect. Part I of the Code with Commentaries, published in 1985, includes most of the "general part" of criminal law: principles of liability, justification, and responsibility; inchoate crimes; and provisions relating to sentencing. Part II of the Code with Commentaries, published in 1980, includes the substantive offenses. For references to additional provisions of the Code included in the Proposed Official Draft, published in 1962, see p. 11 n.1.

Since the publication of the Proposed Official Draft of the Model Penal Code in 1962, most of the States have revised their criminal code; the revision committees commonly prepared and published drafts and commentaries for the use of the state legislature.

James Fitzjames Stephen, A History of the Criminal Law of England (1883), remains the starting point and standard work on the history of English, and therefore American, criminal law. Subsequent scholarship has corrected many of Stephen's statements, but his book is unequaled as a general introduction to the subject and, often, as a source of considerable detail on particular topics.

Joel Feinberg's magisterial multi-volume treatise, The Moral Limits of the Criminal Law is invaluable for discussion of philosophical issues. The four volumes are: 1 Harm to Others (1984), 2 Offense to Others (1985), 3

Harm to Self (1986), and 4 Harmless Wrongdoing (1988).

The Encyclopedia of Crime and Justice (S. Kadish, ed., 1983) contains authoritative articles on many subjects.

Two excellent, although now somewhat dated, discussions of the "general part" of criminal law are J. Hall, General Principles of Criminal Law (2d ed. 1960), and G. Williams, Criminal Law (2d ed. 1961). Williams' book is based largely on the English criminal law. J. Dressler, Understanding Criminal Law (3d ed. 2001) contains valuable discussions of many issues. P. Fitzgerald, Criminal Law and Punishment (1962) is an interesting survey of the criminal law organized along unusual lines.

The essays in H.L.A. Hart, Punishment and Responsibility (1968), contain valuable insights into the nature and function of criminal law. So also do the essays in D. Bazelon, Questioning Authority: Justice and Criminal Law (1988), and S. Kadish, Blame and Punishment (1987) (mostly with respect to more specific issues). L. Katz, Bad Acts and Guilty Minds (1987), has valuable discussions of many of the persistent conundrums of the criminal law. A. Kenny, Freewill and Responsibility (1978), contains an excellent discussion of issues in the areas of purpose, intention, recklessness, etc. A good source of legal and nonlegal readings on many of the basic concepts that the criminal law utilizes—e.g., responsibility, act, intention, negligence, and causation—is Freedom and Responsibility (H. Morris ed. 1961), which has an extensive and useful bibliography.

There is an excellent "hornbook" treatment of criminal law in W. LaFave, Criminal Law (3d ed. 2000). P. Robinson, Criminal Law (1997) is a useful general treatise that contains extensive bibliographies.

The National Commission on Reform of Federal Criminal Laws prepared a Study Draft of a new Federal Criminal Code which was published by the U.S. Government Printing Office in 1970. Published with the Study Draft were two volumes of Working Papers; a third volume was published in 1971. The Working Papers include extensive commentaries prepared by consultants and the staff of the Commission, covering a great many topics of criminal law.

There are many casebooks on criminal law, which contain leading cases and other materials. Although the contents of casebooks are likely to overlap, each has some distinctive material of its own, and their organization of the material may itself provide helpful insights.

Among recently published casebooks are:

R. Bonnie, A. Coughlin, J. Jeffries, & P. Low, Criminal Law (1997);

G. Dix & M. Sharlot, Criminal Law (5th ed. 2002);

J. Dressler, Cases and Materials on Criminal Law (2d ed. 1999);

S. Kadish & S. Schulhofer, Criminal Law and Its Processes (7th ed. 2001);

J. Kaplan, R. Weisberg, & G. Binder, Criminal Law (4th ed. 2000);

P. Johnson & A. Cloud, Criminal Law (7th ed. 2002);

M. Moskovitz, Cases and Problems in Criminal Law (4th ed. 1999);

P. Robinson, Fundamentals of Criminal Law (2d ed. 1995);

S. Saltzburg, J. Diamond, K. Kinports, T. Morawetz, Criminal Law (2d ed. 2000);

R. Singer & M. Gardner, Crimes and Punishment (3d ed. 2001).

S. Beale & N. Abrams, Federal Criminal Law and Its Enforcement (3d ed. 2000), and P. Low & J. Hoffman, Federal Criminal Law (1997) give a close look at federal crimes and issues of federalism that are not treated extensively in the more general casebooks. See also articles in a symposium, The Federal Role in Criminal Law, 543 Annals Am. Acad. Pol. & Soc. Sci. 9 (Jan. 1996).

The Criminal Law Review, published since 1954 by Sweet & Maxwell (London), has met its stated objective of presenting "the latest developments in criminal law in terms which are readable, informative and reliable." 1954 Crim. L. Rev. 1. It regularly contains a number of articles and brief notes on current issues of criminal law in England, which usually are current issues of criminal law in the United States as well.

The Criminal Law Reporter, published weekly by The Bureau of National Affairs in Washington, D.C., provides information about recent developments in criminal law generally.

Page

1   Homicide

A classic analysis of the law of homicide, from a largely utilitarian perspective, is Michael & Wechsler, "A Rationale of the Law of Homicide," 37 Colum. L. Rev. 701, 1261 (1937). Another good analysis, based largely on English law, in which the law of homicide is discussed in the context of debate on capital punishment, is Royal Commission on Capital Punishment, Report (Cmd. 8932) (1953).

E. Abel, Homicide, A Bibliography (1987)

B. Jerath & R. Jerath, Homicide, A Bibliography (2d ed. 1993)

M. Daly & M. Wilson, Homicide (1988)

C. McKanna, Homicide, Race, and Justice in the American West 1880–1920 (1997)

Chavez

On the general problem raised by the *Chavez* and *Singleton* cases, see G. Williams, The Sanctity of Life (1957).

M. Jackson, ed., Infanticide, Historical Perspectives on Child Murder and Concealment, 1550–2000 (2002)

C. Meyer & M. Oberman, Mothers Who Kill Their Children (2001)

Forsythe, Homicide of the Unborn Child: The Born Alive Rule and Other Legal Anachronisms, 21 Val. U. L. Rev. 563 (1987)

10   note 5

On the use of "fictions" in legal reasoning, see generally L. Fuller, Legal Fictions (1967).

11   n. 1

Symposium: The 25th Anniversary of the Model Penal Code, 19 Rutgers L.J. 519 (1988)

Symposium: Toward a New Federal Criminal Code, 2 Buff. Crim. L. Rev. 1 (1998)

note 9

Schroedel, Fiber & Snyder, Women's Rights and Fetal Personhood in Criminal Law, 7 Duke J. Gender L. & Pol'y 89 (2000)

M. Tooley, Abortion and Infanticide (1983)

Note, Taking *Roe* To the Limits: Treating Viable Feticide as Murder, 17 Ind. L. Rev. 1119 (1984)

Page

12	note 10	Teff, The Action for "Wrongful Life" in England and the United States, 34 Int'l & Comp. L.Q. 423 (1985)
		Symposium: The tort-crime distinction, 76 B.U. L. Rev. 1 (1996)
14	note 12	Parness, Crimes Against The Unborn: Protecting The Potentiality of Human Life, 22 Harv. J. on Legis. 97 (1985)
20	note 24	Lindgren, Death by Default, 56 Law & Contemp. Probs. 185 (Summer 1993)
		Note, Physician Liability for Failure to Resuscitate Terminally Ill Patients, 15 Ind. L. Rev. 905 (1982)
22–48		There is an excellent hornbook treatment of criminal procedure in W. LaFave, J. Israel & N. King, Criminal Procedure (3d ed. 2000), and a more extended treatment in their six-volume treatise of the same name (2d ed. 1999). J. Dressler, Understanding Criminal Procedure (3d ed. 2002), is a good general introduction to the subject. The rules and procedures of a federal criminal case are studied in L. Weinreb, Criminal Process (6th ed. 1998). The most important Supreme Court cases are collected in L. Weinreb, Leading Constitutional Cases on Criminal Justice (revised annually).
49	note 25	Terry, Homicide: The Viability of the Year and a Day Murder Rule, 31 How. L.J. 401 (1988)
		Walther, Comment: Taming a Phoenix: The Year-and-a-Day Rule in Federal Prosecutions for Murder, 59 U. Chi. L. Rev. 1337 (1992)
	n.27	Stephen's brother wrote his biography shortly after Stephen's death. L. Stephen, The Life of Sir James Fitzjames Stephen (1895)
52	*Onufrejczyk*	Harrison, Murder without a Body—The Forensic Science Aspect, 1955 Crim. L. Rev. 158 (details of the case)
58	note 29	Edwards, Murder Without a Body—The Legal Aspects, 1955 Crim. L. Rev. 205
60	note 30	Kaye, The Laws of Probability and the Law of the Land, 47 U. Chi. L. Rev. 34 (1979)
		Lushing, Faces Without Features: The Surface Validity of Criminal Inferences, 72 J. Crim. L. and Criminology 82 (1981)

Page

64   note 36   Perkins, The Corpus Delicti of Murder, 48 Va. L. Rev. 173 (1962)

65   Green, The Jury and the English Law of Homicide, 1200–1600, 74 Mich. L. Rev. 413 (1976)

67   Yntema, The Lex Murdrorum, 36 Harv. L. Rev. 146 (1922) (*murdrum*)

69   Simons, Rethinking Mental States, 72 B.U. L. Rev. 463 (1992)

70   note 38   Brown, The Demise of Chance Medley and the Recognition of Provocation as a Defence to Murder in English Law, 7 Am. J. Legal Hist. 310 (1963)

                     Finkelstein, The Goring Ox, 46 Temp. L.Q. 169 (1973) (deodands)

                     Snelling, Manslaughter upon Chance-Medley, 31 Austl. L.J. 102 (1957)

                     Watkin, Hamlet and the Law of Homicide, 100 Law Q. Rev. 282 (1984)

72   Provocation   Ashworth, The Doctrine of Provocation, 35 Camb. L.J. 292 (1976)

                     Dressler, Rethinking Heat of Passion: A Defence in Search of a Rationale, 73 J. Crim. L. and Criminology 421 (1982)

                     Nourse, Passion's Progress: Modern Law Reform and the Provocation Defense, 106 Yale L.J. 1331 (1997)

                     Singer, The Resurgence of *Mens Rea:* I—Provocation, Emotional Disturbance, and the Model Penal Code, 27 B.C. L. Rev. 243 (1986)

77   note 40   Kane, Sticks and Stones: How Words Can Hurt, 43 B.C. L. Rev. 159 (2001)

82   note 49   O'Regan, Indirect Provocation and Misdirected Retaliation, 1968 Crim. L. Rev. 319

87   *Washington*   McCoy, The Homosexual-Advance Defense and Hate Crimes Statutes: Their Interaction and Conflict, 22 Cardozo L. Rev. 629 (2001)

89   note 55   Donovan and Wildman, Is the Reasonable Man Obsolete? A Critical Perspective on Self-Defense and Provocation, 14 Loy. L.A. L. Rev. 435 (1981)

                     Howard, What Colour Is the "Reasonable Man"?, 1961 Crim. L. Rev. 41

                     O'Regan, Provocation and Homicide in Papua and New Guinea, 10 U. W. Austl. L. Rev. 1 (1971)

Page

O'Regan, Sorcery and Homicide in Papua and New Guinea, 48 Austl. L.J. 76 (1974)

Note, The Cultural Defense in the Criminal Law, 99 Harv. L. Rev. 1293 (1986)

92 *Alexander*

M. Blumenthal, R. Kahan, F. Andrews, & K. Head, Justifying Violence: Attitudes of American Men (1972)

99 *Mullaney v. Wilbur*

Allen, *Mullaney v. Wilbur*, the Supreme Court, and the Substantive Criminal Law—An Examination of the Limits of Legitimate Intervention, 55 Tex. L. Rev. 269 (1977)

Underwood, The Thumb on the Scales of Justice: Burdens of Persuasion in Criminal Cases, 86 Yale L.J. 1299 (1977)

106 note 62

Alexander, The Supreme Court, Dr. Jekyll, and the Due Process of Proof, 1996 Sup. Ct. Rev. 191 (1997)

Allen, Structuring Jury Decisionmaking in Criminal Cases: A Unified Constitutional Approach to Evidentiary Devices, 94 Harv. L. Rev. 321 (1980)

Ashford & Risinger, Presumptions, Assumptions and Due Process in Criminal Cases: A Theoretical Overview, 79 Yale L.J. 165 (1969)

Jeffries & Stephan, Defenses, Presumptions and Burden of Proof in the Criminal Law, 88 Yale L.J. 1325 (1979)

109 note 63

Dillof, Transferred Intent: An Inquiry into the Nature of Criminal Culpability, 1 Buff. Crim. L.R. 501 (1998)

110 Murder

G. Falk, Murder, An Analysis of Its Forms, Conditions, and Causes (1990)

R. Flowers & H. Flowers, Murders in the United States (2001) (historical survey)

S. Knox, Murder, A Tale of Modern American Life (1998)

R. Lane, Murder in America, A History (1997)

note 64

Keedy, History of the Pennsylvania Statute Creating Degrees of Murder, 97 U. Pa. L. Rev. 759 (1949)

111 *Caruso*

Brenner, The Impulsive Murder and the Degree Device, 22 Fordham L. Rev. 274 (1953)

Page

123   note 75   Keedy, A Problem of First Degree Murder: Fisher v. United States, 99 U. Pa. L. Rev. 267 (1950)

124   *Wolff*   Comment, Keeping *Wolff* from the Door: California's Diminished Capacity Concept, 60 Cal. L. Rev. 1641 (1972)

134   note 78   Dressler, Reaffirming the Moral Legitimacy of the Doctrine of Diminished Capacity: A Brief Reply to Professor Morse, 75 J. Crim. L. & Criminology 953 (1984)

                           Morse, Undiminished Confusion in Diminished Capacity, 75 J. Crim. L. & Criminology 1 (1984)

                           See bibliography for page 581, note 351.

136   note 80   Gardner, The Mens Rea Enigma: Observations on the Role of Motive in the Criminal Law Past and Present, 1993 Utah L. Rev. 635

139   N. Morris & C. Howard, The Definition of Murder, in Studies in Criminal Law 1–36 (1964)

147   note 90   Comment, *People v. Watson:* Drunk Driving Homicide—Murder or Enhanced Manslaughter?, 71 Cal. L. Rev. 1298 (1983)

150   Felony Murder   Cole, Killings During Crime: Toward a Discriminating Theory of Strict Liability, 28 Am. Crim. L. Rev. 73 (1990)

                           Crump & Crump, In Defense of the Felony Murder Doctrine, 8 Harv. J. L. & Pub. Pol'y. 359 (1985)

178   note 99   Roth and Sundby, The Felony-Murder Rule: A Doctrine at Constitutional Crossroads, 70 Cornell L. Rev. 446 (1985)

179   *Dillon*   Comment, The *Dillon* Dilemma: Finding Proportionate Felony-Murder Punishments, 72 Cal. L. Rev. 1299 (1984)

183   note 100   Gegan, A Case of Depraved Mind Murder, 49 St. John's L. Rev. 417 (1975)

       note 101   Kean, Homicide in Resisting Arrest, 26 Ky. L.J. 50 (1937)

184   Justification and   P. Robinson, Criminal Law Defenses (1984)
       Excuse

                           Dillof, Unraveling Unknowing Justification, 77 Notre Dame L. Rev. 1547 (2002)

                           Dressler, New Thoughts About the Concept of Justification in the Criminal Law: A Critique of Fletcher's Thinking and *Rethinking,* 32 UCLA L. Rev. 61 (1984)

Page

Gardner, The Gist of Excuses, 1 Buff. Crim. L.R. 575 (1998)

Greenawalt, Distinguishing Justifications from Excuses, 49 Law & Contemp. Probs. 89 (Summer 1986)

Greenawalt, The Perplexing Borders of Justification and Excuse, 84 Colum. L. Rev. 1897 (1984)

Kadish, Excusing Crime, 75 Cal. L. Rev. 257 (1987)

Moore, Causation and the Excuses, 73 Cal. L. Rev. 1091 (1985)

Symposium: Justifications, Excuses, and Just Deserts, 33 Wayne L. Rev. 1155 (1987)

| | Defense of Self | S. Uniacke, Permissible Killing (1994) |

191 note 103   Fletcher, The Right and the Reasonable, 98 Harv. L. Rev. 949 (1985)

Hurd, Justifiably Punishing the Justified, 90 Mich. L. Rev. 2203 (1992)

192 note 105   G. Fletcher, A Crime of Self-Defense: Bernhard Goetz and the Law on Trial (1988)

L. Rubin, Quiet Rage: Bernie Goetz in a Time of Madness (1988)

Carter, When Victims Happen to Be Black, 97 Yale L.J. 420 (1988)

193 note 106   Singer, The Resurgence of Mens Rea: II— The Honest but Unreasonable Mistake of Fact in Self Defense, 28 B.C. L. Rev. 459 (1987)

195 notes 111–113   MacCormick, Propter Honoris Respectum: Reasonableness and Objectivity, 74 Notre Dame L. Rev. 1575 (1999)

Nourse, Self-Defense and Subjectivity, 68 U. Chi. L. Rev. 1235 (2001)

197 Retreat   Beale, Retreat from a Murderous Assault, 16 Harv. L. Rev. 567 (1903)

Getman & Marshall, The Continuing Assault on the Right to Strike, 79 Tex. L. Rev. 703 (2001)

206 *Humphrey*   C.P. Ewing, Battered Women Who Kill: Psychological Self-Defense as Legal Justification (1987)

C. Gillespie, Justifiable Homicide: Battered Women, Self-Defense and the Law (1989)

Page

L. Walker, Terrifying Love: Why Battered Women Kill and How Society Responds (1989)

Cippalone, Comment: The Defense of Battered Women Who Kill, 135 U. Pa. L. Rev. 427 (1987)

Faigman, Discerning Justice When Battered Women Kill, 39 Hastings L.J. 207 (1987)

Maguigan, Battered Women and Self-Defense: Myths and Misconceptions in Current Reform Proposals, 140 U. Pa. L. Rev. 379 (1991)

Mahoney, Legal Images of Battered Women: Redefining the Issue of Separation, 90 Mich. L. Rev. 1 (1991)

Romkens, Ambiguous Responsibilities: Law and Conflicting Expert Testimony on the Abused Woman Who Shot Her Sleeping Husband, 25 Law & Soc. Inquiry 355 (2000)

Note, The Battered Woman Syndrome and Self-Defense: A Legal and Empirical Dissent, 72 Va. L. Rev. 619 (1986)

214   note 122   Mosteller, Syndromes and Politics in Criminal Trials and Evidence Law, 46 Duke L.J. 461 (1996)

223   Defense of Property   Green, Castles and Carjackers: Proportionality and the Use of Deadly Force in Defense of Dwellings and Vehicles, 1999 U. Ill. L. Rev. 1

Lanham, Defence of Property in the Criminal Law, 1966 Crim. L.R. 368, 426

230   note 129   The American Law Institute Proceedings 179–200 (1930–31)

242   Duress and Necessity   Christie, The Defense of Legal Necessity Considered from the Legal And Moral Points of View, 48 Duke L.J. 975 (1999)

Dressler, Exegesis of the Law of Duress: Justifying the Excuse and Searching for Its Proper Limits, 62 S. Cal. L. Rev. 1331 (1989)

Glazebrook, The Necessity Plea in English Criminal Law, 30 Camb. L.J. 87 (1972)

Parry, The Virtue of Necessity: Reshaping Culpability and the Rule of Law, Hous. L. Rev. 397 (1999)

243   note 130   Cross, Murder under Duress, 28 U. Toronto L.J. 369 (1978)

Page

Dennis, Duress, Murder and Criminal Responsibility, 96 Law Q. Rev. 208 (1980)

Milgate, Duress and the Criminal Law: Another About Turn by the House of Lords, 47 Camb. L.J. 61 (1988)

248   note 133   N. Morris & D. Rothman, eds., The Oxford History of the Prison (1995)

D. Rothman & N. Morris, eds., The History of Imprisonment (1995)

G. Sykes, The Society of Captives (1971)

Bleich, The Politics of Prison Crowding, 77 Cal. L. Rev. 1125 (1989)

Doré, Downward Adjustment and the Slippery Slope: The Use of Duress in Defense of Battered Offenders, 56 Ohio St. L.J. 665 (1995)

Ergel & Rothman, Prison Violence and the Paradox of Reform, 73 The Public Interest 91 (Fall 1983)

Fingarette, Victimization: A Legalist Analysis of Coercion, Deception, Undue Influence, and Excusable Prison Escape, 42 Wash. & Lee L. Rev. 65 (1985)

Fletcher, Should Intolerable Prison Conditions Generate a Justification or an Excuse for Escape?, 26 UCLA L. Rev. 1355 (1979)

Comment, Prison Escape and Defense Based on Conditions: A Theory of Social Preference, 67 Cal. L. Rev. 1183 (1979)

249   *Ashau*   Comment, *Fedorenko v. United States:* War Crimes, the Defense of Duress, and American Nationality Law, 82 Colum. L. Rev. 120 (1982)

251   Unintentional Injury   G. Erenius, Criminal Negligence and Individuality (1976)

Davis, The Development of Negligence as a Basis for Liability in Criminal Homicide Cases, 26 Ky. L.J. 209 (1938)

Garfield, A More Principled Approach to Criminalizing Negligence: A Prescription for the Legislature, 65 Tenn. L. Rev. 875 (1998)

263   note 136   Brady, Recklessness, Negligence, Indifference and Awareness, 43 Mod. L. Rev. 381 (1980)

Dressler, Does One Mens Rea Fit All?: Thoughts on Alexander's Unified Conception

Page

of Criminal Culpability, 88 Cal. L. Rev. 955 (2000)

270   note 144   Brady, Punishment for Negligence: A Reply to Professor Hall, 22 Buff. L. Rev. 107 (1972)

Hall, Negligent Behavior Should be Excluded from Penal Liability, 63 Colum. L. Rev. 632 (1963)

277   note 150   Michaels, Acceptance: The Missing Mental State, S. Cal. L. Rev. 953 (1998)

284   note 156   Clarke, Law and Order on the Courts: The Application of Criminal Liability for Intentional Fouls During Sporting Events, 32 Ariz. St. L.J. 1149 (2000)

285   Failure to Act   Alexander, Insufficient Concern: A Unified Conception of Criminal Culpability, 88 Cal. L. Rev. 931 (2000)

Hughes, Criminal Omissions, 67 Yale L.J. 590 (1958)

Kirchheimer, Criminal Omissions, 55 Harv. L. Rev. 615 (1942)

Kleinig, Criminal Liability for Failures to Act, 49 Law & Contemp. Probs. 161 (Summer 1986)

Morse, The Moral Metaphysics of Causation and Results, 88 Cal. L. Rev. 879 (2000)

Smith, Legal Liability and Criminal Omissions, 5 Buff. Crim. L.R. 69 (2001)

Symposium, Act & Crime, 142 U. Pa. L. Rev. 1443 (1994)

288   note 159   Freeman, Criminal Liability and Duty to Aid the Distressed, 142 U. Pa. L. Rev. 1455 (1994)

295   *Genovese*   M. Hunt, The Mugging (1972)

297   note 170   Dawson, *Negotiorum Gestio:* The Altruistic Intermeddler, 74 Harv. L. Rev. 1073 (1961)

Dressler, Some Brief Thoughts (Mostly Negative) About "Bad Samaritan" Laws, 40 Santa Clara L. Rev. 971 (2000)

Heyman, Foundations of the Duty to Rescue, 47 Vand. L. Rev. 673 (1994)

Kleinig, Good Samaritanism, 5 Phil. & Pub. Aff. 382 (1976)

Larguier, French Penal Law and the Duty To Aid Persons in Danger, 38 Tul. L. Rev. 81 (1963)

Morse, The Moral Metaphysics of Causation and Results, 88 Cal. L. Rev. 879 (2000)

Page

Murphy, Beneficence, Law, and Liberty: The Case of Required Rescue, 89 Geo. L.J. 605 (2001)

Schroeder, Two Methods for Evaluating Duty to Rescue Proposals, 49 Law & Contemp. Probs. 181 (Summer 1986)

Stewart, How Making the Failure to Assist Illegal Fails to Assist: An Observation of Expanding Criminal Omission Liability, 25 Am. J. Crim. L. 385 (1998)

Woozley, A Duty to Rescue: Some Thoughts on Criminal Liability, 69 Va. L. Rev. 1273 (1983)

304   note 176   Keedy, A Remarkable Murder Trial: Rex v. Sinnisiak, 100 U. Pa. L. Rev. 48 (1951)

Lewis, The Outlook for a Devil in the Colonies, 1958 Crim. L. Rev. 661

Note, The Cultural Defense in the Criminal Law, 99 Harv. L. Rev. 1293 (1986)

305   Causation   H. Hart & A. Honore, Causation in the Law 292–347 (1959)

Lloyd-Bostock, The Ordinary Man and the Psychology of Attributing Causes and Responsibility, 42 Mod. L. Rev. 143 (1979)

Schulhofer, Harm and Punishment: A Critique of Emphasis on the Results of Conduct in the Criminal Law, 122 U. Pa. L. Rev. 1497 (1974)

325   note 194   Note, Causation in the Model Penal Code, 78 Colum. L. Rev. 1249 (1978)

326   Punishment   H.L.A. Hart, Punishment and Responsibility (1968)

J. Michael & M. Adler, Crime, Law and Social Science (1933)

M. Moore, Law and Psychiatry (1984)

N. Morris, The Future of Imprisonment (1974)

P. Robinson & J. Darley, Justice, Liability, and Blame: Community Views and the Criminal Law (1995)

A. Ross, On Guilt, Responsibility and Punishment (1975)

G. Rusche & O. Kirchheimer, Punishment and Social Structure (1939)

C. Ten, Crime, Guilt, and Punishment: A Philosophical Introduction (1987)

Page

A. Von Hirsch, Doing Justice: The Choice of Punishments (1976)

J. Wilson & R. Herrnstein, Crime and Human Nature (1985)

Arenella, Convicting the Morally Blameless: Reassessing the Relationship Between Legal and Moral Accountability, 39 UCLA L. Rev. 1511 (1992)

Barnes, Revenge on Utilitarianism: Renouncing a Comprehensive Economic Theory of Crime and Punishment, 74 Ind. L.J. 627 (1999)

Benn, An Approach to the Problems of Punishment, 33 Philosophy 325 (1958)

Boldt, The Construction of Responsibility in the Criminal Law, 140 U. Pa. L. Rev. 2245 (1992)

Cohen, Moral Aspects of the Criminal Law, 49 Yale L.J. 987 (1940)

Cotton, Back with a Vengeance: The Resilience of Retribution as an Articulated Purpose of Criminal Punishment, 37 Am. Crim. L. Rev. 1313 (2000)

Denno, The Perils of Public Opinion, 28 Hofstra L. Rev. 741 (2000)

Dolinko, Three Mistakes of Retributivism, 39 UCLA L. Rev. 1623 (1992)

Dubber, The Right To Be Punished: Autonomy and Its Demise in Modern Penal Thought, 16 Law & Hist. Rev. 113 (1998)

Dubber, The Victim in American Penal Law: A Systematic Overview, 3 Buff. Crim. L.R. 3 (1999)

Fishman, Old Testament Justice, 51 Cath. U. L. Rev. 405 (2002)

Fletcher, The Place of Victims in the Theory of Retribution, 3 Buff. Crim. L.R. 51 (1999)

Garvey, Punishment as Atonement, 46 UCLA L. Rev. 1801 (1999)

Green, Freedom and Responsibility in the Age of Pound: An Essay on Criminal Justice, 93 Mich. L. Rev. 1915 (1995)

Greenawalt, Dignity and Victimhood, 88 Cal. L. Rev. 779 (2000)

Greenawalt, Punishment, 74 J. Crim. L. & Criminology 343 (1983)

Page

Huigens, The Dead End of Deterrence, 41 Wm. & Mary L. Rev. 943 (2000)

Husak, Holistic Retributivism, 88 Cal. L. Rev. 991 (2000)

Husak, Retribution in Criminal Theory, 37 San Diego L. Rev. 959 (2000)

Kahan, Social Meaning and the Economic Analysis of Crime, 27 J. Legal Stud. 609 (1998)

Kennedy, Making the Crime Fit the Punishment, 51 Emory L.J. 753 (2002)

Massaro, Shame, Culture, and American Criminal Law, 89 Mich. L. Rev. 1880 (1991)

Michaels, "Rationales" of Criminal Law Then and Now: For a Judgmental Descriptivism, 100 Colum. L. Rev. 54 (2000)

Murphy, Does Kant Have a Theory of Punishment, 87 Colum. L. Rev. 509 (1987)

Murphy, Marxism and Retribution, 2 Phil. & Pub. Aff. 217 (1993)

K. Pecarovich, Bibliography on Responsibility, 49 Law & Contemp. Probs. 237 (Summer 1986)

Pillsbury, The Meaning of Deserved Punishment: An Essay on Choice, Character, and Responsibility, 67 Ind. L.J. 719 (1992)

Prittwitz, The Resurrection of the Victim in Penal Theory, 3 Buff. Crim. L.R. 109 (1999)

Quinton, Punishment, 14 Analysis 133 (1954)

Robinson & Darley, The Utility of Desert, 91 Nev. L. Rev. 453 (1997)

Schunemann, The Role of the Victim Within the Criminal Justice System: A Three-Tiered Concept, 3 Buff. Crim. L.R. 33 (1999)

Simons, The Relevance of Community Values to Just Deserts: Criminal Law, Punishment Rationales, and Democracy, 28 Hofstra L. Rev. 635 (2000)

Steiker, Death, Taxes, and Punishment? A Response to Braithwaite and Tonry, 46 UCLA L. Rev. 1793 (1999)

Stewart, Legality and Morality in H.L.A. Hart's Theory of Criminal Law, 52 SMU L. Rev. 201 (1999)

Strauss, Losing Sight of the Utilitarian Forest for the Retributivist Trees: An Analysis of

Page

the Role of Public Opinion in a Utilitarian Model of Punishment, 23 Cardozo L. Rev. 1549 (2002)

Weinreb, Desert, Punishment, and Criminal Responsibility, 49 Law & Contemp. Probs. 47 (Summer 1986)

Wright, The Progressive Logic of Criminal Responsibility and the Circumstances of the Most Deprived, 43 Cath. U. L. Rev. 459 (1994)

330   note 196   Von Hirsch, Commensurability and Crime Prevention: Evaluating Formal Sentencing Structures and Their Rationale, 74 J. Crim. L. & Criminology 209 (1983)

F. Zimring & G. Hawkins, Incapacitation, Penal Confinement and the Restraint of Crime (1995)

331   J. Andenaes, Punishment and Deterrence (1974)

Andenaes, Deterrence and Specific Offenses, 38 U. Chi. L. Rev. 537 (1971)

Andenaes, The Morality of Deterrence, 37 U. Chi. L. Rev. 649 (1970)

Dession, Psychiatry and the Conditioning of Criminal Justice, 47 Yale L.J. 319 (1938)

DiIulio, Help Wanted: Economists, Crime and Public Policy, 10 J. Econ. Persp. 3 (1996)

Kahan, The Secret Ambition of Deterrence, 113 Harv. L. Rev. 413 (1999)

Kahan, What Do Alternative Sanctions Mean?, 63 U. Chi. L. Rev. 591 (1996)

Pillsbury, Understanding Penal Reform: The Dynamic of Change, 80 J. Crim. L. & Criminology 726 (1989)

Posner, An Economic Theory of the Criminal Law, 85 Colum. L. Rev. 1193 (1985)

Shavell, Criminal Law and the Optimal Use of Nonmonetary Sanctions as a Deterrent, 85 Colum. L. Rev. 1232 (1985)

Zimring & Hawkins, Dangerousness and Criminal Justice, 85 Mich. L. Rev. 481 (1986)

334   Capital Punishment   The literature on capital punishment is very large. The following list is a selection.

S. Banner, The Death Penalty (2002)

H. Bedau, The Death Penalty in America (3d ed. 1982)

J. Gorecki, Capital Punishment: Criminal Law and Social Evolution (1983)

Page

T. Sellin, The Death Penalty (1959)

V. Streib, Death Penalty in a Nutshell (2003)

U.S. Dep't of Justice, The Federal Death Penalty System, A Statistical Survey (2001)

W. White, The Death Penalty in the Nineties (1991)

F. Zimring & G. Hawkins, Capital Punishment and the American Agenda (1986)

Denno, Getting to Death: Are Executions Constitutional?, 82 Iowa L. Rev. 319 (1997)

Greenberg, Against the American System of Capital Punishment, 99 Harv. L. Rev. 1670 (1986)

Poulos, Capital Punishment, the Legal Process, and the Emergence of the Lucas Court in California, 23 U.C. Davis L. Rev. 157 (1990)

Radin, Cruel Punishment and Respect for Persons: Super Due Process for Death, 53 S. Cal. L. Rev. 1143 (1980)

Van den Haag, The Ultimate Punishment: A Defense, 99 Harv. L. Rev. 1662 (1986)

355 note 201 Bright & Keenan, Judges and the Politics of Death: Deciding Between the Bill of Rights and the Next Election in Capital Cases, 75 B.U. L. Rev. 759 (1995)

Cobb, Note, Reviving Mercy in the Structure of Capital Punishment, 99 Yale L.J. 389 (1989)

Steiker & Steiker, Sober Second Thoughts: Reflections on Two Decades of Constitutional Regulation of Capital Punishment, 109 Harv. L. Rev. 355 (1995)

Note, Mental Illness as an Aggravating Circumstance in Capital Cases, 89 Colum. L. Rev. 291 (1989)

360 note 203 R. Kennedy, Race, Crime, and the Law (1997)

G. Russell, The Death Penalty and Racial Bias (1994)

Baldus, Pulaski & Woodworth, Comparative Review of Death Sentences: An Empirical Study of the Georgia Experience, 74 J. Crim. L. & Criminology (1983)

Baldus, Pulaski, Woodworth and Kyle, Identifying Comparatively Excessive Sen-

Page

tences of Death: A Quantitative Approach, 33 Stan. L. Rev. 1 (1980)

Carter, When Victims Happen to Be Black, 97 Yale L.J. 420 (1988)

Gross, ABA's Proposed Moratorium: Lost Lives: Miscarriages of Justice in Capital Cases, 61 Law & Contemp. Probs. 125 (1998)

Gross, Race and Death: The Judicial Evaluation of Evidence of Discrimination in Capital Sentencing, 18 U.C. Davis L. Rev. 1275 (1985)

Gross and Mauro, Patterns of Death: An Analysis of Racial Disparities in Capital Sentencing and Homicide Victimization, 37 Stan. L. Rev. 27 (1984)

Kennedy, *McCleskey v. Kemp:* Race, Capital Punishment and the Supreme Court, 101 Harv. L. Rev. 1388 (1988)

361   note 204   Bedau & Radelet, Miscarriages of Justice in Potentially Capital Cases, 40 Stan. L. Rev. 21 (1987)

382   note 215   R. Dworkin, Life's Dominion (1993)

G. Williams, The Sanctity of Life 248–310 [suicide], 311–50 [euthanasia] (1957)

Kadish, Letting Patients Die: Legal and Moral Reflections, 80 Cal. L. Rev. 857 (1992)

Kamisar, Some Non–Religious Views Against Proposed "Mercy-Killing" Legislation, 42 Minn. L. Rev. 969 (1958)

Note, Physician-Assisted Suicide and the Right to Die with Assistance, 105 Harv. L. Rev. 2031 (1992)

     The Open Boat   Mallin, In Warm Blood: Some Historical and Procedural Aspects of Regina v. Dudley and Stephens, 34 U. Chi. L. Rev. 387 (1967)

There is a more romanticized account of the voyage of the Mignonette, the ordeal in the lifeboat, and the aftermath in D. McCormick, Blood on the Sea (1962).

For an account of an "open boat" situation during World War II, see W. Gibson, The Boat (1953).

For a brilliant replay underground (in the year 4300) of *Dudley,* see Fuller, The Case of the Speluncean Explorers, 62 Harv. L. Rev. 616 (1949)

385   Theft   J. Hall, Theft, Law and Society (2d ed. 1952) is a seminal work in the history of the

Page

law of theft and the development of the common law generally. It provided the conception for the historical materials in this Part.

J.C. Smith, The Law of Theft (5th ed. 1984)

386   Bales of Woad

For accounts of the political history of England in this period as well as extensive bibliographies on all aspects of the history, see 7 The Cambridge Medieval History (Decline of Empire and Papacy) 393–485, 881–99 (1932); 8 The Cambridge Medieval History (The Close of the Middle Ages) 362–449, 894–925 (1936). For an account of daily life in this period, see L. Salzman, English Life in the Middle Ages (1926).

For a fuller account of the wool and woolens industry, see E. Lipson, The History of the Woolen and Worsted Industries (1921), including a bibliography. See also W. Ashley, The Early History of the English Woolen Industry (1887); E. Lipson, 1 The Economic History of England 440–510 (the woolen industry), 511–94 (foreign trade) (7th ed. 1937). Lipson discusses later history of these subjects in volumes 2 and 3 of the same work (2d ed. 1934). On Edward IV as a wool merchant and mercantilist generally, see 2 C. Scofield, The Life and Reign of Edward the Fourth 404–28 (1923), which is also useful for general information about the period of the Carrier's Case.

387   n. 4

Maitland's introduction to the Selden Society edition (7 Selden Society) ix–lv (W. Whittaker ed. 1895) discusses at length the provenance and other aspects of The Mirror of Justices.

n. 5

W. Bolland, The Year Books (1921)

J. Dawson, The Oracles of the Law 50–65 (1968)

2 W. Holdsworth, A History of English Law 525–56 (4th ed. 1936)

T. Plucknett, Early English Legal Literature 98–114 (1958)

P. Winfield, The Chief Sources of English Legal History 158–83 (1925), (including a bibliography)

n.6

J. Baldwin, The King's Council in England during the Middle Ages (1913)

Page		
		I. Leadam & J. Baldwin, Introduction to Select Cases Before the King's Council (35 Selden Society) xi–xlvi (1918)
388	n. 7	J. Dawson, The Oracles of the Law 7–34 (1968)
		2 W. Holdsworth, A History of English Law 485–92 (4th ed. 1936) (serjeants)
		Ives, Promotion in the Legal Profession of Yorkist and Early Tudor England, 75 Law. Q. Rev. 348 (1959)
389	n. 8	J. Dawson, The Oracles of the Law 7–34 (1968)
		M. Hemmant, Introduction to Select Cases in the Exchequer Chamber (51 Selden Society) xi–xcvii (1933), and 2 Select Cases in the Exchequer Chamber (64 Selden Society) xi–l (1948)
400	*Wheatly*	Friedman, Crimes of Mobility, 43 Stan. L. Rev. 637 (1991)
404	note 232	Lowe, Larceny by a Trick and Contract, 1957 Crim. L. Rev. 28
408	note 240	Hughes, Sale or Return, Agents, and Larceny, 1963 Crim. L. Rev. 312, 401
		Smith, Larceny and False Pretences, 1958 Crim. L. Rev. 92
412		Brickey, The Jurisprudence of Larceny: An Historical Inquiry and Interest Analysis, 33 Vand. L. Rev. 1101 (1980)
		Edwards, Possession and Larceny, in 3 Current Legal Problems 127 (G. Keeton & G. Schwarzenberger, eds. 1950)
		Scurlock, The Element of Trespass in Larceny at Common Law, 22 Temp. L.Q. 12 (1948)
418	Property	Tigar, The Right of Property and the Law of Theft, 62 Tex. L. Rev. 1443 (1984)
423		Moohr, Federal Criminal Fraud and the Development of Intangible Property Rights in Information, 2000 U. Ill. L. Rev. 683
424	note 259	Jacobson & Green, Computer Crimes, 39 Am. Crim. L. Rev. 273 (2002)
		Lowenstein, Rodriguez & Stockley, Employment–Related Crimes, 36 Am. Crim. L. Rev. 475 (1999)
		Trivedi & Brownstein, Employment-Related Crimes, 39 Am. Crim. L. Rev. 355 (2002)

Page

429		Katyal, Criminal Law in Cyberspace, 149 U. Pa. L. Rev. 1003 (2001)
	note 264	Green, Plagiarism: Norms, and the Limits of Theft Law: Some Observations on the Use of Criminal Sanctions in Enforcing Intellectual Property Rights, 54 Hastings L.J. 167 (2003)
430		Note, Merchant's Responses to Shoplifting: An Empirical Study, 28 Stan. L. Rev. 589 (1976)
433	Intent	Carter, Knowledge, Ignorance and Animus Furandi, 1959 Crim. L. Rev. 613
		Lowe, The Fraudulent Intent in Larceny, 1956 Crim. L. Rev. 78
		Smith, The Fraudulent Intent in Larceny: Another View, 1956 Crim. L. Rev. 238
438	note 280	Howard, Larceny by Accidental Mistake, 36 Austl. L.J. 399 (1963)
		Kerr, The Time of Criminal Intent in Larceny, 66 Law. Q. Rev. 174 (1950)
		Williams, Mistake in the Law of Theft, 36 Camb. L.J. 62 (1977)
446	note 286	Rothschild and Throne, Criminal Consumer Fraud: A Victim-Oriented Analysis, 74 Mich. L. Rev. 661 (1976)
447		Moohr, Mail Fraud Meets Criminal Theory, 67 U. Cin. L. Rev. 1 (1998)
449	Finding	Riesman, Possession and the Law of Finders, 52 Harv. L. Rev. 1105 (1939)
452	Aggravated Theft	R. Matthews, Armed Robbery (2002)
		Note, A Rationale of the Law of Aggravated Theft, 54 Colum. L. Rev. 84 (1954)
454	Extortion	Berman, The Evidentiary Theory of Blackmail: Taking Motives Seriously, 65 U. Chi. L. Rev. 795 (1998)
		Hale, Bargaining Duress, and Economic Liberty, 43 Colum. L. Rev. 603 (1943)
		Helmholz, The Roman Law of Blackmail, 30 J. Legal Stud. 33 (2001)
		Lindgren, The Elusive Distinction Between Bribery and Extortion: From the Common Law to the Hobbs Act, 35 UCLA L. Rev. 815 (1988)
		Lindgren, Unraveling the Paradox of Blackmail, 84 Colum. L. Rev. 670 (1984)
		Symposium, Blackmail, 141 U. Pa. L. Rev. 1565 (1993)

Page

463   Rape

S. Bessmer, The Laws of Rape (1984)

S. Estrich, Real Rape (1987)

M. Gordon & S. Riger, The Female Fear: The Social Cost of Rape (1991)

R. Hall, Rape in America (1995)

D. Russell, Sexual Exploitation (1984)

J. Schwendlinger, Rape and Inequality (1983)

Bottke, Sexuality and Crime: The Victims of Sexual Offenses, 3 Buff. Crim. L.R. 293 (1999)

Bryden, Redefining Rape, 3 Buff. Crim. L.R. 317 (2000)

Bryden & Lengnick, Rape in the Criminal Justice System, 87 J. Crim. L. & Criminology 1194 (1997)

Coughlin, Sex and Guilt, 84 Va. L. Rev. 1 (1998)

Men, Women and Rape, 63 Fordham L. Rev. 125 (1994)

Schulhofer, Taking Sexual Autonomy Seriously: Rape Law and Beyond, 11 Law & Phil. 35 (1992)

465   *Rusk*

L. Bourque, Defining Rape (1989)

479   note 307

Anderson, Reviving Resistance in Rape Law, 1998 U. Ill. L. Rev. 953

Dripps, Beyond Rape: An Essay on the Difference Between the Presence of Force and the Absence of Consent, 92 Colum. L. Rev. 1780 (1992)

Falk, Rape by Fraud and Rape by Coercion, 64 Brook. L. Rev. 39 (1998)

Schwartz, An Argument for the Elimination of the Resistance Requirement from the Definition of Forcible Rape, 16 Loy. L.A. L. Rev. 567 (1983)

489   note 309

Denno, Sexuality, Rape, and Mental Retardation, 1997 U. Ill. L. Rev. 315 (1997)

Schuck, Rethinking Informed Consent, 103 Yale L.J. 899 (1994)

497   note 310

S. Ward et al., Acquaintance and Date Rape (1994) (annotated bibliography)

Husak & Thomas, Date Rape, Social Convention, and Reasonable Mistakes, 11 Law & Phil. 95 (1992)

Page

Pineau, Date Rape: A Feminist Analysis, 8 Law & Phil. 217 (1989)

Schulhofer, The Gender Question in Criminal Law, 7 Soc. Phil. & Pol. 105 (1990)

Note, Rethinking Reasonable Belief Defense to Rape, 100 Yale L.J. 2687 (1991)

498   note 312   S. Box, Power, Crime, and Mystification (1983)

H. Feild, Jurors and Rape (1980)

A.N. Groth, Men Who Rape (1979)

Weiner, Shifting the Communication Burden: A Meaningful Consent Standard in Rape, 6 Harv. Women's L.J. 143 (1983)

499   note 313   Henderson, Review Essay: What Makes Rape a Crime, 3 Berkeley Women's L.J. (1988)

503   note 317   D. Russell, Rape in Marriage (2d ed. 1990)

Sitton, Old Wine in New Bottles: The "Marital" Rape Allowance, 72 N.C. L. Rev. 261 (1993)

Developments in the Law—Domestic Violence, 106 Harv. L. Rev. 1498 (1993)

Note, Abolishing the Marital Exemption for Rape: A Statutory Proposal, 1983 U. Ill. L. Rev. 201

Note, To Have and To Hold: The Marital Rape Exemption and the Fourteenth Amendment, 99 Harv. L. Rev. 1255 (1986)

509   Trial Issues   Berger, Man's Trial, Woman's Tribulation: Rape Cases in the Courtroom, 77 Colum. L. Rev. 1 (1977)

Note, Defense Expert Testimony on Rape Trauma Syndrome: Implications for the Stoic Victim, 42 Hastings L.J. 1143 (1991)

521   note 323   H. Galvin, Shielding Rape Victims in the State and Federal Courts: A Proposal for the Second Decade, 70 Minn. L. Rev. 763 (1986)

524   J. Marsh, A. Geist & N. Caplan, Rape and the Limits of Law Reform (1982)

C. Spohn & J. Horney, Rape Law Reform (1992)

527   P. Brett, An Inquiry into Criminal Guilt (1963)

F. Jacobs, Criminal Responsibility (1971)

J. Marshall, Intention—In Law and Society (1968)

Page

Lynch, The Mental Element in the Actus Reus, 98 Law Q. Rev. 109 (1982)

M. Moore, Act and Crime—The Philosophy of Action and Its Implications for the Criminal Law (1993)

528   Insanity

F. Boland, Anglo-American Insanity Defense Reform (1999)

S. Brakel, J. Parry & B. Weiner, The Mentally Disabled and the Law (3d ed. 1985)

R. Gerber, The Insanity Defense (1984)

S. Halleck, The Mentally Disordered Defendant (1987)

T. Maeder, Crime and Madness (1985)

M. Moore, Law and Psychiatry (1984)

J. Moriarty, The Role of Mental Illness in Criminal Trials (2001), 3 vols. (historical documents): vol. 1, The History of Mental Illness in Criminal Cases: The English Tradition; vol. 2, The Insanity Defense: The American Developments; vol. 3, Competency To Be Tried, Imprisoned, and Executed

N. Morris, Madness and the Criminal Law (1982)

J. Parry & F. Gilliam, Handbook on Mental Disability Law (2002)

M. Perlin, The Jurisprudence of the Insanity Defense (1994)

D. Picquet & R. Best, The Insanity Defense: A Bibiliographic Research Guide (1994)

N. Walker, Crime and Insanity in England (1968)

note 328

MacBain, The Insanity Defense: Conceptual Confusion and the Erosion of Fairness, 67 Marq. L. Rev. 1 (1983)

534

D. West & A. Walk, Daniel McNaughton: His Trial and the Aftermath (1977)

545   note 329

Walker, 1883 and all that, 1966 Crim. L. Rev. 17

546   note 330

J. Allen, Inside Broadmoor (1952)

547   *M'Naghten*

R. Moran, Knowing Right from Wrong (1981)

The defense of insanity is discussed with particular reference to the M'Naghten rules in Royal Commission on Capital Punishment, Report (Cmd. 8932) (1953) at pp. 73–129.

Page

There is also an historical survey of the rules at pp. 397–406.

554   note 335

Platt & Diamond, The Origins of the "Right and Wrong" Test of Criminal Responsibility and Its Subsequent Development in the United States: An Historical Survey, 54 Cal. L. Rev. 1227 (1966)

For a detailed account of the trial of Charles Guiteau, assassin of President Garfield in 1881, who raised the insanity defense unsuccessfully, see Charles E. Rosenberg, The Trial of the Assassin Guiteau (1968).

Snouffer, The Myth of *M'Naghten*, 50 Or. L. Rev. 41 (1970)

555   note 336

F. Boland, Anglo-American Insanity Defense Reform (1999)

Keedy, Irresistible Impulse as a Defense in the Criminal Law, 100 U. Pa. L. Rev. 956 (1952)

Waite, Irresistible Impulse and Criminal Liability, 23 Mich. L. Rev. 443 (1925)

559   note 339

Livermore & Meehl, The Virtues of *M'Naghten*, 51 Minn. L. Rev. 789 (1967)

560   note 340

Reid, The Companion of the New Hampshire Doctrine of Criminal Insanity, 15 Vand. L. Rev. 721 (1962)

Reid, Understanding the New Hampshire Doctrine of Criminal Insanity, 69 Yale L.J. 367 (1960)

Reik, The Doe–Ray Correspondence: A Pioneer Collaboration in the Jurisprudence of Mental Disease, 63 Yale L.J. 183 (1953)

561   *Durham*

D. Robinson, Psychology and Law (1980)

563   note 342

Bonnie & Slobogin, The Role of Mental Health Professionals in the Criminal Process: The Case for Informed Speculation, 66 Va. L. Rev. 427 (1980)

Halleck, The Insanity Defense in the District of Columbia—A Legal *Lorelei,* 49 Geo. L.J. 294 (1960)

Morse, Failed Explanations and Criminal Responsibility: Experts and the Unconscious, 68 Va. L. Rev. 971 (1982)

Comment, Legal and Psychiatric Concepts and the Use of Psychiatric Evidence in Criminal Trials, 73 Cal. L. Rev. 411 (1985)

Page

568   note 343

Bazelon, The Dilemma of Criminal Responsibility, 72 Ky. L.J. 263 (1984)

574   note 345

Reider, Toward a New Test for the Insanity Defense: Incorporating the Discoveries of Neuroscience into Moral and Legal Theories, 46 UCLA L. Rev. 289 (1998)

Slobogin, An End to Insanity: Recasting the Role of Mental Disability in Criminal Cases, 86 Va. L. Rev. 1199 (2000)

575   note 346

Fingarette, The Concept of Mental Disease in Criminal Law Insanity Tests, 33 U. Chi. L. Rev. 229 (1966)

           n. 52

Cross, Reflections on *Bratty*'s Case, 78 Law. Q. Rev. 236 (1962)

Denno, Crime and Consciousness: Science and Involuntary Acts, 87 Minn. L. Rev. 269 (2002)

Hauhart, The Involuntary Action Defense to a Criminal Indictment, 11 N. Ky. L. Rev. 321 (1984)

Holland, Automatism and Criminal Responsibility, 25 Crim. L.Q. 95 (1982)

Moore, Responsibility and the Unconscious, 53 S. Cal. L. Rev. 1563 (1980)

Shapira, Structural Flaws of the "Willed Body Movement" Theory of Action, 1 Buff. Crim. L.R. 349 (1998)

Simester, On the So-Called Requirement for Voluntary Action, 1 Buff. Crim. L.R. 403 (1998)

576   note 349

Hermann, Assault on the Insanity Defense: Limitations on the Effectiveness and Effect of the Defense of Insanity, 14 Rut.-Cam. L.J. 241 (1983)

Morris, The Criminal Responsibility of the Mentally Ill, 33 Syracuse L. Rev. 477 (1982)

Morse, Excusing the Crazy: The Insanity Defense Reconsidered, 58 S. Cal. L. Rev. 777 (1985)

Note, The Guilty But Mentally Ill Verdict and Due Process, 92 Yale L.J. 475 (1983)

579   note 350

Fingarette, Addiction and Criminal Responsibility, 84 Yale L.J. 413 (1975)

Grant, While You Were Sleeping or Addicted: A Suggested Expansion of the Automatism Doctrine to Include an Addiction Defense, 2000 U. Ill. L. Rev. 997

Page

Wald, Alcohol, Drugs, and Criminal Responsibility, 63 Geo. L.J. 69 (1974)

Special Project: Drugs and Criminal Responsibility, 33 Vand. L. Rev. 1145 (1980)

581 note 351   Royal Commission on Capital Punishment, Report (Cmd. 8932) 130–44, 392–96 (1953)

Arenella, The Diminished Capacity and Diminished Responsibility Defenses: Two Children of a Doomed Marriage, 77 Colum. L. Rev. 827 (1977)

Fingarette, Diminished Mental Capacity as a Criminal Defense, 37 Mod. L. Rev. 264 (1974)

582 note 353   Eule, The Presumption of Sanity: Bursting the Bubble, 25 UCLA L. Rev. 637 (1978)

Mandiberg, Protecting Society and Defendants Too: The Constitutional Dilemma of Mental Abnormality and Intoxication Defenses, 53 Fordham L. Rev. 221 (1984)

Comment, The Burden of Proof for Extreme Emotional Disturbance and Insanity: The Deterioration of Due Process, 52 Temp. L.Q. 79 (1979)

584 note 355   D. Paull, Fitness To Stand Trial (1993)

R. Roesch and S.L. Golding, Competency to Stand Trial (1980)

Brakel, Presumption, Bias, and Incompetency in the Criminal Process, 1974 Wis. L. Rev. 1105

Pizzi, Competency to Stand Trial in Federal Courts: Conceptual and Constitutional Problems, 45 U. Chi. L. Rev. 21 (1977)

Winick, Restructuring Competency to Stand Trial, 32 UCLA L. Rev. 921 (1985)

587 *Jackson*   R. Perske, Unequal Justice?: What Can Happen When Persons with Retardation or Other Developmental Disabilities Encounter the Criminal Justice System (1991)

Morse, A Preference for Liberty: The Case Against Involuntary Commitment of the Mentally Disordered, 70 Cal. L. Rev. 54 (1982)

594 note 360   Note, The Eighth Amendment and the Execution of the Presently Incompetent, 32 Stan. L. Rev. 765 (1980)

Note, Insanity of the Condemned, 88 Yale L.J. 533 (1979)

Page

602   note 364

Morris, Dealing Responsibly with the Criminally Irresponsible, 1982 Ariz. St. L.J. 855

Developments in the Law, Civil Commitment of the Mentally Ill, 87 Harv. L. Rev. 1190 (1974)

Note, Commitment Following an Insanity Acquittal, 94 Harv. L. Rev. 605 (1981)

Note, Rules for an Exceptional Class: The Commitment and Release of Persons Acquitted of Violent Offenses by Reason of Insanity, 57 N.Y.U. L. Rev. 281 (1982)

605   note 365

Dybwad and Herr, Unnecessary Coercion: An End to Involuntary Civil Commitment of Retarded Persons, 31 Stan. L. Rev. 753 (1979)

606   note 367

Bruning, The Right of the Defendant To Refuse an Insanity Plea, 3 Am. Acad. Psych. & L. Bull. 238 (1976)

Singer, The Imposition of the Insanity Defense on an Unwilling Defendant, 41 Ohio St. L.J. 637 (1980)

Note, The Right and Responsibility of a Court to Impose the Insanity Defense over the Defendant's Objection, 65 Minn. L. Rev. 927 (1981)

607   note 369

Bazelon, Implementing the Right to Treatment, 36 U. Chi. L. Rev. 742 (1969)

Katz, The Right to Treatment—An Enchanting Legal Fiction?, 36 U. Chi. L. Rev. 755 (1963)

Morris, "Criminality" and the Right to Treatment, 36 U. Chi. L. Rev. 784 (1969)

Symposium, The Right to Treatment, 57 Geo. L.J. 673 (1969)

       note 370

Denno, Life Before the Modern Sex Offender Statutes, 92 Nw. U. L. Rev. 1317 (1998)

610   note 372

R. Simon & D. Aaronson, The Insanity Defense: A Critical Assessment of Law and Policy in the Post-Hinckley Era (1988)

H. Steadman et al., Before and After Hinckley: Evaluating Insanity Defense Reform (1993)

Slovenko, The Insanity Defense in the Wake of *Hinckley*, 14 Rut.-Cam. L.J. 373 (1983)

615   note 373

Symposium, Mental Disability and the Law, 62 Cal. L. Rev. 671 (1974)

Page

616   Infancy   Beschle, The Juvenile Justice Counterrevolution: Responding to Cognitive Dissonance in the Law's View of the Decision-Making Capacity of Minors, 48 Emory L.J. 65 (1999)

Cornwell, Preventing Kids from Killing, 37 Hous. L. Rev. 21 (2000)

Duncan, "So Young and So Untender": Remorseless Children and the Expectations of the Law, 102 Colum. L. Rev. 1469 (2002)

Scott & Steinberg, Blaming Youth, 81 Tex. L. Rev. 799 (2003)

617   note 375   Mlyniec, Juvenile Delinquent or Adult Convict: The Prosecutor's Choice, 14 Am. Crim. L. Rev. 29 (1976)

618   note 378   L. Empey, ed., Juvenile Justice: The Progressive Legacy and Current Reforms (1979)

Ketcham, National Standards for Juvenile Justice, 63 Va. L. Rev. 201 (1977)

620   Intoxication   Hall, Intoxication and Criminal Responsibility, 57 Harv. L. Rev. 1045 (1944)

Robinson, Causing the Conditions of One's Own Defense: A Study in the Limits of Theory in Criminal Law Doctrine, 71 Va. L. Rev. 1 (1985)

Sellers, Mens Rea and the Judicial Approach to "Bad Excuses" in the Criminal Law, 41 Mod. L. Rev. 245 (1978)

Singh, History of the Defence of Drunkenness in English Criminal Law, 49 Law. Q. Rev. 528 (1933)

626   Mistake   Dutile & Moore, Mistake and Impossibility: Arranging a Marriage between Two Difficult Partners, 74 Nw. U. L. Rev. 166 (1979)

Singer, The Resurgence of Mens Rea: II—Honest but Unreasonable Mistake of Fact in Self Defense, 28 B.C. L. Rev. 459 (1987)

629   note 389   Charlow, Wilful Ignorance and Criminal Culpability, 70 Tex. L. Rev. 1351 (1992)

Luban, Contrived Ignorance, 87 Geo. L.J. 957 (1999)

Robbins, The Ostrich Instruction: Deliberate Ignorance as a Criminal Mens Rea, 81 J. Crim. L. & Criminology 191 (1990)

631   Mistake of Law   Alexander, Inculpatory and Exculpatory Mistakes and the Fact/Law Distinction ... , 12 Law & Phil. 33 (1993)

Page

Davies, The Jurisprudence of Willfulness: An Evolving Theory of Excusable Ignorance, 48 Duke L. J. 341 (1998)

Jeffries, Legality, Vagueness and the Construction of Penal Statutes, 71 Va. L. Rev. 189 (1985)

Kahan, Ignorance of Law *Is* an Excuse—But Only for the Virtuous, 96 Mich. L. Rev. 127 (1997)

Parry, Culpability, Mistake, and Official Interpretations of Law, 25 Am. J. Crim. L. 1 (1997)

Perkins, Ignorance or Mistake of Law Revisited, 1980 Utah L. Rev. 473

632   (iii)   Gur-Arye, Reliance on a Lawyer's Mistaken Advice—Should it be an Excuse from Criminal Liability?, 29 Am. J. Crim. L. 455 (2002)

639   Liability without Fault   K. Brickey, Corporate Criminal Liability: A Treatise on the Criminal Liability of Corporations, Their Officers and Agents (1984)

F. Cullen, Corporate Crime Under Attack: The Ford Pinto Case and Beyond (1987)

N. Morris & C. Howard, Strict Responsibility, in Studies in Criminal Law 197 (1964)

M. Spencer & R. Sims, eds., Corporate Misconduct (1995)

Abrams, Criminal Liability of Corporate Officers for Strict Liability Offenses—A Comment on *Dotterweich* and *Park,* 28 UCLA L. Rev. 463 (1981)

Budd and Lynch, Voluntariness, Causation and Strict Liability, 1978 Crim. L. Rev. 74 (1978)

Geraghty, Corporate Criminal Liability, 39 Am. Crim. L. Rev. 327 (2002)

Green, Why It's a Crime To Tear the Tag Off a Mattress: Overcriminalization and the Moral Content of Regulatory Offences, 46 Emory L. J. 1533 (1997)

Levenson, Good Faith Defenses: Reshaping Strict Liability Crimes, 78 Cornell L. Rev. 401 (1993)

Michaels, Constitutional Innocence, 112 Harv. L. Rev. 828 (1999)

Peiris, Strict Liability in Commonwealth Criminal Law, 3 Legal Stud. 117 (1983)

Page

Saltzman, Strict Criminal Liability and the United States Constitution: Substantive Criminal Law Due Process, 24 Wayne L. Rev. 1571 (1978)

Simons, When Is Strict Criminal Liability Just?, 87 J. Crim. L. & Criminology 1075 (1997)

Singer, The Resurgence of *Mens Rea:* III—The Rise and Fall of Strict Criminal Liability, 30 B.C. L. Rev. 337 (1989)

Wiley, Not Guilty by Reason of Blamelessness: Culpability in Federal Criminal Interpretation, 85 Va. L. Rev. 1021 (1999)

Developments in the Law—Corporate Crime: Regulating Corporate Behavior through Criminal Sanctions, 92 Harv. L. Rev. 1227 (1979)

647   Attempts

R. Duff, Criminal Attempts (1996)

Alexander & Kessler, Mens Rea and Inchoate Crimes, 87 J. Crim. L. & Criminology 1138 (1997)

Burkhart, Is There a Rational Justification for Punishing an Accomplished Crime More Severely Than an Attempted Crime, 1986 B.Y.U. L. Rev. 553 (1986)

Keedy, Criminal Attempts at Common Law, 102 U. Pa. L. Rev. 464 (1954)

Robbins, Double Inchoate Crimes, 26 Harv. J. on Legis. 1 (1989)

Sayre, Criminal Attempts, 41 Harv. L. Rev. 821 (1928)

657   note 408

Enker, Mens Rea and Criminal Attempt, 1977 Am. B. Found. Res. J. 845 (1977)

Impossibility

Elkind, Impossibility in Criminal Attempts: A Theorist's Headache, 54 Va. L. Rev. 20 (1968)

Enker, Impossibility in Criminal Attempts—Legality and the Legal Process, 53 Minn. L. Rev. 665 (1969)

Hasnas, Once More Unto the Breach: The Inherent Liberalism of the Criminal Law and Liability for Attempting the Impossible, 54 Hastings L.J. 1 (2003)

Hughes, One Further Footnote on Attempting the Impossible, 42 N.Y.U. L. Rev. 1005 (1967)

Page

Robbins, Attempting the Impossible: The Emerging Consensus, 23 Harv. J. on Legis. 377 (1986)

Simons, Mistake and Impossibility, Law and Fact, and Culpability: A Speculative Essay, 81 J. Crim. L. & Criminology 447 (1990)

Stuntz, Self-Defeating Crimes, 86 Va. L. Rev. 1871 (2000)

658 n. 96 Blair, Constitutional Limitations on the Lesser Included Offense Doctrine, 21 Am. Crim. L. Rev. 445 (1984)

Ettinger, In Search of a Reasoned Approach to the Lesser Included Offense, 50 Brook. L. Rev. 191 (1984)

666 notes 413, 414 Smith, Two Problems in Criminal Attempts, 70 Harv. L. Rev. 422 (1957)

Smith, Two Problems in Criminal Attempts Re-Examined—II, 1962 Crim. L. Rev. 212

Williams, Criminal Attempts—A Reply, 1962 Crim. L. Rev. 300

note 414 Lee, Cancelling Crime, 30 Conn. L. Rev. 117 (1997)

667 note 415 Stuart, Mens Rea, Negligence and Attempts, 1968 Crim. L. Rev. 647

668 Conspiracy P. Gillies, The Law of Criminal Conspiracy (1981)

R. Hazell, Conspiracy and Civil Liberties (1974)

Dennis, The Rationale of Criminal Conspiracy, 93 Law Q. Rev. 39 (1977)

Kadish, Complicity, Cause and Blame: A Study in the Interpretation of Doctrine, 73 Cal. L. Rev. 323 (1985)

Robinson, Imputed Criminal Liability, 93 Yale L.J. 609 (1984)

Tempkin, When Is a Conspiracy Like an Attempt—and Other Impossible Questions, 94 Law Q. Rev. 534 (1978)

669 note 422 Dressler, Reassessing the Theoretical Underpinnings of Accomplice Liability: New Solutions to an Old Problem, 37 Hastings L.J. 91 (1985)

Kadish, Complicity, Cause and Blame: A Study in the Interpretation of Doctrine, 73 Cal. L. Rev. 323 (1985)

Weisberg, Reappraising Complicity, 4 Buff. Crim. L.R. 217 (2000)

Page

Westerfield, The Mens Rea Requirement of Accomplice Liability in American Criminal Law—Knowledge or Intent, 51 Miss. L.J. 155 (1980)

672   *Falcone*

Note, *Falcone* Revisited: The Criminality of Sales to an Illegal Enterprise, 53 Colum. L. Rev. 228 (1953)

683   note 430

Marcus, Conspiracy: The Criminal Agreement in Theory and in Practice, 65 Geo. L.J. 925 (1977)

Orchard, "Agreement" in Criminal Conspiracy, 1974 Crim. L. Rev. 297, 335

688   note 434

Bradley, NOW v. Schiedler: Rico Meets the First Amendment, 1994 Sup. Ct. Rev. 129 (1995)

Lynch, RICO: The Crime of Being a Criminal, 87 Colum. L. Rev. 661, 920 (1987)

Symposium: Law and the Continuing Enterprise: Perspectives on RICO, 65 Notre Dame L. Rev. 873 (1990)

Symposium: RICO: Something for Everyone, 35 Vill. L. Rev. 853 (1990)

698   note 443

Smith, Withdrawal from Criminal Liability for Complicity and Inchoate Offences, 12 Anglo–Am. L. Rev. 200 (1983)

Note, The Withdrawal Defense to Criminal Conspiracy: An Unconstitutional Allocation of the Burden of Proof, 51 Geo. Wash. L. Rev. 420 (1983)

701   note 444

Perkins, The Act of One Conspirator, 26 Hastings L.J. 337 (1974)

704   note 446

Comment, An Analysis of *Wharton's* Rule: *Iannelli v. United States* and One Step Beyond, 71 Nw. U. L. Rev. 547 (1976)

706

Bercusson, One Hundred Years of Conspiracy and Protection of Property: Time for a Change, 40 Mod. L. Rev. 268 (1977)

Sayre, Criminal Conspiracy, 35 Harv. L. Rev. 393 (1922)

Note, Conditional Objectives of Conspiracies, 94 Yale L.J. 895 (1985)

708   note 448

Allen, Criminal Conspiracies in Restraint of Trade at Common Law, 23 Harv. L. Rev. 531 (1910)

716

A. von Hirsch & A. Ashworth, eds., Principled Sentencing (1992)

Page

Grossman, Proportionality in Non-Capital Sentencing: The Supreme Court's Tortured Approach to Cruel and Unusual Punishment, 84 Ky. L.J. 107 (1995–96)

Huigens, Rethinking the Penalty Phase, 32 Ariz. St. L.J. 1195 (2000)

King, Portioning Punishment: Constitutional Limitations on Successive and Excessive Penalties, 144 U. Pa. L. Rev. 103 (1995)

Mascharka, Mandatory Minimum Sentences: Exemplifying the Law of Unintended Consequences, 28 Fla. St. U. L. Rev. 935 (2001)

Olson, Rethinking Mandatory Minimums after *Apprendi*, 96 Nw. U. L. Rev. 811 (2002)

740   Kahan, Some Realism about Retroactive Criminal Lawmaking, 3 Roger Williams U. L. Rev. 95 (1997)

Krent, Should *Bouie* be Buoyed?: Judicial Retroactive Lawmaking and the Ex Post Facto Clause, 3 Roger Williams U. L. Rev. 35 (1997)

741   Ashworth, Interpreting Criminal Statutes, A Crisis of Legality?, 107 Law Q. Rev. 419 (1991)

Jeffries, Legality, Vagueness and the Construction of Penal Statutes, 71 Va. L. Rev. 189 (1985)

Kahan, Lenity and Federal Common Law Crimes, 1994 Sup. Ct. Rev. 345

742   note 459   Livingston, Police Discretion and the Quality of Life in Public Places: Courts, Communities, and the New Policing, 97 Colum. L. Rev. 551 (1997)

744   *Akers*   Difonzo, Parental Responsibility for Juvenile Crime, 80 Or. L. Rev. 1 (2001)

Weinstein, Visiting the Sins of the Child on the Parent: The Legality of Parental Liability Statutes, 64 S. Cal. L. Rev. 859 (1991)

Powell   Denno, Comment: Human Biology and Criminal Responsibility: Free Will or Free Ride?, 137 U. Pa. L. Rev. 615 (1988)

Note, Alcohol Abuse and the Law, 94 Harv. L. Rev. 1660 (1981)

752   Symposium, Comments on the *Griswold* Case, 64 Mich. L. Rev. 197 (1965)

755   *Hardwick*   A. Leonard, Sexuality and the Law (1993)

Page

Sexual Orientation and the Law (R. Achtenberg ed. 1985)

Goodman, Beyond the Enforcement Principle: Sodomy Laws, Social Norms, and Social Panoptics, 89 Cal. L. Rev. 643 (2001)

Richards, Unnatural Acts and the Constitutional Right to Privacy: A Moral Theory, 45 Fordham L. Rev. 1281 (1977)

Project, The Consenting Adult Homosexual and the Law: An Empirical Study of Enforcement and Administration in Los Angeles County, 13 UCLA L. Rev. 643 (1966)

765   note 468   B. Mitchell, Law, Morality, and Religion in a Secular Society (1977)

K. Shienbaum, ed., Legislating Morality (1988)

Becker, Crimes Against Autonomy: Gerald Dworkin on the Enforcement of Morality, 40 Wm. & Mary L. Rev. 959 (1999)

Duff, Harms and Wrongs, 5 Buff. Crim. L.R. 13 (2001)

Dworkin, Devlin Was Right: Law and the Enforcement of Morality, 40 Wm. & Mary L. Rev. 927 (1999)

Green, Feinberg's Moral Limits, and Beyond, 5 Buff. Crim. L.R. 1 (2001)

Harcourt, Joel Feinberg on Crime and Punishment: Exploring the Relationship Between the Moral Limits of the Criminal Law and the Expressive Function of Punishment, 5 Buff. Crim. L.R. 145 (2001)

Hindes, Morality Enforcement Through the Criminal Law and the Modern Doctrine of Substantive Due Process, 126 U. Pa. L. Rev. 344 (1977)

Stewart, Harms, Wrongs, and Set-Backs in Feinberg's Moral Limits of the Criminal Law, 5 Buff. Crim. L.R. 47 (2001)

768   Stephen's Liberty, Equality, Fraternity has been reprinted by the Cambridge University Press with an introduction and notes by R. White (1967)

The debate between Mill and Stephen was rekindled by the Committee on Homosexual Offenses and Prostitution, Report [Wolfenden Report] (Cmnd. 247). Lord Devlin's response, in P. Devlin, The Enforcement of Morals (1965), engendered a broad public debate,

Page

most of it on the side of the committee (and Mill) against Devlin (and Stephen). Lord Devlin includes in his book a bibliography of such comment, at xiii–xiv.

INDEX

References are to Pages

†